MW00590632

THE OXFORD HANDBOOK OF

WISDOM AND THE BIBLE

THE OXFORD HANDBOOK OF

WISDOM AND THE BIBLE

Edited by
WILL KYNES

OXFORD
UNIVERSITY PRESS

OXFORD
UNIVERSITY PRESS

Oxford University Press is a department of the University of Oxford. It furthers
the University's objective of excellence in research, scholarship, and education
by publishing worldwide. Oxford is a registered trade mark of Oxford University
Press in the UK and certain other countries.

Published in the United States of America by Oxford University Press
198 Madison Avenue, New York, NY 10016, United States of America.

© Oxford University Press 2021

All rights reserved. No part of this publication may be reproduced, stored in
a retrieval system, or transmitted, in any form or by any means, without the
prior permission in writing of Oxford University Press, or as expressly permitted
by law, by license, or under terms agreed with the appropriate reproduction
rights organization. Inquiries concerning reproduction outside the scope of the
above should be sent to the Rights Department, Oxford University Press, at the
address above.

You must not circulate this work in any other form
and you must impose this same condition on any acquirer.

Library of Congress Cataloging-in-Publication Data
Names: Kynes, Will, 1981– editor.
Title: The Oxford handbook of wisdom and the Bible / edited by Will Kynes.
Description: New York, NY : Oxford University Press, [2021] | Includes
bibliographical references.
Identifiers: LCCN 2020035227 (print) | LCCN 2020035228 (ebook) |
ISBN 9780190661267 (hardback) | ISBN 9780190661281 (epub) |
ISBN 9780190661298 (ebook)
Subjects: LCSH: Wisdom literature—Criticism, interpretation, etc. |
Wisdom—Religious aspects. | Wisdom—Biblical teaching.
Classification: LCC BS1455.O94 2021 (print) | LCC BS1455 (ebook) |
DDC 223/.06—dc23
LC record available at https://lccn.loc.gov/2020035227
LC ebook record available at https://lccn.loc.gov/2020035228

1 3 5 7 9 8 6 4 2

Printed by Sheridan Books, Inc., United States of America

To Vanessa,
who has embodied the delightful blessings of wisdom in my life.

Get wisdom; get insight: do not forget, nor turn away
from the words of my mouth.
Do not forsake her, and she will keep you;
love her, and she will guard you.
The beginning of wisdom is this: Get wisdom,
and whatever else you get, get insight.
Prize her highly, and she will exalt you;
she will honor you if you embrace her.
She will place on your head a fair garland;
she will bestow on you a beautiful crown.

Proverbs 4:5–9

PREFACE

THE concept of wisdom holds a prominent place in the social and theological imagination of the biblical authors. Wisdom is presented as one of God's defining characteristics (Isa 31:2; Job 12:13; cf. Rom 16:27), present with the deity at creation (Prov 3:19; 8:27–31), the product of obedience to the Torah (Deut 4:6; Ps 119:98), and a divine gift (Prov 2:6; Jas 1:5). It is identified with the fear of the Lord (Prov 1:7; 9:10; Job 28:28; Ps 111:10), righteousness (e.g., Prov 10:31), and life (Prov 13:14), as well as with skill in practical matters, such as spinning yarn (Exod 35:25), sailing ships (Ezek 27:8), proper speech (Prov 12:18; 29:11), and amassing wealth (Ezek 28:4; Prov 8:18). The wise, those who possess wisdom in special measure, are respected for their just judgments (1 Kgs 3:28) and insightful counsel (Jer 18:18). In the New Testament, wisdom is associated with Christ (1 Cor 1:24, 30), and is one of the attributes for which he receives eternal worship (Rev 5:12). The Christian community is expected to be characterized by its own distinctive wisdom (Jas 3:13, 17), different from that of the Greeks (1 Cor 1:22–25).

Within biblical scholarship, the discussion of wisdom and the Bible has been primarily oriented around Wisdom Literature as a category of biblical texts centered around Proverbs, Ecclesiastes, and Job, though sometimes including Psalms and Song of Songs, as well as Sirach and Wisdom of Solomon, and even spreading its "influence" into additional texts across the canon. These texts have been associated with a group called "the wise" in the Hebrew Bible, who are credited with promulgating a "Wisdom" tradition, with its own distinct theological beliefs and literary forms of expression. Therefore, this volume includes chapters on features of Wisdom Literature as a category (Part IV), its relationship to other types of literature in the Hebrew Bible and Second Temple period (Part V), and each of the texts commonly associated with it (Part VI).

However, as becomes evident in a number of these chapters (especially those in Part V), a focus on Wisdom Literature as a category will leave features of the biblical conception of wisdom in the blurry periphery of our vision. The field is currently in the midst of a spirited debate about the value and validity of this category. Oxford Handbooks are designed both to reflect the current state of the discipline and to help shape its future. That makes this an ideal forum in which to carry out this debate. Contributors to this volume represent the full range of opinions on the future of Wisdom Literature, from those who think it should be discarded as a distorting hindrance to the accurate interpretation of the biblical texts associated with it and the concept of wisdom it purports to illuminate, to those who would maintain it for its heuristic value as the encapsulation of distinct features the texts share and a window into the social world behind them.

This volume is not designed to take a particular position in this debate, but it does take advantage of the space the new questions being raised about the Wisdom category has created to think anew about wisdom as a concept. As the introductory chapter explains, the study of Wisdom Literature does not completely comprehend the study of wisdom as a concept in the Bible and related cultures, and yet concept and category remain intertwined, such that their treatment in a common volume is fitting.

Therefore, the first half of the volume focuses on wisdom as a concept. As interpreters have attempted to describe this jewel of biblical thought, they have focused attention on several of its glimmering facets: wisdom's association with skill and success in its advice, its connection to knowledge and revelation in its epistemology, its role in character formation as a virtue, its ligature with creation and covenant in its theology, and its encapsulation of retribution and skepticism in its vision of order. Part I of this volume considers each in turn.

A concept of such significance cannot be understood simply within the constraints of the biblical canon. Part II examines how, dropped into an ancient world already awash with reflection on wisdom, the biblical conception ripples through cultures shaped by the Hebrew Bible. Part III, then, explores the continuing relevance of wisdom in the modern world, both in the three "Religions of the Book" Islam, Judaism, and Christianity, and in a sampling of ideological and contextual perspectives. As in the second half of the volume focused on Wisdom Literature as a category, the contributors who reflect on wisdom as a concept in the three parts in this first half represent a range of views on the validity of the Wisdom category and therefore its value for illuminating the biblical concept of wisdom. Wisdom and Wisdom Literature no longer dance in quite as tight an embrace; how wisdom's steps may change if no longer led by Wisdom Literature and whether Wisdom Literature will even remain on the floor still remain to be seen.

I am grateful to Steve Wiggins at Oxford University Press for initiating and guiding this project to completion. I am also indebted to Katharine J. Dell, Stuart Weeks, and Mark Sneed for offering their insight on the topics to be covered in the volume and its structure. I was incredibly fortunate to be joined in this endeavor by a group of contributors who represent so well the breadth and depth of wisdom. I would also like to thank my research assistant at Samford University, John Pawlik, who worked with the diligence endorsed by Proverbs to help prepare the volume for publication.

CONTENTS

PART III THE CONCEPT OF WISDOM IN THE MODERN WORLD

PART IV THE CATEGORY OF WISDOM LITERATURE

PART V WISDOM LITERATURE AND OTHER LITERATURE

PART VI TEXTS

LIST OF ABBREVIATIONS

ÄAT	Ägypten und Altes Testament
AB	Anchor Bible
ABD	*Anchor Bible Dictionary*. Edited by David Noel Freedman. 6 vols. New York, NY: Doubleday, 1992
ABG	Arbeiten zur Bibel und ihrer Geschichte
ABS	Archaeology and Biblical Studies
ActAnt	Acta Antiqua Academiae Scientiarum Hungaricae
ACW	Ancient Christian Writers
AF	*Archivo di filosofia*
AfO	*Archiv für Orientforschung*
ÄgAbh	Ägyptologische Abhandlungen
AIL	Ancient Israel and Its Literature
AJSR	*Association for Jewish Studies Review*
AnBib	Analecta Biblica
ANESSup	Ancient Near Eastern Studies Supplements Series
ANETS	Ancient Near Eastern Texts and Studies
AnSt	*Anatolian Studies*
AntOr	*Antiguo Oriente*
AOAT	Alter Orient und Altes Testament
AOS	American Oriental Series
ASJ	*Acta Sumerologica*
ASTI	*Annual of the Swedish Theological Institute*
ATANT	Abhandlungen zur Theologie des Alten und Neuen Testaments
ATD	Das Alte Testament Deutsch
ATM	Altes Testament und Moderne
AuOrSup	Aula Orientalis Supplements
BBR	*Bulletin for Biblical Research*
BCOTWP	Baker Commentary on the Old Testament Wisdom and Psalms
BdK	Bibliothek deutscher Klassiker
BEATAJ	Beiträge zur Erforschung des Alten Testaments und des antiken Judentum
BEL	Biblical Encyclopedia Library
BETL	Bibliotheca Ephemeridum Theologicarum Lovaniensium
BHT	Beiträge zur historischen Theologie

Bib	*Biblica*
BibInt	*Biblical Interpretation*
BibInt	Biblical Interpretation Series
BibSem	The Biblical Seminar
BJRL	*Bulletin of the John Rylands University Library of Manchester*
BJS	Brown Judaic Studies
BJSUCSD	Biblical and Judaic Studies from the University of California, San Diego
BKAT	Biblischer Kommentar, Altes Testament
BL	*Bibel und Liturgie*
BLS	Bible and Literature Series
BN	*Biblische Notizen*
BNB	Biblische Notizen Beihefte
BO	*Bibliotheca Orientalis*
BSJS	Brill's Series in Jewish Studies
BTA	Bible and Theology in Africa
BTB	*Biblical Theology Bulletin*
BThSt	Biblisch-theologische Studien
BTS	Biblical Tools and Studies
BZAW	Beihefte zur Zeitschrift für die alttestamentliche Wissenschaft
BZNW	Beihefte zur Zeitschrift für die neutestamentliche Wissenschaft
CBQ	*Catholic Biblical Quarterly*
CBQMS	Catholic Biblical Quarterly Monograph Series
CC	Continental Commentaries
CdE	*Chronique d'Égypte*
CFThL	Clark's Foreign Theological Library, 4th series
CHANE	Culture and History of the Ancient Near East
CM	Cuneiform Monographs
ConBOT	Coniectanea Biblica: Old Testament Series
CSA	Copenhagen Studies in Assyriology
CSHB	Critical Studies in the Hebrew Bible
CTJ	*Calvin Theological Journal*
CurBR	*Currents in Biblical Research*
CurBS	*Currents in Research: Biblical Studies*
CurTM	*Currents in Theology and Mission*
CUSAS	Cornell University Studies in Assyriology and Sumerology
DCLS	Deuterocanonical and Cognate Literature Studies
DJD	Discoveries in the Judaean Desert
DSD	*Dead Sea Discoveries*
EncJud	*Encyclopedia Judaica*. Edited by Fred Skolnik and Michael Berenbaum. 2nd ed. 22 vols. Detroit, MI: Macmillan Reference USA, 2007
ErFor	Erträge der Forschung
ErIsr	*Eretz-Israel*

EvT	*Evangelische Theologie*
FAOS	Freiburger altorientalische Studien
FAT	Forschungen zum Alten Testament
FAT II	Forschungen zum Alten Testament II
FB	Forschung zur Bibel
FCB	Feminist Companion to the Bible
FCB II	Feminist Companion to the Bible, Second Series
FOTL	Forms of the Old Testament Literature
FRLANT	Forschungen zur Religion und Literatur des Alten und Neuen Testaments
FTLZ	Forum Theologische Literaturzeitung
GCT	Gender, Culture, Theory
GMTR	Guides to the Mesopotamian Textual Record
HAR	*Hebrew Annual Review*
HBAI	*Hebrew Bible and Ancient Israel*
HBM	Hebrew Bible Monographs
HBS	Herders Biblische Studien
HCOT	Historical Commentary on the Old Testament
HCS	Hellenistic Culture and Society
HDR	Harvard Dissertations in Religion
HKAT	Handkommentar zum Alten Testament
HS	*Hebrew Studies*
HSTW	The Hebrew Scriptures and Their World
HThKAT	Herders Theologischer Kommentar zum Alten Testament
HTR	*Harvard Theological Review*
HTS	Harvard Theological Studies
HUCA	*Hebrew Union College Annual*
HvTSt	*Hervormde teologiese studies*
IECOT	International Exegetical Commentary on the Old Testament
Int	*Interpretation*
ISBL	Indiana Studies in Biblical Literature
IRM	*International Review of Missions*
JAAR	*Journal of the American Academy of Religion*
JAJSup	Journal of Ancient Judaism. Supplements
JANER	*Journal of Ancient Near Eastern Religions*
JANESCU	*Journal of the Ancient Near Eastern Society of Columbia University*
JAOS	*Journal of the American Oriental Society*
JBL	*Journal of Biblical Literature*
JBTh	*Jahrbuch fur biblische Theologie*
JCS	*Journal of Cuneiform Studies*
JEA	*Journal of Egyptian Archaeology*
JECS	*Journal of Early Christian Studies*

JES	*Journal of Ecumenical Studies*
JHS	*Journal of Hellenic Studies*
JHebS	*Journal of Hebrew Scriptures*
JJS	*Journal of Jewish Studies*
JPSBC	JPS Bible Commentary
JQR	*Jewish Quarterly Review*
JR	*Journal of Religion*
JSJSup	Supplements to the Journal for the Study of Judaism
JSNT	*Journal for the Study of the New Testament*
JSNTSup	Journal for the Study of the New Testament Supplement Series
JSOT	*Journal for the Study of the Old Testament*
JSOTSup	Journal for the Study of the Old Testament Supplement Series
JSRC	Jerusalem Studies in Religion and Culture
JTI	*Journal for Theological Interpretation*
JTISup	Journal of Theological Interpretation Supplements
JTS	*Journal of Theological Studies*
KAT	Kommentar zum Alten Testament
KT	Kaiser Taschenbücher
LAI	Library of Ancient Israel
LCL	Loeb Classical Library
LHBOTS	Library of Hebrew Bible/Old Testament Studies
MBS	Message of Biblical Spirituality
MTSR	*Method and Theory in the Study of Religion*
NAC	New American Commentary
NCB	New Century Bible
NICOT	New International Commentary on the Old Testament
NIDNTTE	*New International Dictionary of New Testament Theology and Exegesis.* Edited by Moises Silva. 5 vols. 2nd ed. Grand Rapids, MI: Zondervan, 2014
NovTSup	Supplements to Novum Testamentum
NRTh	*La nouvelle revue théologique*
NThT	*Nieuw theologisch Tijdschrift*
OBO	Orbis Biblicus et Orientalis
ÖBS	Österreichische biblische Studien
OBS	Oxford Bible Series
OIP	Oriental Institute Publications
OLA	Orientalia Lovaniensia Analecta
ORA	Orientalische Religionen in der Antike
OTE	*Old Testament Essays*
OTL	Old Testament Library
OtSt	*Oudtestamentische Studiën*
OTS	Old Testament Studies
PEGL	*Proceedings of the Eastern Great Lakes Biblical Society*
PG	Patrologia Graeca

PGM	*Papyri Graecae Magicae: Die griechischen Zauberpapyri.* Edited by Karl Preisendanz. 2nd ed. Stuttgart: Teubner, 1973–1974
PNTC	Pillar New Testament Commentary
Proof	*Prooftexts: A Journal of Jewish Literary History*
PRSt	*Perspectives in Religious Studies*
PSAT	Poetologische Studien zum Alten Testament
R&T	*Religion and Theology*
RA	*Revue d'assyriologie et d'archéologie orientale*
RB	*Revue biblique*
ResQ	*Restoration Quarterly*
RevExp	*Review and Expositor*
RevQ	*Revue de Qumran*
RHPR	*Revue d'histoire et de philosophie religieuses*
RivB	*Rivista biblica italiana*
RlA	*Reallexikon der Assyriologie.* Edited by Erich Ebeling et al. Berlin: de Gruyter, 1928–
RSPT	*Revue des sciences philosophiques et théologiques*
RTL	*Revue théologique de Louvain*
RTP	*Revue de théologie et de philosophie*
SAAB	*State Archives of Assyria Bulletin*
SAACT	State Archives of Assyria Cuneiform Texts
SAK	*Studien zur Altägyptischen Kultur*
SANER	Studies in Ancient Near Eastern Records
SAOC	Studies in Ancient Oriental Civilizations
SBAB	Stuttgarter biblische Aufsatzbände
SBLCS	Society of Biblical Literature Commentary on the Septuagint
SBLDS	Society of Biblical Literature Dissertation Series
SBLEJL	Society of Biblical Literature Early Judaism and Its Literature
SBLSCS	Society of Biblical Literature Septuagint and Cognate Studies
SBLStBL	Society of Biblical Literature Studies in Biblical Literature
SBLSymS	Society of Biblical Literature Symposium Series
SBS	Stuttgarter Bibelstudien
SBT	Studies in Biblical Theology
SEÅ	*Svensk exegetisk årsbok*
SemeiaSt	Semeia Studies
SHANE	Studies in the History of the Ancient Near East
SHBC	Smith & Helwys Bible Commentary
SJOT	*Scandinavian Journal of the Old Testament*
SJT	*Scottish Journal of Theology*
SOTSMS	Society for Old Testament Study Monograph Series
SPhiloA	*Studia Philonica Annual*
STDJ	Studies on the Texts of the Desert of Judah
StOR	Studies in Oriental Religions

STR	*Southeastern Theological Review*
StZ	*Stimmen der Zeit*
SubBi	Subsidia Biblica
SVT	Scholia in Vetus Testamentum
SVTQ	*St. Vladimir's Theological Quarterly*
SymS	Symposium Series
TaiJT	*Taiwan Journal of Theology*
TDOT	*Theological Dictionary of the Old Testament.* Edited by G. Johannes Botterweck and Helmer Ringgren. Translated by John T. Willis et al. 8 vols. Grand Rapids, MI: Eerdmans, 1974–2006
TDV	*Turkiye Diyanet Vakfi Ansiklopedisi*
THOTC	Two Horizons Old Testament Commentary
ThTo	*Theology Today*
TJ	*Trinity Journal*
TLZ	*Theologische Literaturzeitung*
TNTC	Tyndale New Testament Commentaries
TQ	*Theologische Quartalschrift*
TS	*Theological Studies*
TSAJ	Texts and Studies in Ancient Judaism
TThSt	Trierer theologische Studien
TUAT.NF	Texte aus der Umwelt des Alten Testaments. Neue Folge
TZ	*Theologische Zeitschrift*
UF	*Ugarit-Forschungen*
USFSJH	University of South Florida Studies in the History of Judaism
VC	*Vigiliae Christianae*
VT	*Vetus Testamentum*
VTSup	Supplements to Vetus Testamentum
WAW	Writings from the Ancient World
WBC	Word Biblical Commentary
WisC	Wisdom Commentary
WLAW	Wisdom Literature from the Ancient World
WMANT	Wissenschaftliche Monographien zum Alten und Neuen Testament
WO	*Die Welt des Orients*
WTJ	*Westminster Theological Journal*
WUNT	Wissenschaftliche Untersuchungen zum Neuen Testament
WW	*Word and World*
YOSR	Yale Oriental Series, Researches
ZÄS	*Zeitschrift für ägyptische Sprache und Altertumskunde*
ZAW	*Zeitschrift für die alttestamentliche Wissenschaft*
ZBK	Zürcher Bibelkommentare
ZTK	*Zeitschrift für Theologie und Kirche*

LIST OF CONTRIBUTORS

John Ahn Associate Professor of Hebrew Bible at Howard University School of Divinity (Washington, D.C.). Trained in ancient Near Eastern and Religious Studies, he is the author/co-editor of *Exile as Forced Migrations* and *Thus Says the LORD: Essays in Honor of Robert R. Wilson.*

James K. Aitken Reader in Hebrew and Early Jewish Studies at the University of Cambridge and a Fellow of Fitzwilliam College. His books include *No Stone Unturned: Greek Inscriptions and Septuagint Vocabulary.*

Arjen Bakker Assistant Professor of New Testament, University of Groningen. He is the author of *The Secret of Time: Reconfiguring Wisdom in the Dead Sea Scrolls.*

Samuel E. Balentine Professor of Old Testament and Director of Graduate Studies at Union Presbyterian Seminary, Richmond, VA. His books include *Have You Considered My Servant Job? Understanding the Biblical Archetype of Patience* and *Wisdom Literature.*

W.H. Bellinger, Jr. Professor of Old Testament at Baylor University. He is the author of *Psalms: A Guide to Studying the Psalter* and *Psalms* in the New Cambridge Bible Commentary (with Walter Brueggemann).

Mark J. Boda Professor of Old Testament at McMaster Divinity College. His books include *Praying the Tradition* and *Exploring Zechariah.*

William P. Brown William Marcellus McPheeters Professor of Old Testament at Columbia Theological Seminary. He is the author of *Wisdom's Wonder: Character, Creation, and Crisis in the Bible's Wisdom Literature* and *Seeing the Psalms: A Theology of Metaphor.*

Jonathan P. Burnside Professor of Biblical Law at the University of Bristol. He is the author of, among other books, *The Signs of Sin: Seriousness of Offence in Biblical Law* and *God, Justice, and Society: Aspects of Law and Legality in the Bible.*

Yoram Cohen Professor of Assyriology in Tel Aviv University. He is the author of, among other books, *Wisdom from the Late Bronze Age.*

Katharine J. Dell Reader in Old Testament Literature and Theology in the Faculty of Divinity, University of Cambridge and a Fellow of St. Catharine's College, Cambridge. She is the author of, among other books, *The Book of Proverbs in Social and Theological Context* and *The Solomonic Corpus of "Wisdom" and Its Influence.*

Paul S. Fiddes Professor of Systematic Theology in the University of Oxford. His books include *The Creative Suffering of God* and *Seeing the World and Knowing God: Hebrew Wisdom and Christian Doctrine in a Late-Modern Context.*

Tova L. Forti Associate Professor of Old Testament at Ben-Gurion University of the Negev. She is the author of *Animal Imagery in the Book of Proverbs* and *"Like A Lone Bird on A Roof": Animal Imagery and the Structure of Psalms.*

Matthew Goff Professor of Hebrew Bible and Second Temple Judaism at Florida State University. He has written several monographs on Wisdom Literature and the Dead Sea Scrolls. His most recent volume is *The Wiley Blackwell Companion to Wisdom Literature*, co-edited with Samuel Adams.

Norman Habel Professorial Fellow at Flinders University, Adelaide, Australia. His recent works include *Discerning Wisdom in God's Creation* and *Being and Earth Being.*

Anselm C. Hagedorn Professor of Hebrew Bible and Ancient Judaism at the University of Osnabrück. He is the author of *Between Moses and Plato: Individual and Society in Deuteronomy and Ancient Greek Law* and *Die Anderen im Spiegel: Israels Auseinandersetzung mit den Völkern in den Büchern Nahum, Zefanja, Obadja und Joel.*

Scott C. Jones Professor of Biblical Studies at Covenant College and author of *Rumors of Wisdom: Job 28 as Poetry.*

Mariam Kamell Kovalishyn Assistant Professor of New Testament at Regent College, Vancouver. She is the co-author of *James: Zondervan Exegetical Commentary Series* (with Craig Blomberg).

Will Kynes Associate Professor of Biblical Studies at Samford University. His books include *An Obituary for "Wisdom Literature": The Birth, Death, and Intertextual Reintegration of a Biblical Corpus* and *My Psalm Has Turned into Weeping: Job's Dialogue with the Psalms.*

Michael C. Legaspi Associate Professor of Classics and Ancient Mediterranean Studies and Jewish Studies at Pennsylvania State University. He is the author of *Wisdom in Classical and Biblical Tradition.*

Tremper Longman III Distinguished Scholar and Professor Emeritus of Biblical Studies at Westmont College. He is the author of *The Fear of the Lord is Wisdom: A Theological Introduction to Wisdom in Israel* and commentaries on Proverbs, Ecclesiastes, and Job.

Ekaterina Matusova Heisenberg Research Fellow at the Institut für antikes Judentum und hellenistische Religionsgeschichte at the University of Tübingen. She is the author of *The Meaning of the "Letter of Aristeas" in Light of Biblical Interpretation and Grammatical Tradition, and with Reference to Its Historical Context.*

John L. McLaughlin Interim Dean and Professor of Old Testament/Hebrew Bible at the University of St. Michael's College. His publications include *An Introduction to Israel's Wisdom Tradition* and *The Ancient Near East: An Essential Guide.*

Suzanna R. Millar Teaching Fellow in Hebrew Bible and Old Testament at the University of Edinburgh. She is the author of *Genre and Openness in Proverbs 10:1–22:16*.

Joachim Friedrich Quack Professor of Egyptology at Heidelberg University. His books include *Die Lehren des Ani: Ein neuägyptischer Weisheitstext in seinem kulturellen Umfeld* and *Einführung in die altägyptische Literaturgeschichte III: Die demotische und gräko-ägyptische Literatur*.

Bennie H. Reynolds III Director of the Office of Institutional Effectiveness and Assistant Professor at the Medical University of South Carolina. He is the author of *Between Symbolism and Realism: The Use of Symbolic and Non-Symbolic Language in Ancient Jewish Apocalypses 333–63 B.C.E.*

Markus Saur Professor of Old Testament at the University of Bonn, and author of *Einführung in die alttestamentliche Weisheitsliteratur*.

Annette Schellenberg Professor of Old Testament at the University of Vienna, Austria. Her books include *Erkenntnis als Problem: Qohelet und die alttestamentliche Diskussion um das menschlich Erkennen* and *Der Mensch, das Bild Gottes? Zum Gedanken einer Sonderstellung des Menschen im Alten Testament und in weiteren altorientalischen Quellen*.

Jonathan Schofer Associate Professor of Classical and Medieval Rabbinic Judaism in the Department of Religious Studies at the University of Texas at Austin. He is the author of *The Making of a Sage: A Study in Rabbinic Ethics* and *Confronting Vulnerability: The Body and the Divine in Rabbinic Ethics*.

Ludger Schwienhorst-Schönberger Professor of Old Testament Studies at the University of Vienna. His books include *Kohelet* (Herders Theologischer Kommentar) and *Ein Weg durch das Leid: Das Buch Ijob*.

Mark Sneed Professor of Bible at Lubbock Christian University. He is the author of *The Politics of Pessimism in Ecclesiastes: A Social-Science Perspective* and *The Social World of the Sages: An Introduction to Israelite and Jewish Wisdom Literature*.

Susannah Ticciati Reader in Christian Theology at King's College London. She is the author of *Job and the Disruption of Identity: Reading beyond Barth* and *A New Apophaticism: Augustine and the Redemption of Signs*.

Amram Tropper Senior Lecturer in Jewish History at Ben-Gurion University. Among other books, he is the author of *Wisdom, Politics, and Historiography: Tractate Avot in the Context of the Graeco-Roman Near East* and *Rewriting Ancient Jewish History: The History of the Jews in Roman Times and the New Historical Method*.

Raymond C. Van Leeuwen Professor Emeritus of Biblical Studies at Eastern University. He is the author of *Context and Meaning in Proverbs 25–27* and *The Book of Proverbs* in the New Interpreter's Bible Commentary.

Jacqueline Vayntrub Assistant Professor of Hebrew Bible at Yale Divinity School. She is the author of *Beyond Orality: Biblical Poetry on Its Own Terms.*

Nathan Wasserman Professor of Assyriology at the Institute of Archaeology, The Hebrew University of Jerusalem. His books include *Style and Form in Old-Babylonian Literary Texts*; *Akkadian Love Literature of the Third and Second Millennium BCE* and *The Flood: The Akkadian Sources, A New Edition, Commentary, and a Literary Discussion.*

Markus Witte Professor of Old Testament at the Humboldt-Universität zu Berlin. He is the author of, among others books, *Hiobs viele Gesichter* and *The Development of God in the Old Testament.*

Benjamin G. Wright III University Distinguished Professor in Religion Studies at Lehigh University. His books include *The Letter of Aristeas: "Aristeas to Philocrates" or "On the Translation of the Law of the Jews"* and *Praise Israel for Wisdom and Instruction: Essays on Ben Sira and Wisdom, The Letter of Aristeas and the Septuagint.*

U. Isra Yazicioglu Associate Professor of Islamic Studies at St. Joseph's University. She is the author of *Understanding the Qur'anic Miracle Stories in the Modern Age.*

Christine Roy Yoder J. McDowell Richards Professor of Biblical Interpretation at Columbia Theological Seminary. She is the author of *Wisdom as a Woman of Substance: A Socioeconomic Reading of Proverbs 1–9 and 31:10–31* and *Proverbs* (Abingdon Old Testament Commentary Series).

CHAPTER 1

··

WISDOM AND WISDOM LITERATURE

Past, Present, and Future

··

WILL KYNES

"History, if viewed as a repository for more than anecdote or chronology, could produce a decisive transformation in the image of science by which we are now possessed." Thus begins Thomas Kuhn's *The Structure of Scientific Revolutions* (1970, 1). The study of biblical wisdom now appears to be in the midst of one of these "decisive transformations," otherwise known as a "paradigm shift."[1] The title of this chapter, "Wisdom and Wisdom Literature," reflects one of the semantic shifts that Kuhn argues often accompany these transformations. That "and" has long been considered conjunctive, with the interpretation of the biblical conception of wisdom inseparable from that of the genre category, Wisdom Literature. Using genre taxonomically, Wisdom Literature reifies the affinities between a set of texts and then collectively associates them with a distinct tradition, theology, social class, and so forth. For example, when Ben Sira asks God to grant his audience "wisdom of heart to judge his people in righteousness" (45:26), Menahem Kister (2004, 14 n. 6) asks, "Would we have identified 'wisdom' in this verse as identical with that of 'wisdom literature' if we had not known that its author was Ben Sira?" The interchangeable use of wisdom as concept and Wisdom as category suggests the Wisdom tradition encompasses the meaning of biblical wisdom. However, interpreters are increasingly exploring the possibility of treating that "and" as disjunctive, such that the concept, biblical wisdom, *and* the category, Wisdom Literature, are recognized to be distinct; related to one another, certainly, but retaining non-coextensive referents.[2]

---

[1] Though, as a discipline within the humanities, biblical studies can withstand inter-paradigm debate in a way in which the sciences in Kuhn's understanding cannot (see Shedinger 2000), the dynamics he identifies surrounding changes in dominant paradigms may still apply, as Shedinger admits in regard to particularly influential paradigms in biblical studies, such as the Documentary Hypothesis (469).

[2] To reflect this semantic shift, throughout this volume Wisdom Literature and Wisdom are capitalized whenever they refer to the category or anything derived from it ("Wisdom thought," "Wisdom tradition," and so forth) to distinguish them from wisdom as a concept. Some would complain that this convention reifies wisdom. I would argue, however, that it reflects the reification that has already occurred.

Interest in biblical wisdom is high, as recent publishing trends indicate.[3] However, confidence in Wisdom Literature as a scholarly category is low. Questions have begun to be raised with increasing frequency and urgency about issues fundamental to the category's definition and interpretation, including its delimitation, the tradition associated with it, and even its usefulness (see Sneed 2011; Dell 2015; Weeks 2016). One scholar has even attempted to write its obituary (Kynes 2019a). And along with these questions, scare quotes have begun to appear around the term, gripping it in uncertainty. Others have jumped to the category's defense (e.g., Schellenberg 2015), but arguments that ideas are alive and well hardly make a strong case for their vitality. Indeed, the most concerning feature of recent Wisdom scholarship has been the increasing reliance on appeals to an ethereal "general consensus" to support its existence (see Kynes 2019a, 34–59).

This all makes the present a particularly exciting time to study biblical wisdom. The field is in what Kuhn would call a "revolutionary phase," in which old paradigms and long-held assumptions may be questioned and new methods and theories proposed and debated. At the heart of these debates is the relationship between Wisdom Literature and the concept of wisdom itself. How have they been related in the past, how are they approached now, and how should they be related in the future?[4]

1.1 WISDOM AS CONCEPT AND CATEGORY

חכמה (hokhmah), the main Hebrew word for wisdom, refers broadly to "a high-degree of knowledge and skill in any domain," and it appears across the Hebrew Bible in contexts that range from women spinning goats' hair into linen (Exod 35:25–26; cf. Prov 31:24) to God creating the world (Jer 10:12; Prov 3:19) (Fox 2000, 32).[5] Ultimately, "wisdom aims at

---

[3] For example, the previous decade has seen the publication of numerous introductions to Wisdom Literature, including Crenshaw 2010; Weeks 2010; Bartholomew and O'Dowd 2011; Penchansky 2012; Saur 2012; Brown 2014; Sneed 2015a; Curtis 2017; Longman 2017; Phillips 2017; Balentine 2018; McLaughlin 2018.

[4] See Markus Witte's discussion in this volume ("Literary Genres of Old Testament Wisdom") of the fundamental engagement of the process of classification with past, present, and future perspectives on the text, and the problems which arise when people attempt to classify texts that originated in a different cultural milieu.

[5] Referencing texts from the Torah, Former and Latter Prophets, and Writings, Michael Fox (2000, 33) lays out the word's semantic breadth, which includes (a) "skill"; (b) "learning"; (c) "perceptiveness"; (d) "cleverness"; (e) "prudence"; and (f) "sagacity." In this volume, Jonathan Schofer ("Wisdom in Jewish Theology") summarizes Maimonides's similar four-fold understanding of חכמה in the Bible: (1) "the apprehension of true realities"; (2) "acquiring arts"; (3) "acquiring moral virtues"; and (4) "the aptitude for stratagems and ruses." See also U. Isra Yazicioglu's chapter in this volume on "Wisdom in the Qur'an and the Islamic Tradition," in which she presents the five aspects of "wisdom" (hikma) that the early qur'anic exegete Muqatil b. Sulayman sees in the Qur'an, which are more closely associated with divine revelation.

a successful life and proves itself to be a life skill," as Markus Witte puts it in this volume.[6] However, when biblical scholars speak about the purported "Wisdom movement," are they referring to a movement in Israel particularly concerned with this concept of wisdom in all its breadth? If so, its appearance in such a broad range of contexts would indicate a similarly broad movement; one which would encompass devotion to the law, as in Deut 4:6 and Ps 19:7, and practical skill, from yarn spinning (Exod 35:25–26) to bronze working (1 Kgs 7:14) (see Van Leeuwen 2010). Similarly, if Wisdom Literature simply referred to literature interested in the concept wisdom, then why would any text that mentions the word be excluded, particularly 1 Kings 1–11, which uses the word "wisdom" (חכמה and its derivatives) twenty-one times, a higher rate than Job (see Whybray 1974, 91; Lemaire 1995, 106–107)? As it is, however, the movement associated with Wisdom Literature has a narrower focus. Norman Whybray's (1974) attempt to "investigate afresh" the meaning of this term across the Hebrew Bible, for example, only ends up reinforcing its restriction by sapiential assumptions, since he considers all non-intellectual usage of the term as "non-significant" (5, 83; see Van Leeuwen 2010, 418). Even aspects of the so-called Wisdom books, such as Proverbs' connections with the law or Job's revelatory climax are disassociated from it.[7]

Thus, with a semantic sleight of hand, the broader biblical conception of wisdom is swallowed up in a narrower scholarly conception of Wisdom Literature imposed upon it, and the wisdom concept is primarily defined by the traits associated with that collection of texts. For instance, despite the concerns James Crenshaw (1969, 130 n. 4) had earlier raised with precisely this terminological confusion, the closest he comes to defining wisdom as a concept in his influential introduction to Old Testament Wisdom (now in its third edition) is clearly shaped by the Wisdom category's intellectual emphasis. Crenshaw (2010, 4) writes:

> The *reasoned* search for specific ways to ensure personal well-being in everyday life, to *make sense* of extreme adversity and vexing anomalies, and to *transmit* this hard-earned *knowledge* so that successive generations will embody it—wisdom—is universal. Until the second century BCE, biblical wisdom was silent about Abraham or any of the patriarchs, Moses, David, prophets, and priests, indeed anything specific to Israel (emphasis mine).

Thus, as Raymond C. Van Leeuwen observes in this volume, "The concomitant *tendency to equate wisdom with select genres, and to restrict wisdom (mostly) to the Wisdom Literature*, meant that the broader biblical presence of wisdom was largely overlooked" ("Theology: Creation, Wisdom, and Covenant"; emphasis original).

[6] For more on the association between wisdom, skill, and success, particularly as mediated through sapiential instruction, see Jacqueline Vayntrub's chapter in this volume, "Advice: Wisdom, Skill, and Success."

[7] In this volume, for example, Witte claims, "Where cosmological knowledge is traced back to a specific divine revelation, that is to say, where vertical communication exists, such as in Enoch's heavenly journeys (1 En. 17–36), it is not a Wisdom genre that is being dealt with, but a prophetic one, or more precisely, an apocalyptic one." He refers to Job as an "inspired wise man."

1.2 PAST

If we are to comprehend the present or anticipate the future, we must, as Kuhn suggests, understand the past. The current revolutionary phase of Wisdom study offers an opportunity to reconsider where the narrower conception of wisdom that defines Wisdom Literature came from and whether it should be retained. It cannot have come from the purported ancient Near Eastern "Wisdom Literature," since grouping these diverse texts, some of which are similar to Proverbs, others to Ecclesiastes or Job, all together as "Wisdom" *resulted* from the preexisting scholarly consensus on the biblical Wisdom corpus, which was already employed in biblical scholarship before those texts had been discovered in the late nineteenth century.[8] This narrower conception is not evidenced amongst early Jewish and Christian interpreters either, since they never exclusively group Proverbs, Job, and Ecclesiastes together or associate them with a distinct conception of wisdom. Instead, they group different texts together for different reasons. This makes these earlier groupings not merely quantitatively but also qualitatively different than the modern Wisdom category.[9]

For example, the Solomonic collection, particularly when Sirach and Wisdom of Solomon are included, may have "emerged as a way to rationalize the affinities readers could discern throughout this 'Solomonic' corpus," as Matthew Goff claims in this volume ("The Pursuit of Wisdom at Qumran"), but that only makes it more significant that the modern Wisdom category excludes one member of that original corpus, Song of Songs, and includes another, Job, not attributed to Solomon.[10] Clearly, Wisdom Literature is an attempt to rationalize different affinities.[11]

When ancient readers employ a narrower conception of wisdom, it also differs from the one used within modern biblical scholarship. Origen, for example, envisions the three Solomonic books as a precursor to Greek philosophy. But he claims this curriculum in "divine philosophy" culminates in the Song of Songs, which "instils into the soul the love of things divine and heavenly," leading "the seeker after wisdom" to "reach out for the things unseen and eternal" (trans. Lawson 1957, 41).[12] The wisdom Origen has in mind is not the practical, humanistic wisdom of the contemporary category.

---

[8] This point has been made by those studying both Egyptian (Williams 1981, 1; Lichtheim 1996, 261) and Mesopotamian (Lambert 1960, 1; Beaulieu 2007, 3) texts. In this volume, Joachim Friedrich Quack raises similar concerns ("Wisdom in Egypt"), while Yoram Cohen and Nathan Wasserman acknowledge that Wisdom is not an emic genre in Mesopotamian literature, but argue for its interpretive value nonetheless ("Mesopotamian Wisdom Literature").

[9] For further documentation of these differences, see Kynes 2019a, 60–81.

[10] For the interpretive implications of the Solomonic corpus, see Katharine J. Dell's chapter in this volume, "Solomon and the Solomonic Collection."

[11] The same can be said for Ephraim Chambers's *Cyclopedia* (1728), which includes Song of Songs and Psalms along with Proverbs, Ecclesiastes, and Job in its "sapiential" category, while acknowledging that Job is at the time also placed in the category of Historical Books.

[12] See Michael C. Legaspi's chapter in this volume, "Wisdom in Dialogue with Greek Civilization."

Similarly, in Berakhot 57b the rabbis associate various texts with a repeated series of different concepts. In the Sifre Emet, Psalms is connected with piety, Proverbs with wisdom, and Job with calamity, while, in the Megilloth, Song of Songs is linked with piety, Ecclesiastes with wisdom, and Lamentations with calamity. The association of both Proverbs and Ecclesiastes with wisdom might suggest a Wisdom category that cuts across these sub-collections, though it would again exclude Job, which, by that logic, would join Lamentations in a Calamity collection. Further, this text also associates Ezekiel with wisdom, which again implies a different understanding of wisdom from that which pervades modern scholarship.[13]

In fact, in many cases, the use of wisdom as a concept in early Jewish and Christian interpretation is even broader than the meaning of חכמה in the Hebrew Bible. As Van Leeuwen observes in this volume, by referring to the Hebrew scriptures' collective ability to "make one wise" (σοφίσαι), 2 Tim 3:15–17 "implies that the entire Old Testament is wise," a view which Augustine and the Western Church would extend to the entire Bible (*De doc. Chr.* 4.5.7). The prologue of Sirach also implicitly refers to the entire canon as "pertaining to instruction and wisdom," since, after reading "the Law and the Prophets and the other books of our ancestors," the prologue says Ben Sira "was himself *also* led to write something pertaining to instruction and wisdom." Further, the rabbinic sages' designation as "the wise" would suggest, as Amram Tropper writes in this volume ("Wisdom in Rabbinic Interpretation"), that their entire output, "including law, midrash, mysticism, theology, magic, medicine, literary narrative and dream-interpretation" could be considered "Wisdom Literature." He argues that "this sweeping range of rabbinic interests implies an understanding of wisdom far broader than the range of conceptions of wisdom found in pre-rabbinic sources,"[14] though one might also conclude that the range of conceptions of wisdom in those earlier sources is broader than we tend to recognize.[15]

However, Ben Sira also provides a narrower view of wisdom by associating it with the Torah (Sir 24:23). Rabbinic sources, such as Leviticus Rabbah, repeatedly treat wisdom as identical with Torah, as well (Fischel 1975, 70).[16] Christian interpreters likewise offer a narrower understanding of wisdom that similarly identifies it with the focal point of their piety,

---

[13] Earlier in the text, the rabbis also associate Solomon with wisdom, but, since they connect Song of Songs with piety (with which David is also associated) and not wisdom, they do not appear to be using Solomonic authorship as an incipient Wisdom classification as some have suggested.

[14] Consistent with the conception of wisdom they apply to their own work, the rabbis at times employ a broader definition of wisdom for classifying texts that incorporates far more books, potentially the Writings as a whole (see y. Mak. 2:4–8; Yalqut Shimeoni Tehillim 702) and perhaps even the entire canon (see, e.g., the Hekhalot literature discussed in Stemberger 2008, 318–319).

[15] Günter Stemberger (2008, 319) similarly claims, "Wisdom literature in the rabbinic world is no longer what it used to be in biblical and Second Temple times. It is no longer a clearly distinguished separate literary genre with a well defined agenda." However, as the Wisdom genre is increasingly considered less clearly distinguished and separate and its agenda less well-defined even within biblical and Second Temple times, the rabbinic view appears to be in closer keeping with its more ancient precedents.

[16] See Tropper's chapter, "Wisdom in Rabbinic Interpretation," in this volume.

Christ, who is spoken of as the wisdom of God in 1 Cor 1:24, 30, and in whom Col 2:3 claims "all the treasures of wisdom and knowledge" are hidden.[17] In this volume, Susannah Ticciati discusses the continued association of wisdom with Christ in Patristic interpretation.

These early Jewish and Christian interpretations may appear to be hopelessly anachronistic impositions of the traits these interpreters most prized onto biblical wisdom. And yet, the scholarly characterization of biblical wisdom that arises in the mid-nineteenth century is hardly immune from the same charge. Franz Delitzsch (1866 [1864], 1:5) characterized Wisdom Literature at the time as the "universalistic, humani[sti]c, philosophical" collection within the Old Testament, independent of Israel's particularistic theocracy, cult, and law. He adopted the category from Johann Bruch, whom he acknowledged was "the first to call special attention to the *Chokma* or humanism as a peculiar intellectual tendency in Israel" in his book *Weisheits-Lehre der Hebräer: Ein Beitrag zur Geschichte der Philosophie* (*Wisdom Teaching of the Hebrews: A Contribution to the History of Philosophy*) published in 1851. However, Delitzsch (1874–1875 [1873], 1:46) had concerns with Bruch's placement of Wisdom "in an indifferent and even hostile relation to the national law and the national cultus [of Israel], which he compares to the relation of Christian philosophy to orthodox theology." As Bruch (1851, ix–x), whose previous work (1839) had focused on Christian philosophy, himself put it, the "wise" in Israel "found no satisfaction in the religious institutions of their nation" and "therefore sought other ways—namely, the way of free thinking—to gain answers about the questions that moved them and to seek their spirit's rest."

This characterization of Wisdom Literature has endured since. Mark Sneed, in this volume ("The Social Setting of Wisdom Literature"), recognizes an enduring "myopic" tendency to view the "wise" as "some idiosyncratic group that was not interested in prophetic literature or the Torah and its commandments or the priestly material." Wisdom Literature continues to be associated with modern values, such as humanism, individualism, universalism, secularism, and empiricism rather than concepts central to Israelite religion (see Miller 2015, 91–93).[18] As Roland Murphy (2002, 1) has observed, the "most striking characteristic" uniting the Wisdom Literature still remains "the absence of what one normally considers as typically Israelite and Jewish."

Michael Fox (2000, 29–30) quotes Eugene Rice's (1958, 2) observation that the concept of wisdom has been "transformed by the changing needs and aspirations of successive epochs, centuries, and even generations," consistently conformed to "the highest knowledge men were capable of and the most desirable patterns of human behavior" and, therefore, "mirrored man's conception of himself, of the world, and of God." Thus, for Jews, wisdom is Torah, while for Christians, it is Christ; "Each community tended to 'decode' canonical wisdom according to their respective commitments" (Berry 1995, 63), what they believed would produce a "successful life," as Witte put it above. Even biblical interpreters, as John Collins (1994, 2) notes, have demonstrated a tendency to apply the

[17] See Mariam Kamell Kovalishyn's chapter, "Wisdom in the New Testament," in this volume.
[18] In this volume ("Theology of Wisdom"), Tremper Longman III challenges the universalistic and cosmopolitan characterizations of the theology of Wisdom Literature that descend from Bruch's work.

"Wisdom" label to "[a]ny form of knowledge that is recognized as good." Unsurprisingly, then, Wisdom Literature, as James Crenshaw (1976, 3) writes, "has stood largely as a mirror image of the scholar painting her portrait."

1.3 PRESENT

As the history of interpretation demonstrates, interpreters' cultural locations inevitably affect how they understand the concept of wisdom and therefore which texts they associate with it. As Witte observes in this volume, "Classifications, even those that are fundamentally timeless, are contingent upon culture and period." Or, as Elisabeth Schüssler Fiorenza (1988, 5) writes, "What we see depends on where we stand." The question now facing interpreters is how to proceed once the subjective nature of their interpretation of wisdom, both as concept and genre category, is acknowledged. In the fragmented and uncertain present state of Wisdom study, three primary approaches are emerging.[19]

1.3.1 The Traditional View

The first, traditional view maintains the understanding of wisdom and Wisdom Literature that reached "general consensus" status during the twentieth century. As Crenshaw (1969, 132) argues, this view orients the definition of biblical wisdom to the accepted Wisdom books. In this volume, Goff makes a more nuanced (and less circular) defense of the traditional category that draws on more recent genre theory that sees genres as "multivocal, fluid, and relational." He argues that, though the Wisdom category is etic and constructed, and therefore "fragile," it provides pragmatic benefit for highlighting significant affinities between texts. He writes, "If one analyzes Proverbs, Job, and Ecclesiastes without classifying them as Wisdom texts, it would still be clear that these three texts have more similarities, despite their extensive differences, with each other than with other books of the Hebrew Bible."

1.3.2 Pan-Sapientialism

Crenshaw feels the need to restrict wisdom to the Wisdom books because a second tendency to expand the category across the canon has long accompanied Wisdom interpretation. This approach began with a proliferation of studies of Wisdom "influence"

---

[19] In his chapter, "The Pervasiveness of Wisdom in (Con)texts," in this volume, John Ahn also sees three approaches emerging, though he characterizes them as the traditional view, the elimination of the category, and an intermediary view that draws on newer approaches while maintaining the traditional view.

in various texts ranging from Genesis to Esther in the mid-twentieth century and has now progressed to a pan-sapiential extreme, in which the whole canon and the heart of the Israelite worldview are associated with the Wisdom movement.[20] This is not mere hyperbole. In *The Philosophy of Hebrew Scripture* (2012, 284–285 n. 26), Yoram Hazony "look[s] forward to a time when most of the Hebrew Bible, if not all of it, will be recognized as 'wisdom literature.'"[21] This recent pan-sapientialism differs in a subtle yet significant way from earlier Jewish and Christian views that the entire canon communicates divinely inspired wisdom, since the wisdom associated with Wisdom Literature is instead rationalistic, humanistic, secular, and philosophical. This is precisely the attraction of pan-sapientialism for Hazony (2012, 284–285 n. 26), who claims texts across the canon "were composed largely in an effort to attain and inculcate worldly wisdom." The language of "Wisdom influence" is particularly telling in this regard. It is the "Wisdom" movement that is said to "influence" texts across the canon while the influence of texts across the canon on the Wisdom Literature is a priori excluded by the defining features of the category as independent of Israel's law, history, and cult.

1.3.3 Sapiential Minimalism

On the opposite extreme, a third approach, which Goff christens "sapiential minimalism" in this volume, questions fundamental features of current Wisdom study and even rejects the category entirely. Concerns about Wisdom Literature have long remained an undercurrent, consistently raised by those, like Delitzsch or Gerhard von Rad, who nevertheless continued to work with the traditional category.[22] However, Stuart Weeks has led the charge in asking more uncomfortable questions, beginning with his book, *Early Israelite Wisdom* (1994), which challenges many of the assumptions surrounding a purported class of "wise men" participating in an international "Wisdom movement." Sneed's article "Is The 'Wisdom Tradition' a Tradition?" (2011) struck a nerve a few years ago, inspiring a session devoted to considering Wisdom's future in the Wisdom in Israel and Cognate Traditions section of the Society of Biblical Literature in 2012 and then the

---

[20] In this volume ("Wisdom Influence"), John L. McLaughlin worries that the many proposals for Wisdom influence put both the distinctive character of Wisdom Literature and the broader analysis of biblical literature in jeopardy, since "if everything is 'Wisdom,' then not only does Wisdom no longer constitute an identifiable body of biblical literature, neither does history, prophecy, etc." See also Crenshaw 2010, 34.

[21] Similarly, J. de Waal Dryden (2018, 261) argues, "The whole of the Hebrew Bible can fit under the umbrella of wisdom," with "all biblical genres as sub-genres of wisdom," and defends a pan-sapiential approach as hermeneutically fruitful for opening up new intertextual readings. Unlike Hazony, Dryden appears to be advocating a return to something closer to the early Christian view of the entire Bible as wisdom, though he defends the modern Wisdom Literature category without acknowledging the presuppositional baggage it brings with it.

[22] Von Rad (1972 [1970], 7–8) questioned whether, as an invention of the scholarly world, the Wisdom category could be "dangerously prejudicing the interpretation of varied material" and has, therefore, "been more of a hindrance than a help."

collected volume *Was There a Wisdom Tradition? New Prospects in Israelite Wisdom Studies* (Sneed 2015b).

Goff's nuanced traditional view and the "minimalist" approach I have developed by building on the work of Weeks and Sneed are not actually that far apart, however (see Kynes 2019a). I agree with Goff that "classification is a core and basic act of the human mind" that "should be acknowledged rather than dismissed," but, precisely for that reason, I would prefer to multiply the genres in which we read each so-called Wisdom text rather than restrict them to this single, fixed, and modernly imposed classification. The Wisdom category may indeed highlight the affinities between texts that Goff identifies, but given the pragmatic value Goff sees in this genre for highlighting those affinities, why not pursue other genres that illuminate other affinities those texts may have with other texts, such as those between Job and Psalms or Proverbs and 1 Kings?[23] The problem, in my view, is not grouping certain texts around a particular interest in wisdom or instruction; it is not even interpreting texts according to modern understandings of wisdom. The problem is projecting a post-Enlightenment conception of wisdom onto a group of biblical texts or even the entire canon without acknowledging it—concealing anachronism in circularly supported historical conjectures about a purported Wisdom movement—and thereby restricting interpretation of biblical wisdom to modern views of what is good.[24]

1.4 FUTURE

Proceeding from this revolutionary phase, Wisdom study would profit in the future from incorporating more readings, first, from before "Wisdom Literature" was developed, and second, from beyond the category's Western cultural context. Rather than restricting the interpretation of these ancient texts to a nineteenth-century conception of wisdom, the approaches of readers before the Wisdom category developed could provide new, ancient insight into the meaning of both the wisdom concept and the texts associated with it. Perhaps their perspectives on the texts—though self-interested like those of modern readers—enabled them to see things that those ostensibly objective interpreters missed or attempted to explain away. Thus, in this volume, after setting aside "the post-Enlightenment presuppositions projected onto the category of

[23] See Kynes 2012, 2019b. For more examples of connections between the three books associated with Wisdom and other texts across the canon and beyond, see Dell and Kynes 2013, 2014, 2019.

[24] It should be acknowledged that restricting the study of wisdom to "biblical" wisdom also imposes an anachronistic category on the texts, since the canon developed after the texts that it includes (see Bowley and Reeves 2003). Some restriction is inevitable to focus the object of study. As a contribution to biblical scholarship, this volume is designed to elucidate the meaning of the concept of wisdom primarily in the texts that came to be known as the Hebrew Bible/Old Testament, with special attention to those texts that have been most closely associated with that concept in that discipline. However, its design also resists restricting the understanding of wisdom exclusively to that corpus by including chapters on wisdom in related ancient and modern cultures and their texts (which is in keeping with Bowley and Reeves's understanding of a more heuristically valuable use of "biblical" in the field [14]).

'Wisdom Literature,'" Jonathan P. Burnside ("Law and Wisdom Literature") comes to a similar conclusion as many early interpreters: Law and Wisdom are complementary, not dichotomous. This is a conclusion with which early interpreters would agree, such as those who interpreted Ecclesiastes in relation to the law during the canonization process (e.g., Targum of Ecclesiastes 1:3; cf. Dell 2013, 23), or attributed Job, with its connections to texts across the Torah, to Moses (b. Baba Batra 15a). In fact, Maimonides follows the Talmudic sages in seeing wisdom as a "verification" of the Torah.[25]

The interpretation of Wisdom should also go beyond Western perspectives. Biblical scholarship has recently begun to appreciate the contributions of various contextual approaches to the text. As Brian Blount (2019, 14) recently argued, differing contextual perspectives allow readers to perceive different aspects of the text's "meaning potential." For this reason, this volume includes essays that consider the concept of wisdom from a variety of contexts, both historical and ideological. For instance, in his chapter on "The Pervasiveness of Wisdom in (Con)texts" in this volume, John Ahn interprets the Wisdom books from an Asian context, which highlights, among other things, how Job, like the Buddha, is tempted by an adversary. This feature is absent from all extant comparable so-called ancient Near Eastern Wisdom texts and minimized in Wisdom interpretation.[26]

1.5 CONCLUSION

This reception-oriented approach is not a flight from the text's original historical meaning or the investigation of the world behind it. Instead, after acknowledging the subjectivity of even critical attempts at objectivity, it multiplies subjective perspectives in order to pursue a more objective perception of that historical meaning between them.[27] For example, research into how ancient Near Eastern scribal practices may illuminate the so-called Wisdom texts will be distorted if it perceives scribal practice exclusively through a modern lens, which reflexively disassociates wisdom from ritual and revelation. In fact, as Sneed argues in this volume, the evidence points not to Wisdom specialists but to scribal curricula in which "Wisdom Literature was integrated with other genres, like erotica, hymns, model letters, etc." Yoram Cohen and Nathan Wasserman similarly acknowledge in this volume ("Mesopotamian Wisdom Literature") that the Mesopotamian concept of wisdom is often associated with divinely revealed knowledge and religious ritual (see, e.g., The Scholars of Uruk, Hear the Advice). This, they say, "broadens for us the significance of the concept of wisdom in Mesopotamian thought."

[25] See Schofer's chapter, "Wisdom in Jewish Theology," in this volume.
[26] For similar contextual approaches, see also Hancock 2019; Masenya and Olojede 2019.
[27] Blount (2019, 12 n. 24) quotes Paul Ricoeur's (1976, 77) comparison of a text to a three-dimensional object "which may be viewed from several sides, but never from all sides at once," and therefore concludes that "the reconstruction of the whole has a perspectival aspect similar to that of a perceived object." For a similar multiperspectival approach, see Kynes 2019a, 107–145, esp. 139–141.

This broader understanding of wisdom will also provide greater relevance for wisdom in the world in front of the text. As von Rad (2001 [1957–1960], 1:428) argues, "Any sound discussion of Israel's wisdom means taking the concept as broadly as it was indeed taken." He laments that wisdom, which "has to do with the whole of life and had to be occupied with all its departments," has been "thought of more or less as the product of an exclusive theological school." Looking before and beyond the Wisdom Literature category underscores that each text it includes is more than a Wisdom book, and that biblical wisdom "has to do with the whole of life," not merely the life of the mind.

The relationship between wisdom and the Bible, which this volume explores, is more complex than common conceptions of the Wisdom category allow. In the past, discussion of the concept of wisdom in the Bible has tended to be classified as a species of the genus Wisdom Literature, with appearance of the concept elsewhere characterized as "Wisdom influence." Thus, handbooks that discuss wisdom in the Bible generally focus on the Wisdom category and have "Wisdom Literature" in their titles.[28] But the structure and title of this volume is intended to communicate that that need not be the case and raise the possibility that this taxonomy should be reversed, if it is persevered at all. The volume is designed both to reflect on the contested nature of the Wisdom Literature category and to take advantage of the opportunities this presents for reconsidering the concept of wisdom more independently from it. Therefore, the first half of the volume is devoted to wisdom as a concept, with essays on its relationship to advice, epistemology, virtue, theology, and order in the Hebrew Bible, its meaning in related cultures, from Egypt and Mesopotamia to Patristic and Rabbinic interpretation, and, finally, in the modern world, including in Islamic, Jewish, and Christian thought, and from feminist, environmental, and other contextual perspectives. The latter half of the Handbook then considers "Wisdom Literature" as a category. Scholars address its relation to the Solomonic Collection, its social setting, literary genres, chronological development, and theology. The category's relation to other biblical literature (law, history, prophecy, apocalyptic, and the broad question of "Wisdom influence") is then discussed before a series of essays address the texts commonly associated with Wisdom Literature. Though the volume's structure gives contributors in the first half devoted to wisdom as a concept the freedom to explore its meaning unfettered by the category's constraints, they embrace this freedom to varying degrees. Some remain within the traditional textual confines of Proverbs, Ecclesiastes, and Job (along with Sirach and Wisdom of Solomon), while others pursue the concept more broadly across the canon. On the other hand, in the latter half of the volume devoted to the category, some emphasize the category's limitations and even question its validity, while others staunchly defend its heuristic value. This reflects well the Kuhnian "revolutionary phase" in which the field now finds itself. The current paradigm can no longer simply be assumed, but a new one has not emerged to claim widespread approval. Though the organization of the volume highlights the independence of wisdom as concept from "Wisdom Literature" as category, seeking

---

[28] E.g., *Wiley Blackwell Companion to Wisdom Literature* (Adams and Goff 2020); *The Cambridge Companion to the Biblical Wisdom Literature* (Dell forthcoming).

to reverse the lack of attention given to this question in the traditional approach, their inclusion together in the same volume reflects their continued interconnection. Time will tell what the future holds for this relationship.

WORKS CITED

Adams, Samuel L., and Matthew Goff, eds. 2020. *Wiley Blackwell Companion to Wisdom Literature*. Hoboken, NJ: Wiley Blackwell.

Balentine, Samuel E. 2018. *Wisdom Literature*. Core Biblical Studies. Nashville, TN: Abingdon.

Bartholomew, Craig G., and Ryan O'Dowd. 2011. *Old Testament Wisdom Literature: A Theological Introduction*. Downers Grove, IL: IVP Academic.

Beaulieu, Paul-Alain. 2007. "The Social and Intellectual Setting of Babylonian Wisdom Literature." Pages 3–19 in *Wisdom Literature in Mesopotamia and Israel*. Edited by Richard J. Clifford. Atlanta, GA: SBL.

Berry, Donald K. 1995. *An Introduction to Wisdom and Poetry of the Old Testament*. Nashville, TN: Broadman & Holman.

Blount, Brian K. 2019. "The Souls of Biblical Folks and the Potential for Meaning." *JBL* 138:6–21.

Bowley, James E., and John C. Reeves. 2003. "Rethinking the Concept of 'Bible': Some Theses and Proposals." *Henoch* 25:3–18.

Brown, William P. 2014. *Wisdom's Wonder: Character, Creation, and Crisis in the Bible's Wisdom Literature*. Grand Rapids, MI: Eerdmans.

Bruch, Johann Friedrich. 1839. *Études philosophiques sur le christianisme*. Paris: Pitois-Levrault.

Bruch, Johann Friedrich. 1851. *Weisheits-Lehre der Hebräer: Ein Beitrag zur Geschichte der Philosophie*. Strasbourg: Treuttel & Würtz.

Chambers, Ephraim. 1728. "Sapiential" in vol. 2 of *Cyclopædia: Or, an Universal Dictionary of Arts and Sciences*. London: printed for James and John Knapton et al.

Collins, John J. 1994. "Response to George Nickelsburg." Paper presented at the annual meeting of the Society of Biblical Literature. Chicago, IL. November 21.

Crenshaw, James L. 1969. "Method in Determining Wisdom Influence upon 'Historical' Literature." *JBL* 88:129–142.

Crenshaw, James L. 1976. "Prolegomenon." Pages 1–60 in *Studies in Ancient Israelite Wisdom*. Edited by James L. Crenshaw. The Library of Biblical Studies. New York, NY: Ktav.

Crenshaw, James L. 2010. *Old Testament Wisdom: An Introduction*. 3rd ed. Louisville, KY: Westminster John Knox.

Curtis, Edward. 2017. *Interpreting the Wisdom Books*. Grand Rapids, MI: Kregel Academic.

Delitzsch, Franz. 1874–1875. *Biblical Commentary on the Proverbs of Solomon*. 2 vols. Translated by M.G. Easton. CFThL 43, 47. Edinburgh: T&T Clark. Original edition: *Salomonisches Spruchbuch*. Leipzig: Dörffling & Franke, 1873.

Delitzsch, Franz. 1866. *Biblical Commentary on the Book of Job*. 2 vols. Translated by Francis Bolton. CFThL 10–11. Edinburgh: T&T Clark. Original edition: *Das Buch Iob*. Leipzig, Dörffling und Franke, 1864.

Dell, Katharine, and Will Kynes, eds. 2013. *Reading Job Intertextually*. LHBOTS 574. New York, NY: Bloomsbury T&T Clark.

Dell, Katharine, and Will Kynes, eds. 2014. *Reading Ecclesiastes Intertextually*. LHBOTS 587. London: Bloomsbury T&T Clark.

Dell, Katharine, and Will Kynes, eds. 2019. *Reading Proverbs Intertextually*. LHBOTS 629. Londan: Bloomsbury T&T Clark.

Dell, Katharine J. 2013. *Interpreting Ecclesiastes: Readers Old and New.* Winona Lake, IN: Eisenbrauns.

Dell, Katharine J. 2015. "Deciding the Boundaries of 'Wisdom': Applying the Concept of Family Resemblance." Pages 145–160 in Sneed 2015b.

Dell, Katharine J., ed. Forthcoming. *The Cambridge Companion to the Biblical Wisdom Literature.* Cambridge: Cambridge University Press.

Dryden, J. de Waal. 2018. *A Hermeneutic of Wisdom: Recovering the Formative Agency of Scripture.* Grand Rapids, MI: Baker Academic.

Fischel, Henry Albert. 1975. "The Transformation of Wisdom in the World of Midrash." Pages 67–101 in vol. 1 of *Aspects of Wisdom in Judaism and Early Christianity.* Edited by Robert L. Wilken. Studies in Judaism and Christianity in Antiquity. Notre Dame, IN: University of Notre Dame.

Fox, Michael V. 2000. *Proverbs 1–9.* AB 18A. New York, NY: Doubleday.

Hancock, Christopher D. 2019. "Proverbs and the Confucian Classics." Pages 203–216 in Dell and Kynes 2019.

Hazony, Yoram. 2012. *The Philosophy of Hebrew Scripture.* New York, NY: Cambridge University Press.

Kister, Menahem. 2004. "Wisdom Literature and Its Relation to Other Genres: From Ben Sira to Mysteries." Pages 13–47 in *Sapiential Perspectives: Wisdom Literature in Light of the Dead Sea Scrolls.* Edited by John J. Collins, Gregory E. Sterling, and Ruth A. Clements. STDJ 51. Leiden: Brill.

Kuhn, Thomas S. 1970. *The Structure of Scientific Revolutions.* 2nd ed. Chicago, IL: University of Chicago Press.

Kynes, Will. 2012. *My Psalm Has Turned into Weeping: Job's Dialogue with the Psalms.* BZAW 437. Berlin: de Gruyter.

Kynes, Will. 2019a. *An Obituary for "Wisdom Literature": The Birth, Death, and Intertextual Reintegration of a Biblical Corpus.* Oxford: Oxford University Press.

Kynes, Will. 2019b. "Wisdom Defined through Narrative and Intertextual Network: 1 Kings 1–11 and Proverbs." Pages 35–47 in Dell and Kynes 2019.

Lambert, W.G. 1960. *Babylonian Wisdom Literature.* Oxford: Clarendon Press.

Lawson, R.P. 1957. *Origen: The Song of Songs: Commentary and Homilies.* ACW 26. Westminster, MD: Newman Press.

Lemaire, André. 1995. "Wisdom in Solomonic Historiography." Pages 106–118 in *Wisdom in Ancient Israel: Essays in Honour of J.A. Emerton.* Edited by John Day, Robert P. Gordon, and H.G.M. Williamson. Cambridge: Cambridge University Press.

Lichtheim, Miriam. 1996. "Didactic Literature." Pages 243–262 in *Ancient Egyptian Literature: History and Forms.* PAe 10. Edited by Antonio Loprieno. Leiden: Brill.

Longman, Tremper, III. 2017. *The Fear of the Lord Is Wisdom: A Theological Introduction to Wisdom in Israel.* Grand Rapids, MI: Baker Academic.

Masenya, Madipoane, and Funlola Olojede. 2019. "Sex and Power(lessness) in Selected Northern Sotho and Yorùbá Proverbs: An Intertextual Reading of Proverbs 5–7." Pages 217–230 in Dell and Kynes 2019.

McLaughlin, John L. 2018. *An Introduction to Israel's Wisdom Traditions.* Grand Rapids, MI: Eerdmans.

Miller, Douglas B. 2015. "Wisdom in the Canon: Discerning the Early Intuition." Pages 87–113 in Sneed 2015b.

Murphy, Roland E. 2002. *The Tree of Life: An Exploration of Biblical Wisdom Literature.* 3rd ed. Grand Rapids, MI: Eerdmans.

Penchansky, David. 2012. *Understanding Wisdom Literature: Conflict and Dissonance in the Hebrew Text*. Grand Rapids, MI: Eerdmans.

Phillips, Elaine A. 2017. *An Introduction to Reading Biblical Wisdom Texts*. Peabody, MA: Hendrickson.

Rad, Gerhard von. 1972. *Wisdom in Israel*. Translated by James D. Martin. Harrisburg, PA: Trinity Press International. Original edition: *Weisheit in Israel*. Neukirchen-Vluyn: Neukirchener Verlag, 1970.

Rad, Gerhard von. 2001. *Old Testament Theology*. 2 vols. OTL. Louisville, KY: Westminster John Knox. Original edition: *Theologie des Alten Testaments*. Munich: C. Kaiser, 1957–1960.

Rice, Eugene, Jr. 1958. *The Renaissance Idea of Wisdom*. Cambridge, MA: Harvard University Press.

Ricoeur, Paul. 1976. *Interpretation Theory: Discourse and the Surplus of Meaning*. Fort Worth, TX: Texas Christian University Press.

Saur, Markus. 2012. *Einführung in die alttestamentliche Weisheitsliteratur*. Darmstadt: WBG.

Schellenberg, Annette. 2015. "Don't Throw the Baby Out with the Bathwater: On the Distinctness of the Sapiential Understanding of the World." Pages 115–143 in Sneed 2015b.

Schüssler Fiorenza, Elisabeth. 1988. "The Ethics of Biblical Interpretation: Decentering Biblical Scholarship." *JBL* 107:3–17.

Shedinger, Robert F. 2000. "Kuhnian Paradigms and Biblical Scholarship: Is Biblical Studies a Science?" *JBL* 119:453–471.

Sneed, Mark. 2011. "Is the 'Wisdom Tradition' a Tradition?" *CBQ* 73:50–71.

Sneed, Mark. 2015a. *The Social World of the Sages: An Introduction to Israelite and Jewish Wisdom Literature*. Minneapolis, MN: Fortress.

Sneed, Mark, ed. 2015b. *Was There a Wisdom Tradition? New Prospects in Israelite Wisdom Studies*. AIL 23. Atlanta, GA: SBL.

Stemberger, Günter. 2008. "Sages, Scribes, and Seers in Rabbinic Judaism." Pages 295–319 in *Scribes, Sages, and Seers: The Sage in the Eastern Mediterranean World*. FRLANT 219. Edited by Leo G. Perdue. Göttingen: Vandenhoeck & Ruprecht.

Van Leeuwen, Raymond C. 2010. "Cosmos, Temple, House: Building and Wisdom in Ancient Mesopotamia and Israel." Pages 399–421 in *From the Foundations to the Crenellations: Essays on Temple Building in the Ancient Near East and Hebrew Bible*. AOAT 366. Edited by Mark J. Boda and Jamie Novotny. Münster: Ugarit-Verlag.

Weeks, Stuart. 1994. *Early Israelite Wisdom*. Oxford Theological Monographs. Oxford: Oxford University Press.

Weeks, Stuart. 2010. *An Introduction to the Study of Wisdom Literature*. New York, NY: T&T Clark.

Weeks, Stuart. 2016. "Is 'Wisdom Literature' a Useful Category?" Pages 3–23 in *Tracing Sapiential Traditions in Ancient Judaism*. Edited by Hindy Najman, Jean-Sébastien Rey, and Eibert J.C. Tigchelaar. JSJSup 174. Leiden: Brill.

Whybray, R.N. 1974. *The Intellectual Tradition in the Old Testament*. Berlin: de Gruyter.

Williams, Ronald J. 1981. "The Sages of Ancient Egypt in the Light of Recent Scholarship." *JAOS* 101:1–19.

PART I

THE CONCEPT OF WISDOM IN THE HEBREW BIBLE

CHAPTER 2

....

ADVICE

Wisdom, Skill, and Success

....

JACQUELINE VAYNTRUB

How should we understand biblical Wisdom Literature, and what makes these texts different than other types of text encountered in the biblical literary tradition? In the following, we will examine: (1) how the scholarly category of biblical Wisdom Literature entails a developmental model of literary development in which the book of Proverbs functions as a paradigmatic text; (2) two salient aspects of this category (vocabulary and genre) and the circular reasoning involved in evaluating texts accordingly; and (3) other literary strategies shared by these texts, including notions of knowledge, its transmission, and survival across generational lines. Beyond a developmental model, a broad category of knowledge production and literary craft help us draw comparisons between texts like Proverbs, Ecclesiastes, Job, Ben Sira, and others. In a variety of ways, these texts build and comment on the ancient Near Eastern literary and social institution of father-to-son instruction. As a literary representation of inter-generational dynamics, the instruction functions as a medium, imparting a blueprint for successful living, in which one generation can assure the survival of the next. In doing so, the advice given in these instructions, and their framing themselves, reflect on the transmission of life-preserving and life-enriching knowledge across generational lines that enable the father to transcend his own individual death and persist in the success of his descendants.

2.1 WISDOM AND CANON

....

One important answer to the question of how to understand biblical Literature is that the distinction of certain texts—Proverbs, Ecclesiastes, Job, perhaps others still, depending on the canon within which one works and the generic limitations imposed—lies with the modern reader, who has inherited an anachronistic category of "Wisdom." A number of scholars have recently shown how "Wisdom Literature" is not a native category but rather a scholarly construct with a deep history. Through this lens, we stand to learn much about both the ancient and modern reception of these texts and how this scholarly category shapes our readings of them.

The Proverbs, Ecclesiastes, Job grouping is reinforced by the Septuagint order of texts, though there the Wisdom corpus includes Song of Songs. This grouping corresponds to the description of Solomon in 1 Kgs 5:9–14 [ET 4:29–34] as the great performer of שיר (shir, "song") and משל (mashal, "proverb"). Unlike the Septuagint, this grouping of texts is not found in the Writings of the Masoretic Text. Instead, we find the grouping of Psalms, Job, and Proverbs (כתבי תא״ס), which has a distinct accent and cantillation system, and the five scrolls-grouping of Song of Songs, Ruth, Lamentations, Qoheleth (Ecclesiastes), and Esther. In the Babylonian Talmud (Baba Batra 14b), the order of biblical texts in the Writings is given as follows: Ruth, Psalms, Job, Proverbs, Qoheleth, Song of Songs, Lamentations, Daniel, Esther, Ezra, and Chronicles. There, Isaiah, Proverbs, Song of Songs, and Qoheleth are grouped together as works written by "Hezekiah and his colleagues," recalling also the ascription on Prov 25:1—presumably here "writing" is not understood as authorship. Elsewhere the grouping of Proverbs, Qoheleth, and Song of Songs is understood by their Solomonic attribution—including Qoheleth, whose Solomonic character is implied by the speaker but never explicitly stated. "Wisdom" as σοφία in Greek is, however, part of the title of two deuterocanonical works: Wisdom of Solomon and Wisdom of Jesus [son of] Sirach (Ben Sira). This designation appears to be part of the ancient reception of these works and their correspondence to a type of wisdom discourse.

A helpful way to understand how Wisdom functions as a scholarly category is to see how scholarship uses this framework to thematize various biblical texts under the broad rubric of Wisdom Literature. In particular, it can be illuminating to examine the assumptions of this scholarly category in texts beyond Proverbs, Ecclesiastes, and Job. In the Anchor Bible commentary on Ben Sira, Alexander Di Lella (Di Lella and Skehan 1987, 23, 32) explains that Wisdom Literature can be characterized as either pretheoretical ("recipe wisdom") or theoretical ("existential").[1] Pretheoretical wisdom, which is exemplified by the book of Proverbs, gives basic advice for everyday living, while theoretical wisdom considers the nature of life and its meaning, a category purportedly typified by Job and Ecclesiastes. In this view of the biblical texts, Proverbs is paradigmatic of basic wisdom, while Ecclesiastes and Job are reflections and advances upon the fundamental discourses of advice-giving. These types of wisdom, pretheoretical and theoretical, are understood on a developmental model, where the former precedes the latter in the unfolding of a culture's literary production, but remarkably, Ben Sira, a later text, is understood to be a "throwback," as it resembles Proverbs in form. Di Lella further explains that Ben Sira, as an example of pretheoretical wisdom, "was not a creative thinker like Job or Qoheleth or a master stylist like the author of The Wisdom of Solomon … he simply employed the forms of expression and literary styles he found ready-made in the Scriptures, especially the Wisdom Literature, of which the book of Proverbs was his overwhelming favorite" (Di Lella and Skehan 1987, 21).

---

[1] A fuller discussion of this issue, from which the following discussion has been paraphrased, can be found in Vayntrub forthcoming.

The binary of "pretheoretical" and "theoretical" wisdom that Di Lella outlines in his Ben Sira commentary reflects a persistent idea in the study of biblical wisdom that can help us understand the way scholars classify, interpret, and even date biblical Wisdom texts. Di Lella concludes that Ben Sira is both imitative of Proverbs, and consequently, an uncreative text which simply repeats those basic Wisdom forms because he subscribes to a concept of how literary cultures develop over time. In this concept, simple, short utterances—a proverb—evolve to longer, more complex forms—poems—to finally more complex prose works. In *Voices of Modernity* (2003), Richard Bauman and Charles Briggs illustrate how the developmental model—the notion that earlier texts are shorter and simpler whereas more evolved texts are longer and more complex—was a way for early modern and modern scholars to favorably evaluate their own literary and intellectual accomplishments in comparison to pre-modern works.[2] This model of "early, short, and simple" versus "later, longer, and complex" maps easily onto Di Lella's characterization of pretheoretical, "recipe," wisdom and theoretical, "existential," wisdom, respectively. The book of Proverbs is considered in the scholarly literature to precede Ecclesiastes chronologically, and even more sharply, its collections of short sentences (Prov 10:1–22:16; 25–29) are widely considered by scholars to be its earliest sections despite any other evidence beyond its formal characteristics.

Following this developmental model, scholars frequently identify Proverbs as the chronologically earliest and foundational form of biblical wisdom. There are two ways in which this model manifests in interpretations of Proverbs among scholars.[3] One view is that the composition of the book of Proverbs has an oral-performance background, and this background is fundamental to understanding its literary forms. For example, Claus Westermann (1995, 109) explains that "The earliest proverbial form is the short, self-contained, single-verse saying," and that these forms have an oral background, yet the writings in Proverbs have already passed a "postdevelopmental stage," as they are hybrids of the original oral form but shaped by their written character. The second view sees Proverbs as the product of a Wisdom school not unlike those schools thought to have produced ancient Egyptian instruction texts.[4] But in both of these perspectives, scholars tend to see the basic literary form of the book of Proverbs, and therefore of Wisdom Literature more generally, as the *mashal*—conventionally translated "proverb."

The term *mashal*, a genre designation, is found in the title heading the book of Proverbs in 1:1 and in the titles of two other sections in the book, in 10:1 and 25:1: משלי שלמה, "The proverbs of Solomon." There is little beyond this, however, to assume that the term is the fundamental Wisdom genre, since it is more commonly attested outside of Proverbs, Ecclesiastes, and Job. The term designates Balaam's speeches in Numbers 23–24, as well as appearing repeatedly in prophetic texts, such as Isaiah (14:4), Jeremiah (24:9), and Ezekiel (12:22; 14:8; 17:2; 18:2; 20:49; 24:3) (see Vayntrub 2019). Despite this, the coincidence of the term as the title for the book of

---

[2] See discussion of this work in Sanders 2009, 15. See also Vayntrub 2019.

[3] These two views are outlined in Vayntrub forthcoming and Vayntrub 2016, 100 n. 13, citing Golka 1993, Rad 1970; for English translation, see Rad 1972, for the oral-origins view of Proverbs.

[4] See von Rad 1972, as discussed in Vayntrub 2016, 100 n. 14.

Proverbs and its Solomonic collections along with the scholarly view that the *mashal* is an originally orally composed and performed form, which is later transmitted literarily, leads to a widespread understanding that it is the fundamental Wisdom form. Beyond this, it is clear that Proverbs functions in the "Wisdom canon" as the paradigmatic text against which all other texts are evaluated.[5] Proverbs is seen to be fundamental, "pretheoretical" wisdom, while Ecclesiastes and Job are more complex deviations in form and content. Within this framework, it is difficult to make the claim that the book of Proverbs, and in particular the "older" collections in chs. 10–29, is anything but paradigmatic of the genre or didactic in its aims.

In short, "Wisdom Literature" is a phenomenon of modern scholarly imagination and organization of ancient forms of expression and literary production, a projection of modern self-fashioning. That which is rational is modern, and therefore forms of knowledge that are more ancient are, by definition, in opposition to modern reason and their literary manifestations. Through this lens, the literary products identified as Wisdom texts are a manifestation of the verbal and cognitive "skill" of their authors and tradents. As we will see, the vocabulary used in Proverbs, Ecclesiastes, Job, as well as discussions of "wisdom" in the biblical texts, range from concrete skill in handicraft to abstract skill in knowledge and speechmaking. The concept of verbal skill itself reflects a scholarly view of such knowledge production as explicitly distinct from and implicitly inferior to the Western philosophical tradition.[6] In this perspective, skill is an abstraction of and tied to the skilled production of material objects.

2.2 VOCABULARY

However, the modern scholarly framework can obscure other aspects that join these texts, namely, the shared compositional features that made them meaningful for their ancient authors and audiences. Scholars frequently point out that these texts share a vocabulary of words for wisdom, knowledge, skill, and advice.[7] As one scholar has noted, "The wisdom books have a characteristic vocabulary," and since this "characteristic vocabulary" is not limited to these texts, they are often used to identify a "wisdom influence in other parts of the Old Testament such as the prophetic writings and the Psalms" (Scott 1971, 121–122).

Indeed, this "characteristic vocabulary" and the frequently intersecting literary form of the father-to-son (or teacher-to-student) instruction can be helpful in grouping together texts in a concrete and meaningful way. However, a quick examination of terms

[5]   According to Norbert Lohfink (2003, 12), Proverbs was the "first-level text" of Wisdom Literature.
[6]   According to Karel van der Toorn (2007, 5), "The authors of antiquity were artisans rather than artists. Our preoccupation with originality would have been foreign to them, nor did they care about intellectual property. What they admired was skill, technical mastery. The texts they produced were often coproductions— if not by a collective of scribes, then by means of a series of scribal redactions."
[7]   A resource for these terms and their valences in Proverbs can be found in Fox 2000 29, 32–33. For this argument, see Murphy 1992, 920; Dell 2006, 856–857.

related to חכמה, such as בינה and תבונה, "understanding, discernment," דעת, "knowledge," and שכל, "sense," recall the scholarly tendency to interpret Proverbs as the paradigmatic Wisdom text. These so-called Wisdom terms occur most frequently in the book of Proverbs, with less frequency in Job, but they can also be found in Psalms and Isaiah (see Vayntrub 2019). Notably, these words are not, in fact, widely attested in Ecclesiastes, foreclosing the possibility of using vocabulary as a consistent guide for identifying a text as belonging to the biblical Wisdom corpus. Beyond simple word statistics, a close study of the terms used in these works can further identify and sharpen the various discourses of skill, advice, and knowledge in the biblical texts.

It seems prudent to begin with the Hebrew term for wisdom itself.[8] This term appears in multiple contexts in the Hebrew Bible, though it should be noted that nowhere does this term appear as a native literary category. The term designates concrete skill, or an abstract concept, a divine quality, or even a personified characteristic. But nowhere in the biblical corpus does it designate text. In Exodus 36, Bezalel's "wisdom" (חכמה), along with the skill of others, is a divine gift of craft and artisanship that enables the construction of the tabernacle. Throughout the passage, the term refers to the concrete skill of handicraft. Elsewhere the term seems to refer to mastery of some area of knowledge, a quality of divine origin. In 1 Kgs 3:12, God gifts Solomon a "wise and discerning mind." In Genesis 41:39, Pharaoh acknowledges that Joseph is the beneficiary of God's wisdom, asserting "there is no one as discerning and wise as you." The "spirit of Yahweh," which Isaiah's messianic figure receives, is one of "wisdom and discernment" (Isa 11:2). Finally, Daniel is said to have "wisdom like that of the gods" (Dan 5:11). Differently, Ecclesiastes and Job do not explicitly present themselves as instructing in the acquisition of wisdom, and instead they examine the fate of the wise, sometimes alongside that of the fool. It is only, unusually, in Proverbs where wisdom constitutes a set of skills that mortals can (and should) acquire through attentiveness to instruction and its discipline. This message is communicated in both the introductory frame of Proverbs (the "motto" in 1:2–7, and chs. 1–9 more generally), as well as in its conclusion in the alphabetic acrostic in 31:10–31 (see Vayntrub 2020).

2.3 CASE STUDY: VOCABULARY OF PROVERBS 1:2–7

Instructions make use of two components to communicate with their audience: (1) the dynamics of the hierarchical and trans-generational relationship (usually, father-to-son); and (2) the juxtaposition and pairing of words in a patterned fashion ("parallelism") to further examine and refine their meaning for the particular message of the

---

[8] See *TDOT* 4:364–385; *Theological Lexicon of the Old Testament (TLOT)*. Edited by Ernst Jenni, with assistance from Claus Westermann. Translated by Mark E. Biddle. 3 vols. Peabody, MA: Hendrickson, 1997 1:418–424.

instruction. In Proverbs 1:2–7 we can see an example of the way patterned speech refines vocabulary for the purpose of the instruction.

Following the attribution to Solomon in 1:1, the initial poetic units of Proverbs open with an examination of the terminology of "wisdom," חכמה, establishing the conceptual parameters for the collections to follow:

> For learning wisdom and discipline
> for understanding words of discernment.

The pairing of חכמה ("wisdom") and מוסר ("discipline") further clarify the relationship between the two. The term מוסר derives from the root יסר, which implies both in usage and etymology instruction through suffering and physical discipline. In Isaiah 8:11, the verb of the same root is used to designate divine instruction alongside disciplining speech: "For Yahweh thus spoke to me with a disciplining hand (היד חזקת) and instructed me (ויסרני) not to go down the path of those people." What does Proverbs 1:2 mean through the pairing of "wisdom" and "discipline"? Is it meant to link the abstract and linguistic with the concrete and physical? The pairing of "wisdom" and "discipline" is resumed in the conclusion of the unit in 1:7, "The fear of Yahweh is the beginning of knowledge, fools abuse wisdom and discipline."[9] In Proverbs 15:33 we find a variation on 1:7, "The fear of Yahweh is the instruction of wisdom, and before success, humility." In 1:7 and 15:33, wisdom and discipline/humility are two sides of the same coin: wisdom brings success, but it is mediated through discipline, which produces humility, physical or psychological. According to Proverbs 1:2–7, one cannot acquire wisdom without discipline, and one cannot remain wise if they lose their discipline; both lead to each other, discipline through humility breeding wisdom, bringing success, and vice versa. The following couplets in vv. 3–4 explain how "wisdom" is to be understood: as the acquisition of character traits leading to behavioral correctness: "discipline leading to insight" (מוסר השכל), a sense of justice, and foresight. From 1:2–4, wisdom is further refined through these qualities and its relationship to discipline, but what role does the already-wise person have in this process? In 1:5, the concept of the "wise person" (חכם) is redefined as one whose education is yet incomplete and who is able to acquire more wisdom through instruction: "A wise one hears and adds a lesson, a discerning one will acquire strategies." While elsewhere in the biblical texts, and even elsewhere in the book of Proverbs, the title "wise" indicates one whose role is to impart lessons, not acquire them, Proverbs 1:2–7 is an example of how what it means to be wise can be subtly redefined in the very texts that appear to be standard representations of wisdom. The language of these texts is dynamic and terms are defined and refined through context as well as the patterning techniques characteristic of Hebrew poetry.

---

[9] See Fox 2000, 68. Many translate "despise" for בוז (King James Version (KJV), Tanakh: The Holy Scriptures: The New JPS (NJPS), Revised Standard Version (RSV)), though "abuse" may be closer to how the Hebrew is used, that is, not merely to "view with contempt" ("despise," *OED*), but to mistreat. See Gen 25:34, "Thus did Esau mistreat (ויבז) his birthright."

2.4 LITERARY FORM

Another criterion for identifying a text as "Wisdom Literature" is its literary form.[10] One scholar explains, "The wisdom psalms may be identified by the presence of typical sapiential forms, the use of particular sapiential saying to provide the structure of the psalm, the syntax of expressions found often also in the books of wisdom, the occasional occurrence of the alphabetic acrostic," as well as a number of common themes (Perdue 1994, 151–152). What is striking about the form criterion is how closely it follows Proverbs as a paradigmatic Wisdom text. For example, full and partial alphabetic acrostics occur in Psalms, and the book of Lamentations is entirely structured through this patterning device. What makes an alphabetic acrostic inherently a Wisdom feature, aside from its occurrence in the final chapter of Proverbs (31:10–31)? Several introductions to biblical Wisdom Literature explicitly identify Proverbs as the most "characteristic" of the category, as the "basic form," and "foundational... teaching the ABCs of wisdom" (Dell 2000, 5; Murphy 2002, 7; van Leeuwen 2005, 638).

Central to these definitions of Wisdom Literature is the notion that its basic underlying, or original form is the single-line proverb.[11] Much of the study of biblical Wisdom Literature is founded on the assumption of a particular approach to genre known as form criticism, in which the essential meaning of a text is reconstructed through identifying the original pristine oral form lying behind the now hybrid or corrupted written realization of this oral form. The reconstructed oral form, for example, the single-line proverb, is meaningful through understanding the lived performance context that gave rise to the literary form. According to Hermann Gunkel, from whom this interpretive framework derives, Wisdom Literature, chiefly represented by the book of Proverbs, had already evolved away from its original literary form, the oral saying or proverb (*Sprichwörter*) into a more complex written composition, *Kunstdichtung* (see Gunkel 2003, 35, 77). A more recent articulation of the form-critical approach to Wisdom Literature is that it "has its roots in traditional insights, continuously adapted to meet new circumstances" (Van Leeuwen 2003, 70). The single-line proverb is understood to be so foundational to biblical wisdom that even the literary form of father-to-son instruction is assumed to be derivative of the basic simple proverb.

There are two important reasons the single-line proverb is assumed to be the foundational Wisdom form from which all other literary forms derive and evolve. The first is explained by the developmental model of literature through which biblical form criticism was formulated: this is the assumption that literary forms begin as short, simple, oral compositions and evolve over time to longer, more complex, written texts. The second reason the single-line proverb persists in biblical scholarship as the imagined foundational Wisdom form is that the biblical genre term, *mashal*, seems to at times designate single-line proverbial statements, and is the genre term governing single-line collections

[10] The following discussion points have been adopted from Vayntrub 2019, 70–102.
[11] "At the beginning [of wisdom texts] stands the one-limbed, single verse saying" (McKane 1970, 3).

in the book of Proverbs (10:1–22:16, 25–29), as well as the entire book (1:1). The use of the term *mashal* in the book's headings, however, seems to have much more to do with its Solomonic attribution—namely, Solomon's famed wisdom and his performance of *mashal* ("proverb") and *shir* ("song") in 1 Kgs 5:12 [ET 4:32]—than a meaningful representation of the collected compositions in the book. Put differently, just because the title mentions *mashal* does not mean that ancient Israelite scribes would have identified all its contents, or any of it, as *mashal* decontextualized from its Solomonic attribution. While *mashal* speeches, both short and long, are attested elsewhere in the biblical text, famously in the story of Balaam in Numbers 22–24 and in a number of prophetic texts, the collection of multiple *meshalim* belongs uniquely to Solomon in the biblical literary tradition. There is little beyond circular reasoning to assume that the *mashal* is the foundational Wisdom form, or that ancient Israelite wisdom begins its life in pithy sayings.

2.5 ADVICE

This is not to say, however, that genre has no place in the study of these texts. Outside of a developmental model, one can observe a number of shared themes in Proverbs, Ecclesiastes, Job, Ben Sira, and perhaps other texts as well, but chiefly in these. Tying these themes together is the framing device of the instruction, and more broadly, the value placed on advice-giving from one character to another. Proverbs includes instructions from father to son in chs. 1–9, and an instruction from a mother to her son, the king, in ch. 31. Ecclesiastes and Ben Sira are framed as instructions from a wise teacher to students, though Ecclesiastes is much more implicitly directed at students and Ben Sira much more explicitly so. In all these cases, the hierarchy (father to son, teacher to student) remains unchallenged, where the speaker, in the socially superior role, transmits knowledge to a subordinate, silent recipient. In Job there is also a social exchange of knowledge of the world and its actors between speakers—Job and his consoling friends, and Job and the Israelite deity—though the social and universal hierarchies are repeatedly challenged.

Instruction, with its framing narrative of knowledge transmission from father to son or teacher to student is not confined to the biblical Wisdom texts; biblical and parabiblical narratives of prophecy, law-giving, and death-bed testament share similar frames and themes. And the literary form of advice-giving, in which fathers or wise teachers impart words to silent, listening sons or students is not unique to the biblical literary tradition. It is widely attested in the ancient Egyptian textual traditions and to a more limited extent in Mesopotamia. However, the vast majority of these ancient Near Eastern instruction texts—Mesopotamian instruction texts, such as the Instructions of Shuruppak and Šimâ Milka, and Egyptian instruction texts, such as the Instruction of Prince Hardjedef, Instruction to Kagemni, the Instruction of Ptahhotep, the Instruction of Amenemope, and the Instruction of Any, as well as the long textual and translation history of the Aramaic Ahiqar—frame their advice as the speech from one individual famed sage to one or more (usually silent) recipients. While Proverbs does this in its very minimalistic attribution of the work to Solomon in 1:1, 10:1, and 25:1, it is both missing the silent, attendant student *and* it is in fact an anthology of multiple instructions, poems, and sayings. While the instructions in chs. 1–9 depict a father-instructor speaking to a present but silent, son-student, these characters remain unnamed—stock figures with no anchor to characters from biblical lore. Proverbs thus radically departs from the ancient Near Eastern convention of instruction texts, consolidating various forms of advice-giving into a single compendium and attributed to the wise speech of Solomon as recounted in his legendary biography in Kings. In fact, Ecclesiastes might be said to follow the ancient Near Eastern literary conventions more closely than Proverbs, as it is framed as Qoheleth's advice to an unnamed silent audience, mediated through a somewhat contradictory frame speaker.

An important aspect of instruction is the character of the sage and their fame. These legendary teachers do more than simply impart advice with authority and gravitas. The advice itself promises to be life preserving and guarantees its adherents material and social success. But it is the very success of the named sages themselves in the broader literary tradition that animate these promises for wealth, health, and fame. Solomon's reputation for excess in wealth, women, and wisdom lies in the background of attributions to him in the titles of Proverbs, Song of Songs, and, to a certain extent, Ecclesiastes—the attribution there is deliberately ambiguous, never identifying the speaker as Solomon but evoking a Solomonic voice in multiple ways, framing itself as the wisdom of a former king of Jerusalem and son of King David who enjoyed great material and social success.

The description in 1 Kgs 5:9 [ET 4:29] of Solomon's vast mind helpfully contextualizes the attribution in Proverbs. It is in the context of Solomon's great capacity for wise speech that the narrator in Kings recounts Solomon's many proverbs and song: "He spoke three-thousand proverbs (*mashal*) and his songs (*shir*) numbered one-thousand and five" (5:12 [ET 4:32]). Solomon's excesses are not limited to wealth and women; they include wise speech, and his "vast mind" can account for his many collected "proverbs," since speech-items, such as sayings and instructions, are described as material objects by the biblical authors and are stored and collected in the לב, or inner cavity of the body. In the instruction in Proverbs 3:1, the son is urged: "Son, do not forget my teaching, and store up my instructions in your mind (לב)." As David Lambert (2016) has noted, as an inner corporeal space or "borderline" in which speech is collected, the לב is in fact a "leaky" organ. He cites, for example, Ecclesiastes 5:1, "Keep your mouth from being rash, and let not your לב be quick to bring forth speech before God," and even more pointedly, how characters' supposed "inner speech"—like Sarah laughing to herself in Genesis 18:12—leaks out to those who hear it.[12]

These spoken nuggets of wisdom are described in Proverbs as objects transmitted, unchanged, from the speaking sage to the attentive and silent student, and sometimes described with protective properties, such as amulets or other types of objects fastened

---

[12] See Lambert's citation of this observation in Niehoff 1992.

around one's neck, head, or fingers (e.g., Prov 3:3; 7:3).[13] Instructions are transmitted from one generation to the next like such an object, whose intact, unaltered qualities are protective for the recipient and extend the legacy of the giver.

2.6 Transmission through Instruction

Without prioritizing Proverbs as the blueprint of the category of Wisdom Literature, we might ask what is nevertheless shared by these texts beyond a consideration of genre and vocabulary? Another way to answer the question is to thematize what these texts *do* for their audience and how their rhetorical features accomplish this. Wisdom texts in their form and content assert *and* reflect upon knowledge of the world, its actors, and their relationships. These texts need not be limited to the corpus as it is classically conceived in the Hebrew Bible (Proverbs, Ecclesiastes, Job) or Old Testament (also Song of Songs, Sirach, and the Wisdom of Solomon), nor should the corpus be limited by particular genres (the *mashal* or instruction, for example) or certain vocabulary. Biblical texts framed as instruction and aimed at advice-giving, either directly to a reading audience (e.g., Proverbs, Ecclesiastes) or to a built-in audience (e.g., Job) are characterized by their *reflection* on the production and transmission of knowledge.

Instruction depicts a particular relationship between individuals across generations. The one who gives the advice—usually the father—imparts life-preserving and enriching knowledge of the world, its actors, and of cause and effect. This advice is often characterized as that which the father himself received from his own father. The one who receives the advice—usually the son—listens silently, collecting the advice fully intact for his own edification, as well as for his future role as father who, too, will give advice to *his* son. Thus, the trans-generational nature of instruction is one of assuring life not only of the individual but of the entire family across multiple generations. There are multiple examples of this in ancient Near Eastern instruction texts, but the simple frame in Proverbs 4:1–9 also supports this point:

> For I was a son to my father,
>> tender and singular before my mother.
> He instructed me and said to me:
> "Let your mind (לב) grasp my words,
>> keep my commands and live."

In the above passage, the trans-generational dimension of advice-giving is explicit: the father explains the provenance of the advice to his son and quotes what he had received from his father, fully intact, including the call to instruction. What is fascinating beyond this is that in this call to instruction, the speaker quotes from his own father, the words

---

[13]   For further discussion, see Vayntrub 2018.

themselves are life-preserving objects. He was instructed to *grasp* his words, to take possession of them as his own, that he might behave accordingly and live. This same verb is used elsewhere for actual objects—in Amos 1:8 for grasping a scepter.

The instruction leverages a presentation of hierarchical relationships, uses specific terminology which depicts a trans-generational passage of knowledge as quasi-objects, and offers promises for survival—a good life, a long life, and a life beyond one's own through progeny. The concept behind this ritual of advice-giving is one of stability in transmission, as the success of the advice is measured by its success in sustaining previous generations of its adherents. In this way, advice-giving has much to do with the so-called "scribal motto" of stable transmission of text, that nothing should be added to its words, and nothing should be taken away from it. While a number of texts under the scholarly rubric of Wisdom Literature, such as Ecclesiastes and Job, might be seen to challenge aspects of instruction—such as the stability of transmission or the validity of immutable hierarchies—they nevertheless work within the constraints of the phenomenon. In sum, instruction functions as a medium to communicate a blueprint for success in life—ranging from basic safeguards and avoiding dangers to strategies for material gains and prominence in the community. The broader connection between skill and wisdom in other texts (e.g., Exod 36) is oriented toward instruction in behavior—speech, social interaction—and worldviews that enable the recipient to prosper.

Works Cited

Bauman, Richard, and Charles L. Briggs. 2003. *Voices of Modernity: Language Ideologies and the Politics of Inequality*. Cambridge: Cambridge University Press.

Dell, Katharine. 2000. *Get Wisdom, Get Insight: An Introduction to Israel's Wisdom Literature*. Macon, GA: Smyth & Helwys.

Dell, Katharine. 2006. "Wisdom in the OT." Pages 869–875 in *The New Interpreter's Dictionary of the Bible*, vol. 5. Edited by Katharine Doob Sakenfeld. Nashville, TN: Abingdon.

Di Lella, Alexander A., and Patrick W. Skehan. 1987. *The Wisdom of Ben Sira: A New Translation with Notes*. AB 39. New York, NY: Doubleday.

Fox, Michael V. 2000. *Proverbs 1–9: A New Translation with Introduction and Commentary*. AB 18A. New York, NY: Doubleday.

Golka, Friedemann W. 1993. *The Leopard's Spots: Biblical and African Wisdom in Proverbs*. Edinburgh: T&T Clark.

Gunkel, Hermann. 2003. "The Literature of Ancient Israel by Hermann Gunkel." Pages 26–83 in *Relating to the Text: Interdisciplinary and Form-Critical Insights on the Bible*. Edited by Timothy Sandoval and Carleen Mandolfo. Translated by Armin Siedlecki. London: T&T Clark.

Lambert, David Arthur. 2016. "Refreshing Philology: James Barr, Supersessionism, and the State of Biblical Words." *BibInt* 24:332–356.

Lohfink, Norbert. 2003. *Qoheleth: A Continental Commentary*. Translated by Sean McEvenue. CC. Minneapolis, MN: Fortress.

McKane, William. 1970. *Proverbs: A New Approach*. Philadelphia, PA: Westminster.

Murphy, Roland E. 1992. "Wisdom in the OT." Pages 920–931 in *The Anchor Bible Dictionary*, vol. 6. Edited by David Noel Freedman. New York, NY: Doubleday.

Murphy, Roland E. 2002. *The Tree of Life: An Exploration of Biblical Wisdom Literature*. 3rd ed. Grand Rapids, MI: Eerdmans.

Niehoff, M. 1992. "Do Biblical Characters Talk to Themselves? Narrative Modes of Representing Inner Speech in Early Biblical Fiction." *JBL* 111:577–595.

Perdue, Leo G. 1994. *Wisdom and Creation: The Theology of Wisdom Literature*. Nashville, TN: Abingdon.

Rad, Gerhard von. 1970. *Weisheit in Israel*. Neukirchen-Vluyn: Neukirchener Verlag.

Rad, Gerhard von. 1972. *Wisdom in Israel*. Translated by James D. Martin. London: SCM Press.

Sanders, Seth L. 2009. *The Invention of Hebrew*. Urbana, IL: University of Illinois Press.

Scott, R.B.Y. 1971. *The Way of Wisdom in the Old Testament*. New York, NY: Macmillan.

Toorn, Karel van der. 2007. *Scribal Culture and the Making of the Hebrew Bible*. Cambridge, MA: Harvard University Press.

Van Leeuwen, Raymond C. 2003. "Form Criticism, Wisdom, and Psalms 111–112." Pages 65–84 in *The Changing Face of Form Criticism for the Twenty-First Century*. Edited by Marvin A. Sweeney and Ehud Ben Zvi. Grand Rapids, MI: Eerdmans.

Van Leeuwen, Raymond C. 2005. "Proverbs, Book Of." Pages 638–641 in *Dictionary for Theological Interpretation of the Bible*. Edited by Kevin J. Vanhoozer. Grand Rapids, MI: Baker Academic.

Vayntrub, Jacqueline. 2016. The Book of Proverbs and the Idea of Ancient Israelite Education." *ZAW* 128:96–114.

Vayntrub, Jacqueline. 2018. "Like Father, Like Son: Theorizing Transmission in Biblical Literature." *HBAI* 7:500–526.

Vayntrub, Jacqueline. 2019. *Beyond Orality: Biblical Poetry on Its Own Terms*. New York, NY: Routledge.

Vayntrub, Jacqueline. 2020. "Beauty, Wisdom, and Handiwork in Proverbs 31:10–31." *HTR* 113:45–62.

Vayntrub, Jacqueline. Forthcoming. "Wisdom in Transmission: Rethinking Proverbs and Sirach." In Sirach and its Contexts: The Pursuit of Wisdom and Human Flourishing. Edited by Gregory Goering, Matthew Goff, and Samuel Adams. JSJSupp. Leiden: Brill.

Westermann, Claus. 1990. *Wurzeln der Weisheit: Die ältesten Sprüche Israels und anderer Völker*. Göttingen: Vandenhoeck & Ruprecht.

Westermann, Claus. 1995. *Roots of Wisdom: The Oldest Proverbs of Israel and Other Peoples*. Translated by J. Daryl Charles. Louisville, KY: Westminster John Knox.

CHAPTER 3

··

EPISTEMOLOGY

Wisdom, Knowledge, and Revelation

··

ANNETTE SCHELLENBERG

THE ancient Israelites' idea of "wisdom" goes far beyond cognitive issues, but they are most essential to it. The intrinsic connection of wisdom with cognitive issues is already reflected in the main Hebrew word to talk about wisdom: חכמה. The English translation "wisdom" reflects that it belongs to the semantic domain of cognition, as do all other words of the root חכם, not only in Hebrew but in Akkadian and other Semitic languages as well (Müller and Krause 1977). Thus, frequently חכמה and other words of the same root are used together with nouns like דעת ("knowledge"), בינה ("insight"), and תבונה ("understanding"), as well as with respective adjectives and verbs that have to do with understanding, learning, and teaching (e.g., Deut 4:6; 1 Kgs 5:9; Isa 11:2; Ezek 28:4; Hos 14:10; Job 28:12; Prov 2:2–3; 3:19–20; 14:6).

The connection of wisdom and cognition can be observed throughout the Hebrew Bible (and beyond), but it is best attested in the sapiential texts widely known as "Wisdom Literature." These texts—their exact demarcation is disputed as is the very definition of "wisdom"—got their scholarly name because they talk about wisdom so often. Questions of cognition are not their only interest, but they all display their authors' epistemological assumptions, with some reflecting on contentious epistemological questions. Furthermore, many of these texts show a clear educational interest (e.g., Prov 1:1–7). Their authors do not only talk about wisdom, they also want to convey it, giving advice to their students who strive to become wise like them.

In the following, the intrinsic connection of the idea of wisdom with cognitive issues shall be explained in more detail. The main focus is on the sapiential texts and, more concretely, their epistemological assumptions and reflections, and how they relate to the idea of wisdom. Obviously, the picture does not remain the same throughout all texts—not only because the very idea of wisdom is so manifold that the connection to cognition can be described from different angles, but also because of historical developments and disagreements among contemporaries. Nonetheless, there are some "threads" that hold the different texts together and make it possible to trace developments.

3.1 EXPERIENCE AND REASONING

Compared to prophetic texts and some other books like Exodus–Deuteronomy, the sapiential books stand out in that they do not claim to contain divine words, revealed to special persons like Moses and the prophets, and handed down through them to the rest of the Israelites (Weeks 2010, 114; Schellenberg 2015, 126–127, 129–130; Schellenberg 2020, 167–168). The sages are not opposed to revelation in general, and in some ways they consider all understanding/wisdom as a gift from God (see below, 3.4 Revelation). When it comes to the concrete process of acquiring knowledge, however, in most cases they assume that it is gained through experience and reasoning, as well as through tradition, which can be understood as condensed experience (see below, 3.2 Tradition).

The prime example for the high esteem of experience and reasoning is the book of Ecclesiastes (Fox 1987; Sciumbata 1996; Frydrych 2002, 69–72; Schellenberg 2002, 161–187; cf. more critically Crenshaw 1998, 212–213; Weeks 2012, 121–125; Gericke 2015, 6–7; on the reason for the different assessments, see below). Repeatedly Qoheleth points out his own observations and reflections, and he even talks about experiments (thus 2:1; 7:23 with the verb נסה pi.; see also 1:13; 2:3; 9:1, etc.). He emphasizes this approach because he often argues against the tradition (see below, 3.3 Skepticism). Without such opposition to the tradition, Ben Sira emphasizes his own experience and independent research, too, pointing out his travels (Sir 34:9–10; 39:4), the leisure he enjoys as scribe (Sir 38:34–39:11; cf. Sir 51:13–30), and observations in nature (Sir 42:15–43:33). Other sages do not stress the empirical approach, but all of them share the esteem of experience and reasoning (Crenshaw 1987, 247–249; Frydrych 2002, 53–56; Goff 2003, 43, 45; Weeks 2010, 114–116, with legitimate qualifications; Leuenberger 2012, with focus on Job and Ecclesiastes; cf. more critically Fox 1987, 145–147; Fox 2007, 670–674).

In the book of Proverbs, the only passage that explicitly points out that one's own observations and considerations are valuable means to become wise is Prov 6:6–11. Here, the Wisdom teacher admonishes his student:

> [6] Go (לך) to the ant, you lazybones; consider (ראה) its ways, and be wise (חכם).
> [7] Without having any chief or officer or ruler,
> [8] it prepares its food in summer, and gathers its sustenance in harvest.
> [9] How long will you lie there, O lazybones? When will you rise from your sleep?
> [10] A little sleep, a little slumber, a little folding of the hands to rest,
> [11] and poverty will come upon you like a robber, and want, like an armed warrior.

Obviously, the teacher already knows what the student could or should learn if he indeed went and had a look at the ants (namely: that it is important to work so that later one can benefit from it). Thus, the two imperatives "go" and "consider" (literally: "see") are rhetorical, because the student could also learn this message by listening to his teacher. Text-internally they are important because they emphasize that the lazybones should get into action. For scholars, they are important because they make explicit that, in the sages' self-understanding, descriptions and admonitions like those of vv. 7–11 are based on experience. Indeed, many of the sapiential sayings and admonitions can be verified by one's own experience—if not always so, at least often (on the problem of generalizations, see below, 3.2 Tradition and 3.3 Skepticism). For example, most people would not want to challenge the claim that one cannot walk on hot coals without scorching one's feet (Prov 6:28); most would agree (or at least wish) that wickedness (often) is followed by contempt (Prov 18:3); and it is easy to find examples of how one's (foolish) words can bring disaster (Prov 13:3; Eccl 10:12). That the sages ordinarily do not point out the empirical basis for their statements probably reflects that in their understanding it is just a given that ordinarily knowledge/wisdom is based on experience and reasoning (if not first-hand, then through tradition). This also explains why (with some few exceptions, see below, 3.5 Conclusions) they do not authorize their teachings with reference to prophetic figures but only with reference to Solomon and other sages and teachers, who acquired their wisdom in exactly the same empirical way.

Interesting from a scholarly perspective is the fact that, side by side with descriptions and admonitions evidently grounded in experience, the sages present others that in a modern understanding are not. For example, most people today would not know how to support empirically the claim that finding a spouse is a sign of being favored by God (Prov 18:22), or that wealth, possessions, and honor are goods given by God (Eccl 6:2). The last example is from Ecclesiastes, notably introduced as something that Qoheleth "saw" (Eccl 6:1). Another interesting example in this regard is Job 13:1–2:

> [1] Look, my eye has seen all this, my ear has heard and understood it.
> [2] What you know, I also know; I am not inferior to you.

Here, Job refers to his own hearing and seeing to emphasize that he knows at least as much as his friends (cf. Job 12:2–3)—a clear confirmation of the sages' high esteem of experience. However, with "all this" he refers back to the previous passage in which he had described God's power in the world, making many statements that in a modern understanding are *not* empirical (e.g., 12:13, 16—wisdom and power are with God; 12:15—droughts are caused by God holding back the water; 12:23—nations are destroyed by God). This example is one of the many indications that for the ancient Israelites the assumption of a divine activity in the world was so common and natural that it was understood as empirically verifiable. (And indeed, for the ancient Israelites God's activity in the world was confirmed over and over again, because their worldview shaped respective experiences.) Thus, sapiential and other writings contain many statements about the power of God and a respective order of the world in which this knowledge is not treated as something extraordinary but assumed to be "readable" by anyone. Even Qoheleth, who stresses his empirical approach so much, often makes "observations" that in a modern understanding have no empirical basis (Crenshaw 1998, 212–213; Schellenberg 2002, 188–191; O'Dowd 2009, 140–141)—hence scholars' disagreement whether his approach is empirical (see above).

For the sages, it is clear that ultimately God is responsible for the "readability" of the world. First, God created humans with the organs that enable sensory perception (experience) and reasoning (Prov 20:12; 29:13; Sir 17:6–7; cf. Exod 4:11; Pss 33:15; 94:9–10). Second, God created the world "with wisdom" or with wisdom being present (Job 28:25–27; Prov 3:19–20; 8:22–31; Sir 1:1, 4, 9; 24:1–9; Wis 8:1, 4; 9:9; cf. Jer 10:12; 51:15; Ps 104:24), which explains both that there is order/wisdom in the world and that humans can detect this order/wisdom (and God's doing) through observing the world and reflecting on it (Schellenberg 2015, 124–125). Thus, unlike others (Isa 47:10; Jer 8:9), the sages normally do not see a contrast between relying on one's own wisdom or cognitive capacities and relying on God.[1] They know that one's own planning or reasoning might be thwarted by God (Job 5:13; Prov 16:9; 19:21; 20:24), and some of them are more pessimistic about humans' cognitive capacities than others (see below, 3.3 Skepticism). Nonetheless, with only a few exceptions,[2] they all agree that it is wise to use one's eyes and ears and brain and foolish not to. Though some sages state that certain people lack the capacity to gain wisdom (Prov 14:6; 17:16; Sir 22:9–10), and they all share the understanding that wisdom is a gift from God, which allows for the thought that this gift is given only to some but not to others (see below, 3.4 Revelation), most of them assume that it is each and every one's own decision whether they become wise or remain a fool.

3.2 TRADITION

For most sages, the decision to become wise also includes listening to others who are already wise. They describe listening and taking advice as a characteristic of the wise (Prov 1:5; 9:9; 12:15; 13:1; Sir 3:29; 6:33–35; 21:15) and admonish their addressees to listen to their teachers and parents, respectively (Job 34:2; Prov 1:8; 4:20; 5:1; 8:33; 22:17; 23:22; Sir 6:23; 51:28; Wis 6:1). In principle, this goes well together with the high esteem of experience and reasoning, at least as long as the sages only hand down knowledge gained this way. In such a case, the only difference is the grade of immediacy, whether the students get the experience first-hand or in a mediated way and whether they do the reasoning independently or follow the paths of others who have drawn their conclusions before them.

In practice, however, the conviction that it is beneficial to listen to the knowledge/wisdom of the teachers often goes hand in hand with a tendency away from experience and independent thinking. For one, this happens when sages understand their teachings as some kind of "doctrine," something that their students must follow. For example, Prov 10:8 formulates that it is wise to accept commandments, and Proverbs 12:1 equates

---

[1] On the exceptions of Prov 3:5–7 and Prov 30:1–9, see below, 3.2 Tradition and 3.4 Revelation; cf. Prov 28:26.

[2] In addition to the two mentioned in the previous note, see Sir 3:21–24, though only with regard to what is hidden.

loving knowledge with loving discipline, disqualifying those who hate being rebuked as brutish. In later sapiential texts, this tendency to understand Wisdom teachings as law gains additional weight in that wisdom is associated with the Torah (Schnabel 1985; Schipper and Teeter 2013). Most famous in this regard is Sirach 24 (esp. vv. 23, 25; see below, 3.4 Revelation), but the development can already be observed in Proverbs 1–9 (Schipper 2012, 230–256; Schipper 2013) and is later continued in the sapiential writings of Qumran (Schnabel 1985, 166–226; Tooman 2013). A clear example is Prov 7:1–4:

> [1] My child, keep my words
> and store up my commandments (מצותי) with you;
> [2] keep my commandments (מצותי) and live,
> keep my teachings (תורתי) as the apple of your eye;
> [3] bind them on your fingers,
> write them on the tablet of your heart.
> [4] Say to wisdom, "You are my sister,"
> and call insight your intimate friend.

In these verses, the teacher not only describes his words as commandments and equates them with (personified) Wisdom, with allusions to Deut 6:6–9 and 11:18–21, he also implies a connection to the Torah. Similarly, Prov 3:1–5 and 6:20–24 exhibit such allusions to Deuteronomy and thus suggest a connection of wisdom with the Torah (Schipper 2012, 230–241; Schipper 2013, 57–63, pointing out small differences within the three passages). In a few verses of Proverbs 1–9, wisdom and one's own reasoning, respectively, are even subordinated to relationship to God—thus in Prov 3:5–7, with the admonition not to rely on one's own insight but to trust in YHWH "with all your heart" (note the allusion to Deut 6:5, etc.; Schipper 2012, 230–233; Schipper 2013, 61, 63) and in Prov 1:7, the motto verse of Proverbs 1–9, with the statement that the fear of YHWH is the beginning of knowledge. With such an understanding of wisdom, students lose the freedom to critically test traditional sayings and admonitions. Instead, some of the sapiential books emphasize the moment of discipline, including rebuke and punishment (Prov 13:24; 23:13–14; 29:15; Sir 6:18–25; 30:1–13, etc.).

Second, even before authoritative claims of sapiential teachers and the association of wisdom with the Torah, tradition often stands in contrast to experience and rational thinking, because in the transmission process individual observations become generalized and are adjusted according to a "coherence theory of truth," as Fox (2007, 675–684) describes it. With that they receive "their validation by virtue of consistency with the integrated system of assumptions that inform the book" and thought system, respectively (Fox 2007, 676). As condensed experience, tradition must generalize— with the price that counterexamples are neglected. As long as everybody is aware of this phenomenon and understands that there are counterexamples, there is no problem with this process. However, as soon as people forget about the counterexamples and take the generalizations as truths, tradition loses its empirical base and accumulates aspects that contrast experience and rational thinking. For some sages this conflict is a problem (see below, 3.3 Skepticism); others find explanations why it is not (see below, 3.4 Revelation).

3.3 Skepticism

That the conflict between tradition and experience poses a problem—or perhaps better: a reason to be skeptical about the tradition—is primarily reflected in the books of Job and Ecclesiastes. The example of Eccl 9:11 shows how much the conflict has to do with the problem of generalizations:

> [11]Again I saw that under the sun the race is not to the swift, nor the battle to the strong, nor bread to the wise, nor riches to the intelligent, nor favor to the skillful; but time and chance happen to them all.

Qoheleth certainly would not question that it is often the case that the swift wins the race and the strong the battle, but he also observes that sometimes the outcome differs from the expectation. This is particularly irritating in cases where the tradition "promises" a good outcome, as sages often do for wise and righteous behavior. Here as well, expectations are sometimes disappointed: like the swift in the race, the wise has no guarantee to be successful in life. In this case, respective observations not only contradict the tradition but also question the world's order (with a nexus of deed and consequence) and God's righteousness.

The books of Job and Ecclesiastes display different reactions on this challenge. In addition to pointing out the limits of wisdom's benefits and admonishing not to exaggerate wise/righteous behavior (Eccl 2:15; 7:16–17; 8:14–15), Qoheleth primarily focuses on the limitations of humans' cognition (Crenshaw 1998, 221; Schellenberg 2002, 75–161; Weeks 2012, 90–101, 159–162; Saur 2016, 64–65). He neither concludes that there is no order in the world (Eccl 1:3–11; 3:1–15; 6:10) nor that God is not good (Eccl 3:11; 5:17–19, etc.) but only that the benefits of wisdom are limited and that humans cannot understand the world and God in all their dimensions. One problem is forgetfulness: though things happen the same way again and again, people forget, and the past (with its patterns) is not remembered (Eccl 1:11; 2:16; 7:24; 9:5). Another problem is death: it brings an end to all cognitive activity—dead people do not know anything (Eccl 9:5, 10)—and limits the benefit of wisdom itself, as even the most wise persons have to die, will not be remembered forever (Eccl 2:15–16; 9:5), and have no control over what happens after their death (Eccl 2:18–21). Generally, humans' cognition is severely limited in that they do not know (and cannot influence) what the future will bring, not only regarding the time after their death (Eccl 2:19; 3:21) but already regarding their own lifetime (Eccl 3:22; 6:12; 7:14; 8:7; 10:14). Experience shows that expectations of tradition can be disappointed: righteous/wicked behavior does not always result in fitting consequences (Eccl 7:15; 8:10, 14; 9:2–3) and life takes unexpected turns (Eccl 5:13; 6:2; 9:11–12; 10:6–7; 11:2).

Repeatedly, Qoheleth combines his statements about the impossibility for humans to know what will happen in the future with the rhetorical question of who could tell them (Eccl 6:12; 8:7; 10:14; cf. 3:22)—probably an indirect attack against people who make such predictions. For Qoheleth, such attempts are foolish (Eccl 6:11; 10:14; 11:4) because they ignore that limited human cognition has much to do with God. The problem with predictions about the future is not only the lack of empirical data but more particularly the involvement of God. As creator of the world, God influences what happens (Eccl 2:26; 5:18; 6:2, 17; 7:13–14, 26; 9:1, 11; 11:5), but humans cannot understand the "logic" behind it; the work of God remains incomprehensible to them (Eccl 3:11; 7:13–14; 8:17; 11:5–6; cf. 1:13–14). Ecclesiastes 3:10–15 is telling for Qoheleth's thinking:

> [10]I have seen the business that God has given to everyone to be busy with. [11]He has made everything suitable for its time; moreover he has put a sense of past and future into their minds, yet they cannot find out what God has done from the beginning to the end. [12]I know that there is nothing better for them than to be happy and enjoy themselves as long as they live; [13]moreover, it is God's gift that all should eat and drink and take pleasure in all their toil. [14]I know that whatever God does endures forever; nothing can be added to it, nor anything taken from it; God has done this, so that all should stand in awe before him. [15]That which is, already has been; that which is to be, already is; and God seeks out what has gone by.

Qoheleth has no doubt that God has created "everything suitable for its time" (Eccl 3:11; cf. 3:1–9) and also that God's creation will endure forever (Eccl 3:14; cf. 1:4)—assumptions that in a modern understanding cannot be verified by experience, but in Qoheleth's view apparently are just a given (see above, 3.1 Experience and Reasoning). What he questions, though, is humans' ability to fully understand God's action (Eccl 3:12), for example the growing of the baby in the mother's womb (Eccl 11:5), why some become rich and others lose everything (Eccl 2:26; 5:18; 6:2), why certain times are pleasant and others are not (Eccl 3:2–11; 7:13–14). Qoheleth seems to assume that this incapacity of humans to understand God's action fully is part of this very action, i.e., that it is caused by God godself. He only once spells this thought out explicitly (Eccl 8:16–17), and once more alludes to it (Eccl 7:29), in a passage that starts with the acknowledgment that, despite his intentions, he could not become wise; wisdom remained remote (Eccl 7:23). Qoheleth's main focus is on the practical consequences of limited human cognition; he admonishes his addressees not to despair but instead to accept the limitations and enjoy the good moments as they come along (Eccl 3:12; cf. 2:24; 3:22; 5:17–19; 7:14; 8:15; 9:7–9).

In the book of Job, the conflict between tradition and experience is exemplified by the figure of Job, who loses his children and health even though he is superlatively righteous. His fate contradicts the traditional expectation that righteous people are blessed with a good life. As representatives of traditional wisdom, Job's friends promptly accuse him of having sinned. They take the traditional expectation as a "law" and conclude from the observation that Job suffers that, in one way or another, he must have behaved wickedly. Thus, not only do they forget that there are counterexamples to every rule, but they also reverse the direction of argumentation, ignoring that other reasons in addition to wickedness might cause misfortune as well. Job, on the other hand, insists that he is innocent. Apparently in some way expecting as well that there should be a nexus of deed and consequence, he concludes that God is unjust (Job 9:24), that God treats him like an enemy (Job 13:24; 16:9; 19:11), and that God has the power to distort the order of the entire world (Job 9:5–7; 12:14–25). Thus, in the dialogues between Job and his friends, the main focus is on content questions like Job's innocence, the world's order, and God's justice.

Nonetheless, like Ecclesiastes, Job also contains epistemological reflections, triggered by the conflict between tradition and experience (Schellenberg 2002, 205–213; O'Dowd 2007, 75–79; O'Dowd 2009, 153–161; Saur 2016, 61–64). Both Job and his friends refer to their own experience (Job 4:8; 13:1; 15:17) to support the validity of their arguments, Eliphaz and Elihu even to experiences of revelations (see below, 3.4 Revelation). Eliphaz, Bildad, and Zophar further back up their opinions with reference to tradition (Job 8:8–10; 15:10, 18; cf. 20:4), whereas Job and Elihu are critical about it, arguing that wisdom is not necessarily a privilege of old age but that all words must be tested (Job 12:11–12; 32:6–9; 34:3). All of them further try to disqualify the arguments of their opponents by questioning whether they have enough understanding (Job 11:5–9; 17:4; 26:3–4; 32:6–9; 34:35; cf. 15:7–9). And finally, like Ecclesiastes, the book of Job also contains reflections on the general limitedness of human cognition. Obviously, this insight is not an argument in the dispute among Job and his friends because it concerns all human beings alike. Rather, as in Ecclesiastes, it serves as an "answer" to the questions triggered by the conflict between tradition and experience. It cannot explain why righteous people have to suffer, etc., but it relieves humans from the need to come up with answers by explaining why such answers are not possible. There are several short statements about the impossibility for humans to understand God throughout the book (Job 9:10–11; 26:14; 36:26; 37:5; cf. 15:7–8). The limitedness of human cognition is unfolded in more detail in Job 28 and Job 38–41. In the speeches from the whirlwind, the focus is on God's doing and the order in the world. With numerous rhetorical questions, God makes it clear to Job that his knowledge is limited. In Job 28, the focus is on wisdom and the question of where it can be found. The text contrasts human technical skills (mining) with their cluelessness about the place of wisdom. Like a refrain it repeats:

> [12] But where shall wisdom be found?
> And where is the place of understanding?
> [13] Mortals do not know the way to it,
> and it is not found in the land of the living. [...]
> [20] Where then does wisdom come from?
> And where is the place of understanding?
> [21] It is hidden from the eyes of all living,
> and concealed from the birds of the air.

Only God knows the way to wisdom (Job 28:23), because as creator God has seen and established wisdom (Job 28:27). As other sapiential texts, Job 28 connects wisdom with creation (see above, 3.1 Experience and Reasoning), but here the gist is not wisdom's recognizability in creation but its exclusive connection with God and hiddenness to all others. Not fully compatible with this insight (and thus often considered a secondary addition), the last verses (Job 28:28) equates wisdom with the fear of YHWH, suggesting that the right relationship with God is a (or rather, the only) way to wisdom.

Besides Ecclesiastes and Job, other sapiential writings include statements about the limitedness of human cognition as well. In some cases, the criticism concerns people who claim to have special access to wisdom and to know more than others (Sir 34:5–7; cf. Job 15:7–8; Prov 30:4; Eccl 6:11–12, etc.). Some texts point out that wisdom is a gift from God, implying or declaring that this gift is given only to some but not to others (see below, 3.4 Revelation). Ben Sira warns against futile attempts to understand what is hidden (Sir 3:21–24) and emphasizes that through revelation in creation (and observations in nature, respectively) humans can understand God only partially (Sir 42:15–43:33; see below, 3.4 Revelation). And some few texts express a general skepticism against wisdom, at least as a human capacity, contrasting it with trust in God. Besides Prov 3:5–7 (see above, 3.2 Tradition), Prov 30:1–9 is particularly noteworthy in this regard.[3] In allusions to prophetic books and the books of Job and Deuteronomy, the speaker of the text, introduced as Agur, declares that he could not acquire any wisdom but is brutishly stupid (cf. Ps 73:22 with a similar line of argumentation). He contrasts his own ignorance with the word of God, which is refined, provides protection, and must not be expanded. The passage concludes with a prayer—extraordinary within sapiential writings—in which Agur asks God for goods that elsewhere in sapiential literature are described as consequences of wisdom. Obviously, the author of this text is most skeptical about wisdom and implicitly argues that a good life can only be achieved by trusting in God (Schipper 2012, 250–255; Schipper 2013; Saur 2014).

3.4 REVELATION

Over the course of time, the concept of revelation gains importance within sapiential epistemology. In addition to Prov 30:1–9, this is most obvious in Proverbs 1–9, the book of Ben Sira, and the Wisdom of Solomon, texts that present Wisdom as a divine female figure who reveals her (and God's, respectively) truths to humans. Without the personification of wisdom, revelation also remains important in some of the sapiential texts from Qumran. Some sages (like Ben Sira) also make connections of wisdom with the Torah—sometimes in descriptions of Woman Wisdom revealing herself, sometimes just generally. In the second case, the main concern is not the aspect of revelation or epistemology as such; rather, the texts try to clarify the relation of wisdom tradition with Torah tradition (see above, 3.2 Tradition).

---

[3] Like Prov 3:5–7 it stands in tension to the rest of Proverbs, and probably belongs to the book's latest additions.

The texts that present Wisdom as a woman most clearly emphasize the revelatory character of wisdom, but they do not introduce this thought. Rather, certain connections between wisdom and revelation can be observed from early times. This is most obvious with the phenomenon of "mantic" wisdom, which is concerned with cosmologic mysteries and their interpretation (Müller 1969; Müller 1972).[4] In the Hebrew Bible, this type of wisdom is primarily attested in later texts, but evidence of the phenomenon at Ugarit suggests an early origin. Joseph and Daniel are the most famous biblical representatives of this type of sage and, for both, the texts state that they received their special skills and insights through God (Gen 40:8; 41:16; Dan 1:17; 2:17–19, 28; 6:4; 10:1; cf. 1 Kgs 3:12; 10:24).

Likewise, even with regard to "educational" wisdom, the sages implicitly assume some revelatory dimension, namely in the sense of general revelation and natural theology, respectively, to use these terms of Jewish-Christian theology (Crenshaw 1987, 252; Perdue 1994, 109–111; Loader 2014, 28–39; Schellenberg, 2020, 165–166). More concretely, this revelatory dimension comes along with the sages' belief that wisdom is a gift from God (Ps 94:10; Job 32:8–9; 38:36; Prov 2:6; Eccl 2:26; Dan 2:21; Sir 1:10, 26; 6:37; 17:7, 11; 39:6; 43:33; Wis 9:17), which cannot be gained through humans' efforts alone but only with God's help. Though in earlier texts this thought is expressed only with regard to God creating humans with organs enabling cognition (Prov 20:12; 29:13; see above, 3.1 Experience and Reasoning), it seems unlikely that the notion that wisdom is given by God and that God made (God's order in) the world "readable" through creating everything in wisdom or with its presence (see above, 3.1 Experience and Reasoning) are late inventions. More likely, the latter formulations are explicit articulations of assumptions that implicitly were present for a long time.

That the concept of revelation has a natural place within sapiential literature is confirmed by the book of Job. Here, it is not Wisdom who is described as revealing herself—rather, Job 28 stresses that wisdom remains hidden to humans (see above, 3.2 Tradition)—but Eliphaz and Elihu refer to revelations in which God or a divine figure appear (Job 4:12–16; 32:18; 33:14–16) and towards the end of the book God speaks directly to Job from the whirlwind (Job 38–41). In Jewish-Christian terminology, these would qualify as special revelation. In Job, however, tellingly they are not described as that extraordinary: Several of the protagonists receive them and they are not mandated to convey the revelations to others.

These last two points are also true in Proverbs 1–9, even though here the concept of revelation is given much more weight. Proverbs 1–9 is the earliest text that presents Wisdom as a female figure—Woman Wisdom, as scholars call her. The roots of this idea are disputed within scholarship, as is whether the authors of Proverbs 1–9 indeed conceptualize Wisdom as a divine figure or hypostasis of God, respectively, or whether they just use the personification as a literary strategy (cf. Woman Folly in Prov 9:13–16; Fox 2000, 331–345; Maier 2007). Despite many open questions, the intention of conceptualizing Wisdom as a divine figure is clear: with the three passages that describe her (Prov 1:20–33; 8:1–36; 9:1–6), the authors of Proverbs 1–9 want to increase further their

---

[4] See also Schipper 2007, who also connects Prov 3:19–20 to this type of wisdom.

students' motivation to follow wisdom's "path." This concern is reflected throughout Proverbs 1–9. Implicitly in dialogue with skeptical voices, the authors stress that it is possible to acquire wisdom, to understand the world's order, to act accordingly, and be protected from the "way of evil" (Prov 2:12). They support their claim with epistemological statements, stressing both that God enables the acquisition of wisdom and that humans must strive for it with all their power (Schellenberg 2002, 219–225). As to be expected in an educational text, the main focus is on the necessity of humans' efforts. But, between admonitions to this effect, the authors also make clear that, ultimately, these efforts are only successful due to divine intervention. Thus, they say explicitly that the world is created "in wisdom" (Prov 3:19–20; cf. 8:22–31) and that wisdom is a gift from God (Prov 2:6). They describe Wisdom as a divine female figure who stands on the streets and invites everyone to listen to her words and "eat" from her "food" (Prov 9:5). Through the concept of revelation, they stress the authority of the sapiential tradition and immunize it against conflicting counter experiences; and through the personification of Wisdom as a woman, they point out her desirability, hoping that their (male) students are drawn to her by *eros*. As in Job, they do not connect the concept of revelation with the thought of exclusivity. On the contrary, Woman Wisdom's revelations occur most public, as already the first few verses about her make clear (Prov 1:20–23):

> [20] Wisdom cries out in the street;
> in the squares she raises her voice.
> [21] At the busiest corner she cries out;
> at the entrance of the city gates she speaks:
> [22] "How long, O simple ones, will you love being simple?
> How long will scoffers delight in their scoffing
> and fools hate knowledge?
> [23] Give heed to my reproof;
> I will pour out my thoughts to you;
> I will make my words known to you."

Woman Wisdom's revelations occur on the streets and squares of the city (Prov 1:20–21; 8:2–3) and they are directed to all, including the simple ones and fools who do not belong to a privy inner circle (Prov 1:22; 8:5; 9:4). Through Woman Wisdom, they have the chance to become wise and profit from all of wisdom's benefits as well (Prov 1:23, 33; 8:5–21; 9:6). The only step they have to take is to seek and love Wisdom, accept her invitation, and follow her advice (Prov 1:23; 8:6, 17, 21, 32–34; 9:4–5).

Like the authors of Proverbs 1–9, Ben Sira is convinced that wisdom/understanding is a gift from God, given to those who strive for it. He unfolds this thought from different angles, emphasizing different aspects (Schellenberg 2002, 225–230). An interesting passage is Sir 42:15–43:33 because here Ben Sira describes what in Jewish-Christian terminology would be labeled general revelation, namely that one can acquire knowledge about God and God's order for the world from observations in that world. As stated above, this thought is present in sapiential epistemology from the beginning, but Ben Sira makes the revelatory aspect explicit. In this passage, he points out the limitations of this "natural" way to learn about God, ending with the statement that God gives wisdom to the righteous (Sir 43:33). Together with observations on Ben Sira's statements about humans in general and Israel in particular, one might interpret this in the sense of a contrast between general and special revelation (Goering 2009, 21–24, 48–49, 65–66, 69–102, 141–142; Wright 2013, 161–162), but it is unclear whether Ben Sira indeed thinks along these categories and would make sharp distinctions between them. What is clear, though, is that elsewhere in his book he describes revelatory processes in a way that in Jewish-Christian theology would qualify as special revelation. Noteworthy in this regard is Sir 17:11, where he alludes to the giving of the Torah at Mount Sinai and parallels "the law of life" with "understanding." This is in line with other passages in the book that closely associate wisdom with the Torah (Schnabel 1985, 8–92; Collins 1997, 54–56; Goering 2009, 89–102; O'Dowd 2009, 176–178; Berg 2013; Wright 2013). The most famous of these is Sir 24:23, 25 (see further Sir 15:1; 19:20), which describes how (the divine Woman) Wisdom sought a place to live and eventually elected Israel. Elsewhere, Ben Sira does not stick to this exclusive association of wisdom with the Torah and Israel. He describes how sages/scribes get their wisdom/understanding through experience (see above, 3.1 Experience and Reasoning), by listening to their teachers (see above, 3.2 Tradition)—according to Sir 24:33 such teachings are themselves comparable to prophecy/revelation—and through God who, if willing, fills them with the "spirit of understanding" (Sir 39:6; cf. 1:6, 10, 26; 6:37; 43:33, etc.). Whereas in some of these passages wisdom/understanding is the object of revelation, elsewhere Ben Sira also describes Wisdom as the revealing subject. Like the authors of Proverbs 1–9, he conceptualizes her as a female figure. Stressing her erotic appeal, he describes how she approaches humans, urges them to cling to her, and reveals her mysteries to those who follow her invitation (Sir 4:11–18; 14:20–15:6; 24; 51:13–21). Ben Sira describes how the differences among humans proceed from God's providence (Sir 33:7–15), implies that fools cannot be awakened from their "sleep" of ignorance (Sir 22:9–10), and, through the association of wisdom with the Torah, suggests it has a special connection to Israel. In many other passages, however, these ideas are not present; rather Ben Sira gives the impression that everybody who works hard enough can acquire wisdom (e.g., Sir 1:10, 26; 6:32; 14:20–15:10). Thus, scholars disagree on how exactly Ben Sira thought about wisdom and its general accessibility. Some emphasize more his particularism (Schnabel 1985, 87, etc.), others more his universalism (Berg 2013; Wright 2013; Schellenberg, forthcoming), while others try to negotiate between them (Marböck 1999, 127–133; Goering 2009).

The picture remains somewhat mixed in the Wisdom of Solomon, the latest of the biblical (including deuterocanonical) Wisdom books, though it clearly tends toward exclusivism. This book also shows a strong educational impetus, telling its addresses that Wisdom reveals herself to those who love and seek her (Wis 6:12–13). At the same time, however, it also includes statements about the exclusivity of wisdom and revelation, respectively. First, the author of the book presents himself as being gifted with special knowledge, thus giving additional authority to his teachings. Alluding to 1 Kings 3, he presents himself as Solomon, pointing out that, after praying, the "spirit of wisdom" came to him (Wis 7:7), God gave him "unerring knowledge of what exists" (Wis 7:17), and, with Wisdom's help—he as well conceptualizes her as a person—he learned not only what is manifest but also what is "secret" (Wis 7:21; cf. 6:22). Second, in the initial part of the book, the author contrasts two groups of people, who in addition to their behavior are distinguished by whether they understand God's "mysteries" (μυστήρια; Wis 2:22). The wicked ones do not.[5] Looking at the fates of different people, they conclude that they can behave unrighteously because evildoing is not punished (Wis 1:16–2:22). Unlike the righteous ones, they do not realize that there is a postmortem final judgment in which the validity of the nexus of deed and consequence will be established (Wis 4:7–5:23). This argument immunizes the tradition against the conflict with experience (see above, 3.3 Skepticism) by expanding the horizon to realms that are beyond experience anyway. At this point, the sapiential argumentation becomes apocalyptic (Burkes 2002), not only through the notion of a final judgment but also through the concept of divine mysteries revealed only to a specific group. The Wisdom of Solomon does not further elaborate this thought but it can also be found in the sapiential writings of Qumran, for example in 4QInstruction, in which the apocalyptic characteristics are even stronger (Goff 2003, 30–126; Goff 2007, 9–68; Berg 2008, 36–94; Berg 2013, 154–156).

3.5 CONCLUSIONS

Different texts from ancient Israel display different epistemologies (Healy and Parry 2007; Gericke 2011). The same is true for different sapiential texts; they do not all share the same epistemology but disagree on essential questions. Some rely more on experience and reasoning, others more on tradition. Some associate wisdom with the Torah, others do not. Some focus on the limitations of human cognition, others stress how easy it is to become wise if one just studies hard enough. Some describe Wisdom as a divine figure who reveals herself to humans and enables them to acquire insight, others understand wisdom as inaccessible for humans. And some, finally, argue that only an elect group of humans get the privilege of such revelation, whereas the majority holds that in cognitive issues there are no privileges but only differences that go back to individual humans themselves.

The sapiential texts mirror how the sages struggle with respective questions and interact with each other. They also mirror historical developments. Most noteworthy in this regard are some of the later sapiential texts' association of wisdom with the Torah (see above, 3.2 Tradition) and some of these texts' assumption that God reveals divine mysteries only to some (see above, 3.4 Revelation). With that, they set aside some epistemological assumptions that were essential in older sapiential texts: first, the high esteem of

---

[5] According to Wis 2:21, their own wickedness "blinds" them, which implies that they could change their behavior and in consequence also get understanding. Apparently, this is not the interest of the author of the book, though. Rather, he focuses on their immoral behavior and ignorance.

experience and independent reasoning (upheld most clearly by Qoheleth but, at least ideologically, also by the other sages) and, second, that all human beings have the same cognitive abilities (and limitations, respectively), so that it is each and everybody's decision whether they become wise, with no human mediator of divine knowledge necessary. These two developments (association of wisdom with the Torah, divine mysteries revealed only to some) are only partially connected—an indication that, as in the beginning, there was not *one* uniform sapiential tradition but room for different opinions side by side.

WORKS CITED

Berg, Shane Alan. 2008. "Religious Epistemologies in the Dead Sea Scrolls: The Heritage and Transformation of the Wisdom Tradition." PhD diss., Yale University.

Berg, Shane Alan. 2013. "Ben Sira, the Genesis Creation Accounts, and the Knowledge of God's Will." *JBL* 32:139–157.

Burkes, Shannon. 2002. "Wisdom and Apocalypticism in the Wisdom of Solomon." *HTR* 95:21–44.

Collins, John J. 1997. *Jewish Wisdom in the Hellenistic Age*. OTL. Louisville, KY: Westminster John Knox.

Crenshaw, James L. 1987. "The Acquisition of Knowledge in Israelite Wisdom Literature." *WW* 7:245–252.

Crenshaw, James L. 1998. "Qoheleth's Understanding of Intellectual Inquiry." Pages 205–224 in *Qohelet in the Context of Wisdom*. Edited by Anton Schoors. BETL 86. Leuven: Peeters.

Fox, Michael V. 1987. "Qohelet's Epistemology." *HUCA* 58:137–155.

Fox, Michael V. 2000. *Proverbs 1–9: A New Translation with Introduction and Commentary*. AB 18A. New Haven, CT: Yale University Press.

Fox, Michael V. 2007. "The Epistemology of the Book of Proverbs." *JBL* 126:669–684.

Frydrych, Thomas. 2002. *Living under the Sun. Examination of Proverbs and Qoheleth*. VTSup 90. Leiden: Brill.

Gericke, Jaco. 2011. "The Epistemologies of Israelite Religion: Introductory Proposals for a Descriptive Approach." *OTE* 24:49–73.

Gericke, Jaco. 2015. "A Comprehensive Philosophical Approach to Qohelet's Epistemology." *HvTSt* 71:1–9.

Goering, Greg Schmidt. 2009. *Wisdom's Root Revealed: Ben Sira and the Election of Israel*. JSOTSup 139. Leiden: Brill.

Goff, Matthew J. 2003. *The Worldly and Heavenly Wisdom of 4QInstruction*. STDJ 50. Leiden: Brill.

Goff, Matthew J. 2007. *Discerning Wisdom: The Sapiential Literature of the Dead Sea Scrolls*. VTSup 116. Leiden: Brill.

Healy, Mary, and Robin Parry, eds. 2007. *The Bible and Epistemology: Biblical Soundings on the Knowledge of God*. Colorado Springs, CO: Paternoster.

Leuenberger, Martin. 2012. "Konsequente Erfahrungstheologien im Hiob- und Qoheletbuch." Pages 33–66 in *Die theologische Bedeutung der alttestamentlichen Weisheitsliteratur: Mit Beiträgen von Martin Leuenberger, Jürgen van Oorschot, Harmut Rosenau, Andreas Scherer und Markus Witte*. Edited by Markus Saur. BThSt 125. Neukirchen-Vluyn: Neukirchener.

Loader, James Alfred. 2014. *Proverbs 1–9*. HCOT. Leuven: Peeters.

Maier, Christl. 2007. "Weisheit (Personifikation) (AT)." *Wibilex*. Permanent link: https://www.bibelwissenschaft.de/stichwort/34659/

Marböck, Johannes. 1999. *Weisheit im Wandel: Untersuchungen zur Weisheitstheologie bei Ben Sira*. BZAW 272. Berlin: de Gruyter.

Müller, Hans-Peter. 1969. "Magisch-mantische Weisheit und die Gestalt Daniels." *UF* 1:79–94.

Müller, Hans-Peter. 1972. "Mantische Weisheit und Apokalyptik." Pages 268–293 in *Congress Volume Uppsala 1971*. VTSup 22. Leiden: Brill.

Müller, Hans-Peter, and Martin Krause. 1977. "חָכַם." *TDOT* 4:364–385.

O'Dowd, Ryan. 2007. "A Chord of Three Strands: Epistemology in Job, Proverbs and Ecclesiastes." Pages 65–87 in *The Bible and Epistemology: Biblical Soundings on the Knowledge of God*. Edited by Mary Healy and Robin Parry. Colorado Springs, CO: Paternoster.

O'Dowd, Ryan. 2009. *The Wisdom of Torah: Epistemology in Deuteronomy and the Wisdom Literature*. FRLANT 225. Göttingen: Vandenhoeck & Ruprecht.

Perdue, Leo. G. 1994. *Wisdom and Creation: The Theology of Wisdom Literature*. Nashville, TN: Abingdon.

Saur, Markus. 2014. "Prophetie, Weisheit und Gebet: Überlegungen zu den Worten Agurs in Prov 30,1–9." *ZAW* 126:570–583.

Saur, Markus. 2016. "Endlichkeit des Erkennens und Endlichkeit des Lebens in der alttestamentlichen Weisheitsliteratur." Pages 53–73 in *Zur Vergänglichkeit und Begrenztheit von Mensch, Natur und Gesellschaft*. Edited by Andreas Bihrer, Anja Franke-Schwenk, and Tine Stein. Edition Kulturwissenschaft 59. Bielefeld: Transkript Verlag.

Schellenberg, Annette. 2002. *Erkenntnis als Problem: Qohelet und die alttestamentliche Diskussion um das menschliche Erkennen*. OBO 188. Göttingen: Vandenhoeck & Ruprecht.

Schellenberg, Annette. 2015. "Don't Throw the Baby Out with the Bathwater: On the Distinctness of the Sapiential Understanding of the World." Pages 115–143 in *Was There a Wisdom Tradition? New Prospects in Israelite Wisdom Studies*. Edited by Mark R. Sneed. AIL 23. Atlanta, GA: SBL.

Schellenberg, Annette. 2020. "'Wisdom Cries Out in the Street' (Prov 1:20): On the Role of Revelation in Wisdom Literature and the Relatedness and Differences between Sapiential and Prophetic Epistemologies." Pages 157–172 in *Scribes as Sages and Prophets: Sapiential Traditions in Wisdom Literature and the Twelve Minor Prophets*. Edited by Jutta Krispenz. BZAW 496. Berlin: de Gruyter.

Schipper, Bernd U. 2007. "Kosmotheistisches Wissen: Prov 3,19f. und die Weisheit Israels." Pages 487–510 in *Bilder als Quellen, Images as Sources: Studies on Ancient Near Eastern Artefacts and the Bible Inspired by the Work of Othmar Keel*. Edited by Susanne Bickel et al. OBO Special Volume. Göttingen: Vandenhoeck & Ruprecht.

Schipper, Bernd U. 2012. *Hermeneutik der Tora: Studien zur Traditionsgeschichte von Prov 2 und zur Komposition von Prov 1–9*. BZAW 432. Berlin: de Gruyter.

Schipper, Bernd U. 2013. "When Wisdom Is Not Enough! The Discourse on Wisdom and Torah and the Composition of the Book of Proverbs." Pages 55–79 in Schipper and Teeter 2013.

Schipper, Bernd U., and D. Andrew Teeter, eds. 2013. *The Reception of "Torah" in the Wisdom Literature of the Second Temple Period*. VTSup 163. Leiden: Brill.

Schnabel, Eckhard, J. 1985. *Law and Wisdom from Ben Sira to Paul: A Tradition Historical Enquiry into the Relation of Law, Wisdom, and Ethics*. WUNT 2/16. Tübingen: Mohr Siebeck.

Sciumbata, M. Patrizia. 1996. "Peculiarità e motivazioni della struttura lessicale dei verbi della 'conoscenza' in Qohelet: Abbozzo di una storia dell'epistemologia ebraico-biblica." *Henoch* 18:235–249.

Tooman, William A. 2013. "Wisdom and Torah at Qumran: Evidence from the Sapiential Texts." Pages 203–232 in Schipper and Teeter 2013.

Weeks, Stuart. 2010. *An Introduction to the Study of Wisdom Literature.* T&T Clark Approaches to Biblical Studies. New York, NY: T&T Clark.

Weeks, Stuart. 2012. *Ecclesiastes and Scepticism.* LHBOTS 541. New York, NY: T&T Clark.

Wright III, Benjamin G. 2013. "Torah and Sapiential Pedagogy in the Book of Ben Sira." Pages 158–186 in Schipper and Teeter 2013.

CHAPTER 4

VIRTUE AND ITS LIMITS IN THE WISDOM CORPUS

Character Formation, Disruption, and Transformation

WILLIAM P. BROWN

"WISDOM" in the biblical literature resists tidy conceptualization. One can, to be sure, identify various marks of wisdom within the Wisdom corpus of the Hebrew Bible, from concrete guidance for success and moral instruction to contemplative reflection on the vagaries of life and the wonder of God and creation (Brown 2014, 24–27). But, given the sheer diversity of the literature, there is no one-size-fits-all definition, and it is even questionable whether Wisdom constitutes a discrete "tradition" (Sneed 2011). Whereas Proverbs, for instance, affirms an inviolable bond between human act and consequence, the example of Job severs the connection, and Qoheleth seems to leave it all to chance. Where Proverbs finds cosmic order, Job finds profound disorder, and Qoheleth discerns only inscrutable mystery. The Wisdom books, moreover, cover the epistemological spectrum from confident certainty to unsettling uncertainty. In short, the three Hebrew Wisdom books do not agree on much. Nevertheless, each book imparts wisdom of some sort.

Defining the "wisdom" of the Wisdom Literature in terms of a common outlook is impossible. Nevertheless, one can carve out something of wisdom's broad domain, at least negatively. Hebrew biblical Wisdom is non-historiographical, non-prophetic, and by and large (but not exclusively) non-cultic in its orientation. Instead of espousing national interests, the Wisdom Literature concerns itself primarily with creation, the family, and the individual. Wisdom's orientation, in the broadest possible terms, is human living, both private and public, within the family and in the world. Drawing from the widely different contexts of human experience, biblical Wisdom is broadly didactic or instructional in its various modes of discourse.

Perhaps the least that can be said conceptually about Wisdom is that Wisdom *imparts* wisdom. While teetering on the tautological, such a claim points to two critically important dimensions: (1) the worth of wisdom, and (2) the goal or *telos* of wisdom. First, wisdom is worthy to be shared, whether widely or selectively. It is part of wisdom's very nature that it is to be given and received, that is, passed on. Second, in the "imparting" of wisdom, there is a broad goal in view, a didactic *telos*, namely human edification, which equips and informs human agency for the challenging, all-encompassing task of living.

4.1 Wisdom and Virtue

One heuristically helpful way of exploring Wisdom's conceptual diversity is, despite recent critiques,[1] the field of "virtue ethics," which serves to highlight the distinctive moral contours of Proverbs, Job, and Ecclesiastes.[2] To demonstrate its heuristic value, a brief review of the field is called for, followed by an examination of the three Wisdom books of the Hebrew Bible. As one might surmise, "virtue ethics" highlights the importance of virtue and, more broadly, moral character in contrast to other approaches that emphasize duties and rules, or utilitarian values and consequences (Hursthouse and Pettigrove 2016). "Virtue" is a trait of human conduct that is both reflective and constitutive of moral character. It refers to an estimable disposition, something more than mere act or behavior. Virtue points, no less, to the self's formation and identity as a moral agent.

The field of virtue ethics has its roots in classical antiquity. Considered its philosophical founder, Aristotle (384–322 BCE) ascribed two functions to the notion of virtue. Virtue enables the self to become "good" and one's "work to be done well" (Aristotle 2011, 1106a15–24). In other words, goodness and excellence, the moral and the practical, are bound inextricably by virtue of virtue! Virtue bears its own efficacy. Aristotle, moreover, claimed that all human virtues are united in having the singular goal (*telos*) of attaining *eudaimonia* or "happiness" (1097b20), in other words, the "good life."[3] Such "happiness" is not to be confused with a generalized feeling or emotion, as implied by its use in contemporary discourse. Rather, *eudaimonia* is a state of fulfilled living embedded in a social context that also contributes to the "common good." Indeed, the exercise of virtue is both the means to and a part of *eudaimonia*. Virtue is tied inseparably to its *telos*.

How the virtues are to be exercised to bring about such "happiness" depends upon the cultivation of a particular virtue, namely the virtue of "practical wisdom" (*phronēsis*)

---

[1] E.g., Barton 2003, 65–74; Hankins 2015, 205–214; Stewart 2016, 11–28, 203–220. The specific critiques offered by Hankins and Stewart will be addressed below. John Barton's claim that the Hebrew Bible is not interested in the development of moral dispositions applies well to the deontological traditions found among the legal and prophetic texts, but it simply misses the mark with respect to the Wisdom corpus, particularly Proverbs. See Stewart's (2016, 14–15) critique.

[2] For general introductions on the intersection between biblical wisdom and virtue ethics, or more broadly character formation, see most recently Ansberry 2016, 181–193. Cf. Brown 1996; Brown 2014.

[3] This is most fully elucidated in Vesely 2019.

or prudence, gained through learning and practice. Practical wisdom, according to Aristotle, is the practical guide to right behavior. It is "a kind of perception" or discernment that guides moral agents to assess situations properly and act accordingly for the sake of human flourishing (1142a26–29). Practical wisdom takes stock of intention and motivation as well as consequence within a given situation. The wise person, the one who possesses practical wisdom, knows how to respond correctly "to the right person, to the right extent, at the right time, with the right motive, and in the right way" (1109a26–30).

Unlike his teacher Plato, Aristotle acknowledged the crucial importance of human emotions in the moral life.[4] The affections or passions (*pathē*) constitute an essential part of human nature and thus are integral to moral conduct: "[T]aking delight and feeling pain make no small contribution to our actions being well or badly done" (1105a5–7). Finally, Aristotle admits that the exercise of virtue is no guarantee for achieving "happiness." *Eudaimonia* is a fulfilled state of existence that lies both within one's control and outside of it. As for the latter, there are "external goods," which are vulnerable to "fate" yet are necessary for achieving "happiness" (1099a31–1099b8). The virtuous person, thus, may never be able to achieve *eudaimonia* fully due to events outside of one's control. "Those fortunes that turn out in the contrary may restrict and even ruin one's blessedness, for they both inflict pains and impede many activities" (1100b28–29).

Beyond Aristotle's own reflections on virtue, one more issue significant for virtue ethics needs to be highlighted, namely the self's unity. Alasdair MacIntyre (2007, 203) writes:

> Unless there is a *telos* which transcends the limited goods of practices by constituting the good of a whole human life, the good of a human life conceived as a unity, it will *both* be the case that a certain subversive arbitrariness will invade the moral life *and* that we shall be unable to specify the context of certain virtues adequately.

MacIntyre's concept of the self is one "whose unity resides in the unity of a narrative which links birth to life to death as narrative beginning to middle to end" (205). Such a narrative, for example, is typically codified in the genre of the obituary. Without this sense of narrative unity, intentions, and beliefs, constitutive components of moral character and conduct are robbed of their integrity. Indeed, for MacIntyre the virtue of "integrity" is by necessity indicative of the context of a whole human life (203). With virtue as its foundation, the moral self bears a narrative morphology; otherwise, life becomes nothing more than a series of discrete episodes, resulting in "a liquidation of the self" (205). In such a segmented state, virtue is rendered meaningless. The self's narrative unity, in other words, has all to do with the *formation* of the self as a moral agent.

Virtue ethics, in short, posits a moral unity of the self, and in so doing stresses character and conduct over action,[5] purpose over consequence, discernment over duty, and the self's unity over discrete experiences and events. Its encompassing question is

---

[4] For a discussion of the "passions and affections" in the Hebrew scriptures, see most recently Lasater 2017, 520–540.

[5] I.e., specific acts of behavior in particular situations or contexts.

"How shall I live?" rather than "How shall I act?" This is not to say that a virtue-based ethic does not give consideration to rules, discrete actions, and their consequences. It does, indeed, but in a way that frames them within the narrative continuity of the moral self.

Given this all too brief introduction, does virtue ethics provide a helpful lens for highlighting the distinctive yet defining moral contours of the Wisdom corpus of the Hebrew Bible? On the one hand, the fact that such literature presents an alternative to the deontologically oriented Torah-based "law" opens the possibility for constructive engagement. On the other hand, that the Wisdom Literature is itself quite divergent ethically suggests that virtue ethics alone may be of limited value for such engagement. Methodologically, there is no one-size-fits-all approach for the Wisdom corpus as a whole. Nevertheless, one must start somewhere, and Proverbs is as good a place as any, since its ethical starting point seems most fully congenial to virtue ethics. As an exploratory venture to determine the value and limitations of a virtue-based ethical approach, beginning with Proverbs, I will examine each Wisdom book according to the following categories: (1) the efficacy of virtue, (2) the shape of "happiness," and (3) the narrativity of the moral self.

4.2 PROVERBS: ETHICS OF FORMATION

In Proverbs, wisdom covers a wide range of virtues, as indicated in the opening collage (1:2–7), followed by various profiles of positive and negative character throughout chapters 1–9. Such virtues include "fear" or reverence of God (יראת יהוה), "righteousness" (צדק/צדקה), and "justice" (משפט)—all moral attributes. Other virtues are more practical in nature: "prudence" (ערמה), "discretion" (מזמה), and "guidance" (תחבלות). They help in achieving the subject's goals. Vices, on the other hand, include "folly" (אולת) or "stupidity" (כסילות), "wickedness" (רשע), "deceit" (מרמה), "pride" or arrogance (√גאה or זדון/זד), and "greed" (√בצע), to name a few. The distinction between virtue and vice, however, can get blurry in some cases. Certain "virtues" of the practical kind are morally ambivalent. מזמה, for example, can be positive ("discretion") or negative ("mischief"), depending on the context.[6] Similarly, ערמה can denote cunning and premeditation, as well as prudence or discretion.[7] The moral valuation of these practical attributes is measured by how and to what end they are employed. Are all virtues intrinsically good? Not so in Proverbs. In short, such a constellation of virtues and vices, and in certain cases their fuzzy boundaries and ambiguities, provides a roadmap (or better "pathway") for the formation of the moral self in Proverbs.

---

[6] For its positive valence, see Prov 1:4; 3:21; 5:2; 8:12; negative, 12:2; 14:17; 24:8. In the negative case, the term is consistently cast as the *nomen regens* in a construct chain that denotes a person's character.

[7] For ערמה, compare Exod 21:14 and Josh 9:4 against Prov 8:5, 12. Cf. its cognate adjective ערום ("crafty") in Gen 3:1.

Since "wisdom" is of central importance in Proverbs,[8] one may query whether it is wisdom or virtue that is irreducibly primary for the ancient biblical sages. On the one hand, the moral trinity of "righteousness, justice, and equity" (Prov 1:3) is deemed teachable and thus a matter of wisdom. On the other hand, the so-called motto of Proverbs given in 1:7 and 9:10 ("The fear of YHWH is the beginning of knowledge/wisdom") suggests that wisdom itself arises from the cardinal virtue of reverence.[9] While this is likely a chicken-or-the-egg issue, it is clear that character formation and wisdom appropriation present a sort of positive feedback loop by which one amplifies the other. Wisdom is demonstrated through the exercise of virtue, and virtue is a matter of learning and understanding. And what is it that drives this amplifying interaction between wisdom and virtue? It is desire (Yoder 2011, 148–162). Like appetite, desire is innate, even while its objects, whether deemed worthy or not, are interchangeable. Through their rhetorical skill, the sages behind Proverbs strive mightily to steer the reader's desire toward wisdom and righteousness and away from folly and greed.

4.2.1 Efficacy of Virtue

Linked inextricably to practical wisdom, the power of virtue in Proverbs is set in sharpest relief by a simple comparison with Psalms regarding one cardinal virtue, "righteousness." In the Psalms, "righteousness" is attributed almost entirely to God (e.g., 5:9 [ET 8]; 11:7a; 31:2 [1]):[10]

> They will receive blessing from YHWH,
>   and righteousness from the God of their salvation.
>   (24:5)[11]

> Your righteousness is like the mighty mountains,
>   your judgments are like the great deep;
>   you save humans and animals alike, YHWH.
>   (36:7 [6])

Indeed, *human* righteousness is rarely mentioned in the Psalms,[12] and when it is, it rarely stands on its own (cf. Pss 111–112). In Proverbs, by contrast, human righteousness bears its own efficacy, even exhibiting salvific import without reference to the deity:

> Treasures gained by wickedness do not profit,
>   but righteousness delivers from death.
>   (Prov 10:2; cf. 11:4b)

---

[8] Wisdom in Proverbs covers everything that can be learned or appropriated in order to develop excellence in skill and moral agency, including the practical, the artistic, and the ethical.

[9] On the other hand, elsewhere in Proverbs "fear" is deemed "understandable" (2:3–5; cf. 15:33; Ps 34:11).

[10] Exceptions are Pss 72:3 ("hills" yielding prosperity); 106:3 ("those who do righteousness"), 31 (Phinehas); 112:3, 9 (cf. 111:3). For "righteousness," see 15:2. Otherwise, the term is most frequently applied to God.

[11] Cf. 40:11 [10]; 51:16 [14]; 71:2.   [12] Only 7:9 [8]; 18:21 [20], 25 [24]; cf. 35:27.

The righteousness of the upright saves them,
> but the treacherous are taken captive by their schemes.

(11:6)

Righteousness guards one whose way is upright,
> but sin overthrows the wicked.

(13:6)

Most telling is Prov 14:32:

The wicked one is overthrown by his evildoing,
> but the righteous one finds refuge in his integrity.[13]

Such a salvific view of human righteousness is unprecedented in the Psalms, even among the so-called Wisdom psalms. In the Psalms, righteousness is predominantly associated with God's wondrous deeds of salvation (e.g., 71:15–16, 19, 24; 98:2). No psalm claims salvific import for the human exercise of righteousness; it is not a virtue but rather a gift. Righteousness in Proverbs, however, is quintessentially a virtue, given its efficacious import. That is to say, righteousness itself saves and protects. In Proverbs, a virtue is robustly consequential for the human subject; it shapes, no less, the person's sphere of destiny (see also 2:10–12).

4.2.2 "Happiness" in Proverbs

The well-lit path that grows ever brighter suggests a salutary *telos*, a fulfilled life. Indeed, the appropriation of wisdom is identified repeatedly with life itself (4:13; 8:35), but what kind of life? While the fulfilled or flourishing life associated with wisdom in Proverbs is multifaceted, certain defining marks are readily identifiable, such as in the following passage concerning personified Wisdom's benefits:

Happy (אשרי) is the one who finds Wisdom,
> the one who attains understanding,
for her income is better than silver,
> and her revenue better than gold.
She is more precious than rubies,
> and the sum of your delights cannot equal her.
Long life is in her right hand;
> in her left hand are wealth and honor.
Her ways are ways of pleasantness,
> and all her paths are well-being.

---

[13] Read בתמו for MT's במותו ("in his death"), which probably arose accidentally through metathesis of the *taw* and *mem* (cf. LXX), contra Clifford (1999, 142–143, 148), who finds the meaning of this emendation "insipid." Clifford wrongly assumes that "refuge" takes God as the subject, as it does in the Psalms.

> She is a tree of life to those grasp her;
> > those who hold her fast are deemed happy.
>
> > (3:13–18)

As a "tree of life," Wisdom offers longevity and prosperity, honor and peace. Her value exceeds the sum total of all material sources of delight and objects of desire (see also 8:11). She offers enduring wealth (8:18; cf. 3:9–10). Elsewhere, Wisdom claims to offer security and ease, a life devoid of fear (1:33). Those who refuse Wisdom, on the other hand, will sooner or later be struck with disaster (1:27; cf. 3:25).

Embracing Wisdom, however, is no single, easy feat. A "wise," and thus fulfilled, life is marked by discipline and diligence (6:4–5; 10:4); it is a life that, on the one hand, eschews laziness and idleness (24:30–34), and, on the other, embraces humility and reverence (e.g., 1:7; 3:5–7). As foils for the virtuous life, Proverbs enumerates seven "abominations" or abhorrent qualities of character or conduct:

> There are six things that YHWH hates,
> > seven that are an abomination to him:
> arrogant eyes, a deceitful tongue,
> > and hands that shed innocent blood,
> a heart that devises wicked plans,
> > feet that run swiftly to evil,
> a lying witness who testifies falsely,
> > and one who stirs up strife among brothers.
> > > (6:16–19)

Cast anatomically, from eyes to feet, and taken together, these vices corporeally fashion the quintessentially immoral agent. Their virtuous opposites include humility, honesty, nonviolence/peace, avoidance of evil, and familial harmony, which also extends to neighborly relations (3:27–30).

The virtuous life, according to Proverbs, begins with individual initiative, as the father repeatedly instructs his listening son: "Get wisdom!" (קנה חכמה; 4:5, 7). But "getting wisdom" is more an exercise of self-love than an act of self-sacrifice:

> To get intelligence is to love oneself;
> > to keep understanding is to prosper.
> > > (19:8)

The sage tries to convince his audience that wisdom is "good for you," that wisdom is to one's benefit, embodied for the sake of "happiness." This is not, however, an exercise in self-aggrandizement. To the contrary, the virtuous individual is one who contributes to the common good, as in the case of giving to the poor: "Happy is the one who is kind to the poor" (14:21b; cf. v. 31; 7:5; 19:17). Indeed, poverty in Proverbs is not always disparaged (16:19; 19:1). Integrity, for example, trumps wealth when it comes to the ethically esteemed life (28:6). Indeed, the only prayer in all of Proverbs is prayer about finding that happy medium between wealth and poverty, that sweet spot of sufficiency (30:7–9). Prosperity is a means not of self-enhancement but of sustenance that fosters trust and dependence upon God.

One more thing about the "happy life" in Proverbs: it is structured androcentrically. The virtuous life serves to guard against the encroachment of the "strange," which presents itself as both temptation and threat, particularly as it is represented in the feminine for a male audience. The so-called "loose woman" (NRSV) is literally the "strange/foreign woman" אשה זרה/נכריה (2:16; 5:3; 7:5; cf. 22:14). Via the male gaze, the stranger is cast as a woman in the form of a *femme fatale* (7:10–21). This object of fatal attraction constitutes the quintessential "other" in Proverbs: an object of both fantasy and fear, including the fear of death (7:27a; cf. 2:18; 22:14).[14] She is, in literary fact, Wisdom's nemesis: they both walk the same streets and occupy their respective homes within the city, inviting their guests to enter (1:20–21; 7:11–12; 8:1–3; 9:1–6, 13–17). They are opposites who share common ground, the same battlefield, as it were, both vying for the reader's allegiance.

Speaking of Wisdom, her real-life counterpart is the "woman of strength" (or "substance," "valor" [אשת חיל]) found in the final chapter of Proverbs (31:10–31). Her profile enfleshes the familial and familiar virtues of Proverbs within the patriarchal household.[15] She models industry and diligence (vv. 13, 15, 18b, 22, 24); idleness is anathema to her (v. 27b). She gives generously to the poor (v. 20), prudently seeks opportunities for profit (vv. 16, 18a), leads without fear (vv. 21, 15), and, yes, honors her husband (vv. 11–12), who enjoys his esteem at the city gates sitting among the elders (v. 23). Like Wisdom herself, she is invaluable to her husband and his household (v. 10b). She is depicted as a domestic warrior, a valiant woman (vv. 17, 25), and her domicile serves as her fortress against all external threats (cf. Wolters 1988, 446–457). It is no coincidence, then, that this "woman of strength" reflects certain virtues that are also commended for males.[16]

4.2.3 Narrativity of the Self

It is no coincidence that the acrostic poem of the "woman of strength" concludes Proverbs. With her poetic profile featured at the end, a meta-narrative arc is established that encompasses most of the book. After the seven-verse prologue, the reader encounters a father addressing his son, stressing the life-over-death importance of heeding parental advice, which includes marrying rightly, on the one hand, and avoiding the "strange woman," on the other. Parental voices, indeed, dominate the first nine chapters of Proverbs, except in those passages in which Wisdom speaks (1:20–33; 8:1–36). Throughout, the common

[14] For a discussion of "otherness" in Proverbs 1–9 with specific focus on its economic and xenophobic underpinnings, see Yee 2003, 135–158.

[15] For a trenchant socioeconomic analysis of the "woman of substance" as a Persian-period woman, see Yoder 2001.

[16] The LXX translation of v. 10 is literally: "Who can find a manly woman (γυναῖκα ἀνδρείαν)?," connoting courage. It may also be worth noting that the word "virtue" has its etymologically androcentric Latin root (*vir* = "man"; *virtus* = "valor").

mode of discourse is direct address or admonition, most typically directed toward the "son," a silent son, in fact, who functions rhetorically as the placeholder for the reader. The reader, in other words, is the listener "interpellated" into such ideologically charged discourse.[17] Because the son never talks, we never know what he is thinking.

The lectures conclude in chapter 9 with a life-determining choice: either accept Wisdom or succumb to Woman Stranger/Folly. Both of their homes are open for business; both of them offer their version of life (9:4–5, 14–17). Will the son choose rightly, unlike the hapless youth in 7:22–23? The answer is not given until the end of the book: the silent son, now grown, is married to the "woman of strength." He sits among the elders at the city gate (31:23), where he finds his voice: "Many women have done valorously (חיל), but you surpass them all!" (v. 29). The narrative unity of the self has reached its conclusion: the mark of his maturity rests, in part at least, on having chosen well.

In her study of the poetics of Proverbs, Anne Stewart (2016) critiques the view that Proverbs can be cast in narrative terms. She rightly notes that Proverbs is "not narrative in literary form" (213, 219), for it does not contain a linear plot (27). Rather, Proverbs features collections of proverbs, admonitions, and lectures, mostly poetic. Hence, imagery, metaphor, emotional appeal, descriptive snapshots, and personification are all integral to Proverbs' didactic toolkit (27–28). Nevertheless, the poetic repertoire of Proverbs in no way precludes the presence of a narrative-like arc that covers the book as a whole, which Stewart actually concedes in her conclusion (212; see also 27 ["narrative elements"]). It is the purposeful arrangement of these blocks and bits of poetry, from the extensive lecture to the terse proverb, that builds to the book's narrative-like resolution in the final chapter. The formation of the self, in other words, is framed in Proverbs by a meta-narrative arc from receptive son to honored husband.

Moreover, under this arc lies a particularly suggestive metaphor that is repeated to the point that it becomes Proverbs' leitmotif: the "pathway." Various virtues, for example, are metaphorically limned as paths (2:8–9, 13, 20; 8:20), so also vices (crooked/twisty paths), which lead to death (2:15, 18). Life is itself a path (v. 19). Wisdom, too, is a path, comprising, in fact, many "paths of well-being (שָׁלוֹם)" (3:17). Proverbs delineates two distinct, nonintersecting paths: the "path" of wisdom (including righteousness, justice, uprightness, etc.) and the "path" of wickedness and folly. The qualities of these two paths are defined in starkly antithetical terms: "The way of the lazy is overgrown with thorns, but the path of the upright is a level highway" (15:19). Or more pointedly:

> But the path of the righteous is like the light of dawn,
> shining ever brighter until the day is set.
> The way of the wicked is like deep darkness;
> they do not know where they will stumble.
>
> (4:18–19)

The metaphor of the pathway itself suggests process and direction. The path of the wicked, by contrast, is "crooked" or twisted (אָקֵשׁ; 2:15; 28:6, 18), perhaps one could say

---

[17] Newsom 1989, 143–144. The term is taken from the Marxist theoretician Louis Althusser.

"segmented," a path without clear direction or unity. For the righteous and the wise, the pathway connotes formation of character, "shining brighter and brighter." As for the wicked, their way is one stumble after another in the dark.

4.3 JOB: ETHICS OF ENCOUNTER

Can a virtue ethics approach be extended to wisdom in the book of Job? If so, it would have to recognize how Job differs ethically from Proverbs. Job, first of all, raises questions that challenge the moral certainties claimed in Proverbs. The prosperity of the wicked, as lamented by Job, presents a stark counter testimony (Job 21:7–34).[18] More broadly, virtue's efficacy seems to be thoroughly emasculated in Job. Finally, the *eudaimonic* ideal, at least as conceived by Job, is given only temporary, if not fleeting, status in Job 29. How, then, can virtue ethics shed light on these Joban "anomalies"?

4.3.1 Virtue's Efficacy?

At the outset, the book's most virtuous and prosperous character is demoralized in a veritable parody of divine providence. In two fell swoops, Job, a man of moral rectitude and the "greatest of all the people of the east" (1:1, 3) is stripped of security, prosperity, and health, not to mention sanity,[19] all the while his moral character is impugned with increasing vehemence by his friends: character assassination conducted in the guise of "comfort" (2:11). But the one thing Job is not stripped of is his "integrity" (2:3, 9; 4:6; 27:5; 31:6). He persists. Job chastises his friends for their rush to judgment and accuses God of committing a travesty of justice, even calling God to court. From Job's perspective, the very efficacy of virtue is thrown into question. It is Job's integrity, after all, that invites trouble in the first place—the height of irony (1:8; 2:3). As such, the Prologue paints a "perversion of moral causality."[20]

Nevertheless, something of virtue resurfaces after the cycles of turgid dialogue have run their course over twenty-five chapters. Chapter 28 features a speculative wisdom poem that opens with rich imagery highlighting the daring nature of exploring remote regions for valuable minerals. But halfway through the poem, the rugged landscape of mining exploration gives way to the hidden topography of wisdom's domain, to which only God knows the way. Nevertheless, a surprising sapiential turn is taken at the end, even as wisdom is deemed inaccessible to humans. The conclusion is not so much an intellectual "let-down," as an anti-speculative subversion: "Truly, the fear of the Lord, that is wisdom, and to depart from evil is understanding" (28:28a). This concluding verse identifies the one and only point of "access" to wisdom that is available to human beings,

---

[18] Cf. Prov 2:22; 3:33; 5:22; 10:25.

[19] Note Job's contradictory discourse in the third cycle of dialogues, particularly in light of 24:18–25 and 27:13–23, both of which stress the certainty of punishment for the wicked and the powerful (contra 21:2–26).

[20] Thanks to ethicist Frederick Simmons for articulating this so pointedly in a personal communication.

namely a disposition of "fear" before God and a dissociation from evil. Because only God can search out wisdom, the wisdom that lies beyond human apprehension, human beings must take their sapiential cue in deference to the God of wisdom. This motto-like statement echoes the proverbial sense of "fear" as the epistemological beginning point of wisdom (e.g., Prov 1:7; 9:10), but with a significant twist. Without wisdom as an object of search and extraction, without wisdom as the prize of heroic exploits, what is left is simply "fear" and the avoidance of evil—*that* is wisdom, no more, no less. Note the difference between the two "mottos":

> Truly, the fear of the Lord, that is wisdom.
> (Job 28:28a)

> The beginning (תחלת) of wisdom is the fear of YHWH.
> (Prov 9:10)

"Fear" in Proverbs constitutes merely the beginning of sapiential formation; it is the point of departure on wisdom's "path." In Job 28, however, there is no path for the appropriation of wisdom; hence, there is no formation or cultivation of wisdom, only "fear" itself. That is to say, "the fear of the Lord" is the beginning *and* the end of wisdom (cf. Sir 1:14, 16, 18); wisdom is reduced to awe of the divine (cf. Job 42:3). In Job 28, wisdom is the virtue of godly "fear." All there is to wisdom is this singleness of virtue: a matter not of discovery but of disposition, not of possession but of practice. In other words, wisdom for human beings is a virtue devoid of Wisdom, that is, wisdom emptied of the kind of wisdom that is cosmically speculative and poetically personified (cf. Prov 8:22–31).

The primacy of "fear" and avoidance of evil in Job 28 recalls Job's own moral stature in the opening verse as one who "feared God and turned away from evil" (1:1b). But the book does not end on this seemingly conclusive note; rather, Job's story continues to lurch forward as if still on a quest—a search for vindication from Job's perspective, yes, but also a quest for something more than simply pious "fear" to provide resolution. The fact that the book's climactic conclusion extends beyond chapter 28 demonstrates both the value and limitation of a virtue-based ethos. From the book's prologue until his oath (chs. 1–31), Job proved himself to be "virtuous but ignorant" (Cooper 1997, 235). This is indubitably (and painfully) clear in Job's final extended discourse (chs. 29–31), which contains an apotheosis of the *eudaimonic* life, now relegated to distant memory.

In chapter 29, Job details his former life of glory within the three human domains of existence: the familial, the communal, and the peripheral.[21] But Job begins with the theological, as he recalls what life was like when "God watched over" him (v. 2), when the "intimate company (סוד) of God graced [his] tent" (v. 4b). Back then Job basked in the company of both *Shadday* and his children (v. 5). Back then Job was the embodied product of his virtues. Back then Job enjoyed great public esteem as both young and old conferred him honor (vv. 8–11, 21–23). Every word from Job's lips was received with deferential silence, welcomed like "spring rain" (v. 23). But it is in the peripheral realm,

---

[21] Vesely (2019) delineates three comparable realms: domestic, public, and marginal.

the world of the marginalized, that Job's virtuous character is best demonstrated, in his estimation. It is precisely *because* Job "delivered the poor," the orphan, and the widow (vv. 12–13), that he was so highly esteemed. It is in the domain of the peripheral that "righteousness" and "justice" are specifically identified (v. 14). In practice, such virtues were demonstrated specifically in service to the most vulnerable. The needy and the poor depended upon him (vv. 15–16a). Job saw himself as the champion of outcasts (vv. 16b–17a). All in all, Job "lived like a king among his troops, like one who comforts mourners" (v. 25), and he looked forward to living large in his longevity (v. 18; cf. 42:17).

4.3.2 Eulogy over *Eudaimonia*

Job's world of honor and hierarchy crumbles in light of his present condition. Once king of the hill, Job is now lord of his ash heap. Cast out from his community, Job is now ridiculed even by the poor (30:1–10, 12–14), an outcast among outcasts. Moreover, once Job's companion, God has turned oppressor and enemy, having "loosed [his] bowstring" (v. 11) and tossing Job "about in the roar of the storm" (v. 22). Job himself has become "needy," without anyone to help him (v. 24). Job's concluding words in chapter 31 take the form of an oath that is meant to prove his innocence/integrity before God and his friends, while at the same time calling God to account. At this point, the poetry of Job is not simply non-*eudaimonist*; it is anti-*eudaimonist*. His final words, in effect, offer a poignant eulogy over the death of *eudaimonia*. Job's concluding discourse, from the nostalgic ruminations of his "glory days" to his climactic oath of innocence (chs. 29–31), effectively buries all sense of happiness born of virtue.

4.3.3 Ethics of Encounter

After the significant detour of Elihu's rebuke (chs. 32–37), the stage is set to move toward a different ethical framework, one derived from YHWH's answer to Job, an answer oriented toward the margins. More than simply a raw demonstration of divine power, the divine speeches are filled with far off encounters that are meant to impart instruction to Job, a sapiential rebuke of the highest order from the divine pedagogue. YHWH's response pulls Job's attention back to the periphery, but to a periphery that lies far beyond his own purview, disrupting his own limited realm of perception. Once again, it is the periphery that holds the key to Job's resolution, as much as it held the key to his righteousness and justice, as noted above (29:14).

Job's encounter with God gives way to other encounters from the margins. Cosmically strange places, from the dwelling place of light to the gates of deep darkness, give way to zoologically strange and monstrous creatures, climaxing with an over-the-top description of Leviathan (40:25–41:26 [41:1–34]). Each creature is given its praiseworthy due, some more than others, whether it is the untamable wild ox, the fearless warhorse, the senselessly fierce ostrich, or the majestically strong Behemoth. Each creature is marked with wild, fierce freedom (O'Connor 2003, 171–179). With each one described in greater detail, Job comes face to face with the other. In God's answer, Job confronts alterity, an encounter marked by difference and dignity. The cumulative result is a creation infused with Otherness.

Is there an ethical perspective to be gained from this theophanic encounter? Or better put, is there an ethical perspective that can more fully account for the climactic, disruptive conclusion of the book of Job than one defined by virtue ethics? Virtue ethics does seem to fall short in Job; it does little to account for the plurality of difference, or in the words of Emmanuel Levinas, the "radical heterogeneity" (1969, 293) that characterizes creation according to YHWH. God's verbal theophany is an intervention that is nothing short of a disruption and dismantling of self-oriented and self-sustaining accounts of morality, such as moral retribution (see Tsevat 1966, 102). The efficacy of virtue and wisdom is replaced by wisdom's inaccessibility and the shock of encounter, beginning with God and continuing with creation in all its bewildering plurality of domains and diversity of creatures. God reveals a creation that privileges alterity over unity and subjects over principles.

Morally, the presence of the other forces a demand upon the self, according to Levinas (1991, 87): "The community with [the other] begins with my obligation to him [sic]." Does God's theophanic discourse make such a comparable claim? Not directly. It is nowhere evident that Job, in his encounter with others, has a moral obligation to these creatures of the wild. Nevertheless, the theophany and its creational extension does set the stage for a distinctly moral outcome, one that answers the question, How shall I live? Specifically, How should Job live?

One particular creature profiled in YHWH's answer, the onager or wild ass, is telling. In his own laments, Job had likened the poor to scavenging onagers in 24:4–8 and 30:1–8. With such association, Job conveys both his pity and his contempt for the poor. But in God's description of the onager, admiration replaces pity:

> Who has set the onager free?
>> Who has loosed the ropes of the wild ass,
> to which I have given the steppe for its home,
>> the salt flats for its dwelling place?
> It scorns the chaos of the city;
>> it does not hear the driver's shouts.
> It roams the mountains as its pasture,
>> while searching for every green thing.
>
> (39:5–8)

In God's eyes, the onager retains its dignity as a quintessentially free, wild creature. The contrast with Job runs deep: as Job reveled in receiving the deferential respect of others (29:23), the onager refuses to hear the "driver's shouts" as it exercises its freedom apart from the city.

Does the transformation of the onager from an object of pity to a subject of dignity transform, in turn, Job's relationship with the "other," such as the poor? One wonders. The issue remains unaddressed in the epilogue. Nothing is said about how Job treated the poor, now that he is more than fully restored. The only hint of transformation is found in the way Job treats his daughters. They become the face of the familiar other, and Job responds accordingly: he gives them "an inheritance along with their brothers" (42:13–15). In so doing Job has disrupted the conventional patriarchal practice of distributing wealth by including his daughters in addition to his sons, enabling them to gain economic independence (cf. Num 27:1–11; 36:1–10). Job shares his inheritance freely, and he does so out of a sense of kinship coupled with pride in his daughters' remarkable differences: they are beautiful and female. His daughters are objects of wonder, as much as the creatures of the wild are in YHWH's answer. Yet in their objectification Job's daughters also become subjects in their own right, as confirmed in Job's treatment of them. An ethics of encounter, as developed by Levinas, highlights Job's encounter with alterity, from the holy Other to beastly others, and finally Job's "other" children, his three daughters, to whom he is morally obligated.

4.3.4   Narrativity of the Self: Job's Integrity

Contrary to attempts to find virtue ethics entirely irrelevant in the case of Job, one cannot deny that Job, unlike Proverbs, is framed literarily as a narrative, a narrative primarily about Job. This literary fact presupposes at some level a narrativity of the self. The question is whether any continuity of Job's character exists from beginning to end. While Job suffers disruption, the epilogue (42:7–17) recalls the story-world of the prologue to certify, among other things, that the latter Job bears some degree of continuity with the former Job. Job remains a patriarch, yet he acts un-patriarchally. Job is restored to wealth, yet he uses that wealth unconventionally.

A virtue ethics approach highlights the degree of continuity that is preserved amid Job's transformation. The one continuing thread throughout the story of Job that prevents Job from devolving into a "segmented" or "liquidated self," to borrow from MacIntyre, or simply into an "event," to borrow from Hankins (2015, 226), is the leitmotif of Job's integrity (Ansberry 2017). Job persists in his "integrity" (תמה; 2:3, 9; 27:5; 31:6). He knows he is innocent and undeserving of what he regards as divine abuse. What, then, is the shape of Job's integrity on the other side of the theophany? Hankins (2015, 20–21) posits that Job discovers himself "undetermined" in the wake of God's answer. A more germane way of putting it is that Job discovers himself to be fundamentally free, as free as the wild creatures he encounters, free enough to reconfigure the socio-economic structure of his new family. Such freedom, it turns out, is reflected in the very "order" of creation, a wild freedom that Job, ironically perhaps, has exhibited all along from the time he uttered his self-curse to the time he gives his self-oath before his friends.

Indeed, Job's integrity is shown to be grounded in his freedom to question the theo-ethical foundations of conventional wisdom, the freedom to charge God with wrongdoing and call God to court, the bold freedom to approach God "like a prince" for a divine accounting (Job 31:37). Nowhere in YHWH's answer is Job's integrity denounced, only his knowledge of things that are "too wonderful" for him, as Job himself admits

(42:3). Like Leviathan, Job's blasphemous mouth breathes fire, incinerating the "wisdom" of his friends (41:11–13 [41:19–21]; cf. 13:12). Like Behemoth, Job is not frightened by the torrent of criticism he receives (40:23). Like the wild ox, Job refuses to be tamed by his friends or by God (39:9). Creation is not a safe place, and neither is Job a "safe" person. If there is any confirmation of Job in his traumatic encounter with YHWH, it is that Job's freedom proves to be inalienable. YHWH's vindication of Job before his friends in 42:7 marks Job's confirmation of his integrity amid his transformation.

4.3.5 *Eudaimonia* **Regained?**

Finally, the epilogue features not only a new life for Job, but a new *way* of life. Job turns unconventional by sharing his inheritance with his daughters. In addition, Job prays on behalf of his friends, who had betrayed him throughout their respective counsels (42:8–9). Perhaps more can be inferred in comparison to Job's former life, as captured in the prologue: Job no longer sacrifices on behalf of his children for fear that they may have "cursed God in their hearts" (1:5). God evidently does not care about that. What Job cares about is the dignity and well-being of all his children, daughters and sons alike, much like God's care of all the creatures of the wild, a gratuitous care in the face of alterity. Wisdom, as a result, becomes filled with awe for the other, from God to animals to daughters (cf. 42:3). Moreover, the epilogue highlights the constructive role of the community in Job's restoration in contrast to the isolationism that runs throughout his discourse (42:11; Hankins 2015, 223). His "comfort" is achieved by the larger community rather than by his three "friends" (2:11; cf. 30:29). The epilogue poses the question that is of primary concern to any virtue ethicist: How does Job live the rest of his life, all 140 years? It is a valid, not inconsequential question, even if it is left to the reader's imagination. The clue is in how Job treats his daughters. Job's longevity is not simply quantitative: the expression "full of days" (ימים שׂבע) also reflects something of Job's satisfaction with his new life (cf. Gen 25:8)—*eudaimonia* regained.

4.4 ECCLESIASTES: "ETHICS" OF ENJOYMENT

Whereas the book of Job turns toward the "other" for its ultimate moral content, Ecclesiastes turns inward toward the self. The language of responsibility and obligation toward others is largely absent throughout Qoheleth's discourse, except when it comes to fearing God. Instead, the sage is obsessed with the question of whether one can secure lasting "gain" (יתרון, 1:3; 3:9), an entirely futile quest in the sage's estimation (2:11; 5:15 [16]). Qoheleth, moreover, is concerned not so much with moral assessment, whether of others or of himself, as he is with what "advantage" (מותר) humans can gain through their conduct (3:19). Qoheleth, in short, is instrumentally self-oriented, one could even say self-absorbed. Whereas the self in Job is thrown into a wondrous, unsettling world of difference, Qoheleth's self is embedded in a monotonous, weary world, the world of הבל,[22] in which human beings are beset with an utter lack of control (Seow 2001, 237–249), a world in which there are no guarantees (9:11–12), a world without wisdom in any summative sense (7:23–28). The link between character and destiny is irreparably severed before the ravages of "time and chance" (9:11).

The human lack of control and its moral implications, in fact, find some degree of correlation in contemporary ethical discourse with what is called "moral luck," which acknowledges that the moral assessment of a human agent frequently depends on factors beyond his or her control (Nelkin 2013)—Aristotle's notion of "external goods" taken to the extreme. The discussion was first introduced by Bernard Williams (1993), who initially regarded "moral luck" as an "oxymoron" (251). The acknowledgment of "moral luck" flies in the face of the conventional understanding of moral assessment that claims that a person is morally assessable only with regard to matters that are under his/her control—what is called the "Control Principle" of ethical theory. But the reality is that realizing our intentions in action, whether successful or not, often depends on factors that lie outside of our control. For some, moral luck (particularly "constitutive" and "causal moral lack") is so pervasive that it can negate the very possibility of moral assessment. According to Nagel (1979, 35), "[T]he area of genuine agency, and therefore of legitimate moral judgment, seems to shrink under this scrutiny to an extensionless point." Nagel goes on to say:

> Eventually nothing remains which can be ascribed to the responsible self, and we are left with nothing but a portion of the larger sequence of events, which can be deplored or celebrated, but not blamed or praised. (37)

The discussion continues among ethicists.

While Qoheleth is no ethicist, he fully acknowledges the arbitrary nature of life, including the moral life. Yet the skeptical sage does not go so far as to cast human agency, moral and otherwise, simply as separate events governed by "time and chance." On the other hand, the sage gives no indication of reading human agency as a product of lifelong formation, as the outcome of the self's narrativity. Nevertheless, the "righteous" and the "wicked," along with the attributes of righteousness and wickedness, remain meaningful categories for him, but only in so far as they highlight the disruptive, nullifying reality of הבל. Qoheleth, for example, finds wickedness displacing justice and righteousness (3:16). Such displacement does not take place simply in the abstract: the righteous, Qoheleth observes, are mistaken for the wicked (8:14). Wickedness and righteousness have traded places, so it seems, and the result is a topsy-turvy moral world, an anti-moral world (7:15). The world of הבל, in other words, is a world that is utterly out of sync with human striving, whether ethical or economic. It is like trying to screw on the lid of a jar that does not fit no matter how hard one

---

[22] Most frequently translated as "vanity" in the sense of futility, but whose basic meaning is that of "vapor" or "breath," connoting, inter alia, a negative valuation. See most recently Sneed 2017, 879–894.

tries. The order of creation, in other words, is not "appropriable for human purposes" (Newsom 2012, 130). For Qoheleth, the effectual distinction between righteousness and wickedness is not only muddied, it is effectively reversed. Moreover, Qoheleth complains that the "same fate" comes to the wise and fool alike, even to humans and animals (2:14–17; 3:19–21; 9:1–3).

4.4.1 Moral Lack

For Qoheleth the issue is not so much "moral luck" as moral lack, or more precisely the lack of moral efficacy. The lack of human control in navigating life is correlated with the lack of moral efficacy in human conduct, which, not coincidentally, also corresponds to wisdom's inaccessibility. Qoheleth does not question the moral assessability of human agents. What he does question is where moral conduct leads: it is a pathway whose destination simply cannot be determined. So has Qoheleth entirely jettisoned the moral life? Not quite. The sage is more nuanced, though enigmatically so:

> Do not be too righteous, and do not act too wise; why should you destroy yourself? Do not be too wicked, and do not be a fool; why should you die before your time? It is good that you should take hold of this, without letting go of that; for the one who fears God shall go forth with both of them.   (7:16–18)

The sage warns against excesses in either direction, wisdom and righteousness, on the one hand, and wickedness and folly, on the other. Although there is much to puzzle over in this passage, it appears that, perhaps ironically, Qoheleth is espousing a third way that opens up a wide latitude for conduct, a way that even extends beyond the conventional notions of righteousness and wickedness, beyond the binary of wisdom and folly. That third way is the fear of God. Yet Qoheleth's third way is also thoroughly pragmatic: avoid both extremes by balancing the admonitions against both extremes. Call it Qoheleth's "iron(ic) mean."

4.4.2 "Ethics" of Enjoyment

Nevertheless, the most constructive point the sage makes is found in his repeated commendation of joy. The heart of it is found in 8:14–15, where Qoheleth makes the leap from his skepticism of virtue to his commendation of enjoyment. After lamenting the fact that righteous people are treated as if they were wicked, and vice versa (v. 14), Qoheleth says this:

> So I commend *enjoyment*, for there is nothing better for people under the sun than to eat, and drink, and to enjoy themselves, for this will go with them in their toil through the days of life that God gives them under the sun.   (8:15)

As a thought experiment, replace "enjoyment" with "righteousness," and the result offers earnest advice from a virtue ethicist:

> So I commend *righteousness*, for there is nothing better for people under the sun than *to act justly and conduct themselves with equity*, for this will go with them in their toil through the days of life that God gives them under the sun.

As for what Qoheleth ultimately commends, enjoyment takes precedence over moral conduct, which is embodied only in fleeting moments. These moments of joy as the source of the "good life" have little to do with the narrative formation of the self. One might say that Ecclesiastes has written the obituary on the narrative unity of the self: the life worth living merely consists of episodic moments of joy. Consequently, there is not much in Ecclesiastes to work with for the virtue ethicist. Nevertheless, Qoheleth comes close to casting enjoyment as its own virtue, specifically a disposition of receptivity: the sage has replaced the *exercise* of virtue with the *reception* of joy. From the vantagepoint of virtue ethics, Qoheleth proves to be hedonic in his orientation without himself being a hedonist. While "the *pursuit* of happiness is doomed" for Qoheleth (Newsom 2012, 131; emphasis original), the *reception* of happiness remains possible despite the collapse of the character/destiny nexus. Qoheleth's mandate, contrary to many scholars, is not so much "seize the day" (*carpe diem*) as "receive the day" (*accipere diem*). Qoheleth's commendations conclude with an appeal to desire, not the desire for wisdom per se, or for that matter righteousness, justice, or equity, but simply the desire of the heart and eyes (11:9). It is an "ethic" so unorthodox that it provoked a decisively deontological response to mark the book's epilogue:

> Fear God, and keep his commandments;
> for that is the end-all for everyone.
>
> (12:13)

Nevertheless, there is one thing that unites the epilogist and Qoheleth, namely the conviction that virtue is not the end-all that it is made out to be. So, too, wisdom. In Qoheleth's hands, wisdom is whittled down to having only minimal value in the encompassing task of living. Stripped of all-encompassing significance, wisdom is relegated to having only slight pragmatic value in a world that is out of human control. But it is in wisdom, tested and tried, that Qoheleth is shown the way to appreciate the value of simple acceptance.

4.5 CONCLUSION

While a virtue-based perspective cannot account for every moral inflection sounded in the Wisdom corpus, it remains a generative starting point, whose limits, in fact, highlight the distinctive sapiential contours of each book. Given its focus on virtue's efficacy and the book's meta-narrative unity, wisdom in Proverbs is most congenial to a virtue-ethics approach, focused as it is largely on the moral efficacy of virtues. Not so, however, for Job and Ecclesiastes. Job opens with a distinctly anti-virtue narrative about a protagonist stripped of his happiness precisely because of his virtuous character. What, then, is left for wisdom? Even as it is "de-moralized" (à la Tsevat), wisdom is concomitantly filled with the awe of alterity: the fear of God in the whirlwind and the unsettling wonder of creation. Nevertheless, the notion of virtue is not entirely dead and buried. While God's answer to Job supersedes an ethics of virtue, it does not entirely replace it. Job's "integrity" remains central from beginning to end, even amid the shock and awe of alterity. That Job is vindicated in the end gives credence to the enduring value of Job's integrity (42:7), but in such a way that effects transformation. Job is a changed man in the end, a transformed patriarch, now that he encounters the inalienable dignity of the alien. How Job is to respond requires a transformed notion of integrity that carries him forward for the next 140 years, "full of days," itself an expression of *eudaimonia*, a liberative form of "happiness," free from patriarchal norms.

Qoheleth is a different beast altogether. The Bible's strangest sage discerns a measure of wisdom precisely in the absence of a totalizing or uniform form of wisdom. While dismantling "virtue supremacy," as it were, Qoheleth does not advocate moral nihilism, and wisely so. Instead, the sage commends a certain mode of living that replaces striving for gain with leading a "nonprofit" form of existence, a life lived, and at times, enjoyed without the expectation that living virtuously guarantees prosperity, much less mastery of one's fate. Qoheleth's *via negativa* creates a space that can be filled with certain virtues, such as simplicity and joyful receptivity. With each Wisdom book, the question still obtains: "How shall I live?" This is the central issue of virtue ethics, and it is the central question of wisdom.[23]

WORKS CITED

Ansberry, Christopher B. 2016. "Wisdom and Biblical Theology." Pages 174–193 in *Interpreting Old Testament Wisdom Literature*. Edited by David G. Firth and Lindsay Wilson. Downers Grove, IL: IVP Academic.

Ansberry, Christopher B. 2017. "Whose Virtues? Which Community? What Rationality? The Resources and Constraints of the Virtue Tradition for Reading Israel's Wisdom Literature." Paper presented at the Annual Meeting of the SBL. Boston, MA, November 21.

Aristotle. 2011. *Nicomachean Ethics*. Translated by Robert C. Bartlett and Susan D. Collins. Chicago, IL: The University of Chicago Press.

Barton, John. 2003. *Understanding Old Testament Ethics: Approaches and Explanations*. Louisville, KY: Westminster John Knox.

Brown, William P. 1996. *Character in Crisis: A Fresh Approach to the Wisdom Literature of the Old Testament*. Grand Rapids, MI: Eerdmans.

Brown, William P. 2014. *Wisdom's Wonder: Character, Creation, and Crisis in the Bible's Wisdom Literature*. Grand Rapids, MI: Eerdmans.

Clifford, Richard J. 1999. *Proverbs: A Commentary*. OTL. Louisville, KY: Westminster John Knox.

Cooper, Alan. 1997. "The Sense of the Book of Job." *Prooftexts* 17:227–244.

---

[23] My thanks to Christine Roy Yoder, Frederick Simmons, and Patricia Vesely for their critical comments on an earlier draft of this essay.

Hankins, Davis. 2015. *The Book of Job and the Immanent Genesis of Transcendence*. Evanston, IL: Northwestern University Press.

Hursthouse, Rosalind, and Glen Pettigrove. 2016. "Virtue Ethics." In *The Stanford Encyclopedia of Philosophy*. Edited by Edward N. Zalta. https://plato.stanford.edu/archives/win2016/entries/ethics-virtue/.

Lasater, Phillip Michael. 2017. "The Emotions in Biblical Anthropology? A Genealogy and Case Study with ירא." *HTR* 110:520–540.

Levinas, Emmanuel. 1969. *Totality and Infinity: An Essay on Exteriority*. Translated by Alphonso Lingis. Pittsburgh, PA: Duquesne University Press.

Levinas, Emmanuel. 1991. *Other than Being, or Beyond Essence*. Translated by Alphonso Lingis. Dordrecht: Kluwer Academic.

MacIntyre, Alisdair. 2007. *After Virtue*. 3rd ed. Notre Dame, IN: University of Notre Dame Press.

Nagel, Thomas. 1979. *Mortal Questions*. New York, NY: Cambridge University Press.

Nelkin, Dana K. Winter 2013. "Moral Luck." In *The Stanford Encyclopedia of Philosophy*. Edited by Edward N. Zalta. https://plato.stanford.edu/archives/win2013/entries/moral-luck/.

Newsom, Carol A. 1989. "Woman and the Discourse of Patriarchal Wisdom: A Study of Proverbs 1–9." Pages 142–160 in *Gender and Difference in Ancient Israel*. Edited by Peggy L. Day. Minneapolis, MN: Augsburg Fortress.

Newsom, Carol A. 2012. "Positive Psychology and Ancient Israelite Wisdom." Pages 117–135 in *The Bible and the Pursuit of Happiness: What the Old and New Testaments Teach Us about the Good Life*. Edited by Brent A. Strawn. Oxford: Oxford University Press.

O'Connor, Kathleen. 2003. "Wild, Raging Creativity: The Scene in the Whirlwind (Job 38–41)." Pages 171–179 in *A God So Near: Essays on Old Testament Theology in Honor of Patrick D. Miller*. Edited by Brent A. Strawn and Nancy R. Bowen. Winona Lake, IN: Eisenbrauns.

Seow, Choon Leong. 2001. "Theology When Everything Is Out of Control." *Interpretation* 55:237–249.

Sneed, Mark. 2011. "Is the 'Wisdom Tradition' a Tradition?" *CBQ* 73:50–71.

Sneed, Mark. 2017. "הבל as 'Worthless' in Qoheleth: A Critique of Michael V. Fox's 'Absurd' Thesis." *JBL* 136:879–894.

Stewart, Anne W. 2016. *Poetic Ethics in Proverbs: Wisdom Literature and the Shaping of the Moral Self*. Cambridge: Cambridge University Press.

Tsevat, Matitiahu. 1966. "The Meaning of the Book of Job." *HUCA* 37:73–106.

Vesely, Patricia. 2019. *Friendship and Virtue Ethics in Job*. Cambridge: Cambridge University Press.

Williams, Bernard. 1993. "Postscript." Pages 251–256 in *Moral Luck*. Edited by Daniel Statman. Albany, NY: SUNY Press.

Wolters, Al. 1988. "Proverbs XXXI 10–31 as Heroic Hymn: A Form-Critical Analysis." *VT* 38:446–457.

Yee, Gale A. 2003. *Poor Banished Children of Eve: Women as Evil in the Hebrew Bible*. Minneapolis, MN: Augsburg Fortress.

Yoder, Christine Roy. 2001. *Wisdom as a Woman of Substance: A Socioeconomic Reading of Proverbs 1–9 and 31:10–31*. BZAW 304. Berlin: de Gruyter.

Yoder, Christine Roy. 2011. "The Shaping of Erotic Desire in Proverbs 1–9." Pages 148–162 in *Saving Desire: The Seduction of Christian Theology*. Edited by J. Henriksen and L. Shults. Grand Rapids, MI: Eerdmans.

CHAPTER 5

....

THEOLOGY

Creation, Wisdom, and Covenant

....

RAYMOND C. VAN LEEUWEN

ALTHOUGH wisdom is usually seen as separate from covenant, a full-orbed, canonical account of wisdom will lead us to consider wisdom and covenant as linked by their common root in creation. Biblical Israel conceived of wisdom as a divine or human capacity rooted and revealed in creation, and implicitly inseparable from covenant as its theological presupposition. Since Walther Zimmerli's 1964 essay, scholars consider wisdom to be rooted in "creation theology," but generally separate wisdom from covenant, because the canonical Wisdom Literature, narrowly speaking, Proverbs, Job, and Ecclesiastes, never mentions the covenants that mark stages in Israel's historical journey. Creation, however, appears to be the condition that makes wisdom and covenant *possible*.

Attempts to define wisdom have produced only partial results, like the six blind men confronting an elephant. Hence, this essay approaches wisdom indirectly, asking, "What are the necessary conditions that make wisdom possible?" and "What does wisdom *do*?" Finally, covenant appears as an implicit but necessary corollary of biblical wisdom.

5.1 CREATION: COSMOS AND HISTORY

....

God created the cosmos with wisdom. Consequently, creation is the universal presupposition for human wisdom, and all that wisdom does, it does in and with creation. Israel's wisdom always has to do with Creator and creation. For Israel, accounts of creation as *origin* concerned "building" the world, but also the resultant cosmos as a "building" that continues throughout time as the normative and provident "house" for God and all creatures. In the ancient Near East (ANE), including Israel, thought was inescapably cosmological, whether explicitly or implicitly (Schmid 1968; Clifford 1994; Knierim 1995). The three Wisdom books explicitly rooted their wisdom in creation.

How are we to understand the relationship of creation and wisdom? How are both related to YHWH? Proverbs 3:19–20; 8:22–31; Job 38 (and Genesis 1 implicitly) all portray creation as God's *building a house with wisdom*. Divine wisdom also *"fills" and provisions the cosmic house with good things* (Van Leeuwen 2010). On a lesser scale, humans create micro-cosmic kingdoms, cities, houses, and *persons* (Ruth 4:11–22; cf. 1QS 8:5–9; 11:8; Matt 12:22–29, 43–45; 1 Cor 3:9–23; Heb 3:1–3; Philo, *De opificio* IV–VI) through literal and metaphoric *house building with wisdom*. This human *imitatio dei* presupposes that creation is in some sense revelatory, that it speaks with the voice of divine, cosmic wisdom (Sommers 2015; see Proverbs 8), and that creatures themselves speak wisdom, rightness (צדקה), and praise (Pss 19:1–4; 50:6; 97:6; 148; Prov 6:6–11; Job 12:7–10; Isa 6:3; cf. Acts 14:15–18; 17:22–29; Rom 1:20; 2:13–16). Human wisdom echoes the divine wisdom in creating a secondary, cultural world (Exod 31:1–3; 1 Kgs 7:14; Prov 24:3–4) within the parameters set by divine wisdom in creation.[1] As an accessible divine "voice," wisdom gave order not just to "nature" in opposition to "culture" (a prevalent modern view), but includes both, so that cosmic wisdom was normative for humans and creatures everywhere (Ps 104:24; Job 12:7–10; von Rad, 1970, 189–228).[2] Human wisdom in every society needs to harmonize cultural developments with the created world and its creatures as given, and with YHWH's laws and norms for reality. Wisdom in creation constitutes the overarching truth-condition for living wisely, and for building a flourishing society in harmony with creation. A foolish culture, as is evident in our technological twenty-first-century world, is one that denies or ignores the requirements of harmony with cosmic order, with its boundaries and limits.

As in ancient cultures generally, biblical "creation" included both *all that exists concretely* and *the laws and norms* for all that exists, *including human culture and its products*. Just as "heaven and earth" and "all that (*concretely*) fills them" (Ps 24:1; Isa 6:3) were created "in the beginning," so also *laws and norms* for creatures existed, from the beginning. In Israel, such socio-cosmic laws and norms were called "rightness" (צדקה, Schmid 1968) or "statute" (חוק, Knierim 1995, 199–200), and "wisdom" (חכמה; Proverbs 8; cf. Deut 4:4–8 on culturally specific positive law).

These were not eternal Platonic "forms," but *stable laws* for "nature"—revealed most dramatically in the "right" heavenly bodies (Pss 50:6; 97:6)—and *dynamic norms* for culture, which allowed freedom within form, life within law, and love within limits (Proverbs 1–9; Van Leeuwen 1997, 66)—a historical freedom that is evident from the historically various Pentateuchal law codes. In contrast, Job 28 portrayed cosmic wisdom as mysterious and beyond human reach. Theologically, both are true: wisdom communicates to humans, and yet has unfathomable depths.

Ecclesiastes famously opens with the declaration that everything is *hevel* ("breath," "mist"). With this thematic metaphor that connotes futility, obscurity, incomprehensibility, evanescence, and so forth, the book asks, in a world of *hevel*, of what advantage is a

---

[1] For the full argument, see Van Leeuwen 2010; Zabán 2012, 19–35.
[2] See especially von Rad 1972, 148 [1970, 193–194], on Job 28, 153–154 [200, cf. 204, 210–211]. Because the English translation is unreliable, I give English and German references, respectively.

person's toil under the sun? The book then proceeds to a poem about cosmic order—"A generation comes and a generation goes, but the earth remains ever constant" (1:4). This poem is generally read in light of the somber view of life that follows. Yet, a contrast is drawn here between the transient cycles of human generation and the stability of the earth. Human generations are cyclical like the flowers of the field (Gen 3:19; Job 10:9, 21; 14:1–2; Isa 40:6–7). In contrast, the earth is stable and irreplaceable; *its* cycles are the ground for all those who come and go upon it—and for the created *goods* that Qoheleth repeatedly tells his readers to embrace.

This wisdom poem reveals something essential about creation that biblical scholarship has neglected: the importance of cyclical time for life and history. The closest parallel to the natural cycles in Ecclesiastes is the short poem that precedes the cosmic covenant after the Flood:

> Through all the days of earth,
> Seed and harvest,
> Cold and hot,
> Summer dry and winter wet,
> Day and night shall not cease.
> (Gen 8:22, my translation)

While the natural cycles of Eccl 1:4–7 are the context for Qoheleth's sober wisdom for humanity, these natural constants are positive; they are simply good, the source of joy in life that Qoheleth recommends. Nature's regularities are praised as God's life-giving servants (Psalm 147). When God sends rain "in its season," both "man and beast" rejoice. Nothing brings people joy so much as the cycles that produce bread and "wine that gladdens the heart of man (אדם)" (Ps 104:15). The followers of YHWH were happy when the barns were full and the children fed, seated like olive saplings around the family table (Ps 128:3; cf. Psalms 126–127).

Knierim (1995, 192–198) demonstrated that Israel's understanding of time was not primarily linear and eschatological. Cosmic, cyclical time was the foundation for linear time. Repetitive, cyclical time was necessary for agrarian life, but it also made history—with its unique and contingent events—*possible*. It was at the spring-time "turning of the year" (תשובת השנה) that kings went to war, and that David instead begot a child with Uriah's wife, Bathsheba, who was the granddaughter of Ahitophel, David's extraordinarily wise counsellor. Not surprisingly, Ahitophel joins Absalom's revolt against David with catastrophic historical consequences (2 Sam 11:1–5; 15:12; 23:34b). These contingencies all concerned permanent, cyclical goods of creation: sex, the begetting of children, loyalty to one's temporal cohort, and battle to possess *the land* securely. Ultimately, historical good and evil, wise and foolish, are determined by human use or misuse of created goods, according to their proper nature or "name" (Genesis 2; Isa 28:23–29), limits, and time (Prov 6:6–11; 25:16–17; Eccl 3:1–15; O'Donovan 1994, 31–52). Proper use of creation is wise; misuse is folly and sin.

Nonetheless, Israel depicted history with a depth and subtlety unsurpassed as to human striving, achievement, and sin, against the backdrop of YHWH's cosmic purposes. In today's historicistic *Zeitgeist*,[3] however, it must be emphasized that the measure of those strivings were the created goods, and the norms of *wisdom* (חכמה) and *righteousness* (צדקה) which obtain for them. As for the terrors of history, if God is not Lord of the cosmos, God cannot save in history (Pss 93–99).

5.2 WISDOM AS A CONCEPT

Against the background of creation, a description of wisdom should account for several conditions that appear constitutive of the biblical usage of "wisdom" and "folly" (חכמה and אולת, respectively, with related terms, Fox 2000, 28–43). Hebrew has a rich repertoire of terms for wisdom and folly, which are often flattened to "wise" and "foolish" in English. Hence, a variety of Hebrew wisdom words underlie our discussion.

Prior to treating the necessary conditions for wisdom, it is necessary to make some linguistic comments. In Hebrew as in English, wisdom, folly, wise, and foolish, are *comparative totality concepts*. For example, divine wisdom encompasses creation in its totality. Likewise, the totality of human actions and "creations" can be wise or foolish. Wisdom words are implicitly *relative* and *comparative* in nature, allowing for "more" or "less" of the quality in play, *relative* to their referents and situation. Thus, a "small elephant" is bigger than a "big mouse," and a simple, honest cobbler is wiser than the "wisest" crook—where the nouns *relativize* the meaning of the adjectives. The "foolishness of God," is wiser than human wisdom (1 Cor 1:25). The snake was "*more clever* than any creature of the field" (ערום, Gen 3:1; cf. Prov 30:24).

It is perhaps this totality aspect of wisdom that has led some scholars to fear that without a strict definition, all of scripture may be labeled "wisdom, and if wisdom can refer to everything, we do not know what wisdom is" (that is, *wisdom's sense*; cf. Longman 2017, 2–3). This view does not follow, for it mistakes a word's *referent* ("everything") for its meaning or *sense*.[4] While *wise* can *refer* to everything, clearly not everything is *wise*. Significantly, 2 Tim 3:15–17 (σοφίσαι) implies that the entire Old Testament is wise! Augustine and the Western Church continued this view that the entire Bible is written wisdom (*De doc. Chr.* 4.5.7).

The referential scope of wisdom is creation itself and creation's *diversity*. *All* of God's creatures are "made *with wisdom*" (בחכמה, Ps 104:24; Berlin 2005). In Hebrew, the "skill"

---

[3] Biblical scholars understand "historicism" variously. I mean it in the classic sense, as the greater or lesser tendency to eliminate *anything constant* in the natural or cultural worlds. See Davaney 2006 for an initial elaboration. I make no objection here to the evolution of species, but insist that without cosmic constants, evolution would not be *possible*.

[4] Loosely speaking, a word's *sense* is its primary meaning as found in a dictionary. A *referent* is something a word or utterance *refers to* or *talks about*. In "The Lord is my rock," for example, "the Lord" is the (metaphoric) *referent* of "rock," though the *sense* (meaning) of rock does not include God. To wisdom's referential scope, compare Bottéro (1992, 105, cf. 107) on divination, "the object of which was virtually the entire earth. In the eyes of the Mesopotamians, *everything* in the world was divinatory."

of sailors is "wisdom" (חכמה, Ps 107:27). The ant's ways are wise, a model for humans (Prov 6:6–11). A snake charmer is "wise" (Ps 58:6), as are funeral singers (Jer 9:16, 19 [ET 17, 20]), metal-workers, and the builders of temples, palaces, and ordinary houses. The holy priestly garments, intended "for glory and beauty," are made by tailors "wise of heart," whom God "has filled with wisdom" for the task (Exod 28:2–3). The totality of human activities can be wise or foolish. As noted above, all these (ought to) act, build, make with the same wisdom that YHWH used to "build" the cosmos.

Among humans, God's gift of wisdom was especially expected of kings (Tavares 2007), as exemplified in the ideal messianic king (Isa 11:1–5) and in Solomon—to wage war (Prov 21:30–31), to do justice and righteousness (1 Kgs 3:9, 12; 2 Chr 1:10–11; Prov 8:15–16; Psalm 72), and to build palace and temple (cf. 1 Kings 5–7; Eccl 2:4–8). Solomon's "wisdom and insight" (1 Kgs 5:9 [ET 4:29]; cf. Prov 8:1) included musical and poetic gifts, as well as a broad knowledge of plants, animals, birds, and fish (1 Kgs 5:12–13 [ET 4:33–34]). Since the king represented the ideal human, the "democratized" royal language of Gen 1:28 and Ps 8:6–9 suggests that the diversity of wisdom finds its home throughout humanity (cf. Prov 28:6, 11; Eccl 4:13).

When we look at basic genres that scholars have labelled "Wisdom," their universal scope again stands out. Indicative "sayings" and imperative "admonitions" are Wisdom's most basic and widespread genres. (I will refer to both as *proverbs*.) Primarily oral in nature, proverbs also appear in literary genres. Their ability to function in multiple situations is another indication of wisdom's total scope. For example, "Out of the wicked comes wickedness'" (1 Sam 24:14 [ET 13]) and "Go to the ant, you sluggard" (Prov 6:6), can fit almost any *foolish* activity or inactivity.

Regarding the totality character of wisdom, two of the most striking recent developments were T.A. Perry's analysis (1993) of the *logical* structure of proverbs and its further refinement in Michael Fox's (2009, 494–498, 597–598) discussion of "disjointed proverbs," of which the "better-than" sayings are a subtype. Neither author explicitly focused on wisdom as a "totality concept," yet their work supports this idea. Perry showed that proverbs implied quadripartite, *hierarchically comparative*, antithetical structures of positive and negative, of good and bad, rooted in cultural values and taboos. Such structures often form enthymemes, logical "gaps," where necessary oppositions are implied but remain unstated. Fox noted that such enthymemes occur in "disjointed proverbs," where seemingly non-congruent parallel lines imply gaps to be filled in by readers, thus making a total set of possibilities explicit.[5]

Proverbial antitheses can also function as *merisms*, that is, bi-polar pairs that imply *all of reality*, or all of the possibilities in an arena marked by the two terms. "Heaven and Earth," for example, indicated the entire creation, as "head to toe" the entire person. In certain saying collections of Proverbs (e.g., 10–15), the regular opposition of "righteous"

---

[5] In Mesopotamian omen and law collections, similar logical gaps were sometimes filled by scribes striving for completeness, even when certain situations were unlikely or impossible in reality (Bottéro 1992, 134–135, 176–177)!

(צדיק) versus "wicked" (רשע),[6] does not mean that the two types are absolutely distinct, and their lines never crossed, but that these limit concepts include the total spectrum of "good" and "bad" human types. Thus, "wisdom" and "righteousness" are totality concepts in two senses. They can refer to any and every human action and to the resultant products; wisdom's and folly's scope is the entire creation. Second, when used as merisms referring to humans, they implicitly include everyone.

The cosmic totality character of wisdom means that only YHWH is ultimately wise. Ultimate wisdom would require total knowledge and insight, and the *power* to do *all* that wisdom wills. Such wisdom belongs only to YHWH, who created the cosmos "with wisdom" and "power" (Jer 10:6–7, 12; Prov 3:19–20). In rare cases, God grants exceptional wisdom and power to humans such as Joseph (Gen 41:33, 38–41), Solomon (1 Kgs 3:5–15; cf. Wisdom of Solomon), or Daniel (Dan 2:20–23). Yet, even the greatest human wisdom suffers severe limits, because no one can experience and know the *totality* of creation and the mysteries embedded in it (Job 11:7–9; 28; Ecclesiastes; von Rad 1972, 97–110 [1970, 131–148]). Humans know not what tomorrow might "birth" (ילד, Prov 27:1); they are afflicted by weakness, injustice, and death (Psalms 39; 49; Ecclesiastes and Job passim). No human possesses the *power* to do all their wisdom might know (2 Sam 15:31; 16:23–17:14; Prov 16:9; 19:21; 21:30–31).

There is yet a third *totality* aspect of wisdom. God's wisdom and power existed from the *beginning* (ראשית), and continues through all *time*, residing in our present world (Proverbs 8; Genesis 1).[7] Cosmic wisdom is master and teacher of reality's creatures (Job 12:7–10), and of the laws and norms that govern creatures and their functions, but also master of *time*, from beginning to end. This third totality claim, that the divine, cosmic wisdom in effect knows and affects "all things"[8] throughout all *time*, is echoed in the lesser claim of human sages, that they have the benefit of *age*, of experience over time, in contrast to inexperienced youth. In general, "gray hair" was a symbol of both age and wisdom (Lev 19:32; Prov 20:29; Job 12:12–13; 15:7–10; 32:4, 6–10; Sir 25:3–6). Wisdom's claims to age are also present in *tradition*, the distilled historical experience and cultural memory of Israel's forebears functioning in the present.

These three totality requirements for wisdom mean that only God is ultimately "wise," that only God possesses wisdom, understanding, knowledge, and strength (חכמה, תבונה, דעת, גבורה) without qualification. The corollary to this theological affirmation is that even the best human wisdom, understanding, knowledge, and strength are limited.

---

[6] In Gen 18:23, 25 and Ps 11:5, these pairs indicate everyone; see Job 3:19a; 9:22b; Matt 5:45 for similar merisms with different terms.

[7] *Genesis Rabbah* 1.1–3 insightfully connects Prov 8:22–30 to Gen 1:1. This appears to be the normative view of creation in the Bible, in spite of remnants of less ultimate views; *pace* Levenson 1988.

[8] Compare the Pauline *ta panta*; Rom 11:33–36; 1 Cor 8:6, and Col 1:15–20, where Christ appears as wisdom active in creation, then and now.

5.3 PRESUPPOSITIONS AND CONDITIONS FOR WISDOM

The presuppositions and necessary conditions for human wisdom in biblical Israel appear to be the following.

5.3.1 Fear of the Lord

This phrase no doubt arose in fitting human dread at the *mysterium tremendum* that is YHWH, the Almighty Creator, as is evident in God's presence at Sinai (Exod 19:16–25; Deut 5:19–30 [ET 22–33]), and in *theophanies* that shatter the earth (Jer 4:22–28; Pss 18:8–16 [7–15]; 97). But the phrase comes to mean generally *Israel's religion as all of life in awe and heartfelt service to God,*[9] both in times of grievous lament or joyful thanksgiving (Job 1:1, 8–10; 2:3; Psalms 25; 86; 103; 111–112).

Epistemologically, Israel's view of creation meant that Israel's experience of reality was unified, without the modern dichotomies of faith and reason, or religion and science. Instead, the "fear of YHWH" was the "beginning of wisdom" (Prov 9:10; cf. Prov 1:7; Job 28:28; Eccl 3:14; 5:6 [ET 5:7]; 8:12–13; 12:13; Pss 111:10; 112:1; Sir 1:16,18),[10] because only a right relation to the Creator enabled one to know creation and its meaning rightly. In the words of von Rad, "For [biblical Israel], experiences of the world were always also God-experiences, and experiences of God were for [Israel] also world-experiences"— yet without a pantheistic confusion of Creator and creation (von Rad 1972, 62 [1970, 87] my translation).

Without a right relation to God the *Creator*, who revealed himself and his Torah to Israel (Psalms 119; 147), it was not possible to gain global wisdom concerning the complex interrelationships of life's varied spheres and creatures, and of the laws and cultural norms which held for their flourishing. Thus, Israel's Torah and Prophets as revealed knowledge and wisdom (Deut 4:5–8; Hos 14:10 [9]; cf. O'Dowd 2009) were a necessary *presupposition* for the generic and conceptual focus on wisdom in the Wisdom Literature. As "the fear of the Lord" was a comprehensive indicator that all of life is religion, one's ultimate love drew one towards God and wisdom, or towards idols and folly (Cf. Proverbs 1–9; Deut 6:4–9; Lev 19:18, 32–34; cf. Sir 1:1–20). One's ultimate love also relativized and limited the love of non-ultimate created *goods*, preventing them from becoming destructive idols. In Proverbs, the desire of a young man for a woman (as wife or

---

[9] Note the "fear the Lord" commands (Deut 6:2,13; cf. 10:12–20) which form an *inclusion* around the *Shema* (6:4–9), and that the *Shema* uses merisms to indicate the totality of life (6:7); cf. Wolters 1984, 15–29, on Prov 31:10–31.

[10] See the data and discussion in *Theologisches Handwörterbuch zum Alten Testament (THAT)* I. Edited by Ernst Jenni, with assistance from Claus Westermann. 2 vols. Munich: Chr. Kaiser Verlag; Zürich: Theologischer Verlag, 1971–1976, 770–778.

"strange woman") was emblematic of humanity's ultimate love and desire for Woman Wisdom or her deadly opposite, Woman Folly (9:13–18). Love of Wisdom was tantamount to the love of God, for though cosmic Wisdom had a certain independence from YHWH, she was not separable from God.

Consequently, the statement, found in each book of the Wisdom Literature, "The fear of the Lord is the beginning of knowledge/wisdom," was the basic *theological and episte-mological* principle of biblical wisdom. For Israel, knowledge of God as *creator enabled* knowledge of creation and humans, and vice versa (von Rad 1972, 53–73 [1970, 75–101]).

5.3.2 Knowledge and Praxis According to the General Patterns of Reality

Biblical wisdom presupposed *knowledge of the general patterns of reality and praxis in harmony with those patterns*. That is, biblical wisdom presupposed a divinely given worldview[11] that, in principle, revealed that the *meaning* of *all things* lay in their relation to God, in their intrinsic, though relative, goodness as *creatures*, and in their mutual relations to one another. Israel's Torah provided this global meaning-context for humanity's limited knowledge and experience of reality's laws, norms, and concrete facts.

Thus, agricultural wisdom required of farmers diligent labor in season, in harmony with the general laws for nature, and with respect to the generic classes of creatures (Prov 6:6–11; 10:4–5; Isa 28:23–29; Vayntrub 2015; Van Leeuwen 2018). Among these cosmic "laws" and patterns was the knowledge that good character and conduct led to good outcomes and well-being (שלום), while wicked character and behavior led to bad outcomes and ultimately death. These *general* patterns of reality had to be mastered and acknowledged, even if they did not always obtain. This was plain to see in the much discussed "Act-Consequence nexus," which, however, admitted of exceptions, when the wicked prospered and the righteous suffered. In spite of exceptions, these general patterns possessed a relative *Eigengesetzlichkeit*, a relatively independent "lawfulness" or even "autonomy"[12] that had to be respected and trusted. Hard work did not always bring prosperity, but that was no reason not to work hard! This general nexus was not exclusive to the Wisdom Literature, but pervaded the biblical writings, appearing in Pentateuchal tales of judgment, in Deuteronomistic and Chronistic narratives, and in Prophetic oracles of judgment or blessing. Nevertheless, insight into general patterns was not enough to make one wise. Acts and consequences are a worldview pattern that runs all through

---

[11] By "worldview" I mean a social group's *committed* basic beliefs about reality, whether explicit, or implicit and tacitly assumed. At a minimum, a worldview answers basic human questions: (1) Where are we in cosmos and time? (2) Who are we? (3) What is wrong? (4) What is the solution? See Naugle 2002.

[12] A more appropriate rendering of the term than "determinism," commonly found in the frequently misleading English translation of von Rad's standard work, *Weisheit in Israel* (1970; cf. 83–85; Eng. 1972, 59–61).

the Hebrew Bible, though some books emphasize general patterns, and others emphasize individuals and exceptions.

5.3.3 Knowledge and Right Action in Relation to Individual Realities

Knowing general patterns did not produce a wise Israelite. General patterns constituted only the ABCs of wisdom. What most sharply distinguished wisdom from folly was right knowledge and fitting praxis regarding concrete individuals. Such individuals include *natural and cultural specifics, situations and relations, and individual creatures, persons, societal and natural groups* (cf. Isa 28:23–29), *and institutions with which humans deal.*

Fortunately, humans deal with people and things whose generic "kind" and "individuality" completely intersect. Thus, no individual something or someone is *totally* unique and unknowable, nor are they totally generic and thus interchangeable (O'Donovan 1994, 76–85, 189–192). Yet, life is lived not only generically, but in the particularities of here and now, of this and that, and of "I and Thou." In the religious-moral spheres of life, with their oppositions of good and bad, righteous and wicked, biblical narratives afforded exceptions to the general norms and patterns of reality, cases where the wicked prospered and the righteous suffered—as many "better-than" proverbs, psalms of lament, and the books of Ecclesiastes and Job especially make clear. The unexpected death of righteous King Josiah defied the patterns laid down by the Deuteronomistic writers. Life's anomalies and peculiarities lead us beyond wisdom's knowledge of the generic patterns of reality to the next requirement of wisdom, engagement with particularity, its graduate school, so to speak.

Wisdom presupposed a *praxis* rooted in the knowledge of *individual* creatures, things, persons, circumstances. That is, wisdom requires *discernment*. Discernment means the ability to distinguish among situations, objects, events, or persons of the same kind, objects whose similarities may obscure crucial differences and render them ambiguous. "Blessings" are good and "curses" bad, but not all blessings or curses are the same (Prov 26:2; 27:14)! In terms of attractiveness, the "strange woman" of Proverbs 1–9 may even be superior to one's wife (cf. 5:15–20; 8:35//18:22). Yet, one entails death, the other life.

What Hans-Georg Gadamer (1960, 38–39) remarks about taste and judgment applies to wisdom: "Both taste and judgment evaluate an object in relation to the whole in order to see whether it fits in with everything else—that is, whether it is 'fitting.' One must have a 'sense' for it—it cannot be demonstrated." Gadamer continues, arguing that in morality and law, the rules are never complete, requiring judgment according to the "concrete instance." It is never enough to apply "general principles." "The individual case," he writes, "is not exhausted by being a particular example of a universal law or concept.... [T]he rule does not comprehend [the special case]."

What Gadamer describes here, aesthetically, morally, and legally, is wisdom in action. Wisdom is characterized by "fittingness." In the context of knowing the general norms and patterns of reality, wisdom *discerns* what is *fitting* in the concrete instance before it, and *acts accordingly*. Biblically, such wisdom is a divine gift (e.g., Prov 2:6), the subjective possession of which varies greatly, with some having a broad wisdom concerning life, others having wisdom in specific areas such as art, sailing, building, singing and more besides, but lacking it in others.

The wisdom problem of knowing the individual is highlighted in several juxtaposed proverbs, such as, "Answer not a fool according to his folly, lest you be like him yourself," and "Answer a fool according to his folly, lest he be *wise in his own eyes*" (Prov 26:4–5). Nothing in the two admonitions tells readers which fool stands before them, or what the situation requires. Yet wisdom must know which is which, to speak or be silent. Here wisdom may reach its limits, not knowing which action is fitting, and standing in danger of oneself becoming a fool. The line between wisdom and folly is often a fine one. Thus, the depth dimension of wisdom is "Be not *wise in your own eyes*; *fear the Lord*; and turn away from evil" (Prov 3:7; cf. 8:11; Ps 111:10; Job 1:1; 1:8; 2:3; Eccl 3:14; 5:6; 8:12–13; 12:13).

It is especially in knowing and dealing with concrete individuals that mature wisdom distinguishes itself. The farmer knows that not all seeds and plants are alike, and each type needs to be treated individually. This field is good for grapes and the other for wheat. One field is better because it has springs (Judg 1:12–15), and one vineyard is better than another (Ahab and Naboth; 1 Kgs 21:1–2). It is not enough to know that humans need work. They must know what kind of work is right for *this* individual, at *this* time, in *this* place, in view of *these* needs, *this* training, and with *these* innate personal gifts. And out of several possible mates, one marries, usually, just one—but why this one and not that one? That is a matter of wisdom or folly, as many have discovered to their bliss or chagrin. As the English proverbs have it, "Happy the wooing that's not long in doing." Yet, "Marry in haste, repent at leisure" (cf. Prov 12:4; 27:15–16; 31:10–31).

The requirement that wisdom know individuals and specific *realia* is not unique to Israel; it is a necessary response to created reality. Levi-Strauss (1966) described the Amazonian aboriginal "science of the concrete," and Aristotle systematized wisdom's knowledge of particulars in his *Nichomachean Ethics*. He says a voluntary act requires an agent "who knows the particular circumstances in which he is acting" and then goes on to specify "the nature and number" of the six circumstances involved in any particular action (*Eth. Nic.* 1111a). More concretely, Aristotle uses the examples of being angry with someone or giving someone money. These acts are easy to do—but to do them well is difficult, he says, since they must be done "to the right person, and to the right amount, and at the right time, and for the right purpose, and in the right way" (*Eth. Nic.* 1109a). More concisely, this issue is formulated in the Hebrew word נאוה ("fitting").[13] Indeed, *fittingness* is the hermeneutical theme of Prov 26:1–12 as a whole.[14] "As rain in

---

[13] What is *fitting*, by semantic extension, is *beautiful* and thus *desirable*, a source of *delight* (Song 1:5; 2:14; 4:3 6:4; note the parallelism with יפה; cf. Prov 5:15–20; 8:11, 17, 30–31, 34–36). For the relation of *fittingness* and beauty, see Nicolaus Wolterstorff 1980, 91–121. The standard work on *fittingness* in the Greco-Roman world is Pohlenz.

[14] For analysis of *fittingness* as the hermeneutical theme of Prov 26:1–12, see Van Leeuwen (1988, 99 and 1997 on the passage) and O'Dowd 2009, 126–136.

Summer, as snow in harvest, so glory for a fool is *not fitting*" (26:1). The principle of *fittingness* is operative even when the predicate *fitting/not fitting* is omitted: "Like a gold ring in the snout of a pig is a beautiful woman without taste (טעם)" (Prov 11:22).

5.3.4 Tradition

Wisdom is *traditional,* passed on from parents to children, master craftsmen to apprentices, and teachers to students. The symbol of tradition is the "path," emblem of good and bad "ways" of traveling through life. It takes many feet to make a path, all seeking the "best way" from the here and now to some goal further on. Paths are literal and metaphorical means of negotiating one's individual and collective (Jer 32:39) journey through reality, from beginning to end (cf. above 5.3.2 Knowledge and Praxis According to the General Patterns of Reality, and 5.3.3 Knowledge and Right Action in Relation to Individual Realities). In an ultimate theological sense, the journey on life's path is motivated by faith, love, and hope towards an ultimate goal at its end (cf. 1 Corinthians 13; Heb 11:1–12:2, where "race" equals "path"). This symbol is as fundamental in Proverbs 1–9 as it is in Genesis 12–25 for Abraham's journey with God to the Promised Land (cf. Gen 12:1–3; Heb 11:8–11), and in Acts, where following Christ was simply called "the way" (9:2; 19:9, 23; 24:14, 22).

5.3.5 Excellence

Wisdom requires that the mentioned requirements be possessed and exercised *with excellence.* As a *comparative* adjective, wisdom may be increased, which, for humans, requires *giftedness* (mysterious, God-given), *training/discipline* (מוסר, Greek, *paideia*), hard *work,* and *love* (Proverbs 1–9). Love for God and "Woman Wisdom" as ultimate good is the motive force that drives one's journey towards life, while love for the "strange woman" and folly is the path to death (Prov 2:16–19; 9:13–18). It is this ultimate love that limits and overcomes the human tendency to love and idolize created goods beyond reason. What we humans, as individuals or groups, *love* drives us on our path towards life or death, as well as towards excellence or folly in lesser matters.

The three basic Wisdom books of the Hebrew Bible each in its own way exercises itself concerning the presuppositions and conditions for wisdom described throughout section 5.3 above. The conflict between Job and his friends, for example, concerns the failure of the friends, who in their focus on the "general patterns" of God's ways with humanity, quite forget that there are exceptions to the rules, individual cases which escape the "wisdom of the wise." Job is one such extraordinary case (cf. John 9). And in terms of that essential requirement of wisdom, "the fear of the Lord," the friends overstep the bounds of their humanity; they lack the humility that comes with fearing God, presuming to take God's place in judging Job, and failing to recognize the divinely set limits of human wisdom. Ironically, it is Job's friends who accuse him of impiety, of failing to fear

God rightly, echoing the *satan's* question, "Does Job fear God *gratis*?" (Job 1:9; 22:4–5). In the end, YHWH chastises the friends and declares that only rebellious Job has "spoken rightly" of God, implying that he has maintained his original integrity and "fear of God" (Job 42:7–8; cf. 1:1, 8–9; 2:3). Job and his friends also argue intensely over who has better "expertise" (*excellence!*) in the ancestral wisdom, in the *traditional* paths set down by their wise forbears long ago (e.g., Job 8:8; 15:8).

5.4 WHAT DOES WISDOM *DO*?

To simply ask, "What topics does wisdom address?" is not an especially fruitful guide to the nature of wisdom. Given the "totality" character of wisdom, *any* topic can be grist for wisdom's mill. And given the use of metaphor in wisdom, to say that Proverbs 1–9 concerns finding or avoiding women is true—but largely misses the point. To gain insight into the nature of wisdom, it is more fruitful to ask, "What does wisdom *do* or *effect*?" In this, I follow the sterling example of Wisdom of Solomon, in which God and Wisdom together teach Solomon, who recounts personified Wisdom's deeds (7:15–9:18), including within Israel's history (passim), something not found in the Hebrew Bible.

5.4.1 Wisdom Solves Problems

Wisdom solves problems that reality presents, often through others who give counsel. The more difficult the problem, the greater the wisdom required. Joab goes to a "wise woman from Tekoa" to return estranged Absalom back to David's court (2 Samuel 14). Lovesick Adonijah consults wise Jonadab for a way to woo Tamar; Solomon solves the harlots' dilemma. A wise architect solves building problems in the context of landscape, materials, physical laws, costs, and the genre of building required (Exodus 31; 35–40; 1 Kings 5–7). An artist considers colors, forms, lines, light, and much more.

In Proverbs 1–9, the young man seeks the "right woman" to love, as opposed to the "strange woman." These women, licit and illicit, are both desirable, and ultimately counterparts of personified Wisdom and Folly. Woman as wife (Prov 5:15–20; 31:10–31), parallels cosmic Lady Wisdom as the ultimate figurative object of love, desire, and delight (8:17, 21, 30–31; 9:1–6; cf. 8:35 and 18:22), in contrast to the "strange woman" and Woman Folly (9:13–18; cf. 2:16; 14:1). These flesh-and-blood women in Proverbs are also emblematic of *any* desirable good (cf. Genesis 3). Like desirable women, created goods are only legitimate within the normative bounds of righteousness and wisdom. Else, even *good* things are "out of order," "out of bounds," foolish, dangerous, *a problem*. Of course, discernment of licit and illicit does not yet solve the problem of which individual licit woman or man might be an appropriate wife or husband.

While wisdom is needed in solving difficult problems of any kind, the king, as ideal human (Psalm 8) is emblematically wise: "The glory of God is to hide a matter (דבר); the glory of kings is to search out (חקר) a matter (דבר). The heavens for height, the underworld for depth, and the heart of kings are unfathomable (אין חקר)" (Prov 25:2–3). Yet, even kings are human: "Water streams, the king's heart—they are in YHWH's hands; he inclines it any way he pleases" (21:1).

5.4.2 Wisdom Negotiates the Spectrum of Relative Goods

Wisdom negotiates the spectrum of relative goods, since these are limited and constantly competing (Job 34:1–4). Fox (2009, 598) even suggests that "the negotiation of values [is] the locus of wisdom." Nothing in this world is absolute or ultimate (Job 9:3–10; cf. Bonhoeffer 1998, 137–162), and humans are subject to cosmic limits of time, strength, knowledge, wealth, beauty, love, and life. How they negotiate these limited goods, especially the goods they primarily *love*, largely determines whether a person, group, or society is "righteous" (צדיק) or "wicked" (רשע—a term sometimes rendered as "godless").[15] The opposition of "righteous" and "wicked" is pervasive in Proverbs 10–15 and 25–27, strongly implying that wickedness is folly, and goodness is wise. Hence, the "fear of the Lord" is often associated with "turning from evil" (Prov 3:7; Job 1:1; 2:3; 28:28). Moreover, "doing good leads to good," while doing bad leads to bad consequences—the so-called act- or character-consequence nexus (von Rad 1972, 124–137 [1970, 165–188]). Humans are also subject to the mysterious constraints of personal, social, and institutional evil, so that wisdom needs also to rank moral *evils*. At times, humans are confronted with options, none of which are *good*. The *righteous* must choose "the lesser evil." It is especially the sub-genre of "better-than" sayings that shows wisdom as a subtle negotiator among things good and bad, by asserting that this or that created "good" is "less good" than its opposite "bad"—if the first "good" is not accompanied by a more "ultimate" (religious-moral) good such as "rightness" or "fear of the Lord" (Prov 15:16–17; 16:8; Eccl 7:2–3).

Wisdom considers the *goods* of creation in their diversity of kinds and ends (i.e., potential "purposes" [O'Donovan 1994, 31–52]) and *discerns* their mutual relations, giving priority to those that are best—*all things considered*.

---

[15] In his *City of God*, Augustine contrasts the City's "love of God" with Rome's "love of domination" (*amor dominandi*) as two ultimate loves that define the historical "path" and culture of the two societies. E. Rosenstock-Huessey (1969) is a twentieth-century instance of such Christian historical analysis of societies.

5.4.3 Wisdom Acts Fittingly in Characteristic Ways

The diversity of things that wisdom does *fittingly* it does in characteristic ways. The wise see things that others do not. They "find a way" where others cannot. Wisdom *knows* things that matter: "The righteous *knows* the needs (נֶפֶשׁ) of *his* animal; but the mercies of the wicked are cruel" (Prov 12:10). Wisdom *knows* the "times," a type of historical knowledge, which sees both the *similarities and differences* between then and now, and acts accordingly (von Rad 1972, 263–283 [1970, 337–363]). Wisdom *knows* its limits; consequently, it trusts the outcome of things to God: "Do not boast about tomorrow, for you do not know what the day will birth (יֵלֶד)" (Prov 27:1). Wisdom perceives relations among things that are significant, but not obvious. And wisdom notes the obvious thing that others ignore to their hurt. Wisdom acts, and is inactive, as cases require. The wise speak well—or are silent. Wisdom delights in beauty and artistic excellence: "As apples of gold in settings of silver…" (Prov 25:11). What wisdom *does* is effective, sometimes surprisingly so: "By patient tact a prince is persuaded, and a 'soft tongue' breaks bone" (Prov 25:15). Human wisdom builds its secondary reality, its cultural "houses" in harmony with the way YHWH has built the world.

Can we say *how* wisdom knows and does these things? Probably not. Wisdom, like so many basic reality functions, is an *inexplicable* gift from God. We can describe it, recognize it, but—like worship, music, or art—never fully grasp it in words. To paraphrase the adage of Michael Polanyi (1966, 4), the wise artist "knows more than she can say."

5.5 COVENANT

The Wisdom Literature famously never mentions the covenants that seemed to define Israel's unique *historical* traditions (e.g., Eichrodt 1967; cf. Genesis 9; 15; 17; Exodus 19–24; 2 Samuel 7; Jeremiah 31).[16] Modern scholarship separated the Wisdom Literature—and thus wisdom itself—from the rest of the Hebrew Bible. This move created a false dichotomy for theology. Biblical religion was *either* covenant, history, and cult, *or* it was wisdom and (perhaps) creation theology. The problem was exacerbated by the nineteenth- and twentieth-century tendency to valorize history and ignore creation as unscientific. The concomitant *tendency to equate wisdom with select genres, and to restrict wisdom (mostly) to the Wisdom Literature*, meant that the broader biblical presence of wisdom was largely overlooked—except for attempts to find Wisdom "influence" and "traditions" here and there.[17] Theologically, wisdom became an anomaly, the product of international influences, and not proper to Israel's Yahwistic religion.

---

[16] W. Eichrodt's great *Theology of the Old Testament* focused on covenant as its organizing principle, which seemed to necessitate his sharp denigration of wisdom's importance (1967, 80–83, 87–91).

[17] The pervasive presence of wisdom in the Qumran scrolls also suffers from similar confusion and neglect.

Yet, relations between covenant and the *wise* creation, and between covenant and human wisdom, need closer scrutiny. Covenant and creation are often seen as almost mutually exclusive (e.g., Schifferdecker 2008, 13–14; 20). Oddly, this view ignores the primal Noahic covenant, which is explicitly a covenant with *creation*. It is also the necessary presupposition for Israel's historical covenants. Without a stable creation, there can be no history (Knierim 1995). Thus, Israelite covenants *presuppose* YHWH's *wise* cosmic sovereignty, even when they do not mention creation. When we look at key moments in the biblical narrative, wisdom and folly play a key role. Of signal importance is Deuteronomy 32, a poem which implicitly presupposes the book's covenantal theology, and where *creation, cult, wisdom, history, and eschatology* (אחרית, 32:20, 28–29; cf. Hosea 14:10 [9]; Jer 9:12 [11]; Ps 107:43) *all play integral roles in Israel's turbulent life before God* (O'Dowd 2009, 91–110).

5.6 THE INTERSECTION OF WISDOM AND COVENANT

Among the conditions for wisdom outlined above, the crucial step to "practical wisdom," is *knowledge of the concrete in its generic and individual aspects*. This is also the most difficult and mysterious. How is it possible to *know* something unique, whether a person or a block of stone set before a sculptor? How is it possible to act *wisely* with something new and not experienced previously? Every "something," however, is both generic—a *kind* of something already known—as well as unique. A block of stone is quickly known generically (marble, granite, or diamond), but to know its *individuality takes time and a certain loving attention*. With individual humans and groups, the problem is yet more complex. Humans are free to act in unexpected ways. Knowing humans requires a *historical* knowledge of past persons, institutions, and events that are both *typical (generic) and individual*. Such knowledge is passed on in tradition and writing. Understanding individual persons and events *in the present* also requires *love and attention*, but more mysteriously, it requires *the other's active self-revelation over time*, something a stone cannot do.

The biblical answer to this problem of knowing *one* God and other humans in their individuality is *covenant*. Biblical covenants govern relationships between individuals and groups through mutual promises, promises to be kept over time. Persons and groups become known through their behavior with one another and with creation's creatures, in accord (or not) with their covenant obligations and promises. Covenants set *limits* ("thou shall not…") and give positive *guidelines* for relationships of "brotherhood," of marriage, of sovereigns and vassals, and notably between YHWH and Israel ("You shall love the Lord your God…. You shall love your neighbor as yourself"). In keeping covenant promises or not, the respective parties come to *know* one another, as they reveal themselves as loving and faithful, or as corrupt and unfaithful. While not all folly is *wicked*, the wickedness of covenant breaking is always *folly*. There is no human *wisdom* without godly *rightness* (צדקה), as defined by the *covenant's wise cultural articulation (positivation) of creation's laws and norms*. Concerning this point, Psalm 119 bears splendid witness—without ever mentioning covenant!

YHWH's making and keeping of covenantal promises, through all the contingencies of history, is the mysterious means through which Israel and the world come to *know* YHWH, as shown by the pervasive *Erkenntnisformel* ("You shall know YHWH") found in Exodus and Ezekiel. When Israel ceases to be *wise*, and becomes *foolish* (Deut 32:28–29; Hos 14:10 [9]; Jer 4:22; 9:12 [11]; Ps 107:43), as a metaphoric "wife," who is unfaithful to her divine "husband," then YHWH laments that his people "do not *know* me" (Hos 5:4; 8:2; 11:3; Jer 2:8; 4:22; 9:3, 6; 22:16). God also laments that "they do not *know* his way," that is, the laws that govern their covenantal relationship (Hos 4:1–3, 6; Jer 5:4; 8:7) in respect to created goods. *God's laws for Israel are culturally specific guides for living wisely in and with the cosmos* (Deut 6:4–9; 10:12–22). They also set limits to behaviors that remove one from the cosmic realm of life in "the land" into the "house" of death (Deut 30:15–20; cf. Prov 2:16–22; 5:3–8; 7:21–27; 9:13–18; 10:30). One enters the realm of death through theft, adultery, coveting, and the pursuit of gods that are not YHWH, who alone brought Israel out of bondage into their law-bound freedom to keep their promises in the land God gave them.

The ultimate criterion for Israel's wisdom is her faithfulness to the covenants she made with YHWH. In the cosmic-historical specifics of dealing with reality over time, Israel reveals who she is with YHWH, *in terms of her use of the God-given land, and of the creatures and humans who dwell in it*. In this lies Israel's greatness and *wisdom*—or her *folly* leading to death by exile. It is God's grace and wisdom to resurrect Judah from the dead (Ezekiel 37), in order to keep God's promises to Abraham and bless all nations (Gen 12:3).

Creation, wisdom, and covenant entail a perennial, unfinished task for Synagogue and Church, of reclaiming the theological integrity of the Hebrew Bible; for Christians, the first Scripture of the Church.[18] Modern scholarship has rightly explored the surface level historical, social, literary, and conceptual *differences* in the Bible. At the deepest level of worldview, however, these writings possess a *coherence* amid their diversity, to guide God's "servants" on their path through creation. Finally, wisdom's delight in creation and Creator returns us to the *fear of the Lord*, which is the *beginning of wisdom* and the *sine qua non* for *covenant-keeping*.

WORKS CITED

Berlin, Adele. 2005. "The Wisdom of Creation in Psalm 104." Pages 71–83 in *Seeking Out the Wisdom of the Ancients: Essays Offered to Honor Michael V. Fox on the Occasion of His Sixty-Fifth Birthday*. Edited by Ronald L. Troxel, Kelvin G. Friebel, and Dennis R. Magary. Winona Lake, IN: Eisenbrauns.

---

[18] Christian Old Testament canons vary at their periphery; the Hebrew Bible is their common, canonical core.

Bonhoeffer, Dietrich. 1998. "Die Letzten und die Vorletzten Dinge." Pages 137–162 in *Ethik*. KT 161. Gütersloh: Kaiser.

Bottéro, Jean. 1992. *Mesopotamia: Writing, Reasoning, and the Gods*. Translated by Zainab Bahrani and Marc Van De Mieroop. Chicago, IL: University of Chicago.

Clifford, Richard J. 1994. *Creation Accounts in the Ancient Near East and in the Bible*. CBQMS 26. Washington, D.C.: Catholic Biblical Association of America.

Davaney, Sheila Greeve. 2006. *Historicism: The Once and Future Challenge for Theology*. Guides to Theological Inquiry. Minneapolis, MN: Fortress.

Eichrodt, Walther. 1967. *Theology of the Old Testament*. 2 vols. Louisville, KY: Westminster John Knox.

Fox, Michael V. 2000. *Proverbs 1–9: A New Translation with Introduction and Commentary*. AB 18A. New Haven, CT: Yale University Press.

Fox, Michael V. 2009. *Proverbs 10–31: A New Translation with Introduction and Commentary*. AB 18B. New Haven, CT: Yale University Press.

Gadamer, Hans-Georg. 1960. *Wahrheit und Methode*. Tübingen: Mohr.

Knierim, Rolf P. 1995. *The Task of Old Testament Theology: Substance, Method, and Cases*. Grand Rapids, MI: Eerdmans.

Levenson, Jon D. 1988. *Creation and the Persistence of Evil: The Jewish Drama of Divine Omnipotence*. San Francisco, CA: Harper & Row.

Lévi-Strauss, Claude. 1966. "The Science of the Concrete." Pages 1–33 in *The Savage Mind*. London: Weidenfeld & Nicholson.

Longman, Tremper, III. 2017. *The Fear of the Lord Is Wisdom: A Theological Introduction to Wisdom in Israel*. Grand Rapids, MI: Baker Academic.

Naugle, David K. 2002. *Worldview: The History of a Concept*. Grand Rapids, MI: Eerdmans.

O'Donovan, Oliver. 1994. *Resurrection and Moral Order*. Grand Rapids, MI: Eerdmans.

O'Dowd, Ryan. 2009. *The Wisdom of Torah: Epistemology in Deuteronomy and the Wisdom Literature*. Göttingen: Vandenhoeck & Ruprecht.

Perry, T. Anthony. 1993. *Wisdom Literature and the Structure of Proverbs*. University Park, PA: Pennsylvania State University Press.

Polanyi, Michael. 1966. *The Tacit Dimension*. Chicago, IL: University of Chicago Press. Repr., 2009.

Rad, Gerhard von. 1970. *Weisheit in Israel*. Neukirchen-Vluyn: Neukirchener Verlag.

Rad, Gerhard von. 1972. *Wisdom in Israel*. Translated by James D. Martin. Harrisburg, PA: Trinity Press International.

Rosenstock-Huessy, Eugen. 1969 (1938). *Out of Revolution: Autobiography of Western Man*. Norwich, VT: Argo Books.

Schifferdecker, Kathryn. 2008. *Out of the Whirlwind: Creation Theology in the Book of Job*. HTS 61. Cambridge, MA: Harvard University Press.

Schmid, Hans H. 1968. *Gerechtigkeit als Weltordnung*. BHT 40. Tübingen: Mohr.

Sommers, Benjamin. 2015. "Nature, Revelation, and Grace in Psalm 19: Towards a Theological Reading of Scripture." HTR 108:376–401.

Tavares, Ricardo. 2007. *Eine königliche Weisheitslehre? Exegetische Analyse von Sprüche 28–29 und Vergleich mit den ägyptischen Lehren Merikaras und Amenemhats*. OBO 234. Fribourg: Academic Press.

Van Leeuwen, Raymond C. 1988. *Context and Meaning in Proverbs 25–27*. SBLDS 96. Atlanta, GA: Scholars Press.

Van Leeuwen, Raymond C. 1997. "The Book of Proverbs." Pages 19–264 in *The New Interpreter's Bible*, vol. 5. Nashville, TN: Abingdon Press.

Van Leeuwen, Raymond C. 2010. "Cosmos, Temple, House in Ancient Mesopotamia and Israel." Pages 399–421 in *From the Foundations to the Crenellations: Essays on Temple Building in the Ancient Near East and Hebrew Bible*. Edited by M.J. Boda and J. Novatny. AOAT 366. Münster: Ugarit Verlag.

Van Leeuwen, Raymond C. 2018. "Wisdom and Agriculture: The Case of the 'Gezer' Calendar." Pages 365–380 in *When the Morning Stars Sang: Essays in Honor of Choon Leong Seow on the Occasion of His Sixty Fifth Birthday*. Edited by Scott C. Jones and Christine Roy Yoder. BZAW 500. Berlin: de Gruyter.

Vayntrub, Jacqueline. 2015. "'Observe Due Measure': The Gezer Inscription and Dividing a Trip around the Sun." Pages 191–208 in *Methodological Epigraphy, Philology, and the Hebrew Bible Perspectives on Philological and Comparative Study of the Hebrew Bible in Honor of Jo Ann Hackett*. Edited by Jeremy M. Hutton and Aaron D. Rubin. Atlanta, GA: SBL.

Wolters, Al. 1984. "Nature and Grace in the Interpretation of Proverbs 31:10–31." *CTJ* 19:153–166.

Wolterstorff, Nicholas. 1980. *Art in Action: Toward a Christian Aesthetic*. Grand Rapids, MI: Eerdmans.

Zabán, Bálint Károly. 2012. *The Pillar Functions of The Speeches of Wisdom: Proverbs 1:20–33; 8:1–36; 9:1–6 in the Structural Framework of Proverbs 1–9*. BZAW 429. Berlin: de Gruyter.

Zimmerli, Walther, 1964. "The Place and Limit of Wisdom in the Framework of the Old Testament Theology." *SJT* 17:146–158.

CHAPTER 6

ORDER

Wisdom, Retribution, and Skepticism

LUDGER SCHWIENHORST-SCHÖNBERGER

6.1 INTRODUCTION

THERE is hardly any biblical book that does not display elements of wisdom in one way or another, considering that wisdom addresses questions of discernment, understanding, and the correct way of life. In regard to theology of creation, the concept of order permeates the entire Old Testament. Genesis 1 describes creation as a kind of order created by God out of chaos. The *Law* (*Torah*), revealed to Israel, aims to maintain the order inserted into creation as a just order in the people of God. Out of Zion shall go the Torah (Isa 2:3; Mic 4:2) as "light for the nations" (Isa 42:6) to overcome the chaos of violence in the world of the nations. *Prophecy* appears when the just order in social life is disregarded or violated (cf. Isa 1:2–4; Mic 3:2). Prophecy too is aware of the connection between society and nature/creation (cf. Amos 5:7–9). A breakdown of social order results in a breakdown of natural order (cf. Hos 4:1–3). It is nevertheless useful to distinguish the Wisdom books, Proverbs, Job, and Ecclesiastes, from the rest of the Bible, since they specifically develop the concept of wisdom and critically reflect on it. In the extended canon of the Septuagint, Sirach and Wisdom of Solomon are also included. Analogous to the five books of the Torah and of the Psalms, one can speak of the five books of Wisdom (Gilbert 2003, 10–13).

Biblical Wisdom Literature represents an epistemological as well as practical approach to life that is fundamentally optimistic. It supposes that recognizing the world's intrinsic order is essentially possible. It further reckons with the basic human capability of ordering life accordingly. The careful yet critical scrutiny of creation enables Wisdom to accumulate knowledge that is normative and directive for human conduct. In its admonition to heed law and justice, it is no less penetrating than the prophetic instructions of the

Bible, establishing a connection between human conduct and its results. It articulates the promise that whoever heeds the call of wisdom will not fail.

This conception of wisdom, which is particularly present in Proverbs, is then reconsidered critically in the books of Job and Ecclesiastes. Both books reflect upon the limitations as well as difficulties and dilemmas (aporia) of human life and perception, leading to their association with a "Wisdom crisis." Yet, they do not represent a radical epistemological skepticism and practical pessimism either. Although these books communicate an awareness of suffering as well as of the limitations of human understanding and action, humanity is not depicted as helpless when facing these realities. In their own unique manner, Job and Ecclesiastes each introduce a decidedly theological perspective on the concept of traditional wisdom. Job and its history of composition particularly allow us to observe a development from the depiction of *experiential wisdom* to that of *revelational wisdom*—we may call this the process of the increased *theologization of wisdom*. Sirach and Wisdom of Solomon, both later than Job and Ecclesiastes, would then complete this process as they take up the aporia and questions that have been introduced in Job and Ecclesiastes to produce a decidedly theological synthesis that unites the sapiential traditions with those of the Prophets and the Torah.

6.2 PROVERBS

6.2.1 The Correspondence of Human Conduct and Its Results: Connective Justice

Sapiential thought, in its fundamental structure as delineated especially in Proverbs, displays a conception of order commonly described with the German term *Tun–Ergehen–Zusammenhang*. According to this conception, the conduct of a human being or a community has a distinct correspondence with the results arising from this conduct. Those who do good will experience good results; those who do evil will encounter adversity, "No harm befalls the just, but the wicked are overwhelmed with misfortune" (Prov 12:21; cf. 14:11; 21:21; 22:8). This correlation applies to the economical (10:4; 12:11; 13:4, 25; 19:15; 20:13; 24:30–34), social (12:24; 19:4, 7), and political (11:14; 14:34–35; 16:12; 20:28; 29:2, 4, 8, 18) dimensions of human life. A number of texts from Proverbs create the impression that this correspondence arises of its own accord, as though it was subject to an immanent regularity (11:5–6, 17; 26:27–28), whereas others clearly state that it is initiated and maintained by God (2:6–8; 3:33–34; 10:29; 15:3, 9, 25; 16:5; 22:12, 23; 24:12). Current research now attempts to reconcile these two aspects through the concept of *connective justice*, which would imply that the underlying conception of order is not static, but dynamic. Order is constituted similar to communication and is maintained through social interaction as expressed by reciprocal deeds, "Whoever confers benefits will be amply enriched, and whoever refreshes others will be refreshed" (11:25).

These reciprocal deeds are carried out within a system of order into which the divine reality is incorporated. In this context, many statements are expressed in the passive voice. The passive expressions leave it open to interpretation whether the reciprocity must be attributed to God, to other humans, or to God *through* human deeds, "A man gets his fill of good from the fruit of his speech; one is repaid in kind for one's deeds" (12:14). Reciprocal thoughts and actions need to be recognized and rehearsed. Sapiential instruction serves the purpose of communicating a set of knowledge in correlation with this conception of order. This knowledge should in turn provide both orientation for everyday life and assistance in dealing with the difficulties that arise with it (3:1–2). The book of Proverbs (cf. the prologue, 1:2–6) is practically a life orientation textbook.

The teaching on human conduct and its direct results is grounded in experience. It is both an expression of the hope that justice will prevail and, to a certain extent, an eloquent contradiction of observable facts. Its emphatic diction might very well serve pedagogic interests. It should be kept in mind, however, that these statements are of such a fundamental and open nature that an eschatological understanding cannot be ruled out either. Sapiential teaching is life coaching in its most comprehensive sense, promising deliverance from an *untimely* and *sudden* death (1:27), but this does not exclude deliverance from *ultimate* death, "Justice saves from death" (10:2; cf. Wis 2–5). Good fortune and salvation, which are promised to those who live righteously, do not necessarily coincide with the superficial realities that are apparent to everybody in everyday life. Rather, they might be understood as a reality that will only set in or become apparent in the future, "He who sows injustice shall reap misfortune" (22:8).

6.2.2 Theology of Creation

The conception of order underlying sapiential thought is rooted in creation theology. "Behind the order stands the divinity, the creator, who has set up his world according to certain laws" (Murphy 1996, 115). God is Creator of the world (3:19; 8:22–31) and of all humans (14:31; 17:5; 20:12; 22:2; 29:13). Social order and natural order correspond to each other. The disruption of social order is accompanied by the disruption of cosmic order. The idea of the integration of society and nature, which can be found both in the Torah (cf. Gen 3; 5–9; Lev 26; Deut 28) and in the Prophets (cf. Amos 1:2; 9:7–15; Hos 4:1–3; Jer 4:25–28), is systematically developed in Wisdom of Solomon (11:2–19:22) along the lines of Israel's history. When the natural order of creation and the distinction between Creator and creation is not acknowledged and maintained as a principle of life (Wis 13), social order becomes corrupted, too, "The upheaval of good values…corruption of souls, reversal of the sexes, disorder in marriage, adultery and licentiousness" (Wis 14:26). Only a life of justice and wisdom ultimately bestows duration on a ruler's reign (Wis 1:1–6:21).

Proverbs 8:22–31 conceptualizes wisdom as a female intermediary of the process of creation. Prior to the creation of the world, she was "acquired" by YHWH (קנה; 8:22 MT) as a beloved wife and "born" or "brought forth" (חיל; 8:24–25) as a beloved child, or "created" (κτίζω; 8:22 LXX) by YHWH. As a "beloved child" (8:30) she was with God at the creation of the world. At the same time, it was her delight to be among the human race (8:31). Pre-existent Wisdom thus takes up the position of an intermediary between God, on the one hand, and the world and its people, on the other. She is the face of God, turned towards the world, "The Lord made me the beginning of his ways *for his works*" (Prov 8:22 LXX). The theological discourse of the other Wisdom books further considers and reflects upon Wisdom's role in creation and salvation. She is no goddess next to God, even though Wis 9:4 describes her as "coadjutor" (πάρεδρος) sitting beside the throne of God. Through her, all things were created (Ps 104:24; Wis 9:2); full of goodness, she rules over everything (Wis 8:1). She is a gift and companion that God sends to all who cry out in longing for her (Prov 2; Wis 7–8). In the guise of the Torah, she established herself "in the holy tabernacle on Zion" (Sir 24:10). The lives of the people of the world and of Israel are touched by her salvation and deliverance (cf. Wis 19; John 1:1–8). The combination of creation theology and the theological concept of pre-existent Wisdom thus establishes and communicates the idea of creational, societal, and historical order.

6.2.3 The Ethics of Love towards God and the Neighbor

The sapiential concept of order includes that of the ordering of love (*ordo amoris*). Even if not mentioned explicitly, the arrangement of individual proverbs and sets of proverbs allows us to recognize that the ethics of Proverbs is directed at the twofold commandment of love towards God and fellow humans (2:5–8, 9–11; 3:1–12, 21–35; 14:21, 27, 31; 19:17; 22:9; 30:1–14). Love towards the neighbor, which includes love towards the enemy (cf. 17:13; 20:22; 24:17, 28–29; 25:21–22), is based upon and measured against love towards self. Its concern both with care for self and care for others (31:19–20) is guided by the quest to find the correct balance. The ethics of Proverbs warns against ruthless egoism (1:10–19; 21:13) as much as against the dangers of thoughtless altruism stemming from a lack of self-respect and ending in self-neglect (6:1–5; 11:15; 22:26–27; 27:13). It is God who ultimately enables human good deeds, achievements, and successes (10:22; 16:1, 3, 9, 33; 19:14; 20:24; 21:30–31). The fitting attitude for humans, however, towards their Creator is one of humility (8:13; 15:33; 16:18–19; 18:12; 21:4; 22:4), trust (3:5–6; 16:20; 18:10; 22:19; 28:25), and reverence (1:7; 3:9–10; 14:2; 15:16, 33; 19:23; 22:4; 23:17; 24:21; 28:14).

6.2.4 Universalism and Faith in YHWH

In treating general questions and difficulties of humanity, sapiential thought displays a universalistic tendency. Great biblical themes of historical theology, such as election, the exodus from Egypt, the gift of the Torah, and the Sinai covenant do not play any direct role in Proverbs. These are only hinted at in a number of verses that are probably to be dated quite late (cf. 30:1–14). Yet established Wisdom is by no means non-religious. It finds itself within a religious scheme of order which is compatible with the Torah and the prophetic books as far as its moral content is concerned. In their original sense, all three corpora deal with law and justice, that is, with human conduct that does justice to God and man. Whoever "does justice" in this sense will also be treated justly by God, "The Lord is far from the wicked, but hears the prayer of the just" (15:29). Divine revelation and divine laws, however, do not appear in their customary sense. Most probably as the result of editorial activity, the motto "Fear of the Lord is the beginning of knowledge" appears at three crucial hinge positions of the book: its beginning, its middle, and its end (1:7; cf. 9:10; 15:33; 31:30). This serves the purpose of ranking knowledge of the divine ahead of knowledge of the world. Skepticism regarding the capacities of human recognition only arises in a limited number of cases. At times, some hints occur, indicating that the natural limitations of human recognition of the divine may be transcended by means of the theology of revelation (cf. 30:1–6). The attribution to Solomon (1:1) places the book within the context of Israel's history. The king is admonished to exercise law and justice, which represents the core values of the Torah and the Prophets, "Open your mouth, judge justly, defend the needy and the poor" (31:9). Only a reign characterized by law and justice can endure (29:14). The young pupil who "turns his ear to wisdom" (2:2) will "understand the fear of the Lord" (2:5) and gain knowledge of God. The wisdom of Proverbs can be considered a particularly Israelite form of ancient Near Eastern thinking about order, which gained its theologically accentuated profile in the course of the history of tradition within the framework of the Torah and the Prophets.

6.3 JOB

6.3.1 Introduction

The book of Job represents a forceful confrontation with the concept of a divine world order. Its discourse takes place in the form of a dramatic dialogue between Job and his friends, who defend the classical concept of divine order. Job, on the other hand, challenges that conception. By the end of the drama, the protagonist arrives at a new and deepened insight into the divine ordering of the world. He is reconciled with himself and with his situation. He declares the battle with God to be closed and is restored. Thus, this discourse, designed as a piece of drama spoken with allocated roles, may be understood as a three-tiered work displaying the levels of *Order—Crisis of Order—Deepened Understanding of God's Maintained Order*.

An extraordinary aspect of the book is that the breakdown of the initial order had not been caused by the protagonist suffering from its consequences. This kindles a quarrel between Job and his friends. The latter maintain that Job is responsible for the consequences that can be observed in his life, but Job declares his innocence. Job's innocence is neither questioned by the narrator of the story, nor by God in his closing speeches.

Job is a righteous man, who has been drawn into deepest misery despite his righteousness. Yet, his words are criticized in God's speeches. This criticism is concerned with the possibilities and limitations of Job's knowledge and insight. In its final form, the book of Job does not fundamentally question the divine world order. It does, however, point out that human attempts to understand this order are subject to limitations. Yet the discourse does not result in a form of radical agnosticism. It does not culminate in aporia, but rather invites the reader to walk the route that Job had to walk. It leads through grief and misery to knowledge of God. At the onset, in a world in which God had been heard of only "by the hearing of the ear," such knowledge was manifestly impossible to attain. Thus, Job's statement in his second answer to the second speech of God, "By hearsay I had heard of you, but now my eye has seen you" (42:5), might be the key to understanding the book (Schwienhorst-Schönberger 2007, 261). The dialectics of God's presence and withdrawal is a decisive feature of the book's final form, which should not be resolved in one direction or the other.

6.3.2 Job, the Long-Suffering Man

In the prologue, the figure of Job is presented as the ideal righteous man, "He was blameless and upright, fearing God and avoiding evil" (1:1). Building on the Hebrew text, the Septuagint adds a fifth trait, explicitly describing Job as "righteous" ($\delta i \kappa a \iota o s$). In his conversation with the Satan, God confirms the narrator's judgment and adds that Job is unmatched in his uprightness (1:8). God speaks of him as "my servant Job" (1:8; 2:3). Job's piety remains unchanged even when the Satan causes him deep distress, "He did not sin, nor did he charge God with wrong" (1:22). Job rejects his wife's suggestion that he relinquish his piety, curse God, and die in light of his affliction (2:9) as being imprudent (2:10). The prologue depicts Job as a suffering servant of God who displays a sapiential attitude in composedly accepting both good fortune and misfortune from God. No word of lament leaves his mouth. In the midst of his affliction, he blesses the name of the Lord (1:21). It is also this Job, the persevering, long-suffering man, who lived on in Christian tradition (cf. Jas 5:11).

6.3.3 Job, the Rebel

A crucial change takes place in the dialogue between Job and his friends. Job curses the day of his birth (3:3) and wishes for death (3:13; 6:9–10). He both questions the concept of just order in the world and the principle of connective justice (the correspondence of conduct and result). God, says Job, "destroys both the innocent (תם) and the wicked (רשע)" (9:22).

Job's friends emphatically object, and attempt to defend a just divine world order. Eliphaz explains Job's affliction through the phenomenon of intrinsic human weakness (4:17–21). He encourages Job to present his case to God (5:8) and appeals to Job's piety (4:6). Bildad energetically rejects Job's words (8:2) and upholds the justice of God, "Does God pervert judgment, does the Almighty pervert justice?" (8:3). He emphatically defends double retribution, "Behold, God will not cast away the upright; neither will he take the hand of the wicked" (8:20). He suspects that Job's children died due to their sins (8:4). He advises Job to turn trustfully to God in prayer. Should he be blameless, God would swiftly restore him (8:5–7). Zophar takes the matter a step further. He, too, adheres to the dogmas of God's justice and of double retribution, but emphasizes that humans can only have partial knowledge of these matters. His speeches display traces of an *epistemological skepticism*. Although he maintains the objective validity of the concept of God's justice, Zophar points out that humans cannot fathom its depths. God alone can offer insight into the "secrets of wisdom." Zophar wishes that Job might benefit from such teaching (11:5–6). Then he would learn that God even overlooks some of his sinfulness (11:6). Zophar calls upon Job to "set his heart aright, stretch his hands towards God and remove iniquity from his hand" (11:13–14). This would enable him to forget his misery and sleep undisturbed (11:16–18). Zophar's speech anticipates God's speeches. God will indeed speak to Job and introduce him into the mysteries of creation. But contrary to Zophar's presupposition, God will not declare Job guilty.

6.3.4 The Poem on Wisdom (Job 28)

Within Job, the Poem on Wisdom (Job 28) has a key position. According to certain structural analyses, it constitutes the center of the book, though its inclusion in the original composition is disputed. Now, however, it resides at the meeting point between the human and godly spheres of the drama. The dialogue between Job and his friends (3–27) culminates in aporia and in a rift between the participants. The Poem on Wisdom, which is formally a part of Job's speech, provides an interval, leading from lament and accusation to reflection, as Job pauses and reflects on the mystery of wisdom. Reflecting *skeptical wisdom*, wisdom here cannot be "found" by humankind, but might well guide behavior, when it follows the fear of God, "God understands the way to her; it is he who knows her place.... To man he said, 'See: the fear of the Lord is wisdom; and avoiding evil is understanding'" (28:23, 28). In his closing sentence, Job refers back to 1:1b. He characterizes his original respectful attitude towards God as the true form of wisdom. He thus anticipates the very perspective that he will gain at the end of God's speeches. In this manner, the Poem on Wisdom conciliates between the "long-suffering Job" of the prologue and the "rebellious Job" of the dialogues. At the same time, it guides the reader on towards God's speeches, and thus to an understanding of wisdom guided by the theology of revelation: wisdom cannot be found by humanity but only received from God.

The path leading away from aporia and alienation, therefore, proves to be the very path leading from experiential wisdom to revelational wisdom. The Poem on Wisdom marks the transition between the "speeches of men" and the "speeches of God." Although the book of Job exhibits a tendency towards a skeptical understanding of wisdom, this does not lead towards a skeptical understanding of revelation, but much rather to revelational wisdom: Its skepticism is directed against a type of optimistic experiential wisdom that presents itself as being epistemologically well versed in divine matters.

6.3.5 The Speeches of Elihu: From Experiential Wisdom to Revelational Wisdom

Elihu's four speeches (32–37) mark exactly this transition. Elihu correctly recognizes that the conflict between Job and his friends cannot resolve the dilemma of suffering. He acts as a prophet and self-confidently represents the concept of revelational wisdom. The explicit reference to his youth (32:6–7) makes it clear that the topic now no longer is knowledge that was acquired through experience in the course of a long life, but divinely revealed knowledge. It is God who teaches humanity (35:11). The youthful king Solomon is a prototype of someone benefitting from knowledge acquired through wisdom. He had recognized that he "could not otherwise possess wisdom unless God gave it" (Wis 8:21). Thus, as a young king he prayed for wisdom, and it was given to him (1 Kgs 3:12; Wis 9). As a likely reference to this, Elihu reminds Job that God often speaks to humans in dreams, but that people often disregard them. Elihu represents the concept of wisdom conveyed by the divine spirit. Wisdom thus finds itself in the proximity of prophecy. Clearly distancing himself from the wisdom of the aged acquired through experience, Elihu speaks of the "spirit" (רוח) in human beings and the breath of the Almighty, which bestows understanding upon them (32:8). Elihu's four speeches, presented without interruption, clearly transcends theologically what has been said by the other three friends. Although he adheres to the concept of God's justice and of just retribution (34:10–12; 35:2; 36:6) just as the three friends had done, he emphasizes that human cannot fully fathom the divine world order. "God is greater than mortals" (33:12), he declares. His works can only be "viewed from afar" (36:25), and "God is great beyond our knowledge" (36:26; cf. 37:5). By the end of his fourth and final speech, Elihu promotes both aspects, God's justice and the incomprehensibility of his works. He concludes that humans cannot stand in high esteem before God on account of their own wisdom, but that it better befits them to fear God (37:23–24). This skepticism concerning Wisdom theology is therefore not to be confused with modern agnosticism, which more or less questions the reality of God. Elihu's skeptical interpretation of traditional Wisdom is rather to be understood as a deeply theologically motivated *relecture*.

In the course of Old Testament history of tradition, wisdom becomes increasingly closely associated with God, with personified Wisdom even described as "coadjutor" or "consort" (πάρεδρος) at God's throne (Wis 9:4). She thus participates in God's mysterious character and is depicted as an otherworldly figure who would come to those who pray piously for her guidance. This development may be understood as the *theologization of wisdom*, of which Elihu's speeches represent an early stage. His speeches most probably are a later addition to the book, emending the friends' experiential wisdom. Job cannot be refuted by human wisdom; only God can solve his problem. Therefore, Elihu declares that the three friends all failed to refute Job, concluding, "God can vanquish him but no mortal!" (32:12–13).

Elihu uses the concept of revelational wisdom to adhere to the traditional belief in a just divine world order and at the same time escape the aporia that this concept causes when it confronts the suffering of a righteous man (32:12). His presentation of his case, however, results in a performative self-contradiction, introducing elements of ambivalence and caricature into his speech. Elihu's prophetically staged performance creates the impression that *he* is able to fulfill the requirements of revelational wisdom as stipulated in his speeches when he challenges Job, "Be silent, and I will teach you wisdom!" (33:33). Elihu himself has previously stated, though, that only God can meet these requirements. He deems himself destined to speak on behalf of God (36:2) and "establish what is right" for his Maker (36:3). He sees himself as a man "perfect in knowledge" (36:4). The divine speeches, following directly afterwards, falsify his claim; God can speak perfectly well for himself.

6.3.6 The Speeches of God

The two divine speeches address two great questions posed in the dialogue. The first deals with creation and its order, the second deals with justice. The *first divine speech* (38:1–40:2) comprises forty rhetorical questions in its first main part (38:4–38) and addresses ten creational themes. The symbolical value of the numbers (4 x 10), representing a totality spreading in all directions, refers to completeness and establishes a connection with the creation narrative. The core statement of part one of the first speech is: YHWH is Creator of the world—not Job! The second main part of this speech (38:39–39:30) describes different wild animals, which are listed in five groups of two each. Its core statement is: YHWH is Lord of the animals—not Job! The first divine speech is to be understood against the background of the creation narrative of Genesis 1, with its leading idea: from chaos to cosmos, from *tohuwabohu* (Gen 1:1) to the House of Life. Original chaos (Gen 1:2) was not completely removed but restrained by God. This chaos is an integral constituent of creational order. Humanity encounters chaotic forces in the cascading waters, in the gloomy night, in the wild animals. God set limitations to chaos, so that it will not engulf his creation, but these restraints are to be kept intact in a constant "battle," which is conducted by YHWH, not Job. As such, God's first speech develops a *deepened and differentiated understanding of order*. That which is chaotic and disordered is an integral part of creation. The concept of creational order presented here thus eclipses an anthropocentric understanding of creation dominated by utilitarian human considerations. The world of the wild animals, removed as it is from human dominion, likewise displays a marvelous order, which is kept in place by God, the "Lord of the animals." This phenomenon, too, practically forces the human observer into awe and wonder. The first speech of God forcefully refutes Job's accusation that the world is chaotic (Job 3). It is ordered marvelously, but this order includes chaos, which is integrated into creation and kept under control by God's mighty rule.

The *second divine speech* (40:6–41:26) deals with the question of justice. Job had made the accusation that the earth was given into the hands of a wicked one (9:24). He had charged God with transgressing the principles of justice, "Both the innocent and the wicked he destroys" (9:22). God decidedly denies the accusation, answering with a rhetorical question, "Would you refuse to acknowledge my right? Would you condemn me that you may be justified?" (40:8). Like the first speech, the second also displays a balanced central position regarding the question of evil in the world. The reality of evil in creation is not denied. But God keeps the dynamics inherent to evil, of a force wishing to destroy all, at bay. The hippopotamus (*Behemoth*: 40:15–24) and crocodile (*Leviathan*: 40:25–41:26 [41:1–34]) represent the forces of evil in ancient Near Eastern mythology. The hippopotamus is a creation of God, just as Job is (40:15). It is a mighty creature, which no human can restrain (40:24). The same is true of the Leviathan (crocodile). Biblical tradition depicts it as a primeval chaos monster (cf. Isa 27:1; Ps 104:26). Yet it does not devour all of creation, because God set a limit to its domain. God's second speech therefore also leads to a differentiated view of divine order. Evil is a reality of the world that God keeps under control, so that creation does not perish under its force.

6.3.7 Job's Answers

Short answers from Job follow each of God's speeches. Both can be understood as an expression of his consent. In his first answer (40:3–5), Job announces that he will henceforth be silent. He declares the end of his confrontation with God, and his willingness to listen to the words of his Teacher. In Job's second answer (42:1–6), the semantic field of "knowledge" or "recognition" is prominent. Job was led to deepened insight that transcends his previous knowledge. The key to understanding the whole book lies in Job's second answer, "By hearsay I had heard of you, but now my eye has seen you" (42:5). The book therefore does not end in agnosticism and skepticism but presents the concept of a deepened knowledge of God. In contrast to the language of the prologue (1:1; 2:3), the epilogue no longer mentions Job's fear of God. Therefore, one could even postulate that Job's experience led him from faith to sight.

6.4 ECCLESIASTES

6.4.1 Introduction

Many scholars consider Ecclesiastes to hold an extraordinary position within the canon. Norbert Lohfink (1998) speaks of it as "the skeptical back door of the Bible" (cf. Michel 1988, 88–89). Sociologically, he considers the book's author to belong to a group of intellectuals, learned men who turn the society's normative cultural knowledge into the object of critical scrutiny.

The book's interpretation is disputed. Its tensions and contradictions have inspired extensive debate (Schwienhorst-Schönberger 2011, 64–69; 2016, 470–473). Though, for example, Qoheleth issues a call to rejoice (11:9), he also describes laughter and joy as folly (2:1–2). The tensions and contradictions cannot be resolved along literary-critical lines, but rather indicate that Qoheleth critically engages with traditional teaching, both of sapiential and prophetical provenance. He often quotes or alludes to traditional sapiential opinions, only to submit them subsequently to critical scrutiny and correct them where necessary (cf. Michel 1988, 27–33). In the book's first postscript, Qoheleth's activity as critical commentator and corrector is aptly described, "Besides being wise, Qoheleth taught the people knowledge, and weighed, scrutinized, and arranged many words" (12:9).

6.4.2 Limitations of Human Knowledge and Actions

Like no other book of the Old Testament, Ecclesiastes makes human cognition into the object of critical reflection. This process is characterized by a twofold movement. First, the subjectivity of the protagonist is more prominent than in any other Old Testament book. Ecclesiastes displays a strong empirical character. Phrases such as "I said in my heart," "I probed," "I examined," "I saw," and "I have found" occur regularly. Qoheleth appears as a figure stepping from tradition and taking a deliberative stance towards it. Second, Qoheleth also points to the limitations of human knowledge and actions. In the context of the world that can be empirically investigated, three areas of limitation are particularly evident: death, the future, and the work of God (Schellenberg 2002, 35–200). Considering death, which every person should anticipate, the differences between the wise and foolish or the righteous and wicked become relative. Arduous striving towards knowledge and possessions proves to be highly questionable (2:12–23; 3:16–22; 9:1–6). In the light of an uncertain future, human activity remains full of risk. However, inactivity is no alternative, either (6:12; 7:14; 8:5–12; 10:13; 11:1–6). The work of God in all its fullness, unfolding in all that happens "under the sun" remains unfathomable to the human mind (8:16–17). It cannot be changed by human endeavor (7:13–14).

These observations of Qoheleth, which critically oppose the optimism of traditional Wisdom, have led scholars to associate the book with skepticism (e.g., Michel 1988, 94). They have also described it as having a pessimistic worldview or representing a philosophy of the absurd (Schoors 2013, 19–24). Some even suggest that Ecclesiastes represented views that directly opposed the biblical message (Michel 1989, 288). An example would be the statement, "Nothing is new under the sun" (1:9), which seems to oppose the prophetical promise that God is doing something new in history (Isa 43:19). Similarly, Qoheleth's advice, "Be not just to excess!" (7:16) seems to promote an ethical relativism in clear opposition to the general biblical ethos.

This contribution does not share the above-mentioned interpretation (for substantiation, see Schwienhorst-Schönberger 2011), but rather understands the skeptical and pessimistic statements of the book in a strictly functional sense. They fulfill the function of deconstructing false, yet common conceptions of human prosperity or good fortune, revealing the hidden nihilism of a superficial optimistic concept of life and clearing the way towards finding true and enduring joy (Schwienhorst-Schönberger 2011, 69, 85).

6.4.3 Qoheleth as Deconstructionist

Qoheleth's procedure in reaching his goal is comparable to *deconstruction*. The book's opening poem contains the famous sentence, "Nothing is new under the sun" (1:9). The ideal reader would associate this with Isa 43:19, which reads, however, "See, I am doing something new!" Prophetic and sapiential circles were in lively intellectual and literary conversation with each other in late post-exilic Jerusalem. It is highly probable that Qoheleth was familiar with eschatological strains of contemporary prophecy. He engages in critical conversation with the proponents of such thought, deconstructing the words from Isaiah and countering their author's intention (Krüger 1996). He thereby demonstrates how the text of Isaiah cancels its own meaning, and in doing so, how it creates a new meaning. Isaiah 43:18 reads, "Remember not the events of the past, the things of long ago consider not; see, I am doing something new! Now it springs forth, do you not perceive it?" If taken seriously, the words "remember not the events of the past" render the phrase "see, I am doing something new" questionable, because someone who had forgotten the past has no means of determining whether something announced as new truly is. Qoheleth therefore does not simply present his statement that "nothing is new under the sun" as a dogmatic assertion that is beyond questioning, but rather proves his statement in a fictitious dialogue. One may therefore suspect that he is here dealing with opinions which we are familiar with from the prophetic tradition (cf. Isa 42:9; 48:6–7; 65:17; Ezek 11:19–20; 36:26–27).

6.4.4 The Ordering of Space and Time

The poems on the cosmos (1:4–11) and on time (3:1–9) frame the royal travesty of 1:12–2:26. The two poems are based upon the concept of order. Contrary to common opinion, the poem on the cosmos does not express futility (Lohfink 1985; Schwienhorst-Schönberger 2011, 155–181). The word "vanity" is significantly absent from this passage. It is not the perpetual cycles of nature that are futile, but the human question of profit (1:3) in light of the enduring quality of the world (1:4). The poem on time functions similarly. It consists of seven strophes of four bicola each, numbering $4 \times 7 = 28$ enumerations, a totality reaching to all four corners of the world. The poem lists good and evil occurrences and assigns each to an appropriate time. It reaches the surprising conclusion, "God has made everything appropriate (beautiful) to (in) its time" (3:11). Reciting the poem lends meaning to that which is seemingly meaningless. Its meaning however only unfolds when the recipient partakes of a consciousness which transcends the good and evil periods enumerated in the poem. Qoheleth introduced such a reality, both transcending and encompassing the contradictions, in the preceding textual unit: God (2:24–26). It is God who "made everything beautiful in its time and had put eternity into human hearts" (3:11) As was the case in Job, traditional sapiential conceptions of order are brought into a crisis in Ecclesiastes, too. In both cases, the crisis is overcome through a mental integration of the difficult experiences and insights that have originally caused the crisis of order. This happens through the introduction of a theological perspective. Here, too, one may cautiously speak of the *theologization of wisdom*.

This becomes particularly clear at a crucial point in the book, which is not wholly uncontested in its interpretation. Ecclesiastes 5:17–18 speaks of human prosperity as a *gift* of God. Verse 19 even takes a further step in calling joy an *answer* of God, "because God answers (עֲנֵה) him in the joy of his heart." According to Ludwig Levy (1912, 99), this verse is of central importance for Qoheleth's impression of God and of life, since it is "the Archimedean point at which the lever is to be fixed for the solution of the supposed contradictions of this curious book" (likewise Lohfink 1990; 2003, 84–85; Bonora 1992, 101–102; Pahk 1996; Schwienhorst-Schönberger 2011, 336–344; cf. Mazzinghi 2001, 389–408).

6.4.5 *Via Media* as an Answer to the Crisis of the Correspondence of Conduct and Result

A skeptical attitude can be identified whenever Qoheleth critically questions exaggerated claims of validity and simplifications of sapiential teaching and scriptural interpretation. His critical attitude towards extreme points of view however does not cause him to relinquish all conceptions of order. It much rather leads towards a novel conception of order in the area of ethics. This novelty may be understood as a *via media*. Qoheleth can thus arguably be seen as a precursor to Ben Sira, who took pains to integrate the criticism in Job and Ecclesiastes into a new synthesis of sapiential teaching.

Torah, Prophecy, and Wisdom all admonish towards a life lived in justice, incorporating the promise of a lengthy and prosperous life into their admonishment, "The Lord loves the righteous" (Ps 146:8). Seen against this background, Qoheleth's call not to be "just to excess" (7:15) might be understood as a provocation. His advice has earned the accusation of clarifying his "bankrupt world view" by "making fun of the concepts of צדיק (righteous) and רשע (evildoer)" (Lauha 1978, 133, 136).

This contribution again does not share this point of view. We encounter no bankruptcy of worldview, but rather a critical, ethical reflection similar to Aristotelian teachings on virtue. Qoheleth recommends the *via media*, the intermediate between two extremes, which, each taken on its own, would lead to destruction. The intermediate is not a compromise characterized by lazy mediocrity, but, in Aristotle's words, the "best and utmost" (*Eth. nic.* 1107a).

Qoheleth's strategy, applied in 7:15–20, is the deconstruction of a given but not thoroughly contemplated understanding. In the sentence, "I have seen all manner of things…the just perishing in their justice, and the wicked living long in their wickedness" (7:15), we may understand the terms צדיק (a just person) and רשע (a wicked person) as contradictory, but also as contrary opposites. All Old Testament texts containing the opposite pair "just / wicked" implicitly understand the pair as *contradictory* opposites. From a moral point of view, there are just and wicked people with no one in between (*tertium non datur*):

the just | the wicked

The sentence may, however, also be understood as containing a *contrary* pair of opposites. Then, the terms "just" and "wicked" are located at the opposite poles of a line. Between them, there is a third element:

FEAR OF GOD

In his advice, "Be not just *to excess* (הרבה)" (7:16), Qoheleth explains that there are different degrees of righteousness, including "too much" and "too little" righteousness. Both are detrimental. This begins the process of correcting the supposed understanding of the reader. Just as one can display "too much" righteousness, one can also have "too much" wisdom, "be not *overwise*" (7:16). Tradition considers Torah observance as wise, and contempt for the Torah as foolish (cf. Prov 9:9; 23:24). Ecclesiastes 7:15–20 probably belongs to a discourse in which צדיק ("just") would tend to mean *in accordance with* the Torah and רשע ("wicked") *in opposition to* the Torah. Considering the contemporary history of the text, these observations point to the early phase of an internal Jewish discourse that centered on the interpretation and validity of the Torah (Bickermann 1937). It would lead to violent clashes shortly after the period when Ecclesiastes was written, during the so-called Maccabean revolt (second century BCE).

The addressee is encouraged to adhere to justice, but not excessively. The meanings of the terms "just" and "wicked" have therefore subtly changed. The word "just" is now no longer synonymous with "morally good," as it was in traditional Wisdom, and "wicked" is no longer synonymous with "morally corrupt." In Eccl 7:15–18 the two words describe a manner of conduct with a moral quality that must be determined. These verses thus represent an explicative discourse, that is, a form of argumentation in which expressions are no longer stated or disputed naïvely, but function as controversial claims. This controversy is then to be dealt with as an independent theme. The fact that Qoheleth deals critically with key concepts of tradition is no indication of his alienation from tradition, but rather of his profound engagement with it. Reflection reveals naïve understandings and may inspire a deepened comprehension of the "intention" of tradition.

Ecclesiastes 7:18b now introduces the decisive third entity, which finds itself in the middle position between the "just" and the "wicked": the God-fearer, "The one who fears God will succeed with both." This implies that the fear of God represents the *correct conduct* regarding the two extremes, both of which are to be rejected, excessive justness and excessive wickedness.

The pericope probably deals with a *hermeneutics of the Torah*. The just seem to be those who practice strict observance of the Torah and justify their conduct in the tradition of the teaching on the correspondence of conduct and result along eudaimonistic lines: whoever keeps the Torah will live long and live well (cf., e.g., Pss 1; 119:137–140; Isa 3:10–11). The "wicked" (largely) reject the Torah as an orientation for their everyday activities and reckon that they can thus act successfully, freed from its restraints. These are the two basic options available in post-exilic Jewish thought. They collide theologically, culturally, and politically during the Hellenistic crisis of the first half of the second century BCE. Ecclesiastes 7:15–18 seems to represent an early phase of this conflict. Qoheleth chooses neither side. He takes up the controversy in order to reach a deeper understanding of the core of the matter.

The conception of a new synthesis is accompanied by a process of internalization. That which is good (טוב), that is, human flourishing or happiness, is transferred inwardly, more decisively than is customary in traditional Wisdom. The connection between happiness and exteriors such as prosperity and longevity is loosened. The inner person (*homo interior*) gains importance. Qoheleth no longer identifies happiness with possessions, but rather with an inner experience that is able to emancipate itself to some degree from externals and the vicissitudes of life (cf. Schwienhorst-Schönberger 2011, 69–82). The book's author is concerned with lasting happiness, with joy that will endure, "And even if man may live many years, he will rejoice *amidst them all* while remembering the dark days—that they, too, are many" (11:8).

6.4.6 Criticism of a Naïve Conception of the Divine Order of Creation

The older conception of wisdom creates the impression that humans can reach happiness through cunning and sensible behavior. In the *royal travesty* (1:12–2:26), Qoheleth takes up the role of a wise and mighty king, in a clear allusion to the story of Solomon (1 Kgs 4–11). He attempts to attain happiness "under the sun" through clever, goal-oriented actions, but his experiment ends in exasperation and disheartenment (2:17). He concludes that the wise king will die just as the fool does (2:14–15) and ultimately will have to leave the fruits of his labor to a successor, who might be wise or foolish. Following the deconstruction of an autonomous understanding of wisdom, as it were, Qoheleth introduces a decidedly theological perspective. At the end of the royal travesty, he recognizes that happiness is a *gift of God* (2:24).

This theological perspective extends throughout Qoheleth's further considerations. The word *God* occurs forty times (!). Contrary to common perception, the book also subscribes to the post-exilic trend of *theologization of wisdom*. Qoheleth's fundamental statements about God are set within the scope of creation theology, with a marked emphasis on the *creatio continua*.

God's creational activity includes contradictions and seeming incompatibilities. Unpleasant and undesirable occurrences are part of all that happens "under the sun." God's presence cannot be denied amidst all of these and humanity is not able to fully comprehend God's actions, "Consider the work of God. Who can make straight what God has made crooked? On a good day enjoy good things, and on an evil day consider: Both the one and the other God has made" (7:13–14). Ecclesiastes emphasizes the inscrutability and mysteriousness of God's ways as does hardly any other biblical book. In doing so, it criticizes a form of wisdom that deems itself able to fathom God's actions, "I saw all the work of God: No mortal can find out the work that is done under the sun. However much mortals may toil in searching, no one finds it out; and even if the wise claim to know, they are unable to find it out" (8:17; cf. 3:11). Likewise, the human categories of *just* and *unjust* reach their limits when God's actions are restricted to one or the other, "Both the just and the wicked God will judge, since a time is set for every affair and for every work" (3:17).

These observations however do not lead Qoheleth into apathy in matters of faith. The *fear of God* is a fourfold motif within the book and is considered to be an attitude placed in human hearts by God himself (3:14). Qoheleth is critical towards offerings in the temple, verbose prayers, and the misuse of vows and sin-offerings. He recommends the fear of God as the religious attitude that should permeate all religious actions and give them all meaning (4:17–5:6). Though the quintessence of all moral actions (7:18), it is no guarantor of success (8:10–15). In the closing poem of the book, Qoheleth calls upon the young man to let his heart be glad and to remember his Creator (11:9–12:1). The second postscript considers the epitome of the book to be the fear of God *and* the observance of his commandments (12:13). The combination of the two aspects transcends the central concerns of the book but is arguably not in complete conflict with its message. The postscript was possibly added to defend Ecclesiastes against the introduction of Sirach as the new school textbook (Lohfink 2003, 11–13). By this means, also, the book found its way into the biblical canon.

6.7 CONCLUSION

The Wisdom books represent a differentiating and integrative understanding of order. The opposite of order is chaos. Creation, as narrated in Genesis 1, however, does not mean that chaos is completely destroyed; on the contrary, it is disempowered by integration into creation. The conceptions of order found in the Wisdom books, range between order and chaos. They are neither naïve nor unaware of the threat to creation order. Humanity as the image of God has the obligation to preserve the order of the world. When the elements of chaos prevail, the destruction of order threatens. The progression of *order, crisis of order, deepened understanding of God's maintained order*, found in the book of Job, can also be used to understand the chronological order of Proverbs, Job, and Ecclesiastes. In Proverbs we find an almost undisputed understanding of order. In Job, however, this conception of order decays. In the revelational horizon opened by the Divine Speeches, a deepened understanding of order appears in which (seemingly) chaotic elements (e.g., wild beasts) of creation are integrated into the powerful and caring action of God. A similar process can be observed in Ecclesiastes. Here the crisis starts in the internal reflection of the subject. Here too, the crisis is overcome by a deepened understanding of God's action and presence in the world, which also includes seemingly contradictory oppositions.

Works Cited

Bickermann, Elias. 1937. *Der Gott der Makkabäer: Untersuchungen über Sinn und Ursprung der makkabäischen Erhebung.* Berlin: Schocken/Jüdischer Buchverlag.

Bonora, Antonio. 1992. *Il libro di Qoèlet.* Rome: Città Nuova.

Gilbert, Maurice. 2003. *Les cinq livres des Sages: Proverbes—Job—Qohélet—Ben Sira—Sagesse.* Paris: Les Éditions du Cerf.

Krüger, Thomas. 1996. "Dekonstruktion und Rekonstruktion prophetischer Eschatologie im Qohelet-Buch." Pages 107–129 in *"Jedes Ding hat seine Zeit": Studien zur israelitischen und altorientalischen Weisheit.* BZAW 241. Edited by Anja Angela Diesel, Reinhard G. Lehmann, Eckart Otto, and Andreas Wagner. Berlin: de Gruyter.

Lauha, Aarre. 1978. *Kohelet* (BK XIX). Neukirchen–Vlyun: Neukirchener.

Levy, Ludwig. 1912. *Das Buch Qoheleth: Ein Beitrag zur Geschichte des Sadduzäismus.* Leipzig: Hinrichsche Buchhandlung.

Lohfink, Norbert. 1985. "Die Wiederkehr des immer Gleichen: Eine frühe Synthese zwischen griechischem und jüdischem Weltgefühl in Kohelet 1,4–11." *AF* 53:125–149.

Lohfink, Norbert. 1990. "Qohelet 5:17–19—Revelation by Joy." *CBQ* 52:625–635.

Lohfink, Norbert. 1998. "Der Bibel skeptische Hintertür: Versuch, den Ort des Buches Kohelet neu zu bestimmen." Pages 11–30 in *Studien zu Kohelet.* Stuttgart: Katholisches Bibelwerk. Repr.; *StZ* 198 (1980):17–31.

Lohfink, Norbert. 2003. *Qoheleth: A Continental Commentary.* Minneapolis, MN: Fortress.

Mazzinghi, Luca. 2001. *"Ho cercato e ho esplorato": Sudi sul Qohelet.* Bologna: Dehoniano.

Michel, Diethelm. 1988. *Qohelet.* EdF 258. Darmstadt: Wissenschaftliche Buchgesellschaft.

Michel, Diethelm. 1989. *Untersuchungen zur Eigenart des Buches Qohelet.* BZAW 183. Berlin: de Gruyter.

Murphy, Roland E. 1996. *The Tree of Life: An Exploration of Biblical Wisdom Literature.* 2nd ed. Grand Rapids, MI: Eerdmans.

Pahk, Johan Yeong. 1996. *Il canto della gioia in Dio: L'itinerario sapienziale espresso dall'unità letteraria in Qohelet 8,16–9,10 e il parallelo di Gilgames Me. iii.* Naples: Istituto Universitario Orientale.

Schellenberg, Annette. 2002. *Erkenntnis als Problem: Qohelet und die alttestamentliche Diskussion um das menschliche Erkennen.* OBO 188. Freiburg: Universitätsverlag Freiburg Schweiz; Göttingen: Vandenhoeck & Ruprecht.

Schwienhorst-Schönberger, Ludger. 2007. *Ein Weg durch das Leid: Das Buch Ijob*. Freiburg: Herder.

Schwienhorst-Schönberger, Ludger. 2011. *Kohelet*. HThKAT. 2nd ed. Freiburg: Herder.

Schwienhorst-Schönberger, Ludger. 2016. "Das Buch Kohelet." Pages 467–479 in *Einleitung in das Alte Testament*. Edited by Christian Frevel. 9th ed. Stuttgart: Kohlhammer.

Schoors, Antoon. 2013. *Ecclesiastes*. HCOT. Leuven: Peeters.

PART II

THE CONCEPT OF WISDOM IN RELATED CULTURES

CHAPTER 7

....

WISDOM IN EGYPT

....

JOACHIM FRIEDRICH QUACK

7.1 THE PROBLEM OF THE GENRE

....

THERE is a problem in defining a category of "Wisdom" texts for ancient Egypt, which is too rarely reflected upon. When the discipline evolved in the nineteenth and early twentieth centuries, Egyptological classifications of texts were strongly influenced by the Hebrew Bible. What resembled the Wisdom category in that corpus got put into an Egyptian "Wisdom" category that was never well defined, especially not according to an emic perspective. Consequently, without much discussion, many Egyptian compositions came to be labeled as "Wisdom" by scholars, resulting in a quite inhomogeneous group, which makes a meaningful analysis rather difficult.[1] This contribution endeavors to counterbalance such tendencies and to pay close attention to the Egyptian genre designations as well as typical formal differentiations.

The category of teachings has a well-defined Egyptian term (*sbꜣy.t*), which is found at the beginning of all well-preserved compositions.[2] Their typical setting is that of a father teaching his son, which serves as a role model for an actual teacher instructing his pupil. The named author (with his titles) serves as an authority for the quality of the teaching as well as a signal for the social setting of potential recipients.

Such an attribution to a specific person is shared with only a few other textual genres, especially prophecies and in some cases laments, while the bulk of Egyptian literary and religious texts lack any indication of authorship. A famous passage in the literary miscellany pChester Beatty IV vv. 3, 5–7, deriving from a school context and dating to the late

---

[1] A recent example is Wyns 2017, 164–171, where even some divinatory compositions have been classified as "Wisdom." Sometimes narrative texts are brought in connection to Wisdom Literature, e.g., Lepper (2008, 299, 304–305) for some sections of P. Westcar.

[2] Good collections of translations are Vernus 2010 (for the pre-demotic texts) and especially for the more recent texts Hoffmann and Quack 2018, 263–341.

nineteenth dynasty (ca. 1200 BCE), enumerates authors with specific names who are considered to be of exemplary quality.[3] For most of them, we know actual compositions ascribed to them that are actually attested as school texts during the New Kingdom. Teachings are attributed to Hardjedef, Khety, Ptahhotep, and Kaïrsu. Neferty is indicated as the speaker of a revelation of the future (put in writing by King Snofru when he hears it). Khakheperreseneb is the speaker of a lament, describing the current bad state of the land and at the same time complaining that he is lacking original ways to express his feelings. For him we have the remarkable situation that several witnesses from the eighteenth dynasty are known,[4] but none for the Ramesside period.[5] While Imhotep is very famous and at this time already received cultic veneration (Quack 2014), no specific composition can safely be attributed to him. Ptahemdjehuti cannot be linked to any known text at the moment.

The specific focus on, on the one hand, authors of instructions, and, on the other, authors who have foretold the future is already plainly indicated in the text itself, which gives the heading "the wise men who foretold what would come about." Some modern scholars have tried to combine these two branches into an overarching genre of "*Spruchliteratur*" (Brunner 1966), while others have stressed the substantial differences between them (Kitchen 1979, 237–240).

We should also keep in mind that indications of specific authors appear also in some other texts that are not designated as *sbꜣy.t*, like the words of Sasobek (pRamesseum I) and the speeches of Khuenanup from the Wadi Natrun. Yet, we cannot be sure if those compositions were still known during the Ramesside period,[6] so it is uncertain if they were deliberately excluded from the list in pChester Beatty IV.

Furthermore, the list in pChester Beatty IV mentions only authors of the distant past. None of the authors of Ramesside teachings (Ani, Amennakhte, perhaps Amenemope)[7] are mentioned. It has to be asked if they were deliberately omitted, or if the list as a composition is older than the Ramesside period (i.e., dating to the eighteenth dynasty). The observation concerning Khakheperreseneb might point towards the second possibility.

Also, Late Egyptian Miscellanies (collections of educational material ranging from administrative letters to eulogies of kings, hymns to deities, and characterizations of professions) go under the heading of *sbꜣy.t*, even though such a title is only rarely really

[3] Simon 2013, 266–271; Vernus 2016, 321–323.

[4] Parkinson 1997; Hagen 2019.

[5] Obviously, this raises the possibility that the passage in pChester Beatty IV ultimately goes back to an eighteenth-dynasty archetype.

[6] There is a well-known passage in a Ramesside ostracon that appears to take up a passage of Khuenanup (Simpson 1958; Guglielmi 1983), but recently the dependence of another passage in that ostracon on its purported source (the Shipwrecked Sailor) has been questioned in favor of something which had developed into a proverb (Winand 2017, 29–30), and a similar question could also be posed for the parallel to Khuenanup.

[7] It is still open to debate whether the instruction of Amenemope dates to the later Ramesside period or postdates it (see Vernus 2013). Laisney (2018, 141–143) dates the oldest manuscript to the end of the twentieth dynasty, which would give a *terminus post quem non*.

attested in the actual manuscripts, most of which do not preserve the very beginning of the roll (Quack in press a).

Onomastica (lexical lists of words) can claim a similar genre; at least the only case with a preserved beginning (the Onomasticon of Amenemope) is explicitly styled as a *sbꜣy.t* (Gardiner 1947, 5; 1*–2*). For modern scholars, it has always been a challenge to come to grips with this identical genre attribution. A potential parallel is the note that King Solomon in his wisdom composed proverbs and wrote about trees and animals (1 Kgs 5:9–14 ET 4:29–34). Some have linked this last activity with onomastica (e.g., Alt 1951), but there have also been skeptical voices (e.g., Fox 1986).

7.2 OTHER SORTS OF "KNOWLEDGE" TEXTS

In Egypt, there are also textual collections of knowledge, especially religious knowledge of arcane things. In contrast to teachings, these compositions do not go under the authorship of a specific individual. In particular, the so-called Amduat (The Book of What Is in the Netherworld) has a long title stressing the relevance of knowing. It has been discussed whether instructions provide precepts for how to behave in life, while the netherworld guides offer direction for post-mortem existence (Hornung 1979). However, the rather negative conclusions of his discussion are based more on an a priori understanding of the netherworld guides as funerary compositions for the king than on the factual evidence of the compositions themselves.

The Ritual for Entering the Chamber of Darkness, rather inappropriately entitled "Book of Thoth" by its editors (Jasnow and Zauzich 2005), must also be considered.[8] The manuscripts date to the Ptolemaic and Roman periods, but the composition is likely to have older roots. This is a quite different sort of wisdom, with a special terminology; the ideal wise man of this composition receives the designation *slꜣ* (with some orthographic variations), which is likely to go back to *sꜣri* "knowledgeable one," otherwise attested as an epithet of the god Thot. There are a few specific human beings indicated as role models. Among them, Nebwenenef is known as high priest of Amun under Ramses II, while Neferhotep and Nebnefer are more difficult to pinpoint. There are still serious problems in understanding many details of this composition,[9] but it is clearly of crucial importance for the question what "wisdom" really meant for cultivated Egyptians. There is one possible direct reference to this composition in one of the traditional teachings, namely that of Amennakht (twentieth dynasty). He recommends frequenting the scriptorium (*pr-ꜥnḫ*)[10] and becoming (in a metaphorical way) a book chest. This is probably the only mention of the scriptorium in a conventional Egyptian teaching, while this institution is

[8] For the understanding of this difficult composition, see especially Quack 2007; Quack 2016/17; Quack in press b.
[9] The latest English translation (Jasnow and Zauzich 2014) is significantly different from the latest German one (Quack in press b).
[10] Against the frequent translation of this term as "house of life," see Quack 2016/17, 227.

of crucial importance in the Ritual for Entering the Chamber of Darkness, which also has sections about books, their organization, and equipment for which the candidate volunteers to care. Such a reference would tally well with other indications (especially the mention of Nebwenenef) that the Ritual for Entering the Chamber of Darkness goes back to a Ramesside archetype. Otherwise, a scribe of the scriptorium is attested much later as the author of a Wisdom composition attested on the Roman-period demotic ostracon BM 50627 (Quack 2016, 155).

There is some formal resemblance between Wisdom maxims and divinatory treatises (Fischer-Elfert 2017). The older compositions (like the Teaching of Ptahhotep in particular) with their casuistic structure show similarity to the conditional clauses typical for Egyptian omen literature.

7.3 Teaching Wisdom

Within the text about the installation of the Vizier transmitted in the tomb of Rekhmire (ca. 1450 BCE), an admonishment given by the king, "it is the taboo of the god to be partial," is followed by a remark, "this is a teaching (sb3y.t)" (Faulkner 1955, 22). Indeed, similar admonishments about not being partial are attested in the Teaching of Ptahhotep, and one of its versions is an exact verbal parallel (Hagen 2012, 189–192). It is quite remarkable that the king singles out just this one point as being a teaching, while many other recommendations do not get any such metatextual note.

Still, the idea of the king actively teaching his high functionaries is also attested elsewhere. During the Amarna period (ca. 1350–1330 BCE), officials proudly indicate having followed the teaching of King Akhenaten (van de Walle 1979; Assmann 1980). Slightly later, in the Edict of Haremhab, the king claims to have instructed the officials that he has installed (Kruchten 1981, 150, 154–155). The vizier Panehsi under Merenptah (ca. 1210 BCE) also indicates that he has been instructed by the king (KRI IV, 90, 6). There are two inscriptions of the late Second Intermediate period (ca. 1600 BCE) that even claim that the owner has been instructed by Thot, the god of wisdom himself (Morenz 1996, 168–173).

Quite relevant for instruction are the duties of the chief teacher of the temple, as transmitted in the book of the Temple (Quack 2002a). They stress ritual performance, recitation techniques, religious geography, customs of the palace, exegesis, and include medical and divinatory texts. What we classify as "Wisdom" texts do not get a clear mention.

7.4 Relations to Funerary Texts

The question of the relation between teachings and autobiographies as inscribed mainly in tombs has received controversial discussions. Many scholars, such as Andrea Gnirs (1996, 207–209) and Pascal Vernus (2010, 24–26), have supposed that Egyptian Wisdom texts have grown out of autobiographies. The latter were supposed to speak about an ideal life conforming in practice to what was recommended on a theoretical level in the Wisdom texts.

Karl Jansen-Winkeln (2004; contra Vernus 2010, 47–49; Buzov 2017), by contrast, has stressed the differences between the two genres. He notes that teachings are part of a this-worldly situation, and carry all necessary information in themselves, while autobiographies have a funerary setting and are embedded in a larger context, mostly of a tomb. He also sees important divergences regarding the typical length of the compositions as well as the existence of emic designations and the basic types of speech; and, according to him, only four of the seven main topics of biographies are well represented in the teachings, and for some situations the recommendations of the teachings are rather the opposite of the behavior praised in the autobiographies. Furthermore, he remarks that Wisdom texts tend to follow the contemporary speech (thus, the later ones are written in Late Egyptian or Demotic), while biographies tend to adhere to classical Egyptian. So, Jansen-Winkeln sees only rare and isolated cases of real interaction between teachings and biographies.

For the relation of funerary inscriptions and Wisdom texts, several pieces of evidence have to be noted. Under King Amenemhet III (late twelfth dynasty, ca. 1800 BCE), the stela Cairo CG 20538, II, ll. 8–20 (inscribed for Sehetepibre) includes a short recension of a teaching that is attested in a long recension in many New Kingdom witnesses (Posener 1976) and now known to be ascribed to a high official named Kaïrsu (Verhoeven 2009). Also, a very fragmentary funerary inscription from the Middle Kingdom (late twelfth dynasty) shows some remnants of what is likely to be a text with a didactic note (Fischer 1982).

In the eighteenth dynasty, there is an autobiographical inscription which presents the life of the tomb owner as a teaching for his children, with a title worded in a way likely reminiscent of the Teaching of Kaïrsu. A substantial part of it is devoted to declarations of guiltless behavior, so it is not so much a teaching in the classical sense of giving admonishment and precepts, but more of presenting a model to be emulated (TT 97; Urk. IV 1408,8–1411,17; Gardiner 1910). Another tomb inscription in the tomb of Ametj (Amos) stays more in the line of normal teaching, with a strong focus on acting according to the ideal of ma‘at, the personified concept of justice, even if the very incomplete preservation of the text renders an analysis difficult (Dziobek 1998, 23–54). It is likely that the text is focused on instructing a future vizier. There are also some references in funerary texts to appropriate parts of Wisdom texts, especially the instruction of Kaïrsu, which is deliberately cited.[11]

---

[11] Both examples cited in Schipper (2018, 25) belong to this category—and it has to be noted that the passage in the instruction itself is likely to be based on funerary models.

7.5 HISTORICAL DEVELOPMENT

While there are compositions ascribed to the Old Kingdom in the indication of their setting, no manuscripts from that time are preserved, and it is debated to which extent to which the ascriptions are pseudepigraphic. For the teaching to Kagemni, set in the period of change from the third to the fourth dynasty (ca. 2550 BCE), only the end is preserved in pPrisse, dating to the late Middle Kingdom (ca. 1800–1700).[12] The instruction of prince Hardjedef (a son of King Kheops; ca. 2500 BCE) is currently only known in a quite fragmentary state mainly from Ramesside period (ca. 1300–1070 BCE) ostraca and a late-period wooden tablet.[13] The very substantial Teaching of Ptahhotep, set under Unas, the last king of the fifth dynasty (ca. 2300 BCE), is fully attested in pPrisse (ca. 1800–1700 BCE) as well as in a slightly earlier quite fragmentary copy in pBM EA 10371+10,435 (ca. 1850 BCE), and several New Kingdom manuscripts (ca. 1550–1070 BCE).[14]

Even during the Middle Kingdom, the manuscript attestations are rather sparse. Several important compositions that are normally ascribed to the Middle Kingdom do not turn up in actual copies before the eighteenth dynasty. This has sparked a recent debate about their real date, and some scholars have proposed that the compositions in question (Teaching for Merikare, Teaching of King Amenemhet, Teaching of Khety, Teaching of Kaïrsu, Teaching of a Man for His Son) were only composed in the eighteenth dynasty (Gnirs 2006; Gnirs 2013; Stauder 2013). At the moment, good arguments are available for keeping the earlier dates (Jansen-Winkeln 2017).

The Ramesside period is a peak of attestation for almost all Wisdom texts, due especially to the large amount of ostraca containing individual sections. They show that a few of the classical Egyptian compositions were very frequently copied. However, the treatment can be quite divergent, and this allows some conclusions about the curricular setting of different teachings in scribal training. These are based partially on the absolute number of preserved manuscripts (especially ostraca), and partially also on attested direct sequence in some manuscripts.

Of the Teaching of Ptahhotep, which is considered by many modern Egyptologists as the most important Egyptian instruction, there are only three ostraca copies (Fischer-Elfert 1997, 18–23), and only one of the Teaching for Merikare (Quack 2006). They can only rarely have been studied at this time and place. By contrast, the Teaching of King Amenemhet I and the Teaching of Khety, both attested in more than two hundred Ramesside ostraca, are likely to have formed part of an obligatory basic curriculum.

---

[12]   Recently, Roccati (2005) has argued that a certain expression in this text indicates a genuine composition of the Old Kingdom.

[13]   A somewhat outdated edition is given by Helck (1984, 1–24). For additional manuscripts, see Fischer-Elfert 2009 with further references. Recently, it has been established that the text up to now considered as §§15–24 of the Teaching of a Man for His Son belongs in fact to the Teaching of Hardjedef.

[14]   For linguistic indications pointing to a pre-Middle Kingdom origin, see Quack 2005, 8–10 and passim; see also Roccati (2014), who supposes an early oral transmission.

Relatively well attested are the Teaching of Kaïrsu and the Teaching of a Man for His Son, probably also the Teaching of Hardjedef. Other compositions (not Wisdom texts) were optional choices.

By contrast, the number of definitely new Wisdom compositions of the New Kingdom is limited. The Teaching of Ani (Quack 1994) is most likely to be dated to the early nineteenth dynasty; it is still attested in manuscripts from the Third Intermediate period. With nine ostraca certainly belonging to it, and two further possible ones, it is rather sparsely attested in comparison with some classical Egyptian texts. The Teaching of Amennakht might be a more specifically local composition circulating in Ramesside Deir el Medineh, attested in about twenty ostraca.[15] The Teaching of Amenemope is somewhat disputed in its date of origin; it might already be post-Ramesside.[16] There is at most one ostracon of it dating to the late Ramesside period (Laisney 2018). Also dating to the New Kingdom is a Wisdom text organized in stichically written self-contained sentences giving prohibitions of certain behavior (Hagen 2005; Gundacker 2015). The text is not ascribed to a named individual, but claimed to be in accordance with ancient writings.

Only a few of the classical texts are still positively attested after the New Kingdom (Hardjedef, Kheti, and Amenemhet). None of the manuscripts is later than the twenty-sixth dynasty (Quack 2020). Also for instructions in Late Egyptian language, there are still a few manuscripts dating to the Third Intermediate and Saïte periods (Amenemope, Ani), but nothing later. While there are some obvious connections with short passages in temple inscriptions of the Greco-Roman period (Hagen 2009; Leitz 2017, 474 n. 12), they could easily be due to prior fluctuations between liturgical compositions and the Wisdom texts, and thus do not constitute evidence for the continued existence of the older Egyptian Wisdom compositions. This gap is a serious problem for efforts to compare classical Egyptian Wisdom texts with Coptic monastic rules, etc. (Eberle 2001).

In the late period, new Wisdom texts make use of the contemporary demotic form of the Egyptian language. A Saïte-period manuscript (pBrooklyn 47.218.135; sixth century BCE) still makes use of the hieratic script and, in general, the Saïte period is likely the time when the classical literature impacted a burgeoning demotic literature (which at that time often was still written in the hieratic script).

For some of the most important Wisdom texts attested in demotic script from the Ptolemaic period onwards, like the Teaching of Khasheshonqy and the Great Demotic Wisdom Book (often called papyrus Insinger after its best preserved manuscript), there are reasons for attributing their origins to the Saïte period (Quack 2002b). From the Roman period, there are quite a number of manuscripts of Wisdom compositions, mainly due to the preservation of substantial papyrus finds linked with temples. In particular, the Great Demotic Wisdom Book is attested in a relatively high number of papyrus copies. Still, in this time the total number of narrative manuscripts is far higher than the total number of Wisdom manuscripts, even if the number of copies per composition is clearly higher for the Wisdom texts.

---

[15] For the manuscripts, see Dorn 2004; Dorn 2013; see also the controversy over the actual author in Sikora 2015.

[16] See the edition of Laisney 2007 and the discussion by Vernus 2013.

For some time periods, certainly the New Kingdom until the Saïte period, we have to note a co-occurrence of recent and received texts. It has to be asked what their respective status was, especially during the Ramesside period, when the much-copied classics went side by side with more rarely copied new compositions. Were the "classics" considered the core part of Wisdom tradition, and new compositions like the Teaching of Ani just a supplement for topics less covered in the older texts? Or were the older ones still kept as schooling material but largely replaced by the newer ones in reading by adults? The Teaching of Amenemope, in any case, achieved a status as a relatively much copied work in the early first millennium BCE.

7.6 Textual Transmission

The textual transmission of most compositions is relatively closed, even if the normal amount of variants in the manuscripts is encountered. The Ramesside ostraca (which dominate our impression) at most show only individual deviations from an overall fixed model. However, there are some noteworthy exceptions that demonstrate deep-seated redactional work. For the Teaching of Ptahhotep, the completely preserved copy in pPrisse (late Middle Kingdom) constitutes very much a strand of its own, contrasting with all other (fragmentary) witnesses from the Middle and New Kingdom. They show differences in the sequence of the individual maxims, and quite substantial variations in the actual wording of sentences, sometimes going almost as far as recommending the opposite sort of behavior. This case, which is the only one where we have several pre-New Kingdom manuscripts of an instruction, should warn us for other teachings that the *textus receptus* of the New Kingdom versions is not necessarily a faithful successor to older models.

Another remarkable case is the late composition of the Great Demotic Wisdom Book attested most completely in pInsinger. Most of the at least twelve different papyri of this composition can still be traced back to a common model, even though variations in reading and sometimes even presence of individual lines are not rare. But there is at least one manuscript, pCarlsberg 2, which has so deep-seated divergences in reading and also a substantially abbreviated text that it has to be considered a fully different edition. Perhaps even more extreme is the case of the Teaching of Ani, where all papyrus manuscripts represent, as far as can be discerned, quite different recensions.

7.7 Compositional Form

A Wisdom text normally begins with a prologue setting the situation of the teaching.[17] This can be quite short, giving no more than name and titles of the teaching authority, as well as of the addressees. In other cases, longer narrative sections can occur. The

---

[17] Compare Römheld 1989.

prologue of the Teaching of Ptahhotep is fairly detailed, as he complains about the afflictions of old age and asks the king for permission to raise his son as assistant and future successor. Even longer is the introduction of the Teaching of Khasheshonqy, which tells about the life of its author, how he ended up in prison and asked for writing tools in order to teach his son in written form. These are the only cases where any sort of official control over the production of teachings is positively attested. Otherwise, little is known about any official assignment for compositions[18] or control of circulation.

Some Wisdom texts also have elaborated epilogues. The epilogue of the Teaching of Ptahhotep, where the valor of good listening is extolled, is well known. The final part of the Teaching of Ani is more unusual, with its dialogue between father and son about the question whether behavior can be taught or is predestined.

The compositional form of the older Egyptian teachings is the maxim-structure, where a certain topic is addressed in relatively few sentences. Most especially in the Teaching of Ptahhotep, a casuistic construction "if you…" is dominant. Some late compositions (Amenemope, the Great Demotic Wisdom Book, and another, still unpublished demotic teaching) make use of explicit numbering of the chapters.

The very fragmentary Teaching of pRamesseum 2 (late Middle Kingdom) seems to make use of loosely organized sentences. Also, the Prohibitions of the New Kingdom attest single (negated) sentences without a clear logical succession.

In the late period, two different tendencies can be observed. On the one hand, there are compositions like the Great Demotic Wisdom Book which have organized sections with headings, but no longer a casuistic structure. Rather, the general topic of a section is traced through mostly self-contained sentences—sometimes general statements, sometimes recommendations to do or to refrain from certain actions. On the other hand, there are texts like the Teaching of Khasheshonqy that contain just individual sayings (sometimes continued with pronominal references over two or three lines) without any larger order beyond word association. Several of them could be popular proverbs. In the frame story, there is even an explicit justification for the lack of larger order by claiming that the author was refused a papyrus roll and had to make do with pottery sherds as a writing support.

It is important to note that loosely organized sayings without clear overall structure are definitely later than works organized into well-contained maxims. This is of potential relevance for assessing the situation in the Hebrew Bible. There, the usual model is that compositions of loosely organized isolated sayings are considered to be older than those which (like Prov 1–9) build larger units. The attested situation for Egyptian Wisdom compositions does not support such a model.

---

[18] A possible case is pChester Beatty IV, vv. 6, 13–14. where the scribe Khety is said to have written a teaching on order of the king.

7.8 Social Setting(s)

Normally, modern scholarly research assumes a single line of development for Egyptian Wisdom texts. Some claim that there is a global development from a higher to a lower social setting (Brunner 1991). By contrast, I would rather stress the existence of different strands, with also different intended audiences. Some compositions are more intended for the top elite or people aspiring to it, others for a "middle class." This leads to a different economic outlook.

For the Middle Kingdom, this can be illustrated by three different teachings which have sometimes been thought to represent three different steps of the same career (Fischer-Elfert 1999). The Instruction of Khety (also called "satire of the trades")[19] spends the better part of its content on demonstrating how each profession except that of a scribe is disagreeable. Its teaching sections clearly reflect the situation of somebody who is still being instructed at school, and also serving as an errand boy for higher-ranking functionaries. Another text which stands out by the explicit anonymity of its author (Teaching of a Man for His Son) shows the level of a medium-ranking functionary who already has some responsibility in making decisions and settling disputes. Finally, the Teaching of Kaïrsu (formerly known as Loyalist Instruction) is addressed to people who are relatively close to the king, and who have subordinates and tenant-farmers. Here, loyalty towards the king is the main topic of the first part, while the second recommends not burdening the poor tenants overmuch, lest they desert their fields and thus undermine the livelihood of their master.

In the New Kingdom, the divergent outlook of different teachings can be felt even more clearly. The Instruction of Amenemope recommends cancelling the larger part of outstanding debts. This admonition tallies well with the substantial amount of titles of the teacher as well as his son, showing that he was at the upper echelon of the grain tax administration and could afford some generosity without risking his own lifestyle.[20] By contrast, Ani recommends not to give away charitably, but to lend money with interest. This also tallies well with the situation of the author, who is a simple scribe at a less important temple.

These quite divergent audiences can at least equally well be established for the Late period. In the Great Demotic Wisdom Book, a whole section stresses that one should provide for one's community, if one has the economic means for it. By contrast, Khasheshonqy's teaching is deeply steeped in cynicism, and mainly aims at showing the harsh realities of life and how best to deal with them. From the introduction,[21] we know that he was a minor priest who had serious economic problems, so that eventually he set

---

[19] Last edition Jäger 2004; important discussion Widmaier 2013.

[20] I fully disagree with the position of Washington 1994 that Amenemope was mainly addressed to the poor.

[21] For this, see Quack in press c (incorporating two previously unknown fragments).

out to get support from an old friend (which ultimately led to his imprisonment because he became embroiled in a conspiracy against the king).

Normally, the social setting which is thought relevant can be recognized from the titles ascribed to the teaching authority. The position of the teacher and the experiences usually linked with it serve as warrant for the quality and appropriateness of the teaching. The Wisdom texts claiming an origin in the Old Kingdom are ascribed to princes or viziers, thus really the top elite. In the Middle and New Kingdom, and probably also the Late period, the social spectrum becomes larger, encompassing high functionaries as well as lower ranks.

A special small group is constituted by teachings ascribed to a king. Currently, there are two such texts known. One is a teaching that a king (whose name is lost in a lacuna of the papyrus) has written for his son and successor Merikare, who is known as one of the last rulers of the Heracleopolite period (ninth–tenth dynasty; late third millennium BCE; Quack 1992). It contains extensive advice about how to deal with internal issues (including potential troublemakers) as well as the coexistence of an independent state in southern Egypt and the problem of nomadic incursions into the Egyptian delta. The other is the Teaching of Amenemhet I for Sesostris I, which warns the recipient not to trust others, illustrating that with the description of a murderous attack. While a royal setting for Wisdom literature is much rarer than in the Hebrew Bible, these specific compositions fit it much better (Wilke 2006; Quack 2017, 22–29).

7.9 BASIC CONTENTS

The teachings do not so much transmit an abstract concept as concrete cases. The aim is to have success in life, either a successful career with the prospect of reaching a high position of authority (and rich income), or at least to make ends meet and go along without being hassled too much by superiors. A somewhat classical formulation about the teaching as "profit for the one who hears, but woe to the one who transgresses it" is found already in the Teaching of Ptahhotep (49–50) and taken up with some variation in Amenemope (3, 11–12), but also in the Book of the Temple in the instruction to the chief teacher (Quack 2002a, 163, 170).

An important part of the teachings is given to behavior during professional life: dealing with superiors, in some of the teachings also with inferiors, and sometimes advice about economic options. Private life is also covered, especially interactions with women, often the wife, sometimes also the mother. There is also advice about choosing friends and trustworthy companions. Some texts also give recommendations about providing a tomb, and occasionally implementing a funerary cult. Only from the New Kingdom onwards do teachings for non-royal persons touch upon topics of cult and veneration of the gods. From these times onwards, the free will of a deity also gets increasingly stressed, culminating in the "paradoxical" chapter endings in the Great Demotic Wisdom Book, which describe that the opposite of the regular outcome of behavior can

also occur. By contrast, normally a conception of an automatic link of act and consequence is supposed in modern scholarship for the older teachings.

On the surface, especially the older teachings give the impression of being relatively
utilitarian and not all that religious. Beginning with an article by Adrian de Buck (1932),
who mainly based his study on the Teaching of Ptahhotep, *ma'at* was considered a fundamental religious concept permeating all Wisdom texts. It has to be remarked critically
that a concept of *ma'at* as justice and world order has been built up in recent decades by
Egyptologists and is in some need of deconstruction. Specifically concerning Wisdom
texts, several teachings do not use the term at all (Quack 1994, 71–72). In others it does
occur, but normally in the clearly circumscribed area of juridical disputes. It hardly
seems a good indication of a specifically religious outlook.

In the texts, the abstract expression "the god" is quite frequent and its relevance has
been much discussed (Quack 1994, 72–74). Sometimes it has been considered as the sign
of a monotheistic outlook of the authors standing in opposition to the polytheism of an
uneducated populace. It is more likely that the term was deliberately left vague by the
authors of the texts so that readers would have an option to fill in their personal favored
deity.

We also have to ask to which degree the teachings are sources of Egyptian ethics.
There have been some efforts to bring the Teaching of Ptahhotep together with classics
of philosophical ethics like Aristotle, Cicero, and Kant (Junge 2003). Such an approach
hardly does justice to the Egyptian material. Overall, many topics covered in the teachings are of limited relevance for ethics in general. Often, they are more about good man-
ners, and not rarely the behavior proposed, while useful in view of private success, can
hardly be called an ethical model.

7.10   RELATIONS TO OTHER CULTURES

The relation of the Egyptian teachings to Wisdom texts of the Hebrew Bible has been
much discussed (e.g. Bryce 1979; more specifically focused on terminology, Shupak 1993).
By far the most important case is the Teaching of Amenemope, which is likely to be a
rather direct model for the biblical passage Prov 22:17–23:11.[22] Also, the Maxims of Ani
have some connections with the biblical proverbs, especially warnings concerning the
strange woman (Quack 1994, 212–215). Otherwise, proposed connections often remain
relatively vague and are limited to overall similarities of the genre.

The Teaching of Ben Sira must also be taken into consideration. It contains a section
(38:24–39:11) about different professions that is likely to go back ultimately to the
Egyptian Teaching of Khety (Jäger 2004, 305–317). Similarities to passages in the Great
Demotic Wisdom Book have also been pointed out, though the question of the direc-

---

[22] For the quite intense modern discussion, see the bibliographical references in Quack 2017, 23 n.
174, and additionally Reichmann 2016, 57–111.

tion of possible contacts hinges on the chronology for the Egyptian text (whose real date of composition is not easy to ascertain).

There is a clear interaction with the Aramaic wisdom of Akhiqar. On the one hand, the original text might be influenced by some sayings from Egyptian Wisdom texts. On the other hand, fragments of a demotic version of the tale of Akhiqar are preserved, and probably belong to the same manuscript as fragmentary Wisdom sayings (Quack in press e). Some sayings documented in at least parts of the Akhiqar tradition can also be found in the Teaching of Khasheshonqy (Lichtheim 1983, 13–22).

Miriam Lichtheim has also seen connections between the Demotic Egyptian Wisdom compositions and Greek gnomologies (Lichtheim 1983, 24–28). For these, specific points of contact are much more difficult to establish.

7.11 PERSPECTIVES FOR FURTHER RESEARCH

Much work still needs to be done on the purely philological level. For several important compositions (especially the instruction of Ptahhotep and the Great Demotic Wisdom Book), an adequate and up-to-date edition, translation, and commentary is still lacking. Large-scale comparisons of the main topics of Wisdom texts and their relation to real life in Egypt are rare.

While there have been some recent efforts to apply modern literary theory to Egyptian narrative texts, nothing comparable has been done for Wisdom texts, perhaps because "Wisdom texts" are not an important part of "modern" literature. Probably more could be learned by comparison with other traditional societies.

The overall concept of wisdom in ancient Egypt certainly needs a more detailed investigation that begins with emic terms. This paper has focused on instructions, a genre which can be easily distinguished by its typical title and global coherence of contents and structure. A rather loose group of other texts that have often also been lumped together under the general heading of "Wisdom" do not share this coherence and would rather render the image less clear. Still, we have to keep in mind that the term "to know" and other expressions we would associate with wisdom are not particularly frequent in the instructions, but occur a lot more often in the other "knowledge texts" mustered above. It will be a task for the future to see if meaningful subcategories within the rather broad field of "Wisdom" can be established.

WORKS CITED

Alt, Albrecht. 1951. "Die Weisheit Salomos." *TLZ* 76:139–144.
Assmann, Jan. 1980. "Die 'loyalistische Lehre' Echnatons." *SAK* 8:1–32.
Brunner, Hellmut. 1966. "Die 'Weisen,' ihre 'Lehren' und 'Prophezeiungen' in altägyptischer Sicht." *ZÄS* 93:29–35.

Brunner, Hellmut 1991. *Die Weisheitsbücher der Ägypter: Lehren für das Leben*. 2nd ed. Zürich: Artemis.

Bryce, Glendon E. 1979. *A Legacy of Wisdom: the Egyptian Contribution to the Wisdom of Israel*. Lewisburg, PA: Bucknell University Press.

de Buck, Adriaan. 1932. "Het religieus Karakter der oudste egyptische Wijshed." *NThT* 21:329–342.

Buzov, Emil 2017. "The Relation between Wisdom Texts and Biographical Inscriptions in Ancient Egypt." *Journal of Egyptological Studies* 5:45–53.

Dorn, Andreas. 2004. "Die Lehre Amunnachts." *ZÄS* 131:38–55.

Dorn, Andreas. 2013. "Zur Lehre Amunnachts: ein Join und Missing Links." *ZÄS* 140:112–125.

Dziobek, Eberhard. 1998. *Denkmäler des Vezirs User-Amun*. Heidelberg: Orientverlag.

Eberle, Andrea. 2001. *Ethos im koptischen Mönchtum: Christliches Gedankengut oder kulturelles Erbe Altägyptens?* Wiesbaden: Harrassowitz.

Faulkner, R.O. 1955. "The Installation of the Vizier." *JEA* 41:18–29.

Fischer, Henry George. 1982. "A Didactic Text of the Late Middle Kingdom." *JEA* 68:45–50.

Fischer-Elfert, Hans-Werner. 1997. *Lesefunde im literarischen Steinbruch von Deir el-Medineh*. Kleine ägyptische Texte 12. Wiesbaden: Harrassowitz.

Fischer-Elfert, Hans-Werner. 1999. *Die Lehre eines Mannes für seinen Sohn: Eine Etappe auf dem „Gottesweg" des loyalen und solidarischen Beamten des Mittleren Reiches*. ÄgAbh 60. Wiesbaden: Harrassowitz.

Fischer-Elfert, Hans-Werner. 2009. "Ein neuer Mosaikstein im Hordjedef-Puzzle (§7): (Ostrakon Berlin P. 12383)." Pages 118–127 in Kessler et al. 2009.

Fischer-Elfert, Hans-Werner. 2017. "Cross-genre Correspondences: Wisdom, Medical, Mathematical and Oneirological Compositions from the Middle Kingdom to the Late New Kingdom." Pages 149–161 in *(Re)productive Traditions in Ancient Egypt: Proceedings of the Conference Held at the University of Liège, 6th–8th February 2013*. Edited by Todd Gillen. Liège: Presses universitaires de Liège.

Fox, Michael V. 1986. "Egyptian Onomastica and Biblical Wisdom." *VT* 36:302–310.

Gardiner, Alan H. 1910. "The Tomb of Amenemhet, High-Priest of Amon." *ZÄS* 47:87–99.

Gardiner, Alan Henderson. 1947. *Ancient Egyptian Onomastica*. Oxford: Oxford University Press.

Gnirs, Andrea M. 2006. "Das Motiv des Bürgerkriegs in Merikare und Neferti: Zur Literatur der 18. Dynastie." Pages 207–265 in *jn.t ḏr.w: Festschrift für Friedrich Junge*, vol. 1. Edited by Gerald Moers, Heike Behlmer, Katja Demuß, and Kai Widmaier. Göttingen: Lingua Aegyptia, Seminar für Ägyptologie und Koptologie.

Gnirs, Andrea. 1996. "Die ägyptische Autobiographie." Pages 191–241 in *Ancient Egyptian Literature: History and Forms*. Edited by Antonio Loprieno. Leiden: Brill.

Gnirs, Andrea M. 2013. "Zum Verhältnis von Literatur und Geschichte in der 18. Dynastie." Pages 127–86 in *Vergangenheit und Zukunft: Studien zum historischen Bewusstsein in der Thutmosidenzeit*. Edited by Susanne Bickel. Basel: Schwabe.

Guglielmi, Waltraut. 1983. "Eine 'Lehre' für den reiselustigen Sohn." *WO* 14:147–166.

Gundacker, Roman. 2015. "The Prohibitions—Ein Kompendium negativer Lehrsätze." Pages 315–328 in *Texte aus der Umwelt des Alten Testaments neue Folge Band 8: Weisheitstexte, Mythen und Epen*. Edited by Bernd Janowski and Daniel Schwemer. Gütersloh: Gütersloher Verlagshaus.

Hagen, Fredrik 2005. "*The Prohibitions*: A New Kingdom Didactic Text." *JEA* 91:25–164.

Hagen, Fredrik. 2009. "Echoes of 'Ptahhotep' in the Greco-Roman Period?" *ZÄS* 136:130–135.

Hagen, Fredrik. 2012. *An Ancient Egyptian Literary Text in Context: The Instruction of Ptahhotep*. OLA 218. Leuven: Peeters.

Hagen, Fredrik. "New Copies of Old Classics. Early Manuscripts of *Khakheperreseneb* and *The Instruction of a Man for his Son*." *JEA* 105 (2019):177–208.

Helck, Wolfgang 1984. *Die Lehre des Djedefhor und die Lehre eines Vaters an seinen Sohn.* Kleine ägyptische Texte 8. Wiesbaden: Harrassowitz.

Hoffmann, Friedhelm, and Joachim Friedrich Quack. 2018. *Anthologie der demotischen Literatur: Zweite, neubearbeitete und erheblich erweiterte Auflage.* Einführungen und Quellentexte zur Ägyptologie 4. Berlin: LIT.

Hornung, Erik. 1979. "Lehren über das Jenseits." Pages 217–224 in Hornung and Keel 1979.

Hornung, Erik, and Othmar Keel, eds. 1979. *Studien zu altägyptischen Lebenslehren.* Edited by Erik Hornung and Othmar Keel. Fribourg: Fribourg University Press; Göttingen: Vandenhoeck & Ruprecht.

Jäger, Stephan, 2004. *Altägyptische Berufstypologien.* Lingua Aegyptia Studia Monographica 4. Göttingen: Seminar für Ägyptologie und Koptologie.

Jansen-Winkeln, Karl. 2004. "Lebenslehre und Biographie." *ZÄS* 131:59–72.

Jansen-Winkeln, Karl. 2017. "Zur Datierung der mittelägyptischen Literatur." *Orientalia* 86:107–134.

Jasnow, Richard, and Karl-Theodor Zauzich. 2005. *The Ancient Egyptian Book of Thoth: A Demotic Discourse on Knowledge and Pendant to the Classical Hermetica.* 2 vols. Wiesbaden: Harrassowitz.

Jasnow, Richard, and Karl-Theodor Zauzich. 2014. *Conversations in the House of Life: A New Translation of the Ancient Egyptian Book of Thot.* Wiesbaden: Harrassowitz.

Junge, Friedrich 2003. *Die Lehre Ptahhoteps und die Tugenden der ägyptischen Welt.* OBO 193. Freiburg: Universitätsverlag; Göttingen: Vandenhoeck & Ruprecht.

Kessler, Dieter, Regine Schulz, Martina Ullmann, Alexandra Verbovsek, and Stefan J. Wimmer, eds. 2009. *Texte—Theben—Tonfragmente: Festschrift für Günter Burkard.* ÄAT 76. Wiesbaden: Harrassowitz.

Kitchen, Kenneth A. 1979. "The Basic Literary Formulations of Ancient Instructional Writings in Egypt and Western Asia." Pages 235–282 in Hornung and Keel 1979.

Kruchten, Jean-Marie. 1981. *Le Décret d'Horemheb: Traduction, commentaire épigraphique, philologique et institutionnel.* Brussels: Université de Bruxelles.

Laisney, Vincent Pierre-Michel. 2007. *L'Enseignement d'Aménémopé.* Rome: Pontifical Biblical Institute.

Laisney, Vincent Pierre-Michel. 2018. "L'ostracon du Caire d'Aménémopé retrouvé (JE 96555)." *Orientalia* 87:137–146.

Leitz, Christian. 2017. *Die regionale Mythologie Ägyptens nach Ausweis der geographischen Prozessionen in den späten Tempeln.* Wiesbaden: Harrassowitz.

Lepper, Verena M. 2008. *Untersuchungen zu pWestcar: Eine philologische und literaturwissenschaftliche (Neu-)Analyse.* Wiesbaden: Harrassowitz.

Lichtheim, Miriam 1983. *Late Egyptian Wisdom Literature in the International Context: A Study of Demotic Instructions.* OBO 52. Freiburg: Universitätsverlag; Göttingen: Vandenhoeck & Ruprecht.

Morenz, Ludwig D. 1996. *Beiträge zur Schriftlichkeitskultur im Mittleren Reich und in der 2. Zwischenzeit.* ÄAT 29. Wiesbaden: Harrassowitz.

Parkinson, Richard B. 1997. "The Text of *Khakheperreseneb*: New Readings of EA 5645, and an Unpublished Ostracon." *JEA* 83:55–68.

Posener, Georges. 1976. *L'enseignement loyaliste: Sagesse égyptienne du Moyen Empire.* Centre de Recherches d'Histoire et de Philologie de la IVe Section de l'Ecole pratique des Hautes Etudes 2; Hautes Études Orientales 5. Genève: Librairie Droz.

Quack, Joachim Friedrich 1992. *Studien zur Lehre für Merikare*. Göttinger Orientforschungen, 4. Reihe: Ägypten 23. Wiesbaden: Harrassowitz.

Quack, Joachim Friedrich. 1994. *Die Lehren des Ani: Ein neuägyptischer Weisheitstext in seinem kulturellen Umfeld*. OBO 141. Freiburg: Universitätsverlag; Göttingen: Vandenhoeck & Ruprecht.

Quack, Joachim Friedrich. 2002a. "Die Dienstanweisung des Oberlehrers im Buch vom Tempel." Pages 159–171 in 5. *Ägyptologische Tempeltagung Würzburg, 23.–26. September 1999*. Edited by Horst Beinlich, Jochen Hallof, Holger Hussy, and Christiane von Pfeil. ÄAT 33/3. Wiesbaden: Harrassowitz.

Quack, Joachim Friedrich. 2002b. "Zur Chronologie der demotischen Weisheitsliteratur." Pages 329–342 in *Acts of the Seventh International Conference of Demotic Studies, Copenhagen, 23–27 August 1999*. Edited by Kim Ryholt. CNI Publications 27. Copenhagen: Museum Tusculanum.

Quack, Joachim Friedrich. 2005. "Ein neuer Zugang zur Lehre des Ptahhotep?" *WO* 35:7–21.

Quack, Joachim Friedrich. 2006. "Das Deir el-Medine-Ostrakon der Lehre für Merikare." *ActAnt* 46:181–184.

Quack, Joachim Friedrich. 2007. "Die Initiation zum Schreiberberuf im Alten Ägypten." *SAK* 36:249–295.

Quack, Joachim Friedrich. 2014. "Imhotep—der Weise, der zum Gott wurde." Pages 43–66 in *Persönlichkeiten aus dem Alten Ägypten im Neuen Museum*. Edited by Verena Lepper. Petersberg: Michael Imhof.

Quack, Joachim Friedrich. 2016. *Einführung in die altägyptische Literaturgeschichte III: Die demotische und gräko-ägyptische Literatur*. Einführungen und Quellentexte zur Ägyptologie 3. 3rd ed. Berlin: LIT.

Quack, Joachim Friedrich. 2016/17. Review of *Conversations in the House of Life: A New Translation of the Ancient Egyptian Book of Thot*, by Richard Jasnow and Karl-Theodor Zauzich. *Enchoria* 35:215–230.

Quack, Joachim Friedrich. 2017. "Ägyptische Einflüsse auf nordwestsemitische Königspräsentationen?" Pages 1–65 in *Herrschaftslegitimation in Vorderorientalischen Reichen der Eisenzeit*. Edited by Christoph Levin and Reinhard Müller. ORA 21. Tübingen: Mohr Siebeck.

Quack, Joachim Friedrich. In press a. "Modellbriefe als Mittel der Schreiberausbildung im Alten Ägypten." In *Modelle*. Edited by Susanne Deicher and Christian Loeben.

Quack, Joachim Friedrich. In press b. "Das Ritual zum Eintritt in die Kammer der Finsternis." In *Texte zur Wissenskultur*. Edited by Bernd Janowski and Daniel Schwemer. TUAT.NF 9. Gütersloh: Gütersloher Verlag.

Quack, Joachim Friedrich. In press c. "Neue Fragmente der einleitenden Erzählung der Lehre des Chascheschonqi." *Enchoria* 36.

Quack, Joachim Friedrich. 2020. "Eine spätzeitliche Handschrift der Lehre des Cheti (Papyrus Berlin P 14423)." Pages 233–251 in *Ein Kundiger, der in die Gottesworte eingedrungen ist: Festschrift für den Ägyptologen Karl Jansen-Winkeln zum 65. Geburtstag*. Edited by Shih-Wei Hsu, Vincent Pierre-Michel Laisney, and Jan Moje. Münster: Zaphon.

Quack, Joachim Friedrich. In press e. "Die demotischen Fragmente der Erzählung und der Sprüche des Ahiqar." In *Elephantine in Context*. Edited by Reinhard Kratz and Bernd U. Schipper.

Reichmann, Sirje. 2016. *Bei Übernahme Korrektur? Aufnahme und Wandlung ägyptischer Tradition im Alten Testament anhand der Beispiele Proverbia 22–24 und Psalm 104*. AOAT 428. Münster: Ugarit-Verlag.

Römheld, K.F. Diethard. 1989. *Die Weisheitslehre im Alten Orient: Elemente einer Kompositionsgeschichte*. BNB 4. Munich: Manfred Görg.

Roccati, Alessandro. 2005. "Note letterarie—II: Imparare a memoria nell'età menfita." *ZÄS* 132:161–165.

Roccati, Alessandro. 2014. "Dating Ptahhotep's Maxims (Note Letterarie VI)." *Orientalia* 83:238–240.

Schipper, Bernd U. 2018. *Sprüche (Proverbia) 1–15. Teilband 1: Proverbien 1,1–15,33*. BKAT XVII, 1. Göttingen: Vandenhoeck & Ruprecht.

Shupak, Nili. 1993. *Where Can Wisdom Be Found? The Sage's Language in the Bible and in Ancient Egyptian Literature*. Fribourg: Universitätsverlag; Göttingen: Vandenhoeck & Ruprecht.

Sikora, Uwe. 2015. "Amunnacht, Sohn des Ipuy als Autor der *Lehre des Amunnacht*: Ein Artefakt ägyptologischer Beschreibungspraxis." Pages 191–207 in *Text: Wissen—Wirkung—Wahrnehmung: Beiträge des vierten Münchner Arbeitskreises Junge Ägyptologie (MAJA 4), 29.11. bis 1.12.2013*. Edited by Gregor Neunert, Henrike Simon, Alexandra Verbovsek, and Kathrin Gabler. Göttinger Orientforschungen 4. Reihe: Ägypten 59. Wiesbaden: Harrassowitz.

Simon, Henrike. 2013. *"Textaufgaben": Kulturwissenschaftliche Konzepte in Anwendung auf die Literatur der Ramessidenzeit*. Hamburg: Buske.

Simpson, William Kelly. 1958. "Allusions to *The Shipwrecked Sailor* and *The Eloquent Peasant* in a Ramesside Text." *JAOS* 78:50–51.

Stauder, Andréas, ed. 2013. *Linguistic Dating of Middle Egyptian Literary Texts: Dating Egyptian literary Texts, Göttingen, 9–12 June 2010*. 2 vols., vol. 2. Lingua Aegyptia. Studia Monographica 12. Hamburg: Widmaier.

Verhoeven, Ursula 2009. "Von der 'Loyalistischen Lehre' zur 'Lehre des Kaïrsu': Eine neue Textquelle in Assiut und deren Auswirkungen." *ZÄS* 136:87–98.

Vernus, Pascal. 2010. *Sagesses de l'Égypte pharaonique: Présentation, traduction et notes. Deuxième édition révisée et augmentée*. Arles: Actes Sud.

Vernus, Pascal 2013. "La datation de L'*Enseignement d'Aménemopé*: Le littéraire et le linguistique." Pages 191–236 in *Linguistic Dating of Middle Egyptian Literary Texts: Dating Egyptian literary Texts, Göttingen, 9–12 June 2010*. 2 vols., vol. 1. Edited by Gerald Moers, Kai Widmaier, Antonia Giewekemeyer, Arndt Lümers, and Ralf Ernst. Lingua Aegyptia. Studia Monographica 11. Hamburg: Widmaier.

Vernus, Pascal 2016. "L'écrit et la canonicté dans la civilisation pharaonique." Pages 271–347 in *Problems of Canonicity and Identity Formation in Ancient Egypt and Mesopotamia*. Edited by Kim Ryholt and Gojko Barjamovic. CNI Publications 43. Copenhagen: Museum Tusculanum Press.

Walle, Baudoin van de. 1979. "Les textes d'Amarna se réfèrent-ils à une doctrine morale?" Pages 353–362 in Hornung and Keel 1979.

Washington, Harold C. 1994. *Wealth and Poverty in the Instruction of Amenemope and the Hebrew Proverbs*. Atlanta, GA: Scholars.

Widmaier, Kai. 2013. "Die *Lehre des Cheti* und ihre Kontexte: Zu Berufen und Berufsbildern im Neuen Reich." Pages 483–557 in in *Linguistic Dating of Middle Egyptian Literary Texts: Dating Egyptian literary Texts, Göttingen, 9–12 June 2010*. 2 vols., vol. 1. Edited by Gerald Moers, Kai Widmaier, Antonia Giewekemeyer, Arndt Lümers, and Ralf Ernst. Lingua Aegyptia. Studia Monographica 11. Hamburg: Widmaier.

Wilke, Alexa F. 2006. *Kronerben der Weisheit: Gott, König und Frommer in der didaktischen Literatur Ägyptens und Israels*. FAT II 20. Tübingen: Mohr Siebeck.

Winand, Jean. 2017. "(Re)productive Traditions in Ancient Egypt: Some Considerations with a Particular Focus on Literature and Language(s)." Pages 19–40 in *(Re)productive Traditions in Ancient Egypt: Proceedings of the Conference Held at the University of Liège, 6th–8th February 2013*. Edited by Todd Gillen. Liège: Presses universitaires de Liège.

Wyns, Valérie. 2017. "The State Ideology of the Ptolemies: Origins and Influences." *CdE* 92:137–174.

CHAPTER 8

....

MESOPOTAMIAN WISDOM LITERATURE

....

YORAM COHEN AND NATHAN WASSERMAN

8.1 ORIGINS AND DISTRIBUTION

....

MESOPOTAMIAN Wisdom Literature is one of the oldest literary genres of cuneiform literature and can easily boast of being the earliest written Wisdom Literature in the world.[1] The Wisdom composition The Instructions of Šuruppak (written in Sumerian) is found in manuscripts dating to as early as ca. 2500 BCE. Mesopotamian Wisdom Literature is also one of the most long-lived genres of cuneiform literature: Wisdom Literature compositions were continuously copied and studied to the very end of cunei-

[1] A general bibliographical comment: Lambert's 1960 *Babylonian Wisdom Literature* (hereafter, BWL) is still essential, although nowadays obviously dated. The major compositions found in Lambert's book have benefited from up-to-date editions (cited below under respective works). Translations of important Wisdom compositions can be found in Foster 2005 and Hallo and Younger 1997 (hereafter, COS 1). Sumerian Wisdom was collected and given new editions by Alster (1997 and 2005). Denning-Bolle 1992 is a good, although not comprehensive, literary study of Mesopotamian Wisdom. Collective studies dedicated to the genre of ancient Near Eastern Wisdom and its socio-historical setting, e.g., Clifford 2007, Perdue 2008, and Oshima 2018b, reflect the renewed interest in ancient Wisdom Literature during the past decade or so. The *Electronic Text Corpus of Sumerian Literature* (hereafter, ETCSL: http://etcsl.orinst.ox.ac.uk/) offers many editions with translations of the Sumerian materials; note its treatment of the disputation poems. The *Sources of Early Akkadian Literature* (SEAL: http://www.seal.uni-leipzig.de/) presents a comprehensive collection of Akkadian literature (editions and translations), including many new (and, alas, mostly fragmentary) Wisdom works; see also Streck and Wasserman 2014; Streck and Wasserman 2016. Wisdom Literature recovered outside of Babylonia (in Ugarit, Hattuša, and Emar) was edited by Cohen 2013; see also Viano 2016. A thorough treatment of the disputation poems, along with the editions of several newly discovered works is found in Jiménez 2017. For the Mesopotamian Wisdom heritage in Greek and Roman sources, specifically proverbs and fables, consider Adrados (1999/2003).

form civilization, at the closing centuries of the first millennium BCE. And far from remaining frozen, the corpus of Wisdom Literature was continuously augmented by new works composed across time. More than thirty distinct Sumerian and Akkadian compositions (some in bilingual formats) can be defined as Wisdom compositions: some are short, of no more than a few stanzas, others run over hundreds of verses.

The distribution of Wisdom Literature was not limited to the scribal centers of Babylonia and Assyria. Wisdom Literature was transmitted across the ancient Near East, reaching its widest distribution during the second half of the second millennium: Wisdom Literature was at home in Syria, at Ugarit and Emar, in Anatolia at Hattuša, and even in Elam. The reception of Mesopotamian Wisdom Literature in the western parts of the cuneiform world saw its translation into Hittite and Hurrian (Cohen 2013).

8.2 Approaching Mesopotamian Wisdom Literature: Genre, Role, and Key Themes

As such a prolific literary form, there is no denying the importance of Wisdom Literature, yet to find an all-inclusive genre definition is challenging. It must be acknowledged that the ancient Mesopotamians did not give a collective title to Wisdom compositions, hence Wisdom Literature lacks an emic definition, unlike some works, such as incantations, which were recognized as distinct genres. The Mesopotamian concept of wisdom (in Akkadian *nēmequ* or *uznu*, lit. "ear," and in Sumerian GEŠTUG, lit., "ear"), which can also denote manual skill or craftsmanship (Sweet 1990), is not used to classify the works we are interested in, although it appears in some. Wisdom is used either as an epithet of a god (such as Marduk in Ludlul Bēl Nēmeqi), or it can be bestowed by the god on his chosen sage (such as in Hear the Advice, where Wise Ea bestows wisdom to Šūpû-amēlu).

By itself, the lack of an internal definition does not preclude an etic definition that is set by our own criteria or tastes. To illustrate, today we differentiate between myths and hymns, but in Mesopotamia both were given the title *zamārum*, "Song." Yet, even if we employ our own criteria, it remains difficult to decide what can be called Wisdom Literature. The variety of compositions—proverbs, fables, instructions, admonitions, disputation poems, and long reflective deliberations—do not exhibit a typical set of stylistic devices or a consistent literary structure that can single them out as a distinct literary genre (Cohen 2013, 7–19, with previous literature; Wasserman 2016). Despite these difficulties, there are ways to help us approach Wisdom Literature and appreciate its qualities.

One way to approach Mesopotamian Wisdom compositions is to study the role that this type of literature played within its socio-historical context. We can begin with the classroom. Scholars have argued that Sumerian proverbs were collected into a large corpus, now called The Sumerian Proverb Collection, in order to provide schooling material for training junior scribes in scribal schools (Veldhuis 2000; Taylor 2005). Longer Wisdom compositions, such as The Instructions of Šuruppak or the didactic poem The Farmer's Instructions, are also regarded as constituting part of student training in the Sumerian language. In later periods, when Akkadian became more prominent as a written language, the school curriculum changed accordingly, and Akkadian Wisdom compositions, such as Counsels of Wisdom and Ludlul Bēl Nēmeqi were added to the students' workload. It can be argued that schooling activities themselves contributed to the appreciation of Wisdom Literature as a distinct form of literature. Indeed, finding different Wisdom compositions repeatedly written on the same tablet by novice scribes (Kleinerman 2011) can lead us to deduce that they were learnt together and considered, by the very fact of their collection, as related, hence as forming a distinct literary genre, even if not explicitly stated.

Wisdom Literature was not limited to the school environment; its social setting was wider. It certainly was appreciated among Mesopotamian literary circles for both its antiquity and sapiential content. Wisdom compositions were attributed to sages of old, such as the royal advisor, Sidu. Many Wisdom works, some of which will be discussed below, such as select chapters of The Sumerian Proverb Collection, The Ballad of Early Rulers, and The Farmer's Instructions, were considered to be written by Sidu (Cohen 2018). Other scholars are also attributed as authors of various Wisdom compositions (Lambert 1962). The professional class at the service of king and court, such as expert diviners or exorcists, by inventing complex family trees, associated themselves with such illustrious and ancient authors of Wisdom Literature. A list of ancient kings and their sages from Uruk further enhanced the standing of these professionals (Lenzi 2008). They deemed themselves as endowed with wisdom, sometimes defined as secret or ancient, and alluded to themselves as "wise" or "expert" (Sweet 1990, 60–61). In this instance, the concept of wisdom was not the practical advice found in proverbs and instructions common to the genre of Mesopotamian Wisdom Literature. Rather it was specialized knowledge, of divine origin, handed down through the ages, relating to divination and exorcism.

It is very likely that members of this professional class were also responsible for composing some of the more elaborate Wisdom compositions, such as Ludlul Bēl Nēmeqi and The Babylonian Theodicy (Beaulieu 2007). The association of the source of wisdom with the divine (see, e.g., The Scholars of Uruk; George 2009, 78–112), further bolstered the appreciation of Wisdom Literature among the literate class of Mesopotamia (Klein and Samet 2015). Indeed, the Wisdom composition Hear the Advice goes as far as to pronounce that the god Ea himself granted wisdom to the father who will deliver advice to his son (see also The Farmer's Instructions below, 8.3 Proverbs and Instructions). And lastly, the mythological and ritual traditions in Mesopotamia gave place to the Seven Sages (called *apkallu*s), among whom Adapa is the most famous. They were semi-divine figures associated closely with Ea, the god of wisdom and Sage of the Gods, appearing in ritual texts and deemed to hold special powers and possess primeval knowledge (Fechner 2016). Although these figures do not feature in Mesopotamian Wisdom Literature, their role in religious practices broadens for us the significance of the concept of wisdom in Mesopotamian thought.

To conclude, Wisdom Literature was considered as an ancient source of veritable wisdom. Its status as an elite form of literature is surely what earned its quotation in exegetical texts (Frahm 2011) and what lead to its select citation in official letters (e.g., Hurowitz 2002–2005).

Another way to define Mesopotamian Wisdom Literature is to try to identify its overarching key theme: an overall concern of Wisdom Literature is human destiny. By human destiny we mean the way to attain a good or moral life and the possibility of attaining it. Wisdom Literature lays out traditional percepts and conservative attitudes for the individual in respect to the divine order and social hierarchy, which, if followed, promise a prosperous life, family harmony, and social standing. Although it is not said so explicitly, maintaining the divine order and social hierarchy is the mark of the wise person. Hence, the sum of all instructions and percepts given in Wisdom Literature, if taken together, allows us to understand how the concept of wisdom was perceived in Mesopotamia. Because wisdom was never offered an independent evaluation or articulation, as one finds in the book of Proverbs, or valued as a divine being, such as the Egyptian Maat, it is through the prism of literary works that we can judge its worth in Mesopotamian society.

Incidentally, this appreciates the instructive value of Wisdom Literature in the ancient classroom. It can be understood as a social discourse, which presumes common values and relays cultural coordinates to its receivers—students of the scribal school, who later become administrators and judges, businessmen and merchants, and even generals and the royalty. Consequently, Wisdom Literature can be viewed as a central tool for preserving and propagating the hegemonic ideology of ancient Mesopotamian civilization.

Concurrently, Mesopotamian Wisdom Literature also conveys a completely contrasting attitude towards human destiny. It expresses an existential principle of the finality of life and a nihilistic notion according to which nothing is of eternal value. It argues that because death is unavoidable, it is best to enjoy life while it lasts. Thus, Wisdom Literature offers a critique of the prevalent power structure of traditional society and questions (although obliquely) what we call the retribution principle by asking, if one behaves morally toward fellow humans and piously prays to one's god, as traditional wisdom recommends, then why is one not met with justice? This attitude appears in several works, such as The Ballad of Early Rulers and Hear the Advice. It also forms the base upon which Wisdom works of an existential nature, such as the Babylonian Theodicy, were built.

The articulation of this notion was not limited to Wisdom Literature. Its echo resounds in the Epic of Gilgamesh, when the barmaid Siduri urges Gilgamesh to enjoy life while he can and Utnapišti, the survivor of the flood, tells the hero to give up the quest for immortality and recognize the finality of life (George 2003, 278–279; 696–699). Where stands the difference between Wisdom Literature and wisdom-like themes in epic or myth? This is a complicated question which brings us again to the question of the definition of genre. We can say that in Mesopotamian Wisdom Literature the concern over human destiny, as we have seen, is conveyed—if at all—by a loose plot or weak narrative frame whose chief characters are almost cardboard cutouts (such as "the sage," "father," or "son"). Thus, human destiny remains general and not specifically related to either a narrative or a hero. The result is what some would call moralistic or didactic literature.

Our discussion will now proceed with a closer examination of Mesopotamian Wisdom, as we take care to highlight the key themes of Wisdom Literature and where the occasion calls for, its socio-historical setting. The body of works chosen here is arranged according to loose genre subcategories as follows: proverbs and instructions, Vanity Theme works, Existential works, disputations poems, and, lastly, satire and parody.

8.3 PROVERBS AND INSTRUCTIONS

The Sumerian Proverb Collection (Alster 1997; Alster 2007; ETCSL 6, according to which the proverbs below are cited) is a modern name given to an extensive set of proverbs, known from the Old Babylonian period (ca. 2000–1595 BCE). The corpus, written in Sumerian, was organized according to more or less consistent chapters (or collections), with some holding many dozens of proverbs. As explained above, it was argued that the setting and motivation of studying and copying these proverbs was primarily curricular—to train students in their study of Sumerian in the scribal school.

The subject matter of the proverbs is varied, but most wish to convey practical or ethical wisdom (Klein and Samet 2015). Some proverbs in The Sumerian Proverb Collection can be grouped thematically. For example, in one collection, some twenty proverbs focus on the destiny of the destitute (2.14–35). In many of the proverbs, animals (either domestic or wild) feature as stand-ins for human types in typical situations. Consider these two examples: "The dog understands 'Take it!', but it does not understand 'Put it down!'" (5.81) or "A fox trod on the hoof of a wild bull, (asking), 'It didn't hurt, did it?'" (5.65).

Like proverbs worldwide, some Sumerian proverbs can read like truisms; for example, "Fire in a reed house cannot be extinguished" (Alster 2007, 90). Yet others offer a sharper, critical view of reality, such as "A poor man chewing at silver" (2.31), which means that a poor man can never make any savings, because all he earns goes to feed him. Other proverbs convey deeper existential insights. Consider, for example, "He who keeps fleeing, flees from his own past" (3.141).

Some proverbs, however, do not look much like proverbs in the traditional sense of the word. They may convey didactic counsels, such as, "Putting unwashed hands in one's mouth is disgusting" (3.161), or describe experiences typical of novice scribes at the school: "You are a scribe and you don't know your own name! Shame on you!" (2.37), or "What kind of a scribe is a scribe who does not know Sumerian?" (2.47).

In a number of cases, select proverbs from The Sumerian Proverb Collection appear in other types of works (epic, hymns, and more), which is an indication of their use and distribution (COS 1.175). After the Old Babylonian period, proverbs were still collected, and, when written in Sumerian, an Akkadian translation was often provided (e.g., BWL

225–262; Frahm 2010). Such proverb collections circulated outside of Mesopotamia, where they were translated into Hittite (at Hattuša—the capital of the Hittite Empire) and into Hurrian (at Ugarit on the Syrian coast) (Cohen 2013, 199–212).

Another type of Wisdom Literature related to proverbs is the didactic poem that delivers instructions. The instructions are framed by a narrative of the wise man (king, elder, or father) delivering instructions to his junior. The instructions are articulated as either single sentences, in other words, proverbs, or as short pericopes.

A prime example of this type of Wisdom compositions is the earliest and one of the longest-lived Wisdom compositions—The Instructions of Šuruppak (Alster 2005, 31–220; ETCSL 5.6.1; COS 1.176). The composition (written in Sumerian but also attested in Akkadian and Hurrian translations) begins with an exposition (ll. 1–13):

> In those days, in those far remote days, in those nights, in those far-away nights, in those years, in those far remote years, in those days, the intelligent one, the one of elaborate words, the wise one, who lived in the land, Šuruppak... gave instructions to his son, gave instructions to his son Ziusudra (Sumerian version) / Utnapištim (Akkadian version).

After the exposition, come the instructions, which are practical in nature. Here is an example of a few: "Don't buy an ass that brays; it will split your yoke!" (l. 14) or "You should not place your house next to a public square: there is always a crowd(?) there" (l. 18). Sometimes, they may be admonishing: "You should not boast in beer halls like a deceitful man" (l. 67). Some are more metaphorical: "The palace is a mighty river; its inside is goring bulls: what flows in is never enough to fill it and what flows out can never be stopped" (ll. 94–96).

A similar work is The Farmer's Instructions (Civil 1994; ETCSL 5.6.3), also written in Sumerian. In this text, the father, a farmer, delivers advice to his son. The advice is mostly practical—how to seed a field, plough and water it—although it ends with a declaration that the source of the instructions is divine—from the god Ninurta, with the implicit understanding that success in agriculture is related to pious behavior. The work appeared in literary catalogs with other Wisdom works and was included in The Series of Sidu (see above), hence for the ancients it belonged to the type of works discussed here.

The Counsels of Ur-Ninurta (Alster 2005, 221–240; COS 1.177), a similar composition, contains divergent types of advice and instruction, some pertaining to the ethical–religious domain. The work, based on a reconstruction of several manuscripts, delivers instructions that seem to be aimed at the faithful population of King Ur-Ninurta, whose rule is celebrated at the beginning of the piece.

The Akkadian Counsels of Wisdom (BWL 96–107), like The Instructions of Šuruppak, also contains advice from father to son. The work was intended perhaps to be a manual of sorts for the education of future administrators (Lenzi 2018), although some of the sayings also appear in other Wisdom works, hence they were not specifically composed for this text.

Another Akkadian composition is the Advice to a Prince (sometimes called Fürstenspiegel; BWL 110–115; Cole 1996, no. 128; Foster 2007, 35). The piece, which may have had a political purpose, was composed under the possible influence of Wisdom instructions: an anonymous ruler is given a set of instructions meant to protect the rights of ancient cult centers under his power.

The most elaborate work in the instruction genre is the Akkadian piece Hear the Advice (sometimes called The Instructions of Šūpê-amēli; Cohen 2013, 81–128). It is known almost entirely from manuscripts arriving from the western parts of the cunei-form world—Emar, Ugarit, and Hattuša (where it exists in a bilingual version, Akkadian and Hittite). It too begins with the father (named Šūpû-amēlu, "most-illustrious man"), who, after receiving wisdom from the god of wisdom and magic, Ea, delivers practical advice to his son. But when the father finishes, his son replies, negating the instructions by introducing wisdom of a different kind, which makes use of the Vanity Theme (see below 8.4 Vanity Theme Works).

To conclude, instructions are Wisdom compositions that are dialogical and illocu-tionary, aware of their own speech. They assume a discursive bond between the speaker, who is conscious of the importance of his own words, and his listener, who may either accept (implicitly) the value of the speaker's words, as in The Instructions of Šuruppak, or reject them, as in Hear the Advice, as will be seen below. We will find this dialogue-type employed again in Wisdom Literature—in complex works such as The Babylonian Theodicy (see below 8.5 "Existential Works") and The Dialogue of Pessimism (see below 8.7 Satire and Parody).

8.4 VANITY THEME WORKS

At the core of a number of Mesopotamian Wisdom works stands the Vanity Theme. It provides a counter-argument to the traditional wisdom encountered in the proverbs and instructions by advocating the rejection of all material gains and enjoying life while it lasts, because only the gods have eternal life. Thus, it incorporates two well-known lit-erary motifs—*memento mori* and *carpe diem*. The simplest articulation of this theme is found in a number of short Sumerian compositions, collectively called as NÍG-NAM NU-KAL ("Nothing is of Value"; Alster 2005, 266–287), which repeat the refrain "nothing is of worth, but life itself is sweet." They celebrate life through a number of verses, and remind the readers of their own mortality.

Another work to feature the Vanity Theme is Enlil and Namzitarra (Alster 2005, 327–338; Cohen 2013, 151–164; cf. Cooper 2017; ETCSL 5.7.1; known in bilingual manuscripts). In this short Wisdom tale, the protagonist, a priest called Namzitarra, rejects a material reward from the god Enlil given for his good deeds, saying to the god:

> To where will I take your silver, your lapis lazuli gems, your sheep? The days of man-kind are approaching (i.e., his death), day after day—so it (life) will diminish, month after month—so it will diminish, year after year—so it will diminish, […]—so it will diminish, 120 years—so will be the limit of mankind's life … from that day till now as long as mankind lived!

The Vanity Theme also appears in Hear the Advice (discussed above) as the reply of the son to the father's useful instructions. The son says:

> My father, you built a house, you elevated high the door; sixty cubits is the width of your (house). But what have you achieved? Just as much as [your] house's loft is full so too its storage room is full of grain. (But) upon the day of your death (only) nine bread portions of offerings will be counted and placed at your head.... Few are the days in which we eat (our) bread, but many will be the days in which our teeth will be idle,
> Few are the days in which we look at the Sun, but many will be the days in which we will sit in the shadows. The Netherworld is teeming, but its inhabitants lie sleeping. Ereškigal (the goddess of the Netherworld) is our mother and we her children.

In Hear the Advice, as in Enlil and Namzitarra, the futility of material things and wealth is stressed, because they cannot be enjoyed in the Netherworld.

Perhaps the work that most poignantly expresses the Vanity Theme is the Ballad of Early Rulers (Cohen 2013, 129–150; ETCSL 5.2.5; known in bilingual manuscripts). It opens by stating that the fates of man are determined by the god Ea. It then supplies a list of illustrious heroes of the past, some known from Mesopotamian epic or historiography, in order to illustrate that in spite of their deeds, they are all dead and gone. Hence the conclusion is to enjoy life:

> The fates are determined by Ea,
> The lots are drawn according to the will of the god... Where is Alulu who reigned for 36,000 years?
> Where is Etana who went up to heaven?
> Where is Gilgamesh who sought (eternal) life like (that of) [Zius]udra?... Where is Enkidu who [proclaimed] (his) strength throughout the land?
> Where is Bazi? Where is Zizi?
> Where are the great kings of which (the like) from then to now
>   are not (anymore) engendered, are not born?
> Life without light—how can it be better than death?
> Young man let me truly instruct you about your god (i.e., his eternal nature).
> Repel, drive away sorrow, scorn silence!
> In exchange for this single day of happiness, let pass a time of silence lasting
>   36,000 years.
> May [Siraš] (the beer-goddess) rejoice over you as if over (her) son!
> This is the fate of humanity.

This nihilistic theme, as we will next see, appears as a literary device to propel the message of a number of works which can be defined under the broad title of existential, in that they deal with questions of reward and punishment, the purpose of life, and human mortality.

8.5 Existential Works

Several Wisdom works are concerned with the relationship between man and god, tackling a basic tenet of religion—divine reward and punishment, or the problem of theodicy (van der Toorn 2003; Uehlinger 2007; Cohen 2015; Oshima 2018a). The articulation of this question is put forward by an individual speaking in the first person, the "just sufferer," who tries to understand his lot in life. A somewhat related expression of this concern appears in the so-called Letter Prayers (e.g., COS 1.164–165), which, however, can be defined as individual prayers, or personal laments, rather than Wisdom Literature, because of their straightforward request for salvation.

In the Sumerian Man and His God (Klein 2006; ETCSL 5.2.4; COS 1.179), after the sufferer is rejected from his social circle and suffers physical ailments, he offers a lament to his god. He prays for forgiveness, admitting that "they say—the wise men—a word true and right, 'Never has a sinless child been born to its mother, a mortal has never been perfect, a sinless man has never existed from old!' " The confession of sin, although its nature remains unclear (perhaps the transgression of religious taboos), leads to salvation.

A similar work, written in Akkadian, called The Dialogue between a Man and His God, (Lambert 1987; COS 1.151) is structured around a similar frame: suffering, a confession of sin, lament and prayer, and eventual salvation. Although both works utilize themes from the world of prayers, supplications, and incantations, their existential questioning of the problem of the "just sufferer" allows us to consider them as Wisdom Literature.

The most sophisticated of the "Just Sufferer" poems is Ludlul Bēl Nēmeqi ("Let me Praise the Lord of Wisdom"; BWL 21–62; COS 1.153; Annus and Lenzi 2010; Oshima 2014).[2] This five-hundred-line poem is justly one of the more celebrated pieces of Babylonian literature. The large number of manuscripts (over fifty, but not all are complete, and some are scribal exercises) offer a testimony to the popularity of the work among the literati of Assyria and Babylonia. The poem also gained a learned commentary to explain many of its difficult words. Unlike the anonymous voice of the "Just Sufferer" poems, the name of the individual who narrates the poem is given. He is called Šubši-mešre-Šakkan. Whether or not Šubši-mešre-Šakkan was the actual author of the work remains an open question, although there is some evidence that he was a historical figure who lived ca. 1300 BCE.

The poem expresses its message through a narrative. It begins with Marduk forsaking Šubši-mešre-Šakkan. He is rejected by family and friends, has lost favor with the king, and night and day suffers both physical and physiological ailments (I 77–80; II 86–89):

> I, who once strolled like a lord, have now learned to crawl,
> Being proud, I turned into a slave,
> I ended up a loner although of many a kin,

---

[2] The interest in Ludlul Bēl Nēmeqi is never waning, but given our limited space here, we can mention only the latest studies: Pongratz-Leisten 2010; Lenzi 2012; Noegel 2016; and Greenstein 2017.

As I walk through streets, fingers are pointed at me...
My gate was locked and my watering place was barred,
My hunger enduring, my throat constricted,
Food—as if it were stinkweed—I swallow down,
Beer—sustenance of mankind—sickens me.

In his miserable state, Šubši-mešre-Šakkan experiences dreams which foretell of his salvation. Finally, he is saved by Marduk, with his apparent realization that he had sinned against the god. Marduk restores the protagonist to his social standing and rids him of his illness (III 96–99):

The throat which was constricted and choking as if on a block,
He (Marduk) healed and had it sing its songs as a flute.
The throat, which choked not being able to receive in [food],
Its swelling went down and he opened its blockage.

The narrator is further revived as he enters the temple of Marduk in Babylon. His recovery is then celebrated by the people of Babylon as if witnessing a miracle. The poem closes with a call to worship Marduk.

The poem at first glance may be considered a hymn to Marduk. However, it deeply questions the problem of theodicy, or divine retribution. Its theological conclusion is that one is forced to realize that, as in Job, one cannot fully understand divine judgment (II 33–38):

I indeed believed that these things (proper rites and behavior) would satisfy a deity.
(However), what is good for oneself is a crime for the god,
And what is bad in one's mind is good for his god.
Which person could know the plan of the gods in heaven?
Who would comprehend the counsel of the gods of the deep sea?
How could mankind know the way of the god?

The theme of suffering is explored much more bitingly in The Babylonian Theodicy (sometimes called The Babylonian Job; BWL 63–91; COS 1.154; Oshima 2013; Oshima 2014), a dialogue-form composition taking place between the sufferer (called Saggil-kīnam-ubbib) and his friend. Through alternate speeches, the two contend on the problem of theodicy. The sufferer questions divine retribution, rejecting pious and even moral behavior, because nothing promises material gains or social standing. He sees how the wicked prosper while the just and pious suffer. He chooses to adopt the life of the rogue, as he stands no chance to survive in this unjust world (ll. 52–55, 70–71, and 133–135):

Now the rich man, whose wealth is multiplied—
Did he pay out rich gold to the goddess Mami?
Have I held back offerings? I pray to (my) god,

I have dedicated regular offerings of (my) goddess *according to her command*...
Treading on the road to success are those who have neglected the god,
Poor and weak are those who pray to the goddess...
I will abandon (my) home [...],
I will desire no property [...],
I will disregard cultic duties, trample on religious rites...
House to house I will enter in order to banish my hunger.

The friend, on the other hand, promises the sufferer that the evil eventually will be punished, urging him to put his trust in the gods, although their ways are incomprehensible to mankind. The poem ends with the sufferer acknowledging that his situation is the result of his former sinful behavior (Oshima 2014), which brought about his abandonment by his personal god and subsequently his misfortune. After this realization, he pleads that the king lead the people back to true faith in the gods.

8.6 DISPUTATION POEMS

Disputation poems (Vanstiphout 1990; Vanstiphout 1992; Jiménez 2017) are poetic compositions with a tripartite structure. The first part is the introduction. It sets the scene in mythical times, when the world was created, introducing two opposing protagonists. The second part, which forms the main body of the work, is a back-and-forth engagement between the two protagonists. The third part is the declaration of the winner of the disputation, either by the gods or by the king.

The protagonists of the disputations are non-human: animals (Bird and Fish; ETCSL 5.3.5; Ox and Horse; BWL 175–185), trees (Date Palm and Tamarisk; Cohen 2013, 177–198; Date Palm and Vine; Jiménez 2017, 231–287), metals (Copper and Silver; ETCSL 5.3.6), work tools (Hoe and Plough; ETCSL 5.3.1), and even the seasons (Winter and Summer; ETCSL 5.3.3). The scene in the disputations is static (cf. however, the Bird and Fish): with no change in the narrative line, the two protagonists exchange their self-proclaimed arguments of supremacy. This lack of development in the plot is the main distinction between disputations and fables. Disputations, therefore, were rhetorical compositions, celebrating eloquence. Disputation poems were focused on the question of who among the two contestants is more beneficial to humankind and the gods. As such, these works were neither practical nor moralizing.

The genre was much appreciated in ancient Mesopotamia: at least six Sumerian and eight Akkadian disputations are known to date and they are attested by dozens of manuscripts spanning from the Old Babylonian period to the end of cuneiform literature. Here is a typical exchange between two protagonists, in this example, the Date Palm and the Tamarisk (Cohen 2013, 182–183):

(The Date Palm spoke:) "You—Tamarisk—are a tree of no use. Why are your branches, O Tamarisk, fruitless? (On the other hand), our fruits are fit for the royal table! The king eats and the crowd says 'They are my gift.' Thanks to me the orchard cultivator gains a profit and he provides it to the queen. The mother raises her baby—it eats the gift of my resources and grows up..."

(The Tamarisk responds:) "My flesh is the flesh of the gods (i.e., the wood out of which the divine statue is made). Your excellent assets—like a maid who brings and presents her finished product to her mistress—what is worthy and good you will bring to me (as offerings to the divine statue)...What is mine in the king's palace? The king eats upon my table, out of my cup the queen drinks, with my spoon the warriors eat, in my trough the baker kneads the dough..."

8.7 SATIRE AND PARODY

A number of works resist easy classification and some would not deign to call them Wisdom Literature. However, we can consider them as belonging to our discussion because they question the accepted social order of gods and men, attacking the very themes we have met, though with a humorous voice, resulting in sarcasm or irony (Foster 1974; Foster 2007, 36–40).

The most notable work of this category is the Dialogue of Pessimism (BWL 139–149; COS 1.155; sometimes named in modern literature as *Arad Mitanguranni*, "Slave—Listen to Me!"). It is structured as an exchange between a master and his slave. Whenever the master wishes to embark upon a task (hunting, marrying, conducting business, starting a revolt), the slave supports his intentions with words of positive or instructive wisdom, such as found in proverbs and instructions. But when the master reneges on his words, the slave, in order to buttress his master's desires, brings about negative or pessimistic wisdom, reminiscent of the Vanity Theme found in the son's speech in Hear the Advice. It is as if, similar to The Babylonian Theodicy, the reader is presented with the two faces of Mesopotamian Wisdom, both expressed by the slave. Indeed, some of the replies of the slave have been identified as quotes from Mesopotamian literature, Wisdom Literature included (cf. ll. 79–86 below with Ludlul Bēl Nēmeqi III 33–38 quoted above; see, e.g., Hurowitz 2007; Samet 2010; Wasserman 2011, 8–9; Metcalf 2013). Consider the following dialogue between the master and his slave (ll. 62–69):

(MASTER:)   "Slave, listen to me!"
(SLAVE:)   "Yes—My Master—yes."
(MASTER:)   "I will give out loans as a creditor!"
(SLAVE:)   "Give out loans, My Master, [give out!] The man who gives out loans—his grain remains his grain, while his interest multiplies!"
(MASTER:)   "No—Slave—I will not give out loans as a creditor!"

(SLAVE:)   "Don't give out loans, My Master, don't give out! Giving out loans is like the love [of a woman!] Being repaid is like having children: your grain will be eaten away, you will be cursed and the interest on your grain will disappear!"

The concluding exchange sees the master asking his slave what he deems worthwhile (ll. 79–86):

(MASTER:)   "Slave, listen to me!"
(SLAVE:)   "Yes—My Master—yes."
(MASTER:)   "Now what is of worth (in this life)?"
(SLAVE:)   "To have my neck and your neck broken, and to be thrown into the river is of worth! Who is so tall to reach the sky? Who is so wide to cover the earth?"
(MASTER:)   "No—Slave—I will kill you and send you off first!"
(SLAVE:)   "But then once I am gone would My Master survive more than three days!?"

The work can be considered satire, not because of its subject matter, which is serious—an existential debate, in a sense, like Ludlul Bēl Nēmeqi or The Babylonian Theodicy—but because of the reversal of roles. It is not the figure of power who holds the keys to knowledge, but rather the servile one (Metcalf 2013), the slave, in whom we can see the precursor to the Aesopic figure. Thus, the dialogue satirizes the traditional view on the source of wisdom of old, considered as generated by the gods and passed on through the fathers (Greenstein 2007).

A somewhat similar approach to the source and use of wisdom is found in The Poor Man of Nippur (Gurney 1972; Foster 2005, 931–936; Ottervanger 2016). This is a folktale with a universal appeal: it tells of a destitute fellow, a master-trickster, who takes his revenge on a figure of authority—the pompous major of the city of Nippur.

Animal fables are a well-known literary technique for creating satire. The Fable of the Fox (BWL 186–209; Kienast 2003; Jiménez 2017, 39–57, 377–395) is a composition whose plot is very poorly understood because of its state of preservation, despite its many manuscripts. We meet four animal figures—lion, wolf, fox, and dog—metaphorically standing as representatives of the social order, which engage one against the other (Liverani 2011). The exaggerated voice of the dialogues, as far as they can be understood, leads us to view this work as a sort of mock-epic that ridicules human characteristics.

In some of the disputation poems that we have treated above, a parodic voice can be detected: a few poems consciously mimic the style and literary patterns found in epic and Wisdom Literature. One such example is The Series of the Spider (Jiménez 2017, 291–323): two insignificant animals (insects or rodents?) argue in front of the spider over who is more worthy among them. The absurd situation is heightened by use of poetic language found in epic literature, reinforced by quotes from The Babylonian Theodicy. A recently discovered fable, The Story of the Poor Forlorn Wren (Jiménez 2017), recounts the victory of a tiny bird, the wren, over the eagle—a story with a didactic purpose told through an amplified fictional situation.

At the Cleaner's (Wasserman 2013; COS 1.156) is a dialogue between a fuller and his boastful client. The client gives complex washing instructions to the fuller, but he rejects them. The structure of the composition, which is full of technical jargon taken from the world of laundry, resembles instructions, such as The Farmer's Instructions, or the disputation poems, only in a reversal of roles: the layman gives instructions to the expert. Furthermore, the subject matter—instructions for washing clothes—reveals the parodic intention of the dialogue, accentuated even more when the fuller evokes the god Ea, calling him "Lord of wisdom."

8.8 CONCLUSION: ASSESSMENT AND AFTERMATH

Proverbs, instructions, Vanity Theme compositions and existential works, disputation poems, and satires or parodies are all different literary forms, although not entirely unrelated, which were grouped here under a wide genre, Wisdom Literature. Each form could have benefited from a separate treatment as a distinct genre, and yet we chose to accentuate the key themes which weave these works into one multicolored literary fabric of Mesopotamian Wisdom Literature.

As we have shown, there is no clear boundary between the various subcategories of the genre: individual proverbs are found in the didactic instructions; the Vanity Theme negates the conventional wisdom of instructions and proverbs; existential works question divine retribution in order to reflect upon the meaning of life; and satire and parody use the various subcategories of Wisdom Literature to offer the reader a critical perspective on what has probably become clichéd wisdom over the ages.

This chapter has allowed us to appreciate the development of Mesopotamian Wisdom and its remarkable literary complexity. A genre which began from collecting proverbs or stringing instructions within a father-to-son narrative frame developed to include a variety of literary forms. Perhaps it utilized to the fullest the literary and rhetorical potentials of the dialogue-form (van der Toorn 1991). The dialogue enabled the concurrent presentation of the two major themes of Wisdom Literature: setting practical advice against questioning the very purpose of life.

Mesopotamian Wisdom was certainly a major part of cuneiform literature, and it also had an impact, so it can be argued, on other ancient non-Mesopotamian literatures. Wisdom Literature is one of the few Mesopotamian genres that show undeniable thematic relations, and close, sometimes even exact verbatim, parallels with Egyptian, Ugaritic, and Aramaic (in the Wisdom of Ahiqar) literatures and, notably, with the Bible. This is evident in particular throughout Proverbs, Job, and Ecclesiastes. The relationship between the biblical Wisdom books and Mesopotamian Wisdom (as well as Egyptian Wisdom Literature), discussed over a century, is still a matter of contention among scholars (e.g., Samet 2015a; Greenstein 2017). The ways by which this type of literature reached biblical literature is far from clear and all kinds of direct and indirect modes of transmission and reception have been suggested, depending on one's view regarding the time and place of the composition of the relevant books or verses. Regardless of the different suggestions and with all known difficulties, Wisdom works which are now better known, especially those which include the Vanity Theme, are to be considered serious contenders for being the primary forces to have left their mark on biblical Wisdom Literature (Lambert 1995). Perhaps the clearest example is Ecclesiastes, whose indebtedness to Mesopotamian Wisdom themes rather than to Greek philosophy, as has been repeatedly assumed in the literature, can be demonstrated rather clearly (Samet 2015a; Samet 2015b).

The transmission of ancient Near Eastern literature, including Wisdom tradition, to early Greek literature was argued most famously by West (1997). The relation between the disputation poems (such as the Date Palm and the Tamarisk/Vine) and fables (such as the Poor Man of Nippur and the Fable of the Fox) and the Aesopic tradition (and later European fables), Arabic, and Persian works has been discussed in the past (e.g., Jason 1979; Vanstiphout 1988; Reinink and Vanstiphout 1991). However, much remains to be done to reach the full potential scope of this line of investigation (see for now Adrados 1999/2003). This involves as a first stage the reconstruction and recovery of the Mesopotamian sources, many of which are still lying in museums and collections worldwide waiting their identification (e.g., Jiménez 2017). More advanced stages must involve a concentrated effort undertaken by scholars from many fields in order to unravel as much as possible the complicated threads of the transmission of Wisdom Literature.

In this respect, although it can be argued that Wisdom Literature was susceptible to transmission east and west, because of its very nature of voicing inclusive human issues, some scholars, for this very reason, have viewed with concern the search for the exact routes of transmission of Wisdom compositions, especially in regard to proverbs and fables (e.g., Haubold 2013, 26–29). A more nuanced approach to the issue of transmission therefore seeks to highlight the shared themes of Wisdom compositions of the ancient Near East (the biblical Wisdom books included) and the Eastern Mediterranean (Cohen 2017; Ayali-Darshan 2018), rather than pinpoint their origin. And a less constraining approach to Wisdom Literature as a specific and tightly defined genre has also led to a better appreciation of key Wisdom themes within a wider scope of literature, such as epic, for example, in the Epic of Gilgamesh (George 2007; Wasserman 2011) and in the Iliad (Haubold 2013).

WORKS CITED

Adrados, Francisco Rodríguez. 1999/2003. *History of the Graeco-Latin Fable.* Mnemosyne, bibliotheca classica Batava, Supplementum 201, 207 and 236. Leiden: Brill.

Alster, Bendt. 1997. *Proverbs of Ancient Sumer.* Bethesda, MD: CDL.

Alster, Bendt. 2005. *Wisdom of Ancient Sumer.* Bethesda, MD: CDL.

Alster, Bendt. 2007. *Sumerian Proverbs in the Schøyen Collection*. CUSAS 2. Bethesda, MD: CDL.

Annus, Amar, and Alan Lenzi. 2010. *Ludlul bēl nēmeqi: The Standard Babylonian Poem of the Righteous Sufferer*. SAACT 7. Winona Lake, IN: Eisenbrauns.

Ayali-Darshan, Noga. 2018. "'Do Not Open Your Heart to Your Wife or Servant' (Onch. 13:17): A West-Asiatic Antecedent and Its Relation to Later Wisdom Instructions." Pages 95–103 in Oshima 2018b.

Beaulieu, Paul-Alain. 2007. "The Social and Intellectual Setting of Babylonian Wisdom Literature." Pages 3–19 in Clifford 2007.

Civil, Miguel. 1994. *The Farmer's Instructions: A Sumerian Agricultural Manual*. AuOrSup 5. Barcelona: Editorial Ausa.

Clifford, Richard J., ed. 2007. *Wisdom Literature in Mesopotamia and Israel*. SymS 36. Atlanta, GA: SBL.

Cohen, Yoram. 2013. *Wisdom from the Late Bronze Age*. WAW 29. Atlanta, GA: SBL.

Cohen, Yoram. 2015. "The Problem of Theodicy—The Mesopotamian Perspective." Pages 243–270 in *Colères et repentirs divins: Actes du colloque organisé par le Collège de France, Paris, les 24 et 25 avril 2013*. Edited by Jean M. Durand, Lionel Marti, and Thomas Römer. OBO 278. Fribourg: Academic Press; Göttingen: Vandenhoeck & Ruprecht.

Cohen, Yoram. 2017. "Les Neiges d'Antan: 'Early Rulers' and the Vanity Theme in Mesopotamian Wisdom Literature and Beyond." *AntOr* 15:13–35.

Cohen, Yoram. 2018. "Why 'Wisdom'? Copying, Studying, and Collecting Wisdom Literature in the Cuneiform World." Pages 41–59 in Oshima 2018b.

Cole, Steven. 1996. *Nippur IV: The Early Neo-Babylonian Governor's Archive from Nippur*. OIP 114. Chicago, IL: The Oriental Institute.

Cooper, Jerrold. 2017. "'Enlil and Namzitarra' Reconsidered." Pages 37–53 in *The First Ninety Years: A Sumerian Celebration in Honor of Miguel Civil*. Edited by Lluís Feliu, Fumi Karahashi, and Gonzalo Rubio. SANER 12. Boston, MA: de Gruyter.

Denning-Bolle, Sara J. 1992. *Wisdom in Akkadian Literature: Expression, Instruction, Dialogue*. Leiden: Ex Oriente Lux.

Fechner, Josephine. 2016. "Weiser (sage)." *RlA* 15:46–51.

Foster, Benjamin R. 1974. "Humor and Cuneiform Literature." *JANESCU* 6:69–85.

Foster, Benjamin R. 2005. *Before the Muses: An Anthology of Akkadian Literature*. 3rd ed. Bethesda, MD: CDL Press.

Foster, Benjamin R. 2007. *Akkadian Literature of the Late Period*. GMTR 2. Münster: Ugarit-Verlag.

Frahm, Eckart. 2010. "The Latest Sumerian Proverbs." Pages 155–184 in *Opening the Tablet Box: Near Eastern Studies in Honor of Benjamin R. Foster*. Edited by Sarah C. Melville and Alice L. Slotsky. CHANE 42. Leiden: Brill.

Frahm, Eckart. 2011. *Babylonian and Assyrian Text Commentaries: Origins of Interpretation*. GMTR 5. Münster: Ugarit-Verlag.

George, Andrew R. 2003. *The Babylonian Gilgamesh Epic: Introduction, Critical Edition, and Cuneiform Texts*. Oxford: Oxford University Press.

George, Andrew R. 2007. "The Epic of Gilgamesh: Thoughts on Genre and Meaning." Pages 37–66 in *Gilgamesh and the World of Assyria: Proceedings of the Conference Held at the Mandelbaum House, the University of Sydney, 21–23 July 2004*. Edited by Joseph Azize and Noel Weeks. ANESSup 21. Leuven: Peeters.

George, Andrew R. 2009. *Babylonian Literary Texts in the Schøyen Collection*. CUSAS 10. Bethesda, MD: CDL.

Greenstein, Edward. 2007. "Sages with a Sense of Humor: The Babylonian Dialogue between a Master and His Servant and the Book of Qohelet." Pages 55–65 in Clifford 2007.

Greenstein, Edward. 2017. "The Book of Job and Mesopotamian Literature: How Many Degrees of Separation?" Pages 143–158 in *Subtle Citation, Allusion, and Translation in the Hebrew Bible*. Edited by Ziony Zevit. Sheffield: Equinox.

Gurney, Oliver. 1972. "The Tale of the Poor Man of Nippur and Its Folktale Parallels." *AnSt* 22:149–158.

Hallo, William W., and K. Lawson Younger, Jr. eds. 1997–2002. *The Context of Scripture*. Leiden: Brill.

Haubold, Johannes. 2013. *Greece and Mesopotamia: Dialogues in Literature*. New York, NY: Cambridge University Press.

Hurowitz, Victor A. 2002–2005. "An Overlooked Allusion to Ludlul in Urad-Gula's Letter to Assurbanipal." *SAAB* 14:129–132.

Hurowitz, Victor A. 2007. "An Allusion to the Šamaš Hymn in The Dialogue of Pessimism." Pages 33–36 in Clifford 2007.

Jason, Heda. 1979. "The Poor Man of Nippur: An Ethnopoetic Analysis." *JCS* 31:189–215.

Jiménez, Enrique. 2017. *The Babylonian Disputation Poems: With Editions of the Series of the Poplar, Palm and Vine, the Series of the Spider, and the Story of the Poor, Forlorn Wren*. CHANE 87. Leiden: Brill.

Kienast, Burkhard. 2003. *Iškar šēlebi: Die Serie vom Fuchs*. FAOS 22. Stuttgart: Franz Steiner.

Klein, Jacob. 2006. "Man and His God: A Wisdom Poem or a Cultic Lament?" Pages 123–144 in *Approaches to Sumerian Literature: Studies in Honour of Stip (H.L.J. Vanstiphout)*. Edited by Piotr Michalowski and Niek Veldhuis. CM 35. Leiden: Brill.

Klein, Jacob, and Nili Samet. 2015. "Religion and Ethics in Sumerian Proverb Literature." Pages 295–321 in *Marbeh Hokmah: Studies in the Bible and the Ancient Near East in Loving Memory of Victor Avigdor Hurowitz*. Edited by Shamir Yona, Edward L. Greenstein, Mayer I. Gruber, Peter Machinist, and Shalom M. Paul. Winona Lake, IN: Eisenbrauns.

Kleinerman, Alexandra. 2011. *Education in Early 2nd Millennium BC Babylonia: The Sumerian Epistolary Miscellany*. CM 42. Leiden: Brill.

Lambert, Wilfred G. 1960. *Babylonian Wisdom Literature*. Oxford: Clarendon Press.

Lambert Wilfred G. 1962. "A Catalogue of Texts and Authors." *JCS* 16:59–77.

Lambert, Wilfred G. 1987. "A Further Attempt at the Babylonian 'Man and His God.'" Pages 187–202 in *Language, Literature, and History: Philological and Historical Studies Presented to Erica Reiner*. Edited by Francesca Rochberg-Halton. AOS 67. New Haven, CT: American Oriental Society.

Lambert, Wilfred G. 1995. "Some New Babylonian Wisdom Literature." Pages 30–42 in *Wisdom in Ancient Israel: Essays in Honour of J.A. Emerton*. Edited by John Day, Robert, P. Gordon, and Hugh G.M. Williamson. Cambridge: Cambridge University Press.

Lenzi Alan. 2008. "The Uruk List of Kings and Sages and Late Mesopotamian Scholarship." *JANER* 8:137–169.

Lenzi, Alan. 2012. "The Curious Case of Failed Revelation in Ludlul Bel Nemeqi: A New Suggestion for the Poem's Scholarly Purpose." Pages 36–66 in *Mediating Between Heaven and Earth: Communication with the Divine in the Ancient Near East*. Edited by Carly L. Crouch, Jonathan Stökl, and Anna E. Zernecke. LHBOTS 566. London: T&T Clark.

Lenzi, Alan. 2018. "'Counsels of Wisdom' as 'White-Collar' Wisdom in First Millennium Ancient Mesopotamia." Pages 60–69 in Oshima 2018b.

Liverani, Mario. 2011. "Portrait du héros comme un jeune chien." Pages 11–26 in *Le jeune héros: recherches sur la formation et la diffusion d'un thème littéraire au Proche-Orient ancien: actes du colloque organisé par les chaires d'Assyriologie et des Milieux bibliques du Collège de France, Paris, les 6 et 7 avril 2009*. Edited by Jean M. Durand, Thomas Römer, and Michaël Langlois. OBO 250. Fribourg: Academic Press; Göttingen: Vandenhoeck & Ruprecht.

Metcalf, Christopher. 2013. "Babylonian Perspectives on the Certainty of Death." *Kaskal* 13:255–267.

Noegel, Scott B. 2016. "Suffering Ambiguity in Ludlul Bēl Nēmeqi: On Erudition, Ideology, and Theology in Tablet I." *BO* 73:613–636.

Oshima, Takayoshi. 2013. *The Babylonian Theodicy: Introduction, Cuneiform Text and Transliteration with a Translation, Glossary and Commentary*. SAACT 9; Publications of the Foundation of Finnish Assyriological Research 9. Winona Lake, IN: Eisenbrauns.

Oshima, Takayoshi. 2014. *Babylonian Poems of Pious Sufferers: Ludlul Bēl Nēmeqi and the Babylonian Theodicy*. ORA 14. Tübingen: Mohr Siebeck.

Oshima, Takayoshi. 2018a. " 'When the Godless Thrives and a Wolf Grows Fat': Notions of the Prosperity of the Impious in Ancient Mesopotamian Wisdom Texts." Pages 189–215 in Oshima 2018b.

Oshima, Takayoshi, ed. 2018b. *Teaching Morality in Antiquity: Wisdom Texts, Oral Traditions, and Images*. Tübingen: Mohr Siebeck.

Ottervanger, B. 2016. *The Tale of the Poor Man of Nippur*. SAACT 12. Winona Lake, IN: Eisenbrauns.

Perdue, Leo G. 2008. *Scribes, Sages, and Seers: The Sage in the Eastern Mediterranean World*. FRLANT 219. Göttingen: Vandenhoeck & Ruprecht.

Pongratz-Leisten, Beate. 2010. "From Ritual to Text to Intertext: A New Look on the Dreams in Ludlul Bel Nemeqi." Pages 139–157 in *In the Second Degree: Paratextual Literature in Ancient Near Eastern and Ancient Mediterranean Culture and Its Reflections in Medieval Literature*. Edited by Philip Alexander, Armin Lange, and Renate Pillinger. Leiden: Brill.

Reinink, Gerrit J., and Herman L.J. Vanstiphout. 1991. *Dispute Poems and Dialogues in the Ancient and Mediaeval Near East: Forms and Types of Literary Debates in Semitic and Related Literatures*. OLA 42. Leuven: Peeters.

Samet, Nili. 2010. "The Tallest Man Cannot Reach Heaven; the Broadest Man Cannot Cover Earth—Reconsidering the Proverb and Its Biblical Parallels." *JHS* 10:2–13.

Samet, Nili. 2015a. "Religious Redaction in Qohelet in Light of Mesopotamian Vanity Literature." *VT* 65:1–16.

Samet, Nili. 2015b. "The Gilgamesh Epic and the Book of Qohelet: A New Look." *Bib* 96:375–390.

Streck, Michael, and Nathan Wasserman. 2014. "Mankind's Bitter Fate: The Wisdom Dialog BM 79111+." *JCS* 66:39–47.

Streck, Michael, and Nathan Wasserman. 2016. "On Wolves and Kings: Two Tablets with Akkadian Wisdom Texts from the Second Millennium BC" *Iraq* 78:241–252.

Sweet, Ronald. 1990. "The Sage in Akkadian Literature: A Philological Study." Pages 45–66 in *The Sage in Israel and the Ancient Near East*. Edited by John G. Gammie and Leo. G. Perdue. Winona Lake, IN: Eisenbrauns.

Taylor, Jon. 2005. "The Sumerian Proverb Collections." *RA* 99:13–38.

Toorn, Karel van der. 1991. "The Ancient Near Eastern Literary Dialogue as a Vehicle of Critical Reflection." Pages 59–75 in *Dispute Poems and Dialogues in the Ancient and Mediaeval Near East*. Edited by Gerrit J. Reinink and Herman L.J. Vanstiphout. OLA 42. Leuven: Peeters.

Toorn, Karel van der. 2003. "Theodicy in Akkadian Literature." Pages 57–89 in *Theodicy in the World of the Bible*. Edited by Antti Laato and Johannes C. de Moor. Leiden: Brill.

Uehlinger, Christoff. 2007. "Das Hiob-Buch im Kontext der altorientalischen Literatur-und Religionsgeschichte." Pages 97–163 in *Das Buch Hiob und seine Interpretationen: Beiträge zum Hiob-Symposium auf dem Monte Verita vom 14.–19. August 2005*. Edited by Thomas Krüger et al. Zürich: Theologischer Verlag Zürich.

Vanstiphout, Herman L.J. 1988. "The Importance of the 'Tale of the Fox.'" *ASJ* 10:191–227.

Vanstiphout, Herman L.J. 1990. "The Mesopotamian Debate Poems: A General Presentation. Part I." *ASJ* 12:271–318.

Vanstiphout, Herman L.J. 1992. "The Mesopotamian Debate Poems: A General Presentation. Part II: The Subject." *ASJ* 14:339–367.

Veldhuis, Niek. 2000. "Sumerian Proverbs in their Curricular Context." *JAOS* 120:383–399.

Viano, Maurizio. 2016. *The Reception of Sumerian Literature in the Western Periphery*. Antichistica 9; Studi orientali 4. Venice: Ca'Foscari.

Wasserman, Nathan. 2011. "The Distant Voice of Gilgameš: The Circulation and Reception of the Babylonian Gilgameš Epic in Ancient Mesopotamia. Review article of A.R. George, The Babylonian Gilgamesh Epic. Introduction, Critical Edition and Cuneiform Texts, Oxford (Oxford University Press), 2003." *AfO* 52:1–14.

Wasserman, Nathan. 2013. "Treating Garments in the Old Babylonian Period: 'At the Cleaners' in a Comparative View." *Iraq* 75:255–277.

Wasserman, Nathan. 2016. "Weisheitliteratur (Wisdom Literature). A. In Mesopotamien." *RlA* 15:51–52.

West, Martin L. 1997. *The East Face of Helicon: West Asiatic Elements in Greek Poetry and Myth*. Oxford: Clarendon Press.

CHAPTER 9

....

WISDOM IN THE DEAD SEA SCROLLS AND EARLY JEWISH INTERPRETATION

....

ARJEN BAKKER

THE topic of wisdom has become a major theme in Dead Sea Scrolls scholarship in the last two decades. This is mainly the result of the publication in the 1990s of a number of fragmentary texts from Qumran Cave 4 that share literary features with biblical Wisdom Literature and have for this reason been classified as sapiential texts in the editions and translations. However, even before the publication of the Cave 4 materials it was evident that Wisdom was an important category in the newly found compositions. Texts from Cave 1 such as the Rule of the Community (1QS) and the Thanksgiving Hymns (1QH^a) are replete with Wisdom terminology and have the highest esteem for the pursuit and attainment of knowledge. The main question is how to situate the various forms of wisdom we encounter in the Dead Sea Scrolls within the broader landscape of Judaism in the Hellenistic and early Roman periods.

Building on recent developments in scholarship, this article argues that the Qumran sapiential texts cannot be separated off from the broader corpus on account of their literary form. In order to better understand the intricate wisdom concepts that are being developed in these compositions, we have to study the multitude of fragmentary texts side by side without insisting on strict distinctions in terms of literary genre or provenance (i.e., sectarian vs. non-sectarian). This will lead to the observation that rather than continuing the biblical Wisdom tradition, texts found at Qumran perform a reinterpretation of Wisdom within the context of the broader intellectual culture of Judaism. To appreciate this wider framework of early Jewish interpretation, it is important to look across the linguistic boundaries of Hebrew, Aramaic, and Greek. Only by cultivating this broader outlook can we gain more clarity on the ways in which intellectual traditions from the Second Temple period reverberate in late antiquity.

9.1 Questions of Classification

The discovery of Qumran texts that resemble biblical Wisdom Literature obviously raises the question of the relation between these two corpora. Are these texts really continuing the Wisdom tradition that we already encounter in books of the Hebrew Bible? In order to address this question, we have to take a closer look at issues of taxonomy, not only in terms of literary genre, but also regarding the supposed sectarian or non-sectarian provenance of the texts.

The editors of the Dead Sea Scrolls had to find ways of categorizing the newly discovered fragmentary manuscripts. The editors had to sort thousands of fragments and reconstruct manuscripts that included many texts that were previously unknown to modern scholars (Tigchelaar 2010). Evidently, when characterizing and labelling the texts, familiar categories, especially those deriving from form-critical scholarship of the Hebrew Bible, were used (Najman and Tigchelaar 2014). When it became clear that certain fragmentary texts shared formal features with compositions such as Proverbs, Job, Qohelet, and Ben Sira, it was only too natural to label these as Wisdom compositions. Nonetheless, it was also apparent that these works had features that did not fit within the traditional frame of Wisdom Literature.

The category of Wisdom Literature is a modern scholarly construct (Weeks 2016). Biblical scholars had developed this category on the basis of a set of characteristics shared by some texts in the Hebrew Bible: terminology related to wisdom and knowledge, literary forms associated with pedagogy, and a worldview that centered on the notion of a perfectly ordered creation. Texts that had been unearthed in Mesopotamia and Egypt made use of similar literary forms and presented a worldview and concepts that corresponded to those found in biblical Wisdom Literature. For this reason, scholars argued that these writings were part of an international literary tradition that functioned in the education of scribal elites. These basic parameters have been much discussed. It has proved difficult to clearly define criteria and delineate the corpus. Some scholars have even argued that the category of Wisdom Literature should be abandoned altogether (Kynes 2019).

The sapiential texts from Qumran further complicate the discussion on the category of Wisdom Literature. It is obvious that the biblical Wisdom books were considered of great importance by the authors of the Qumran texts: the typical terminology of biblical Wisdom is applied profusely and its literary forms are emulated. However, this terminology is imbued with meanings that are alien to classical Wisdom and, although we can recognize aspects of a worldview that is focused on cosmic order, the conceptual framework in which these notions are embedded is rather different. Moreover, the literary genres associated with Wisdom Literature are mixed with genres known from other types of literature (Kister 2004).

The provenance of the Qumran sapiential texts is a matter of dispute, namely whether or not these texts were sectarian. The label "sectarian" here refers to texts that were

composed by the communities that owned the Dead Sea Scrolls. The nature and structure of these communities, as well as their relation to the site of Qumran and the school
of the Essenes, continue to be debated (Goodman 1995; Mason 2007; Collins 2010). But
despite the lack of consensus and clarity, many scholars still presume that it is possible
to differentiate between sectarian and non-sectarian texts and argue that the Wisdom
texts from Qumran belong to the non-sectarian division. Other scholars claim that the
same texts *are* sectarian. This bifurcation of views has led to an impasse in scholarship
on Qumran Wisdom to the point that it is difficult to have a meaningful conversation
between scholars working on either side of the fence, since they read the fragments in
radically different ways.

When the fragments resembling biblical Wisdom were first studied, the Qumran-
Essene hypothesis and the sectarian nature of the community were still largely taken
for granted. John Strugnell, who was responsible for editing the largest and most widely
attested Wisdom text found at Qumran (4QInstruction), assumed in an early publication that this text contained moral teachings of the Qumran sect (Strugnell et al. 1956).
However, when he published the official edition of the 1Q and 4Q manuscripts of
4QInstruction, he had changed his view and claimed that this was a non-sectarian composition that was composed before the sect had been founded (Strugnell et al. 1999).

This reversal of opinion results from a major shift in the categorization of the Dead
Sea Scrolls that began in the late 1970s (Newsom 1990; Dimant 2011; Tigchelaar 2012).
In the early years after the discoveries, scholars generally assumed that all previously
unknown texts were products of the Qumran community. But the gradual publication
of new texts revealed a large variety among the compositions. Many of these texts did
not display the sectarian markers that scholars had come to associate with the community's literary production. Since the biblical texts were obviously not composed by this
community, why would there not be other (non-biblical) texts in their library that also
had been composed by others?

The fragmentary Wisdom texts by and large do not employ terminology that refers
to the communities of the Damascus Document and the Community Rule. Moreover,
4QInstruction, the most important of the Wisdom texts, gives advice on issues relating to property, marriage, and offspring. By contrast, the Community Rule describes
how members renounce private property. The absence of women in the Rule has been
taken by many scholars as an indication that the members were unmarried, just like the
Essenes described by Philo and Josephus. For these reasons, it was argued that the sapiential texts from Qumran were not composed by the sectarian community, but were
merely copied and preserved as part of their library. These texts would then be the products of Wisdom teachers representing an ongoing sapiential tradition that was part
of the "mainstream" intellectual world of Second Temple Judaism (Harrington 1996;
Collins 1997; Goff 2007; Lange 2010; Kampen 2011).

Scholars arguing for the non-sectarian provenance of the Qumran Wisdom
texts do recognize the shared terminology in sectarian texts such as the Rule of the
Community and the Thanksgiving Hymns. This is usually explained as influence of
the sapiential texts on the sectarian texts: the sectarian composers had 4QInstruction

in their library and adopted its terms and concepts. The problem with this line of reasoning is that we have no way of proving that the sapiential texts were actually composed prior to the sectarian ones. The only argument for dating these compositions earlier is the assumption that they had not been written by the sect and must therefore have been written before its foundation. But there is no reason to exclude the possibility that the community adopted contemporaneous compositions from the outside. Moreover, our criteria are rather shaky. There is a significant degree of terminological overlap. Why could this vocabulary only be used to prove literary dependence and not shared provenance?

For precisely this reason, other scholars have argued that the sapiential texts from Qumran are literary products of the community. Both Devorah Dimant (2011) and Menahem Kister (2009) have pointed to a large number of distinctive phrases and concepts that are shared by the Qumran Wisdom texts and compositions that are typically associated with the community. In their judgment, the pervasive presence of sectarian vocabulary in the Wisdom texts indicates that these should indeed be regarded as sectarian. The divergent classifications of the Wisdom texts make discussion between scholars on either side of the divide difficult. Since context is so crucial for the interpretation of fragmentary texts, scholars who classify the Wisdom texts as sectarian are in some sense reading entirely different compositions than those scholars who classify the same texts as non-sectarian.

This impasse can be overcome by recognizing that the strict dichotomy of sectarian and non-sectarian compositions cannot ultimately be sustained, and is an obstacle to research that casts a wider net on Jewish Wisdom traditions in the Greco-Roman period. The absence of sectarian features in a text does not necessarily mean that it was written by a different group, since vocabulary and style can also be dictated by literary genre. Moreover, we can never be sure that the lost portions of a text did not contain sectarian features. But more fundamentally, there is a problem with our criteria and our categories. For in order to define which texts are sectarian and which texts are not, we need to have a clear notion of what we mean by "sectarian," what the sect looked like, and in which ways it deviated from other Jewish communities. Scholarship has no clarity on these issues at present. The publication of the entire corpus of the Dead Sea Scrolls is relatively recent and further research will certainly result in clearer answers to these questions. But if we impose preliminary distinctions on the corpus, we will continue to follow the circular paths that we have ourselves created.

9.2 REINTERPRETING WISDOM

In order to understand the concept of wisdom in the Dead Sea Scrolls all texts should be studied in conjunction, whether they have been labelled as Wisdom compositions or not, and whether they have been classified as sectarian or non-sectarian. It is questionable whether the Qumran sapiential texts can be seen as representatives of an ongoing tradition of Wisdom Literature that is cultivated by circles of scribes. Rather, as Menahem Kister observes, "The continuity of the biblical wisdom tradition, often presumed because of the similarity in terminology or phraseology, is just as often an illusion" (Kister 2004, 19). What we see in the scrolls is rather a reinterpretation of biblical Wisdom Literature within new conceptual frameworks and within the broader context of the interpretive culture of Second Temple Judaism.

One of the main aspects of this new version of wisdom is that it is hidden and not available to everyone. Whereas in the book of Proverbs Lady Wisdom raises her voice and cries out by the city gates (Prov 8:1–3), the texts from Qumran tend to assume that wisdom is concealed and that only a select group of initiates have access. Throughout 4QInstruction the addressee is called a *mebin*, someone who understands, and is told: "your ear has been opened for the secret of being (*raz nihyeh*)." The meaning of the enigmatic phrase *raz nihyeh* is much disputed and will briefly be discussed below. But the elements of secrecy and the need of initiation are obvious and an important aspect of wisdom in the scrolls.

To a large extent this secret knowledge is focused on understanding the meaning of scriptures. This meaning is not accessible to just anyone who reads the text, but has to be teased out by the right person, within the right community, and with the right method. Wisdom consists in uncovering the "hidden things" (נסתרות) of the scriptures. The texts from Qumran are replete with references to biblical texts and allude to specific interpretations. This approach to interpreting the scriptures is very much in line with what James Kugel (1998) observed about interpretation in ancient Judaism more generally: the text is fundamentally regarded as cryptic and needs to decoded by the reader. This suggests that Wisdom features in the Dead Sea Scrolls may often attest to reinterpretation rather than to the continuation of a tradition.

A good example is the term *mebin*. The form occurs in Proverbs to describe someone who understands situations and has insight into wisdom teachings. The occurrence of this form in Proverbs may have influenced its usage in 4QInstruction but it is important to recognize the discontinuity in usage. In Proverbs the term never functions as a form of address for the disciple, while 4QInstruction consistently addresses its audience as *mebin*. How can this new usage of the term be explained?

In Proverbs we encounter the admonition, "And now, sons (בנים), listen to me." In fragmentary Qumran texts we find a remarkable variation on this form: "And now, understanding one/ones (*mebin/mebinim*), listen to me" (4Q303, 4Q525). The authors used the admonition from Proverbs, but interpreted the plural בנים not as "sons" but as a participle of the verb בין, "to understand," and applied it in the *hifil* pattern (Kister 2000). The same twist occurs in a wordplay in Ben Sira: "Wisdom educates her sons (בניה) and she admonishes all those who understand her (מבינים בה)" (Sir 4:11). It seems that a similar reinterpretation of sapiential terminology lies behind the usage of *mebin* as a form of address in 4QInstruction. Throughout Proverbs the student of wisdom is addressed as son (בני, בנים). But 4QInstruction discerns a deeper meaning behind this trope: the student of wisdom is someone who understands secrets and mysteries (Bakker 2020).

The sapiential features of Qumran texts should be seen in the broader context of rewriting, interpreting, and emulating authoritative writings. The communities behind these manuscripts did not study the Wisdom books of the Bible separately, but in conjunction with other texts. This is precisely how Ben Sira describes the daily occupation of the sage:

> ...who devotes his soul,
> and who thinks about the Law of the Most High.
> He will seek out the wisdom of all the ancients,
> and he will be occupied with prophecies.
> He will preserve the narrative of famous men,
> and he will penetrate into the twists of illustrations.
> He will seek out the obscurities of proverbs,
> and he will be engaged with the riddles of illustration.
> (Sir 38:34–39:3, transl. Wright, NETS)

The pursuit of wisdom is not restricted to the study of proverbs and riddles, but is also directed towards prophecies and, most prominently, the Torah. The recycling and reinterpretation of terminology and literary forms from biblical Wisdom Literature should be seen in this context. In the course of the Second Temple period a collection of canonical writings emerged, and although this was not a closed canon, it is clear that these writings were held in reverence and were scrutinized. The content of wisdom is determined to a large extent by these writings, or more precisely, by the interpretation of these writings and the correct understanding of their hidden meaning. But it is important to emphasize that other books that never became part of the Bible were studied as well.

The Law of Moses obviously takes a central place in this interpretive enterprise. Ben Sira places the Torah at the top of his list of holy writings and elsewhere he famously states that all the fruits of wisdom are embedded "in the book of the covenant of the Most High, a Law that Moses commanded us" (Sir 24:23). There is an elaborate and ongoing discussion on the relationship between Wisdom and Law (Schipper and Teeter 2013). Many scholars argue that Torah became incorporated into Wisdom traditions. But Wisdom from the late Second Temple period cannot be separated from the broader interpretive culture and literary production of Judaism. In terms of authority, it is no doubt more correct to say that wisdom "is subsumed by Torah" (Tooman 2013, 227; cf. Kister 2004). But we should note that the processes of reinterpretation are reciprocal and that various forms of literature leave their mark on the ways in which the entire textual corpus is read.

The concept of Torah is extremely difficult to pin down and it is not clear to what extent "the Law of the Most High" or the "Law that Moses commanded us" are to be identified with the books of the Pentateuch, or with a more abstract notion of divine law (Levenson 1987). In order to get a better grasp of the entanglement of Torah and wisdom, it is helpful to examine the way in which both are intertwined with practice and observance. This is exemplified in a beautiful way in a passage that praises the wise with a series of beatitudes and concludes:

> Happy is the man who has reached wisdom,
>> and walks in the law of the Most High,
>>> and sets his heart to her ways.
> He controls himself in her punishments,
>> and always willingly accepts her afflictions.
> He does not forsake her in the distress of [his] cruci[ble],
>> and at the time of anguish he will not leave her.
> He does not forget her [on the day] of terror,
>> and in humbling himself, he will not despise her.
> Rather, he meditates on her continually,
>> and in his distress he speaks about [her].
>> (4Q525 2 ii 3–6)

Wisdom and law are placed on an equal footing and the sage lives by their instructions. He is educated by holding fast to wisdom and any unfortunate events in his life are regarded as admonishment or trial. This implies that wisdom is not only seen as an object of knowledge, but also as an agent in the world: she inflicts suffering on the sage in order to train him and purify him, like metal in a crucible.

According to 4Q525 the sage constantly meditates on wisdom. There is a direct allusion here to Joshua 1:8, "This book of the Law shall not depart out of your mouth, you shall meditate on it day and night" (NRSV). This verse had a great impact and is also reflected in Psalm 1, Ben Sira 6, and the Rule of the Community (1QS VI 6). It is reused in a remarkable way in 4QInstruction, which tells the *mebin*:

> [Day] and night meditate on the mystery of being,
>> and study continuously
> And then you will know truth and iniquity,
>> wisdom and [foll]y you will un[dersta]nd.
>> (4Q417 1 6–7)

The phrase "mystery of being" (*raz nihyeh*) occurs frequently in 4QInstruction and is also attested in the Rule of the Community and 4QMysteries. It is one of the most elusive concepts in the Dead Sea Scrolls. The allusion to Joshua 1:8 indicates that *raz nihyeh* relates to the Torah, and the same can be inferred from 4QInstruction's many allusions to the Pentateuch, its discussion of legal matters (Schiffman 2004), and its reference to Mosaic revelation (4Q418 184 1).

The concept of the "mystery of being" is similar to the concept of wisdom in Proverbs and Job in the sense that it organizes the cosmos and society (Lange 1995). But there is a much stronger emphasis on temporality in *raz nihyeh*: it is the hidden force behind history and causes situations to develop and change both on a small scale and on a large scale. The use of various forms of the root היה ("to be," "to happen") in the Dead Sea Scrolls attests to an intricate reflection on the concept time and the phrase *raz nihyeh* could also be translated as the "secret of time" (Bakker 2021).

The *raz nihyeh* can be examined by studying the words of Moses and the prophets and by uncovering their hidden meaning. But other mantic techniques provide access to the mystery of being as well, especially astrology. More than once the *mebin* is told to study horoscopes in order to understand the hidden structures of social relationships (Morgenstern 2000; Schmidt 2006). The *raz nihyeh* is the hidden plan of God and allows insight into the divisions and workings of good and evil in the world. There is a close correspondence between the vocabulary and concepts in 4QInstruction and in the Treatise of the Two Spirits, in columns III and IV of 1QS (Lange 1995; Tigchelaar 2001). This indicates that the teachings of these texts are related and can be mutually illuminating. But *raz nihyeh* refers to a broader concept that encompasses all possible forms of knowledge.

The instructions to the *mebin* are repeatedly reinforced by the statement: "as He has opened your ear for the mystery of being." The teachings presented are accessible to someone who was given insight into heavenly mysteries. But this divine gift to the *mebin* does not release him from the obligation to acquire knowledge himself. To the contrary, throughout 4QInstruction the addressees are incited to study and gather knowledge, whatever the circumstances:

> If you are poor, do not say "I am poor so w[hy] should I study wisdom?"
> Bring your shoulder under all instruction,
>   and with every [...] refine your mind,
>   and with abundance of insight your thoughts.
> Study the mystery of being,
>   and consider all the ways of truth,
>   and all the roots of iniquity you must contemplate.
> Then you will know what is bitter for a man,
>   and what is sweet for a person.
>   (4Q416 iii 12–15 *par* 4Q418 9+9a–c 13–16)

As in the passage from 4Q525 quoted above, the pursuit of wisdom is presented as a continuous exercise in which the sage is tested and in which his mind is purified. The command in Joshua 1:8 to meditate on the law day and night is taken literally and the students are admonished to study continuously, by day and by night. In another fragment from 4QInstruction the ideal of the uninterrupted pursuit of knowledge is exemplified by angels who chase after insight without ever becoming tired or hungry (4Q418 69 ii). The students of wisdom are admonished to follow this example. The wisdom they pursue lies beyond the limits of human comprehension and for this reason they are required to transcend human limitations, such as the need for food and rest, in order to chase after knowledge continually. The pursuit of heavenly wisdom requires a transformation on the part of the sage in order to become more like the angelic example (Bakker 2016).

9.3 WISDOM AND PRAYER BEYOND THE HEBREW-GREEK DIVIDE

Intellectual developments in the broader Greco-Roman world may cast light on some of the innovations in the concepts of wisdom we encounter in the Dead Sea Scrolls. Hindy Najman (2017) has pointed out that, while it is commonplace in scholarship to study parallels and direct points of contact between ancient Near Eastern Wisdom texts and biblical Wisdom, scholars have been much more reluctant to explore correspondences between the Dead Sea Scrolls and contemporaneous writings in Greek. This is surprising since these literatures were produced in chronological and geographical proximity, much closer, in fact, than the biblical and ancient Near Eastern Wisdom writings. There is abundant evidence of cultural contacts, including the Greek manuscripts discovered in the Qumran caves.

The Greek text Wisdom of Solomon is one of the most obvious points of departure in comparing Hebrew and Greek expressions of wisdom. Scholars generally date this text sometime between the early first century BCE and mid-first century CE and locate the composition in Egypt. Isaac Seeligmann (2002) has pointed to a number of close correspondences between Wisdom of Solomon and passages from the Dead Sea Scrolls, especially from the Hodayot. He highlights, for example, the language of mystery in the context of divine retribution (Wis 2:22), the notion that the sages share in the lot of the holy ones (Wis 5:5), and the dichotomy between human ignorance and heavenly knowledge, which can only be bridged by mediation of a divine spirit (Wis 9:13–18). These and other correspondences between the Qumran scrolls and passages from the Septuagint lead Seeligmann to the conclusion that there must have been contacts between sectarian circles in Judea and Jewish communities in Alexandria.

The similarities between Wisdom of Solomon's concept of wisdom and *raz nihyeh* are indeed striking. Both are presented as principles of retribution that ensure the reward of the righteous and the punishment of the wicked (Collins 2003). But the correspondences are even more intimate. Particularly striking is the emphasis on time and the knowledge of history, which is based on the correct interpretation of prophecies:

> And if anyone longs for wide experience, she knows the things of old and infers the things to come; she understands the subtleties of sayings and the solutions of riddles; she has foreknowledge of signs and wonders and the outcomes of seasons and times.   (Wis 8:8 NRSV)

The Greek composition describes wisdom as a spirit that permeates all of creation (7:22–8:1). She is not only an object of knowledge but also a force in the cosmos and an agent that drives history forward and guides events, for example the exodus from Egypt. Wisdom also has prophetic knowledge: she comprehends the things of old and the things to come (cf. 1Q27 1 i; Kister 2004, 32–33), she understands sayings and riddles, and foresees signs and wonders. All of this is remarkably similar to *raz nihyeh* in the Dead Sea Scrolls. But whereas Seeligmann regarded these as sectarian ideas that were transmitted from Judea to Egypt, current developments in research suggest a different model of explanation.

As I have argued in the first section, it is not so easy to draw a line between sectarian and non-sectarian texts from Qumran, and the idea that certain texts were written in an environment that might be called "sectarian" does not imply that ideas or practices of these communities were not shared along a broader basis in Judaism. Hindy Najman (2007) illustrates this point with respect to practices of prayer, divine inspiration, and philosophical contemplation. She places the writings of Philo of Alexandria alongside compositions that were found in Qumran and examines over-lapping notions of revelation. She questions the strict distinctions that are generally drawn in scholarship between Jewish communities speaking Greek and Jewish com-munities speaking Hebrew and Aramaic, and she emphasizes multilingualism and the fact that Jews writing in different languages inhabited a shared world and inherited shared traditions and practices.

Najman demonstrates the sharing of traditions across Hebrew and Greek boundar-ies with the examples of ecstatic prayer among the Therapeutae in Egypt that can be compared to liturgical communion with angels in the writings from Qumran. Philo of Alexandria describes the Therapeutae as a community that has withdrawn to the coun-tryside and lives a life entirely devoted to study and prayer. Once every fifty days they celebrate festivals at which they sing hymns of praise in perfect harmony while dancing throughout the night and experiencing mystic rapture. In a similar way, members of the *yahad* feel that they join the ranks of the angels in giving praise, and they experi-ence heavenly light in their otherworldly worship. It has been pointed out that these themes in the Thanksgiving Hymns and the Songs of the Sabbath Sacrifice have echoes in liturgical and mystical traditions of late antique Judaism (Chazon 2000). If we find overlapping concepts in the Dead Sea Scrolls, in Philo of Alexandria, and in Judaism of the rabbinic period, it becomes very difficult to regard these as marginal and sectarian.

Although certain concepts and practices of wisdom may have been restricted to spe-cific circles and communities, it is important not to lose sight of broader and overlapping structures that are embedded in processes of interpretation, textualization, and forma-tion of liturgical traditions. A clear example of the intertwining of wisdom, Torah, the recitation of scriptures, and the performance of glorification is a text known as Psalm 154. This hymn has been preserved in translation in Syriac manuscripts and has also been discovered at Qumran. In this text the revelation of Torah and wisdom have a clear pedagogical purpose:

> For wisdom was given to make the glory of the LORD known
>> And to tell his great deeds, she was made known to humankind.
> To make simpletons know his might,
>> and to instruct senseless people concerning his greatness.
> Those who are far away from her doors,
>> those who are banished from her entries...
> From the gates of the righteous her voice is heard,
>> and from the assembly of the pious her song.
> When they eat in abundance she is spoken of,
>> and when they drink in community together.
>> (11QPsalms[a] XVIII 3–6, 10–12)

The last verses emphasize the communal dimension: wisdom is present in the liturgi-cal community, and the shared meals of the pious are the primary occasion for convers-ing about wisdom. There is an obvious parallel here with Mishnah Avot 3:3, which says that when three people are eating together and speak words of Torah, it is as if they were eating at the divine table (Kister 2009). The preservation of this hymn both in Qumran and in Syriac indicates the wider circulation of this text, despite arguments for its sectarian origin. The parallel in the Mishnah suggests a much broader liturgical context for the practice of devoting shared meals to conversations about wisdom and Torah.

9.4 Conclusion

The discussion on classifications of the Dead Sea Scrolls is based on the important insight that not all texts found at Qumran were composed by the same communities. At the same time, it should be recognized that it is extremely difficult to establish criteria for categorizing texts, especially when scholarly reconstructions of the communities behind these texts are still in a continuous state of flux. Taking into account that texts in the Qumran collections may have been written in distinct communities, it is nonetheless worthwhile to study the texts alongside each other.

The fragmentary state of most manuscripts implies that we need some kind of context for interpreting the fragments, and the presence of similar terminology across various compositions suggests they can cast light on one another. Additionally, the texts need to be placed in the broader landscape of Jewish literature from the period, of which most works that have been preserved are in Greek. The often-assumed dichotomy between Jewish writings in Greek and Hebrew, which partly originates in theological considerations, should be abandoned in order to make place for an approach that appreciates the different cultural contexts, but at the same time recognizes the shared practices of interpretation and explores the points of contact between distinct forms of literature.

The discovery of the scrolls made the world of ancient Jewish Wisdom a much larger world. We can see the omnipresence of Wisdom across Jewish traditions as it is integrated with Torah, revelation, and prayer. The emphasis on mystery and the hidden structures of time is shared by Wisdom texts from Qumran and from the Hellenistic world. Wisdom as a way of thinking permeates a variety of traditions across genres and opens up new pathways for what will emerge as Torah study and Jewish Law. These Wisdom tendencies are manifest across Hebrew, Greek, and Aramaic traditions. One could not underestimate the centrality and importance of wisdom, both as a concept and as a reinterpreted tradition, as we have now learned from the discovery of the scrolls.

Works Cited

Bakker, Arjen. 2016. "Sages and Saints: Continuous Study and Transformation in *Musar le-Mevin* and *Serekh ha-Yahad*." Pages 106–118 in *Tracing Sapiential Traditions in Ancient Judaism*. Edited by Hindy Najman, Jean-Sébastien Rey, and Eibert J.C. Tigchelaar. JSJSup 174. Leiden: Brill.

Bakker, Arjen. 2021. *The Secret of Time: Reconfiguring Wisdom in the Dead Sea Scrolls*. STDJ. Leiden: Brill.

Chazon, Esther G. 2000. "Liturgical Communion with the Angels at Qumran." Pages 95–105 in *Sapiential, Liturgical and Poetical Texts from Qumran*. Edited by Daniel Falk, F. García Martínez, and Eileen M. Schuller. STDJ 35. Leiden: Brill.

Collins, John J. 1997. "Wisdom Reconsidered in Light of the Scrolls." *DSD* 4:265–281.

Collins, John J. 2003. "The Mysteries of God: Creation and Eschatology in 4QInstruction and the Wisdom of Solomon." Pages 287–305 in *Wisdom and Apocalypticism in the Dead Sea Scrolls and in the Biblical Tradition*. Edited by Florentino García Martínez. Leuven: Peeters.

Collins, John J. 2010. *Beyond the Qumran Community: The Sectarian Movement of the Dead Sea Scrolls*. Grand Rapids MI: Eerdmans.

Dimant, Devorah. 2011. "The Vocabulary of the Qumran Sectarian Texts." Pages 347–395 in *Qumran und die Archäologie: Texte und Kontexte*. Edited by Jorg Frey, Carsten Claussen, and Nadine Kessler. Tübingen: Mohr Siebeck.

Goff, Matthew. 2007. *Discerning Wisdom: The Sapiential Literature of the Dead Sea Scrolls*. SVT 116. Leiden: Brill.

Goodman, Martin. 1995. "A Note on the Qumran Sectarians, the Essenes and Josephus." *JJS* 46:161–166.

Harrington, Daniel. 1996. *Wisdom Texts from Qumran*. London: Routledge.

Kampen, John. 2011 *Wisdom Literature*. Grand Rapids, MI: Eerdmans.

Kister, Menahem. 2000. "Some Observations on Vocabulary and Style in the Dead Sea Scrolls." Pages 137–165 in *Diggers at the Well: Proceedings of a Third International Symposium on the Hebrew of the Dead Sea Scrolls and Ben Sira*. Edited by Takamitsu Muraoka and John Elwolde. STDJ 36. Leiden: Brill.

Kister, Menahem. 2004. "Wisdom Literature and Its Relation to Other Genres: From Ben Sira to *Mysteries*." Pages 13–47 in *Sapiential Perspectives: Wisdom Literature in Light of the Dead Sea Scrolls*. Edited by John Collins, Gregory Sterling, and Ruth Clements. STDJ 51. Leiden: Brill.

Kister, Menaham. 2009. "Wisdom Literature from Qumran." Pages 299–319 in *The Qumran Scrolls and Their World*, vol. 1. Edited by Menaham Kister. Jerusalem: Yad Ben-Zvi. (Hebrew)

Kugel, James L. 1998. *Traditions of the Bible: A Guide to the Bible as It Was at the Start of the Common Era*. Cambridge, MA: Harvard University Press.

Kynes, Will. 2019. *An Obituary for "Wisdom Literature": The Birth, Death, and Intertextual Reintegration of a Biblical Corpus*. Oxford: Oxford University Press.

Lange, Armin. 1995. *Weisheit und Prädestination: Weisheitliche Urordnung und Prädestination in den Textfunden von Qumran*. STDJ 18. Leiden: Brill.

Lange, Armin. 2010. "Wisdom Literature and Thought in the Dead Sea Scrolls." Pages 455–478 in *The Oxford Handbook of the Dead Sea Scrolls*. Edited by John Collins and Timothy Lim. Oxford: Oxford University Press.

Levenson, Jon D. 1987. "The Sources of Torah: Psalm 119 and the Modes of Revelation in Second Temple Judaism." Pages 559–574 in *Ancient Israelite Religion*. Edited by Paul Hanson, S. Dean McBride, and Patrick D. Miller. Philadelphia, PA: Fortress Press.

Mason, Steve. 2007. "Essenes and Lurking Spartans in Josephus' Judean War: From Story to History." Pages 219–261 in *Making History: Josephus and Historical Method*. Edited by Zuleika Rodgers. JSJSup 110. Leiden: Brill.

Morgenstern, Matthew. 2000. "The Meaning of בית מולדים in the Qumran Wisdom Texts." *JJS* 51:141–144.

Najman, Hindy. 2007. "Philosophical Contemplation and Revelatory Inspiration in Ancient Judean Traditions." *SPhiloA* 19: 101–111.

Najman, Hindy. 2017. "Jewish Wisdom in the Hellenistic Period: Towards the Study of a Semantic Constellation." Pages 459–472 in *Is There a Text in This Cave? Studies in the Textuality of the Dead Sea Scrolls in Honour of George J. Brooke*. Edited by Ariel Feldman, Maria Cioată, and Charlotte Hempel. STDJ 119. Leiden: Brill.

Najman, Hindy, and Eibert J.C. Tigchelaar. 2014. "A Preparatory Study of Nomenclature and Text Designation in the Dead Sea Scrolls." *RevQ* 26:305–325.

Newman, Judith. 2018. *Before the Bible: The Liturgical Body and the Formation of Scriptures in Early Judaism*. Oxford: Oxford University Press.

Newsom, Carol. 1990. "'Sectually Explicit' Literature from Qumran." Pages 167–187 in *The Hebrew Bible and Its Interpreters*. Edited by William H. Propp. Winona Lake, IN: Eisenbrauns.

Schiffman, Lawrence H. 2004. "Halakhic Elements in the Sapiential Texts from Qumran." Pages 89–100 in *Sapiential Perspectives: Wisdom Literature in Light of the Dead Sea Scrolls*. Edited by John Collins, Gregory Sterling, and Ruth Clements. STDJ 51. Leiden: Brill.

Schipper, Bernd, and D. Andrew Teeter, eds. 2013. *Wisdom and Torah: The Reception of "Torah" in the Wisdom Literature of the Second Temple Period*. JSJSup 164. Leiden: Brill.

Schmidt, Francis. 2006. "'Recherche son thème de géniture dans le mystère de ce qui doit être': Astrologie et prédestination à Qoumrân." Pages 51–62 *in Qoumrân et le judaïsme du tournant de notre ère*. Edited by André Caquot, André Lemaire, and Simon Claude Mimouni. Leuven: Peeters.

Seeligmann, Isaac L. 2002. "δεῖξαι αὐτῷ φῶς." *Textus* 21:107–128.

Strugnell, John et al. 1956. "Le travail d'édition des fragments manuscrits de Qumrân." *RB* 63:4–67.

Strugnell, John, Daniel Harrington, and Torleif Elgvin. 1999. *Qumran Cave 4 XXIV: Sapiential Texts; Part 2. 4QInstruction (Mûsār lĕ Mēvîn): 4Q415 ff. With a Re-edition of 1Q26*. DJD 34. Oxford: Clarendon.

Tigchelaar, Eibert J.C. 2001. *To Increase Learning for the Understanding Ones: Reading and Reconstructing the Fragmentary Early Jewish Sapiential Text 4QInstruction*. STDJ 44. Leiden: Brill.

Tigchelaar, Eibert J.C. 2010. "Constructing, Deconstructing and Reconstructing Fragmentary Manuscripts: Illustrated by a Study of 4Q184 (4QWiles of the Wicked Woman)." Pages 26–47 in *Rediscovering the Dead Sea Scrolls: An Assessment of Old and New Approaches and Methods*. Edited by Maxine Grossman. Grand Rapids, MI: Eerdmans.

Tigchelaar, Eibert J.C. 2012. "Classifications of the Collection of Dead Sea Scrolls and the Case of *Apocryphon of Jeremiah C*." *JSJ* 43:519–550.

Tooman, William A. 2013. "Wisdom and Torah at Qumran: Evidence from the Sapiential Texts." Pages 203–232 in *Wisdom and Torah: The Reception of "Torah" in the Wisdom Literature of the Second Temple Period*. Edited by Bernd U. Schipper, and D. Andrew Teeter. Leiden: Brill.

Uusimäki, Elisa, 2016. *Turning Proverbs towards Torah: An Analysis of 4Q525*. Leiden: Brill.

Weeks, Stuart. 2016. "Is 'Wisdom Literature' a Useful Category?" Pages 3–23 in *Tracing Sapiential Traditions in Ancient Judaism*. Edited by Hindy Najman, Jean-Sébastien Rey, and Eibert J.C. Tigchelaar. JSJSup 174. Leiden: Brill.

Wright, Benjamin G. "Wisdom Literature." To appear in *Early Judaism and Its Modern Interpreters: Second Edition*. Edited by Matthias Henze and Rodney Werline. Atlanta: SBL.

CHAPTER 10

···

WISDOM IN DIALOGUE
WITH GREEK
CIVILIZATION

···

MICHAEL C. LEGASPI

ONE of the most significant reference works to appear in the last twenty-five years is an ambitious four-volume anthology that makes an impressive array of ancient texts and inscriptions accessible to biblical scholars. The title of this monumental work, *The Context of Scripture* (Hallo 1997–2017), advertises an assemblage of materials that are essential to an understanding of the Bible's "context." The work features texts and inscriptions from Ugarit, Egypt, Mesopotamia, and Anatolia, including many that have been important to the study of Wisdom. Yet, tellingly, it does not include any materials from the Aegean world. The clear implication is that, when it comes to the Hebrew Bible, Greek civilization is not a part of "the context of scripture." The situation is different, of course, when the category of "scripture" is broadened to include Hellenistic Jewish writings and the books of the New Testament, but Greek writings have not played as significant a role in the comparative, historical-critical analysis of the Hebrew Bible as their ancient Near Eastern counterparts have. In the case of biblical Wisdom texts, this is at least mildly surprising, especially given the wide influence of Greek texts and authors on notions of wisdom in Western culture. Yet, to a great degree, the course of modern scholarship in the late nineteenth and early twentieth centuries favored the use of Near Eastern rather than Greek texts and inscriptions to illuminate the backgrounds of biblical Wisdom Literature. At one level, this is understandable. In the time between the French Revolution and the second World War, biblical interpreters gained unprecedented access to the lost peoples and cultures of Egypt, Mesopotamia, and the Levant. Scholars and explorers unearthed texts, deciphered scripts, and reconstructed languages with close geographical relations and strong historical connections to the peoples and lands of the Hebrew Bible. Egyptian, Ugaritic, and Babylonian compositions, to say nothing of the discoveries at Qumran, revolutionized the study of Genesis, Proverbs, and the exploration of suffering and piety in the book of Job. With the rise of scientific archaeology, epigraphy, Egyptology, and Assyriology, biblical scholars now had a wealth of sources by which to illuminate the language, forms, and ideas of Wisdom Literature. They were in a position to understand, in an entirely new way, how the wisdom of Solomon compared to "the wisdom of all the people of the east and all the wisdom of Egypt" (1 Kgs 5:10 [ET 4:30]).

The fact that the peoples of the Aegean were not included in this biblical comparison lends oblique support to the strategy of looking east and southwest to reconstruct a venue for the ancient, cross-cultural dialogue in which Solomon and fellow Israelites apparently participated. Nevertheless, both classicists and biblical scholars have shown that contacts between Near Eastern and Aegean civilizations had important reflexes for the development of art, architecture, language, and religious forms. In an influential and important work published first in German in 1984 and then translated into English, Walter Burkert (1992) documented the influence of eastern peoples on the Greeks in the Homeric epoch spanning the eighth and seventh centuries BCE. This influence was evident not only in artifacts and commercial goods but also in the adoption of the Semitic alphabet, scribal technologies and practices, and, importantly, various religious and literary *topoi* as well. What Burkert set out to challenge in his book was the long-standing habit of studying ancient Greece in isolation, as an organic, more or less self-contained culture that evolved in ways particular to its own Hellenic genius. This habit, he argues, was the result of developments in German scholarship in the eighteenth and nineteenth centuries, including a Herderian "romantic nationalism" which understood cultures largely in terms of their unique animating spirits. Burkert also points, in this connection, to the assimilation of Greece and Rome to an Indo-European rather than Semitic cultural-linguistic tradition. With *Black Athena* (1987–2006), Martin Bernal sought, famously and controversially, to challenge the notion of an "Aryan" Greece by emphasizing its debts to and points of contact with Egyptian and West Semitic peoples.

Turning specifically to Israel, the redoubtable Cyrus Gordon (1962) argued that Israel and Greece sprang from the same roots. Denying that Greece was a "hermetically sealed Olympian miracle" and that Israel was a "vacuum-packed miracle from Sinai," Gordon identified the two as close relatives, or, to use an architectural metaphor, as "parallel structures built upon the same East Mediterranean foundation" (9). Both developed in the second half of the second millennium BCE, in the wake of events associated with the "Amarna Age," with the result that obvious differences between Greek and Israelite works are best understood within a broader context of shared language and culture (Gordon 1955, 46). It is not merely difference that deserves our attention, but similarity as well. In more recent works, scholars have continued to make the case for Greece as a companion civilization to Israel, one with which fruitful comparisons can and should be made. Much like Gordon, John Pairman Brown (1995) adduces a wide variety of evidence, chiefly philological, which supports an understanding of Greece and Israel as two similar, complementary civilizations emerging in the early part of the Iron Age. Both flourished by means of citadels surrounded by rain-watered fields, employed iron weapons and alphabetic scripts, and produced writings befitting the free societies that they had created on the edges of the wider ancient Near Eastern cultural sphere—with Israel landlocked just inside it, and sea-faring Greece just beyond its western edge (Brown 2003, 6–9). Jan Bremmer (2008) and Thomas Römer (2015) have also explored the value of Greek parallels for understanding loanwords, mythological elements, literary tropes, and social and religious institutions in the Hebrew Bible. For the most part, though, scholars working in this vein have not integrated comparative studies of wisdom into larger, eastern Mediterranean contextualizations of Greek and Israelite civilizations (a valuable and notable exception is the essay by Sara J. Denning-Bolle [1987]).

10.1 ATHENS AND JERUSALEM

This is remarkable because Israel and Greece have, for centuries, been paired as parallel sources of wisdom that furnish an essential, even defining dialectic within Western culture, variously represented as the tension between sacred and secular, religion and science, faith and reason. Even Brown, who looks at ancient Israel and Greece as a philologist and ancient historian, resorts to the old duality, seeing Greece and Israel ultimately in terms of faith and reason (2003, 44–48). The dualism is indeed an old one. In antiquity, Jews and Greeks were thought to espouse comparable wisdoms. Theophrastus, pupil of and successor to Aristotle, famously described the Jews as a "nation of philosophers" (φιλόσοφοι τὸ γένος) in his lost treatise on piety (Stern 1974, 10). Beginning at least with Aristobulus of Alexandria, the famed exegete and philosopher of the second century BCE, Jews identified the formidable figure of *sophia* (σοφία) personified in LXX Proverbs 8 with the same wisdom propounded by Plato, Pythagoras, the Stoics, and the Peripatetics (Holladay 1995, 153–155, 181). Philo, of course, saw wisdom as a point of contact, indeed a point of convergence between the biblical tradition and Greek philosophy (*De virtutibus* 65; *De specialibus legibus* 2.165–166). In the early church, Tertullian rejected philosophy and turned the pairing into an opposition between "Jerusalem" and "Athens," whereas others like Clement and Justin Martyr understood the Greek quest for wisdom in more conciliatory terms, as a preparation for the Christian Gospel among the pagans (Clement, *Stromata* 1.5) or as evidence of God's bestowal of a "generative word" (σπερματικός λόγος) on all humans (Justin Martyr, *Apology* I, 44). In his commentary on Song of Songs, Origen describes Greek philosophy itself as an ordered pursuit of knowledge that was borrowed from Israel and from Solomon in particular. The Greeks divided this pursuit into three branches: moral philosophy, the study of nature, and the contemplation of unseen realities. Yet Origen maintains that Solomon did this long before the Greeks did when he wrote about ethics and virtue in Proverbs, the things of nature in Ecclesiastes, and, in allegorical fashion, communion with God in Song of Songs (Origen 1957, 39–41).

Later Christians continued to see biblical writings and Greek pagan literature as parallel (though unequal) sources of moral inspiration and intellectual insight. Basil of Caesarea, for example, wrote that, in spite of their theological shortcomings, the writings of Hesiod and Homer should be valued. According to Basil, Hesiod exhorts young men to undertake the rough and steep path to moral improvement, and "all Homer's poetry is an encomium of virtue" (*On Greek Literature*, 5). Thus, Homer became a staple in the education of young men in the Byzantine Empire. Byzantine philosophers also studied and commented on Aristotle and Neoplatonic authors like Plotinus, even as they maintained, at the same time, a distinction between the useful but limited "outer wisdom" of Greek pagans and the orthodox "inner wisdom" of the theological tradition (Louth 2007, 319–322). In the Latin West, Thomas Aquinas effected a lasting synthesis of Christian doctrine and Greek philosophy. He opens the *Summa contra gentiles*, for example, with a discussion of wisdom that draws on Proverbs 8, Aristotle's *Metaphysics*, 1 Corinthians 3, and a statement of Jesus from John 18—in that order. Though the rediscovery of Greek learning in the Renaissance yielded a style and method of appropriating ancient philosophy that differed from that of the scholastics, it ultimately reinforced the pairing of Greek and biblical texts as sources for wisdom in modern culture. Erasmus is famous for championing a form of Christian piety (what he called *philosophia Christi*) that was based as much on study of the Scriptures and the church fathers as on a deep immersion in classical literature. Almost as if to parallel Solomon's four thousand proverbs and songs (1 Kgs 5:12 [ET 4:32]), Erasmus compiled and commented on over four thousand sayings from classical authors in his famous *Adages*. Nothing was more natural for Erasmus and fellow humanists than to think of wisdom as something that was available to learned inquirers in both classical and biblical texts.

Erasmus is a convenient figure by which to mark the beginnings of an early modern classical-biblical synthesis that would last well into the eighteenth century. This synthesis was undergirded, for a time, by the notion that Plato learned his wisdom from the likes of Pythagoras, Orpheus, and Hermes Trismegistus who, in turn, inherited their wisdom from Moses or even earlier biblical luminaries (Walker 1972, 1–3). Even when scholars discredited this historical sequence on philological grounds and abandoned the notion of a *prisca theologia* or "ancient theology" underlying both classical and biblical wisdoms, classical erudition and biblical interpretation remained essential to the stewardship of a common cultural inheritance. Students at early modern European universities, for instance, studied Greek and Latin authors in the arts faculty before undertaking advanced biblical study in the theology faculty (or, alternatively, pursuing law and medicine in those faculties; see Legaspi 2010, 28–33). In this way, the complementarity of Greco-Roman civilization and biblical study was an institutional reality as well as a cultural ideal. The pairing, however, was not always placid. In the wake of criticisms directed against the historical veracity, textual integrity, and Mosaic authorship of the Pentateuch in the seventeenth century—carried out famously by Baruch Spinoza and Richard Simon—the cultural prestige of the Bible declined. It became possible, in a new way, to honor both the moral teachings of the Bible (Spinoza) and to uphold its doctrinal content (Simon) while at the same time criticizing it as an ancient and imperfect text that is the product of its own time and place. When compared to the considerable corpus of Greek and Roman philosophers, poets, orators, dramatists, and historians, the collection of Hebrew texts in the Old Testament seemed, in this new light, to be small and inferior.

It was against the backdrop of the cultural devaluation of the Bible that Robert Lowth, in his famous lectures on Hebrew poetry at Oxford between 1741 and 1750, plotted a new direction for the study of the Bible in relation to its classical counterparts. Lowth conceded that biblical compositions might indeed be found wanting when analyzed according to classical canons of taste, eloquence, and refinement. Yet when understood as models of *Hebrew* poetry, as examples of a poetic style particular to the ancient Hebrews, they shine forth in sacred splendor. Lowth, a skillful reader of classics in his own right, believed that the pairing of classical and biblical had become detrimental to the latter (Legaspi 2010, 107–115). To maintain the Bible's reputation as a book both sublime and wise, he surgically separated the Hebrew Bible from its conjoined, classical twin, freeing it to "live" independently. As denizens of an even remoter antiquity, the Hebrews possessed wisdom in a "rude and unfinished state," but the parallelistic sayings of the sages made the transmission of wisdom pleasant and effective (Lowth 1829, 200). When analyzed as a Greek drama and compared to the works of Sophocles and Aeschylus, the book of Job is "lame and imperfect"; yet, when understood according to Hebrew poetic genius, it is beautiful, perfect, and without rival in Hebrew literature (Lowth 1829, 280–281).

Lowth's strategy of separation carried the day. When the great classicist Friedrich August Wolf arrived at university in 1777 and defiantly refused to enroll in theology, matriculating instead as *studiosus philologiae*, he defined a moment when "philology broke free of theology" (Burkert 1992, 2). As Anthony Grafton (1991, 214–243) has shown, the break was not absolute: Wolf's ground-breaking work on Homer was modeled on the Pentateuchal criticism of Johann Gottfried Eichhorn. Nevertheless, Wolf and fellow philhellenists like Wilhelm von Humboldt charted a path for classical studies that was oriented away from theology and biblical studies and toward a recovery of Greek civilization in its own right. Biblical scholars, for their part, sought to understand biblical Wisdom Literature in terms of internal Israelite developments and Near Eastern parallels. They thus disdained formal comparisons of biblical books with Greek compositions. For example, Eichhorn and W.M.L. de Wette, in their Old Testament introductions, dismiss attempts to see the book of Job as an epic poem or a Greek-style tragedy. Despite the fact that Egyptian and Mesopotamian advice literature were unknown at the time, nineteenth-century scholars were already predisposed to understand the "international" character of wisdom in terms of "Oriental," rather than Aegean parallels (Smend 1995, 264). One vestige of the old biblical-classical pairing that did survive into the nineteenth century, however, was the tendency to treat biblical Wisdom books as examples of or contributions to "philosophy." It was certainly possible to see Ecclesiastes, which was often dated to the post-exilic period, as a text with affinities for Epicureanism and skeptical philosophies (more on this below), but the idea that Wisdom books were "philosophical" did not, by and large, yield sustained comparisons between them and texts from Greece's archaic or classical periods. To be sure, the dating of Proverbs to the early monarchic period and the tendency to date Job even earlier made such comparisons seem unpromising or even irrelevant, but scholarly motivations were not merely historiographic. A more pressing concern in the nineteenth century, as Will Kynes

(2016) has argued, was to understand the possible role of Wisdom Literature as an authentic Israelite source for a "universalistic, humanistic, and philosophical" religion that was "independent of Israel's particularistic theocracy, cult, and law" (97). The real dialogue, then, was not with Greek philosophers but with German ones.

An example from the early twentieth century illustrates the way in which the study of Wisdom reflected a similar tension for Jewish scholars. Educated at the University of Prague, Moriz Friedländer (1844–1919) served as secretary for a Jewish relief organization in Vienna called the Israelitische Allianz. More an activist, perhaps, than a scholar, he wrote on a wide variety of scholarly topics with the aim of advancing the cause of liberal Judaism (Brenner 1999). Friedländer (1898) entered contemporary debates about the origins of Gnosticism, arguing that it was a pre-Christian movement that developed among Jews in Hellenistic Alexandria. Friedländer saw Hellenized, diasporic Judaism, with its universalistic aspirations and its embrace of Greek culture and Gnostic ideas, as an older and more genuine form of Judaism than Palestinian, Pharisaic Judaism. In 1904, Friedländer published a book entitled *Griechische Philosophie im Alten Testament: Eine Einleitung in die Psalmen- und Weisheitsliteratur*, in which he argued that the Wisdom Literature was itself a product of Palestinian Jewish contact with Greek culture after Alexander. He dates Proverbs and Job to the beginning of the third century and Ecclesiastes to the end of that century, connecting them to a worldwide "Sturm und Drang" period and identifying them with a modernized "Mosaismus" that would become a true world religion in the work of later interpreters like Philo (14). Job and Proverbs reflect the impulses of a vigorous Hellenistic culture and the authors' laudable attempts to embrace its elevated understanding of God and its valorization of reason, while, at the same time, rejecting atheism (Job) and achieving a *via media* between old and new (Prov 4:27: "Turn neither to the right nor to the left"). By Qoheleth's time, though, the new philosophy had cooled and become commonplace, the subject of too many books (Eccl 12:12: "Of making many books there is no end"). Like the authors of Job and Proverbs, Qoheleth steers a middle course between hyper-righteous reaction (Eccl 7:16: "Do not be too righteous, and do not act too wise") and uncritical acceptance of the new philosophy, which, by the Hasmonean period, had degenerated into a vulgar, nihilistic Epicureanism. Qoheleth thus counsels moderate enjoyment of God-given pleasures and constant awareness of divine judgment. As for earlier German Protestants, the Wisdom Literature was, for Friedländer, the site of negotiation between a particularistic Jewish tradition and a philosophical Greek universalism.

10.2 HEBREW AND GREEK THOUGHT

Before turning to specific treatments of Israelite Wisdom texts and putative Greek counterparts in recent times, it is necessary to mark a distinctive way in which the old juxtaposition of classical and biblical re-emerged in the inter-war period, despite a parting of the ways between classicists and biblical scholars. Burkert (1992, 4) notes that in this period German scholars tended to approach ancient cultures in terms of internal form and style, as self-contained entities, downplaying the role of foreign influences in their development. As he notes, there were exceptions to this hermeneutical approach, but the prevailing mood was isolationist and comparative rather than diffusionist and integrative. The resurgence of this approach, which hearkened back to the Romantic, *völkisch* ("nationalistic") tendencies of the early nineteenth century, may be counted among the effects of Oswald Spengler's bombshell, *The Decline of the West*, initially published in German in 1918 (*Der Untergang des Abendlandes*) and translated into English in 1926. The details of Spengler's historical analysis, many of which have been criticized and contested, need not be rehearsed here. What is important to note, however, is that Spengler saw world history as a venue for self-particular cultures that, though distinct from one another, nevertheless undergo the same organic processes of development (aging from "spring" to "summer" to "autumn") before reaching a "winter" in which these cultures, having exhausted their own internal possibilities, become technologically advanced but decadent "civilizations" that then die their own natural deaths (21, 31, table I). Classical civilization reached its winter in the fourth century; according to Spengler, Western civilization did so in the nineteenth century (32). Spengler denied a doctrine of progress, a simple linear movement of a generalized humanity from ancient to medieval to modern to something even better. By doing so, he made it possible to see the outlines of Western civilization in sharp relief and to understand it as a peculiar kind of ("Faustian") endeavor (159). On this view, Western civilization is distinct from classical culture and civilization and distinct, too, from a "Magian" culture that included Judaism and Christianity but ultimately culminated in classical Islamic civilization (183).

Spengler's highly influential book helped to shape a mid-century discourse among scholars of the Bible and ancient Near East, one that featured attempts to understand what made Hebrew thought and culture distinctive over and against its classical counterparts. It also included efforts to show, contra Spengler's relegation of Judaism to a spent Magian civilization, that Hebrew thought has indeed been relevant to Western culture. This discourse did not concern itself with historical connections between biblical and classical texts but rather with a holistic, intellectual-historical study of ancient modes of thought and their contributions to the modern world. In an influential, two-volume work originally published in Danish in 1920 and entitled, *Israel: Its Life and Culture* (1926–1940), Johannes Pedersen argues that Hebrew thought is not logical and discursive but sensory and immediate, oriented toward totalities, images, and action. On this account, wisdom is not theoretical or contemplative but rather a skill by which one produces the thought that yields the right result (1926, 127). In 1952, Norwegian biblical scholar Thorleif Boman published a study of Hebrew thought, *Das Hebräische Denken im Vergleich mit dem Griechischen* (the English translation *Hebrew Thought Compared with Greek* appeared in 1960). The work became widely influential, as it was translated into English and Japanese and appeared in five German editions, the last in 1968. Boman's book was indebted to the work of Pedersen. Yet, as Boman's title suggests, it was not merely a study of ancient Israel but an effort to recover a mode of Hebrew thought in opposition, specifically, to Greek thought. It is not only the title that is binary but the chapters as well: for example, static or dynamic thought; perception through appearance or by way of impression; spatial or temporal orientations toward reality; logical thinking or psychological understanding. The first member of each of these pairs describes the Greeks, and the second describes the Hebrews; thus: "rest, harmony, composure, and self-control—this is the Greek way; movement, life, deep emotion, and power—this is the Hebrew way" (Boman 1960, 205). James Barr (1961, 46–79) criticized Boman extensively and, perhaps, definitively in *The Semantics of Biblical Language*, arguing that putative distinctions between Hebrew and Greek *thought* cannot be based merely on differences in the two *languages*.

Barr took aim not only at Boman and Pedersen but also at an Anglophone phenomenon: the biblical theology movement. Barr's targets erred by using philology to prove the existence of a distinctive Hebrew mentality, but others approached the concept of distinctiveness without attaching philosophical significance, for example, to Hebrew verbal tenses or the etymology of λόγος. In his famous 1946 essay on the scar of Odysseus passage (*Od.* 19) and the *Aqedah* (Gen 22:1–19), Erich Auerbach (2003, 14–15) drew attention to essential differences between Homeric and biblical literature, arguing that the former is intended to delight and bewitch the senses whereas the latter, "fraught with background," stakes a "tyrannical" claim to truth that banishes all other perspectives. According to Auerbach, the two are touchstones for the representation of reality in the greater Western literary tradition, a version of Athens and Jerusalem in the aesthetic rather than theological realm. In the year that Auerbach's essay appeared, a group of scholars including Henri Frankfort and Thorkild Jacobsen published *The Intellectual Adventure of Ancient Man*, which later appeared under the title *Before Philosophy* in 1949. Focusing on ancient Babylon and Egypt, the authors explain the nature of primitive "mythopoeic" thought in these two cultures. However, the final chapter, "The Emancipation of Thought from Myth," takes up Hebrew and Greek thought. In it, the authors assert that the Israelites developed an exalted, abstract conception of the one God that emboldened them to reject myths and images that fell beneath God's dignity. By virtue of "moral courage" the Israelites rose above their neighbors, but by virtue of "intellectual courage" the Greeks went even farther in their rejection of myth (Frankfort et al. 1949, 247–248). Focusing on the pre-Socratic philosophers, the authors claim that the Greeks ultimately transposed ultimate questions to the realm of critical reflection. Reality and the world were, for the first time, fully open to human reason. They quote Heraclitus to this effect: "Wisdom is one thing. It is to know the *thought* by which all things are steered through all things" (Frankfort et al. 1949, 255). In positing a distinction between Hebrew and Greek thought, mid-century authors did not always resort specifically to concepts of wisdom (or indeed to interpretations of Wisdom Literature) to register what they regarded as essential differences. Yet, as the scope of their investigations and the generality of their conclusions make clear, their interests were not antiquarian but dialectical. The goal was to see classical tradition, essentialized as "Greek thought," and biblical tradition, identified with "Hebrew thought," in relation to modern culture and to one another. Put differently, these were attempts to understand the

Western intellectual inheritance by attending to the distinctive wisdoms of the Greeks and the Hebrews. Boman and Auerbach saw them as complementary. Henri Frankfort saw them as alike but unequal. But all thought it necessary to engage them both at a time when the future of a Western civilization descended from the two appeared to hang in the balance.

These mid-century treatments reflect, among other things, special anxieties about the prospects of modern culture and its traditional foundations. While attempts to isolate the character of Hebrew thought in connection with these anxieties did not disappear entirely in the second half of the twentieth century, the vogue for comparative thought seemed, for the most part, to pass. Newer approaches, owing in part to Barr's (1961) criticism of philosophically oriented philology, abandoned a quest for Wisdom that is intelligible chiefly in lexicographic terms or in terms of some putative ancient (even primitive) Israelite mindset. Many scholars focused instead on the relation of Wisdom to other Israelite traditions and institutions, notably monarchy, prophecy, cult, and apocalypticism. Hartmut Gese (1958, 2), for example, staked out a distinctive position when he described Wisdom, intramurally, as an alien body within the Old Testament. In *Wisdom in Israel*, Gerhard von Rad (1972, 10) noted a flagging interest in the comparison of Israelite wisdom "with the wisdom of neighboring cultures." Accordingly, von Rad examined the place of Wisdom, as his title indicates, "in" Israel and not outside of it, arguing that Wisdom, which developed in a school setting, nevertheless bore an integral relation to traditional Yahwism. When, in recent decades, scholars have turned to extramural comparisons of Wisdom Literature and Greek civilization, they have done so in very focused ways. Instead of large-scale comparisons involving "Hebrew thought" or the like, scholars have tended to take up narrower questions regarding the relation of the Greeks to the Wisdom books of the Hebrew Bible.

10.3 ECCLESIASTES

The question of Greek influence on Ecclesiastes has been a durable and much contested topic in the history of the book's interpretation. While some argue that Qoheleth was a philosopher directly engaged with Hellenistic traditions and schools of thought (Braun 1973), others like R.N. Whybray (1998, 245) maintain that Qoheleth is best understood as a Jewish theologian whose views fall squarely "within the boundaries of the essential features of Judaism." Christoph Uehlinger (1997) argues for a third option: to understand Qoheleth not simply in terms of Judaism or Hellenism but against the background of ancient Near Eastern cultures of the Persian and Hellenistic periods. More specifically, Uehlinger characterizes Qoheleth's "philosophy of joy" as a "scarlet thread" that runs throughout the book and suggests a very particular *Sitz im Leben*: the philosophical banquet or symposium (230–235). Keenly conscious of death, Qoheleth writes or speaks as a kind of symposiarch who calls for enjoyment of life. That the book of Ecclesiastes has also been understood as a pessimistic work is a testament to the book's obscurity, the difficulty involved in identifying it with one definite idea or outlook. One possible point of connection to Greek thought that has proven attractive to many is philosophical skepticism and the extent to which Qoheleth may or may not be identified with it.

In a survey of works examining skepticism within the Hebrew Bible, William Anderson (1999, 239–245) describes notable attempts by Robert Davidson (1983), James Crenshaw (1980), and others to identify a skeptical tradition in ancient Israel. As Anderson points out, the very word "skeptic" is of Greek origin (225). Anderson draws on the work of Jonathan Barnes (1990), a scholar of ancient Greek philosophy, to arrive at a loose definition of skepticism as a "disposition which attacks dogmatic assertions (of truth or absolute knowledge) with doubt and questions" (233). With a definition as broad as this one, Anderson is able to affirm that many biblical books, including Ecclesiastes, are skeptical by virtue of their doubting spirit and apparent rejections of dogma. To illuminate the specific question of *Greek* influence on skeptical biblical texts, though, one would have to undertake a more specific comparison. Johannes Pedersen (1930), for example, considers whether or in what sense Ecclesiastes might be an example of "Israelite skepticism" when compared to specific schools of Greek thought. There are a number of Greek philosophical approaches that recommend themselves for comparison with Ecclesiastes. The continual flowing of rivers to a sea that is never full (Eccl 1:7) and the pairing of opposites in the catalogue of times (Eccl 3:1–8) recall Heraclitus's statements on the constancy of change and the perpetual conflict of opposites (339). Ecclesiastes 3 also has affinities for Zeno and Stoic teachings, specifically the embeddedness of human life within a fixed natural order and, indeed, the wisdom of living in conformity with such order (340). Pedersen points thirdly to Epicureanism, which denies the immortality or transcendence of the human soul and prescribes the attainment of ἀταραξία ("freedom from disturbance") through moderate pleasures; so, too, does Qoheleth (340–341).

Instead of proving that Greek philosophy contributed to the skeptical outlook of Ecclesiastes, however, these similarities demonstrate, for Pedersen, how little these philosophies actually have in common with the biblical book. When it comes to social conventions, certain dogmatic claims about the metaphysical realm, or the pursuit of wealth and power, Stoics and Epicureans, as well as Cynics and followers of Heraclitus, might well adopt skeptical attitudes. Yet, Pedersen argues, their goals were constructive, and their outlooks were fundamentally optimistic: to embrace flux and struggle as divine goods (Heraclitus) and to insulate the individual against the turbulences of a troubled world and to cultivate the health and happiness of the soul (Stoicism, Epicureanism, Cynicism; 341–344). By contrast, Pedersen writes that Qoheleth is a teacher of despair: "his wisdom is resignation" (322). Ecclesiastes is not so much an example of Greek skepticism as of radical pessimism. The author of Ecclesiastes may have been influenced by Hellenistic philosophy in a very general way, but, if so, it served only to distort the faith of Qoheleth and to wreak "destructive effects" on the "foreign civilization" of the Jews (363). Pedersen's analysis is another example of the tendency to see Greek and Jewish traditions as distinct cultural organisms. Yet even when such a tendency is not necessarily at work, it has proven difficult to establish a tight correspondence between Greek skepticism and Ecclesiastes.

Jonathan Barnes (1999), mentioned above, used his expertise in Greek philosophy to evaluate whether Ecclesiastes reflects the influence of Greek skepticism. Barnes turns specifically to Pyrrho and the detailed exposition of his philosophy by Sextus Empiricus. The essential requirement of skepticism in the Pyrrhonian tradition is the suspension of judgment ($\epsilon\pi o\chi\acute{\eta}$) for philosophical reasons; it is the decision to withhold belief with respect to a specific question or set of questions because there are objectively valid (not simply personal) reasons for doing so. Though many statements within Ecclesiastes comport well with a skeptical attitude, Barnes denies that the book, taken as a whole, meets the requirements of Pyrrhonian skepticism. The author does not provide reasons for withholding belief on occasions when he claims that humans cannot know things. To confess ignorance and to suspend judgment for specific reasons are two different things. Additionally, Qoheleth functions too often in the role of a teacher with a definite lesson for him to ring true as a Greek skeptic. Though Pedersen (oddly) does not include Pyrrho or Sextus Empiricus in his essay on "Israelite skepticism" and Barnes (sensibly) does in his essay, the two come to remarkably similar conclusions: Qoheleth is not a skeptic but a pessimist. According to Pedersen, he despairs of meaning and satisfaction and settles for prudence in an unpredictable world (Pedersen 1930, 326). According to Barnes, Qoheleth is not pessimistic about the attainment of knowledge but pessimistic, rather, about its usefulness (112).

Another Greek figure who has been connected to the Wisdom Literature of the Hebrew Bible is the sixth-century BCE poet Theognis of Megara. The collection of elegiac verse that was transmitted under his name (*Theognidea*) contains contributions from a variety of poets, but a portion of the collection addressed to Theognis's friend Kyrnos is usually attributed to Theognis himself. In his book on Ecclesiastes and skepticism, Stuart Weeks (2012, 134–136) points out similarities between the writings of Theognis and Qoheleth. Theognis adopts a posture toward human toil reminiscent of Qoheleth, noting that, for reasons beyond human control, effort does not always produce the desired results. Life is a hardship to be endured, but humans should relish what joy they can while they are young and vigorous. For Weeks, the similarity raises a useful point about skepticism. When part of the biblical canon, this advice seems skeptical and radical, but it "seems much less unusual when it is considered in the context of ancient literature more broadly" (136). No one regards Theognis as a skeptic. With respect to the question of skepticism, then, Theognis is a useful negative example, much as Pyrrho is for Barnes, albeit in a different way.

10.4 PROVERBS

Ecclesiastes, however, is not the only book that has invited comparison with Theognis. John Pairman Brown (1995), following M.L. West, sees in the Theognis collection evidence for a westward diffusion of the proverb form, from the Near East to Greece and eventually to Rome (291). Similarities between the book of Proverbs and the proverbs of

Theognis suggest a common literary form, a shared outlook, and similar socio-political settings. Elegiac couplets resemble biblical *meshalim* in length and structure. Common themes in the collections include the need to accumulate wealth justly, surround oneself with honest companions, pursue an enlightened self-interest, and reckon honestly with instances of injustice in the world. Brown also cites couplets of Theognis that are close parallels to specific biblical proverbs (5:15; 14:20; 16:18; 19:21; 27:1), all of which reinforce the idea that the well-to-do "good" man must also stay within his limits and avoid pride, ambition, and impiety. Brown also notes the prominence of imagery, metaphors, and advice related to gold in both collections (299–308). According to Brown, the development of gold-economies, again spreading from east to west, facilitated international trade and cultural diffusion, but it also produced new classes of unscrupulous plutocrats. What one finds in Proverbs and in the advice offered by Theognis are prescriptions that reflect the experience of landed aristocrats seeking to live by a wisdom that produces wealth honestly, one that is superior to "gold" and all that "gold" represents (Prov 8:19–20). Here, then, is a different, non-philosophical variety of skepticism.

Given the prominence of ethical topics in the book of Proverbs, it makes sense that scholars have turned to Athenian moral philosophy to search for illuminative parallels. Those who have done so have not pursued lines of historical inquiry but have instead compared Greek ethics to Proverbs for what are commonly referred to as "heuristic" purposes. To what extent, if any, does a comparison with Greek figures help to clarify the intellectual framework of an anthology that contains no explicit theory? The very language of academic investigation—"ethics," "heuristic," and "theory"—reflects a heavy debt to Greek categories (also a Greek word). The intuition, then, that an explicit comparison with Greek philosophy might bring the moral philosophy of Proverbs into clearer scholarly focus would seem to be a sound one. Michael Fox (2007) argues that three of Socrates's most important and controversial ethical principles also underlie ethical teaching in Proverbs. These include the claims that "virtue is knowledge," "no one does wrong willingly," and "all virtues are one." If Fox is right, then the ethical enterprise in Proverbs is a heavily intellectual one, with tremendous value placed on education and the attainment of knowledge.

Turning to Aristotle, Christopher Ansberry (2010) sees Aristotelian ethics as a better analogue to the ethical theory of Proverbs than what Fox identifies with Socratic ethics. Ansberry argues, rightly, that Aristotle attributed a greater role to character in ethical performance than to knowledge per se and that, accordingly, he emphasized habituation and instruction in ethical formation in ways that resemble the sages of Proverbs. One might also add that the eudaimonism of Aristotle may be closer to the outlook of Proverbs than previously acknowledged (Schwáb 2013, 91–93). Yet, as Ansberry (2010, 169) points out, key differences must also be recognized. There is no notion of a "golden mean" in Proverbs, and Aristotle's catalog of virtues in *Nicomachean Ethics* does not include biblical virtues like mercy and loyalty. In a comprehensive, comparative discussion of ethical thought in Greek philosophy and the Hebrew Bible, Seizō Sekine (2005, 171–196) devotes a chapter to virtues as enumerated by Aristotle and the book of Proverbs. Like Ansberry, he indicates significant overlaps while noting differences.

Proverbs says very little about bravery, liberality, magnificence, and high-mindedness, whereas Aristotle has nothing to say about humility and faith (Sekine 2005, 184–189). According to Sekine, ethics in Proverbs is framed by a belief in divine retribution, whereas Aristotle's ethics is not.

10.5 JOB

Turning to the book of Job, Katharine Dell (1991) has made the case for it as an example of skeptical literature. Dell dates the book to the fourth century, just before the conquests of Alexander, and therefore denies any direct Greek influence on the author of Job. Nevertheless, she argues that the book had its origins in a small, philosophically minded group of sages "which can be likened to the milieu of the Greek sceptics" (215). Just as the latter practiced a principled suspension of judgment in the face of dogmatic assertions by rival philosophers, the author of Job has created a work in which the withholding of belief is essential to a larger, ironic aim. Dell sees skepticism in the speeches of Job, a man who refuses to assent to his friends' propositions concerning God, justice, and piety. More significantly, Dell sees skepticism in the literary form of the work itself: the juxtaposition of elements (prologue/epilogue, dialogues, God's speeches, Job's humble response) manifestly in tension with one another prevents the reader from arriving at a firm judgment about the meaning of Job's ordeal. The point of the book, which Dell describes as a "parody," is to unsettle belief by "misusing" conventional literary forms. The identification of Job as a parody, then, is a second way in which Dell forges a connection with the Greeks. Though the book of Jonah is, for Dell, the example of a parody closest to Job, she also regards parallels with Greek parodies (for example, by Aristophanes) as instructive. In turning to ancient Greece to understand Job by means of formal parallels and conceptual similarities rather than direct lines of historical influence, Dell follows a very old tradition.

Instead of the parody, though, it was epic and Greek drama that were thought to yield the closest analogues to Job. As Ann Astell (1994) demonstrates in her fine book on medieval understandings of Job, interpreters read Job as an epic and a purveyor of what she calls "epic truth." Along with the *Iliad*, *Odyssey*, and *Aeneid*, the book of Job was thought to illustrate how humans, though weak and mortal, may nevertheless master their lower selves and reach their divinely appointed ends as beings with immortal souls (1–10). The notion that Job is best understood in terms of a Greek tragedy is also an old one. As early as the fifth century, Theodore of Mopsuestia suggested that the book of Job was an imitation of a Greek tragedy. The suggestion proved to be a durable one (see, for example, Gordon 1962, 299–300). As noted above, it was something of a commonplace in early modern studies of Job. More recently, the suggestion has been renewed on form-critical grounds (see Mies 2003). Of all the Greek tragedies, the Prometheus trilogy of Aeschylus has most often been linked to Job (note, however, the attempt of Horace Kallen [1918] to show that Job is a Euripidean drama). Like Job, Prometheus in

Prometheus Bound suffers at the hands of a supreme divine power. He believes that the punishment that Zeus has decreed for him is unjust. Though chained to a rock, he will not acquiesce in spirit nor divulge a secret that has the power to undo Zeus. As in the book of Job, there is very little action. The drama is one of ideas, an examination of the contest between a higher power and authority on the one hand and the knowledge, integrity, and compassion of the subordinate on the other. In response to the defiance of Prometheus, Zeus unleashes a storm on Prometheus as the play draws to a close. As it stands, the play bears clear similarities to Job, but because only fragments of the two remaining plays in the trilogy (*Prometheus Unbound* and *Prometheus the Fire-Carrier*) have survived, the full trajectory of the Aeschylean story must remain a matter of conjecture. While the parallel has proven attractive, uncertainty about the dating of Job makes it difficult to advance non-circular historical arguments regarding the relation of Job to any of the classical Greek tragedies.

Similarly, the *sui generis* character of the book's structure, the considerable disorder of chapters 22–31, and uncertainty about the exact compositional history of the book of Job all make it difficult to identify the formal elements of Greek tragedy in the book without performing certain feats of imagination and emendation. No less important than historical or formal considerations are the perspectives that the two works take on justice, human suffering, and the nature of divine authority. For the great classicist Gilbert Murray (1968), the book of Job shows that, whereas the "democratic Greek instinctively cared more for Law and Justice . . . the Oriental, accustomed to the rule of a despot or monarch, cared most for obedience to the supreme Power" (95). For biblical scholar William Irwin (1950, 101–102), though, the book of Job and its subtle intimations of hope represent a far wiser, more profound understanding of suffering than what one sees in the defiance of Prometheus: "With all its greatness, Aeschylus' answer to man's most poignant question seems, by contrast, adolescent."

10.6 Conclusion

This survey of attempts to coordinate biblical Wisdom Literature to Greek civilization is, in many ways, a limited one. It is limited in scope, both with respect to topics and to specific works discussed. It has no doubt left a great many worthy and important things out of account. More consequentially, it is limited in its understanding. It is helpful to remember that wisdom is a difficult and elusive thing to understand. There is a great deal to commend Sekine's (2005, 1–5) suggestion that classical and biblical authors, though different in essential respects, were nevertheless united in their experience of wonder, the strange condition of being impressed, somehow, by reality (see also Brown 2014). As Socrates, Plato, and Aristotle all affirmed, wonder is philosophically generative. That the experience of wonder should yield a search for understanding, a pursuit of wisdom, is fitting. A survey like this one may point to the literary vestiges of such pursuits, but it does little to capture the vital realities behind them. If it fails in this respect, it also fails in one other way. The two-sidedness of the wisdom discourse considered here, one composed of a dialogue between the "classical" and the "biblical," is itself exceedingly difficult to understand (see Legaspi 2018). It is hard to do it justice. The familiarity of the pairing conceals its extraordinariness. The encounter of Greek thought with biblical tradition was certainly, from the point of view of later observers, a historical accident, but the continuation of a dialogue between them over the centuries was not a historical necessity. It might have been otherwise. One may well wonder at this, too. In describing the relation of classical pursuits of wisdom to biblical ones, one sooner or later confronts what is probably an unanswerable question. To ask why the two have traveled so far in one another's company is to ask why Western civilization is what it is and not something else. It is to wonder, finally, why peoples in various periods have aspired to dwell in Athens, or in Jerusalem, or, stranger still, in both places at once.

WORKS CITED

Anderson, William H.U. 1999. "What Is Skepticism and Can It Be Found in the Hebrew Bible?" *SJOT* 13:225–257.

Ansberry, Christopher B. 2010. "What Does Jerusalem Have to Do with Athens? The Moral Vision of the Book of Proverbs and Aristotle's *Nicomachean Ethics*." *HS* 51:157–173.

Astell, Ann W. 1994. *Job, Boethius, and Epic Truth*. Ithaca, NY: Cornell University Press.

Auerbach, Erich. 2003. *Mimesis: The Representation of Reality in Western Literature*. Translated by Willard R. Trask. Princeton, NJ: Princeton University Press. Orig. 1946. *Mimesis: dargestellte Wirklichkeit in der abendländischen Literatur*. Bern: Francke.

Barnes, Jonathan. 1990. *The Toils of Scepticism*. Cambridge: Cambridge University Press.

Barnes, Jonathan. 1999. "L'Ecclésiaste et le scepticisme grec." *RTP* 131:103–114.

Barr, James. 1961. *The Semantics of Biblical Language*. Oxford: Oxford University Press.

Bernal, Martin. 1987–2006. *Black Athena: The Afroasiatic Roots of Classical Civilization*. 3 vols. New Brunswick, NJ: Rutgers University Press.

Boman, Thorleif. 1960. *Hebrew Thought Compared with Greek*. Translated by Jules L. Moreau. Philadelphia, PA: Westminster Press, 1960. Orig. 1952. *Das Hebräische Denken im Vergleich mit dem Griechischen*; Göttingen: Vandenhoeck & Ruprecht.

Braun, Rainer. 1973. *Kohelet und die frühhellenistische Popularphilosophie*. Berlin: de Gruyter.

Bremmer, Jan. 2008. *Greek Religion and Culture, the Bible and the Ancient Near East*. JSRC 8. Leiden: Brill.

Brenner, Michael. 1999. "Gnosis and History: Polemics of German-Jewish Identity from Graetz to Scholem." *New German Critique 77*: 45–60.

Brown, John Pairman. 1995. *Israel and Hellas*. 3 vols. Berlin: de Gruyter.

Brown, John Pairman. 2003. *Ancient Israel and Ancient Greece: Religion, Politics, and Culture*. Minneapolis, MN: Fortress.

Brown, William P. 2014. *Wisdom's Wonder: Character, Creation, and Crisis in the Bible's Wisdom Literature*. Grand Rapids, MI: Eerdmans.

Burkert, Walter. 1992. *The Orientalizing Revolution: Near Eastern Influence on Greek Culture in the Early Archaic Age*. Translated by Margaret E. Pinder and Walter Burkert. Cambridge, MA: Harvard University Press, 1992. Orig. 1984. *Die Orientalisierende Epoche in der griechischen Religion und Literatur*. Heidelberg: Winter.

Crenshaw, James L. 1980. "The Birth of Skepticism in Ancient Israel." Pages 1–19 in *The Divine Helmsman: Studies on God's Control of Human Events Presented to Lou H. Silberman*. Edited by James L. Crenshaw and Samuel Sandmel. New York, NY: KTAV.

Davidson, Robert. 1983. *The Courage to Doubt: Exploring an Old Testament Theme*. London: SCM.

Dell, Katharine J. 1991. *The Book of Job as Sceptical Literature*. BZAW 197. Berlin: de Gruyter.

Denning-Bolle, Sara J. 1987. "Wisdom and Dialogue in the Ancient Near East." *Numen* 34: 214–234.

Fox, Michael. 2007. "Ethics and Wisdom in the Book of Proverbs." *HS* 48:75–88.

Frankfort, Henri, H.A. Frankfort, John A. Wilson, and Thorkild Jacobsen. 1949. *Before Philosophy: The Intellectual Adventure of Ancient Man. An Essay on Speculative Thought in the Ancient Near East*. Baltimore, MD: Penguin. Orig. 1946. *The Intellectual Adventure of Ancient Man*. Chicago, IL: University of Chicago Press.

Friedländer, Moriz. 1898. *Der vorchristliche jüdische Gnosticismus*. Göttingen: Vandenhoeck & Ruprecht.

Friedländer, Moriz. 1904. *Griechische Philosophie im Alten Testament: Eine Einleitung in die Psalmen- und Weisheitsliteratur*. Berlin: Georg Reimer.

Gese, Hartmut. 1958. *Lehre und Wirklichkeit in der alten Weisheit: Studien zu den Spruchen Salomos und zu dem Buche Hiob*. Tübingen: Mohr.

Gordon, Cyrus. 1955. "Homer and the Bible: The Origin and Character of East Mediterranean Literature." *HUCA* 26:43–108.

Gordon, Cyrus. 1962. *Before the Bible: The Common Background of Greek and Hebrew Civilisations*. New York, NY: Harper and Row.

Grafton, Anthony. 1991. *Defenders of the Text: The Traditions of Scholarship in an Age of Science, 1450–1800*. Cambridge, MA: Harvard University Press.

Hallo, William W., ed. 1997–2017. *The Context of Scripture*. 4 vols. K.L. Younger, associate editor. Leiden: Brill.

Holladay, Carl R., ed. 1995. *Fragments from Hellenistic Jewish Authors*. Vol. III: *Aristobulus*. Atlanta, GA: Scholars Press.

Irwin, William. 1950. "Job and Prometheus." *JR* 30:90–108.

Kallen, Horace. 1918. *The Book of Job as a Greek Tragedy*. New York, NY: Moffat, Yard, and Company.

Kynes, Will. 2016. "The Nineteenth-Century Beginnings of 'Wisdom Literature,' and Its Twenty-First-Century End." Pages 83–108 in *Perspectives on Israelite Wisdom: Proceedings of the Oxford Old Testament Seminar*. Edited by John Jarick. London: Bloomsbury T&T Clark.

Legaspi, Michael C. 2010. *The Death of Scripture and the Rise of Biblical Studies*. New York, NY: Oxford University Press.

Legaspi, Michael C. 2018. *Wisdom in Classical and Biblical Tradition*. New York, NY: Oxford University Press.

Louth, Andrew. 2007. *Greek East and Latin West: The Church AD 681–1071*. Crestwood, NY: St. Vladimir's Seminary Press.

Lowth, Robert. 1829. *Lectures on the Sacred Poetry of the Hebrews*. Translated by G. Gregory. Boston, MA: Crocker & Brewster. Orig. 1753. *De sacra poesi Hebraeorum: praelectiones academiae Oxonii habitae*. Oxford: Clarendon.

Mies, Françoise. 2003. "Le genre littéraire du livre de Job." *RB* 110:336–369.

Murray, Gilbert. 1968. *Aeschylus: The Creator of Tragedy*. Oxford: Clarendon.

Origen. 1957. *The Song of Songs: Commentary and Homilies*. Translated by R.P. Lawson. Westminster, MD: Newman Press.

Pedersen, Johannes. 1926–1940. *Israel: Its Life and Culture*. 2 vols. London: Cumberlege. Orig. *Israel, I–II: Sjæleliv og samfundsliv* [1920] and *Israel, III–IV: Hellighed og guddommelighed* [1934]. Copenhagen: Branner og Korch.

Pedersen, Johannes. 1930. "Scepticisme israélite." *RHPR* 10:317–370.

Römer, Thomas. 2015. "The Hebrew Bible and Greek Philosophy and Mythology—Some Case Studies." *Semitica* 57:185–203.

Schwáb, Zoltán S. 2013. *Toward an Interpretation of the Book of Proverbs: Selfishness and Secularity Reconsidered*. JTISup 7. Winona Lake, IN: Eisenbrauns.

Sekine, Seizō. 2005. *A Comparative Study of the Origins of Ethical Thought: Hellenism and Hebraism*. Lanham, MD: Rowman & Littlefield.

Smend, Rudolf. 1995. "The Interpretation of Wisdom in Nineteenth-Century Scholarship." Pages 257–268 in *Wisdom in Ancient Israel: Essays in Honour of J.A. Emerton*. Edited by John Day, Robert P. Gordon, and H.G.M. Williamson. Cambridge: Cambridge University Press.

Spengler, Oswald. 1926. *The Decline of the West: Form and Actuality*. Translated by Charles Francis Atkinson. New York, NY: Knopf. Orig. 1918. *Der Untergang des Abendlandes: Umrisse einer Morphologie der Weltgeshichte*. Vienna: Braumüller.

Stern, Menahem, ed. 1974. *Greek and Latin Authors on Jews and Judaism*, vol. 1. Jerusalem: Israel Academy of Sciences and Humanities.

Uehlinger, Christoph. 1997. "Qohelet im Horizont mesopotamischer, levantinischer und ägyptischer Weisheitsliteratur der persischen und hellenistischen Zeit." Pages 155–235 in *Das Buch Kohelet: Studien zur Struktur, Geschichte, Rezeption und Theologie*. Edited by Ludger Schwienhorst-Schönberger. Berlin: de Gruyter.

Von Rad, Gerhard. 1972. *Wisdom in Israel*. Translated by James D. Martin. Nashville, TN: Abingdon.

Walker, D.P. 1972. *The Ancient Theology: Studies in Christian Platonism from the Fifteenth to the Eighteenth Century*. Ithaca, NY: Cornell University Press.

Weeks, Stuart. 2012. *Ecclesiastes and Scepticism*. LHBOTS 541. London: T&T Clark.

Whybray, R.N. 1998. "Qoheleth as Theologian." Pages 239–265 in *Qohelet in the Context of Wisdom*. Edited by Anton Schoors. Leuven: Leuven University Press.

....

CHAPTER 11

WISDOM IN THE
NEW TESTAMENT

....

MARIAM KAMELL KOVALISHYN

WISDOM is not an obvious genre in the New Testament. For one reason, in the Second Temple period, Wisdom Literature gained apocalyptic overtones. Whereas early Wisdom Literature appeared to concern itself with issues of this earthly life, by the Wisdom of Solomon and 1 Enoch we have a clear concern with eschatological judgment and hints of an eternal life, at least for the righteous. Also, Wisdom is personified in the Hebrew Bible, a character who works alongside YHWH in creation and to teach Israel the way of God, almost a semi-divine character (Proverbs 8). While some see her suggesting a separate deity, James Dunn (1989, 176) argues that she remains a *personification* of an aspect of God, such as his involvement with his creation, but never a separate character. Wisdom teaches and trains, disciplines and corrects the righteous as they walk in obedience before God, a personification depicting God's work in the world.

In the New Testament, in places such as the Synoptics or Colossians, Jesus appears to take on some of the aspects of personified Wisdom. James, meanwhile, is the clearest example of Wisdom Literature we see in the New Testament. One can find interest in the ideas around "wisdom" clustered in certain books, particularly Matthew, 1 Corinthians, and Colossians.[1] But a study like this is interested in more than just the appearance of wisdom-related terms. The reader needs to be sensitive to the themes and echoes of wisdom in the New Testament. In this essay, we will explore the way wisdom appears in the various New Testament texts, and see how the New Testament authors use wisdom to shape Christian community.

---

[1] "The noun σοφία occurs c. 50x in the NT, incl. 17x occurrences in 1 Corinthians (relative to book length, it is esp. freq. in Colossians, 6x). The adj. σοφός is found 20x, incl. 11x in 1 Corinthians and 4x in Romans, while the negative ἄσοφος only in Eph 5:15 (contrasted with σοφός)" (*NIDNTTE*, 4:334). While helpful data, to look only at these instances would be to commit the world-concept fallacy.

11.1 SYNOPTIC GOSPELS

For reasons of space, this essay will deal with the final form of these three Gospels, but mention must inevitably be made to Q. Much scholarship (see, particularly, Kloppenborg 1987) has focused on sorting sapiential versus apocalyptic layers in Q, a misguided question, given the far greater consensus that Wisdom and apocalyptic are not two contrasting traditions that can be separated, but two closely interrelated traditions (see, e.g., Rowland 2017, 134, citing Stone 1976). Horsley and Tiller (2012, 163–164) critique this scholarly tendency, which viewed the sapiential elements as more primitive layers in Gospel construction, with apocalyptic sayings added later. This dichotomy, however, between Wisdom and apocalyptic, whether in sayings or in theology, has largely been abandoned. Since Q scholarship is dominated by this older perspective, it seems of greater value to examine the Synoptic Gospels in their final form. For simplicity's sake, we will mostly deal with the texts that refer to wisdom explicitly.

The gospel of Mark does not unambiguously deal with wisdom concepts. The only clear reference to "wisdom" comes in Mark 6:2 (par. Matt 13:54), when Jesus amazes his audience at the synagogue in Nazareth who then ask, "Where did this man get all this? What is this wisdom ($\sigma o \varphi i a$) that has been given to him? What deeds of power are being done by his hands!"[2] Because his family was familiar to them and he had grown up there, the wisdom Jesus showed when teaching was dismissed by his audience who chose to reject him. This rejection of God's wisdom revealed in Jesus is a common theme throughout the Synoptics.

But alongside others' rejection of Jesus, Mark highlights Jesus's secrecy about his identity. Grant Macaskill (2017, 65) notes how Mark's "Messianic secret" and the explanation of the parable of the sower in Mark 4 echo the language of wisdom and mystery from the Qumran scroll 4QInstruction. The way that the term $\mu \upsilon \sigma \tau \acute{\eta} \rho \iota o \nu$ functions in Mark, and particularly the way that Jesus calls his followers to understand what those outside their community cannot, parallel the ways the Persian loanword $r \bar{a} z$ occurs in the Scrolls to indicate "a body of wisdom that has been revealed specifically to the community and that is constitutive of their special identity as 'the wise.'" When the mystery has been revealed to a community by divine disclosure, that community also gains the responsibility to guard and pass it on to others within the community. When Jesus observes in Mark 4:11 (par. Luke 8:10; Matt. 13:11), "To you has been given the secret ($\tau \grave{o}$ $\mu \upsilon \sigma \tau \acute{\eta} \rho \iota o \nu$) of the kingdom of God, but for those outside, everything comes in parables" and then quotes Isa 6:9–10, he makes clear that his disciples form a community that is being granted a wisdom that not everyone is willing or able to receive. The parables are intended, according to Mark, both to teach *and* obscure. While many of us may be inclined to hear "mystery" language and think of apocalyptic and revelation, Macaskill's reference to 4QInstruction helps us see how inner-community understanding of a

---

[2] The NRSV is used for all biblical citations in this essay.

revealed mystery can be a sign of wisdom teaching. Jesus teaches those with ears to hear how to be his community of wisdom.

This inner-community nature of understanding can also be seen in the saying found in Luke 10:21 (par. Matt 11:25), when Jesus prays, "I thank you, Father, Lord of heaven and earth, because you have hidden these things from the wise and the intelligent and have revealed them to infants; yes, Father, for such was your gracious will." Leslie Baynes (2017, 21) notes, "Revelation of secrets or mysteries is the heart of the apocalyptic endeavor, and typically they are divulged only to those deemed wise. Wisdom is elusive; it must be sought; it is a gift from God, and only a few will receive it" (cf. 2 Bar. 48:3; Wis 6:22). The placement of Luke's saying, however, adds a humorous note: the disciples return from their ministry thrilled with the power that they were able to exercise, assuming they have indeed progressed in status, but Jesus calls them "$\nu\eta\pi\acute{\iota}o\iota\varsigma$" ("infants"). In doing so, Jesus subverts the expectations regarding progress in esoteric knowledge. The community is the location of wisdom, but Jesus reveals that those who are weak are the truly wise. And those who think they are wise outside of the community remain blind.

From the outset, Luke makes clear Jesus's right and qualification to create such an inner community. Luke twice refers to Jesus's wisdom in his childhood, framing the temple incident (Luke 2:41–50). Luke 2:40, which concludes the infancy narratives and introduces the child Jesus, observes, "the child grew and became strong, filled with wisdom ($\pi\lambda\eta\rho o\acute{\upsilon}\mu\epsilon\nu o\nu$ $\sigma o\phi\acute{\iota}\alpha$); and the favor of God was upon him." Then, in Luke 2:52, which concludes the temple narrative wherein Jesus sat among the teachers and learned, Luke again writes, "And Jesus increased in wisdom ($\pi\rho o\acute{\epsilon}\kappa o\pi\tau\epsilon\nu$ [$\acute{\epsilon}\nu$ $\tau\hat{\eta}$] $\sigma o\phi\acute{\iota}\alpha$) and in years, and in divine and human favor." The summary of Jesus's childhood is his growth in wisdom tied to divine favor, framing an episode in which Jesus reveals his knowledge of the law. This concurs with "the Jewish view that wisdom is closely associated with knowledge of the law" (*NIDNTTE* 2014, 4:335). Jesus's wisdom revealed itself in his youthful desire to be at the temple and learn the law from its experts.

Of the synoptics, Matthew bears the strongest sapiential imprint, which is best seen by comparing its shared tradition with Luke. For instance, when Luke 7:35 states, "Nevertheless, wisdom is vindicated by all her children ($\kappa\alpha\grave{\iota}$ $\acute{\epsilon}\delta\iota\kappa\alpha\iota\acute{\omega}\theta\eta$ $\acute{\eta}$ $\sigma o\phi\acute{\iota}\alpha$ $\acute{\alpha}\pi\grave{o}$ $\pi\acute{\alpha}\nu\tau\omega\nu$ $\tau\hat{\omega}\nu$ $\tau\acute{\epsilon}\kappa\nu\omega\nu$ $\alpha\grave{\upsilon}\tau\hat{\eta}\varsigma$)," Matt 11:19b concludes, "Yet wisdom is vindicated by her deeds ($\kappa\alpha\grave{\iota}$ $\acute{\epsilon}\delta\iota\kappa\alpha\iota\acute{\omega}\theta\eta$ $\acute{\eta}$ $\sigma o\phi\acute{\iota}\alpha$ $\acute{\alpha}\pi\grave{o}$ $\tau\hat{\omega}\nu$ $\acute{\epsilon}\rho\gamma\omega\nu$ $\alpha\grave{\upsilon}\tau\hat{\eta}\varsigma$)." Luke depicts John and Jesus as children of wisdom who, despite rejection by those around them, will be vindicated as wise. This vindication will also, by default, reveal the folly of those who reject them. In contrast, in Matthew, Jesus is closely related to Wisdom itself. It is Jesus's own deeds under suspicion, and Jesus's own vindication will be brought through the realization of the wisdom of his action. Contextually, he has just condemned several cities for their failure to see his deeds as his vindication: "Then he began to reproach the cities in which most of his deeds of power had been done, because they did not repent" (11:20). Those who fail to recognize the wisdom of his deeds face condemnation.

Moreover, Matthew reveals an even stronger Wisdom connection in Jesus's call in 11:29–30: "Take my yoke upon you, and learn from me; for I am gentle and humble in heart, and you will find rest for your souls. For my yoke is easy, and my burden is light." This is a clear echo of Sirach 51 and the search for and celebration of Wisdom found there. The sage encourages his readers, "Put your neck under her [Wisdom's] yoke, and let your souls receive instruction; it is to be found close by. See with your own eyes that I have labored but little and found for myself much serenity" (51:26–27). Instead of encouraging people to take on the yoke of Wisdom, Jesus instead usurps her place by offering his own teaching that brings life. Both teachers begin with a call to "draw near" (Matt 11:28, δεῦτε πρός με; Sir 51:23, ἐγγίσατε πρός με) and issue the call to rest within a yoke, but whereas Sirach points to Wisdom, Jesus calls people to himself.

This same variation of Wisdom's role happens in the woe passages in Luke 11 and Matthew 23. In the Lukan version, Jesus warns: "Therefore also the Wisdom of God said, 'I will send (διὰ τοῦτο καὶ ἡσοφίατοῦθεοῦ εἶπεν· ἀποστελῶ) them prophets and apostles...'" (Luke 11:49–50). In Matthew, however, Jesus himself does the sending: "Therefore I send you (διὰ τοῦτο ἰδοὺ ἐγὼ ἀποστέλλω) prophets, sages, and scribes, some of whom you will kill and crucify, and some you will flog in your synagogues and pursue from town to town, so that upon you may come all the righteous blood shed on earth" (Matt 23:34–35a). Matthew also changes Wisdom's future promise to Jesus's present action: Jesus has the authority to declare such an event and condemnation. "A saying of Wisdom has become a saying of Jesus" (Burnett and Bennema 2013, 998). This warning is similar to the one issued in Luke 11:31 (par. Matt 12:42), again for the people's failure to recognize Jesus as more than simply "wise." In Luke 21:15 we can finally see the Lukan Jesus acting in this manner, for he promises his disciples that when the trials of the end come, "I will give you words and a wisdom that none of your opponents will be able to withstand or contradict." Thus, it is not only Matthew who presents Jesus as acting as the Wisdom of God would be expected to act. Jesus teaches in line with Wisdom traditions, but more than simply as a Wisdom teacher: he acts as Wisdom herself.

The way that Jesus seems to take on the character of Wisdom has led many to speculate about a Wisdom Christology. Matthew's Jesus makes the claims of Wisdom for himself, calling others to his yoke and teaching the way of life as he presents the Law anew (see Lillie 1989, 136). Karen Jobes (2000, 226–227) notes that in the quest to pair Jesus with Sophia, some have "regendered" Jesus as the female "Sophia," with "Jesus as the incarnate Wisdom-Sophia of God that was presented to show the feminine principle of God as an acceptable complement to the masculine metaphors of son and king." She argues, however, that this does disservice to the truth of the incarnation, unintentionally undermining the *humanity* of Jesus. Rather than a Sophia Christology, it is more appropriate to speak of Christ as the revelation of God and thus the revelation of the *wisdom* of God. Throughout Scripture, wisdom is how God interacts with his creation, teaching them who God is and how they should live, so it is not surprising that "the self-revelation of God in Jesus" would include God's wisdom (Boerman 2017, 9). Jesus *is* God, therefore the one who reveals the wisdom of God.

In the Synoptics, Jesus's teaching is the way of wisdom, hidden from those who think they are wise apart from Jesus. But Helmut Koester (1990, 160) warns that while the forms of Jesus's teaching in the Synoptics fit a wisdom genre, "[t]he behavior which Jesus requests is a demonstration of the kingdom's presence, i.e., of a society which is governed by new principles of ethics. This not only ascribes a kerygmatic quality to the ethical demands of Jesus, it presents Jesus as a prophet rather than a teacher of wisdom." Jesus's teaching is best categorized, therefore, as both prophetic and sapiential: "it shares wisdom's basic task: the interpretation of human existence as lived out in the intense historicity of everyday life," but is also a prophetic social critique with content "quite unconventional by wisdom standards" (Patterson 1993, 206–207). The one who "hears these words of [Jesus] and puts them into practice is like a wise man (φρονίμῳ) who built his house on the rock" (Matt 7:24). Wisdom is revealed by Jesus, but it subsequently must be embodied by those who *live* accordingly in the Christian communities. Intellectual assent alone has no place in Jesus's paradigm. As the ultimate revelation of God's wisdom, the responsibility to pay heed and obey his warnings falls to his hearers to be people with "ears to hear" and obey, just as with the prophets before.

11.2 JOHN

John's presentation of Jesus is not centered on Jesus as a wisdom teacher. The language of "wisdom" (σοφία, etc.) does not appear at all in this Gospel. The prologue, however, has strong overtones of Wisdom Literature, such that Raymond Brown (1964, cxxv) went so far as to argue that "in John, Jesus is personified Wisdom." While Brown's comment is an overstatement, the presence of wisdom overtones should not be ignored merely because the vocabulary does not appear. The lack of wisdom terminology is not a problem if the language and imagery borrow from Wisdom Literature.

Regarding the prologue, likely itself an independent hymn incorporated into the Gospel (see Witherington 1994, 283), the use of λόγος is proposed as an alternative title for Wisdom, linking Jesus to a pre-existent Sophia. The prologue is clearly influenced by Proverbs 8 and Genesis 1, the former an exposition of the latter but adding Wisdom as an active agent in the creation narrative. Elizabeth Johnson (2002, 96–97) argues:

> The Prologue to [John's] Gospel, which more than any other scriptural text influences the subsequent development of Christology, actually presents the prehistory of Jesus as the story of Sophia: present "in the beginning," an active agent in creation, descending from heaven to pitch a tent among the people, rejected by some, giving life to those who seek, a radiant light that darkness cannot overcome.   (John 1:1–18)

Additionally, Wisdom cannot be overcome by darkness, just as the darkness could not quell the λόγος. In Jewish tradition, "God's 'Word' and 'Wisdom' are sometimes linked," observes Larry Hurtado (2003, 366), thus the speculation that the λόγος in John 1:1–18 is reflective of the Jewish tradition of personified Wisdom is reasonable.

Nevertheless, John seems to be going out of his way to show Jesus as *more than* Wisdom. For example, the early Jewish Similitudes of Enoch 42:2 expands Wisdom's story in a way highly reminiscent of the λόγος in John: "Wisdom went out in order to dwell among the sons of men, but did not find a dwelling; wisdom returned to her place and took her seat in the midst of the angels." Experiencing rejection from her own people, Wisdom returned to God. John's prologue, in contrast, observes, "He was in the world, and the world came into being through him; yet the world did not know him. He came to what was his own, and his own people did not accept him" (John 1:10–11). Jesus *stayed*, however, and "to all who received him, who believed in his name, [Jesus] gave power to become children of God" (1:12). This contrast should lead us to be cautious of mere equation, because John advances the description in new ways (contra Kling 2013). Jesus proves more effective than Wisdom was, able to abide rejection and remain to bring about transformation.

More importantly, "the stark statement in John 1:1, 'the Word was God,' takes us noticeably beyond Wisdom tradition . . . . [A]s Dodd observed, the evidence indicates that in this Jewish Wisdom tradition, a statement such as 'Wisdom was God' was apparently 'unthinkable'" (Hurtado 2003, 367). Ben Witherington (1994, 287) concurs about the shocking import of John 1:1: "the whole of this Gospel must be read in light of this very first verse for it means the deeds and words of Jesus are the deeds and words of a divine being, and not a created supernatural being either, for he existed prior to all of creation." The Gospel of John thus emphasizes the divinity of the Son from the very beginning. The prologue also serves to introduce key terms for the Gospel such as "light" and "life," which remain after the emphasis on the λόγος disappears.

In John's Gospel, we see Jesus teach in expanded forms, such as in the Tabernacles discourse, and these blocks have extended Wisdom references. Much like the contrast above with the *Similitudes*, in John 7:28–29 Jesus depicts himself as having been sent by God. Catherine Cory (1997, 100–101) observes that the next step of the discourse also has Wisdom overtones:

> Concerning where he is going, the Johannine Jesus announces, "You will seek me, but you will not find me" (John 7:34)—another allusion to the Wisdom/Sophia traditions. This "seeking and not finding" motif runs through the whole of the Tabernacles discourse and plays a significant role in the Johannine presentation of Jesus as personified Wisdom.

Wisdom controls access to herself and does not let herself be found by the unworthy. In much the same way, John plays with the image that the Jewish leaders "sought" Jesus in order to kill him, but they were unsuccessful until Jesus allowed them to find him (see Newton 2012).

Like in the Synoptics, although Jesus takes up the ideas of Wisdom and light and revelation, he is more than Wisdom or Logos. Jesus is the fulfillment of the festivals, of shepherding imagery (cf. Ps 23), as well as of wisdom teaching. Imagery of seeking and finding, descending and ascending, revealing and concealing, these help us to draw on all possible resources to understand who Jesus is. But resonance points us to see how he is *more than* any of the allusions. Everything given to reveal God could be seen to culminate in Jesus, without him being limited to any one of the images. Like Wisdom, he required pursuit and was found by those he deemed worthy, and he also dealt with rejection from those who ought to learn from him. John's Jesus is more than one aspect or revelation of God. He was both "with God" and he "was God," and he called people to himself as "the way, the truth, and the life" (John 14:6).

11.3 PAUL

In the New Testament, the σοφία word group is most prominent in 1 Corinthians 1–4, where variants occur twenty-six times, the highest concentration in the New Testament. The conceptual world of Wisdom, however, is most prominent in the epistles to the Colossians and Ephesians, particularly the creation hymn in Colossians 1. While other letters also refer to wisdom or wisdom themes, these will be the focus of our exploration in Paul, who sees wisdom inextricably tied up with the crucified and resurrected Christ.

Before turning to the main epistles, some see the Philippian hymn as echoing language of personified Wisdom. There is a significant linguistic parallel between Wis 7:26, wherein Wisdom is described as εἰκὼν τῆς ἀγαθότητος αὐτοῦ ("an image of his goodness"), and Phil 2:6, that Jesus was ἐν μορφῇ θεοῦ ("in the form of God"). "The designation of Christ as being 'in the form of God' and 'being equal to God' (Phil 2:6) draws upon the thought of Wisdom being near to God, sharing in God's nature and existing before creation" (Schnabel 1993, 970). While there may be echoes, this sort of equation falls into danger of parallelomania, for nowhere is Wisdom *equated* with God the way that Paul equates Jesus with God in this hymn (see Fee 2000, 266).

First Corinthians begins with a lengthy exposition wherein Paul seeks to overturn the church's preoccupation with worldly power and wisdom and dispel their penchant for factions. Rather than expressing loyalty to any one leader on the basis of how well they "perform" on worldly standards, such as speech or wealth, Paul warns them that they fail to understand God's wisdom so long as they hold to those metrics. The wisdom of God uses the weak to perform great deeds, the poor to display God's wealth, the things not well known to make God's name known, and the cross as the ultimate power and wisdom of God. While it may seem odd that he argues against factions with an exposition on the wisdom of God, John Polhill (1983, 325) observes, "The key to Paul's interplay between these twin themes of faction and wisdom is his conviction that the Spirit unites (see chap. 12). Where the Spirit of God is present, who alone reveals the divine wisdom, there can be no factions." Wisdom comes from God and brings unity of purpose and identity in the crucified Christ. Paul juxtaposes the worldly wisdom of the Corinthians with the wisdom of God: their ongoing sinfulness and fighting reveals that they are celebrating a worldly perspective.

Paul, however, ministers from a godly perspective, taking "care to perform his ministry in accordance with the divine reversal of values. Therefore, he is not concerned to appear impressive (2:1–5)" (Grindheim 2002, 693). Rather, he cautions the Corinthians that they need to participate in the reversal: "Do not deceive yourselves. If you think that you are wise in this age, you should become fools so that you may become wise" (1 Cor 3:18). Wisdom cannot be attained by those who continue to value worldly markers of status, wealth, beauty, or rhetorical brilliance. In contrast, those who are wise will not fight for status or preeminence but seek the unity and holiness of the body (individual and communal), serving one another as the Spirit guides. Paul thus gives the church a litmus test for wisdom: where there is factionalism, pride, and fights for status, God's wisdom is absent. Instead, the church is to look to the *crucified* Christ for their understanding of wisdom: "Christ the power of God and the wisdom of God" (1:24), whose humility and crucifixion redefined wisdom for humanity.

Moreover, wisdom comes as a gift of revelation by the Spirit to those who understand that God works through weakness and humility (also the theme of the end of 2 Corinthians). "In response to the congregation's apparent assumption that wisdom is a human characteristic or possession, ... [Paul's] proclamation is itself the *revealed* wisdom of God (2:10)" (Johnson 1993, 276). Paul consistently focuses on the cross and on Christ crucified as revealing the power and wisdom of God, something they could not discern on their own. Wisdom can only come by revelation from God. Matthew Goff (2017, 180–181) observes a similar teaching style in a Qumran text: "Like the *mebin* of 4QInstruction, the Corinthians are students whose spiritual progress depends upon their comprehension of the mysteries conveyed to them by their teacher Paul" who brings to them "the revelation of heavenly knowledge." Revelation is required, without which wisdom cannot be obtained. But submission to the correct teacher is also required, an instructor who can explain the revelation received. Even while Paul begins his epistle in celebration of the gifting and revelation that the Corinthians have received from the Spirit, he is clear that they misunderstand that revelation and therefore require his instruction to bring clarity and unity. The mystery of God, the wisdom of God, is revealed in Christ crucified, but true wisdom does not just know the mystery, it requires a similarly shaped life in Christ's followers. Roy Ciampa and Brian Rosner (2010, 95) warn that "Christians in all walks of life must live in ways that are consistent with" this message. One's acceptance of wisdom is revealed by living a cruciform life in service of others.

With its grand hymn of creation (1:15–20), Colossians celebrates Christ in language reminiscent of Wisdom in Proverbs 8 and other creation hymns. "There is no passage in the New Testament, apart from the Prologue to the Fourth Gospel and Heb. 1:3, whose roots can be traced so clearly to Jewish Wisdom literature as the hymn in Col. 1:15–20" (Schweizer 1982, 246). The debate focuses on verse 15: "He is the image of the invisible God, the firstborn of all creation" (ὅς ἐστιν εἰκὼν τοῦ θεοῦ τοῦ ἀοράτου, πρωτότοκος πάσης κτίσεως) is clearly reminiscent of earlier Wisdom hymns, pairing together images of Wisdom's preeminence in creation from Proverbs 8 with her emanation from God from Wisdom 7, wherein the line from 7:21 is again particularly apt, that Wisdom is the "image of his goodness" ($\epsilon\grave{\iota}\kappa\grave{\omega}\nu\ \tau\hat{\eta}s\ \mathring{a}\gamma\alpha\theta\acute{o}\tau\eta\tau os\ a\mathring{\upsilon}\tauo\hat{\upsilon}$). John Anthony Dunne (2011, 5), however, warns that divergence in language should make us wary of overstating connections: "One area of particular dissimilarity arises from one of the key terms of the hymn, $\pi\rho\omega\tau\acute{o}\tauoкos$. This is especially so because Wisdom (i.e., 'Lady Sophia') is never called $\pi\rho\omega\tau\acute{o}\tauoкos$, since the term implies firstborn *son*." Although Wisdom may assert preeminence in creation, she always remains an image, a reflection, a mirror, a first-of-creation. Similarly, Paul's view of how Christ participates in mediating creation—originating and sustaining—surpasses any of the descriptions given of Wisdom's participation (see Fee 2000; Dunne 2011). This does not "preclude the idea that Wisdom traditions have influenced the composition of the 'hymn,' especially as it relates to Christ's involvement in creation" (Dunne 2011, 7), it merely urges caution against importing Wisdom ideas without allowing Paul to take them in unexpected directions. Paul echoes Wisdom language, but he *surpasses* it in his description of Christ, as he includes also Davidic and regal imagery (Dunne 2011, 8). To limit Christ in the Colossian hymn to a personification of Wisdom is to limit Paul's Christology.

However, Colossians itself is an example of New Testament sapiential, or paraenetic, literature (see van Broekhoven 1996, 44–46, for a summary of research). One place this has taken research is the implications of wisdom readings of the household codes of Colossians (and Ephesians). Andrew Lincoln (1999, 93) asks, "Does the household code of Colossians have anything in common with the Christ-hymn?" Indeed, against the "other-worldly and ascetic wisdom" that the Colossians are celebrating, Paul "sets his own version of apostolic Christian wisdom" (Lincoln 1999, 103). Paul sets forth a coherent philosophy that includes how to live together as a Christian community. Christ is head of the body, the Church, and he is also "Lord of the household . . . the place in which the consequences of Christ's lordship are made most visible to the surrounding world" (Lincoln 1999, 106). How Christ reigns in the household illustrates how Christ is also Lord of the cosmos, the polis. The cosmic Lordship of the Christ-hymn is made practical in the wisdom of how believers live with one another.

When Ephesians adopts the household code from Colossians, the author makes this Lordship even more explicit. Rather than remaining with the traditional teaching regarding households, Ephesians blends wisdom and apocalyptic traditions through the mystery at the heart of the household. "In Ephesians, . . . mysteries are part of cosmology and the point of departure for reflecting on everything. In the same way that *4QInstruction* is described as a sapiential document motivated by an apocalyptic worldview, so too one might say the same of Ephesians 5:21–6:9" (Wold 2017, 232). The mystery of Christ's Lordship and union with the Church is the apocalyptic reality to which the household is but a reflection. Therefore Lincoln (1999, 108) concludes, "Having a Lord in heaven does not direct attention away from the earthly. Rather it is meant to provide the motivation for taking earthly relationships with all seriousness and living distinctively within them." Both Colossians and Ephesians take seriously the Lordship of Christ and, in their own ways, strive to teach the converts the implications of this cosmic Lordship in their daily relationships.

Paul sought to shape his communities in line with the revealed wisdom of Christ. Always the Gospel is at the heart of his teaching, and this upends any ideas people may import. The mystery people long sought access to has been revealed in Christ. The foolishness of the cross teaches us the wisdom of God, and the subsequent cosmic Lordship of Christ transforms the daily lives of those who encounter him.

11.4 THE REST OF THE NEW TESTAMENT

Wisdom ideas and style continue to be influential in other New Testament books. Allusions are probable in Hebrews, the epistle of James is the most evident example of a Wisdom text in the New Testament, the binary vision of 1 John echoes Wisdom's two ways, and Revelation presents us with revealed wisdom in apocalyptic form. In these books, the focus is on Wisdom Literature's ideological influence.

Hurtado (2003, 366 n. 31) observes that there is a likely allusion to Wis 7:25 in Heb 1:3, but as with the Philippians 2 debate, the strength of Hebrews' equation of Jesus as embodying the "imprint" ($\chi\alpha\rho\alpha\kappa\tau\acute{\eta}\rho$) of God is unmatched by Wisdom's description as an "emanation" ($\dot{\alpha}\pi\acute{o}\rho\rho o\iota\alpha$) in the older text. The warnings against apostasy throughout the sermon, however, compare to the warnings of punishment to those who go astray in other Wisdom judgments. The idea that unfaithfulness to covenant life leads to punishment would be familiar to readers of contemporary Wisdom Literature.

James is universally recognized as the New Testament's Wisdom epistle, even while there are debates about its apocalyptic elements (see, e.g., Penner 1996; Kamell 2017). Again, if these two genres are not taken to be oppositional, then the debate is simply one of balance. Ever since Martin Dibelius (1975) labelled it as "paraenesis," James has remained categorized as Wisdom. One of James's key claims is that wisdom is $\ddot{\alpha}\nu\omega\theta\epsilon\nu$, "from above," in stark contrast to that which is earthly. Language of "above" and "coming from above" indicate divine origin (Moo 1985, 133), providing a cosmological contrast to what is earthly and lacking the divine perspective. Wisdom comes from God alone and provides the ability to live according to God's way. Wisdom thus also acts as the intermediary between God and humanity, teaching much as Lady Wisdom does in earlier Wisdom texts. She reveals the truth about the $\kappa\acute{o}\sigma\mu os$ so that God's people can discern reality and live according to God's ways rather than according to their own limited vision (see Kamell 2017). James is at home in Wisdom Literature, focusing on practical themes of wealth and poverty, human mercy and divine mercy, pride and envy, and trust in God. The wise person will worship God alone, rather than being torn by their desires and worldly values, and this will be revealed in the peaceful nature of their relationships.

First John shows a bias toward a Wisdom theme that developed into its own tradition of the Two Ways (see, e.g., Didache). The dichotomy between righteousness and sinfulness is even starker than in James, and 1 John cycles around the necessity of loving one's neighbor (practically) to be able to love God. To obey God's law involves love, not mere rote actions. Bennie Reynolds (2017, 344) claims that "the Jewish, apocalyptic character of 1–3 John—and especially 1 John—can be illuminated by comparing their binary oppositions with similar examples found in Jewish texts from Hellenistic times," such as in the Epistle of Enoch, the Wisdom conclusion to the apocalyptic text. The duality of 1 John also matches that of Wisdom writings such as Proverbs or Sirach, where one is either righteous or wicked as shown by one's deeds, but the cosmic scope has been amplified. This epistle of John teaches its hearers that they will reveal whether they love God (or not) in their choices to (or not to) love their neighbor and obey the commands of God.

Finally, the ultimate apocalyptic text of the New Testament, Revelation, also has strong Wisdom elements. Loren Stuckenbruck (2017, 358–359) calls Revelation "a Disclosure of Wisdom," and argues that an:

> overview of "wisdom" in the Apocalypse demonstrates that, although the term occurs only four times, its significance is interwoven with the message of the book as a whole. To proclaim wisdom among the features of the Lamb (5:12) and of God (7:12) is to locate the true perception of things in a faith-based reality that contrasts with the world that the recipients of the revelation are presumed to experience. This reality expresses itself in a worship and devotion that does not falter when confronted by a system thoroughly caught up in a web of deception.

This wisdom "embraces reality as a whole," and calls for the reader to engage in "a process of active discernment" (359). As in Wisdom Literature, merely gaining revelation is not enough. Readers are called to understand "the true nature of the situation, . . . heeding the prophetic *demand* for an appropriate response" (Bauckham 1986, 94). Revelation upends worldly notions of power with the wisdom of the crucified lamb (5:6, 9, 12), which leads to worship of the Lamb rather than the powers that contend against him. In chapter 7, wisdom is again linked to correct worship. But the uses in 13:18 and 17:9 "challenge the audience to gain insight" regarding their own context (Stuckenbruck 2017, 352). In Revelation, therefore, wisdom functions both to instruct right worship but also to provoke the reader to engage in their own pursuit of wisdom. In this way, then, wisdom functions to transform people's perspective such that it also transforms how they live and worship.

Thus, throughout the conclusion of the New Testament, wisdom continues to function both as a genre and as a theme. When it is a genre, we still see overlaps with apocalyptic revelation, but focused on the practical nature of wisdom shaping the daily lives of average people in their relationships at home, church, and work. As a theme, it is often tied with worship and a true picture of reality, in contrast to the "cleverly devised myths" (σεσοφισμένοις μύθοις; 2 Pet 1:16) of sinful people. Wisdom leads to single-minded, faithful worship of God that is lived out in one's peaceable relations.

11.5 CONCLUSION

In conclusion, given the way discussions have often progressed particularly in Gospel studies, we need to be wary of making a strong distinction between apocalyptic literature and Wisdom Literature. "Modern scholarship has barely faced up to the problem of the interface between apocalypticism and wisdom. This question is reaching some urgency in New Testament Studies, which have begun to flounder on the old paradigm with its watertight compartments and the presumed opposition of apocalyptic and wisdom" (Scott 1993, 245). To continue to function as if these are two opposed genres will continue to lead New Testament studies astray.

Secondly, the link between wisdom and right worship should continue to gain focus. Stuckenbruck's article on Revelation provides a vision of the relationship between wisdom and worship and practical life, but this connection is not limited to that book. The Epistle of James, 1 Corinthians, Jesus's saying in Matt 11:19b that "wisdom is vindicated by her deeds," or the more parabolic statement in Matt 12:33 that "a tree is recognized by its fruit," all bear witness to the link between wisdom and life. Wisdom comes from God alone, and it teaches God's people how to live such that they can worship him in truth and deed. Wisdom inverts the worldly categories of class, status, wealth, and power, pointing instead to a crucified Lord (cf. 1 Corinthians, but also the Gospels), who is now in charge of the entire cosmos (see Colossians, Revelation). Wisdom is hidden from those who presume to be able to evaluate using worldly categories, but she is given to those whom the world has rejected, much as the world rejected the Savior who embodied God's wisdom to his world. Wisdom can no longer be discussed apart from the Crucified Lamb.

Wisdom has never been humanity's to own, but is given by God and thus leads to worship of God. But worship of God, according to New Testament Wisdom teaching, means that God's people become shaped in alignment with the crucified Christ, serving one another in humility and unity. Ultimately, David Ford (2003, 4–5) is correct when he observes that wisdom "asks not only about meaning, interpretation, and truth but also, inextricably, about living life before God now and about how lives and communities are shaped in line with who God is and with God's purposes for the future. In short, it is about lived meaning directed towards the kingdom of God." Wisdom is the lived faithfulness of the people of God, revealed to and empowered in them by the Spirit. How God's people respond to Christ's calls for obedience reveal whether they participate in the Wisdom of God.

WORKS CITED

Bauckham, Richard. 1986. "Approaching the Apocalypse." Pages 88–98 in *Decide for Peace: Evangelicals and the Bomb*. Edited by Dana-Mills-Powell. Basingstoke: Marshall Pickering.
Baynes, Leslie A. 2017. "Jesus the Revealer and the Revealed." Pages 15–30 in Reynolds and Stuckenbruck 2017.

Boerman, Daniel. 2017. "The Self-Revelation of God in Jesus." *CTJ* 52:9–36.

Burnett, F.W., and C. Bennema. 2013. "Wisdom." Pages 995–1000 in *Dictionary of Jesus and the Gospels*. Edited by Joel B. Green, Jeannine K. Brown, and Nicholas Perrin. Downers Grove, IL: IVP Academic.

Brown, Raymond E. 1964. *The Gospel According to John*, vol. 1. AB 29. Garden City, NY: Doubleday.

Ciampa, Roy E., and Brian S. Rosner. 2010. *The First Letter to the Corinthians*. PNTC. Grand Rapids, MI: Eerdmans.

Cory, Catherine. 1997. "Wisdom's Rescue: A New Reading of the Tabernacles Discourse (John 7:1–8:59)." *JBL* 116:95–116.

Dibelius, M. 1975. *James*. Translated by Michael A. Williams. Hermeneia. Philadelphia, PA: Fortress.

Dunn, James D. 1989. *Christology in the Making: A New Testament Inquiry into the Origins of the Doctrine of the Incarnation*. 2nd ed. Grand Rapids, MI: Eerdmans.

Dunne, John Anthony. 2011. "The Regal Status of Christ in the Colossian 'Christ-Hymn': A Re-evaluation of the Influence of Wisdom Traditions." *TJ* 32:3–18.

Fee, Gordon. 2000. "Wisdom Christology in Paul: A Dissenting View." Pages 251–279 in *The Way of Wisdom: Essays in Honor of Bruce K. Waltke*. Edited by J.I. Packer and Sven K. Soderlund. Grand Rapids, MI: Zondervan.

Ford, David. 2003. "Jesus Christ, the Wisdom of God." Pages 4–21 in *Reading Texts, Seeking Wisdom: Scripture and Theology*. Edited by David. F. Ford and Graham Stanton. London: SCM.

Goff, Matthew. 2017. "The Mystery of God's Wisdom, the Parousia of a Messiah, and Visions of Heavenly Paradise: 1 and 2 Corinthians in the Context of Jewish Apocalypticism." Pages 175–192 in Reynolds and Stuckenbruck 2017.

Grindheim, Sigurd. 2002. "Wisdom for the Perfect: Paul's Challenge to the Corinthian Church (1 Corinthians 2:6–16)." *JBL* 121:689–709.

Horsley, Richard A., and Patrick A. Tiller. 2012. *After Apocalypticism and Wisdom: Rethinking Texts in Context*. Eugene, OR: Cascade Books.

Hurtado, Larry W. 2003. *Lord Jesus Christ: Devotion to Jesus in Earliest Christianity*. Grand Rapids, MI: Eerdmans.

Jobes, Karen. 2000. "Sophia Christology: The Way of Wisdom?" Pages 226–250 in *The Way of Wisdom: Essays in Honor of Bruce K. Waltke*. Edited by J.I. Packer and Sven K. Soderlund. Grand Rapids, MI: Zondervan.

Johnson, E. Elizabeth. 1993. "Wisdom and Apocalyptic in Paul." Pages 263–283 in Perdue, Scott, and Wiseman 1993.

Johnson, Elizabeth A. 2002. *She Who Is*. 10th anniversary ed. New York, NY: Crossroads.

Kamell, Mariam J. 2017. "James and Jewish Apocalyptic Thought." Pages 389–406 in Reynolds and Stuckenbruck 2017.

Kling, Sheri D. 2013. "Wisdom Became Flesh: An Analysis of the Prologue to the Gospel of John." *CurTM* 40:179–187.

Kloppenborg, John S. 1987. *The Formation of Q*. Philadelphia, PA: Fortress.

Koester, Helmut. 1990. *Ancient Christian Gospels: Their History and Development*. Philadelphia, PA: Trinity Press International; London: SCM.

Lillie, Betty Jane. 1989. "Matthew's Wisdom Theology: Old Things and New." *PEGL* 9:124–137.

Lincoln, Andrew T. 1999. "The Household Code and Wisdom Mode of Colossians." *JSNT* 74:93–112.

Macaskill, Grant. 2017. "Apocalypse and the Gospel of Mark." Pages 53–77 in Reynolds and Stuckenbruck 2017.

Moo, Douglas J. 1985. *The Letter of James*. TNTC 16. Leicester: Inter-Varsity Press.

Newton, Bert. 2012. *Subversive Wisdom: Sociopolitical Dimensions of John's Gospel*. Eugene, OR: Wipf & Stock.

Patterson, Stephen J. 1993. "Wisdom in Q and Thomas." Pages 187–221 in Perdue, Scott, and Wiseman 1993.

Penner, Todd C. 1996. *The Epistle of James and Eschatology: Re-reading an Ancient Christian Letter*. JSNTSup 121. Sheffield: Sheffield Academic.

Perdue, Leo G., Bernard Brandon Scott, and William Johnston Wiseman, eds. 1993. *In Search of Wisdom: Essays in Memory of John G. Gammie*. Louisville, KY: Westminster John Knox.

Polhill, John B. 1983, "The Wisdom of God and Factionalism: 1 Corinthians 1–4." *RevExp* 80:325–339.

Reynolds, Benjamin E. 2017. "Apocalyptic Revelation in the Gospel of John." Pages 109–128 in Reynolds and Stuckenbruck 2017.

Reynolds, Benjamin E., and Loren T. Stuckenbruck, eds. 2017. *The Jewish Apocalyptic Tradition and the Shaping of New Testament Thought*. Minneapolis, MN: Fortress.

Reynolds III, Bennie H. 2017. "Demonology and Eschatology in the Oppositional Language of the Johannine Epistles and Jewish Apocalyptic Texts." Pages 327–345 in Reynolds and Stuckenbruck 2017.

Rowland, Christopher. 2017. "Paul as an Apocalyptist." Pages 131–153 in Reynolds and Stuckenbruck 2017.

Schnabel, Eckhard J. 1993. "Wisdom." Pages 966–972 in *Dictionary of Paul and His Letters*. Edited by Gerald F. Hawthorne, Ralph P. Martin, and Daniel G. Reid. Downers Grove, IL: InterVarsity.

Schweizer, Eduard. 1982. *The Letter to the Colossians: A Commentary*. Translated by A. Chester. Minneapolis, MN: Augsburg Fortress.

Scott, Bernard Brandon. 1993. "The Gospel of Matthew: A Sapiential Performance of an Apocalyptic Discourse." Pages 245–262 in Perdue, Scott, and Wiseman 1993.

Stone, Michael E. 1976. "Lists of Revealed Things in the Apocalyptic Literature." Pages 414–452 in *Magnalia Dei: The Mighty Acts of God: Essays on the Bible and Archaeology in Memory of G. Ernest Wright*. Edited by F. M. Cross, W. E. Lemke, and P. D. Miller. Garden City, NY: Doubleday.

Stuckenbruck, Loren T. 2017. "The Book of Revelation as a Disclosure of Wisdom." Pages 347–359 in Reynolds and Stuckenbruck 2017.

Van Broekhoven, Harold. 1996. "Praise and Paraenesis in Wisdom Literature and Colossians." *PEGL* 16:41–51.

Witherington, Ben, III. 1994. *Jesus the Sage: The Pilgrimage of Wisdom*. Minneapolis, MN: Fortress.

Wold, Benjamin. 2017. "Apocalyptic Thought in the Epistles of Colossians and Ephesians." Pages 219–232 in Reynolds and Stuckenbruck 2017.

CHAPTER 12

WISDOM IN PATRISTIC INTERPRETATION

*Scriptural and Cosmic Unity in Athanasius's
Exegesis of Proverbs 8:22*

SUSANNAH TICCIATI

In late antiquity, both within the church and beyond, talk of wisdom was (among other things) a way of negotiating the relation between God and creation. This negotiation took a bewildering variety of forms. Consider the Origenist and Philonic hypostasized Wisdom, identified with the mediating figure of the Logos, and its modalist rejection; the Valentinian identification of Sophia as an inferior emanation of the Most High God, and Irenaeus's counter-identification of Wisdom with the Holy Spirit of God; the Arian distinction of the Wisdom proper to God from that changeable Wisdom that becomes incarnate in Christ, and Athanasius's divine Wisdom incarnate; the rabbinic identification of Wisdom with Torah; or Augustine's rejection of the speculations of the Platonists in favor of the humble wisdom of the path trodden by the incarnate Christ. However, running through (almost) all of these accounts is something that we, in our fragmented twenty-first-century world, have arguably lost: an account of the unity of the cosmos held in being by God. Wisdom language was a way of articulating that unity.

Proverbs 8 was at the center of these diverse debates about wisdom. In the "Arian" controversy of the fourth century, Prov 8:22 was the chief scriptural battleground, all parties to the controversy starting out from the assumption that the figure of Wisdom who speaks in the verse is to be identified with the Logos or Son, christologically understood. The patterns of scriptural argumentation draw attention to another unity, corresponding to that of the cosmos, that we have also arguably lost: the unity of Scripture. This unity is exhibited by a practice of intertextual reading that pervades not only the "Arian" controversy, but practically all patristic interpretation: in the West and the East, in "Antiochene" as well as "Alexandrian" interpretation, in the works of those pronounced heretical and of those pronounced orthodox, and across a considerable time span, well into the Middle Ages. This practice involves the interpreting of a particular verse of Scripture in intertextual relation with other verses of Scripture from across the canon, whatever the genre of the passage from which they are taken, and whatever their "original" historical context. It is so pervasive that it is largely taken for granted in the scholarly literature—despite being quite alien to historically and literarily trained modern exegetes.[1]

In this essay I will focus on Athanasius's treatment of Prov 8:22 in the context of the "Arian" controversy[2]—as a window onto wisdom in patristic interpretation, and more specifically, onto the cosmic and scriptural unity articulated in this period in the language of wisdom. This is an apt focus for several reasons. First, substantially, it is the status of the figure of Wisdom that is under dispute in the controversy. Second, exegetically, the verse under consideration is from a paradigmatic Wisdom book. Third, hermeneutically, the assumption at the heart of the controversy that Wisdom is to be christologically identified intensifies the alienness for us today of the intertextual practice prevalent in the period, and thus makes the controversy all the better a window onto what is distinctive about that practice. Fourth, in the profusion of diverse scriptural citations in his treatment of Prov 8:22, Athanasius is representative (even paradigmatic) of that hermeneutical practice.[3]

The essay will begin by describing the practice of intertextual reading, shared by all parties to the dispute, that makes the identification of the figure of Wisdom in Proverbs with Christ a natural one. It will then briefly outline the common cosmological assumptions corresponding to the intertextual practice. In a second and third section, it will focus specifically on Athanasius's *Orationes contra Arianos*, drawing out his distinctive account of the *skopos* of Scripture and his particular understanding of cosmic unity in Christ. Thus far the essay will have succeeded, by way of close description, in merely heightening what is alien in fourth-century practice. In a fourth section—the pivotal one—it will seek to make sense of what it has described by way of a shift in hermeneutical perspective. To anticipate, it will argue that Athanasius's goal is not to tell us what Scripture means, but "to speak as Scripture speaks."[4] Athanasius, I will argue, enacts a wisdom hermeneutic. Specifically, I will suggest that the unity of Scripture, for

---

[1] Frances Young (1997) is a noteworthy exception. She offers a helpful and sympathetic cultural contextualization of the fathers' intertextual reading practices against the backdrop of their belief in the unity of Scripture. While acknowledging that we might learn from them, she nevertheless takes it as read that many aspects of their practice would be unthinkable today (Young 1997, e.g. 31 n. 3; 116). In the following, I will offer an analysis that diverges from hers in significant ways.

[2] His treatment is to be found in *Orationes contra Arianos*. For the critical edition, see Hansen, Metzler, and Savvidis 1998 and 2000. The English translation I have followed is Schaff and Wace 1994.

[3] Kannengiesser (1999, 73) catalogues the large number of scriptural quotations (according to biblical book) in the section of Athanasius's *Contra Arianos* dedicated to Prov 8:22. In this citational practice, he claims, Athanasius is representative of many Christian writers from the second century to the second half of the seventh. He gestures to the simultaneous difficulty and importance of retrieving the practice for today (1999, 74).

[4] James (2016) offers an illuminating account of Origen of Alexandria's hermeneutic in these terms. I extend his analysis to Athanasius.

Athanasius, is akin not so much to that of a cohesive plot as to that of an interconnected set of proverbs. In the light of this shift in perspective, the themes of the earlier sections will be revisited and freshly elucidated.

It will not be within the scope of the essay to examine anti-Nicene ways of making sense of the intertextual practice they share with Athanasius. It would be quite a task to disentangle what is shared from what is distinctive, and to work out how that which is shared is transformed by what is distinctive in each author. The essay will not, however, constitute an apology for Athanasius's doctrine over against that of his opponents. It aims simply to offer a coherent account of his hermeneutic in a way that makes sense of what was previously alien. We can imagine that something comparable would be possible in the case of his opponents, too. Thus, unlike in some other scholarly accounts,[5] the primary contrast the essay draws is not between "the heretical" and "the orthodox," but between the twenty-first century and the fourth century—with an eye to patristic interpretation more widely, and its distinctive use and interpretation of wisdom.

12.1 PROVERBS 8:22 AND SCRIPTURAL INTERTEXTUALITY

Κύριος ἔκτισέ με ἀρχὴν ὁδῶν αὐτοῦ εἰς ἔργα αὐτοῦ. (Prov 8:22 LXX)
The Lord created me a beginning of his ways for his works.

To identify the Wisdom in whose mouth Proverbs puts these words with Christ, and thus to envisage Christ as speaking these words, is likely to strike any modern exegete as an anachronism.[6] But this identification is at the bedrock of the "Arian" controversy, assumed by pro-Nicenes and anti-Nicenes alike. It is hard for the modern exegete, even one who takes seriously the doctrinal outcome of that controversy, not to regard its exegetical underpinnings as precarious to say the least, and thus not to endeavor to divorce the doctrinal outcome from its exegetical context. Whether it is possible to salvage the emergent Nicene doctrine of the Trinity at the expense of the exegesis is questionable. But be that as it may, the practice of identifying the speaker here with Christ, despite the differences in time and genre etc., is—precisely in its flouting of modern common sense—a window onto the different presuppositions with which the fourth-century controversialists were operating. The purpose of this first section is briefly to describe the intertextual reading practice (and its corresponding cosmological assumptions) from which the christological identification follows.

---

[5] See, e.g., Pollard 1959 and (less polemically) Boersma 2016.
[6] With reference to Athanasius, but in a slightly different connection, Young remarks that "Ancient literary criticism did not grasp the notion of an anachronistic reading, because it was essentially about reader reception and response" (Young 1997, 36).

Athanasius and his anti-Nicene opponents[7] alike assume that the Bible is a unity,[8] and thus that verses from one location can be read alongside verses from other locations, in mutual interpretation of one another. Indeed, the way in which Athanasius's *Contra Arianos* are structured is premised upon this assumption: from the end of the first oration, Athanasius proceeds by treating specific verses, most of them ones that have functioned as anti-Nicene "proof-texts."[9] Thus, he treats Phil 2:9–10, Ps 44:7–8 LXX, Heb 1:4, Heb 3:2, Acts 2:36, and so on. Each is read not only in the context of the others, but in the context of many other scriptural verses that Athanasius draws in along the way. What unites the proof-texts is a linguistic pattern of describing Christ (who is assumed to be the referent in various Old Testament cases, too) in a way that might be taken to imply his creatureliness—something that speaks in favor of the anti-Nicenes, but which Athanasius must account for differently. He does so by way of the other verses he draws on (in the case of Phil 2:9–10, this includes John 17:5, Ps 17:10, 14 LXX, Col 1:15, and Matt 11:27; *Ar.* 1.38–39), which are not simply offered as counter-proof-texts, but which are used both to show up inconsistencies in the anti-Nicene logic and to develop an alternative logic.

This promiscuous intertextuality is what has led to the shared conclusion, now a premise in the present controversy, that it is Christ who speaks in Prov 8:22. Paul names Christ the Power and Wisdom of God in 1 Cor 1:24. Khaled Anatolios deftly shows how the debate in which Athanasius is embroiled in this work hinges on the way in which 1 Cor 1:24 and Rom 1:20 are related: is Christ to be identified with or distinguished from the eternal Wisdom of Rom 1:20?[10] While the precise status of Christ as Wisdom is in question, Christ's identification as Wisdom is so much taken for granted that it need not even be argued for. Thus, when it comes to Prov 8:22, the debate is again about the status of Christ as Wisdom, not the presupposed identification. Anyone who would depart from the latter would have to dismantle a strong and dynamic network of signs, effectively creating for themselves a new Bible. As we are beginning to see, however, the differences between Athanasius and his opponents turn on the way they wield further intertextual linkages, such that one might consider the pro-Nicene and anti-Nicene arguments as inventions of different scriptural semiotic networks, with different arterial links and capillaries, creating alternative routes through the one Bible. The method is shared, even while the results diverge.

---

[7] Athanasius's explicit targets in this work are specifically Arius (whose *Thalia* he cites in *Contra Arianos* [*Ar.*] 1.5) and Asterius (whom he names in *Ar.* 1.30). Anatolios (2013) argues that the work, written in the early 340s, is implicitly concerned to position Athanasius in a contemporary debate involving Asterius, Marcellus of Ancyra, and Eusebius of Caesarea, but that Athanasius hides the different voices so as to create an oversimplified opposition between "orthodoxy" and "heresy."

[8] As Young shows, this unity was a "dogma" among the Fathers. She goes on to explore its effect on their exegesis (Young 1997: Part I).

[9] I use this term neutrally. For a negative assessment of "proof-texting" in the Arian controversy, see Dowling 2010. By contrast, Young suggests, with reference to Athanasius's appeal to the *skopos* of Scripture (to be discussed below under 12.2 *Skopos*), that "his argument [was] quite different from a simple text-slinging match" (Young 1997, 35).

[10] Anatolios 2013, esp. 507.

While Athanasius and his opponents differ on how precisely to relate the creator God, creation, and the Wisdom by which God creates, they nevertheless share some basic, minimal cosmological assumptions that underlie their intertextual practice. The Bible's unity corresponds to the unity of creation, to which God has imparted Wisdom. That Wisdom, with God before creation (even if, for Arius, as the first of all creatures), is the same Wisdom that becomes flesh in Christ for the salvation of creation. Proverbs and the New Testament speak of the same Wisdom. They share a creational context, and thus can be meaningfully read together in the context of that unified creation. Wisdom is the principle of unification. For our modern historical and scientific imaginations, which distend the cosmos into almost incommensurable historical time periods, or into evolutionary epochs that make Christ's particular life an insignificant drop in the ocean, this creational coherence is hard to appreciate other than mythologically. A different sort of imagination fuels the fourth-century theologians. This is more readily given spatial articulation (if we think, for example, in Stoic terms of the Logos pervading the universe), and in turn, semiotic articulation (consider the semiotic connections drawn between divergent aspects of the one creation in their intertextual reading practice).

In the next two sections I will describe Athanasius's distinctive inflection and articulation of this shared intertextual hermeneutic and its corresponding cosmology. Only in the fourth section will I frame what he is doing in terms of the wisdom hermeneutic that promises to make sense of what otherwise seems so alien.

12.2 Skopos

Reworking a well-known hermeneutical principle,[11] Athanasius appeals to the *skopos* ("scope") of Scripture. This is his articulation of the unity of the Bible, and is thus the principle that undergirds the possibility of reading each verse in relation to any of the others. It is, in his words, a "rule" ($\kappa\alpha\nu\acute{\omega}\nu$) for the right reading of Scripture (*Ar.* 3.28). Here is his full rendition:

> [T]he scope ($\sigma\kappa\sigma\pi\acute{o}s$) and character of Holy Scripture, as we have often said, is this—it contains a double account of the Saviour; that He was ever God, and is the Son, being the Father's Word and Radiance and Wisdom; and that afterwards for us He took flesh of a Virgin, Mary Bearer of God, and was made man. And this scope is to be found throughout inspired Scripture[.]   (*Ar.* 3.29)

---

[11] See Young 1997, 35 for some helpful historical background. She draws attention to another significant term Athanasius uses alongside *skopos*: the $\delta\iota\acute{\alpha}\nu\sigma\iota\alpha$ (mind or sense) of Scripture. She cites occurrences in *De decretis*, but he also uses it in *Contra Arianos*, e.g., at *Ar.* 2.55.

There is much literature devoted to Athanasius's *skopos*, with a variety of suggestions as to how it is best defined.[12] Most consider it to be something close to the overall intention of Scripture. Without yet offering my own closer definition, or paying attention to the content Athanasius gives it, we might ask about the feasibility of identifying such a unitive intention. On the face of it, such an endeavor might be thought to be doomed to failure in the light of the plurality of biblical books and authors, innumerable layers of redaction, and manifold historical contexts of production and distribution. As we are rightly reminded by modern exegetes, the Bible (τὰ βιβλία, plural of βιβλίον, "book") is more like a library than a book. What sense is there in seeking a single scope? We might liken Athanasius's project to that of the now out-of-fashion biblical theology which in order to unite the various (and conflicting) perspectives into one overarching theology had to conform them to its (arbitrarily chosen) agenda, thus making it an unavoidably ideological endeavor. Whether this is the right analogy for what Athanasius is up to is something that will be brought in question over the course of this essay.

Athanasius's definition of the scope of Scripture is a summary of the incarnation, read through the lens of the absolute distinction he maintains between creator and creation. He has, in turn, established the latter christologically, in part through an understanding of the Word's or Wisdom's role in creation and in salvation. In *Contra Arianos* 2, Athanasius argues by way of a concatenation of scriptural texts that the Son is not a work. On the shared assumption of the identification of Wisdom—itself used interchangeably with the Word—with the Son, Athanasius draws on Ps 103:24 LXX, "In Wisdom hast Thou made them all," and John 1:3, "All things were made through Him, and without Him was not anything made," to argue that the Son, as the Wisdom by which God creates all things, cannot be numbered among those things. If he were, the question would arise by what further wisdom he was created (*Ar.* 2.5). Wisdom is ranged squarely on the divine side of the distinction between creator and creation; there is no derivative Wisdom, or Wisdom by participation (as, according to *Ar.* 1.5, Arius would have it), in addition to the Wisdom proper to God. Athanasius distinguishes between "offspring" (γεννήματος), as "proper" (ἴδιος) to the essence of its source, and "work" (ποίημα) as external to it, identifying the Son or Wisdom robustly as offspring of the Father (*Ar.* 2.2).

The flipside of the unequivocal identification of the Son as eternal, divine Wisdom is the reading of all those scriptural passages that imply the creaturehood of the Son in terms of what Athanasius calls "the Word's human Economy" (ἡ κατὰ τὸν ἄνθρωπον οἰκονομία τοῦ λόγου, *Ar.* 2.9). This other pole of the christologically focused absolute distinction is staked out at the very beginning of *Contra Arianos* 2 by way of John 1:14, on the one hand complementarily paired with John 1:1 as a reference to the other pole, and on the other hand ranged with a number of anti-Nicene proof-texts, among them Prov

[12] See, e.g., Pollard (1959, 23), who opts for "general drift"; Ernest (1993), who describes it as the "theological unity" of Scripture (Ernest 1993, 342), and suggests the meaning (in certain contexts) of "authorial intent" (Ernest 1993, 344); Torrance (1995), who in the context of a nuanced semiotic analysis emphasizes the meaning of "objective reality signified" (Torrance 1995, 239); and Boersma (2016), who uses "scope," "intention," and "overall purpose" interchangeably.

8:22. John 1:14 thus becomes a lens through which to read these more difficult verses in terms of the human economy (*Ar.* 2.1). In this way, Athanasius (anticipating the Chalcedonian Definition) establishes an absolute distinction running *through* Christ, not *between* Christ and the Father (as Arius would have it). He thereby also rules out a mediating figure that straddles God and creation (as Asterius and Eusebius of Caesarea would have it).

These verses help to establish and consolidate Athanasius's *skopos* even as they are being read through its lens. The latter hermeneutical vector is clearly in play in Athanasius's employment and peculiar adaptation of a well-known contemporary rhetorical strategy, in which he invites the reader to ask after the "person" ($\pi\rho\delta\sigma\omega\pi\sigma\nu$), "time" ($\kappa\alpha\iota\rho\delta s$), and "purpose" ($\pi\rho\hat{\alpha}\gamma\mu\alpha$) of the passage at hand (see, e.g., *Ar.* 1.54 and 1.55).[13] His definition of the scope is, we could say, his summary of the range of answers that might be given to these questions. Conversely, to ask these questions is to apply the scope to a particular passage. Thus, in response to an anti-Nicene reading of Heb 1:4, Athanasius concludes, "had they known the person ($\pi\rho\delta\sigma\omega\pi\sigma\nu$), and the subject ($\pi\rho\hat{\alpha}\gamma\mu\alpha$), and the season ($\kappa\alpha\iota\rho\delta s$) of the Apostle's words, they would not have expounded of Christ's divinity what belongs to His manhood" (*Ar.* 1.55). In terms of the scope, the person is either the eternal Son of God or the Son of Man. The time is either "before" or "after" the incarnation, the temporal prepositions also metaphorically signifying the distinction between the eternal processions on the one hand, and the temporal economy on the other hand. When a purpose is specified, it is "for us" or "for our sakes," referring to the time of salvation; when, by contrast, the eternity of God is in question, no purpose is specified.

When Athanasius finally arrives at his exegesis of Prov 8:22 proper (*Ar.* 2.44), he has already established such a tightly woven context for the verse, that his exegesis (while counterintuitive both to the anti-Nicenes and indeed to us today) is the most natural exegesis. As he says: "We have gone through thus much before the passage in the Proverbs, resisting the insensate fables which their hearts have invented, that they may know that the Son of God ought not to be called a creature, and may learn rightly to read what admits in truth of a right explanation" (*Ar.* 2.44).

I will expound Athanasius's exegesis of Prov 8:22 in terms of his threefold pursuit of the "person, time, and purpose" of the verse. In respect of the person (which he asks after in *Ar.* 2.44), it should be obvious from the foregoing that Athanasius will conclude that "he created" refers not to "the Essence of His Godhead" but to "His manhood and Economy towards us" (*Ar.* 2.45).[14] Given his christological rendering of the absolute distinction, it cannot do otherwise: "created" cannot be used of Wisdom qua eternal Wisdom.[15] But he consolidates this reading by reference to Prov 9:1, "Wisdom made

---

[13] Boersma (2016, 13–15) offers a good summary of this strategy and its link with the *skopos*. He refers the reader to Clayton 1988 for a full discussion in historical context.

[14] Athanasius is not the first to read the verse in this way; Marcellus of Ancyra precedes him. But his treatment is the most extensive.

[15] Once the anti-Nicene use of $\kappa\tau\iota\sigma\mu\alpha$ for the Son as creature had been established, it became impossible to use the verb $\kappa\tau\iota\zeta\omega$ ("to create") more flexibly (Williams 2001, 152).

herself a house," read through John 1:14. The implication (in respect of the time) is that we are dealing with the temporal economy. The other potential solution, which he entertains more generally at the beginning of *Contra Arianos* 2, is to allow the subject matter to dictate the meaning of the term "created"—thus interpreting it as "begat"—rather than to conform the subject matter to the term (*Ar.* 1.3–4). At *Ar.* 2.44 he passes over this possibility in favor of the incarnational reading that has been enabled by the momentum-gathering *skopos*.

In respect of the purpose, Athanasius notes that "he created" goes together with a reason: "for the works." He continues, "And this is usual with divine Scripture; for when it signifies the fleshly origination of the Son, it adds also the cause for which He became man; but when he speaks… anything of His Godhead, all is said… with an absolute sense" (*Ar.* 2.53). He compares Prov 8:22 again with John 1:14, where he understands "And dwelt among us" as the reason (*Ar.* 2.53). The reason, in each case, is the "renovation" of creatures. This makes way for Athanasius's understanding of "a beginning of His ways" as the beginning of the new creation, inaugurated by Christ as the Way (John 14:6) and the Beginning (Col 1:18) (*Ar.* 2.65). To be in Christ is to be a new creation (2 Cor 5:17). In this sense, the "Economy of Christ's manhood" is the economy of salvation. He distinguishes between Christ as only begotten, in which he stands apart from all creatures as utterly unique, and Christ as Beginning or first-born, in which he is connected with other creatures as the one who paves the way for their redemption (*Ar.* 2.48).

Finally, if Prov 8:22 and 23 refer to the Economy, Athanasius allows Prov 8:25, "Before all the hills He begets me," to refer to the eternal Son, noting the lack of purpose associated with the verb "begets" (*Ar.* 2.56, 60). Rather than regarding this shift in person as awkward, he understands the distinction between verbs to underscore his fundamental distinction between "creature" and "offspring."[16]

12.3 COSMIC UNITY IN CHRIST

Throughout the last section, Athanasius's practice of reading verses from across the canon in illuminating interrelationship with one another has been evident. In particular, Prov 8:22 gains its sense from its placement within a carefully constructed network of scriptural verses, which is simultaneously generative of and ordered by Athanasius's definition of Scripture's *skopos*. Such a practice will seem to the modern exegete both arbitrary and ideologically driven: the verses have been ripped out of their native historical and literary contexts, with no eye to authorial intention or genre, and made to

[16] As noted by Boersma (2016, 16–17), who is following Kannengiesser and Clayton, Athanasius offers an alternative interpretation of Prov 8:22 in *Ar.* 2.78–82 as referring to the eternal Wisdom which is "created" in its image in creatures. This otherwise surprising shift is explained, I would argue, by a recognition of the inextricable connection between the incarnate Christ and all other creatures (for whose sake he became incarnate). To talk about Christ in the economy, for Athanasius, is to talk about the economy of the whole creation (as I will argue below).

mean something else by way of an ecclesially imposed canon and doctrinal agenda. The fact that an anti-Nicene reading would be equally viable according to the same method gives the lie to the orthodox resolution.

What might seem arbitrary to a twenty-first-century onlooker, however, is not so to the fourth-century controversialist. Scriptural unity is underpinned and underwritten by a cosmic unity located in Christ. For both Arius and Athanasius, the Wisdom through which God creates is the same Wisdom that becomes incarnate in Christ (whether that Wisdom be proper to the Father, as Athanasius would have it, or itself created, as Arius would have it). Doctrinally committed twenty-first-century Christians might want to make an analogous claim, but the connection between the cosmic claim and the historically produced scriptures is much more remote for them. To believe that the Wisdom to which the New Testament witnesses is itself speaking in Proverbs, and moreover prophetically of the incarnation (as at least Athanasius argues), is hard to take seriously while also taking seriously the diverse historical circumstances in which Proverbs and, say, John's Gospel were produced. To make a connection between them can only be to impose one's own ideological agenda on them from without, at the expense of their own historically located agendas. The upshot of this view is that the cosmic christology of the fourth century can only be received as mythological-by-contrast-with-historical. At best such mythology can be demythologized to yield acceptable conceptual insights that make no claim on history.

By the end of the essay my aim is to have brought into question the set of assumptions that leads us to receive the claim of cosmic unity in Christ as myth. In the meantime, the present section will fill in the detail of Athanasius's particular vision of cosmic unity in Christ.

As we saw in the previous section, Christ, as "the beginning of ways," is the one who makes way for the renovation of creation, ushering in the new creation. But as Athanasius clarifies, Christ is not first-born simply "in point of time." He is so in his "condescension" ($\sigma\upsilon\gamma\kappa\alpha\tau\dot{\alpha}\beta\alpha\sigma\iota\varsigma$) to creation (*Ar.* 2.62), being created as "the Way" for its sake (*Ar.* 2.65). He is not, as first-born, just the first of many new creatures (on a level with those creatures), but because also the only begotten is the one *in whom* all is made new (2 Cor 5:17, cited in *Ar.* 2.65). The economy of his humanity is in this strong sense the economy of salvation: he is not just the initiator or facilitator of salvation, but *is* salvation, insofar as his flesh is not just his own but is bound up with the whole of creation. Recall Athanasius's question about "purpose." Definite purpose is lacking when Christ's divinity is in view, but present when his humanity is in view, its creation being "for us" or "for our sakes." Again, this is not to be taken loosely. Christ's humanity is tightly bound up with the whole of creation, having no rationale apart from that creation, and thus being inseparable from it: the rest of creation is implied in Christ's humanity. In the words of Athanasius: in "his taking of manhood,...He collects together the tribes of Israel"; and "whereas he was created for us, all things may now be created in Him" (*Ar.* 2.53). Again, "God created Him for our sakes, preparing for Him the created body, as it is written, for us, that in Him we might be capable of being renewed and deified" (*Ar.* 2.47).

This tightly knit, interconnected character of new creation in Christ is not a feature of the new creation by contrast with the old. The incarnation is for the sake of the renovation of a creation already created in Wisdom—in the one who becomes incarnate. Commenting on Prov 8:25, "Before all the hills he begets me," Athanasius argues from the fact that Wisdom was begotten "before all" that it must be "other than all things" (*Ar*. 2.60). His argument does not simply rely on the elision between "all the hills" and "all things," but on the premise, recalled from earlier, that "no one creature was made before another, but all things originate subsisted at once together (ἀθρόως ἅμα) upon one and the same command" (*Ar*. 2.60). This is a startling claim. One could not emphasize more pithily the oneness of creation. Earlier, Athanasius had claimed (in implicit comment on Genesis 1) that "each [creature] has its origination with all the rest, however it may excel others in glory" (*Ar*. 2.48), and elaborated: "And from the visible creation, we clearly discern that His invisible things also . . . are not independent of each other; for it was not first one and then another, but all at once were constituted after their kind" (*Ar*. 2.49). His vision of creation is as an interconnected whole.

This has implications, moreover, for the role of the incarnation within creation. If creation is to be considered as an inseparable whole, then the crucial distinction made by the Word's taking flesh will not be between the time before and the time after the incarnation (or Jesus's human life), but between the eternity of the Word and the Word's human economy, in which the whole of creation is bound up. To be sure, Athanasius does not do away with the significance of the temporal distinction. Thus, when tackling Heb 1:4, he interprets the time (καιρός) of which the apostle speaks, by appeal to Heb 1:1, as the time of God's Son by contrast with the time of the prophets. But when he later presses the καιρός question in discussion of Heb 3:1–2, he distinguishes between "things before creation" and "when 'the Word became flesh,'" and again between "the Essence of the Word [or] His natural generation from the Father" and "His descent to mankind and High-priesthood which did 'become'" (*Ar*. 2.7), and finally between "the Word's human Economy" and "His Essence" (*Ar*. 2.9). From this vantage point, the incarnation is not a moment in time, but God's condescension to and transformation of the whole creation. While the incarnation is for the sake of creation's *renovation*, insofar as it is the making new of *all* things, we cannot get behind the new creation to something more basic. "Old creation" is an abstraction. While the incarnation is not thereby rendered necessary for creation, the hypothesis of a creation without Christ becomes unthinkable.

New creation, for Athanasius, just is creation. This emerges in his discussion, alluded to above, of Christ as "first-born" by contrast with "only begotten." As we would by now expect, the distinction is one between essence (only begotten) and economy, in which the Word, by its condescension (συγκατάβασις), has become the first of many brethren (Rom 8:29) (*Ar*. 2.62). Athanasius draws out the distinction by posing the question of purpose. "Only begotten" is said "absolutely" (ἀπολελυμένως), while "first-born" is said "because of brethren," and more all-encompassingly, because it "has again the creation as a reason (αἰτία) in connection with it" (*Ar*. 2.62); and he goes on to cite Col 1:16. Athanasius sums up: "Not then because He was from the Father was He called 'First-born,' but because in Him the creation came to be" (*Ar*. 2.63). The economy of the Word has here become, more than the economy of salvation, the economy of creation, whose very existence depends on the Word's condescension.

12.4 SPEAKING AS SCRIPTURE SPEAKS

This is a compelling vision. But is it compelling to the twenty-first-century reader? Proverbs 8:22 can be read in connection with John 1:14 and Col 1:16 (and sundry other verses from across both testaments) because they are all ultimately about Christ, who is both the Wisdom by which God created all things, and the one in whom that same Wisdom became incarnate. Christ is, on this account, the subject matter of Scripture, its *skopos*, authorizing Athanasius's promiscuous intertextuality. Such a claim is most easily made by appeal to the divine author, perhaps in tandem with an appeal to divinely inspired human authorship. But this smacks of historical docetism to the twenty-first-century reader: the subject matter of the divine (or divinely inspired human) author trumps the other historically bound subject matters about which Scripture's human authors might have been speaking. Put differently, the canonical context for reading Prov 8:22 trumps its local literary and historical context. The cosmic Christ is myth not history.

In the present section—the pivotal one for the essay as a whole—I will offer an alternative account of Athanasius's hermeneutic, one that will enable me to argue that the above summary involves a category mistake: Athanasius's intertextuality is grounded not in an assumption about common subject matter, but in the practice of discerning appropriate contexts.[17] This will make way for the more specific claims of the sections to follow, concerning cosmic unity in Christ and Athanasius's *skopos*. To anticipate, cosmic unity in Christ does not mean that everything is contained in some mythical godlike human, who thereby becomes the totalizing content of Scripture, but rather that creation, patterned after divine Wisdom, has the human Christ as its finite node of interconnectedness. Second, Athanasius's *skopos* is not the subject matter of Scripture; it is an instruction regarding the contexts in which Scripture is to be read (or better, uttered).[18] In semiotic terms (see Peirce 1998, 13), Christ as the God-man is not Scripture's object (or referent) but its interpretant.

In order to understand what Athanasius is up to in his appeal to the *skopos* of Scripture, with its presupposition of cosmic unity in Christ, we need to investigate his wider hermeneutical goals, which turn out to be quite different from those of a twenty-first-century exegete.

---

[17] Cf. James 2016, discussed below.

[18] My account diverges here from Young's, which aligns the διάνοια with the referent of a text (in distinction from its mode of expression). This becomes clear in Young 1997, ch. 6, entitled "Reference and Cross-Reference." Earlier, when discussing Athanasius, she identifies the *skopos* with the "overarching plot" (Young 1997, 43).

We can begin to flesh out Athanasius's hermeneutic by returning to his threefold question concerning person, time, and purpose. When he asks this of Prov 8:22, his goal is to determine in what "sense" (νοῦς) the verse might be appropriately spoken (*Ar.* 2.44). That his concern is precisely with contexts of right speech is underlined by his repeated use in this section of verbs of speech (λέγω and φημί). To clarify, Athanasius's question is not, "What is the verse about?" (after which he might then determine whether it is true), but "How might the verse be truly spoken?" To establish person, time, and purpose is thus to establish the appropriate use(s) of a verse, or the appropriate context(s) in which it might be spoken.

Keeping this hermeneutical goal in mind allows one to make sense of much of Athanasius's interpretive practice. For example, in *Ar.* 2.17, in continued wrestling with the Arian-friendly verse Acts 2:36, and in particular the fact that it speaks of Christ as "made," Athanasius investigates "parallel phrases . . . to find what the usage (συνήθεια) is of divine Scripture" (*Ar.* 2.17). He shows, with reference to Gen 27:37, in which Jacob is "made lord" over Esau, how "made" may be used not of essence but relatively. He concludes that Christ is "made lord" not as Word (implying that the Word is a work) but relative to us (*Ar.* 2.18). Similarly, in 2.45–46, in exegesis of "He created" in Prov 8:22, he distinguishes in scriptural usage between calling something a "creature" (κτίσμα) and using the verbal expression "he created" (ἔκτισε) of something, enumerating examples of the former in which essence is signified, but going on to show that the verb does not (typically) "denote the essence and mode of generation" (*Ar.* 2.46), but "something else as coming to pass" (*Ar.* 2.45), citing Ps 101:19 LXX; Ps 50:12 LXX; Eph 2:15, etc. (each of which has to do with renewal). This "rule" is then applied to Prov 8:22. A further example can be found in *Ar.* 2.3, in which Athanasius seeks to show that a term should be understood in keeping with the nature of what it is used to describe, rather than the other way round, giving examples in which children are called servants and vice versa. Again, in *Ar.* 1.13, he shows that certain (trademark Arian) prepositional phrases ("was not," "when," "before") are characteristically used of creatures, but never of the Son, who instead is spoken of as "ever," mapping the creator/creature distinction by way of these verbal markers.

By plotting these scriptural patterns of speech, Athanasius develops rules for understanding how words are being used in controverted cases. From the way in which a word or phrase is used in other, analogous instances, he can hypothesize how it is to be appropriately spoken in the instance at hand. In other words, he hypothesizes an appropriate context for the latter. Thus, to take one of the above examples, "ἔκτισε" is typically or habitually used in the context of creaturely renewal; thus one may hypothesize that Prov 8:22 is also appropriately spoken in that context (i.e., in the context of Wisdom's human economy), rather than in the context of a determination of Wisdom's essence. In corroboration of this account of his practice, Athanasius on several occasions appeals explicitly to the "custom" (ἔθος) of Scripture to speak in certain ways (*Ar.* 2.53, 3.18, and 3.30).

Mark Randall James (2016), in a doctoral dissertation on the scriptural hermeneutics of Origen of Alexandria, makes a compelling case that Origen's hermeneutical goal is to speak as Scripture speaks, both by the repetition of its own utterances in new contexts, and by the invention of analogous utterances for analogous contexts. James (2016, 176–177) shows how Origen searches for "the underlying rules of scriptural language," or "the habits of scripture," picking out two related terms that Origen uses to denote such habits, both of which we have met in Athanasius: συνήθεια and ἔθος.[19] James goes on to argue that an important part of learning scriptural wisdom is, for Origen, "learning to discern contexts" for the appropriate use of scriptural speech (James 2016, 196). In the light of my analysis above, I propose that Athanasius's hermeneutic can be fittingly described in similar terms.[20]

The ramifications of this conclusion for a twenty-first-century assessment of Athanasius's hermeneutic are profound. The modern exegete is oriented to the past, to uncovering historically situated meaning controlled by authorial intention or (at least) by original context of production. If a scriptural pericope is to have meaning for the present-day reader, that meaning will have to be derived from the original meaning in a second stage of interpretation, perhaps by the application of analogy. Athanasius, by contrast, does not first try to determine what a scriptural verse means, but asks how (i.e., in what contexts) it might be appropriately spoken. The latter question frees the interpreter from the assumption of a singular meaning, but without (relativistically) multiplying possible meanings beyond measure. To ascertain by way of a scriptural habit the appropriate contexts in which a scriptural verse might be uttered is not to determine what it means in advance, but to offer guidelines for the determination of its meaning on hypothetical future occasions. In short, by asking not after the "what" (meaning) but after the "how" (context), Athanasius pluralizes meaning, emphasizing possible futures for Scripture's interpretation regulated by scriptural habits of speech. On this account, there is no competition between an "original" meaning and meanings for later readers. Each can be an appropriate use of Scripture's speech for a particular occasion, as long as the habit of Scripture is wisely discerned and appropriated in each case. Note also that there is no privileging here of "original context." The latter is just one of the occasions on which the habit of Scripture must be discerned and followed.

What, then, about Athanasius's practice of "promiscuous intertextuality," as I put it earlier? This, too, is illuminated by the above account. If Athanasius's goal is to discern appropriate contexts of use, then his interpretation of diverse scriptural verses in the light of one another does not entail any a priori assumptions about how the verses are

[19] Torrance (1995) devotes a substantial discussion to the significance of Athanasius's use of such terms, naming in addition ἰδίωμα and τάχις, and offering the paraphrase "characteristic biblical usage" (which he equates with one sense of σκοπός). He comments: "[Athanasius] has so steeped himself in all the sacred Scriptures, assimilated their forms of speech and thought, and attained such a mastery of their general tenor, that he can quickly discern the distinctive slant of a particular passage and ring out its natural and proper meaning without artifice" (Torrance 1995, 237).
[20] Cf. Anatolios (2004, 63), who observes that in his anti-Arian polemic Athanasius is "not simply making an abstract theological argument on some neutral ground," but is operating "[w]ithin the context of the linguistic field of the Scriptures." His aim is to follow the scriptural linguistic correlation between God and his Wisdom, and his accusation is that "the 'Arians' are tearing asunder that scriptural correlation."

related. This would be the case if he selected them on the basis of their similar content, assuming that they have a common subject matter. Such would represent the premature unification of Scripture that arguably goes on in some so-called biblical theologies. Rather, if the connections drawn have to do with habits of speech, then they are more minimal and more flexible, capable of accommodating great diversity in subject matter. All that must be assumed is that each verse drawn upon has itself an appropriate context of use, or alternatively put, that it may be spoken wisely, contributing to wise habits of speech. That this itself is not a negligible assumption will be shown in the following section, in which its theological underpinnings will be articulated. But it is nevertheless quite a different assumption from the one normally attributed to those who follow Athanasius in this practice—one that renders them historically docetic.

Before turning to the theological underpinnings, I will make one further hermeneutical observation. The practice of discerning appropriate contexts of utterance, while alien to much twenty-first-century exegetical practice, nevertheless becomes recognizable when we think about how we naturally interpret the Wisdom books, and paradigmatically the book of Proverbs. To interpret a proverb is typically to ask when, where, and how it might be appropriately spoken. What are the contexts in which one should "answer a fool according to his folly" (Prov 26:5) and what are those in which one should not (Prov 26:4)? When is it right to interpret one's suffering as retribution (as Bildad misguidedly counsels Job to do in Job 4:7–8)? Athanasius, we might say, applies this wisdom hermeneutic across the whole canon. This is not to say that he cannot be alert to other genres within the canon; it is a claim, rather, about the character of canonical unity. While the canon contains many genres—narrative, legal, epistolary, etc.—Scripture as a whole has, for Athanasius, the kind of loose coherence of a set of proverbs, rather than the tighter sequential coherence of a plot or the more formal character of a legal code. If that is true, then it is perhaps no accident that the pivotal verse in his exegetical controversy with Arius, Asterius, and others is drawn from Proverbs, nor that the doctrinal focus of the controversy is the precise manner in which Christ is to be named Wisdom.

12.5 Revisiting Christological Unity

In the caricature summary at the beginning of the last section, I accounted for Athanasius's intertextuality by appeal to Scripture's common subject matter: the cosmic Christ. In light of the alternative hermeneutic outlined above, how might this summary be rewritten? We might try the following: the warrant for Athanasius's intertextuality is the cosmic Christ as ultimate *context* for the appropriate utterance of scriptural language. This is an improvement, but it is not quite right. Near the end of the previous section, we uncovered the non-negligible assumption that all the verses of Scripture have appropriate contexts of use, or may be spoken wisely. Might it be the case that Christ is the warrant that such contexts arise, and will continue to arise for future utterers? How might that be, if so?

To assume that a scriptural verse may be appropriately spoken in multiple contexts is to assume that analogies can be found between multiple different worldly situations, which is to assume, in something like the way Athanasius does, that the world is interconnected. It does not fragment into incommensurable worlds across which communication is impossible. Put differently, it is to assume that the world is patterned according to some kind of unifying wisdom. This wisdom is reflected in the habits of Scripture, which retain their pertinence in the most diverse of circumstances. To speak Scripture wisely is to pattern oneself on that wisdom, contributing to its unfolding over time. For Athanasius, Christ is the guarantor of the world's wisdom; indeed Christ *is* that wisdom. To trust that Scripture will continue to yield wisdom over time is, for him, to trust in the sustaining and renewing wisdom of the Word, in whom all things hang together.

On this account, Christ is not the mythical content of all Scripture, but the guarantor of the possibility of its wise utterance in varying historical circumstances. If Christ in this way underpins history's interconnectedness, he does so not by homogenizing diverse historical circumstances, but by enabling analogies to be drawn between them—which is in fact a possibility that any historian must presuppose in the doing of history.

This might all sound quite acceptable as long as we do not have the human Christ in mind. But what about Athanasius's strong claims concerning the Word's human economy, which for him is to be equated with the economy of our salvation, and indeed (if only implicitly) with the economy of creation? In what way does creation find its interconnectedness in the human Christ? It is easy to understand the unity of creation in Christ in "container" terms, Christ as the ideal creature containing all creaturely perfection, and thus the ideal content of all creaturely life. This is not only to dissolve the finite particularity of Christ (as that which distinguishes him from other creatures), but thereby to conflate his divinity and humanity, insofar as his humanity is made to do the work of his infinite divine nature. Christ, as the content of all creaturely life, also becomes the total subject matter of Scripture. In short, the mythical cosmic Christ returns. Instead, Athanasius invites us to envisage Christ in the economy as the nodal point of its interconnectedness, all lines intersecting in his life. His particularity is thereby respected, but is brought into relation with myriad other creatures in their different particularities.[21] Translating it hermeneutically, this amounts to the habit of speaking all scriptural utterances in the company of utterances concerning Jesus's life, as well as in the company of each other in the light of their different connections with that life. This is just the practice of intertextual reading we have observed in Athanasius.

---

[21] In this description I go beyond Athanasius's own language, translating it into contemporary terms. For the contrast between Christ as container and Christ as one who relates to all others, cf. Bauckham and Williams 1987.

12.6 Revisiting *Skopos*

Moreover, Athanasius's *skopos* can be understood as an articulation of just this wisdom of scriptural speech in the company of Christ. To recall:

> [T]he scope and character of Holy Scripture, as we have often said, is this—it contains a double account of the Saviour; that He was ever God, and is the Son, being the Father's Word and Radiance and Wisdom; and that afterwards for us He took flesh of a Virgin, Mary Bearer of God, and was made man. And this scope is to be found throughout inspired Scripture[.]   (*Ar.* 3.29)

Athanasius is misunderstood here if he is understood to be saying that Christ, the God-man, is what Scripture is at every point about. This would be highly reductionist, closing down Scripture's wisdom for future generations rather than opening it up. Rather, Athanasius's scope is an instruction regarding the contexts in which scriptural speech might be appropriately uttered. Specifically, and first in negative terms, no context is appropriate that confuses or conflates the divine and the creaturely in Christ. As we have seen above, to do so is to end up with the mythical cosmic Christ, who trumps the other potential finite contents of Scripture. Ironically, then, Athanasius's *skopos* seeks precisely to guard against that which is attributed to him by our typical twenty-first-century exegete. Positively, Christ embodies an absolute distinction between the divine and the creaturely in his person. To respect this distinction hermeneutically means to respect finite creaturely contexts of utterance in their distinction from one another, not presupposing how a particular utterance will be spoken in advance (and thus what it will mean). To relate each new utterance to the economy of the human Christ is to relate it to the economy of salvation, which is to enhance its distinctiveness against the backdrop of the interconnectedness of the whole.[22]

12.7 Conclusion

Κύριος ἔκτισέ με ἀρχὴν ὁδῶν αὐτοῦ εἰς ἔργα αὐτοῦ. (Prov 8:22 LXX)
The Lord created me a beginning of his ways for his works.

The significance of this verse in the "Arian" controversy does not lie merely in the use of the verb κτίζω of personified Wisdom, as this coincides with the clear New Testament

---

[22] In this account, I part company both with Young, who understands the *skopos* as the overarching plot of Scripture (Young 1997, 43), and who (as we noted above) makes scriptural *reference* central; and also with Torrance, who also links *skopos* (on one of its two levels of meaning) with reference, and ultimately identifies it with Jesus Christ (Torrance 1995, 239). On my account, by contrast, *skopos* is about logic rather than subject matter.

identifications of Christ as Wisdom. At stake is the character of the wisdom in which creation coheres, to which all parties in the controversy give christological articulation. We have examined Athanasius's account of this coherence, with particular reference to his practice of scriptural intertextuality. This is not to presume that Arius or Asterius, or other anti-Nicenes, would not have their own compelling theologies that accounted for their own variants of that practice. Such an exploration being beyond the bounds of this essay, it remains to gather together the threads of Athanasius's vision, and I will do so with reference to its wisdom character.

For Athanasius, the Wisdom in which everything was created results in creation's thoroughgoing interconnectedness. New creation recapitulates this interconnectedness now threaded through the node of the economy of the Word, the human Christ. Athanasius's double *skopos* enshrines the rule that this interconnectedness not be short-circuited: each new occasion requires the discernment of further, particular connections—both with the life of Christ, and with other finite creatures, and with each in the light of the other—which will also mean to make appropriate distinctions. To discern interconnectedness is to practice wisdom. Indeed, it is to be patterned after the Wisdom in which these connections subsist.

To interpret Scripture wisely means to learn its habits of speech, which will mean patiently discerning distinctions and connections between its many verses as these crystallize on each new occasion its words are to be uttered. To short-circuit its intertextual connections would be to fail to discern differences in context, and thus to harden Scripture's habits into a priori rules. This wisdom hermeneutic likens the unity of the canon more to the unity of a collection of proverbs than to the unity of an overarching narrative or that of a formal legal code. Like the Wisdom Literature, it guides one in the discernment of patterns, being itself patterned on the wise creation. If Athanasius is anything to go by, to discover wisdom in patristic interpretation is to rediscover a scriptural and cosmic unity that has become elusive in our contemporary, fragmented world.

Works Cited

Anatolios, Khaled. 2004. *Athanasius. The Early Church Fathers.* Edited by Carol Harrison. London: Routledge.

Anatolios, Khaled. 2013. "'Christ the Power and Wisdom of God': Biblical Exegesis and Polemical Intertextuality in Athanasius's *Orations against the Arians.*" *JECS* 21:503–535.

Bauckham, R. and Williams, R. 1987. "Jesus—God with Us." Pages 21–39 in *Stepping Stones.* Edited by Christina Baxter. London: Hodder and Stoughton.

Boersma, Hans. 2016. "The Sacramental Reading of Nicene Theology: Athanasius and Gregory of Nyssa on Proverbs 8." *JTI* 10:1–30.

Clayton, Allan Lee. 1988. "The Orthodox Recovery of a Heretical Proof-Text: Athanasius of Alexandria's Interpretation of Proverbs 8:22–30 in Conflict with the Arians." PhD diss., Southern Methodist University.

Dowling, Maurice. 2010. "Proverbs 8:22–31 in the Christology of the Early Fathers." *Perichoresis* 8:47–65.

Ernest, James E. 1993. "Athanasius of Alexandria: The Scope of Scripture in Polemical and Pastoral Context." *VC* 47:341–362.

Hansen, D., K. Metzler, and K. Savvidis. 1998. *Athanasius Werke 1/1.2, Orationes I et II contra Arianos*. Berlin: de Gruyter.

Hansen, D., K. Metzler, and K. Savvidis, K. 2000. *Athanasius Werke 1/1.3, Oratio III contra Arianos*. Berlin: de Gruyter.

James, Mark Randall. 2016. "Learning the Language of Scripture: Origen, Wisdom, and Exegetical Inquiry." PhD diss., University of Virginia.

Kannengiesser, C. 1999. "Lady Wisdom's Final Call: The Patristic Recovery of Proverbs 8." Pages 65–78 in *Nova Doctrina Vetusque: Essays on Early Christianity in Honor of Fredric W. Schlatter, S.J.* Edited by D. Kries and C. Brown Tkacz. New York, NY: Peter Lang.

Peirce, Charles Sanders. 1998. *The Essential Peirce: Selected Philosophical Writings*, Vol. 2: *(1983–1913)*. Edited by The Peirce Edition Project. Bloomington, IN: Indiana University Press.

Pollard, T.E. 1959. "The Exegesis of Scripture and the Arian Controversy." *BJRL* 41:414–429.

Schaff, Philip, and Henry Wace, eds. 1994. *Athanasius: Select Works and Letters*, vol. 4 of *Nicene and Post-Nicene Fathers*, Series 2. Peabody, MA: Hendrickson Publishers.

Torrance, T.F. 1995. "The Hermeneutics of Athanasius." Pages 229–288 in *Divine Meaning: Studies in Patristic Hermeneutics*. Edinburgh: T&T Clark, 1995.

Williams, Rowan. 2001. *Arius: Heresy and Tradition*. 2nd ed. London: SCM.

Young, Frances. 1997. *Biblical Exegesis and the Formation of Christian Culture*. Cambridge: Cambridge University Press.

CHAPTER 13

WISDOM IN RABBINIC INTERPRETATION

AMRAM TROPPER

Iɴ rabbinic literature, the sages of the rabbinic movement who flourished in Roman Palestine and Sassanian Babylonia are called "חכמים" or "the wise." As wise men, rabbinic sages viewed their wisdom as the sort attained through natural means such as the interpretation of the Bible and the reception of traditional lore. Prophecy, in rabbinic eyes, had long ago given way to biblical interpretation, hallowed tradition, and legal reasoning.[1] Hence, as the naturally amassed wisdom of "the wise," all of rabbinic literature may be defined as Wisdom Literature.

Needless to say, however, viewing all of rabbinic literature as Wisdom Literature is unhelpful since, other than highlighting that rabbinic sages were called "the wise," it sheds little light on the rabbis or their literature. Moreover, contemporary Wisdom scholarship focuses primarily on specific biblical and Second Temple works, such as Proverbs, Ecclesiastes, Job, and Ben Sira, and the rabbinic epithet "the wise" has little bearing on any of these pre-rabbinic works. The literature of "the wise" encompasses a staggeringly wide array of fields and disciplines, including law, midrash, mysticism, theology, magic, medicine, literary narrative, and dream-interpretation; this sweeping range of rabbinic interests implies an understanding of wisdom far broader than the range of conceptions of wisdom found in pre-rabbinic sources.[2]

Since rabbinic literature *as a whole* is too vast and unwieldly to reveal much about pre-rabbinic conceptions of wisdom or works such as Proverbs and Ben Sira, let us home in on some rabbinic uses of the term "wisdom" instead. A cursory investigation of the term "wisdom" in rabbinic literature already reveals a span of conceptions of wisdom far narrower than the broad understanding of wisdom implied by rabbinic literature as a

---

[1] The transition from the prophetic to the rabbinic era is described in Seder Olam 30 (ed. Milikowsky 2013, vol. 1, 322) as follows: "from here on out, 'incline your ears and listen to the words of the sages' (*Proverbs* 22:17)." For further references, see Tropper 2013, 26 n. 8.

[2] See Stemberger 2008, 295.

whole. At one extreme, some rabbinic sources envision wisdom much like Ben Sira did. Linking wisdom to Torah (e.g., Sir 24:23), Ben Sira apparently viewed universal wisdom as a natural revelation granted to all humanity and Torah as a special wisdom bestowed only upon Israel.[3] Similarly recognizing the existence of a universal gentile wisdom independent of Torah, the following citation from Lamentations Rabbati seems to set forth a comparable interpretation of wisdom:

> "Her king and her leaders are amongst the gentiles [where] Torah is not [to be found]" (Lamentations 2:9). If a man should say to you there is wisdom amongst the gentiles, believe him for it is written "I will make the wise vanish from Edom and understanding from Esau's mountain" (Obadiah 1:8). [However, if he should say] there is Torah amongst the gentiles, do not believe him for it is written "Her king and her leaders are amongst the gentiles [where] Torah is not [to be found]."[4]

Other rabbinic sources, such as the citation below from Sifre Deuteronomy, also acknowledge the existence of a universal gentile wisdom but discourage its study:

> "Recite them" (Deuteronomy 6:7): Make them central (to your life) and do not make them tangential by having no discussion without them and by not mixing them with other matters as did a certain person—lest you say (since) I have learned the wisdom of Israel, I will go and learn the wisdom of the nations, hence another verse says "to walk in them" (Leviticus 18:4) and not to be without them.[5]

At the opposite extreme, some rabbinic sources identify wisdom with rabbinic law[6] or even with talmud, the advanced dialectical analysis of the Mishnah. In the following parallel sources from Tosefta and Babylonian Talmud Bava Metzi'a, wisdom is alternatively identified as rabbinic law and as talmud:

Tosefta Bava Mezti'a 2:30:[7]	Babylonian Talmud Bava Metzi'a 33a:
And who is his teacher?	Our rabbis taught: The aforementioned teacher is
...Rabbi Meir says: the teacher who taught him **wisdom**, not the teacher who taught him **Bible**.	the teacher who taught him **wisdom** and not the teacher who taught him **Bible** and **Mishnah**, [these are the] words of Rabbi Meir.
Rabbi Judah says: Anyone from whom most of his **talmud** derives.	Rabbi Judah says: Anyone from whom most of his **wisdom** derives.

---

[3] This interpretation of Ben Sira's conception of the relationship between wisdom and Torah was compellingly presented in Schmidt Goering 2009. See also Adams 2008, 203–204; Weeks 2010, 91; Wright 2013, 157–159; Beentjes 2016, 11–17.

[4] Lamentations Rabbati 2:9 (ed. Buber 5659, 114). See Schmidt Goering 2009, 78 n. 27. See also Babylonian Talmud Berakhot 58a; Babylonian Talmud Megillah 16a. Many rabbinic sources seem to share a similar view of wisdom alongside Torah. See, for example, Mishnah Avot 3:13; 3:17; 3:18. (Cf. Rosen-Zvi 2016, 177–178.)

[5] Sifre Deuteronomy 34 (ed. Finkelstein 1993, 61–62). See also Sifra 13, 11 (ed. Weiss 1862, 86a–b) and the position attributed to Rabbi Ishmael in Babylonian Talmud Menaḥot 99b. (Cf. Hirshman 1999, 133–134.)

[6] See Lieberman 1992, 47; Tropper 2004, 58; Rosen-Zvi 2016, 175.

[7] See also Tosefta Horayot 2:5.

In the Tosefta's earlier source, Rabbi Meir identifies wisdom as rabbinic (or extra-biblical) law while in the Babylonian Talmud's later source, he implicitly equates wisdom with talmud.[8] In the same vein, the correlation of wisdom with talmud is also intimated in the Babylonian version of Rabbi Judah's position, where the Tosefta's "talmud" is replaced with "wisdom."

Betwixt the extreme rabbinic conceptions of wisdom, some rabbinic sources, such as the citation below from the Mekhilta de Rabbi Simeon Bar Yohai, seem to view wisdom and Torah as largely synonymous:

> "And the sound of the horn [grew louder and louder]" (Exodus 19:19): It is the way of the world that the longer a sound goes on, it weakens. However, He who spoke and the world came into being is not so, for the longer his sound (or voice) goes on, it strengthens; the longer the children of Torah go on, their understanding settles as it says "wisdom is in the aged" (Job 12:12).[9]

Although these varied rabbinic conceptions of wisdom lack close biblical precedents, they are loosely reminiscent of some biblical passages. For example, the existence of a universal gentile wisdom, explicitly acknowledged by the rabbis, is already posited in the reference to the wisdom of the Kedemites and Egyptians in 1 Kgs 5:10 [4:30], the wisdom of the gentile kings cited in Proverbs,[10] and the wisdom of the gentile protagonists of Job. Similarly, long before the rabbis, Deut 4:6 and Ezra 7:25 already linked wisdom to law, when the former referred to observance of God's laws and rules as "your wisdom and discernment to other peoples" and the latter had King Artaxerxes call upon Ezra to enlist his divine wisdom when appointing officials to enforce and teach God's laws. Yet despite their shared elements, rabbinic conceptions of wisdom extend far beyond earlier biblical conceptions. No biblical text prefers Torah study to instruction in gentile wisdom and rabbinic texts explore the relationship between wisdom and law in far more detail than any biblical text. In other words, as wisdom continued to evolve through rabbinic times, the rabbis extended, developed, and transformed the variegated pre-rabbinic conceptions of wisdom.

One expansive way to illuminate the rabbinic interpretation of wisdom is to map out the nuances and details of the rabbis' diverse notions of wisdom against pre-rabbinic conceptions. An alternative and more focused course, and the one pursued below, approaches Wisdom as a literary genre (or mode).[11] If the Wisdom literary genre is defined as a host of family resemblances in form and content shared by a handful of pre-rabbinic writings,[12] then it seems that one rabbinic composition, Mishnah Avot, should

[8] See Lieberman 1988, 168.
[9] See Mekhilta de-Rabbi Simeon Bar Yohai, Yitro 19:19 (ed. Epstein and Melamed 1955, 144). See also Kugel 1997, 28; Horovitz 2011, 72–74, 78, 180–183, 273; Stemberger 2008, 295; Rosen-Zvi 2016, 175.
[10] See Prov 30:1; 31:1.
[11] On Wisdom as a literary mode, see Sneed 2015a, 39–42. See also Fox 2015, 69–86.
[12] See Collins 1998, 1; Tropper 2004, 56; Dell 2015, 145–160; Sneed 2015a, 59–62. For current purposes, it is irrelevant whether one views the qualities of Wisdom Literature as family resemblances or the privileged properties of a prototypical exemplar (see Miller 2015, 94–95).

be viewed as a late member of the Wisdom literary trajectory.[13] In light of Avot's presence on a literary continuum with ancient Hebrew Wisdom, I hope to show how Ben Sira paved the way for various features and innovations of Avot, which, in turn, enriched the rabbinic interpretation of wisdom.

13.1 Avot As Mishnah, Hebrew Wisdom, and a Greco-Roman Succession

Avot is a tractate of the Mishnah and, in line with mishnaic practice, Avot cites sayings attributed to rabbinic sages of the tannaitic period (ca. 60–220 CE). Avot, however, is also an unusual mishnaic tractate because it also cites numerous sages from Second Temple times and, more importantly, its contents are quite unlike the legal materials which comprise the bulk of the Mishnah. In contrast to mishnaic law, Avot's didactic sayings are akin to the style and substance of ancient Hebrew Wisdom Literature, to works such as Proverbs and Ben Sira.

With respect to style, numerous literary traits connect Avot to ancient Hebrew Wisdom. For example, Avot cites and paraphrases passages from Proverbs and Ben Sira.[14] Avot employs literary techniques often employed in Wisdom Literature such as riddles, numerical sayings, lists, anadiplosis, anthology, dialogue, and metaphor.[15] Moreover, the hallmark of Hebrew Wisdom, the bipartite sentence (or proverb), leaves traces throughout Avot as attested by the following examples: "Make for yourself a teacher and possess for yourself a friend" (1:6); "Love work and hate lordship" (1:10); "Say little and do much" (1:15); "Be a tail to lions and not a head to foxes" (4:15); "Look not at the pitcher but at what is in it" (4:20).[16]

With respect to substance, numerous themes of ancient Wisdom Literature appear in Avot such as the search for life's secrets, reward and punishment, and self-evident intuitions about mastering life,[17] though ethics receives more attention than any other traditional Wisdom theme. Avot portrays kindness as one of the three pillars of the world (1:2); extols disinterested righteousness (1:3); exhorts the opening of one's house to the poor (1:4); urges one to select worthy companions and a virtuous way of life (1:6–7); commends truthful testimony (1:9); praises the pursuit of peace and love of humanity (1:12); counsels how to avoid transgression (3:1); cautions one to cherish other people's honor and property (2:10, 2:12, 4:12); and calls upon one to receive every person with

---

[13] See Tropper 2004, 51 (with references in n. 2); Rofé 2006, 416–418; Stemberger 2008, 301–304; Horovitz 2011, 71–72; Hurovitz 2012, 87–91; Rosen-Zvi 2016, 183; cf. Fischel 1975, 74–75.

[14] See Mishnah Avot 1:17 and Prov 10:19; Mishnah Avot 4:4 and Sir 7:17; Mishnah Avot 4:19 and Prov 24:17.

[15] See Tropper 2004, 61 with references in n. 51.

[16] See Tropper 2004, 64–75; Sharvit 2006, 20–32.

[17] See Tropper 2004, 57–58.

joy and a pleasant countenance (1:15, 3:12). In sum, Avot, like earlier books of Hebrew Wisdom, embodies a "language craft" (Alter 1985, 164), a synthesis of Wisdom themes and an artistic literary format (Tropper 2004, 57). As such, Avot emerges as a late member of the Wisdom literary genre or, in other words, the nature and extent of the similarities between Avot and earlier works of Wisdom warrant close comparison.

Comparisons highlight both similarities and differences and it is noteworthy that the prominence of Torah in Avot is unparalleled in earlier Wisdom Literature.[18] Although Torah plays a role in some earlier Wisdom compositions, Avot elevates Torah to new heights by establishing the study of Torah and the observance of its precepts as fundamental Jewish values. Avot depicts Torah as a pillar of the world (1:2) and the instrument through which it was created (3:14), as a crown of the Jewish people (4:13) and the purpose of their creation (2:8). Torah is not to be viewed as an inheritance that is acquired without effort (2:12), rather it is to be toiled after constantly (2:15, 4:10), sought even in distant places (4:14), established in one's home (1:4), discussed at one's dinner table (3:3), studied on the road (3:4), and carefully preserved in one's memory (3:8, 5:12). Torah is to be honored and cherished (1:4), and its observance will be rewarded (2:7, 14–16). Through its depiction of Torah, Avot recasts earlier understandings of both Torah and Wisdom through the lens of rabbinic ideology.[19]

In wedding artistic language to ethical instruction or medium to message, Avot's synthesis of form and content creates an aesthetic that evokes the imagination and inculcates ideas deep within the mind. Echoing Wisdom Literature's hope to mold character with the help of poetic language and vivid imagery, Avot's artistic prose, its language craft, was also designed to form character. However, in addition to the timeless verities of the biblical sage, Avot sought to form the character of the new, rabbinic Jew.[20]

The first four of Avot's five chapters present an anthology of Wisdom sayings attributed to rabbinic and proto-rabbinic sages while chapter five is comprised of similarly non-legal though mostly anonymous materials organized in a descending numerical order. The central structuring principle of chapters one through four is the chain of transmission and the chain prominently opens the tractate as follows: "Moses received the Torah from Sinai and transmitted it to Joshua, and Joshua to the elders, and the elders to the prophets, and the prophets transmitted it to the Men of the Great Assembly" (1:1). This opening statement constructs the earliest stages of the transmission of the Torah, i.e. the five books of Moses and extra-biblical oral traditions, from its initial reception on Mount Sinai until the early Second Temple period. The chain of transmission then explicitly structures the first two chapters of Avot, tracing the history of the Torah's transmission via a teacher-disciple schema from biblical times until the early tannaitic period. Chapters three and four continue the chronological theme until the end of the

---

[18] See Tropper 2004, 58; Rofé 2006, 418; Horovitz 2011, 72–74; Hurovitz 2012, 90; Rosen-Zvi 2016, 182–184.

[19] For a new interpretation of the rabbinic house of study and other rabbinic instructional settings, see Mandel 2017, 171–211.

[20] See Tropper 2004, 85–87.

tannaitic period but are structured along generational lines rather than by a teacher-disciple pattern. Avot's chain is not a straightforward reflection of historical realty but rather a rhetorical construct designed to establish the continuity of the rabbinic enterprise with earlier Jewish sages and leaders, thereby grounding rabbinic teachings in the ancient past.

There is no pre-rabbinic Jewish precedent for a teacher-disciple chain of transmission extending over a number of generations nor is there any precedent in ancient Wisdom Literature for a collection of named-sayings by multiple authors. However, both of these unprecedented literary features appear in the Greco-Roman Successions literary genre. Successions, which emerged within philosophical academies during the second century BCE, ascribed the origin of a philosophical school to a sage from the distant past and then portrayed each successive academy head as the disciple of his immediate predecessor. Successions were scholastic (or doctrinal) in nature since they outlined the transmission of proper doctrine over the course of time and thereby served to ground the traditions of a school in the hallowed past. Yet, since the links in succession lists were the heads of philosophical academies, Successions were also supposed to reflect the line of the legitimate institutional authority of an academy. In time, Successions spread beyond philosophy to other intellectual traditions and gradually became the standard way in which one portrayed the history of an intellectual discipline in the Greco-Roman world. Successions also included attributed maxims (entitled *chreiai*) and so the synthesis of a chain of transmission with a collection of attributed Wisdom sayings in Avot is in tune with the standard format for depicting the history of an intellectual discipline during tannaitic times.[21]

In short, when Avot was composed in third-century Roman Palestine,[22] its editor drew inspiration from three distinct spheres: Hebrew Wisdom, Greco-Roman Successions, and rabbinic culture. Reinventing Hebrew Wisdom as named sayings in a succession list, the editor infused his novel creation with the values and worldview of the ambient rabbinic setting.

13.2 Avot and Ben Sira

As noted above, Avot cites (or lightly paraphrases) a passage from Ben Sira and, more generally, Avot echoes the didactic style and Wisdom themes of Ben Sira (and its predecessor, Proverbs). These echoes of Ben Sira are sufficiently prominent to link the two works together, but they do not indicate that Avot closely hews to Ben Sira's image. In point of fact, Avot refashions Ben Sira's form and content in entirely new ways. For example, Avot often appends third legs to the bipartite sentences typical of Ben Sira (and

---

[21] See Tropper 2004, 157–188. On the literary matrix of tannaitic texts which influenced the formation of Avot's chain of transmission, see Tropper 2013, 23–67.

[22] See Tropper 2004, 88–116.

Proverbs)[23] and Avot amplifies the role of Torah far beyond the role it was assigned in Ben Sira. In short, as distinct moments in a shared literary trajectory, Avot and Ben Sira form discrete points on a literary continuum with both robust similarities and pointed differences.

In light of the Wisdom literary continuum, I would like to suggest that comparisons of Avot to earlier Wisdom Literature reveal that Ben Sira sometimes served as the missing link between Proverbs and Avot. Ben Sira, in other words, laid the groundwork for certain features and innovations of Avot. For example, whereas Torah played a minimal role in Proverbs, Torah's enhanced role in Ben Sira eased the way for its central role in Avot. Thinking about Ben Sira as a pivotal moment on the continuum from Proverbs to Avot, I hope to further illuminate Avot's variation on Hebrew Wisdom by showing four ways in which one section of Ben Sira, the Praise of the Fathers, set the stage for Avot.

The Praise of the Fathers in chapters 44 through 50 of Ben Sira lauds illustrious figures from the past in chronological order,[24] from Enoch and Noah through the early Second Temple leaders, Zerubbabel, Joshua son of Jehozadak and Nehemiah. Simeon the High Priest appears in chapter 50 as the final ancestor eulogized and this Second Temple high priest was apparently identified as Simeon the Righteous by the rabbinic sages.[25] Prior to Ben Sira, no book of Hebrew Wisdom included an extensive discussion of history or surveyed the past via encomia of "the fathers of the world." Hence the first way Ben Sira's Praise of the Fathers illuminates Avot involves its merging of Wisdom and history. By introducing the Praise of the Fathers into Hebrew Wisdom Literature, Ben Sira inspired Avot's similar synthesis of the chain of transmission and Wisdom sayings.

In contrast to Avot, however, Ben Sira's Praise of the Fathers is not structured around a chain of transmission. Unlike a chain of transmission, Ben Sira's Praise of the Fathers does not presuppose a teacher-disciple schema nor underscore the transmission of a lore nor trace the leadership of a scholastic institution.[26] Nonetheless, the chronological ordering of hallowed elders from the past in a Hebrew Wisdom composition, a phenomenon found for the first time in Ben Sira and echoed later on in Avot, suggests that Ben Sira inspired Avot. In other words, Avot's entwining of Wisdom materials with a chronological sketch of revered ancestors apparently stems from Ben Sira's Praise of the Fathers. However, when Ben Sira's synthesis of Wisdom and history was translated into the scholastic setting of the rabbinic movement, Avot recast it in the image of Greco-Roman Successions, a literary genre which wed the succession list to named sayings. In sum, while Ben Sira supplied the ultimate inspiration for interweaving Hebrew Wisdom with a chronological overview of notable ancestor, Greco-Roman Successions supplied the immediate literary paradigm for Avot's synthesis of attributed sayings and a scholastic chain of transmission.

---

[23] See Tropper 2004, 75–80; Stemberger 2008, 302. Cf. Gilbert 2016, 160–171.

[24] The chronological order is broken for the retrospective evocation of Enoch, Joseph, Shem, Seth, and Adam in 49:14–19.

[25] See Moore 1927, 359. More generally, see Tropper 2013, 29, 140–142, 199–212.

[26] See Tropper 2004, 165–172; Schmidt Goering 2009, 104–108; Gilbert 2014, 334–339; Gilbert 2016, 158.

The second way Ben Sira's Praise of the Fathers sheds light on Avot relates to a simple yet significant issue: the tractate's title "Avot" (אבות) or "Fathers." The term "fathers" appears three times in the course of Avot, but in all three cases it appears incidentally, serving a local literary purpose with no broader ramifications for the tractate or its title.[27] By contrast, the term "fathers" makes two prominent appearances at the head of Ben Sira's Praise of the Fathers. The term appears first in the Praise of the Fathers's official title, "Praise of the Fathers of Antiquity,"[28] and then once again in the very first passage of the Praise of the Fathers, "I will now praise men of good deeds, our fathers in their generations" (Sir 44:1). In context, both of these appearances associate the term "fathers" with a chronological overview of esteemed ancestors. Hence, when drawing from Ben Sira the idea to join a survey of early fathers with Wisdom materials, Avot apparently elicited the title "Fathers" as well.[29] Since the titles of most mishnaic tractates are comprised of a single word, Ben Sira's "Fathers of Antiquity" or "our fathers in their generations," was presumably shortened to "Fathers."

The third way Ben Sira's Praise of the Fathers illuminates Avot involves Avot's portrayal of Simeon the Righteous. After Avot's opening mishnah traces the transmission of the Torah from Sinai all the way to the prophets and the men of the Great Assembly, Avot 1:2 reveals that "Simeon the Righteous was of the remnants of the Great Assembly." This portrayal is unusual because all the other tradents in Avot are linked to their predecessors with the verb "received" (קבל) or with its counterpart, "transmitted" (מסר). Thus, for example, "Moses *received* the Torah from Sinai and *transmitted* it to Joshua...and the prophets *transmitted* it to the men of the Great Assembly" (1:1); "Antigonus of Sokho *received* [the Torah] from Simeon the Righteous" (1:3); and "Rabban Yohanan ben Zakkai *received* [the Torah] from Hillel and from Shammai" (2:8). Rather than receiving the Torah from his immediate predecessors, however, Simeon the Righteous is portrayed as a remnant of the Great Assembly. The Great Assembly emerges in Avot 1:1 as an early Second Temple institution which had "received" the Torah from its predecessors, and Avot 1:2 divulges Simeon's affiliation with this Great Assembly. In relating Simeon's institutional affiliation in lieu of his reception of the Torah, Avot 1:2 breaks the literary mold enlisted throughout the chain of transmission and one wonders what triggered this literary divergence. Since no earlier source describes Simeon the Righteous as a member of the Great Assembly,[30] what prompted Avot to describe Simeon as a remnant of the Great Assembly rather than as a tradent who had "received" the Torah from his predecessors?

The rationale for portraying Simeon the Righteous as a remnant of the Great Assembly and at the end of an era stems, I believe, from Simeon the High Priest's presence at the

[27] See Mishnah Avot 2:2 (cf. Sir 44:16), 5:4, 5:5.

[28] This title does not appear in all the textual witnesses and hence may not be authentic (see Corley 2008, 164 n. 50). Yet even if inauthentic, the title may well have been interpolated by rabbinic times.

[29] Cf. Lerner 1987, 263–264; Tropper 2004, 187–188.

[30] Moreover, no earlier source even mentions the Great Assembly and the tannaitic conception of the Great Assembly was apparently modeled on the assemblies of Nehemiah 8–10. See Tropper 2013, 23–67.

tail end of Ben Sira's Praise of the Fathers. Simeon the High Priest is the only figure in the Praise of the Fathers not mentioned in the Bible, and yet he is proudly featured at the end of Ben Sira's list of worthy ancestors. Though Ben Sira probably concluded the Praise of the Fathers with Simeon the High Priest because Simeon, his contemporary, was the last great figure he considered worthy of including in the Praise of the Fathers, rabbinic readers of Ben Sira were likely to view Simeon the High Priest's location in the Praise of the Fathers as indicative of his historical significance. Coming at the end of a long list of great historical figures from the past, Simeon the High Priest is easily construed as the final representative of a former age; since Simeon is the only ancestor mentioned who lived after Nehemiah, the rabbis would have probably viewed him as a late member of the Jewish leadership of Nehemiah's days, i.e. as a remnant of the (imagined) institution they called the Great Assembly.[31] In short, it seems that Simeon the High Priest's suggestive location at the end of Ben Sira's Praise of the Fathers prompted Avot to portray Simeon the Righteous as a remnant of the Great Assembly.

The fourth way Ben Sira's Praise of the Father paints Avot in a new light relates to Avot's chronological focus. After quickly sketching the history of the transmission of the Torah from Moses till the early Second Temple period, Avot's very first Wisdom saying is attributed to the men of the Great Assembly. Immediately afterwards, Avot continues with Simeon the Righteous, a remnant of the Great Assembly, citing a saying attributed to him as well. Following Simeon, Avot then traces the transmission of Torah down through the Second Temple period and beyond:

> 1:1: Moses received the Torah from Sinai and transmitted it to Joshua, and Joshua to the elders, and the elders to the prophets, and the prophets transmitted it to the men of the Great Assembly. They said three things... 1:2 Simeon the Righteous was of the remnants of the Great Assembly. He used to say... 1:3: Antigonus of Sokho received [the Torah] from Simeon the Righteous. He used to say... 1:4: Yose ben Yoezer of Zeredah and Yose ben Yohanan of Jerusalem received [the Torah] from him. Yose ben Yoezer of Zeredah said... 1:5: Yose ben Yohanan of Jerusalem said... 1:6: Joshua ben Perahyah and Mattai or Arbela received [the Torah] from them. Joshua ben Perahyah said... 1:7 Mattai of Arbela said... 1:8: Judah ben Tabbai and Simeon ben Shatah received [the Torah] from them. Judah ben Tabbai said... 1:9: Simeon ben Shatah said... 1:10: Shemaiah and Avtaylon received the Torah from them. Shemaiah said... 1:11: Avtalyon said... 1:12: Hillel and Shammai received [the Torah] from them. Hillel said... 1:15: Shammai said... 2:8: Rabban Yohanan ben Zakkai received [the Torah] from Hillel and from Shammai. He used to say ....[32]

---

[31] Since the rabbis mistakenly thought that the Persian era only lasted thirty-four years into the Second Temple period, they could easily imagine that Simeon the Righteous was a remnant of Nehemiah's Great Assembly and also lived into Hellenistic times. See Tropper 2013, 208–209. See also n. 30 above.

[32] Mishnah Avot 1:1–2:8 according to MS Kaufmann. On the interpolation of the house of Gamaliel (skipped over here) into the chain of transmission, see Tropper 2004, 21–24.

In short, Simeon the Righteous assumes a prominent role at the head of Avot. Avot's first Wisdom saying is attributed to Simeon's institutional affiliation, the Great Assembly, and Simeon himself is the first named tradent attributed a saying. Simeon's prominent role in Avot's opening is striking because Simeon is also the final patriarch lauded in Ben Sira's Praise of the Fathers. Simeon's opposing locations at the end of the Praise of the Fathers and at the head of Avot strongly suggest, in my opinion, that Avot was composed as the Praise of the Fathers's sequel (or update). In commencing with Simeon the Righteous and his Great Assembly (after quickly sketching the biblical background), Avot took off exactly where Ben Sira's Praise of the Father's had left off. Since Ben Sira had focused on the patriarchs leading up to Simeon, Avot did not. Indeed, after Moses and Joshua, Avot mentions no patriarch by name until Simeon the Righteous. Having served as the final patriarch in Ben Sira's list, Simeon was the natural choice to kick off the next chapter in Jewish history, i.e. Avot's list of Second Temple and tannaitic sages.

In sum, Avot is an unusual tractate of the Mishnah, a rabbinic adaptation of the Greco-Roman Successions and a late member of the Wisdom literary trajectory. Comparisons to earlier Wisdom Literature reveal that Avot not only echoes Wisdom themes and artistic forms, but also develops some of these literary features in new directions. Sometimes Avot builds upon Ben Sira, as it does when linking Wisdom to Torah, and I have argued above that four features of Avot stem from Ben Sira's Praise of the Fathers. The Praise of the Fathers modeled the synthesis between Wisdom and history which Avot transformed into a Greco-Roman Succession. The prominent use of the term "fathers" in the Praise of the Fathers inspired Avot's title. The location of Simeon the High Priest at the tail end of the Praise of the Fathers prompted Avot's conception of Simeon as a remnant of the Great Assembly and also triggered the idea to place Simeon at the head of the rabbinic sequel to the Praise of the Fathers. Each of these four developments is significant in its own right but as a group they underscore the benefits of interpreting Avot in light of earlier Wisdom Literature.

13.3 Avot as Wisdom

As a late member of the Wisdom literary trajectory, Avot drew inspiration from earlier works of Hebrew Wisdom like Ben Sira, but as a product of the rabbinic movement of the early Roman Empire, Avot recast pre-rabbinic notions of wisdom in line with a new institutional context and historical setting. Imagining wisdom anew within the rabbinic disciple circles of Roman Palestine, Avot Hellenized and Romanized wisdom while rabbinizing and politicizing it.

Though ultimately inspired by Ben Sira to entwine Wisdom and history, Avot, as noted above, enlisted the Greco-Roman Successions format when integrating attributed sayings into a scholastic chain of transmission. Further signs of Greco-Roman culture appear elsewhere in Avot as well. For example, the witty reflection attributed to Hillel in Avot 2:6—"Moreover, he saw a skull floating on the face of the water and said to it: 'On account of drowning others, they drowned you. In the end, those who drowned you shall be drowned'"—is a fine illustration of a Greco-Roman cynicizing *chreia*.[33] Similarly, the series of questions and counterintuitive answers attributed to Ben Zoma in Avot 4:1— "Who is wise? He who learns from every man .... Who is mighty? He who subdues his evil inclination .... Who is rich? He who rejoices with his lot .... Who is honored? He who honors humanity..."—is highly reminiscent of Stoic ethics and similar paradoxical Stoic formulations.[34] In a related vein, the five-part saying attributed to Rabbi Tarfon in Avot 2:15—"The day is short, and the work is great, the laborers are sluggish, and the recompense is great, and the master of the house is urging"—is a rabbinic adaptation of the five-part aphorism attributed to Hippocrates: "Life is short, the craft (of medicine) long, opportunity fleeting, experience treacherous, judgment difficult."[35] Avot's use of Greek loanwords from legal (4:11), military (4:11), and architectural contexts (4:16) reflects close familiarity with some prominent features of Greek-speaking society in the eastern provinces of the Roman Empire and the notion that "equinoxes and geometry (i.e. mathematics) are appetizers for wisdom" (3:18) is reminiscent of Quintilian's claim that children be taught geometry (i.e. mathematics) because "it exercises the mind, sharpens the wits and generates quickness of perception."[36] In addition, the call to "pray for the welfare of the kingdom since, but for the fear of it, each one of us would have swallowed his neighbor alive" (3:2), is a typical sentiment for a provincial who appreciated the benefits of the Pax Romana. In short, by framing wisdom in terms drawn from the ambient Greco-Roman context, Avot Hellenized and Romanized Hebrew wisdom.

Whereas Avot's ties to Greek and Roman culture are sometimes hard to detect, its rabbinizing program is evident throughout. From beginning to end, Avot attributes statements to rabbinic or proto-rabbinic sages and alongside traditional Wisdom themes, Avot spotlights the study of Torah, the fulfillment of its precepts and ethical behavior. Expanding Torah's role far beyond its role in Ben Sira, Avot unabashedly weds Wisdom to Torah, setting forth the values which crystalized within the rabbinic study houses of Roman Palestine. For example, the very first saying in Avot—"Be deliberate in judgment, raise up many disciples and make a fence for the Torah" (1:1)—addresses the three central rabbinic leadership roles: that of judge/arbitrator,[37] teacher,[38] and legislator/jurist. In mapping out the fundamental elements of rabbinic public service, Avot's opening saying serves as a programmatic statement for the rabbinic movement.[39] In addition, in light of the centrality of discipleship and the house of study within this movement, Avot

---

[33] See Tropper 2004, 179 n. 74.

[34] See Seneca, *Ad Lucilium epistulae morales* 2.5–6; Cicero, *Paradoxa Stoicorum* 6.42–52. Though Avot never mentions any Stoic philosopher by name, it exhorts one "to study what to respond to an Epicurean" (Avot 2:14).

[35] Hippocrates, *Aphorisms* 1.1 (with Jones's translation, slightly modified). See also Tropper 2004, 174 n. 56.

[36] Quintilian, *The Orator's Education* 1.10.34–35. See also Tropper 2004, 173 n. 53.

[37] See Avot 1:8–9; 4:8.

[38] See Avot 1:4, 6, 11, 16; 2:5; 4:12, 20; 5:14–15.

[39] See Tropper 2013, 24–26.

exhorts every Jewish man to transform his home into a study house (1:4); to make for himself a rabbinic teacher (1:6, 16); to fear his teacher (4:12); to warm himself by the fire of his teachers (2:10); and to study Torah regularly (1:15) and ever more intensively (1:13). Insofar as rewards are concerned, Avot assures that the study of Torah secures one a place in the afterlife (2:7). In short, in reworking Wisdom within a rabbinic setting, Avot synthesized the Wisdom themes of old with rabbinic piety, theology, and scholasticism.

Furthermore, wisdom in Avot does not stem from parents,[40] communal elders,[41] kings,[42] or bureaucrats, but from specific "fathers." These fathers, moreover, are not merely revered ancestors, like the fathers in Ben Sira's chronological overview, but links in a chain of transmission. Across the generations, the sages of Avot's chain of transmission were purportedly entrusted with passing down the Torah (along with its extra-biblical traditions), and the Wisdom sayings attributed to these sages, by association, bolstered their authority and that of their rabbinic colleagues and heirs. Avot ascribes Wisdom sayings to the rabbis and proto-rabbis who passed on the Torah and only to them. Traditional repositories of knowledge in the home and community as well as other religious groups or sects, such as Sadducees and Jesus followers, were all excluded from Avot's chain of transmission. Avot portrays the rabbinic movement as the only true heir to Moses and the prophets, so from Avot's point of view, any and all other Jewish groups broke off at some point from the mainstream path of rabbinic Judaism.[43] Hence, by enhancing the rabbinic movement's claim to represent authentic Jewish practice, belief, and leadership, wisdom assumed a novel political role.

In sum, while echoing the ancient language craft of Hebrew Wisdom, Avot introduced new values and literary forms. While articulating a rabbinized Wisdom, Avot refracted the ambient Greco-Roman setting. In updating Ben Sira's historical sketch, Avot sought to empower the rabbinic movement. In seeking to mold rabbinic character, Avot redefined the good life.

WORKS CITED

Adams, Samuel L. 2008. *Wisdom in Tradition: Act and Consequence in Second Temple Instructions*. Leiden: Brill.

Alter, Robert. 1985. *The Art of Biblical Poetry*. New York, NY: Basic Books.

Beentjes, Pancratius C. 2016. "The Book of Ben Sira: Some New Perspectives at the Dawn of the 21st Century." Pages 1–19 in *Goochem in Mokum: Wisdom in Amsterdam*. Edited by George J. Brooke and Pierre Van Hecke. Leiden: Brill.

Babylonian Talmud = *Talmud Bavli*. Vilna: Romm, 1880–1886.

Buber, Salomon, ed. 5659 [1899]. *Lamentations Rabbati*. Vilna: Romm.

---

[40]   See Prov 1:8.

[41]   See Job 12:12.

[42]   See 1 Kgs 5:10 [4:30]; Prov 1:1; and the references in n. 11 above.

[43]   See Tropper 2013, 190–195.

Cicero. 1968. *Paradoxa Stoicorum*. Trans. H. Rackham. Vol. 4. Cambridge, MA: Harvard University Press and William Heinemann.

Collins, John J. 1998. *Jewish Wisdom in the Hellenistic Age*. Edinburgh: T&T Clark.

Corley, Jeremy. 2008. "Sirach 44:1–15 as Introduction to the Praise of the Ancestors." Pages 151–181 in *Studies in the Book of Ben Sira: Papers of the Third International Conference on the Deuterocanonical Books, Shimeʿon Centre, Pápa, Hungary, 18–20 May, 2006*. Edited by Géza G. Xeravits and Jósef Zsengellér. Leiden: Brill.

Dell, Katharine J. 2015. "Deciding the Boundaries of "Wisdom: Applying the Concept of Family Resemblance." Pages 145–160 in Sneed 2015b.

Epstein, Jacob N., and Ezra Z. Melamed, eds. 1955. *Mekhilta de-Rabbi Simeon Bar Yohai*. Jerusalem: Mekize Nirdamim.

Finkelstein, Louis, ed. 1993. Sifre Deuteronomy = *Siphre ad Deuteronomium*. New York, NY: Jewish Theological Seminary of America.

Fischel, Henry A. 1975. "The Transformation of Wisdom in the World of Midrash." Pages 67–101 in *Aspects of Wisdom in Judaism and Early Christianity*. Edited by Robert L. Wilken. Notre Dame, IN: University of Notre Dame Press.

Fox, Michael V. 2015. "Three Theses on Wisdom." Pages 69–86 in Sneed 2015b.

Gilbert, Maurice. 2014. *Ben Sira: Recueil d'études—Collected Essays*. Leuven: Uitgeverij Peeters.

Gilbert, Mauric. 2016. "*Pirqé Avot* and Wisdom Tradition." Pages 155–171 in *Tracing Sapiential Traditions in Ancient Judaism*. Edited by Hindy Najman, Jean-Sébastien Rey, and Eibert J.C. Tigchelaar. JSJSup 174. Brill: Leiden.

Hippocrates. 1979. *Aphorisms*. Translated by W.H.S. Jones. Vol. 4. Cambridge, MA: Harvard University Press; London: William Heinemann.

Hirshman, Marc. 1999. *Torah for the Entire World*. Tel-Aviv: Hakibbutz Hameuchad [Hebrew].

Horovitz, Ben-Tzion. 2011. *From Corpus to Corpus—The Integration of the Book of Proverbs into the Tannaic Literature, against the Background of the History of the Israeli Wisdom Literature*. PhD diss., Hebrew University [Hebrew].

Hurovitz, Victor Avigdor. 2012. *Proverbs: Introduction and Commentary*, Vol. 1: *Chapters 1–9*. Tel Aviv: Am Oved; Jerusalem: Hebrew University [Hebrew].

Kugel, James. 1997. "Wisdom and the Anthological Temple." *Prooftexts* 17:19–32.

Lerner, Myron B. 1987. "The Tractate Avot." Pages 263–276 in *The Literature of the Sages*, Part I. Edited by Shmuel Safrai and Peter J. Tomson. Assen/Maastricht: Van Gorcum; Philadelphia, PA: Fortress.

Lieberman, Saul. 1988. *Tosefta = The Tosefta According to Codex Vienna, with Variants from Codex Erfurt, Genizah Mss. And Editio Princeps (Venice 1521), Zeraʿim—Nezikin*. New York, NY: Jewish Theological Seminary of America; *Tosephta Based on the Erfurt and Vienna Codices*. Edited by M.S. Zuckermandel. Pozevolk: Yissakhar Yizhak Meir, 5641.

Lieberman, Saul. 1992. *Tosefta Ki-fshuṭah: Zeraʾim*. Jerusalem: The Jewish Theological Seminary of America and the Maxwell Abbell Publication Fund.

Mandel, Paul D. 2017. *The Origins of Midrash: From Teaching to Text*. Leiden: Brill.

Milikowsky, Chaim, ed. 2013. Seder Olam = *Seder Olam: Critical Edition, Commentary and Introduction*. 2 vols. Jerusalem: Yad Izhak ben Zvi and The Rabbi David Moses and Amalia Rosen Foundation.

Miller, Douglas B. 2015. "Wisdom in the Canon: Discerning the Early Intuition." Pages 87–113 in Sneed 2015b.

Mishnah = *Faksimile Ausgabe des Mischnacodex Kaufmann A 50 (5728)*. Reprint. Hague: Veröffentlichungen der Alexander Kohut-Gedächtnisstiftung, 1929. Jerusalem: s.n.

Moore, George Foot. 1927. "Simeon the Righteous." Pages 348–364 in *Jewish Studies in Memory of Israel Abrahams*. New York, NY: Jewish Institute of Religion.

Quintilian. 2001. *The Orator's Education*, vol. 1. Translated Donald A. Russell. Cambridge, MA: Harvard University Press; London: William Heinemann.

Rofé, Alexander. 2006. *Introduction to the Literature of the Hebrew Bible*. Jerusalem: Carmel [Hebrew].

Rosen-Zvi, Ishay. 2016. "The Wisdom Tradition in Rabbinic Literature and Mishnah *Avot*." Pages 172–190 in *Tracing Sapiential Traditions in Ancient Judaism*. Edited by Hindy Najman, Jean-Sébastien Rey, and Eibert J.C. Tigchelaar. JSJSup 174. Brill: Leiden.

Schmidt Goering, Greg. 2009. *Wisdom's Root Revealed: Ben Sira and the Election of Israel*. Leiden: Brill.

Segal, Moshe Zvi, editor. 1972. Ben Sira = *Sefer Ben-Sira Ha-shalem*. Jerusalem: Bialik Institute.

Seneca. 1979. *Ad Lucilium Epistulae Morales*. Vol. 1. Translated by Richard M. Gummere. Cambridge, MA: Harvard University Press; London: William Heinemann.

Sharvit, Shimon. 2006. *Language and Style of Tractate Avoth through the Ages*. Beer-Sheva: Ben-Gurion University of the Negev [Hebrew].

Sneed, Mark R. 2015a. "'Grasping after the Wind': The Elusive Attempt to Define and Delimit Wisdom." Pages 39–67 in Sneed 2015b.

Sneed, Mark R., ed. 2015b. *Was There a Wisdom Tradition? New Prospects in Israelite Wisdom Studies*. AIL 23. Atlanta, GA: SBL.

Stemberger, Günter. 2008. "Sages, Scribes and Seers in Rabbinic Judaism." Pages 295–319 in *Scribes, Sages, and Seers: The Sage in the Eastern Mediterranean World*. Edited by Leo G. Perdue. Göttingen: Vandenhoeck & Ruprecht.

Tropper, Amram. 2004. *Wisdom, Politics, and Historiography: Tractate Avot in the Context of the Graeco-Roman Near East*. Oxford: Oxford University Press.

Tropper, Amram. 2013. *Simeon the Righteous in Rabbinic Literature: A Legend Reinvented*. Leiden: Brill.

Weeks, Stuart. 2010. *An Introduction to the Study of Wisdom Literature*. London: T&T Clark.

Weiss, I.H., ed. 1862. Sifra = *Sifra de-Vei Rav*. Vienna: Jacob Schlossberg.

Wright III, Benjamin G. 2013. "Torah and Sapiential Pedagogy in the Book of Ben Sira." Pages 157–186 in *Wisdom and Torah: The Reception of "Torah" in the Wisdom Literature of the Second Temple Period*. Edited by Bernd U. Schipper and D. Andrew Teeter. JSJSup 163. Leiden: Brill.

PART III

THE CONCEPT OF WISDOM IN THE MODERN WORLD

CHAPTER 14

....

WISDOM IN THE QUR'AN
AND THE ISLAMIC
TRADITION

....

U. ISRA YAZICIOGLU

He [God] grants wisdom unto whom He wills:
and whoever is granted wisdom has indeed been granted abundant good,
but none bears this in mind except those with insight.

(Qur'an 2:269)[1]

THE qur'anic passage above, well known among Muslims, highlights three characteristics of wisdom. First, wisdom is granted by God to whomever God wills. Given that from a qur'anic perspective everything happens according to God's will, it is worth asking why wisdom is specially highlighted here. Second, the verse states that wisdom is abundant goodness, which raises the question: What is so good about wisdom? Third, the verse suggests that not all will seek or cherish wisdom, highlighting the relational character of wisdom. How is wisdom particularly relational? Taking these three questions as central, I shall discuss the place of wisdom in the Qur'an and in various interpretive traditions of Islam, such as qur'anic exegesis and Islamic spirituality, theology, and jurisprudence, with special attention to several important Muslim thinkers and sages in the classical and contemporary era, such as al-Ghazali, Rumi, Ibn al-'Arabi, and Said Nursi. Needless to say, this relatively short article is far from being representative of wisdom in the entire Islamic tradition, but offers general highlights to introduce various streams of thought on the subject.

---

[1] Unless otherwise noted, translations of qur'anic passages are from Muhammad Asad 1984 with occasional minor modification.

14.1 BACKGROUND AND ASSUMPTIONS

The narrator's voice throughout the Qur'an is God, who is understood as addressing people through the Prophet Muhammad, who claimed to have received the text from God through the angel Gabriel over a period of about twenty-three years (610–32 CE). The Qur'an bears some similarity to the Bible in terms of content, referring, for example, to the same figures, such as Adam, Abraham, Moses, and Jesus. One interpretation of this fact is that the Qur'an was somehow assembled from biblical and post-biblical traditions, which has been almost the default assumption for a long time in Western Islamic studies. Another interpretation considers the similarities as a sign of a shared origin, God, which is how the Qur'an presents itself and is the Muslim view. As a Muslim theologian puts it, "Islam does not believe that it has inherited their teachings through temporal and historical transmission, for a prophet owes nothing to anyone and receives everything from Heaven" (Nasr 2002, 18). Since explanations of origin will always involve an existential decision, this essay will leave such decisions to the reader and instead focus on the qur'anic text and its reception by Muslim interpreters. Throughout the essay, I treat the Qur'an as a separate unit in itself, and, while acknowledging similarities with other traditions, I resist a hierarchical model that deems the Qur'an as "derivative" of biblical literature.

Two qur'anic terms used in this essay that are quite different than the biblical usage also require clarification. First is the term "prophet." In qur'anic discourse, Muhammad is the final prophet of God, and the term prophet/messenger refers to human beings chosen by God to communicate divine guidance for humanity, calling them to belief in one God and life after death, worship, and just conduct. In the Qur'an, prophethood is a universal phenomenon, not limited to a particular region or race. From the first human, Adam, to Muhammad, God has sent countless prophets to various peoples throughout time (Q 3:33; 40:78, etc.). Second, the term "revelation" (*wahy*) refers to the messages directly given by God to the prophets to convey.

14.2 WISDOM IN ARABIC AND QUR'ANIC USAGE

In classical Arabic, the word for wisdom, *ḥikma*, is traced to the root *ḥ-k-m* and related to *ḥukm*, which means to judge. Its meaning is also sometimes related to *iḥkam*, which means "to prevent, curb; be strong." Therefore, wisdom is also defined as preventing harm and guiding to good. When ascribed to a human being, it also communicates that the person is balanced and just (Kutluer 1998, 503).

Within the qur'anic context, *ḥikma* is used in a variety of ways. In one of the earliest texts on qur'anic terminology that has reached us, the qur'anic exegete Muqatil

b. Sulayman (d. 150/767),[2] lists five aspects (*wujuh*) of wisdom he sees in the Qur'an (Kutluer 1998, 503):

1. Commands and guidelines set by God. For instance, "And so, [men] when you divorce women and they are about to reach the end of their waiting-term, then either retain them in a fair manner or let them go in a fair manner. But do not retain them against their will in order to hurt [them]: for he who does so sins indeed against himself. And do not take [these] messages of God in a frivolous spirit; and remember the blessings with which God has graced you, and all the revelation and the wisdom (*ḥikma*) which He has bestowed on you from on high in order to admonish you thereby" (Q 2:231; see also Q 3:48, 4:113).
2. As understanding and knowledge. For instance, in regards to John the Baptist, "We [God] granted him wisdom (*ḥukma*) while he was yet a little boy" (Q 19:12).
3. As prophethood. For instance, in regards to Prophet David, "And We strengthened his dominion, and bestowed upon him wisdom and sagacity in judgment" (Q 38:20).
4. As interpretation of the Qur'an (as in 2:269, quoted in the epigraph).
5. The Qur'an itself. For instance, "That is from the wisdom thy Lord has revealed unto thee" (Q 17:39).[3]

Wisdom is related to revelation in some form throughout the Qur'an. Indeed, the noun wisdom is mentioned in the Qur'an twenty times, with half of the occurrences referring explicitly to revelation (*kitab*). God is said to have bestowed revelation and wisdom on all prophets (see Q 3:79, 81). There are also specific references to certain prophets who have been given wisdom and revelation, such as Jesus: "Now when Jesus came [to his people] with all evidence of the truth, he said: 'I have now come unto you with wisdom, and to make clear unto you some of that on which you are at variance: hence, be conscious of God, and pay heed unto me'" (Q 43:63).[4] In addition, the noun wisdom is mentioned in the Qur'an in conjunction with several different topics (Kutluer 1998, 503–504):

1. Sovereignty (*mulk*). Three times: e.g., "We granted revelation and wisdom unto the House of Abraham, and We did bestow on them a mighty sovereignty" (Q 4:54).
2. Counsel (*maw'iẓa*). Once: "Call thou [all mankind] unto thy Sustainer's path with wisdom and goodly exhortation and argue with them in the most kindly manner" (Q 16:125).

---

[2] Maintaining a common practice in Islamic Studies, I give two dates, first referring to an "after hijra" (AH) date according to the Muslim calendar: hijra, 622 CE, referring to a major transformation during Muhammad's ministry and the first year of the Muslim calendar. The second date refers to the common era.

[3] Translation is from *The Study Quran* (2015) edited by Nasr et al.

[4] Similar comments are made about Mary (Q 3:47–48), David (Q 38:20), and Muhammad (e.g., Q 4:113; 17:39).

3. Goodness (*khayr*). Once, as wisdom being abundant goodness (Q 2:269, as quoted in the epigraph).
4. Sign (*aya*), which is a key term in the Qur'an referring to the signs of God in nature and/or in the revelation. Once: "And bear in mind all that is recited in your homes of God's signs and [His] wisdom" (Q 33:34).

In the Qur'an, therefore, the prophets are the primary conveyers of wisdom. There is also a person mentioned in the Qur'an, Luqman, who is not explicitly called a prophet but is noted as having been granted wisdom (Q 31:12). Not much is known about Luqman historically, but "it is most likely that he was a pre-Islamic [ancient] Arabian sage revered during the time of Muhammad" (Nasr et al. 2015, 1002). Only a minority of exegetes claim that he was a prophet; others consider him a sage, who is a follower of revelation given to a previous prophet (Nasr et al. 2015, 1002). In a space of eight verses, the Qur'an narrates his wise advice to his son (Q 31:12–19). In this advice, Luqman emphasizes belief, which should be lived out in gratitude, patience, and humility. He encourages his son to worship one God only and notes that idolatry (*shirk*) is a major injustice. He also counsels him to be grateful to God for his own good, knowing that such gratitude is not needed by God. One should also be grateful to his parents, to be constant in prayer, enjoin goodness and forbid evil, and be patient in what befalls him. Finally, he advises his son to be humble in his interaction with people, avoid false pride, and be modest in bearing and voice.

Commenting on Luqman's wisdom, Rashid al-din Maybudi (2015, 388), a twelfth-century exegete (and author of the longest Sunni commentary in Persian) says:

> Know that wisdom is correct activity or correct speech. Correct activity is to preserve the balance of interaction with self between fear and hope, with the people between tenderness and cajolery, and with the Real between awe and intimacy. Correct speech is that you do not mix levity with the mention of the Real, you preserve reverence, and you connect the end of every talk with its beginning. The wise man is he who puts everything in its own place, does each work as is worthy of that work, and ties each thing to its equal.

Luqman's wisdom as explained by Maybudi suggests that wisdom is the ability to know the truth (that there is one God, that gratitude is for your own soul only, etc.) and express it in attitude and action (by being balanced in joy and seriousness, between fear and hope, etc.). Given that Luqman is the only non-prophet to be mentioned as having been given wisdom, he unsurprisingly emerges in the Islamic tradition as an exemplary sage. Extra-qur'anic stories about Luqman's wisdom appear in Islamic literature. Luqman also appears in pre-Islamic Arab literature. The pre-Islamic stories present him as a wise man with insightful ideas about life and action (Kutluer 1998, 505). In contrast, Islamic traditions talk about his wisdom as that of a God-conscious sage (e.g., Tustari 2011, 138).

In addition to the use of wisdom as a noun in the twenty verses described above, the root *ḥ-k-m* from which wisdom derives, is used more than two hundred times in the Qur'an. Around a hundred of these describe God as being All-Wise (*ḥakīm*). Additionally, there are many instances where the word wisdom does not appear directly, but the wisdom of creation and wisdom behind God's actions is explicated, a point to which we will return later. After this brief introduction to wisdom in the Qur'an, let us now turn to our first question: why is wisdom a unique bestowal from God?

14.3 Part 1: Wisdom as a Unique Bestowal

> God has bestowed upon thee from on high this divine writ and wisdom
> and has imparted unto thee the knowledge of what thou didst not know.
> And God's favor upon thee is tremendous indeed.   (Q 4:113)

From a qur'anic perspective, *everything* happens through God's power and will, including a leaf falling (Q 6:102, 25:2, 39:62, 40:62, etc.). Nevertheless, a number of things in the Qur'an are emphasized as being specifically related to God's will, such as guidance, revelation, forgiveness, sustenance, and, of course, wisdom. Why are certain things specially mentioned as granted by God if all is from God anyway? To answer this question, it will be helpful to look at some theological considerations.

In Islamic disciplines, ranging from theology to mysticism, God is the causer of all causes (*musabbib al-asbab*) and the creator of all events (Chittick 1989, 44). To offer a simplified example: when a flower grows in water, it is not the water that gives life to it, rather God gives life to the flower through the water. Water is merely the apparent cause, with no power to create, while the real cause of the flower's growth is God. Water and life are regularly connected by God and this apparent causal arrangement is maintained by Him for a wise purpose (see 14.4.2 below) (Mermer 2017, 76–77). These apparent causes act both like a "screen" and a "veil" at the same time. They are screens in the sense that the glimpses of divine qualities, such as power, knowledge, and wisdom, are displayed on them. Yet, apparent causes are also like a veil in that they hide the presence of divine agency from the heedless who may not see the beauty in them (see 14.4.2 below). While many things in the universe are veiled through these apparent causes, there are a number of things in the universe that are not "veiled" under regular patterns or with apparent causes. These are things that are crucial for human beings, like mercy and life, whose association with God's will does not need veiling (Nursi 1997, 151; cf. Ibn al-'Arabi's view in Chittick 1989, 45). From this theological perspective, therefore, the reason why wisdom is singled out as a gift granted by God in the Qur'an may be because it is among the things that are crucial for a well-lived life.

In the reception history of the Qur'an, many exegetes and interpreters took note of the special feature of wisdom as a gift that is not granted through apparent causes. That is, it cannot be obtained through hard work or intelligence (though, of course, one can ready oneself to receive wisdom, as will be discussed in the third part). In that sense, wisdom is unique like revelation; it is granted to whomever God wishes and cannot be reproduced or imitated. Indeed, in exegetical works, the connection between revelation and wisdom is well noted.

Tafsir literature is exegesis of the Qur'an, often composed in the form of line-by-line running commentary. Many of the exegetes who wrote such commentaries highlighted and explored the connection between prophethood and wisdom. For instance, Muhammad Ibn Jarir al-Tabari (d. 310/923), a famous early exegete of the Qur'an, defines wisdom as the understanding of the message the prophet of God has brought. He also notes that it is through wisdom that one distinguishes between truth and false-hood and that is why *ḥikma* ("wisdom") comes from the same root as *ḥukm* ("judg-ment"). Another classical exegete, al-Harizmi al-Zamakhshari (d. 538/1144), defines wisdom as putting revelation into practice (Kutluer 1998, 504). Putting revealed truths into practice requires wisdom likely because the complexities of lived reality require dis-cernment in applying principles of truth and ethics.

Another important exegete and theologian, Fakhr al-din al-Razi (d. 606/1210), regards wisdom as the tool with which one comprehends revelation. Commenting on the qur'anic command, "Call thou [all mankind] unto thy Sustainer's path with wisdom and goodly exhortation and argue with them in the most kindly manner" (Q 16:125), al-Razi (1934, 67–68) glosses wisdom "as knowledge with clear evidence" (cited in Kutluer 1998, 504). Hence, the Prophet invites people to God's path with clear evidence.

Finally, in his Sufi commentary, Sahl b. 'Abd Allāh Tustari (d. 283/896) summa-rizes common interpretations of wisdom, including those mentioned above (Tustari 2011, 36):

> Mujāhid and Ṭāwūs said, "Wisdom is the Qur'ān," as He [God] says in Sūrat al-Naḥl, *Call to the way of your Lord with wisdom* [16:125], meaning the Qur'ān. Ḥasan said, "Wisdom is the understanding of the Qur'ān, and wisdom is prophethood," as He says in Sūrat Ṣād, *and gave him wisdom* [38:20], meaning prophethood (*nubuwwa*). And God said [concerning] David, *And God gave him kingship and wisdom* [2:251] meaning prophethood, along with the Book. Qatāda said, "Wisdom is understand-ing the religion of God, Mighty and Majestic is He, and following the Messenger of God"; Suddī said: "Wisdom is prophethood"; Zayd b. Aslam said, "Wisdom is the intellect (*'aql*)"; while Rabī' b. Anas said, "Wisdom is the fear of God, Exalted is He." Ibn 'Umar said, "Wisdom is [to be found in] three things: a clear verse (*āya muḥkama*), the Sunna put into practice and a tongue which is articulate with the Qur'ān."

In sum, many exegetes regard wisdom as closely linked to prophethood and revela-tion. According to the Qur'an, God grants revelation as a pure grace onto whomever He chooses and revelation goes beyond usual powers given to a human. Indeed, the Qur'an repeatedly challenges its audience to attempt to produce similar revelation on their own: "If you have doubts about the revelation We have sent down to Our servant, then produce a single *sura* (chapter) like it—enlist whatever supporters you have other than God—if you truly [think you can]" (Q 2:23). Similarly, "Say, [Muhammad], 'Even if all mankind and jinn came together to produce something like this Qur'an, they could not produce anything like it, however much they helped each other'" (Q 17:88; see also 10:38, 11:13, 52:33–34).

Why is revelation unique like this? According to many Muslim scholars and sages, it is because only revelation fully explains the meaning and purpose of existence that would otherwise remain hidden. As a late Muslim exegete and theologian, Bediuzzaman Said Nursi (d. 1960), puts it, "[W]hile being apparently open, the doors of the universe are in fact closed" (Nursi 2004, 422). That is, while it may seem as if human beings can figure out the meaning of the universe on their own, in reality the "riddle" of existence can only be solved through revelation sent by God through the prophets. Intellect is needed in the process of understanding reality but is not sufficient on its own. Only through a revelation from the Creator and Sustainer of all can humans start to understand reality. Without cues from God, who has infinite and comprehensive vision, human reason is like an illiterate person looking at a text who sees it but does not understand it or even recognize that it is a text (Nursi 2004, 143–145; see also Chittick 1989, 179–180).

The unique connection between revelation and wisdom, therefore, is due to their enlightening perspective on reality. If, from a qur'anic perspective, wisdom is the ability to "read" the universe as a meaningful discourse, what meanings are disclosed in that reading? In exploring this question, we shall also unpack why wisdom is so precious within Islam.

14.4 PART 2: WISDOM REVEALS PRECIOUS TREASURE

> Do you not see that all that is in the heavens and the earth praise God, even the birds as they spread out their wings? Each [of them] knows indeed how to pray unto Him and to glorify Him; and God has full knowledge of all that they do. (Q 24:41)
>
> God said: "I was a hidden treasure, I wanted to be known, so I created the creation."
>
> *al-hadith al-qudsi*

In the act of reading, one ascends, so to speak, from the scribbles and shapes on the page to the meanings expressed by them. Similarly, qur'anic reading of the universe is about ascending from the seen world to the unseen, discovering meanings expressed in the creation. Why is this act of reading the world such an abundant good for humanity? It seems that the qur'anic answer is two-fold. First, such wisdom uncovers the treasure of the beautiful names of God in creation, thereby enabling humanity to discover unending power and beauty through the transient world. Second, through this qur'anic wisdom one discovers that humanity is made for an eternal future.

14.4.1 Wisdom and the "Treasures" of the Beautiful Names of God

The "beautiful names" or "perfect attributes" of God (*al-asma al-ḥusna*), such as All-Powerful, All-Knowing, All-Merciful, All-Wise, the Loving, the Forgiver, the Majestic, and the Punisher, are mentioned throughout the Qur'an repeatedly. Everything in creation, including nature, history, and human life, points to these qualities of God. The created beings, in their beauty and decay, in their apparent power and weakness, reveal these names, the eternal Creator's power, knowledge, compassion, and beauty (e.g., Q 16:70; 22:5). Thus, everything praises God in its own way (e.g., Q 12:105; 17:44; 41:53).

In a saying attributed to Prophet Muhammad and used extensively in Islamic spirituality, God is quoted as saying, "I was a hidden treasure. I wanted to be known and I created the creation" (Schimmel 1992, 74). Wisdom is seeing the world as revealing the treasures of the beautiful qualities/names of God. While the concept of the beautiful names of God has been recognized as crucial in the Qur'an and expounded upon earlier in the tradition, Muhyiddin Ibn al- 'Arabi (d. 638/1240) is credited for bringing a renewed emphasis on the beautiful names of God. Ibn al- 'Arabi notes that the reality of things is grounded in the beautiful names of God. The world is transient in itself but manifests the eternal One's knowledge, power, wisdom, compassion, and so on at each moment. For Ibn al-'Arabi, Nursi, and others, the universe is "the macro-Qur'an" (*al-Qur'an al-kabir*). Just as the Qur'an revealed to the Prophet talks about who God is, the "Qur'an of the universe" "talks about" the Creator's beautiful qualities (Chittick 1998, 3–16; Mermer and Yazicioglu 2017, 54–59). Nursi (2004, 270–271) suggests that even the sciences will find their perfection only if their origins in the beautiful names of God are recognized:

> The reality of the universe and of all beings is based on the Divine Names. The reality of every being is based on one Name or on many. All sciences and arts are also based on and rely upon a Name. The true science of wisdom is based on the Name of All-Wise, true medicine on the Name of Healer, and geometry on the Name of Determiner, and so on.

Seeing the world as a sign of the perfect qualities of God is valuable because it means that passing things disclose enduring meanings. A beautiful flower eventually withers away, but through its existence and decay, it signified that its beauty is from the unending source of beauty that created both it and the other flowers that replace it (Nursi 2004, 87, 710–711). Wisdom given through revelation, therefore, is abundant goodness because it leads humanity to see how transient reality spells out the inscriptions of the source of undying beauty.

14.4.2 God's Wisdom in Nature

As noted earlier, God is described as All-Wise [*ḥakim*] more than one hundred times in the Qur'an; the All-Wise is regarded as one of the beautiful names of God. The Qur'an repeatedly invites its audience to reflect on the world to witness God's wisdom. Nature is one locus of manifestation of divine wisdom. The Qur'an attracts attention to intentionality and purposefulness in nature, such as the benefits in wind and rain or the purposeful growth of a baby in stages, and shows them as signs of divine wisdom and power. In the theological tradition (*kalam*), God's wisdom has been understood as His knowing and creating things with purpose (Ozervarli 1998, 511). Muslim thinkers as well as scientists have talked about the details of natural structures as disclosing the Creator's wisdom (Iqbal 2007, 16–26). They noted the placement of wise and beneficial results in balanced and intricate ways within the living beings and the rest of the world as revealing comprehensive divine knowledge and wisdom. Moreover, qur'anic references to wisdom in creation encouraged impressive Muslim developments in science during the classical and medieval periods (Landau 1958). Contemporary Muslim approaches continue to value studying nature to appreciate God's wisdom.

Classical theologians defined divine wisdom in the relations of created beings. The classical theologian al-Maturidi notes that wisdom has the connotation of "putting things to their proper place" and in that sense relates to divine justice as well (Ozervarli 1998, 511). Ibn al-ʿArabi says in his *Futuhat al-Makkiya*, God's name "the All-Wise" "has a face toward the Knowing (*al-ʿalim*) and a face toward the Governing (*al-mudabbir*), for the Wise has two properties: It determines the property of the places of affairs and it determines the actual putting of the things to their places" (I 389.31; quoted in Chittick 1989, 174).

Reflecting on the universe so as to appreciate divine wisdom has opened up rich discussions about natural causality in the Islamic tradition, as can be seen in the works of various theologians, such as al-Ghazali's arguments against Aristotelian Muslim thinkers. Theologians and mystics tend to caution against getting stuck in "apparent causes" by attributing the wisdom seen in the natural order to the things themselves. They emphasize that God does not need natural causes to create; rather He employs them to reveal His wisdom. For instance, God does not need water to create life but He maintains a consistent link between water and life so that his wisdom can be displayed in it. Divine wisdom, thereby, becomes manifest in water being sent down as rain, in the ability of roots to soak up the water, and so on (Yazicioglu 2013, 146). The affirmation of a need for rain in a frame sustained by the divine wisdom and plan does not mean that rain itself is inherently necessary for God to be able to create life. After all, lifeless rain lacks the necessary qualities—such as knowledge, planning, mercy, and power—to account for the life created through it. Hence, God does not need water to create life, but he connects water and life to display his wisdom and other attributes. The world being structured with apparent causes also makes it possible for human beings to arrange their lives accordingly. For instance, because God maintains a consistent link between water and plant growth, human beings know to water plants if they want them to grow. Various theologians and sages, including Ghazali, Ibn al-ʿArabi, Rumi (d. 672/1273), and Nursi, suggest that the wise person honors the apparent causes as divine missives while knowing that only God makes things happen (Chittick 1989, 177; Schimmel 1992, 78; Yazicioglu 2013, 145–146).

Furthermore, God's maintenance of a causal order not only serves as a screen on which divine qualities manifest but also as a veil (Chittick 1989, 45). Apparent causes veil heedless human beings from unjustly complaining about God. For instance, a heedless person who does not see the beauty of death as transition from this world to the next will focus on the veil of the sickness and blame sickness as the cause of a loved one's death, rather than complaining about the real cause of death, God's will. Divine wisdom requires veiling the "hand of Divine power" from misguided perceptions through natural causality (Nursi 2004, 300–301).

14.4.3 God's Wisdom in Destiny

Divine wisdom manifests also in history, in personal and social realms. Indeed, belief in destiny and trust in God's wisdom has been emphasized as a pillar of faith in the Qur'an and the theological tradition (Yazicioglu 2017, 130–133). While a person or community may not always understand the particular wisdom behind what is happening to them, their lives are traced with divine wisdom. Discernment is necessary to recognize manifestations of divine wisdom in life. After all, as the Qur'an says, sometimes people like things that are bad for them and dislike things that are good for them, and "God knows and you do not know" (Q 2:216, also see 24:19). The story of Prophet Joseph, the longest narrative in the Qur'an, exemplifies how the fate of societies and individuals are wisely planned by God (Q 12). There is also the story of Prophet Moses's journey with a mysterious servant of God who commits shocking offenses that turn out to be part of a wise divine plan (Q 18:60–82). The story is also used in the Sufi tradition as signifying the need for a spiritual teacher in the path to understanding. In Islamic tradition, God's wisdom is also indicated in the reasons for which humanity was created, which brings us to the connection between wisdom and eternal life.

14.4.4 Divine Wisdom and Life after Death

> If the [inscriptions] of the heavens and the earth is for the sake of itself,
> Then there is no wisdom in it.
> But if there is no wise (Creator), what is this orderly arrangement?
> And if there is a wise (Creator), how is His action devoid (of meaning)?
>
> (Rumi, *Mathnawi* IV: 2998–3000)[5]

---

[5] Nicholson's translation (1989) was used with slight modification in brackets introduced in light of Celebi's translation (1946).

A related consequence of qur'anic wisdom valued within Islam is the discovery of life after death. The Qur'an presents life after death as a necessary component of reality indicated by this world. Various Muslim thinkers and sages noted the connection between wisdom and life after death. The wise person realizes that this world is a foretaste of eternal life. The One who made this existence to display His beautiful names will of course take human being from this transient life to continue to witness eternal divine beauty. Such is the requirement of divine wisdom (Nursi 2004, 70–102). Indeed, as noted in Rumi's verses above, Muslim sages saw God's wisdom displayed in the visible arrangement of the world as indicating that humans are created for more than just a transient life. Wisdom is knowing that the world reveals the eternal one. Anything else is not real wisdom because what is the point of anything if we are doomed to transience? (Rumi, *Mathnawi* II: 3200). The wise arrangement of the world is not futile; it is a sign pointing beyond itself to the eternal meanings of the beautiful names of God. The same wisdom shows that human life is also for a larger purpose and is meant for eternity. The One who creates a tree with such wise details and attaches many fruits and flowers would of course not make human life without an enduring purpose. Divine wisdom requires that human life is meant for more than just this fleeting world (Nursi 2004, 77–87). The Wise and Caring God who arranges for the needs of our stomach will of course arrange for the intense yearning of the human heart for eternity (Nursi 2004, 120). Similarly, when one considers the beauty and pleasures of the world, it is clear that, as Nursi (2004, 87, emphasis added) says:

> [T]he adornments of this world are not simply for the sake of enjoyment or admiration. For if they yield pleasure for a time, they cause pain for a longer time with their cessation. They give you a taste and whet your appetite, but never satiate you. For either the life of the pleasure is short, or your life is short, too brief for you to become satiated. These adornments of high value and brief duration must, then, be for the sake of instruction in *wisdom*, for arousing gratitude .... They are, then, for other exalted goals beyond themselves.

The wise person is thus the one who sets his heart on the eternal and sees beyond the surface.

14.4.5 Competing Claims for Wisdom

Muslim scholars who identified revelation as a source of wisdom were of course aware of competing claims about wisdom that placed wisdom outside of revelation. One such claim came from classical traditions of philosophy, especially Greek thought. Starting in the eighth century (second century of the Muslim calendar), successive Muslim caliphs sponsored an extensive translation project in Baghdad's "House of Wisdom" (*bayt al-ḥikma*). During this period, many scientific, philosophical, and cultural texts from various cultures—Indian, Greek, Persian, and so on—were translated into Arabic. Thus, *ḥikma* accrued a special meaning; referring to insights from other traditions and cultures that did not necessarily link to revelation or any transcendent reality. It also became used as a term for philosophy structured along Aristotelian and Platonist lines as well as for study of nature or natural philosophy. Such developments both signaled openness and tension in the Islamic intellectual tradition.

Openness to learning from other cultures seems to have been underpinned by a trust in one God—that all wisdom comes from One source, and insight cannot be a monopoly of one culture or race. A saying attributed to Prophet Muhammad supported such openness: "Wisdom [or 'knowledge' in alternate versions] is the lost item of the believer, he recovers it wherever he finds it."[6] At the same time, given that wisdom in these contexts did not always align with revelation and even at times contradicted it, there have been discussions about the authenticity of non-revealed wisdom. Such tension between the wisdom of revelation and of other sources is visible in exegetical, philosophical, and spiritual traditions. Rumi claims that if one misses the breakthrough brought by the prophets, what appears as wisdom is in fact futility. He emphasizes the Qur'an as the source of true wisdom: "the wisdom *of the Qur'an* is the lost item of the believer, and everyone recognizes their lost property" (*Mathnawi* II: 2910, italics added).

In contrast, Ibn Rushd, a Muslim philosopher and jurist writing in the thirteenth century, made a case for the importance of Aristotelian philosophy, even suggesting that a philosophically trained mind could arrive at the same truth that the prophets of God bring. Ibn Rushd, however, rejected any contradiction between these two sources of wisdom. His apologetic work is thus tellingly entitled: "Book of Decisive Treatise and Determining the Connection between Revelation and Wisdom" (*Kitab Faṣl al-Maqal wa tafriq ma bayn al-sharīʻah wa al-ḥikma min al-ittiṣal*).

Others emphasized the link between reason and revelation by arguing for the need for both. A tenth-century exegete, linguist, and thinker, Raghib al-Isfahani, for instance, glosses the qur'anic passages that mention revelation and wisdom together as suggesting the need for both revelation and reason. For, if there was no revelation, the intellect would be confused, if there was no intellect, revelation would be of no use (Kutluer 1998, 508). Some Muslim philosophers of the Ishraqi school also contrasted "Greek wisdom" (*hikmat-i Yunani*) with "Yamanite wisdom" (*hikmat-i yamani*), which represented the wisdom granted through the mystical path (Schimmel 1975, 262).

14.4.6 Islamic Jurisprudence and Wisdom

Islamic jurisprudence recognizes two main sacred sources, the Qur'an and the *sunna*, and covers a vast area of human life, including rituals, family law, business law, and

---

[6] This tradition is invoked by many Muslims in the contemporary period as well. See, for instance, the renowned African-American Muslim scholar and leader W.D. Muhammad's approach in Lawrence 2007, 164–168.

dietary guidelines.[7] Muslim exegetes of the Qur'an often considered wisdom as related not only to the revelation but also to the life example (*sunna*) of the "messenger of God," Muhammad. Indeed, Imam al-Shafi'i (d. 204/820), an early and foundational figure for Islamic jurisprudence, interprets the wisdom given to Muhammad alongside scripture in Q 4:113 ("God has bestowed upon thee from on high this divine writ [*kitab*] and wisdom") as the exemplary life and sayings of Muhammad (al-Shafi'i 1961, 75–76). During the formation period of various schools of Islamic jurisprudence, al-Shafi'i offered a compelling argument for the significance of *sunna* and prophetic sayings (*hadith*) for understanding the Qur'an and applying its injunctions.

In order to extend the application of an explicit sacred guideline in these two sources to new situations, many jurists sought to identify the "wisdom" behind an injunction in the Qur'an or the prophetic tradition. Therefore, in the context of Islamic law, "wisdom" acquired a technical meaning. For instance, jurists identified the "wisdom" for prohibition of alcohol in the Qur'an as the protection from intoxication, and thus inferred that all other intoxicants, such as drugs, are prohibited in sacred law.

While they sought to identify the "wisdom" behind obligations or prohibitions in the sacred sources, Muslim jurists also recognized that this wisdom may not always be easy to identify or even be completely hidden. In order to avoid arbitrariness, Muslim jurists restricted the use of the perceived wisdom of a divine command as a basis for extending it to new circumstances. Hence, they distinguished the wisdom (*hikma*) behind a ruling from the real reason (*'illa*) behind a ruling. For instance, the Qur'an allows shortening of prayers during travel. The "wisdom" behind this permission seems to be the difficulty of travelling. However, given that the permission is explicitly linked to travelling in the Quran, they identified the "real reason" as travel itself. Thus, they inferred that even if the journey is an easy one, the permission to shorten the daily prayers will stand. Similarly, they noted a "wisdom" behind the prohibition of alcohol may be a health benefit, however, being unhealthy may not be the "reason" for it being prohibited. Therefore, one may not declare everything unhealthy, such as excessive sugar, as religiously forbidden.

While being cautious in making use of their perception of "wisdom" behind a commandment, Muslim jurists still considered trying to understand the overall wisdom of sacred guidelines important. The protection of five things have been identified as the aim of the sacred law (*maqasid al-sharia*): life, intellect, lineage, religion, and property. They also noted that the sacred law is given to humanity for bringing justice, compassion, and purpose as opposed to injustice, cruelty, and absurdity. Anything that goes against these aims, even if they are clothed in religious justifications, are actually distortions of the sacred law (Koca 1998, 514–515).

---

[7] Much of Islamic law is independent of state sanction, that is, what is inferred as God's commands, such as prohibitions against drinking alcohol or lying in selling a product, do not have to have a state authority to be considered part of the sacred law.

14.4.7 Theological Debates on God's Wisdom

Muslim theologians also debated about wisdom in a different context: divine wisdom in relation to divine will and power. The Qur'an contains statements that indicate purpose and wisdom in God's act of creating everything in the best way (Q 32:7). Similarly, God creates with truth (*bi al-haqq*) (Q 64:3), which can be interpreted as creation being molded according to a just and meaningful purpose. Similarly, God has not created the world in vain (*batila*) (Q 38:27). Based on such passages, theologians of various schools agree on God being infinitely wise. They all deny the possibility of injustice or absurdity in divine actions. They note that sometimes things may appear unjust or frivolous to us on the surface, but claim that, in reality, either in themselves or in their results, everything has a meaningful purpose (Ozervarli 1998, 512).

The early Muslim theologians debated, however, the relation between divine wisdom and divine will. The debate arose partly because of the qur'anic passages that highlight the absolute freedom of God (as in, "He cannot be called to account for whatever He does, whereas they [human beings] will be called to account"; Q 21:23). A minority of theologians, the Mutazilites, argued that God cannot act without a wise purpose (*'illah*). Others, Asharite and Maturidi theologians, disagreed by saying that no external criteria, not even a wise purpose, can constrain divine freedom; God does as He wills. Mutazilites accused their opponents of imputing frivolity to divine will. In reality, the latter affirmed that God's wisdom is manifest in creation and nothing is created in vain. They simply did not recognize any external purpose as a necessitating factor for divine action; God does not need any means to achieve any end or any external reason to act. The purposes in God's actions do not pertain to himself but to his creatures and the order He set for them. Similarly, according to Ibn al-'Arabi, who takes a different approach to the Qur'an than these scholastics, the act of the Pre-eternal Being cannot be expected to be bound to any motivating factor; He acts freely as He wishes (Ozervarli 1998, 513).

Given the fact that the Mutazilite theologian Qadi Abd al-Jabbar also notes that ultimately God's actions cannot be necessitated by any reason, the implications of the theological debate regarding wisdom and the will of God might seem unclear. In reality, the emphasis on the absoluteness of God's will, which transcends any human criteria of judgment, has an implication: surrender to God's will. In turn, this attitude of surrender produces a markedly different attitude toward the problem of evil in traditional Islam than in Western thought (Nasr 2002, 10).

This absolute view of divine will also influenced a medieval Muslim debate on "the best of all possible worlds." Abu Hamid al-Ghazali (d. 505/1111), a major theologian (usually associated with the Asharite school), claimed that "there is not in possibility anything more wonderful than what is" (*laysa fil imkan abda min ma kana*). The statement opened up a debate among theologians across centuries on the themes of divine power and possibility, divine will and necessity, and divine justice and obligation. For our purposes of understanding divine wisdom in relation to divine will and reason in Islamic theology, it will be helpful to attend to the debate a bit more closely.

14.4.8 God's Wisdom and Power

One side of the debate focused on divine power and possibility. To Ghazali's critics, the possibility of a better world seemed so obvious (e.g., people could be richer, harsh climates could be milder) that to deny this possibility seemed an assault on divine power (Ormbsy 1984, 135–150). The defenders of Ghazali's statement answered that the term "possibility" (*imkan*) in the statement was misunderstood. Ghazali would concede that a more wonderful world than this world may be possible in that it may be conceived by the mind. Yet it is not possible because of an "extrinsic factor," divine will. The perfection or the wonderfulness of the world is not an inherent quality of the world itself. Rather, God's will and wisdom renders the world as wonderful. For instance, being blind is an imperfection but it helps appreciation of vision. Hence, blindness is "perfectly" placed by divine wisdom as a necessary precondition for the appreciation of healthy vision (Ormsby 1984, 79).

Another concern about "the best of all possible worlds" claim relates to divine justice and obligation. To explain his claim, Ghazali said that if there were a possible world and God withheld it, then this would be "miserliness contrary to Divine generosity and injustice contrary to the Divine justice." This view, the critics said, put a limit on God's will, as if God had to follow an external criterion of optimum good. The defenders of Ghazali's view replied by saying that it had nothing to do with the theory of the optimum (*aslah*). For divine wisdom can necessitate something contrary to the optimum and make it good, such that sickness may be suitable for someone.[8] Interestingly, Ghazali distances himself from the Mutazilite view here, saying that while God does everything with His wisdom, "things divine are too exalted in their majesty to be weighed on the scales of the Mutazilites" (Ormsby 1984, 263). In sum, despite their arguments, theologians agreed on the conclusion that things are just and perfect because God willed them, and since nothing exists apart from God's will, then this existing world is the best possible and perfect as it exists. Similar to the previous section's ending, such a conclusion may be a bit surprising, making us wonder what the contention was in the first place if they all agreed that whatever God does is wisdom. I take their debate as a reminder that accepting God's wisdom does not preclude discussing what appears to be unwise or imperfect and exploring in what ways such imperfections in the world can be wise. More importantly, it suggests that appreciation of divine wisdom goes beyond an intellectual formula and is ultimately an existential stance (Ormsby 1984, 263). Indeed, according to some Muslim scholars, understanding revelation and embracing wisdom requires a particular spiritual attitude, which brings us to the relational aspect of wisdom.

---

[8] As a Muslim mystic from Egypt, Ibn Ataillah (709/1309) notes, "[S]ometimes He [God] gives while depriving you, and sometimes He deprives you in giving" (Schimmel 1978, xv). That sickness can be a means of great blessings (such as remembering God's care, appreciating things taken for granted, being mindful of the eternal life, and so on), has been noted by various Muslim sages and exegetes. For example, see Nursi's (1996, 266–285) "Treatise for the Sick."

14.5 PART 3: WISDOM AS RELATIONAL

> Repeat wisdom as much as you want
> If you are unfit for it, it is far away from you.
>
> (Rumi, *Mathnawi* II: 318)

Whether in the narrations related from the highly regarded Imam Ali (d. 40/661), the close companion and son-in-law of Prophet Muhammad, who was praised as having been gifted wisdom, or in wisdom sayings attributed to later sages like Ibn Ataillah (d. 709/1309), the relational character of wisdom has been emphasized in Islamic spirituality. I use "relational" in the sense that the nature of a thing emerges in one's interaction with that thing. Wisdom is appreciated only by people who are ready for it. In fact, many Muslim sages considered wisdom to be kept hidden from those who are unprepared. Prophet Jesus, whose wise prophetic counsels were in circulation in Islamic literature from early on, warns not to offer pearls of wisdom to those unable to understand it (Khalidi 2001, 88). What prepares one for wisdom? The willingness to clear the ego.

To receive wisdom, one needs to be willing to confront the illusionary perspective of one's ego. As long as the ego's claim of self-sufficiency persists, one cannot have the wisdom of seeing reality as manifesting the hidden treasures of God (Chittick 1983, 30–35). In Islamic spirituality, ego (*nafs*) is often used to represent the deluded self, sometimes translated as the "lower self." In its default state, the ego deludes itself by claiming to be self-sufficient and independent of its Creator. Ego resists its purpose as a sign pointing to the Absolute; it perceives itself to be the source of its existence and power. So long as a person remains in that state and does not cleanse the ego, there is no share of wisdom; even if one hears wisdom, one cannot get it (Schimmel 1975, 112–113).

The point is not to destroy the ego but to cleanse it. Once cleansed of its illusions, the ego helps in the path to wisdom. Indeed, Nursi (2004, 557–571; Turner 2011, 190–196) regards the ego, or the "I," as part of the momentous trust God gives to humanity in the Qur'an (Q 33:72). The selfhood or ego given to humans is to be used as a yardstick to relate to the beautiful names of God and ultimately the divine self. Through the "I," humans are given the capacity to know, will, build, love, and so on, so that they can relate these accidental qualities to the absolute qualities of the Absolute Knower, Creator, and Loving One. The analogy between human self and the divine is just a heuristic tool, though, to be used as a means to know God. If the ego gets stuck in illusion by supposing to own the "I," then it leads to betrayal of that purpose. When in that state of betrayal, according to Nursi (2004, 558):

> [T]he "I" is in absolute ignorance. Even if it knows thousands of branches of science, with compounded ignorance it is most ignorant. For when its senses and thoughts yield the lights of knowledge of the universe, those lights are extinguished because they do not find [within the ego any support with which] to confirm, illuminate, and perpetuate them.

Thus, whoever polishes the mirror of the heart sees more of divine wisdom. The same information becomes futility or knowledge depending on whether one perceives it in the name of ego or of the Creator (Mermer and Ameur 2004, 138–139).

Wisdom, then, is given to those who are willing to let go of the illusions of the ego and admit their existential neediness and poverty. Hence, for instance, Ibn Ataillah al-Iskandari, the famous author of the small, widely studied book of aphorisms known as *Wisdoms* (*ḥikam*), laid great emphasis on admitting one's neediness and dependence on God. He also emphasized going beyond the surface, as in *ḥikma* 42 (Ibn Ataillah 1978, 57):

> Travel not from creature to creature,
> otherwise you will be like a donkey at the mill:
> Roundabout he turns, his goal the same as his departure.
> Rather, go from creatures to the Creator:
> "And that the final end is unto thy Lord."

Sincerity is also needed to receive wisdom. According to a tradition attributed to Prophet Muhammad and widely used in Islamic spirituality, if one practices what one knows, God teaches one what one does not know. This *ḥadith* may explain why wisdom is relational and cannot be appreciated by everyone. What is the point of knowing if one is not going to live accordingly? Does one who does not act according to wisdom really know wisdom? In a symbolic tale about a peasant and a philosopher, Rumi denounces the person who knows much but lacks wisdom because his knowledge does not make a difference in his life (*Mathnawi* II: 3176–3197).

14.6 CONCLUSION

In sum, wisdom is a crucial qur'anic concept that has been discussed in richly variegated ways in the Islamic tradition, including in qur'anic exegesis and Islamic theology, philosophy, law, and spirituality. Wisdom is the understanding of reality in light of revelation as signifying the eternal one and acting in accordance with such understanding. As Molla Sadra, a sixteenth-century Muslim thinker defined it, wisdom is knowing things as they are. It is to know the truth that existence, which is pure good, relies on (Kutluer 1998, 508). If so, whoever has been granted such understanding has indeed been given access to much good.

WORKS CITED

Asad, Muhammad. 1984. *The Message of the Qur'an*. Gibraltar: Dar al-Andalus.
Chittick, William. 1983. *Sufi Path of Love: The Spiritual Teachings of Rumi*. Albany, NY: SUNY Press.
Chittick, William. 1989. *The Sufi Path of Knowledge*. Albany, NY: SUNY Press.

Chittick, William. 1998. *The Self-Disclosure of God: Principles of Ibn al-'Arabi's Cosmology*. Albany, NY: SUNY Press.

Iqbal, Muhammad. 2007. *Science and Islam*. Westport, CT: Greenwood.

al-Iskandari, Ibn Ataillah. 1978. *The Book of Wisdom*. Translated by Victor Danner. New York, NY: Paulist.

Khalidi, Tarif. 2001. *The Muslim Jesus*. Cambridge, MA: Harvard University Press.

Koca, Ferhat. 1998. "Hikmet, Fıkıh." *TDV* 17:514–518.

Kutluer, Ilhan. 1998. "Hikmet." *TDV* 17:503–511.

Landau, Rom. 1958. *Arab Contribution to Civilization*. San Francisco, CA: American Academy of Asian Studies.

Lawrence, Bruce. 2007. *The Qur'an: A Biography*. New York, NY: Atlantic Monthly Press.

Markham, Ian S., and Zeyneb Sayilgan, eds. 2017. *The Companion to Said Nursi Studies*. Euguene, OR: Pickwick.

al-Maybudi, Rashid al-din. 2015. *Unveiling of the Mysteries and the Provision of the Pious*. Selections translated by William C. Chittick. Amman: Aal-al Bayt Institute.

Mermer, Yamina Bouguenaya. 2017. "The Concept of God in the *Risale-i Nur*." Pages 69–86 in Markham and Sayilgan 2017.

Mermer, Yamina Bouguenaya, and Redha Ameur. 2004. "Beyond the Modern: Sa'id al-Nursi's View of Science." *Islam and Science* 2:119–160.

Mermer, Yamina Bouguenaya, and Isra Yazicioglu. 2017. "Said Nursi's Qur'anic Hermeneutics." Pages 51–66 in Markham and Sayilgan 2017.

Nasr, Seyyed Hossein. 2002. *The Heart of Islam: Enduring Values for Humanity*. New York, NY: Harper Collins.

Nasr, Seyyed Hossein, Caner Dagli, Maria M. Dakake, Joseph E.B. Lumbard, and M. Rustom. 2015. *The Study Qur'an: A New Translation and Commentary*. New York, NY: Harper Collins.

Nursi, Bediuzzaman Said. 1996. *Flashes*. Translated by Sukran Vahide. Istanbul: Sozler Yayinevi.

Nursi, Bediuzzaman Said. 2004. *Words*. Translated by Sukran Vahide. Istanbul: Sozler Yayinevi.

Ormbsy, Eric. 1984. *Theodicy in Islamic Thought: The Dispute over al-Ghazali's "Best of All Possible Worlds."* Princeton, NJ: Princeton University Press.

Ozervarli, Sait. 1998. "Hikmet, Kelam." *TDV* 17:511–514.

al-Razi, Fakhr al-Din. 1934. *Tafsīr al-kabīr*. Vol. 7. Egypt: Al-Maṭbaʿah al-Bāhiyah al-Miṣrīya.

Rumi, Mawlana Muhammad Jalal al-din. 1989. *Mathnawi*. Translated by Reynold A. Nicholson. Lahore: Islamic Book Service.

Rumi, Mawlana Muhammad Jalal al-din. 1946. *Mesnevi*. Translated into Turkish by Veled Celebi. http://www.dar-al-masnavi.org.

Schimmel, Annemarie. 1975. *Mystical Dimensions of Islam*. Chapel Hill, NC: University of North Carolina Press.

Schimmel, Annemarie. 1978. Preface to *The Book of Wisdom and Intimate Conversations*, by Ibn 'Ata'illah and Kwaja Abdullah Ansari with introduction, translation, and notes by Victor Danner and Wheeler M. Thackston, New York, NY: Paulist.

Schimmel, Annemarie. 1992. *I Am Wind, You Are Fire*. London: Shambhala.

al-Shafii, al-Imam Muhammad ibn Idris. 1961. *Al-Risala fi usul al-fiqh*. Translated by Majid Khadduri. Cambridge: Islamic Texts Society.

Turner, Colin. 2011. *Islam: The Basics*. 2nd ed. Abingdon: Routledge.

al-Tustari, Sahl b. 'Abd Allah. 2011. *Tafsir al-Tustari*. Translated by Annabel Keeler and Ali Keeler. Amman: Aal-al Bayt Institute & Fons Vitae.

Yazicioglu, Isra. 2013. *Understanding the Qur'anic Miracle Stories in the Modern Age*. University Park, PA: Pennsylvania State University Press.

Yazicioglu, Isra. 2017. "A Graceful Reconciliation: Said Nursi on Free Will and Destiny." Pages 129–145 in Markham and Sayilgan 2017.

CHAPTER 15

···

WISDOM IN JEWISH
THEOLOGY

···

JONATHAN SCHOFER

WISDOM (*hokhmah*) in Jewish theology from the medieval period to the present has been articulated in two key ways. The first, well established in Maimonides's twelfth-century CE treatise *The Guide for the Perplexed*, understands wisdom to be an exemplary human quality, which is defined largely through reference back to its appearances in the biblical book of Proverbs. The second, articulated extensively in the thirteenth-century CE work, *The Zohar*, presents Wisdom as the second of the *sefirot* in the Kabbalistic understanding of the deity. Here, wisdom is primarily a facet of God in divine emanation, which is also received by human beings through traditional study of Torah. This chapter examines the role of wisdom in Jewish theology emphasizing these two distinct strands. New developments, building upon the Kabbalistic strand, appeared in the eigthteenth and nineteenth centuries through the innovations of Hasidism. In the twentieth century, Martin Buber's encounter with Hasidism brought a distinct combination of the two conceptions of wisdom, with a philosopher's gathering of mystical tales articulating an innovative and at times counterintuitive picture of wisdom. Also, for Emmanuel Levinas, wisdom is a crucial element in guiding rational consideration of relations with others.[1]

---

[1] The sources treated in this chapter were originally written in Judeo-Arabic, Hebrew, Aramaic, German, and French. I will cite standard English translations for all, with the modification that all quotations of biblical verses will be from the JPS *TaNaKh*, to avoid confusion that can arise from each translator rendering biblical terms and verses differently from the others.

15.1 WISDOM AS A VIRTUE IN MEDIEVAL PHILOSOPHY: MAIMONIDES'S *THE GUIDE OF THE PERPLEXED*

Moses Maimonides (1135–1204 CE) is by many standards the greatest philosopher of Judaism, and his major work, *The Guide of the Perplexed*, the greatest work of Jewish philosophy (for general background, see Seeskin 2005). *The Guide of the Perplexed* does not initially focus on virtues, but in the third and final part of the work, Maimonides turns to discuss standards and ideals for human action, with a focus on the divine commandments. In the concluding chapters of Part 3, Maimonides discusses virtues, completing the *Guide of the Perplexed* with a chapter on wisdom. The primary focus of *The Guide of the Perplexed*, though, is to elaborate the meanings, for a person who is both Jewish and a philosopher, of terms that may convey that God has human qualities, in light of Maimonides's desire to reject the corporeality of God absolutely. He does not want to say that these depictions of God are simply an embarrassment for the philosopher, but rather that they have distinct meanings, which he exposits. The most complex and important of these parts of the Jewish Scriptures concern creation in Genesis 1 (which he refers to as, "the *Account of the Beginning*") and Ezekiel's vision of the chariot in Ezekiel 1 (which he refers to as, "the *Account of the Chariot*"). At the opening of *The Guide of the Perplexed*, Maimonides states, "The first purpose of this Treatise is to explain the meanings of certain terms occurring in books of prophecy" (1:Introduction; 1963, 5), and later he specifies, "the chief aim of this Treatise is to explain what can be explained of the *Account of the Beginning* and the *Account of the Chariot*" (3:Introduction; 1963, 415). The attention to wisdom, then, is neither a primary focus of *The Guide of the Perplexed* nor simply peripheral. Maimonides aims to clarify the use of *hokhmah* or wisdom throughout the Jewish Scripture with an emphasis ultimately on the usage in the prophetic words of Jer 9:22–23.

Maimonides opens this chapter by writing, "The term wisdom [*hokhmah*] is applied in Hebrew in four senses." The four are: (1) "the apprehension of true realities," (2) "acquiring arts," (3) "acquiring moral virtues," and (4) "the aptitude for strategems and ruses" (3:54; 1963, 632). This fourfold definition is the result of exegesis, and examining his citations of biblical verses can show the degree to which his philosophy is connected with philology and specifically the plain sense of biblical Hebrew. Maimonides derives the first sense, "the apprehension of true realities," from two verses that attribute to wisdom, as such, a value that is comparable to or greater than precious metals, one by Job and one in Proverbs: "But where can wisdom be found; where is the source of understanding?" (Job 28:12 JPS), and "If you seek it as you do silver, and search for it as for treasures" (Prov 2:4, referring to wisdom named in Prov 2:2). He observes that the adjectival use of the root can mean "skillful," as in the skills needed to build the Tabernacle, and Maimonides cites two verses from Exodus to exemplify "acquiring arts" as the second definition: "And let all among you who are skilled (*hakham-lev*) come and make all that the LORD has commanded" (Exod 35:10), and "And all the skilled (*hakhmat-lev*) women spun with their own hands, and brought what they had spun, in blue, purple, and crimson yarns, and in fine linen" (Exod 35:25). When Maimonides supports his third definition, "acquiring moral virtues," he may have less clear justification than for the first two definitions, at least by a plain sense of the scriptural verses. He first quotes a verbal use of the root used in Ps 105:22 that describes Joseph's instruction to the elders of Egypt when the Egyptian Pharaoh placed Joseph in a position of power. The book of Genesis itself states that the Pharaoh identifies Joseph's wisdom (Gen 41:39, also Gen 41:33), and that the Pharaoh later instructed Egyptians to follow Joseph's guidance (Gen 41:55). Perhaps presuming this narrative, Psalm 105 states that Joseph was empowered by the king, "to discipline his princes at will, to teach his elders wisdom" (Ps 105:22). For this moral sense of wisdom, Maimonides also cites a verse from Job that challenges whether the elderly have wisdom or understanding. God has wisdom, courage, counsel, and understanding, says Job, but, "Is wisdom in the aged? And understanding in the long-lived?" (Job 12:12). Finally, Maimonides attends to the verbal use of the root in the words of the Egyptian king who turns to persecute the Israelites at the start of Exodus, noting that the word can mean "aptitude for stratagems and ruses" rather than qualities linked with truth, skill, or morality: "And he said to his people, 'Let us deal shrewdly (nithakkemah) with them, so that they may not increase; otherwise in the event of war they may join our enemies in fighting against us and rise up from the ground'" (Exod 1:10; see also his use of 2 Sam 14:2).

From this basis, Maimonides observes that the term "wise" can be applied to a number of different cases: "one possessing the rational virtues, one possessing the moral virtues, to everyone skilled in a practical art, and to one possessing ruses in working evil and wickedness." He specifies, though, that "one who knows the whole of the Law" is wise "in respect of the rational virtues comprised in the Law and in respect of the moral virtues included in it" (3:54; 1963, 633). More specifically, wisdom by way of the Talmudic sages, in Maimonides's view, gains a complementary relation to Torah: "according to them, the science of the *Torah* is one species and wisdom is a different species, being the verification of the opinions of *Torah* through correct speculation." Wisdom as the "verification" of what is found in Torah, demanding "correct speculation," becomes for Maimonides a crucial virtue culminating his study.

The later stages of Maimonides's treatment of wisdom frames wisdom as preparatory for the achievement of kindness, justice, and equity as exemplified by God, and here he addresses wisdom in the context of the prophecy of Jeremiah. Maimonides sets out four kinds of "perfection" related to one's possessions, health, moral virtues, and rational virtues as well as knowledge of God. Based on Jeremiah, Maimonides frames wisdom as the possession of moral virtues, and as such valued but not the greatest perfection: "Thus said the LORD: Let not the wise man glory in his wisdom; Let not the strong man glory in his strength, Let not the rich man glory in his riches" (Jer 9:22). All of these—wisdom, strength, and wealth—are for Maimonides important but not the ultimate end. Rather, Maimonides follows Jeremiah as the prophet continues: "But only in this should one glory: in his earnest devotion to Me. For I the LORD act with kindness, justice, and equity in the world. For in these I delight—declares the LORD" (Jer 9:22–23). Wisdom, then, is "preparations made for the sake of this end" (3:54; 1963, 634–638; see also the discussion in Seeskin 2005, 184–188).

15.2 Wisdom as a *Sefirah* in Medieval Mysticism: *The Zohar*

The Zohar is the greatest work of medieval Kabbalah and medieval Jewish mysticism more generally. The date and authorship of *The Zohar* are topics of vast scholarship, but a basic understanding is that the text was written in the late thirteenth century CE, likely by Moses de Leon alone or with those in his circle of mystics, and in Spain in a Christian context (a discussion of date and authorship can be found in *The Zohar*, 2004, liv–lix; and resources on Kabbalah more generally are in Idel 1988, 1–34). *The Zohar* is a mystical exegesis of the Pentateuch, with an Introduction that also is articulated through Kabbalistic interpretations of scripture. The role of wisdom in *The Zohar* is quite different than in Maimonides's *The Guide for the Perplexed*. A distinct feature of Kabbalah is the theological doctrine of the *sefirot*, and within the ten *sefirot*, *hokhmah* or wisdom has a prominent place as the second in elevation. The *sefirot* designate, in Moshe Idel's definition, "manifestations that are either part of the divine structure or directly related to the divine essence, serving as its vessels or instruments; almost universally, these powers number ten" (Idel 1988, 112). The *sefirot* set out an arrangement of divine emanation from an unending source, through "crown" (*keter*) and then "wisdom" (*hokhmah*) as the highest two *sefirot*, and then down through the rest to the indwelling presence in the world (*shekhinah*). Wisdom or *hokhmah*, then, is one of the two highest *sefirot*, and as such is among the two furthest from human beings. The Introduction to *The Zohar* tends to discuss wisdom, and its relation to "crown" or *keter*, somewhat separately from the discussion of the lower *sefirot*. In other words, the dynamics of *keter* and *hokhmah* are often treated as related to each other, in the upper realms of the *sefirot*, with symbolism that is distinct: "Beyond, there is no question," conveys that beyond the third *sefirah*, "understanding" (*binah*), the emanations of wisdom (as second) and crown (as first) are unknowable (1:1b; 2004, 5).

The imagery used to discuss wisdom emphasizes secret knowledge. Rabbi Simeon opens an exposition by quoting from the book of Isaiah: "Lift high your eyes and see: Who created these? He who sends out their host by count, Who calls to each by name: Because of His great might and vast power, not one fails to appear" (Isa 40:26). The rabbi asks the question, what is the meaning of, "Who created these?" He says that the prophet Elijah told him that God revealed the meaning "on High." This meaning, conveyed in *The Zohar* through depicting a rabbi of late antiquity quoting Elijah, is: "Concealed of all Concealed" or crown (*keter*), "verged on being revealed, it produced at first a single point, which ascended to become thought." This point is the *sefirah* of wisdom or *hokhmah*. *The Zohar* continues, "Within, it drew all drawings, graved all engravings, carving within the concealed holy lamp a graving of one hidden design." The holy lamp is another image for *hokhmah*, which gives rise to "the hidden design" of the next *sefirah*, *binah* or understanding, which in turn is "a deep structure emerging from thought" (1:2a; 2004, 7–8). *Binah* gives rise to the lower *sefirot*, and knowledge of them is more accessible. Just a little later in the pages of *The Zohar*, Rabbi Simeon exposits a later part of Isa 40:26—"Because of His great might and vast power"—also to portray wisdom: "His great might" is wisdom as "First of rungs, to which all desires ascend, ascending there secretly." For Rabbi Simeon, "God's vast power," the next component of Isa 40:26, is taken to be *binah* as the next *sefirah* (1:2b; 2004, 11).

Wisdom as one of the *sefirot* is, for *The Zohar*, crucial to God's creation. *The Zohar* portrays Rabbi Yudai interpreting the opening words of the scripture—"When God began to create (*be-re'shit bara' 'elohim*) the heavens and the earth" (Gen 1:1)—to emphasize that wisdom gives rise to the next *sefirot*, which then flow into the "ocean" of the indwelling presence, *shekhinah* as the tenth of the *sefirot*. *The Zohar* says, "Rabbi Yudai said, 'What is *be-re'shit*? With Wisdom." He continues, "This is the Wisdom on which the world stands—through which one enters hidden, high mysteries. Here were engraved six vast, supernal dimensions, from which everything emerges, from which issued six springs and streams, flowing into the immense ocean." The six "dimensions" and "springs and streams," then, are the six *sefirot* following wisdom, leading to the indwelling presence of *shekhinah* (1:3b; 2004, 17).

For the Kabbalah of *The Zohar*, then, wisdom is a crucial element in a theology of emanation. Wisdom is the second of the ten points of emanation, difficult for humans to know, and crucial to divine creation. It is through wisdom that divine emanation flows to the more accessible *sefirot*, and above wisdom are the crown and the unending source.

15.3 HUMAN RECEPTION OF WISDOM IN MEDIEVAL MYSTICISM: *THE ZOHAR*

For *The Zohar*, wisdom appears as a human quality attained through study and diligence, which is directly connected to the role of wisdom in the emanation of the *sefirot*: a mystic's cultivation of wisdom through study activates and is empowered by the *sefirah* of wisdom. An elaborate treatment of wisdom and its importance for the Kabbalistic mystic appears in the commentary in *The Zohar* to the book of Exodus, and specifically God's giving the manna to the Israelites in Exod 16:4: "And the LORD said to Moses, 'I will rain down break for you from the sky.'" Within this Kabbalistic discussion, wisdom is compared with human food, both as nourishing and as given by the deity. The key verse for discussing wisdom is Eccl 7:12. The relevant section of Ecclesiastes is as follows:

7:11: Wisdom is as good as a patrimony, and even better, for those who behold the sun.

7:12: For to be in the shelter of wisdom is to be also in the shelter of money, and the advantage of intelligence is that wisdom preserves the life of him who possesses it.

The Zohar highlights the point "wisdom preserves the life of him who possesses it," and links that imagery with the manna as preserving the life of Israel, to present a distinct picture of study, asceticism, mysticism, and wisdom.

To do so, *The Zohar* envisions a sequence that characterizes the emanation of the *sefirot* in a threefold manner: first, the unending source to crown (*keter*) is called "The Holy Ancient One" as primordial; second, the indwelling presence (*shekhinah*) that is most proximate to human beings is named here as the "Orchard of Holy Apples." The metaphor of a field filled with apple trees conveys this *sefirah* being filled with the emanation of the higher *sefirot*. Third, the *sefirot* in between, including wisdom (*hokhmah*), are called "the Short Tempered One," whose opposing and complementing features such as loving-kindness and judgment contrast with the pure compassion of the unending source (*Zohar* 2007, 321 n. 432, 331 n. 470). Emanation "trickles" as "dew" and is also characterized as nourishing food:

> Come and see: Every single day dew trickles from the Holy Ancient One to the Short-Tempered One, and the whole Orchard of Holy Apples is blessed. Some of that dew is drawn to those below, and holy angels are nourished by it ....
>
> Rabbi Simeon said, "Some people are nourished by it now. And who are they? These Companions, engaging in Torah day and night ....
>
> Companions engaging in Torah are nourished from another, higher place. What is it? As it is written: 'Wisdom preserves the life of him who possesses it...' (Eccl 7:12)—a higher place"   (*Zohar* 2:61a–62a; 2007, 331–332).

For the Kabbalistic mystics, or "Companions," traditional study ("engaging in Torah") carried out with extreme intensity ("day and night") is a manner of making contact with, and being nourished by, divine emanation. Ecclesiastes states, "Wisdom preserves the life of him who possesses it," and for the Zohar "wisdom" comes from the study of Torah, and this study generates nourishing divine emanation, which "preserves the life" of the diligent mystic.

This nourishing through wisdom as Torah study has an ascetic dimension, as the Companions "eat" this "food" rather than "food of the body":

> Rabbi Eleazar said to him [to Rabbi Simeon], "If so, why are they weaker than other inhabitants of the world. They should be stronger and more powerful!"
>
> He [Rabbi Simeon] replied..., "Highest food of all is food of the Companions, those engaging in Torah, who eat food of spirit and soul-breath—not eating food of the body at all—namely, from a high place, precious beyond all, called Wisdom. Therefore, the body of the Companions is weaker than inhabitants of the world, for they do not eat food of the body at all. They eat food of spirit and soul-breath, from a distant, supernal place, most precious of all. So that food is refined of the refined, finest of all. Happy is their portion, as is written, 'Wisdom preserves the life of him who possesses it...' (Eccl 7:12)! Happy is the share of the body that can be nourished by food of the soul!"   (*Zohar* 2:61a–62a; 2007, 332–333)

The Kabbalistic mystics or "Companions," then, are devoted to "eating" only the "food" that comes from the high "place" or *sefirah* of Wisdom. Their bodies are weaker than those of other humans, but they eat "food of spirit and soul-breath" that is refined, and, as stated through the words of Ecclesiastes, preserves their lives. The *sefirah* of Wisdom, then, sustains Torah study. Torah study both demands night and day attention, and refraining from food, and as such includes ascetic discipline. The result is that the mystic is devoted to study as the reception of emanation from the "most precious of all," Wisdom.

Maimonides's *Guide of the Perplexed* and *The Zohar*, then, exemplify two peaks of medieval Jewish theology and were foundational works for later Jewish thought and practice. The contrast between the two, in genre and in content, is notable. Maimonides defines wisdom with respect to biblical verses, offers four definitions, refines those definitions for his philosophical reflection, and then upholds wisdom as a human quality central to rational and moral virtues. *The Zohar* employs its mystical exegesis of Jewish scripture to convey the role of wisdom as the second of the *sefirot*, the emanation that gives forth to the lower and more accessible points of emanation, and the place of wisdom in the very process of God's creation of the world. *The Zohar*, moreover, considers wisdom in two roles: the *sefirah* that is crucial to divine emanation, and a human quality generated by the study of Torah with ascetic discipline that is nourished by that emanation.

15.4 WISDOM IN EIGHTEENTH- AND NINETEENTH-CENTURY HASIDISM

The influence of both *The Guide of the Perplexed* and *The Zohar* in the centuries following the Jewish Middle Ages is tremendous, and key elements have been studied by Moshe Idel (1988, 46, 80, 97, 99, 147–148, 180). Arguably the most significant development of wisdom in Jewish theology appears in the mystical movement of Hasidism, starting in the eighteenth century, both for its intrinsic features and for the influence of Hasidism upon the twentieth-century philosopher, Martin Buber. It is in Buber's encounter with Hasidism that the mystical, the philosophical, and the truly modern meet for Jewish thought as influencing the current day. In the eighteenth and nineteenth centuries, Hasidic leaders built upon the Kabbalistic understanding of wisdom, yet let go of the specific description of wisdom as a *sefirah* to describe their mystical techniques and their methods of gaining mystical union with the deity (for more resources on Hasidism and also Buber's presentation of Hasidism, see Idel 1995, 130; also Green 1987, 127–156).

The Baal Shem Tov, or Besht (1700–1760 CE) was the founder of Hasidism. He created a major shift in Jewish mysticism that generated immense influence. The mystical teachings of the Besht employ "wisdom" to give authority to mystical practices of "the combinations of the letters" and speaking "in accordance with the divine spirit" as known (according to the Besht's picture of Jewish history) by the tannaitic rabbis named in the Mishnah of 200 CE. The Besht teaches that if a person "is strongly united to the holiness, he is able to elevate profane things to [the level of] holiness by means of the lore of combinations of letters which is known to the holy and divine Besht, blessed be his memory, and to his disciples, who possess the holy spirit." The Tannaim, he says, "were in the possession of the divine spirit and they possessed this wisdom in a perfect manner." In fact, he says, "they were all worthy on account of their cleaving to the supernal holiness" (Idel 1995, 56).

Another Hasidic account of wisdom is part of what Idel calls, "the most elaborate presentation of the way to achieving mystical union with God by cleaving to the Torah." R. Shneur Zalman of Lyady (1745–1813) writes, "The Torah and the Holy one, blessed be he, are one. The meaning of this is that the Torah, which is the wisdom and will of the Holy one, blessed be he, and his glorious essence are one, since he is both the knower and the knowledge" (Idel 1988, 246). This equation of Torah with God, and of the "wisdom and will" of God with God's "essence," is a distinct stance. R. Shneur Zalman of Lyady also articulates this stance, using the Kabbalistic term of the *Eiyn Sof*, the unending source of divine emanation that precedes *keter* or crown on the hierarchy, when discussing Torah study: "The Torah is absorbed by his intellect and is united with it and they become one. This becomes nourishment for the soul and its inner life from the giver of life, the blessed *Eiyn Sof*, who is clothed in this wisdom and this Torah that are [absorbed] in it [the soul]" (Idel 1988, 246). Wisdom is figuratively clothing for the unending source of divine presence at its highest levels.

The transformation of *The Zohar* from a medieval source of mystical expression to a centerpoint of study for later mystics can be seen in the nineteenth-century use of "wisdom" by R. Isaac Yehudah Yehiel Safrin (1806–1874), who created a commentary to *The Zohar*. His own work of commentary, he writes, was aided by the mystical practice of weeping in order to gain revelations and knowledge of secrets. He articulates this by quoting from Proverbs: "The words a man speaks are deep waters, A flowing stream, a fountain of wisdom" (Prov 18:4). R. Isaac Yehudah Yehiel Safrin says, "By much weeping, like a well, and suffering I became worthy to be transformed into 'a flowing stream, a fountain of wisdom'; but afterward I became like dust and wept before the Creator of the universe like a spring" (Idel 1988, 86). Here the Hasidic mystic become *a fountain of wisdom*, quoting from scripture, in order to write commentary to the mystical medieval *Zohar*.

15.5 WISDOM IN TWENTIETH-CENTURY JEWISH PHILOSOPHY: MARTIN BUBER

An elaborate consideration of wisdom in twentieth-century Jewish philosophy appears in the work of Martin Buber, one of the greatest Jewish philosophers of the century. Buber's discussions of wisdom appear in his collections of Hasidic tales, which themselves emerge through the intersection of Buber's thought and his meetings with Jews in Hasidic communities. The picture of wisdom in these tales is creative and at times counterintuitive, often emphasizing the connection between knowing worldly foolishness and true wisdom.

Hasidism, through Buber, became a point of study for those beyond Hasidic communities. Buber's methods of gathering Hasidic materials and expositing their significance did not become the model for historical scholarship, as Idel emphasizes (1995, 2–30), but they are important for Buber's own intellectual outlook. For Buber, Hasidism is crucial for "modern man" to understand, because Hasidism has "the powerful tendency, preserved in personal as well as communal existence, to overcome the fundamental separation between the sacred and the profane" (Buber 2016, 5). For Buber, Hasidism "understands and proclaims" that there is "no essential distinction between sacred and profane spaces, sacred and profane times, between sacred and profane actions, and between sacred and profane conversations." Then, "the holy can blossom forth" every moment (Buber 2016, 8). The modern world, beyond Hasidism, needs to learn this from Hasidism, for Buber, and this is his point in gathering his "tales" of Hasidic leaders and expositing their outlooks. The "tales," moreover, contain vivid portrayals of wisdom.

The accounts of wisdom in Buber's "tales" of Hasidic leaders exemplify a common feature of the "tales" in general, which is a sense of surprise and somewhat shocking unexpected stances. The "tales" present wisdom as an intellectual ideal that combines practical knowledge and timing with religious values, but frequently in unexpected ways. "Wisdom" according to the "tales" often is not what either secular knowledge conventionally conveys or what a standard understanding of religious values teaches. Other times, we find popular versions of the imagery articulated in more speculative terms in Kabbalistic sources through the imagery of the *sefirot*.

The speculative imagery of *The Zohar* and the role of wisdom or *hokhmah* in creation appear in Buber's *Tales of the Hasidim* through an exposition by a student of the Besht, focusing on biblical words that Buber presents as, "In wisdom hast Thou made them all." This verse is probably from the Psalms, "How many are the things that You have made, O Lord; You have made them all with wisdom; the earth is full of your creations" (Ps 104:24). Wisdom is, in this exposition of the verse, "the rung before creation," which is a motif that may come from *The Zohar* and its account of the *sefirah* of *hokhmah* giving rise to the next series of *sefirot*. Wisdom in this Hasidic teaching, told by the philosopher Buber, is "a thought which cannot be made manifest" yet also "gives rise to creation." Wisdom also, however, in a way that is counterintuitive from consideration of Maimonides and *The Zohar*, is "nothingness." This "nothingness" is a key stage in the change from chaos—probably presuming the opening of Genesis 1—to creation. The Hasidic teaching begins with a sense of apparent paradox: "Nothing in the world can change from one reality to another, unless it first turns into nothing, that is, into the reality of the in-between stage." This stage is the "rung of nothingness," which is "just before creation." Nothingness is the chaos that is "a force which precedes creation." And all this is wisdom, which is what God uses to make the world (Buber 1947, 1:104).

Another account of wisdom builds from an exegesis of words from Ecclesiastes. The core verse is, "It is better to listen to a wise man's reproof than to listen to the praise of fools" (Eccl 7:5), but the story also cites the opening words of the book, "Utter futility!" or "Vanity of vanities" (Eccl 1:1). A tale of a student of a student of the Besht emphasizes that an audience found the Hasidic leader's teaching "peculiar." At the beginning, the rabbi "assumed office" and "preached on the seven worldly wisdoms on the first seven Sabbath-days, one wisdom on each Sabbath. From week to week, the congregation grew more surprised at this peculiar choice of subject for a sermon," but no one questioned or challenged him. Following these seven Sabbaths, on the eighth he quotes Eccl 7:5. He interprets, "It is good to hear the rebuke of a wise man who has heard and understood the song of fools, that is, the seven worldly wisdoms, which—compared to the teachings of God—are a song of fools." For those who know the foolish false wisdoms, then the choice "to choose the wisdom of the Torah" becomes clear (Buber 1947, 1:184–185). Here, the counterintuitive practices of the Hasidic leaders ultimately teach "the wisdom of Torah." The Hasid teaches that one needs to know the values of "fools" and the "worldly wisdoms" in order to see that they are "vanity of vanities" and not worth following. For this reason he engaged in "peculiar" teaching for seven weeks. On the eighth, through this exegesis of verses from Ecclesiastes, he integrates his teaching with values of scripture, seeking "wisdom of Torah" with experience of the world.

In Buber's *Tales of the Hasidim*, the emphasis on a connection between knowing worldly foolishness, and true wisdom, appears again in a story of another student of a student of the Besht. This Hasid is asked, what is the meaning of a tradition people know: "With regard to that passage in the Scriptures which states that King Solomon was wiser than all other men, it has been observed: 'Even wiser than fools.'" The Hasidic rabbi states that Solomon was so wise that he could even "hold true converse with fools, and impress their hearts until they recognized" their foolishness. Since a fool "considers himself wiser than anyone else, and no one can convince him that he is a fool," then Solomon's ability both to be wise and also to understand, speak with, and persuade those who are foolish, is distinct (Buber 1947, 1:224). In this case, the experience of the truly wise exemplar enables teaching. Solomon as wise not only could teach those who sought wisdom, but also those who did not.

Another student of a student of the Besht, according to Buber's retelling, conveys the relation between the wisdom of those who are "at home in the rooms" of the deity, perhaps those who engage in regular Torah study and prayer, and those who are not. The "parable of the wood-cutter" tells of a poor man who "had a great longing to see the king face to face." He gained employment at the palace and successfully cared for the stoves and heating: "The king enjoyed the good, living warmth. It was better than what he had had, and he asked how this came about." He learned of the poor man and offered him a wish, and the man wished "to see the king every once in awhile." Then the palace workers made a window to the living room, so the poor man "could look through and satisfy his longing." The prince once "said something which displeased" the king and "was punished by a year's banishment" from the king. Mourning, he found the window of the poor man. The man told the prince, "You are at home in the rooms of the lord and eat at his table. All you need to do is govern your speech wisely. But I have neither wisdom nor learning, and so I must perform my lowly service that I may sometimes see the lord's face" (Buber 1947, 1:235–236). The king in the parable is God. What exactly do the prince and the poor man represent? Probably the prince is the person with skills and access to Torah study, which enable proximity to God as long as he can "govern" his "speech wisely." For those without that wisdom or learning, there are other ways to perform Jewish service to gain contact with God. Wisdom here, then, is both the wisdom that accompanies Torah study, and the wisdom to speak appropriately in the context of that study and devotion.

Wisdom in Buber's *Tales of the Hasidim* appears, then, in the context of stories of Hasidic rabbis. The relationship between these portrayals of wisdom and Buber's own view is central to the consideration of Buber's purpose in gathering and presenting his tales. As Idel emphasizes, Buber knew the historical methods of his time, and he chose to depart from them in ways that he found necessary to convey what he found important in Hasidism (Idel 1995, 2–30). Buber presents his tales organized through the name of the Hasidic leader at the center of them, but analyses of social context and of historical change are minimal. Buber's stance as a philosopher and the words of those who tell the tales blend. Buber chose to preserve the form of the tale for many of his writings, though he has some pieces in which he summarizes positions of Hasidic Judaism in his own words. His large collections of tales, though, appear as a genre in between Buber's own words and a historically sensitive treatment of another culture. Buber appears to have been quite intentional in this, neither becoming a Hasid nor a historian of Hasidism, but rather calling upon "modern man" to consider the value of Hasidic genres of expression and Hasidic teachings in order to overcome the split between the sacred and the profane. In the accounts of wisdom found in Buber's tales, worldly foolishness is not separate from sacred wisdom, but rather the truly wise know the foolishness of the world, both to know truly the words of the Jewish Bible, and also to be able to teach those who are foolish. The wise in learning must be wise in everyday speech or they may be "banished" from God's presence. Even at the theological level of divine creation, chaos and nothingness are necessary precursors to creation itself, a distinct wisdom.

15.6 WISDOM IN TWENTIENTH-CENTURY JEWISH PHILOSOPHY: EMMANUEL LEVINAS

Buber's tales are not the only reflection on wisdom in modern Judaism. Complex reflections on wisdom can also be seen in the work of Emmanuel Levinas, a phenomenological philosopher. As in the medieval period, twentieth-century Jewish thought includes both mystical and analytic forms of considering wisdom. Levinas turns to wisdom at the end of his work, *Otherwise than Being* (2004). His account of wisdom, in very different forms of expression than the ones considered above, carries several of the same themes. Wisdom is a quality of philosophy, which is linked closely with both speech and justice. The key words from Levinas are: "Philosophy circumscribes the life of the approach and it measures obligations before the third party with justice and knowledge, with wisdom" (168–169). In order to understand this use of wisdom, and its relation to philosophy, Levinas's concepts of "the third party" and of "the approach" are crucial.

Levinas's "third party" generates "the birth of the question: What do I have to do with justice?" The third party is "a neighbor of the other, and not simply his fellow." The response to the other, then, is conditioned by the third party: "The other stands in a relationship with the third party, for whom I cannot entirely answer, even if I alone answer, before any question, for my neighbor." In this picture, then, one does not respond to an other in isolation, but as part of larger relationships. There is a "distance" that is placed "between me and the other and the third party." This distance and this complex set of relationships mean that responsibility is in relation to justice (2004, 157). Levinas's "approach" is part of his account of language and the relation between "saying" and "the said." If language can "exceed the limits of what is thought" in part because language can imply meaning distinct from "that which comes to signs" and from "the logical definitions of concepts," then the words of poetry and prophecy ("the poetic said" and "the prophetic said") can yield unending interpretation. "The approach," then, is a "saying" that is "a relationship," which "overflows the theme it states" (169–170).

To return to wisdom: "Philosophy circumscribes the life of the approach," meaning that philosophy conditions the forms of saying and "said" in a context in which language has these excessive possibilities for meaning, and it does so with wisdom. Philosophy also "measures obligations before the third party," setting out the demands of justice, also with wisdom (for other references to wisdom, see 2004, 161, 162). As was evident in the philosophy of Maimonides, for Levinas wisdom is not a primary focus, but wisdom becomes a key element in guiding rational consideration of relations with others.

15.7 CONCLUSION

In conclusion, six points are central to the uses of wisdom in Jewish theology from the Middle Ages to the present.

First, Jewish conceptions of wisdom regularly build from the Jewish Bible.

Second, the Jewish framing of wisdom as a virtue of human beings, combining intellectual ability and practical efficacy, is articulated most extensively in Maimonides's *The Guide for the Perplexed*, where wisdom both is valued for its own sake and supports loving-kindness, judgment, and righteousness. This philosophical understanding of wisdom, grounded in biblical interpretation, established one of the two major approaches to wisdom from the medieval period forward.

Third, in Kabbalistic theology, wisdom is first and foremost a point of divine emanation, the second of the *sefirot* and among the least accessible to human beings. Wisdom is often discussed alongside "crown" (*keter*) as associated with the highest points of the divine emanation, and close to the unending source. Wisdom is crucial to the divine creation of the world, and even to the creation of the lower *sefirot* themselves. In *The Zohar*, human attainment of wisdom comes through intensive study of traditional materials, or Torah, with ascetic intensity: a day and night endeavor that even substitutes for ordinary food through mystical nourishment.

Fourth, in Hasidism of the eighteenth and nineteenth centuries, the mystical understanding of wisdom is separated from the detailed depictions of the *sefirot* and also given new intensity: wisdom authorizes mystical techniques as emerging from as well as yielding true knowledge of the divine.

Fifth, in the modern period, the meeting of Hasidism, philosophy, and modernity in Buber's philosophy brings portraits of wisdom that disrupt common assumptions: Buber's tales show true wisdom to be related with, for example, foolishness in ways that worldly profane life and sacred learning are unexpectedly connected. Levinas, in contrast, maintains an account of wisdom as a guide for philosophy and for considering one's relations with others that does not take up Buber's embrace of the unconventional.

Sixth, and finally, even the very genres through which wisdom is defined and explained vary tremendously. Maimonides in *The Guide for the Perplexed* aims to give a rigorous definition, even to lead the reader through a process of defining that begins with four definitions based on four kinds of uses in biblical verses, and then refines the definition from there for his philosophical purposes. *The Zohar*, by contrast, only exposits wisdom through mystical exegesis of biblical verses, and does not give definitions with analytic prose. Buber's tales, as yet another variation, combine parables, biblical verses, and counterintuitive depictions of religious leaders to offer standards for wisdom that both preserve traditional values and generate a complexity that aims to enable wisdom to respond to the pervasive foolishness found in the world.

Works Cited

Buber, Martin. 1947. *Tales of the Hasidim*. Translated by Olga Marx. New York, NY: Schocken Books.

Buber, Martin. 2016. *Hasidism and Modern Man*. Edited and translated by Maurice Friedman. Princeton, NJ: Princeton University Press.

Green, Arthur. 1987. "Typologies of Leadership and the Hasidic *Zaddiq*." Pages 127–156 in *Jewish Spirituality: From the Sixteenth Century Revival to the Present*. Edited by A. Green. New York, NY: Crossroad.

Idel, Moshe. 1988. *Kabbalah: New Perspectives*. New Haven, CT: Yale University Press.

Idel, Moshe. 1995. *Hasidism: Between Ecstasy and Magic*. Albany, NY: State University of New York Press.

Levinas, Emmanuel. 2004. *Otherwise than Being: Or Beyond Essence*. Translated by Alphonso Lingis. Pittsburgh, PA: Duquesne University Press.

Maimonides, Moses. 1963. *The Guide of the Perplexed*. Translated with an Introduction and Notes by Shlomo Pines. Chicago, IL: The University of Chicago Press.

Seeskin, Kenneth, ed. 2005. *The Cambridge Companion to Maimonides*. New York, NY: Cambridge University Press.

The Zohar: Pritzker Edition, vol. 1. 2004. Translation and Commentary by Daniel Matt. Stanford, CA: Stanford University Press.

The Zohar: Pritzker Edition, vol. 4. 2007. Translation and Commentary by Daniel Matt. Stanford, CA: Stanford University Press.

....

CHAPTER 16

WISDOM IN CHRISTIAN THEOLOGY

....

PAUL S. FIDDES

16.1 TWO DIMENSIONS OF WISDOM

....

"WISDOM" has become a significant theme in the making of recent Christian theology, and where it appears there is usually some reference to the Wisdom Literature of the Hebrew Bible. It is not always clear, however, whether—or how much—this tradition has had a shaping influence on the theology being created; despite due acknowledgments to a historic debt, theologians may in fact be more dependent on the *phronēsis* ("practical wisdom") of Aristotle or the *prudentia* ("prudent wisdom") of Aquinas. I intend in this essay to recognize a dual dimension of wisdom which marks Hebrew Wisdom Literature, to employ it as an interpretative tool in the analysis of some contemporary thinking, and to propose its adoption in a wisdom theology that may be appropriate for a late modern world and a scientific culture. I am concerned here with two aspects of wisdom that we might call "observation" and "participation" (Fiddes 2015, 9–11).

As they show themselves to us in their writings, the Hebrew wise are fairly confident that they can cope with experience through careful observation of how things are. From their own experiments in living, and from the reports of others back through the generations, they can deduce the reasonable thing to do in any particular circumstances. Their technique is to collect and pass on deductions from experience, on the assumption that the natural and human world is amenable to being understood by patient investigation, built up over many years (von Rad 1972, 24–50, 74–82; Crenshaw 1998, 10–15). Their observations are fixed in proverbs, riddles, and lists of natural phenomena, by which they begin to bring some order to a vast area of investigation. As we shall see, this sense of mastery of the world is modified by a strong note of cautiousness and humility, but generally, when the wise have to cope with a situation, to "steer" their way through the maze of events, they appeal to the guidelines gleaned from experience; these represent order won from the chaos of life (Prov 1:1–6). For convenience, I will name this approach "Wisdom A."

Alongside the wisdom of observation we find a second portrayal of wisdom in the Hebrew Wisdom Literature. What we might call "Wisdom B" is the appearance of a personified figure of Wisdom, usually depicted as an intelligent and enticing woman who walks along the paths of the world. Lady Wisdom is out on the road of life, issuing an invitation to those who are foolish to come and live and learn with her. She cries out her invitation in the streets and in the marketplace, like a Wisdom teacher setting out a prospectus, inviting pupils into her school; "You who are ignorant," she cries, "turn in here" (Prov 9:4, cf. Prov 8:1–5) (Whybray 1965, 76–80; Perdue 1994, 77–100; Joyce 2003, 93–99). This Wisdom danced on the earth at the beginning of creation when God made the mountains and the seas; she played on the earth and delighted in the company of newly created human beings (Prov 8:30–31). This Wisdom walks through the world here and now, following the path of the sun from its rising to its setting on the far horizon (Sir 24:1–22; see Fiddes 2015, 176–184); she seeks for somewhere to dwell, longing for those who will make their home with her. She looks for those who will walk with her, for "her ways are ways of pleasantness, and all her paths are peace" (Prov 3:17).

While Wisdom A is a hard and disciplined skill, resulting in a great deal of uncertainty (as we shall see) alongside knowledge, this Wisdom B is available, offering herself to human beings (Wis 6:16–17). The point of the image is to hold out a promise of having a *relationship* with Wisdom, to be in tune with the wisdom that shapes the world, to walk with her and dwell with her. Alongside the wisdom of observation, there is thus a wisdom of participation. Using a later image, there is a spirit of wisdom with which the wise can be filled (Wis 7:23–8:1). Participation in the life of wisdom is also participation in God, since Lady Wisdom is presented as keeping company with God, knowing God intimately. Indeed, rather than a quasi-independent hypostasis or even a goddess, Wisdom is portrayed as an extension of God's own personality, and recent feminist theology has laid stress upon her gender as female.

This has led some scholars to propose that there are two totally different kinds of wisdom in view, a human wisdom and a divine wisdom. There is, they suppose, a practical wisdom, collecting guidelines from experience, and there is "theological" wisdom that only God bestows as a gift (Ringgren 1947, 93–94; von Rad 1972, 144–157). Lady Wisdom would then be a kind of mediator of transcendent reality, a bridge between divine and human life. But this, I suggest, is a total misreading of the pictures of wisdom. Lady Wisdom is a thoroughly practical woman; she is depicted as a Wisdom teacher, looking for pupils to instruct in the art of seeing the world properly. She appears then to be a personification both of divine wisdom and of the Wisdom teacher, encouraging pupils to gain the skills of wisdom by which to "steer" through the world. Above all, God is represented in the Wisdom texts as exercising a highly *practical* kind of wisdom in creating and sustaining the world. In the poem of Job 28, for example, just like the practical wisdom of the wise, God's wisdom as creator is a matter of observing and handling the world. God's surveying of wisdom is synonymous with God's operation upon the world in creation. It was when God gave "weight," "measure," "decree," and "way" to the elements (vv. 25–26) that he did corresponding things to wisdom: he "surveyed" it, "counted" it, "established" it, and "searched it out" (v. 27). When God gave proportion to the world, that *was* his searching out of wisdom, and so to know wisdom is to handle the world successfully. While human wisdom is bound to be limited, it is not of a different kind from divine wisdom.

Wisdom A and B are thus not two wisdoms but one, displaying two different *aspects* of wisdom. On the one hand, wisdom comes from observation, from the careful collecting of evidence; it is a skill requiring discipline and humility, or the "fear of the Lord." On the other hand, wisdom has a personal, relational quality, symbolized by the figure of Lady Wisdom; wisdom is learning to be attuned to creation and to its creator, vibrating with its rhythms of life, living in sympathy with others. The wise live in a world where they are always receiving the offer to participate in God's own wisdom, seeing the world as God sees it. Practical and relational wisdom thus belong together, each assisting the other.

We might say that in their concept of *ḥokmah* ("wisdom") the writers of ancient Israelite Wisdom Literature offer, in effect, a unique integration of what was to be called *phronēsis* and *sophia* in other conceptual traditions. Aristotle proposed *phronēsis* as the virtue of practical reason, the capacity to make moral judgments and to regulate other virtues and skills in a particular situation (*Eth. Nic.*, 1140a.20, 1140b.6). He distinguished this both from *technē* (or exercise of a skill that can secure success in life) and from *sophia*, by which he meant the ability to discern what is ultimately real, lasting, universal, and true (*Eth. Nic.*, 1141a.19–20). The approximate counterpart of Aristotle's *sophia* in the Western, Latin Christian tradition was often named *sapientia* ("wisdom"). It indicated a knowledge of God as the final reality, and was characterized by contemplation and a disposition in which knowing and loving God were inseparable. Its context was the monastery and a life of prayer, and its main tool was a spiritual reading of scripture (*lectio divina*). While the Christian idea of wisdom (*sapientia*) was to some extent influenced by Aristotle's *sophia* (largely assuming, for instance, that the ultimate reality to be contemplated was timeless and unchanging), it derived more directly from the *sophia* of the New Testament, where Christ is identified as the true "wisdom of God" (e.g., 1 Cor 2:1–10; Col 2:1–3), and the Holy Spirit can inspire wisdom within those who seek to have "the mind of Christ" (1 Cor 2:14–16). Indeed, the New Testament seems to show a distinct hostility here towards the *sophia* of Greek philosophy, as a form of human self-aggrandizement, and the positive celebration of *sophia* in early Christian thinking is grounded in the wisdom of the Hebrew Bible.

With the growth of the universities from the twelfth century onward, however, another mode of knowing God appeared which may be called *scientia*. Characterized by speculation and a disposition of knowing *about* God, its context was the lecture room, and its main tool was a dialectic of question and answer. It may appear that wisdom (*sapientia*) was being pitched against science (*scientia*), but it is more usual now to recognize blurred edges between these two spheres. Thomas Aquinas, for instance, has often been regarded as the archetypal representative of *scientia*, while Bonaventure has been nominated as representing *sapientia*. Thus, in Aquinas wisdom takes form as a cardinal virtue, *prudentia*, bearing resemblance to the *phronēsis* of Aristotle. But it is clear that Aquinas was also a "sapiential" theologian, exhibiting a strong contemplative streak by rooting *prudentia* in wisdom as an intellectual virtue, which is itself suffused by the love of God (*Summa Theologiae*, 2a2e. 45, 3; 2a2e. 47, 2).

In recent theological writing, the appeal to "wisdom" is sometimes a renewal of Christian *sapientia*, as seems to be the main emphasis in the project of David Ford to recover a Christian wisdom for living in the twenty-first century. Ford claims, "The richest wisdom has been found in God's love of creation for its own sake and a responsive human love of God for God's sake and of other people for their own sake" (Ford 2007, 380). At the same time, present-day theology has shown increasing interest in *phronēsis*, and response to the dominance of *scientia* has taken the form of a stress on "practice" over against "theory" (MacIntyre 1985, 187; Kelsey 1992, 123–129; Kelsey 2009, 1:211–14, 311–21), which is perceived to be in the same area as *phronēsis*, or practical wisdom (Treier 2006, 61–64, 95–98). It is often stressed that Christian *phronēsis* is utterly dependent on Christian *sophia* (or *sapientia*), so that *phronēsis* is seen as a gift from God, and "is nurtured by the Spirit in response to prayer" (Treier 2006, 54–57).

Stemming from Hebrew Wisdom writing, then, it has been possible to recognize two trends of approach to knowing God, which might be combined in one disposition of life, though showing different emphases in different contexts. This duality at times has been expressed as *prudentia* and *sapientia*, or *phronēsis* and *sophia*, or empirical and poetic wisdom (Deane-Drummond 2000, 20), or everyday (quotidian) wisdom and cosmic wisdom (Kelsey 2009, 1:225–226). Stress on the first of each pair has been typical of the Western intellectual tradition, and the second takes central place in the "sophiology" of Eastern theologians such as Vladimir Solovyov and Sergius Bulgakov. I suggest the most helpful way to characterize these trends is as a wisdom of "observation" and "participation," but in any case they should not be polarized as "human" and "divine," though this has regrettably happened in the theological tradition. My argument is that both distinguishing and blending these two forms of wisdom is essential for theology.

16.2 Wisdom and Contemporary Culture

In recent years, theologians have appealed to the concept of wisdom and the tradition associated with it to meet a particular problem which late modern thinking has identified in the confident world view which stems from the Enlightenment (Kelsey 2009, 1:85–90; Fiddes 2015, 60–66, 167–174). In modernity the human self has been encouraged to impose itself on the world, to dominate the natural environment through the intellect, and to place itself at the center of a totality built around the self. This is a problem of "observation"; the "seeing" of the world and others has become an attempt to control them. This kind of observation has, it is now perceived, led to exploitation of others and alienation from nature (Derrida 1978, 90–92; Derrida 1973, 60–62; Arendt 1998, 250–285; Levinas 1998a, 188–191, 295–297). Late modern thinking has sought to replace a totalizing, completed self with the self as an elusive project in a process of *becoming* itself through attention to others and through construction by its social context.

For philosophers of religion, philosophers with an interest in religion, and theologians, wisdom has become a key concept in this shift in the concept of the self. Wisdom has been associated with terms such as "embodiment," "connectedness," "interwovenness," and "participation" (Grey 1993, 81–88; Hardy 1999, 231–332, 242–245). Theology, of course, adds to the relation between the self and the world a relation with God, who is no longer envisaged as sanctioning the dominating self as the image of God in the way that past theology has often celebrated.

Counter to an observation of the world that seeks to control, the Hebraic-Christian Wisdom tradition has seemed to offer a different kind of "observation," one which fosters sympathy and synergy (Wisdom A). For instance, the Jewish philosopher Emmanuel Levinas and the Christian philosopher Paul Ricoeur have both located a necessary shift in the way that the self sees the world in their commentaries on Job. In his reflections, Levinas (1998b, 122) takes as a key verse the question posed by YHWH to the hapless Job: "Where were you when I laid the foundations of the earth?" (Job 38:4). From a late modern perspective, Levinas reads Job as exemplifying a critique of the dominating self of modernity. YHWH's question, he maintains, limits the freedom of the ego-self, understanding it in the sense that "you have come late to the world," and affirming that "the subjectivity of a subject come late into a world which has not issued from his projects does not consist in projecting, or in treating this world as one's project." The question, he proposes, can also be read as a "record of truancy" (Levinas 1998c, 180), as if to say "Where were you when you were needed?" Self and subjectivity is thus established through responsibility to the other, and in the face of the human other we catch a trace of the God who withdraws from the world to leave us to respond to the absolute demand of the neighbor. Similarly, Ricoeur (1969, 321; cf. Ricoeur 1995, 138) urges that our life-stories can be "refigured" by the story of Job, since the observation of the vast diversity of creation in the poem calls for "the sacrifice of [Job's] claim by himself to form a little island of meaning in the universe, an empire within an empire."

From the analytic tradition of philosophy, Eleanor Stump (2010, 177–226, 432–435) finds the narrative of Job to be a paradigm for using a range of other narratives to explore the condition of human suffering. Such stories, she argues, expose the inscrutability of a human heart and the complexity of a human life, which only the omniscient mind of God can fully comprehend, so that the loss of the heart's desires can only be redeemed when those desires have been reconfigured into the *deepest* desire, which is for God.

All these philosophers find that the claim of the self to mastery runs up against the "otherness" of the world, in its extent and multiplicity, and that this experience is captured in the ancient wisdom of Job. Wisdom in that poem is said to be at least partly hidden to human beings (Job 28:20–21), but in my view this is not because it is a divine quality which God has concealed in heaven. I suggest that wisdom is hidden because of the extent, multiplicity, and complexity of the world under observation (Clines 2003, 76, citing Fiddes 1996, 177–182; Fiddes 2015, 233–238). God knows *wisdom* because only God knows the *world* perfectly; wisdom is presented as an object which God surveys, counts, establishes, and searches out (Job 28:23–27) (Clines 2006, 922–923; Fiddes 2015, 234–235). Wisdom is thus not just observation of the world, but a humble way of looking, expressed in the ancient dictum of knowing "the fear of the Lord." Ricoeur (1969, 86) picks up Job's accusation that God is looking at him with hostile intent (Job 7:17–19), but suggests that Job finally discovers that this experience is "always inscribed within a relationship in which the absolute Seeing continues to be the foundation of truth for the view that I have of myself... this Seeing preserves the reality of my existence."

The second dimension of wisdom (Wisdom B) proves an attractive way for theology to oppose the dominance of the seeing eye which alienates the observer from the world. The figure of Wisdom personifies the divine observation of the world in which human beings, especially the wise, are called to participate. Three passages from different stages of the Wisdom movement present wisdom as a female figure who is active on a cosmic scene and who makes herself available to human beings; significantly, she is also some kind of supreme observer of the world. We find these portrayals in Prov 8:22–31, Sir 24:1–22, and Wisdom of Solomon 6–9. In the last passage, she is portrayed as one who "spans the world... from end to end" and is "all-surveying" (Wis 7:23). She knows and understands all things (Wis 9:11), and shares with God the faculty of being a "witness" and one who "sees clear" into the heart and tongue of human beings (Wis 1:6 NEB). This portrait of an observer is in continuity with the picture of Wisdom in the earlier two passages, since she is portrayed in all three cases as treading the path of the sun on its daily circuit, and so is given a significant attribute of the sun in the culture of the ancient Near East, namely that of being the great observer or over-seer of everything that takes place in the world (Fiddes 2015, 175–203). Her "mythology" is simply the mytho-poetic image of the circuit of the sun. While some commentators have identified this Wisdom as an independent hypostasis, it is generally agreed that she is a personified attribute of God, or, as Karl Barth (1957, 428–429) puts it, the "self-explanation" of God. Though colored by language not only about the sun but about goddesses such as Isis in the ancient Near East, she is neither goddess nor sun-god but the very wisdom of God.

Von Rad (1972, 1=155–1=156) postulates, based on a parallel with Maat in Egyptian Wisdom, that the figure of Wisdom is not a personification of a divine attribute at all, but is the "orderliness" which God has implanted in creation, "something which... now mysteriously inhabits it," and which could also be described as "world reason" or "meaning." In this theory, however, von Rad has unfortunately separated practical wisdom from the wisdom of God, and David Kelsey (2009, 1:173) responds to this deficiency by offering a more nuanced version of von Rad's theory. When order is discerned, it is "localized, ad hoc and patchy," only to be formulated in "rules of thumb." This is an "ambiguity of the observable scene," and humility is required in looking at it (1:211). Kelsey's point is that God's gift in creation is the quotidian, or everyday reality, "gratuitously given to each human creature and each human creature gratuitously given to the quotidian." This is the context into which we are born, a network of relations in which we engage in practices of interaction with the natural world, other humans, and God (1:193). He asserts that God "relates to [Woman Wisdom] and to all creatures through her" and "her relation back to God is a trope for the how creation generally ought to relate to the Creator." What matters, he maintains, "is to stress the relationships in which she stands" (1:225). Woman Wisdom is a trope, then, for the way that God relates to the world and the way that world relates to God, living in tune with the call to wisdom.

If this is the reality for which Lady Wisdom stands, then it is odd that Kelsey refuses to name this wisdom as an attribute of God. In the situation he describes, we are surely participating in a self-giving movement of God which is aptly pictured in the dancing and traveling of a divine Wisdom herself. The wisdom with which we observe the world is a sharing in God's vision of things, and the feminine terms in which Wisdom is described makes clear that this is a sympathetic and not a dominating manner of looking. Elizabeth Johnson (1992, 178), while sensitive to the danger of type-casting women with a fixed range of general characteristics, nevertheless finds the image of "Holy Wisdom, the mother of the universe" to be a way of renewing language about God, embedding it in the historic experience of women, and freeing it from patriarchy and hegemony. The inner dynamic of the maternal symbol associated with wisdom ("Mother-Sophia"), she affirms, departs from the idea associated with classical theism that God creates the world while remaining unrelated to it (180–181).

16.3 Wisdom and a Creation Theology

It is to a theology of creation that Wisdom thinking has made the most obvious contribution in recent years. Kelsey (2009, 1:162) has stressed that the ancient Hebrew Wisdom Literature offers a version of the creation story "whose narrative logic is [its] own," and which is not "bent under the narrative logic of the stories of God relating to reconcile." His point is that while there are three basic "plotlines" in the Bible, relating to creation, reconciliation, and consummation, a theology of creation has often been elided into the last two, and not been allowed to make its own impact. The Wisdom Literature reflects on the human person's God-relatedness in the most ordinary, day-to-day situations, in order to appreciate God's ongoing providential activity. Nevertheless, Kelsey accepts that the three plotlines overlap and even intermesh with each other, and other theologians have found the identification of Wisdom with the person of Christ to offer an integration between the themes of creation and redemption without simply subsuming the one to the other (Gunton 1999, 256–261). The suffering of Christ as the wisdom of God, for example, might be seen as continuous with, or even to include, the suffering of other forms of life within the process of evolution (Deane-Drummond 2000, 57–70).

The concept of wisdom, indeed, seems to offer a way of developing the doctrine of creation in the context of the new sciences of physics and biology. In the first place, this is because the sapiential model of creation acknowledges the complexity of the natural and human world, and so opposes the loss of complexity in previously reductionist philosophies of science. Here we are concerned with the dimension of wisdom as observation of the world (Wisdom A), and in the ancient Wisdom tradition we find a recognition of uncertainty about the ability to reduce phenomena to easy formulas, such as that of retribution. Alongside confidence in "steering" one's way through life, there is a strong note of caution. For all the hard discipline, the Wisdom teacher was prepared to recognize an element of the unpredictable in all calculations; there are unknown factors which the wise person must reckon with (von Rad 1975, 97–112; Crenshaw 1998, 123–125, 189–190). The multiplicity and variety of the world order with which the wise engage can never be completely mastered, and always has the capacity to surprise (Prov 30:18–19). The wise are aware of the uncertainties that arise out of the very material they are dealing with. There is a hiddenness about wisdom, but not because it is concealed somewhere— for instance in heaven. It is hidden because of the complexity of the world, its vast scope, on which the wise can never get a complete grip.

Now it is in this situation that talk about God gets started. There are unknown factors with which the wise must reckon, and in this context it becomes appropriate to talk about God. In a significant group of sayings in Proverbs, something which cannot be calculated in experience is recognized, and in this connection the name of YHWH, God the Lord, is invoked—referring to YHWH's presence or purpose or activity (Prov 16:1, 2, 3, 9, 20, 33; 19:14, 21; 20:12, 24; 21:30, 31). This humble approach to life can take the form of admonitions about "the fear of the Lord," and the primary meaning of this phrase "the fear of the Lord" is a humility in the midst of calculations. The point in the sayings that combine a sense of human limitation with a reference to YHWH is not that God suddenly intervenes to trip the wise man up, or that God *only* acts where there are "gaps" in human knowledge. Rather, the sayings affirm that God has the perfect wisdom to operate successfully in *all* areas, *including* those where human wisdom falters through lack of grasp on the situation, and the moments when a sense of the limits of wisdom is sharpest are only reminders of what is always the case, points of focus. We find that the limitation of the Wisdom method arises out of the very material with which the wise concern themselves; so we can picture this limit not as a boundary *beyond* which God is, but as a continual extension of the known into the unknown. It is a question of complexity and multiplicity, of limitation consisting in the "limitless" scope of things that cannot be grasped. What defeats wisdom is not a boundary, but boundlessness. In this boundless expanse, God is immanent as we are not (Prov 30:1–4).

A theology of creation informed by wisdom can thus enter into dialogue with the new physics and biology today, which show more cautious claims about the knowledge that can be discovered by science than earlier approaches fostered. This does not support any kind of cosmological "proof" for God, but opens opportunities for theology to develop its language and concepts in relation to the reality of the world in which it works, and for theology to urge ethical responsibility on science in terms of care for the natural world. Scientific enterprise today is aware of a range of different types of complexity (Niekerk and Buhl 2004, 1–20), which has curious echoes with ancient Wisdom Literature. The first type, often called "chaos," arises from the reaction of non-linear systems to initial conditions. We find events to be unpredictable and surprising because certain formative factors are hidden from us, or we find it difficult to measure them. A second kind of complexity arises from actual uncertainty, or indeterminacy. At the microscopic level of sub-atomic particles, in the "quantum" world, most researchers accept—despite Einstein—that there is a real indeterminism. Third, modern science recognizes a complexity arising from interaction within the whole community of the natural world, not just among human beings. Finally, there is a complexity that belongs to open possibilities (Prigogine 1997, 29). Not only systems but the future is open, continually under construction. So-called scientific laws now sketch out a range of possibilities, all of which are valid and which issue in different kinds of reality.

The four types of complexity do, of course, overlap with each other, and together they create a sense of limitation about human knowledge. The Wisdom writers of ancient Israel knew, in their own way, about the limits that a complex world imposes, and it was in this context that talk about God got going. They affirmed that God was unlike human observers in seeing everything; nothing is hidden from the divine gaze, as a psalm (possibly influenced by Wisdom thinking) confesses: "you saw me when my unformed limbs were being made in the womb" (Ps 139:16). The modern sense of complexity and uncertainty is a similarly fruitful context for thinking about God as creator and sustainer of the universe, exercising a divine purpose, and I suggest that the corresponding and appropriate concept of God is as *complex* Being. Thus Christian wisdom in the present day will be concerned with attunement to a creator who is certainly one God, but essentially *triune*. Talk about God properly conceives God as both self-existent and *actus purus*, but this need not imply either self-sufficiency or *actus simplex*. As Keith Ward (1982, 216) suggests, "It is quite coherent . . . to suppose that God, while indivisible, is internally complex."

The appropriateness of talking about God as complex in a world of inexhaustible phenomena will also become clear if we think about complexity from the perspective of language. Thinkers such as Jacques Derrida (1988, 148) point out that the whole world around us can be envisaged as a system of signs—or signifiers—which we "read" in order to make sense of our place in the world and through which we relate to others. Presence, whether of the subject or object, is the result of the movement of *différance*— of continual relation to the other who/which is absent and of the interplay between signs (44). This is the complexity of the world from a semiotic standpoint: "the finiteness of a context is never secured *or simple*, there is an indefinite opening of every context, an essential nontotalization" (137). Because of the open boundaries of texts to each other, the subject is unstable, not possessing the "solid substance" of an older metaphysics of presence, and yet this very instability is the ground for the agency and moral responsibility of the "singular" self.

Modern science and late modern semiotics thus provide us with complementary accounts of a complex world, which is (in Derrida's words) "a space that exceeds the calculable programme" (116). Science locates this complexity in physical factors, while late modern semiotics locates it in the network of signs that constitutes the "real." This is in line with ancient Wisdom thinking which considers wisdom to be a body of knowledge which is something to be "found," knowledge which waits exploration within the world order itself, an area of knowledge corresponding to the world, or the world as an object of study.

Theology and philosophy of religion has found appeal to wisdom to be an apt way of addressing a situation in which the discoveries of modern biology have been applied to technology, producing business enterprises whose motor is commercial gain and which threaten the environment and particularly its diversity (Deane-Drummond 2000, 1–5, 218–220). While pure science is aware of complexity and the limitations of knowledge, applications often lose this cautious and humble approach to the world. Aquinas had already developed a link between wisdom, prudence, and charity (exemplified in friendship) in handling the materials of the world, so that practical action was always guided by a wisdom rooted in love of the Good. The philosopher Mary Midgely (1989, 74–80) insists that at the heart of all knowledge must be a quest for the goodness to which creation is moving, so that observation of the world is also a stance of contemplation, reflecting on the implications of our technology. Wisdom, for her, is about the formation of moral character at the same time as gaining information about the world.

The second dimension of wisdom is participation (Wisdom B). The figure of Lady Wisdom dancing at the dawn of creation and walking through the world in the present is a poetic image for the way that humble observation of the world can become participation in the movements of creativity and love at the center of creation. Creation is to be understood theologically as immersion into the complexity of the being of a triune God (Fiddes 2015, 146–149, 161–166). When the concept of three "persons" (*hypostases*) in God is allowed to be defined by relationships, as in the early Fathers, and is detached from any notion of "beings," even in the subtle modern version of "centres of consciousness," then talk of a triune God ceases to be a language of observation and becomes one of participation (Fiddes 2000, 34–46). It only makes sense in terms of involvement in the complex network of relationships in which God happens. Indeed, from a trinitarian perspective, the world with its complexity of signs exists within the "difference" which is God, in a communion of love which is entirely characterized by difference. Eternal relations in God can only be conceived and experienced through finite relations in the world.

It is this complex life of God, matching the complex life of the world, that science and semiotics explore, finding late modern versions of the complex world discerned by the wise of ancient Israel. The triune God enjoys a richness of life which results precisely from the infinite difference between Father, Son, and Spirit (Balthasar 1990, vii–ix), and this God is committed unconditionally to the world of signs for which room is made within the fellowship of the divine life. Any idea that God acts in the world must thus connect with the complexities of indeterminism and interaction, as science conceives them. A creator who makes a world in which complexity arises from the indeterminate and the uncertain, in which chance plays a major role, gives considerable freedom to creation: such a God gives the world its own freedom to be self-organizing and self-creating. This means giving the world freedom to make its own mistakes and to develop its own tragedies. A God like this must be patient and vulnerable, willing to work with the long, painful process of growth and to have at least short-term purposes frustrated.

The action of such a God, arising from the divine "seeing" of the world, will thus not be unilateral but cooperative. It will not be coercive, but seeking to achieve the purpose of love through persuasion. We can then conceive of God's influencing created beings, or luring them with love, to cooperate with divine aims. There is no mechanical causality here, no inevitable link between cause and effect. According to this vision of the Trinity, this divine persuasion is based in attraction, in the attractiveness of *movements* of love, rhythms of a kind of "dance" into which we are swept up (Johnson 1992, 220–223), so that our actions follow the same divine purpose. Created beings are offered, or presented with, aims through being engaged in the purposeful flow of the divine love.

Conversation with ancient Hebrew thinking about wisdom thus prompts us to conceive of a divine *telos* or purpose which is appropriate to a complex world. Wisdom is an awareness of complexity through careful observation, and is sensitive to patterns in the growth of the world—a "feeling for the organism," as Celia Deane-Drummond (2000, 223–225) puts it, drawing on the work of a plant geneticist who witnesses to the need for attunement to nature.

16.4 WISDOM AND THE DOCTRINE OF A TRIUNE GOD

We have already necessarily been exploring the doctrine of a triune God in developing a theology of a complex creation. For Christian theologians, the creator God cannot be other than the triune God. But the concept of wisdom has further impacts on the doctrine of the Trinity, corresponding once again to the two dimensions of wisdom I have identified.

The wisdom of observation (Wisdom A) recognizes that wisdom is hidden through the complexity and multiplicity of the world, not because wisdom is a purely divine entity concealed in heaven; wisdom is elusive because it is a body of knowledge coterminous with the inexhaustible creation. Moreover, while God's observation of the world is infinitely superior to that of the wise, they are engaged in the same activity. As is made clear everywhere in the Wisdom Literature, human and divine wisdom are not totally different operations (Clines 2006, 915–917). There is only one wisdom, though God employs it with more notable success than humans. This approach to wisdom stands against any doctrine of the Trinity which involves the concept of mediation, such as that a word (*logos*) or wisdom (*sophia*), which is the eternal self-expression of the source of all reality, is needed to make a link with physical creation, whether in creation or redemption (so Gunton 1998, 43–64).

Irenaeus among the early Fathers gives us the picture of the Father creating with "two hands," the Word and the Spirit, identifying the Word with the Son and the Spirit with Wisdom (*Against Heresies*, 4.20.1). Dogmatic implications developed, as the figure of Christ, who is portrayed in the New Testament as a mediator in *relationship* between a righteous God and sinful human beings (1 Tim 2:5, Heb 9:15),was reconfigured as a mediator between God the Father and a physical creation. As early as Justin Martyr, we find the assumption that there are two spheres of reality—a world of unchanging, intellectual Being and a world of transient, material Becoming where everything passes away (*First Apology* 60; *Dialogue with Trypho* 60–61). It was almost irresistible for early Christianity, moving out from Palestine into a Greco-Roman milieu, to take up these popular philosophical ideas and put Christ into the available role of the Logos or World Soul, mediating between two ontological realms, or bridging an abyss between two completely different worlds which otherwise could have no contact with each other.

Although this scheme seems to make the Holy Spirit redundant, as only one mediator is needed, the image of mediator has persisted in Christian thinking ever since, promoting a dualistic view of reality. The Hebrew Wisdom tradition makes clear that there is no ontological gulf that needs to be crossed between God and the world. My discussion of this tradition has shown that while God as uncreated is of course infinitely *different* from what God has created, God is not *separated* from it. For a doctrine of the Trinity, this means replacing mediation with participation. In accord with the picture of Lady Wisdom, the Son or Logos comes forth from the Father, as does the Spirit, not to link a remote God with the world as in the mediation model, but so that the world can share in the movements of self-giving within God, participating in the flowing movement of love between the Father and the Son in the ever-surprising newness of the Spirit. In accord with this kind of model, feminist theologians have emphasized that woman's experience is of a relational world, and that wisdom is characterized by "connection." We have, however, moved from "Wisdom A" to its implications for "Wisdom B" (wisdom as participation), which now requires further exploration.

The female figure of Wisdom often called "Lady Wisdom" or "Woman Wisdom" (*ḥokmah, sophia*) is best understood in early Jewish literature as an extension of the personality of God, similar to the other major extensions of "word" and "spirit," together with veilings of the divine glory in "masks" such as the cloud, the name, the Angel of the Lord, and (in later Judaism), the *shekinah* or "dwelling" (Johnson 1942, 17–35). As I have suggested already, the personification takes on the characteristics of the sun moving on its circuit, an image which also underlies a number of goddess myths of the period. The personification expresses the invitation of Wisdom to commune with her, and so with God. In the Wisdom of Solomon this aspect of personal fellowship offered to the wise is accentuated by two features—a coloring from the figure of Isis, who also entices devotees into communion with her, and an identification of Wisdom with "spirit." The author thus brings together the nature of Wisdom as observer ("all-surveying") with a suffusing of creation that is associated with the image of spirit (breath or wind), claiming that "in wisdom there is a spirit intelligent and holy, unique in its kind yet made up of many parts, subtle, free-moving, lucid, spotless, clear, working no harm, loving what is good…all-powerful, all-surveying, and permeating all intelligent, pure and delicate spirits" (Wis 7:22–25 NEB).

This presentation of Wisdom is not, of course, a proto-trinitarianism, but it does evoke a complexity within the being of God that is later to take form in the Christian doctrine of Trinity, as three *hypostases* in one essence. Thus the female gendering of Wisdom is of interest to theologians, not necessarily feminist, who want to deconstruct patriarchal discourse about God and to increase the range of analogies for a God whom they cannot speak about literally. Exactly how "Wisdom" might fit into a Trinity of persons traditionally named Father, Son, and Spirit has however proved contentious. The historical record shows that the association of Wisdom with the "spirit" of God, and both with female gender, soon disappeared. There was a loss of feminine imagery for Spirit, a suppression of Wisdom (and the feminine *sophia*) in favor of the masculine *logos*, and a transfer of feminine language in liturgy to the Virgin Mary (Schüssler Fiorenza 1994, 150–154, 163–168; Ruether 2005, 110–111, 234–238). The doctrine of the Trinity was finally established with a normative form of masculine imagery—Father, Son, Spirit; although there has been an awareness that this cannot be literal language, it fails to profit positively from the particular experiences of women in the making of analogies for God.

Some recovery of feminine imagery is made with such women theologians of the Middle Ages as Hildegard of Bingen (1998, 100–101), who draws on the biblical image of Wisdom as making a circuit of the cosmos like the sun, portraying this as a divine embrace of all created realities: "Oh energy of Wisdom, you circle circling, encompassing all things in one path possessed of life" (*O Virtus Sapientiae*). This Wisdom (*sapientia*), also called love (*caritas*), and portrayed as feminine is present with God from the beginning; she is the "eye of God which forsees and contemplates all things" (Hildegard 1994, 191). Hildegard makes, however, no special association between Wisdom and Spirit, although this has been reaffirmed by a number of modern female theologians (Johnson 1992, 94, 131–133; Deane-Drummond 2000, 113–152).

Some feminist theologians have in fact warned against the attempt to import a feminine figure of Wisdom (Sophia) into the Trinity, as being simply a projection of male sexual fantasies. Wisdom speculation arose, they point out, in elite male circles and served their interests, underwriting the giving of instruction by the authoritative "father" figure in family and society (Ruether 2005, 90–97). Interest in Sophia, some protest, eclipses what should be a proper concern of feminist liberation theology—namely the gospel of the poor at the heart of Jesus's teaching, which is certainly a gospel for women (Schottrof 1995, 347–360). Other female theologians propose that, as long as the patriarchal context of the development of wisdom is recognized, the feminine imagery of Sophia may still help in the present age to widen discourse about God and undermine hierarchy, which will serve the interests of liberation (Schüssler Fiorenza 1994, 157–162; Johnson 1992, 103, 191–193).

The best way forward in placing personified Wisdom within the Trinity may be to avoid restricting wisdom to any one "person." Augustine proposed that wisdom, together with love, was characteristic of all three persons (*De Trinitate*, 15.27–28). Johnson (1992, 123) replaces the names Father, Son, and Holy Spirit, with "Mother-Sophia," "Jesus-Sophia," and "Spirit-Sophia," working inductively from experience of the Spirit and believing that "this starting point stems from the pattern of women's experience of birthing new life, caring for those they love, creating poetry and resisting constriction." Her intention to bring language both of wisdom and the feminine into the whole doctrine of God, rather than isolating it in one person, echoes the "sophiology" of Eastern theology.

For Solovyov (1995, 118–119, 128–132), the divine essence is Sophia, and as the act of God's love for self and others she is also the self-revelation of all three persons. She is a kind of divine "world," or the environment in which the three persons exist, a world composed of all things in unity, an "organism" of "All-Unity" that holds together all God's ideas about everything. For Bulgakov, Solovyov's successor in wisdom theology, this Sophia gives herself away, allowing herself to be diminished, as a *created Sophia* comes into being along with the creation of the physical universe and is embodied in the world as the soul of the world. The two Sophias—created and uncreated, in the world and in God—are somehow, mysteriously, one: "the all in the Divine World, in the Divine Sophia, and the all in the creaturely world, in the creaturely Sophia, are one and are identical in content (although not in being)." The biblical image for this oneness, he suggests, is the picture of wisdom in Proverbs 8, in the world and at the side of God in creation (Bulgakov 2008, 126). Sophia thus acts as intersection between God and the world, but not in the manner of a mediator bridging two opposed realms. She is the state of "reciprocating orientation," or "receiving and reciprocal love" (Bulgakov 2005, 29). In Western theology, a similar affirmation of wisdom as the essence of God, marked by mutuality, is made by Hans Urs von Balthasar (2004, 160).

Finding wisdom to be characteristic of all three "persons" in God should correct the tendency in doctrines of the Trinity to attribute divine activity in the cosmos to the Spirit alone (Moltmann 2005, 98–103). It should also help to resolve what has been often regarded as the puzzling relationship between the work of the Spirit within the Christian community and in the wider world beyond. Following the sapiential vision of a complex world engaging in a complex God, every part of the created world is participating in the movements of love and justice in God that Christian theology calls *hypostases*, or distinct modes of being. From experience of these movements, the Christian confession has been that they are like a Father sending out a Son on a mission in the world to create and redeem life, like a Son responding in love and obedience to a Father, and like a Breath or Wind (Spirit) that always opens up these relations to new depths and a new future. Of course, in different circumstances these mutual flows of giving and receiving love will be experienced in ways that lead to different gendering, including analogies like "mother" and "daughter."

Now, the immersion of creation into this triune web of relations is confirmed by the attributing of wisdom to all three movements of being, since wisdom, as we have seen, must include the dimension of practical wisdom (*phronēsis*) and so involvement with the finite world. The Christian community will thus have its own distinct—though not exclusive—way of engaging in the "flow" of the Trinity, understood as relational movements of being that can only be known by participation, and which are characterized by wisdom. The church's participation is shaped by its practices of reading Scripture and receiving sacraments ordained by Christ; above all it is formed by knowing Wisdom in the historical form of Jesus Christ.

16.5 A WISDOM CHRISTOLOGY

The first aspect of wisdom (Wisdom A, observational) is in view in the widely accepted verdict of New Testament scholarship that Christ appears as the messenger or prophet of wisdom in the early material called "Q" by scholars. In this collection of sayings of Jesus, which is presumed to underlie Matthew and Luke, Jesus is presented as the rejected last and greatest messenger of wisdom (Suggs 1970, 27–28, 40–48; Witherington 2000, 221–233). He is supremely one of those of whom the Wisdom of Solomon says, "[Wisdom] enters into holy souls, and makes them God's friends and prophets" (Wis 7:27). In dispute with the lawyers, Jesus recalls: "Therefore the wisdom of God said, 'I will send them prophets, sages and scribes, some of whom you will kill and crucify'" (Luke 11:49; cf. Matt 23:34). As M.J. Suggs (1970, 18) argues, Jesus here distinguishes himself from Wisdom herself, to whom the oracle is assigned. As the envoy of Sophia, Jesus speaks as a wise man, drawing conclusions from his careful observation of the world around, drawing on inherited wisdom sayings and framing his teaching in parables and startling metaphors. At the same time, since Jesus's wisdom teaching is in service of urging the imminent coming of the Kingdom of God, he also appears in the Gospel narrative as an eschatological prophet.

This kind of picture of Jesus reinforces a modern "functional" Christology, in which Jesus *acts* on behalf of God in an exceptional way. In feminist theology, it also lends support to those who aim to develop a Christology based on Jesus, the "prophet of Sophia," as a liberator of the oppressed, including women. So Ruether (1983, 135–138) understands Christ as neither essentially male or female but as "liberated humanity." The alternative approach is to concentrate on reform of a doctrine of God through emphasis on "Jesus-Sophia" as the feminine side of divinity. Although the difference between the two approaches often seems to be a matter of emphasis and convergence (so Ruether 2005, 306–308), the latter takes us into the area of Wisdom B, in which Jesus is portrayed as Wisdom incarnate, making participation in God possible.

The evangelist Matthew thus seems to take a step beyond Q. Even if Q were *implying* that Jesus is more than a mere envoy of wisdom (Witherington 2000, 217), Matthew makes clear that Jesus is also wisdom in person. In the saying about Wisdom sending her messengers, Matthew has adapted the Q text to make Jesus himself the one who sends them out: "Therefore, I send you prophets, sages ...." Feminist theologians have detected here a potential for associating Christ directly with a feminine Wisdom, while exposing an actual shift in early Christian thought from a conceptual framework in which Jesus is the prophet of a female Sophia to one in which Jesus as Wisdom himself is the son of a divine Father (see Matt 11:25–27; Schüssler Fiorenza 1994, 151–154).

There seems, however, no reason why "prophet of a Sophia-God" and "Son of a Father-God" might not both be used in a compatible way to open up discourse about a God who, as ultimate mystery, eludes all human language. One advantage with wisdom language in Christology is that, just as with the intimate relation between Wisdom

A and B in ancient Hebrew wisdom, applying wisdom to Jesus assists a movement between a functional and an ontological Christology. Wolfhart Pannenberg (1968, 334–337) has maintained that since persons are always in a process of becoming, and since being is inseparable from doing, someone who acts consistently and uniquely for God, and is fully open to God, will be "one with the being of God." In wisdom terms, the Jesus who is unfailingly the prophet of Sophia will participate in the being of the God who is Sophia. Another way of stating this fusion of two dimensions of wisdom is that Christ, whose life is inseparable from the movement in the Trinity which can be recognized as "sonship," comprehends in himself the inexhaustibility of wisdom which can be gleaned by observation of the world (Fiddes 2015, 345–346).

This approach to sapiential Christology seems preferable to the wisdom Christology of Bulgakov, based on the two-nature scheme of Chalcedon. He proposes that in the incarnate Christ the two natures, divine and human, are a unique synergy or harmony between the uncreated and created Sophias (Bulgakov 2008, 226–230). But, since the divine Sophia is—in Bulgakov's view—the same as the created Sophia, the result seems to be a monophysite Christology, identifying the person of Christ simply with a single divine nature (Gallaher 2016, 106–108). Bulgakov's theology does, however, make clear another advantage of a wisdom Christology, that it links Christ with the whole cosmos, and enables us to see the cross of Jesus as a lens into the healing of all creation. The Apostle Paul's affirmation of Christ as the wisdom of God, in the sense of embodying God's wise economy of salvation in the world through God's own exposure to suffering, is thus extended into the community of the world beyond human beings alone. As Deane-Drummond (2000, 244) puts it: "Christ as Wisdom more readily appropriates the spatial dimension in cosmic redemption compared with other temporal descriptions of Christ as Lord of History."

Christology thus brings to a focus the part that wisdom can play in a theology which aims to articulate the relation of God to the world in creation and redemption, while taking seriously our contemporary cultural awareness of the fragility of the self. The figure of Christ, both prophet of Sophia and God's Wisdom, expresses the integration of wisdom as observation (A) and participation (B) for which I have been contending. By combining them we may thus begin to answer the lament of the modernist poet T.S. Eliot (1969, 147) that wisdom has been "lost in knowledge."

WORKS CITED

Arendt, Hannah.1998. *The Human Condition*. 2nd ed. Chicago, IL: University of Chicago Press.

Balthasar, Hans Urs von. 1990. *Mysterium Paschale*. Translated by Aidan Nichols. Edinburgh: T&T Clark.

Balthasar, Hans Urs von. 2004. *Theo-Logic: Theological Logical Theory*, vol. 2: *Truth of God*. Translated by Adrian J. Walker. San Francisco, CA: Ignatius.

Barth, Karl. 1957. *Church Dogmatics*, vol. 2: *The Doctrine of God*. First Half-Volume. Translated by T.H.L. Parker, W.B. Johnston, Harold Knight, and J.L.M. Haire. Edinburgh: T&T Clark.

Bulgakov, Sergei. 2005. "Protopresbyter Sergii Bulgakov: Hypostasis and Hypostaticity: Scholia to The Unfading Light." Translated by Anastassy Brandon Gallaher and Irina Kukota. *SVTQ* 49:5–46.

Bulgakov, Sergei. 2008. *The Lamb of God*. Translated by Boris Jakim. Grand Rapids, MI: Eerdmans.

Clines, David. 2003. "'The Fear of the Lord Is Wisdom' (Job 28:28): A Semantic and Contextual Study." Pages 57–92 in *Job 28: Cognition in Context*. Edited by Ellen Van Wolde. Leiden: Brill.

Clines, David. 2006. *Job 21–37*. WBC 18A. Nashville, TN: Nelson.

Crenshaw, James L. 1998. *Old Testament Wisdom: An Introduction*. Revised and Enlarged. Louisville, KY: Westminster John Knox.

Deane-Drummond, Celia E. 2000. *Creation through Wisdom: Theology and the New Biology*. Edinburgh: T&T Clark.

Derrida, Jacques. 1973. *Speech and Phenomena, and Other Essays on Husserl's Theory of Signs*. Translated by David Allison. Evanston, IL: Northwestern University Press.

Derrida, Jacques. 1978. *Writing and Difference*. Translated by Alan Bass. London: Routledge.

Derrida, Jacques. 1988. *Limited Inc*. Evanston, IL: Northwestern University Press.

Eliot, T.S. 1969. *The Complete Poems and Plays*. London: Faber & Faber.

Fiddes, Paul S. 1996. "'Where Shall Wisdom Be Found?' Job 28 as a Riddle for Ancient and Modern Readers." Pages 171–90 in *After the Exile: Essays in Honour of Rex Mason*. Edited by John Barton and David J. Reimer. Macon, GA: Mercer University Press.

Fiddes, Paul S. 2000. *Participating in God: A Pastoral Doctrine of the Trinity*. London: Darton, Longman and Todd.

Fiddes, Paul S. 2015. *Seeing the World and Knowing God: Hebrew Wisdom and Christian Doctrine in a Late-Modern Context*. Oxford: Oxford University Press.

Ford, David. 2007. *Christian Wisdom: Desiring God and Learning in Love*. Cambridge: Cambridge University Press.

Gallaher, Brandon. 2016. *Freedom and Necessity in Modern Trinitarian Theology*. Oxford: Oxford University Press.

Grey, Mary. 1993. *The Wisdom of Fools? Seeking Revelation for Today*. London: SPCK.

Gunton, Colin. 1998. *The Triune Creator: A Historical and Systematic Study*. Grand Rapids, MI: Eerdmans.

Gunton, Colin. 1999. "Christ, the Wisdom of God: A Study in Divine Activity." Pages 249–262 in *Where Shall Wisdom Be Found? Wisdom in the Bible, the Church and the Contemporary World*. Edited by Stephen G. Barton. Edinburgh: T&T Clark.

Hardy, Daniel W. 1999. "The Grace of God and Earthly Wisdom." Pages 231–48 in *Where Shall Wisdom Be Found? Wisdom in the Bible, the Church and the Contemporary World*. Edited by Stephen G. Barton. Edinburgh: T&T Clark.

Hildegard of Bingen. 1994. *Book of the Rewards of Life*. Translated by B.W. Hozeski. New York, NY: Garland Press.

Hildegard of Bingen. 1998. *Symphonica*. 2nd ed. Edited and translated by Barbara Newman. Ithaca, NY: Cornell University Press.

Johnson, Aubrey. 1942. *The One and the Many in the Israelite Conception of God*. Cardiff: University of Wales Press.

Johnson, Elizabeth A. 1992. *She Who Is: The Mystery of God in Feminist Theological Discourse*. New York, NY: Crossroad.

Joyce, Paul. 2003. "Proverbs 8 in Interpretation." Pages 89–101 in *Reading Texts, Seeking Wisdom*. Edited by David Ford and Graham Stanton. London: SCM.

Kelsey, David. 1992. *To Understand God Truly: What's Theological about a Theological School.* Louisville, KY: Westminster John Knox.

Kelsey, David. 2009. *Eccentric Existence: Theological Anthropology.* 2 vols. Louisville, KY: Westminster John Knox.

Levinas, Emmanuel. 1998a. *Totality and Infinity: An Essay on Interiority.* Translated by Aphonso Lingis. Pittsburgh, PA: Duquesne University Press.

Levinas, Emmanuel. 1998b. *Otherwise Than Being, or Beyond Essence.* Translated by Alphonso Lingis. Pittsburgh, PA: Duquesne University Press.

Levinas, Emmanuel. 1998c. "Postface." Pages 165–182 in *Job and the Excess of Evil.* Edited by Philippe Nemo. Translated by Michael Kigel. Pittsburgh, PA: Duquesne University Press.

MacIntyre, Alasdair. 1985. *After Virtue: A Study in Moral Theory.* 2nd ed. London: Duckworth.

Midgely, Mary. 1989. *Wisdom, Information, Wonder: What is Knowledge For?* London: Routledge.

Moltmann, Jürgen. 2005. *God in Creation: An Ecological Doctrine of Creation.* Translated by Margaret Kohl. London: SCM.

Niekerk, Kees van Kooten, and Hans Buhl. 2004. *The Significance of Complexity: Approaching a Complex World through Science, Theology and the Humanities.* Aldershot: Ashgate.

Pannenberg, Wolfhart. 1968. *Jesus—God and Man.* Translated by L. Wilkins and D. Priebe. London: SCM.

Perdue, Leo G. 1994. *Wisdom and Creation: The Theology of Wisdom Literature.* Eugene, OR: Wipf and Stock.

Prigogine, Ilya. 1997. *The End of Certainty: Time, Chaos and the New Laws of Nature.* New York, NY: The Free Press.

von Rad, Gerhard. 1972. *Wisdom in Israel.* Translated by James D. Martin. London: SCM.

Ricoeur, Paul. 1969. *The Symbolism of Evil.* Translated by E. Buchanan. Boston, MA: Beacon.

Ricoeur, Paul. 1995. *Figuring the Sacred: Religion, Narrative, and Imagination.* Edited by Mark I. Wallace. Translated by David Pellauer. Minneapolis, MN: Fortress.

Ringgren, Helmer. 1947. *Word and Wisdom.* Lund: Haken Ohlssons.

Ruether, Rosemary Radford. 1983. *Sexism and God-Talk: Towards a Feminist Theology.* London: SCM.

Ruether, Rosemary Radford. 2005. *Goddesses and the Divine Feminine: A Western Religious History.* Berkeley, CA: University of California Press.

Schottroff, Luise. 1995. "Itinerant Prophetesses." Pages 347–360 in *The Gospel behind the Gospels: Current Studies on* Q. Edited by Ronald A. Piper. NovTSup 7. Leiden: Brill.

Schüssler Fiorenza, Elisabeth. 1994. *Jesus: Miriam's Child, Sophia's Prophet: Critical Issues in Feminist Christology.* London: SCM.

Solovyov, Vladimir. 1995. *Lectures on Divine Humanity.* Translated by Peter Zouboff. Revised and edited by Boris Jakim. New York, NY: Lindisfarne.

Stump, Eleanor. 2010. *Wandering in Darkness: Narrative and the Problem of Suffering.* Oxford: Clarendon.

Suggs, M. Jack. 1970. *Wisdom, Christology and Law in Matthew's Gospel.* Cambridge, MA: Harvard University Press.

Treier, Daniel J. 2006. *Virtue and the Voice of God: Towards Theology as Wisdom.* Grand Rapids, MI: Eerdmans.

Ward, Keith. 1982. Rational Theology and the Creativity of God. Oxford: Blackwell.

Whybray, R.N. 1965. *Wisdom in Proverbs.* London: SCM.

Witherington, Ben III. 2000. *Jesus the Sage: The Pilgrimage of Wisdom.* Minneapolis, MN: Fortress.

CHAPTER 17

....

PERSONIFIED WISDOM
AND FEMINIST
THEOLOGIES

....

CHRISTINE ROY YODER

WISDOM personified as a woman strides across time and texts. For centuries and in different contexts and types of literature, Jews and Christians adapted traditions about her to instruct and inspire their communities. She appears first in Proverbs 1–9, a biblical Wisdom text from the early Second Temple period. The books of Sirach, Wisdom of Solomon, and 1 Enoch develop her further,[1] as do several texts from Qumran.[2] Christians drew from these traditions to teach about the person and work of Jesus Christ,[3] and later associated personified Wisdom also with the Holy Spirit and with Mary, the mother of Jesus.[4] In Judaism, descriptions in the Talmud and midrash of the *Knesseth Yisra'el*, the community of Israel, reflect features of personified Wisdom, as do medieval Kabbalistic depictions of *Shekhinah*, the female indwelling presence of God (e.g., Devine 2014). Clearly, Wisdom who walked into Proverbs and built her house came to stay. Praised variously as prophet and teacher, tree of life, Torah, sheer delight, beloved companion, generous host, mother, reflection of God, and fashioner of all

---

[1] Wisdom (a feminine noun in Hebrew) is not personified explicitly in Job 28 and Baruch 3:9–4:4. However, both texts describe wisdom as distinct from God—not as a divine attribute—and evoke details that are consistent with the personifications of Wisdom elsewhere, including her presence during creation, the motif of "seek and find" combined with paths and ways, and the favorable comparison of wisdom to precious gems and metals. Arguably, whereas other texts illustrate the accessibility of Wisdom (e.g., Proverbs 1–9, Sirach 24), Job 28 and Bar 3:9–4:4 suggest her elusiveness (see, e.g., Sinnott 2005).

[2] 4Q185, 4Q525, 11QPs^a. See, e.g., Crawford 1998; Brewer-Boydston 2012; Baumann 2014. Personified Wisdom also figures prominently in works by the philosopher Philo, and in Christian and non-Christian gnostic writings (e.g., Good 1987).

[3] See, e.g., Johnson 1985; Witherington 1994; Deutsch 1996; Douglas 2016; McAlister 2018.

[4] For more on the association of personified Wisdom with Mary, see, e.g., Ruether 2005, 220–48; Deane-Drummond 2005.

things, personified Wisdom and the many traditions about her have proven resilient and generative.

Feminist theologians have been instrumental in reclaiming the manifold traditions about Wisdom and the significance of her story for communities of faith. Feminist theological approaches emerged explicitly[5] in the late 1960s amid the civil rights and Black Power movements in the United States, anti-colonial and nationalist movements in many parts of the world, and global student protests (Kwok 2004, 25). A diverse endeavor from its inception—intercultural, interdisciplinary, and multi-faith[6]—feminist theologies are part of the broader feminist movement committed to building a world where women and all people flourish. Hallmarks of that world, as discerned through over-lapping themes of liberation and inclusion voiced especially by Asian, Latina, African-American, and white women, include: equality and empowerment of women in societies and religions; recognition of women's agency; women's full participation in decision-making; respect for women's bodies; valuing the work done by women both culturally and economically; esteem for women's ideas, stories, practices, and memories; access to education for everyone; the availability of resources to enable communities to thrive; and treating the natural world with dignity (Jones 2011, 4–5). Building that world is tire-less work. It requires activism at the highest levels of government and in everyday, local interactions. Building that world also demands challenging and transforming the language, categories, and processes that women use to make sense of their lives and the world (Jones 2011, 5).

While remarkably diverse, feminist theologians share certain commitments and habits of mind.[7] They focus particularly on women in religious life, and privilege as resources women's experiences and insights. Alert to the power of symbols and speech to shape systems, they examine how faith communities understand the Divine and the relationship of the Divine to humankind and the natural world. They explore religious interpretations of what it means to be a human being, a self, and how faith communities construct and organize gender. They uncover sexist arrangements of power and author-ity. They analyze symbols of faith. They call attention to the misogyny and suppression of women inscribed in sacred texts, doctrines, traditions, and ecclesiastical structures (Schüssler Fiorenza 2014, 16). They challenge universal claims and categories—includ-ing that of "woman" itself—insisting instead that knowledge is contextual and rooted in experience. And they propose ways in which faith communities might reinterpret and transform their symbols, stories, structures, and practices to be just and life-giving for women and all people.

Many feminist theologians consider personified Wisdom essential to these efforts and have gone to great lengths to recover and reclaim the traditions about her—most if

---

[5] For overviews of the history and development of feminist theologies and feminist biblical studies, see Isherwood and McEwan 1993; Clifford 2001; Parsons 2004; Schüssler Fiorenza 2014.

[6] For pioneering work in Jewish feminist theology, see Plaskow 1990; and in Buddhist feminist theology, see Gross 1993.

[7] Serene Jones (2011, 5–9) more fully describes these and related "plays of mind" shared by feminist theologians.

not all of which are largely unknown to contemporary believers, particularly in the West.[8] The diverse and compelling ways these scholars engage personified Wisdom and her theological implications are too numerous and substantial to describe here. Therefore, to be suggestive of this work and its import, this essay focuses in two ways. First, I examine the traditions about personified Wisdom principally in the biblical (i.e., Job 28, Proverbs 1–9) and apocryphal/deuterocanonical texts (i.e., Sirach, Baruch, and Wisdom of Solomon). And, second, I explore how those traditions have been generative in Christian feminist theological discourse with regard to four matters: (1) possible sources for the initial personification of Wisdom in Proverbs 1–9; (2) Wisdom's preeminent relationship with God and roles in the creation of the cosmos; (3) Wisdom's relationship with humankind and the natural world; and (4) implications of personified Wisdom for understanding the nature and scope of knowledge, that is, epistemology. The essay concludes with a brief reflection about how the "where" of personified Wisdom, as much as the "who," is instructive in the effort to build a world where women and all people flourish.[9]

17.1 SOURCES FOR THE PERSONIFICATION OF WISDOM IN PROVERBS

Personification, or the animation of objects, creatures, or abstract concepts with human characteristics (Preminger and Brogan 1993, 902), is common in the Hebrew Bible, especially in its poetry. Prophets, for example, portray cities and lands as women.[10] Heaven and earth, mountains and hills, seas and rivers are witnesses (e.g., Isa 1:2; Deut 32:1). The glory of God stands as a rear guard (Isa 58:8). Steadfast love and faithfulness are divine heralds (Ps 89:14). Justice and peace kiss (Ps 85:10). Wine is a mocker and strong drink is a brawler (Prov 20:1). A type of metaphor, personification draws from an animate "source" to describe an inanimate "target"—an object or abstraction. What might be the source(s) of personified Wisdom? What figure, role, or image contributed to her personification, which is unique to Israel in the ancient Near East?[11] Feminist theologians typically consider these questions from one of three approaches, which are not mutually exclusive. Each approach has implications for Israel's constructions of gender and notions of the Divine.

---

[8] A widespread view, for example, is that the early identification of Christ as Wisdom faded and eventually disappeared with the growth of Christian traditions and, especially, the christological controversies of the fourth century CE (e.g., Engelsman 1979, 141; Cady, Ronan, and Taussig 1986, 12, 16, 59–60; Johnson 2002, 100). But see challenges to that assumption (e.g., McAlister 2018).

[9] I take my cue from Virginia Fabella (1988) who observes that Asian women focus more on "where" Jesus Christ is than "who" he is.

[10] See, e.g., Babylon in Isaiah 47; Zion in Isaiah 52–53; and Samaria in Ezekiel 23.

[11] Contrary to the long-held argument that Saying 13 of Aramaic Ahiqar contains a reference to personified Wisdom (Bledsoe 2013).

The first approach looks to ancient Near Eastern goddesses for parallels to personified Wisdom. Proposals include the Mesopotamian goddess Ishtar (Boström 1935), Egyptian Maat (e.g., Schroer 1996; Baumann 1998), a Hellenized form of the Egyptian goddess Isis (e.g., Fox 1995), and Asherah (e.g., Hadley 1995; McKinlay 1996). At issue are the ways in which characteristics and actions of Wisdom in Proverbs 1–9 resemble those of divine beings, including her presence before and participation during the creation of the world; the benefits of health, wealth, honor, and security she grants to those who embrace her; her inspiration of just leadership around the world; and her movement between divine and earthly realms. The personification of Wisdom may suggest that Israel imagined YHWH to have a female counterpart and companion as was typical of gods in other ancient Near Eastern cultures. Alternatively, Wisdom may have originated as a manifestation of God's own wisdom.

The second approach seeks the sources for personified Wisdom in the social and religious roles of Israelite women generally. The argument is that the personal, human imagery attributed to Wisdom in Proverbs mirrors that of other female figures in the Hebrew Bible. Claudia Camp (1985), for instance, identifies six female motifs that contribute to the "matrix of meaning" produced by personified Wisdom: wife, lover, harlot or adulteress, wise woman, the woman who uses indirect means to effect God's ends, and the woman who authenticates written tradition. Other scholars propose the models of wise and counseling women (Schroer 1995), mothers, hosts, prophets (Baumann 1996, 289–291), and teachers (Fox 2000, 340–341). Viewed in this way, personified Wisdom reflects the agency, authority, and roles of women in Israelite culture and elevates them as quintessential expressions of wisdom for young men, the primary students of the Wisdom tradition.

The third approach also looks for Wisdom's origins in women's roles but does so in a specific social-historical context. The authors of Proverbs 1–9, that is, based the personification of Wisdom on activities and perceptions of women in their historical setting. I argue elsewhere, for example, that Wisdom in Proverbs reflects some of the socioeconomic circumstances and activities of real, albeit exceptional, women in the early post-exilic or Persian period, including the measurement of her "worth" in economic terms, and her skillful and lucrative management of a business[12] and thriving household (Yoder 2001). Such an argument requires the study of biblical and extrabiblical evidence for what women may or may not have been doing at a certain historical moment. It also takes seriously that women's realities and constructions of gender vary across time and place. The result is a more localized or situated analysis of personified Wisdom that highlights how real women's lives and work may be either venerated or objectified to serve timely pedagogical and theological purposes.

The question of Wisdom's origins is complicated by the fact that Wisdom is one of two female personifications in Proverbs 1–9. Wisdom has a negative counterpart, namely, the "strange" woman or Folly. The two women stand literarily shoulder to shoulder; poems about them alternate across the chapters and culminate in an extended description of

---

[12] E.g., סחר ("merchant profit"; 3:14).

each that together form a diptych in Proverbs 7–9.[13] Despite this literary coupling and the women's many shared characteristics,[14] interpreters have largely investigated the sources of each personification separately. Their pairing remains nonetheless important. The two women are male projections, dialectical opposites who embody and perpetuate certain stereotypes of women as either wholly good or wholly bad. Moreover, the two women symbolically frame the world of young men, the intended audience of Proverbs 1–9: a young man's choice between the two women renders him either a beneficiary or, due to no fault of his own other than stupidity, a victim. The pedagogy offers no relief to women. Rather, it is a reminder and caution. Such gender assumptions and mythic conceptions of women are woven deeply into the social and religious symbolism of many cultures and persist to this day (Newsom 1989).

In the end, the sources of personified Wisdom are likely a combination of divine and human figures and roles. Careful tracings of her pedigree by feminist theologians and others helpfully uncovers and pulls the textures of that combination into relief, and provides insight into Israel's constructions of gender, the religious and social realities of women, and conceptions of the Divine.

17.2 Personified Wisdom's Preeminent Relationship to God and Role in the Creation of the World

Persistent in the traditions about Wisdom is her existence prior to God's creation of the world. In the beginning, Wisdom was. She is preeminent: first, superior, surpassing. Wisdom herself testifies to this in Prov 8:22–31, repeating various prepositions (e.g., "before"), negative expressions (e.g., "when there were no"), and phrases (e.g., "at the beginning") to underscore the point. "I was there," she declares, at God's side daily, before God "at all times" (vv. 27–31). Sirach adapts the theme, stating that God created Wisdom "before all other things" and lavishly poured her out on God's works (1:4–10); she "came forth from the mouth of the Most High" and covered the earth like a mist (24:3–4). Wisdom of Solomon similarly praises Wisdom as the one who is with God, knows God's works, and was present when God made the world (9:9–10). The texts leave no room for debate. Wisdom was, and was with God, from the beginning.

While Wisdom's preexistence is clear, the exact relationship between God and Wisdom at the beginning is less so. The texts refuse to settle on one description of it,

---

[13] For personified Wisdom, see Prov 1:20–33; 3:13–18; 4:5–9; 5:15–20; 7:4–5; 8:1–9:6, 11; for the "Strange" woman or personified Folly, see 2:16–19; 5:1–14; 6:20–35; 7:1–27; 9:13–18.

[14] For example, both women seek the young man's attention; persuade with speech (e.g., Prov 1:20–33; 7:14–21; 8:4–36); move about in city streets and squares (1:20–21; 7:10–12; 8:2–3); offer wealth and luxuries (e.g., 3:7, 16; 7:16–17; 8:18–19); and reside in affluent houses (7:8, 27; 9:1–6). They also both extend the same initial invitation to the naïve to "turn in" to their homes for what prove to be quite different feasts (9:4, 16; Yoder 2009, 109).

engaging in a dialogue across time that surrounds the two with mystery and wonder. Did God "find" or "acquire" Wisdom during creation, suggesting she was already there (e.g., Job 28:23–28; Prov 8:22a; Bar 3:32, 36)? Or did God "birth" or "create" Wisdom as the first creative act (e.g., Prov 8:24–25; Sir 1:4, 9; 24:8–9)? Did God find and then "appoint" or "anoint" her (e.g., Prov 8:23a)? Or is God identified with Wisdom from the first—Wisdom as the very breath of God's power and emanation of divine glory (Wis 7:25)? This back-and-forth in the texts, combined with frequent use of cryptic language, suggests the details of Wisdom's beginning with God are beyond words and human understanding. Multiple metaphors—acquiring, birthing, anointing, creating—provide glimpses of what is otherwise inexpressible.

Similarly unsettled but no less pivotal is Wisdom's role in the creation of the cosmos. Brief mention in Prov 3:19 that God "by wisdom" established the earth and heavens suggests she is the instrument or means of God's creation, perhaps the structure or frame of God's handiwork. Five chapters later, Wisdom paints the world's creation with vivid brushstrokes and declares, "I was at God's side 'āmôn" (8:30). The Hebrew term has baffled interpreters for millennia. Was she an artisan or architect? A trusted companion? A little child? From the earliest manuscript traditions, all three are possibilities. A quite different image comes from Sirach, who likens Wisdom to water that pours over creation, enfolds the world as a mist, surges over riverbanks, and saturates everything (1:9; 24:3, 23–29). And Wisdom of Solomon, informed by Greek philosophy, renders Wisdom the "fashioner of all things" (7:22; cf. 8:6) and "active cause of all things" (8:5).

These and other traditions about personified Wisdom were invaluable to early Christians seeking to put words to the cosmic significance and mystery of Jesus Christ. What Judaism long claimed about Wisdom became a lens through which to perceive the preeminence of Christ, his intimate relationship with God, his role in the creation of the cosmos and its governance—that is, Christ's divinity and ontological relationship with God. Paul, for example, declares Jesus to be the wisdom of God (1 Cor 1:24; cf. v. 30) and the one "through whom all things are and through whom we exist" (1 Cor 8:6). Other texts depict Christ as the image of the invisible God, the firstborn of all creation (Col 1:15; cf. 2 Cor 4:4), and the reflection of God's glory (Heb 1:3; cf. 2 Cor 4:6). The prologue to the book of John introduces Jesus as the Logos (Word) "in the beginning with God" (1:2) and the one through whom all things came into being (1:3); that introduction played a crucial role in the church's eventual affirmation of the Trinity (Malcom 2010, 239–240) and, at the same time, very nearly eclipsed or absorbed personified Wisdom, as feminist theologians emphasize. Numerous explicit and implicit parallels across the New Testament recognize the male Jesus Christ as female Wisdom—preeminent, companion and agent with God in the creation of the world, and provider and sustainer of the structures of creation.

The identification of Christ as Wisdom upends long-held assumptions about gender and the Divine. For far too long, Christian theologians and communities have used the maleness of Jesus Christ, a part of his historical identity (just like his race, class, Jewish faith, and so on), to reinforce a patriarchal image of God—an image that is fortified further by the hierarchical father-son/God-Christ metaphor. Regarding God as male in turn fuels the reification of men or, as Mary Daly (1993, 19) famously stated, "If God is male, then the male is God." Indeed, the assumption that men are closer to and more like God has such deep roots in the doctrine of Christology, it is arguably the doctrine most often used to exclude and repress women (Johnson 2002, 151). After all, the fact that Jesus was a man must surely mean that a "particular honor, dignity, and normativity accrues to the male sex" (Johnson 1993, 119). The identification of Jesus as Wisdom, however, breaks the stranglehold of male metaphors for the Divine and offers ways of understanding Christ and the Trinity that are more inclusive, just, and life-giving for women and all marginalized gendered and sexualized identities. No longer is Jesus's male gender construed as essential to his divinity and identity, his preeminence, or his intimate relationships to God, humanity, and the cosmos. Accordingly, no longer should structures and systems derived from that notion persist.

17.3 WISDOM'S RELATIONSHIPS TO HUMANITY AND THE NATURAL WORLD

Aspects of Wisdom's relationship to humanity also prove fruitful for feminist theologies. Wisdom personifies "fear of the LORD,"[15] namely, a reverence for God that compels participation in God's work in the world, insists on justice, and cultivates individual and communal flourishing. Wisdom cries out on street corners as a prophet, admonishing the naïve, arrogant, and willfully ignorant to lay aside their immaturity and learn (e.g., Prov 1:20–31; 8:1–5). She speaks honestly (e.g., Prov 8:6–9). She holds to paths of justice and courage (e.g., Prov 8:20).[16] She teaches that to honor God is to honor the most vulnerable in the world—the poor, the widow, and the orphan[17]—and she inspires leaders to use their power to make just and equitable decisions and decrees (Prov 8:15–16). Wisdom also privileges the secrets and wonders of the natural world in her teaching, pointing to the wisdom and integrity that the ant and the root reveal to those who pay attention (e.g., Prov 6:6–11; Wis 7:15–22). Certainly, Wisdom's paths are not always easy to follow (e.g., Sir 4:17–19; 6:18–28). But she promises to sustain those who do. She offers abundant bread, fruits, mixed wine and meat, and an always-open invitation to her table (e.g., Prov 9:1–6; Sir 1:16–17; 24:19–22).

[15] In Proverbs, for example, "fear of the LORD" is a resounding refrain: the phrase is found fourteen times (1:7; 2:5; 8:13; 9:10, and so on), and the imperative "fear the LORD!" occurs twice (3:7; 24:21). "Fear of the LORD" also forms an *inclusio*, or literary frame, around Proverbs 1–9 (1:7; 9:10) and the whole book (1:7; 31:30).

[16] A concept that is not unique to Wisdom Literature, "fear of the LORD" motivates just behavior even and especially when human laws and regulations are ineffective or silent, including fair business practices, respect for and deference to the elderly, care for the physically disabled, and support and protection of families. Without "fear of the LORD," the threads that weave together moral, equitable relations easily fray or unravel (Fox 2000, 69–71).

[17] For examples of proverbs about God's solidarity with the poor, see Prov 14:31; 17:5; 19:17; 22:2.

In concert with profound responsibility, "fear of the LORD" engenders human flourishing. Wisdom declares that she is joy itself: "I was delight day by day, rejoicing before YHWH all times, rejoicing in YHWH's inhabited world. My delight is in humanity" (Prov 8:30–31; cf. Sir 4:11–13). She who strides across the vault of heaven and traverses the depths of the abyss (Sir 24:5) is "the center of a matrix of relationships" (O'Connor 1988, 68), a mediator, shaper of communities, and vital bridge connecting God, human beings, and the cosmos. Those in her company awaken to the interconnectedness of God's creation, glimpse its marvels, align with the deep structures of things, and thrive. Recurrent in the texts about personified Wisdom are the motifs of happiness and celebration of her many benefits, including health, long life, prosperity, and honor (e.g., Prov 3:13–18; Bar 4:4; Sir 14:20; 15:6). She is the mother of all good things (Wis 7:12).

The early Christian identification of Jesus Christ as Wisdom, as the embodiment of Wisdom's transformative work, means women can and should see a female face reflected in his incarnation and ministry. Emmanuel, God-with-us, is neither contained nor constrained by Jesus's male identity; rather, Christ as Wisdom is inclusive of and beyond male and female (see Coakley 2013). This makes the good news far more accessible and inviting to women. Like Wisdom, Jesus manifests God's activity in the world in ways that confront and topple oppressive systems. Prophet and wise teacher, Jesus spoke truths in proverbs and parables that challenged everyone—especially the naïve, arrogant, and willfully ignorant—to see God's creation and their lives in it differently. He stood with and cared for the poor, marginalized, and outcast, manifesting compassionate responsibility and God's solidarity with the oppressed. He carved out paths of justice and peace for the sake of the flourishing and joy of all creation. And he invites and provides the welcoming feast of life-renewing bread and wine to his disciples. Jesus as Wisdom continued and gave new expression to Israel's testimony about God's sustaining work in the world.

Feminist theologians observe that traditions about personified Wisdom likewise helpfully inform understandings of the Holy Spirit. Wisdom of Solomon was the first to call Wisdom the πνεῦμα σοφίας ("spirit of Wisdom," 7:7), and to describe her as "the breath of the power of God" and "pure emanation of the glory of the Almighty" (7:25). That portrait, in combination with other traditions about personified Wisdom, lends much-needed potency to rather stereotypical conceptions of the Spirit as female (Johnson 2002, 148–149; cf. Fiddes 2014, esp. 159–167). First, Wisdom has cosmic reach and intimate connection to all of creation. At home in both the heavenly and earthly realms, transcendent and immanent, she observes everything and "pervades and penetrates all things" (Wis 7:24). Her power and scope are vast—from one end of the earth to the other (Wis 8:1)—while, at the same time, she knows all that is quiet, secret, wild, and deep in the world (Wis 7:22). Second, Wisdom moves. Many are the metaphors across the texts that suggest her mobility: exhaled by the Divine as breath and word (Sir 24:3), walking along paths (Proverbs 1–9), pervading the world as mist and cloud (Sir 24:2–4), flowing and overflowing as water and rivers (Sir 24:23–29), and piercing as eternal light (Wis 7:26, 29). "More mobile than any motion" (Wis 7:24), Wisdom strides over boundaries and borders to invite all people to learn from her. Finally, as noted above,

Wisdom mediates relationships between God, human beings, herself, and the world. She is the welcoming, joyful presence who inspires delight in the presence of God and one another. Indeed, for Wisdom of Solomon, she is the source of holy friendship and justice-making: "in every generation she passes into holy souls and makes them friends of God, and prophets" (7:27). Wisdom as Spirit is the mysterious force that enlivens, disturbs, sustains, and makes possible partnership with God and a world marked by justice and solidarity.

17.4 WISDOM AND KNOWING

Many of the ways that feminists and feminist theologians think about the nature and scope of knowledge resonate with traditions about personified Wisdom. To begin, the texts portray Wisdom as an extraordinary gift from God, a manifestation of God's desire for relationship with humanity (e.g., Sir 1:1; Wis 8:17–21). Wisdom is available to everyone, though some are sure to refuse or squander her instruction.[18] Conceived of as gift, it follows that no one obtains Wisdom on her own. No one earns or achieves Wisdom through sheer force of will, status, or identity. No person or group possesses or owns Wisdom. Becoming wise is an inherently relational phenomenon, a divine response to the human search for understanding. The refrain "seek and find" in the texts about her highlights this dynamic. A person seeks Wisdom, searches for her as for hidden treasures (e.g., Prov 2:4; Sir 4:11; 6:27), cries out and prays to God for her (Wis 7:7), watches and listens. For her part, Wisdom travels the world in search of her companions, calling out and coming alongside them on their paths (e.g., Sir 24; Wis 6:12–16; Bar 3:36). Those who seek Wisdom and Wisdom herself expend great energy to find one another. Yet in the end their meeting is a gift.

Cosmic in reach, Wisdom is also immanent. She has a place in the world. The texts capture the particularity—the contextuality—of Wisdom's expression in various ways. Proverbs describes her moving about a bustling city where she builds a seven-pillared house (Proverbs 1–9; cf. Wis 6:14). Sirach tells how Wisdom traversed creation in search of a place to abide ("over waves of the sea, over all the earth, over every people and nation," 24:6), only to eventually pitch her tent at God's command in Jerusalem and minister in the Temple (24:1–12). And Sirach and Baruch situate her within Israel as the embodiment of Torah (Bar 4:1; Sir 24:23–29). Indeed, Wisdom so desires a place to dwell that, as 1 Enoch tells it, she withdraws to heaven diminished after being unable to find a home on earth (42:1–2). The immanent or indwelling characteristic of Wisdom is amplified further by depictions of her as a tree: a "tree of life" in Prov 3:18, and Sirach's subsequent glorious expansion of that image (24:12–22). Wisdom so portrayed is organic and slow-growing, deeply rooted in a place, changing with the seasons, nourished or

---

[18] Scoffers, mockers, and fools, for example, are notorious for refusing instruction (e.g., Prov 1:7, 20–31; 13:1; 15:12; 28:26).

depleted by the elements, life-giving and beautiful, and manifest in ways both cultivated and wild. Said differently, Wisdom is manifest locally, worked for and wondrous,
ancient and unfolding.[19]

Feminist theologians highlight two other claims in the Wisdom texts about the nature
and scope of knowledge as particularly empowering for women. First, the Wisdom tradition values human experience as an essential resource for making sense of the world.
The daily, ordinary hubbub in which Wisdom first beckons (Prov 1:20–21) is an arena
of revelation and ethical import—from interactions with others, to household tasks, to
marketplace transactions, to decisions about time and money and speech. No moment
is too slight to matter or spark insight; no insect is too small to be exceedingly wise
(Prov 6:6–11; cf. 30:24–28). The Wisdom tradition thus emboldens human agency in
the search for knowledge, accents the everyday with theological and moral significance,
and honors the hard-earned learnings of elders and artists and creatures—those with
honed skills and street smarts. Second and relatedly, the tradition describes education
as a holistic endeavor, a process that engages the body and its diverse faculties of discernment and evaluation, including the senses, emotions, desires, appetites, and loves.[20]
Coming to know or, said better, to love Wisdom is therefore far more than cognitive
achievement. It is a valuing and orientation of the whole fleshly self in the world in ways
that make possible personal and communal flourishing.

In closing, I suggest that the "where" of personified Wisdom, as much as the "who,"
is also instructive in the effort to build a world where women and all people flourish.
Persistent across the texts about Wisdom is the question of "where" she can be found.
Where, after all, is the place of understanding (e.g., Job 28:12, 20)? The replies vary. At
times, Wisdom locates herself at the centers of power, authority, and community: the
city gates and high places as in Proverbs, or the Temple as in Sirach. At times, Wisdom
is nowhere to be found, not at all in the land of the living (e.g., Job 28; Bar 3:9–4:4).
But frequently the texts describe Wisdom as either on the move or lingering in liminal
spaces. She calls out along pathways and from intersections; she stands near, in, or just
outside city gates; she beckons from beside doorways and on thresholds (e.g., Prov 1:20–21;
8:1–3). She crosses over horizons, and journeys over oceans and lands—heedless of
boundaries and borders (Sir 24:5–7). She migrates, pitching her tent as she journeys in
search of a place to abide (Sir 24:1–12). Where exactly is Wisdom to be found? Taken
together, the texts convey mystery and the enduring challenge of finding her. At the
same time, the texts suggest that the search for wisdom does well to begin in the margins,
the edges, between the familiar and the not-yet known—the very places and spaces that
feminist theologians survey and illumine for the sake of human flourishing.

---

[19] Johnson (1993, 133) captures the tension of Wisdom's transcendence and immanence in her
description of Jesus's incarnation: "Jesus-Sophia personally incarnates Wisdom's gracious care in one
particular history, for the benefit of all, while she lays down a multiplicity of paths in diverse cultures by
which all people may seek and, seeking, find her."

[20] For recent work on the senses, emotions, and desire in Wisdom Literature, see, e.g., Yoder 2016;
Tilford 2017.

WORKS CITED

Baumann, Gerlinde. 1996. *Die Weisheitsgestalt in Proverbien 1–9*. FAT 16. Tübingen: Mohr-Siebeck.

Baumann, Gerlinde. 1998. "A Figure with Many Facets: The Literary and Theological Functions of Personified Wisdom in Proverbs 1–9." Pages 44–78 in *Wisdom and the Psalms: A Feminist Companion to the Bible (Second Series)*. Edited by Athalya Brenner and Carole R. Fontaine. FCB II 2; Sheffield: Sheffield Academic.

Baumann, Gerlinde. 2014. "Personified Wisdom: Contexts, Meanings, Theology." Pages 57–75 in *The Writings and Later Wisdom Books*. Edited by Nuria Calduch-Benages and Christl M. Maier. Atlanta, GA: SBL.

Bledsoe, Seth A. 2013. "Can *Ahiqar* Tell Us Anything about Personified Wisdom?" *JBL* 132:119–137.

Boström, Gustav. 1935. *Proverbiastudien: Die Weisheit und das fremde Weib in Spruche 1–9*. Lunds Univeristets Arsskrift 30, 3. Lund: Gleerup.

Brewer-Boydston, Ginny. 2012. "'They Walk in Wisdom or Folly': The Intensification of Wisdom and Folly from Proverbs to the Dead Sea Scrolls." *PRSt* 39:319–334.

Cady, Susan, Marian Ronan, and Hal Taussig. 1986. *Sophia, the Future of Feminist Spirituality*. New York, NY: Harper and Row.

Camp, Claudia V. 1985. *Wisdom and the Feminine in the Book of Proverbs*. BLS 11. Sheffield: JSOT/Almond.

Clifford, Anne M. 2001. *Introducing Feminist Theology*. Maryknoll, NY: Orbis.

Coakley, Sarah. 2013. *God, Sexuality, and the Self: An Essay "On the Trinity."* Cambridge: Cambridge University Press.

Crawford, Sidnie White. 1998. "Lady Wisdom and Dame Folly at Qumran," *DSD* 5:355–366.

Daly, Mary. 1993. *Beyond God the Father: Toward a Philosophy of Women's Liberation*. Rev. ed. Boston, MA: Beacon Press.

Deane-Drummond, Celia. 2005. "Sophia, Mary and the Eternal Feminine in Pierre Teilhard de Chardin and Sergei Bulgakov." *Ecotheology* 10:215–231.

Deutsch, Celia M. 1996. *Lady Wisdom, Jesus, and the Sages: Metaphor and Social Context in Matthew's Gospel*. Valley Forge, PA: Trinity.

Devine, Luke. 2014. "How *Shekhinah* Became the God(dess) of Jewish Feminism." *Feminist Theology* 23:71–91.

Douglas, Sally. 2016. *Early Church Understandings of Jesus as the Female Divine: The Scandal of the Scandal of Particularity*. New York, NY: Bloomsbury.

Engelsman, Joan Chamberlain. 1979. *The Feminine Dimension of the Divine*. Philadelphia, PA: Westminster.

Fabella, Virginia. 1988. "A Common Methodology for Diverse Christologies?" Pages 108–117 in *With Passion and Compassion: Third World Women Doing Theology*. Edited by Virginia Fabella and Mercy Amba Oduyoye. Maryknoll, NY: Orbis.

Fiddes, Paul S. 2014. "Wisdom and the Spirit: The Loss and Remaking of Relationship." *PRSt* 41:151–167.

Fox, Michael V. 1995. "World Order and Maꜥat: A Crooked Parallel." *JANES* 23:37–48.

Fox, Michael V. 2000. *Proverbs 1–9: A New Translation with Introduction and Commentary*. AB 18a. New York, NY: Doubleday.

Good, Deirdre J. 1987. *Reconstructing the Tradition of Sophia in Gnostic Literature*. SBLMS 32. Atlanta, GA: Scholars Press.

Gross, Rita M. 1993. *Buddhism after Patriarchy: A Feminist History, Analysis, and Reconstruction of Buddhism*. Albany, NY: State University of New York.

Hadley, Judith M. 1995. "Wisdom and the Goddess." Pages 234–243 in *Wisdom in Ancient Israel: Essays in Honour of J.A. Emerton*. Edited by J. Day, R.P. Gordon, and H.G.M. Williamson. Cambridge: Cambridge University Press.

Isherwood, Lisa, and Dorothea McEwan. 1993. "An Introduction to Feminist Theology and the Case for Its Study in an Academic Setting." *Feminist Theology* 1:10–25.

Johnson, Elizabeth A. 1985. "Jesus, the Wisdom of God: A Biblical Basis for Non-Androcentric Christology." *ETL* 61:261–294.

Johnson, Elizabeth A. 1993. "Redeeming the Name of Christ—Christology." Pages 115–137 in *Freeing Theology: The Essentials of Theology in Feminist Perspective*. Edited by Catherine Mawry LaCugna. New York, NY: Harper

Johnson, Elizabeth A. 2002. *She Who Is: The Mystery of God in Feminist Theological Discourse*. 2nd ed. New York, NY: Crossroad.

Jones, Serene. 2011. "Feminist Theology and the Global Imagination." Pages 1–34 in *The Oxford Handbook of Feminist Theology Online*. Edited by Sheila Briggs and Mary McClintock Ferguson. Oxford: Oxford University Press.

Kwok, Pui-Lan. 2004. "Feminist Theology as Intercultural Discourse." Pages 23–39 in *The Cambridge Companion to Feminist Theology*. Edited by Susan Frank Parsons. Cambridge: Cambridge University Press.

Malcom, Lois. 2010. "On Not Three Male Gods: Retrieving Wisdom in Trinitarian Discourse." *Dialog* 49:238–247.

McAlister, Shannon. 2018. "Christ as the Woman Seeking Her Lost Coin: Luke 15:8–10 and Divine Sophia in the Latin West." *TS* 79:7–35.

McKinlay, Judith. 1996. *Gendering Wisdom the Host: Biblical Invitations to Eat and Drink*. JSOTSup 216. Sheffield: Sheffield Academic.

Newsom, Carol A. 1989. "Women and the Discourse of Patriarchal Wisdom: A Study of Proverbs 1–9." Pages 85–98 in *Gender and Difference in Ancient Israel*. Edited by Peggy L. Day. Minneapolis, MN: Augsburg Fortress. Repr. pages 85–98 in *Women in the Hebrew Bible: A Reader*. Edited by Alice Bach. New York, NY: Routledge, 1999.

O'Connor, Kathleen M. 1988. *The Wisdom Literature*. MBS 5. Collegeville, MN: Liturgical.

Parsons, Susan Frank, ed. 2004. *The Cambridge Companion to Feminist Theology*. Cambridge: Cambridge University Press.

Plaskow, Judith. 1990. *Standing Against Sinai: Judaism from a Feminist Perspective*. San Francisco, CA: HarperSanFrancisco.

Preminger, Alex, and T.V.F. Brogan, eds. 1993. *The New Princeton Encyclopedia of Poetry and Poetics*. Princeton, NJ: Princeton University Press.

Ruether, Rosemary Radford. 2005. *Goddesses and the Divine Feminine: A Western Religious History*. Berkeley, CA: University of California Press.

Schroer, Sylvia. 1995. "Wise and Counselling Women in Ancient Israel: Literary and Historical Ideals of the Personified Hokmah." Pages 67–84 in *A Feminist Companion to Wisdom Literature*. Edited by Athalya Brenner. FCB 9. Sheffield: Sheffield Academic.

Schroer, Sylvia. 1996. *Die Weisheit hat ihr Haus gebaut: Studien zur Gestalt der Sophia in den biblischen Schriften*. Mainz: Matthias-Grünewald.

Schüssler Fiorenza, Elisabeth, ed. 2014. *Feminist Biblical Studies in the Twentieth Century: Scholarship and Movement*. Atlanta, GA: SBL.

Sinnott, Alice M. 2005. *The Personification of Wisdom*. SOTSMS. Burlington, VT: Ashgate.

Tilford, Nicole. 2017. *Sensing World, Sensing Wisdom: The Cognitive Foundation of Biblical Metaphors*. Atlanta, GA: SBL.

Witherington, Ben. 1994. *Jesus the Sage: The Pilgrimage of Wisdom*. Minneapolis, MN: Augsburg Fortress.

Yoder, Christine Roy. 2001. *Wisdom as a Woman of Substance: A Socioeconomic Reading of Proverbs 1–9 and 31:10–31*. BZAW 304. Berlin: de Gruyter.

Yoder, Christine Roy. 2009. *Proverbs*. Abingdon Old Testament Commentaries. Nashville, TN: Abingdon.

Yoder, Christine Roy, ed. 2016. *The Senses in Israelite Wisdom Literature*. HBAI 5.1.

CHAPTER 18

....

WISDOM IN NATURE

....

NORMAN HABEL

Who put Wisdom in the clouds?

(Job 38:36)

WHEN God takes Job on his eco-tour of the cosmos (chs. 38–39), he poses the challenging question—one among many similar questions—Who put Wisdom in the clouds? A reader who is uninformed about the locations of Wisdom according to the wise of the ancient—or modern—world, might automatically reply: God!

A close reading of relevant texts discloses the insight that wisdom, among the many ways in which its presence is characterized, is an innate dimension of all domains of nature, whether animate or inanimate. This dimension is discerned by the wise, the scientists of the ancient world, by close observation of nature.

One tradition among the wise is to "acquire" wisdom, whether by personal observation or by embracing the wisdom truth of mentors. Acquired wisdom, however, needs to be distinguished from innate wisdom, the theme of this analysis. Von Rad, in chapter 9 of his work *Wisdom in Israel* (1972, 145–157), speaks of "Wisdom immanent in the world." My analysis explores this insight afresh, taking into account my own original reading of pivotal texts.

18.1 INNATE WISDOM TERMINOLOGY

....

To appreciate the textual analysis which follows, it is wise to identify some of the key terms relevant for this investigation, terms I have discussed in detail elsewhere (Habel 2015). These terms reflect the modus operandi of the wise in relation to nature.

18.1.1 "Observe"—ראה

Like all good scientists, the wise are expected to discern through "observation" and rational analysis. This practice is abundantly clear in the following passage: "Go to the ant, *observe* its ways and be wise" (Prov 6:6). In this example the wise person "observes" or "watches critically" a specific phenomenon of nature: the ant. As the wider use of this verb indicates, the process of "observing" is more than a chance "seeing." The task is to "observe" closely and discern the "way," the determining characteristic of that phenomenon.

18.1.2 "Discern"—בין

While the noun "discernment" is found in parallel with "wisdom" in some passages, such as Prov 4:7, the verb בין refers to a process of distinguishing one factor from another. The aim of discernment is, more specifically, to determine the "way" (דרך) and/or the "place" (מקום) of a particular phenomenon of nature.

18.1.3 "Acquire"—קנה

To "acquire" wisdom is the mission and task of every student of wisdom (Prov 4:7) The wise over the centuries observed the behavior of humans and society, observations that led to an accumulation of acquired wisdom known as proverbs. Acquiring wisdom could also be achieved by observing and analyzing nature where Wisdom may be discerned as an innate force.

18.1.4 "Place"—מקום

In the ordering of things on Earth, in the thinking of the Wisdom school, everything has its "place." In Job 28 the "place" of things is made explicit. The rocks of Earth, for example, are the "place" of sapphires. Precious gems have a "place" in stones (Job 28:6); gold has its "place" in the Earth (Job 28:1); Earth has its "place" in the cosmos (Job 14:18; 18:4) and the East wind has its "place" in the heavens (Job 27:23).

18.1.5 "Way"—דרך

Just as the term מקום has Wisdom significance, so too does the key term דרך, which is usually translated "way." In Wisdom contexts we hear about the "way" of the eagle in the sky and the "way" of a snake on a rock (Prov 30:18).

Every phenomenon of nature has its own inner formative force, its driving characteristic, its דרך (Habel 2003, 286). This concept of דרך ("way") is crucial for an understanding of the basic Wisdom interpretation of nature in the ancient world. The דרך of something is the wisdom programmed into its nature as part of the ecosystem.

18.1.6 "Law"—חק

While this term for "law" may refer to law in society, it may also refer to a "law" in nature. In Job 28:26 the term is parallel with דרך ("way"), the innate nature/wisdom of natural phenomenon. In Job 38:33, Job is challenged to grasp how the laws (חקות) of the sky/space impact on Earth.

18.2 LOCATING INNATE WISDOM

Perhaps the most obvious explication of this phenomenon is found in Job 28, where the ultimate question is posed: Where can Wisdom be found?

The significance of this chapter was demonstrated in the Netherlands when an entire conference was dedicated to the topic of "Job 28: Cognition in Context" (see Habel 2003). For a more detailed analysis of Job 28, see *Finding Wisdom in Nature* (Habel 2014, ch. 3).

Crucial for an understanding of this chapter in Job is the Wisdom school concept of "place" (מקום), the locus or habitat of a phenomenon/factor in the ecosystem network of the universe.

In Job 28, the poet recognizes the essential מקום of everything in the universe and even asks the question: Where is the מקום of Wisdom itself? The answer to that question might seem to be obvious: the source or the original מקום of Wisdom is within God. In the course of this poem, however, the Wisdom poet leads us on a search that ends in another location—the world of nature!

The opening verse of the poem immediately focuses on the question of the מקום of various phenomena in creation, entities such as silver and gold: Truly, there is a source for silver and a place (מקום) for the gold they refine (Job 28:1). As indicated above, everything has its appointed "place" in the order of creation, and more specifically on Earth. By establishing that precious commodities have a specific "place" in the design of the universe, the poet prepares the way for posing the ultimate question about the "place" of Wisdom, the most precious find of all (Job 28:12).

The crucial question about the location of Wisdom in Job 28:12–14 is made explicit in Job 28:20:

> But Wisdom, where does she originate?
> Where is the "place" of Discernment?

In this version of the refrain, the "place" of Wisdom in the cosmos is linked to the mystery of its origin. The "place" of Wisdom is a wonder that harks back to its very origins at the time of creation.

In the final verses of Job 28, we learn that God is the one who first undertook a successful search for Wisdom. As the divine Sage-cum-Scientist, God searched far and wide across Earth to find Wisdom. Unlike like other deities of the ancient world who claimed to possess great wisdom, the God discerned by the Wisdom school undertakes the ultimate search for Wisdom.

In the ancient Near East, the God Ea was known as "the wisest of the gods who knew every sort of thing." The wisdom of Marduk was considered a mystery never understood by humans. And the sun god Shamash was not only wise and mighty, "he was his own counsellor" (Kalugila 1980, 30–45). While the wisdom deities of the ancient Near East possess wisdom and apply it in a variety of ways, the scientists of the Wisdom school discern God as a primordial scientist who "seeks and discerns Wisdom" in nature.

The "place" where the God of the Wisdom school begins to search for Wisdom is not a distant realm among the gods or the council of heaven. The "way" of Wisdom that God the observing "scientist" discerns is not the "mind" of God or a personal divine capacity. Rather:

> God discerned (בין) her way (דרך),
> and came to know her place (מקום),
> for God looked to the ends of Earth
> and observed (ראה) everything under heaven.
> (Job 28:23–24)

God searches to the ends of Earth including every domain "under heaven." God reads the entire landscape of the planet. The "place" of Wisdom is on/in Earth!

When we finally reach the climax of the poem, God discovers Wisdom in nature. God's discovery of Wisdom, however, is not a recent event. God discerned the presence of Wisdom at the very beginning, during the process of creation. It is specifically when God is creating meteorological domains that God the scientist discerns Wisdom. These specific domains, it would seem, are representative of all the domains of nature:

> When God fixed the *weight* of the wind
> and meted out the waters by *measure*,
> when God made a *rule* (חק) for the rain
> and a *way* (דרך) for the thunderstorm,
> then God observed (ראה) her and appraised her,
> established her and probed her.
> (Job 28:25–27)

So, the primary question here is not: who put Wisdom in the clouds, but rather, who first discerned Wisdom in the clouds?

A significant dimension of God's search for Wisdom lies not in the specific domains themselves, but in that feature of these domains where Wisdom is to be found. The use of the technical terms דֶּרֶךְ and חֹק indicates that God is discerning the innate character of these phenomena—whether they be the wind, the waters, the storm clouds, or the rain. God does not merely observe a given phenomenon. God "discerns" its "way" (דֶּרֶךְ), its inner code, its innate character. By discerning the "ways" of these phenomena of nature, God discovers innate Wisdom. Wisdom, then, is not separate from these phenomena of nature, but an innate dimension of nature. God discovers Wisdom as an inner code, a "network of forces" or "laws" in nature!

It is striking that this understanding of these "laws" of nature was anticipated by the scientists of ancient times. Significantly a "law" of nature was viewed as "intelligent," as the innate Wisdom or knowledge of a given phenomenon that guided its behavior. Wisdom, then, is a powerful code innate in all the domains of nature, a code that today is understood as integral to the laws of nature.

The search for Wisdom in the laws of nature, the network of codes that govern and balance the forces of nature—from gravity and anti-gravity to summer and winter—persists as a challenge for the scientists and thinkers of today, whether they are geologists or astrophysicists.

Given the specific "place" of Wisdom in Job 28, we may well consult meteorologists and climate scientists about the innate laws of nature in our atmosphere—our clouds—and ask whether the excessive use of greenhouse gases by humans has upset the network of forces innate in the ecosystems of the weather (cf. Habel 2013).

18.3 INNATE WISDOM IN LIVING CREATURES

This portrait of Wisdom as innate in nature helps us to re-read a range of other texts where this phenomenon is identified but its significance rarely explored. An excellent example is Prov 6:6–8, which refers to the "way" of the ant:

> Go to the ant, you lazybones!
> *Observe* its *way* and be wise!
> Without having any chief
> or officer or ruler,
> it prepares its food in summer,
> and gathers its sustenance in harvest.
> (Prov 6:6–8)

The Wisdom in an ant colony is, according to these ancient scientists, an inner capacity to function as a corporate body without any hierarchy—without any bosses or leaders—a mystery that modern scientists still find fascinating. Another dimension of ant Wisdom, according to this ancient scientist, is the instinctual/intellectual capacity of ants to gather food in summer and store it for the winter when conditions for finding food are difficult. The Wisdom embedded in the ant enables it to anticipate the future and plan ahead (Habel 2013, 3).

It may seem surprising that ants were chosen by the wise as an exemplar of Wisdom in living creatures on our planet. But modern scientists share this fascination with these tiny insects. Tim Flannery, for example, in his chapter on "super-organisms," also explores the amazing capacity of ants, especially attine ants, to construct complex ecosystems we might well call societies, even agricultural societies (Flannery 2010, 15).

The wise in ancient times called this interconnected and programmed intelligence of ants the "way" or the innate Wisdom dimension of the ant. And as Flannery outlines, this inner capacity is apparent in all areas of the ant ecosystem—from the ingenious techniques used to locate and prepare a new habitat to the sophisticated practices developed for the agriculture of fungus. These innate capacities may have developed over millions of years, but they testify to a deep dimension of such creatures in nature that may still be designated their innate Wisdom (Habel 2013, 3–4).

The author of Proverbs 30 explores a range of mysteries both in society and in nature. He claims that he lacks the capacity to understand the mysteries that surround him (Prov 30:1–3), the innate way/Wisdom he has observed. There are four innate things in nature, he declares, that are too wonderful to comprehend:

> The way of an eagle in the sky,
> the way of a snake on a rock,
> the way of a ship on the high seas,
> the way of a man with a girl.
> (Prov 30:18–19)

This ancient scribe recognizes the mystery innate in nature and natural behavior, a mystery designated as the "way"—a mystery also known as Wisdom. The mystery of Wisdom in nature is also proclaimed in subsequent verses:

> Four things on Earth are small
> yet they are exceedingly wise;
> the ants are a people without strength
> yet they provide their food in the summer;
> the badgers are a people without power
> yet they make their homes in the rocks;
> the locusts have no king,
> yet all of them march in rank;
> the lizard can be grasped in the hand
> yet it is found in king's palaces.
> (Prov 30:24–28)

Wisdom is clearly not confined to humans, but is present as the "way," the driving characteristic of all living creatures, regardless of how small they are. Wisdom is the life-force that determines the identity and behavior of all living beings.

When, in his speeches, God leads Job into the kingdom of the wild, the sufferer is confronted by the "ways" of creatures in the wild. The assumption in this context is that all such creatures have an innate Wisdom that enables them to survive in the wild.

One creature, however, seems to demonstrate the opposite—the ostrich. She is a creature with grand plumage and high spirits but she, according to popular tradition, leaves her eggs on the ground, lets them get hot in the dust and be crushed by wild beasts. She also treats her young harshly, as if they were not hers (Job 38:13–16). The reason given is that אלוה ("God") deprived her of Wisdom and withheld her portion of discernment (Job 39:17).

The ostrich is here presented as the exception that proves the rule. The implication is quite clearly that all living creatures are imbued with innate wisdom or discernment. In the preceding verses the ibex is portrayed as a nurturing mother, quite the opposite of the ostrich. The ibex has the innate Wisdom needed to determine the time of birth and how to watch over her young so that they grow into healthy animals who can leave home and be self-sufficient (Job 39:1–4).

The wild ass has the Wisdom needed to survive in the salt flats of the wilderness, find sustenance without a taskmaster and the capacity to laugh at the furor of the city (Job 39:5–8). The wild ox (Job 39:9–11) stands as a testimony to the Wisdom of creatures who know they are not subject to the mandate to dominate found in Gen 1:26–28 (Habel 2001). Even the horse, who may appear to have been domesticated and dominated by humans, exhibits the fierce spirit of the wild (Job 39:19–25).

Hawks are explicitly said to soar through the sky and spread their wings on high because of their inner "discernment" or Wisdom. Similarly, the eagle has the innate knowledge required to dwell on rocky crags and build a nest safely in the heights (Job 39:26–30). Birds like the eagle, and animals like the ibex, are testimony to Wisdom innate in living creatures.

We know, however, that the ostrich is neither careless about her eggs nor cruel to her chicks, that she does not leave her eggs on the ground for the sun to heat them. The dominant female has an innate Wisdom to choose where her eggs should be laid to keep them safe. The male sits on the eggs from late afternoon to sunrise the next day. The Joban poet, it seems, has selected—tongue in cheek—an example of Wisdom absent in nature that is found in local tradition to highlight the issue of innate Wisdom.

Celia Deane-Drummond, in her discussion of natural wisdom in evolutionary biology, returns to the example of the ant and asks whether we are now better informed than the "way" of the ant. She distinguishes between natural Wisdom and cosmic design, which implies a deliberate designer. She concludes:

> Natural wisdom by contrast puts more emphasis on the process of the evolutionary searchlight scanning forms of biological diversity. Convergence across all traits simultaneously has not yet been found, for the way/wisdom of each species is unique.
> (Deane-Drummond 2006, 70)

The Wisdom school would also argue that each species has its own unique "way," its innate Wisdom. From each species we can learn new dimensions of the Wisdom embedded in all life forms.

18.4 Innate Wisdom in the Cosmos

Job's experience of Wisdom innate in living creatures is preceded by a profound experience of Wisdom in the domains of the cosmos, an experience that might well be called his "ecological conversion."

God's opening words confront Job with the "design" (עֵצָה) of the cosmos, a cosmic master-plan Job has ignored because of his obsession with injustice on Earth (Job 38:1–2). God's reference to the "design" of the cosmos in his opening words indicates that Job is being confronted with the big picture and, in particular, how the many dimensions of the cosmos combine to form the ecosystem of the universe. Inherent is this picture are the beginnings of cosmic ecology.

In stage one of Job's tour of the cosmos, God begins with a striking question that some scholars view as pure sarcasm. But is it?

> Where were you when I laid Earth's foundations?
> Tell me if you have gained Discernment?
> Who fixed its dimensions? Surely you know!
> (Job 38:4–5)

Rather than view this passage as mere sarcasm, I believe it is possible to recognize in this question an ancient scientist's challenge to explore the primal impulses, the innate Wisdom, in the cosmos. God asks Job whether he has the "discernment" or the research skills of the Wisdom school necessary to explore the origins of Earth. Discernment (בִּינָה) is a critical skill required of the wise, the scientists of old. God is challenging Job to find the Discernment/Wisdom required to explore a primal impulse of the cosmos—the origin of Earth.

Later, God challenges Job to locate the designated "places" or sources of light and darkness in the design of the cosmos, once again locating Job in the primordial:

> Surely you know, for you were born then,
> and the number of your days is great.
> (Job 38:21)

The narrator-mentor views a return to the beginning as a necessary process for discovering the precise "place" of darkness in the cosmos, and the inner nature or "way" of light. In contemporary terms, the nature of light and darkness is a primal mystery that leads scientists to probe the beginnings of time and space. And, in terms of cosmic ecology, we are acutely conscious that distant light from the beginnings of time continues to interact with our planet, enabling us to live, move, and have our being. It is specifically in the primordial world of creation that God, the wise scientist, discerns the "place" of Wisdom, as we noted above in Job 28:25–27.

Job is also asked to explore light and darkness, forces beyond the control of humans like Job, in terms of their respective locations in the cosmos. The laws of nature, reflected in the movement of light and darkness, control the potentials of the wicked as well as the patterns of life on Earth. The narrator presents the laws of nature—rather than an intervening God—as a factor in the fate of humans, demonstrating that ecology and ethics are interrelated.

Just as challenging for a would-be scientist like Job are the domains that exist in the depths of the cosmos:

> Have you penetrated the sources of Sea,
> or walked through the recesses of the Deep?
> Have the gates of Death been revealed to you?
> Have you seen the gates of Death's gloom?
> Have you discerned the expanses of Earth?
> Tell me if you know all this?
> (Job 38:16–18)

Just as scientists today seek to penetrate the extremities of the cosmos, the limits of outer space, and the depths of dark matter, so Job is challenged to locate the extremities of space, light and darkness. Especially significant is the question of whether Job has "discerned" the expanses of Earth including the "way" and the "place" of light and darkness (Job 38:19) or whether he can discover the "way" of lightning and the "way" of the thunderstorm (Job 38:24–25).

The reference to "way" in connection with both lightning and thunder recalls the narrator's account of how God found Wisdom in the rules governing the phenomena of the weather, including the "way" of the thunderstorm (Job 28:26). In Job 38, Job is confronted with the mystery of innate knowledge: that dimension of each domain of nature—including the domains of the Weather—that guides its role in the cosmic ecosystem.

Job is also led to observe the world of space, its constellations and laws. The narrator's knowledge of this domain of the cosmos may well surprise us even today:

> Can you bind the fetters of the Pleiades
> or loosen the reins of Orion?
> Can you lead out Mazzaroth in its season
> or guide the Bear with her sons?
> Do you know the "laws" of the sky?
> Can you establish its order on Earth?
> (Job 38:31–33)

Job's initial challenge is to probe traditional knowledge of the constellations. It is one thing to observe and wonder at their design and pattern in the sky; it is quite another to contemplate how these constellations in space are controlled by a Wisdom that is beyond human ingenuity. The narrator views the skies as a domain filled with both mystery and mythology, the scientific and the spiritual.

Even more stunning, perhaps, is the question posed about the "laws" (חקות) of the skies (Job 38:33). The focus is clearly on Wisdom as science, not on some deity who controls the heavens or manipulates the stars. We might identify the laws in the skies governing the cosmos with contemporary understandings of gravity and related astral forces. Just as Wisdom is found by God in the "laws" of nature associated with the weather (Job 28:25–26), Job is challenged to discern the same Wisdom functioning in the laws of space.

The narrator-mentor asks whether these laws can be employed to establish an ordered domain on Earth: a genuine mystery of ancient ecology or astrophysics. This question relates to the very core of ecology as a science. How do the laws of one domain inter-relate with those of another domain? How do the laws of space interact and affect the modus operandi of planet Earth? How do the laws of the cosmos relate to each other to facilitate the operation of the universe and the place of Earth in that universe? How does the cosmos function?

In short, Job is confronted with one of the great mysteries of astrophysics, the cosmic ecology of time and space and the function of Wisdom in that ecology.

18.5 WISDOM THE PRIMAL BLUEPRINT

If we now turn to the famous Wisdom text in Proverbs 8, in the light of our preceding analyses of Wisdom in nature, we are confronted with another dimension of the relationship of Wisdom with nature. Pivotal for our appreciation of this insight is a close reading of the opening verses, Prov 8:22–23:

> YHWH acquired (קנה) me first,
> his way (דרך) before his works.
> From of old, from antiquity I was established,
> from the first, from the beginnings of Earth.

Wisdom introduces herself as the "way" that God "acquires" before any of the works of creation. Wisdom is the primal "way," the primordial dimension or impulse in the pre-creation universe. The verb translated "acquired" (קנה) is the standard term employed in Proverbs for acquiring Wisdom (see Prov 4:3, 7). The repeated injunction of the Wisdom teacher is to "acquire Wisdom"! The aim of the wise is to "acquire" Wisdom as an essential skill for a positive life.

Given this context, it seems logical to understand this term in the standard way (cf. Lenzi 2006, 692). God "acquires" Wisdom and in so doing is portrayed as a primordial sage, the ideal "scientist," the one who introduces the modus operandi of the wise as primal and powerful. God is introduced as the first student in the Wisdom school.

Crucial for an appreciation of the nature and role of Wisdom in this text and else-where is the designation of Wisdom as the "way" (דרך) that precedes the "works" of cre-ation. As indicated previously, the "way" (דרך) of something refers to its *bildende Kraft*, its own inner formative force or, as I suggest, its driving characteristic (Habel 2003, 286). The דֶּרֶךְ of something is its essential nature as part of the cosmos.

In Proverbs 8, דֶּרֶךְ is identified as the primordial formative force or factor that precedes the works of creation. Scholars have long sought to discern precisely what this primal dimension might be. McKane (1970, 351) declares, "I would hold with von Rad that the intention here is to emphasize the vast intelligence of Wisdom by assigning to her an architectonic function in the ordering of the world."

McKane's recognition of Wisdom's "architectonic function" is consistent with the approach of von Rad (1972, 156–157) and others who speak of Wisdom as "primeval order," "world reason," or cosmic design. "Cosmic blueprint" is an appropriate description of the essential nature of wisdom as a primordial factor "acquired" by God for the design and creation of the cosmos (see Habel 2015, ch. 4).

Wisdom is introduced in Proverbs 8 as the primordial "way," the cosmic blueprint essential to the design and creation of the universe. This reading of the text eliminates any need to identify prior mythological figures or factors in the portrayal of Wisdom as the "way." Von Rad (1972, 153–155), who explores possible ancient prototypes such as the Egyptian goddess Ma'at, ultimately finds no direct dependence on ancient mythology. Lenzi argues there may, however, be a polemic against the mythology of the Enuma Elish, where Marduk is called the Sage (2006, 706).

In Proverbs 8, however, Wisdom is not a deity; Wisdom is a force/factor that precedes all creation. Wisdom as a primordial blueprint reflects a dynamic understanding of the physical universe that extends beyond the primordial into the present. This dimension of innate Wisdom is not a memory of ancient mythology, but a dynamic natural force discerned by the scientists of old.

18.6 CONCLUSION

Who put Wisdom in the clouds? According to the scientists of the ancient world, Wisdom is an innate dimension of clouds, crabs, and every other domain of nature, whether animate or inanimate.

A modern scientist, like Tim Flannery, may give a different name to this mystery, this innate dimension of nature, but the phenomenon discerned by the wise of ancient times remains a pivotal focus of research among scientists of today.

Especially significant is the ecological dimension of this phenomenon where the innate "wisdom" of one part of nature interacts with the "wisdom" of other realms of nature. The question Job faced was not only whether Wisdom was in the clouds, but how the "laws/wisdom" of space affect the modus operandi of Earth!

Innate Wisdom extends from the ant to the atmosphere, from the antelope to astrophysics! Ultimately, God is portrayed as the primal scientist who discerns Wisdom in nature during the process of creation (Job 28:25–27) and acquires Wisdom as the cosmic blueprint for the "works" of creation (Prov 8:22–23).

Godwit Wisdom

Some years ago
I was seated on a grassy area by a shoreline
on a bay in Auckland, New Zealand.
As I waited and watched I observed
hundreds of bar-tailed godwits gather
from all around the island.
All day they raced around in a feeding frenzy
communicating with extreme agitation.
Suddenly,
they heeded a signal deep within each of them,
began to circle round
and form a spiral of spinning life.
Slowly the spiral swirled out to sea
and the godwits set out across the ocean.
They fly across vast waters,
through storms over the equator,
on their way to a chosen location in Siberia
where they feed, breed and nurture their young
before they return.
At that moment I could sense their Wisdom—
the Wisdom of flight and the Wisdom of memory—
encoded in their spirit.
I discerned an amazing intelligence
of fellow Earth beings,
guiding themselves non-stop
to a place across the ocean
more than ten thousand kilometres away!
As they vanished into the distance
I had sense of sheer wonder.
I had discerned Wisdom in nature,
the innate force driving their evolution
over millions of years.

Works Cited

Deane-Drummond, Celia. 2006. *Wisdom and Wonder: Conversations in Science, Spirituality and Theology*. Philadelphia, PA: Templeton Foundation Press.

Flannery, Tim. 2010. *Here on Earth: An Argument for Hope*. Melbourne: Text Publishing.

Habel, Norman. 2001. "Is the Wild Ox Willing to Serve You? Challenging the Mandate to Dominate." Pages 179–189 in *The Earth Story in Wisdom Traditions: Earth Bible*, vol. 3. Edited by Norman Habel and Shirley Wurst. Sheffield: Sheffield Academic Press.

Habel, Norman. 2003. "The Implications of God Discovering Wisdom in Earth." Pages 281–298 in *Job 28: Cognition in Context*. Edited by Ellen van Wolde. Leiden: Brill.

Habel, Norman. 2013. "The Way of Things! Earth-Wisdom and Climate Change." Pages 1–10 in *Climate Change Cultural Change: Religious Responses and Responsibilities*. Edited by Anne Elvey and David Gormley-O'Brien. Melbourne: Mosaic.

Habel, Norman. 2014. *Finding Wisdom in Nature: An Ecological Reading of the Book of Job*. Sheffield: Sheffield Phoenix.

Habel, Norman. 2015. *Discerning Wisdom in God's Creation: Following the Way of Ancient Scientists*. Northcote: Morning Star.

Kalugila, Leonidas. 1980. *The Wise King: Studies in Royal Wisdom as Divine Revelation in the Old Testament and its Environment*. Gleerup: AMS.

Lenzi, Alan. 2006. "Proverbs 8:22–31: Three Perspectives on Its Composition." *JBL* 125:687–714.

McKane, William. 1970. *Proverbs: A New Approach*. OTL. London: SCM.

Rad, Gerhard von. 1972. *Wisdom in Israel*. Nashville, TN: Abingdon.

....

CHAPTER 19

THE PERVASIVENESS OF WISDOM IN (CON)TEXTS

....

JOHN AHN

19.1 OPENING

....

In recent years, the scholarly debate on Wisdom Literature has been sharp. In fact, this entire tradition has now been questioned (Sneed 2011; Kynes 2015). The once prized scholarly position on assessing this distinctive canonical collection has been challenged. Time will tell if the category of Wisdom will indeed succumb to this challenge, meet its obituary, or a timely measured response prevail.

Currently, there are at least three positions on the study of Wisdom (see Sneed 2015). The first is the preservation of tradition, where scholars continue to argue for a distinctive corpus of texts called Wisdom Literature (e.g., Crenshaw 2010). The second, new position suggests eliminating the category of Wisdom altogether (Kynes 2019). The third is an intermediary position that pushes for newer approaches without completely abandoning the traditional Wisdom category (Schellenberg 2015). This essay falls on the border, between the second and third views, pushing the boundary of Wisdom Literature.

Critical scholars often begin with the inquiry: What is Wisdom? Within Wisdom, they include Proverbs, Job, and Ecclesiastes. In the Greek or Septuagint context, the tradition adds the Song of Songs, Sirach, and Wisdom of Solomon. Scholars note that they can spot Wisdom when they see or hear it. In fact, most specialists, and even generalists alike, are usually well versed in correctly identifying Wisdom books. Below are ten texts. Which Wisdom text is each from?

1. Life and death are the decree of heaven.
2. Son, always keep in mind the age of your parents. It is an occasion for joy.

3. In good years most of the young people behave well. In bad years most of them abandon themselves to evil.
4. We are all human beings (men). Why is it that some men become great and others become small?
5. Better is bread when the heart is happy, than riches with sorrow.
6. Do not bear witness with false words, nor support another person with your tongue.
7. If the shoot is not right it will not produce the stalk, nor create seed.
8. Treat not lightly the word of a king: let it be healing for thy flesh.
9. More than all watchfulness, watch the mouth.
10. I have lifted sand, and I have carried salt; but there is nothing which is heavier than rage.

None of these passages are from the Hebrew Bible/Old Testament (HB/OT). The first two are from the Chinese philosopher Confucius (sixth century BCE). The next two are from Mencius (fourth–third century BCE). Texts 5–6 are Egyptian proverbs, 7–8 are Sumerian proverbs, and the last two are Aramaic proverbs. The construct of Wisdom is not limited to the Hebrew Bible or the ancient Near Eastern context. In fact, the category, if it exists, is really quite pervasive, found in various cultures and textual traditions.

19.2 A Brief History on Wisdom Scholarship in Context

As early as 1935 (Hewat 1935a; Hewat 1935b), biblical scholars have cross examined comparative works of the ancient Near East with the Far East to better understand Wisdom Literature (Horton 1972; Ogden 1981; Heard 1996; Perera 2008; Polish 2008; Vermander 2011). Marvin Pope's (1977) Song of Songs commentary is a particularly significant contribution. He brilliantly uses Indian love poems to help biblical scholars better understand the Hebrew and ancient Near Eastern imagery in the book. Other more recent examples are Martin Buss's (2001, 61–68) comparison of Qoheleth to the Indian philosopher Nagarjuna.

The study of Wisdom Literature took further formal shape after World War II. It generated further widespread scholarly activity into the 1960s and 1970s. By the mid- and late 1980s, in North America, Wisdom found its own distinctive hermeneutical construct (Sheppard 1980) within the Writings (Fox 2009; Fox 2014). Not surprisingly, however, not one established and recognized specialist attempted to reengage parallel texts from the Far East. The critical question is: Why didn't they? Was it because Elizabeth G.K. Hewat, a woman, introduced foreign ideas? Was her methodology or conclusion deemed inferior? The fact of the matter is, Wisdom Literature scholars have had little or no command of Sanskrit, Pali, Chinese, or other East Asian languages that generated other Wisdom texts, which discouraged such comparisons.

Subject matters in the Pentateuch (Van Seters 2015) and the Prophets (Wilson 1980), including the themes of "promise made to the ancestors," "covenants," and "legal or cultic matters," are all non-factors in the Wisdom collection. Proverbs, Job, and Ecclesiastes rarely reference priestly or Deuteronomic agendas, including narratives, genealogies, itinerary lists, and even the rights to the land. Rather, the genres in Wisdom, which include short sayings, artistic proverbs, admonitions, riddles, fables, allegories, disputes, example stories, and confessions (Gottwald 1985, 565; cf. Murphy 1981, 48–82) capture the experiences of everyday common people. There is a deliberate distancing from revelation and received ideologies that framed past canonical consciousness. Wisdom's new center was humanity—an inclusive outlook on all of humanity—which was also the hallmark of Chinese philosophical and ethical texts by the sixth century BCE.

As early as the twelfth century BCE, Chinese philosophy taught that the Chou dynasty's (1111–249 BCE) replacement of the Shang (yin) dynasty (1751–1112 BCE)—in order to establish a new mandate of heaven—resulted from the Shangs' neglect of moral laws and virtues. Because they fostered imbalance in society rather than harmony, the Chous would add fresh and original thoughts to counter-balance those established by the Shangs. As the antithesis, their contributions would be framed as yang. With the two dominant cultural traditions in paradox, or the original cultural yin-yang (thesis and antithesis), the synthesis would become the influencers of all power, culture, and present and future ideologies. This dramatic shift in critical understanding advanced "humanism," reaching new heights in right governance, action, and speech. It furthermore freed Chinese epistemology from superstitious religious indoctrinations. In short, Wisdom Literature may have functioned in a parallel manner, countering the thesis established by the priestly/Deuteronomistic traditions.

19.3 PROBLEMS

The principal problem in Wisdom scholarship is "context." That is, the isolation and exclusive examination of the ancient Near Eastern context (e.g., Hallo and Younger 2002; Younger 2016) without understanding or being versed in the broader contexts that envelope the Middle East. In other words, when it comes to the context of ancient Near Eastern and biblical studies, we have not been critical enough (Larson and Deutsch 1988).

The secondary problem, as noted in passing, is that sapiential texts are not concerned with priestly or Deuteronomistic issues but humanity's most pressing problem: "human suffering." When human suffering is overly theologized; it becomes almighty "theodicy." Theodicy overwhelms and overshadows humanity. Humanity is taken out of the equation. The topics shift to God's goodness, God's omnipotence, and the construct or reality of evil.

The authors of the sapiential tradition appear to have sensed the need for a sharp break from past canonical responses to addressing human suffering. The consideration of state-lessness, liminality, and vulnerability, both individually and collectively, had to go beyond the same-old complex of creation, exodus, guidance in the wilderness, and fulfillment of the promised land. Turning to the Prophets or Torah for humanity's solution lacked inno-vation. Humanity had to offer humanity new insights. In the eyes of the sapiential writers, the priestly and the Deuteronomic traditions failed in their attempts to address human suffering. They offered "sin" and "repentance" as the cause and alleviation from suffering.

Some of the Wisdom authors and tradents, like those who produced Proverbs, do not appear ready to abandon the received tradition. Job and Ecclesiastes, however, move boldly, rejecting this older outdated ideology. Interestingly, these authors based their new-found ideas not on scriptural writings of their received tradition, but other Far Eastern canonical writings. These and other sources, I will argue, likely became the basis for borrowing and composition of Wisdom Literature in the fifth to second centu-ries BCE. But first, a discussion on the sociological trajectories that inspired each book, raising the issue that they are primarily responses to the collapse of the nation, which resulted in the forced migrations of its peoples.

19.4 PROVERBS

Proverbs puts particular emphasis on the "king-sages," such as Solomon (1:1; 10:1), Hezekiah (25:1), and Lemuel (31:1). Their words become the basis for sound governance with expectations placed on those training to govern. A similar cadre is also at the very center of Confucius's *Analects*, compiled between the fifth and third centuries BCE.

One of the salient features of Proverbs is the feminine characterizations of Lady Wisdom, the Adulterous/Strange Woman, and the Noble Woman (Prov 31) (Harris 1990; Yoder 2001). A new commentary on Proverbs by Alice Ogden Bellis (2018) offers a rich multivalent reading by women of various cultural backgrounds, which provides a col-lective feminist perspective. From the traditional point of view, a parallel has long been acknowledged in the Exaltation of Inanna collected by Enheduanna, the high priestess and daughter of Sargon, Akkad's ruler (Hallo and van Dijk 1968). The very act of women scribes or scholars discovering female voices in feminized Wisdom texts may have been normative among the elites or educated. But what is unique to ancient Israel is the emphasis placed on the capable woman-wife in Prov 31:10–31.

The capable woman has taken on a life of her own, being compared to a superwoman in modern settings. However, the imagery is a social reconstruction of the reality of restoration. That is, from a collective return migrations point of view—incorporating communities from Persia, Egypt, the coastlands, and the wilderness—the final chapter in Proverbs restores the image of a collapsed city-state (province) of Yehud. The closing section of Proverbs attempts to inspire and restore Jerusalem during the early and middle return migrations period. She, the capable woman, symbolizes the city-state (cf. Daughter Zion in Lamentations). She rebuilds her enterprise by, first, providing food, clothing, and shelter for her people. She then establishes security and invests and offers promises of prosperity to the people even after the tragedy of human suffering of war and displacement and forced resettlements. Interestingly, men are not the initiators of restoration. They brought forth war and turmoil, with added internal conflicts within the return migrations communities concerning inter-marriage (Ezra-Nehemiah). Like the counter-narratives to support the inclusive Egyptian point of view over against the Persian, Abraham's intermarriage to Hagar (an Egyptian), Joseph's to Asneth (Egyptian), Moses's to a Midianite and then a Cushite woman (African), and Boaz's to Ruth (Midianite), the Persian era policy, driven by Ezra, to remove all foreign women and their children (Canaanite or indigenous) appears to be questioned and sharply challenged by the tradent(s) of Proverbs 31. The capable wife ("who can find?") is inclusive. She speaks out and judges righteously (Prov 31:8–9). The restoration of the city-state begins with the family, beginning with "her."

19.5 JOB

The book of Job has recently received attention as "a contest of moral imaginations" (Newsom 2003), a testing ground for psychological readings (Boss 2010), an exemplary example of reception history or history of consequences (Seow 2013), and even as a refutation of retributive theology (Fox 2018). Yet, it continues to be read as a drawnout debate on the divine-human relationship, especially pertaining to the problem of evil (Greenstein 2009), theodicy, or, more broadly, "human suffering" (Janzen 2008; Crenshaw 2011). Liberation scholars have read Job as in favor of the preferential treatment of the poor (Gutiérrez 1987); while others continue to read the book in the framework of ancient Near Eastern texts like Ludlul Bel Nemeqi, which is a direct address against the Kassite kings (Oshima 2015).

Historically, literarily, and socially, all of Job's dialogues may reflect tragedy striking a nation, in particular, the Southern Kingdom of Judah in 597, 587, and 582 BCE (Ahn 2012a), with textual emendations from later periods (see Pope 1965; Habel 1985, 40–42). Those three events led to the complete collapse and removal of a nation. In this historical and social context, Job's literary features are best read as the synecdoche of an entire second generation reflecting and responding to the aftermaths of a collapsed nation. Each of the three cycles of the dialogue with the three friends symbolically represents each historical social displacement (and resettlement). Job forcefully says that sin has no bearing on his (or his generation's) predicament. He will not repent because he believes he did nothing wrong. The pathos in exile or forced migration (Fiddian-Qasmiyeh 2014) is not related to sin. His three friends say otherwise. Each in his own righteousness sees sin as the cause for Job's destruction.

The concept of sin was widely accepted among first generation exilic/forced migration tradents. That sinful ideology is passed down to the next generation, down to the third or fourth generations (Deut 5:8)—the actual duration of exile or forced migra-tions (Ahn 2012b)—is a remnant of an anti-Judeo-Babylonian point of view. Those who were left behind in Judah viewed the diaspora as judgment and required repentance to return. But not so with Job and those of the second and subsequent generation Judeo-Babylonians/Persians. There was no need to return. The diaspora became home. They completely rejected this outdated ideology in favor of assimilating into a new context. Moreover, the sin-repentance dichotomy was rejected since it made those who were born in Babylon sinful. Rightfully, Job never repents. He stands steadfast by advanc-ing the ideology that each generation is responsible for its own (sinful) action, best described in the sour grape imagery (Jer 31:29; Ezek 18:2–3).

In the end, Job is held in the right—as God agrees with Job—and his three friends are all wide of the mark. In fact, they sinned by holding onto and applying such a degrading concept to a person suffering. By rejecting the construct of sin as the cause of the forced migration, Isaiah 43, a second-generation Judeo-Babylonian text,[1] sheds considerable new light. God brought the new (second and subsequent) generation into being, into existence in a new land, as the carriers and conduits of a new memory and story (Ahn 2015a). They are loved and precious in God's sight. The new directive is "to forget the former things and behold the new" (Isa 43:17–18). They become the bearers of monotheism and tradents of a new canonical consciousness. However, the question of why human suffering occurs, even among and within the next generation, is never fully addressed or resolved.

In Babylonia, during the forced migrations period (597–538 BCE), there were at least three socio-economic classes: the "in-group," the upper- and skilled-class descendants of the 597 BCE displacement, the "out-group," the poor, the descendants of the 587 BCE displacement, and the "outcasts," the third group, descendants of the 582 BCE displace-ment. This third group likely represented the "mixed peoples of the land." During the time of Gedaliah, the pro-Deuteronomic policy of integration and peoples practicing inter-marriage to re-populate in order to survive by producing economic output for the Babylonians was likely encouraged. But with Gedaliah's sudden murder in 582 by nation-alists or zealots, this last group was also forcibly taken to Babylon while another group voluntarily fled to Egypt (Jeremiah 43). When the 582-group arrived in Babylon, they were especially singled out by the 597- and 587-groups. In fact, in the LXX rendering of Ezekiel 15, the 582-group is blamed for the complete collapse of the nation (Ahn 2015b).

Dealing with and providing a strategy for how to cope with suffering beyond mere words or simply enduring it is wanting in Job. Even YHWH's speeches, which emerged orally in Babylonia, do not offer much substance. God's rhetorical responses to the challenges Job posed further subjugates humanity. The central theme of individual and collective suffering in Job mirrors the social conditions of the underclasses (587- and 582-groups) that contin-ued to suffer by the irrigation canals of Babylon. Without ever assimilating into mainstream culture like Daniel and his three friends in Babylon, Ezra, Nehemiah, and Esther in Persia, or Joseph and Moses in Egypt, the underclasses suffered, as presented by the suffering servant in Second Isaiah (Terrien 1966). The vicarious suffering of Job is rightfully read

[1] On second-generation consciousness, see Ahn 2010, 159–222.

intertextually with the suffering servant passages in Second Isaiah (Kynes 2013). Indeed, there is strong agreement among scholars that the prologue (Cho 2017) and the sudden happy ending (Ngwa 2004) constitutes an "epic prose substratum" (Sarna 1957) which was likely reworked (Hurvitz 1974) during the late period of the restoration (return).

19.6 ECCLESIASTES

In Ecclesiastes, every deed, matter, or affair is "ephemeral," "chasing after the wind." Even appropriated time, seemingly predictable, composed in a string of infinitive constructs ("a time to x and a time to y"), ends unpredictability. That is, the final two lexemes "war and peace" (Eccl 3:8) are nouns, breaking the pattern of the infinitives—thereby asking the reader to re-examine, re-assess, and redress the entire pattern of the positives and negatives along the lines of grammatical structural integrity, which governs the semantics. In other words, although time may establish order, "a time to be born, a time to die, a time to plant and uproot" (Eccl 3:1), war disrupts everything. War destroys set time. However, the "absurd" or "chance" in humanity, existentialism, suggests that even in such times, within a stratified caste system expounded by suffering—toil and labor—as spoils of war in forced migration, somehow life is to be rediscovered, restored, and even enjoyed (Seow 1997). With a clear reference to generational consciousness at the outset (1:4), Ecclesiastes entertains the important constructs of thesis (yin) and antithesis (yang). Chapter 3 sets life's most sentimental complexities in juxtaposition rather than merely observing them as cultural memory of a failed monarchy (cf. Barbour 2012). "A time to scatter stones and time to gather them," (3:5) is at the center of the poem, echoing the reality of forced and return migrations (exile and return).

19.7 SOCIOLOGICAL SUMMARY OF PROVERBS, JOB, AND ECCLESIASTES

Proverbs, then, is a first-generation response to the exile or forced migrations of the nation, providing a clear-cut answer as to why it occurred: obedience versus disobedience. Job, a second-generation response, suggests the reasons are more complicated, rejecting the doctrine of sin as the cause for the people's religious and social suffering. Ecclesiastes, a third-generation response, is a collective attempt at a resolution that the scattered communities in Persia, Egypt, the Coastlands, and in the Wilderness or Yehud, may never fully know why God permitted the destruction of the nation and its institutions (monarchy/skilled elites [597], temple/priesthood [587], and all the peoples of the land [582]). The goal of the sages' teachings may have been a synthesized road map for proper conduct, which, in turn, was an attempt to foster a moral society, advancing civility for peaceful co-existence among the return migrants from diverse locales. With heated debates on citizenship and resident alien status, marriage and inter-marriage, old and new land rights, all the more complicated by Persian hegemony and Egyptian cultural influences, reviving and restoring the ancient collapsed citadel, Jerusalem, and its walls did little to truly restore Yehud's old center. Although Wisdom texts on the surface may appear to deflect such conflicts, noticeable concepts like "righteousness," "economic fairness," "kindness to the poor," among others, foster idealized values by attempting to return to some established form of systemic political and social order.

In the end, the medium for salvation is no longer a fixation on the Mosaic or Davidic covenants. Both forms were markers of ideological hubris, which inevitably led to the collapse of the northern and southern kingdoms. In their place, is "wisdom" and "knowledge," which incorporates righteousness, fairness, and decency—partners to humanism and a precursor to human dignity. Past scholars have debated whether such instructions were limited to the elites or open to the masses. The cadre of sapiential authors would reply, both. And by no means was ancient Israel's humanism antithetical to religious education. In fact, to re-establish and re-foster a new ideal society, real or imagined, it began with "the fear of the Lord" (Longman 2017, see also Longman's contribution to this volume). A late interpolation, this closing thought attempts to re-align the final shape of the text canonically to be more like Israelite scripture than like its ancient Far Eastern influences.

19.8 ANCIENT FAR EASTERN CONTEXTS THAT INFLUENCED ANCIENT NEAR EASTERN CONTEXTS

In what follows, the pervasive nature of sapiential writings is offered. The geographical poles that situate the ancient Near East are Africa and Asia. Because sound scholarly contributions on African/Africana parallels are in circulation (see Dube and West 2000; Dube 2001; Page 2009; Akoto-Abutiate 2014; Mbuvi 2017),[2] this piece is limited to Asia or more appropriately, the ancient Far East.[3] Fundamentally, the cultures of the Far East influenced the Persians of Central Asia and vice versa.

In the fourth century BCE, after Alexander the Great's quest into India in 326 BCE, conquering much of Persia, Bactria, and Afghanistan, he and his army went beyond the Khyber Pass, into the Indus Valley, and eventually into the Punjab region. As the Greek army finally turned back, the vacuum left by Alexander's withdrawal from Punjab created an opportunity for a solider named Chandragupta Maurya to take full advantage. He rose to power, fostering the idea of an ideal Indian king. He expanded trade, agriculture,

[2] Not to be confused with African American parallels; see Felder 1991; Brown 2004; Byron and Lovelace 2016.
[3] Not to be confused with Asian American parallels; see Foskett and Kuan 2006; Kim and Yang 2019.

currency, and built cities by clearing forests. After his death, his son, King Bindusāra, continued his father's policies of trade, including open dialogue and political unity with the Seleucid rulers of Persia and Bactria (Fenton et al. 1988, 142–145). In other words, trade and regional influences of exchange of ideas, stories, material goods, and spices crossed into the Middle East from India (McLaughlin 2010). According to Thomas McEvilley (2002), it is erroneous to see little or no connection between Greek and Indian philosophies. If Indian philosophy is involved, Chinese philosophy must also be further factored. This then, opens up possibilities for ancient Far Eastern influence on biblical texts.

19.9 Proverbs and Chinese Philosophy

Proverbs, much of which is attributed to Solomon, has parallels in the *Analects* by the Chinese sage-kings, who were the important practitioners of learning for delivering sound governance. Only with full learning and practice will the sage-king govern in peace. The *Analects* by Confucius (551–479 BCE) is technically a collection of sayings from the sage himself, other teachers, disciples, and especially well-regarded governors, rulers, and kings (emperors). The *Analects* focuses on five subject matters: rectification of names, the means, heaven, way, and humanity (*jen*). The rectification of names is the correspondence of words and actions, thoughts and deeds. By means, balance is discovered, as in the yin and yang—the passive and active cosmic forces or elements that produce harmony (Hegel's dialectic: thesis, antithesis, synthesis—albeit 1,200 years earlier). Heaven refers to the mandate or order of heaven (*T'ien-ming*), which is best understood as natural laws that guide society and civilization. Heaven has a pattern for proper way and action (moral law). These laws are not based on death and re-birth or providence and predestination, but active good words and virtuous deeds. Thus *jen*, humanity, an original contribution from Confucius, is at the very center of Confucianism and "proper" (*li*) society. That Chinese wisdom moved away from prayers for rain to a knowledge-based irrigation system for cultivation was a fundamental shift in epistemological advancement.

To be a true *chün-tzu* or noble, virtuous person, one must be responsible for every activity and action. *Jen* can be described as virtue, but this virtue is oriented not merely individually but also collectively. The part and whole are one: "wishing to establish his own character, he also establishes the character of others, and wishing to be prominent himself, he also helps others to be prominent" (6:28; Chan 1963, 31). *Jen* is grounded in *chung* and *shu*—consciousness and altruism as parallels for "wisdom" and "goodness" in Wisdom Literature.

In the *Analects*, the speakers include Yu Tzu (a pupil, whose private name was Jo, 538–457 BCE), Tzu-Chang (Chuan-sun Shih, 503–450 BCE), Wang-sun Chia (commander in chief of the state of Wei), Tseng-Tzu, Tzu-Kung, and Duke Ting (ruler of Confucius's native state of Lu, 509–495 BCE), among others. Tzu is an honorific title given to students of Confucius, who collected, emended, and passed down the text. Like the collection of kings and sages found in Proverbs, the words of rulers or governors frame important sections of the *Analects*. Could Proverbs's formatting be a canonical borrowing from the *Analects*? Biblical scholars need to investigate these and other structural and textual parallels. The subject matters in the *Analects* deal with a host of topics also found in Proverbs, including filial piety, education and learning, destiny, knowledge and wisdom, humanity, nature, righteousness, the superior (wise) and foolish person, virtue, business ethics, governing a nation, and individual and collective words and actions for good conduct. Below are selected texts for comparison.

Analects	Proverbs
1:6 Young men should be filial when at home and respectful to their elders when away from home. They should be earnest and faithful. They should love all extensively and be intimate with men of humanity. When they have any energy to spare after the performance of moral duties they should use it to study literature and the arts (wen). (Chan 1963, 20)	1:8–9 My son, hear the instruction of your father and do not forsake the teaching of your mother. For they are a graceful wreath around your head, a necklace about your throat. 1:2 For learning about wisdom and instruction, understanding words of insight. 2:9 Then you will understand righteousness and justice and equity, every good path.
4:18 Confucius said: "In serving his parents, a son may gently remonstrate with them. When he sees that they are not inclined to listen to him, he should resume an attitude of reverence and not abandon his effort to serve them. He may feel worried but does not complain." (Chan 1963, 28)	15:5 A fool despises a parent's instruction but the one who heeds admonition is prudent. 4:1 Listen, children, to a father's instruction, and be attentive, that you may gain insight.
4:21 Confucius said: "The superior man wants to be slow in words but diligent in action." (Chan 1963, 28)	10:19 When words are many, transgression is not lacking, but the prudent are restrained in speech.
7:26 Confucius fished with a line but not a net. While shooting he would not shoot a bird at rest.[4]	1:17 For in vain is the net baited while the bird is looking on.
16:4 Confucius said: "There are three kinds of friendship which are beneficial and three kinds which are harmful. Friendship with the upright, with the truthful, and with the well informed is beneficial. Friendship with those who flatter with those who are meek and who compromise with principles, and with those who talk cleverly are harmful. (Chan 1963, 45)	18:24 Some friends play at friendship but a true friend sticks closer than one's nearest kin. 17:9 One who forgives an affront fosters friendship, but one who dwells on disputes will alienate a friend. 16:28 A perverse person spreads strife, and a whisperer separates close friends. 22:24 Make no friends with those given to anger And do not associate with hotheads.
17:3 Confucius said: "Only the most intelligent and most stupid do not change."[5]	10:21 If the wise go to law with fools, there is ranting and ridicule without relief.

[4] The saying is a reference to fair play, without taking advantage or cutting the corners. See Chan 1963, 32 n. 105.

[5] Chan (1963, 46) notes that according to Wang Ch'ung Chia I (201–169 BCE) and Han Yu those who are intelligent are born good, the most stupid are born evil, and rest of humanity are born neutral.

Mencius (371–289 BCE) is recognized as the second great sage in Chinese philosophy. The notable difference between Confucius and Mencius is that Mencius viewed goodness in humanity. He taught that goodness must be bound in love. He went further than Confucius and redefined *jen* as steadfastness/love and righteousness. Righteousness, as in Proverbs, is a guiding principle for his teaching. Mencius judged that righteousness could lead to a (peaceful) revolution, however. He advanced the idea of protest and revolt against all forms of ill governance, especially when there is corruption and evil, even against a recognized or established leader or state.

Mencius	Proverbs
4A:10. Mencius said, "It is useless to talk to those who do violence to their own nature, and it is useless to do anything with those who throw themselves away. To speak what is against propriety and righteousness is to do violence to oneself. To say that one cannot abide by humanity and follow righteousness is to throw oneself away. Humanity is the peaceful abode of men and righteousness is his straight path. What a pity for those who leave the peaceful abode and do not live there, and abandon the straight path and do not follow it!" (Chan 1963, 74)	2:11 Prudence will watch over you; and understanding will guard you. 2:12 It will save you from the way of evil, from those who speak perversely, 2:13 who forsake the paths of uprightness to walk in the ways of darkness, 2:14 who rejoice in doing evil and delight in the perverseness of evil; 2:15 those whose paths are crooked, and who are devious in their ways.... 2:20 Therefore walk in the way of the good, and keep to the paths of the just. 2:21 For the upright will abide in the land, and the innocent will remain in it; 2:22 but the wicked will be cut off from the land, and the treacherous will be rooted out of it.
6A:16 Mencius said, "There is nobility of Heaven and there is nobility of man. Humanity, righteousness, loyalty, faithfulness, and the love of the good without getting tired of it constitute the nobility of Heaven, and to be a grand official, a great official, and a high official—this constitutes the nobility of man. The ancient people cultivated the nobility of Heaven, and the nobility of man naturally came to them. People today cultivate the nobility of Heaven in order to seek for the nobility of man, and once they have obtained the nobility of man, they forsake the nobility of Heaven. Therefore their delusion is extreme. At the end they surely lose [the nobility of man] also." (Chan 1963, 60)	11:4–5 Riches do not profit in the day of wrath, but righteousness delivers from death. The righteousness of the blameless keeps their ways straight, but the wicked fall by their own wickedness. 3:3 Do not let loyalty and faithfulness forsake you; bind them around your neck, write them on the tablet of your heart. 20:28 Loyalty and faithfulness preserve the king, and his throne is upheld by righteousness.

Mencius	Proverbs
6A:6 Mencius said: "If you let people follow their feelings (original nature), they will be able to do good. This is what is meant by saying that human nature is good. If man does evil, it is not the fault of his natural endowment. The feeling of commiseration is found in all men; the feeling of shame and dislike is found in all men; the feeling of right and wrong is found in all men. The feeling of commiseration is what we call humanity; the feeling of shame and reverence is what we call propriety *li* ; and the feeling of right and wrong is what we call wisdom. Humanity, righteousness, propriety, and wisdom are not drilled into us from the outside. We originally have them with us. Only we do not think [to find them]. Therefore it is said: 'Seek and you will find it, neglect and you will lose it.'" (Chan 1963, 54)	2:20 Therefore walk in the way of the good, and keep to the paths of the just. 11:27 Whoever diligently seeks good seeks favor, but evil comes to the one who searches for it. 18:13 If one gives answer before hearing, it is folly and shame. 23:29 Who has woe? Who has sorrow? Who has strife? Who has complaining? Who has wounds without cause? Who has redness of eyes? 2:10 For wisdom will come into your Heart, and knowledge will be pleasant to your soul. 8:19 I love those who love me, and those who seek me [wisdom] diligently find me.

19.10 JOB AND BUDDHISM

Buddhist teachings on suffering are identifiable in Job. Beyond Sankara's four levels of knowledge—verbal knowledge, deluded knowledge, empirical knowledge, and supreme (*paramarthika*) knowledge, which produces a unique state of consciousness called *samadhi* in the Upanishads (Radhakrishnan and Moore 1957, 37–96)—the rise and culmination of the Buddha's teachings are best understood as a response to and separation from (classic) Hinduism (Fenton et al. 1988, 131–141). Is this what the tradents of the Israelite Wisdom tradition were also attempting to accomplish as a new collection of texts?

As in many ancient Near Eastern (con)texts, the earliest account of Siddhartha Gautama (563–483 BCE), the Buddha, and his teachings, were written down five centuries after his death. In short, after Siddhartha reached the age of twenty-nine, a mythopoetic construction of reality notes that he left the protected gates of his royal abode to experience the world. The successive experiences of seeing an aged old man, a sick man, and a dead man shocked Siddhartha, awakening his being, propelling him to confront and rectify humanity's suffering. At first, he practiced renunciation and self-mortification like the Hindu sages. He bid farewell to his wife and son, put on the yellow robe of the mendicant monk, and lived in abject deprivation—on one grain of rice per day. After he roamed northeast India for six years, he arrived at a powerful conclusion: extremism as a way to the truth was to be rejected. He ate, bathed, and sat under a bodhi tree to meditate. In a state of deep meditation, he witnessed all past lives with a final temptation by Mara, evil (desire and death). He withstood all her temptations in order to arrive at "emptiness," nirvana, a path to ending humanity's suffering. His enlightenment through consciousness offered a new message of a path out of suffering to non-existence (Radhakrishnan and Moore 1957, 272–346). To cease to exist is the goal of Buddhism.

The Buddha's teaching begins with a series of sermons for his disciples. They include: (1) all existence is *dukkha*, suffering; (2) all suffering is caused by *trishna*, craving or desire; (3) all suffering can end; (4) and the way to liberation for suffering comes through the eightfold path. These four noble truths lead to the correct path, the middle way. In addressing suffering, the book of Job has several ancient Near Eastern parallels (Gray 1970; Wikander 2010), but, like the Buddha, Job too was tempted by an adversary, which is closer to the narrative experience of Shakyamuni, the Buddha, than any extant ancient Near Eastern literature. Suffering and death are central topics in Job. The dialogue's three cycles may symbolically represent the repeated cycles of death and re-birth that is common in Hinduism and Buddhism. There are traces of Job's vulnerability and integrity (see Ing 2017). It is difficult to assess fully if Job's suffering ever ceased. Only in the prose setting, the epilogue, do we hear that Job was restored. In the dialogue, his final words are set by the tradent: "The words of Job are ended" (31:40). This is suggestive that the original text of Job, the poetic cycle, ended in a highly technical non-existence state. Job performed his duties with propriety (31:9–40). The virtuous deeds (karma) merit Job to arrive at a state of complete emptiness, enlightenment (nirvana), and thus "cease to exist." Perhaps, this is how the poetic text of Job was meant to end—in a Far Eastern context.[6] But because those who received the text and tradition were unfamiliar with this eastern framework, and further propelled by canonical consciousness, they added Elihu's speeches, followed by the divine responses, and eventually the prose "happy ending," creating multiple conclusions to reshape the original (con)text.

19.11 ECCLESIASTES AND CHINESE PHILOSOPHY

Although careful readers of Ecclesiastes have noticed the Ying-Yang principle, the teachings of Lao Tzu and Chuang Tzu are less familiar. Below are parallel sayings from their teachings that echo Ecclesiastes 3. They resonate with the pessimism and learning that is attributed to Qoheleth.

2. When the people of the world all know beauty as beauty,
There arises the recognition of ugliness.
When they all know the good as good,
There arises the recognition of evil.
Therefore:

---

[6] In the War Scrolls (2:11), Uz (Job 1:3) is clearly defined as a region or place "beyond (east of) the Euphrates," which would situate Job somewhere beyond modern-day Uzbekistan.

Being and non-being produce each other;
Difficult and easy complete each other;
Long and short contrast each other;
High and low distinguish each other;
Sound and voice harmonize each other;
Front and back follow each other.
There the sage manages affairs without action (*wu-wei*)
And spreads doctrines without words.
All things arise, and he does not turn away from them.
He produces them, but does not take possession of them.
He acts, but does not rely on his own ability.
He accomplishes his task but does not claim credit for it.   (Chan 1963, 140)

20. Abandon learning and there will be no sorrow.
How much difference is there between "yes sir" and "of course not?"
How much difference is there between "good" and "evil"?
What people dread, do not fail to dread.
But alas, how confused, and the end is not yet.
The multitude are merry, as though feasting on a day of sacrifice,
Or like ascending a tower at springtime.
I alone am inert, showing no sign (of desires)
Like an infant that has not yet smiled.
Wearied, indeed, I seem to be without a home.
The multitude all possess more than enough.
I alone seem to have lost all.
Mine is indeed the mind of an ignorant man,
Indiscriminate and dull!
Common folks are indeed brilliant;
I alone seem to be in the dark.   (Chan 1963, 149–50)

In the teachings of Chuang Tzu (399–295 BCE), nature takes center stage. For example:

He does not quarrel over right or wrong and mingles with conventional society
....Above he roams with the Creator, and below he makes friends with those who
transcend life and death and beginning and end.   (Chan 1963, 177)

"...The wind blows in a thousand different ways," replied Tzu-chi, "but the sounds
are produced in their own way. They do so by themselves. Who is there to rouse
them to action?"   (Chan 1963, 180)

The sage has the sun and moon by his side. He grasps the universe under the arm. He
blends everything into a harmonious whole, casts aside whatever is confused or
obscured, and regards the humble as honorable. While the multitude toil, he seems to
be stupid and non-discriminative. He blends the disparities of ten thousand years into
one complete purity. All things are blended like this and mutually involve each other.
                                                                    (Chan 1963, 189)

It should be noted that Chuang Tzu's ideas have inspired much of Chinese landscape painting and poetry. In Ecclesiastes, various aspects of nature, such as the sun (e.g., 1:3, 9, 14; 2:11, 17, 19, 20, 22; 3:16), moon and stars (12:2), sea (1:7), wind (e.g., 1:6, 14, 17; 2:11, 17, 26), water (2:6; 11:1), and shadow (6:12; 8:13), among others, are all treated with integral regard.

The section on "Great Teacher" from Chuang Tzu offers additional insights and comparative material with Ecclesiastes. Mo Tzu, Han Fei Tzu, and others can also add new light. Confucianism, Taoism, and other original Chinese thought did not remain exclusively in China. It migrated and spread, through cultural diffusion into Southeast Asia and to Japan through Korea as well as into the Near East (Lazaridis, et al. 2016, 419–424). Indian philosophy, especially the laws of Manu (Radhakrishnan and Moore 1957, 172–192), offers additional opportunities for further textual exploration.

19.12 OPEN-ENDED CLOSING

The pervasiveness of Wisdom can be limited and bound by form and provenance, historical and social contexts. Conversely, it can be open and fluid, reaching various contexts and texts. The most distinctive aspect of all sapiential texts, universally, is the emphasis on humanity. Indeed, humanity is at the center of all sapiential texts. From acknowledging a collapsed nation in the sixth century BCE, to rebuilding a society (in literary stages), this article has pushed the boundaries of Wisdom Literature's spheres of influences to include ancient Chinese and Indian philosophical (con)texts.

Peter Ackroyd (1968, 31) notes that the sixth century BCE was a dynamic age, which included Taoism in China, the Upanishads of pre-Buddhism, Hinduism in India, Zoroastrianism in Iran, Orphic-Pythagorean thought in Greece, and the exilic Hebrew prophets. Perhaps he could have added Wisdom Literature, which extends into the Greco-Persian period and beyond. Through the learned tradents of the Hebrew Bible in Persia during the time after Alexander the Great, humanism, originally at home in Indian and Chinese ideologies, made its way into the Hebrew Bible's sapiential writings. These authors and tradents did not neglect their immediate wider contexts. Modern and contemporary critical biblical scholars have the opportunity to be open minded, embrace the new, and further foster critical biblical scholarship with attention to wider and broader contexts. If not, Wisdom's obituary is fully justifiable.

WORKS CITED

Ackroyd, Peter. 1968. *Exile and Restoration*. OTL. Philadelphia, PA: Westminster.

Ahn, John. 2010. *Exile as Forced Migrations*. BZAW 417. Berlin: de Gruyter.

Ahn, John. 2012a. "Forced Migrations Guiding the Exile: Demarcating 597, 587, 582." Pages 173–189 in *By the Irrigation Canals of Babylon: Approaches to the Study of the Exile*. Edited by John J. Ahn and Jill Middlemas. LHBOTS 526. New York, NY: T&T Clark.

Ahn, John. 2012b. "Exile." Pages 196–204 in *The Dictionary of the Old Testament: Prophets*. Edited by Mark Boda and J. Gordon McConville. Downers Grove, IL: IVP.

Ahn, John. 2015a. "Story and Memory." Pages 332–343 in *The Oxford Encyclopedia of the Bible and Theology*. Edited by Samuel Balentine. Oxford: Oxford University Press.

Ahn, John. 2015b. "Ezekiel 15: A משל." Pages 101–120 in *The Prophets Speak on Forced Migrations*. AIL 21. Edited by Mark Boda, Frank Ritchel Ames, John Ahn, and Mark Leuchter. Atlanta, GA: SBL.

Akoto-Abutiate, Dorothy BEA. 2014. *Proverbs and the African Tree of Life: Grafting Biblical Proverbs to Ghanaian Eve Folk Proverbs*. Leiden: Brill.

Barbour, Jennifer. 2012. *The Story of Israel in the Book of Qohelet*. Oxford: Oxford University Press.

Bellis, Alice Ogden. 2018. *Proverbs*. WisC 23. Collegeville, MN: Liturgical Press.

Boss, Jeffrey. 2010. *Human Consciousness of God in the Book of Job*. London: T&T Clark.

Brown, Michael Joseph. 2004. *Blackening of the Bible: The Aims of African American Biblical Scholarship*. Harrisburg, PA: Trinity Press International.

Buss, Martin. 2001. "A Projection for Israelite Historiography: With a Comparison between Qohelet and Nagarjuna." Pages 61–68 in *The Land That I Will Show You: Essays on the History and Archaeology of the Ancient Near East in Honor of J. Maxwell Miller*. Edited by M. Patrick Graham and J. Andrew Dearman. JSOTSup 343. Sheffield: Sheffield Academic.

Byron, Gay, and Vanessa Lovelace, ed. 2016. *Womanist Interpretations of the Bible: Expanding the Discourse*. Atlanta, GA: SBL.

Chan, Wing-Tsit. 1963. *A Source Book in Chinese Philosophy*. Princeton, NJ: Princeton University Press.

Cho, Paul K. 2017. "Job 2 and 42:7–10 as Narrative Bridge and Theological Pivot." *JBL* 136:857–877.

Crenshaw, James L. 2010. *Old Testament Wisdom: An Introduction*. 3rd ed. Louisville, KY: Westminster John Knox.

Crenshaw, James L. 2011. *Reading Job: A Literary and Theological Commentary*. Macon, GA: Smyth & Helwys.

Dube, Musa W., ed. 2001. *Other Ways of Reading: African Women and the Bible*. Atlanta, GA: SBL.

Dube, Musa W., and Gerald West, ed. 2000. *The Bible in Africa: Transactions, Trajectories, and Trends*. Leiden: Brill.

Felder, Cain Hope, ed. 1991. *Stony the Road We Trod: African American Biblical Interpretation*. Minneapolis, MN: Fortress.

Fenton, John Y., Norvin Hein, Frank E. Reynolds, Alan L. Miller, Niels C. Nielsen, and Grace G. Burford. 1988. *Religions of Asia*. 2nd ed. New York, NY: St. Martin's.

Fiddian-Qasmiyeh, Elena, Gil Loescher, and Katy Long, eds. 2014. *The Oxford Handbook of Refugee and Forced Migration Studies*. Oxford: Oxford University Press.

Foskett, Mary F., and Jeffrey Kah-Jin Kuan, eds. 2006. *Ways of Being, Ways of Reading: Asian American Biblical Interpretation*. St. Louis, MO: Chalice.

Fox, Michael V. 2009. *Proverbs 10–31*. AB 19B. New Haven, CT: Yale University Press.

Fox, Michael V. 2014. "From Amenemope to Proverbs: Editorial Art in Proverbs 22,17–23,11." *ZAW* 126:76–91.

Fox, Michael V. 2018. "The Meanings of the Book of Job." *JBL* 137:7–18.

Gottwald, Norman K. 1985. *The Hebrew Bible: A Socio-Literary Introduction*. Philadelphia, PA: Fortress.

Gray, John. 1970. "The Book of Job in the Context of Near Eastern Literature." *ZAW* 82:251–269.

Greenstein, Edward L. 2009. "The Problem of Evil in the Book of Job." Pages 333–362 in *Mishneh Todah: Studies in Deuteronomy and Its Cultural Environment in Honor of Jeffrey H. Tigay.* Edited by Nili Sacher Fox, David A. Glatt-Gilad, and Michael J. Williams. Winona Lake, IN: Eisenbrauns.

Gutiérrez, Gustavo. 1987. *On Job: God-talk and the Suffering of the Innocent.* Translated by Mathew J. O'Connell. Maryknoll, NY: Orbis.

Habel, Norman C. 1985. *The Book of Job.* OTL. Philadelphia, PA: Westminster.

Hallo, William W., and J.J.A. van Dijk. 1968. *The Exaltation of Inanna.* New Haven, CT: Yale University Press.

Hallo, William, and K. Lawson Younger, eds. 2002. *The Context of Scripture,* vols., 1–3. Leiden: Brill.

Harris, Rivkah. 1990. "The Female 'Sage' in Mesopotamian Literature (with an Appendix on Egypt)." Pages 3–18 in *The Sage in Israel and the Ancient Near East.* Edited by John G. Gammie and Leo G. Perdue. Winona Lake, IN: Eisenbrauns.

Heard, R. Christopher. 1996. "The Dao of Qoheleth: An Intertextual Reading of the Daode Jing and the Book of Ecclesiastes." *Jian Dao* 5:65–93.

Hewat, Elizabeth G.K. 1935a. "The Hebrew and Chinese Wisdom: A Comparative Study on the Book of Proverbs and the Analects of Confucius." *IRM* 24:506–514.

Hewat, Elizabeth G.K. 1935b. "The Hebrew and Chinese Wisdom: A Comparative Study on the Book of Proverbs and the Analects of Confucius." PhD diss., University of Edinburgh.

Horton, Ernest, Jr. 1972. "Koheleth's Concept of Opposites: Compared to Samples of Greek Philosophy and Near and Far Eastern Wisdom Classics." *Numen* 19:1–21.

Hurvitz, Avi. 1974. "The Date of the Prose-Tale of Job Linguistically Reconsidered." *HTR* 67:17–34.

Ing, Michael. 2017. *The Vulnerability of Integrity in Early Confucian Thought.* New York, NY: Oxford University Press.

Janzen, Waldemar. 2008. *Deconstructing Theodicy: Why Job Has Nothing to Say to the Puzzle of Suffering.* Grand Rapids, MI: Brazos.

Kim, Uriah Y., and Seung Ai Yang, ed. 2019. *T&T Clark Handbook of Asian American Biblical Hermeneutics.* London: Bloomsbury T&T Clark.

Kynes, Will. 2013. "Job and Isaiah 40–55: Intertextualities in Dialogue." Pages 94–105 in *Reading Job Intertextually.* LHBOTS 574. Edited by Katharine Dell and Will Kynes. New York, NY: Bloomsbury T&T Clark.

Kynes, Will. 2015. "The Modern Scholarly Wisdom Tradition and the Threat of Pan-sapientialism: A Case Report." Pages 11–38 in Sneed 2015.

Kynes, Will. 2019. *An Obituary for "Wisdom Literature": The Birth, Death, and Intertextual Reintegration of a Biblical Corpus.* Oxford: Oxford University Press.

Larson, Gerald James, and Eliot Deutsch, eds. 1988. *Interpreting across Boundaries: New Essays in Comparative Philosophy.* Princeton, NJ: Princeton University Press.

Lazaridis, Iosif, et al. 2016. "Genomic Insights into the Origins of Farming in the Ancient Near East." *Nature* 536:419–424.

Longman, Tremper, III. 2017. *The Fear of the Lord is Wisdom.* Grand Rapids, MI: Baker Academic.

Mbuvi, Andrew M. 2017. "African Biblical Studies: An Introduction to an Emerging Discipline." *CurBR* 15:149–178.

McEvilley, Thomas. 2002. *The Shape of Ancient Thought: Comparative Studies in Greek and Indian Philosophies.* New York, NY: Allworth.

McLaughlin, Raoul. 2010. *Rome and the Distant East: Trade Routes to the Ancient Lands of Arabia, India, and China.* London: Continuum.

Murphy, Roland E. 1981. *Wisdom Literature: Job, Proverbs, Ruth, Canticles, Ecclesiastes, and Esther.* FOTL 13. Grand Rapids, MI: Eerdmans.

Newsom, Carol A. 2003. *The Book of Job: A Contest of Moral Imaginations.* Oxford: Oxford University Press.

Ngwa, Kenneth. 2004. *The Hermeneutics of the "Happy" Ending in Job 42:7–17.* BZAW 354. Berlin: de Gruyter.

Ogden, Graham S. 1981. "Numerical Sayings in Israelite Wisdom and in Confucius." *TaiJT* 3:145–176.

Oshima, Takayoshi. 2015. *Babylonian Poems of Pious Sufferers: Ludlul Bel Nemeqi.* ORA 14. Tübingen: Mohr Siebeck.

Page, Hugh R., Jr., ed. 2009. *The Africana Bible: Reading Israel's Scriptures from Africa and the African Diaspora.* Minneapolis, MN: Fortress.

Perera, Makawitage. 2008. "Was Qoheleth Influenced by Early Buddhism? Dhammapada of the Pali Canon as a Point of Departure." PhD diss., Leuven University.

Polish, Daniel. 2008. "The Buddha as Lens for Reading Kohelet/Ecclesiastes." *JES* 43:370–382.

Pope, Marvin. 1965. *Job.* AB 15. New York, NY: Doubleday.

Pope, Marvin. 1977. *Song of Songs.* AB 7C. New York, NY: Doubleday.

Radhakrishnan, Sarvepalli, and Charles Moore, eds. 1957. *A Source Book in Indian Philosophy.* Princeton, NJ: Princeton University Press.

Sarna, Nahum. 1957. "Epic Substratum in the Prose of Job." *JBL* 76:13–25.

Schellenberg, Annette. 2015. "Don't Throw the Baby Out with the Bathwater: On the Distinctness of the Sapiential Understanding of the World." Pages 115–143 in Sneed 2015.

Seow, Choon L. 1997. *Ecclesiastes.* AB 18C. New York, NY: Doubleday.

Seow, Choon L. 2013. *Job 1–21.* Illuminations. Grand Rapids, MI: Eerdmans.

Sheppard, Gerald T. 1980. *Wisdom as a Hermeneutical Construct: A Study in the Sapientializing of Old Testament Traditions.* BZAW 151. Berlin: de Gruyter.

Sneed, Mark. 2011. "Is the 'Wisdom Tradition' a Tradition?" *CBQ* 73:50–71.

Sneed, Mark, ed. 2015. *Was There a Wisdom Tradition? New Perspectives in Israelite Wisdom Studies.* AIL 23. Atlanta, GA: SBL.

Terrien, Samuel. 1966. "Quelque remarques sur les affinités de Job avec le Deutéro-Esaïe." Pages 295–310 in *Volume du Congrès: Genève 1965.* VTSup 15. Leiden: Brill.

Van Seters, John. 2015. *The Pentateuch: A Social Science Commentary.* 2nd ed. London: Bloomsbury T&T Clark.

Vermander, Benoît. 2011. "Sagesse et révélation: Réflexion théologique à partir de la Chine." *RTL* 42:53–74.

Wikander, Ola. 2010. "Job 3:8: Cosmological Snake-Charming and Leviathanic Panic in an Ancient Near Eastern Setting." *ZAW* 122:265–271.

Wilson, Robert R. 1980. *Prophecy and Society in Ancient Israel.* Philadelphia, PA: Fortress.

Yoder, Christine Roy. 2001. *Wisdom as a Woman of Substance: A Socioeconomic Reading of Proverbs 1–9 and 31:10–31.* BZAW 304. Berlin: de Gruyter.

Younger, K. Lawson, ed. 2016. *The Context of Scripture,* vol. 4: *Supplements.* Leiden: Brill.

PART IV

THE CATEGORY OF WISDOM LITERATURE

CHAPTER 20

SOLOMON AND THE SOLOMONIC COLLECTION

KATHARINE J. DELL

People came from all the nations to hear the wisdom of Solomon; they
came from all the kings of the earth who had heard of his wisdom.

1 Kgs 5:14 [ET 4:34]

KING Solomon is the key figurehead associated with wisdom in its broadest sense—his
reputation for wisdom is unsurpassed; his authority is stamped on the Wisdom collections and his sagacity becomes legendary both within the Hebrew Bible and beyond it.
In this chapter I wish to explore, first, the character of Solomon especially in relation to
his own reputation for "wisdom" as gleaned from the sources that tell of his life; sources
that vary in the extents of their historical veracity and literary idealization of the son and
heir of David. Second, I will explore Solomon's key role within the "Wisdom" collection
that bears his name and his growing reputation within and outside this collection as
authoritative wise man par excellence.

20.1 THE CHARACTER OF SOLOMON

20.1.1 Solomon: The "Historical" Character in 1 Kings 1–11

The character of Solomon as he is first introduced to us in the pages of 1 Kings is in
many ways an idealized figure.[1] According to the author(s) of these texts,[2] his crowning

---

[1] There has been a recent interest in character and characterization in Wisdom Literature, following
in particular the work of William Brown (1996). Building on Brown's work, see Dave Bland 2015. There
has also been recent work on character within narrative—e.g., Bar Efrat 1989; Phelan 2005.

[2] Suggestions as to possible authors of this narrative section of 1 Kings include a separate author of a
"Succession Narrative" (at least for the first two chapters) as suggested by Leonhard Rost (1982 [1926])
and a Deuteronomistic author or redactor who stitched these chapters into the much longer whole of
Joshua to 2 Kings (Noth 1981) which has led to many scholarly variations.

achievements are the building of the Jerusalem temple, his governance over a prosperous and sizeable "united" kingdom of Israel, his lavish wealth, and, last and perhaps most significant, his wisdom with which he is filled as a gift of God. The account of Solomon's reign in Kings is highly positive, idealized even, and yet, towards the end of it, there is a note of criticism and recognition of errors made.[3] No king is perfect, but by comparison to most of the other Davidic kings, Solomon is a wise role model and closer to perfection than most (see Dell, 2020).

20.1.1.1 *Solomon's Birth and Accession*

The first mention of Solomon comes in 2 Sam 5:14, when he is part of a list of sons and daughters born to King David, but his story is really taken up in 2 Sam 12:24, where his conception and birth is described, and the first thing we are told about Solomon is that "The Lord loved him." Solomon is at the climax of the Succession Narrative, which tells the winding tale of the struggle over who should succeed King David.[4] Through the machinations of his mother and the prophet Nathan, Solomon is nominated as the preferred candidate (1 Kings 1). In 1 Kgs 1:15–21 Bathsheba is received by King David and she reminds him of his promise to make Solomon his successor. This is the first mention of any such promise, and one cannot help wondering whether there is an element of auto-suggestion here, Bathsheba perhaps taking advantage of an elderly man to "remind" him of a promise he may not have made. In a less cynical vein, such a promise might have been made but not recorded. David acts quickly to assure Bathsheba that Solomon will not only succeed him but that he will start to rule during David's declining years (1 Kgs 1:29–30). Solomon is taken down to Gihon, where there is a spring, riding on David's mule, in order to be anointed king there by Zadok the priest and Nathan the prophet (1 Kgs 1:38–40). This is David's authorization for Solomon to sit on his throne and rule in his place. The people follow the lead of their priests and prophets and proclaim Solomon king even when Adonijah is still on the throne (1 Kgs 1:18, 43). If we are to attribute this section to the authors of a "Succession Narrative" telling of these events, we might posit that they may well have been Solomon's supporters, possibly scribes from the court of Solomon himself, writing up the history of the accession after the event in order to favor Solomon and cast him in a good light. Here we begin to see the problem of an idealized account over historical veracity. It is interesting though that the Chronicler writing some years later mentions none of this rivalry for the throne.[5] In 1 Chronicles 28 Solomon is announced by David as his successor, primarily in the context of being the one who will build the temple in Jerusalem. Here God promises to establish Solomon's kingdom forever if he keeps God's commandments. Solomon is duly anointed king and

---

[3] As chiefly argued by Walter Brueggemann (1990); followed by his book, *Solomon: Israel's Ironic Icon of Human Achievement* (Brueggemann 2005).

[4] Rost 1982. There have been many subsequent discussions of the extent of this possible narrative and recent questionings of its isolation from the rest of the broader narrative of Israel's history.

[5] By "the Chronicler" I refer to the author of 1 and 2 Chronicles (who may or may not be the same author as that of Ezra and Nehemiah). See discussion in Williamson 1982.

all the leaders of Israel and its warriors pledge allegiance. This is the same "history" from a rather different angle.[6]

20.1.1.2 *Solomon's Wisdom*

Already in the 1 Kings account we start to form an impression of Solomon's fairness in dealing with his opponents, notably his initial sparing of Adonijah (1 Kgs 1:53), but in 1 Kings 3 his wisdom is confirmed.[7] He first makes a political marriage with the Egyptian Pharaoh's daughter (Dell 2010). It is mentioned that Solomon loved the Lord, walking in the statutes of his father and his role as temple builder is confirmed. At Gibeon he has a dream and asks God for the discernment to rule well—he asks for keynote qualities that we associate with Wisdom: "an understanding mind to govern your people, able to discern between good and evil" (1 Kgs 3:9; cf. Prov 1:2; 8:16). This request is approved by God who is impressed that Solomon asked neither for wealth nor for success over his enemies (1 Kgs 3:10–11). Thus, God grants Solomon "a wise and discerning mind" (v. 12) and, largely because he did not ask, God also gives Solomon riches (the usual product of wisdom; see Prov 8:17–19) and longevity (also a benefit of following wisdom's path; see Job 42:16–17). This account is also paralleled in Chronicles (2 Chron 1:1–13).

This dream is realized later in 1 Kings 3, as Solomon fulfills one of the king's roles as judge in a public assembly. He is asked to solve an argument between two women (described as prostitutes) as to whose is the living baby. Both women had borne children, but one child had died and one woman accused the other of swapping the living and the dead child when the mother was asleep. When Solomon suggests that the only solution is to cut the child down the middle and give the women half each, the real mother reveals herself in preferring to spare the baby's life and give him to the other woman rather than see him die. Solomon is then able to proclaim that he has discovered the true mother of the child. This execution of justice stuns the people by its wisdom and its proof of Solomon's God-given endowment.

Solomon's wisdom is praised as "vast as the sand on the seashore" (5:9 [ET 4:29]). Egypt is mentioned for its wisdom as are the people of the east. Egypt was the real center of wisdom at that time and we have many instructions and other documents still extant that are the products of that genre (see the essay by Joachim Quack in this volume). Babylon too had its Wisdom tradition, inherited from the Sumerians (see the essay by Yoram Cohen and Nathan Wasserman in this volume). The East was famed for its wisdom—possibly a reference to Babylon.

We are then told that Solomon composed three thousand proverbs (5:11 [ET 4:32])—a link perhaps with the book of Proverbs.[8] This is many more than exist in Proverbs, in fact. There may be some exaggeration in the round numbers here. Songs

---

[6] On the rather different presentation of Solomon by the Chronicler, see Braun 1973; Braun 1976. Also, Dillard 1980.

[7] First Kings 3–11 is a separate section for those following the Succession narrative argument, but does this make an unnatural break in the narrative, which might be better taken as a whole?

[8] See Kynes (2019) on the significance of such connections between 1 Kings 1–11 and Proverbs.

are also mentioned, and of course another traditional attribution to Solomon is the Song of Songs or Song of Solomon, which is about love between a man and a woman (Dell 2005). Interestingly, Jewish tradition relates that Solomon composed the Song of Songs in his youth, Proverbs in middle age, and Ecclesiastes when he was old and gray (Canticles Rabbah 1:1). Further, we are told that he had knowledge of the natural world, of fish and animals, birds and reptiles, such that people would flock to hear him speak (5:13–14 [ET 4:33–34]). This suggests a kind of encyclopedic knowledge. We know a type of listing from Egypt called onomastica, used in educational contexts, in which varieties of species are listed—maybe there is a parallel here.[9] None of this is mentioned by the Chronicler, by the way, who is largely focused on Solomon's role as temple builder (cf. 1 Kings 6–8) (Van Seters 1997).

20.1.1.3 *The Queen of Sheba's Visit*

Another insight into Solomon's wisdom is given in the description of the visit from the Queen of Sheba, who comes to test King Solomon with hard questions (10:1–10). She is probably on a trade mission—she is also wealthy and she is clearly very much Solomon's intellectual equal. Solomon successfully answers all of her questions and so passes her test. Interestingly, we are in the realm of riddles and word-play here, arguably a different form of wisdom from the proverbs and listing described in 1 Kings 5 and the administrative skill of 1 Kings 3.[10] The Queen of Sheba is impressed by Solomon's wisdom, his temple, and his opulence. Indeed, she expresses to him that he far exceeded her expectations and she blesses his God's choice of king. She gives him gold from Ophir, spices and precious stones, almug wood, and musical instruments. In return he grants her every desire and gifts in return. Her visit seems mainly to underline Solomon's wealth, power, beneficence, and wisdom. The Chronicler echoes the account in 2 Chronicles 9.

It is only at the end of the account in 1 Kings 11 that we encounter criticisms of Solomon (all of which are omitted by the Chronicler).[11] We are told of his penchant for foreign women and that his foreign wives influenced him in old age to go after other gods (11:1–8). Solomon builds a high place for Chemosh the Moabite god and so elicits God's anger. From this comes the threat to divide the kingdom so that Solomon's descendants will from this point onwards only rule over one part of it (11:9–13). This was to be Judah, the southern kingdom which, for much of the century that followed, was the less powerful of the two kingdoms. The account in Kings ends on a positive note—Solomon's wealth and wisdom are mentioned again in 11:41, that wisdom being God-given. After his death he gets a good verdict from the authors of his story—he had a long and prosperous reign and was given a good burial in Jerusalem with his father David (11:42–43).

[9] This goes back to a form-critical suggestion by von Rad (1966).
[10] So traditionally argued by R.B.Y. Scott (1960).
[11] See Knoppers 1997b; Hays 2003.

20.1.2 Scholarly Questioning of the Tradition of Solomon's Historicity and Wisdom

20.1.2.1 *Historicity*

It is clear that the account of Solomon's reign in 1 Kings 1–11 is in many ways an idealized picture and that it is written with hindsight. A major issue in scholarship is what the nature of "historical writing" is from the Solomonic period—is the text purely an ideological construct of a later age (Gelinas 1995) or can something of the historical Solomon be retrieved from this account? For many scholars in the 1960s and 1970s, an ever-expanding Israelite state under Solomon that could be reconstructed by appeal to Egyptian parallels in relation to court administration and the schooling of upper-class scribes was a reality (Heaton 1974; Ahlström 1982). Von Rad (1966, 203) spoke of a Solomonic "enlightenment" when he wrote, "In short, the time of Solomon was a period of 'enlightenment,' of a sharp break with the ancient patriarchal code of living."[12] Since those decades, this theory is thought to have been overstated (Crenshaw 1987) and it has been replaced by an increasing skepticism about Solomon's historical existence, his supposed wisdom, and whether an Israelite state in the ninth century bore any resemblance to Egyptian parallels (Weeks 1994).

The first issue to discuss is a literary one—do we have an older separate account of the reign that has been incorporated into a longer, Deuteronomic account as on the traditional view? Or are we to attribute the entire account to the Deuteronomists of the seventh to sixth centuries BCE? Would the Deuteronomists have penned such an idealistic account in Kings with only a mild critique, or was it they who added the critique to an existing eulogy? Were the Deuteronomists idealizing a particular status quo in an account that might or might not have come down to them but then offering their own critique (Brueggemann 1990)? The Deuteronomistic history is well known for its tension between pro- and anti-monarchical stances. There is a general suspicion amongst scholars of narrative as a factual medium. As Brueggemann (1990, 118) writes, "whatever happened historically is cased in a narrative form, which makes factuality precarious." Brueggemann sees the account in Kings as stereotypical, bound by literary convention and probably already accreting legendary elements. This leads him to pursue a line that looks at the socio-political processes that may have formed the text rather than at the text itself. As a result, he sees this period under Solomon as a "novum," a time of transition in which a rather different Israelite state emerged, one that brought wisdom under royal patronage and made it part of the establishment in the same way as occurred in Egypt. He prefers to speak in literary rather than historical terms, but it has to be remembered that the Deuteronomists are presenting a history, and, as history, their work should, even if later and ideological, give a meaningful and substantial account of the past. The Deuteronomic Historian furthermore refers to other documents, such as the

---

[12] This view was taken up by E.W. Heaton (1974).

"book of the acts of Solomon" (1 Kgs 11:41), within the narrative, suggesting some inter-action of the authors with external sources, a method any good historian would follow.

The second issue is a more historical one in relation to archaeological evidence. A scholarly movement in archaeology has posed significant questions about the extent and veracity of evidence linking up with the Solomonic period, accompanied by some serious redating of strata (following Finkelstein's "low chronology"). This has been countered in some quarters too (Knoppers 1997a). While it is now widely agreed that significant amounts of written epigraphic data seem to come mainly from the eighth century BCE, does that nullify the account of a great kingdom prior to that date? Did the golden age as presented in the text in fact exist? Even if the account is ideological, is that not the common way of presenting material both in other Israelite and in extra-biblical sources? Selectivity and exaggeration in presenting a view one wishes to promote is nothing new (Provan et al. 2003). The question is whether we should seek to establish a fact—such as Solomon's reign—by archaeology alone before recourse to the text or whether we should take the text at face value. As Provan (2003, 250) writes:

> The general paucity of the archaeological record with regard to the Solomonic period is, of course, well known, and has come to have an important place in recent discussion of Israelite history that tends to ask for corroboration of the text before the text is taken seriously rather than asking whether evidence shows that the text should *not* be taken seriously.   (Emphasis original)

Provan therefore, unlike Brueggemann, is taking the text seriously as a historical docu-ment; while literary evidence does not necessarily equal historical proof, that does not mean that all literary references are false.

20.1.2.2 *Wisdom*

While the description of Solomon's wisdom in 1 Kgs 5:9–14 [ET 4:29–34] may need to be taken with an ideological pinch of salt as an exaggeration, it is interesting that his wis-dom is such a major theme of the account. R.B.Y. Scott (1960) identified three types of wisdom in the Kings account: (1) Skill in government; (2) Forensic wisdom; (3) Wisdom as knowledge and intellect. He sees them as a development one from another, but I think rather that these categories simply reflect different aspects of wisdom. Crenshaw argued that these types of wisdom did not correspond with that found in Proverbs, but this is to work with too narrow a view of what wisdom is and, following Albrecht Alt (1951), I would add the category of nature wisdom.[13] Kynes (2019) has recently helpfully shown the many intertextual connections of Solomon's wisdom in Kings with the "Wisdom Literature," building on Scott's three categories. Kynes (2019, 61–62) writes, "The Solomonic attribution invites Proverbs into the complex intertextual network represented in the description of the wise king in 1 Kings, which provides a definition of wisdom in which politics and

---

[13]   As I argued in relation to the categorization of Wisdom psalms (Dell 2004)—an interaction with the natural world and issues around creation are inherent to the Wisdom genre and so other material that concerns these issues should be incorporated under a broad definition.

prophecy, intellect and piety, the secular and the sacred intersect." The question why this wisdom emphasis is made in the Kings account undercuts the more socio-political views of Brueggemann (1990) that it was legitimation of the reign, the temple, and the administration that was at the center of concern, with the wisdom emphasis affirming the official class. Rather, it was perhaps more of a matter of Solomon's personality and his not inconsiderable reputation as a wise king that led to this emphasis. That is how the historical personage was remembered in literary terms. This emphasis is reinforced by his authoritative role in the headings to Wisdom books and in the "royal testament" of Ecclesiastes to which I shall turn below in 20.2.1.2 (Ecclesiastes). First, though, how is Solomon remembered in the canon outside the key Wisdom texts?

20.1.3 Solomon in the Biblical Canon

Brueggemann (2005), in the book that follows up his seminal article, confirms Solomon's status as Israel's wisest king through the voice of the canon of Scripture and beyond, rather than simply from the Kings account. He speaks in terms of "imaginative retell-ing" that gradually made Solomon's influence and reputation greater over time. Again, the ideology of the text is key, "whereby certain interests have been imposed upon the tradition of ancient Israel" (Brueggemann 2005, 15–16). He emphasizes the influence of the canon in creating "the most celebrated figure in Jerusalem" out of a modest chieftain through acts of "critical faithful imagination" (Brueggemann 2005, 78). While he can be criticized for overstating this ideological case, where Solomon reappears in the canon does provide insight into both the figure and the wisdom associated with him.

I have already mentioned that Chronicles clearly promotes the picture of Solomon as temple builder over against any other emphasis. However, the Chronicler also repeats the encomium for Solomon's wisdom (2 Chron 9:1–9, 22–23), without its demonstra-tion by the judgment between the two women. In some ways the portrayal of Solomon as temple builder extraordinaire reduces the richness of our picture of this multifac-eted character, as of course does the removal of any negative press.[14] Solomon is first mentioned by the Chronicler in 1 Chron 3:5 (cf. 14:4) in relation to his birth. Then he re-emerges in 1 Chron 22; 23:1; 28; 29 and 2 Chron 1–9; 33:7. He is clearly not as interesting and central to the Chronicler as King David is. For example, in 1 Chron 22:5 David makes preparations for the temple since Solomon is considered too young and inexperienced, and one gets the impression that Solomon could not have failed in this task as every-thing was planned by his predecessor in advance of his own building project.

The sister work to Chronicles, Nehemiah, also mentions Solomon, though in a nega-tive vein as having a poor reputation in relation to his foreign wives (Neh 13:26). This is a key concern of this text that calls on Israelite men to "unmarry" their foreign wives or, preferably, not marry foreigners in the first place. Also within the canon we find two psalms attributed not to David but to Solomon—Psalms 72 and 127 (Dell, forthcoming).

---

[14] Although, recently Jeon (2013) has emphasized Solomon's faults in Chronicles.

This is interesting for the fact that these are not generally classified as Wisdom psalms, although Psalm 127 has a greater claim to the category. Elsewhere Jer 52:20, probably penned by Deuteronomists, refers to the temple furnishings made in Solomon's reign, but not to his wisdom.

In the New Testament, Solomon in all his glory is compared to lilies in both Matthew (6:29) and Luke (12:27). This is a striking visual image summoning up ideas of the wealth and luxury of his reign rather than his reputation for wisdom, although of course the two aspects generally went together. Luke 11:31 also makes this point. Matthew 1:6–7 mentions Solomon in a genealogy of Christ, and 12:42 mentions the Queen of Sheba coming to listen to Solomon's wisdom. In John 10:23 the temple's "portico of Solomon" is mentioned, and in Acts 7:47 it was recalled that Solomon built a house for the Lord. These references tell us little, but they certainly indicate that Solomon was regarded as a historical figure of some note by that time.

20.2 THE SOLOMONIC COLLECTION

20.2.1 Solomon as a Wisdom "Authority"

As David is to the Psalms, so is Solomon to the so-called "Wisdom Literature." He is the "implied" author, according to the text, of Proverbs, Ecclesiastes, and the Wisdom of Solomon, and he is mentioned in the title of Song of Songs, potentially as its author as well. In each case, this attribution is more likely to be a literary connection than a historical fact. While it is clear, as we have seen above in section 20.1 (The Character of Solomon), that the Solomon of Kings had a reputation for wisdom and probably was some kind of inspirational figure for the sages and scribes who practiced wisdom on a day-to-day basis, I suspect, with many scholars (so Brueggemann 2005), that the attribution of these books to him is honorific. Let us look more closely at the attributions.

20.2.1.1 *Proverbs*

In Proverbs there are three attributions, two directly to King Solomon (1:1; 10:1) and one to the "men of Hezekiah who copied" his proverbs (25:1). The beginning of the book is where one would most expect an attribution of authorship. The mention is part of a prologue in 1:1–7 that sets out the purpose of the book. Treating this prologue as a unit, it is clear that Solomon's wise authority is a key part of this purpose and quest for wisdom that is described. However, it is perhaps more surprising that there is a second attribution in 10:1, which is a clear marker of a different section. In fact, 10:1–22:16 is thought to be a separate and older section. It could be that some of the sayings in this earlier collection, particularly those that concern the king and courtly behavior, originated with Solomon or at his court. However, a family or tribal setting is also possible for those that treat everyday topics. We also have to distinguish between the original coining of a proverb and the writing-down stage; even if proverbs originated elsewhere, there were sages at the courts of kings who probably wrote them down. This most likely happened at Solomon's court or at that of a later king—the latter is more likely if the attribution to Solomon himself is honorific. Perhaps the most interesting attribution of the three is in Prov 25:1, covering the section in Proverbs 25–29 which is another sayings collection, similar to 10:1–22:16. This time the officials of King Hezekiah are said to have copied the proverbs of Solomon. Hezekiah was king in the seventh century BCE, two centuries after Solomon. There was a certain revival of national life under his rule which came to a climax in the reign of Josiah some time later. Hezekiah is in some ways a second Solomon, certainly for the Chronicler (Throntveit 2003). We could be seeing a distinction in this superscription between the literary production of proverbs in the seventh century BCE and the original oral product as indicated by the other superscriptions. Clearly these proverbs were felt to be important enough for someone to gather them together, and that had to be a group with courtly connections because they were the literati of the time. They had the leisure to reflect, learn, write, and perform archival functions in the preservation of documents and literature. It is interesting that the reference is to copying the proverbs of Solomon so that Solomon also gets a third mention as the father of the proverbs enterprise. Whatever the historical nature of these attributions, they are functioning in a literary way to unite material across the canon of scripture. As Kynes (2019, 50) writes, "Just as Proverbs' superscription invites the book to be read according to the wisdom attributed to Solomon in 1 Kings, so the variegated presentation of wisdom in that account draws other texts across the canon into the interpretation of Proverbs."

20.2.1.2 *Ecclesiastes*

Ecclesiastes is not directly attributed to Solomon, but the reference to "son of David, king in Jerusalem" (1:1) suggests him strongly, such that Solomon has been widely seen, since antiquity, as the author of the book. There is more than simply this attribution, which also appears again in 1:12 with slight variation, suggesting a time span: "*when king over Israel in Jerusalem.*" There is also the "royal testament" section of 1:12–2:26[15] in which the author—probably Qoheleth (1:1)—takes on the persona of a king, who in his great wealth and wisdom clearly is meant to evoke Solomon. The purpose of the section seems to be to test the worth of the Wisdom quest. Here Qoheleth reveals himself as the "wise man" interested in "all that is done under heaven." In Solomonic guise, Qoheleth devises a series of tests to try to find enjoyment in life, and each one fails. He tries great works, building himself fine houses and vineyards, gardens, and parks full of trees. Singers and concubines are also part of the attempt to satisfy himself. This shows that the references to the son of David and then the royal testament may all be part of a royal guise (Koh 2006), a "test" of the worth or worthlessness of wisdom.

The passage continues as Qoheleth tests wisdom, madness, and folly. He decides that wisdom is on the whole to be preferred to folly just as light is preferable to darkness. But then he relativizes it all by musing on death, the great leveler, which makes all human

---

[15] The precise parameters of this section are debated.

striving pointless. It is all very well acquiring great wisdom, but what distinguishes the wise man from the fool when they are both dead? Why try to be wise in the first place? Nor is the wise man remembered after his death (although this one is because he wrote a book that was preserved!). One conclusion is in 2:11—the toil was in fact "vanity" (הבל) and led to no real gain "under the sun." Perhaps Qoheleth's mistake was to do all of this for himself and his own gratification. Although, indirectly, as King Solomon, he would be doing it all for his people, it was perhaps more in the service of his greatness than for their benefit. There is perhaps a lesson here in the diminishment of wisdom in the context of power and perceived greatness. In some ways, the author of Ecclesiastes is undercutting the great Solomon myth. And yet there is a second answer in v. 24, a moment of optimism that states that eating and drinking and finding enjoyment in toil is probably the best answer. Enjoyment is a gift of God, and in v. 26 the one who pleases God will gain all good things. But is this not also vanity? The author is teasing us with possible scenarios—the Solomonic example is simply part of the wider musings on the meaning of life and of the attempt to live by wisdom.

20.2.1.3 *Song of Songs*

The Song of Songs mentions Solomon a total of six times, but only the first time is it an attribution, "The Song of Songs which is Solomon's" (1:1 NRSV). First Kings 4 mentions that Solomon composed songs as well as other genres, as does Sir 47:14. So it is the opening verse of the book (1:1) that is usually taken as a heading and ascription of the work to the most famous wise King (1 Kgs 10:23). The attribution could, however, indicate that the book was by Solomon, dedicated to him, concerning him, in his style, or belonging to him. It is generally thought that "by Solomon" or "belonging to" him is most appropriate, the latter not directly assigning authorship. Once again, this communicates Solomonic legitimization rather than strictly authorial concerns, although it is clear that from early times the Song was literally attributed to the wise king. Rabbi Jonathan, for example, deduced that the Song was Solomon's first achievement. He wrote, "When a man is young he composes songs; when he grows older he makes sententious remarks; and when he becomes an old man he speaks of the vanity of things" (Canticles Rabbah 1:1). Either the attribution was made to gain the book some kind of approval, possibly in relation to canonization, or the link with Solomon may have been made on the basis of traditions about his life, notably in relation to his numerous wives and concubines (1 Kgs 11:1–3; cf. Song 6:8–9). Also, references to Solomon's supposed interest in flora and fauna (1 Kgs 4:32–33), exotic spices from abroad (1 Kgs 4:13–14), and to the images of wealth and luxury (1 Kings 9–10) all connect the account of Solomon's reign to the Song of Songs, where all feature abundantly. A distant historical connection to Solomon cannot be ruled out.

The other mentions of Solomon in the third person (1:5; 3:7, 9, 11; 8:11–12) could be seen to relate him to the plot as a character, possibly used as some kind of role play by the lovers, or to deliberately evoke the wise king (Dell 2005), or even to denote Solomon and the Shunammite woman (Abishag) as the lovers themselves (the relationship described in 1 Kgs 1:3–4). There are other references to "the king" who may or may not be the same person and many references to riches, including the description of Solomon's wedding palanquin as having "posts of silver, its back of gold, its seat of purple" (cf. Ps 45:13–15). The associations with Solomon in the Song are rather like those in Ecclesiastes—he is a hidden figure who comes in and out of the shadows of the text. In my own view, he is more prominent in the Song than in Ecclesiastes. Robert Gordis (1968) argued that the royal wedding song goes back to Solomon's reign; Childs (1979) preferred to see Solomonic elements in the Song as an editorial layer added to confirm the book's Wisdom status. It does seem that in going beyond simply an attribution the book seeks to associate itself in a more integrated way to wisdom's wisest patron, Solomon.

20.2.1.4 *Other Texts*

There are a few mentions of Solomon in other texts, notably among the Deuterocanonical works ("Apocrypha"). I have already mentioned Ben Sira, where in the "famous men" passage Solomon is represented (47:12–22) and noted for his wisdom: "Your songs, proverbs, and parables, and the answers you gave astounded the nations" (Sir 47:14). This book is not attributed to Solomon in any way although it contains many proverbs and other Wisdom genres. In 2 Macc 2:8–12 Solomon is recalled a few times, though only in the context of the place of consecration of and building of the temple. Solomon prays and offers sacrifice and the fire of God consumes the sacrifice as a sign of the consecration of the site. Similarly, 1 Esd 1:3 and 2 Esd 7:108; 10:46 mention Solomon, all focused on his role as dedicator of the temple. Perhaps the most significant link to Solomon is made by the "Wisdom of Solomon," which purports to be the advice of King Solomon but very clearly betrays the concerns of a later age. It is a first-century BCE work thought to have been produced in Egypt and influenced by Greek ideas and written in Greek. There is a key section (chs. 6–9) where Solomon speaks about wisdom, enjoining the mighty of the earth to seek and find it. The book also shows a concern with Wisdom pursuits—such as a curriculum of the kind of astronomical knowledge the wise of the time were supposed to know (7:17–20)—but the overriding interest of the book is in the personification of wisdom. It could not have been written by Solomon and so was attributed to him in a symbolic way to add more weight to the content of the book in pseudonymous style. In the New Testament, Solomon is mentioned several times (see above 20.1.3). His splendor is said to be less than the lilies of the field (Matt 6:29; Luke 12:27), and his wisdom less than Christ's (Matt 12:42; Luke 11:31). In John 10:23 and Acts 7:47, Solomon is referred to for his temple building rather than his wisdom.

Solomon was a popular figure for early Jewish interpreters and he frequently appears in the rabbinic writings. Many legends grew up about him, including a story that Solomon was at one time temporarily deposed by a powerful demon and wandered the streets as a beggar, atoning for his sins of greed and foreign wives, mixing with his people and testing their worth. This was based on Eccl 1:12, which arguably states that the son of David "had been" king in Jerusalem, suggesting that he was no longer, or at least that he had a period away from the throne.

20.2.2 Concluding Remarks

It is clear that Solomon is depicted as the father of wisdom and that the quest for wisdom and writings illustrating wisdom took some inspiration from him. This presentation and the references to him link the family of Wisdom books together, and yet it is not a grouping that corresponds directly to "Wisdom Literature" as defined by scholarship since the nineteenth century (Kynes 2018) because it does not include Job. In Job there is no mention of Solomon and no attribution (Dell 2016). This rather is an older grouping of texts—a Solomonic collection within the Writings of the Hebrew Bible with tentacles reaching beyond the canon into Deuterocanonical works. The rabbis clearly took up the authorial associations and gave them some import, and this grouping held significance until other groupings came into vogue. There is a question whether the attributions are just honorific or whether they indicate rather more. Solomon is certainly the symbolic figure who links this family of texts together and communicates wisdom across the canon (Dell, 2020). As one reads one text with Solomonic associations so it informs a reading of another text with similar associations and this can take us beyond the "Wisdom" boundaries into the narrative books and beyond, as this article has shown.

The interest shown in Solomon in the history of interpretation is a subject too vast to cover comprehensively here, so a sampling will have to suffice. The visit of the Queen of Sheba is related in the Qur'an in a brief passage (27:15–44) that suggests that the pious (now Muslim) King Solomon summoned her to see him on hearing a report of her worship of other gods. This becomes an opportunity for a further demonstration of his wisdom, as he "tests" her in two ways. First, he disguises her throne, which was brought secretly to Jerusalem. This she recognizes, thus demonstrating her intelligence. But second, Solomon sits on a throne set on glass, which looks to the queen like water. She lifts her robes because of the water and uncovers her ankles. Thus, she is deceived and humiliated and so converted to Islam in submitting to God (Allah).

There is also an Ethiopic version of this same account, which follows the biblical tale in having Sheba come to Solomon on hearing of his wisdom but describes her as a sun-worshipper whom the Israelite Solomon persuades back to the Creator, the God of Israel. In this version, Solomon deceives her into sharing his tent and they eventually have a son together, Menelik, who becomes king and founder of the royal dynasty in Ethiopia.

A more recent Solomonic tradition has surfaced in freemasonry from the mid-eighteenth century in England. Solomon as temple builder inspired the imagery that is crucial to the idea of the "mason" rebuilding a defeated society after the Thirty Years War in Europe. In addition, Solomon's wisdom appealed to the sense of secret knowledge known only to the initiated which included myths and rituals but also ethical ideals.

With the Masonic movement inspired by works written in the 1720s and 1730s we find an interesting link to the time when Handel was working on his oratorio, *Solomon*, in the 1740s. (Rooke 2012). Handel was writing in a time when consolidation of the reign was important after the Jacobite rebellion (first performance 1749), and Solomon as a strong, wealthy, and wise king was a natural subject for an oratorio that would flatter George

II, the King of England at the time. Handel elaborated on three aspects of Solomon's reign, known to us from 1 Kings—his happy marriage to his adoring Egyptian queen, the daughter of the pharaoh of Egypt; his juridical wisdom in judging between the right of two prostitutes to a baby; and his foreign relations with the Queen of Sheba, who admires him both as a man and as a wise king. Fascinatingly, all three parts emphasize Solomon and his relationships with women. The Song of Songs is used in Part 1 of the oratorio to express the love of king and queen. Solomon's juridical wisdom is stressed in Part 2 in the court scene with the women, but also before that in the justification of his eventual killing of Adonijah as just and divinely legitimated. Part 3 stresses the wisdom of both Solomon and Sheba and focuses on her admiration for Solomon's splendor and wealth. She compares herself in her final recitative and air to a flower brought into bloom by Solomon's spring rain. There is no critique of Solomon here—the oratorio's depiction is as idealized as most of 1 Kings. Solomon's greatness is stressed over everything else. The image of Solomon anointed king by Zadok the priest and Nathan the prophet in Handel's famous anthem of 1727 has rung down the centuries in the coronation ceremonies of successive kings and queens of the British Isles. This is how tradition remembers him—as the wisest of Israel's kings, an inspiration to those who follow his kingly path and figurehead for the path of wisdom that we should all seek to follow.

WORKS CITED

Ahlström, Gösta W. 1982. *Royal Administration and National Religion in Ancient Palestine.* SHANE 1. Leiden: Brill.

Alt, Albrecht. 1951. "Die Weisheit Salomos." *TLZ* 76:139–144.

Bar-Efrat, Shimon 1989. *Narrative Art in the Bible.* JSOTSup 70/BLS 17. Worcester: Almond.

Bland, Dave. 2015. *Proverbs and the Formation of Character.* Eugene, OR: Cascade.

Braun, Roddy L. 1973. "Solomonic Apologetic in Chronicles." *JBL* 92:501–516.

Braun, Roddy L. 1976. "Solomon, the Chosen Temple Builder: The Significance of 1 Chronicles 22, 28, and 29 for the Theology of Chronicles." *JBL* 95:581–590.

Brown, William P. 1996. *Character in Crisis: A Fresh Approach to the Wisdom Literature of the Old Testament.* Grand Rapids, MI: Eerdmans.

Brueggemann, Walter. 1990. "The Social Significance of Solomon as a Patron of Wisdom." Pages 117–132 in *The Sage in Israel and the Ancient Near East.* Edited by John G. Gammie and Leo G. Perdue. Winona Lake, IN: Eisenbrauns.

Brueggemann, Walter 2005. *Solomon: Israel's Ironic Icon of Human Achievement.* Columbia, SC: University of South Carolina Press.

Childs, Brevard S. 1979. *Introduction to the Old Testament as Scripture.* Philadelphia, PA: Fortress.

Crenshaw, James L. 1987. "Wisdom Literature: Biblical Books." Pages 401–409 in *The Encyclopaedia of Religion.* Edited by Mircea Eliade et al. New York, NY: Free Press.

Dell, Katharine J. 2004. "'I Will Solve My Riddle to the Music of the Lyre (Psalm XLIX 4 [5])': A Cultic Setting for Wisdom Psalms?" *VT* 54:445–458.

Dell, Katharine J. 2005. "Does the Song of Songs Have Any Connections to Wisdom?" Pages 8–25 in *Perspectives on the Song of Songs/Perspektiven der Hoheliedauslegung.* Edited by Anselm C. Hagedorn. Berlin: de Gruyter.

Dell, Katharine J. 2010. "Solomon's Wisdom and the Egyptian Connection." Pages 23–37 in *The Centre and the Periphery: A European Tribute to Walter Brueggemann*. Edited by Jill Middlemas, David J.A. Clines, and Else Holt. Sheffield: Sheffield Phoenix.

Dell, Katharine J. 2016. "Ecclesiastes as Mainstream Wisdom (without Job)." Pages 43–52 in *Goochem in Mokum/Wisdom in Amsterdam: Papers on Biblical and Related Wisdom Read at the Fifteenth Joint Meeting of The Society of Old Testament Study and the Oudtestamentisch Werkgezelschap, Amsterdam July 2012*. Edited by George J. Brooke and Pierre Van Hecke. OtSt 68. Leiden: Brill.

Dell, Katharine J. 2020. *The Solomonic Corpus of "Wisdom" and Its Influence*. Oxford: Oxford University Press.

Dell, Katharine J. Forthcoming. "The Two "Solomon" Psalms: Psalm 72 and 127 in the Light of the Solomonic Attribution." *Psalms and the Use of the Critical Imagination: A Festschrift in Honour of Professor Susan Gillingham*. Edited by Katherine Southwood and Holly Morse. LHBOTS. London: Bloomsbury T&T Clark.

Dillard, Raymond B. 1980. "The Chronicler's Solomon." *WTJ* 43:289–300.

Gelinas, M.M. 1995. "United Monarchy—Divided Monarchy: Fact or Fiction?" Pages 227–237 in *The Pitcher Is Broken: Memorial Essays for Gösta W. Ahlström*. Edited by S.W. Holloway and L. Handy. JSOTSup 190. Sheffield: Sheffield Academic.

Gordis, Robert. 1968. *Koheleth: The Man and His World*. New York, NY: Schocken.

Hays, J. Daniel. 2003. "Has the Narrator Come to Praise Solomon or to Bury Him? Narrative Subtlety in 1 Kings 1–11." *JSOT* 28:149–174.

Heaton, E.W. 1974. *Solomon's New Men: The Emergence of Ancient Israel as a National State*. London: Thames & Hudson.

Jeon, Yong Ho. 2013. *Impeccable Solomon? A Study of Solomon's Faults in Chronicles*. Eugene, OR: Pickwick.

Knoppers, Gary N. 1997a. "The Vanishing Solomon: The Disappearance of the United Monarchy from Recent Histories of Ancient Israel." *JBL* 116:19–44.

Knoppers, Gary N. 1997b. "Solomon's Fall and Deuteronomy." Pages 392–410 in *The Age of Solomon: Scholarship at the Turn of the Millennium*. Edited by Lowell K. Handy. Leiden: Brill.

Koh, Yee Von 2006. *Royal Autobiography in the Book of Qoheleth*. BZAW 136. Berlin: de Gruyter.

Kynes, Will. 2018. "The Wisdom Literature Category: An Obituary." *JTS* 69:1–24.

Kynes, Will. 2019. "Wisdom Defined through Narrative and Intertextual Network: 1 Kings 1–11 and Proverbs." Pages 35–47 in *Reading Proverbs Intertextually*. Edited by Katharine Dell and Will Kynes. LHBOTS 629. New York, NY: Bloomsbury T&T Clark.

Noth, Martin. 1981. *The Deuteronomistic History*. JSOTSupp 15. Sheffield: Sheffield Academic.

Phelan, James 2005. *Living to Tell about It: A Rhetoric and Ethics of Character Narration*. Ithaca, NY: Cornell University Press.

Provan, Ian, V. Phillips Long, and Tremper Longman, III. 2003. *A Biblical History of Israel*. Louisville, KY: Westminster John Knox Press.

Rad, Gerhard von. 1966. "The Beginnings of Historical Writing in Ancient Israel." Pages 166–204 in *The Problem of the Hexateuch and Other Essays*. London: SCM.

Rooke, Deborah. 2012. *Handel's Israelite Oratorio Libretti: Sacred Drama and Biblical Exegesis*. Oxford: Oxford University Press.

Rost, Leonhard. 1982. *The Succession to the Throne of David*. Sheffield: Almond Press. Translation of *Die Überlieferung von der Thronnachfolge Davids*. BWANT 42. Stuttgart: Kohlhammer, 1926.

Scott, R.B.Y. 1960. "Solomon and the Beginnings of Wisdom in Israel." Pages 262–279 in *Wisdom in Israel and in the Ancient Near East*. Edited by M. Noth and D. Winton Thomas. VTSup 3. Leiden: Brill.

Throntveit, Mark A. 2003. "The Relationship of Hezekiah to David and Solomon in the Books of Chronicles." Pages 105–121 in *The Chronicler as Theologian: Essays in Honor of Ralph W. Klein*. Edited by M. Patrick Graham, Steven L. McKenzie, and Gary N. Knoppers. London: T&T Clark International.

Van Seters, John. 1997. "The Chronicler's Account of Solomon's Temple Building: A Continuity Theme." Pages 283–300 in *The Chronicler as Historian*. Edited by M. Patrick Graham, Kenneth G. Hoglund, and Steven. L. McKenzie. Sheffield: Sheffield Academic.

Weeks, Stuart 1994. *Early Israelite Wisdom*. Oxford: Clarendon Press.

Williamson, H.G.M. 1982. *1 and 2 Chronicles*. NCB. Grand Rapids, MI: Eerdmans.

CHAPTER 21

....

THE SOCIAL SETTING OF WISDOM LITERATURE

....

MARK SNEED

THE question of the social setting of the biblical Wisdom Literature is an interesting one in that this type of literature seeks to exclude its social background as much as possible (cf. Sneed 1998, 41). Wisdom Literature, by its very nature, ostensibly portrays itself as universal in its appeal.[1] The notion of a parochial or sectarian wisdom is almost by definition oxymoronic. Any wise saying or parable worth its weight should apply to everyone, no matter the nationality. A parochial truth, we might say, is no truth at all!

So, what we find in the biblical Wisdom Literature is a lack of reference to specifically Israelite or Jewish identity markers. One will search in vain for clear references to the Torah or any of the Israelite covenants (Mosaic or Davidic), or the patriarchs, or significant Israelite events, like the Exodus. Several scholars (e.g., Crenshaw 2010, 11, 24–25, 229) have argued that this "anomaly" indicates that the Wisdom writers were not totally Yahwistic and represent a particular social group, the sages, whose literature was written to offer a different perspective, even worldview, from that reflected in the rest of the Hebrew Bible.[2] But this is to fail to understand this particular characteristic of the Wisdom Literature as a literary convention. A convention is what identifies a particular genre over against another, what makes one genre distinguishable from another. The use of a literary convention per se does not necessarily indicate a particular group membership (see Sneed 2011; Sneed 2015b).

Other ancient Near Eastern Wisdom Literature also partakes in this convention. For example, the Instruction of Ptahhotep, an early Egyptian example of Wisdom Literature, makes few references to Egyptian mythology. It even fails to specify a particular deity when the gods are mentioned. There are few if any nationalistic concerns as well. Again, Wisdom Literature usually focuses on persons in terms of their daily, mundane existence

---

[1] This is fundamentally a rhetorical and ideological move; see Eagleton 1991, 56–58.

[2] All of this is based on the argument from silence. On the often fallacious character of this form of argumentation, see Sneed 2015b.

and avoids nationalistic or historical perspectives. Mesopotamian Wisdom Literature is the same. For example, the Babylonian Counsels of Wisdom is also fairly generic, with references to deities, like Ea and Shamash, which is no surprise since wisdom and justice are concerns of Wisdom Literature generally. The work betrays no interest in Babylonian history or events. So, for literature that deliberately avoids ethnic and group identifiers, how does one identify its authors?

21.1 IDENTIFYING THE "WISDOM WRITERS"

Biblical scholars often refer to the authors of the biblical Wisdom Literature as the "Wisdom writers," which is rather tautological, and suggests their identity is a great mystery. However, there really is no real question about their general identity. They had to be scribes, though what type of scribe could be open to debate. Of course, all of the composers and copyists of the books in the Hebrew Bible were scribes. Identifying them as such is also tautological except that it becomes significant if one also maintains that the same scribes who composed the Wisdom Literature also composed the other types of literature in the Hebrew Bible. This assumption goes against the consensus view. Viewing the authors of the Wisdom Literature as the same authors who composed the other genres or modes of literature prevents one from myopically segregating their literature from the other types. It prevents viewing the Wisdom Literature as the product of some idiosyncratic group that was not interested in prophetic literature or the Torah and its commandments or the priestly material (see Sneed 2018; Sneed forthcoming). To treat it in such a myopic way truly distorts the nature of the literature and misrepresents the group that produced it.

Scholars often refer to "Wisdom teachers," "Wisdom scribes," or "Wisdom schools," but this is a purely scholarly construction and perhaps a projection of the Greek philosophical schools back upon ancient Israel (see Fox 2015, 69). There is no evidence for a scribal teacher who only taught Wisdom Literature. In fact, in the curricula of the various ancient Near Eastern scribal schools, Wisdom Literature was integrated with other genres, like erotica, hymns, model letters, etc. (see Carr 2005; Sneed 2011; Sneed 2015a, 67–182; cf. van der Toorn 2007).

Part of the difficulty of identifying the biblical Wisdom writers is that their works are technically anonymous, as is typical also of the rest of the Hebrew Bible and the ancient Near Eastern Literature. Superscriptions, when they appear, are there simply to buttress their authority. With the biblical Wisdom Literature, it is not until we get to Sirach that an individual is indicated as the sole author of a Wisdom text. And, Ben Sira, its author, identifies both himself and his audience as scribes (Sir 38:24). In ancient Egypt, the most famous Wisdom genre is the instruction, and, of course, these are often identified as either compositions by a vizier of the Pharaoh or a Pharaoh himself, though most Egyptologists are skeptical about the credibility of these claims; the attributions more likely simply bolster the authority of the works. Egyptologists are quite confident that these texts were composed by scribes for scribes, whether to serve pedagogical or other purposes. The same is true for Mesopotamian Wisdom texts. Their real authors are not identified, except for the Babylonian Theodicy, whose stanzas form an acrostic that spells out its author's name. Though we do not usually know the authors, we do know the scribes who copied and studied these texts because of the colophons on the clay tablets that identify them. Why the biblical Wisdom Literature, as well as the other kinds of biblical literature, never identifies, even fictitiously, its authors or the scribal nature of its compositions is a mystery. Perhaps it was that the authors wanted their material to be publicized beyond scribal circles, i.e., it was meant for public reading as well as instruction for novice scribes. Or, since the material was largely internal, the scribal nature and original purpose of the literature was simply assumed, and so the scribes who composed the texts did not think they needed any identification or clarification on this matter.

Some have also questioned whether Israel in fact had schools where Wisdom books could be studied. While there is little direct evidence, Chris Rollston (2010) has argued that there had to be some kind of centralized educational institution to train Israelite scribes. This is indicated by evidence for the standardization of Hebrew, which could not have occurred if scribes were independent (95). Of course, these schools were probably more like the Islamic *madrasa*, which did not necessarily need permanent locales but could have involved available rooms at the Temple or palace or even the homes of scribes (see Lemaire 1984, 278). These scribes would pass their skills on to their sons in their homes or other places, with perhaps a neighborhood boy or two. Still, these homeschools, as the standardization evidence suggests, were controlled by the monarchy in some way.

21.2 WISDOM LITERATURE AS PART OF THE SCRIBAL CURRICULUM

What we know for certain is that Wisdom Literature was used in the training of scribes throughout the ancient Near East, including Egypt, Mesopotamia, Asia Minor, and Syro-Palestine. The appropriate question is how would Wisdom Literature be important for the training of Israelite scribes? One cannot know for certain, but the following reasons seem likely. First, the study and copying of proverbs was helpful in both learning to write Hebrew, including mastering calligraphy, building vocabulary, and comprehending grammar. The typical ancient Near Eastern scribal curricula included the study of proverbial material in the earliest stages. For example, in the Old Babylonian period, young scribes at Nippur were trained in two phases (Veldhuis 2000, 383–387). In the first, students copied lexical texts; this activity imparted the writing system and introduced Sumerian vocabulary. At the end of the first phase, tablets with proverbs were used, and their contents prepared students for studying Sumerian in the second phase, which involved the actual reading of texts. Archaeologists have also found Sumerian clay tablets with lexical lists on one side and matching proverbs on the other (Alster 1997, xviii).

That scribal training began early on with proverb study makes sense because the sentences (the short sayings found in the collections in Prov 10:1–22:16; 25–29) or epigrams (a better English term; they are not true proverbs because they do not appear to have been current among the general populace) are one of the smallest genres in the Hebrew Bible (normally two cola or a bicolon).[3] A novice scribe could master this genre before going on to more complex genres.[4]

Second, studying proverbs not only taught literary skills; it most likely also taught rhetorical skills. Bendt Alster (1997, xix) maintains that the proverb collections functioned as a source for rhetorical phrases used in debates. But, of course, this function would be true also for the study of literature proper. Even today the more well-read a person is, the better speaker she usually is.

Third, it had a moral function. Wisdom Literature was never studied alone or in an isolated fashion. When one examines the curricula of the ancient Near Eastern scribal schools, one sees that other types of literature were studied in conjunction with Wisdom Literature (see Sneed 2015a). These types include literature like epics (Gilgamesh), creation accounts, hymns, erotica, omen texts, etc. Also, the study and copying of business or practical texts was usually part of the scribe's training. Mathematics, surveying, and music were studied as well. There were no scribal schools with Wisdom teachers where only Wisdom Literature was taught. Wisdom Literature was only one component, though certainly a very important one, in the training of scribes. From this perspective, the distinctiveness of Wisdom Literature points to its function within the scribal curriculum and training. Like other ancient Near Eastern Wisdom Literature, the biblical Wisdom Literature focuses largely on the domain of ethics and mores. Even for the more speculative books, like Job and Ecclesiastes, which focus on mitigating the problem of evil and suffering in the world, their ultimate aim is to provide advice for surviving and being successful in daily living, which has a heavy moral component.

Apparently, it was universally held that young scribes needed study in morality. It is not that the moral principles contained in the Wisdom Literature were first taught to a scribe when studying, say, the book of Proverbs. Consider the very first epigram in its earliest collection:

> A wise son pleases his father,
> Whereas a foolish son is sorrow to his mother   (10:1)[5]

---

[3] The problem is that we do not know for certain whether the sentences were actually used orally outside the small circle of scribes who composed and studied them. They were unlikely cited in conversation or debate, except among the scribes themselves (see Waltke 2004, 56), because they are epigrams (wise sayings coined by famous or elite persons). The superscriptions (1:1; 10:1; 22:17; 24:23; 25:1; 30:1; 31:1) identify them as such (composed by Solomon, "wise men," King Lemuel's mother, and Agur). Actual folk proverbs would not need such superscriptions because they would be current, and thus, common knowledge (for the full defense of this position, see Sneed 2019).

[4] Though Jacqueline Vayntrub (2016) rightly argues that the book of Proverbs itself cannot be used to extrapolate ancient Israelite pedagogy, this does not mean that Proverbs must be precluded from having served as part of Israel's scribal curriculum.

[5] All Hebrew citations are my own translation.

This teaches the importance of both being wise and bringing honor to one's parents. These are values that all Israelite children would undoubtedly have been taught at home as part of their early socialization. Thus, the early values inculcated in novice scribes when they were children are reinforced by the Wisdom Literature.

Fourth, beyond linguistic proficiency, it had an aesthetic function. It is not just morality or social mores that the Wisdom Literature reinforces. It also puts these moral principles in a pretty package. The sentences, in particular, are aesthetic delights. So, learning the basics of Hebrew poetry, in which all the biblical Wisdom Literature, as well as its ancient Near Eastern parallels, are written, and the subtleties of parallelism would have also served some purpose in the training of scribes. What purpose would that be? Scribes often assumed very practical roles of simply copying texts or serving as notaries or witnesses to contractual agreements. Would knowing the intricacies of Hebrew parallelism from epigrams that reinforced moral principles aid a scribe in his profession? Likely not. Understanding the intricacies of Hebrew poetry serves no practical function, as far as particular scribal skills.[6] However, it would have served a social function connected to the social class that the sages occupied. But before discussing this purpose, we need to discuss the Israelite social stratification broadly and the place that scribes occupied within it.

21.3 ISRAELITE SOCIAL STRATIFICATION

By the time that scribes were important officials or professionals working within ancient Israel or Judah, the nation(s) had become highly stratified into three main social classes. First, there was a governing class that consisted of the king, his family, and high officials, like the military commander and high priest. During the colonial periods, this class would be occupied by the priesthood and nobles. Directly below this class but attached to it would be the retainer class. As the name suggests, this class would serve the needs of the governing class and would include royal butlers, bakers, and cooks, as well as soldiers and lower level priests. Scribes would also be included in this stratum. One could not refer to this layer as a true middle class because it was not independent of the ruling class, which is what distinguishes our modern middle class (see Sneed 1999). The closest stratum to a form of middle class would have been merchants, but there is no indication that this was a sizeable group. The lowest stratum would consist mainly of peasants, though some peasants were wealthy. The most vulnerable would be widows, orphans, aliens, the poor in general, and the Levites (after Josiah's removal of local shrines). Slaves also formed their own social class, but their situation was probably better than that of the most vulnerable.

---

[6] Anne Stewart (2016, 1–69) argues, however, that Proverbs intentionally uses poetry to aid in the moral formation of its intended student audience.

21.4 The Wisdom Writers as Retainers

The composers of the biblical Wisdom Literature indirectly reflect their social location as retainers. On the one hand, this literature certainly did not arise from the lower classes (contra Golka 1993; Kimilike 2008).[7] That they were not peasants and part of the lower classes is indicated inferentially by the education level necessary in order to be able to compose high literature such as one finds in the case of biblical Wisdom Literature. Sociologists sometimes view level of education as a criterion for identification within a particular social class (Vander Zanden 1990, 166). Their education placed the scribes within a very elite and selective circle of individuals within ancient Israel. This is why Chris Rollston, who has done extensive research on the character of Israelite scribalism, argues that Israelite scribes would have been ranked very highly within Israelite society (2010, 85–90). Ranking or status signifies prestige, an important variable in social stratification, but it can impinge upon social class identity (more on this below under 21.5 Honor or Prestige). In ancient Egypt, literacy was 1 to 5 percent (Wente 1995, 2214), and we can assume the rate for ancient Israel would have been similar and would have largely been restricted to scribes. This meant that scribalism would have been considered highly valuable by the Israelite monarchy. Also, the education that scribes received provided them with career opportunities (messengers, diplomats, notaries, accountants, surveyors, officials, copyists, etc.) that were inaccessible to the vast majority of other Israelites.

That the Wisdom composers (or scribes) were not among the poor peasants or lower classes is also indicated by the way they refer to the poor as if they did not belong to that stratum. For example, Qoheleth refers to the "tears of the oppressed" (4:1) as though he were not among their number. Qoheleth also assumes that his audience would have typically been slave owners (7:21). Relatedly, several of the sentences in Proverbs assume that the poor are lazy (e.g., Prov 10:4), which is a notion with which the poor would not have likely concurred (see Sneed 2017a). Of course, this could be explained as due to the pedagogical intent of steering the novice scribes toward discipline in the continuation of their studies so that they avoid poverty. Yet it still implicitly indicates the social class of the intended audience.

Also, the doctrine of retribution, which the Wisdom Literature assumes as axiomatic, even for books that question it but do not completely reject it, like Job and Ecclesiastes, is inherently elitist and ideological.[8] It is the karmic notion that the wise and pious will live long and prosper, while the wicked and foolish will die young and fail. While many scholars have demonstrated that the doctrine is not held rigidly in all cases (e.g., Van Leeuwen 1992, 25–36), this does not detract from its function to legitimate the status quo, which makes it a quintessentially conservative mechanism.

---

[7] The first truly sociologically theoretical survey of this issue was Sneed 1994.

[8] Identifying a perspective or idea that is supposedly connected to a particular social class is known as class culture; see Sneed 1996.

One could also argue that the doctrine is held to more vigorously in Proverbs for the pedagogical purpose of motivating young scribes to take their studies seriously for success. But, again, this does not mitigate its ideological underpinning of a highly stratified society existing at the time the Wisdom books were composed. Even the quintessential skeptic, Qoheleth, though denying the doctrine's validity in its traditional formulation (7:15), also reformulates the doctrine into a notion that transcends the traditional definitions of righteousness/wickedness and wisdom/folly: God-fearing/non-God-fearing (2:26; 3:14; 5:6; 7:18; 8:12–13; see Sneed 2003).[9] Qoheleth's concept of God-fearing/non-God-fearing is apparently neither righteousness/wickedness, nor wisdom/folly, all in their traditional senses. Rather, Qoheleth attempts to create a new category beyond all these, but that still partakes in retribution. Thus, the doctrine of retribution is preserved after all!

On the other hand, the composers of the biblical Wisdom Literature were not among the wealthiest stratum of society, though earlier interpreters often categorized them as such.[10] Ranking these authors as upper class is not nuanced enough. An indication of this less-than-upper-class status is found in the sages' valuation of wisdom over wealth, even asserting that poverty is preferential to wealth if riches create ill effects within the family:

> Better a meal of vegetables and love there,
> Than a fatted cow and hatred there.   (Prov 15:17)

While the sages value wealth, they do not rank it as highly as would an aristocrat generally. But, simultaneously, the coining of this epigram also indicates that the sages were elitist because it does not resonate with the sentiments of the truly poor: they might prefer the fatted cow. The sages, thus, are comfortable enough to rank wisdom over wealth but not uncomfortable enough to avoid a certain naivety about the crushing reality of true poverty.

The Wisdom composers are also not among the most powerful, usually. While in ancient Ugarit scribes could rise in ranks to become mayors of cities, and Egyptian scribes could assume very high ranking, this does not appear to have been common in ancient Israel. The Israelite scribes' general lack of fundamental power is indicated more clearly in their oblique criticism of those with real power (e.g., Prov 16:14; 17:2; 21:22). Again, Qoheleth expresses this the most explicitly (e.g., 8:4–7). The scribes no doubt held power, especially if they served as governmental officials, which was a popular option for a scribe as indicated

---

[9] For a comprehensive treatment of the social location of Qoheleth, see Sneed 2012.

[10] E.g., von Rad 1972, 15–17; Gordis 1971, 162, 176; for Proverbs, Gottwald 1985, 574; for Qoheleth, Lang 1979, 118, 120–121; Müller 1978, 256, 258; Crüsemann 1984, 57–77; for Job, Clines 1995, 125; more recently, for Proverbs, Perdue 2008, 100. Some have intuitively sensed a lower-than-upper-class location for the authors of the Wisdom Literature but never use the terminology of a retainer class: for Proverbs: "upper-middle class elite" (Kovacs 1978, 448–450); "the wise belong to a privileged class" (Crenshaw 1990, 211–212); for Qoheleth, the author was not necessarily well-to-do, but his students were (Crenshaw 1987, 50).

by the many references to royal and temple scribes in Israel as well as the rest of the ancient Near East. But their power was always derived from the governing class that they served. This meant that they represented the governing class to the lower classes and in many ways served as its buffer (see Lenski 1984, 246). But scribes rarely held absolute power.

21.5 Honor or Prestige

In addition to social class, another factor is very important for understanding the biblical Wisdom Literature: prestige or honor. This is the German *Stand*, which is distinct from social class and power, though certainly related. Prestige is the social ranking of an individual, how much respect a person attracts to herself. These three variables, power, wealth, and prestige, resonate and reinforce each other. A person with wealth tends to have more power and prestige, but not always. For example, a mafia don has much wealth and power but only has prestige among his "family" members, not the general public, who would view him as corrupt and abusive. But usually the three variables correlate in mutual reinforcement, increasing a person's status.

Status is involved in the compensation the scribal retainer guild wielded in constructing their identities over against the other classes that have been mentioned. In the sentences in Proverbs, when a comparison is made between values, honor almost always takes priority over any other value. Even where it appears that honor might take second place to survival, honor usually ranks supreme. Consider Prov 12:9:

> Better to be dishonorable and own a slave,
> Than to play the great man and lack bread.

Here it is better to be disreputable yet wealthy, indicated by a slave-owning status, than to pretend to be a wealthy person and yet actually be destitute. In honor/shame cultures, one is allowed to boast about oneself, as long as it can be backed up with evidence. Here in this epigram, that is not the case. Actually, this person in the end becomes more dishonorable as a hypocrite than the man who makes no pretense about his lack of respectability yet is comfortable financially. Thus, this epigram is really comparing two kinds of dishonor and ranking one above the other.

The following epigram is more typical:

> Better a little with righteousness,
> Than much income without justice.   (Prov 16:8)

Here piety is ranked above wealth, which certainly resonates with the scribal attempts to compensate for their lack of wealth over against the members of the governing class. Of course, within the broader Israelite society, piety would at least be acknowledged by all as preferable to wealth. But for the scribes, piety was their particular means by which to accrue higher status, and they took this to another level.

A final example from Proverbs is 26:4–5, the notorious alignment of two apparently contradictory epigrams:

> Do not answer a fool according to his folly, lest you be like him.
> Answer a fool according to his folly, lest he become wise in his own eyes.

Understanding the honor culture of the Israelites helps resolve this conundrum (see Sneed 2015a, 272–274). The two epigrams assume a public challenge and riposte situation, much like the contexts of duels in the nineteenth-century United States. How one responds to an insult depends on the social status of the combatants. If the sage is of superior status (e.g., a retainer before a poor peasant), the insult can safely be ignored (v. 4). But if the two combatants are of equal status or the lower-status insulter will not give up his attack, then the sage must respond or lose face (be shamed) (v. 5). He must put the fool in his place!

Though at first glance unexpected, Ecclesiastes also is concerned with honor; it focuses specifically on how honor does not accrue always to those who are wise or pious. The world does not operate as it should, according to Qoheleth. For example, in 6:1–2 he is alarmed about the Ptolemies' disenfranchisement of one of his wealthy country-men (see Lauha 1981, 400–401), whom God gives wealth and honor but not the ability to enjoy them. He calls this a "grievous illness" or "worthless." The latter term translates הבל, which is used thirty-eight times in the book, and functions as its leitmotif. It speci-fies the lack of value, thereby expressing the notion of futility or worthlessness. This lack of value in the world causes Qoheleth to resign himself to another value, simple pleasure (Maussion 2005, 501–510), inspiring his carpe diem ethic (2:24; 3:12–13, 22; 5:18–20; 8:15; 9:7–10; 11:7–10), which, though it has liabilities, is preferable to disappointment con-nected to human striving after profit (see Sneed 2017b, 893–894).

The honor/shame paradigm is reflected also in Job in that Job's loss of all his wealth simultaneously meant that he lost his status as well (29:7–12; 30:9–12) (see Bechtel 1997, 255–256). This shows how wealth and status often correlate, even if not completely. Also, Job's challenging of God is eventually returned with God's riposte in the divine speeches (see Sneed 2015a, 337–339). Someone of God's stature could certainly afford to ignore Job's pleas, but God finally has enough and shames and humiliates Job in the divine speeches for challenging the deity's justice. That Job understood God's response as dressing him down is indicated in his emphatically deferential responses, including his "repentance" (40:3–4; 42:1–6).

21.6 THE FOCUS ON ETHICS AND AESTHETICS

As retainers, the scribes' identity could never be constructed in terms of fundamental power or great wealth. Rather, their identity appears to have been conceived through their expertise in wisdom and piety. In Pierre Bourdieu's *Distinctions* (2010), he argues that social classes construct themselves over against other classes in the perennial competition for supremacy. Using statistics from vast surveys in 1960s France, Bourdieu discerned two common strategies for the petite-bourgeoisie, what we would call the middle class. Since this class lacks the required wealth to compete within the actual bourgeoisie or the upper class, they had to focus on other variables. Instead of economic capital, which they lacked, they compensated by focusing on cultural capital.[11] For example, artists, who are inherently members of the petite-bourgeoisie, actually vaunt the lack of utility of their productions—art for art's sake—in order to project an elitist notion of art that focuses more on form than substance. The more abstract the art is and the less utilitarian, ironically, the more valuable it is financially, which the truly rich are eager to purchase. Professors also compensate for their lack of economic capital by their specialization in their respective fields, and, as experts, they cannot be easily ignored by the bourgeoisie. School teachers also often compensate by what Bourdieu calls "aristocratic asceticism," focusing on their morality and integrity as opposed to wealth or social connections in constructing their identity (Bourdieu 2010, 217).

This helps explain two things about the book of Proverbs. The first is its focus on form over substance in the design of the sentences (epigrams). Robert Alter (1985, 163–184) has demonstrated the literary sophistication of this small but widespread genre. The sentences' brevity, in fact, is part of their aesthetic effect. The bicolon structure of the sentences provides the framework for a wide range of creativity that essentially functions as a resonation between the cola. This degree of sophistication is not characteristic of folk proverbs. The principles that the sentences convey are usually banal, not profound: be wise, honor parents, value wisdom over wealth, etc. But the nice package in which the scribe encapsulates them truly distinguishes them and demonstrates that the scribes who composed the Wisdom Literature had a taste for literary aesthetics, which is a type of wisdom:

> Let the wise hear and increase learning,
> And let the insightful attain wise counsel,
> For understanding an aphorism and enigma,
> The words of the wise and their riddles.   (Prov 1:5–6)

Secondly, it explains the fixation, almost obsession, that the biblical (as well as the ancient Near Eastern) Wisdom Literature has for morality and ethics. This reveals a focus on "aristocratic asceticism" among the scribes who composed and studied the Wisdom Literature. In other words, the scribes appear to identify themselves over against the other social classes in ancient Israel by means of their moral and social discipline, by their piety and integrity.[12] It is what they could do better than Israelites from other

---

[11] On cultural versus economic capital, see Bourdieu 1993.

[12] Other groups within the retainer class, such as the cultic professions, including priests and prophets, would have used the same strategy.

classes. On the one hand, the governing class often must resort to Machiavellian tactics in order to govern and can afford to dispense with morality when it is advantageous. On the other hand, for the poor, who are perennially fatigued and hungry, practicing the nuances of morality is not usually a priority. Survival is the name of the game with them.

Thus, the focus on formality, especially literary aesthetics, and ethics in the biblical Wisdom Literature distinguishes its original composers and readers from both the governing class above and the poor below. The wise who composed our Wisdom Literature identified themselves over against both the peasants beneath them and their superiors above them. Their form of compensation for their lack of economic capital was to focus and develop their literary skills, which brought them much respect and admiration from the other classes. But by focusing on developing personal piety and integrity, they could attain a form of social leverage that they could muster when negotiating the social terrain (see Sneed 2019).

21.7 WISDOM AND GENDER

Another important social variable reflected in the biblical Wisdom Literature is gender. The intended audience is clearly male; the addressee's gender in both Proverbs and Ecclesiastes is identified: "my son." It is no surprise that there is no "Mister Wisdom" who woos females to come follow after him. There also is no "Ode to the Virtuous Man" that would correlate with the description on the ideal wife in Prov 31:10–31. There are also epigrams that value the attainment of a good woman (e.g., Prov 18:22) but not the reverse. The book of Proverbs contains four epigrams (19:13; 21:9; 21:19; 27:15–16) about the stereotypical, nagging wife, but no male corollary. The Wisdom books exude a clear androcentric perspective.

But what about Woman Wisdom (and the closely related Virtuous Woman [Prov 31:10–31])? She has often been positively evaluated by many feminist biblical scholars.[13] Claudia Camp (1985, 116, 120, 286, 290–291; cf. Camp 1990, 190–194) believes her to be a symbolic replacement of the then-defunct monarchy (in the Persian period when Proverbs reached its final form); with her, the home becomes prominent, and she helps promote egalitarian values.Similarly, Silvia Schroer (1995, 68, 71) believes Woman Wisdom is a post-exilic figure who "is the one and only acceptable feminine image of God in ancient Israel." She shares elements of the goddess figure. Also, Christine Roy Yoder (2003) connects Woman Wisdom with the Virtuous Woman in Prov 31:10–31, whom she argues reflects elite Persian period women generally, even if the portrait is from a male perspective. And, finally, Carol Meyers (2013, esp. 191) draws on Prov 31, among a number of texts and archaeological evidence, to argue that Israelite women, especially peasants, were not subordinated to men to an extent justifying the term "patriarchal society."

[13] See the article by Christine Roy Yoder in this volume.

However, Woman Wisdom is, in fact, perhaps the most androcentric figure in the entire Hebrew Bible. Other feminists agree. Carol Newsom (1989) argues that Woman Wisdom, couched in the voice of the father, essentially serves to ground patriarchal authority in the transcendent realm. And referring to both the figures of Woman Wisdom and the Virtuous Woman, Carol Fontaine (1995, 25) maintains they "may be inversely proportional to the truth of real women's lives. That is, such fine figures may just as easily be an index of women's lack of power and status as a reflection of a gentler, kinder social reality for women."

Woman Wisdom's seduction of young men infers that the only ones who might be attracted to her will be masculine; thus, wisdom, at least in the highly refined sense that Proverbs defines it, is the prerogative of males only (see Sneed 2007). The ideal Israelite woman could and should have been wise, but she could never attain the type of scribal wisdom that Proverbs lauds and propagates (1:6), since females were excluded from this vocation.[14] This would be largely true for most males as well. Only a select group of elite males were trained as scribes in ancient Israel.

That the sages were androcentric cannot be denied, but whether they were misogynistic as well is open for debate. Ben Sira (26:12; 42:14) comes very close, but for Qoheleth, who in 7:23–29 appears to describe women as a trap, the evidence is less clear. Both notable Wisdom experts Choon-Leong Seow (1997, 262–263) and Katharine Dell (2013, 91–94) have argued that this woman is not women in general but perhaps Woman Folly; however, I am not convinced.

21.8 WISDOM AND AGE (IMPLIED/INTENDED AUDIENCE)

A final social variable that needs discussing is age, particularly the age and maturity of the implied audience. While scholars used to assume that the intended audience of the book of Proverbs was mainly young men (e.g., 1:4), most today also recognize that for parts of the book, like the long introduction of chs. 1–9, the intended or implied audience might be more sophisticated. Stuart Weeks (2007) has most persuasively made this case. Yet, the sentence collections could certainly have served to train new scribes because the genre is so short. There are epigrams, however, that assume that the reader might be older, either already married (e.g., Prov 5:15) or even selecting a wife for a son (e.g., 19:14). There are also epigrams that are more relatable to grandparents than young scribes (e.g., 17:6). Ecclesiastes also indicates a young male audience (11:9), though his book was probably reserved for more advanced studies.

[14] While there were a few female scribes in ancient Mesopotamia (see Harris 1990, 3–17) and Egypt, there is no evidence of any among the Israelites. The role of prophetess appears to be the one legitimate professional role outside of the domestic setting which Israelite women could assume. This would mean that the Israelite scribes were similar to the priests in generally excluding females within their guild.

Recently, scholars have attempted to pinpoint the implied audience of Proverbs, but there is no consensus. Michael Fox (2000, 80–81) interprets בני/בנים "sons" literally, even if by convention. Fox also views the original audience as "the king's men," at least for chs. 10–29, whom he does not believe were scribes (Fox 1996, 234–239; Fox 2009, 504–505; cf. Ansberry 2011, 49, 69–70, 184–190). Richard Clifford (2017) refers to an original scribal audience but argues that the compositional history of Proverbs indicates that its intended audience was broadened apparently to a general public, much like Leviticus's redactional history indicates a pivot from priests alone to a broader readership. Author Keefer (2017) argues that the "wise" are the intended audience, not the "youths," whereas Timothy Sandoval (2007) argues that neither group is clearly in mind but a more subtly constructed audience.

21.9 SUMMARY

Though the biblical Wisdom Literature does not easily reveal its social setting, largely due to rhetorical and ideological reasons, significant features of that setting emerge with a little teasing. Wisdom Literature throughout the ancient Near East, including ancient Israel, was used in the training of young scribes (Proverbs implies a possible mature audience as well) for both linguistic and rhetorical proficiency but also for training in morality. The honing of aesthetic skills and the fixation on ethics reflected in the biblical Wisdom Literature (perhaps a similar phenomenon in the broader ancient Near East?), might have been a way that the scribal guild constructed its identity over against the other classes in Israelite stratification. The guild's forte was cultural, not economic, capital, and its perspective was also heavily androcentric. The biblical Wisdom Literature reveals both its composers' and audience's retainer-class status as well as their search for high prestige, which reflects the concern for honor and shame that was part of Israelite society as a whole.

WORKS CITED

Alster, Bendt. 1997. *Proverbs of Ancient Sumer: The World's Earliest Proverb Collections*, vol. 1. Bethesda, MD: CDL.

Alter, Robert. 1985. *The Art of Biblical Poetry*. New York: Basic Books.

Ansberry, Christopher B. 2011. *Be Wise, My Son, and Make My Heart Glad: An Exploration of the Courtly Nature of the Book of Proverbs*. BZAW 422. Berlin: de Gruyter.

Bechtel, Lynn M. 1997. "Shame as a Sanction of Social Control in Biblical Israel: Judicial, Political, and Social Shaming." Pages 232–258 in *Social-Scientific Old Testament Criticism: A Sheffield Reader*. BibSem 47. Edited by David Chalcraft. Sheffield: Sheffield Academic.

Bourdieu, Pierre. 1993. *The Field of Cultural Production*. European Perspectives. New York, NY: Columbia University Press.

Bourdieu, Pierre. 2010. *Distinction: A Social Critique of the Judgement of Taste*. Translated by Richard Nice. Routledge Classics. London: Routledge.

Camp, Claudia V. 1985. *Wisdom and the Feminine in the Book of Proverbs*. BLS 11. Sheffield: Almond.

Camp, Claudia V. 1990. "The Female Sage in the Biblical Wisdom Literature." Pages 185–203 in Gammie and Perdue 1990.

Carr, David M. 2005. *Writing on the Tablet of the Heart*. Oxford: Oxford University Press.

Clifford, Richard J. 2017. "Proverbs 1–9 as Instruction for a Young Man and 'Everyman.'" Pages 129–141 in *"When the Morning Stars Sang": Essays in Honor of Choon Leong Seow on the Occasion of his Sixty-Fifth Birthday*. Edited by Scott C. Jones and Christine Roy Yoder. BZAW 500. Berlin: de Gruyter.

Clines, David J.A. 1995. *Interested Parties: The Ideologies of Writers and Readers of the Hebrew Bible*. JSOTSup 205; GCT 1. Sheffield: Sheffield Academic Press.

Crenshaw, James L. 1987. *Ecclesiastes*. OTL. Philadelphia, PA: Westminster.

Crenshaw, James L. 1990. "The Sage in Proverbs." Pages 205–216 in Gammie and Perdue 1990.

Crenshaw, James L. 2010. *Old Testament Wisdom: An Introduction*. 3rd ed. Atlanta, GA: Westminster John Knox.

Crüsemann, Frank. 1984. "The Unchangeable World: The "Crisis of Wisdom" in Koheleth." Pages 57–77 in *God of the Lowly: Socio-Historical Interpretations of the Bible*. Edited by Willy Schottroff, and Wolfgang Stegemann. Translated by Matthew J. O'Connell. Maryknoll, NY: Orbis Books.

Dell, Katharine J. 2013. *Interpreting Ecclesiastes: Readers Old and New*. CSHB 3. Winona Lake, IN: Eisenbrauns.

Eagleton, Terry. 1991. *Ideology: An Introduction*. London: Verso.

Fontaine, Carol R. 1995. "The Social Roles of Women in the World of Wisdom." Pages 24–49 in *Feminist Companion to Wisdom Literature*. Edited by Athalya Brenner. FCB 9. Sheffield: Sheffield Academic.

Fox, Michael V. 1996. "The Social Location of the Book of Proverbs." Pages 227–39 in *Texts, Temples, and Traditions: A Tribute to Menahem Haran*. Edited by Michael V. Fox. Winona Lake, IN: Eisenbrauns.

Fox, Michael V. 2000. *Proverbs 1–9*. AB. New York, NY: Doubleday.

Fox, Michael V. 2009. *Proverbs 10–31*. AB 18B. New Haven, CT: Yale University Press.

Fox, Michael V. 2015. "Three Theses on Wisdom." Pages 69–86 in *Is There a Wisdom Tradition? New Prospects in Israelite Wisdom Studies*. AIL 23. Edited by Mark Sneed. Atlanta, GA: SBL.

Gammie, John, and Leo Perdue, eds. 1990. *The Sage in Israel and the Ancient Near East*. Winona Lake, IN: Eisenbrauns.

Golka, Friedemann W. 1993. *The Leopard's Spots: Biblical and African Wisdom in Proverbs*. Edinburgh: T&T Clark.

Gordis, Robert. 1971. *Poets, Prophets, and Sages*. Bloomington, IN: Indiana University.

Gottwald, Norman. 1985. *The Hebrew Bible—A Socio-Literary Introduction*. Philadelphia, PA: Fortress.

Harris, Rivkah. 1990. "The Female 'Sage' in Mesopotamian Literature (with an Appendix on Egypt)." Pages 3–17 in Gammie and Perdue 1990.

Keefer, Arthur. 2017. "A Shift in Perspective: The Intended Audience and a Coherent Reading of Proverbs 1:1–17." *JBL* 136:103–116.

Kimilike, Lechion Peter. 2008. *Poverty in the Book of Proverbs: An African Transformational Hermeneutic of Proverbs of Poverty*. BTA 7. New York, NY: Lang.

Kovacs, Brian. 1978. "Sociological-Structural Constraints upon Wisdom." Ph.D. Diss., Vanderbilt University.

Lang, Bernhard. 1979. "Ist der Mensch hilflos? Das biblische Buch Koheleth, neu und kritisch gelesen." *TQ* 159:109–204.

Lauha, Aare. 1981. "Kohelets Verhältnis zur Geschichte." Pages 393–401 in *Die Botschaft und die Boten: Festschrift für Hans Walter Wolff zum 70. Geburtstag.* Edited by Jörg Jeremias and Lothar Perlit. Nekirchen-Vlykn: Neukirchener Verlag.

Lemaire, André. 1984. "Sagesse et ecoles." *VT* 34:271–281.

Lenski, Gerhard. 1984. *Power and Privilege: A Theory of Stratification.* New York, NY: McGraw-Hill, 1966. Repr., Chapel Hill, NC: University of North Carolina.

Maussion, Marie. 2005. "Qohélet VI 1–2: 'Dieu ne permet pas ….'" *VT* 55:501–510.

Meyers, Carol. 2013. *Rediscovering Eve: Ancient Israelite Women in Context.* Oxford: Oxford University Press.

Müller, Hans-Peter. 1978. "Neige der althebräischen 'Weisheit.'" *ZAW* 90:238–263.

Newsom, Carol. 1989. "Woman and the Discourse of Patriarchal Wisdom: A Study of Proverbs 1–9." Pages 142–160 in *Gender and Difference in Ancient Israel.* Edited by Peggy L. Day. Minneapolis, MN: Fortress.

Perdue, Leo G. 2008. *The Sword and the Stylus: An Introduction to Wisdom in the Age of Empires.* Grand Rapids, MI: Eerdmans.

Rad, Gerhard von. 1972. *Wisdom in Israel.* Translated by James D. Martin. Nashville, TN: Abingdon.

Rollston, Christopher A. 2010. *Writing and Literacy in the World of Ancient Israel: Epigraphic Evidence from the Iron Age.* ABS 11. Atlanta, GA: SBL.

Sandoval, Timothy J. 2007. "Revisiting the Prologue of Proverbs." *JBL* 126:455–473.

Schroer, Silvia. 1995. "Wise and Counseling Women in Ancient Israel: Literary and Historical Ideals of the Personified *HOKMÁ.*" Pages 67–84 in *Feminist Companion to Wisdom Literature.* Edited by Athalya Brenner. FCB 9. Sheffield: Sheffield Academic.

Seow, C.L. 1997. *Ecclesiastes.* AB 18C. New York, NY: Doubleday.

Sneed, Mark. 1994. "Wisdom and Class: A Review and Critique." *JAAR* 62:651–672.

Sneed, Mark. 1996. "The Class Culture of Proverbs: Eliminating Stereotypes." *SJOT* 10:296–308.

Sneed, Mark. 1998. "The Social Location of the Book of Qoheleth." *HS* 39:41–51.

Sneed, Mark. 1999. "A Middle Class in Ancient Israel?" Pages 53–69 in *Concepts of Class in Ancient Israel.* USFSHJ; HSTW 201. Atlanta, GA: Scholars.

Sneed, Mark. 2003. "A Note on Qoh 8,12b–13." *Bib* 84:412–416.

Sneed, Mark. 2007. "'White Trash' Wisdom: Proverbs 9 Deconstructed." *JHebS* article 7, http://www.jhsonline.org/cocoon/JHS/a066.html.

Sneed, Mark. 2011. "Is the 'Wisdom Tradition' a Tradition?" *CBQ* 73:50–71.

Sneed, Mark. 2012. *The Politics of Pessimism: A Socio-Literary Perspective.* AIL12. Atlanta, GA: SBL.

Sneed, Mark. 2015a. *The Social World of the Sages: An Introduction to Israelite and Jewish Wisdom Literature.* Minneapolis, MN: Fortress.

Sneed, Mark. 2015b. "'Grasping after the Wind': The Elusive Attempt to Define Wisdom." Pages 39–67 in *Is There a Wisdom Tradition? New Prospects in Israelite Wisdom Studies.* AIL 23. Edited by Mark Sneed. Atlanta, GA: SBL.

Sneed, Mark. 2017a. "Lazy, Idle; Laziness, Idleness in the HB/OT." In *Encyclopedia of the Bible Online.* 2017. Berlin: de Gruyter, https://www.degruyter.com/view/EBR/key_7f59c79a–fd3c–4dc4–9255–4c7ec3d0390e.

Sneed, Mark. 2017b. "הֶבֶל as 'Worthless' in Qoheleth: A Critique of Michael V. Fox's 'Absurd' Thesis." *JBL* 136:879–894.

Sneed, Mark. 2018. "Methods, Muddles, and Modes of Literature: The Question of Influence between Wisdom and Prophecy." Pages 30–44 in *Riddles and Revelations: Explorations into the Relationship between Wisdom and Prophecy in the Hebrew Bible*. LHBOTS 634. Edited by Mark J. Boda, Russell L. Meek, and Rusty Osborne. London: Bloomsbury T&T Clark.

Sneed, Mark. 2019. "A Taste for Wisdom: Aesthetics, Moral Discernment, and Social Class in Proverbs." Pages 111–126 in *Imagined Worlds and Constructed Differences*. Edited by Jeremiah Cataldo. LHBOTS 677. London: Bloomsbury T&T Clark.

Sneed, Mark. Forthcoming. "Inspired Sages: *Massa'* and the Confluence of Wisdom and Prophecy." In *Scribes as Sages and Prophets*. BZAW 496. Edited by Jutta Krispenz. Berlin: de Gruyter.

Stewart, Anne W. 2016. *Poetic Ethics in Proverbs: Wisdom Literature and the Shaping of the Moral Self*. Cambridge: Cambridge University Press.

Toorn, Karel van der. 2007. *Scribal Culture and the Making of the Hebrew Bible*. Cambridge, MA: Harvard University Press.

Van Leeuwen, Raymond C. 1992. "Wealth and Poverty: System and Contradiction in Proverbs." *HS* 33:25–36.

Vander Zanden, James W. 1993. *Sociology: The Core*. New York, NY: McGraw-Hill.

Vayntrub, Jacqueline. 2016. "The Book of Proverbs and the Idea of Ancient Israelite Education." *ZAW* 128:96–114.

Veldhuis, Niek. 2000. "Sumerian Proverbs in their Curricular Context." *JAOS* 120:383–387.

Waltke, Bruce K. 2004. *Proverbs 1–15*. NICOT. Grand Rapids, MI: Eerdmans.

Weeks, Stuart. 2007. *Instruction and Imagery in Proverbs 1–9*. New York, NY: Oxford University Press.

Wente, Edward. 1995. "The Scribes of Ancient Egypt." Pages 2211–2221 in vol. 4 of *Civilizations of the Ancient Near East*. Edited by Jack M. Sasson. New York, NY: Charles Scribner's Sons.

Yoder, Christine Roy. 2003. "The Woman of Substance (אשת חיל): A Socioeconomic Reading of Proverbs 31:10–31." *JBL* 122:427–447.

CHAPTER 22

....

LITERARY GENRES OF OLD TESTAMENT WISDOM

....

MARKUS WITTE

22.1 ON THE PATH TO A LITERARY GENRE

22.1.1 Fundamental Aspects of Classification

Amongst the basic tools humans have for finding their way in the world and shaping their own lives belongs the classification of phenomena.[1] The continual conscious or unconscious comparison, ordering, and grouping of experiences and perceptions provides the foundation for life and survival in an often-inscrutable world. Classification here encompasses, in equal measure, natural phenomena, societal behavior, and manufactured items. Individual patterns of order reflect specific geographical, societal, and linguistic characteristics. Classifications, even those that are fundamentally timeless, are contingent upon culture and period. The more nuanced and complex the life of humanity and the perception of reality become, the more diverse the objects that are classified and the criteria according to which they are classified.

Classification serves not just to secure existence and form identity, however; rather, it is a prerequisite for, and an aspect of, communication. The classification of literature as a complex form of communication thus entails nuanced orders of categorization. Whenever a written text comes into being, this goes hand in hand with the allocation of that work to specific groups of texts. And so, already at the end of the third millennium

[1] I warmly thank Josephine Draper (Oxford/Berlin) for the translation of this article from German into English.

and in the early second millennium BCE, classifications of (for the most part anonymously written and anonymously passed down) texts into specific textual groups (e.g.,
prayers, rituals) is evidenced for the ancient Near East and Egypt. Primarily linguistic,
structural, situational, thematic, and pragmatic criteria are used for this. In the field of
ancient Greek and Roman literature, increasingly authorial criteria—that is, criteria that
are focused on (putative) authors—also appear. Occasionally, the texts themselves offer
relevant information on their own textual category, usage, purpose, author, or tradents
in a heading or colophon. Archives, libraries, and schools located in the vicinity of palaces and temples make a significant contribution to this literary classification. In these
institutions, a specific canon of textual categories is established, with a view to various
different social and functional areas (the everyday, cult, politics, the law, entertainment,
knowledge). Individual real or fictional authors are assigned a paradigmatic significance. Individual genres thereby receive an authoritative and normative character.

The same criteria for classification that are found in Mesopotamia, Egypt, and Greece
are generally seen for the field of Israelite-Jewish literature, even though the archaeological evidence of archives, libraries, and schools in pre-Hellenistic Israel und Judah
is disputed. Nevertheless, details in the Hebrew Bible, sociological considerations, and
the textual findings from Elephantine (fifth century BCE) suggest that in pre-Hellenistic
Judaism too, there were equivalent institutions. The findings from Tell Deir 'Alla in the
East Jordan Valley also point in this direction, in that the building on whose walls the
Aramaic Balaam inscription (eighth century BCE) was written could have been a school
(Blum 2016).

Since the Persian and Hellenistic period, at the latest, one has been able to find in
Judaism: (1) inner-textual statements on textual categories, situations of use, and writers
(cf. Ps 7:1; Prov 1:1; Eccl 1:1; Lam 1:1 LXX); (2) extra-textual statements on authors and
genres (cf. 11Q5 27:2–11; Sir 47:8–9, 14–17); and (3) locations of systematic collections of
literature (cf. 2 Macc 2:13–15 and the Dead Sea Scroll discoveries).

22.1.2 Phases of Old Testament Genre Research

The allocation of a specific text to a concrete genre, like any classification, fundamentally
touches upon three temporal periods: it takes place always from the perspective of looking back on the text that has been produced, it aims at attaining present understanding,
and it establishes a pattern for future texts and future understanding. Therefore, the literary classification that is made is subject to transitions in language and in understanding. Definitions of genres are never static, and should not be either, if they wish to keep
their orientating and normative function. Different genre classifications may be useful
at different times. A particular problem arises when classifying texts as communication
in written form when the texts to be classified originate from a different linguistic region
and a different cultural milieu from the person who is doing the classification. These transitions and problems, which are fundamentally conditional upon culture and hermeneutics, are reflected in a variety of ways in the history of Old Testament genre research.

Modern classification of biblical literature—and thereby also of the Wisdom texts of the Old Testament—has its foundations in the discussion on genre typology that took place in the eighteenth century. The lectures given by Oxford professor of rhetoric Robert Lowth on the sacred poetry of the Hebrews (1753) were ground-breaking here. Based on the triad of *epic*, *lyric*, and *drama* that dominated in the eighteenth century and originated in the genre typology of Greek and Roman literature, Lowth presented Proverbs, Ecclesiastes, and Ben Sira, as well as alphabetic psalms, under the heading "משלים *sive carmina didactica* [didactic songs]." Lowth identified the individual saying (משל), or more precisely, the parable and aphorism, as the basic form of didactic poetry. He distinguished didactic poetry from dramatic poetry, his classification for Job, prophetic poetry (נבואה), and lyric, sub-divided into elegy (קינה), ode (שיר), and hymn (שיר) (cf. Witte 2018). The goal of his lectures was to extol the aesthetic substance of biblical poetry and promote its communication to contemporary readers. Characteristic of Lowth's typology is that, on the one hand, he draws on genre identifications that originate in the writings of the Hebrew Bible itself, and, on the other hand, he takes his primary criteria for determining the genres (*genera* and *species*) from Greek and Roman poetry. Lowth's comparison of biblical poetry with Homer, Sophocles, Pindar, and Horace moves entirely in the footsteps of the focus on paradigmatic authors that was already undertaken in antiquity itself.

It was at this point that criticism came from Johann Gottfried Herder. Herder, who, alongside Johann David Michaelis, contributed significantly to the dissemination of Lowth's lectures throughout Europe, accused Lowth of classifying biblical poetry according to a schema that was alien to it. According to Herder, when determining a genre, it is not only the identifications contained within a text that must be taken into account, but, above all, the living world that the individual texts stem from. In his unfinished work *Vom Geist der Ebräischen Poesie* (1782/83), which shares with Lowth's lectures an interest in the aesthetics of the biblical texts, Herder tried to derive two basic genres of Hebrew poetry from the Israelite culture and mentality: (1) the *saying* (משל), understood as figurative speech, and (2) the *song*. Herder at the same time differentiated figurative speech according to *function* and *time*: "In der Bilderrede spricht Einer; er lehret, straft, tröstet, unterrichtet, lobpreiset, sieht die Vergangenheit und enthüllet die Zukunft" (Herder 1879–1880 [1783], 22). This definition then results, *sociologically* speaking, in assigning the use of the משל to teachers of wisdom and prophets, and, *functionally* speaking, in the distinction between paraenesis, paraclesis, interpretation, and doxology. The contrast to Lowth can be seen, for example, in Herder's identification of the book of Job as an Eastern "*Consessus* einiger Weisen" ("assembly of wise men") (Herder 1879–1880 [1782], 314).

Herder's admonition to understand Hebrew poetry in its ancient Near Eastern context defined further nineteenth-century genre research. After medieval and modern-era poetry from the Near and Middle East had been made accessible by William Jones (1777), and its fruits spread by Johann Gottfried Eichhorn, the classification of Hebrew literature within the context of Levantine and Near Eastern literature was strongly influenced by the extensive textual findings in Egypt and Mesopotamia. Thus, in the field of

Wisdom Literature especially, the genre typology that had existed from the second half of the nineteenth century onwards, which had focused on classical antiquity, was gradually superseded by an Eastern paradigm. Thanks to the discovery of archives and libraries in Babylon, Ur, and Nineveh, it gained entirely new momentum.

Within the program of his biblical literary history, Hermann Gunkel (1906/1913) brought the comparison between the biblical texts and the literature of Mesopotamia and Egypt to a synthesis. At the same time, Gunkel arrived at an epoch-defining identification of three essential genre parameters: (1) linguistic structure, (2) content, and (3) socio-cultural use (*Sitz im Leben*). Gunkel's literary-historical synthesis was accompanied by Hugo Gressmann's compilation of important comparison texts from the ancient Near East. Gressman's anthology (1906/1926), which was organized according to geographical area and genre, for the first time offered easy access to a representative selection of Egyptian, Babylonian-Assyrian, North Semitic, and ancient South Arabian texts, among which were Egyptian collections of sayings and instructions (such as the Instruction of Amenemope, important for the tradition history of Prov 22:17–24:22), Mesopotamian Wisdom sayings, didactic dialogues, and fables, and the Aramaic Ahiqar sayings. With their programme of writing literary history as genre history and as cultural history, Gunkel and Gressmann were standing on the shoulders of Herder and Ernst Meier (1856). At the same time, they paved the way for pivotal genre-historical and religious-historical compilations such as *Ancient Near Eastern Texts Relating to the Old Testament* (1955, 1969), *Texte aus der Umwelt des Alten Testaments* (1982–2001, 2004–2018), and *The Context of Scripture* (1997–2002, 2016), which likewise offered a selection of ancient Near Eastern texts classified by genre, linguistic region, and cultural area.

Further research, right up to the present day, has worked tirelessly with Gunkel's criteria—and on his program of a biblical literary history, which, despite isolated attempts, has not been satisfactorily implemented. The comparative material, enormously increased since the first half of the twentieth century thanks to the discoveries of the archives at Elephantine, Ugarit (*Rash Shamra*), and Qumran, and developments in linguistics and literary studies in the second half of the twentieth century, can be read as comprehensive commentaries on Gunkel's tripartite typology. Attempts to distinguish between linguistic structure and content more strongly than Gunkel did have not proved successful. Attempts to use the terms form and genre synonymously have been equally unrewarding. Thus, when determining a genre, form and content cannot be strictly separated from one another, and form and genre are not identical. The term *form* denotes the linguistic structure of a specific text. The term *genre*, on the other hand, refers to the over-arching paradigm to which texts with comparable linguistic features, content, and uses can be assigned. Thus, it would be more accurate to speak of Gunkel's approach as "genre criticism" than "form criticism" (cf. Barton 1992; Blum 2003). However, in more recent research, the objective of genre determination has shifted relative to Gunkel. Gunkel aimed at locating individual genres within the *oral* tradition, reconstructing original usage, and identifying original institutions. Contemporary genre research focuses on the question of *literary* genres and the functions these have within the individual texts (cf. Knierim and Tucker in Murphy 1981, x).

There are primarily three factors responsible for this shift away from the background of a text towards the text itself:

1. the *literary-aesthetic view* that grew concurrently to Gunkel, classically demonstrated in Richard G. Moulton's *Literary Study of the Bible* (1896), which devotes itself above all to the poetic and rhetorical structures of a text and the effects it has upon the reader;
2. *redaction-critical research*, which, proceeding from the "final text," traces the literary and material profile of the successive *Fortschreibungen* ("revisions") of a text;
3. the recognition of the categorial *difference between oral and written texts* and the methodological difficulty connected with reconstructing the, presumably preceding, oral tradition on the basis of a written text.

We are currently seeing another shift in the line of enquiry of genre criticism, thanks to the particular interest in the *reception aesthetics* and *reception history* of biblical texts. In other words: Gunkel's question concerning the *Sitz im Leben* of a genre has been joined by questions concerning its *Sitz in der Literatur* ("location in the literature") and *Sitz in der Welt der Leser* ("location in the world of the reader") (cf. Melugin 2003).

22.2 CHARACTERISTICS OF A WISDOM GENRE

22.2.1 General and Specific Parameters of a Genre

If one still focuses on Gunkel's criteria, taking into consideration more recent linguistic and literary knowledge, then three *general parameters* for determining an oral or written genre may be specified:

1. *Communication level.* Communication between people (*horizontal communication*) is distinguished from communication between people and a deity (*vertical communication*). In the latter case, if the direction is from the person to the deity, one could be dealing with a prayer; if the direction is from the deity to the person, perhaps an oracle or a blessing.
2. *Morphological, syntactic, and morpho-syntactic phenomena.* For example, an imperative or a conditional clause.
3. *Function.* For example, to instruct, thank, admonish, inform, interpret, praise, standardize, or regulate.

However, there are also three *specific* parameters that must be added to the three general parameters:

1. *Content* and *subject*;
2. Specific *words* (*lexemes*) and *word combinations* (*syntagms*);
3. Concrete *situation* of use, that is, the sociological location and context.

These three parameters bear a mutual relation to one another:

Parameters of a genre		
communication level	language (morphology, syntax)	function
↕	↕	↕
content and subject	language (lexemes, syntagms)	situation

Stylistic devices, including phenomena frequently investigated in more recent research, such as allegory, metaphor, and paranomasia, rhythm, or "poetry" and "prose," are certainly central factors when it comes to describing and differentiating texts. However, it is not characteristics of a genre that are at issue here, even if certain genres are primarily poetic or prosaic in nature or more strongly marked stylistically than others. Studies on poetics or rhetoric go alongside genre research, but they do not replace it (cf., e.g., König 1900; Watson 1984; Alonso Schökel 1988; Fokkelman 1998; Luchsinger 2010). The same goes for the practice that emerged out of structuralism of breaking down a text into *movements* and *segments*, where the true *plot* and literary *genre* of a text are extracted from the interplay of those elements, as well as from the use and deliberate misuse of traditional forms (cf. Habel 1985; Dell 1991, 109–157).

22.2.2 General and Specific Parameters of a Wisdom Genre

Essential *general characteristics* of a Wisdom genre are:

1. horizontal communication;
2. formulations in the imperative, adhortative or deliberative, or questions;
3. a function that is instructive (didactic, paraenetic), incites reflection (is discursive, confrontational, critical, meditative), or one that combines these (resultative), which focuses on the act of persuasion (persuasive) and motivates one to a particular action or is directive—that is, schooling.

In addition, there are *specific characteristics*:

1. content that encompasses human life in its entirety;
2. words and phrases that make reference to knowledge, teaching and learning, reasoning, ethics, and orientation in the world;

3. a positioning in situations and institutions that aim at upbringing and education, such as family and—in a broad sense—school. One must bear in mind here that the notion of the "school" was subject to multiple social and regional changes throughout the course of the history of Israel and Judah. Thus, in the shadow of the collapse of the Judean Kingdom in 587 BCE and the growing Jewish diaspora in the Persian and Hellenistic period came a shift from the training of scribes at the royal court towards the education of learned writers (*literati*) in the vicinity of the Second Temple, emerging houses of learning, and synagogues (*catechetical wisdom*).

With regard to the specific parameter of the content of a Wisdom genre, it is ultimately the *understanding of wisdom* itself that is of crucial significance. Though in the Old Testament—as too in ancient Greek literature—the term wisdom (חכמה, σοφία) denotes, primarily in a technical sense, artisanal knowledge and craftsmanship (cf. Exod 31:1–5), this corresponds, in a broader sense, with an ability to differentiate and a skill in orientation that is based on experience and tradition, through which humans cope with life. In this regard, wisdom aims at a successful life and proves itself to be a life skill. Its point of departure is the observation of nature and of culture. Close perception (בין, νοέω) is regarded as intelligence (בינה, ἐπιστήμη/σύνεσις/φρόνησις). Wisdom is condensed experience that is passed down over generations and carefully adapted to new circumstances. Out of experience, which leads to an intense familiarity (ידי, εἰδέναι) with something, grows wisdom and knowledge (דעת, σύνεσις/αἴσθησις, γινώσκειν). The conceptual background here is the notion that God the Creator or God the Originator has given a just order to the world. Compliance with this reveals the "way of life" (Prov 6:23) to the individual and to the community and promises justice and happiness in every relationship. A constituent of this is the conviction that a close connection exists between a person's actions and how they fare (*the act–consequence connection*), and that within society, there is a web of social responsibilities. A synthetic perception of reality dominates; that is, deed and consequence, individual and community, are viewed in close relation. Justice (צדקה, δικαιοσύνη) appears as a benchmark for how to act, and as a harmonious and beneficial social sphere: he who lives justly—that is, he who acts appropriately in relation to the community in which he lives—experiences justice. The connection between justice and life (חיים, ζωή) is fundamental for wise existence (cf. Prov 11:19; 12:28; 21:21). Justice, as a central concept and a central theme of Wisdom in the Old Testament and Early Jewish scriptures, thus denotes a salvific community.

To be wise (חכם, σοφός) was to observe oneself and one's environment precisely, to be open to new experiences, to listen to the instructions of one's forefathers and to align one's life and behavior with the just world order. If wisdom is a processual summation of life experience, then he who pays no heed to an accurate perception of his living environment and who disregards the experience of past traditions appears stupid (כסיל, ἄφρων/ἀσεβής) and foolish (אויל, ἄφρων/ἀσεβής). The notion of a wisdom that rests upon experience and is based in an order of creation that pervades the cosmos is something the Old Testament and Early Judaism share with the entire ancient Near East and

Egypt. The domain of such an interpretation of reality is all spheres of human life in the family and society, but also the natural environment and the entire cosmos. Thus, wisdom can be broken down into *education in the skills of life* and *cosmological knowledge*, the latter including astronomical and theological knowledge. There can be overlaps between the two areas. From a functional point of view, they meet with regard to orientation in space and time. As concerns education in the skills of life, it is the earth and the present, including the (recent) past and (near) future that are the focus. By contrast, in the field of cosmological knowledge, it is the heavens as well as protology and eschatology that are central. Where cosmological knowledge is traced back to a specific divine revelation, that is to say, where vertical communication exists, such as in Enoch's heavenly journeys (1 Enoch 17–36), it is not a Wisdom genre that is being dealt with, but a prophetic one, or more precisely, an apocalyptic one. The wise man appears here in the guise of the apocalyptist. In between these two is the inspired wise man, as he appears in later redactions of Job or in the stylization of Daniel, as well as in esoteric doctrines from Qumran (cf. Job 4:12–21; 32:8, 18; Dan 1:4; 4QInstruction; 4QBook of Mysteries), where he is even more clearly outlined.

Parameters of a wisdom genre		
horizontal communication	imperative, adhortative, question	schooling
↕	↕	↕
justice, life, time	שכל* , למד* , יסר* , ידע* , הכם* , בין *	family, "school," synagogue

22.3 LITERARY GENRES IN WISDOM

If one proceeds from these outlined parameters of a Wisdom genre and from the final form of the writings of the Old Testament and Early Judaism, then *two major literary genres* of Wisdom can be distinguished: the *instructional book* (*Lehrbuch*) and the *commentary*. In the Old Testament, only the instructional book is represented, in the form of Proverbs, Ecclesiastes, Ben Sira, and Wisdom of Solomon. While Proverbs and Ecclesiastes, in the versions found in the Hebrew Bible, originate in the third century BCE, the Hebrew book of Ben Sira came into being around 180 BCE, its Greek translation between 132 and 117 BCE, and the Greek original of Wisdom of Solomon between 30 BCE and 30 CE. The book of Job, often classified as Wisdom literature, contains many sapiential genres and also has a strong didactic tendency, but it is a work *sui generis* (cf. Dell 1991, 63–88; Witte 2018).

22.3.1 The Instructional Book

The instructional book takes the form of an editorial compilation of different small compositions that are, however, consistently didactic in their orientation. These include, *instruction, didactic poem,* and *didactic dialogue.* The structure of the instructional book is provided by:

1. headings, which can contain original generic terms or elements of a genre determination (cf. Prov 1:1; 25:1; the superscription of the Bileam-inscription from the Tell Deir ʿAlla [Blum 2016, 29] and the epilogue of the book Qohelet in Eccl 12:9–11);
2. a call to attention, or the instructor's opening formula (שמעו בני/שמע בני, ἄκουε υἱέ/ἀκούσατε παῖδες), in which one or even several pupils are addressed as son/ child and are called upon to listen attentively (cf. Prov 1:8; 4:1; Sir 3:1);
3. formulaic recapitulations (the "summary appraisal"; cf. Prov 1:19; Job 18:21).

In both Proverbs and Ecclesiastes, the introductory verse characterizes the entire respective work as the *teachings of a king* (Prov 1:1; Eccl 1:1), as is documented in Egypt in the Old and Middle Kingdom already with the Instruction for Merikare and the Instruction of Amenemhet (Lichtheim 1973, 97–109, 135–139). The tradition-historical background is the concept, documented in the entire ancient Near East right up into the Hellenistic period, of a wise king. Its biblical ideal is Solomon (cf. 1 Kgs 5:9–14 [ET 4:29–34]; 10:1–7), and so to him was attributed—in some cases already within the Bible itself—the instructional books Proverbs, Ecclesiastes, and Wisdom of Solomon, as well as Song of Songs (cf. Kingsmill 2016) and the Psalms of Solomon, which are also particularly characterized by wisdom.

22.3.1.1 *Instruction*

Instruction directly addresses a party in need of teaching, who is either called upon using the imperative to adopt a way of behaving and acting that is beneficial for life or is led through persuasion and self-reflection to the knowledge of what should or should not be done. One could ascribe the two forms of instruction two different pedagogical concepts as well: an indicative concept, where the Wisdom pupil is the subject of the acquisition of insight, and an imperative concept, where the Wisdom pupil is the object of education (מוסר, παιδεία) (cf. Schipper 2018, 45). In its explanatory, admonitory, and/or cautionary main section, the instruction can contain a description (cf. Prov 5:3–6) or an example story (cf. Prov 7:6–23, par. 4Q184). Special stylistic devices of instruction are the rhetorical or didactic question (cf. Eccl 2:19), the question and answer game (cf. Prov 23:29–30), or the riddle (חידה cf. Prov 30:4). The latter is occasionally considered a genuine Wisdom genre, especially as the term חידה (in the Septuagint: πρόβλημα/αἴνιγμα) appears within the Bible as a genre label (cf. Prov 1:6; Sir 8:8 [par. שיחה]; 39:9[G]; 47:17 [H]).

Old Testament instruction finds its nearest relatives in Egyptian *life teachings* (Egyptian *sebayt*), handed down and composed from the Old Kingdom (2655–2310 BCE) into the Ptolemaic period (323–331 BCE), though teachings are also documented from the Mesopotamian region (cf. the Instructions of Shuruppak [Lambert 1960, 92–95]).

22.3.1.2 *Treatise, Diatribe, and Protreptic*

When instruction assumes a strongly argumentative and discursive character, it may be labeled a treatise. A characteristic form of treatise is offered by Qoheleth's reflections, which exhibit a specific argumentation in four stages: the starting point is shaped by *questions* on the nature of humanity. These are correlated with his own *observations* and *experiences* in nature and culture—therefore, in Ecclesiastes, the notion of "seeing" (ראה) is found time and again alongside the already mentioned notions of perception (ידע, בין). Through the *citation* of contrasting traditional Wisdom phrases, a *conclusion* is drawn, generally formulated as a negation, which answers the question posed at the outset (cf. Eccl 1:3, 4–11). Considering its time of origin and potential contact with Greek philosophy (cf. Müller 2003; Schwienhorst-Schönberger 2004, 104–109), the genre of Ecclesiastes may potentially be influenced in its entirety by the lectures of Hellenistic popular philosophers, which, in the modern genre typology for ancient literature, are identified as *diatribe*.

By contrast, thanks to their manner of espousing wisdom, the instructions in the first two parts of Wisdom of Solomon can be grouped under the genre of *protreptic*, famous from Greek and Roman literature. Sub-genres here include *encomium* (*song of praise*, Wis 6:22–11:1), the *example list* (Wis 9:18–11:1), and *syncrisis* (*comparison*, Wis 11:2–14; 16:1–19:17) (cf. Schmitt 2000).

22.3.1.3 *Testament*

The testaments that developed in the Hellenistic-Roman period represent a special form of purely literary instruction. These are generally not classed as Wisdom Literature; however, by virtue of the characteristics presented above, and above all due to their paraenetic tendency, they can be classified as Wisdom-based with respect to genre. The fictional speaker, usually a well-known figure from the biblical tradition, looks back on his life up until that point from within the setting of a farewell or impending death. He gives his children ethical instructions and dares to take a glance into the future. The label testament refers back to the heading (διαθήκη/*testamentum*) that some of these pseudepigraphical texts bear. Alternatively, these texts can also be labeled *farewell speeches* or *legacy speeches*. Models from within Israelite-Jewish literature include:

1. the words placed in the mouth of the dying Jacob, addressed to his twelve sons, in Genesis 49, which, in their final form, can be read as partly eschatologized tribal sayings (for example, the speech to Judah in Gen 49:8–12, which is to be interpreted as messianic);

2. Moses's blessing of the twelve tribes of Israel in Deuteronomy 33, which corresponds on a macro-compositional, structural, and motif level with the blessing of Jacob;

3. the farewell speeches of Joshua (Joshua 23), Samuel (1 Samuel 12), and David (1 Chronicles 28–29). Farewell speeches from the Jewish literature of the Hellenistic period are found in Tobit 4 and 14, 1 Macc 2:49–70, and Jub 22:10–23:8; 36:1–18. Characteristic of testament literature in a narrower sense, which above all is showcased by the Testament of the Twelve Patriarchs, extant only in Greek in complete form, is the mixture of Jewish ethics and a pagan doctrine of virtue. Thus, each individual speech given by a son of Jacob is dedicated to one particular emotion or one particular virtue. By contrast, the Aramaic fragments of the Testament of Qahat (4Q542) and the Visions of Amram (4Q543–548) remain strongly in the group of genuinely Israelite-Jewish traditions.

22.3.1.4 *The Didactic Poem*

The didactic poem describes a particular action or behavior that is qualified as being wise or foolish. Sometimes it takes a personified form, for example, in the guise of Lady Wisdom or Lady Folly. After an introduction, which is initiated by the person speaking, Lady Wisdom or Lady Folly vies for supporters in a speech that is predominantly formulated in the first person (cf. Prov 1:20–33; 8:1–36; 9:1–18). The actual impulse towards correct behavior and action arises either indirectly or directly when, in a concluding section, the consequences are stated, which will be orientated towards either wisdom or folly, as the case may be (cf. Prov 1:32–33; 8:32–36; 9:6, 18; Job 28:28).

A further-developed form of the didactic poem is constituted by the *hymns to (cosmic) wisdom* in Ben Sira 24 and in Wis 6:22–11:1 (cf. also Sir 51:13–30). Although in both these texts, the influence of Hellenistic Isis *aretalogies* from both Stoic and—in the case of Wisdom of Solomon—Platonic philosophy can be seen, both texts are firmly anchored in Israelite-Jewish Wisdom and are profiled as *Jewish* instructional books by virtue of the identification of wisdom and Torah (cf. Sir 24:23 and, as a precursor, Deut 4:5–6), or wisdom and the Exodus tradition (cf. Wis 11–19). With the "Praise of the Fathers" (Ben Sira 44–49) and the description of the dealings of σοφία in pre- and early history (Wisdom 10), Ben Sira and Wisdom of Solomon also offer poems that have a modified Wisdom element and a didactic function, whose origins, in terms of genre history, lie in poetic *historical summaries* ("historical psalms") (cf. Psalms 78; 105; 106; Nehemiah 9) and in pagan *encomium*.

Last to be counted as part of the genre of didactic poetry are individual *Wisdom psalms* or *meditations* that display an exclusively horizontal, self-reflexive communication structure (such as Psalms 1 and 37; but not, however, Psalms 19; 49; 73; and 119) and owe their name to their location in the psalter, although from a genre point of view, they would be better considered proverbs. Conversely, *prayers* are found in the instructional books, that is, a ritual-liturgical major genre characterized by vertical communication whose true place would be in an anthology of psalms (cf. Prov 30:5–7; Sir 23:1–6; 36:1–22; 51:12a–o, 13–30 [H]; Wis 8:21–9:18). Their inclusion in an instructional book shows that for Jewish wise men of the Hellenistic period, prayer was an object and means of Wisdom-based guidance.

22.3.1.5 *Didactic Dialogue*

Instruction, in particular, treatise, can contain individual dialogical elements, if, for example, positions of a fictional opposite party are cited (cf. Ecclesiastes; Wisdom of Solomon). However, on the whole, a monologue structure dominates. In an instructional book that is stylized as didactic dialogue or as a didactic conversation, however, various conversational partners are explicitly mentioned, who give speeches with stylistically and thematically independent profiles. The conversational partners can be introduced in a narrative manner, and the speeches can be of differing lengths. A defining characteristic of didactic dialogue is its discursive and confrontational disposition. It aims at persuasion or rebuttal of the conversation partner, and, ultimately, at the education of the reader. The speeches in a didactic dialogue often bear a polemic and apologetic character, which is why they can also be classified as *disputation speeches*. The speeches found between Job and his three friends, Eliphaz, Bildad, and Zophar, in the Job poem (Job 3–28) provide the basic pattern—the speeches of Elihu (Job 32–37), despite their direct addressing of Job by name, are ultimately monologues that are better labeled treatises (see above 22.3.1.2 Treatise, Diatribe, and Protreptic). At the same time, these very speeches within the Job poem exhibit a mixture, subversion (*parody*), and coining of genres that is unique within literary history in this form (cf. Fohrer 1983; Hartley 1988, 37–43; Dell 1991). Due to their tackling of traditional convictions of the divine world order, of the act-and-consequence connection in operation or of justice, this form of critical Wisdom can, from a literary historical perspective, be ascribed as *Auseinandersetzungsliteratur* (*problem literature*) or *theodicy-analagous poetry*, which are also documented in Egypt and Mesopotamia. Dorothea Sitzler (1995) speaks aptly here of *Vorwurfdichtung* (*blame poetry*). Recent translations of select Egyptian and Mesopotamian texts from this textual group have been offered by Wilfried G. Lambert (1960), Miriam Lichtheim (1973–1980), and Yoram Cohen (2013).

In contrast, the Greek didactic dialogue in the so-called Letter of Aristeas (first century BCE, embedded within the framework of a symposium and held between the Egyptian King Ptolemy II and the Jewish wise men who came to Alexandria as translators of the Torah, more strongly exhibits the character of a simple juxtaposition of Wisdom-based aphorisms. In these conversations, the Jews show themselves to be learned men who, due to their special wisdom, can compete with Greek philosophers, without abandoning the fundamental tenets of their Jewish religion (cf. 3.2, *Aristobulus*). From *the point of view of its genre*, Aristeas's letter is not a letter, but rather a narratively framed Wisdom text, even if, in the reception history, it was predominantly understood as the foundation myth (aetiology) of the Septuagint.

22.3.1.6 *The Saying*

Both instruction and didactic poetry, as well as didactic dialogue, are *poetic* in their design. Their smallest common component, as Lowth and Herder already elaborated in detail, is the saying (מָשָׁל, παραβολή/παροιμία). At the same time, מָשָׁל literally means *allegory* (*parable*), because, in this linguistic mode of expression, a concrete experience is viewed as a reference to a universal one, or of a reality that stands behind this experience, and, to a certain extent, a linguistic *equivalence* is established. In the books of the Old Testament, it is almost exclusively two-part sayings that are found. These are constructed using *parallelismus membrorum*, following the basic law of Hebrew poetry; the essential elements of the members (cola, stichoi) of a verse, which in Hebrew are predominantly connected by the copula ו, are correlated in terms of form and content. This correlation can be *synonymous*, in as much as the thought expressed in the first part of the verse is repeated using similar words in the second part of the verse—the copula connecting both parts of the verse should then be translated using "and" (cf. Prov 10:18). However, the correlation can also be *antithetical*, inasmuch as the assertion expressed in the first part of the verse is contrasted with an opposite assertion—in this case, the copula that connects both parts of the verse is to be translated using "but" (cf. Prov 14:34). Finally, the thought expressed in the first part of the verse can be continued by means of a thought that expands upon it, so that a type of *synthetic* parallelism exists, and the copula fulfills the function of a consecutive or final conjunction (cf. Prov 16:3). This classification of parallelisms also has its origins in Lowth. Since then, it has been expanded upon repeatedly—among other things, by *parabolic* or *comparative* parallelism, where the two cola split into a figurative half and a concrete half (cf. Prov 10:26), and by *climactic* (*repetitious* or *tautological*) parallelism, where there are normally three parts to the verse, and these continue a thought in stages, retaining a key word throughout (cf. Prov 30:33). This system of classification into three or five forms of parallelism has, despite criticism—especially of the designation of the synthetic parallelism, which is less clearly definable formally—proved itself. Due to more recent approaches in communication theory and linguistics, particularly speech act theory, being taken into consideration, it has been fully differentiated with regard to pragmatics and semantics (Luchsinger 2010, 120–158).

Considering that wisdom, in the ancient Near Eastern and Old Testament sense, is based predominantly on the summation of experiences, the synoptic view of as many aspects of a phenomenon as possible and the categorization of social roles and of manifestations found in the animal and plant worlds, the *parallelismus membrorum* is particularly well suited to the task of tying knowledge together in a linguistically very dense form and boiling it down to its essence in one *aphorism* (cf. Krüger 2003). It shapes the character of Israelite-Jewish poetry so strongly—and not only in the field of Wisdom— that it was also preserved in the Greek translations of Hebrew texts and was used in writings originally composed in Greek, such as in Wisdom of Solomon, for example. By contrast, the unknown Jewish author, active between 50 BCE and 50 CE, of the Wisdom sayings that have been handed down under the name of the Greek poet Phocylides (sixth century BCE) employed classical hexameter.

The early research into genre history strove at length to illuminate the *oral precursor* to individual Wisdom sayings (aphorisms). It made a distinction between the popular proverb and the artificially constructed saying and, using broad-based ethnological comparisons that transcended cultural boundaries, sought to locate the proverbial wisdom of Israel within the context of a universal human knowledge (cf. Westermann 1990). The justification for this comparison arises from the fact that proverbial wisdom is widespread across the entire ancient Near East, ancient Egypt, and ancient Greece. Contemporary research that is interested in form and genre, however, concentrates predominantly on the exact delineation of the linguistic and stylistic character of the *literary* sayings found in the Wisdom books, and on the elaboration of the poetological and material specifics of Israelite-Jewish sayings in the context of their immediate geographical and temporal neighbors. Three textual groups are assigned particular significance here: firstly, the Egyptian Wisdom books dating from the Ptolemaic period and written in Demotic, particularly Papyrus Insinger from the late Ptolemaic period (cf. Lichtheim 1980, 184–217); secondly the Aramaic Story of Ahiqar (seventh/sixth century BCE; cf. Weigl 2010); and thirdly, ancient Greek proverbial wisdom (Theognis, Mimnermus, seventh to fifth century BCE; cf. Gerber 1999), which—after classification in the fifth/fourth century BCE—found expression in the proverb (παροιμία) and aphorism (γνώμη), in the situational maxim (ἀπόφθηγμα) and in counsel (ὑποθήκη).

The following *types of saying* in Old Testament Wisdom Literature can be differentiated according to linguistic, content-related, and pragmatic criteria (cf. Murphy 1981, 4–5, 172–185):

1. Phenomena, behaviors, and their consequences are expressed using the *sentential saying (Aussagespruch)* or *dictum (Wahrspruch)*, or the *declaratory aphorism*, and sometimes also simply juxtaposed (the *contrastive saying*). Instruction as to how to act results indirectly (cf. Prov 11:30; 21:21; 26:27; Eccl 2:14; 7:11; 11:4). In terms of genre history, the sentential saying or dictum could have grown out of the single-line proverb (cf. Judg 8:2b, 21aβ; 1 Kgs 20:11b). A special type of sentential saying, characterized by its content, is the *God-fearing saying*, which recognizes the value of fear before God for a successful life (cf. Prov 10:27; Sir 10:22).

2. The *comparative saying* or the *comparative* טוב ("better than") *saying* establishes what is more advantageous for life. Here too, instruction as to how to act is only implicitly present (cf. Prov 17:1; Eccl 4:6; 7:1; 9:18).

3. The *numerical saying* consists of a title line and a subsequent enumeration (list). The first line names the common characteristic of the objects described, and the number of them that possess this characteristic. The list enumerates the individual objects and describes the specific way in which they reflect the common characteristic (cf. Prov 30:24–28). The *simple numerical saying* names just one number in the title line (cf. Prov 30:24); the *progressive numerical saying* contains two numbers, the second of which is one greater than the first (cf. Prov 30:18–19). From a genre history perspective, the background to the numerical saying is probably the riddle question and occult notions of the special significance and symbolism of individual numbers. Analogous to the numerical saying are onomastica, encyclopedic lists in which manifestations from the animal and plant world, but also meteorological and astronomical phenomena, are compiled

according to specific formal and material traits. As with the numerical saying, profound knowledge is believed to be imparted and reality disclosed through the compilation of phenomena. Onomastica are documented above all in ancient Egypt, are encountered in poetry, broadly developed, in Hellenistic cosmological didactic poetry (cf. Aratus, *Phaenomena*), and are found in the Bible, with dramatic modification, in the divine speeches in Job (cf. Job 38–39; 40:15–41:26).

4. The *admonition* is formulated in the imperative or vetative, and, in contrast to the sentential saying and to the comparative saying, contains an explicit instruction for action (*directive*). Usually, the admonition is coupled to a rationale (כִּי "for"; פֶּן "lest") that includes a motivation for the behavior that is being demanded and/or an indication of its consequences. When positive in form, the admonition appears as *counsel* (cf. Prov 22:17–19; Eccl 11:1–2), and when negative, as a *warning* (cf. Prov 22:22–23; Eccl 7:9, 16–17).

5. The *beatitude* is introduced by the interjection אַשְׁרֵי/μακάριος "Blessed is / Fortunate is / O the happiness of" (Prov 3:13; Eccl 10:17; Sir 14:20). It represents the strongest form of counsel. The instruction for action is given implicitly, in that a particular way of acting or behaving is declared to be blessed, and thus imitation is recommended. The beatitude is probably a genuine Wisdom genre, but it is also found outside the true Wisdom books (cf. Ps 1:1; Isa 30:18; Ps. Sol. 6:1; 4Q525 f2ii + 3:3).

Wisdom sayings can be differentiated further based on the situation in which they are used and based on their sphere of knowledge. So, a Wisdom saying from the domain of ethos enjoins one to practice correct social behavior. In cosmology, it interprets nature and its phenomena. In theology, it articulates the question about the justice of God (*theodicy*).

Even though the individual Wisdom saying forms the foundation of the Old Testament instructional books, as the elements of the structure described above show, these are not simply collections, where sayings or series of sayings from different contexts are strung together arbitrarily—though this assessment may hold true for the Sumerian collections of sayings (*COS* 1.174: 563–567). Already the partial compositions that underlie Proverbs and Ben Sira at an older stage are constructed according to specific linguistic, stylistic, thematic, and functional traits. The instructions in the first and second main sections of Wisdom of Solomon (1:1–6:21; 6:22–11:1) and the contrastive and creative juxtaposition of traditional Wisdom sayings with personal observations and conclusions in Ecclesiastes give consistent evidence of the compositional design of a single author.

22.3.1.7 *The Didactic Story*

The most important narrative genre of Wisdom Literature is the didactic story composed in artful prose. It aims at imparting fundamental knowledge, as well as the intellectual and ethical consequences that are to be gathered therefrom. In view of its pedagogical orientation, the didactic story converges with instruction and treatise. Its prosaic structure and its concentration on one particular central motif, which is articulated through scene and dialogue and is focused on one specific goal, is like a novella. At its heart is often a Wisdom-based aphorism, which can be poetic in form (cf. Job 1:21; Tob 4:13). Such aphorisms can be labeled a nucleus of the didactic story and of the narrative theology conveyed within it. As in the novella, a theological or ethical problem is unfolded in the didactic story, using the example of an extraordinary incident, and led to its resolution. In the process, the reader is called to active participation more intensely than in other narrative genres, whether through being provoked to an opinion by the problematization of a belief considered incontrovertible in the tradition, or through the narrator directly addressing readers with a question.

In Israelite-Jewish literature, this genre is represented most notably by the Job novella (Job 1:1–5*, 13–21; 42:11*, 12–17)—which originally came into being as a standalone work—and the book of Jonah. Literary historical parallels from the surrounding world of the Old Testament are, for example, the Akkadian Tale of the Poor Man of Nippur and the Story of Ahiqar, placed around the Ahiqar sayings at a later date (cf. Müller 1994).

A specific, short form of the didactic story is the *fable*, where the chief characters are animals or plants. Little represented in the Old Testament (cf. Judg 9:8–15; 2 Kgs 14:9), the fable is encountered more frequently in Sumerian and classic Greek and Roman Wisdom Literature.

The stories of Ruth, Esther, and Tobit also bear features of a Wisdom text, as do passages in the story of Joseph (Genesis 37–50), the book of Daniel (Daniel 1–6; Daniel 13 [Susanna]), and the Genesis Apocryphon (1Q20 XIX:10–XX:32), though none of these are pure didactic stories. As the book of Jonah shows, didactic stories could also be handed down as initially standalone (small) instructional books.

22.3.2 The Commentary

The commentary, which is here regarded as a major Wisdom genre due to its horizontal communication structure and propensity for instruction, offers an exposition that pertains to one specific text and, in contrast to ancient Israelite-Jewish literature, is no longer performed within the text itself, in the style of a redactional update, but stands literarily independent alongside a text that is viewed as authoritative.

Extra-textual exposition of Scripture is almost a genuine Wisdom genre itself according to the definition above in 22.2 (Characteristics of a Wisdom Genre). However, if one disregards the commentary-like paraphrasing of Exodus in the third part of Wisdom of Solomon (11:2–19:22) and Ben Sira's occasional scriptural expositions and "Praise of the Fathers" (Sirach 44–49), it is only documented in Early Jewish exegetical writings that were not canonical. Among these belong texts that differ greatly in formal and linguistic design, as well as in their socio-cultural provenance, for example:

1. The exegetical work of *Aristobulus* (second century BCE), which is composed in Greek and survives only in fragments.

2. The continuous and thematic *pesharim* on individual prophetic books and individual psalms (first century BCE), written in Hebrew and discovered in Qumran. The continuous *pesharim* from Qumran reveal an interesting shift from the point of view of genre typology, inasmuch as a prophetic text marked by vertical communication is interpreted using a didactic text that is marked by horizontal communication.

3. The extensive commentaries of *Philo of Alexandria* (ca. 25 BCE to ca. 50 CE). Like the *Aristobulus* fragments, these are characterized by allegory, popular in the Hellenistic exegesis of Homer, and by philosophical erudition.

22.4 A Look Ahead to Further Research

Classifications are never absolute (cf. above 22.1 On a Path to a Literary Genre). Important areas for the future research on genres of Wisdom Literature touch on social history, cultural history, methodology, and hermeneutics.

In terms of *social history*, the focus must be on an even more specific historical placement of the circles of dissemination of Wisdom traditions and of the linguistic forms these choose to employ. In this regard, classical, historically oriented genre research once again gets full credence.

In terms of *cultural history*, further correlation with Wisdom genres in the pagan literature of the Persian and, most notably, the Hellenistic period is due. The Hellenistic period is *the* epoch in which the Old Testament Wisdom books find their quintessential form. Textual areas of focus for the comparison must therefore include the Egyptian Wisdom texts of the Ptolemaic period, transmitted in Demotic, and pagan Greek Wisdom. The latter pertains especially to the Israelite-Jewish Wisdom books that have come down to us in Greek, which, by virtue of the Septuagint, also constitute a part of pagan Greek literary and genre history. This could lead, without losing sight of the Near Eastern parallels, to a methodologically directed new resurrection of the dialogue between biblical "philosophy" and Greek philosophy (cf. Moulton 1896, 253 and Legaspi's chapter in this volume), such as is prefigured in *Aristobulus*, for example, when he sets Pythagoras, Socrates, and Plato in relation to Moses (Frag. 4.4) (cf. Collins 1997; Kaiser 2003b; Kaiser 2008).

Methodologically speaking, cooperation between studies on the Old Testament, New Testament, patristics, and rabbinics means we can expect elucidation of the common originating environment of Wisdom Literature, the cross-connections between the circles of Wisdom transmission and the specific, religiously influenced transformations of individual genres (cf. Küchler 1979; von Lips 1990; Collins 1997; Löning 2002; Kaiser 2003a).

In the field of *hermeneutics*, the following are still in need of clarification: (1) the pragmatics of Wisdom genres, taking into consideration their dynamics and their process-driven character; (2) the anthropological and psychological dimension of individual genres; and (3) the significance of the Wisdom genres in the Old Testament for contemporary epistemological and ethical discourse.

WORKS CITED

Alonso Schökel, Luis. 1988. *A Manual of Hebrew Poetics*. SubBi 11. Rome: Pontificio Istituto Biblico (reprint 2000).

Barton, John. 1992. "Form Criticism." *ABD* 2:838–841.

Blum, Erhard. 2003. *"Formgeschichte*—A Miseleading Category? Some Critical Remarks." Pages 32–45 in *The Changing Face of Form Criticism for the Twenty-First Century*. Edited by Marvin A. Sweeney and Ehud Ben Zvi. Grand Rapids, MI: Eerdmans.

Blum, Erhard. 2016. "Die altaramäischen Wandinschriften vom Tell Deir 'Alla und ihr institutioneller Hintergrund." Pages 21–52 in *Metatexte: Erzählungen von schrifttragenden Artefakten in der alttestamentlichen und mittelalterlichen Literatur*. Edited by F.-E. Focken and M.R. Ott. Berlin: de Gruyter.

Cohen, Yoram. 2013. *Wisdom from the Late Bronze Age*. WAW 34. Atlanta, GA: SBL.

Collins, John J. 1997. *Jewish Wisdom in the Hellenistic Age*. OTL. Louisville, KY: Westminster John Knox.

Dell, Katharine J. 1991. *The Book of Job as Sceptical Literature*. BZAW 197. Berlin: de Gruyter.

Fohrer, Georg. 1983. "Form und Funktion in der Hiobdichtung (1959)." Pages 60–77 in *Studien zum Buche Hiob (1956–1979)*. 2nd ed. BZAW 159. Berlin: de Gruyter.

Fokkelman, J.P. 1998–2004. *Major Poems of the Hebrew Bible, at the Interface of Prosody and Structural Analysis*. 4 vols. Assen: Van Gorcum.

Gerber, Douglas E. 1999. *Greek Elegiac Poetry: From the Seventh to the Fifth Centuries BC. Tyrtaeus, Solon, Theognis, Mimnermus*. LCL 258. Cambridge, MA: Harvard University Press.

Gressmann, Hugo, ed. 1926. *Altorientalische Texte zum Alten Testament*. 2nd ed. Berlin: de Gruyter.

Gunkel, Hermann. 1906. "Die israelitische Literatur." Pages 51–102 in *Die Kultur der Gegenwart: Ihre Entwicklung und ihre Ziele, I/VII. Die orientalischen Literaturen*. Edited by P. Hinneberg. Berlin: Teubner.

Gunkel, Hermann. 1913. "Die Grundprobleme der israelitischen Literaturgeschichte (1906)." Pages 29–38 in *Reden und Aufsätze*. Göttingen: Vandenhoeck & Ruprecht.

Habel, Norman C. 1985. *The Book of Job: A Commentary*. OTL. London: SCM.

Hartley, John E. 1988. *The Book of Job*. NICOT. Grand Rapids, MI: Eerdmans.

Herder, Johann Gottfried. 1879–1880. *Vom Geist der Ebräischen Poesie: Eine Anleitung für die Liebhaber derselben und der ältesten Geschichte des menschlichen Geistes. Erster Theil (1782. ²1787) Zweiter Theil (1783. ²1787)*. Edited by B. Suphan. Herders Sämmtliche Werke 11–12. Berlin: Weidmann.

Jones, W. 1777. *Poeseos Asiaticae Commentariorum libri sex cum appendice recudi curavit Io. G. Eichhorn*. Leipzig: Weidmannus & Reichius.

Kaiser, Otto. 2003a. *Anweisungen zum gelingenden, gesegneten und ewigen Leben: Eine Einführung in die spätbiblischen Weisheitsbücher*. FTLZ 9. Leipzig: Evangelische Verlagsanstalt.

Kaiser, Otto. 2003b. *Zwischen Athen und Jerusalem: Studien zur griechischen und biblischen Theologie, ihrer Eigenart und ihrem Verhältnis*. BZAW 320. Berlin: de Gruyter.

Kaiser, Otto. 2008. *Vom offenbaren und verborgenen Gott: Studien zur spätbiblischen Weisheit und Hermeneutik*. BZAW 392. Berlin: de Gruyter.

Kingsmill, Edmée. 2016. "The Song of Songs: A Wisdom Book. " Pages 310–335 in *Perspectives on Israelite Wisdom*. Edited by J. Jarick. LHBOTS 618. London: Bloomsbury T&T Clark.

König, Eduard. 1900. *Stilistik, Rhetorik, Poetik in Bezug auf die Biblische Literatur komparativisch dargestellt*. Leipzig: Dieterisch.

Krüger, Thomas. 2003. "Erkenntnisbindung im Weisheitsspruch: Überlegungen im Anschluss an Gerhard von Rad." Pages 53–66 in *Weisheit in Israel*. Edited by D.J.A. Clines, H. Lichtenberger, and H.-P. Müller. ATM 12. Münster: LIT.

Küchler, M. 1979. *Frühjüdische Weisheitstraditionen: Zum Fortgang weisheitlichen Denkens im Bereich des frühjüdischen Jahweglaubens.* OBO 26. Freiburg: Universitätsverlag.

Lambert, Wilfried G. 1960. *Babylonian Wisdom Literature.* Oxford: Clarendon; rev. reprint Winona Lake, IN: Eisenbrauns, 1996.

Lichtheim, Miriam. 1973–1980. *Ancient Egyptian Literature.* 3 vols. Berkeley, CA: University of California Press.

Lips, Hermann von. 1990. *Weisheitliche Traditionen im Neuen Testament.* WMANT 64. Neukirchen-Vluyn: Neukirchener Verlag.

Löning, Karl, ed. 2002. *Rettendes Wissen: Studien zum Fortgang weisheitlichen Denkens im Frühjudentum und im frühen Christentum.* AOAT 300. Münster: Ugarit Verlag.

Lowth, Robert. 1815. *De Sacra Poesi Hebraeorum Praelectiones Academicae Oxonii habitae subiicitur metricae Haranae brevis confutatio et oratio Crewiana* (1753). Cum notis et epimetris Io. Dav. Michaelis suis animadversionibus adjectis edidit E.F.C. Rosenmüller. Leipzig: Weigel.

Luchsinger, Jürg. 2010. *Poetik der alttestamentlichen Spruchweisheit.* PSAT 3. Stuttgart: Kohlhammer.

Meier, Ernst Heinrich. 1856. *Geschichte der poetischen National-Literatur der Hebräer.* Leipzig: W. Engelmann.

Melugin, Roy F. 2003. "Recent Form Criticism Revisited in an Age of Reader Response." Pages 46–64 in *The Changing Face of Form Criticism for the Twenty-First Century.* Edited by M.A. Sweeney and E. Ben Zvi. Grand Rapids, MI: Eerdmans.

Moulton, Richard G. 1896. *The Literary Study of the Bible: An Account of the Leading Forms of Literature Represented in the Sacred Writings.* London: Isbister and Company.

Müller, Hans-Peter. 1994. "Die Hiobrahmenerzählung und ihre altorientalischen Parallelen als Paradigmen einer weisheitlichen Wirklichkeitswahrnahme." Pages 21–39 in *The Book of Job.* Edited by W.A.M. Beuken. BETL 114. Leuven: Peeters.

Müller, Hans-Peter. 2003. "Kohelet im Lichte der frühgriechischen Philosophie." Pages 67–80 in *Weisheit in Israel.* Edited by D.J.A. Clines, H. Lichtenberger, and H.-P. Müller. ATM 12. Münster: LIT.

Murphy, Roland E. 1981. *Wisdom Literature: Job, Proverbs, Ruth, Canticles, Ecclesiastes, and Esther.* FOTL XIII. Grand Rapids, MI: Eerdmans; repr. 1983.

Schipper, Bernd U. 2018. *Sprüche (Proverbia): 1-15.* BKAT 17. Göttingen: Vandenhoeck & Ruprecht.

Schmitt, Armin. 2000. "Der Gegenwart verpflichtet. Literarische Formen des Frühjudentums im Kontext griechisch-hellenistischer Schriften." Pages 21–46 in *Der Gegenwart verpflichtet: Studien zur biblischen Literatur des Frühjudentums.* BZAW 292. Berlin: de Gruyter.

Schwienhorst-Schönberger, Ludger. 2004. *Kohelet.* HThKAT. Freiburg: Herder.

Sitzler, Dorothea. 1995. *"Vorwurf gegen Gott": Ein religiöses Motiv im Alten Orient (Ägypten und Mesopotamien).* StOR 32. Wiesbaden: Harrassowitz.

Watson, Wilfred G. E. 1984. *Classical Hebrew Poetry: A Guide to Its Techniques.* Sheffield: Sheffield Academic; repr. 2001.

Weigl, Michael. 2010. *Die aramäischen Achikar-Sprüche aus Elephantine und die alttestamentliche Weisheitsliteratur.* BZAW 399. Berlin: de Gruyter.

Westermann, Claus. 1990. *Wurzeln der Weisheit: Die ältesten Sprüche Israels und anderer Völker.* Göttingen: Vandenhoeck & Ruprecht. English translation: *Roots of Wisdom: The Oldest Proverbs of Israel and Other Peoples.* Louisville, KY: Westminster John Knox, 1995.

Witte, Markus. 2018. "Die literarische Gattung des Buches Hiob: Robert Lowth (1710–1787) und seine Erben (2007)." Pages 37–64 in *Hiobs viele Gesichter: Studien zur Komposition, Tradition und frühen Rezeption des Hiobbuches.* FRLANT 267. Göttingen: Vandenhoeck & Ruprecht.

CHAPTER 23

THE CHRONOLOGICAL DEVELOPMENT OF WISDOM LITERATURE

MARKUS SAUR

23.1 FORMATION AND HISTORICAL CLASSIFICATION OF HEBREW WISDOM WRITINGS

WHAT applies to large parts of the Old Testament writings can also be proven for the Old Testament Wisdom Literature, namely that the texts have gone through a lengthy process of formation and editing. Before this is explained in detail, however, the question of the oldest attainable stages of the Wisdom tradition and the beginnings of its literarization must be discussed (cf. Carr 2005, 111–134). The sayings in Proverbs particularly suggest that preliminary oral stages precede the literary form of Wisdom (cf. Whybray 1994, 129). These oral forms of wisdom can no longer be reconstructed in view of an ancient cultural area; they can only be comparatively deduced. A comparative cultural study shows that in African kings' sayings, for example, there are sayings comparable to those in Proverbs (Westermann 1990; Golka 1993). For the origin of such sayings, a condensation of everyday experiences among the common people can be assumed, where the sayings in turn are used to interpret everyday situations. Even in contemporary Western societies, sayings are not first learned by reading literary collections of them, but they are heard again and again, for example in childhood, are gradually memorized, and are then again used and passed on orally. It is not unlikely that such oral processes also preceded the inscription of Wisdom sayings in ancient Israel and Judah, and accompanied them in parallel.

That wisdom first has to do with the condensation of experience, which is made teachable and learnable in such sayings, was emphasized in particular by Gerhard von Rad (cf. 1970, 13–27). As soon as the transition from orality to writing has taken place in view of this condensation of experience, wisdom resides in the hands of appropriate educational institutions (cf. Lemaire 1981, 72–85; Carr 2005, 112–122). Writing and reading will have been taught and learned here. In any case, teachers and students are familiarized with a certain *set* of norms and behaviors, and thus introduced to the wisdom worldview (cf. Carr 2005, 126–134). The basis of this view of the world is the conviction that deed and consequence correspond, and that through human activity a form of social interaction is set in motion that has retroactive effects on the people involved, but also has consequences for their social environment (cf. Assmann 1990, 60–69, 283–288; Janowski 1994).

However, the contents of the sayings suggest that not only educated *literati* stand behind them, but that the reality of life of broader sections of the population is reflected in the sayings. Especially the sayings with agricultural or handicraft references were certainly passed on in other social contexts before they found their way into the written collections of sayings.

When and where the outlined oral and early literary processes have their time and place can no longer be determined exactly. However, it is likely that the collecting and writing of individual sayings and groups of sayings extended over a longer period of time. The superscriptions in Prov 10:1 and Prov 25:1 show that besides a first collection of Solomonic sayings, there was also a second collection of Solomonic sayings compiled by the men of Hezekiah. Here parallel processes of formation between orality and textuality will have to be assumed (cf. Carr 2005, 3–14).

23.2 PROVERBS

According to Prov 1:1, the book of Proverbs contains sayings of Solomon, son of David, king of Israel, which the superscription in Prov 10:1 repeats in abridged form. Against the background of these superscriptions, it seems obvious at first glance to place the beginnings of the book in the tenth century BCE, and to understand the book as a Wisdom writing of the royal court of Solomon. However, this assessment is contradicted by the superscription in Prov 25:1, according to which Solomon's sayings are also present in the following, but these sayings were compiled by the men of Hezekiah, the king of Judah. This is of great importance for the reconstruction of the formation of Proverbs: The compilation of sayings, expressed in Prov 25:1 with the Hebrew root העתק *hi.*, which locates this process at the end of the eighth century BCE in the surroundings of Hezekiah, makes it clear that the literarization of the sayings extended over several centuries and cannot be understood as a temporally narrowly limited process of the tenth century BCE (cf. Schipper 2018, 7).

There are no reliable sources for the hypothesis of a Solomonic empire and a court with an appropriate staff of officials or an established teaching organization, as it would have to be assumed for the extensive collection of sayings in Prov 10:1–22:16 (cf. Schmid 2008, 59–61). The depictions in 1 Kings 1–11, 1 Chronicles 29, and 2 Chronicles

1–9 were written more than half a millennium after Solomon's reign (cf. Japhet 1993, 23–27; Römer 2005, 98–100). They are obviously an idealized conception from later historians, who could only rely to a limited extent on earlier sources (cf. Römer 2005, 104–106). In addition, epigraphic findings challenge the assumption of larger textual complexes emerging at this time. The most extensive non-Old Testament Hebrew text which has survived from the tenth century BCE is the Gezer calendar (cf. Renz 1995, 30–37), which is very short, with a total of nineteen words, which suggests that in this phase of Israel's history, it is not yet possible to assume extensive literary production.

This has consequences for the book of Proverbs and for understanding the superscriptions in Prov 1:1, 10:1, and 25:1, which refer to Solomon. These superscriptions do not give any historical information about authorship, but authorize the collections by their reference to Solomon, who is increasingly shaped over the course of the first millennium BCE into an exemplary sage. This image of Solomon has earlier roots, but is then developed primarily in 1 Kings 3 and 5 and is reflected in the superscriptions of Proverbs as well as in the implicit Solomonization of Ecclesiastes and the later Wisdom of Solomon. None of these writings date back to the tenth century BCE, but each of them is attributed to the wise King Solomon, so that an ensemble of Solomonic books is created. Against this background, it cannot be assumed that Proverbs is a Wisdom document from the tenth century BCE. The reference to the collecting activity of the men of Hezekiah in Prov 25:1 rather suggests that the book is the product of a longer formation process.

The two large Solomonic collections in Prov 10:1–22:16 and in Proverbs 25–29 mainly consist of concise individual sayings. An experience is condensed in them, which is recorded in the form of a statement. In their pragmatics, these statements are directed at the recipients. Readers of these sayings are integrated into the process of the constitution of meaning; they must interpret the statements and derive certain orientations for action from them. The stylistic short form and the areas of everyday rural and urban life dealt with in the sayings speak in favor of seeking the beginnings of the two Solomonic collections in the period of the monarchy, and to assume as a *terminus a quo*, following Prov 25:1, the eighth century BCE (cf. Schmid 2008, 79–80). However, this is only the starting point of a broader redactional and editorial process. It can be assumed, for example, that theological markings such as the reference to "the fear of the Lord" in Prov 15:33 were entered at a later date in order to establish structures throughout the book. In addition to such *Fortschreibungen* within the Solomonic collections, the other collections also show that the book's formation process goes far into post-exilic times.

Following Prov 10:1–22:16; 25–29, the collections in Prov 22:17–24:22 and Prov 24:23–34 attract attention in the first instance. Both collections are delimited by their own superscriptions: Prov 22:17 refers to "words of wise men," and Prov 24:23 follows Prov 22:17 with the phrase "these as well are for sages." These two collections of sapiential words interrupt the context of the Solomonic collections, and were likely added to the composition later. The proverbial material handed down in Prov 22:17–24:22; 24:23–34 were included in the Solomonic framework in the course of the composition of the book of Proverbs and thus were also implicitly Solomonized. This is coherent within the logic of the composition of the book, although the structure and background of the collections indicate that there are other texts here than in the two Solomonic collections.

For the larger of the two collections in Prov 22:17–24:22, a connection between the Hebrew and an Egyptian text is often assumed due to conceptual and literary correlations to the Egyptian Wisdom instruction of Amen-em-ope. However, the significance of the correlations must be precisely examined, and the question must be answered whether, on the basis of the available analogies, a literary dependence of the Hebrew text on Egyptian instruction can be assumed (cf. Schipper 2005, 240–247). Based on the compositional history of the book of Proverbs, however, it can be assumed that Prov 22:17–24:22 was embedded in the book only after the two Solomonic collections and thus at the earliest in the late period of the monarchy. However, it could well have been written earlier as a separate text.

In view of the smaller collection in Prov 24:23–34, which can be delimited by its own superscription in Prov 24:23 and the new superscription in Prov 25:1, the comparatively low-profile superscription following Prov 22:17 is striking (cf. Whybray 1994, 145–147). This identifies Prov 24:23–34 as a more recent text compared to the previous collection. The close connection between the two collections can be observed on the basis of a characteristic in Prov 24:30–34 and Prov 23:29–35: In Prov 24:30–34, no single saying becomes tangible, but a process of cognition formulated from the perspective of the first person is recorded, which leads to the sequence of sayings in vv. 33–34. A similar, even more condensed sequence can be found in Prov 23:29–35, where introductory questions, answers, observations, and admonitions on abusing wine form a thematic context that falls outside the context of Prov 22:17–24:22. These longer literary forms stand out from the individual sayings of the Solomonic collections, within which thematic clusters can also be found (cf. Scoralick 1995), but no longer reflective texts. This may be a significant development in Wisdom Literature. While the older collections of sayings condense experience in the short form of a saying (משל), the more recent collections show tendencies towards the expansion of this form. The process of experience implicitly behind a concise saying is now explicitly presented and executed. Thus, the process of cognition in Prov 24:30–34 comes from observing the overgrown field and the run-down vineyard, and leads to the instruction formulated in vv. 33–34, which is recorded as a statement, and whose ethical pragmatics must be explored. The task of the constitution of meaning thus lies, as with the short proverbs, on the part of the recipient, but is limited and guided in a certain direction by the preceding observations of the exemplary sage.

The elucidation of the cognitive and educational process from which the Wisdom sayings come and what they are meant to convey also determines the other collections in the book. While the center of the book, Proverbs 10–29, consists mostly of short proverbs, which are only occasionally transformed into longer sequences or reflections, expanded forms characterize the introduction of the book in Proverbs 1–9 as well as the two collections of the words of Agur in Proverbs 30 and the words to Lemuel in Proverbs 31. Within these framing collections, primarily in Prov 30:10–31:9, mainly smaller Wisdom sequences appear, while in Proverbs 1–9, Prov 30:1–9 and Prov 31:10–31 more extensive reflections and Wisdom speeches are transmitted.

The words of Agur are introduced in Prov 30:1–9 with a reflection consisting of sapiential, prophetic, and psalmistic elements, which cannot belong to the oldest material of the book of Proverbs due to their tradition-historical breadth alone (cf. Saur 2014). The same applies to the final acrostic poem in Prov 31:10–31, which is probably shaped by influences from the Phoenician cultural sphere and seems to allude to the Greek word for wisdom, σοφία, in v. 27 with the Hebrew form צופיה (cf. Mathys 2004, 29–30)—both clearly point back to the fourth or third century BCE.

Proverbs 1–9 consistently contain longer reflective texts which justify the virtue of wisdom and at the same time warn of the dangers of a turn towards the so-called "Foreign Woman." The introductory sequence in Prov 1:2–6 leads directly to the insight in v. 7 that the fear of God is the beginning of knowledge. This tangible connection of wisdom and fear of God reflects an understanding of wisdom that is more theologically determined than is the case for the collections in Proverbs 10–29. Above all, the speeches of personified Wisdom in Prov 1:20–33; 8; and 9:1–6 cannot be located tradition-historically in the pre-exilic period, as can be shown, for example, in Prov 8:22–31, where different older ideas of creation theology converge, identifying Proverbs 8 as a comparatively late text (cf. Baumann 1996, 111–152). The terminus a quo of Proverbs 1–9 lies in the Persian period. The connections to the final text in Prov 31:10–31 (cf. Whybray 1994, 159–162) make it probable, however, that Proverbs 1–9 experienced revisions and *Fortschreibungen* until the Hellenistic period (cf. Schipper 2018, 94). The introductory chapters of Proverbs are therefore to be understood as a deliberate and subsequent thematic opening, which on the one hand is intended as a hermeneutic key to help interpret the following individual sayings and collections of sayings, but on the other hand also substantiates their claim to validity against the background of fundamental questions regarding wisdom.

This results in the following picture for the chronological classification of the book of Proverbs: The book is based on the older, pre-exilic collections of sayings in Prov 10:1–22:16 and Proverbs 25–29, which can be traced back to the middle period of the monarchy. The insertion of the late pre-exilic collections Prov 22:17–24:22; 24:23–34 creates the core and basic stock of the book in Proverbs 10–29, which is then surrounded by a post-exilic framework: Proverbs 30 and Prov 31:1–9 extend the large Solomonic collection by two further collections of royal instructions, which, however, with the mention of Agur and Lemuel, refer beyond Israel and Judah and thus indicate a broad horizon of the constituent groups (cf. Schipper 2018, 12), which were probably active in the Persian period. With the final acrostic poem in Prov 31:10–31 and the reflections and Wisdom speeches in Proverbs 1–9, a framework is set around the earlier collections of royal instructions at the end of the formation process of the book of Proverbs in Hellenistic times.

23.3 JOB

Fundamental for the literary-historical classification of the book of Job is the distinction between the story of Job in Job 1–2; 42:7–17, and the poetic parts of the book in Job 3:1–42:6. While the narrative can be understood largely as a literary unity, a complex process of formation is reflected in Job 3:1–42:6. To be distinguished here are the lament of Job in Job 3, the dialogue of Job with his three friends Eliphaz, Bildad, and Zophar in Job 4–27, the Wisdom hymn in Job 28, Job's challenge to God in Job 29–31, Elihu's speeches in Job 32–37, and God's speeches in Job 38:1–42:6 with the short answers of Job in Job 40:1–5 and 42:1–6. Job's answers are surprising against the background of the phrase in Job 31:40b, according to which no more words of Job could be expected after Job 31—such text signals indicate different stages in the formation of the book.

However, the Elihu speeches in particular point to a multi-level redactional process of the poetic parts of the book. That there is no mention of Elihu outside of Job 32–37 is surprising at first in view of Job 42:7–10, where Eliphaz, Bildad, and Zophar are explicitly mentioned in v. 9. The fact that Elihu does not appear here could have something to do with the fact that God's judgment that the other friends did not speak properly in v. 7 is not valid for him. More likely, however, Elihu is not mentioned here because the author of Job 42:7–10 simply did not have access to the as yet unwritten Elihu speeches and could therefore only refer to Job's three other friends. The language of Job 32–37 with its Aramaisms also suggests that the Elihu speeches were only later embedded in the book. Elihu's interpretation of suffering as divine pedagogy reveals the effort to mediate between Job and his friends in their aporetic dialogue.

The Wisdom hymn in Job 28 points in a similar direction; it stands out in its poetic structure from Job's previous discourses with his friends and the following challenge to God. The text, which is divided into stanzas in v. 12 and v. 20 by repeating the question of the place of wisdom and which, at the end in v. 28, recommends the fear of the Lord as wisdom, is to be interpreted in form and content as an independent poem within the book, corresponding to the idea of fear of God, as it is also witnessed in Prov 1:7; 15:33; 31:30; Eccl 12:13; and Ps 111:10. As with the above-mentioned texts, Job 28 also probably belongs to the Hellenistic epoch and was likely written in the third century BCE.

If the Elihu speeches and the Wisdom hymn are now deduced as the latest layers of the text of Job, alongside Job's lament and his discourses with his friends and his challenge to God, what remains are God's speeches to Job in Job 38:1–42:6. Because of the answers given here by Job (40:1–5; 42:1–6), which are in tension with the phrase in Job 31:40b, it can be assumed that redaction-critically, God's speeches from the whirlwind can be distinguished from Job 3–31 and may have originated after Job 3–31, but before Job 28 and 32–37, and thus probably date back to the late Persian period in the fourth century BCE.

No clear boundaries separate Job 3 and Job 29–31, which frame Job's discourses with his friends, from the discourses in Job 4–27, though Job in Job 3 and Job 29–31 does not deal with his friends, but with himself and with God. But the parts of the text are very closely interwoven and clearly follow one another: Job's lament in Job 3 leads to the disputes with his friends in Job 4–27, whose failure inspires his turn towards God in Job 29–31. In Job 3–31, however, there are very different accentuations in the image of the world, of God, and of humanity, which suggest that a multi-layered redactional process can be expected here, which can only be reconstructed if the individual texts and their theological tendencies are precisely analyzed. Such analyses show that the different redactional levels within the texts mirror a discourse about the sovereignty of God, his justice, and the lowliness of humanity (cf. Witte 1994, 193–221; van Oorschot 2007), which ultimately constitutes the theological core of the book. That this discourse will have been conducted in Persian times is suggested by the linguistic, formal, and content-related references of the texts to the language of the Psalms, whose genres and themes are received by the authors of Job, which in principle, however, would also be conceivable at an earlier or later date. Due to the formal proximity of the reflective texts in Job to those in Proverbs, and against the background of the observation that especially the introductory chapters of Proverbs react to the criticism of Wisdom that is articulated in the core of Job, it seems reasonable to assume a literary-historical development from Job 3–31 to Proverbs 1–9, and thus to see Job 3–31 as a text that is earlier, from the Persian period, in comparison to the Hellenistic texts in Proverbs 1–9.

The problems of redactional criticism regarding the poetic parts of the book in Job 3:1–42:6 (cf. Schmid 2010, 11–18) are to be distinguished from the question of the composition of the book. There is much to suggest that the literary composition of the narrative and poetic revisions of the Job material initially took place independently of one another and were only linked together at a later stage. The conceptual pattern of the righteous sufferer can be traced beyond the Old Testament, as the Akkadian poem Ludlul bēl nēmeqi shows (cf. Schmid 2010, 56–62). The literary connection between the Hebrew Job narrative and the poetic parts of the book takes place above all in Job 2:11–13, where the three friends of Job are introduced, and in Job 42:7–10, where the three friends are reprimanded by God and excused by Job. With these narrative links, the depiction of Job as a patriarch in Job 1–2 is connected with the city-dweller Job from Job 3–31, and thus the Job material circulating in different forms in post-exilic Judah is transformed into a major literary complex. Analogies to this collection of traditions are offered in the narrower context by Proverbs, which also brings together various collections in one book, and in the wider context by the Pentateuch, whose image of the patriarchs in Genesis 12–36 is in conspicuous correspondence with the depiction of Job in Job 1–2 (cf. Schmid 2010, 65). Hellenistic influences can hardly be recognized here. The location of Job in the land of Uz in Job 1:1 rather suggests the authors' broad horizon, which is characteristic for the Persian period. The connection of the Job traditions from Job 1–2; 42:7–17; and Job 3–31 could therefore have already taken place in the fourth century BCE, the answers of God from the whirlwind in Job 38:1–42:6 were soon added, before finally the Elihu speeches in Job 32–37 and the Wisdom hymn in Job 28 conceptually linked the book of Job with other sapiential ideas and texts. These last redactional steps likely date back to the third century BCE, in which the framework of Proverbs and the epilogues of Ecclesiastes were also written.

23.4 ECCLESIASTES

The superscription of Ecclesiastes guides readers in a certain interpretive direction: according to Eccl 1:1, the book contains the words of Qoheleth, the son of David, the king in Jerusalem. The Solomonization, only implicitly carried out with this superscription, connects Ecclesiastes with Proverbs, but maintains a certain distance by omitting the name Solomon. Without a doubt, however, the book should be understood as a Wisdom writing. Thus, the numerous individual sayings that Qoheleth voices and incorporates in his arguments show how deeply Qoheleth is rooted in the sapiential tradition (cf. Crenshaw 1988, 38).

At the end of the book there are two epilogues that, together with the superscription, form a frame around the text. In Eccl 12:9–11, the book's anchoring in proverbial Wisdom is explicitly emphasized when Qoheleth is characterized as a sage who taught the people knowledge and heard, tested, and arranged sayings. In Eccl 12:12–14, on the other hand, a new accent is set with a warning against the many books being made, and fear of God and obedience to the commandments come to the fore (cf. Crenshaw 1988, 192). This builds bridges with texts outside Ecclesiastes. The exhortation to the fear of God corresponds with texts such as Prov 1:7, Job 28:28, and Ps 111:10, which see in the fear of God the beginning of wisdom. Both the superscription and the two epilogues speak of Qoheleth in the third person, which stands in a certain contrast to much of the text, within which Qoheleth unfolds his reflections from a first-person perspective. This becomes clear from Eccl 1:12, where after the introductory reflection in Eccl 1:3–11, the first large section follows in which Qoheleth appears as a wise king who develops his insights from experience (cf. Leuenberger 2011, 253–278).

Searching within the book for further textual signals of its redaction history apart from the framing by superscription and epilogues, the inclusion between Eccl 1:2 and Eccl 12:8 with the declaration of vanity is of particular importance. This is an inner frame around Qoheleth's reflections, which does not place them in a horizon outside of the book, but thematically sets a starting and an end point, which is connected with many thought processes within the book.

Whether the text enclosed by Eccl 1:2 and 12:8 can be further subdivided is controversial (cf. Schwienhorst-Schönberger 2011, 46–53). A certain foundation seems to exist in Ecclesiastes 1–3 (cf. Michel 1989, 1–83). Formally, the compositions in these chapters stand out with respect to each other, as the differences between the stereotypical poem on time in Eccl 3:1–8, 9 and the following two reflections in Eccl 3:10–15 and Eccl 3:16–22 show. The same applies to the coexistence of the introductory reflections in Eccl 1:3–11 and the "royal fiction" in Eccl 1:12–2:26. In the further course of the text there are longer reflections in Eccl 4:1–12:7, in which, however, individual words and sayings are occasionally incorporated, some of which are in tension with one another. Thus, in Eccl 7:3 and Eccl 7:9, grief and joy are judged very differently, as in Eccl 7:12 and Eccl 9:11 the economic benefits of wisdom are judged differently. In research, this juxtaposition of formally different and tensioned text elements has led to the search for different textual layers in the book of Ecclesiastes and, in view of its formation, to assume a process of *Fortschreibung* (cf. Rose 1999, 533–545). In contrast to redaction-historical models of formation, however, there is a growing view that Eccl 1:2–12:8 should be read as literary unity that goes back to one author (cf. Schmid 2008, 35). The tensions within the text are understood as "polar structures" (cf. Loader 1979, 1–3, 124–133) and deliberate comparisons that aim to involve the reader in the process of the constitution of meaning (cf. Krüger 2000, 32–39; Schwienhorst-Schönberger 2011, 68–69). Like the sayings in Proverbs, the book of Ecclesiastes focuses on the interpretive cooperation of its recipients, but no longer formulates its insights supra-individually and generally, as is the case in Proverbs, but shows how insights and knowledge can be gained on the path of experience.

Based on linguistic evidence, it can be shown that the book cannot be one of the earliest texts of the Old Testament, even if the superscription suggests this at first glance. The Aramaisms and hapax legomena as well as the preference for abstract word formations with regard to nouns give Qoheleth's language its own character (cf. Schoors 1992, 223). The Persian loanwords in Eccl 2:5 (פתגם) and 8:11 (פרדסים) are particularly meaningful, and thus the Persian period, in which linguistic mediations from Persian into Hebrew are first conceivable, is to be assumed as *terminus a quo* for the book's formation. The use of language and forms from proverbial Wisdom also indicates that Ecclesiastes could not have appeared until the fifth or fourth century BCE at the earliest, especially since it not only adopts these proverbial features, but, like Job, also enters into a discourse with the convictions reflected in Proverbs. While the constituent groups behind Proverbs count on the interpretability of the world and assume that knowledge of the world can be learned and understood, Qoheleth demonstrates with his empirical approach that experience, which is also the basis of proverbial Wisdom, may be suitable for opening up options for dealing with everyday life, but experience is unable to comprehend the world and its functional mechanisms as a whole. In the relative chronology of Old Testament Wisdom Literature, Qoheleth thus stands at Job's side, even though his problematization of man's cognitive possibilities has completely different features in style and content than the book of Job.

In its socio-economic background, Ecclesiastes shows indications of the Persian economic system (cf. Seow 2008, 216). However, what can be described for the Persian period may also apply in part to the Hellenistic period—especially the feeling of incomprehensibility of complex processes in a world that has become inscrutable (cf. Gehrke 2003, 74–78; Schwienhorst-Schönberger 2011, 103). The political framework conditions have great importance for an epoch's attitude to life; however, a change in these conditions generally does not cause radical breaks in mentality and attitude to life. Rather, earlier views and ways of thinking are confronted with new perspectives and expanded in agreement or contradiction. Thus, Persian loanwords and allusions to the economic organization of the Persian period are conceivable even in Hellenistic times, especially since the Hellenistic political elite were quite prepared to tie in with the economic conditions in the Orient, and economic mechanisms survived the change from the Persians to the Greeks (cf. Lohfink 1998 [1981], 71–82; Gehrke 2003, 46–61; Schellenberg 2013, 42).

Basically, the formation of Ecclesiastes is quite conceivable in the Persian period (cf. Seow 1997, 12–15). However, the probable influence of the Hellenistic attitude to life on the book and its presumed influence by a Greek form of discourse, the so-called *diatribe* (cf. Schwienhorst-Schönberger 2011, 57–59), lead in current research to the conclusion that it was written in Jerusalem in the third century BCE (cf. Crenshaw 1988, 50; Krüger 2000, 39). The book cannot be much later because its *terminus ad quem* likely lies in the second or first century BCE due to its appearance at Qumran (cf. Schwienhorst-Schönberger 2011, 112).

23.5 WISDOM PSALMS

The development of Old Testament Wisdom Literature described in the preceding sections, from the earlier collections of the book of Proverbs to Ecclesiastes and its peculiarities, is once again depicted *en miniature* within the Psalter and its Wisdom psalms. This is not surprising when the Psalter is understood as a "kleine Biblia" (Luther 1528) in which the central theologies of the Old Testament can be found.

Which psalms are to be determined as Wisdom psalms and what their peculiarities are, however, is controversial. The debate about the Wisdom psalms has been conducted primarily from a form-critical perspective. However, Hermann Gunkel's (Gunkel and Begrich 1933, 22–23) classical criteria for delimiting a literary genre produce no results with regard to the Wisdom psalms. Gunkel himself therefore speaks of "wisdom poetry" and sees a certain "type of poetry" behind the texts (Gunkel and Begrich 1933, 381–397). Sigmund Mowinckel (1955, 208–217) follows this less specific terminology when he speaks of "learned psalmography" instead of Wisdom psalms.

In more recent debate, Norman Whybray (1995, 160) has observed that Wisdom psalms should be identified by their proximity to the Old Testament Wisdom books. It is quite possible to find texts that fulfill this criterion. Characteristic for Wisdom Literature are individual sayings, which can be found in Proverbs, but which are also used in Job and Ecclesiastes. Such sayings can also be found within the Psalter. For example, in Psalm 127, several individual sayings appear, and the initial verses of Psalm 128 read like a compilation of sayings. Their similarity to Proverbs is unmistakable, and it is entirely conceivable that the Psalmists compiled such smaller texts from earlier sayings traditions and included them in their collection.

In Job and Ecclesiastes, the interpretability of the world is fundamentally problematized, due to existential affliction and empirical analysis, respectively. Corresponding problematizations can be found within the Psalter, particularly in Psalms 49 and 73 (cf. Witte 2014, 67–115; Saur 2015), where the Psalmists, like Qoheleth, lament the transience of life, and, like Job, deplore the disintegration of the nexus between deed and consequence (cf. Kynes 2012, 161–179). It is remarkable that these texts correspond to Psalm 37, which in many places refers to individual sayings, and thus at first seems to belong in the vicinity of Proverbs 10–29, but ultimately speaks very emphatically of trust in YHWH and is thus close to a level of theologically accentuated wisdom, as in Proverbs 1–9 (cf. Witte 2014, 39–65; Saur 2016).

In literary history, the collections in which these Wisdom psalms are transmitted have been subjected to continuous redaction and *Fortschreibung*. This applies both to the first group of Korah psalms, at the end of which Psalm 49 sets an individual closing point, and to the group of Asaph psalms, which opens with the individual reflection in Psalm 73. Psalm 37 is not quite as strikingly positioned in the first collection of Davidic psalms, but it emphasizes that the deed-consequence nexus is valid, and thus reacts within the Psalter in advance to the problematizations that follow in Psalms 49 and 73 (cf. Saur 2016). While Psalm 128 is anchored in the older Wisdom tradition and could have pre-exilic roots, Psalms 49 and 73 belong to the Hellenistic period. If Psalm 37 actually reacts to Psalms 49 and 73 with its affirmation of the deed-consequence nexus, it must also have originated in the Hellenistic epoch. This applies similarly to the late Psalms in which sapiential ideas, references to the fear of God, and orientation towards the Torah are combined, as is to some extent the case for Psalms 111–112. Psalms 111–112 are compositionally connected with Psalm 119, where sapiential thinking and Torah orientation are closely related. Conceptually, this should also apply to Psalm 1, which, as its opening text, prefaces the Psalter with a Wisdom-based hermeneutic key. Psalms 1, 111, 112, and 119 thus move in the context of texts such as Proverbs 1–9, Job 28, and Eccl 12:12–14, all of which belong to Hellenistic times and testify to a form of wisdom which no longer has its basis in human experience, but in divine revelation. The convergence of wisdom and Torah discernible here is further enhanced in Ben Sira, where in Ben Sira 24 both theological core areas are connected and merged.

23.6 BEN SIRA

While the Wisdom texts presented so far were written and transmitted in Hebrew, things are more complicated for the book of Jesus Ben Sira. The sapiential aphorisms, the instructions, and the poems of Ben Sira show that the book is rooted in the Jewish sapiential tradition and participates in its language and forms. This is particularly evident in several poems on Wisdom, reminiscent of the corresponding texts from Job 28 and Proverbs 1–9. What is new about these Wisdom poems, however, is the tendency to combine wisdom and Torah, which points to the fact that in Ben Sira, the reader is confronted with a tradition-historically later text when comparing central *theologumena* of Ben Sira with the profiling of these *theologumena* in the later Wisdom writings in the Hebrew canon (cf. Witte 2015, 59–82).

The formation of Ben Sira can only be reconstructed to a limited extent due to the difficult transmission of the text. Most experts take the Hebrew text as the oldest stage and attempt to reconstruct an older version of the book from it. Whether the formation of the book can be explained in terms of compositional history or of literary and redaction history remains to be seen (cf. Witte 2015, 7–9). In terms of form, Ben Sira is a sapiential instruction that deals primarily with Jewish tradition (cf. Witte 2015, 39–58).

The historical dating of Ben Sira can be based on the book's prologue. Here one of the few exact dates within a Wisdom writing can be used for the reconstruction of the period of the book's formation. In v. 27 of the prologue, Jesus Ben Sira's grandson states that he came to Egypt in the thirty-eighth year of King Ptolemy Euergetes, that is, in 132 BCE. It is likely that the translation was done within this time frame. The Hebrew book must have been written two generations earlier, probably at the beginning of the second century BCE, and transmitted with the help of the translation of the Greek-speaking Jewish diaspora in Egypt. If these chronological assumptions are correct, Ben Sira is a Wisdom writing, which is not too distant chronologically from the late texts of the books of Proverbs, Job, and Ecclesiastes, as well as the late Wisdom psalms. The formal correlations and theological interdependencies between these writings and Ben Sira have been intensively studied in recent years (cf. Witte 2015, 225–262). It has been shown that the book is in a chronological series with the Hebrew Wisdom writings in form and content, but that it presupposes them and reacts to them. Ben Sira marks the conclusion of Hebrew Wisdom Literature in the first millennium BCE. Its translation into Greek already points in the direction of the later Wisdom writings from Judaism, which, like the Wisdom of Solomon, were no longer written in Hebrew but in Greek. In this context, however, the fact that the community of Qumran also transmitted the Hebrew Wisdom writings, worked on sapiential topics, and wrote its own Wisdom texts should not be overlooked, as can be seen from the collection 4QInstruction from the first century BCE (cf. Goff 2007, 12–13; Goff 2013, 12–14).

23.7 A Short History of Old Testament Wisdom Literature

Starting from the preceding considerations, a history of Old Testament Wisdom Literature can now be reconstructed in summary, extending from the middle period of the monarchy to Hellenistic times.

The beginnings of sapiential thinking and forms of sapiential language can be found in the sapiential sayings, whose characteristic is a conciseness that favors both the teachability and learnability of this form of Wisdom. It is not demonstrable, but it can be assumed that the written form of this Wisdom in the form of sayings and collections of sayings had its place in educational contexts. The older collections transmitted in Proverbs, found in Proverbs 10–29, may have been collected in written form in their core—which was, however, continuously redacted—since the middle period of the monarchy, whereby the oldest sapiential material is to be found in the two Solomonic collections. In these collections, Wisdom is not only a phenomenon of the educated and upper class, but has probably been anchored in large sections of the population, as the sayings that deal with agricultural and handicraft topics suggest in particular. The fact that the literarization of the sayings took place in the context of the palace and was thus bound to central institutions is suggested by Prov 25:1, which mentions the "men of Hezekiah," the king's officials, who collected the sayings. The use to which these collections were put at the royal court can no longer be determined. It is noteworthy, however, that in close temporal proximity to these collection efforts, during the period in the eighth and seventh century BCE, in which Assyria exerted a considerable cultural influence on Judah, the preservation of traditions assumed greater importance there as well, as the library of Assurbanipal with its collections of the knowledge of that time particularly shows. The collections in Prov 22:17–24:22 and Prov 24:23–34 clearly indicate that, with the compilation of the two Solomonic collections of sayings, the literary history of Wisdom was by no means complete, but had only just begun. The integration of the two later collections into the horizon of the Solomonic collections shows the high integrative power of Wisdom, which at that time was, at its core, proverbial Wisdom, and was oriented towards an experience-based coping with everyday life. The conceptual core of this proverbial Wisdom is the assumption that there is a nexus between deed and consequence, and that the actions of each individual are located in a social framework. Here it must have come to a gradual expansion of the cognitive claims of the constituent groups of Wisdom, who were no longer concerned solely with coping with everyday situations with the help of individual sayings, but who recognized a basic law in the nexus they purported to see between deed and consequence, with whose help they tried comprehensively to interpret reality as a whole.

In Wisdom Literature this pattern of thinking appears again in Persian times, but now in a fundamental debate about the question of the validity of the deed-consequence nexus and the possibilities of the interpretability of the world. Already in Proverbs, a voice is heard in Prov 30:1–9 which, directly following the large collections of sayings in Proverbs 10–29, questions human cognitive abilities. And Job is the first literary work in which human limits are explored with full existential force in the form of both the narrative and the simultaneously emerging poetic parts of the book. The social and geographical location of Job in both the narrative and the poetic parts of the book may point to the Persian period, in which the book's constituent groups express fundamental aporia regarding the understanding of God's action in literary forms. That the questions of a hidden, evading, and ultimately inaccessible God were also discussed and literarized outside of the Wisdom writings is evident in texts like Genesis 22 or Isaiah 6, whose image of God is as dread-inducing as the one in Job.

The questions of the Persian period are already addressed within Job, when both the Elihu speeches and the Wisdom hymn make literary contributions to the discussion, which examine human limits and the purposes of God's cosmic action. The divine answer in Job 38–41 is the link between the older of the poetic parts of the book and the presumably Hellenistic positions. The inscrutability and inaccessibility of God is put into a wider horizon by theological extensions of God's areas of power. This is exactly what can be observed in this phase of the literary history of Wisdom in Proverbs, whose introductory chapters react to the problematization of Wisdom and try to secure the basic concern of the constituent groups to be able to understand the world with the help of wisdom in the form of a personified Wisdom that accompanies creation from the beginning. The very concrete and everyday wisdom is placed here from the outset in a theologically highly speculative horizon, which, at least to some extent in Prov 31:10–31, is brought back to everyday life, when the woman of the final verses, although reminiscent of personified Wisdom from Proverbs 1–9, is at the same time also portrayed as a practical and powerful manager of her family business.

Both the late *Fortschreibungen* of Job and the introductory and final chapters of Proverbs lead to the Hellenistic period, when the Wisdom psalms also appear, in which wisdom and Torah converge and thus prepare for the theological program of Ben Sira. This is most evident in Psalm 119, which in turn is anticipated by Psalms 111–112 as well as Psalm 1, and thus forms a Wisdom network that defines the Psalter as a whole. On another level are the problematizing Psalms 49 and 73 and the strangely affirmative Psalm 37, which, with its clear distinction between the wicked and the righteous and its adherence to the deed-consequence nexus is close to Proverbs 1–9. Together with Psalms 49 and 73, Psalm 37 represents the Hellenistic discourse between the books of Ecclesiastes, Job, and Proverbs within the Psalter.

The Hellenistic book of Ecclesiastes occupies a special position, which problematizes human cognitive abilities, but at the same time recognizes human limits relatively calmly, as opposed to the emotional highs and lows of Job. Qoheleth summarizes his thoughts at the same time as Proverbs 1–9 and Job 28 and 32–37 are formulated. Ecclesiastes 1:1 and 12:9–11 make it clear that the constituent groups of the book of Ecclesiastes want to connect their text with those writings in that, on the one hand, they both carry out an implicit Solomonization of Ecclesiastes based on Prov 1:1 and profile Qoheleth as a teacher of proverbial Wisdom. The connection of wisdom, Torah, and fear of God, which becomes tangible in Psalm 119 and Ben Sira, determines the second epilogue of Ecclesiastes in 12:12–14. With its themes of the fear of God and obedience to the commandments, it takes a rather unexpected perspective on the book, but at the same time anchors the ever more established ways of thinking of Wisdom also within Ecclesiastes, which now speaks of the fear of God (cf. Job 28:28; Prov 1:7; Ps 111:10) and obedience to the commandments (cf. Proverbs 2; Psalm 119; Ben Sira 24). In Hellenistic times, traditional strands of different origins converge here on the literary-historical level. Wisdom, which comes from human experience and aims at coping with everyday life, becomes a revealed wisdom, which is now to be understood as a comprehensive knowledge of coping with life in fear of God and in obedience to divine instruction. The sapiential texts from Qumran (cf. 4QInstr) and the sapientially influenced hymns of the New Testament (cf. John 1:1–18; Phil 2:6–11; Col 1:15–20), then, demonstrate that wisdom and Wisdom Literature continued to develop beyond the Hebrew Bible (cf. Leuenberger 2011, 279–312).

Works Cited

Assmann, Jan. 1990. *Maʾat: Gerechtigkeit und Unsterblichkeit im Alten Ägypten*. Munich: Beck.

Baumann, Gerlinde. 1996. *Die Weisheitsgestalt in Proverbien 1–9: Traditionsgeschichtliche und theologische Studien*. FAT 16. Tübingen: Mohr Siebeck.

Carr, David M. 2005. *Writing on the Tablet of the Heart: Origins of Scripture and Literature*. Oxford: Oxford University Press.

Crenshaw, James L. 1988. *Ecclesiastes: A Commentary*. OTL. London: SCM Press.

Gehrke, Hans-Joachim. 2003. *Geschichte des Hellenismus*. Oldenbourg Grundriss der Geschichte 1A. 3rd ed. Munich: Oldenbourg.

Goff, Matthew J. 2007. *Discerning Wisdom: The Sapiential Literature of the Dead Sea Scrolls*. VTSup 116. Leiden: Brill.

Goff, Matthew J. 2013. *4QInstruction*. WLAW 2. Atlanta, GA: SBL.

Golka, Friedemann W. 1993. *The Leopard's Spots: Biblical and African Wisdom in Proverbs*. London: T&T Clark.

Gunkel, Hermann, and Joachim Begrich. 1933. *Einleitung in die Psalmen: Die Gattungen der religiösen Lyrik Israels*. Göttingen: Vandenhoeck & Ruprecht.

Janowski, Bernd. 1994. "Die Tat kehrt zum Täter zurück: Offene Fragen im Umkreis des 'Tun-Ergehen-Zusammenhangs.'" *ZTK* 91:247–271.

Japhet, Sara. 1993. *I & II Chronicles: A Commentary*. OTL. Louisville, KY: Westminster John Knox.

Krüger, Thomas. 2000. *Kohelet (Prediger)*. BKAT 19 (Sonderband). Neukirchen-Vluyn: Neukirchener Verlag.

Kynes, Will. 2012. *My Psalm Has Turned into Weeping: Job's Dialogue with the Psalms*. BZAW 437. Berlin: de Gruyter.

Lemaire, André. 1981. *Les écoles et la formation de la Bible dans l'Ancien Israël*. OBO 39. Göttingen: Vandenhoeck & Ruprecht; Fribourg: Presses Universitaires.

Leuenberger, Martin. 2011. *Gott in Bewegung: Religions- und theologiegeschichtliche Beiträge zu Gottesvorstellungen im alten Israel*. FAT 76. Tübingen: Mohr Siebeck.

Loader, James A. 1979. *Polar Structures in the Book of Qohelet*. BZAW 152. Berlin: de Gruyter.

Lohfink, Norbert. 1998. "*melek, šallîṭ* und *môšēl* bei Kohelet und die Abfassungszeit des Buchs." Pages 71–82 in *Studien zu Kohelet*. Edited by Norbert Lohfink. SBAB 26. Stuttgart: Verlag Katholisches Bibelwerk.

Luther, Martin. 1528. "Vorrede zum Psalter." Pages 32–37 in *Luther Deutsch 5: Die Schriftauslegung*. Edited by Kurt Aland. 2nd ed. 1963. Göttingen: Vandenhoeck & Ruprecht.

Mathys, Hans-Peter. 2004. "Die tüchtige Hausfrau von Prov 31,10–31: Eine phönizische Unternehmerin." *TZ* 60:23–42.

Michel, Diethelm. 1989. *Untersuchungen zur Eigenart des Buches Qohelet: Mit einem Anhang von Reinhard G. Lehmann: Bibliographie zu Qohelet*. BZAW 183. Berlin: de Gruyter.

Mowinckel, Sigmund. 1955. "Psalms and Wisdom." Pages 205–224 in *Wisdom in Israel and in the Ancient Near East*. Edited by Martin Noth and D. Winton Thomas. VTSup 3. Leiden: Brill.

Oorschot, Jürgen van. 2007. "Die Entstehung des Hiobbuches." Pages 165–184 in *Das Buch Hiob und seine Interpretationen: Beiträge zum Hiob-Symposium auf dem Monte Verità vom 14.–19. August 2005*. ATANT 88. Edited by Thomas Krüger, Manfred Oeming, Konrad Schmid, and Christoph Uehlinger. Zurich: Theologischer Verlag.

Rad, Gerhard von. 1970. *Weisheit in Israel*. Neukirchen-Vluyn: Neukirchener Verlag.

Renz, Johannes. 1995. *Die althebräischen Inschriften*, vol. 1: *Text und Kommentar*. Handbuch der althebräischen Epigraphik 1. Darmstadt: Wissenschaftliche Buchgesellschaft.

Römer, Thomas C. 2005. *The So-called Deuteronomistic History: A Sociological, Historical and Literary Introduction*. London: T&T Clark.

Rose, Martin. 1999. *Rien de nouveau: Nouvelles approches du livre de Qohéleth*. OBO 168. Göttingen: Vandenhoeck & Ruprecht; Fribourg: Presses Universitaires.

Saur, Markus. 2014. "Prophetie, Weisheit und Gebet: Überlegungen zu den Worten Agurs in Prov 30,1–9." *ZAW* 126:570–583.

Saur, Markus. 2015. "Where Can Wisdom Be Found? New Perspectives on the Wisdom Psalms." Pages 181–204 in *Was There a Wisdom Tradition? New Prospects in Israelite Wisdom Studies*. Edited by Mark Sneed. AIL 23. Atlanta, GA: SBL.

Saur, Markus. 2016. "Frevler und Gerechte: Überlegungen zum theologischen Ort von Psalm 37." Pages 375–392 in *Nächstenliebe und Gottesfurcht: Beiträge aus alttestamentlicher, semitistischer und altorientalistischer Wissenschaft für Hans-Peter Mathys zum 65. Geburtstag*. Edited by Hanna Jenni and Markus Saur. AOAT 439. Münster: Ugarit-Verlag.

Schellenberg, Annette. 2013. *Kohelet*. ZBK 17. Zürich: Theologischer Verlag.

Schipper, Bernd U. 2005. "Die Lehre des Amenemope und Prov 22,17–24,22: Eine Neubestimmung des literarischen Verhältnisses." *ZAW* 117:53–72, 232–248.

Schipper, Bernd U. 2018. *Sprüche (Proverbia) 1: Proverbien 1,1–15,33*. BKAT 17.1. Göttingen: Vandenhoeck & Ruprecht.

Schmid, Konrad. 2008. *Literaturgeschichte des Alten Testaments: Eine Einführung*. Darmstadt: Wissenschaftliche Buchgesellschaft.

Schmid, Konrad. 2010. *Hiob als biblisches und antikes Buch: Historische und intellektuelle Kontexte seiner Theologie*. SBS 219. Stuttgart: Verlag Katholisches Bibelwerk.

Schoors, Anton. 1992. *The Preacher Sought to Find Pleasing Words: A Study of the Language of Qoheleth*. OLA 41. Leuven: Peeters.

Schwienhorst-Schönberger, Ludger. 2011. *Kohelet*. HThKAT. 2nd ed. Freiburg im Breisgau: Herder.

Seow, Choon Leong. 1997. *Ecclesiastes*. AB 18C. New York, NY: Doubleday.

Seow, Choon Leong. 2008. "The Social World of Ecclesiastes." Pages 189–217 in *Scribes, Sages, and Seers: The Sage in the Eastern Mediterranean World*. Edited by Leo G. Perdue. FRLANT 219. Göttingen: Vandenhoeck & Ruprecht.

Scoralick, Ruth. 1995. *Einzelspruch und Sammlung: Komposition im Buch der Sprichwörter Kapitel 10–15*. BZAW 232. Berlin: de Gruyter.

Westermann, Claus. 1990. *Wurzeln der Weisheit: Die ältesten Sprüche Israels und anderer Völker*. Göttingen: Vandenhoeck & Ruprecht.

Witte, Markus. 1994. *Vom Leiden zur Lehre: Der dritte Redegang (Hiob 21–27) und die Redaktionsgeschichte des Hiobbuches*. BZAW 230. Berlin: de Gruyter.

Witte, Markus. 2014. *Von Ewigkeit zu Ewigkeit: Weisheit und Geschichte in den Psalmen*. BThSt 146. Neukirchen-Vluyn: Neukirchener Verlag.

Witte, Markus. 2015. *Texte und Kontexte des Sirachbuchs: Gesammelte Studien zu Ben Sira und zur frühjüdischen Weisheit*. FAT 98. Tübingen: Mohr Siebeck.

Whybray, Roger N. 1994. *The Composition of the Book of Proverbs*. JSOTSup 168. Sheffield: Sheffield Academic.

Whybray, Roger N. 1995. "The Wisdom Psalms." Pages 152–160 in *Wisdom in Ancient Israel: Essays in Honour of J.A. Emerton*. Edited by John Day, Robert P. Gordon, and H.G.M. Williamson. Cambridge: Cambridge University Press.

CHAPTER 24

···

THEOLOGY OF WISDOM

···

TREMPER LONGMAN III

24.1 IS THERE A DISTINCT WISDOM THEOLOGY?

···

IN the thinking of a previous generation, a theology of Wisdom would be something of a misnomer.[1] After all, they thought, Wisdom was distinct from other traditions in the Hebrew Bible (covenant, law, redemptive history, prophecy, cult) in its subdued interest in God. Rather than revelation, the sages derived their wisdom primarily, if not exclusively, from human reflection. As Otto Eissfeldt (1965, 47) put it, "The basis for the commendation of wisdom and piety is purely secular and rational." C. Westermann (1995, 130) similarly stated:

> The proverbs as such have a universal character. Proverbs can surface anywhere among humankind.... [Proverbs mentioning God] have no specifically theological foundation in an explicitly theological context. Rather, they speak of God in such a manner as would any person without stepping outside of everyday secular discourse.[2]

Of course, as one reads a book like Proverbs, it is hard to ignore numerous references to God (e.g., "Fraudulent scales are an abomination to Yahweh, but an accurate weight brings his favor," Prov 11:1),[3] even if certain proverbs come across as just so much good

---

[1] The focus of this chapter is on Wisdom Literature, particularly the books of Proverbs, Ecclesiastes, and Job. The concept of wisdom is more pervasive throughout the Hebrew Bible than in just these three books, and the characteristics of Wisdom theology described here is relevant for this broader concept as well.

[2] See also Brueggemann 1972, 81–83.

[3] Translations from Proverbs come from Longman 2006.

advice when isolated from their broader context (e.g., "Expectation delayed makes the heart sick; longing fulfilled is the tree of life," Prov 13:12). But this school of thought that separated Wisdom from the rest of the biblical traditions in its approach to theology responded by arguing that later redactors of Proverbs introduced this theological dimension to the book which was originally secular (McKane 1965; McKane 1992, 1–22; see also Whybray 1965, 72).

Even though this perspective has been thoroughly and, in the opinion of many, effectively critiqued (see Bostrom 1990, 36–39; Schwab 2013), remnants of this viewpoint continue to exist. For example, William Brown (2014, 3), one of the most accomplished interpreters of Wisdom today, has recently stated:

> Ancient Israel's sages had no qualms incorporating the wisdom of other cultures. Biblical wisdom seeks the common good along with the common God. Wisdom's international, indeed universal appeal constitutes its canonical uniqueness. The Bible's wisdom corpus is the open door to an otherwise closed canon.[4]

One is left to wonder whether such a viewpoint is motivated by the desire for a less exclusive, more ecumenical understanding of God in the canon, otherwise filled with a very specific, particular theology that is different than that found in other cultures.

Of course, these scholars are certainly correct to note that Wisdom in the Hebrew Bible has its own particular nuance. Their mistake, in the opinion of others,[5] was to create too large a distinction between Wisdom and the rest of the Hebrew Bible. As other chapters in this volume demonstrate, Wisdom does share a special relationship with other ancient Near Eastern texts. Indeed, the book of Kings praises Solomon's wisdom by comparing him favorably with "the wisdom of Egypt" (1 Kgs 5:10 [ET 4:30]), an evaluation that presumes that the wisdom of Egypt was worthwhile. One could not imagine a comparable statement in the Hebrew Bible about Egyptian priests or Assyrian prophets. Then, too, Wisdom Literature does indeed look to human experience and reflection on mistakes as sources of wisdom. Further, we must also acknowledge that allusions to redemptive-history, covenant, law, and cultic matters are not as explicit as in other parts of the Hebrew Bible. Finally, it is true that those books associated with wisdom do appeal to creation as a foundation for knowledge of God in a way that might appeal to those who might think wisdom is available for all in spite of their lack of commitment to the specific God YHWH.[6]

But, in my opinion, the citation of these traits associated with wisdom to depict a "common God" that seeks a "common good" misses the very heart of wisdom, which, according to the biblical text can only be found through a relationship with a very specific deity named YHWH. I turn now to demonstrate the fundamental nature of the "fear

---

[4] See also Fiddes 2013 and the summary statement in Perdue 2007, 344.
[5] For instance, Kynes 2019.
[6] Note Walther Zimmerli's (1964, 148) often-quoted comment that "wisdom thinks resolutely within the framework of a theology of creation."

of God" to biblical wisdom. I will do so by focusing on the three books most associated with wisdom in the Hebrew Bible: Proverbs, Ecclesiastes, and Job.[7]

24.2 WHAT IS WISDOM THEOLOGY?

24.2.1 The Theology of Proverbs

As mentioned above, much of Proverbs strikes modern readers as not much more than the type of practical advice one might find from someone like Benjamin Franklin or Yogi Berra:

> Those who love discipline love knowledge;
>> and those who hate correction are dullards.
> The good person obtains favor from Yahweh,
>> and he will condemn the scheming person.
> No one will stand fast by wicked acts,
>> but the root of the righteous cannot be disturbed.
> A noble woman is a crown for her husband,
>> but like rot in his bones is a disgraceful woman.   (Prov 12:1–4)

Granted, YHWH makes the occasional appearance as in v. 2 in this passage, but most proverbs seem to be nothing more than means of shaping a person's emotional intelligence.[8]

To conclude, however, that Proverbs is only dimly interested in God and his relationship with his people would be a mischaracterization of the book that could only arise from not understanding its overall structure. In the first place, the preface to the book announces that the "fear of the Lord" provides the basis of all wisdom, and, in the second place, the metaphor of Woman Wisdom signals that wisdom only results from a proper relationship with God, while all folly results from idolatry.

24.2.1.1 The Fear of the Lord

In keeping with the convention of ancient Near Eastern instructions,[9] Proverbs begins with a preamble (1:1–7) that introduces the book's purpose among other matters. While

---

[7] Recent studies have questioned the utility of the generic label Wisdom Literature as it has been applied to these three books over the past century plus (since at least Bruch 1851). For instance, see the provocative work by Sneed (2015) as well as the work of Kynes (2019). See Longman 2017, 276–282 for an attempt to defend the generic categorization.

[8] The term "emotional intelligence" became popular with the publication of Goleman 1995. One is emotionally intelligent if they are able to do or say the right thing at the right time. Goleman cited studies indicating that such social skills correlated well with success in life defined as having and maintaining good relationships with people as well as getting and keeping a job.

[9] Particularly Egyptian sḇyt texts, including the Instruction of Amenemope, which is often compared with the book of Proverbs. See Longman 2009, 464–505.

citing the practical value of wisdom as well as its ethical nature (1:3b), the preamble concludes by announcing the theological basis of its contents:

> The fear of Yahweh is the beginning of knowledge,
>> but fools despise wisdom and discipline.   (1:7)

With variations ("knowledge" [דעת] sometimes replaces "wisdom" [חכמה], for example), this formula recurs a number of times throughout the book (1:29; 2:5; 3:7; 8:13; 10:27; 14:2, 26, 27; 15:16, 33; 16:6; 19:23; 22:4; 23:17; 24:21; 28:14; 29:25; 31:30), thus signaling its importance for the very definition of wisdom in the book.

Indeed, by stating that the fear of the Lord is the "beginning" (ראשית) of wisdom Proverbs affirms that a person cannot be considered wise unless they have such a relationship with God. That would be true whether "beginning" should be taken in a foundational or in a temporal sense (or both). This phrase alone indicates that wisdom is a theological concept at its very heart. The specification that this fear is specifically "of YHWH" undercuts any attempt to make wisdom a universal or cosmopolitan idea in spite of some surface similarities with ancient Near Eastern wisdom.

But what is meant by "fear" and why would the author choose "fear" over other possible states of mind, for instance "the love of YHWH"? We should begin by admitting the difficulty in capturing the proper nuance of the Hebrew word יראה in an English word. Contenders would run the gamut from "respect" to "awe" to "fear" to "horror." However, "respect" seems too weak for the context as well as too formal. "Horror," on the other end of the spectrum, would seem counterproductive since horror would not enhance relationship between a person and God, which is clearly a desired outcome of the sages.

That leaves "awe" and "fear" as possibilities. In one respect, either will do. Awe incorporates fear and includes reverence and wonder before something or someone sublime. But for my tastes, the traditional "fear" remains the best choice of translation because, while awe leads primarily to contemplation, fear is a more primal emotion and connects better to obedience. And this connection is important because Proverbs makes much of the relationship between wisdom, יראה, and obedience.

יראה is not just an emotion or a state of mind; it leads to action. We see this clearly in the book of Ecclesiastes (for more see 24.2.2 The Theology of Ecclesiastes below), where the unnamed second wise man at the end urges his son to "יראו God and keep his commandments" (12:12–13). In Proverbs, those who have the יראה of YHWH will obey the advice that comes from the sages. Indeed, the connection is explicitly made in specific texts:

> Those who walk in virtue fear Yahweh,
>> but those who go the wrong way on his path despise him.   (14:2)
> With covenant love and faithfulness guilt is atoned for,
>> and with the fear of Yahweh there is turning away from evil.   (16:6)

For these reasons, while "awe" is not misleading, the English word "fear" serves best, as long as we understand that this is a fear that does not make a person run away, but rather leads to relationship and obedience. But so can love. That said, fear is the more appropriate emotion to lead to another desired wisdom virtue, namely humility. Proverbs often warns against pride and encourages its opposite, humility.

> The fear of Yahweh is wise discipline,
>   and humility comes before glory.   (15:33)
> The reward of humility, the fear of Yahweh,
>   is wealth, honor, and life.   (22:4)

The opposite of the fear of God that leads to obedience in the advice of the sages is to be "wise in one's own eyes" and do what one wants to do and thus embrace evil.

> Don't be wise in your own eyes.
>   Fear Yahweh and turn away from evil.   (3:7)
> Do you see people who are wise in their own eyes?
>   There is more hope for a fool than for them.   (26:12)

Fear leads to humility and a turning to God's wisdom rather than one's own ideas of what defines right attitudes and behavior. Fear leads to a posture that allows a person to learn from their mistakes as they receive criticism (correction) from others:

> The discipline of Yahweh, my son, do not reject,
>   and do not loathe his correction.
> For the one whom Yahweh loves he will correct,
>   even like a father who treats his son favorably.   (3:11–12)

In summary, wisdom begins with fear of the Lord that leads to obedience. Fear breeds humility, not pride that seeks autonomy (being wise in one's own eyes). The wise person who fears God will be open to instruction from God and his agents (the sages). Fear also opens one up to being criticized and learning from correction rather than being doomed to keep repeating mistakes.

24.2.1.2 *Embracing Woman Wisdom*

The book of Proverbs reveals the pervasive theological nature of its wisdom in yet another important way—through the figure of Woman Wisdom. We first encounter her in the second discourse of the book (1:20–33). The narrator introduces her as speaking in a public place (an emphasis that will be repeated in chs. 8 and 9), and when she speaks in the remaining verses of her first discourse, she demands that her implied audience of young men enter into a relationship with her. She disdains their rejection ("because I invited you, but you rejected me; I extended my hand, but you paid no attention," 2:24). She threatens them that she will ignore them when they decide to turn to her later when they are in trouble (2:26–32) and ends by reminding them of the rewards of entering into a relationship with her ("those who obey me will dwell securely; they will be untroubled from the horror of evil," 2:23).

A little later in the discourses, the fatherly sage also urgently appeals to his sons to develop an intimate relationship with Woman Wisdom:

> Acquire Wisdom;
> acquire Understanding.
> Don't forget,
> and don't divert from the speeches of my mouth.
> Don't abandon her, and she will guard you.
> Love her, and she will protect you.
> ....
> Esteem her highly, and she will embrace you.
> She will honor you, if you embrace her.   (4:5–6, 8)

While here the father hints at the erotic nature of the relationship, in a later discourse this tone becomes more explicit as the father urges the son to, "Say to Wisdom, 'You are my sister' " (7:4), a term of intimacy with which we are familiar from the Song of Songs (e.g., 4:10).

A truly wise person has an intimate relationship with this woman named Wisdom and none other, as we learn from perhaps the most crucial chapter in the book of Proverbs. Proverbs 9 stands at the end of the first part of the book with its speeches or discourses (chs. 1–9) and just before the anthology of proverbs that forms its second part (chs. 10–31). Before reading the advice in the form of proverbs that follows, the sages demand that the reader make a choice between relationship with Woman Wisdom or Woman Folly:

> Wisdom built her house;
> she erected her seven pillars.
> She slaughtered her slaughter, mixed her wine.
> She also arranged her tables.
> She sends her maidens; she issues an invitation
> from the pinnacle of the heights of the city:
> "Whoever is immature—turn aside here,"
> she says to those who lack heart.
> "Come, eat my food,
> and drink the wine I mixed.
> Abandon immaturity and live.
> March on the path of understanding."   (9:1–6)

> Woman Folly is boisterous;
> she is immature but does not even know it.

> She sits at the doorway of her house,
>   on a seat at the heights of the city.
> She invites those who pass by on the path,
>   those going straight on their way.
> "Whoever is immature—turn aside here,"
>   she says to those who lack heart.
> "Stolen water is sweet;
>   food eaten in secret is pleasant."
> But they do not know that the departed are there,
>   that those invited by her are in the depths of Sheol.   (9:13–18)

Notice the symmetry between the two units. Both have houses on "the heights of the city." Both have meals that they offer to the immature who go by on the path. Indeed, their initial appeal is identical, "'Whoever is immature—turn aside here,' she says to those who lack heart" (vv. 4 and 16).

But differences between the descriptions appear as well. Wisdom's house is grand and magnificent (the significance of the symbolic number seven). She has prepared her meal with care and then sends out her maidens to invite the guests. Her intention is to grant understanding to the immature. Folly's house is not described, but she lounges by the door and calls lazily to those going by. She offers food, but we do not hear about its preparation. She may not even have prepared a meal; it is described as secret. Finally, the narrator informs the reader that her intention is not to grant understanding, but to kill. Those who accept her invitation to dine will end up among "the departed," in Hebrew, the *rephaim* (רפאים), the denizens of Sheol, the underworld.

Again, both women invite the same group of men to a meal. The men are those who, according to v. 15 "pass by the path... going straight on their way." The path/way is a pervasive metaphor throughout Proverbs (particularly chs. 1–9) for the journey of life. The wise path is smooth, lit, and leads straight to life, while the foolish path is crooked, dark, filled with snares and traps, and leads to death (Prov. 3:6; 4:1–19; 11:5; 12:28; 14:12; 16:25; 21:8; 22:5). The meal itself is a metaphor for intimate relationship: to dine with someone is to enter into a deeper relationship. The author intends the readers/hearers of Proverbs 9 to make a choice. Will they dine with Woman Wisdom or Woman Folly?

The narrator clearly pushes the men to choose Wisdom and not Folly. There is a grandeur and dignity to the description of Wisdom's house and her meal. Her promise of maturity and understanding rings true. The same cannot be said of Folly. Her boisterous tone signals a lack of discipline; her sitting at the doorway a kind of laziness. In contrast to the public nature of what Wisdom offers, Folly entices by offering "stolen water" and a "secret" meal. But, as we have already mentioned, her meal leads to death not life.

But who are these women? What do they represent? As we explore this question, we come to understand how they contribute to the theological dimension of wisdom in the book of Proverbs. The question also takes us back to Proverbs 8, which is the longest sustained depiction of Woman Wisdom found in the book.

Once again, Wisdom is introduced in terms of her location that, as we saw in ch. 9, highlights her public stance as well as the height of her location (8:1–3). Here too she appeals to the immature to listen to her (vv. 4–6) because what she says and who she is embodies the virtues of wisdom itself. She espouses virtue and nobility; she rejects evil and perverse speech, while she imparts advice and resourcefulness (vv. 7–14). Kings and nobles are singled out as particular beneficiaries of a relationship with her, presumably because their wise rule would benefit their subjects (vv. 15–16). A relationship with her brings benefits of prosperity (vv. 17–21).

The most difficult, and well-known, part of her description comes in vv. 22–31, where Wisdom describes her involvement with creation. She boasts of her antiquity, being begotten (v. 22) even before the earth itself. Thus, she observed the very creation of the earth. But her connection with creation exceeds that of observation. She may well have participated in the creation process. This assertion depends on the translation of the enigmatic אמון of v. 30, which could be taken as "craftsperson," thus implying a contribution to the creation of the world.[10]

The chapter then ends (vv. 32–36) with a final appeal by Wisdom to pay attention to her. She bolsters her invitation by telling her audience that they will be happy and they will find life as opposed to those who do not heed her. These will instead find death.

Now we are in a position to address the issue of the identity of Woman Wisdom as well as Woman Folly. The key to the identity of Wisdom is the location of her house on the heights of the city. There is only one house that occupies this position in the real world of the ancient Near East, including Israel, and that is the temple, the place where the divine presence makes itself known. As Psalm 48 proclaims in its opening: "Great is the Lord, and most worthy of praise, in the city of our God, his holy mountain. Beautiful in its loftiness, the joy of the whole earth, like the heights of Zaphon is mount Zion." Thus, at a minimum, Woman Wisdom personifies YHWH's wisdom. Therefore, in ch. 9, to choose to dine with Woman Wisdom is to choose to learn from YHWH himself. But perhaps we can go even further and say that Woman Wisdom represents YHWH himself by means of synecdoche.

But if the location of Woman Wisdom's house on the heights leads us to this conclusion, what then of Woman Folly, whose house is also on the highest point of the city? She too represents deity, but in this case all the false gods and goddesses that were a temptation to Israel that potentially lured them away from the worship of their true God.

Note then how the figure of Woman Wisdom accentuates the theological dimension of wisdom in the book. Wisdom comes from a relationship with YHWH; folly from a relationship with other deities, false gods. The very concept of wisdom is theologically rich, even in later contexts where God is not mentioned at all. In other words, we are to carry this theological understanding of wisdom into Proverbs 10–31.

Let's consider two later proverbs that do not mention YHWH:

> Wise women build their houses
> but dupes demolish theirs with their own hands....

---

[10] For a defense of this translation in the light of alternatives, see Longman 2006, 196 n. h.

In the mouth of a dupe is a sprig of pride,
  but the lips of the wise guard them   (14:1, 3).[11]

Both proverbs are rather typical antithetical parallelisms that contrast wisdom with folly. On the one hand, we have women whose wisdom builds up their households and wise people who are disciplined in speech over against, on the other hand, foolish women (dupes) whose folly destroys their households and those whose speech demonstrates the vice of pride. While these two proverbs are practical and ethical on the surface, when read in the context of the whole book, in particular through the hermeneutical prism of chs. 1–9 with the concluding choice it presents, we can also see their theological dimension. In other words, women who build their houses and those who guard their lips are dining with Woman Wisdom. They have and demonstrate a proper relationship with YHWH. But those who demolish their houses and those who speak with pride are acting like those who have chosen to dine with Woman Folly. In other words, they act like idolaters.

24.2.2 The Theology of Ecclesiastes

We turn next to the book of Ecclesiastes, which like Proverbs concerns wisdom, but unlike Proverbs focuses on noting the limitations of wisdom for humanity. In spite of the differences, however, we will now see that Ecclesiastes and Proverbs share the same fundamental conclusion concerning the nature of wisdom and its source. The book of Ecclesiastes speaks of and reflects on human relationship with God quite frequently. But what does the book actually say about God? How does the book compare to the rest of the Hebrew Bible and in particular other books associated with wisdom?

Scholars have come to quite drastically different views on this subject. On the one hand, certain scholars have followed a tradition that can be traced back to the Targums (Levine 1978) and early church fathers like Gregory Thaumaturgos (Jarick 1990) that read the book as presenting a view of God that was robustly positive and in keeping with the rest of the Hebrew Bible.[12] A close examination shows that this approach results from what most will see as an overly simplistic and misleading interpretation. Others see the book as consistently negative about God and his relationship to humanity. James Crenshaw (1980, 15), for instance, believed that Qoheleth, the main speaker, was the epitome of the skeptical tradition in the Hebrew Bible: "Israel's skeptics severed a vital nerve at two distinct junctions. They denied God's goodness if not his very existence, and they portrayed men and women as powerless to acquire essential truth." Both these perspectives fail to make a distinction that is crucial for understanding the book of Ecclesiastes

---

[11] I am skipping v. 2 because it explicitly mentions YHWH ("Those who walk in virtue fear Yahweh, but those who go the wrong way on his path despise him").

[12] Though achieved differently, such interpretations may be found in Kaiser 1979; Whybray 1982; Ogden 1987; Fredericks 1993.

and its theological message. There are two speakers with two different viewpoints on God and human relationship with him.

In the main body of the book, we hear the voice of Qoheleth (1:12–12:7). He speaks in the first person, searches for the meaning of life "under the sun," and repeatedly concludes that life is "meaningless." He tries to locate meaning in pleasure (2:1–11), work (2:18–23; 4:4–6), wisdom (2:12–17), wealth (5:9–6:8 [ET 5:10–6:8]), and more. He fails to find meaning because of death (3:16–22; 12:1–7), injustice in this life (7:15–22; 8:10–15), and because, while God has made everything for its proper time (3:1–8), he has not let his human creatures discern that right time (3:9–15).

The second speaker provides an introduction (1:1–11) to Qoheleth's autobiographical speech and, even more importantly, analyzes Qoheleth's thought for the benefit of his son (12:8–14). In this concluding reflection, the second wise man, often referred to as the frame narrator,[13] both affirms Qoheleth's basic perspective as true of life under the sun, but then gives his son what might be called an "above the sun" perspective:

> The end of the matter. All has been heard. Fear God and keep his commandments, for this is the whole duty of humanity. For God will bring every deed into judgment, including every hidden thing, whether good or evil.   (12:13–14)[14]

Since there are two speakers in the book, we must examine their theologies separately. We begin with Qoheleth and then proceed to the frame narrator's message concerning God. We will then see how the book connects the two theologies.

If one selects certain verses and treats them in isolation from the context, it is possible to conclude that Qoheleth has a positive view of God in keeping with the rest of the canon. God is a giver of all good gifts (2:26), is sovereign over everything (7:13–14), is our Creator (12:1), and is the one to whom we owe our very existence (12:7).

But reading these verses in the context of Qoheleth's whole speech leads to the conclusion that God was at best distant and unconcerned about humanity. In the first place, Qoheleth only refers to God by his generic name Elohim (אלוהים), not his personal or covenantal name YHWH (יהוה). Qoheleth does affirm God's sovereignty (3:9–18; 7:13–14; 8:16–9:1; 11:5), but this sovereignty calls into question God's concern for his people. God has a plan but does not reveal it to his people, including those, like Qoheleth, who want to know it (3:11; 8:16–17; 11:5). There will be judgment in the future, but Qoheleth does not expect to find justice there (3:16; 9:1). There is, after all, no afterlife according to Qoheleth (3:18–21). Qoheleth finds no comfort in God as he faces the chaos and uncertainties of life.

This idea of a distant, and perhaps threatening, God is also found in his most sustained reflection on God:

---

[13] Since his words "frame" Qoheleth's in the book. The label, as far as I can see, was coined by Fox (1977).

[14] Translations of the book of Ecclesiastes come from Longman 1998.

Watch your step when you go to the house of God. Draw near to listen rather than offer the sacrifice of fools. For they do not know that they are doing evil. Do not be quick with your mouth, and do not let your heart rush to utter a word before God. For God is in heaven and you are on earth. Therefore, let your words be few. For dreams come with much work, and the voice of the fool with many words. When you make a vow to God, do not delay to fulfill it, for there is no pleasure in fools. You, however, fulfill what you have vowed. It is better that you do not make a vow than that you make a vow and not fulfill it. Do not let your mouth cause your flesh to commit sin. And do not say to the messenger that it was a mistake. Why should God be angry with your words and destroy the work of your hands? For when dreams multiply, so do meaningless words. Instead, fear God.

(4:17–5:6 [ET 5:1–7])

While there have been attempts to read these verses as urging reverence and thoughtful care as one approaches a powerful God, more likely Qoheleth here despairs that the universe is overseen by a God who does not seem to care much about earthly concerns ("God is in heaven and you are on earth"). Even though Qoheleth ends this reflection on God with the appeal that his hearers "fear God" (5:6 [ET 5:7]), context in this and similar passages (7:15–18; 8:12–13) indicates that Qoheleth has something different in mind than the writers of Proverbs (see 24.2.1 The Theology of Proverbs above) or the second wise man (12:13), to whose theology we now turn.[15]

Whatever the compositional history of the book of Ecclesiastes,[16] the present form of the book concludes not with Qoheleth's voice, but with the words of a second wise man who speaks to his son about Qoheleth. In 12:8–12, he certainly does not totally reject Qoheleth's message—after all, he thought it important enough to expose his son to it—but his approval is tepid at best. Perhaps he believes Qoheleth is right to conclude that life is meaningless under the sun. But even if the second wise man's stance in relation to Qoheleth is debatable, we are left in no doubt about the lesson that he wants his son (with whom the reader should identify) to take away from the exposure to Qoheleth's thought. The book ends with this clear demand: "Fear God and keep his commandments, for this is the whole duty of humanity. For God will bring every deed into judgment, including every hidden thing, whether good or bad" (12:13–14).

In this final call, we see the main theological message of the book of Ecclesiastes, and that message ends up sounding very similar to what we found in the book of Proverbs. This call to "fear God" is different than that given by Qoheleth, who encouraged distance for a distant and potentially threatening deity. The frame narrator's call to fear God leads to obedience in the light of a future judgment.

---

[15] For more, see Longman 2015.

[16] It used to be fashionable to delineate different redactional layers of the book (e.g., Siegfried [1898], who identified nine (!) different redactors), but today there is more of a tendency to interpret the book as a final literary whole no matter how it came to the form in which we know it today (see the critique given in Bartholomew 1998).

24.2.3 The Theology of Job

Both Proverbs and Ecclesiastes urge their readers to "fear God." What is the message of the third book often associated with wisdom, namely Job?

Theories of Job's compositional history abound. Were the prose parts (chs. 1–2; 42:7–17) the original, while the poetry of the rest of the current book was added later? And perhaps the different poetical parts (the debate with the three friends [chs. 3–27], the wisdom poem [ch. 28], and the Elihu speech [chs. 32–37]) were added at different times rather than as a group? Again, we find a variety of theories offered in recent scholarship, and one of them might actually be correct, though all are admittedly speculative.

These theories often come with the belief that the authors of these different parts had conflicting ideas about God and his relationship to humanity. Loren Fisher, for one, believes the author of Job's poetry intended to critique the author of the prose story, who presented a Job who was passively pious in the face of his suffering. Fisher (2009, ix) clearly prefers the poetic Job: "I want to thank the poet of Job 3–26 whose anger burned against the ancient story of Job, and whose fairy poem was extinguished by wrapping it in the ancient story of Job."[17] He advocates keeping the two Jobs separate from each other.

Carol Newsom (2003), in her brilliant and provocative study of Job, believes that the book as we have it is full of "dialogical" or competing voices. She recognizes that in the final form of the book, it is "not only plausible that God, the great authority figure, would represent the perspective of the author, but the structure of the book itself also seems designed to lead the reader through an education of the moral imagination" (18). Still she makes it obvious that she thinks that this authoritarian voice at the end which quiets the debating human voices is a poor ending and prefers not to "privilege" the author's viewpoint and stay with "a polyphonic text" (21). That the divine speeches at the end do not resonate with the sensibilities of many modern scholarly readers can also be seen in another school of thought that interprets Job's two responses (40:3–5; 42:1–6) not as submission but rather as a final and irreverent protest (e.g., Curtis 1979).

But even though there is a history of composition to the book, the form of the book as we have it in the Hebrew Bible has a coherent theological message that is brought to a closure by the divine voice that speaks at the end. And, when we read the book as a whole, that message is consonant with the main theme shared by Proverbs and Ecclesiastes, as they urge their readers to "fear God."

The book opens by introducing Job as "innocent and virtuous, fearing God and turning away from evil" (1:1).[18] In other words, Job displays the characteristics of the wise person advocated by the book of Proverbs. He also receives the benefits, such as wealth and a harmonious family, that Proverbs typically associates with the wise person (8:18–19; 10:4–5; 20:7; 22:29).

[17] Penchansky (1991) and Zuckerman (1991, 47) express similar views.
[18] Translations from the book of Job are from Longman 2012.

After describing Job, the scene shifts to heaven, which the author depicts on analogy with an ancient Near Eastern royal court. "The accuser," one of the attendants of God, the king in the court, challenges Job's motivation for his piety. Is Job pious just for the benefits that piety brings him? Thus, the author of the book sets up a "thought experiment" in which Job's suffering becomes an occasion for a debate about the source of wisdom. Job's complaint (ch. 3) initiates a response from his three friends with interaction from Job (4–27), followed by a monologue by Job (28–31), and then finally the surprise appearance of Elihu (32–37). All this before the dramatic appearance and speeches of YHWH.

The bulk of the book, therefore, finds the human participants setting themselves up as sages who offer passionate diagnoses for why Job suffers along with urgent prescriptions for a solution. The three friends famously offer a theology of retribution where they blame Job's pitiful condition on his purported sin and encourage him to repent to return to the prosperity that he enjoyed at the beginning of the story. Job responds by rejecting their diagnosis, and charges that his suffering is unjust. Thus, he believes that the way forward is to meet with God and set him straight. While first he doubts that such an approach would be possible (9:11–24), he grows in confidence that he can effectively challenge God (31:35–37).[19]

Before we leave the subject of Job's response, we briefly need to pay attention to the special problem of Job 28. While some scholars believe otherwise (e.g., Newsom 2003, 169), the most natural reading is that Job is the speaker of this beautiful poem. The issue arises because here Job asserts what will be the conclusion of the book: wisdom is found in the fear of God. In the poem, he extols human ability to extract precious metals and gems from the earth through tremendous ingenuity and effort, while contrasting it with the inaccessibility of wisdom. He finally concludes that wisdom is only with God and gained through a relationship with God characterized by fear (28:20).

With this conclusion we might expect the book to come to a resolution, but instead Job goes on to continue to complain about his present state and to protest his innocence (chs. 29–31). Perhaps the best explanation for what appears to be an awkward insertion of this clear-sighted anticipation of the end is provided by Alison Lo (2003), who points out that it well reflects the psychology of a sufferer, who may have a moment of clarity and then quickly sink back into anguish.

After Job's last speech, the reader's expectations are further frustrated, as, instead of hearing God's response, yet one more human voice is heard, that of Elihu. While at first he claims to have a view different and more compelling than the three friends, when he speaks, he ends up mouthing the same platitudes about suffering and sin as the three friends. Thus, though he claims a more "spiritual" authority for his viewpoint (38:6–10), his wisdom, like that of all the human participants, is inadequate for the task, and he is ignored by all.

---

[19] This growing confidence may be rooted in a wrong-minded sense that there was someone in heaven who might intercede between him and God (16:18–22; 19:23–25). Based on what Elihu says, he may be thinking of a member of God's heavenly court (33:23–30). For more on this, see Longman 2012, 262–263.

At this point, God makes his appearance in a storm. God does not explain himself to Job or give him a reason why he suffers. Rather, he asserts his power and wisdom and upbraids Job for questioning his justice (40:8). He asserts his power by subjecting Job to a series of questions that Job cannot answer concerning his creation and maintenance of the cosmos (38:4–38) as well as his care and provision for animals beyond humans' ability to control (38:39–39:30; 40:15–41:34). In terms of wisdom, God illustrates how he is the one to dole out that trait as he speaks of the ostrich as a creature from whom he withheld wisdom while giving it speed (39:13–18).

Job responds twice (40:3–5; 42:1–6), ultimately choosing to end his challenge and become silent before God. He assumes this posture without knowing that God would stop his suffering, as the deity does in the epilogue, which immediately follows (42:7–17).

What is the upshot of this story? Job did not turn from God in the face of his suffering but pursued him for answers. He never got the answer or the response that he hoped for, but still, in the light of his deeper knowledge of God ("my ear had heard a report of you, but now my eyes have seen you," 42:5), he stayed in relationship with God. Though the phrase is not found in the story's conclusion, Job's stance at the end illustrates what it means to "fear God," a fear which has matured from the beginning of his story through his experience of suffering.

24.3 WHERE DOES THE WISDOM OF DEUTEROCANONICAL LITERATURE FIT IN?

The deuterocanonical literature ("apocrypha") provides valuable insight into how Jewish thought developed in the Second Temple period. Thus, a few words about the two books commonly associated with wisdom are appropriate here. Ecclesiasticus (also known as Ben Sira or Sirach) and the Wisdom of Solomon continue to develop many of the themes found in Proverbs, Ecclesiastes, and Job, as well as other books from the narrower canon that treat the concept of wisdom.

Most notable is the even more explicit connection drawn between wisdom, the fear of the Lord, and the law. According to Sir 19:20, "Fearing the Lord is the whole of wisdom, and all wisdom involved doing the Law." We also hear that "those who keep the Law become masters to their thoughts; fearing the Lord leads ultimately to wisdom" (Sir 21:11).

This connection between wisdom and obedience is also reflected in the continued use of the figure of Woman Wisdom in these books. Sirach 15 observes that "whoever has a firm hold on the Law will possess Wisdom.... She will come to meet them like a mother, and she will await them like a young bride. She will feed them bread of understanding and will give them water of wisdom to drink" (15:2–3). A similar connection between Woman Wisdom and obedience is found in the Wisdom of Solomon as illustrated by 6:17–18: "The real beginning of wisdom is to desire instruction with all your heart. Love for instruction expresses itself in careful reflection. If you love Wisdom, you will keep her laws. If you are attentive to her laws, you can be assured that you will live forever."

Thus, the theological nature of wisdom becomes even more pronounced during the period between the Testaments.[20] We turn finally to a consideration of wisdom in the New Testament and its relationship to what came before.

24.4 WISDOM IN THE NEW TESTAMENT

We have observed that the consistent message of the Hebrew Bible is that true wisdom is found in God and that humans can only acquire wisdom through a relationship with God characterized by "fear." With that background, Paul states that his goal for those to whom he ministers is that "they may have the full riches of complete understanding, in order that they may know the mystery of God, namely Christ, in whom are hidden all the treasures of wisdom and knowledge" (Col 2:2–3). In other words, "understanding" comes through a relationship with Christ who is the epitome of God's wisdom (see also 1 Cor 1:18–2:16).

Thus, we are not surprised that the Gospels present Christ as profoundly wise. Even in his youth, people recognized his wisdom (Luke 2:40–52). When he started his ministry, he primarily taught in parables, the teaching vehicle for the sage, and his teaching was received as far outstripping that of any other (Matt 13:54–57; Mark 6:2–4) (see Witherington 1994).

Notably, some New Testament writers make an association between Jesus and Woman Wisdom.[21] Matthew quotes Jesus as making such an association when he responds to the criticism of some Jewish leaders by saying "but wisdom is proved right by her deeds" (Matt 11:19), while both the opening of John (1:1–5) and Colossians (1:15–17) utilize language from the description of Woman Wisdom (particularly Prov 8:22–31) as they speak of Jesus. The message for Christians is, therefore, that true wisdom is found in a relationship with Jesus and they must accordingly live in the "fear of the Lord" that leads to obedience. Interestingly, the book of James advises readers that, if they are not wise, "they should ask God, who gives generously to all without finding fault, and it will be given to you" (1:5) along with giving practical advice that sounds very similar to the book of Proverbs on topics like speech and control of emotions (1:19–20, 26; cf. Prov 8:32–34; 11:16, etc.) and planning (4:13–17; cf. Prov 16:1, 3, 9).

[20] For more on wisdom in deuterocanonical literature and also in the Dead Sea Scrolls, see Longman 2017, 219–242.

[21] The word "association" is intentionally chosen. The New Testament authors are not identifying Jesus as Woman Wisdom as if Proverbs 8 is some type of prophecy of Jesus. We have argued that Woman Wisdom is a personification of God's attribute of wisdom standing for God himself. Thus, the New Testament presents Jesus as an incarnation or embodiment of God's wisdom.

24.5 CONCLUSION

The study of wisdom over the last number of decades raised questions about the nature of the theology of Wisdom. Did Wisdom Literature have a theology and if so how did it relate, if at all, to the theology of the rest of the canon?

An examination of the three books that have the most sustained interest in wisdom in the Hebrew Bible revealed a pervasive theological dimension focused on the concept of the "fear of the Lord." While there is no denying that Wisdom has different emphases than other parts of the Hebrew canon, there is no question that it presents a picture of God and God's relationship to humanity that fits well within the whole. Rather than a cosmopolitan and universal God that could be embraced by those not in a relationship with the God of Israel, a close study of the canonical forms of the books of Proverbs, Ecclesiastes, and Job urge a relationship of fear, trust, and obedience with YHWH, the particular God of Israel.

WORKS CITED

Bartholomew, Craig G. 1998. *Reading Ecclesiastes: Old Testament Exegesis and Hermeneutical Theory*. AnBib 139. Rome: Pontifical Biblical Institute.

Bostrom, Lennart. 1990. *God of the Sages: The Portrayal of God in the Book of Proverbs*. Stockholm: Almqvist and Wiksell.

Brown, William P. 2014. *Wisdom's Wonder: Character, Creation, and Crisis in the Bible's Wisdom Literature*. Grand Rapids, MI: Eerdmans.

Bruch, Johann. F. 1851. *Weisheits-Lehre der Hebräer: Ein Beitrag zur Geschichte der Philosophie*. Strassburg: Truettel and Wurtz.

Brueggemann, Walter. 1972. *In Man We Trust: The Neglected Side of Biblical Faith*. Atlanta, GA: John Knox.

Crenshaw, James L. 1980. "The Birth of Skepticism in Ancient Israel." Pages 1–19 in *The Divine Helmsman: Studies on God's Control of Human Events*. Edited by James L. Crenshaw and Samuel Sandmel. New York, NY: KTAV.

Curtis, John. 1979. "On Job's Response to Yahweh." *JBL* 98:497–511.

Eissfeldt, Otto. 1965. *The Old Testament: An Introduction*. New York, NY: Harper and Row.

Fiddes, Paul S. 2013. *Seeing the World and Knowing God: Hebrew Wisdom and Christian Doctrine in a Late-Modern Context*. Oxford: Oxford University Press.

Fisher, Loren R. 2009. *The Many Voices of Job*. Eugene, OR: Cascade Books.

Fox, Michael V. 1977. "Frame-Narrative and Composition in the Book of Ecclesiastes." *HUCA* 48:83–106.

Fredericks, Daniel C. 1993. *Coping with Transience: Ecclesiastes on the Brevity of Life*. Sheffield: JSOT Press.

Goleman, Daniel. 1995. *Emotional Intelligence*. New York, NY: Bantam Books.

Jarick, John. 1990. *Gregory Thaumaturgos' Paraphrase of Ecclesiastes*. SBLSCS 29. Atlanta, GA: Scholars Press.

Kaiser, Walter. 1979. *Ecclesiastes: Total Life*. Chicago, IL: Moody.

Kynes, Will. 2019. *An Obituary for "Wisdom Literature": The Birth, Death, and Intertextual Reintegration of a Biblical Corpus*. Oxford: Oxford University Press.

Levine, Etan. 1978. *The Aramaic Version of Qohelet*. New York, NY: Sepher-Hermon.

Lo, Alison. 2003. *Job 28 as Rhetoric: The Analysis of Job 28 in the Context of Job 22–31*. VTSup 97. Leiden: Brill.

Longman III, Tremper. 1998. *Ecclesiastes*. NICOT. Grand Rapids, MI: Eerdmans.

Longman III, Tremper. 2006. *Proverbs*. BCOTWP. Grand Rapids, MI: Baker.

Longman III, Tremper. 2009. "Proverbs." Pages 464–505 in *The Zondervan Illustrated Bible Backgrounds Commentary*, vol. 5. Edited by John Walton. Grand Rapids, MI: Zondervan.

Longman III, Tremper. 2012. *Job*. BCOTWP. Grand Rapids, MI: Baker.

Longman III, Tremper. 2015. "The 'Fear of God' in the Book of Ecclesiastes." *BBR* 25:13–22.

Longman III, Tremper. 2017. *The Fear of the Lord Is Wisdom: A Theological Introduction to Wisdom in Israel*. Grand Rapids, MI: Baker Academic.

McKane, William. 1965. *Prophets and Wise Men*. London: SCM.

McKane, William. 1992. *Proverbs: A New Approach*. OTL. London: SCM.

Newsom, Carol A. 2003. *The Book of Job: A Contest of Moral Imaginations*. Oxford: Oxford University Press.

Ogden, Graham S. 1987. *Qoheleth*. Sheffield: JSOT Press.

Penchansky, David. 1991. *The Betrayal of God: Ideological Conflict in Job*. Louisville, KY: Westminster John Knox.

Perdue, Leo G. 2007. *Wisdom Literature: A Theological History*. Louisville, KY: Westminster John Knox.

Schwab, Zoltan S. 2013. *Toward an Interpretation of the Book of Proverbs: Selfishness and Secularity Reconsidered*. JTISup 7. Winona Lake, IN: Eisenbrauns.

Siegfried, Carl. 1898. *Prediger und Hoheslied*. HKAT. Gottingen: Vanderhoeck.

Sneed, Mark. 2015. "'Grasping after the Wind?': The Elusive Attempt to Define and Delimit Wisdom." Pages 39–67 in *Was There a Wisdom Tradition? New Prospects in Israelite Wisdom Studies*. Edited by Mark Sneed. AIL 23. Atlanta, GA: SBL Press.

Westermann, Claus. 1995. *Roots of Wisdom*. Edinburgh: T&T Clark.

Whybray, Roger N. 1965. *Wisdom in Proverbs: The Concept of Wisdom in Proverbs 1–9*. London: SCM.

Whybray, Roger N. 1982. "Qoheleth, Preacher of Joy." *JSOT* 23:87–98.

Witherington, Ben, III. 1994. *Jesus the Sage: The Pilgrimage of Wisdom*. Minneapolis, MN: Fortress.

Zimmerli, Walther. 1964. "The Place and Limit of the Wisdom in the Framework of the Old Testament Theology." *SJT* 17:146–158.

Zuckerman, Bruce. 1991. *Job the Silent: A Story in Historical Counterpoint*. Oxford: Oxford University Press.

PART V

WISDOM LITERATURE AND OTHER LITERATURE

CHAPTER 25

....

WISDOM INFLUENCE

....

JOHN L. McLAUGHLIN

THE people responsible for Israel's Wisdom traditions lived and worked within the larger context of ancient Israelite society. As such, one would expect to see points of contact between the Israelite Wisdom Literature preserved in the Bible and the other components of that collection. Indeed, scholars have proposed Wisdom influence in portions of the Pentateuch, the Deuteronomistic History, the Prophets, the Psalms, and other biblical books. Recognizing that the efforts of ancient Wisdom writers are reflected outside the traditional Wisdom books (Proverbs, Job, Ecclesiastes, and the deutero-canonical Ben Sira and Wisdom of Solomon) indicates that the sages played a greater role in ancient Israelite society than those Wisdom books alone suggest. But if all such proposals are correct, then the Wisdom Literature risks losing its distinctive character within the Bible—if everything is "Wisdom," then not only does Wisdom no longer constitute an identifiable body of biblical literature, neither does history, prophecy, etc. However, the point of this essay is not to evaluate such proposals (but see the other entries in this section of the Handbook plus McLaughlin 2018, 141–170), but rather to consider the methodological principles necessary for assessing them.

Possible Wisdom influence outside the Wisdom Literature rests upon two major principles. First, since the sages in ancient Israel did not operate in a vacuum, there will probably be some overlap with other literature in the Hebrew Bible. However, in and of themselves, points of overlap do not necessarily mean that the Wisdom Literature was the point of origin. Shared or even similar material could simply be the result of a shared cultural, social, and historical context. On the other hand, an individual point of overlap might indicate "contact" with the Wisdom traditions, in as much as it uses a distinctively Wisdom element but not in the same way that the Wisdom Literature does. In contrast, "Wisdom influence" constitutes intentional use of elements drawn from the Wisdom Literature in a manner that is consistent with that source.

The second principle underpinning the search for Wisdom influence is that despite its shared ancient Israelite context, some aspects of the Wisdom traditions were distinctive enough that their literary output can be classified as "Wisdom Literature." It is impossible to consider Wisdom influence without a Wisdom tradition to serve as the source of that influence. It is necessary, however, to have some criteria by which to determine whether points of overlap with other types of biblical literature are evidence of actual influence or simply a matter of a shared context or incidental contact.

25.1 A BRIEF REVIEW OF PREVIOUS SCHOLARSHIP

Before presenting such criteria, it will be helpful to review briefly some significant developments in previous scholarship identifying Wisdom influence outside the traditional Wisdom books. The seminal work in this regard is by James Crenshaw (1969), who lists five criteria for identifying Wisdom influence: (1) Distinguishing among four types of wisdom (juridical, natural, practical, and theological) each of which has its own goal, stance, and method; (2) distinctive forms or terms; (3) reflecting the same nuance as in the recognized Wisdom books; (4) recognizing the negative attitude towards wisdom elsewhere; and (5) noting historical development within the Wisdom tradition itself. Norman Whybray (1974, 71–76) notes the importance of Wisdom subject matter, forms, and vocabulary, then focuses on the latter in his own analysis. Donn Morgan (1981, 13–29) acknowledges the role of Wisdom vocabulary and perspectives, but he goes beyond simply itemizing such elements outside the Wisdom Literature to stress the degree to which a non-Wisdom book reflects the Wisdom tradition, distinguishing between general "contact" and more extensive "influence" (27). Roland Murphy (2002, 98–102) looks for an accumulation of recognizable/typical Wisdom vocabulary, forms, and topics that reflect a didactic purpose. Focusing on the Joseph Story in Genesis 37–50, Lindsay Wilson (2004, 36–37) acknowledges the importance of "wisdom-like elements" but emphasizes the need to assess the extent of their distribution throughout the entire narrative in order to evaluate whether or not they perform a central function in the text. Finally, Simon Chi-Chung Cheung (2015, 28–50) identifies Wisdom psalms based on "a ruling wisdom thrust," established by devices that create an "intellectual tone" and result in "a didactic speech intention."

25.2 CRITERIA FOR ESTABLISHING WISDOM INFLUENCE

Building upon and synthesizing the preceding scholarship, the following presents three criteria for determining Wisdom influence outside the established biblical Wisdom books. First, a work must contain Wisdom elements, namely specific Wisdom terms, forms, or content. Second, these elements must be used in the same way as in the Wisdom Literature. Third, a text should contain a number of Wisdom elements distributed throughout the work, preferably with different elements combined together. The following expands upon these three criteria and illustrates their application to a variety of texts outside the accepted Wisdom books.

25.2.1 Wisdom Elements

25.2.1.1 *Vocabulary*

The first criterion for determining Wisdom influence in the Hebrew Bible calls for elements that are characteristic of the Wisdom tradition as reflected in the established Wisdom books. The first element that one should look for is Wisdom vocabulary. Unfortunately, there is no clear consensus as to what exactly constitutes Wisdom vocabulary, with proposals varying widely. At one extreme, R.B.Y. Scott (1971, 121–122) lists seventy-seven words to consider in determining Wisdom influence, but without providing any justification. Moreover, some are fairly common words (e.g., דרך, "way, path"; חוס, "hurry"; לב, "heart, mind," etc.) and others seem more at home in the cult (e.g., חטא, "sinner") or the courtroom (e.g., ריב, "dispute"). Whybray (1974) is at the other end of the spectrum, both in terms of the number of Wisdom terms that he accepts and the justification for them. For instance, based on a careful enumeration of words that occur primarily in Proverbs, Job, or Ecclesiastes but rarely in other books, he identifies nine terms that are "exclusive" to the Wisdom tradition and therefore indicative of Wisdom influence outside those three Wisdom books (142–149).[1] These are supplemented by ten terms that he considers "characteristic" of the Wisdom tradition, in that they are significantly more frequent in the Wisdom books than elsewhere (134–140).[2] Whybray contrasts these two lists with twenty-three words that are found a number of times in both Wisdom and non-Wisdom texts, and therefore are not indicative of Wisdom influence (124–134).

Whybray's third category includes a number of terms that scholars often appeal to as indicative of the Wisdom tradition but that actually occur less frequently in the Wisdom books than elsewhere, such as ירשא, "happy, blessed" (10x in Wisdom Literature vs. 35x elsewhere), וב *bîn*, "understand" (38x vs. 52x), לשמ, "proverb," although it has many other meanings (10x vs. 29x), and הצע, "plan, counsel" (19x vs. 69x). But this is not simply a matter of statistics, with the relative number of occurrences determining characteristic Wisdom terms. Sometimes Whybray discounts a term because its frequency is only slightly greater in the Wisdom books, such as סעכ, "vexation" (13x vs. 12x). He also excludes some words that are more frequent in the Wisdom texts because they are not widely distributed among those books. This includes ויבמ, which occurs as the adjective

---

[1] The terms are בינה ("insight"), בער ("stupid"), כסיל ("foolish"), ליץ ("scoffer"), לקח ("teaching"), נבון ("intelligent"), סכל ("foolish"), ערום ("shrewd, cunning"), and תושיה ("success").

[2] They are אויל ("fool"), אולת ("foolishness"), חנף ("godless"), חקר ("searching"), עקש ("perverted"), ערמה ("cunning"), פתי ("simple"), שכל (hiphil: "understand"), תבונה ("understanding"), and תוכחת ("reprimand, reproach").

"intelligent" equally (six times) in Wisdom and non-Wisdom books, but the former are all in Proverbs. Similarly, לבה ("breath, vapor") is found forty-six times in Job, Proverbs, and Ecclesiastes compared to just twenty-seven times elsewhere, but because thirty-eight of the former are in Ecclesiastes, the term is characteristic of that book, not the Wisdom tradition in general. Other times, anticipating the second criterion above, namely that elements need to be used in the same way as in the established Wisdom texts, Whybray eliminates a word found more frequently in the Wisdom books because it has a different nuance there than elsewhere, as in the case of מוסר (34 vs. 16x), which refers primarily to human correction in the context of education in Proverbs and once in Job, compared to divine punishment of Israel elsewhere, including three times in Job. This different nuance in the Wisdom books in contrast to the term's use elsewhere, combined with the word's absence from Ecclesiastes, means that it cannot be used to demonstrate Wisdom influence.

Whybray's minimalistic approach to determining Wisdom vocabulary is valuable in that it highlights terms that are distinctive to the Wisdom tradition. However, it risks excluding words that are not distinctively Wisdom terms but are still characteristic of the Wisdom Literature. While the latter cannot establish Wisdom influence on their own, they can still be used in conjunction with other features that are more typical of the Wisdom Literature.

25.2.1.2 Forms

Another Wisdom element that can help determine Wisdom influence in non-Wisdom texts is literary forms. Once again, they too need to be distinctive to the Wisdom tradition in order to indicate Wisdom influence by themselves. There are some forms that occur frequently in the Wisdom books but are so general that they are not uniquely Wisdom forms. For instance, rhetorical questions and similes clearly serve a didactic function within the Wisdom Literature, but they are not exclusive to those texts or even to literature in general. They are also common in everyday speech, so they do not in themselves demonstrate Wisdom Literature. Similarly, the Wisdom Literature, especially Proverbs, regularly exhorts the reader or listener to perform certain actions, but this too is common to non-Wisdom discourse, so exhortations cannot be the sole basis for considering a work reflective of Wisdom. Lists are also common to the ancient and modern worlds, although in the Wisdom books they reflect an underlying attempt to categorize human experience and therefore better understand it. Even the basic proverb is not conclusive in this regard, especially since a true proverb, by definition, has entered into common usage apart from its original context. Only if a proverb is used in a way that goes beyond a simple popular saying can it suggest Wisdom influence, but this evidence is not persuasive in and of itself. In short, some forms cannot establish Wisdom influence on their own, but they are still useful for identifying Wisdom influence. Their presence alongside more distinctive Wisdom forms in non-Wisdom contexts, especially when they display a didactic intent, can support an argument that such works display Wisdom influence.

There are, however, a number of forms that are very much characteristic of the Wisdom tradition, such that their appearance elsewhere constitutes a stronger argument for Wisdom influence. A full discussion of Wisdom forms is well beyond the scope of this essay (cf. the contribution by Markus Witte in this Handbook and McLaughlin 2018, 35–40), but a review of some of the more distinctive ones will be helpful. The instruction is found ten times in Proverbs and reflects the Egyptian instruction. It consists of three elements: a direct address to "my son," which reflects the use of "father" and "son" to indicate a teacher and pupil, plus a command to "hear," "listen," etc., to the teaching; this is followed by motives for listening, and ends with the actual teaching. The full form does not appear outside the Wisdom Literature, but components of the form might indicate Wisdom influence if their use reflects the nuances in the Wisdom Literature (see further below under 25.2.2 Wisdom Usage).

Another characteristic Wisdom form is the graduated numerical saying, also known as the x/x + 1 saying because it starts with a number followed by the next highest number on successive lines (e.g., "three ... four," "five ... six," etc.). This form occurs six times in Proverbs (five of them clustered in Proverbs 30), once in Job and four times in Ben Sira.[3] The progression from one number to the next was common in the ancient world (e.g., Hos 6:2; Mic 5:5), but only the Wisdom texts and Amos 1–2 use the actual x/x + 1 formula. Some use this to argue for Wisdom influence in Amos, but, as we will see below (25.2.2 Wisdom Usage), it is used differently in the prophetic book.

The appeal to tradition is another form that is indicative of Wisdom (e.g., Job 8:8–13; 12:7–12; 15:17–35; 20:4–29). It contains the actual appeal, a statement of the tradition in question, and an application to a situation. The final element is reflected in the "summary appraisal" form that Brevard Childs (1967, 128–136) considered indicative of Wisdom in Isa 14:26–27; 17:14; 28:29. Yet another Wisdom form is the allegory, an extended metaphor in which elements of the composition stand for separate elements outside the allegory, as in Prov 5:15–23, where the reader is exhorted to drink from his own well but not let others drink from it, with the well metaphorically representing his wife and its water sexual intercourse.

25.2.1.3 *Themes and Motifs*

A third element that can indicate a connection between the Wisdom tradition and other literature is the actual content of the Wisdom books. If themes or motifs that are central concerns of the sages appear elsewhere, that too could be a sign of Wisdom influence. However, as with terminology and forms, some of those issues might also be shared with other elements of ancient Israelite society, and so cannot be used alone to establish a connection with the Wisdom tradition. For instance, the theory of retribution, the belief that the good are blessed and the bad are punished, is a recurrent motif in Proverbs and a central concern of the book of Job. This was an issue for the larger community as well, which in particular is reflected in the Israelite legal tradition, with many of the laws explicitly indicating the punishment that should follow specific crimes (e.g., Exod 22:1–20; Lev 20:1–16, etc.; cf. the curses and blessings in Deut 27–28). Similarly, the Wisdom

---

[3] Prov 6:16–19; 30:5–16, 18–19, 21–23, 24–28, 29–31; Job 5:19–22; Sir 25:7–11; 26:5–6, 28–29; 50:25–26.

Literature shares a concern for social justice with the prophetic tradition, where it also figures prominently.

On the other hand, there are Wisdom themes that are more distinctive of the Wisdom approach. In keeping with the Wisdom method of reflecting upon common human experience, the sages offer observations on human affairs with an eye to what is conducive to proper relationships with others and the world around them. This can be expressed in a number of ways. Sometimes it is simply a matter of making brief observations about human behavior, as in Prov 13:7; 15:1, etc. Other proverbs draw an analogy between nature and human affairs, such as Prov 26:1; 26:17. Both approaches lead to some characteristic Wisdom themes, which are sometimes developed at great length. Foremost is the value of wisdom itself, with attendant exhortations to seek it out, reflections on the benefits it brings to one's life, and the negative consequences that result from ignoring it. At the same time, the analogies with nature emphasize the order and structure inherent in the natural world, implying a comparable order within human affairs that people should seek to follow.

These points are reinforced by the motif of the two ways or paths. Here the sages contrast the wise person and the fool or the righteous and the wicked, with the wise and foolish often conflated or even explicitly identified with the righteous and wicked, respectively. The details may vary from one text to another, ranging from reflections on how these opposites act, or their reasons for doing so, or the ultimate effect of their actions. Extrapolating from these two ways can mean an emphasis on representative examples of one or the other path. But this is not always black and white. For instance, while a wealthy person might be held up in one text as an example of someone who succeeds by acting wisely (e.g., Prov 12:27), elsewhere the rich are condemned for exploiting the poor (e.g., Prov 28:6). One group of people who are consistently condemned are loose or adulterous women. Granted, adultery is condemned in the legal material, but in Wisdom the emphasis is not on the act of sexual congress but rather the effect, namely that by leading men, especially young men, away from wisdom the loose woman leads to death.

To summarize, the first criterion for establishing Wisdom influence outside of the main Wisdom corpus is identifying Wisdom elements in the target text. These include terms, forms, and topics or themes that are distinctively representative of Israel's Wisdom traditions. The same issues arise with respect to each of these three elements. First of all, not every proposed Wisdom word, form, or theme is actually a quintessential Wisdom element, so each one must be reviewed to determine whether or not it meets this criterion. Second, these elements must be derived directly from the Wisdom Literature in order to avoid a "chain-reaction effect." For instance, Gerhard von Rad (1984, and later Wilson 2004) found Wisdom influence in the Joseph story (Genesis 37–50), after which others appealed in part to the Joseph story to support their identification of Wisdom influence in the Succession Narrative, and the books of Esther and Daniel (see Whybray 1968; Talmon 1963; Olojede 2012, respectively). Similarly, while some psalms can justifiably be considered to reflect Wisdom influence, it is methodologically problematic to invoke aspects from any of those psalms that are not also found in the Wisdom Literature in an attempt to establish Wisdom influence in a third text. Third, there are elements that are characteristic of the Wisdom Literature but are also found frequently in other types of material. In such cases, those elements do not in themselves indicate Wisdom influence, but they can be appealed to in conjunction with other uniquely Wisdom elements. Fourth, some elements are so central to the Wisdom Literature that by themselves they reflect contact with Israel's Wisdom traditions. But even these cannot be used in isolation to establish other works as Wisdom texts. A single element is insufficient to establish intentional use of the Wisdom traditions, to say nothing of whether that element is used elsewhere in the same way as in the Wisdom Literature. Therefore, rather than just appealing to individual Wisdom elements, the other two criteria must also be employed before Wisdom influence can be established.

25.2.2 Wisdom Usage

Just because a text outside the established Wisdom books contains one or more Wisdom elements does not automatically constitute true Wisdom influence. Similarity to Wisdom does not, by itself, indicate intentional use of the Wisdom traditions. Some Wisdom vocabulary, forms, or themes could easily "spill over" into the general populace. As a result, people can use words without being aware of the full nuances involved; people today might allude to "existentialism" or "communism" without any real knowledge of their original philosophical or political meaning. So too with Wisdom forms; modern speakers might repeat proverbs coined by Benjamin Franklin without knowing that they appeared in *Poor Richard's Almanack*, or even that the latter existed. Moreover, as noted above, a true proverb is so by virtue of popular usage, whereas those in the book of Proverbs have been collected together into a single text. The collection may have been intended in part as a resource for people to draw from as needed, but at the same time, by being in the collection, the sayings repeat various topics throughout the book, so that the combined proverbs become mutually interpretative.

Furthermore, a speaker may appropriate a word, form, or motif from one type of literature and adapt it to his or her own purposes, but that does not make that person a member of the group most commonly identified with that form or motif. For instance, Amos uses a priestly call to worship to attack the Israelites' cultic activities (e.g., Amos 5:4–5) and parodies the priestly acceptance of a sacrifice (Amos 5:21–24), but that does not make him a priest. Similarly, he uses the word הוֹי (Amos 5:18; 6:1), which is rooted in funerary orations (McLaughlin 2001, 89–94), to convey the certainty of their coming destruction without Amos being an actual mourner. Moreover, a person can even use a group's forms and content against that very group, either as a critique of the group or as a challenge for it to live up to what it professes, as Isaiah does with respect to Wisdom (McKane 1965, 65–112; Jensen 1973).

Therefore, it is essential to assess in every case whether Wisdom elements found outside the Wisdom books reflect concrete Wisdom usage. Does a term have the same nuance as Proverbs, Job, or Ecclesiastes? Is a form used in the same way? Does a theme or motif function didactically as in those books? A few examples of how each of the three elements is used in traditionally non-Wisdom books will illustrate these points.

25.2.2.1 *Vocabulary*

Samuel Terrien (1962, 112–113) proposed that three different vocabulary items demonstrate Wisdom influence in Amos. First, he characterizes נכחה in Amos 3:10 as "a favorite term of wisdom" (112; see also Wolff 1973, 56–59; Wolff 1977, 193; Crenshaw 1967, 46), but the word only occurs twice in Proverbs compared to six times elsewhere. More importantly, even allowing this point for the sake of argument, the term has a different nuance in Prov 8:9 and 24:26, where it refers to speech, in contrast to action in Amos 3:10. Second, Terrien acknowledges that the word סוד occurs in a variety of biblical texts but focuses on the fact that it only has the sense "intimate secret" in Wisdom texts (five in Proverbs and four in Job, plus four in Sirach) and Amos 3:7. However, he fails to account for the verb גלה in Amos, which otherwise is only linked to סוד in Prov 11:13; 20:19; 25:9, all of which speak negatively of humans betraying a secret, in contrast to Amos's positive image of God conveying heavenly secrets. Finally, the noun אף only occurs with the verb טרף in Amos 1:11; Job 16:9; 18:4, making it a "sapiential idiom" for Terrien (113). But the Wisdom texts combine the words differently: in Job 16:9, divine anger tears at Job whereas in Job 18:4, Job is said to tear at himself. Not only is there not a common Wisdom "idiom" in Job, but in Amos 1:11, the usage is different still, in that one nation tears at another.

In contrast, there are certainly instances when a term is used in a manner consistent with the Wisdom usage. For example, apart from Gen 3:1, where it is used of the serpent, the adjective ערום ("shrewd") appears only in Wisdom books, twice in Job and eight times in Proverbs, and the serpent's "shrewd" awareness of how to acquire "insight" (שכל in v. 6) is consistent with the Wisdom usage. Similarly, כסיל ("foolish") occurs sixty-five times in Proverbs and Ecclesiastes, plus Pss 49:11; 92:7; 94:8, making it one of Whybray's (1974, 146) "exclusive" Wisdom terms. In Psalms 49 and 92 it occurs in the context of the contrasting fates of the righteous and the wicked, while in Psalm 94 it initiates a direct address to the wicked, trying to convince them of their folly in not recognizing their coming destruction. Not only do all three psalm verses reflect the Wisdom usage of the term in conjunction with a Wisdom motif, but the third one is also similar to Lady Wisdom's call to the "foolish" alongside the "simple" in Prov 1:22; 8:5 (plus "scoffers" in 1:22), and the argument in Ps 94:9 echoes Prov 20:12 (Whybray 1974, 146).

25.2.2.2 *Forms*

The book of Amos also provides us with a clear instance of a Wisdom form that is not used in the same way as the Wisdom writers. Terrien (1962, 109–110) and Wolff (1973, 34–44; 1977, 95–96, 138) pointed to the x/x + 1 formula (described above) in the Oracles Against the Nations as evidence that Amos was influenced by the Wisdom tradition. But while Amos 1–2 is the only place outside the Wisdom books where the actual x/x + 1 formula appears, Amos does not use it the way that the Wisdom writers do. The latter always enumerate things up to the x + 1 number, and the individual items listed often do not have a common point of reference; in fact, the final element frequently includes a surprising twist (see Prov 30:18–19; 29–31). This reflects the didactic purpose of the wise, namely to bring people into the pedagogical process by challenging the reader or listener to determine what the connection is among the diverse components. In contrast, despite the reference to "three transgressions...and for four" in Amos 1:3, 6, 9, 11, 13; 2:1, 4, each of those oracles only lists one offense, while Amos 2:6–8 lists more than four. As such, the use of the x/x + 1 formula in Amos 1–2 does not reflect either the form or the function of the formula in the Wisdom Literature. There is no itemization of only four items and therefore no surprise element connected to the fourth item, and as a result there is no attempt to engage the reader into drawing a connection among diverse items, since only one is mentioned. At most, Amos may have had a passing familiarity with this distinctive Wisdom form, but he uses it in a decidedly non-Wisdom way. As such, it does not constitute Wisdom "influence" as defined earlier, but at most indicates a general awareness of the form but not its specifically Wisdom function.

Another example of a non-Wisdom nuance for a Wisdom form involves the teacher's call to attention from the beginning of the instruction genre. James Boston (1968, 198–200) suggests that the call to "give ear" (האזינו) and "hear" (תשמע) in Deut 32:1 indicates Wisdom influence in the Song of Moses (Deuteronomy 32), as do Morgan (1981, 77) and Wilson (2009, 153) for the same words in the reverse order in Isa 1:2. A double call for attention is common in biblical literature, but Boston (200) points to the terminology in Deut 32:1 as indicative of a teacher's appeal to "the wisdom of his own words without reference to any divine authority." Similarly, Morgan and Wilson note Wisdom vocabulary and the analogy with nature in Isa 1:3. However, in both places the call is addressed to the heavens and the earth, which is more reflective of the prophetic trial motif, while the content of what follows is not the typical Wisdom reflection on general human experience but rather Israel's particular experience of Yahweh.

Nevertheless, Wisdom forms are used elsewhere in ways that are consistent with their original Wisdom usage. For instance, the direct address by the teacher from the beginning of the instruction (and elsewhere) sometimes does indicate Wisdom influence. The commands to "give ear," "hear," "pay attention" and "hear" in Isa 28:23 are consistent with Wisdom usage, being followed by a parable about a farmer that combines didactic questions and Wisdom terminology in vv. 24–28 and a summary appraisal in v. 29, indicating that the farmer's ability is the result of Yahweh's wisdom. The summary-appraisal form also appears in Isa 14:26 and 17:14. In addition, there are a number of true allegories in Ezekiel (e.g., Ezek 16; 19:2–9, 10–14; 23), enough that he is called "a maker of allegories" (ממשל משלים; Ezek 20:49). Similarly, proverbial sayings are found in more than one prophet (Isa 2:22; 10:15; 29:16; Jer 2:26; 3:20; 6:7; 17:11; 24:5, 8, etc.), while Jeremiah frequently uses rhetorical questions (e.g., 2:14, 31; 3:5; 8:4; 30:6; 31:20). These prophets always use those forms didactically, like the sages, not for their own sake but to support their specific messages. For instance, Jeremiah's appeals to nature and human affairs would have elicited his audience's agreement, which he could then use as a springboard to argue that their own actions were contrary to that shared perspective (Brueggemann 1973; Hobbs 1974).

The third Wisdom element, namely themes or motifs, can also be paralleled elsewhere without reflecting actual Wisdom usage. But first, one must be sure that it actually is a

Wisdom theme. For example, Terrien (1962, 110–111) argues that divine interaction with Sheol is restricted to Prov 15:11 and Job 26:6 (plus Ps 139:7, which he incorrectly identifies as a Wisdom psalm), which then influenced the same idea in Amos 9:2. However, Yahweh intervenes in Sheol in pentateuchal, historical, psalmic, and prophetic texts.[4]

In addition, some parallels to significant Wisdom motifs do not actually reflect how that motif is used in Wisdom texts. For instance, creation plays an important role in the thought of Second Isaiah, but rather than contemplating the order embodied in the created world as the Wisdom Literature does, in Second Isaiah the emphasis is on Yahweh as the creator of the universe in contrast to the powerless Babylonian gods. Another example is the attempt to read the woman (Eve) in Genesis 3 in light of the female seductress who leads to death in Proverbs (Blenkinsopp 1966, 53–54). But the Wisdom seductress is usually an adulteress or a foreigner, or both, while Eve is neither. Because she and the man (later Adam) are the only humans who exist, she cannot be a foreign woman, and, in fact, she is Adam's own wife. Moreover, she is not a temptress; she simply gives some of the fruit "to her husband, who was with her" (Gen 3:6), with no indication of seduction on her part. Further, it is not her actions alone that ultimately result in death but the pair's joint effort in eating the fruit. Thus, the woman in Genesis 3 is very different than the wanton women about whom the Wisdom writers warn. Readers could well reflect on the two women in relationship to each other in light of their combination in the larger Hebrew Bible, but that is very different from the author of Genesis consciously using the Proverbs motif in such a way as to constitute Wisdom influence. In fact, the significant differences between the two women argue for the opposite conclusion.

On the other hand, Jeremiah appeals to the order found in creation to further his prophetic message, often using Wisdom forms to do so, thus providing examples of Wisdom themes used as the Wisdom writers did. Jeremiah contrasts how various birds know their "time" with Israel's lack of knowledge (8:7), asks rhetorical questions concerning the stability of snow creating mountain streams in contrast to Israel's lack of fidelity (18:14), and appeals to the "fixed order" of day and night as a reflection of divine faithfulness (31:35–37). In addition to such appeals to order in creation, he also uses straightforward analogies with the natural world to further his message, such as comparisons between the freshness of both a well and Jerusalem's wickedness (Jer 6:7) and a link between a partridge hatching another's egg and those who become wealthy through injustice (Jer 17:11), drawing the conclusion that both Jerusalem's wickedness and unjust wealth will not be of lasting benefit.

The "two ways" theme that is so common in the Wisdom material, namely the contrast between sets of opposites, such as the righteous and the wicked or the wise and the foolish, also appears in a variety of non-Wisdom locations. Jeremiah 17:5–8, for instance, contrasts those who trust in mortals and those who trust in the Lord, with each pair described through an analogy with nature: a desert shrub and a tree by a flowing stream. This is reflected in Psalm 1 as well, which contrasts the righteous with the wicked: the

---

[4] Deut 32:22; 1 Sam 2:6; Pss 30:3; 49:16; 86:13 (cf. Pss 18:5, 16; 56:13; 103:4; 116:3, 8); Ezek 26:20; 31:16; Hos 13:14; Jon 2:3, 7.

latter are like chaff (v. 4), whereas the former are once again like a fruitful tree by a stream (v. 3), a motif also found in the Egyptian Instruction of Amenemope. So, too, Psalm 37 focuses on the wicked's oppression of the righteous as well as their respective fates, namely punishment and reward.

The preceding paragraphs demonstrate Wisdom influence on individual verses in Jeremiah (plus Psalms 1 and 37, to which I return below), in as much as they contain distinctively Wisdom forms and themes used in the same way as they are employed in the Wisdom Literature. But in the case of Jeremiah especially, these occur in distinct passages separated from one another, and do not demonstrate a pervasive Wisdom influence on the book as a whole, or even on longer passages within Jeremiah. For that we must turn to the third criterion for demonstrating Wisdom influence.

25.2.3 The Number, Variety, and Distribution of the Elements

The third criterion for establishing Wisdom influence is whether or not the extra-Wisdom text contains a number of different Wisdom elements distributed throughout the work. A small amount of one kind of Wisdom element in only one location does not constitute strong evidence of conscious Wisdom influence rather than random similarity. The greater the number, variety, and distribution of Wisdom elements, the easier it is to establish that they play a central function, creating what Cheung (2015, 29) calls "a ruling wisdom thrust."

However, many biblical books are so big that it is practically impossible for Wisdom elements to appear as extensively as required to achieve this effect, even if such books do contain a significant number of different Wisdom elements in different sections. It was noted above that Jeremiah used Wisdom forms, like rhetorical questions and proverbs, and Wisdom motifs, such as appeals to human affairs and to nature, especially its inherent order, and the two ways of trust in humans and in God. To these one can add questions and answers (1:11–12, 13; 24:3) and lists (15:3), as well as a shared concern with the Wisdom tradition for retribution, social justice, and true wisdom. But while these clearly indicate contact between isolated verses in Jeremiah and the Wisdom tradition, they are neither numerous enough nor extensive enough to establish Wisdom influence for the book as a whole.

Nevertheless, at times diverse Wisdom elements are sufficiently clustered in a passage to establish Wisdom influence on that passage. The combination of commands for attention, a parable, and a summary appraisal form in Isa 28:23–29 were discussed earlier (cf. another parable and application in Isa 5:1–7). Similarly, Psalm 49 opens with the instruction's call to "hear" and "give ear," followed by the teaching in vv. 5–20. It includes Wisdom terminology such as "wisdom," "understanding," (v. 3) and "incline my ear," the latter action directed towards the Wisdom forms "proverb" and "riddle" (v. 4; cf. Prov 1:6). The teaching section makes comparisons between humans and animals in vv. 12, 14, 20, while their shared destiny in the latter two verses echoes Eccl 3:19–21. Finally, Ps 49:13 uses the application component of the appeal to tradition form. Psalm 37 also contains several Wisdom forms, such as prohibitions (vv. 1–2, 8b), admonitions (vv. 3, 4, 5–6, etc.), a better saying (v. 16), and a proverb (v. 21), complemented by appeals to the author's own experience and observations (vv. 25–26, 35–36). The psalm reflects the Wisdom dichotomy between the wicked and the righteous, including their respective punishment and reward, and its relativization of wealth echoes the book of Proverbs (cf. Ps 37:16–17, 21–22, 25–26 with Prov 10:2; 11:28, etc.); the correlation between Ps 37:16 and Prov 16:8 is especially striking. Finally, while acrostics are not exclusive to the Wisdom Literature, the appearance of successive letters of the Hebrew alphabet in every second line of the poem reinforces the Wisdom tenor that the other elements create.

Some shorter biblical books contain a number of varied Wisdom elements throughout. Habakkuk 1–2 comprises a dialogue concerning theodicy, utilizing words that only occur together elsewhere in Wisdom books: רע ("evil") and עמל ("wrongdoing") (Hab 1:13; Eccl 4:8); ריב ("strife") and מדון ("contention") (Hab 1:3; Prov 15:18; 17:14; 26:20–21, plus Jer 15:10, which also deals with theodicy); חמס ("violence"; Hab 1:2, 3, 9; 2:8, 17) and בוגד ("treacherous"; Hab 1:13; 2:5) only occur together in Prov 13:2; and Sheol and the root שבע ("be sated, have enough") are only linked in Hab 2:5 and Prov 27:20 and 30:16. In addition, תוכחת ("argument"; NRSV "complaint"; Hab 2:1), as well as the combination of משל ("proverb"; NRSV "taunt") and מליצה חידות ("mocking riddle") in Hab 2:6 also suggest a Wisdom background. Finally, the book never mentions Israel, Judah, Jerusalem, or such typical prophetic motifs as election and covenant (see Gowan 1968).

Comparably, Phyllis Trible (1963, 249–257) identifies multiple Wisdom contacts in Jonah, including an international outlook rather than a specific historical context, didactic reflection on nature leading to an analogy between a bush and the human sphere (4:10–11), and an effort to educate rather than amuse, while Katherine Dell (1996, 96–100) proposes literary and thematic (e.g., theodicy) points of contact between Jonah and Job. In addition, the book lacks explicit reflections of Israel's religious history, but contains Wisdom concerns such as the fear of the Lord (Jon 1:9, 16), nature (1:4, 15, 17; 2:10; 4:6–8), and opposition to both evil (1:2, 3:8, 10; 4:6) and anger (4:1–4, 9). As a result, George Landes (1978) considers the book to be a prophetic example story with possible Wisdom contacts.

25.3 Conclusion

Biblical scholars have proposed numerous instances of possible Wisdom influence outside the parameters of the generally accepted biblical Wisdom books. If all these proposals are correct, the extent of such Wisdom influence would be so great that the Wisdom Literature would be at risk of losing its distinctive character. It is important, therefore, to have explicit criteria for evaluating proposed points of Wisdom influence. This essay has proposed three overlapping criteria to that end: (1) the presence of distinctive Wisdom elements, namely vocabulary, forms, and content; (2) Wisdom usage, wherein these elements are used in the same way and with the same nuances as in the Wisdom Literature; and (3) the presence of a number of different Wisdom elements distributed through a significant portion of the work in question. The preceding has elaborated each of these criteria and then applied them to individual biblical texts, demonstrating how the criteria can establish both Wisdom influence and its absence.

These criteria are not meant to be applied in isolation from each other, but rather are designed to reinforce one other. Rather than just counting up the number of Wisdom elements or confirming that they do or do not reflect Wisdom usage and nuance, it is important to consider the cumulative weight of a number of different Wisdom indicators. Doing so can result in different levels of Wisdom influence. The most basic level is parallels to the Wisdom traditions that are general enough that it is not possible to determine decisively whether they are drawn from the Wisdom traditions themselves or from a shared Israelite culture and context. Second, some items might point to a connection to the Wisdom Literature but not actual Wisdom usage. Third, there can be unquestionable Wisdom influence, with peculiar Wisdom elements that clearly reflect the Wisdom tradition's underlying didactic intent. At the same time, more than one of these levels can be found in different places in a single biblical book, while in some shorter works, such as individual psalms, there may be enough indicators of wisdom influence to justify labelling that work an actual Wisdom text. Which, if any, of these levels of Wisdom influence is present in a specific non-Wisdom text can only be determined by a careful evaluation of that text in light of the established criteria.

As noted at the beginning, such full evaluation of specific texts is beyond the scope of this essay, but the preceding has presented some evidence both for and against Wisdom influence in non-Wisdom biblical books. For example, many of the negative examples have been drawn from the book of Amos, and I have examined them and others in much greater detail elsewhere (McLaughlin 2014), where I determined that the proposed Wisdom elements in Amos were either not actually distinctive to the Wisdom Literature or were not used in the same way as in the Wisdom books. On the other hand, I have also summarized above how works such as Psalms 37 and 49 combine all three kinds of Wisdom elements, namely vocabulary, forms, and themes, in a way that is consistent with how each element is used in the Wisdom Literature. This constitutes such extensive Wisdom influence that each psalm can be considered a Wisdom text in its own right (for fuller treatments of both psalms, see Cheung 2015, 52–100; McLaughlin 2018, 154–155). These summary treatments of possible Wisdom influence in the Hebrew Bible are supplemented by the other entries in this section of the Handbook, plus McLaughlin 2018, 141–170.

Works Cited

Blenkinsopp, Joseph. 1966. "Theme and Motif in the Succession History (2 Sam. XI 2ff) and the Yahwist Corpus." Pages 44–57 in *Volume du Congrès: Genève, 1965*. Edited by G.W. Anderson, P.A.H. de Boer, G.R. Castellino, Henry Cazelles, E. Hammershaimb, H.G. May, and W. Zimmerli. VTSup 15. Leiden: Brill.

Boston, James R. 1968. "Wisdom Influence upon the Song of Moses." *JBL* 87:198–202.

Brueggemann, Walter. 1973. "Jeremiah's Use of Rhetorical Questions." *JBL* 92:358–374.

Cheung, Simon Chi-Chung. 2015. *Wisdom Intoned: A Reappraisal of the Genre "Wisdom Psalms."* LHBOTS 613. London: Bloomsbury T&T Clark.

Childs, Brevard S. 1967. *Isaiah and the Assyrian Crisis*. SBT 2/3. Naperville, IL: Allenson.

Crenshaw, James L. 1967. "The Influence of the Wise on Amos: The 'Doxologies of Amos' and Job 5, 9–16; 9, 5–10." *ZAW* 79:42–52.

Crenshaw, James L. 1969. "Method in Determining Wisdom Influence Upon 'Historical' Literature." *JBL* 88:129–142.

Dell, Katharine J. 1996. "Reinventing the Wheel: The Shaping of the Book of Jonah." Pages 85–101 in *After the Exile: Essays in Honour of Rex Mason*. Edited by John Barton and David J. Reimer. Macon, GA: Mercer University Press.

Gowan, Donald E. 1968. "Habakkuk and Wisdom." *Perspective* 9:157–166.

Hobbs, T. Raymond. 1974. "Jeremiah 3:1–5 and Deuteronomy 24:1–4." *ZAW* 86:23–29.

Jensen, Joseph, O.S.B. 1973. *The Use of* tôrâ *by Isaiah: His Debate with the Wisdom Tradition*. CBQMS 3. Washington, D.C.: The Catholic Biblical Association of America.

Landes, George M. 1978. "Jonah: A Māšāl?" Pages 137–158 in *Israelite Wisdom: Theological and Literary Essays in Honor of Samuel Terrien*. Edited by John G. Gammie, Walter A. Brueggemann, W. Lee Humphreys, and James M. Ward. Scholars Press Homage Series. Missoula, MT: Scholars Press.

McKane, William. 1965. *Prophets and Wise Men*. SBT 44. London: SCM.

McLaughlin, John L. 2001. *The* marzēaḥ *in the Prophetic Literature: References and Allusions in Light of the Extra-Biblical Evidence*. VTSup 86. Leiden: Brill.

McLaughlin, John L. 2014. "Is Amos (Still) among the Wise?" *JBL* 133:281–303.

McLaughlin, John L. 2018. *An Introduction to Israel's Wisdom Traditions*. Grand Rapids, MI: Eerdmans.

Morgan, Donn F. 1981. *Wisdom in the Old Testament Traditions*. Atlanta, GA: John Knox.

Murphy, Roland E. 2002. *The Tree of Life: An Exploration of Biblical Wisdom Literature*. 3rd ed. Grand Rapids, MI: Eerdmans.

Olojede, Funlola O. 2012. "Sapiential Elements in the Joseph and Daniel Narratives vis-à-vis Woman Wisdom: Conjunctions and Disjunctions." *OTE* 25:351–368.

Rad, Gerhard von. 1984. "The Joseph Narrative and Ancient Wisdom." Pages 292–300 in *The Problem of the Hexateuch and Other Essays*. London: SCM.

Scott, R.B.Y. 1971. *The Way of Wisdom in the Old Testament*. New York, NY: Collier Books.

Talmon, Shemeryahu. 1963. "'Wisdom' in the Book of Esther." *VT* 13:419–455.

Terrien, Samuel. 1962. "Amos and Wisdom." Pages 108–115 in *Israel's Prophetic Heritage: Essays in Honor of James Muilenburg*. Edited by Bernhard W. Anderson and Walter J. Harrelson. New York, NY: Harper & Brothers.

Trible, Phyllis. 1963. "Studies in the Book of Jonah." Ph.D. diss., Columbia University.

Whybray, R.N. 1968. *The Succession Narrative*. SBT 2/9. London: SCM Press.

Whybray, R.N. 1974. *The Intellectual Tradition in the Old Testament*. BZAW 135. Berlin: de Gruyter.

Wilson, Lindsay. 2004. *Joseph, Wise and Otherwise: The Intersection of Wisdom and Covenant in Genesis 37–50*. Paternoster Biblical Monographs. Carlisle: Paternoster Press.

Wilson, Lindsay. 2009. "Wisdom in Isaiah." Pages 145–167 in *Interpreting Isaiah: Issues and Approaches*. Edited by David Firth and H.G.M. Williamson. Downers Grove, IL: Intervarsity.

Wolff, Hans Walter. 1973. *Amos the Prophet: The Man and His Background*. Edited by John Reumann. Translated by Foster R. McCurley. Philadelphia, PA: Fortress Press.

Wolff, Hans Walter. 1977. *Joel and Amos: A Commentary on the Books of the Prophets Joel and Amos*. Edited by S. Dean McBride, Jr. Translated by Waldemar Janzen, S. Dean McBride, Jr., and Charles A. Muenchow. Hermeneia. Philadelphia, PA: Fortress.

CHAPTER 26

....

LAW AND WISDOM LITERATURE

....

JONATHAN P. BURNSIDE

THE relationship between Law and Wisdom Literature, as scholars usually think of them, is slippery.[1] This is partly because we do not know much about how Law actually functioned in biblical Israel.[2] Accordingly, no matter how confident we may be about how scribes, sages, or "Wisdom schools" operated in Israel (though, in fact, these subjects are themselves strongly contested), assumptions about how any of them interfaced with Law, as it was practiced, are speculative.[3] To this uncertainty, we can add lack of consensus among scholars as to what wisdom and, indeed, Wisdom Literature itself means (Weeks 2010, 85). By contrast, there is a general consensus among scholars about what Law is, though the problem here is that Law is defined in positivistic terms as a matter of "rules." This is unhelpful, especially when the phenomenon of Torah, as described in the Hebrew Bible, is broader than a positivist portrait suggests. It further problematizes the relationship between Law and Wisdom Literature because it exaggerates any difference there may be. The relationship between Law and Wisdom Literature must be examined afresh.

This chapter begins by looking at the standard bifurcation in biblical studies that sees Law and Wisdom as separate—even opposed—categories. I shall argue that this dichotomous approach is unsatisfactory in view of the many correlations that exist between Law and Wisdom. The remainder of the chapter will then pursue a correction to the

---

[1] Thanks to Dr. Will Kynes (Samford), Prof. Bernard Jackson (Manchester), and Prof. Julian Rivers (Bristol) for their responses to an earlier draft of this paper. The usual disclaimers apply.

[2] E.g., Wilson (1993, 91): "To put the matter...bluntly, we still do not know how law worked in ancient Israel."

[3] Weinfeld's (1972) account of the role of scribal circles in shaping Law remains influential, despite scholarly reservations (e.g., Crenshaw 1976, 22; Fontaine 1982, 12). Fitzpatrick-McKinley (1999, 181) overstates the case, claiming the morality of biblical law was only "compelling" to "the scribal elite." For an overview of relevant scholarship, see Jackson (2006, ss. 2.1–2.6).

standard dichotomy by proposing a paradigm change that sees Law and Wisdom as complementary.

26.1 THE DICHOTOMY BETWEEN LAW AND WISDOM IN BIBLICAL STUDIES

Although scholarly definitions of Wisdom can be extremely broad, they still manage to exclude any formal alignment with Law.[4] If it is true that "[t]he task of the wise man is to uncover the hidden order of the world and to understand the experience of humans within that wider context," including "societal order" (Dell 2006, 413), one might have thought this definition would include discussion of Law. But such is not the case. Wisdom may have many facets, but Law is seemingly not one of them. The result is a dichotomy that sees Law and Wisdom as separate, and even opposed, categories. This is so deeply entrenched that even recent works designed to introduce students to the subject of biblical law explicitly deny any connection with Wisdom (e.g., Westbrook and Wells 2009, 33). Even a recent state-of-the-art overview, such as the 2015 *Oxford Encyclopedia of the Bible and Law*, has no entry on Wisdom, nor does it refer to Wisdom in its leading article on "Biblical Law" (Wells 2015).

This bifurcation between Law and Wisdom reflects, in part, long-standing source-critical debates regarding their respective origins. Thus, Erhard Gerstenberger's (1965, 49) influential account of the relationship between Law and Wisdom located the original setting of the "universal and timeless" biblical "rules" in Wisdom Literature, due to Wisdom's apparent concern for "the welfare of society in general." Although Gerstenberger claimed "a common background for wisdom maxims and legal commandments" (50), Law and Wisdom were separate entities. Some commandments were absorbed into the Wisdom Literature whilst others, he averred, were transplanted from the "family ethos" to a "secondary cultic setting" where they played out as Law (51). Whilst criticized by Dale Patrick (1985, 23) and Westbrook (1994, 20), Gerstenberger's assumptions frequently recur in scholarly analyses (e.g., Otto 1988; Marshall 1993, 12–13; Carr 2011, 419).

Joseph Blenkinsopp's (1995, 20, 93) argument is somewhat similar to preceding accounts but is notable for projecting onto biblical Israel a nineteenth-century model of legal evolution where codification is harnessed to the rise of the modern nation state. Thus Law—in the form of "law codes"—is said to emerge "with the passage from tribal society to state"; a model that is then said to apply to "early Israel" (99). Law and Wisdom are presented as two great, but separate, streams. Eventually, both legal and sapiential traditions flow together, though this is a late development. When Law and Wisdom do meet, as in Deuteronomy, Blenkinsopp claims that Law changes, under the influence of

---

[4] See the summary of scholarly definitions in Dell 2000, 1–13.

Wisdom, from "a purely objective and extrinsic reality" to an internal activity that "unites learning and piety" (118). Blenkinsopp here plays off the objective versus the subjective; the letter versus the spirit and basic knowledge versus lofty erudition. Behind this fairly standard opposition between Law and Wisdom lurks a latent antinomianism.

Why do scholars assume that Law and Wisdom do not mix? Our answers must be speculative but a (non-exhaustive) list might include the following: (1) the influence of legal positivism, which defines Torah in terms of rules, in contrast to Wisdom, which, however it is defined, is understood as a non-rule normative standard; (2) the intuitive assumption that Law is essentially concerned with coercion and with making people do what they may not want to do, usually under threat of punishment, in contrast to Wisdom, which is generally not seen as coercive; (3) the notion that Law is given by God whereas Wisdom is discovered by means of human searching; (4) the lack of references in Wisdom Literature to the idea of covenant, which is so central to Law; and (5) an emphasis on creation theology in Wisdom studies, which marginalizes Torah (Weeks 2010, 116–117).

However, these assumptions that Law and Wisdom do not mix are problematic. If these explanations are anywhere along the right lines, questions may be raised regarding the basis of a dichotomous approach. First, I have argued that it is anachronistic to define Torah purely in terms of Benthamite rules, since this amounts to a projection of modern ideas about law onto the ancient texts (Burnside 2018; Burnside 2019b). Torah is an accumulated phenomenon that integrates legal precept, judicial decision narrative and prophecy (Burnside 2011, xxx–xxxii).

Second, it is similarly reductive to understand Law primarily in terms of coercion and punishment. There is a strong element of voluntariness in narrative accounts of the Giving of the Law; indeed, the covenant between YHWH and Israel is presented as a precise moment in time when a people consciously resolved to obey their sovereign (Exod 24:3); an assent that legal positivists, including Jeremy Bentham, thought was extremely rare. Law shares with Wisdom the idea of persons choosing to live well.

Third, it is not possible to distinguish between Law and Wisdom based on a simple contrast between "revealed" and "concealed" since the narrative account of the Giving of the Law at Mount Sinai emphasizes the concealed qualities of Torah. YHWH's face is hidden in regard to Israel in a variety of ways (Exod 19:16–20). Revelation is given in the context of concealment. This is true even for Moses, who alone enjoys proximity to YHWH's Presence. Moreover, the face of the lawgiver is hidden when delivered by Moses himself because Moses's own face is transfigured (Exod 34:29). In sum, biblical law is not only an icon of revealed law; it is also an icon of concealed law (see further Burnside 2019b, and below, 26.3 Towards a Complementary Understanding of Law and Wisdom).

Fourth, the Wisdom Literature's lack of references to legal terminology is also questionable. Absence of evidence is not evidence of absence. In addition, there are no shared criteria among scholars regarding what would count as evidence: what is "clearly implied" for one reader is "deliberate rejection" for another. Thus, the mere appearance of the name of YHWH in Proverbs does not strike Barton (2016, 32) as showing that "all the supposedly normative features of 'Yahwism'" including "Moses, law, [and] covenant...are thereby implied." By contrast, Markus Witte (2014, 82) argues that "factual and structural theological interpretative lines of the Torah" may still be present in Job, even though the book itself does not contain terms such as "torah" (תורה) and "covenant" (ברית). Likewise, David Noel Freedman (1999, 92) claims, in regard to Psalm 119, that the mere omission of much of Israelite history and theology should not be taken as rejection, since the function of all such traditions exist "only to explain, support, or exalt Yahweh's unique, unparalleled revelation... *tôrâ*." Moreover, if, say, covenantal vocabulary is present, but without "any explicit concept of covenant" (Weeks 2016, 8), should that vocabulary be dismissed as irrelevant? Some scholars would suggest so. More clarity is needed regarding what standard is being applied and whether such criteria are appropriate for the creative enterprise of writing and redaction (for more, see below, 26.2 New Approaches to the Relationship between Law and Wisdom).

Finally, an emphasis on creation theology in Wisdom studies could just as well find a privileged place for Torah as a peripheral one. Weeks (2016, 15) acknowledges: "What Israelite wisdom does...is in response to a divine command [in Creation]." Modern approaches to biblical law have themselves emphasized how "Creation, law and wisdom texts...share a fundamental belief in a comprehensive ordering of reality" (McConville 2013, 630). I have argued that Torah is rooted in God's purpose in creation and so must be understood in regard to the divine ordering of creation (Burnside 2019a). Summarizing this approach, Gordon McConville (2013, 631) concludes that: "Torah and wisdom together are tasks given to human beings as part of the divine intention to establish a human society characterized by justice and righteousness."

Consequently, although there are a number of possible reasons why biblical scholars have assumed that Law and Wisdom do not mix, these assumptions can be challenged. This, in turn, leads us to question whether the bifurcation between Law and Wisdom should be the default position in biblical and theological studies.

26.2 NEW APPROACHES TO THE RELATIONSHIP BETWEEN LAW AND WISDOM

Questioning this bifurcation links up with a growing appetite among scholars to explore possible relationships between Law and Wisdom, as part of the recent interest in Wisdom scholarship "to build...bridges and to recover some important understandings that had become displaced or underplayed" (Weeks 2016, 6; similarly Otto 2007, 1). Scholars have recently moved beyond attempted reconstructions of the history of laws and proverbs to explore semantic, literary, and conceptual connections between Law and Wisdom that exist outside legal and proverbial collections. However, these developments do not in themselves undermine the dichotomy; they may, in fact, even reinforce it, as we shall see. Nevertheless, they are straws in the wind that need to be caught and considered.

First, Reinhard Müller (2013) finds a contrast between Joseph and Solomon (who both receive wisdom from God) and the judges of Deut 1:9–18 (whose wisdom, he thinks, is self-acquired and therefore non-spiritual because the candidates were already thought to possess it). Second, Witte (2014) builds on the work of Manfred Oeming (2001), who identified links between Law and Wisdom in Job 31 (e.g., correspondence between the ban of images [Deut 5:8] and worshipping sun and moon [Deut 4:19; 17:2–3] with Job 31:24–27), to propose various intersections and motifs between Job 31 and Deuteronomy 32. Third, Bernd Schipper (2013) finds points of contact between Law and Wisdom in Proverbs, building on the work of Franz Delitzsch and Michael Fishbane. In particular, he shows how Prov 3:1–5, 6:20–24, and 7:1–5 allude to Deut 6:6–8 (paralleled in Deut 11:18–21). Finally, a number of scholars have mined the relationship between Torah and Ecclesiastes, not only in regard to Eccl 12:13b (obviously) but, less obviously, the relationship between Eccl 5:5, 11:9, and Num 15:22–31, 39 (Kynes 2014).

Although more could be said regarding these proposals, and others like them, suffice it to say that scholars are making fresh, intertextual, discoveries between Law and Wisdom not only in areas where they might be expected (such as Proverbs, following the pioneering work of Weinfeld [1972]) but further afield (including Job), as well as narratives (Genesis; 1 Kings). Although the question of what counts as a valid intertextual connection remains contested, evidence of intertextuality allows for more complex readings of the relationship between Law and Wisdom. Indeed, both Müller and Witte posit interactions between different sorts of Law and different kinds of Wisdom. We do not need to follow these arguments in all their particulars to find in these semantic and linguistic analyses the possibility of further stimulating lines of inquiry, as follows.

First, Müller's observation that there is more than one way to acquire wisdom raises questions about how plural forms of epistemology might have mapped onto different ways of doing justice. This suggests new ways of relating Law and Wisdom. Müller's view of plurality presents a contrast between "divine" and "self-acquired" wisdom, though one could equally suggest plurality in acquiring divine wisdom directly from God. Certainly, the modus in the case of the seventy elders (Num 11:24–30) is arguably different from that described for Solomon. How might a plural epistemology relate to the range of authorities tasked with adjudication, including Levites, priests, prophets, and kings, as well as elected judges? Such varied offices give rise to different ways in which divine knowledge can be communicated, including divination, intuition, prophecy, and reason. The different adjudicatory authorities reflect different modes of divine knowledge, each of which has a role to play in adjudication and each of which has potential for being institutionalized to varying degrees (Burnside 2011, 131–133).

Second, Schipper's argument that Proverbs brings the father's מצות ("commands") and the mother's תורות ("instructions") closer to the commandments and instruction of YHWH merits further consideration. One implication of this is that the parents stand, as it were, in the place of YHWH, whilst the child stands in the place of Moses (though Schipper does not quite put matters this way himself). Among other implications for how Law and Wisdom are understood, both in terms of concepts and as forms of communication, this suggests, as I have argued, that, in semiotic terms, Moses's delivery of

Torah to the people on Mount Sinai with a shining face (Exod 34:29) signifies that he now stands in the place of YHWH in giving Torah to Israel (Burnside 2019b). This has the knock-on effect of casting the people in Moses's role.

This means that Israel is invited to behave concerning Moses as Moses did in relation to YHWH on the mountain. Moses waits expectantly for YHWH (Exod 24:12); he prepares to receive Torah (Exod 24:16–17), fasts (Exod 34:28), and worships (Exod 24:1). He even engages in a daring exchange with YHWH in Exodus 32–33 that results in YHWH initiating another covenant that repairs the breach between the Israelites and God (Exod 34:10) and leads to fresh law (Exod 34:11–26). Torah is explicitly given in the context of intercession, discussion, rational argument, and strategic risk-taking. There is also room for protest of a kind (e.g., Exod 32:11–14). The same model of engagement is found when Moses receives divine revelation in the Tent of Meeting (Exod 33:7–11) (Burnside 2019b). All this means that the people are to engage actively in dialogue, reflection, and meditation on Torah. Indeed, this is what they are explicitly commanded to do (Deut 6:7). If Moses's encounter with God on Mount Sinai is both highly participatory and paradigmatic for all Israel, it raises the possibility that every discussion of Torah among the people, including as they "walk by the way" (Deut 6:1) has cultic significance.[5] The paradigm of Moses's encounter with God could apply even to parental instruction within the home. Teaching the commandments (Deut 6:1) might thus evoke the dynamic of YHWH's teaching Moses on Sinai. This suggestion is consistent with Schipper's parallel between Proverbs and Deuteronomy. Schipper's reading also fits the connotative significance of Moses's encounters with YHWH at the Tent of Meeting (e.g., Exod 33:11; Num 12:6–8), especially if this was Moses's own personal tent, used for revelatory purposes. In ancient Israelite culture, the tent is, of course, the place of habitation and conversation. In sum, we can make connections between Law and Wisdom by considering the semiotic significance of how Torah was given to Israel.

We conclude this brief survey of recent developments in Law and Wisdom by considering Will Kynes's (2016, 101) proposal that, in future, we should treat "wisdom as a concept instead of a genre." This would be a new development for our understanding of Law and Wisdom. Thomas Krüger's (2014, 51–52) analysis of Deut 4:5–8 suggests that this text might be a good place to start relating law and wisdom, as concepts. The passage presents this relationship not abstractly, but through the particular, namely, the hope that the nations will see Israel's obedience to Torah as virtuous. Elsewhere in Deuteronomy, Deut 1:13–17, 16:19, and 34:9 stress wisdom as a pre-requisite for rightly interpreting law, whilst Deut 29:3 [ET 4] and 30:6 "express doubts about whether the Israelites have such wisdom and offers possibilities to acquire such wisdom" (Krüger 2014, 47 n. 35). It is at this point that law and wisdom, as concepts, link up with broader "prophetic statements about the change or renewal of the human heart by God (Jeremiah 31; Ezekiel 36, etc.) [which] address the same problem" (Krüger 2014, 47 n. 35). Outside the Pentateuch, Psalms 19 and 119 offer fertile ground. Questions we can ask of law and wisdom—as

---

[5] Biblical quotations are drawn from the New Revised Standard Version (NRSV) translation of the Holy Bible, unless otherwise noted.

concepts—include: Do these psalms infer that only law mediates wisdom? Is there another source of wisdom besides Torah? And does law, in Psalms 19 and 119, mediate the same virtues as wisdom does elsewhere? (Krüger 2014, 46).

All these examples of semantic, literary, and conceptual connections have the potential to undermine the dichotomy between Law and Wisdom. But not necessarily. They can equally be seen, by biblical scholars, as reinforcing the bifurcation. Intertextuality cuts both ways. They could pave the way for a complementary approach, which sees connections between Law and Wisdom, not simply a chasm. However, if those connections are not understood as integral to the original text but are, rather, later additions (usually, legal additions to earlier Wisdom texts),[6] such intertextuality merely restates the dichotomy in its own way. The latter response is particularly problematic because it suggests that biblical scholarship is underpinned by a presupposition that is so strong that it is non-falsifiable, namely, that if there is a connection between Law and Wisdom, then this must be late.

I propose, then, that these emerging trends in Law and Wisdom scholarship are not random straws blowing in the wind. Rather, they point in a particular direction that, in turn, indicates the need for change. They give added force to the need to question the dichotomy between Law and Wisdom and raise the possibility that this default position does not do justice to the texts. They even suggest that the underlying assumption that there is a dichotomy is wrong. Consequently, I propose that the emerging trends in Wisdom scholarship identified in this section point towards the need for a paradigm shift in biblical studies. A change of paradigm within a discipline is never comfortable but, sometimes, it is necessary. This is one such case. If we took, instead, the presumption that Law and Wisdom are complementary as our starting-point, a lot of findings would fall into place. Law and Wisdom are not opposed. They are complementary; they speak to each other and they relate to each other.

26.3 TOWARDS A COMPLEMENTARY UNDERSTANDING OF LAW AND WISDOM

Along with burgeoning interest in semantic and linguistic studies, a further development in Wisdom studies has been the application of cognitive linguistics, along with cognitive studies generally, to Wisdom Literature (e.g., Van Wolde 2003). The application of cognitive linguistics to Law and Wisdom adds further weight to my proposal for a paradigm shift.

---

[6] E.g., Weinfeld (1972, 260–261) argues for the relative priority of Proverbs over Deuteronomy whilst Fishbane (1977, 284) argues for the reverse. Carr (2011, 415–421) thinks that the strongest examples of intertextuality favor an earlier date for Proverbs, though he accepts that, in weaker examples, "the cases for direction of dependence are progressively less clear" (417).

I begin with Jackson's pioneering application of the insights of semiotics and associated theories of cognition to biblical law over the last twenty-five years. His resulting
model of "wisdom-laws" (2006) remarkably relocates discussion of the nature, origin,
and purpose of biblical law from a modern-style, positivist, and forensic milieu to a
Wisdom context. Although Jackson himself uses his approach to propose his own theories regarding the history and sources of biblical law, it is fair to say that locating biblical
law in a Wisdom context provides strong evidence that we should understand Law and
Wisdom in complementary terms. This is because, for Jackson, law assumes the social
knowledge which is presented, or advocated, in the Hebrew Bible as wisdom.

Put briefly, Jackson's approach assumes, inter alia, that many early biblical laws take
the form of "self-executing" rules, viz. rules formulated to reduce the need for third-
party adjudication. Importantly, the cognitive structures that go into reading "wisdom-
laws" are narrative, not semantic (2006, 24–25). Rules that we read semantically
(or literally) cover all cases that may be included under their language whereas rules
that we understand narratively (or imagistically) apply only to the typical cases that they
bring to mind. This is because the narrative image represents the "core" of the message.
The further the real-life case is from the "typical case," the less likely it is that the rule
applies and the more room there is for negotiation between the parties (2000a, 75–82).
Applying the "eye for eye, tooth for tooth" formula in Exod 21:24–25 to a one-eyed man
would not be a valid application of the law, since taking the eye of this non-typical
offender would leave him blind (see Jackson 2000a, 85–86). The question is whether the
dispute is sufficiently similar to the picture evoked by the rule to justify its use to resolve
the problem. Significantly, questions of relative similarity evoke intuitive judgments
of justice to a greater degree than literal interpretations (Jackson 1995a, 82ff). Finally,
the images suggested by narrative are drawn from social knowledge;[7] in that sense,
"wisdom-laws" function as a "restricted code."[8]

What is "wisdom-like" about such "wisdom-laws"? Quite a lot, which is why Jackson's
method is a strong pointer towards a complementary approach to Law and Wisdom. We
can identify the following (though this list is not exhaustive):

1. Jackson draws on Carole Fontaine's (1982) detailed analysis of "proverb performance" (i.e., how proverbial sayings are transmitted in a given social interaction)
   in selected biblical texts (e.g., Judg 8:2, 21; 1 Sam 16:7; 24:14; 1 Kgs 20:11;
   Fontaine 1982, 76–138; see Jackson's [2006, 34–35] discussion of Judg 8:1–3). This
   shows how, inter alia, traditional wisdom functions to restore social order.
   Jackson (2006, 37–38) argues that, like such proverbs, "wisdom-laws" provide a
   model for conflict resolution and settling disputes. For example, the "wise

---

[7] That is, our knowledge of social situations that is informed by our social and historical context and
which we normally take for granted (see Jackson 2000b, 45).

[8] A restricted code is "one where meanings are embedded in a particular social context, and where
as a result language needs to be less explicit, since values and understandings are shared (and known to
be shared), and therefore do not require explicit statement" (Jackson 2006, 25). Jackson derives the term
from Basil Bernstein.

woman" of Tekoa uses a traditional saying (2 Sam 14:14) to resolve a dispute. At the same time, she also presents what can be termed a "hard case" in the biblical laws of homicide inasmuch as the typical case presupposes that the death of the killer will not extinguish the family line.

2. This preference for resolving disputes "on the spot" and avoiding litigation resonates with the social ideology of Prov 25:7–9, which shows a clear "anti-institutional bias" that is directed against adjudicatory institutions (Jackson 1992, 65). Wisdom plays a key role in dispute resolution (Jackson 1992, 65–67; Jackson 1995b, 1762–1765; Jackson 2006, 58–59).

3. By providing instructions for individuals to sort out their own affairs, "wisdom-laws" are in keeping with the tendency of Proverbs to address the individual citizen, as opposed to Israel as a whole.[9]

4. By addressing the citizen qua citizen, rather than formal institutions like courts, "wisdom-laws" also fit the anti-institutional rhetoric found in Proverbs (e.g., Prov 6:6–8; Jackson 1992, 1).

5. Like "wisdom-laws," proverbial wisdom deploys "images...familiar to the culture (or subculture) in which the saying circulates" (Fontaine 1982, 152). Scholars have long noted that the brevity of the folk proverb means that it is "virtually unintelligible apart from the context of its use" (Fontaine 1982, 19). Fontaine (1982, 152) herself describes how proverbs provide a cognitive challenge to "break the cultural and linguistic code of the form...and supply its immediate contextual referents." This is the very definition of a "restricted code" (Jackson 2006, 66). Similarly, Weeks (1994, 159) observes that: "Proverbs moralizes, and encourages its readers to pursue certain ideals or patterns of behaviour, but assumes that they will know about them already." The same is said of "wisdom-laws" (Jackson 2006, 66).

6. Related to the previous point, there are many Wisdom connections, at the level of social stereotypes, between the laws and Wisdom Literature, such as the stereotypes of the Hebrew slave (Exod 21:2; cf. Prov 22:7) and the nocturnal thief (Exod 22:1–2 [ET 2–3]; cf. Job 24:14, 16).[10]

7. "Wisdom-laws" provide resources for dealing with untypical cases that fall outside the paradigm but which are still thought, for whatever reason, to be sufficiently close to the narrative typification. This arises because the casuistic formula "if X..." should not be read as "if X and only X" (Jackson 2015, 77, 79); accordingly, narrative readings may sometimes extend beyond what is covered by a semantic reading. This is, again, close to the cognitive function of proverbs. Weeks (2016, 18) thinks that "Proverbs 1–9 sees the Law as a route, *via* wisdom, for individuals to acquire the knowledge of the choices that they should make, even in situations that are not explicitly addressed by the Law." There could

---

[9] Though this is not to ignore the public dimension of Wisdom, nor the ways in which Lady Wisdom addresses a collectivity of persons; e.g., Proverbs 8–9.

[10] For a full list, see Jackson 2006, 42–43.

hardly be a better description of how paradigm cases form the basis of adjudication in situations where the case at hand falls outside the paradigm.

8. By evoking intuitive judgments of justice, "wisdom-laws" recall Martha Nussbaum's (1986, 301) account of Aristotelian "practical wisdom," one of the characteristics of which is the need for "[g]ood judgement... [which] supplies both a superior concreteness and a superior responsiveness or flexibility."

9. Finally, although wisdom has been understood by scholars as both a genre and a concept, Jackson directs our attention to the significance of wisdom as a value. Areas of overlap between Law and wisdom at the level of value include: (i) keeping disputes out of the courts; (ii) avoiding contentiousness; (iii) internalizing wisdom; and (iv) the value of reproof, among others (Jackson 2000b, 32).

It should be noted that Jackson's particular argument in *Wisdom-Laws* is advanced only in regard to the *Mishpatim* (2006, 30), although, in his earlier work, Jackson (1995b, 1761) suggested "[a]ll laws presented as such in the Pentateuch are 'wisdom-laws,' but to be understood within a developing concept of wisdom." The question arises how far Jackson's ideas extend beyond the *Mishpatim*. Jackson's series of studies on the book of Ruth (e.g., 2015) represents a significant extension of his thesis; Ruth, he argues, reflects a situation where "wisdom-laws" operate on the basis of negotiable social custom, without, for the most part, reference to the formulations found in the Pentateuch. This has the potential to refine yet further our understanding of the relationship between Law and Wisdom.

As far as "wisdom-laws" in the Pentateuch are concerned, my own work has shown the usefulness of thinking in terms of "wisdom-laws" across different legal collections. Examples include the food laws of Lev 11:3–23 and Deut 14:3–20 (Burnside 2016), the case of the Sabbath-breaker (Num 15:32–36; Burnside 2010a), and laws of siege warfare (Deut 20:19–20; Burnside 2011, 173–176), among others. I have also argued that the "wisdom-law" approach also applies to biblical narratives, including the relationship between laws of asylum (Exod 21:12–14) and the Davidic succession narrative (1 Kings 1–2) (Burnside 2010b). This body of research raises the question of how the various social stereotypes that we find in Wisdom Literature inform and underlie the narrative paradigms that we find in biblical law (e.g., the relationship between the typology of "a glutton and a drunkard" in Prov 23:19–22 and Deut 21:20c; Burnside 2003, 51–55). If we embrace a change of paradigm, and explore the complementary nature of the relationship between Law and Wisdom, we can expect to find further, and deeper, connections between texts conventionally constructed as Law, narrative, and Wisdom. To date, explorations of the relationship between Law and Wisdom have tended to focus on the relationship between Deuteronomy and Wisdom, as though all that might be said about the relationship between different legal collections and Wisdom should be refracted through Deuteronomy or "Deuteronomic ideas" (Weeks 2016, 18). Jackson's (2006, 41–42) discovery of multiple substantive connections between the *Mishpatim* and Wisdom shows the need to extend the discussion into other legal collections as well. For example, the enmity theme of Exod 23:4–5 recalls Prov 10:12, 26:21, and, conversely, concern for the "neighbor" in Exod 21:35; 22:6, 8, 9, 10, 13, 25 evokes Prov 27:10.

A change of paradigm would also cause us to embrace the implications of the fact that written Law contains evidence of what Walter Ong (1982, 115) has termed "oral residue." Residual orality occurs when previously oral-based cultures are exposed to the technologies of literacy and writing, but have not fully interiorized their use in their daily lives (Ong 1982, 11; see also Jackson 1995a, 78–88). It means that earlier patterns of cognition, associated with orality, persist within literacy (Jackson 2000a, 41). As far as the *Mishpatim* is concerned, Jackson (2006, 93–113) has argued that this oral residue is not completely overlaid, even when the stage of writing has been reached. I have highlighted the prevalence of oral residue in a range of texts outside the *Mishpatim* (Burnside 2020) and suggested that the food laws of Leviticus 11 and Deuteronomy 14 provide an example, not only at the stage of writing, but also (in the context of Leviticus) at an advanced stage of legal reasoning as well (Burnside 2016, 236). This is significant because the use of restricted code, narrative paradigms, and social stereotypes—all of which are features of biblical law, as we have seen—are also indicators of an oral-based culture (Jackson 2006, 434). Wisdom itself, as is often observed, is strongly associated with orality and oral-based forms of cognition. Consequently, examining these indicators more closely will also provide further evidence of the complementary nature of the relationship between Law and Wisdom.

Similarly, a complementary relationship between Law and Wisdom may also be discerned in regard to literary presentation. Increasing attention has been paid to the intricate literary structures found in biblical law (e.g., Lev 24:13–23 and Leviticus 20; see Burnside 2006; Burnside 2015) as well as to the semiotic and cognitive assumptions that lie behind them (Jackson 2006, 447–448). Such ornate literary examples are consistent with the aesthetic literary values of Wisdom (e.g., Prov 25:11). This too is a matter for further exploration.

Finally, we should also consider the significance, for Law, of Wisdom's own reflections upon the relationship between the knowable and the unknowable (e.g., Job 5:9; cf. 11:7; Job 25:2–3; cf. 36:26). Of course, Torah belongs to the realm of the revealed and knowable (e.g., Deut 29:29 [ET 28]). But, at the same time, it is given in the context of hiddenness. As noted above, the face of the lawgiver, both YHWH and Moses, is hidden, even in the act of giving the law (Burnside 2018). Revelation is given in the context of concealment. This is significant in a host of ways that underline the sapiential quality of Torah. Apart from anything else, it signifies that engaging with Torah involves a posture of openness towards that which is presently unknown, as well as the limitations of what is presently known, including the mystery of YHWH's Name and character.

For example, YHWH's pronouncement of his Name in Exod 34:6–7 is the greatest disclosure of YHWH's nature and character in the whole of the Hebrew Bible, but this fullness of revelation, so to speak, is formally presented in terms of just seeing YHWH's "back," since Moses cannot see YHWH's face and live (33:20). In the very context of the giving of the law, while Moses carries the two tablets of stone he has carved himself (Exod 34:4), we find engagement with precisely the issue of the limitations of human knowledge of God. This alternation between the knowable and the unknowable is as much a feature of the giving of Torah as it is of the concept of wisdom. As the doyen of

Wisdom studies, Gerhard von Rad (1972, 109), wrote: "The fear of God not only enabled a man to acquire knowledge but also...kept awake in the person acquiring the knowledge the awareness that his intellect was directed towards a world in which mystery predominated." In Torah, no less than in Wisdom, we confront the mystery of God.

26.4 RECASTING THE RELATIONSHIP BETWEEN LAW AND WISDOM

Questioning the dichotomous approach to Law and Wisdom does not entail collapsing them into one another. To claim that Law and Wisdom are complementary necessarily involves the claim that there is still some distinction between them. There are differences that survive my critique of the dichotomous approach (see above, 26.1 The Dichotomy between Law and Wisdom in Biblical Studies) and these, remaining, distinctions are worth preserving.

Some are implied by the texts themselves. First, Deut 16:19 contains a warning against bribery, underlining the fallibility of even those judges who were appointed on the basis of their reputation for wisdom (Deut 16:18; cf. 1:13–18). Clearly, as Müller (2013, 27) has already pointed out, it takes more than wisdom and experience to serve as a judge; one also needs Torah.

Second, Deut 4:5 also implies a distinction between Law and wisdom as concept if not also Wisdom as category. When Moses exhorts the people to observe YHWH's "statutes and ordinances" (חקים ומשפטים; Deut 4:5), a spur to their obedience is that "this will show your wisdom and discernment (חכמתכם ובינתכם) to the peoples, who, when they hear all these statutes (כל החקים) will say, 'Surely this great nation is a wise and discerning people (עם־חכם ונבון)!'" (Deut 4:6). "Statutes and ordinances" are here aligned with "wisdom and discernment" but they are distinct. Verse 6 attributes to the laws, when they are obeyed, the qualification (in semiotic terms) of being wise, which even outsiders will recognize. Law is like Wisdom, if it is recognized as wise, but not all wisdom is legal.

A third distinction between Law and Wisdom is implied by the way in which the latter overtly presents itself in a contradictory—even paradoxical—manner. The obvious example, at least as far as Proverbs is concerned, is Prov 26:4–5:

> Answer not a fool according to his folly, lest you be like him yourself.
> Answer a fool according to his folly, lest he be wise in his own eyes.

Of course, it is possible to find apparent conflicts and differing formulations between laws in various biblical sources, including laws relating to homicide (Exod 21:30; Num 35:31–32), kidnapping (Exod 21:16; Deut 24:7), slavery (Exod 21:2; Lev 25:39–40), and expectations regarding vicarious punishment (Exod 20:5–6; Ezek 18:1–4). This prompts us to consider whether the purpose of canonization was to encourage closer study of these issues. This, in turn, links up with broader pedagogic traditions in rabbinic thought and literature, which encourage the ability of the individual to entertain contradictory ideas (Lancaster 2000, 194). Certainly, rabbinic interpretation excels in identifying and then explaining away apparent inconsistencies in the text, supported by a linguistic theology best summed up in the Talmudic adage אלו ואלו דברי אלהים חיים ("these and these [apparent contradictions] are the words of the living God"; BT Eruvin 13b). That said, there does not seem to be an equivalent to Prov 26:4–5 in Torah, and for good reason. It is not appropriate for Law to overtly present contradictory rules that co-exist side by side and which claim equal authority. This difference in presentation between Law and Wisdom is significant.

Fourth, this difference in presentation raises the question as to whether Law and Wisdom are, in addition, distinct in terms of their rhetorical strategies. There is a world of difference between commandments that are given by a divine sovereign (first directly and, later, through an intermediary) in the shattering context of a theophany and domestic instructions given directly by parents to their children. From a semiotic perspective, it is clearly a matter of the utmost significance that these instructions are communicated by different forms of authority, and by different means.

Fifth, difference in rhetorical strategies raises the further question as to whether there may also be a difference between Law and Wisdom in terms of their social functions. Here I am at my most tentative. Any difference in social function is unlikely to be at the level of a difference between the collective and the individual since the commandments of Torah are themselves expressed in the singular and many of the laws of the *Mishpatim* (or "Covenant Code"), for example, are concerned with disputes between individuals. Nor can any potential difference be between formal social control (Law) and informal social control (Wisdom), since both Law and Wisdom in the Bible have interests that go well beyond mere social control. But there may be a difference between norms that are rhetorically and socially appropriate for providing national goals and direction and those that are rhetorically and socially appropriate for day-to-day living. To give an historical example from the United Kingdom during the Second World War (at a time when we could fairly say the state did have clear national purpose), this is the difference between the national goal of defeating the Axis powers, which might involve a well-known government decree such as "Dig for Victory," and the day-to-day gardening instructions that enabled citizens to grow their own food in order to "Dig for Victory." In terms of their social function, the difference between a decree and its realization may map onto the difference between Law and Wisdom.

In the context of biblical Israel, her national goal and vocation is expressly set out in terms of her being "a kingdom of priests and a holy nation" (Exod 19:6). Torah molds Israel into a nation and contains specific decrees that will enable her to fulfill this national goal and collective vocation. Wisdom may particularly concern the specifics of how to fulfill that vocation. Using the "Dig for Victory" decree as an example (which is likewise a national objective that is also aimed at every individual), it is Wisdom that turns gardens into communal allotments, runs them well and grows lots of the right crops so as to impact positively on the main goal. To put it yet another way, Wisdom may be the realization, or the fulfillment, of Torah. Law presents us with the paradigm and Wisdom is concerned with the question of how we apply it. This proposed distinction need not be a sharp one. Indeed, seeing Law and Wisdom in terms of paradigm and application may even help to explain why law, in the Bible, assumes the social knowledge which is presented, or advocated, as wisdom. We might even speak of this as a distinction of degree and not of type in which Law and Wisdom fall at different points on a spectrum of normativity.

Putting matters thus has some resonance with Craig Bartholomew's (2016, 25) view that Wisdom and Law operate side-by-side in "a 'carved' creation order" (drawing on Raymond Van Leeuwen). Here, "cultural and personal exhortation is grounded in the reality of the created world with its inbuilt normativity" (Van Leeuwen 1990, 116). This in turn is consistent with the argument I have made elsewhere that, in an ideal but also in a practical sense, Wisdom and Law together form a seamless web of normativity in biblical Israel. Whilst Law is incomplete, its purpose is to instruct in Wisdom, which is complete (Burnside 2011, 472). Just as we need to think about Law in counter-cultural and difficult ways, so we also must be prepared to think of Wisdom in creative ways, treating them both as complementary modes of access to a single normative reality. This means that there are Law-like elements in Wisdom as well as Wisdom elements in Law. Law is more like Wisdom than we have allowed it to be and Wisdom is also more like Law. Yet neither is embedded in the other. Law and Wisdom are complementary and cognate sources of normativity that have distinctive features.

26.5 CONCLUSION

The dichotomous approach to Law and Wisdom that has dominated biblical studies distorts our understanding of the traditions of both Law and Wisdom, as well as the more unified biblical tradition as a whole. Given the many correlations between Law and Wisdom that can now be identified, a paradigm shift to an approach that sees Law and Wisdom as complementary is now needed. We must look anew at the relationship between the concepts of Law and Wisdom in the Hebrew Bible with the post-Enlightenment presuppositions projected onto the category of "Wisdom Literature" laid aside. This is a key task. The relationship between Israel's Law and Wisdom is crucial to re-evaluating the concept of wisdom because Law has hitherto been excluded, by definition. A paradigm shift in the relationship between Law and Wisdom is thus central to our understanding of both.

WORKS CITED

Bartholomew, Craig. 2016. "Old Testament Wisdom Today." Pages 3–33 in Firth and Wilson 2016.
Barton, John. 2016. "Ethics in the Wisdom Literature of the Old Testament." Pages 24–37 in Jarick 2016.

Blenkinsopp, Joseph. 1995. *Wisdom and Law in the Old Testament*. Rev. ed. Oxford: Oxford University Press.

Burnside, Jonathan P. 2003. *The Signs of Sin: Seriousness of Offence in Biblical Law*. LHBOTS 364. Sheffield: Sheffield Academic.

Burnside, Jonathan P. 2006. "Strange Flesh: Sex, Semiotics and the Construction of Deviancy in Biblical Law." *JSOT* 30:387–420.

Burnside, Jonathan. 2010a. "'What Shall We Do with the Sabbath-gatherer?' A Narrative Approach to a 'Hard Case' in Biblical Law (Num. 15:32–36)." *VT* 60:45–62.

Burnside, Jonathan. 2010b. "Flight of the Fugitives: Rethinking the Relationship between Biblical Law (Exod. 21:12–14) and the Davidic Succession Narrative (1 Kings 1–2)." *JBL* 129:418–431.

Burnside, Jonathan. 2011. *God, Justice and Society: Aspects of Law and Legality in the Bible*. Oxford: Oxford University Press.

Burnside, Jonathan. 2015. "The Medium and the Message: Necromancy and the Literary Context of Leviticus 20." Pages 41–62 in *Text, Time and Temple: Literary, Historical and Ritual Studies in Leviticus*. Edited by Leigh M. Trevaskis, Francis Landy, and Bryan D. Bibb. Sheffield: Phoenix.

Burnside, Jonathan. 2016. "At Wisdom's Table: How Narrative Shapes the Biblical Food Laws and Their Social Function." *JBL* 135:223–245.

Burnside, Jonathan. 2018. "Jeremy Bentham and the Problem of the Authority of Biblical Law." Pages 53–78 in *Research Handbook in Law and Religion*. Edited by Rex Ahdar. Cheltenham: Edward Elgar.

Burnside, Jonathan. 2019a. "Biblical Law and Natural Law." Pages 181–203 in *Research Handbook on Natural Law*. Edited by Jonathan Crowe and Constance Lee. Cheltenham: Edward Elgar.

Burnside, Jonathan. 2019b. "The Hidden Face of the Law-Giver: Revelation and Concealment in the Giving of the Law at Mount Sinai." Forthcoming in Pages 103-120 in *Ben Porat Yosef: Studies in the Bible and Its World*. Edited by Michael Avioz, Yael Shemesh, and Omer Minka. Münster: Ugarit-Verlag.

Burnside, Jonathan. 2020. "Write That They May Judge? Applying Written Law in Biblical Israel." Pages 127–147 in *Write That They May Read: Studies in Literacy and Textualization in the Ancient Near East and in the Hebrew Scriptures*. Edited by Daniel I. Block, David C. Deuel, C. John Collins, and Paul J. N. Laurence. Eugene, Oregon: Pickwick.

Carr, David M. 2011. *The Formation of the Hebrew Bible: A New Reconstruction*. New York, NY: Oxford University Press.

Crenshaw, J.L. 1976. "Prolegomenon." Pages 1–35 in *Studies in Ancient Israelite Wisdom*. Edited by J.L. Crenshaw. New York, NY: Ktav Publishing House.

Dell, Katharine. 2000. *"Get Wisdom, Get Insight": An Introduction to Israel's Wisdom Literature*. London: Darton, Longman, and Todd.

Dell, Katharine J. 2006. "Wisdom." Pages 409–419 in *The Oxford Handbook of Biblical Studies*. Edited by J.W. Rogerson and Judith M. Lieu. Oxford: Oxford University Press.

Firth, David G., and Lindsay Wilson. 2016. *Exploring Old Testament Wisdom: Literature and Themes*. London: Apollos.

Fishbane, Michael. 1977. "Torah and Tradition." Pages 275–300 in *Tradition and Theology in the Old Testament*. Edited by Douglas A. Knight. Philadelphia, PA: Fortress.

Fitzpatrick McKinley, Anne. 1999. *The Transformation of Torah from Scribal Advice to Law*. LHBOTS 287. Sheffield: Sheffield Academic.

Fontaine, Carole R. 1982. *Traditional Sayings in the Old Testament*. Sheffield: Almond.

Freedman, David Noel. 1999. *Psalm 119: The Exaltation of Torah*. Winona Lake, IN: Eisenbrauns.

Gerstenberger, Erhard. 1965. "Covenant and Commandment." *JBL* 84:38–51.

Jackson, Bernard S. 1992. "Practical Wisdom and Literary Artifice in the Covenant Code." Pages 65–92 in *The Jerusalem 1990 Conference Volume*. Edited by B.S. Jackson and S.M. Passamaneck. Atlanta, GA: Scholars.

Jackson, Bernard S. *Making Sense in Law: Linguistic, Psychological and Semiotic Perspectives*. Liverpool: Deborah Charles Publications, 1995a.

Jackson, Bernard S. 1995b. "Modelling Biblical Law: The Covenant Code." *Chicago-Kent Law Review* 70:1745–1827.

Jackson, Bernard S. 2000a. *Studies in the Semiotics of Biblical Law*. LHBOTS 314. Sheffield: Sheffield Academic.

Jackson, Bernard S. 2000b. "Law, Wisdom and Narrative." Pages 31–51 in *Narrativity in Biblical and Related Texts*. Edited by G.J. Brooke and J.-D. Kaestli. Leuven: Leuven University Press.

Jackson, Bernard S. 2006. *Wisdom-Laws*. Oxford: Oxford University Press.

Jackson, Bernard S. 2015. "Ruth, the Pentateuch and the Nature of Biblical Law: In Conversation with Jean Louis Ska." Pages 75–111 in *The Post-Priestly Pentateuch*. Edited by Federico Giuntoli and Konrad Schmid. Tübingen: Mohr Siebeck.

Jarick, John, ed. 2016. *Perspectives on Israelite Wisdom: Proceedings of the Oxford Old Testament Seminar*. LHBOTS 618. London: Bloomsbury T&T Clark.

Krüger, Thomas. 2014. "Law and Wisdom according to Deut. 4:5–8." Pages 36–54 in Schipper and Teeter 2013.

Kynes, Will. 2014. "Follow Your Heart and Do Not Say It Was a Mistake: Qoheleth's Allusions to Numbers 15 and the Story of the Spies." Pages 15–27 in *Reading Ecclesiastes Intertextually*. LHBOTS 587. Edited by Katharine Dell and Will Kynes. London: Bloomsbury T&T Clark.

Kynes, Will. 2016. "The Nineteenth-Century Beginnings of 'Wisdom Literature.'" Pages 83–108 in Jarick 2016.

Lancaster, Brian L. 2000. "The Psychology of Oppositional Thinking in Rabbinic Biblical Commentary." Pages 191–203 in *Jewish Ways of Reading the Bible*. Edited by George J. Brook. Oxford: Oxford University Press.

Marshall, J.W. 1993. *Israel and the Book of the Covenant: An Anthropological Approach to Biblical Law*. Atlanta, GA: Scholars.

McConville, Gordon. 2013. "Biblical Law and Human Formation." *Political Theology* 14:628–640.

Müller, Reinhard. 2013. "The Blinded Eyes of the Wise: Sapiential Tradition and Mosaic Commandment in Deut. 16:19–20." Pages 9–33 in Schipper and Teeter 2013.

Nussbaum, Martha. 1986. *The Fragility of Goodness: Luck and Ethics in Greek Tragedy and Philosophy*. Cambridge: Cambridge University Press.

Oeming, Manfred. 2001. Hiobs Monolog—der Weg nach innen. Pages 57–75 in *Hiobs Weg: Stationen von Menschen im Leid*. BThSt 45. Edited by Manfred Oeming, and Konrad Schmid. Neukirchen-Vluyn: Neukirchener.

Ong, W. 1982. *Orality and Literacy*. London: Methuen.

Otto, Eckart. 1988. *Wandel der Rechtsbegründungen in der Gesellschaftsgeschichte des antiken Israel: Eine Rechtsgeschichte des "Bundesbuches" Ex. XX 22–XXIII 13*. Leiden: Brill.

Otto, Eckart. 2007. "A Hidden Truth Behind the Text or the Truth of the Text: At a Turning Point in Biblical Scholarship Two Hundred Years after De Wette's Dissertation Critico-Exegetica." Pages 19–28 in *South African Perspectives on the Pentateuch: Between Synchrony and Diachrony*. Edited by J.H. le Roux and E. Otto. New York, NY: T&T Clark.

Patrick, Dale. 1985. *Old Testament Law*. London: SCM.

Rad, Gerhard von. 1972. *Wisdom in Israel*. London: SCM.

Schipper, Bernd U. 2013. "When Wisdom Is Not Enough! The Discourse on Wisdom and Torah and the Composition of the Book of Proverbs." Pages 55–79 in Schipper and Teeter 2013.

Schipper, Bernd U., and D. Andrew Teeter, eds. 2013. *Wisdom and Torah: The Reception of "Torah" in the Wisdom Literature of the Second Temple Period*. Leiden: Brill.

Van Leeuwen, Raymond. 1990. "Liminality and Worldview in Proverbs 1–9." *Semeia* 50:111–144.

Van Wolde, Ellen. 2003. *Job 28: Cognition in Context*. Leiden: Brill.

Weeks, Stuart. 1994. *Early Israelite Wisdom*. Oxford: Clarendon Press.

Weeks, Stuart. 2010. *An Introduction to the Study of Wisdom Literature*. New York, NY: T&T Clark.

Weeks, Stuart. 2016. "The Place and Limits of Wisdom Revisited." Pages 3–23 in Jarick 2016.

Weinfeld, Moshe. 1972. *Deuteronomy and the Deuteronomic School*. Oxford: Oxford University Press.

Wells, Bruce. 2015. "Biblical Law." Pages 39–50 in *The Oxford Encyclopedia of the Bible and Law*. Edited by Brent A. Strawn. Oxford: Oxford University Press.

Westbrook, Raymond. 1994. "What Is the Covenant Code?" Pages 15–36 in *Theory and Method in Biblical and Cuneiform Law: Revision, Interpolation and Development*. Edited by B.M. Levinson. Sheffield: Sheffield Academic.

Westbrook, Raymond, and Bruce Wells. 2009. *Everyday Law in Biblical Israel*. Louisville, KY: Westminster John Knox.

Wilson, R.R. 1993. "The Role of Law in Early Israelite Society." Pages 90–99 in *Law, Politics and Society in the Ancient Mediterranean World*. Edited by B. Halpern and D. W. Hobson. Sheffield: Sheffield Academic.

Witte, Markus. 2014. "Job in Conversation with the Torah." Pages 81–99 in Schipper and Teeter 2013.

CHAPTER 27

HISTORY AND WISDOM LITERATURE

SUZANNA R. MILLAR

"Wisdom" as a corpus of biblical texts with an associated tradition in ancient Israel has sometimes been defined in opposition to "history" (e.g., von Rad 1962, 355–459). However, this dichotomy can be challenged, with the traditions seen instead as interconnected. Indeed, evidence of "Wisdom" has been found in several historical[1] texts: the stories of Adam and Eve, Joseph, the Succession Narrative, Solomon, and Esther. This chapter will consider these texts as they interact with wisdom, and will discover points of intriguing interplay around themes of human ingenuity and divine intervention.

27.1 "Wisdom Influence" in Historical Texts

27.1.1 Historical Questions

First, though, it is worth sketching the background for the study of "Wisdom influence," both in historical and methodological terms. Scholars have suggested that Wisdom texts are rooted historically in the "Wisdom tradition," the "Solomonic Enlightenment," and the royal court. Each of these hypotheses is influential, but debatable.

Wisdom texts are said to belong to the *Wisdom tradition* of Israel's sages. The sages were allegedly a particular professional group, distinct from comparable groups like priests and prophets (cf. Jer 18:18). They apparently had a "unified worldview"

---

[1] These texts are not straightforwardly "historical" by modern standards. We will bypass this issue here.

(Crenshaw 2010, 25), which came to expression in Wisdom Literature (preeminently, Proverbs). If "Wisdom" is found in the historical books, it is argued, it is through the influence of this tradition. However, this idea has been seriously questioned. Wisdom Literature does not have a completely distinctive worldview, but shares much with other genres. And these various genres did not stem from different social groups, but had shared scribal origins (Carr 2005; Sneed 2011).

Searching for a historical origin for the hypothesized tradition, scholars suggested an "Enlightenment" during the reign of Solomon (seminally von Rad, e.g., 1966a). Allegedly, in this period of economic prosperity and strengthening international relations, Israelite thought increased in sophistication, and was influenced by Egypt. Alt (1976) argued, for example, that Solomon's nature proverbs (1 Kgs 5:13 [ET 4:33]) drew on Egyptian onomastica. In this new sophisticated climate, the focus shifted from miraculous divine interventions to human ingenuity. A new enlightened historiography allegedly emerged, bearing traces of this Wisdom consciousness. However, few scholars nowadays subscribe to the "Solomonic Enlightenment" hypothesis. The references to wisdom in the Solomonic narratives are historically suspect. Very little archaeological or epigraphic evidence points towards a developed state at this time, and the postulated correspondences with Egypt have little support (Weeks 2000, 110–131).

One potential Egyptian connection with particular relevance concerns the *royal court*. In Egypt and Mesopotamia, "Wisdom" texts (primarily Instructions) are often located in the court, depicting a king or vizier passing on wise words to his heir. These may have been penned by royal officials to educate others in their profession. Correspondingly, it is argued that "courtly" biblical texts are likely to be connected to Wisdom. However, this is false reasoning. Wisdom authors are not synonymous with royal courtiers. Indeed, Wisdom may sometimes stem from folk tradition (e.g., Golka 1993), and courtiers may have been trained with more than just Wisdom (Carr 2005).

We will see that each of these points has influenced the scholarly discussion of Wisdom in historical texts. Given the concerns raised here, however, caution is needed.

27.1.2 Methodological Questions

Methodologically, scholars often try to correlate Wisdom Literature with historical narratives according to their vocabulary, themes, and theology. "Wisdom influence" is found when certain themes are present (e.g., universalism, anthropocentrism, morality), or others are absent (e.g., nationalism, cult, revelation).

This method has proliferated discoveries, such that "Wisdom influence" has spread across the canon (Kynes 2015). By incorporating many other texts, the meaning of "Wisdom" has expanded, the category becoming so broad as to include almost anything. Alarmed by this dilution, some have argued for increased methodological rigor, and stricter criteria to judge Wisdom influence (Crenshaw 1969; McLaughlin in this volume). A more fundamental problem, however, lies in what is assumed by this method: that "Wisdom Literature" forms a unified, distinctive corpus. The very fact that so much wisdom is found elsewhere problematizes this. Almost every biblical theme can be found somewhere in the Wisdom books, and almost every theme thought distinctive of Wisdom Literature can also be found elsewhere. Wisdom texts may be fruitfully categorized into other groupings (Kynes 2019), and without the undergirdings (discussed above) of a Wisdom tradition, Solomonic Enlightenment and court context, Wisdom Literature lacks historical rooting.

Therefore, this chapter will not look for evidence of "Wisdom influence" in the historical texts as such. Instead, it offers an intertextual approach, which views the historical narratives in relation to the biblical Wisdom books, considering both as products of a shared scribal tradition. I will read the historical narratives with a horizon of expectation formed primarily by Proverbs. Proverbs presents certain themes with confidence, as though unaware of potential problems that might arise. But problems do arise, as is evident in the misgivings of Job and Ecclesiastes. The historical books grapple with these same issues, at times bringing them closer to Job and Ecclesiastes, at time forging distinctive paths. Putting aside the notion of "Wisdom influence," "Wisdom" can nonetheless be a helpful lens for reading.

27.2 Human Wisdom and Divine Intervention in the Wisdom Literature

27.2.1 Human Wisdom

Two thematic clusters are particularly pertinent: human wisdom and divine intervention. We will find these themes reverberating through our historical texts. First, human wisdom. Wisdom and ethics are intimately interwoven in Proverbs: the wise person is also righteous and vice versa. Taken at face value, actions can be neatly categorized into wise and righteous versus foolish and wicked. However, different proverbs have different perspectives, which are not adjudicated. Tensions emerge for the careful reader, which the book does not resolve. We will later see similar tensions in the historical narratives, pressed further and problematized. I note four themes in particular below.

(a) How should we judge eloquent speech? The wise in Proverbs pay attention to words (1:6), and speak persuasively (16:21, 23). At the same time, though, the forbidden woman is known for her "smooth words" (2:16, 7:5), and lips that "drip honey" (5:3). The persuasive speech of the educated may prove as substanceless as wind (Job 8:2; 16:3–4). (b) If speech is ambiguous, what of silence? On the one hand, Proverbs commends silence—it is the "prudent" who are "restrained in speech" (Prov 10:19; cf. Eccl 5:1–7; Job 13:5). On the other hand, Proverbs condemns deception (Prov 14:5, 25; 24:28). Not discussed, however, is withholding information (cf. Job 31:33–34). The ethical ambivalence of silent deception will be pressed by our historical texts. (c) Several proverbs commend just governance (e.g., Prov 8:15; 29:4). But what constitutes justice? Depending on circumstances, the king's "messengers of death" (16:14) may enact rightful retribution (16:10; 20:8, 26; cf. Job 29:17) or flagrant corruption (Prov 28:15–16). Ecclesiastes will lament this latter temptation, for "on the side of [the] oppressors is power" (Eccl 4:1). (d) Finally, ambivalence hovers around desire, and around its objects: women and wealth. Wealth is offered by Woman Wisdom (Prov 8:18, 21), and she is to be desired more than precious stones (3:15; 8:11). But wisdom cannot guarantee wealth (as is painfully shown by the poverty of Job). Indeed, the foolish, forbidden woman lavishly displays her finery (Prov 7:16–17), and she must certainly not be desired (6:25; cf. Eccl 7:26).

Different proverbs, then, have different stances, revealing tensions to the perceptive reader. These tensions are pushed by Job and Ecclesiastes—and, I will suggest, by the historical narratives too.

27.2.2 Divine Intervention

A second thematic cluster concerns the role of God. (e) God is often described as "behind the scenes" in these texts. Wisdom Literature does not authenticate itself through divine revelation; it is not "thus says YHWH" but "our fathers have sought out" (Job 8:8). Divine involvement is understated; parting seas and pillars of fire are lacking. But God is not absent either. In Proverbs, God is mentioned enough to suggest his persistent presence, but not enough to be everywhere obvious (and, of course, God makes a dramatic whirlwind appearance in Job).

(f) God's behind-the-scenes agency may be evident in the "act-consequence connection": the righteous are rewarded, the wicked are punished. God may regulate and sustain this moral order, but his direct activity is not often stated. This may suggest an intrinsic causality where actions inevitably bring certain results (Koch 1983). With poetic justice, act and consequence correlate in degree and kind—one who digs a pit will fall into it (Prov 26:27; cf. Eccl 10:8). Lamentably though—as testified by Job's righteous suffering—the connection sometimes unravels.

(g) This understated theology has implications for anthropology too, offering humans both freedom and responsibility (Brueggemann 1972a). Proverbs encourages readers to trust human knowledge, and to act from their own sagacity. The assumption, though, is that YHWH remain the foundation of human wisdom (Prov 1:7a). If he does not, tensions may emerge. Proverbs occasionally acknowledges these tensions, but quickly quashes them: "Many are the plans in a man's mind, but the purpose of YHWH will stand" (Prov 19:21; cf. 16:1, 9; 20:24; 21:30–31). Pressing this further, Ecclesiastes and Job ruminate on human futility in the face of divine inscrutable power (Eccl 3:11, 8:17; Job 38–41).

27.3 ADAM AND EVE (GENESIS 2–3)

Let us turn to selected historical texts, with the foregoing themes within our horizon of expectation. Five stories are particularly relevant: Adam and Eve, Joseph, the Succession Narrative, Solomon, and Esther.

The story of Adam and Eve (Genesis 2–3) has sometimes been connected with the Wisdom tradition (e.g., Carr 1993; Schmid 2017). Traditional Pentateuchal scholarship considers this a J text, composed in the tenth century BCE. This places it around the time of the alleged Wisdom flourishing of the Solomonic Enlightenment. However, the Solomonic Enlightenment hypothesis has shortcomings (noted above, 27.1.1 Historical Questions). Furthermore, the dating of Genesis 2–3 is disputed: part or all of it may have been composed significantly later than the tenth century.[2]

Thematically, it is supposedly an indicator of Wisdom that the text is concerned for creation. Wisdom and creation are often intertwined in the Hebrew Bible (Proverbs 8; Job 28) and across the ancient Near East (e.g., Enuma Elish, Atrahasis). In Genesis 2–3, the quest for knowledge is central.

27.3.1 Human Wisdom

The term "wisdom" (חכמה) does not appear in Genesis 2–3, but the theme is established through "the knowledge of good and evil" (2:9, 17), which elsewhere describes a virtue of the wise (2 Sam 14:17; 1 Kgs 3:9; Sir 39:4). Its precise meaning in Genesis 2 is disputed. Some suggest that it refers to loss of sexual innocence. The verb to "know" (ידע) can suggest sexual "knowledge," and here it precipitates Adam and Eve's awareness of nakedness (3:7). However, this does not account for the "good and evil," which suggests moral discernment. If so, then wisdom is closely connected to ethics, as is the case in Proverbs. Proverbs lauds the one who discerns his ethical choices (14:8), following good (11:27), and turning from evil (4:27).

Like Proverbs, Genesis 3 suggests the desirability of moral discernment, here symbolized by a tree: "Eve saw that the tree was good for food, and a delight (תאוה) to the eyes, and . . . desirable (נחמד) to make one wise" (3:6) (להשכיל). If this verse were in Proverbs, the action described might be considered praiseworthy. Indeed, the final term, "to make one wise" (להשכיל), is positively construed throughout the book (e.g., Prov 1:3; 16:20; 17:8). Proverbs even uses the same images and terms as this verse. Food and fruit metaphors express wisdom's bounty (e.g., Prov 16:24; 18:20; 25:11). What the righteous delight in (their תאוה) will be given to them (10:24; 11:23; 13:12), and the wise will have desirable (נחמד) goods (21:20).

But Proverbs is also aware of desire's underside. Not all delights are commendable (תאוה in Prov 18:1; 21:25–26; נחמד in 1:22; 6:25; 12:12), and people crave unwholesome food (20:17; 23:1–8; 25:16). Lady Folly is sumptuously alluring, with lips that drip honey (5:3), offering illicit love (7:18). The history of interpretation of Genesis 3 maximizes this negative desire. Eve, though her craving is for wisdom, is transformed into a Lady Folly—a temptress who exploits the hapless man, and ultimately leads him to death (Gen 3:22–24; cf. Prov 7:22–23). Returning to the themes set out above, it is around (d)—women and desire—that Genesis 2–3 comes into ambivalent contact with Proverbial wisdom.

---

[2] For example, Carr (1993) suggests that an early creation story celebrating wisdom acquired a subversive anti-wisdom addition in the late pre-exilic or early exilic period.

27.3.2 Divine Intervention

The irony is that the desire for wisdom should lead to life. This is explicit in Proverbs, in keeping the pervasive act-consequence connection (e.g., Prov 3:16; 8:35; 13:14). So too in Genesis, the trees of knowledge and life stand together in the garden (Gen 2:9), and when the humans eat from the former, God assumes they will seek the latter (3:22). But Genesis inverts the outcome. In Proverbs, searching for wisdom provides access to the tree of life (Prov 3:18); in Genesis it bars the way to it (Gen 3:22–24; cf. 2:17). Indeed, after attaining knowledge, the humans are reminded of their finitude, and their lives become hardship and toil (Gen 3:17–19)—a pessimistic anthropology shared by Ecclesiastes (2:22–23; 3:20; 12:7) and Job (10:9).

Proverbs is generally enthusiastic about independent human wisdom. To be "shrewd" (עָרוּם) is commended (e.g., Prov 13:16; 14:8, 15). But Proverbs assumes this wisdom is born from trust and humility, fear of YHWH (e.g., 1:7; 9:10; 15:33). Any wisdom which diverges is unequivocally quashed (21:30). Genesis 3 dramatizes this confrontation, with much more attention to the possibility and ambiguity of dissent. "Shrewdness" now characterizes the serpent (עָרוּם, 3:1), and "to become wise" opposes God (3:6). As in Proverbs, Genesis 3 extinguishes the opposition, now cutting the humans off from the tree of life.

But the consequences are bittersweet: the humans *do* attain knowledge, even becoming "like God" (3:5). In their autonomous search, humans have encroached upon divine territory. Across the ancient Near East, humans are differentiated from divinities by their limited wisdom and their mortality. In this story, humans attain quasi-divine wisdom (3:5). And, fearful that they should receive immortality too, God bars them from the tree of life (3:22). The relationship between human and divine (theme g) is fraught, with God problematizing the act-consequence connection (theme f), bringing death to the search for wisdom.

27.4 JOSEPH (GENESIS 37–50)

A second text often connected with Wisdom is the story of Joseph (Genesis 37–50; seminally von Rad 1966b, followed by, e.g., Coats 1973; Wilson 2004). Again, this was partially premised on historical context, which von Rad alleged to be the "Solomonic Enlightenment." He found within the text the new "spiritual self–consciousness" of the period, with its focus on the human's "potentialities and his limitations, his psychological complexity and profundity" (1966b, 293). Furthermore, its setting in Egypt suggested to him Solomon's internationalization movement, and possible influence from Egyptian Wisdom. And the court setting, with Joseph as an exemplary political leader, hinted at a possible function of the text to educate courtiers (von Rad 1966b; Coats 1973). However, few scholars nowadays follow this dating, the Egyptian setting says nothing about actual connections with Egypt, and Joseph's character (as we will shortly see) is far from a Wisdom ideal.

27.4.1 Human Wisdom

Pharaoh declares Joseph to be an איש נבון וחכם "discerning and wise man" (Gen 41:39). Some scholars take this as an interpretive crux for his character, and consider him to fulfill Proverbs' ideals of wisdom. Four relevant features are often drawn out: speech (theme a), silence (theme b), governance (theme c), and women (theme d). In each case, though, the line between wisdom and folly is blurry.

First, Joseph's speech. Pharaoh pronounces Joseph's wisdom after Joseph gives a long, eloquent address (Gen 41:29–36). For von Rad, this fulfills Proverbs' prediction that skilled words will bring the speaker before kings (Prov 22:29; cf. Sir 8:8; von Rad 1966b, 294). But eloquent speech is not a sure sign of wisdom (note the forbidden woman's "smooth words," Prov 2:16; 7:5). In Proverbs, good speech is characterized by timeliness and appropriateness (15:23; 25:11), restraint (10:19; 17:27), and righteousness (10:20, 31). The Joseph story draws no attention to these features. Indeed, it begins with Joseph's untimely loquacity: blurting out his dreams leads to his enslavement (Genesis 37).

If Joseph's speech is ambiguous, so is his silence. The "silent man" is a common ideal in Wisdom Literature of the ancient Near East and Israel (Prov 10:19; 12:23). Von Rad accordingly argues, "In his relationship with his brothers, Joseph is the very pattern of the man who can 'keep silence,' as described in Egyptian wisdom-lore" (von Rad 1966b, 295). This presumably refers to Joseph's non-disclosure of his true identity (Gen 42:7). However, there is a fine line between non-disclosure and deception; and the latter is prohibited (Prov 24:28; 26:18–19; 26:24–26). Wisdom Literature further commends silence through controlling the emotions: being "cool in spirit" (Prov 17:27) and having a "tranquil mind" (Prov 14:30). Accordingly, Joseph is sometimes held as a model of Proverbial self-control. And, to be sure, he turns away (Gen 42:24), leaves the room (43:30–31), or sends everyone out (45:1) before he weeps. But weep he does, and so loudly that the whole household hears (45:2; cf. 45:14–15; 46:29; 50:1)! Hardly a model of silent restraint.

Politically, Joseph offers advice about how to deal with the ensuing famine. He acts with the foresight and prudence advocated by Proverbs (6:6–8; 20:4), storing up one-fifth of Egypt's produce for the hard years (Gen 41:34–36; 47:23–26). Perhaps he thus "demonstrates to future administrators the proper procedure for using power" (Coats 1973, 290). However, it is unclear whether Joseph really is idealized here. There is a blurry line between effective, strict governance and downright cruelty. Joseph sells grain to the hungry—perhaps a laudable act (Prov 11:26b). But he only acquires this grain through heavy taxation (condemned in Prov 11:26a; 29:4), and when the people cannot buy it back, he takes them into slavery (Gen 47:21). His policies are arguably far from Proverbs' advocated generosity (e.g., 14:31; 19:17; 28:15–16), and are closer to Ecclesiastes's lamented oppressions (Eccl 4:1; 5:7 [8]).

These first three traits seem problematic when matched against the ideal of Proverbs. The fourth is perhaps closer to the ideal: Joseph's avoidance of "foreign women." Proverbs warns of the adulteress who seduces naive young men (Prov 5:20–23; 7:6–27; 22:14; 23:27–28), just like Potiphar's wife who makes advances on Joseph (Genesis 39).

Both these women are brazen and persistent in speech (Prov 7:11, 21; Gen 39:7, 10, 12). But unlike the young man in Proverbs 7, Joseph is not enticed; indeed, he flees (Gen 39:12). There is certainly thematic similarity here, but the strength and significance of the connection has been questioned. Adultery is a common trope across literature, and is not restricted to Wisdom. Furthermore, Joseph rejects the woman because of loyalty to his master (39:8–9), a motivation not mentioned in Proverbs. And the just consequences of Proverbs 7 face a cruel twist in Genesis 39—Joseph is punished for his piety (v. 20).

Joseph, then, has an ambiguous relationship with the ideal of Proverbs. When he speaks, he is eloquent (theme a), but the political advice he offers may be cruel (theme c). When he is silent, he deceives his brothers (theme b), and when he flees seduction, he is jailed (theme d).

27.4.2 Divine Intervention

If Joseph's story does not wholly conform to Proverbs' ideals of virtue, does it conform to Proverbs' theology—in the role of God "behind the scenes" (theme e), the "act-consequence connection" (theme f), or the tension between human and divine (theme g)?

At times, God's role is explicit. In contrast to wisdom in Proverbs, which is primarily acquired through human learning and instruction, Joseph's wisdom is a divine endowment. He is "discerning and wise" precisely because he has "the spirit of God" in him, and "God has shown [him] all this" (41:38–39). He receives revelations of dreams (Genesis 37) and dream interpretations (Genesis 40–41), such as do not figure in biblical Wisdom books.[3] But if it is God who reveals the plan to Joseph, it is not explicitly he who executes it. Joseph says that God will bring the famine (41:32), but his hand is hidden when it occurs. And with one anomalous exception (Gen 46:1–4),[4] God does not appear directly. The story takes place at a "secular" level, driven by human activity. And yet God's activity is sensed "behind the scenes." He regulates the characters' fates: he is "with Joseph," bringing him success (39:2–3, 21, 23) and blessing his house (39:5), perhaps as the divine overseer of the act-consequence connection. Lindsay Wilson (2004, 262) accordingly argues that God "is actively at work ordering situations and events so as to make all things come right for his chosen people and purposes."

At two climactic points, Joseph explicitly acknowledges God's control, which overrides human efforts. In both instances, he draws a contrast between the purposes of his brothers and of God: "It was not you who sent me here, but God" (45:8); "you meant evil against me, but God meant it for good" (50:20). Human actions are allowed to take place, but their intended consequences are overridden. Several proverbs are comparable here (Prov 16:1, 9; 19:21; 20:24; 21:30–31), leading von Rad (1966a, 297) to speculate that Gen 50:20 might be "a wisdom-saying which has been adapted for the purpose of the story."

---

[3] Dreams seem to have been important for Babylonian mantic wisdom. They are occasionally mentioned in Job (4:13–15; 7:13–14; 33:15–22).

[4] This passage may belong to a different source text.

God's role, then, has interesting correlations with that in Wisdom books. It is explicit in revelation, but only implicit in the unfolding of events (theme e). It possibly manifests itself in the act-consequence connection (theme f), and emerges in tension with human efforts (theme g)—a conflict powerfully dramatized by the narrative.

27.5 The Succession Narrative (2 Samuel 9–20, 1 Kings 1–2)

The "Succession Narrative" (2 Samuel 9[5]–20, 1 Kings 1–2) tells of the struggle between David's sons to succeed him. Its composition is often dated to the early monarchy period—the time of the alleged Enlightenment, when Wisdom is thought to have flourished. It is sometimes considered a ground-breaking work of enlightened historiography, concerned not with God's direct interventions, but with everyday human affairs (von Rad 1966a; Brueggemann 1972b). Much of the story is set in the royal court, with royal advisers appearing several times (e.g., 2 Sam 15:12; 16:20–17:14). Whybray accordingly hypothesized that it was a didactic narrative, functioning to educate courtiers by enacting proverbial wisdom. In his view, it was intended "to show how the precepts of the wisdom schools were to be worked out in real situations in the very court in which the pupils would spend their lives" (Whybray 1968, 80).

27.5.1 Human Wisdom

Three pairs of characters exemplify relevant aspects of human wisdom. The first is Bathsheba and Nathan. Bathsheba is sometimes characterized as a temptress; a foreign "Woman who brings death" (Blenkinsopp 1966, 52–55) in the manner of Eve, Potiphar's wife, and the forbidden woman of Proverbs 7. She is thought to be brazen—provocatively bathing where she could be seen, seducing David towards folly. However, the narrative (2 Sam 11:1–5) is so concise that the reader is hard-pressed to find her culpable. Indeed, when Nathan subsequently appears, he blames David alone. Nathan weaves an eloquent parable, luring David into condemning himself (2 Sam 12:5–7). This persuasive cunning is often seen as indicative of Wisdom speech. But subsequently Nathan continues in the manner of a prophet (12:10–15), complexifying a simple ascription of the story to "Wisdom."

Bathsheba and Nathan reappear at the end of David's story as political co-conspirators, intent on securing Solomon's accession (1 Kings 1–2). They succeed through persuasive rhetoric, "reminding" David of a promise he allegedly made to Solomon. The text, however, has recorded no such promise, and it may be an invention, intended to dupe

[5] The beginning point of this narrative is disputed.

the confused aging monarch. If so, then Proverbs' advocacy of eloquence is followed, but its prohibition of deception is not.

The second pair is the women of Tekoa and Abel. Equally as persuasive in their language are the so-called "wise women" of Tekoa and Abel (2 Sam 14:1–24; 20:14–22; see esp. Camp 1981). Living away from Jerusalem, they may represent Wisdom independent of the court. Like Nathan before her, the woman of Tekoa offers a parable, which convinces David to change course. The woman of Abel confronts Joab, and persuasively negotiates with the people "in her wisdom" (20:22) (בחכמתה). Both women may speak with proverbs (14:14 and 20:18; Camp 1981, 18–21): a popular Wisdom form designed to clinch the case. Persuasive speech, however, is not the sole preserve of Wisdom. Camp likens the woman of Tekoa's speech to a prophet's and the woman of Abel's to a military commander's (1981, 21–24).

Furthermore, despite the persuasiveness of their advice, its true sagacity is suspect. The woman of Tekoa begins with deception: she pretends to be a mourner and fabricates a judicial case. And her advice to invite Absalom home is politically dubious. It does not heal the rift between father and son, and it prepares the way for Absalom's rebellion. The woman of Abel's advice is morally suspect: while it protects her people, it advocates the ruthless beheading of Sheba, who has taken sanctuary in the city. Such moral-military conundrums are out of the purview of Proverbs.

A final pair are the rival counsellors, Ahitophel and Hushai (2 Samuel 15–17). Their encounter is characterized by eloquent verbal jousting (Park 2009; Gordon 2014). While Ahitophel's advice is concise and to the point, Hushai weaves an elaborate speech, with similes, metaphors, and other stylish flourishes. Hushai's verbosity wins out, emphasizing the efficacy of elegant rhetoric. At the same time, though, the narrative pokes fun at this rhetorical enterprise: Hushai's advice *sounds* wise, but is intentionally substanceless, designed to mislead Absalom. These are the "smooth words" of folly, leading the man to his death (Prov 7:21–23). If Hushai's wisdom purposely goes against Proverbs' aspiration to effective governance (Prov 11:14), Ahitophel's goes against Proverbs' morality. Ahitophel advises Absalom to go into his father's concubines (2 Sam 16:21), violating Proverbial propriety towards parents and women. It resembles Jonadab's "wise" (חכם) advice preceding the rape of Tamar (2 Sam 13:3), and David's taking of Bathsheba. In each case, women are used in the power games of royal folly.

Overall, then, while all of these characters speak with eloquence (theme a), they sometimes speak with deception (theme b) or injustice (theme c). Women (theme d) may be paragons of wisdom (Tekoa and Abel), but they also tempt men into foolishness.

27.5.2 Divine Intervention

Ahitophel's wisdom is likened to an "oracle of God" (2 Sam 16:23). But, ironically, he is opposed by God: "YHWH had commanded to defeat the good (טובה) counsel of Ahitophel, in order that YHWH might bring disaster (רעה) to Absalom" (2 Sam 17:14).

Whatever the humans reasons for Ahitophel's failure, the more important reason is theological. The tension between human and divine wisdom, voiced in Proverbs (Prov 16:1, 9; 19:21; 20:24; 21:30–31), is exacerbated here. Strikingly, "good" (טובה) is associated with Ahitophel, and "bad" (רעה) with YHWH. This subverts readers' expectations, confusing the criteria for true wisdom, and problematizing human perception. Occasionally, David seems to recognize these human limitations (Brueggemann 1972b). Against seemingly wise advice towards self-preservation, he twice declares that the inscrutable divine plan will prevail (2 Sam 15:25–26; 16:11–12).

This inscrutable plan is enacted "behind the scenes," as has been argued for the Wisdom books. Only three times is YHWH's direct activity reported: 2 Sam 11:27; 12:24; 17:14. The last of these we have just considered. In the first, YHWH is displeased with David, and in the second, he loves Solomon. Attention is on YHWH's sentiments and relationships, not on his intervention. For Brueggemann (1972a, 18), God is thus "much more the *creator of a context* for human freedom and responsibility than a *disruptor of events*" (emphasis original).

If YHWH is active, it may be through regulating the act-consequence connection. Von Rad suggests a "tightly drawn chain of causality which links sin with suffering" throughout the story (1966a, 196; cf. Whybray 1968, 60–62). The punishments are suited to the crimes, like those of the Proverbial digger, who falls into his own pit (Prov 26:27). David takes Uriah's wife on the rooftop, so his concubines are taken on a rooftop; David brings death to Uriah's house, so death enters his own house. However, these consequences are not motivated by intrinsic causality, but are punishments foretold by a prophet (2 Sam 12:9–12). And the narrative is not straightforwardly structured towards the success of the righteous and downfall of the wicked. David remains king desite his moral failings, and the story climaxes with Solomon's accession regardless of righteousness.

God's work in the Succession Narrative, then, sometimes manifests itself through the act-consequence connection (theme f). But this connection is uncertain, and the more prevalent impression is of hidden, inscrutable activity (theme e), in the face of which human wisdom must concede ignorance and defeat (theme g).

27.6 SOLOMON (1 KINGS 1–11)

This brings us to consider Solomon (1 Kings 1–11). Wisdom pervades Solomon's story (Scott 1976; Parker 1992; Lemaire 1995), leading to the eponymous "Solomonic Enlightenment" hypothesis. However, the narrative is historically questionable, and it may consist of multiple redactional layers. Scott (1976) suggests a three-stage development, with the passages most exuberant about Solomon's wisdom as post-exilic additions. Conversely, Alt (1976) sees these passages as the earliest historical kernel, later tempered by Deuteronomistic redaction. In this chapter so far, we have considered historical narratives in light of Wisdom. But here we can also read Wisdom in light of the historical narratives. Proverbs is legitimized by its Solomonic ascription. Ecclesiastes begins with a Solomonic persona,[6] and seriously questions the value of his wisdom.

27.6.1 Human Wisdom

Solomon's wisdom is central to his story, particularly as it manifests itself in governance (theme c), and in his relationships with wealth and women (theme d). In 1 Kings 1–10, his wisdom is legendary (3:1–15; 5:9–14 [ET 4:29–34]; 10:1–13), the greatest of all times and places (1 Kgs 3:14, 5:10 [ET 4:30]; cf. Eccl 1:16). But in 1 Kings 11, he faces a rapid demise. This may lead us to reassess the preceding material, and when we do, problematic hints emerge within Solomon's wisdom. Ecclesiastes pushes at this underside, demonstrating wisdom's ultimate "vanity" (הבל).

At the start of his reign, Solomon is Eve-like, desiring wisdom to "discern between good and evil" (1 Kgs 3:9; cf. Gen 3:5–6). Eve is consequently barred from the tree of life. But Solomon (in line with Proverbs) is granted length of days—and riches and honor to boot (Prov 3:15–16; 1 Kgs 3:11–14). The luxurious depictions of Solomon's wisdom, wealth, and prestige are seen by many as unambiguously positive.

However, there are persistent disconcerting notes, akin to Proverbial folly. Claudia Camp (2000, 145–146) argues that "1 Kings 1–11 draws on [Proverbs'] symbolic portrayals of Woman Wisdom (love of whom leads to life) *and Woman Stranger/Folly (whose embrace brings death)* . . . to structure and thematize the narrative" (emphasis added). Indeed, "Woman Stranger" (or the "foreign woman" נכריה, Prov 5:20; 6:24; 23:27) will bring about Solomon's eventual demise (1 Kgs 11:3). This ending refracts back, coloring the references to "foreignness" earlier in the story with an ominous hue. Solomon's wisdom comes after his marriage to an Egyptian princess (3:1–3); is compared to that of "all the people of the east and all the wisdom of Egypt" (5:10 [ET 4:30]); and is celebrated by the foreign Queen of Sheba (10:1–10). Solomon builds with foreign labor and foreign materials (e.g., 1 Kgs 5:22–23 [ET 8–9]). To Camp (2000, 172), this all suggests "a kind of fatalism, a prediction of the foreignness that will subvert Solomon's wisdom."

Of course, "foreign women" are not exclusive to Wisdom Literature. Indeed, the foreign marriages in 1 Kgs 11:1–8 closely correspond to the condemnation in Deuteronomy (7:1–5). And elsewhere too, Solomon's actions are judged, not by the standards of Wisdom, but by the standards of law (Parker 1992). Solomon's initial receipt of wisdom comes with the Deuteronomistic proviso that he must "walk in my way, keeping my statutes and my commandments" (1 Kgs 3:14). This also correlates with Solomon's just governance: he is granted "an understanding mind to govern/judge (לשפט) [God's] people" (3:9; cf. 10:9).

It is debatable how far Solomon, in his wisdom, achieves this, for there is a fine line between necessary force (Prov 16:14; 19:12; 20:2, 8, 26) and unnecessary cruelty (Prov

---

[6] The Solomonic identity of this figure has recently been challenged by Jennie Barbour (2012), who argues that it is a composite of multiple kings.

28:15–16). First, even before Solomon's accession, David tells him to "act according to [his] wisdom" (1 Kgs 2:6; cf. 2:9) by executing his enemies. Accordingly, Solomon sends out Benaiah son of Jehoiada—his personal "messenger of death" (Prov 16:14). Solomon may have found these executions politically necessary, but their legitimacy is suspect (Walsh 1995, 483–485).

Second, Solomon's wise justice is exemplified when two prostitutes come to him, fighting over one living child. He suggests bisecting the child, at which the true mother reveals herself by her horror. Commentators and narrator agree that this was a wise solution (1 Kgs 3:28). But there may be sinister undertones—not least the blood-curdling brutality of Solomon's suggestion. Furthermore, the protagonists are prostitutes, who are viewed with unease by Proverbs and Deuteronomy alike (Prov 7:10, 23:27; Deut 23:19 [ET 18]), perhaps suggesting the persistent intermingling of Solomon's wisdom with the chaotic and foreign.

Third, there are signs of injustice in Solomon's double implementation of forced labor. Immediately after the first instance (5:27–32 [ET 13–18]) comes a reference to Egypt (6:1), recalling the forced labor suffered there (cf. Exod 1:11). The second instance (this time conducted by foreign workers) has still less justification (9:15–22). It is for Solomon's personal projects, rather than for the common or divine good.

Fourth, Solomon amasses wealth such that he "excelled all the kings of the earth in riches and in wisdom" (10:23). The "happy confluence of wealth and wisdom" (Camp 2000, 179) evident in Proverbs, is superficially present here. However, it is also problematized. Solomon acquires gold and silver (10:14–22, 25, 27), and horses from Egypt (10:26–29), thus violating two of the three prohibitions in Deuteronomy's law of kingship (Deut 17:16–17). When, immediately afterwards, Solomon acquires foreign wives (1 Kgs 11:1), the final prohibition is broken, and his demise ensues. A later Wisdom writer will reflect on Solomon's extravagant wealth (Eccl 2:1–11)—all acquired with wisdom (2:3)—and will find it to be vanity (2:11).

The narrator reminds us several times of Solomon's great wisdom. On closer analysis, however, this wisdom is suspect. In his assassinations and forced labor, the justice of his governance is unclear (theme c), and his wisdom and wealth are persistently undercut by the allure of foreignness and women (theme d). This will ultimately be his undoing.

27.6.2 Divine Intervention

In the Solomon account, we do not find a tension between human initiative and divine intervention (as we have seen elsewhere; theme g), but rather, human violation of divine laws. God's hidden providence, thought to characterize Wisdom writings (theme e), is not present here either. Rather, God's activity is clear. Solomon's wisdom is a gift from God, granted through a dream vision (3:8–15). Wisdom's divine origin is reiterated (3:28; 5:9, 26 [ET 4:29; 5:12]; 10:6–9, 24), and the story is concerned with cultic matters (the temple). Notably, when Ecclesiastes retells Solomon's story, these divine origins are replaced with empirical derivation (e.g., Eccl 1:13). The story assumes a connection between

Solomon's wisdom and wealth, but neither of these are straightforward or unproblematic. Nor is this the intrinsic causality of the act-consequence connection (such as is suggested for Proverbs; theme f). Rather, both wisdom and wealth are gifts from God.

27.7 ESTHER

Our final text is the book of Esther, which Talmon influentially argued constitutes a "historicized wisdom-tale," enacting Wisdom motifs in narrative form (Talmon 1963; cf. van Uchelen 1974; Loader 1978). Others, however, vehemently oppose this view. Crenshaw (1969, 141) asserts "it is difficult to conceive of a book more alien to Wisdom Literature than Esther." And similarly Fox (1991, 143): "Esther is not affiliated with Wisdom by even the broadest definition." Esther is unlike our other texts, as it cannot stem from the Solomonic Enlightenment (depicting events five hundred years later). But it is like them in being set in the royal court. Talmon (1963) accordingly suggests it teaches the skills of the wise courtier, and Wills (1990) categorizes it as a "wisdom court legend." Talmon further notes several significant lacks in Esther, which he suggests link it to Wisdom: divine intervention (discussed below, 27.7.2 Divine Intervention), Jewish religiosity or history, and contemporary Jewry outside Persia. However, the historical survival of the Jewish people is essential to Esther's plot, and Talmon's argument here is dubious.

27.7.1 Human Wisdom

"Wisdom" does not explicitly appear in the characterizations in Esther. Nonetheless, some interpret the characters as idealized Wisdom figures. Talmon (1963, 440) argues that the writer was not interested in the dramatic personae as such, but in the virtues and vices they represent. They are static character types, like those in Proverbs, without complexity or meaningful development. Ahasuerus represents "the witless dupe"; Mordecai and Esther "the righteous wise"; and Haman and Zeresh "the conniving schemer" (441). However, while the characters are distinctive and sometimes exaggerated, they are not one-dimensional. This is especially true of Esther herself. She is complex and psychologically real, and develops through the story.

Fox (1991, 196–205) tracks this as a move from passivity to activity to authority. At the start, Esther is passive, with little independent agency. Like the Proverbial paragon of the good youth, she obeys her elders and does not question authority (e.g., Prov 10:17, 19:20). She submits to Mordecai (2:10, 20), allows herself to be taken into the king's palace (2:8), and follows her overseer's advice (2:15). But there is a fine line between humble submission and naive passivity. Esther follows Mordecai's commands to conceal her ethnicity. While this is necessary for the plot, its rationale is undisclosed and it may violate Proverbs' prohibition of deception. When in the harem, her feminine beauty is central: she has "a beautiful figure and is lovely to look at" (2:7), and she is treated to "six months with oil of myrrh and six months with spices and ointments" (2:12). Subsequently, she offers sexual favors to the king (2:14). If we are to compare Proverbs here, the opulence of myrrh, spices, and sexuality are known only in the bedroom of the forbidden woman (Prov 7:17–18). Reading Esther through Proverbs may thus reveal an unwise positioning of the naive youth.

The balance of power shifts in Esther 4:15–17: Esther commands Mordecai and he obeys. She then skillfully unfolds a multi-stage plan, twice plying the king with food, wine, and flattery. She reveals her request with rhetorical polish, highlighting its personal and national implications (7:3) and playing into the king's ego (7:4), before her dramatic condemnation: "A foe and enemy! This wicked Haman!" (7:6). If eloquent speech is Wisdom's remit, then Esther reveals herself as a sage. But eloquence is ambiguous, for the Strange Woman too knows "smooth words." Accordingly, some think Esther exploits her sexuality here. Remarkably, Talmon (1963, 452) himself (though arguing for Esther as a paragon of virtue) cites Proverbs 5 and 7 as parallels. But, like Eve and Bathsheba, Esther is unfairly vilified. The text does not comment on her physical appearance here, and nothing suggests provocative sexuality.

In ch. 9, Esther assumes authority. She loses her subservient, circumlocutionary tone through a forceful instruction: "Let the Jews who are in Susa be allowed tomorrow also to do according to this day's edict" (9:13), which is to say, let them kill anyone who might pose a threat (cf. 8:11). This characterization is morally disturbing. As Fox (1991, 203) comments, "Esther's personality has evolved into the near-opposite of what it was at the start. Once sweet and compliant, she is now steely and unbending, even harsh." Proverbs is wary of foreigners, but such annihilation wildly escalates its unease.

Esther, then, is not a static paragon of wisdom, but a much more complex, dynamic hero. She uses her words persuasively (theme a), her silence deceptively (theme b), her political position forcefully (theme c), and her femininity ambiguously (theme d).

27.7.2 Divine Intervention

This book lacks any mention of God. This goes far beyond Proverbs, in which the divine presence is evident, even if understated. Nevertheless, interpreters have found God "behind the scenes" in Esther, drawing it closer to Proverbs. For example, faced with Esther's reluctance, Mordecai says "if you keep silent at this time, relief and deliverance will rise for the Jews from another place (4:14) "(ממקום אחר). This "other place" is often taken as a veiled reference to God, and it does offer tantalizing hints. However, this is not a necessary extrapolation—it may instead be a comment on the tenacity of the Jewish people and their resilience through crisis. Mordecai subsequently ponders, "Who knows whether you have not come to the kingdom for such a time as this?" (4:14)—his "who knows" raising the tentative possibility of providence. In response, Esther calls a fast (4:16). Fasting is usually coupled with prayer, but, notably, prayer is not mentioned here. The author may be avoiding explicit mention of a religious practice. We find no confident assurance of "God under the surface," but only a tentative hope.

Further evidence for divine causality is sometimes found in the implicit order-ing of events. Van Uchelen (1974) suggests that this "order mentality" is a sure sign of Wisdom thought. There are many coincidences throughout the book—too many, it is argued, to be pure chance. A Jewish queen happens to emerge when one is needed (4:14); the account about Mordecai happens to be read to the king (6:1–2); the king happens to see Haman fling himself on Esther (7:8). More could be cited (Fox 1991, 240–243). Additionally, the act-consequence connection is apparent: the wicked suf-fer, the righteous prosper; all without explicit divine intervention (Talmon 1963, 443–449). And the punishment eminently fits the crime. Just like the one who digs a pit and falls into it (Prov 26:27), Haman builds a gallows and is hung upon it. Conversely, the rewards he wants for himself are given to his enemy (cf. Eccl 2:26). However, such delicious ironies are not unique to Wisdom, but are found in literature the world over. And their comic effect in Esther is quite different from their serious warning in Proverbs.

Esther, then, goes beyond Proverbs. While acts do often lead to consequences (theme f), it is far from obvious that God regulates this connection. He seems so far behind the scenes (theme e) that one might suspect him of leaving the theater.

27.8 CONCLUSION

These five narratives—Adam and Eve, Joseph, the Succession Narrative, Solomon, and Esther—have a complex relationship with Wisdom. Each has distinctive purposes and concerns, which I have not fully dealt with here. Nevertheless, each can be fruitfully read through a Wisdom lens, formed by Proverbs, Job, and Ecclesiastes. When read with this horizon of expectation, the texts reveal themselves to grapple with the same issues—particularly concerning human wisdom and divine intervention.

Four features of human wisdom have suggested themselves. These features are intro-duced with confidence in Proverbs, but are complexified here. (a) Several characters offer elegant speeches, in line with Proverbs' advocation of sagacious words: Joseph, Nathan, the women of Tekoa and Abel, Ahitophel and Hushai, Esther. However, these characters have dubious morals and goals, challenging whether eloquence constitutes true wisdom. (b) Nor is silence a sure sign of wisdom. Joseph and Esther remain silent about their true identities. While this is necessary for their plots, it amounts to decep-tion. And deception occurs elsewhere too: in the Succession Narrative, Hushai deceives Absalom, and the woman of Tekoa, Bathsheba, and Nathan may all deceive David. (c) In governance, there is a fine line between necessary harshness and unwarranted cruelty. Proverbs presents it as though cases easily fall on one side or the other, but the histori-cal books ambiguate this. Is it right for the woman of Abel to execute Sheba, or Solomon his enemies? Is Joseph justified in enslaving the people, Solomon in putting them to forced labor, or Esther in permitting their slaughter? (d) Several of these narratives (and their interpreters) betray anxiety about the lure of luxury and the foreign seduc-tress (cf. Proverbs' forbidden woman). Joseph manages to resist her advances, while

Solomon succumbs. Eve, Bathsheba, and even Esther are all placed by interpreters into this "temptress" mold, luring wise men towards folly.

Three theological themes have emerged too. (e) These stories show a spectrum of divine involvement—from Esther (where God's work is not mentioned), through Joseph and the Succession Narrative (where it is under the surface) to Solomon and Adam and Eve (where it is explicit). The medial position is most commonly associated with "Wisdom." (f) This spectrum of divine agency is also found in the diverse approaches to the "act-consequence connection." The connection in these narratives shuns predictability. Sometimes, it is problematic—such as the link in Genesis 2–3 between wisdom and death, and the ambiguous value of Solomon's wealth, wisdom, and wives. (g) In Proverbs, nascent tensions emerge between divine and human agency. In the historical narratives, these tensions are exasperated. Characters like Eve, Joseph's brothers, and Ahithophel overreach themselves in ingenuity, asserting their own plans against God's. It is, however, always God's plan that prevails.

WORKS CITED

Alt, Albrecht. 1976. "Solomonic Wisdom." Pages 102–112 in Crenshaw 1976.

Barbour, Jennie. 2012. *The Story of Israel in the Book of Qohelet: Ecclesiastes as Cultural Memory*. Oxford: Oxford University Press.

Blenkinsopp, Joseph. 1966. "Theme and Motif in the Succession History (2 Sam XI 2ff) and the Yahwist Corpus." Pages 44–57 in *Volume de Congrès International Pour l'étude de l'Ancien Testament, Genève 1965*. VTSup 15. Leiden: Brill.

Brueggemann, Walter. 1972a. *In Man We Trust: The Neglected Side of Biblical Faith*. Richmond, VA: John Knox Press.

Brueggemann, Walter. 1972b. "On Trust and Freedom: A Study of Faith in the Succession Narrative." *Interpretation* 26:3–19.

Camp, Claudia V. 1981. "The Wise Women of 2 Samuel: A Role Model for Women in Early Israel?" *CBQ* 43:14–29.

Camp, Claudia V. 2000. "Reading Solomon as a Woman." Pages 144–186 in *Wise, Strange and Holy: The Strange Woman and the Making of the Bible*. JSOTSup 320. Sheffield: Sheffield Academic.

Carr, David M. 1993. "The Politics of Textual Subversion: A Diachronic Perspective on the Garden of Eden Story." *JBL* 112:577–595.

Carr, David M. 2005. *Writing on the Tablet of the Heart: Origins of Scripture and Literature*. Oxford: Oxford University Press.

Coats, George W. 1973. "The Joseph Story and Ancient Wisdom: A Reappraisal." *CBQ* 35:285–297.

Crenshaw, James L. 1969. "Method in Determining Wisdom Influence upon 'Historical' Literature." *JBL* 88:129–142.

Crenshaw, James L., ed. 1976. *Studies in Ancient Israelite Wisdom*. New York, NY: Ktav Publishing House.

Crenshaw, James L. 2010. *Old Testament Wisdom: An Introduction*. 3rd edn. Louisville, KY: Westminster John Knox.

Fox, Michael V. 1991. *Character and Ideology in the Book of Esther*. Columbia, SC: University of South Carolina Press.

Golka, Friedemann. 1993. *The Leopard's Spots: Biblical and African Wisdom in Proverbs.* Edinburgh: T&T Clark.

Gordon, Robert P. 2014. "A Battle of Wits and Words: Hushai, Ahithophel and the Absalom Rebellion (2 Samuel 16–17)." Pages 99–114 in *Approaches to Literary Readings of Ancient Jewish Writing.* Edited by Klaas Smelik and Karolien Vermeulen. Leiden: Brill.

Koch, Klaus. 1983. "Is There a Doctrine of Retribution in the Old Testament?" Pages 57–87 in *Theodicy in the Old Testament.* Edited by James L. Crenshaw. London: SPCK.

Kynes, Will. 2015. "The Modern Scholarly Wisdom Tradition and the Threat of Pan-Sapientialism: A Case Report." Pages 11–38 in *Was There a Wisdom Tradition? New Prospects in Israelite Wisdom Studies.* Edited by Mark Sneed. AIL 23. Atlanta, GA: SBL.

Kynes, Will. 2019. *An Obituary for "Wisdom Literature": The Birth, Death, and Intertextual Reintegration of a Biblical Corpus.* Oxford: Oxford University Press.

Lemaire, André. 1995. "Wisdom in Solomonic Historiography." Pages 106–118 in *Wisdom in Ancient Israel: Essays in Honour of J.A. Emerton.* Edited by John Day, Robert P. Gordon, and H.G.M. Williamson. Cambridge: Cambridge University Press.

Loader, J.A. 1978. "Esther as a Novel with Different Levels of Meaning." *ZAW* 90:417–421.

Park, Song-Mi Suzie. 2009. "The Frustration of Wisdom: Wisdom, Counsel, and Divine Will in 2 Samuel 17:1–23." *JBL* 128:453–467.

Parker, K.I. 1992. "Solomon as Philosopher King? The Nexus of Law and Wisdom in 1 Kings 1–11." *JSOT* 53:75–91.

Rad, Gerhard von. 1962. *Old Testament Theology,* vol. 1: *The Theology of Israel's Historical Traditions.* Translated by D.M.G. Stalker. Edinburgh: Oliver and Boyd.

Rad, Gerhard von. 1966a. "The Beginnings of Historical Writing in Ancient Israel." Pages 166–204 in *The Problem of the Hexateuch and Other Essays.* Edinburgh: Oliver and Boyd.

Rad, Gerhard von. 1966b. "The Joseph Narrative and Ancient Wisdom." Pages 292–300 in *The Problem of the Hexateuch and Other Essays.* Edinburgh: Oliver and Boyd.

Schmid, Konrad. 2017. "The Ambivalence of Human Wisdom: Genesis 2–3 as a Sapiential Text." Pages 275–286 in *"When the Morning Stars Sang": Essays in Honor of Choon Leong Seow on the Occasion of His Sixty-Fifth Birthday.* Edited by Scott C. Jones and Christine Roy Yoder. Berlin: de Gruyter.

Scott, R.B.Y. 1976. "Solomon and the Beginnings of Wisdom in Israel." Pages 262–279 in Crenshaw 1976.

Sneed, Mark. 2011. "Is the 'Wisdom Tradition' a Tradition?" *CBQ* 73:50–71.

Talmon, Shemaryahu. 1963. "'Wisdom' in the Book of Esther." *VT* 13:419–455.

Uchelen, N.A. van. 1974. "A Chokmatic Theme in the Book of Esther: A Study in the Structure of the Story." Pages 132–140 in *Verkenningen in een Stroomgebied: Proeven van Oudtestamentisch Onderzoek.* Edited by M. Boertien et al. Amsterdam: University of Amsterdam.

Walsh, Jerome T. 1995. "The Characterization of Solomon in First Kings 1–5." *CBQ* 57:471–493.

Weeks, Stuart. 2000. *Early Israelite Wisdom.* Oxford: Oxford University Press.

Whybray, R.N. 1968. *The Succession Narrative.* SBT 2.9. London: SCM.

Wills, Lawrence M. 1990. *The Jew in the Court of the Foreign King.* HDR 26. Minneapolis, MN: Fortress Press.

Wilson, Lindsay. 2004. *Joseph Wise and Otherwise.* Eugene, OR: Paternoster.

CHAPTER 28

PROPHECY AND WISDOM LITERATURE

MARK J. BODA

In his 1960 Society of Biblical Literature and Exegesis presidential address, R.B.Y. Scott (1961, 1) spoke on the Bible as the "Book of the Knowledge of God." He traced three distinct approaches to the knowledge of God within the Hebrew Bible, using as his point of departure Jer 18:18 with its list "of the authority of the priestly *tôrah*, of the sage's counsel, and the prophet's word" (2–3). Although acknowledging points of interaction between these various approaches, he concluded that "the ways to the knowledge of God represented by prophet, priest, and sage remain distinct" (3), going so far as to point to the very canonical divisions of Torah, Prophets, and Writings as related to, respectively, priest, prophet, and sage (5). Scott's view expressed here was not radical in his time, but represented the result of a century of research on the development of Israelite religion and society.

In Scott's later treatment of the Wisdom tradition, *The Way of Wisdom* (1971), one can see the same proclivity to distinguish between prophet and sage in chapter 5: "Prophecy and Wisdom" (101–135). He begins this chapter with a review of the history of the relationship between the two traditions from the pre-monarchial age until after the exile, concluding that "prophecy and wisdom were markedly distinct cultural and religious phenomena, each with its own history concurrent with the other's," pointing to the fact that there "was constant interaction between the two, and sometimes conflict" (113). In general terms he argues that "the prophet speaks from the standpoint of revelation, the wise man from that of reason working from the data of experience and observation" and that the prophet exhorts people "to hear, decide, and obey. The wise man summons them to understand and to learn. He does not demand, but seeks to persuade and instruct" (113–114). Furthermore, prophets and sages possess differing theological perspectives, with the prophets' God "the living, active, personal deity who had confronted them in the moment of their call," while the "secular" sages "did not have (or at least did not show) any theological interest" and the "religious group of sages" had "a theological basis" in general Wisdom theology that was (at least originally) "anthropocentric," while "prophetic theology was theocentric" (115–116). The practical concerns and objectives of these two groups also differ, with the prophets calling for the nation to believe and respond with reference to the unique covenant relationship between Israel and Yahweh, while sages focused on "individuals, offering counsel based on social experience and their own reflections about the nature of the world and of the good life of men," such that "Wisdom had no national or religious frontiers" (17–18). Prophets and sages used distinct literary and rhetorical forms, with the prophets favoring the oracle with its introductory "Thus speaks Yahweh" and the sages employing a variety of forms (proverbs, precepts, riddles, parables, allegories, hortatory discourses, debates, soliloquies) that emphasized "knowledge and rational understanding; indifference to a religion of revelation through supernatural events, sacred history, and cultic observance; and the contrast between two ways of life" (120).

Scott admits some similarities between the two groups: membership in "the intellectually active and articulate stratum of society," use of "the potent mysteries of language as their primary tool," and criticism of "cultic religion and its ceremonies" (123). He then proceeds to identify points of "influence" of the one group upon the other, showing how Wisdom influenced prophecy through the use of vocabulary and forms in prophetic works (124–129), and then how prophecy influenced Wisdom as seen in the increasingly "religious note" of texts like Proverbs 1–9, Job 28, 38–42 (129–132).

Scott's work is not revolutionary, but rather reflects the status quo of that moment in the history of Hebrew Bible research. But as we look back at his summary of the results of research, we cannot help but notice some significant problems. The fundamental problem is first seen in Scott's observation of the impact of prophecy on Wisdom, which is only compounded by the two chapters which follow in the volume, both of which are entitled "Wisdom in Revolt." These considerations of Wisdom Literature reveal that very little of what Scott included within the "wisdom tradition" actually reflects the kind of wisdom that distinguishes it from the prophetic tradition. It appears then that the Wisdom tradition of Scott's making is nothing short of a caricature that can only be sustained by embracing a developmental model that excises the majority of the literary artifacts often associated with the tradition. The same may be said for the prophetic tradition Scott presented. Wisdom elements can be found at various points in the prophetic tradition, and not only in texts which are criticizing wisdom, but also those employing it in normative ways either in form or vocabulary.

This evidence raises questions about the practice of categorization within the Hebrew Bible research guild. Part of this is related to the enduring legacy of Hermann Gunkel's form-critical enterprise (e.g., Gunkel and Begrich 1933). Gunkel established the important link between literary genre and social setting, described in James Muilenburg's 1968 presidential address to the Society of Biblical Literature (1969, 4): "We therefore encounter in a particular genre or Gattung the same structural forms, the same terminology and style, and the same Sitz im Leben." In his introduction to Form Criticism, Gene Tucker (1971, 9) echoed this feature of Gunkel's approach: "each genre originates in a particular setting or Sitz im Leben and . . . this setting can be recovered through a study of the genre itself," before citing Gunkel: "Every ancient literary type originally belonged to a quite definite side of the national life of Israel" (15).

Muilenburg's (1969, 5) critique is often cited, as he focused on "a proclivity among scholars in recent years to lay such stress upon the typical and representative that the individual, personal, and unique features of the particular pericope are all but lost to view." But there is a greater issue that needed to be recognized, that is, the identification of the "same structural forms, the same terminology and style" with "the same *Sitz im Leben*." What was not recognized was the fact that "the same *Sitz im Leben*" could be linked to different structural forms/terminology/style, or that the "same structural forms, the same terminology and style" could be linked to different *Sitze im Leben*. Tucker (1971, 9) seems to understand the difficulty of this singular approach to setting when he states:

> Careful study often reveals that a particular story or speech has been alive in more than one setting. In the speeches of the prophets, for instance, one finds genres which originated in the worship or the court or elsewhere. So those speeches reflect at least three distinct settings: the background in cultic, legal or other institutions; the prophetic speech itself as an event in the life of the prophet and of Israel; and the situation in which the speech was collected and perhaps edited.

This problem of the link between form and setting is also evident in the closely related discipline of Tradition Criticism.[1] Particularly useful as illustration is the work of Odil Hannes Steck (1977, 183–214) and his description of "Theological Streams of Tradition" which are strikingly similar to the work of R.B.Y. Scott above. Steck identified four dominant streams of tradition (*Traditionsströme*): the cultic, sapiential, prophetic, and Deuteronomic/Deuteronomistic. All of these streams are related to social groups, with the first two found in the urban setting of Jerusalem and the latter two in the rural context of Judah. Steck (1977, 197–198) notes:

> Distinctive, long-lasting intellectual movements of this kind are not borne by individuals but only by groups in which the tradition streams are kept in flux through transmission, learned discussion, and development of new witnesses to the tradition. For carrying out their activities and training their successors these groups need fixed meeting places and durable, more or less established institutions.[2]

As with form criticism, so with tradition criticism a link was established between literary artifact and social group. Of course, the problem not only lies in the interpenetration of the sapiential and prophetic we have noted above, but also the presence of not only the cultic/priestly (see Leuchter and Hutton 2011), but especially the Deuteronomic/Deuteronomistic throughout the Hebrew Bible as revealed in Pan-Deuteronomism (see Schearing and McKenzie 1999).

The real challenge of the categorization of Wisdom and its distinction from prophecy is readily seen as one seeks to understand the books often associated with wisdom in light of texts from historical contexts that predate and postdate the Hebrew Bible. Comparisons between Israelite literature and broader ancient Near Eastern texts revealed similar

---

[1] Form Criticism was often treated as the vehicle by which the traditions were passed on from generation to generation.

[2] Walter Brueggemann (1979) identifies two trajectories: one urban, one rural; the first status quo, Davidic/Royal, and the second revolutionary, Mosaic (see Knight 2006, 313).

features. However, it was regularly noted that the material that was similar to Wisdom arose from circles and in texts that were connected very closely with the cult and liturgy, as well as divinatory practices (Beaulieu 2007, 3–19). These connections led many to question the sociological reality of a Wisdom class or school and instead shift the focus to what Stuart Weeks (1994, 157) identified as a "scribal elite" who were responsible not only for these texts associated with wisdom but also with other types of texts now represented in the Hebrew Bible. Mark Sneed (2018) has taken this insight further by focusing on this scribal elite and explaining the differences in genre in terms of scribal modes of thinking, rather than distinct sociological groups. While it is difficult to critique this, since the only extant evidence is a scribal product, one does have to wonder where these "modes" arose originally. This genesis, however, need not be simplistically associated with sociological groups.

Will Kynes (2019) has pointed a way forward for reflection on texts that we often identified as "Wisdom," and that way forward is through giving attention to the variety of intertextual links that exist between these texts and various other texts. In this way he shifts the focus from those responsible for the texts' origination to a more creative hermeneutical interplay between production and reception of texts. Genre identification is a process by which we read texts in light of other texts, and a more flexible approach to this process gives attention to the variety of texts that inform the reading of any given text rather than enforcing the strictures required in traditional genre identification.[3]

The focus of this particular article is on the intersection between texts traditionally identified as Wisdom and texts associated with prophecy. Within the Jewish tradition, books associated with prophecy include not only what has come to be known as the Writing Prophets or the Latter Prophets, but also the Former Prophets, a section of the Hebrew Bible that is often associated with historiography and even the Torah (Primary History). For the sake of space, this article will focus on the intersection between a sample from the "Wisdom" corpus (Proverbs, Job, Ecclesiastes, and Song of Songs, and texts associated with this corpus elsewhere in the Hebrew Bible) and the Latter Prophets (Isaiah, Jeremiah, Ezekiel, and the Twelve [Hosea–Malachi]), beginning with an investigation of the theme which Scott used to drive a wedge between the two corpora over a half century ago.

28.1 REVELATION IN WISDOM AND PROPHECY

Since the question of "revelation" has played such a key role in the early distinctions between the identity of Wisdom and Prophecy, I will focus my attention on this particular theme and the way it creates connection rather than disconnection between

---

[3] For the discussion of the genre of Wisdom Literature, see, e.g., Sneed 2015; Boda, Meek, and Osborne 2018.

the texts traditionally associated with wisdom and those traditionally associated with prophecy in the Hebrew Bible.

The first indication of the revelatory nature of traditions associated with wisdom arises outside the classic corpus of Wisdom books, that is, in the narrative traditions often associated with wisdom concerning Joseph, Daniel, and Solomon. Joseph is associated with wisdom first of all in the role he plays as one who is able to interpret dreams in the wake of the failure of Egypt's "sages" (חכמים) in Gen 41:8.[4] Having successfully interpreted Pharaoh's dream, Joseph counsels Pharaoh to "look for a man discerning and wise, and set him over the land of Egypt" (41:33). These qualities, "discerning and wise" (נבון וחכם), are identical to qualities associated with the key wisdom figure of Solomon in 1 Kgs 3:12 (חכם ונבון), and are qualities noted throughout the book of Proverbs (e.g., 10:13; 16:21; 17:28; see Mathews 1995, 761). When Pharaoh considers the best candidate to fill this role, he describes the person differently to his servants, as one "in whom is a divine spirit" (41:38). Then he turns to Joseph and identifies him as the best "discerning and wise" candidate because "God has informed you of all this" (41:39). Pharaoh thus links the qualities of "discerning and wise" with the presence of a revelatory divine spirit within Joseph.

Similar evidence can be culled from the court story of Daniel (cf. Mastin 1995, 161–169). There we see some evidence of an initial ability in wisdom as Dan 1:4 identifies the qualities of the youths who were deported to the Babylonian court as those who were "showing intelligence (שׂכל) in every branch of wisdom (חכמה), endowed with understanding (ידעי דעת) and discerning knowledge (מביני מדע)." In addition, they were placed in a program where they would be "taught" (למד) the literature and language of the Chaldeans. However, Dan 1:17 points to a divine endowment of wisdom as "God gave them knowledge and intelligence in all literature and wisdom," showing a divine source for an ability which the narrator tells us would distinguish them as "ten times better than all the magicians and conjurers who were in all his realm" (1:20). When the king demands both the content and interpretation of his dream, these Chaldeans, who are identified as "the wise men of Babylon" (2:4, 12, 14, 18, 27, 48), state that such revelation is only available for the "gods, whose dwelling place is not with flesh" (2:11). Daniel's praise for God's revelation to him in 2:20–23 makes clear the revelatory nature of the wisdom he has received. A similar episode is related in Daniel 4, and when Daniel provides the interpretation of the dream, the king identifies in Daniel "a spirit of the holy gods" (vv. 5, 6 [ET 8, 9]). In Daniel 5 the queen identifies Daniel as one "in whom is a spirit of the holy gods" (v. 11; cf. v. 14), and this spirit is described as "an extraordinary spirit" (רוח יתירה) in v. 12. Possession of this spirit is linked to various activities of wisdom and insight throughout vv. 11, 12, and 14 and later in Dan 6:3 to the activities of governance.

---

[4] For connections between the Joseph story and wisdom, see Fox 2001; Wilson 2004; Longman 2017, 84–85; Steinmann 2018.

And finally, Solomon, the figure which lies at the heart of traditions concerning wisdom in the Hebrew Bible, is described in a similar way to these other two court figures.[5] First Kings depicts Solomon's wise ability as surpassing all his contemporaries as he provided insightful advice, creative arts, and scientific discovery through his proverbs, songs, and catalogues of nature. These activities attracted international visitors to hear his wisdom (1 Kgs 5:10–14 [ET 4:30–34]). This description, however, is preceded by the statement, "Now God gave (נתן) Solomon wisdom (חכמה) and very great discernment (תבונה) and breadth of mind (רחב לב), like the sand that is on the seashore" (5:9 [ET 4:29]). And that gift of wisdom is provided in Solomon's initial encounter with God at the beginning of his reign in 1 Kings 3. There Solomon confesses his lack of knowledge to lead the nation (1 Kgs 3:7, 9) and asks God "to give (נתן) your servant a listening heart (לב שמע) to judge your people to discern between good and evil." This request is granted by God in 3:10–12 as God grants (נתן) him "a wise and discerning heart" (לב חכם ונבון), using the same vocabulary connected with Joseph in Gen 41:33. First Kings 3:16–28 shows Solomon's immediate ability for wise discernment, summarized by the narrator in 3:28: "When all Israel heard of the judgment which the king had handed down, they feared the king, for they saw that the wisdom of God was in him to administer justice."

All three of these figures who are closely associated with wisdom in the Hebrew Bible are identified as youth who are given an endowment of divine wisdom rather than acquiring wisdom over a lifetime of experience and learning. This is clearly not revelation from below but revelation from above and is akin to the revelatory mode often associated with the prophetic tradition and books in the Hebrew Bible.

What we see in these three figures associated with wisdom, however, is not an outlier. Turning to the opening chapter of Proverbs, one finds an immediate challenge to the caricature of wisdom as revelation from below. Following the prologue in 1:1–7 and the opening parental voice in 1:8–19, a new voice can be heard, that of Wisdom itself. Addressing the "naïve ones…simple-minded…scoffers…fools" (v. 22). Wisdom speaks in vocabulary which dominates the Wisdom books (knowledge, reproof, counsel), but in vv. 23–24 combines this with vocabulary that dominates the prophetic books:

> [23] Turn (שוב) to my reproof,
> Behold (הנה), I will pour out my spirit on you;
> I will make my words known to you.
> [24] Because I called and you refused,
> I stretched out my hand and no one paid attention;
> …
> [28] Then they will call on me, but I will not answer;
> They will seek me diligently but they will not find me.

---

[5] See André Lemaire (1995), who highlights how 1 Kings 3–11 "confirms beyond the shadow of a doubt the central role which [wisdom] plays in the biblical historiography of the reign of Solomon" (110).

Employing the common prophetic word for repentance (שׁוּב), Wisdom invites its listeners to respond to wise counsel. The description of the audience's refusal to respond followed by divine reciprocation is strikingly similar to passages within the prophetic books, including Isa 1:15; Jer 11:11; 14:12; Ezek 8:18; Mic 3:4; and especially Zech 7:11–13. And the message of repentance is followed in Prov 1:23 with the promise to send forth a spirit to the audience, a promise associated with the impartation of the divine spirit throughout the prophetic books, including Isa 44:3; Ezek 11:19; 36:26, 27; 37:14; 39:29; Joel 3:1, 2 [ET 2:28, 29]; Zech 12:10.[6] The pouring out of this spirit in Prov 1:23 is followed by a reference to revelation in the following clause: "I will make my words known to you," employing a verb associated with divine speech through the prophets (e.g., Isa 5:5; Jer 16:21; Ezek 20:5; Trible 1975).[7]

Central to the first introduction to the figure of Wisdom in the book of Proverbs is a depiction that is strikingly similar to vocabulary and themes usually associated with prophetic books.[8] And this depiction highlights the revelatory nature of wisdom in a way that does not suggest it is somehow distinct from prophecy, that is, that it comes from below rather than from above.

This evidence, however, does not stand alone in Proverbs. In the very next passage in the book we find a clear declaration that "the Lord gives (נתן) wisdom, from his mouth is knowledge and understanding" (2:6). Such a gift of wisdom is a common theme throughout the proverbial literature of Proverbs 10–31, as God imparts and reveals wisdom to humanity (e.g., Prov 16:1; 19:21; 21:1; 28:5; 29:18).

The concluding sections of Proverbs also contain language often associated only with the revelatory tradition of prophecy. The opening superscriptions of Proverbs 30 and 31 read similarly:

דִּבְרֵי אָגוּר בִּן־יָקֶה הַמַּשָּׂא נְאֻם הַגֶּבֶר	Prov 30:1	The words of Agur the son of Jakeh, the oracle. Declaration of the man:
דִּבְרֵי לְמוּאֵל מֶלֶךְ מַשָּׂא אֲשֶׁר־יִסְּרַתּוּ אִמּוֹ	Prov 31:1	The words of King Lemuel, an oracle which his mother taught him:

Unlike earlier superscriptions in Prov 1:1, 10:1, and 25:1 where the term מָשָׁל appears, 30:1 and 31:1 are similar to 22:17 in employing "words of" (דברי). Uniquely in 30:1 and 31:1 the term "oracle" (משא) follows. This latter term is one associated elsewhere usually with prophets or prophetic material, appearing in Isa 13:1; 14:28; 15:1; 17:1; 19:1; 21:1, 11,

---

[6] Contra Bruce Waltke (2004, 1:199 n. 17), who translates this as "my thoughts," not wanting to "mislead many English readers into associating the thought with Isa. 44:3 and Joel 2:28 (3:1)."

[7] Scott Harris (1995, 67–109), notes how Wisdom teachers in Prov 1:20–33 draw especially on Jeremiah 7, 20, and Zechariah 7 for the portrayal of wisdom, suggesting strong affinities with the prophetic tradition.

[8] See further Alan Lenzi (2006, 711–714), who argues for allusions to prophetic calling passages also in Prov 8:22–31 (Exod 3:14; Isa 48:16), which shows that "Wisdom is implicitly a messenger sent by Yahweh to humanity and therefore can communicate to mortals her unique cosmological knowledge" (713).

13; 22:1; 23:1; 30:6; Jer 23:33–38; Ezek 12:10; Nah 1:1; Hab 1:1; Zech 9:1; 12:1; Mal 1:1; 2 Kgs 9:25; 2 Chron 24:27; Lam 2:14 (Boda 2006). This connection to the prophetic tradition is developed further by the appearance of the phrase in 30:1: "declaration of the man" (נאם הגבר). The word נאם is ubiquitous throughout prophetic literature, functioning with the divine name ("declaration of YHWH/Lord") as a prophetic messenger formula in many prophetic speeches (e.g., Isa 1:24; Jer 1:8; Ezek 5:11; Zech 1:3). Its use in Prov 30:1 alongside the term "oracle" (משא) reminds one of the Latter Prophets. But its use with a human ("declaration of the man"; נאם הגבר) also brings to mind other prophetic traditions within the Hebrew Bible. This phrase is found three other times in the Hebrew Bible, twice in the Balaam texts of Numbers (24:3, 15) and once in 2 Sam 23:1, with נאם occurring five further times in these texts all in connection with human figures who are portrayed as revelatory figures. Balaam is the one "who hears the words of God . . . knows the knowledge of the Most High . . . sees the vision of the Almighty," while David is one through whom "the Spirit of Yahweh spoke," on whose was tongue was "his word" and to whom "the Rock of Israel spoke." Thus, although the use of נאם in Prov 30:1 is different from that found in the Latter Prophets, the variant formulation here is still connected with revelatory figures associated with prophecy.[9]

This evidence from Proverbs highlights clear intertextual links between what is often identified as the traditional expression of wisdom in the Hebrew Bible (Proverbs) and the prophetic tradition. And interestingly this evidence appears at the beginning and end of this book, suggesting that those responsible for the final form of Proverbs saw this as an important emphasis that is essential to wisdom as opposed to being an aberration (see Moore 1994).

This evidence of special revelation as key to Proverbs calibrates our interpretive senses to other signs of revelatory figures and experience in the books traditionally associated with wisdom. If one is able to embrace the conclusions of John Calvin, Robert Gordis (1965, 104–116), and Choon Leong Seow (2011), who follow most medieval Jewish interpreters,[10] the figure of Elihu (Job 32–37) plays a key role in preparing readers for the encounter between God and Job in chapters 38–41. Elihu confronts the wisdom expressions of the three friends and Job in his opening speech in chapter 32. He declares in 32:18:

> I am full of words, the spirit (רוח) within me constrains me; Behold, my belly is like unvented wine, like new wineskins it is about to burst. Let me speak that I may get relief; Let me open my lips and answer.

The language used here is strikingly similar to that of the prophet Jeremiah in Jer 4:19; 20:9; 23:9. Reference to the "spirit" (רוח) here is a further development of a theme developed earlier in this speech, where he points to the value of acquiring wisdom directly from the deity through the spirit and breath that has enlivened him:

---

[9] See also Markus Saur (2014), who highlights the key role of Proverbs 30 in drawing in prophetic and prayer traditions to solve the problems with traditional Wisdom sources raised by books like Ecclesiastes and Job.

[10] See the superb review in Seow 2011.

it is a spirit (רוח) in mortals, and the breath (נשמה) of the Almighty, gives understanding. (32:8)

This theme is continued in his next speech (33:3–4) as he traces his wisdom to the spirit and breath of God that grant him life:

> My words are *from* the uprightness of my heart,
> And my lips speak knowledge sincerely.
> The Spirit (רוח) of God has made me,
> And the breath (נשמה) of the Almighty gives me life.

This connection between spirit and revelation can be found throughout the prophetic tradition of the Hebrew Bible. Zechariah reviews the history of this connection by referring to "the words which Yahweh of hosts had sent by his spirit through the former prophets" (7:12). This link between prophecy and the divine spirit can be discerned throughout the Hebrew Bible (Num 11:25, 29; 1 Sam 10:5–6, 10; 19:20–21, 24; 2 Sam 23:2; 1 Kgs 18:12; 22:21–23//2 Chr 18:20–22; 1 Kgs 22:24; 2 Kgs 2:9, 15, 16; Neh 9:30). And the prophetic books regularly link spirit and prophecy (Isa 61:1, 2; Ezek 2:2; 3:12, 14, 24; 8:3; 11:1, 5, 24; 37:1, 9, 10; 43:5; Joel 3:1–2 [ET 2:28–29]; Mic 3:8; Hag 2:5; Zech 4:6; cf. Isa 59:21; Ezek 13:3; Zech 13:2).

Elihu thus reveals a key conduit for discovery of wisdom, which is direct revelation rather than the patient acquisition of knowledge through experience and learning past tradition. Furthermore, Elihu's emphasis can also be discerned at times even within the preceding speeches of his four elders as reference is made to a spirit providing an answer (Job 20:3) or God breaking in with special revelation (11:5–6a; 15:2–3, 8–10). At times there is skepticism over whether such spirit knowledge is useful (15:2–3) or such claims to divine revelation are legitimate (15:8–10). Reference to revelation through a spirit in Eliphaz's opening speech in 4:12–21, which may refer to an experience he had or that another such as Job had, does provide a key theme which is debated throughout the speeches which follow.[11]

Even if one rejects Elihu as a legitimate source of wisdom and interprets references to revelatory means of wisdom as negative in the friends' speeches, one cannot deny the normativity of the direct revelatory encounter between God and Job in chapters 38–41. The conclusion to the wisdom struggle throughout the book of Job is reached with the appearance of God to speak directly to Job and shape his response to the issue under discussion. And it is this encounter with God that prompts the concluding response of Job in 42:1–6, as indicated by his allusions to the divine speeches, as well as his concluding statement prior to his declaration of repentance: "I had heard of you by the hearing of the ear; but now my eyes have seen you" (42:5). The "hearing of the ear" refers to a knowledge mediated through tradition, while "my eyes have seen you" refers to the powerful encounter with God in chapters 38–41. Often the encounter between God and humanity

---

[11]   See the full discussion of the role of this key passage in Brown 2015.

is associated with the prophetic tradition, that is, those who are granted access to the divine council where they hear God and receive messages to be mediated to humanity (1 Kgs 22:19–21; Isa 6; Ezek 1, 10; cf. Jer 23:18, 22). But here we find a non-prophetic person who is encountered directly by God and through this experience gains divine wisdom. This occurs at the climax of the book, which brings resolution to the complications introduced throughout the book, as Job's final speech in 42:1–6 and the concluding narrative in 42:7–17 confirms. Therefore, it reveals the superiority of revelatory experience over traditional means of acquiring wisdom represented in the debate cycles of the elder sages.

Intertextual links between Wisdom and Prophecy have proven helpful in challenging our common caricature of Wisdom, that is, that wisdom in the Hebrew Bible is largely anthropocentric, a search for truth and meaning apart from divine revelation and illumination. The shaping of two key books associated with wisdom points to the importance of special revelation to the acquisition of wisdom. Such special revelation forms a bracket around the book of Proverbs and can be discerned at various intervals throughout the intervening material. And special revelation lies at the climax to the book of Job and is key to the resolution of the crisis in Wisdom of the book.

There are points of difference between the two traditions, however. The tradition of the spirit as conduit for revelatory wisdom in Job, especially in the speeches of Elihu, points to the creational nuance of the Wisdom tradition. That is, while the spirit in the Wisdom tradition is dominated by depictions of the enlivening spirit and breath of God from creation traditions such as Genesis 2, a dynamic that means that such wisdom is available to all humanity and not merely social functionaries, such as kings, judges, priests, and especially prophets, the spirit in the prophetic tradition is dominated by depictions of the spirit as a heavenly entity which enables revelation more so than the impartation of life.[12] This does not lessen the importance of revelation in Wisdom contexts, nor elevate the role of the prophetic. It reveals the importance of the revelatory in these key books of the Hebrew Bible with sensitivity to their unique contributions to the theme.

28.2 Theophany and Theodicy in Wisdom and Prophecy

In the above section we have considered the importance of revelation within the matrix of two books associated with wisdom, Proverbs and Job. At the climax of that revelation we have noted the importance of the theophany of God. This theophanic appearance has often been noted as a key feature of Job and central to the resolution of theodicy in the book. Theodicy, however, is considered at many other points within the Hebrew Bible, ranging from the patriarchal narratives regarding Sodom in Genesis (ch. 18), to

---

[12] The creational dimension of the spirit, however, can be discerned in prophetic literature, e.g., Isa 42:5; Zech 12:1, but not for the acquisition of revelation. There is also hope for a democratization of the spirit beyond social functionaries, e.g., Joel 3:1–2 [ET 2:28–29].

the Deuteronomistic History as a whole (Noth 1943, 43–152; cf. Noth 1981), and, as we will soon see, to prophetic literature. By grouping these texts within particular, separate literary and cultural traditions, there has been a tendency to lose the opportunity for interconnective insight.

The power of traditional groupings to hinder interpretation can be showcased by consideration of theophanic texts within the Twelve. Because of the superscription of Habakkuk and its placement among the Twelve prophets within the Latter Prophets of the Hebrew Bible, it is not surprising that much interpretation focuses on the connection between Habakkuk and the prophetic corpus. But the book of Job provides key data for reading the book of Habakkuk.[13] Habakkuk parallels Job's predicament as the prophet struggles with the justice of the people's predicament. Habakkuk's cries in chapter 1 are similar to Job's laments and protests. The testimony of Habakkuk in 3:16–19 in the wake of the theophany of YHWH is akin to that of Job in 42:1–6. While most have taken this into account, there is a tendency to see this as odd, reflecting some other non-prophetic influence such as cultic (e.g., Nogalski 2011, 645) or Wisdom traditions (e.g., Gowan 1976, 12–16), while if we allow for intertextuality to drive our generic categorization, we open up a world of interconnection and rereading in light of literary witnesses that transcend traditional literary and social boundaries.

Habakkuk, however, does not stand alone among the Twelve in its presentation of theophany and theodicy. Amos contains a series of interactions between the prophet and the deity. This begins with the visions in Amos 7–8 in which Yahweh shows the prophet three different scenes, first, a locust-swarm (7:1–3), second, a fire (7:4–6), third, a plumb line (7:7–9), and finally a basket of summer fruit (8:1–3). The first two visionary experiences elicit a response from the prophet that resonates with the theodicy tradition encountered in Job and Habakkuk, as the prophet intercedes with: "Lord Yahweh, please pardon/stop! How can Jacob stand, for he is small?" (7:2, 5). In these two initial cases Yahweh reverses his decision to judge. In the third and fourth cases, however, the prophetic intercession is absent, suggesting that the prophetic concern over theodicy has been silenced. It is at this point, then, that we find a description of the powerful theophany of Amos 9. As in Job and Habakkuk, it appears in a rhetorically climactic position at the end of the book. While Amos is clearly associated with the Israelite context, the theophany expands the presentation of God and especially leverages creational language through the final doxology of judgment. Reading Amos 9 in light of Job takes us back to the creational emphasis of Job which prepares the way for the theophany. Furthermore, this creational emphasis matches the international emphasis of Amos 9, which parallels what is often considered the unique redemptive-historical event of Israel's exodus from Egypt with similar movements by other ancient people groups, including the Philistines and Arameans (9:7). Reading Amos 7–9, then, in light of Job and Habakkuk, we find the creative interlinking of theophany and theodicy, which provides a way forward out of suffering.

---

[13] See Timmer 2018 and my response (Boda 2018).

Finally, the book of Zechariah begins with the promise that if the people will return to YHWH that he would return to them (Zech 1:1–6a). The people's positive response in 1:6b sets up the visionary sequence of 1:7–6:15, which begins with the declaration of Yahweh's return in 1:16 (suffix conjugation of שוב). This declaration comes in the midst of a visionary experience which takes place at the entrance to the divine abode (the deep) and introduces language that reminds one of the opening chapters of Job in the heavenly courts where Yahweh dwells and heavenly beings gather from their patrols. Language connected with these opening chapters of Job also appear in visions 4, 5, and 8,[14] suggesting the importance of the Joban tradition to the formation of the structure of the vision sequence (see Boda 2016, 21–22). Notably, at the outset of the visionary material one finds a lament uttered by the angel of YHWH, which questions the delay over the restoration: "how long will you have no compassion for Jerusalem and the cities of Jerusalem with which you have been indignant these seventy years?" (1:12). It is the angelic beings who have gathered for the appearing of YHWH and references to these beings and even some humans experiencing the presence of Yahweh reappear in visions 4, 5, and 8. While one can learn much structurally from the connections between the visions in Zechariah and those in texts traditionally associated with the prophetic tradition, such as Jeremiah, Amos, and Ezekiel (Boda 2014), attending to intertextual links to Job brings out dynamics from the lament-theophany dimension associated with Joban wisdom that then connects the reader to the Habakkuk and Amos traditions.

28.3 Conclusion

One of the deficiencies of the classic genre approach to biblical literature, particularly through its connections to form and tradition criticism, has been the limitations it has often placed on which texts are deemed appropriate to bring into conversation with other texts. Even when texts beyond the identified genre are connected, the artificial literary wall that has been created forces the interpreter to emphasize differences between the two texts because of their lack of membership in the dominant genre group and the associations of their authors with purported distinct sociological groups. Intertextual studies have gone a long way to fostering connections beyond texts from traditional generic groupings, but there is much more work to be done.

The value of shifting away from formal approaches to genre and embracing an intertextual approach can be seen in this case study of the intersection of texts often associated with Wisdom and Prophecy. Bringing these texts into closer connection highlights the creational and international quality of prophetic literature. Prophetic literature

---

[14] הלך ("patrol," *hithpael*): Zech 1:10, 11; 6:7 ("throughout the earth," בארץ); cf. Job 1:7; 2:2 ("throughout it," בה, with the referent the preceding בארץ); השטן ("the accuser"): Zech 3:1, 2; cf. Job 1:6, 7, 8, 9, 12; 2:1, 2, 3, 4, 6, 7; שוט ("roam," *polel*): Zech 4:10 ("throughout all the earth," בכל־הארץ); cf. Job 1:7; 2:2 *qal* ("throughout the earth," בארץ); יצב ("present oneself," *hithpael*): Zech 6:5 ("before the Lord of all the earth," על־אדון כל־הארץ); cf. Job 1:6; 2:1 ("before Yahweh," על־יהוה).

has often been interpreted as more restricted to a "redemptive-historical" perspective focused on the interests of Israel and Judah and, through them, the nations. Addresses to the nations are interpreted as indirect encouragements for Israel and Judah. While this cannot be denied, this makes little sense of the positive hope attached to the nations even in the midst of judgment (e.g., Isa 19:18–25; Zech 14:16–17). It also does not take seriously the interest of the prophetic corpus in the cosmos, drawing on creation for much of its imagery, envisioning the impact of Israel's failure on the cosmos, and projecting a future renewal of the cosmos alongside the redemption of Israel. This then makes sense of certain texts within the prophetic corpus which are often treated as "eschatological" or "apocalyptic" for which the international and cosmic are essential.

Bringing these texts into closer connection also highlights the revelatory nature of Wisdom Literature as wisdom from above. It expands the conduits of revelation beyond some particular prophetic class to include all humanity, even a farmer like Job. This takes us back to a figure like Amos who is identified as a common man, a sheepherder from Tekoa, or to Zechariah, who is identified in tradition as from a priestly family, not unlike Ezekiel and Jeremiah.

This data should encourage us to embrace an intertextual hermeneutic not restricted by traditional genre categories and in doing so these Wisdom texts have greater potential to speak in creative ways.

Works Cited

Beaulieu, Paul-Alain. 2007. "The Social and Intellectual Setting of Babylonian Wisdom Literature." Pages 3–19 in *Wisdom Literature in Mesopotamia and Israel*. Edited by Richard J. Clifford. Leiden: Brill.

Boda, Mark J. 2006. "Freeing the Burden of Prophecy: Maśśā' and the Legitimacy of Prophecy in Zech 9–14." *Bib* 86:338–357.

Boda, Mark J. 2014. "Writing the Vision: Zechariah within the Visionary Traditions of the Hebrew Bible." Pages 101–118 in *"I Lifted My Eyes and Saw": Reading Dream and Vision Reports in the Hebrew Bible*. Edited by Lena-Sofia Tiemeyer and Elizabeth Hayes. LHBOTS 584. London: T&T Clark.

Boda, Mark J. 2016. *The Book of Zechariah*. NICOT. Grand Rapids, MI: Eerdmans.

Boda, Mark J. 2018. "Wisdom in Prophecy: A Response." Pages 246–256 in Boda, Meek, and Osborne 2018.

Boda, Mark J., Russell L. Meek, and William R. Osborne. 2018. *Riddles and Revelations: Explorations into the Relationship between Wisdom and Prophecy in the Hebrew Bible*. LHBOTS 634. New York, NY: Bloomsbury T&T Clark.

Brown, Ken. 2015. *The Vision in Job 4 and Its Role in the Book: Reframing the Development of the Joban Dialogues*. Studies of the Sofja Kovalevskaja Research Group on Early Jewish Monotheism. Tübingen: Mohr Siebeck.

Brueggemann, Walter. 1979. "Trajectories in Old Testament Literature and the Sociology of Ancient Israel." *JBL* 98:161–185.

Day, John, Robert P. Gordon, and H.G.M. Williamson, eds. 1995. *Wisdom in Ancient Israel: Essays in Honour of J.A. Emerton*. Edited by Cambridge: Cambridge University Press.

Fox, Michael V. 2001. "Wisdom in the Joseph Story." *VT* 51:26–41.

Gordis, Robert. 1965. *The Book of God and Man: A Study of Job*. Chicago, IL: University of Chicago.

Gowan, Donald E. 1976. *The Triumph of Faith in Habakkuk*. Atlanta, GA: John Knox.

Gunkel, Hermann, and Joachim Begrich. 1933. *Einleitung in Die Psalmen: Die Gattungen der Religiösen Lyrik Israels*. 2nd ed. Göttingen: Vandenhoeck & Ruprecht. English translation: *Introduction to Psalms: The Genres of the Religious Lyric of Israel*. Mercer Library of Biblical Studies. Macon, GA: Mercer University, 1998.

Harris, Scott L. 1995. *Proverbs 1–9: A Study of Inner-Biblical Interpretation*. Edited by Michael V. Fox. SBLDS 150. Atlanta, GA: Scholars Press.

Knight, Douglas A. 2006. *Rediscovering the Traditions of Israel*. 3rd ed. SBLStBL 16. Atlanta, GA: SBL.

Kynes, Will. 2019. *An Obituary for Wisdom Literature: The Birth, Death, and Intertextual Reintegration of a Biblical Corpus*. Oxford: Oxford University Press.

Lemaire, André. 1995. "Wisdom in Solomonic Historiography." Pages 106–118 in Day et al. 1995.

Lenzi, Alan C. 2006. "Proverbs 8:22–31: Three Perspectives on Its Composition." *JBL* 125:687–714.

Leuchter, Mark, and Jeremy Michael Hutton. 2011. *Levites and Priests in History and Tradition*. AIL 9. Atlanta, GA: Brill.

Longman, Tremper. 2017. *The Fear of the Lord Is Wisdom: A Theological Introduction to Wisdom in Israel*. Grand Rapids, MI: Baker Academic.

Mastin, Brian A. 1995. "Wisdom and Daniel." Pages 161–169 in Day et al. 1995.

Mathews, K.A. 1995. *Genesis 11:27–50:26*. NAC. Nashville, TN: Broadman & Holman.

Moore, Rick D. 1994. "A Home for the Alien: Worldly Wisdom and Covenantal Confession in Proverbs 30,1–9." *ZAW* 106:96–107.

Muilenburg, James. 1969. "Form Criticism and Beyond." *JBL* 88:1–18.

Nogalski, James D. 2011. *The Book of the Twelve: Micah–Malachi*. Smyth & Helwys Bible Commentary. Macon, GA: Smyth & Helwys.

Noth, Martin. 1943. *Überlieferungsgeschichtliche Studien*. Halle: Niemeyer.

Noth, Martin. 1981. *The Deuteronomistic History*. JSOTSup 15. Sheffield: JSOT.

Saur, Markus. 2014. "Prophetie, Weisheit und Gebet: Überlegungen zu den Worten Agurs in Prov 30,1–9." *ZAW* 126:570–583.

Schearing, Linda S., and Steven L. McKenzie. 1999. *Those Elusive Deuteronomists: The Phenomenon of Pan-Deuteronomism*. JSOTSup 268. Sheffield: Sheffield Academic Press.

Scott, R.B.Y. 1961. "Priesthood, Prophecy, Wisdom, and the Knowledge of God." *JBL* 80:1–15.

Scott, R.B.Y. 1971. *The Way of Wisdom in the Old Testament*. New York, NY: Macmillan.

Seow, Choon Leong. 2011. "Elihu's Revelation." *Theology Today* 68:253–271.

Sneed, Mark R. 2015. *Was There a Wisdom Tradition? New Prospects in Israelite Wisdom Studies*. AIL 23. Atlanta, GA: SBL.

Sneed, Mark R. 2018. "Methods, Muddles, and Modes of Literature: The Question of Influence between Wisdom and Prophecy." Pages 30–44 in Boda, Meek, and Osborne 2018.

Steck, Odil Hannes. 1977. "Theological Streams of Tradition." Pages 183–214 in *Tradition and Theology in the Old Testament*. Edited by Douglas A. Knight and Walter J. Harrelson. Philadelphia, PA: Fortress.

Steinmann, Andrew E. 2018. "Daniel as Wisdom in Action." Pages 123–145 in Boda, Meek, and Osborne 2018.

Timmer, Daniel C. 2018. "Where Shall Wisdom Be Found (in the Book of the Twelve)?" Pages 146–163 in Boda, Meek, and Osborne 2018.

Trible, Phyllis. 1975. "Wisdom Builds a Poem: The Architecture of Proverbs 1:20–33." *JBL* 94:509–518.

Tucker, Gene M. 1971. *Form Criticism of the Old Testament*. Philadelphia, PA: Fortress.

Waltke, Bruce K. 2004. *The Book of Proverbs*. 2 vols. NICOT. Grand Rapids, MI: Eerdmans.

Weeks, Stuart. 1994. *Early Israelite Wisdom*. Oxford Theological Monographs. Oxford: Oxford University Press.

Wilson, Lindsay. 2004. *Joseph Wise and Otherwise: The Intersection of Wisdom and Covenant in Genesis 37–50*. Paternoster Biblical Monographs. Carlisle: Paternoster.

CHAPTER 29

··

APOCALYPTIC AND WISDOM LITERATURE

··

BENNIE H. REYNOLDS III

"APOCALYPTIC Literature" and "Wisdom Literature" are broad designations that represent widely recognized categories of inquiry in the fields of ancient Judaism, early Christianity, and beyond. The fact that I have introduced both of them in quotation marks indicates, however, that each must be disambiguated and more narrowly defined in order to produce a valuable comparison. The relationship between the two has been a prominent topic of study over the last five decades. For example, the two categories have animated to a significant extent the so-called "quest for the historical Jesus" as well as related examples of source- and tradition-criticism of the gospels in the fields of New Testament and Early Christianity (see the discussion in Macaskill 2007, 1–9). In the study of ancient Judaism, scholars have invested significant effort over several decades in attempts to understand what role Wisdom might have played in the development of apocalypticism and apocalyptic literature in early Hellenistic times. More recently, scholars have reconsidered the relationship and most no longer approach it with the driving question: "Whence the apocalypses?" The interaction between key features and ideas expressed in the Wisdom Literature and Jewish apocalyptic literature is now treated as more of a two-way street. How one characterizes the relationship depends, in part, on the chronological boundaries of the study since both literary genres and social movements are fluid and evolve over time.

This essay proceeds in three sections. First, I outline some working-definitions and assumptions for apocalypses and for the genres of Wisdom Literature after making some programmatic statements about how I understand literary genres. Second, I offer the reader an impressionistic overview of some of the most significant differences, similarities, interactions, and evolutions that one can observe when comparing apocalyptic literature with Wisdom Literature. Finally, I sketch out some of the large shifts and developments in scholarly thought about the relationship between Wisdom Literature and Jewish apocalyptic literature and offer some observations about where things stand today.

29.1 GENRE

I begin with a statement about genre because, as I will later discuss, one of the most contentious issues in the modern study of Wisdom and apocalyptic literature is the question of whether heuristic categories put us at an advantage or disadvantage when analyzing the literary data.

Genres are always scholarly impositions upon literary data—even in situations where a text makes explicit claims about its own genre. In the worst cases, scholars treat genres as independently existing, immutable Platonic forms. Thus, it is important to highlight the more modest and utilitarian goals of genre analysis along the lines articulated by Adena Rosmarin. For her, genre is "the critic's heuristic tool, his chosen or defined way of persuading his audience to see the literary text in all its previously inexplicable and 'literary' fullness and then to relate this text to those that are similar or, more precisely, to those that may be similarly explained" (Rosmarin 1985, 25).

For religious studies specialists (and for humanists more generally), critical comparison is the interpretive tool par excellence (see, e.g., Freidenreich 2004, 80–101; Smith 2004, 19–25). Ideally, one might compare each unique literary work to all other literary works, each ceramic vessel unearthed by archaeologists individually to all other ceramic vessels, each painting to all other paintings. But beyond the practical difficulties of dealing with impossibly large amounts of data, the avoidance of typologies (with all their built-in artificialness) is no less dangerous than reifying them. Thomas Pavel (2003, 202) assesses the trade-off well:

> With all their instability, generic notions are irreplaceable. Attempts to speak about literature in terms of a single all-encompassing category that would make generic concerns obsolete (the "masterpiece" of the Romantics, the "poem" of the New Critics, and the "text" of poststructuralist criticism) leave aside something essential. Genre is a crucial interpretive tool because it is a crucial artistic tool in the first place.

In other words, writers always operate under artistic and cultural constraints. Most of those constraints are unacknowledged and writers probably experience the majority of their influences unconsciously. Even when writers acknowledge and confront generic constraints, they cannot overcome them entirely. As Mark Sneed (2015, 60) has remarked in conversation with Jacques Derrida's famous essay "The Law of Genre" (1980), "If a person wants to do something new generically, then it cannot be entirely new or else it would not be understood. One can never transcend generic conventions completely, though the always partially successful attempt makes for interesting effect." The value of literary genres (and, thus, quasi-artificial groupings of texts) is that they allow us to see more clearly the fine distinctions between texts that share general similarities. They allow us to *attempt* to understand the conventions that shaped literary production at any particular time and within any particular culture.

29.1.1 Wisdom

Like many important *topoi* in the study of ancient Mediterranean religions, Wisdom is problematic to the extent that some of the earliest and most influential descriptions of its conceptual boundaries were formulated based on a small portion of the ancient evidence that is available nowadays. The boundaries of "Wisdom Literature" as it is typically understood were drawn first around canonical and deuterocanonical biblical literature, specifically the books of Proverbs, Ecclesiastes, Job, Ben Sira, and Wisdom of Solomon. Will Kynes (2016) has recently demonstrated that the notion of a distinct "Wisdom Literature" in more or less its current form was developed in the middle of the nineteenth century and owes considerably to the work of Johann Bruch.

Scholars nowadays tend to treat Wisdom Literature as a widespread genre in the ancient Near East, reaching far beyond biblical literature. But the boundaries drawn around a core of biblical literature have not been significantly revised in light of the considerable evidence available from neighboring cultures. As Kynes (2016, 85) points out, it has long been noted by Egyptologists and Assyriologists that the term "Wisdom Literature" was adopted into their fields from biblical scholars. I tend to view this transfer more as a contribution from biblical scholars than an imposition. After all, the term Wisdom Literature has not been uncritically adopted by Egyptologists and Assyriologists, who generally demonstrate little compunction to imitate biblical scholars. Nevertheless, in light of the formal similarities between a large constellation of texts from across the ancient Near East, it would be preferable to revisit our definitions from a deliberately cross-cultural perspective.

In light of what we know about the modern development of the genre(s) of Wisdom Literature, Kynes and others (to greater and lesser extents) have expressed skepticism about whether the category might be more trouble than it is worth—preventing rather than facilitating learning (see, for example, the many excellent contributions in Sneed 2015). Kynes also acknowledges that drawing specific conclusions from his findings about the origins of "Wisdom Literature" runs the risk of committing the genetic fallacy that an idea's origins can be used to confirm or contradict its truth. Precisely to this point, there are reasons to suspect that, notwithstanding Kynes's important discoveries, the notion of "Wisdom Literature" (and the associated cultural assumptions and expectations) was not derived purely from nineteenth-century tendentiousness.

In the second century, a Bishop named Melito recorded a list of Hebrew books that was later preserved by the fourth-century historian Eusebius. Melito describes the book of Proverbs as "Solomon's Proverbs or Wisdom" (*Ecclesiastical History*, 4.26). The description of Proverbs as Σολομῶνος Παροιμίαι ἡ καὶ Σοφία is interesting because the book consistently begins with the words משלי שלמה in Hebrew and παροιμίαι Σαλωμῶντος in Greek translation, both of which mean "proverbs of Solomon." In other words, already in ancient times Proverbs was so thoroughly associated with "wisdom" that unlike every other scriptural book he listed, Melito felt compelled to give it the alternate designation. Similarly, Eusebius reports Hegesippus's claim that he, Iranaeus, and many other early Christian writers were accustomed to calling Proverbs ἡ πανάρετος σοφία "the All-Virtuous Wisdom" (*Ecclesiastical History*, 4.22). At least one confirmation of Hegesippus's claim is found in 1 Clement 57. But importantly, the title "All-Virtuous Wisdom" was not reserved exclusively for Proverbs among ancient writers. It is sometimes also applied to Ben Sira and to the Wisdom of Solomon (Toy 1899, v). In addition, medieval *Tosefot Baba Batra 14b* describes Proverbs as *sefer ḥokmah* "Book of Wisdom."

To be sure, labels such as these *do not* indicate that a clearly defined Wisdom genre was conceptualized in ancient or medieval times or even that the group of biblical texts that we typically regard as "Wisdom" were normally read together. But we also cannot ignore that interpreters have long noted the disproportionate frequency of use of the Hebrew word *ḥokmah* in Proverbs, Job, and Ecclesiastes and the Greek analogue σοφία in Ben Sira and the Wisdom of Solomon. Approximately two-thirds of all the uses of the root חכם (or the word σοφία) in the books of the Hebrew Bible and the Apocrypha are found in those five books. This is not a modern discovery and it undoubtedly affected how the books were understood. But the writers/editors of ancient Wisdom texts themselves provide the most powerful indications of the influence of Wisdom genres (or, we may say, conventions) in the ancient world. Indeed, it is precisely the ease of cultural and literary appropriation that can be observed between specific ancient Near Eastern texts (for example, Amenemope and Proverbs) that speaks so forcefully in favor of the concept of Wisdom genres (Fox 2015, 81). The self-evident compatibility of specific literary works both across and within the individual cultures of the ancient Near East suggests that it should not be abandoned.

Biblical scholars have long used the category of Wisdom expansively to describe a literary genre (or, genres), a general approach to life (a philosophy, so to speak), various discrete technical skills, and more. James Crenshaw (2010, 12) offers an influential definition that embraces this diversity:

> Formally, wisdom consists of proverbial sentence or instruction, debate, intellectual reflection; thematically, wisdom comprises self-evident intuitions about mastering life for human betterment, gropings after life's secrets with regard to innocent suffering, grappling with finitude and quest for truth concealed in the created order and manifested in feminine persona.

For Crenshaw, Wisdom Literature is found where the formal and thematic features he lists are combined.

I am generally persuaded by Michael Fox (2000, 17) that whatever diversity exists around the edges of Wisdom Literature and whatever sub-classifications one might fairly make within, when we are speaking about formal literary expression in the ancient Near East, there are two genres of Wisdom books: didactic wisdom (i.e., "instruction") and critical (or speculative) wisdom. The first genre is the most widespread and the most formally coherent. One could, with relative ease, mix and match sayings between Egyptian texts such as Instruction to Kagemni, Instruction of Ptahhotep, Instruction of Any, Instruction of Amenemope, Instruction of Ankhsheshonq, and Papyrus Insinger, Mesopotamian texts such as Instruction of Šuruppak and Instruction of Šupe-Ameli, and Jewish texts such as Proverbs, Ecclesiastes, Ben Sira, Wisdom of Solomon, 4QInstruction, 4QBeatitudes, Mysteries, and Pirqe Abot. Indeed, as I have already mentioned, we know that some of these texts *did* borrow liberally from one another and that at least some grew anthologically over time. The second Wisdom genre is more difficult to define than the first. Fox (2000, 17) characterizes its contents by their common endeavor to "reflect and comment *on* doctrines and values found in didactic Wisdom literature rather than directly inculcating them." Examples of this genre include the Jewish text Job, the Mesopotamian text Ludlul bēl nēmeqi, and the Egyptian texts Tale of the Eloquent Peasant, Dispute between a Man and His Ba, and Admonitions of Ipuwer.

29.1.2 Apocalypses and Apocalypticism

Apocalypse, as a distinctive genre of literature, begins to appear much later than Wisdom Literature and perhaps for this reason our notions of its development and internal coherence are clearer and more comprehensive. In 1832, Friedrich Lücke compared the New Testament book of Revelation to other, primarily Jewish, literary works that share significant similarities in terms of both form and content in his *Versuch einer vollständigen Einleitung in die Offenbarung des Johannes* [*Towards a Comprehensive Introduction to the Revelation of John*], and the modern scholarly study of *Apokalyptik* was born. Significantly, for several decades following this origin, this corpus of primarily Jewish texts continued to be collected and analyzed as *background* for later canonical Christian literature. In other words, neither the individual literary works nor the genre were typically evaluated on their own merits.

A turning point in the study of apocalypses came when Klaus Koch (1970, 23) put a finer point on the most important methodological considerations for understanding the texts as literature: "If we are to succeed at all in the future in arriving at a binding definition of apocalyptic [*Apokalyptik*], a starting point in form criticism and literary and linguistic history is, in the nature of things, the only one possible." As we shall see, the focus of genre analysis for apocalypses is no longer centered around "arriving at a binding definition of *Apokalyptik*." But Koch's insistence on privileging form criticism has been highly influential in defining which texts, more or less, are most usefully considered together.

John J. Collins took up Koch's methodological imperatives and has produced comparative literary work that has defined the field for his generation. Collins spearheaded a working group within the Society of Biblical Literature that spent several years comparing evidence from ancient Jewish and Christian texts (Collins 1979). They established a working definition of apocalypse that enjoys consensus support among scholars (DiTommaso 2007, 238–247; Reynolds 2011, 31–32). The definition is not, however, an end in itself. It represents a protocol for how to gather relevant evidence. It helps group data sets that are neither too small to be representative nor too large to maintain internal consistency. According to this definition, an apocalypse is:

> A genre of revelatory literature with a narrative framework, in which a revelation is mediated by an otherworldly being to a human recipient, disclosing a transcendent reality which is both temporal, insofar as it envisages eschatological salvation, and spatial, insofar as it involves another, supernatural world.   (Collins 2016, 5)

In addition to this formal definition, Collins and the SBL working group called attention to the fact that apocalypses generally appear in two basic types (or, two basic story plots): otherworldly journeys (in which a visionary is, for example, transported through the realms of heaven) and historical reviews (in which, for example, an inspired visionary recounts important events on earth from its beginnings until its end).

In addition to their typical forms, many apocalypses share a common set of features. For example, the texts are often pseudepigraphic (written in the name or voice of a famous figure from the past). They also regularly describe history in neatly organized and distinctly labeled periods—often within the context of *ex eventu* (after-the-fact) prophecies. Often has it been suggested that symbolic language is a hallmark—even a formal feature—of apocalypses, but studying the poetics of apocalypses shows that while some apocalypses use symbolic language, many use other poetic techniques to accomplish similar ends (Reynolds 2011). Apocalypses feature robust angel/demonologies and many devote considerable attention to eschatological events, especially as concerns the judgment of the wicked and the resurrection (even angelification) of the righteous in the next world. Nevertheless, eschatology is not always a major feature of apocalypses and tends to be foregrounded to a much greater extent in the historical apocalypses. Apocalypses are often characterized by ideas and motifs that are both predestinarian and dualistic. In other words, apocalyptic views of the cosmos, of humans, of otherworldly/divine beings, and of ethics generally reflect a kind of binary thought that "emphasizes clarity at the expense of nuance and ambiguity" (Newsom 2014, 213). Examples are readily available in the contrasts between light and darkness, evil and righteousness, heaven and earth, and so on, found in apocalypses. Apocalypses always claim to disclose hidden knowledge and, in doing so, make special claims as authoritative literature. The genre also places special emphasis on the roles played by scribes and books, distinctively foregrounding scribes' "privileged access to knowledge" (Newsom 2014, 212). Finally, as Seth Sanders (2017, 129–152) has recently emphasized, the apocalypses contain the first known examples of Jewish literary use of "scientific knowledge." Sanders mounts a compelling argument that the form of visionary revelation unique to apocalypses provided Jewish writers in Hellenistic times with a motif that allowed them to incorporate the methods of "exact knowledge" known from Babylonia into Jewish traditions without abrogating the received "systematic knowledge" of the Priestly literature in the Torah.

The typical features of apocalypses highlighted above are important because they form a matrix by which we can compare the thought found in formal (literary) apocalypses to the apocalyptic thought (i.e., apocalypticism) that emerges from other contemporary literary genres. For example, while texts like the War Scroll (1Q33) and the *pesharim* do not share the literary form of apocalypses, they espouse a worldview that contains significant overlap with the worldview found in literary apocalypses. This raises the issue of terminology. Initially, the German noun *Apokalyptik* functioned as a kind of clearinghouse for all things apocalyptic. The English adjective "apocalyptic" was pressed into similar (and uncomfortable) service. Indeed, it was sometimes used as multiple parts of speech. Koch recognized that literary types and historical movements should be distinguished in our terminology and Paul Hanson (1976, 28–34) built on those distinctions, offering three terms for three distinct concepts that became influential: "apocalypse" as a literary type, "apocalypticism" as a social ideology, and "apocalyptic eschatology" as a set of ideas and motifs. These terms have won general approval, though in my own work, I modify the final category to simply "apocalyptic" in recognition of the fact that the most prominent ideas and motifs found in the apocalypses are hardly limited to eschatology. When some of those ideas and motifs turn up in other literary genres, we might say they provide evidence of "apocalypticism," and we might label the text with the adjective "apocalyptic," but not the noun "apocalypse," which we reserve for literary works that fit our formal typology.

29.2 SOME DIFFERENCES, SIMILARITIES, INTERACTIONS, AND EVOLUTIONS

29.2.1 Form

From a purely formal perspective, there is little overlap between the Wisdom genres and apocalypses. The most basic formal feature of apocalypses is that their narrative frameworks depict supernatural revelations that divulge knowledge about the organization of the cosmos or the history of the world from its beginning until its end. In other words, they take the form of (1) depictions of other-worldly journeys or (2) visions uncovering a wide expanse of history. In many cases the revelations are mediated by otherworldly beings. In contrast, no instruction is presented within the context of a divine revelation. To the contrary, many instructions emphasize that the knowledge crucial for life is plainly available to anyone who will carefully observe the world around them: "Does not wisdom call, and does not understanding raise her voice? On the heights, beside the way, at the crossroads she takes her stand; beside the gates in front of the town, at the entrance of the portals she cries out" (Prov 8:1 NRSV). Of course, one finds a more complicated image around the "fuzzy edges" of the genres. The book of Job presents a sort of anti-apocalypse in the theophany in chapters 38–41. Unlike the otherworldly journey scenes in 1 Enoch, in which the protagonist is taken up to heaven and shown the organization of the cosmos, the deity appears on earth and chastises Job repeatedly for his ignorance of the inner-workings of the earth.

It should also be noted that while Ben Sira does not present a revelation, he differs from many instructions to the extent that he considers revealed knowledge to be a source of wisdom (in this case, the Mosaic Torah, not revelatory visions): "All this is the book of the covenant of the Most High God, the law that Moses commanded us as an inheritance for the congregations of Jacob. It overflows, like the Pishon, with wisdom" (24:23–25a). Many are quick to point out that Ben Sira does not consider all revealed knowledge to be legitimate. While apocalypses often present knowledge discovered though the interpretation of dream visions, Ben Sira rejects this knowledge: "Divinations and omens and dreams are unreal" (34:5). It is less frequently emphasized that Ben Sira adds, "unless they are sent by intervention from the Most High" (34:6). In my view, this caveat is a rather classic formulation of the principle that "magic is forbidden, except for *our* magic, which is *legitimate religion*," so familiar from encounters between European explorers/missionaries and the indigenous peoples they considered "primitive" or "savage" on foreign shores (see, e.g., Chidester 1996).

From among the Dead Sea Scrolls we now have several more didactic texts that join Ben Sira in their appeal to revealed knowledge as a source of wisdom. 4QInstruction is discussed in more detail below in 29.3 (Wisdom as Progenitor of Apocalypse). 4QBeatitudes (4Q525) blends form, language, and motifs that are prominent in Proverbs with the admonition that wisdom is found in revealed scripture: "Blessed is the man who has obtained wisdom. He walks in the law of the Most High and prepares his heart for her wisdom" (4Q525 2+3 ii 3–4). The macarism form (see Prov 3:13; 8:32, 34; 14:21; 16:20; 20:7; 28:14; 29:18), the personification of wisdom, and the collocation "walking in the way" (Prov 1:15; 2:20) all point to the influence of Proverbs. But the appeal to the "law of the Most High" appeals to the Mosaic Torah. To be sure, from a formal perspective, texts like Ben Sira, 4QInstruction, and 4QBeatitudes are not presenting revelations. They are easily distinguished from formal apocalypses. But they do illustrate the ways in which the worldviews associated with the Wisdom genre of instruction evolved. And in the case of 4QInstuction and Mysteries (1Q27, 4Q299–301), they demonstrate the influence of apocalypticism within Jewish Wisdom Literature.

Another important formal distinction between instructions and apocalypses is that instructions are typically poetic texts comprised of many short, discrete sayings that could easily be removed from their literary context without loss of meaning. In other words, many if not most individual Wisdom sayings are self-contained, even if they are sometimes combined into more extended arguments. Generalizations are more difficult for critical (speculative) Wisdom texts, but dialogues are a prominent formal feature. In this regard, we find a prominent example of the dialogue form so familiar from speculative Wisdom texts like Job incorporated into an apocalypse that transparently questions the justice of God in the wake of the destruction of Jerusalem in 70 CE: 4 Ezra. Indeed, 4 Ezra 4 is strikingly similar to the Job theophany (38–41) in its dialogic style:

> Then the angel that had been sent to me, whose name was Uriel, answered and said to me, "Your understanding has utterly failed regarding this world, and do you think you can comprehend the way of the Most High?" Then I said, "Yes, my lord." And he replied to me, "I have been sent to show you three ways, and to put before you three problems. If you can solve one of them for me, then I will show you the way you desire to see, and will teach you why the heart is evil."   (4 Ezra 4:1–4)

This brief look at *some* of the formal features of apocalypses and the Wisdom genres has shown that while the forms are typically distinct, they are not entirely mutually exclusive. Form marks important boundaries, but those boundaries are porous.

29.2.2 Dating and Distribution

The genres of Wisdom Literature are much older and much more widely distributed (at least before the modern era) than the apocalypse genre. Well-developed examples of instructions are attested as early as the Old Kingdom (mid- to late third millennium BCE) in Egypt and around the same time in Mesopotamia (e.g., Sumerian versions of Šuruppak). As one might expect, speculative Wisdom appears somewhat later but is attested by the beginning of the second millennium BCE. Judahite Wisdom texts do not appear until much later (naturally, since Judah does not appear on the scene until much later). Precise dates cannot be assigned to the oldest biblical Wisdom texts, but dates from the late Persian or early Hellenistic period are likely for Proverbs, Ecclesiastes, and Job. Portions of Proverbs are certainly older still. The same could be true for Job. Ben Sira can be dated to the early second century BCE and Wisdom of Solomon to the middle of the first century CE. 4QInstruction, 4QBeatitudes, and Mysteries all probably date to the second century BCE and Pirqe Abot was completed no later than the early third century CE.

By contrast, apocalypses are first attested in the Judahite literature of early Hellenistic times. Otherworldly journeys appear first with the Astronomical Book (1 Enoch 72–82) dating to the early third century BCE (possibly slightly earlier) and the Book of Watchers (1 Enoch 1–36) likely also dating to the third century. Historical apocalypses begin to appear in the second century BCE with Daniel 7, 8, 10–12, the Animal Apocalypse (1 Enoch 85–90), and the Apocalypse of Weeks (1 Enoch 93:1–10, 91:11–17). The genre is adopted (and adapted) by Christian writers. The earliest and most prominent example is, of course, the late first-century CE Apocalypse of John (Revelation). The Shepherd of Hermas follows in the second century CE. Jewish writers continued to produce literary apocalypses, and 4 Ezra and 2 Baruch represent prominent examples from the late first century CE, with the Apocalypse of Abraham following not too far behind.

29.2.3 Binary Logic

Binary logic is a widespread feature of both apocalypses and Wisdom texts. In both instances binary logic functions to express clarity at the expense of nuance (see Newsom 2014, 213). The poetic bi-cola typical of Wisdom instructions often present contrasting sides of a coin. For example, Prov 11:18 contrasts the wicked and the righteous: "The wicked earn not real gain, but those who sow righteousness get a true reward." The binary logic characteristic of apocalypses is often referred to as "dualism." The binary juxtapositions found in apocalypses are rarely packaged so succinctly, but there are examples, such as Dan 12:10: "None of the wicked shall understand, but those who are wise shall understand." We may sometimes be able to distinguish degrees within binary divisions, but a substantive difference between the binary logic that is found in the Wisdom genres and the "dualism" at home in apocalypses is elusive. While Israelite culture always featured notions of malevolent and benevolent spirts, the dualism of apocalyptic literature organizes the material to develop etiologies of evil and to construct a supernatural opponent for God (Newsom 2014, 214). I view "apocalyptic dualism" as a trope by which a range of binary thinking is used to express a distinctive concern for order, particularly in demonological and eschatological contexts, oftentimes providing theological resources for navigating real or imagined conflicts (Reynolds 2017, 327–345, esp. 331–334). Most Wisdom texts do not have "demonological and eschatological contexts," though notably a few found in the Qumran library do. In these cases, we might say that the Wisdom genres transition from a more basic binary logic towards "dualism" under the influence of apocalyptic thought.

29.2.4 Order

"Order" is critically important for both the Wisdom genres and for apocalypses. But one must exercise caution when observing this similarity because the *reasons* they emphasize order and the manner in which they articulate order can be quite distinct. In Wisdom Literature, the order of the universe is apparent from creation and takes on both natural and ethical components (Kampen 2011, 7). For brevity's sake, let us draw an example from the most famous articulation of natural order in the biblical Wisdom Literature: "For everything there is a season, and a time for every matter under heaven; a time to be born and a time to die; a time to plant and a time to pluck up what is planted" (Eccl 3:1–2). The ethical order of the universe is no less apparent: "Pride goes before destruction, and a haughty spirit before a fall. It is better to be of a lowly spirit among the poor than to divide the spoil with the proud" (Prov 16:18–19). Didactic Wisdom holds that careful observation of the natural and ethical orders in the world can allow a person to work "with the grain" of the universe, so to speak. Understanding the order of the world leads to prosperity and peace. Speculative Wisdom texts question the validity of the order or the extent to which it can be known. But they ultimately suggest that in the end, the order that can be observed works out reliably.

Order is no less important for apocalypses, but it functions differently. All the main historical schemes in Second Temple apocalypses "share the view that history is not a random succession of events with no discernable goal. Rather, though disaster may follow disaster, the course of history was long ago determined and its time measured out" (Himmelfarb 2010, 44). While texts from the Wisdom genres *sometimes* appeal to revealed knowledge to understand the natural and ethical order of the world, apocalypses *always* reveal cosmic order by means of revelation. For example, the writer of 2 Baruch admonishes, "For the Mighty One has indeed made known to you the sequence of the times that have passed and of those that are yet to be in the world, from the beginning of its creation right up to its end" (56:2). In some cases, this order is derived from an otherworldly journey into the clockwork of the heavens and in others from a dream vision of world history interpreted by an angel. Both Wisdom texts and apocalypses claim that the events of the world are not random—but there is a difference. In the Wisdom genres, earthly events follow an orderly *pattern*. In the apocalypses, events follow an orderly *script* (literally a "script," e.g., written on the heavenly tablets in 1 Enoch 81:1–2). As the genres interact with one another in Hellenistic times, some Wisdom texts (see the discussion of 4QInstruction below, 29.5 The Importance of the Dead Sea Scrolls) begin to transition their notion of patterned order to the apocalyptic concept of scripted order.

This essay cannot provide an account—even in brief—of all the most prominent features that reveal similarities, differences, interactions, and evolutions between Wisdom Literature and apocalyptic literature. A more exhaustive survey would also include discussions of eschatology, otherworldly beings/characters, determinism/predestination, "the wise" (and other figures/groups assigned common or conventional sobriquets), time, universalism, ethics, and more. I hope that this brief overview of key concepts has illustrated some general tendencies while giving appropriate recognition to the porous borders that distinguish Wisdom Literature and apocalyptic literature.

29.3 Wisdom as Progenitor of Apocalypse?

Modern investigations into the relationship between apocalyptic literature and Wisdom Literature are generally traced back to the work of Gerhard von Rad, which has more to do with his stature as a scholar than the amount of attention he devoted to the topic. Scholarly associations between wisdom and apocalypticism go back to at least the middle of the nineteenth century, when Ludwig Noack described apocalypticism as originating out of a kind of "Weisheitslehre" of the Hellenistic period (Goff 2014, 52). Of the more than four hundred pages of the second volume of his *Old Testament Theology*, von Rad allots only about eight to the topic. Von Rad entertains the possibility that either prophecy or Wisdom might have been formative for *Apokalyptik*, but one can sense that he was more concerned with the negative evidence against prophecy than the positive evidence for Wisdom:

> In view of its keen interest in the last things and of the significance it attaches to visions and dreams, it might seem appropriate to understand apocalyptic literature as a child of prophecy. To my mind, however, this is completely out of the question . . . . The decisive factor, as I see it, is the incompatibility between apocalyptic literature's view of history and that of the prophets. The prophetic message is specifically rooted in the saving history, that is to say, it is rooted in definite election traditions.
> (von Rad 1965, 303)

In other words, if, according to the apocalypses, the history of the world has always been neatly scripted and perfectly determined in advance, the contents of nearly all of Israel's prophetic oracles are rubbish.

So, having ruled out prophecy as the seedbed of *Apokalyptik*, von Rad turns to the concept of knowledge as the link between Wisdom and "apocalyptic." Knowledge in biblical Wisdom Literature is derived and formulated independently from, as von Rad calls it, the "saving history" (*Heilsgeschichte*) and comes closer to the ways that apocalypses interact with astronomy, calendars, meteorology, geography, oneiromancy, and so forth. A critical problem with von Rad's thesis is that he downplays the extent to which features of "mantic wisdom" (divination) are themselves related to prophecy (VanderKam 1997, 338). In spite of the fact that von Rad's theory was not widely adopted, his claims resulted in debates that have proven fruitful for the field (DiTommoso 2007, 381).

In the debates that resulted from von Rad's work, Hans-Peter Müller (1969) argued for a connection between *Apokalyptik* and "mantic wisdom," the thought-world and literature of divination (especially as found in Mesopotamia). Indeed, Müller considered the book of Daniel a sort of microcosm of the transition from "mantic wisdom" to apocalypticism in the Jewish imagination. The "sage" of chapters 1–6 transforms into the seer of apocalyptic visions in chapters 7–12 (Müller 1972, 279–280). For Müller, prominent features of apocalyptic books, such as eschatology, determinism, claims to special enlightenment, the use of symbols, and pseudonymity, are best explained against the backdrop of Mesopotamian divination (280–290).

Most specialists accept, to one degree or another, that the thought-world of divination played some role in the development of ancient Jewish apocalypses. But some limitations to Müller's theory must be considered. For example, even though James VanderKam (1984, 62) agrees with Müller's broad thesis and argues that 1 Enoch's protagonist is in some sense derived from the Mesopotamian legendary king Enmeduranki (founder of a guild of diviners known as the *bārûs*), he is quick to caution that, "However similar Mesopotamian divination and Jewish apocalypticism may be in some respects, they certainly have not produced comparable literature." Indeed, not only do the generic forms of omens and apocalypses not cohere, VanderKam also emphasizes that, for example, the *content* of Mesopotamian dream omens is often entirely incongruent with the content of dreams recorded in Jewish apocalypses. The only exception he notes is the suggestion of otherworldly travel in [d]Ziqīqu (cf. 1.69, 1.82) (60).

Others have leveled more pointed critiques at Müller's theory (and to a lesser extent at VanderKam's). Andreas Bedenbender (2002, 190–191) expresses astonishment that one might associate a figure like Daniel with the mantic sages of the ancient Near East since the role that Daniel plays as interpreter of mysterious, symbolic dreams is basically unheard of in the extant literature from Egypt and Mesopotamia, where "kings were seen as the chosen tools of the gods." Bedenbender suggests that while mantic sages consistently based their interpretations of omens on learned skills, Daniel bases his interpretations of dreams on direct revelation, passively receiving correct interpretations directly from the deity. Of course, whether or not the writers/editors of Daniel might have had formal knowledge of the texts and practices associated with Mesopotamian divination says nothing about their intention to style their protagonist in that light. Even if they knew next to nothing about Mesopotamian divination, they could have had reasons to portray Daniel as a dream interpreter.

Sanders (2017, 134) offers a more measured critique, acknowledging that at least some of the evidence from Daniel is equivocal and emphasizing that Daniel is presented as both an insider and an outsider to the Babylonian court. Sanders also points out what is perhaps the more significant issue for comparing apocalyptic literature with Wisdom Literature: "The category of mantic wisdom is not recognized in Assyriology, nor is there evidence that it was a native category of Mesopotamian scholars" (134). In other words, even if there are parallels between concepts, terminology, or practices found in Jewish apocalypses and Near Eastern omen literature, what would that have to do with "wisdom"?

The evidence connecting apocalypses to the arts of divination is significantly removed from the literary forms and attendant worldviews given expression in books like Proverbs, Ecclesiastes, and Ben Sira. It is true that both omen literature and Wisdom instructions depend on careful observations. Omens are based on the careful observation of elements of the natural world (or of physical actions and events set in motion by the diviner). The diviner might read the heavenly writing (astronomy), the condition of a sheep's liver (hepatoscopy), or the movements of oil poured on water (lecanomancy). In contrast, Wisdom instructions are based on the careful observations of human behaviors and consequences, which were not supposed to encode messages from the gods. Both types of observational practices belong to the realm of scribal arts. And both remind us that we still know far too little about the roles of scribes in the ancient Near East.

29.4 CONTRIBUTIONS OF THE SBL WISDOM AND APOCALYPTICISM GROUP

An important development in the study of Wisdom and Apocalypticism was the formation of a formal study group at the Annual Meeting of the Society of Biblical Literature in 1994. In an influential programmatic essay for the group, George Nickelsburg (2005, 18) characterized its work as, in part, to "clarify the nature and interrelationship of the wisdom, prophetic, and eschatological components in Jewish apocalyptic writings." Given that Wisdom texts have a much longer history than apocalypses, it is understandable that the group's first objective was phrased as an investigation of the sources and influences of apocalypses. But, it would have been preferable to articulate the group's objective in accord with the thesis of Nickelsburg's essay, which admits the possibility of observing influences and cultural transmissions in both directions (20).

Nickelsburg is particularly keen to highlight the dangers associated with the terms wisdom and apocalypticism from a methodological perspective. In other words, he fears that in an attempt to understand the relevant texts, we have defined them in a way that constrains them. The concern is reflected in his thesis: "The entities usually defined as sapiential and apocalyptic often cannot be cleanly separated from one another because both are the products of wisdom circles that are becoming increasingly diverse in the Greco-Roman period. Thus, apocalyptic texts contain elements that are at home in wisdom literature, and wisdom texts reflect growing interest in eschatology" (20).

Nickelburg's essay (unintentionally) represents a complimentary approach to one published around the same time by Collins (1993). While Collins reaches similar conclusions

about the difficulty of parsing Wisdom features and apocalyptic features in period literature (arguing convincingly that the supposed intrinsic incompatibility of Wisdom and
apocalypticism used to undergird source-criticism of the gospels, is unfounded), he has
more confidence in the "scholarly abstractions and heuristic categories" that Nickelsburg
(2005, 36) suspects are too often confused with "flesh and blood realities."

29.5 THE IMPORTANCE OF THE DEAD SEA SCROLLS

The Qumran library has contributed its share of confusion to the study of Wisdom and
apocalypticism, though primarily because such a large corpus of texts came to light
simultaneously and only slowly did we appreciate the finer distinctions among many
of them (see, e.g., García Martínez 1998, 163). But the scrolls have also provided us with
invaluable data for understanding how the worldviews associated with Wisdom and
apocalypticism could interact in Hellenistic times. Indeed, while Ben-Sira's appeal to
revealed knowledge and Wisdom of Solomon's eschatology might have appeared anomalous in the corpus of Wisdom Literature known before the discovery of the scrolls, we
can now see those works within a much wider context.

Questions of genre are particularly thorny when dealing with Qumran scrolls because
many exist is such a poor state of preservation. I will not attempt to adjudicate here the
arguments about which Qumran texts belong to the Wisdom genres (see Matthew Goff's
Chapter 37: "The Pursuit of Wisdom at Qumran" in this volume), but will instead focus on
an example that engenders little disagreement: 4QInstruction (1Q26, 4Q415–418, 4Q423).

Goff (2014, 56) highlights why the text is at home among Wisdom instructions: "The
composition is explicitly pedagogical, written by a teacher to a student, who is called a
mebin ('understanding one'), and its literary style is characterized by didactic admonitions." The following lines could be seamlessly added to virtually any instruction known
from the ancient Near East:

> Do not sate yourself with food when there is no clothing, and do not drink wine
> when there is no food. Do not seek after delicacies when you lack bread. Do not
> esteem yourself highly for your poverty when you are (anyhow?) a pauper, lest you
> bring into contempt your (own way) of life.   (4Q416 2ii 18b–21a)

But 4QInstruction also presents its readers with some perhaps unexpected content in its
emphasis on the revelation of eschatological, dualistic knowledge. The following section
could not be so easily sewn into any Wisdom instruction in the ancient Near East:

> [And by day and by night meditate upon the mystery that is to] come, and study (it)
> continually. And then you will know the truth and iniquity, wisdom [and foolish]ness
> you will [recognize], every ac[t] in all their ways, together with their punishments

in all ages everlasting. And the punishment of eternity. Then you will discern between the [goo]d and the [evil according to their] deeds. For the God of knowledge is the foundation of truth and by the mystery that is to come he has laid out its foundation.   (4Q417 ii 6–9)

Goff (2003, 40–41) summarizes the situation that confronts the modern reader: "Biblical wisdom promotes the acquisition of knowledge through perception of the natural order. The addressee of 4QInstruction, however, learns about the world through the contemplation of revealed knowledge. In terms of pre-Christian Jewish literature, the epistemology of 4QInstruction has its closest parallels in the apocalypses." Armin Lange persuasively argues that this innovation can be explained as a natural outgrowth or evolution of Wisdom thought in Israel. Lange (2010, 456) sees the appeal to revealed knowledge in 4QInstruction as a response to the perennial "crises" that affected carefully constructed systems of thought "[w]hen new experiences of reality did not agree with the order of the universe construed by the sages." Job and Ecclesiastes both serve as examples of negotiating those crises in earlier times but they are ultimately minority opinions in Lange's view. A more mainstream solution is a turn towards the Torah: wisdom as the ethical and natural order of the universe revealed to Israel on Mount Sinai. This solution was not perfect because it would have been self-evident that Torah-adherence did not always result in prosperity. And so a further synthesis of thought, borne witness by, for example, 4QInstruction, solves the ongoing crisis by eschatologizing Torah wisdom: "Now the course of history as well as the cosmological and eschatological conflict between good and evil become part of the sapiential order of the universe" (Lange 2010, 458–459). This rhetorical shift was effective because the eschatologizing of Torah wisdom places it outside the bounds of disconfirmation—beyond the reach of another "crisis."

Rather than seeing 4QInstruction as a distinct break from "classical" Judahite Wisdom known from Proverbs, Lange see it as a creative approach to preserving the sapiential worldview expressed in the book of Proverbs at a moment when cultural experiences and expectations have shifted. One should remember, though, that while this type of evolution seems to have been effective, it was hardly inevitable. One can find examples of the evolution of traditional Wisdom instruction in both Egypt and Mesopotamia without a comparable epistemological development.

29.6 CONCLUSION

Jonathan Z. Smith (1975, 131) observed over forty years ago, "One of the more vexing problems in contemporary Biblical scholarship is that of determining the relationship between Wisdom and Apocalypticism." This observation is no less accurate today. But we are now asking new and different questions because we have made progress along the way. For example, the field no longer works with the assumption that because apocalypses are comparatively late they are fundamentally derivative. As pertains to ancient Judaism, two questions are currently of primary importance: (1) how shall we understand and describe "Wisdom," and (2) how did Jewish apocalypticism and its attendant literary genre shape the evolution of Wisdom thought and Wisdom Literature in late Hellenistic times? The relationship between Wisdom and apocalypticism is also significant for understanding nascent Christianity and its literature, though scholars are currently more likely to find synthesis than antithesis at the heart of the relationship. In my view, a fruitful, if indirect, avenue for understanding the relationship between Wisdom and apocalyptic literature is to devote additional attention to understanding scribalism in the ancient Near East and in Second Temple Judaism. Lange's thesis about the eschatologization of Torah wisdom is, in this regard, a very suggestive direction. While we nowadays reject Smith's specific conclusions about the history of Wisdom and apocalyptic literature ("Apocalypticism is Wisdom lacking a royal court and patron"), his observation that both are essentially scribal phenomena, the product of learned rather than popular expressions, remains salient more than four decades later (Smith 1975, 155–156).

WORKS CITED

Bedenbender, Andreas. 2002. "Jewish Apocalypticism: A Child of Mantic Wisdom?" *Henoch* 24:189–196.

Chidester, David. 1996. *Savage Systems: Colonialism and Comparative Religion in Southern Africa.* Charlottesville, VA: University of Virginia Press.

Collins, John J., ed. 1979. *Apocalypse: The Morphology of a Genre.* Semeia 14. Missoula, MT: Scholars Press.

Collins, John J. 1993. "Wisdom, Apocalypticism, and Generic Compatibility." Pages 165–185 in *In Search of Wisdom: Essays in Memory of John G. Gammie.* Edited by Leo G. Perdue. Philadelphia, PA: Westminster John Knox.

Collins, John J. 2014. *The Oxford Handbook of Apocalyptic Literature.* Oxford: Oxford University Press.

Collins, John J. 2016. *The Apocalyptic Imagination: An Introduction to Jewish Apocalyptic Literature.* 3rd ed. Grand Rapids, MI: Eerdmans.

Crenshaw, James L. 2010. *Old Testament Wisdom: An Introduction.* 3rd ed. Louisville, KY: Westminster John Knox.

Derrida, Jacques, and Avital Ronell. 1980. "The Law of Genre." *Critical Theory* 7:55–81.

DiTomasso, Lorenzo. 2007. "Apocalypses and Apocalypticism in Antiquity (Part I)." *CurBR* 5:235–286.

Fox, Michael V. 2000. *Proverbs 1–9.* AB 18A. New York, NY: Doubleday.

Fox, Michael V. 2015. "Three Theses on Wisdom." Pages 69–86 in *Was There a Wisdom Tradition? New Prospects in Israelite Wisdom Studies.* Edited by Mark R. Sneed. AIL 23. Atlanta, GA: SBL.

Freidenreich, David M. 2004. "Comparisons Compared: A Methodological Survey of Comparisons of Religion from 'A Magic Dwells' to *A Magic Still Dwells.*" *MTSR* 16:80–101.

García Martínez, Florentino. 1998. "Apocalypticism in the Dead Sea Scrolls." Pages 162–192 in *The Encyclopedia of Apocalypticism.* Edited by John J. Collins. New York, NY: Continuum.

Goff, Matthew. 2003. *The Worldly and Heavenly Wisdom of 4QInstruction*. STDJ 50. Leiden: Brill.

Goff, Matthew. 2014. "Wisdom and Apocalypticism." Pages 52–68 in Collins 2014.

Hanson, Paul D. 1976. "Apocalypticism." Pages 28–34 in *The Interpreter's Dictionary of the Bible Supplement Volume*. Edited by Keith Crim. Nashville, TN: Abingdon.

Himmelfarb, Martha. 2010. *The Apocalypse: A Brief History*. Blackwell Brief Histories of Religion Series. Chichester: Wiley-Blackwell.

Kampen, John. 2011. *Wisdom Literature*. Grand Rapids, MI: Eerdmans.

Koch, Klaus. 1970. *Ratlos vor der Apokalyptik: Eine Streitschrift über ein vernachlässigtes Gebiet der Bibelwissenschaft und die schädlichen Auswirkungen auf Theologie und Philosophie*. Gütersloh: Mohn.

Kynes, Will. 2016. "The Nineteenth-Century Beginnings of 'Wisdom Literature,' and Its Twenty-First-Century End?" Pages 83–108 in *Perspectives on Israelite Wisdom: Proceedings of the Oxford Old Testament Seminar*. Edited by John Jarick. LHBOTS 618. London: Bloomsbury T&T Clark.

Lange, Armin. 2010. "Wisdom Literature and Thought in the Dead Sea Scrolls." Pages 455–478 in *The Oxford Handbook of the Dead Sea Scrolls*. Edited by T.H. Lim and J.J. Collins. Oxford: Oxford University Press.

Macaskill, Grant. 2007. *Revealed Wisdom and Inaugurated Eschatology in Ancient Judaism and Early Christianity*. Leiden: Brill.

Müller, Hans-Peter. 1969. "Magisch-mantische Weisheit und die Gestalt Daniels." *UF* 1:79–94.

Müller, Hans-Peter. 1972. "Mantische Weisheit und Apokalyptik." Pages 268–293 in *Congress Volume, Uppsala 1971*. VTSup 22. Leiden: Brill.

Newsom, Carol A. 2014. "The Rhetoric of Jewish Apocalyptic Literature." Pages 201–217 in Collins 2014.

Nickelsburg, George W.E. 2005. "Wisdom and Apocalypticism in Early Judaism: Some Points for Discussion." Pages 17–37 in Wright and Wills 2005.

Pavel, Thomas. 2003. "Literary Genres as Norms and Good Habits." *New Literary History* 34:201–210.

Rad, Gerhard von. 1965. *Old Testament Theology*. Vol. 2. New York, NY: Harper & Row.

Reynolds, Bennie H., III. 2011. *Between Symbolism and Realism: The Use of Symbolic and Non-Symbolic Language in Ancient Jewish Apocalypses 333–63 BCE*. JAJSup 8. Göttingen: Vandenhoeck & Ruprecht.

Reynolds, Bennie H., III. 2017. "Demonology and Eschatology in the Oppositional Language of the Johannine Epistles and Jewish Apocalyptic Texts." Pages 327–345 in *The Jewish Apocalyptic Tradition and the Shaping of New Testament Thought*. Edited by Benjamin E. Reynolds and Loren T. Stuckenbruck. Minneapolis, MN: Fortress.

Rosmarin, Adena. 1985. *The Power of Genre*. Minneapolis, MN: University of Minnesota Press.

Sanders, Seth L. 2017. *From Adapa to Enoch: Scribal Culture and Religious Vision in Judea and Babylon*. TSAJ 167. Tübingen: Mohr Siebeck.

Smith, Jonathan Z. 1975. "Wisdom and Apocalyptic." Pages 131–156 in *Religious Syncretism in Antiquity: Essays in Conversation with Geo Widengren*. Edited by Birger A. Pearson. Missoula, MT: Scholars Press.

Smith, Jonathan Z. 2004. *Relating Religion: Essays in the Study of Religion*. Chicago, IL: University of Chicago Press.

Sneed, Mark R., ed. 2015. *Was There a Wisdom Tradition? New Prospects in Israelite Wisdom Studies*. AIL 23. Atlanta, GA: SBL.

Toy, Crawford Howell. 1899. *A Critical and Exegetical Commentary on the Book of Proverbs.* ICC. Edinburgh: T&T Clark.

VanderKam, James C. 1997. "Mantic Wisdom in the Dead Sea Scrolls." *DSD* 4:336–353.

VanderKam, James C. 1984. *Enoch and the Growth of an Apocalyptic Tradition.* CBQMS 16. Washington, D.C.: Catholic Biblical Association of America.

Wright, Benjamin G., III, and Lawrence M. Wills, eds. 2005. *Conflicted Boundaries in Wisdom and Apocalypticism.* Atlanta, GA: SBL.

PART VI

TEXTS

CHAPTER 30

··

PROVERBS

··

SAMUEL E. BALENTINE

"IT is thus written, because it is thus in life." Ralph Waldo Emerson's (Ferguson and Slater 1980, 64) description of folkloric wisdom provides an apt introduction to the book of Proverbs. Nuggets of wisdom, rooted in stories and experiences long since forgotten, fossilize into truths that are passed from generation to generation. They can be taught and learned, as the instructions in Proverbs 1–9 make clear, and when utilized as strategies for dealing with typical and recurring situations in life, such as those suggested in Proverbs 10–31, they ensure both moral integrity and material prosperity. Biblical wisdom is by no means restricted to Proverbs, but it presumes an authoritative status there that is essentially inscrutable. Pupils are expected to obey their teachers, not argue with them: "My son, accept my words and store up my commands" (2:1; unless otherwise noted, biblical translations are from the CEB). They are disciplined to a pedagogy of monologue, not dialogue.

On close inspection, however, Emerson's description is apt but insufficient for understanding the wisdom of Proverbs. The motivation for obedience to proverbial truth, according to ancient Israel's sages, is not primarily historical precedent, but the transcendent authority of God, who is the inspiration for the search for knowledge and the source and substance of the knowledge towards which wisdom aspires. "It is thus written, because it is thus in life," to which the sages would add, it is thus in life, because God "laid the foundations of the earth with wisdom" (Prov 3:9). The most important lesson to be learned is itself therefore reducible to a single certainty that informs all of the wisdom sayings in this book: "The beginning of wisdom is the fear of the Lord; the knowledge of the holy one is understanding" (9:10; cf. 1:7).

This chapter will address five major interpretive issues in Proverbs: (1) composition history, (2) literary forms, (3) socio-political context, (4) moral reasoning and ethical conduct, and (5) thematic coherence.

30.1 COMPOSITION AND COMPILATION

A proverb originates in daily life, not as a statement of a universal truth, but instead as a solitary discernment about an individual's specific experience. Its vocabulary, form, and pertinence derive from a social context in which a majority of people share a common set of values. Inside such a community, the discernment conveys a relative and recognizable truth that requires no explanation. Outside a defined community, however, the saying may have little or no relevance. We need only consider a saying like Prov 11:22—"Like a gold ring in a pig's nose is a beautiful woman who lacks discretion"—to understand that its meaning is embedded in imagery that is culture-specific.

Individual, autonomous maxims can be preserved orally for limited periods of time, but they do not attain the currency of proverbial wisdom that is generally applicable in diverse cultures across time until they become part of a literary compilation. The earliest known collections of proverbs come from Mesopotamia (The Instruction of Šuruppak, ca. 2600–2550 BCE; Alster 1974; Veldhuis 2000) and Egypt (The Instruction of Prince Hardjedef, ca. 2450–2300 BCE; Lichtheim 2006). Both sources are part of the ancient Near Eastern trajectory of Wisdom Literature antecedent to Proverbs. In the words of the nineteenth-century English statesman Lord John Russell, "a proverb is the wit of one, and the wisdom of many" (cited in Mieder 1993, 13).

When individual proverbs are gathered into a collection, becoming the wisdom of many, they are detached from their original setting and therefore from the context in which their meaning and function had particular resonance. As part of a compilation, they are now conveyed as propositional truths that presuppose silent consent from all instructed by them. In the words of an anonymous nineteenth-century editorialist, "[A proverb] commends itself, mainly by sparing us the trouble of reflection" (cited in Mieder 1993, 25). The wisdom they promulgate assumes that a shared reasoning process between teacher and student will result in conformity to a moral code that advances agreed-upon social and political objectives. Who determines the nature of these objectives? What authority legitimizes them and monitors their effectiveness? Because a compilation is a literary production, its author(s) will come from the educated elite of the society, not from those whose survival depends on managing the vicissitudes of daily life; its objectives will be to reinforce and sustain status quo values, not to call them into question. We may suppose that a similar process of collecting maxims and purposing them for the maintenance of a normative moral code was also at work in the composition and compilation of the book of Proverbs.

The final form of the book is as follows, with all but one of the major text units introduced by a title or superscription:

1:1–9:18	"The proverbs of Solomon King David's son, from Israel" (1:1);
10:1–22:16	"The proverbs of Solomon" (10:1);
22:17–24:22	"The words of the wise" (22:17);
24:23–34	"These are also the sayings of the wise" (24:23);

25:1–29:27	"These are also proverbs of Solomon, copied by the men of Hezekiah, king of Israel" (25:1);
30:1–33	"The words of Agur, Jakeh's son" (30:1);
31:1–9	"The words of King Lemuel, which his mother taught him" (31:1);
31:10–31	An untitled poem, structured as an acrostic (alphabetic) hymn, praising the "competent wife."

The different introductions to Proverbs indicate that this book, like its ancient Near Eastern antecedents, is a compilation of texts that have been stitched together over time. That parts are attributed to Solomon (1:1; 10:1; 25:1) is more a recognition of his legendary embodiment of "the spirit of wisdom" exemplified by Moses and Joshua than a claim that he authored these texts (Deut 34:9; cf. 1 Kgs 2:6; 3:3–28; 5:9–14 [ET 4:29–34]; 10:1–25; Weeks 2007, 39–41).[1] The long legacy of Solomon's wisdom is evident both within this book, in its inclusion of the "copy work" attributed to Hezekiah's officials (25:1), who would have been active some two centuries after Solomon's death, and in biblical (Eccl 1:1) and deuterocanonical books that extend the memory of Solomon's wisdom into the first century CE (Sir 47:12–17; Wisdom 7–9) and well beyond (on Francis Bacon's appeal to the "glory of [Solomon's] inquisition of truth" in seventeenth-century natural philosophy, see Harrison 1998, 137–138; Gaukroger 2001, 73). A part of this legacy connects Solomon's wisdom with that of other sages in the Eastern Mediterranean world (1 Kgs 5:15–32 [ET 5:1–18]), which suggests that a collection called "the proverbs of Solomon" will likely draw upon an international Wisdom discourse. The book of Proverbs confirms this. The section introduced as the "words of the wise" (22:17–24:22) shows a creative dependence on the second-millennium Egyptian text The Instruction of Amenemope (see, e.g., Washington 1994; Clifford 1999, 199–216; Fox 2009, 757). Both "the words of Agur, Jakeh's son" (30:1–33) and "the words of King Lemuel" (31:1–9) are attributed to a foreigner from Massa (מַשָּׂא), a region in Arabia. We may deduce from this variegated collection that in ancient Israel, as in every place where *Homo sapiens* ("wise persons") lived, the pursuit of wisdom was instinctive.

To read Proverbs front to back, following the sequence of chapters preserved in its final form, is to recognize that this book has a complex compositional history spanning centuries. Although there are no confirmable historical markers, scholars typically locate the Solomonic collections (10:1–22:16; 25:1–29:27) in the latter part of the First Temple period (eighth–seventh century BCE). This earliest form was then enlarged by the addition of other collections, with the framing pieces (chs. 1–9 and 31) likely added in the early Persian period (538–333 BCE). The Septuagint (LXX) sequences parts of the collection differently (22:17–24:22 → 30:1–14 → 24:23–34 → 30:15–33 → 31:1–9 → 25:1–29:27 → 31:10–31), an indication that the final form of the book remained in flux during the Hellenistic period (323–31 BCE).

This collection of "proverbs," "words," and "sayings," wisdom added to wisdom over the span of at least four centuries, represents ancient Israel's participation in an

---

[1] For Solomon as the *addressee* rather than the author, see Miles 2004.

international intellectual economy. In the Western world, we tend to think *philosophia* (φιλοσοφία, "love of wisdom") begins with Plato and Aristotle in ancient Greece. As the entry point into the Hebrew Bible's Wisdom Literature, Proverbs is a reminder that the quest to understand the nature of the world and the purpose of life transcends geographical and cultural boundaries. To cite Emerson once again, "Proverbs are the poetry, the Solomon, the Socrates of the people" (Gilman and Orth 1982, 160). Proverbs 18:15a describes this universal drive straightforwardly: "The mind of an intelligent person goes about acquiring knowledge" (author's translation).

30.2 LITERARY FORMS

The book of Proverbs comprises a variety of literary forms, as will be discussed below, but fundamental to all of them is poetic language (Bartholomew and O'Dowd 2011, 47–52; Stewart 2016, 29–69). In contrast with prose, which narrates a story by describing the major characters, placing their speeches and actions in a logical sequence, and moving a discernible plot line from beginning to end, poetry privileges imagery and imagination. It vivifies ideas and concepts by employing metaphors, similes, comparisons and contrasts, rhetorical questions, figurative language, and other forms of artful diction. Its objective is rhetorical persuasion; it succeeds by seduction rather than coercion.

Inasmuch as proverbs seek to educate and enlighten, it is instructive to reflect on their pedagogy (see further below, 30.4 Moral Reasoning and Ethical Conduct). The sages do not legislate obedience or prophesy the future, administer the prescriptive rites and rituals of the cult, or command mastery of historical details. Instead, they invite their students to examine life for what it is and for what it is not, to reflect on the known, the unknown, and the unknowable, all for the purpose of learning how to disambiguate life's puzzles, or at least how to live in accord with its irresolvable mysteries. In so doing, the sages do not speak with one voice, but from multiple, diverse, and frequently contradictory perspectives. Proverbs represents but one of the voices in the constellation of ancient Israel's Wisdom Literature (along with Job, Ecclesiastes, Sirach, and Wisdom of Solomon), and even its canonized form, as discussed above, is a compilation of perspectives in search of an elusive coherence (see below, 30.5 Thematic Coherence). The variety of its literary forms is case in point.

The most distinctive literary form in Wisdom Literature is the "proverb" (משל). The word appears in the title of the first two collections (1:1; 10:1), which illustrate the various forms proverbs take. The first collection consists of ten speeches (1:8–19; 2:1–22; 3:1–12; 3:21–35; 4:1–9; 4:10–19; 4:20–27; 5:1–23; 6:20–35; 7:1–27) couched as instructions, admonitions, warnings, and rebukes from a teacher, variously characterized, whose personal authority should persuade the hearer to heed the counsel offered. Prov 1:8–19 exemplifies parental advice to a child: "My son, don't let sinners entice you, child, . . . don't go on the path with them . . . because their feet run to evil" (vv. 10, 15, 16). If children accept this counsel, they will follow the "good course" of "righteousness and justice as well as equity"

(2:9); they will "find wisdom" and "gain understanding" (3:13); and their reward will be a long life of "well-being" (3:2), a "glorious crown" (4:9) that symbolizes the nobility of a virtuous life. Alternatively, a child may be tempted to heed the siren call of seduction, personified as the "mysterious woman" whose "slick words" (2:16) "drip honey" (5:3) but ensnare the one who partakes in "disgrace" that cannot be erased (6:33). Imbedded within these ten speeches are the words of another teacher, personified now as Woman Wisdom, who counters the "mysterious woman," first by mocking those who refuse Wisdom's invitation (1:20–33), then by delighting in those who are wise enough to "keep to [her] ways" (8:32), enter into her house, and feast on the food and wine at her bounteous table (9:5).

The 375 proverbial sayings in the second collection (10:1–22:16) exemplify a more succinct literary form, typically one-line maxims, divided into parallel halves, that advocate inviolable truths by means of three primary rhetorical strategies. The dominant form of the sayings in Proverbs 10–15 utilizes an *antithetical parallelism* to draw a sharp contrast between two different ways of living, for example:

wise/foolish: A wise child makes a father glad, but a foolish child brings sorrow
                to his mother. (10:1)
diligent/lazy: A hard worker is in charge, while a lazy one will be sentenced to
                hard labor. (12:24)

The sayings in Proverbs 16–22 are more often conveyed by a *synonymous parallelism* in which a truth is stated in the first half of the line, then essentially repeated with similar words in the second half, for example: "A false witness won't go unpunished, and a liar will not escape" (19:5). A variation of this form, often labeled *progressive* or *synthetic parallelism*, states a truth in the first half of the line, then extends or intensifies its meaning in the second half, for example: "Gray hair is a crown of glory; it is found on the path of righteousness" (16:31). Integral to each of these types of one-line sayings is the assumption that an unambiguous truth is plain to see. It does not need to be argued and compliance need not be commanded. Simple assertion, buttressed by the wisdom of collective experience, conveys its own imperative.

Scattered within and beyond these two collections are additional literary forms.

1. *"Better-than sayings"* teach that one thing is preferable to another (e.g., 12:9: "Better to be held in low regard and have a servant, / than to be conceited and lack food").

2. *Conditional sentences* use an "if-then" construction to accent the connection between deed and consequence (e.g., 25:16: "If you have honey, eat just the right amount; / otherwise, you'll get full and vomit it up").

3. *Rhetorical questions* invite agreement with assumed answers (e.g., 26:12: "Do you see people who consider themselves wise? / There is more hope for a fool than them").

4. *Numerical sayings* catalogue social and natural phenomena, thus widening the perspective for understanding (e.g., 6:16–19: "There are six things that the Lord hates / seven things detestable to him . . .").

5. *Metaphors* and *similes* offer poetic analogies that engage and revitalize the imagination (e.g., 25:11: "Words spoken at the right time are like gold apples in a silver setting").

A previous generation of scholarship made much of the difference between the longer speeches that dominate in Proverbs 1–9, which are framed by a distinctive theological linkage between "the beginning of wisdom" and the "fear of the Lord" (1:7; 9:10), and the shorter sentence forms that dominate in the other collections of the book, which convey primarily empirical and practical observations (Schwáb 2013, 30–61). The sentence forms were widely regarded as exemplars of older, "secular" wisdom, which was rooted in Near Eastern antecedent traditions. The speeches, on the other hand, were thought to be ancient Israel's later theologized adaptation of international Wisdom discourse. This distinction has largely collapsed for multiple reasons, two of which merit brief discussion.

First, ancient Near Eastern texts routinely connected wisdom with the gods who created the world and endowed it with principles of order and justice. Sumerian texts from the third millennium BCE report that Enki/Ea, the god of wisdom who organizes the earth, sent Adapa, the first of seven antediluvian "super sages" (*apkallu*), to teach the arts of civilization (*me*) to human beings. In the postdiluvian age, Ziusudra (known in Mesopotamian texts as Atrahasis, "extra wise," and Utnapishtam) resumes Adapa's role as the divine sage who has access to the wisdom that keeps the world operating in accord with the god's design (Izreẻl 2001; Espak 2015). In Egyptian Wisdom texts and iconography, the goddess of truth and justice (Maat) sets the moral order of the cosmos to which humans must conform, if they are to live successfully (Hornung 1982; Assmann 1990; Teeter 1997). In short, there was no "secular" understanding of life in the ancient world. Every aspect of one's existence from birth to death to afterlife was inextricably tied to divine decision. The notion that "the beginning of wisdom is the fear of the Lord" (9:10) may be a distinctively Israelite conception (see below, 30.5.2 "The Fear of the Lord is the Beginning of Knowledge"), but it draws upon a religious worldview that has deep roots in contiguous cultures.

Secondly, neither in ancient Near Eastern Wisdom texts nor in Proverbs is there a strong distinction between "practical" wisdom and "religious" wisdom. According to Sumerian texts, the one hundred-plus arts of civilization (*me*) created and transmitted by the gods to human beings included a wide assortment of practical skills in areas such as music, metalworking, weaving, and building (Kramer 1963, 116). Adapa, for example, demonstrates the technique of baking and fishing to the people of Eridu (Dalley 2000, 184). Alongside these practical skills, however, the gods also dispensed wisdom concerning the cultic prescriptions for proper worship. One version of the Sumerian tale, The Death of Gilgamesh, reports that Gilgamesh received from Ziusudra the rites of Sumer, such as hand and mouth washing, which he brought back to Uruk in order to restart civilization after the flood. Learning how to reverence the gods, no less than learning how to bake, fish, and build, was one of the arts essential for a prosperous life.

In Proverbs, the "fear of the Lord" is not only the beginning of wisdom in an abstract theological sense, it is also the source of very pragmatic benefits, such as longevity (10:27), "confidence" (14:26), and material prosperity (15:16; 22:4). Moreover, "YHWH sayings" are not limited to Proverbs 1–9 but occur throughout the book (e.g., 16:1, 2, 9; 17:3; 20:24, 27; 21:31; 28:5, 25; 29:25, 26; Dell 2006, 90–124), a repeating reminder that wise and moral behavior—"righteousness, justice, and integrity" (1:9; 2:9)—is necessarily generated, informed, corrected, and sustained by devotion to the God who tuned the world to these requisite virtues.

30.3 Socio-Political Context

The discrete collections and the various literary forms are indicative of the different social and political contexts in which proverbial material functioned in ancient Israel. Two primary contexts may be singled out.

30.3.1 Family Setting

The speeches in Proverbs 1–9 reflect a *family setting* in which a parent endeavors to shape a child's intellectual and moral development. The sages likely adapted these speeches from Egyptian instructional texts in which an elderly vizier passes on practical wisdom and personal advice to the son who will succeed him (e.g., Weeks 2007, 4–32). The thirty-seven maxims in the Instruction of Ptahhotep (ca. 2014–1650 BCE), for example, exhort the son to practice virtues such as humility, truthfulness, and generosity (for the text, see Lichtheim 2006, 1:61–76).

In Proverbs, this domestic setting for wisdom reflects the dynamics of Israel's pre-state period, when parents were the locus of authority for a child's education and character formation. Persistent appeals, such as, "My son, pay attention to my wisdom. Bend your ear to what I know" (5:1), impart longstanding communal values. The template for these values is 1:2–7, which serves as an introduction to both the first collection and to the book as a whole:

> [2] For learning about wisdom (חכמה) and instruction (מוסר), for understanding words of insight(בינה), [3]for gaining instruction (מוסר) in wise dealing, righteousness (צדק), justice (משפט), and equity (מישרים); [4]to teach shrewdness (ערמה) to the simple, knowledge (דעת) and prudence (מזמה) to the young— [5] let the wise also hear and gain in learning (לקח) and the discerning acquire skill (תחבלות), [6]to understand a proverb and a figure, the words of the wise and their riddles.[7] The fear of the Lord is the beginning of knowledge (דעת); fools despise wisdom (חכמה) and instruction (מוסר). (NRSV)

To become productive and responsible members of society, all persons—the "simple," the "young," even the "wise" (1:4–5)—should acquire and develop the following (for further discussion, see Fox 2000, 28–43):

1. "Wisdom" (חכמה, v. 2), "knowledge" (דעת, vv. 4, 7), and "understanding" (בינה, v. 2). In the broadest sense, "knowledge" is information—anything a person acquires through thinking or experience. "Understanding" is discernment, the result of a cognitive process of analyzing and interpreting information to clarify meaning lying beneath its surface. "Wisdom" is a combination of knowledge elevated to expertise and understanding enacted in moral and ethical behavior. To acquire wisdom is to be able to weigh all options, decide which is morally compelling, and to act accordingly. The link between knowledge, understanding, wisdom, *and* moral/ethical conduct is critical. As Fox (2015, 76 n. 10) puts it, "חכמה has no moral valence outside wisdom literature. Wisdom literature alone claims that there is no wisdom that is not in accord with ethical and religious principles" (see below on "righteousness," "justice," and "equity").

2. "Instruction" (מוסר, vv. 2, 3, 7) and "learning" (לקח, v. 5). מוסר is the "instruction," "discipline," or "correction" the teacher gives to the student. It is authoritative, because it comes from a superior to an inferior, and compliance is obligatory, because the learner (the child) is morally bound to submit to the teacher (the parent). "Learning" has to do more with how wisdom is communicated than with how it is acquired. The word usually connotes erudition or eloquence. Those who obtain wisdom aspire to communicate truth persuasively.

3. "Righteousness" (צדק, v. 3), "justice" (משפט, v. 3), and "equity" (מישרים, v. 3). All three terms relate to ethical behavior, although with slightly different nuances. "Righteousness" is the quality ascribed to one whose life in community with others complies with a normative code of ethics. The term closely aligns with "equity," which conveys the sense of being "straight" or "upright," and by extension, being "honest" and "truthful." "Justice" is a broad term that applies to every aspect of the moral vision that requires ethical behavior in all areas of life, individual and communal, economic and political. Where justice is present, it must be secured and sustained. Where it is lacking, it must be restored and reinforced.

4. "Shrewdness" (ערמה, v. 4) and "prudence" (מזמה, v. 4). ערמה refers to cunning or guile, which for the wise means having the maturity to see ultimate objectives clearly and craft the right strategy to accomplish them. The Hebrew root from which "prudence" derives (זמם) means "plan" or "devise." In the context of teaching the young, it is the exhortation to beginners to think for themselves, to be confident about their capacity to seek and obtain wisdom wherever it may be found (cf. Prov 8:12).

5. "Skill" (תחבלות, v. 5). To acquire "skills" in the context of Wisdom thought means to have the capacity to steer a successful course through whatever obstacles may lie ahead. The LXX translates the line as, "The discerning will acquire *direction*

($\kappa\upsilon\beta\acute{\epsilon}\rho\nu\eta\sigma\iota\nu$)," and understands the term to be associated with the Hebrew words "rope" (of a ship); (חבל), "sailor" (חבל), and "mast" or "rigging" (חבל). The nautical imagery suggests "navigational skills," or in common parlance, "learning the ropes" (McKane 1970, 266; Fox 2000, 37).

Wisdom comprised of the virtues above and learned in a familial context should be enacted in all areas of life, including, for example, neighborliness (3:27–31), marital fidelity (5:15–20), money lending (6:1–3), and diligent labor (6:6–11). The taproot of the learning and insight required to navigate each of these areas successfully is the wisdom that comes from devotion to God (1:7; 2:6; 9:10). Thus, the parent's instruction, like that of Woman Wisdom, the parental character who personifies the very wisdom of God (1:20–33; 8:1–36; 9:1–17), makes a common appeal: "Don't reject the instruction of the Lord, my son; don't despise his correction. The Lord loves those he corrects, just like a father" (3:11–12).

30.3.2 Royal or Court Setting

The Solomonic collection (10:1–22:16), "the words" (22:17–24:22) and "sayings" (24:23–34) of the wise, and the other proverbs "copied by the men of Hezekiah, king of Judah" (25:1–29:27) reflect a *royal* or *court setting* for instruction in wisdom (Ansberry 2010). Envisioned is the historical period of the monarchy, when the center of power and authority in Israel shifted from the family to the state, the official responsibility for education from the parent to an elite group of scribes and sages who served—and prospered—at the king's pleasure. Particularly indicative of this setting is a collection of twenty-four "royal proverbs" (e.g., 14:28; 16:10; 22:11; 29:2; Fox 2009, 500) that express appreciation for the king's good will, confidence in his justice, and the rationale for obedience to his rule (cf. the negative views of foreign rulers in later Wisdom writers, e.g., Eccl 8:2–4 and Sir 36:1–12). The national and international affairs of state required that those who served the king be educated in a wide range of matters, including, table etiquette (23:1–8); the administration of impartial justice for the accused (e.g., 15:27; 17:15; 18:5); economic justice, especially the obligation to the poor and disenfranchised (e.g., 14:3; 17:5; 19:17); and the cult (e.g., 15:8; 21:27; 28:9).

The king himself should wear wisdom like a crown (25:2), thus modeling the wisdom required in his court (16:10–15). He is expected to invite instruction and to be receptive to critique (28:3, 15–16; 29:4, 12, 14), but his wisdom, authority, and wrath, the near equal of God's, brooks no dispute, hence the warning: "My child, fear the Lord and the king, and do not disobey either of them" (24:21, NRSV; cf. 14:35; 16:14; 19:12; 20:2). According to the Lemuel collection (31:1–9), the king is subject to the admonitions of his mother, who warns him that excessive consumption of alcohol will compromise his ability to speak clearly on behalf of the poor and needy who appeal for justice.

By and large, court wisdom promotes a politically and theologically conservative perspective on the world, reflecting the sages' institutional status. Through antithetical proverbs, they envision a world where choices are clear and their consequences unambiguous. One is *either* righteous *or* wicked, wise *or* foolish, and the rewards for choosing either path of life are predictably etched into the cosmic order by God, whom the king faithfully serves. There is little room and virtually no encouragement in court wisdom for questions or dissent. Edifying speech is prized (e.g., 10:11, 21; 15:4; 16:21, 23, 24), for "the lips of the wise know what is acceptable" (10:32), but best of all, especially in the face of moral complexities, is silence (10:19; 11:12b; 12:23; 13:3; 17:28), rooted in the abiding truth that the one who trusts God's inscrutable wisdom is safe (14:26; 16:3, 20; 18:10; 29:25), whatever the limits of human understanding (16:1, 9; 19:21; 21:30–31). There is sparing acknowledgment that the system of rewards and punishments sometimes seems upside-down (30:21–23; see Van Leeuwen 1992; Hatton 2008) and that what is incomprehensible may drive one more to lament than praise (30:1–4), but such thoughts are placed on the lips of foreigners, perhaps a subtle suggestion that their wisdom may have merit but is not the norm. On this point, however, we remember that the sages who speak in Proverbs are not the only voices sitting at wisdom's table. Job (represented as another foreigner, Job 1:1) will advance the lament and the protest that is muted in Proverbs; Qoheleth will press this lament to its outermost boundaries, where skepticism demands a hearing. To quote a Sumerian proverb, "That which bowed down its neck (in submission) puts its breast forward (in defiance)" (Alster 1997, 7 [1.7]).

30.4 MORAL REASONING AND ETHICAL CONDUCT

The moral vision of Proverbs and the ethics it generated in ancient Israel has received significant attention during the last two decades. Some have found resonance with Socratic epistemology and its ethics of virtue (Fox 2007a; Fox 2007b; Fox 2009, 934–945, 963–976; cf. Frydrych 2002, 53–82, 127–168), others with Aristotelian principles of intellectual virtue and moral character (Ansberry 2010). Some have appropriated Proverbs for an examination of character ethics and the concept of the self as a moral agent (Brown 1996; Brown 2014), others have argued that the concept of the moral self in Proverbs is a window into the moral culture of the sages who produced the book (Stewart 2016). Such approaches continue to be generative and will perhaps seed a comprehensive and integrated assessment of epistemology and ethics in Wisdom Literature.[2] As an introduction to the current state of the discussion, we may (1) identify salient aspects of moral reasoning in Proverbs and (2) consider their significance from two perspectives: the teacher and the student.

---

[2] See the chapter by William Brown on virtue and by Annette Schellenberg on epistemology in this volume.

30.4.1 Salient Aspects of Moral Reasoning

Moral *reasoning* is a *thinking* process. One thinks about what to do or say in a particular situation, considers the available options and the probable consequences of choosing one over another, and then enacts the decision. The process presupposes the thinker's autonomy; a person is free to consider a situation from an unlimited range of perspectives, free to choose for themselves what is wise or foolish; in *moral* terms, what is good or bad. Within the Hebrew Bible's corpus of Wisdom texts, we may think of Job discussing, debating, and disagreeing with the decisions his friends urge on him, or Qoheleth, who repeatedly engages in a debate with himself about what is or is not "pointless" (הבל; e.g., "I said to myself," 1:16; 2:2, 15, 17; 3:18). In Proverbs, there is no active debate or discussion. Only the teacher has a voice; the student never speaks (with the possible exception of Agur in Prov 30:1–4) and is never explicitly presented as thinking for himself. The student is expected to agree with his teacher's thinking.

Moral reasoning in Proverbs is *a hierarchical process* that vests authority in parents, who expect obedience from their children, in masters, who control the fortunes of their slaves, in kings, who rule over their citizens, and above all in God, whose sovereign wisdom seeds and sustains a moral pedagogy that is embedded in the natural order of the world (Fox 2007b, 675–679). In this pedagogical system, teachers determine the syllabus, select the topics students are required to study, frame the challenges and the choices these topics present, and offer instruction meant to persuade students to agree with a thinking and reasoning process that has predetermined what is wise or foolish. In advance of any decision the student may make, the teachers have decided what will conform with established truth and will be rewarded accordingly. The student's role in this system is to learn by rote to think as the teacher thinks.

The instruction in Proverbs 5 concerning the "mysterious woman" (cf. 2:16–22; 6:20–35; 7:1–27) exemplifies how a teacher guides the student's thinking process toward an acceptable outcome. The student must choose between loyalty to two women, one "strange" or "mysterious" (5:3, זרה), the other the "wife of your youth" (5:18, אשת נעורך). Both women are enticing, one offering the sweetness of honey and the smoothness of oil (5:3), the other the satiation of flowing spring waters (5:15). What are the moral criteria for the choice the student must make? How is he to know whether honey is better than water, whether the sweetness of taste is better than the slaking of thirst? At one level, the options seem morally neutral; one is neither more nor less right or good than the other. The student could learn by trial and error; he could test for truth by experimenting with both women. Or, as the teacher urges, the student could accept, without empirical proof, the a priori moral valuations of his learned superior: the sweetness of the strange woman is in truth "bitter as gall" (5:3), "her steps lead to the grave" (5:5), "her paths wander" (5:6), and those who follow her are not only "stupid," they also identify themselves in God's eyes as "wicked" and "evil" (5:21–23). The teacher assesses the other woman, the student's wife, to be undeniably lovely, graceful, and sexually satisfying (5:18–19); to choose her is not only to make the right decision, it is also to join oneself with those blessed by God (5:18). The teacher's opening summons to the student—"Pay attention to my wisdom" (5:1a)—signals at the outset that the process of moral reasoning in this matter has already concluded; all that remains is for the student to obey one accompanying imperative: "Bend your ear to what I know" (5:1b).

The hierarchical reasoning process privileges *obedience over autonomy, conformity to axiomatic truth over intellectual exploration*, and a *static concept of knowledge over innovative thinking* (cf. Fox 2007b, 676; Stewart 2016, 197–200). No doubt such emphases reflect the socio-political context of the sages who composed and compiled Proverbs (see above, 30.3 Socio-Political Context). As members of the intellectual elite who enjoyed the privileges of royal patronage, they had little incentive to challenge regnant modes of enquiry, traditional patterns of conduct, or institutionalized moral paradigms for right and wrong. Their primary objective was not moral revolution but moral harmony (on "coherence theory" as an epistemological model in Proverbs, see Fox 2007b, 675–684; Fox 2009, 967–976).

Beyond their general conservatism, however, the sages understood the acquisition of knowledge to be the *embodiment of a moral virtue*—the "fear of the Lord" (see the discussion below, 30.5.2 "The Fear of the Lord is the Beginning of Knowledge")—that transcends and transforms all conventional human constructs of reality. The teacher's lesson in Proverbs 2 outlines the steps of the learning process:

> Turn your ear toward wisdom (חכמה),
>   and stretch your mind toward understanding (תבונה).   (v. 2)
>
> Then you will understand the fear of the Lord (יראת יהוה),
>   and discover the knowledge (דעת) of God.   (v. 5)
>
> The Lord gives wisdom (חכמה);
>   from his mouth come knowledge and understanding (דעת ותבונה).   (v. 6)
>
> Then you will understand righteousness and justice (צדק ומשפט),
>   as well as integrity (מישרים), every good course.   (v. 9)
>
> Wisdom (חכמה) enters your mind,
>   and knowledge (דעת) will fill you with delight.   (v. 10)

Moral reasoning is a thinking process that makes knowledge a virtue and virtue an intellectual piety that finds "favor and approval in the eyes of God and humanity" (3:4).

30.4.2 Perspectives on Moral Reasoning from the Teacher and the Student

Although Proverbs envisions moral reasoning as a "cooperative effort of child, parents, and God" (Fox 2000, 132), we may suspect that the cooperation was not necessarily reciprocal. Teachers (and God) expect cooperation from their students, but the hierarchical prototype for learning minimizes any comparable expectations students might have of their teachers. *From the vantage point of the teachers*, control of the learning process, especially the indisputable certainty they claim for their evaluations of right and wrong, provides the stability the society and its institutions (both political and religious) needs in order to flourish (Prov 16:12; 20:28; 25:5; 29:12, 14). Questions left unanswered or answers that evoke endless debate create unnecessary confusion, which in turn may paralyze the body politic. Moral ambiguity invites ethical indecision. In Socratic terms, if one cannot *know* what is good, then one cannot *do* what is good.

From the vantage point of students, cooperation is exemplified by submission and quietude. To acquire the wisdom they seek, they must subordinate their curiosity to the teacher's authoritative conclusions; they must conform their thinking to the teacher's moral norms. In sum, they must learn to fit in with the status quo as determined and sustained by an imposed social hierarchy. Reversals of the power structure that assigns to everyone a predetermined place in the moral order are unacceptable:

> At three things the earth trembles,
>   at four it can't bear up:
> at a servant when he becomes king
>   and fools when they are full of food;
> at a detested woman when she gets married
>   and a female servant when she replaces her mistress.   (30:21–23)

Deviations from what proverbial wisdom declares right and good, for example, a slave becoming a king or a servant succeeding her mistress, are evidence of unchecked hubris. Were students to claim to know more than their teachers, they would obstruct God's purposes and place themselves among the morally loathsome (תועבה; CEB: "detestable") who deserve divine punishment (16:4–5; cf., e.g., 3:32; 6:16–19; 11:20; 12:22).

From the student's perspective, we may wonder whether this paradigm for moral reasoning leaves any room for autonomous thinking. If teachers are the privileged stewards of the wisdom of the ages, if they manage a behind-the-curtain decision-making process that conveys settled truth, then what moral agency do students have? How do students "grow in wisdom" (1:5) if their education, framed in the hierarchical imagery of a parent-child relationship, constrains their maturation by never treating them as more than juveniles (cf. Stewart 2016, 199–200)? What capacity for independent thinking do students have if they can only agree with pre-thought ideas, if they can only enact ethical decisions based on a reasoning process in which they have not actively participated?

Proverbs does not address moral reasoning from the student's perspective. Its vantage point is that of the sages who convey wisdom with uninhibited authority that invites neither interruption nor interrogation. Since theirs is the only voice that counts in this reasoning process, they expect their students to accept their truth. From the sages' perspective, the *homo sapiens*, the "wise person," is the *homo docilis*, the "docile" or "submissive" or perhaps in a more charitable understanding, the "teachable person" (Frydrych 2002, 128). We belated readers of Proverbs, also addressed by the rhetorical logic of the book as students seeking wisdom, may flinch at the expectation that we will circumscribe our intellectual journey by submitting to truth that transcends our reasoning. Proverbs seems to anticipate this potential resistance, exemplified in its own textual world by Job and Ecclesiastes, with its reminder that human agency and divine sovereignty are not mutually exclusive.

> To people belong the plans of the heart [לב, "mind"],
>> but the answer belongs to God.
> People plan their path [לב אדם יחשב דרכו; literally, "a person's mind plans his course"]
>> but the Lord secures his course   (16:1, 9; cf. 19:21; 28:26)

30.5 Thematic Coherence

Because of its anthological character, scholars generally concede that Proverbs lacks any overarching thematic coherence. Superscriptions identify the beginning and ending of different sections, as noted previously; thematic emphases frame certain sections (e.g., "the fear of the Lord" in chs. 1–9) and cluster together in others (e.g., righteousness and wickedness in 10:1–15:33; kingship in 16:10–15, 28:1–29:27; Heim 2001). Repetitions, catchwords, and other rhetorical devices create sophisticated literary sub-units within the collection (e.g., chs. 25–27). For all these structural and thematic markers, however, the book itself seems intentionally to thwart the search for a rationale that explains its final arrangement.

The absence of a unifying structural design should not, however, be understood as a deficiency. Proverbs' "sweet disorder" (Fox 2009, 481) introduces an important characteristic of intellectual discourse in the sapiential tradition: the quest for wisdom was a process of thinking about thinking that resisted closure, for knowledge was itself always a moving target, a journey more than a destination. In its final form, Proverbs illustrates this in various ways.

30.5.1 The Intellectualization of Piety vs. the Piety of Intellectualization

The *intellectualization of piety* (Proverbs 10–31) is combined with, not separated from, the *piety of intellectualism* (Proverbs 1–9). Wisdom in Proverbs develops in stages. The short maxims in Proverbs 10–29 constitute the earliest stage, when the pursuit of wisdom was primarily an intellectual exercise in thinking about pragmatic matters. It was not thinking divorced from trust in God's overarching providence and provision, but it did not assume that piety could substitute for prudence. To be safe from danger, one should avoid conflict (14:16); to be prosperous, one should protect things of value (21:20) and secure one's inheritance for posterity (17:2); to gain the respect and favor of others, one should be honest and forthright in all relationships (15:21, 24); to be persuasive in disagreements, one should develop verbal skills (10:13; 16:21). In sum, the wisdom in Proverbs 10–31 affirms the importance of the human capacity to think through the issues of life and resolve them satisfactorily without direct divine intervention, even if only in a limited way (on "intellectualized virtue" in Proverbs, see Fox 2009, 943–945).

The ten lessons in Proverbs 1–9 represent a second stage in the development of Israelite wisdom, which foregrounds piety rather than human intellect, dedication to God rather than acquisition of knowledge, and moral virtue rather than material prosperity. Proverbs 3:5–10 provides an apt illustration: to be safe from danger one should certainly avoid conflict, but more important is the security that comes from trusting God (3:5); to attain knowledge by human reasoning enables good choices when navigating the obstacles in life, but the better part of wisdom is the humility to recognize that it is God who clears the way forward (3:6); to have confidence in one's ability to effect change is admirable, but reverence for God mitigates self-glorification (3:7–8); to secure wealth for future generations is always smart, but the wise will recognize abundance as a summons to honor God (3:9–10). Devotion to God does not deny the role of human agency in the intellectual economy of life, but it does render it subordinate to a higher power.

The sages who added Proverbs 1–9 to the Solomonic collection provided the first commentary on the intellectualization of piety in ancient Israel. From their perspective, a proper understanding of wisdom required the "fear of the Lord" (more on this below, 30.5.2 "The Fear of the Lord is the Beginning of Knowledge"). In so doing, these sages were modeling the very intellectual process they were critiquing. In Aristotelian terms, they were engaged in the most excellent, god-like activity imaginable, "thinking on thinking" (ἡ νόησις νοήσεως; *Metaph.* 12.9.34 in Barnes 1984, 1698). Even as they advocated piety as a pre-condition for obtaining wisdom, they were engaging in an intellectual exercise that subjected observations about the way the world works to their own rigorous review and analysis.

30.5.2 "The Fear of the Lord is the Beginning of Knowledge"

"The fear of the Lord is the beginning of knowledge" (Prov 1:7, NRSV; cf. Prov 9:10; 15:33; Job 28:28; Ps 111:10; Sir 1:14, 16, 18, 20, 27; 19:20; 21:11). The sages who provided the Prologue in 1:2–7 understood it to be the key for interpreting not only chapters 1–9 but also the entire book. The concluding verse of this Prologue could be interpreted as the elusive thematic thread that ties the discrete sections into a unified whole: "Wisdom begins with the fear of the Lord." The three iterations of this maxim in Proverbs (1:7; 9:10; 15:33) affirm essentially the same truth: the starting point for obtaining wisdom is an awareness of God's presence that evokes what Plato and Aristotle called the pathos of "wonder" (τὸ θαυμάζειν).[3] "It is owing to their wonder," Aristotle writes, "that men . . . first began to philosophize [i.e. to become lovers of wisdom]; they wondered

---

[3] For the connection between wisdom and wonder, see Brown 2014.

originally at the obvious difficulties, then advanced little by little and stated difficulties about greater matters, e.g., about the phenomena of the moon and those of the sun and the stars, and about the genesis of the universe" (*Metaph.* 1.2.982b in Barnes 1984, 1554; cf. *Theaet.* 155d). Wonder is the catalyst for curiosity. For the Greeks, the objective was to acquire knowledge of "original causes" (*Metaph.* 1.3.24), a quest that at its farthest extension probed for the "genesis" of the cosmos. For the sages in ancient Israel, the explanation for the world's genesis was available in a simple assertion, "In the beginning, God created the heavens and the earth" (Gen 1:1). Their curiosity evoked another question, "What is good for humans to do in the limited number of days they live under the heavens?" (Eccl 2:3). The question is explicitly posed only by Qoheleth. Providing an answer to the question is the objective of the sages who compiled the book of Proverbs: fear God, seek wisdom, and walk in the path of righteousness and justice (Prov 1:3; Fox 2007a, 76–77).

Is a sense of God's presence available to everyone equally, as the sages suggest in the prologue (1:4–5), then repeatedly throughout the ten lectures (e.g., 1:20–22; 8:1–5; 9:4), or are some excluded by choice or design (e.g., 1:24–31; 8:35–36; 9:13–18)? Proverbs 1–9 entertains the questions and answers by affirming a tautology: "the fear of the Lord is the beginning of knowledge" (1:7, NRSV); "the beginning of wisdom is the fear of the Lord" (9:10). What Proverbs 1–9 regards as axiomatic—wisdom is available to all who seek wisdom, all who seek wisdom will find wisdom—the Solomonic collection (Proverbs 10–29) presents as a truth bifurcated by reality: the wise are not foolish, the foolish are not wise; the righteous are not wicked, the wicked are not righteous; the good is not evil, the evil is not good; the gracious are not greedy, the greedy are not gracious (see the antithetical proverbs in chs. 10–15).

Given the debate engendered by these two stages in the growth of wisdom, perhaps it should not surprise that a later scribe appends a fatigued lament:

> I'm tired, God,
>   I'm tired, God, and I'm exhausted.
> Actually, I'm too stupid to be human,
>   a man without understanding.
> I haven't learned wisdom,
>   nor do I have knowledge of the holy one.   (Prov 30:1–3)

And yet still another appendix (31:10–31) counters despair by reaffirming the motto of the book. The "woman of strength" (אשת חיל, v. 10; NRSV) embodies the virtues Proverbs promotes from beginning to end. Like Woman Wisdom in Proverbs 9, the woman of strength has built a home that offers joy and prosperity to everyone at her table—her husband, her children, and her servants (31:11–15; cf. 9:1–6 and 3:13–18). With the same hands that provide for her household, she "reaches out to the needy . . . [and] the poor" (31:19–20; cf. 3:16). She speaks kindness and wisdom (חכמה, 31:26). Such a woman, Proverbs concludes, and all who like her "fear the Lord," "is to be praised" (31:30).

30.5.3 Proverbs' God

God never speaks in Proverbs, a characteristic that distinguishes this book and Wisdom Literature in general from the Pentateuch and the prophets (the divine speeches in Job 38–41 are a notable exception; see further, Boström 1990; Frydrych 2002, 83–95, 170–176; Waltke 2004, 67–75; Lucas 2015, 243–250). In the Pentateuchal narrative, God is a major character who intervenes directly by speech and action in the unfolding drama. In prophetic literature, prophets typically introduce their speeches with the phrase, "Thus says the Lord," a messenger formula that signals they have come from God's presence and deliver God's words, not their own. When compared with these parts of the Hebrew Bible, Proverbs can justifiably be called humanistic literature; its primary focus is not on divine revelation but on human acquisition of knowledge and its ethical imperatives for everyday life. Even so, at likely the latest editorial stage of the book, sages spliced into the ten lectures a series of interludes (1:20–33; 3:13–20; 8:1–31; 9:1–18; Fox 2000, 326–330) that personify wisdom as a woman whose words summon people into the proximate presence of God. Woman Wisdom speaks wisdom that transcends human wisdom (cf. Sir 24:1–33; Wisdom 6–19). In doing so, she both identifies herself with God and distinguishes herself from God.

Wisdom's speech in Proverbs 8 plays a central role in these reflections. In the first half of her speech (vv. 1–21), Wisdom describes herself as a teacher in search of students. She travels throughout cities and towns, palaces and temples (vv. 1–3), inviting all who will listen—the dull and the bright; the privileged and the disadvantaged—to heed her lessons about life, for what she has to offer is more valuable than gold (vv. 4–11). She identifies herself, "I am Wisdom" (חכמה, v. 12a), and proclaims her own virtues, "prudence" (ערמה), "knowledge" (דעת), and "discretion" (מזמה, v. 12), each of which the Prologue introduces as essential for learning wisdom, as discussed above (30.3.1 Family Setting). Because she exemplifies the "fear of the Lord" (v. 12a), she possesses the counsel and competence that enables kings and rulers to govern with righteousness (צדק, vv. 14–16). She loves those who love her; their material prosperity is a reciprocal endowment of her riches and honor (vv. 17–21).

The most commented on part of Wisdom's speech, vv. 22–31, offers a striking correspondence between Wisdom's genesis and the creation of the cosmos as described in Genesis 1. This part of the speech is also the most complex and ambiguous. Wisdom is primordial, pre-existent, and preeminent, thus on some level coeval with God (vv. 22–29). Born before creation itself, Wisdom asserts that she was growing up "alongside" God (v. 30), perhaps even a full participant with God in the creative act ("as a master of crafts," v. 30). However, Wisdom also affirms that her genealogy begins with God. The first of God's creative acts, she comes from God and thus is subordinate to God. Adding to the ambiguity surrounding Wisdom's relationship to God, the phrase, "The Lord *created* (קנני) me" (v. 22) can also be translated "The Lord *acquired* me," which would indicate that even for God wisdom was not an inherent or essential attribute. Like the learner sitting at the teacher's feet, God acquires wisdom through some supernatural cognitive process. Fox (2000, 294) puts it this way:

Though the author may not realize it, the underlying assumption is that prior to creation God was in stasis, his power only potential. He brought his power to actuality by acquiring wisdom. He acquired wisdom by creating it, drawing it from within, from the infinite potential for being that is inherent in Godhead.

These difficulties call attention to the generative complexity of the mosaic that is Proverbs. Thinking about thinking was and remains an ongoing process of discernment about truths that are graspable but elusive.

In the midst of such ambiguity, however, another aspect of Woman Wisdom's speech is critical. In vv. 30–31, Wisdom speaks of mutual delight and laughter in her relationship to God. "I was daily *his* delight,"[4] Wisdom says, "playing (משחקת) before him all the time," indicating that God enjoys playing with Wisdom like a parent delights in rolling around on the floor with a laughing child (cf. Jer 31:20; Isa 66:12). As much as God has fun playing with Wisdom, Wisdom enjoys playing with God and with humans (v. 31). Wisdom's speech ends with an accent on happiness: "Happy (אשרי) are those who keep to my ways.... Happy (אשרי) are those who listen to me" (8:32b, 34a; cf. 3:12–13).

For all its riddles and enigmas, its complex integration of wisdom and piety, its thick explication of moral reasoning, in short, its incoherent coherence, Proverbs invites its readers and learners to frolic in the pursuit of wisdom. To paraphrase Aristotle (*Metaph*.12.9.34), even the gods enjoy thinking about thinking.

WORKS CITED

Alster, Brendt. 1974. *The Instructions of Shuruppak*. CSA 10. Copenhagen: Akademisk Forlag.

Alster, Brendt. 1997. *Proverbs of Ancient Sumer: The World's Earliest Proverbs Collections*. 2 vols. Bethesda, MD: DL Press.

Ansberry, Christopher B. 2010. "What Does Jerusalem Have to Do with Athens? The Moral Vision of the Book of Proverbs and Aristotle's *Nicomachean Ethics*." HS 51:157–173.

Assmann, Jan. 1990. *Ma'at Gerechtigheit und Unsterblichkeit im alten Ägypten*. Munich: Beck.

Barnes, Jonathan, ed. 1984. *The Complete Works of Aristotle*. The Revised Oxford Translation, vol. 2. Princeton, NJ: Princeton University Press.

Bartholomew, Craig G., and Ryan P. O'Dowd. 2011. *Old Testament Wisdom Literature: A Theological Introduction*. Downers Grove, IL: InterVarsity Press.

Boström, Lennart. 1990. *The God of the Sages: The Portrayal of God in the Book of Proverbs*. ConBOT 29. Stockholm: Almqvist & Wiksell International.

Brown, William P. 1996. *Character in Crisis: A Fresh Approach to the Wisdom Literature of the Old Testament*. Grand Rapids, MI: Eerdmans.

Brown, William P. 2014. *Wisdom's Wonder: Character, Creation, and Crisis in the Bible's Wisdom Literature*. Grand Rapids, MI: Eerdmans.

Clifford, Richard J. 1999. *Proverbs. A Commentary*. OTL. Louisville, KY: Westminster John Knox.

---

[4] The pronoun "his" is not present in the Hebrew, but cf. LXX, "It is I [Wisdom] who was the one in whom he [God] took delight."

Dalley, Stephanie. 2000. *Myths from Mesopotamia: Creation, The Flood, Gilgamesh and Others.* Rev. ed. Oxford: Oxford University Press.

Dell, Katharine J. 2006. *The Book of Proverbs in Social and Theological Context.* Cambridge: Cambridge University Press.

Espak, Peter. 2015. *The God Enki in Sumerian Royal Ideology and Mythology.* Wiesbaden: Harrassowitz.

Ferguson, Alfred R., and J. Slater, eds. 1980. *The Collected Works of Ralph Waldo Emerson. Vol II: Essays: First Series.* Cambridge, MA: Harvard University Press.

Fox, Michael V. 2000. *Proverbs 1–9: A New Translation with Introduction and Commentary.* AB 18A. New Haven, CT: Yale University Press.

Fox, Michael V. 2007a. "Ethics and Wisdom in the Book of Proverbs." *HS* 48:75–88.

Fox, Michael V. 2007b. "The Epistemology of the Book of Proverbs." *JBL* 126:669–684.

Fox, Michael V. 2009. *Proverbs 10–31. A New Translation with Introduction and Commentary.* AB 18B. New Haven, CT: Yale University Press.

Fox, Michael V. 2015. "Three Theses on Wisdom." Pages 69–86 in *Was There a Wisdom Tradition? New Prospects in Israelite Wisdom Studies.* Edited by Mark R. Sneed. AIL 23. Atlanta, GA: SBL.

Frydrych, Tomáš. 2002. *Living under the Sun: Examination of Proverbs and Qoheleth.* VTSup 90. Leiden: Brill.

Gaukroger, Stephen. 2001. *Francis Bacon and the Transformation of Early-Modern Philosophy.* Cambridge: Cambridge University Press.

Gilman, William H., and Ralph H. Orth, eds. 1982. *The Journals and Miscellaneous Notebooks of Ralph Waldo Emerson,* vol. 15. Cambridge, MA: Harvard University Press.

Harrison, Peter. 1998. *The Bible, Protestantism and the Rise of Natural Science.* Cambridge: Cambridge University Press.

Hatton, Peter T.H. 2008. *Contradiction in the Book of Proverbs: The Deep Waters of Counsel.* Aldershot: Ashgate.

Heim, Knut M. 2001. *Like Grapes of Gold Set in Silver: An Interpretation of Proverbial Clusters in Proverbs 10:1–22:16.* BZAW 273. Berlin: de Gruyter.

Hornung, Erik. 1982. *Conceptions of God in Ancient Egypt.* Ithaca, NY: Cornell University Press.

Izre'el, Shlomo. 2001. *Adapa and the South Wind: Language Has the Power of Life and Death.* Winona Lake, IN: Eisenbrauns.

Kramer, Samuel N. 1963. *The Sumerians: Their History, Culture, and Character.* Chicago, IL: University of Chicago Press.

Lichtheim, Miriam. 2006. *Ancient Egyptian Literature: The Old and Middle Kingdoms.* Berkeley, CA: University of California Press.

Lucas, Ernest C. 2015. *Proverbs.* THOTC. Grand Rapids, MI: Eerdmans.

McKane, William. 1970. *Proverbs: A New Approach.* OTL. London: SCM.

Mieder, Wolfgang. 1993. *Proverbs Are Never Out of Season: Popular Wisdom in the Middle Age.* Oxford: Oxford University Press.

Miles, J.E. 2004. *Wise King—Royal Fool: Semiotics, Satire and Proverbs 1–9.* JSOTSup 399. London: T&T Clark International.

Schwáb, Zoltán S. 2013. *Toward an Interpretation of the Book of Proverbs: Selfishness and Secularity Reconsidered.* JTISup 7. Winona Lake, IN: Eisenbrauns.

Stewart, Anne W. 2016. *Poetic Ethics in Proverbs: Wisdom Literature and the Shaping of the Moral Self.* Cambridge: Cambridge University Press.

Teeter, Emily. 1997. *The Presentation of Maat: Ritual and Legitimacy in Ancient Egypt.* SAOC 57. Chicago, IL: Oriental Institute of the University of Chicago.

Van Leeuwen, Raymond C. 1992. "Wealth and Poverty: System and Contradiction in Proverbs." *HS* 33:25–36.

Veldhuis, Niek. 2000. "Sumerian Proverbs in Their Curricular Context." *JAOS* 120:383–399.

Waltke, Bruce K. 2004. *The Book of Proverbs: Chapters 1–15.* NICOT. Grand Rapids, MI: Eerdmans.

Washington, Harold C. 1994. *Wealth and Poverty in the Instruction of Amenemope and the Hebrew Proverbs.* SBLDS 142. Atlanta, GA: Scholars Press.

Weeks, Stuart. 2007. *Instruction and Imagery in Proverbs 1–9.* Oxford: Oxford University Press.

CHAPTER 31

··

ECCLESIASTES

··

TOVA L. FORTI

31.1 ECCLESIASTES AND THE BIBLICAL WISDOM TRADITION

THE biblical Wisdom tradition, as primarily exemplified in Proverbs, Job, and Ecclesiastes, is distinct from other biblical genres. Only a few sayings in Ecclesiastes include ritual terms ("offering" in 4:17 and 9:2; "vows" in 5:1–6).[1] Ecclesiastes also betrays little historical sensitivity or context, with no definite allusions to historical events or political policies. Nonetheless, scholars have sought to define the book's socio-historical *Sitz im Leben*, imbuing those passages that present archetypes of kings (4:13–16) and vague allusions to social conditions (e.g., 5:12–16 [ET 5:13–17]; 6:1–6) with historical-contextual significance, often related to the national catastrophe of the fall of Jerusalem, the traumatic memory of exile, the post-exilic period under the Achaemenid government, or the impact of the Ptolemaic state mercantilism on the upper class in Judea.[2] However, the absence of any explicit mention of historical circumstances or reference to formative national-historical events makes it difficult to contextualize Ecclesiastes within any Israelite historiographical setting.

Within the biblical Wisdom tradition itself, Qoheleth's style is easily distinguishable from that of Proverbs, with its didactic aim to maintain social harmony and stability. Qoheleth, in contrast, teaches to cope with the uncertainties of life and acknowledge undesirable conduct, including antisocial and immoral behavior, as an unavoidable phenomenon in human experience. Since Qoheleth denies the existence of any "advantage" of one person over another—rich over poor, good over evil, or just over unjust—when

[1] Translations of biblical verses are from the JPS Tanakh (1985), with my emendations.
[2] See, e.g., Whybray 1989, 8–14; Seow 1997, 21–23; Krüger 2004, 19–21. On "collective/cultural/social memory," see Barbour 2012.

confronted with humanity's ignorance as to the causes of death and suffering, the narrator assumes the role of a skeptical, disillusioned sage (Holm-Nielsen 1975–1976, 41). Ecclesiastes is also formally distinctive insofar as it communicates primarily personal observations and reflections rather than transmitting traditional teaching as does Proverbs (Collins 1997, 14).

As the book of Ecclesiastes is mainly concerned with reflections and meditations on existential problems and the meaning of life, it is categorized as part of the literary genre of Speculative Wisdom. In this vein, the book issues contemplative-skeptical pronouncements with regard to universal existential questions and dogmatic issues such as just retribution and divine punishment. Notably, however, Qoheleth upends orthodox ideas of divine justice, presenting a version of the message *carpe diem* that urges the reader to enjoy life in the face of the inevitability of death.

The word חכמה itself refers to practical knowledge, skill, cleverness, guile, insight, general intelligence, and wisdom (Crenshaw 1988, 72). Qoheleth uses the word to refer to both the faculty of reason and the knowledge which can be gained thereby (Fox 1989, 79). In Ecclesiastes, the concept of wisdom denotes the ability to articulate a sense of order in the world that is informed by a principle of retributive justice.

Although the author of Ecclesiastes has a clear idea of what is conveyed by the words "wise" and "wisdom," the book displays ambivalence towards wisdom itself. Qoheleth's style, outlook, and conclusions regarding the meaning of life radically challenge the conventional thought of his time. Qoheleth maintains an ongoing open and uninhibited inner dialogue, raising theological and philosophical questions of human existence and governance by moral laws. The book is dominated by a polarity in which the tools of wisdom are employed both to praise and to cast doubt on the worth of wisdom itself, as Qoheleth uses the "weapons of the ḥokmâ against the ḥokmâ" (Loader 1979, 131). Thus, for example, Qoheleth states: "I found that wisdom is superior to folly as light is superior to darkness; a wise man has eyes in his head, whereas a fool walks in darkness" (2:13–14a), but also: "for as wisdom grows vexation grows; to increase learning is to increase heartache" (1:18). The author frequently presents the advantages of wisdom in the form of a proverb, as in 7:12a: "For to be in the shelter of wisdom is to be also in the shelter of money" (cf. 7:19). But he then goes on to deny them when positing his view of human experience: "The fate of the fool is also destined for me; to what advantage, then, have I been wise?" (2:15). Qoheleth thus simultaneously both presupposes and attacks the conventional wisdom as represented by Proverbs.

Qoheleth employs an essentially empirical methodology; he seeks both to derive knowledge from experience and to validate ideas experientially (Fox 1989, 80). He does not deny the utility of wisdom; he merely recognizes its weaknesses and failings: "For sometimes a person whose fortune was made with wisdom, knowledge and skill, must hand it on to be the portion of somebody who did not toil for it. That too is futile, and a great evil" (2:21). The wisdom Qoheleth seeks to impart to its audience is thus realistically aware of its own limitations in view of the certainty of death and the uncertainties of life (Krüger 2004, 5).

31.2 QOHELETH: NAME AND AUTHORSHIP

The word קהלת, "Qoheleth," is not a name or moniker, but rather denotes a role. It may indicate a professional title or office, comparable to other feminine participles with a similar function, such as ספרת, "scribe" (Ezra 2:55; Neh 7:57) and פכרת הצביים, "gazelle-tender" (Ezra 2:57; Neh 7:59). The Hebrew meaning of the term derives from the root קהל, denoting an assembly or congregation (cf. קהלת יעקב in Deut 33:4), and can therefore be understood to mean "assembler." This understanding probably gave rise to the LXX's translation Ἐκκλησιαστής, namely a member of the ἐκκλησία ("assembly").

The epilogue of the book (12:9–14) identifies Qoheleth as a חכם, "sage," who "continued to instruct the people" and "listened to and tested the soundness of many maxims" (12:9). His role vis-à-vis the people is that of a learned figure offering teachings publicly or to a group of students gathered around him, and it can be inferred that this earned him the title "Qoheleth." The practice of public teaching is hinted at in Prov 1:20–21 and 8:1–3, in which Wisdom personified goes about the city streets preaching and instructing (Fox 2004, 3). The concepts of assembly and gathering also lend themselves to interpretation in the sense of collecting and transmitting sayings and teachings (cf. Prov 25:1), the role of Qoheleth described in 12:9 (e.g., Rashi, Rashbam, Ibn Ezra).

The individual referred to as Qoheleth has traditionally been identified with Solomon on the basis of the two superscriptions presented in 1:1 and 1:12. Although the name Solomon is not mentioned, the designation "son of David, king in Jerusalem" (1:1) suggests his identification with Solomon, who was the only son of David to have ruled in Jerusalem over all Israel (1:1; 1:12; cf. 1 Kgs 11:42). The earliest recorded claim of Solomonic authorship is that of Gregory Thaumaturgos (213–270 CE). A similar tendency can be seen among early Jewish literary circles (e.g., Song Rab. 1:1 §10). Based on the date of the work's composition, however, these traditions of Solomonic authorship are not accepted by modern scholars.

There is likely, however, an intentional pseudepigraphal link between Solomon and Qoheleth. In 1 Kings 8, The root קהל occurs several times in reference to Solomon gathering the people to hear his oration at the dedication of the newly constructed temple (vv. 1, 2, 14, 22, 55). Furthermore, Qoheleth's descriptions of his abundant wealth, royal achievements, and wisdom correlate with the figure of Solomon, the archetypal wise and wealthy king (e.g., 1 Kgs 3:12–13; 5:9–14; 1 Chr 29:25; 2 Chr 1:12).

The royal description of Qoheleth goes beyond the implied identification with Solomon. Qoheleth's self-aggrandizing descriptions of his accomplishments: "I built," "I planted," "I constructed," "I acquired," "I amassed," and "I grew rich" (2:4–11), are typical of the "résumé style" evident in West Semitic royal inscriptions (Seow 1997, 128). The list of the king's accomplishments details construction of buildings, gardens, and irrigation pools, and possessions of herds, flocks, and male and female slaves. Mention of silver and gold is reminiscent of the descriptions of Solomon's wealth in 1 Kgs 10:14–25 and 1 Chr 9:27.

However, while the tone of such extra-biblical inscriptions is usually unmitigatedly boastful, such statements here lead to the surprising conclusion offered in 2:11: "Then my thoughts turned to all the fortune my hands had built up, to the wealth I had an won—and oh, it was all futile and pursuit of wind; there was no real value under the sun." This perspective throws the figure of Qoheleth into the role of a skeptic philosopher rather than the magnificent monarch. Though the mention of Qoheleth's prodigious wisdom in 2:9 may refer to God's gift of wisdom to Solomon in 1 Kgs 3:9–13, 5:9–14, and 10:24 (cf. Ecc 12:9–11), the philosophical mode of Qoheleth's thought remains unprecedented.

Reference to the author in both the third person in the book's title (1:1) and in the first person (1:12) evinces a literary convention well-established in other biblical texts (see Amos 1:1; Jer 1:1, 4). Scholars debate whether the initial superscription is an addition by an editor or redactor, who may have added the Epilogue (12:9–14) as well, or a literary framing device. Fox (2004, 82–83) contends that these verses are a retrospective framing of the work by the original author of the book, who interpolates his voice in 1:2, 7:27, and 12:8 as well.

In sum, the references to Qoheleth (1:1, 12), traditionally identified with Solomon, are more appropriately the subject of a literary-critical discussion than of an investigation into the book's historical context and dating. It seems more obvious that the author of the book, through considerations of fictive teaching authority, placed his own reflections into Qoheleth's mouth, thereby reserving the possibility of distancing himself from Qoheleth (Krüger 2004, 40). The enigmatic and elusive identity of the author—was he a wealthy king, a teacher, or a philosopher?—might be "a deliberate playing with literary conventions" (Fox 1997, 83–106).

31.3 LANGUAGE AND STYLE

Ever since commentators began to adopt a critical approach to biblical literature in the seventeenth century, the idiosyncratic character of Qoheleth's language has been a major argument for assigning a late date to the book. The thesis advanced by Hugo Grotius in his preface to *Annotationes ad Qohelet* (1644; quoted in Schoors 1992, 1:1) that "the book contains too many words which are not found anywhere except in Daniel, Ezra, and the Chaldean interpreters" has been generally accepted by modern scholarship.

The grammar and vocabulary of Qoheleth's Hebrew differs considerably from that of the classical Hebrew of most biblical works. The frequent use of Aramaic loanwords and grammatical and syntactical forms, Persian words (פרדס, פתגם), and late Hebrew words found only in the Mishna indicate a post-exilic date for the composition of Qoheleth (Barton 1908, 52–53). Since these linguistic developments most probably occurred in the period when Aramaic became the lingua franca in administration and commerce in the western part of the Persian empire, several scholars have even posited that the book was originally composed in Aramaic and only later translated into Hebrew (e.g., Torrey 1948–1949) based on its high density of Aramaisms and unusual use of the definite article among other factors. This claim has been contested by other scholars (e.g., Gordis 1968,

59–62), who suggest instead that the book was written in Hebrew by a writer whose native speech was Aramaic. Fredericks (1988, 267), however, offers earlier (pre-exilic) instances of those features that had been held to be unique to late Hebrew, and concludes that Ecclesiastes, though late, was deliberately written in archaic Hebrew language.

Schoors's (1992; 2004) two-volume study on the language of Qoheleth has demonstrated that the Hebrew of the book definitely represents a late stage in the development of Biblical Hebrew, belonging to a dialect referred to by scholars as Late Biblical Hebrew. Typical features of Late Biblical Hebrew are the exclusive use of אני instead of אנכי and some grammatical traits such as the interchange of the relative forms אשר and ש. Another late development of Biblical Hebrew favored by the author is the usage of abstract forms ending in וֹן, such as חשבון, חסרון, יתרון, and שלטון, and in וּת, such as ילדוּת, and הוללוּת, שכלוּת, סכלוּת, שפלוּת.

Seow (1997, 13) argues that the high frequency of Aramaic expressions in the book, particularly economic and commercial terms such as יתרון ("surplus"), חסרון ("deficit"), חשבון ("account"), and נכסים ("assets") likely indicates a date of composition in the fifth century BCE. However, Qoheleth's familiarity with conditions of prosperity may indicate the living conditions of the Jews in the Hellenistic period (third–second century BCE) no less than those of the fifth century BCE.

Some have not limited their linguistic investigation to the chronological problem but have instead taken a broader approach linking Qoheleth's linguistic peculiarities to the philosophical genre of the book and the author's personal style (Gordis 1946, 84; Gordis 1949–1950, 106). Much of the book of Ecclesiastes employs literary forms and genres found in previous Wisdom Literature, such as proverbial sayings, advisory maxims, and observations encapsulating truths on human and divine conduct in the world. However, there can be no doubt about the distinctiveness of the text's meditative style, as philosophical prose is previously unknown in ancient Israel. Syntactically, this style is characterized by a string of sentences connected through coordinating and subordinating conjunctions.

Qoheleth formulates his ideas a priori, employing an essentially empirical methodology. The advice Qoheleth offers is firmly rooted in his own personal experience, "the soil out of which his wisdom grows" (Longman 1998, 19). He sets up a wide variety of expressive modes for his personal observations and introduces his perceptions while sketching a procedure for investigation, e.g., "I set my mind to study and to probe with wisdom all that happens under the sun" (1:13; cf. 1:17; 9:1).

31.4 PROVERBIAL SAYINGS AND KEY-WORDS IN ECCLESIASTES

The identification of proverbs within the work is often unclear, since they are mostly embedded in the narrator's flow of observational reflections. Thus the apparent proverb, "a twisted thing cannot be made straight, a lack cannot be made good" (1:15), follows a clause in the first-person autobiographic style: "I observed all the happenings beneath the sun, and I found that all is futile and pursuit of wind" (1:14).

Special proverbial forms used in Ecclesiastes include the comparative proverb (3:19; 7:6; 9:12) and the numerical proverb (6:6; 7:19, 28; 11:2), as well as the "better-than" (טוב) proverb, which creates an analogical relation between two terms, declaring the first item mentioned to be qualitatively superior to the second. For example: "A good name is better than fragrant oil, and the day of death than the day of birth" (7:1). At a higher level of complexity, the inequality is buttressed by a clause or clauses that specify the reason and/or particular circumstances of the difference in merit or value. For example: "It is better to go to a house of mourning than to a house of feasting; for that is the end of every man, and a living one should take it to heart" (7:2). This system of argumentation typically enables the reader to reconsider the expected relation between the two options. However, Qoheleth plays ironically with this form—instead of using the motive clause to strengthen the advantage of A over B, he employs the oppositional *waw* to limit the main assertion pronounced in the opening clause. Thus, for example: "Wisdom is better than valor; but a poor man's wisdom is scorned, and his words are not heeded" (9:16; cf. 9:18). The "better-than"-proverbs assess the relative value of wisdom, emphasizing the qualified and vulnerable nature of its utility (Forti 2005, 235–255).

An understanding of Qoheleth's unique vocabulary is key to appreciating the book and its message. Although many of these keywords occur elsewhere in the Bible, their context and semantic connotations distinguish Ecclesiastes from other books.[3] The following terms are among the most favored in Qoheleth, occurring as both verbs and related forms: הוללות ("madness"), חלק ("portion, share, possession"), חשבון ("account of things, sum, reckoning"), מה-יתרון ("what advantage"), עמל ("toil"), שמחה ("enjoyment, pleasure"), מעשה ("work, event"), and כשר ("succeed"). The ambiguous meaning of certain keywords encourages readers to play an active role in interpreting them (Ingram 2006, 37). This is the case especially with regard to two of the most prominent repeated terms in the work, הבל, "ephemerality," and רעות/רעיון רוח, "pursuit of wind."

The noun הבל is used seventy-three times in the Hebrew Bible, thirty-eight of which are in Ecclesiastes. The basic meanings of this term are: breath, air, vapor, and breeze, all insensible or intangible substances that leave no mark (Isa 57:13; Ps 62:10; 144:4; Job 7:16). The LXX has rendered this word ματαιότης "nonsense, emptiness," which has been followed by the Vulgate with the translation *vanitas*, from which the English word "vanity" derives (Schoors, 2013, 40–47). The particularly modern problem with the word "vanity" as a translation of הבל is that it does not evoke the fleetingness or emptiness connoted by "air" or "vapor." Those who translate הבל as "vanity" therefore tend to mistakenly see Qoheleth "as a pious moralist who chides people for pursuing worldly frivolities rather than spiritual values" (Fox 2004, xix). הבל is mainly used metaphorically in the Hebrew Bible, its main connotations are:

---

[3] See, e.g., Fox 2004, xvii–xxi; Schoors 2004, 2:3–196, 423–470.

1. Ephemerality: This sense is clearly indicated by Qoheleth in 6:12: "Who can possibly know what is best for a man to do in life—the few days of his fleeting life (יְמֵי חַיֵּי הֶבְלוֹ)?" (cf. Ps 39:6–7, 12).

2. Futility: This aspect of the meaning of הבל focuses on the disparate relationship between human beings' labor and their profit. So, for example, 2:15: "So I reflected: 'The fate of the fool is also destined for me; to what advantage, then, have I been wise?' And I came to the conclusion that that too was futile."

3. Absurdity: In 8:14, Qoheleth employs the word as part to describe the injustice and irrationality of the human condition, in which individuals often meet a fate opposite to what they deserve (Fox 1999, 27–49).

Due to the multifaceted meaning of the word הבל, translations must take context into account. In all cases, however, the term הבל pronounces an explicit or implicit value judgement on the nature of existence as a whole. The expression "all is הבל" (1:2 and 12:8) encapsulates Qoheleth's larger position with respect to the events of human life (Schweinhorst-Schönberger 1996, 291–292).

The compound phrase רעות רוח/רעיון רוח "pursuit of wind" is difficult to define precisely, since רעות can mean pursuit, shepherd, desire, or thought, while רוח can denote wind, spirit, or desire (Fox 2004, xx). The terms רעות רוח (2:11, 17, 26; 4:4, 6; 6:9) and רעיון רוח (4:16) are used interchangeably, and are almost always paired with הבל or עמל. Following the etymology of רעה "to pasture, tend, graze," scholars have opted for translations such as "to desire," or "to strive after" (e.g., Gordis 1968, 210).

31.5 ECCLESIASTES IN ITS ANCIENT NEAR EASTERN CONTEXT

Scholars have demonstrated distinctive literary and even phraseological parallels between Ecclesiastes and Babylonian texts that, though insufficient to demonstrate direct literary dependence, nevertheless evoke the possibility of indirect intellectual influence. One Mesopotamian source that evinces striking commonalities with Ecclesiastes (esp. 4:9–12 and 9:7–9) is the Epic of Gilgamesh. The inevitability of death and transience of human life is thematically dominant in both works. Confronting the futility of fame and fortune, Gilgamesh pursues immortality, eventually settling for an appeal to the walls he built in Uruk as his lasting legacy in the face of death (Standard Version Tablet 11.6 in Dalley 2000, 120). Elsewhere, Gilgamesh says to his companion Enkidu (Jastrow and Clay 1920, ll. 140–143):

Who is there, my friend, who can climb to the sky? Only the gods dwell forever with the Sun-god (or: in sunlight). As for man, his days are numbered. Whatever he may do, it is but wind.

Scholars have noted the similarity of this statement to Qoheleth's observation about God being in heaven and humans on earth (Eccl 5:1). More significant, however, is the parallel between "wind" (*šaru*) in Gilgamesh and הבל in Ecclesiastes as a metaphor for the meaninglessness of humanity's pursuit of exploits (van der Toorn 2001, 504).

Another striking parallel has been noted by Aaron Shaffer (Shaffer 1967, 246–250; Shaffer 1969, 138–139, 159–160), who identifies a traditional saying about the strength of a triple cord in the Sumerian composition Gilgamesh and the Land of the Living. Here, the protagonist Gilgamesh attempts to persuade his friend Enkidu to embark upon a dangerous journey with him:

> Two men will not die; the towed boat will not sink,
> A tow-rope of three strands shall not be cut.
> (Version A, II. 103–104)

Qoheleth's proverb in praise of companionship: "Two are better off than one...and a threefold cord is not readily broken" (4:9, 12), would therefore seem to quote the Gilgamesh Epic, in either the Old Babylonian or Neo-Assyrian version.

The most well-known and closest parallel between Gilgamesh and Ecclesiastes is Siduri's advice to Gilgamesh. Having met Gilgamesh in the course of his quest for immortality, she discourages him from such futile ambitions and offers him instead a philosophy of life, urging him to seize the day:

> But you, Gilgamesh, let your belly be full,
> Enjoy yourself always by day and by night!
> Make merry each day, dance and play all night!
> Let your clothes be clean,
> Let your head be washed, may you bathe in water!
> Gaze on the child who holds your hand,
> Let your wife enjoy your repeated embrace!
> (George 1999, 162 [Meissner tablet, iii, 6–13])

Qoheleth echoes this counsel:

> Go, eat your bread in gladness, and drink your wine in joy; for your action was long ago approved by God. Let your clothes be always freshly washed; and your head never lack ointment. Enjoy happiness with a wife you love .... (9:7–9)

In both texts, the injunction *carpe diem* is juxtaposed to the wisdom-*topos* of death's inevitability. In both, enjoyment of life's pleasures is offered as an answer to this fact, albeit a partial one (Anderson 2014, 171).

Against the broader backdrop of ancient Near Eastern literature, Qoheleth's skeptical ruminations on life are unexceptional. Scholars have associated Qoheleth with the genre of ancient Near Eastern pessimistic Wisdom Literature, which includes the Babylonian Dialogue of Pessimism (dated ca. 1200–1000 BCE), which records a discourse between a master and his slave about what is good in life. The literary structure of this text is a vacillation between action and inaction in routine courses of life (traveling to the palace, dining, hunting, setting up a home, loving a woman, etc.), leading to paralysis. The slave's words merely reflect the master's changing moods (Lambert 1960, 140). This inner conflict reflects that of the master vis-à-vis the fickle nature of life (Anderson 2014, 169). The versatility the slave displays in affirming both the positive and negative aspects of a situation is reminiscent of Qoheleth's own style. Thus, for example, the poem often called the Catalogue of Times (Qoh 3:1–8) presents both positive and negative actions as counterbalancing one another, epitomizing "opportune circumstances in which it is wise to act in a certain way, even one that involves an apparent loss" (Fox, 2004, 22).

A Babylonian fragmental text entitled Counsels of a Pessimist also echoes the theme of life's transience so central to Ecclesiastes: "[Whatever] men do does not last forever. Mankind and their achievements alike come to an end" (K 1453, Plate 30, ll. 9–10; Lambert 1960, 109). Qoheleth likewise proclaims: "Who can possibly know what is best for a man to do in life—the few days of his fleeting life?" (6:12; see also 2:11). Another motif common to the two works is human anxiety as a cause of nightmares. Qoheleth describes the restless and overworked mind that accompanies the tired and aching body of the laborer: "All his days his thoughts are grief and heartache, and even at night his mind has no respite. That too is futile" (2:23). At the same time, the Babylonian text enjoins: "Do [not] let evil sleep afflict your heart; banish misery and suffering from your side; misery and suffering produce a dream" (K 1453, Plate 30, ll. 17–19; Lambert 1960, 109). The motif of the dream is also mentioned explicitly in Ecclesiastes: "For dreams come with much brooding" (5:2a). Both texts associate the concept of dreams with the sense of anxiety, rather than portraying them as a mantic device as ancient cultures often did.

The sentiments and thoughts discussed above are not exclusive to Mesopotamian literature; close parallels to a number of Egyptian texts are evident as well, both with respect to their terminology and literary genre. Though Egyptian literature reflects a highly developed, uniquely Egyptian tradition regarding the afterlife, one clearly distinct from Mesopotamian and Israelite views, commonalities still abound. The inscriptions known as the Harper's Songs, carved on tomb walls and mortuary stelae, question the reality of an afterlife and urge the living to enjoy life while it lasts (Lichtheim 1973, 1:193–197). The most eloquent expression of this message can be found in the Harper's Song from the Tomb of King Intef (Middle Kingdom, ca. 1600 BCE). Here, as in Qoheleth, the concept of *carpe diem* follows a negative assessment of human achievement and skepticism regarding the afterlife:

> Hence rejoice in your heart! . . .
> Follow your heart as long as you live!
> Put myrrh on your head, dress in fine linen,
> Anoint yourself with oils fit for a God.
> (ll. vi, 10–14; Lichtheim 1973, 1:196)

The theme of life's transitory nature as well—"a generation passes, another stays, since the time of the ancestors" (ll. vi, 2)—evokes Eccl 1:4: "One generation goes, another comes, but the earth remains the same forever." Both texts note that human beings take nothing to the afterlife. The Egyptian song reads: "Lo, none is allowed to take his goods with him, / Lo, none who departs comes back again!" (vii, 2; Lichtheim 1973, 1:197) parallel to Qoheleth: "As he came out of his mother's womb, so must he depart at last, naked as he came. He can take nothing of his wealth to carry with him" (5:14 [ET 15]).

The concept of hedonism coupled with skepticism is reflected in other Egyptian texts, notably in the Dispute between a Man and His Ba. This text traces the story of a man who suffers from life and longs for death, but is terrified of being abandoned by his *ba*, which represents one's vital forces and the ability to act, close to נפש ("soul") in Biblical Hebrew, since this would mean total spiritual annihilation as opposed to the resurrection and immortal bliss that he envisages. He therefore implores his *ba* to remain with him and not to oppose him in his longing for death. The *ba* urges him to stop complaining and to enjoy life (Lichtheim 1973, 1:163). Throughout this debate, one can discern conflicts and contradictions typical of the thoughts of a person in great pain and distress (Shupak, forthcoming).

Like the protagonists of the Egyptian speculative Wisdom Literature, Qoheleth also debates with his heart. The closest phrasing to that found in Egyptian literature appears in 1:16: "I spoke to my heart saying" (cf. 2:1, 15; 3:17–18). Here, however, the heart plays a passive role rather than functioning independently as an entity distinct from the person. The heart in Ecclesiastes appears as a seat of contemplation rather than a conversation partner. Still, both the *ba* and the Harper's Songs and the author of Ecclesiastes take a skeptical and unorthodox approach vis-à-vis the fate of human beings after death, urging the person to instead enjoy life (3:18–22; 9:7–9; cf. 2:24; 3:12, 22; 11:9–10).

Notwithstanding the above comparison, direct influence or deliberate assimilation of Egyptian Wisdom models in Ecclesiastes is uncertain. The pattern of conversation between a man and his heart or soul is only a literary tool employed by the ancient sages to illustrate "a universal phenomenon of human emotional distress; while feeling alone and alienated from society, nothing is left over but to address his/her heart or soul" (Shupak, forthcoming).

31.6 QOHELETH AND GREEK PHILOSOPHY

Scholarly awareness of the educational and cultural impact of the Hellenistic world on Israelite society, and especially on the elite families in Jerusalem, has prompted the search for parallels to Hellenistic philosophical ideas in Ecclesiastes. Several scholars have taken for granted the Hellenistic character of the book, relying mainly on the date of its composition, closely preceding Sirach (190–180 BCE) and the Maccabean revolt.

Qoheleth's contemplative approach and personal intellectual engagement, set out at the beginning of the book—"I set my mind to study and to probe with wisdom all that happens under the heavens" (1:13)—has been interpreted as a function of "the open spirit of world citizenship typical of the Ptolemaic period" (Lohfink 2003, 4). Several commentaries and studies have detected thoughts, ideas, and key terms common to both Qoheleth and various branches of Greek philosophy, especially Epicureanism and

Stoicism. Rainer Braun (1973) finds expressions and ideas analogous to those in Greek literature in almost half of the verses of Qoheleth. He argues that the presuppositions of Qoheleth's rhetoric and motifs, empirical methods, unbiased questions, and personal individualistic-cosmopolitan self-understanding were all influenced by Greek popular philosophy and the literary training of early Hellenism (178). Charles Whitley (1979, 165–175) detects Epicurean influence on Qoheleth's views on life and existence. The conception of death as complete oblivion in Qoheleth—"for there is no action, no reasoning, no learning, no wisdom in Sheol, where you are going" (9:10b)—is shared by Epicurus: "Death is deprivation of sensation . . . when death comes, then we do not exist" (cited by Whitley 1979, 167).

Robert Gordis (1968, 51–58) counters the widely held view that Qoheleth was influenced by the Stoics, especially in the determinism of the Catalogue of Times (Eccl 3:1–9). Although Qoheleth, like the Stoics, emphasizes the predestination of events, this principle was held by most ancient philosophic thinkers, and the Stoics were far from sharing Qoheleth's convictions that the truth was forever unknowable to man, or that pleasure is the ideal object of human striving (Gordis 1968, 52). Gordis also argues against scholarly efforts to equate the characteristic vocabulary of Ecclesiastes with Cynic-Stoic terminology, such as הבל and τῦφος, "illusion," or רעות רוח and κηνὴ δόξα, "empty notion." Thus, according to Gordis, while Qoheleth might have been familiar with the popular doctrines of the schools that formed the intellectual climate of his age, what is truly remarkable about Qoheleth is "his completely original and independent use of these ideas to express his own unique world view" (56).

Many other scholars, emphasizing the differences over the similarities, doubt whether Ecclesiastes betrays any direct influence of Greek philosophy at all (e.g., Loretz 1964, 45–134; Schwienhorst-Schönberger 1996, 232–332). Recent scholarship has tended to shy away from unequivocal claims regarding Qoheleth's familiarity with classical Greek texts, noting the lack of explicit citations of Hellenistic thought in the work (Jarick 2014, 95). Still, when comparing the Greek text of Qoheleth in the Septuagint with classical Greek writings, we might acknowledge the possibility, as regards keywords, that the translator chose analogous vocabulary from Greek literature. The term μόχθος, used for עמל, "toil," for example, resonates with the cognate expression used by the Athenian tragedians (Jarick 2016, 106).

In sum, Ecclesiastes is the biblical book closest to the Hellenistic genre of philosophy and intellectual contemplation of fundamental human issues (Fox 2004, xi). However, Qoheleth's thought cannot be attributed to any particular Greek philosopher or school. The links with Greek culture are too unspecific to enable solid claims of direct influence.

31.7 Structure and Unity

The question of overarching structure and cohesiveness in Ecclesiastes remains one of the most pressing issues in modern scholarship. Scholars have wrestled with how to view the organization of the book and divide it into coherent sections, either on a conceptual-thematic basis or through a reconstruction of the author's logical progression. The endeavor to subdivide the work into manageable segments can be seen prominently in commentaries, which must produce easily digestible chunks for readers (e.g., Murphy 1992, xxxv–xli), but commentaries rarely agree on the divisions themselves. While there is broad agreement that the book contains an epilogue (12:9–14), and that verses 1:1–11 may constitute an introduction, any further attempt to subdivide the large middle section between these extremes tends to flounder.

Addison Wright's (1968, 313–334) structural division of Ecclesiastes into thematic has elicited the approval of many commentators. He proposes a complex hierarchical design based on repeated keywords that delimit units as follows:

Initial poem (1:2–11);

1. Qoheleth's investigation of life (1:12–6:9);
2. Qoheleth's conclusions (6:10–11:6);
   a. Introduction (6:10–12);
   b. Man cannot find out what is good for him to do (7:1–8:17);
   c. Man does not know what will come after him (9:1–11:6);

Concluding poem (11:7–12:8);
Epilogue (12:9–14).

However, Wright's proposal has come under attack (Fox 1999, 148–149). James Crenshaw (1988, 40–42), for example, argues that the key-phrases are not always present at the end of the unit and that the plan does not match the content of the work. Furthermore, he disputes the uniformity of the units' lengths. Choon-Leong Seow (1997, 46–47) presents an alternative division, which divides the book into two roughly equal halves (1:2–6:9; 6:10–12:8). He subdivides each into two large blocks, alternating in emphasis between reflection (1:2–4:16; 6:10–8:17) and ethics (5:1–6:9; 9:1–12:8). However, within the thematic discussions of each chapter he labels smaller units as well. There are also scholars who argue for a structure based on internal, self-contained logical progression, rather than hierarchical division. Michael Fox (2004, xvi) argues that despite the lack of any organizing principle, the book displays a deep cohesiveness.

Over the years, scholars have studied the reflective passages in detail. Gary Salyer (2001, 173), for example, argues that since the narrative framework articulated in the autobiographical passages engulfs the Wisdom-style aphorisms interspersed throughout the text, the latter are perceived by the reader as part of Qoheleth's overarching narrative. Eric Christianson (1998, 36–37) notes the stylistic distinctiveness of the autobiographical reflective narratives in Ecclesiastes, acknowledging that they convey the narrator's innermost reflections. He contends that without the "I," Qoheleth's narration would lack the cohesive power that enables us to speak of Qoheleth as a unified, albeit multifaceted, persona.

Others, however, believe that Ecclesiastes comprises a loose collection of separate units. Longman (1998, 22) writes: "Close study shows that Qohelet's thought rambles, repeats . . . and occasionally contradicts itself. Such a lack of order, though, far from detracting from the message of the book actually contributes to it." However, Longman ultimately does outline a structure of the book following Qoheleth's autobiographical speech:

1. Autobiographical introduction (1:12);
2. "Solomon's" quest for the meaning of life (1:13–2:26);
3. The quest continues (3:1–6:9);
4. Qohelet's wise advice (6:10–12:7).

The looseness of the book's structure has led William Brown (2000, 15) as well to remark that "seeking structure in Qoheleth's turbid discourse is, frankly, an exercise in frustration." And yet the work evinces a clear sense of progression that suggests a more than haphazard composition. All scholars acknowledge an "envelope" surrounding the book as a whole in the הבל phrases in 1:2 and 12:8. There is a clear distinction between the editorial comments (1:1; 12:9–14) and the internal bulk of poetic reflections (1:3–12:7). The reader encounters a set of prominent, recurring themes and ideas: death, futility, human transience, time and chance, gain (שכר) and lot or portion (חלק), work and toil, wealth and poverty, wisdom and folly, hedonism, pleasure and happiness, divine justice, and God's relation to human beings (Whybray 1997, 63–83; Krüger 2004, 1–5).

Three lyrical poems are incorporated into the book's narrative sequence: The first (1:4–11) tells of the permanence of the physical earth versus human transience; the Catalogue of Times (3:1–8) contrasts constructive and destructive deeds and events, asserting that everything has its proper occasion; the final poem (12:1–7) describes figuratively the process of human aging and death. This poem has often been understood as an allegory, in which each image represents one part of the deteriorating body.

The book has a highly circuitous manner of presentation, characterized by repetition and revolution of topics that seem to push the narrative back toward its beginning: "For everything that moves forward, there is a force tugging in the opposite direction" (Horne 2003, 378). Sections scholars designate as conclusions do not really conclude anything. Some musings contradict one another. Topics change suddenly, suggesting the beginning of a new section, but then allusion is made to the original theme. Some verses are cross-thematic, eliding key subjects together, though not necessarily as a summary. Some topics are pursued over lengthy stretches of the book, "not in straight-line of thought but in an associative continuation" (Zimmerli 1974, 226–227).

While the thought of Qoheleth cannot be neatly divided into large thematic portions, general consensus does exist with respect to certain smaller sections. Thomas Krüger (2004, 5) suggests that these smaller units should be studied both as self-contained elements and as part of their larger context. Commentators often try to justify their divisions with various criteria such as a unified theme or common key terms. While always insightful, these divisions are often intuitively uncompelling. Fox (2004, xvi) posits important criteria for any convincing subdivision: "The test of any inferred structure or design is whether it matches the reader's experience—that is, whether it emerges from your own reading, and whether awareness of it helps you organize the book's thoughts and deepens your understanding of its message."

In my view, the problem of uncertain boundaries is often solved by the concept of "Janus sayings" (Dell and Forti 2016, 115–128). These are passages that function as a textual pivot point, seemingly closing one section and opening the following one at the same time. We argue that the placement of the Janus saying enhances the thematic continuity between apparently separate units and enables us to read the book effortlessly.[4] More than as a tool for mere free association, Janus sayings are deliberately employed by Qoheleth as linking devices in an overarching planned design for the presentation of his ideas.

31.8 READING CONTRADICTIONS

Ecclesiastes's apparent lack of internal consistency was not lost on ancient readers (Holm-Nielsen 1975–1976, 38–95; Dell 2013, 9–36).[5] In rabbinic sources, we encounter two primary arguments against admitting Ecclesiastes into the canon of divinely inspired texts: (1) the book contradicts itself (b. Šabb. 30b), and (2) the views expressed incline to heresy (Qoh. Rab. 1:3; 11:9; Num. Rab. 161b). While the Rabbis were concerned with contradictions both within the book and in relation to the Torah (see Wright 1883, 3–27, 470–474), early Christian exegetes such as Jerome noted "inconvenient" passages, which were usually attributed to opponents to the truth as later, inauthentic interpolations (Dell 1994, 301–329).

Diverse voices are heard in the book. Sometimes the narrator refers to himself as Qoheleth in the first person; at other times he refers to Qoheleth in the third person. Beyond the confused style, a more serious literary problem arises from the dissonance between conservative, orthodox statements regarding the human condition and skeptical observations that contradict those traditional beliefs. Carl Siegfried (1898, 2–12) has attributed the skeptical voice to the original author, which he dubs the חכם "sage," and the conservative views to one or several pious glossators or editors, referred to as the חסיד, "pietist." Hans Wilhelm Hertzberg (1963), on the other hand, invokes the interpretive principle of the "Zwar-AberTatsache" to resolve contradictory propositions by relating them to different objects or perspectives. Thus, although in 8:11–14 Qoheleth observes that the righteous live long and the wicked die young, there are nevertheless exceptional cases where the opposite principle holds.

---

[4] For example, Qoh 6:11–12, which links 5:9–6:10 [ET 5:10–6:10] and 7:1–14; 8:1, which links 7:23–29 and 8:2–4; 10:1, which links 9:13–18 and 10:2–3 (Dell and Forti 2016, 115–128).

[5] For a survey of different approaches to the contradictions in Ecclesiastes, see Fox (1989, 23–25).

Such a systematic approach to harmonizing apparent contradictions in Ecclesiastes can already be discerned among medieval Jewish commentators. Ibn Ezra (1089–1164), for example, claims that the same term כעס, "vexation," is judged differently in different situations. While "vexation abides in the breasts of fools" (7:5:9b), this refers only to constant anger. This does not contradict Qoheleth's commendation of anger in 7:3a: "Vexation is better than revelry," since the wise man's anger is not permanent but timely and temporary (Zer-Kavod 1973, 28–31). In a similar vein, Rashbam (twelfth century) attempts to sort out logical incongruities by drawing semantic distinctions. With regard to pleasure for example, Qoheleth is said to repudiate frivolous and extravagant pleasure (שמחה, שחוק) but to affirm happiness (also called שמחה), which means contentment in one's lot. Since the merrymaking of fools is motivated by hedonistic passion, which causes sin, the negative connotation of שחוק is associated with them.

Modern scholars have taken updated approaches to harmonization. Some (Podechard, McNiele, and Barton) have developed the hypothesis of additions and glosses, namely statements of ideas that both bear directly on the central issues of the book and contradict the material considered authentic. This procedure presents us with the dilemma: How can we determine which statements are authentically Qoheleth's and which are later additions (Fox 1989, 23)?

A different resolution of the book's inconsistencies can be found in the hypothesis of quotations, which posits that the author has deliberately created a debate within the work by quoting standard, traditional views that contradict one another (see, e.g., Whybray 1981, 435–451). Under this assumption, the text takes the form of a dialogue with either a genuine or fictional interlocutor.

The conflicting points of view in the book's discourses can also be viewed as a dialogue between Qoheleth and his inner self, where contradictory terms and values that he juxtaposes represent the competing, equally legitimate motivational forces that inform the human process of decision-making (Forti 2005, 236). Indeed, Qoheleth's ambivalent attitude toward life might be most authentically expressed as a series of contradictions, and this method is especially effective in stimulating his audience to reflect upon contradictory phenomena in human experience.

All biblical texts suffer more than one reading, and Ecclesiastes is no exception. Notwithstanding the biblical literary-interpretive approach proffered by Fox (1981, 53–61 [53]), in which "the primary task of exegesis is ascertaining the text's meaning, which is to be identified with the authorial intention," such an investigation into Ecclesiastes reveals deep-seated ambiguity and indeterminacy. Ambiguity—as opposed to ambivalence—intentionally lends itself to an enhanced role for the reader, precisely because the indeterminacy "permits, even requires, the reader to determine meaning" (Ingram 2006, 13). The challenge then is not so much in pinning down one true meaning as in navigating between different and even opposing attitudes towards the meaning of life that different readers may find. Any attempt to judge between readings necessarily enters a subjective arena of exegesis where one must contend not only with the meanings of particular words, but with the significance gleaned from the immediate context and even the work as a whole (Dell and Forti, 2019:481–489).

31.9 CONCLUSION

The increasing diversity of methods and literary approaches for interpreting the Bible (e.g., reader response criticism, rhetorical criticism, feminist interpretation, ideological criticism, etc.), have added fresh insights into the text of Ecclesiastes and its contextual world. The selected issues treated in this entry endeavor to reflect a careful combination of a linguistically focused approach and a conceptual and ideational discussion through identification of key words and key themes—both highlighting the social context and cultural worldview of the author. This perspective sets the stage for our forthcoming commentary on Ecclesiastes (Dell and Forti, forthcoming), which is designed to reflect a collaboration between authors from divergent cultural and religious backgrounds, each bringing her own hermeneutical considerations, theological perspectives, and aspects of cultural contextualization. It is this type of interpretation that the rich, complex, and multivalent text of Ecclesiastes invites.

WORKS CITED

Anderson, William H.U. 2014. "Ecclesiastes in the Intertextual Matrix of Ancient Near Eastern Literature." Pages 157–175 in *Reading Ecclesiastes Intertextually*. Edited by Katharine Dell and Will Kynes. LHBOTS 587. London: Bloomsbury T&T Clark.

Barbour, Jennie. 2012. *The Story of Israel in the Book of Qohelet: Ecclesiastes as Cultural Memory*. Oxford: Oxford University Press.

Barton, George A. 1908. *A Critical and Exegetical Commentary of the Book of Ecclesiastes*. Edinburgh: T&T Clark.

Braun, Rainer. 1973. *Kohelet und die frühhellenistische Popularphilosophie*. BZAW 130. Berlin: de Gruyter.

Brown, William P. 2000. *Ecclesiastes*. Int. Louisville, KY: Westminster John Knox.

Christianson, Eric S. 1998. *A Time to Tell: Narrative Strategies in Ecclesiastes*. JSOTSup 280. Sheffield: Sheffield Academic.

Collins, John J. 1997. *Jewish Wisdom in the Hellenistic Age*. Edinburgh: T&T Clark.

Crenshaw, James L. 1988. *Ecclesiastes*. OTL. London: SCM.

Dalley, Stephanie. 2000. *Myths from Mesopotamia*. Oxford: Oxford University Press.

Dell, Katharine J. 1994. "Ecclesiastes as Wisdom: Consulting Early Interpreters." *VT* 44:301–329.

Dell, Katharine J. 2013. *Interpreting Ecclesiastes: Readers Old and New*. Winona Lake, IN: Eisenbrauns.

Dell, Katharine J., and Tova Forti. 2016. "Janus Sayings: A Linking Device in Qoheleth's Discourse." *ZAW* 128:115–128.

Dell, Katharine J., and Tova Forti. 2019. "Enjoying the Tension: Reading Qoh 2:25 in the Context of Qoh 2:24–6." *VT* 69:481–489.

Dell, Katharine J., and Tova Forti. Forthcoming. *Ecclesiastes*. IECOT. Stuttgart: Kohlhammer.

Forti, Tova. 2005. "The Fly and the Dog: Observations on the Ideational Polarity in the Book of Qoheleth." Pages 235–255 in *Seeking Out the Wisdom of the Ancients: Essays Offered to*

Honor Michael V. Fox. Edited by Ronald L. Troxel, Kevin G. Friebel, and Dennis R. Magary. Winona Lake, IN: Eisenbrauns.

Fox, Michael V. 1981. "Job 38 and God's Rhetoric." *Semeia* 19:53–61.

Fox, Michael V. 1989. *Qohelet and His Contradictions*. BLS 18. Sheffield: Almond.

Fox, Michael V. 1997. "Frame Narrative and Composition in the Book of Qohelet." *HUCA* 48:83–106.

Fox, Michael V. 1999. *A Time to Tear Down & A Time to Build Up: A Reading of Ecclesiastes*. Grand Rapids, MI: Eerdmans.

Fox, Michael V. 2004. *Ecclesiastes*. JPSBC. Philadelphia, PA: JPS.

Fredericks, Daniel C. 1988. *Qoheleth's Language: Re-Evaluating Its Nature and Date*. Lewiston, NY: Mellen.

George, Andrew. 1999. *The Epic of Gilgamesh: A New Translation*. London: Lane.

Gordis, Robert. 1946-1947. "The Original Language of Qohelet." *JQR* 37:67–84.

Gordis, Robert. 1949-1950. "The Translation Theory of Qoheleth Re-Examined." *JQR* 40:103–116.

Gordis, Robert. 1968. *Koheleth—The Man and His World*. New York, NY: Schocken (orig. 1955).

Hertzberg, Hans Wilhelm. 1963. *Der Prediger*. KAT 17/4–5. Gütersloh: Mohn.

Holm-Nielsen, Svend. 1975-1976. "The Book of Ecclesiastes and the Interpretation of It in Jewish and Christian Theology." *ASTI* 10:38–96.

Horne, Milton. 2003. *Proverbs—Ecclesiastes*. SHBC. Macon, GA: Smith & Helwys.

Ingram, Doug. 2006. *Ambiguity in Ecclesiastes*. LHBOTS 431. New York, NY: T&T Clark.

Jarick, John. 2014. "Ecclesiastes among the Comedians." Pages 176–188 in *Reading Ecclesiastes Intertextually*. Edited by Katharine Dell and Will Kynes. London: Bloomsbury T&T Clark.

Jarick, John. 2016. "Ecclesiastes among the Tragedians." Pages 155–166 in *Goochem in Mokum: Wisdom in Amsterdam*. Edited by George J. Bruuke and Pierre van Hecke. OtSt 68. Leiden: Brill.

Jastrow, Morris, and A.T. Clay. 1920. *An Old Babylonian Version of the Gilgamesh Epic*. YOSR IV:3. New Haven, CT: Yale University Press.

Krüger, Thomas. 2004. *Qoheleth: A Commentary*. Translated by O.C. Dean. Hermeneia. Minneapolis, MN: Fortress Press.

Lambert, Wilfred G. 1960. *Babylonian Wisdom Literature*. Oxford: Clarendon Press.

Lichtheim, Miriam. 1973–1980. *Ancient Egyptian Literature*. 3 vols. Berkeley, CA: University of California Press.

Loader, James A. 1979. *Polar Structures in the Book of Qohelet*. New York, NY: de Gruyter.

Lohfink, Norbert. 2003. *Qoheleth*. Translated by Sean McEvenue. CC. Minneapolis, MN: Augsburg Fortress.

Longman, Tremper, III. 1998. *The Book of Ecclesiastes*. NICOT. Grand Rapids, MI: Eerdmans.

Loretz, Oswald. 1964. *Qohelet und der alte Orient*. Freiburg: Herder.

Murphy, Roland E. 1992. *Ecclesiastes*. WBC 23A. Nashville, TN: Thomas Nelson.

Salyer, Gary D. 2001. *Vain Rhetoric: Private Insights and Public Debate in Ecclesiastes*. Sheffield: Sheffield Academic.

Schoors, Anton. 1992. *The Preacher Sought to Find Pleasing Words: A Study of the Language of Qoheleth*, Part I: *Grammar*. OLA 41. Leuven: Department Orientalistiek and Peeters.

Schoors, Anton. 2004. *The Preacher Sought to Find Pleasing Words: A Study of the Language of Qoheleth*, Part II: *Vocabulary*. OLA 143. Leuven: Department Orientalistiek and Peeters.

Schoors, Anton. 2013. *Ecclesiastes*. HCOT. Leuven: Peeters.

Schwienhorst-Schönberger, L. 1996. *"Nicht im Menschen gründet das Glück" (Koh 2, 24): Kohelet im spannungsfeld jüdischer Weisheit und hellenisticher Philosophie.* HBS 2. Freiburg: Herder.

Seow, C.L. 1997. *Ecclesiastes.* AB 18C. New York, NY: Doubleday.

Shaffer, Aaron. 1967. "The Mesopotamian Background of Qohelet 4:9–12." *ErIsr* 8:246–250 (Hebrew).

Shaffer, Aaron. 1969. "A New Light on the 'Three-Ply Cord.'" *ErIsr* 9:138–139, 159–160 (Hebrew).

Shupak, Nili. Forthcoming. "Conversation with One's Heart or Soul in Wisdom Literature." In *Ve-'Ed Ya'aleh (Gen 2:6): Essays in Biblical and Ancient Near Eastern Studies Presented to Edward L. Greenstein.* Edited by Peter Machinist et al. University Park, PA: Eisenbrauns.

Siegfried, Carl G. 1898. *Predisger und Hoheslied.* Göttingen: Vandenhoeck & Ruprecht.

Toorn, Karl van der. 2001. "Echoes of Gilgamesh in the Book of Qohelet?" Pages 503–514 in *Veenhof Anniversary Volume: Studies Presented to Klaas R. Veenhof on the Occasion of His Sixty-Fifth Birthday.* Edited by W.H. van Soldt. Leiden: Nederlands Instituut voor Het Nabue Oosten.

Torrey, Charles C. 1948–1949. "The Question of the Original Language of Qohelet." *JQR* 39:151–160.

Whitley, Charles F. 1979. *Koheleth: His Language and Thought.* BZAW 148. Berlin: de Gruyter.

Whybray, R. Norman. 1981. "The Identification and Use of Quotations in Ecclesiastes." Pages 435–451 in *Congress Volume: Vienna, 1980.* Edited by J.A. Emerton. VTSup 32. Leiden: Brill.

Whybray, R. Norman. 1989. *Ecclesiastes.* NCB. Grand Rapids, MI: Eerdmans; London: Marshall, Morgan & Scott.

Whybray, R. Norman. 1997. *Ecclesiastes.* JSOT. Sheffield: Sheffield Academic (orig. 1989).

Wright, Addison. G. 1968. "The Riddle of the Sphinx: The Structure of the Book of Qohelet." *CBQ* 30:313–334.

Wright, Charles H.H. 1883. *Book of Koheleth.* London: Hodder & Stoughton.

Zer-Kavod, Mordechai. 1973. "Qoheleth." In *Five Megilloth.* Da'at Miqra. Jerusalem: Mossad Harav Kook (Hebrew).

Zimmerli, Walter. 1974. *"Das Buch Kohelet: Traktat oder Sentenzensammlung?"* VT 24:221–230.

CHAPTER 32

....

JOB

....

SCOTT C. JONES

32.1 JOB THE RIGHTEOUS, JOB THE PATIENT, AND JOB THE ATHLETE

....

ALREADY in the book of Ezekiel, the figure of Job appears alongside Noah as part of an ancient tradition. Job is idealized as one of the consummate righteous men who, if YHWH were not so determined, might otherwise save the house of Israel by his right-eousness (צדקה, Ezek 14:14, 20). In the New Testament, too, Job is a paragon, but this time of "patience" (ὑπομονή, Jas 5:11). The patience of Job, which is still axiomatic in current parlance, was a theme in early Jewish testamentary literature, including the Greek com-position commonly known as the Testament of Job, where Job is praised for his patient endurance (Attridge 2013; Balentine 2015).

Job is often paired with Abraham in early Jewish literature, since both are called "God-fearers" who are exemplary in their righteousness (Gen 22:12; Job 1:1; t. Sotah 6:1; T. Abraham 15:4–5; Weinberg 1994). But while Abraham was the consummate pious Israelite, most held that Job was a God-fearing Gentile (Baskin 1983; Baskin 1992). In addition to their comparable piety, Job was commonly said to be a contemporary of Abraham or Moses. The longer ending of the Greek book of Job in 42:17 identifies him as descendant of Esau (thus an Edomite) who was converted to Abrahamic religion. To symbolize this conversion, Jobab, as he was formerly known (Gen 36:33), became Job. Given the typical portrayal of Job as a patriarch, the rabbis often held that the book was composed by Moses (b. B. Bat. 15a–16b), and that theory may have been promi-nent even at Qumran, where one Hebrew manuscript containing portions of Job 13–14 was written using an old-style script (4QpaleoJob[c] = 4Q101). All other Qumran manu-scripts written in this script are from the Pentateuch or Joshua (Skehan, Ulrich, and Sanderson 1992, 155).

The Testament of Job, which likely dates to the first century CE, portrays Job as an ideal athlete, who wrestled with Satan and won (T. Job 4:10; 27:1–5). The theme persists in Christian literature at least through late antiquity, even informing literary works from the Renaissance such as Milton's brief epic, *Paradise Regained* (Lewalski 1966), and it reverberates in chilling ways in proto-Nazi literature such as Kurt Eggers's *Das Spiel vom Job dem Deutschen*, published in 1933 (Jones 2015).

32.2 JOB, THE INNOCENT SUFFERER, AND THE JUSTICE OF GOD

Interpreters in the modern West have tended to emphasize Job's role as an iconic innocent sufferer so that the book of Job is portrayed more as a trial of God's justice than a test of Job's fortitude, righteousness, or patient endurance. The question of God's justice is not a new one, nor is it particularly Western. However, the word "theodicy," coined by Gottfried Wilhelm Leibniz (1710), is a recent invention, and its theoretical inclination is at home in modernity. The term theodicy is now freely applied to Job as a description of its purpose: to justify the ways of God to humans in the face of suffering and evil (Illman 2003). In connection with this tendency, the figure of Job is often viewed as a kind of "Everyman"—a symbol of any human who suffers inexplicable tragedy. Interestingly, this portrayal of Job runs against the grain of the initial prose description of him as utterly unique in terms of piety and wealth (Job 1:1–3; Clines 1994, 20; Fox 2011, 147–148).

Scholars have offered numerous answers to the question of whether the God of the book of Job can be justified in light of the discontinuity that the book presents between the hero's deeds and the suffering he endures (Oeming 2018). For example, Matitiahu Tsevat (1966) famously argued that God is neither just nor unjust; rather, the book makes the world a-moral. Janzen (2018) suggests that an apparent disconnect between deeds and consequences does not invalidate God's justice, for God's justice is at core characterized by a generosity of divine movement beyond any quid pro quo. Still others do not attempt to argue for God's justice, concluding that Job's God is a brutal sadomasochist who wants to be revered for his power (Greenstein 2009). It is clear that any answer to the question of theodicy in Job depends in large part on how one construes the nature of justice.

Others have underscored that the book is not interested in offering a theoretical explanation for suffering but instead points beyond theodicy to a dialogical relationship with a transcendent Creator (Burrell 2008). In my estimation, one of the book's greatest innovations is the author's imagining of a system of justice outside the deity, to which the deity is accountable. As Bruce Zuckerman (1991, 113) says, "What makes Job's prosecution of God so outrageous from a legal standpoint is that it endeavors to bypass the power that makes the legal system work[;] . . . the most fundamental rule of law in the Ancient Near East [is that] God *is* the Law." However one answers the question of Job's relationship to modern reflections on divine justice, the figure of Job has long served as an exemplary sufferer that audiences are to identify with. Already in the Qumran

Hodayot, the author alludes to Job's sufferings so that his community would relate themselves to Job in his trials but also see themselves as those who have persisted through suffering and, like Job after the whirlwind, are enlightened with wisdom (Szpek 2005, 366–367).

32.3 THE HEBREW BOOK OF JOB
AS A LITERARY WORK

The book of Job is, as Edward Greenstein (2007a, 83) notes, "a drama of words." Yet the language of this literary masterpiece is often as puzzling as it is inspiring. This is due in part to the relative rarity of its diction, including the 160 or so terms that are unique to Job in the Hebrew Bible. Martin Luther (1960, 252) could say in 1524 that "The language of this book is more vigorous (*reisig*) and splendid (*prächtig*) than that of any other book in all the Scriptures" and yet recount six years later that during their translation efforts of that same year, he, Melanchthon, and Aurogallus "hardly could complete three lines in four days" (*Sendbrief vom Dolmetschen*, 1530; see Raeder 2008, 398).

Recent studies have offered that Job was very likely written using an economic or "conservative" style of spelling as part of a conceit that the book is ancient. This spelling practice also results in several cases of "visual poetry" throughout the work (Seow 2011a). Dovetailing with this, Greenstein (2003a) explains the use of foreign— especially Aramaic—elements in the poetry of Job as an intentional poetic feature. The book's linguistic "foreignness" is part and parcel of the author's depiction of the book's speakers and setting as Transjordanian in origin (Greenstein 2007a, 88). Whatever one's view of the book's language and spelling, its artistry is rich and multifaceted (Seow 2013, 74–87), and it is worthy of Victor Hugo's praise as "one of the greatest masterpieces of the human mind" (Uzanne 1892, 570).

A masterpiece though it is, Job does not fit neatly into any category, and there have been a wide array of views on its literary genre, ranging from lament to apocalypse (see survey in Mies 2003). Whatever its original state may have been, the received form of the book in the Hebrew Bible is a composition consisting of many genres—a kind of "supergenre"—in which all the parts are in dialogue with one another and where none rightly describes the whole. Some scholars have even seen the book's generic innovation as a necessary outworking of the complex aesthetic problem its author seeks to solve (Hoffman 1996). Carol Newsom (2016, 243) comments insightfully on the tension between the book's parts: "Had the author of the canonical book of Job wished to write a seamlessly coherent literary version of the Job story, he undoubtedly could have done so. Instead, he has produced a work that requires the reader to negotiate both its centrifugal and centripetal forces in a manner that makes simple coherence not only impossible but undesirable."

In some respects, Job has its closest Near Eastern counterparts in dialogue literature like The Babylonian Theodicy. Yet Job is not so much a dialogue as it is dialogical
(Newsom 2003; Stordalen 2006). It sets various voices in conversation with one another
for critical reflection, but unlike the later Socratic dialogues, it lacks a sense of progression and does not arrive at a satisfactory conclusion. Job is not at ease in any traditional
category and is truly sui generis—one of a kind.

32.4 THE BOOK OF JOB AS "WISDOM LITERATURE"

Beyond the particular issue of genre, there is the general issue of whether Job is properly
considered to be "Wisdom Literature." Its inclusion in the present volume follows common scholarly convention, but not all are convinced that Job is mainstream Wisdom
Literature (Dell 1991, 57–108) or that "Wisdom Literature" is even a helpful moniker
(Kynes 2015). It must be admitted that Job stands outside of the widely attested threefold list of "Solomonic" books—Proverbs, Ecclesiastes, and Song of Songs—and that
Job came into its own as "Wisdom Literature" precisely when the theory of Solomonic
authorship for those three books began to dissolve. The book of Job does focus in a concentrated way on wisdom in chapter 28, but the largest parts of the book are more closely
related to Babylonian compositions which were not thought of as belonging to a distinct
genre of "Wisdom." Thus "Wisdom" is an etic, rather than an emic, category for Job and
for much of the ancient Near Eastern literature that is closest to it. That said, its literary
proximity to Proverbs and Ecclesiastes in the Hebrew tradition (b. B. Bat. 14b) and in
Western canons means that it is not likely to be dislodged from its connection to those
two books in particular and to "Wisdom Literature" in general.

32.5 ANCIENT NEAR EASTERN LITERATURE AND THE BOOK OF JOB

There are five main texts that are commonly compared to Job in one way or another—
one in Sumerian and four in Akkadian (see Newsom 2003, 72–89; Seow 2013, 51–56). It
must be noted that these are only comparable in some way to the poetic portions of the
book, not to the narrative frame.

The five texts are: (1) The Sumerian text from Nippur, "Man and His God." The tablet
dates to ca. 1700 BCE, though the composition was already known in the third millennium (Kramer 1960). (2) The Old Babylonian (ca. 2003–1595 BCE) text AO 4462, called
"Dialogue between a Man and His God" (Foster 2005, 148–150). (3) The Babylonian text

now known by its first line in Akkadian, Ludlul bēl nēmeqi (= "I Will Praise the Lord of Wisdom") (Foster 2005, 392–409; Oshima 2014, 3–114, 169–342), which was likely written in the thirteenth century BCE (4) An Akkadian hymn to Marduk text from Ugarit (RS 25.460) that has obvious connections with Ludlul bēl nēmeqi and is roughly contemporaneous with it. Benjamin Foster (2005, 410–411) calls it "A Sufferer's Salvation." (5) The "Babylonian Theodicy," which takes the form of a dialogue between a sufferer and a friend and which likely dates somewhere between 1400–800 BCE (Foster 2005, 914–922; Oshima 2014, 115–168, 343–375).

It is important to note at the outset how closely several of these are connected to incantations and magic. Marduk, the "Lord of Wisdom" (*bēl nēmeqi*), was an expert in exorcism, which is why the composition praises him and appeals to him for healing. RS 25.460 was found in the library of an incantation-priest and likewise addresses Marduk. The "Babylonian Theodicy" is a dialogue written in twenty-seven stanzas of eleven lines each, in which each line in any stanza begins with the same syllable. Taken together, the initial syllable from the twenty-seven stanzas is an acrostic that identifies the author as the incantation-priest, Saggil-kinam-ubbib. Beyond the artistry of the compositions, then, these facts underscore that such literature was the product and currency of a small and esoteric group of literary elite.

The Sumerian text, "Man and His God," is an extended lament in which an unnamed sufferer pleads with his personal god to intercede for him and relieve his physical, emotional, and social suffering. After confessing his guilt and pleading for deliverance, the god accepts his prayer and removes the demons that plague him. The Akkadian text "Dialogue between a Man and His God" is similarly a lament expressed by a man who pleads before the statue of his personal god to forgive his sins and restore his health and who receives a positive response. Both texts assume, like Job's friends (but unlike Job himself), that suffering in the form of illness was a punishment for sin, whether known or unknown. All one can do is praise and confess until the gods respond.

Since its discovery in 1875, Ludlul bēl nēmeqi has been compared to Job. At that time, only Tablet II of the work was known, and the comparison seemed so apt that it was dubbed "The Babylonian Job." As more tablets came to light, however, the narrative of the text changed somewhat, so that its original English editor stated that it was better thought of as "The Babylonian *Pilgrim's Progress*" (Lambert 1960, 27). The text is a long poetic monologue by one Šubši-mešrê-Šakkan, which opens and closes with a hymn to Marduk, who is the lord of *nēmequ*, which is to say, practical wisdom, including magic. The framework of the whole text is the presentation of Marduk as a dialectical deity—one who both strikes and heals. The sufferer's journey is one of the discovery of Marduk's sovereignty over all the personal gods that leads to the glorification of the cult of Marduk as the cosmic ruler (Moran 2002). Behind apparent inscrutability is Marduk's plan. The theology of RS 25.460 is similar, though much shorter and less developed. Ludlul perhaps compares most favorably to Job, since both seem to revel in words and literary artistry. Yet in form and content Ludlul is more like a hymn of thanksgiving (Weinfeld 1988). Job, like others texts in the Hebrew Bible, presents YHWH as a dialectical deity who both inflicts and heals (Job 5:18; cf. Deut 32:39; Isa 30:26; Hos 6:1). Perhaps from a long view, Job's journey from being an ideal devotee of YHWH in the prologue to once again being a servant of YHWH after the whirlwind speeches may be considered similar to the religious journey of Šubši-mešrê-Šakkan. But the theology of the central figure in Ludlul is closer to that of Job's friends than to Job as the emblematic sufferer.

The Babylonian Theodicy is in many respects the closest ancient Near Eastern analogue to Job. The sufferer dialogues with a friend, and each has a different position on the relationship between piety and present circumstance. While the sufferer suggests that piety seems to have done him no good, the friend argues that the strategy of the gods is impenetrable, and he encourages the sufferer to continue to seek divine healing. Like Job, the dialogue comes to no real conclusion, and some of the viewpoints in the final stanzas seem ill-fitting to their speaker (see Foster 2005, 921 n. 3). Even with their similarities, however, there are significant differences. The comparison between Job and the Theodicy applies only to the dialogue portion in Job chapters 4–28 and not to the rest of the book. The exchange between the sufferer and the friend is much more polite, and while the sufferer questions the effectiveness of his piety, he never seeks to put the gods on trial, as Job does. Finally, the acrostic structure is much closer to Psalm 119 than anything in Job.

Gerald Mattingly (1990) has proposed that this group of texts is best called "pious sufferer" texts, rather than "righteous sufferer" texts, due to the fact that the sufferer in this literature typically believes that his own sin has brought about his current condition, even if he does not know what that sin is. Job, however, is different. Job is righteous (the prologue tells us that is precisely why he suffers), and throughout the book, Job declares his own righteousness. Texts like "Dialogue between a Man and His God" and Ludlul end with the sufferer's healing, yet Job's body is never said to have been healed in the biblical book. Like these "pious sufferer" texts from the ancient Near East, Job does not know why he suffers. But a key difference is that the remoteness of the divine plan, emphasized both by Job's friends and the friend in The Babylonian Theodicy, is laid bare in the prologue of Job, as the audience is admitted into the celestial court. Much of the tension involved in experiencing the book rests on this dramatic irony.

32.6 THE CAST OF CHARACTERS, AND A FAIRYTALE BEGINNING (JOB 1–2)

Though the opening narrative of Job is integral to the interpretation of the whole, it is commonplace to pit the narrative frame against the poetic middle. Indeed, referring to it as a "prologue" and to the narrative ending as the "epilogue" reinforces the apparent centrality of the non-narrative portions. There is some debate over the relationship of the narrative and the poetry in the book's development, each having a different literary effect if one comes before the other (see Newsom 2002, 134).

Some scholars have gone so far as to argue for two different characterizations of Job that arise from two different literary strata. These correspond roughly (though not entirely) to the book's prose and poetic portions: the book of Job the Patient (chs. 1–2, 27–28, 42:7b–17) and the book of Job the Impatient (chs. 3–26; 29:1–42:6) (Ginsberg 1967; Ginsberg 1971). The tension is so pronounced that it has led most scholars to reconstruct a different prehistory for the prose and poetic portions of the book. Some have compared the Joban narrative, now commonly referred to as a "folk tale" (*Volkssage*), to Canaanite epics like Kirta and Aqhat, suggesting that the prose tale is derived from an original Joban epic (Sarna 1957). All such characterizations have, wittingly or unwittingly, made modern scholars feel compelled to choose to take either the prose or poetry more seriously than the other.

Despite the fact that it introduces "the assumptions upon which the entire book is based and according to which everything that follows is to be understood" (Weiss 1983, 14), most have not taken the prose introduction all that seriously (Fox 2011, 145). That is not, however, universally the case. David Clines (1985) has argued that though the opening narrative seems naive, it is really *pseudo*-naive—its apparent simplicity and lack of subtlety covers over a much deeper and more thoughtful narration that can be interpreted in continuity with the poetic portions of the book. Alan Cooper (1990) and Susanne Gillmayr-Bucher (2007) have bolstered Clines's argument, pointing to the intricate strategies and multiplicity of voices that characterize the narrative. According to Cooper (1990, 71–73), the prologue offers three ways of looking at God's relation to humanity's actions: (1) predictable causality, (2) causality but not predictability, and (3) neither causality nor predictability. He concludes that the prologue intentionally presents all three as possibilities, depending on the reader's point of view. If, as both Clines and Cooper suggest, reading the prologue is like looking in a hermeneutical mirror, then it is perhaps as revealing of the current lines of both lay and scholarly interpretation as it is of the prologue itself that the narrative's apparent order, stability, and wholeness (so Newsom 2002, 125) are often seen as hopelessly idealistic illusions that must be deconstructed through irony (see Fox 2011, 146). Furthermore, most interpreters seem naturally to sympathize with the view that a human's actions have predictable consequences that flow causally from them—the view that Cooper (1990, 71) assigns to Job's friends and the שטן.

The שטן—commonly called "Satan" (NRSV, NIV)—has an important role in the Joban prologue, though he is strangely absent in the epilogue. The reception of this figure as "Satan," as known from the New Testament and beyond, is as real as any historical reconstruction of the figure that is at work in what is likely a Persian period narrative. However, the שטן in Job is not identical to the group of concepts that readers often associate with the term "Satan" (Breytenbach and Day 1999, 726–732). It seems that what is now thought of as a personal name—"Satan"—was originally a title or job description: "*the* שטן" or "*the* Adversary." The Adversary's role was one of casting doubt on the status quo or, as one might say, "playing the Devil's advocate." The context was primarily legal, and the role extended to appearances during deliberations of the divine council, as in Job 1:6 (Weiss 1983, 35–42; Seow 2013, 272–274). Newsom (2003, 125) fittingly describes the Adversary as "the narrative embodiment of the hermeneutic of suspicion."

After YHWH calls attention to the exemplary nature of Job's religion in 1:8, the Adversary questions whether Job really serves God חנם, since he has been protected from what would make him stumble. In response, YHWH agrees to allow Job's integrity to be tested, and he removes the first "hedge," giving the Adversary permission to do what he wishes with Job's possessions. The meaning of the term חנם is a matter of some dispute, but its interpretation is likely one of the keys to interpreting the entire book (Janzen 2018, 52–60, 69). Common glosses are "for nothing," "for no reason," and "without cause." Though the term occurs only twice in the prologue, it is often translated differently in each case: normally "for nothing" when spoken by the Adversary in 1:9 and "for no reason" when spoken by YHWH in 2:3. However, it seems best to gloss both instances as something like "without benefit" (Linafelt and Davis 2013). Thus the Adversary implies in 1:9 that Job is only gaming the system and serving YHWH for some benefit he will receive. And YHWH implies in 2:3 that the experiment so far has not produced any benefit, since Job's persistence in his integrity has left the situation unchanged.

The Adversary's line of questioning assumes the possibility of conflict between Job's outer and inner lives. Though the focus here on interiority jibes with modern sensibilities, the overwhelming focus in ancient Near Eastern religion was on deeds, not the inner life of a person. This inner life, however, is the basis for the Adversary's instigation of the Joban experiment and his "wager" (as Goethe's *Faust* characterizes it) with YHWH. But Job himself introduces the idea in 1:5, when he goes so far as to offer prophylactic sacrifices for his children in case they cursed God "in their hearts." The degree to which the book investigates this interiority is, in my estimation, a point of innovation. Equally innovative is the Adversary's implication that Job is pious only to receive some benefit from God. Thus, the ideal promoted here by the Adversary (and perhaps the author) is piety for piety's sake. This sounds remarkably like a Kantian ethic of doing good for its own sake, while all other motives are corrupt. But "people do not do religion *not* to get some benefit" (Snell 2011, 96). While none of this, then, is entirely new, such viewpoints were not as commonplace in ancient Near Eastern religion as modern readers might be inclined to believe. While human motives were commonly thought to be accessible only to the gods and not to humans themselves (e.g., Prov 15:11), the author(s) of Job construct(s) an entire composition around the theme and draw(s) the audience into the process of investigation as voyeurs.

Bereft of his possessions and having passed the first test, Job loses another of his "hedges," as YHWH now allows the Adversary access to Job's flesh and bones, though not his life-force (2:6). With this second test, the book moves one layer deeper into Job's interiority. Job's bodily suffering provokes the only speech of Job's unnamed wife in the entire book: "Bless God and die!" (2:9). The word ברך, commonly translated "bless," sometimes functions as a euphemism with the opposite meaning, "curse." However, in its six occurrences in the Joban prologue, which of these two possible meanings is intended is not self-evident (Linafelt 1996). Yet the choice one makes has enormous implications for the interpretation of Job, and especially for its characterization of Job's wife (see Low 2013). Is she a sympathetic figure, as she seems to be in the Old Greek expansion of Job 2:9 and in the Testament of Job, where she even disgraces herself by selling her hair in exchange for food (T. Job 24:1–25:10)? Or is she a temptress who is "the Devil's helper" in undermining Job's piety, as Augustine said (Seow 2007)? And just as

Job had wondered whether his children had sinned "in their hearts" (1:5), the narrator seems to raise the same possibility for Job by specifying only that Job did not sin "with his lips" (2:10). Thus, the question of Job's interiority has not yet been resolved.

32.7 Arguments, Insults, and Soapbox-Speeches (Job 3–31)

The poetic portions of Job open with what is indisputably a curse (קלל, 3:1). By expressing his pain in this way, the ideal and unparalleled "fairy tale" figure of Job in the prologue "becomes one of us" in chapter 3 (Fox 2011, 147). Job's malediction is not directed against God but against his own "day." While Job's body was the subject of a celestial experiment in the second half of the prologue, now he imagines it to be the very center of the cosmos (Jones 2013, 846). His outburst portrays himself and the world-order as so closely intertwined that his death-wish coincides with the undoing of the entire cosmos (cf. Jer 20:14–18).

Job's three friends, introduced in the prologue and there noted for their silent sympathy (2:11–13), can no longer hold their tongues (4:1). From this point until Job's closing monologue in chapters 29–31, they respond to Job in the same order—Eliphaz, then Bildad, then Zophar—and in three rounds (chapters 4–14; 15–21; and 22–28). Despite the differences between Job and his friends, their viewpoints overlap so much at some points that their speeches (or parts of them) seem to have been assigned to the wrong person. Some scholars, for example, attribute 4:12–21 to Job rather than Eliphaz (most recently, Brown 2015). On the whole, the three friends differ markedly from Job in taking their epistemological starting point not from their own personal experience but from the tradition (Greenstein 2007b). Repeatedly, they claim to have "searched out" the tradition in the wisdom of the sages and found it to establish their point of view (e.g., 5:27; 8:8; 15:10, 17–18).

Job, however, is unimpressed. He claims that the friends are unreliable, while he himself is in the right (6:29). He is equally unimpressed with God, who created humans as slave labor and terrifies them until their death (7:1–16). God's gaze does not watch and protect but investigates and incriminates (7:17–21). Bildad contests Job's claim that God perverts justice and reminds him that if he is indeed righteous, he has nothing to fear (8:1–22). Job admits that his desire to enter into a dispute (ריב) with God is not feasible (9:2–3), but claims the fault lies with God. For God would simply overpower Job, making him guilty even when he was innocent and refusing to hear his testimony (9:4–20). It is God who would ensure that Job did not receive a fair trial. Job is so in awe of God's numinous terror that he imagines he could only dispute with God through an arbitrator (מוכיח, 9:33) who could hold both him and God to account. The legal metaphor becomes prominent here and remains important throughout the book. Job's desire to initiate litigation with God is highly unconventional, and it may well be a critical reflection upon

Isa 1:18–20, pointing out what he sees as a logical weakness in the prophetic use of the legal metaphor. Namely, "How can he hope for a fair trial, if God is to be both his opponent and his judge?" (Roberts 1973, 165). His appeal to a mediator may be akin to the Mesopotamian appeal to a personal god to intercede on one's behalf with the national god. Job is certain that God knows he is innocent (10:7), and yet God would pile up witnesses against him and attack him repeatedly (10:16–17). And so Job imagines himself as a fetal misbirth, wishing to return to the chthonic depths whence he came (10:18–22).

Zophar wishes that Job's tendency to multiply words would be met by a theophany in which God would demonstrate how multi-faceted wisdom is (11:1–6). For the wisdom of God is unsearchable, beyond the bounds of spatial dimensions (11:7–9). Job's only hope is to pray and rid himself of any wickedness (11:13–15).

Job, however, mocks the friends' collective "wisdom" (12:1), and he himself takes on the role of the sage to deconstruct their roles as sages. For God often thwarts counselors (12:17), and age does not guarantee wisdom (12:12). Rather, Job appeals to his ear, his palate, and his eyes (12:12; 13:1), and in his exchanges with his friends, he does not hear, taste, or see wisdom. Their utterances are "proverbs of dust" (13:12). Job insists on taking his life into his own hands (13:14) and on arguing with God (13:3). Job's claim in 13:15 is as difficult to interpret as it is important to the book's interpretation. The Masoretic text preserves two traditions that seem to have opposite meanings. As the text is written (*ketiv*: לא), Job has no hope. But as the Masoretic tradition would have it read (*qere*: לו), he does have hope. The tradition of interpretation is mixed, but most have seen it as "an affirmation of unshakeable faith amid suffering and even the possibility of death" (see discussion in Seow 2013, 641). My own inclination is to interpret Job as saying that even if God were to kill him, he still holds on to hope that he may argue his case posthumously. Job's speech in chapter 14 is likewise characterized by a tension vis-à-vis hope, as elsewhere throughout the book (see Mies 2006). Job notes the fragility of mortality, as humans fade quickly like a flower (14:1–2). Some plants need only the scent of water to re-bloom (14:7–9), yet this is not the case with mortals (14:10–12). Or is it? Interpreters through the centuries have taken Job 14:14 to claim life after death. So the Greek reads, "If a person dies, he will live." Though the Hebrew text poses this as a question that expects a negative answer, the theme of hope lives on in Job 14 not only through various renderings amongst the early versions, but also through the "afterlife" of the poem (Seow 2010). Whatever the historical author of Job meant for his character to say, the themes of hope and the afterlife continue to crop up and refuse to go away. And yet Job's final speech in the first cycle ends with his declaration that God "destroys human hope" (14:19), and concludes with the word "mourns" (14:22).

The second cycle of speeches (chs. 15–21) begins with Eliphaz accusing Job of undermining piety (15:4). Job's own mouth and lips condemn him (15:6). Eliphaz claims authority for all three of Job's companions, once again, by appeal to their connection to ancient tradition (15:10, 18). He counts Job among the wicked, who rush at God like a warrior (15:25). Like those who challenge God directly, Job will not flourish (15:28–35). For Job, the "comfort" the friends came to provide (cf. 2:11) has in fact produced more misery and toil (16:2). Their words have destroyed his body, which now offers its own testimony against him (16:8). Here, as elsewhere, parts of Job's disintegrating body participate in his continuing legal case (Erickson 2013). Though Eliphaz has accused Job of playing the warrior, he points out that it is God who, as a warrior, has attacked him (16:9–14; Jones 2013, 849–853). Job continues to look for an arbitrator, now specified as being celestial (16:19–21). He rehearses his bodily and social dislocation (17:1–11), consigning not only his body to Sheol, but with it, his hope (17:15–16). Bildad objects to being thought of as an ignorant beast (18:3; cf. Ps 73:22), and he narrates the doomed fate of the wicked.

Job's response in chapter 19 is among the most famous parts of the book. Once again, he focuses on divine violence and his status as a social outcast, so that even his own family has disowned him (19:13–19). Only his skin will stick by him (19:20). And yet he wants to be rid of his flesh, too, since it represents decay, and therefore guilt (Erickson 2013: 307–308). He wants a permanent record, hewn into a mountain with an iron stylus (19:23–24; cf. the Bisitun inscription). Ostracized from all other relatives, he proclaims that there is a kinsman-redeemer (גאל) who will testify on his behalf even after he is dead (19:25). But, remarkably, he will also behold God after his flesh has been peeled from his body (19:26–27). The text of this passage is exceedingly difficult, producing widely divergent interpretations. Early Christian interpreters cited this passage in Greek as proof of bodily resurrection (1 Clem 26:3). Just as Job's fractured body somehow transcends its own limitations to see God, so also have the themes of hope and survival—and even resurrection—survived in the book of Job, despite occasional attempts to dismiss it as theologically secondary (Breed 2014, 163–189).

Zophar retorts with a lengthy description of the God-ordained inheritance of the wicked. Their apparent flourishing during their lifetime will be overshadowed by their ruinous demise and the misfortune reserved for their heirs (cf. Pss 37, 73). Job, however, claims that this is not, in fact, the case: "How often is the lamp of the wicked extinguished, and [how often] does their calamity befall them?" (21:17). Job believes that calamity is not meted out on the day of disaster (21:30). The friends' attempts to console Job amount to nothing other than infidelity (21:34). Thus ends the second cycle of speeches.

The third round of speeches (chs. 22–28) again begins with Eliphaz, and it confirms the impression that little progress is made in these dialogues. The rhetoric has become so heated that the arguments have run off the rails. The third cycle has caused a great deal of difficulty for interpreters, because here more than elsewhere, the content of some speeches do not fit their speaker. Furthermore, while the structure of the friends' speeches has been regular to this point, Bildad's is unusually short (25:1–6) and Zophar lacks a final speech altogether. Furthermore, Job's last retort (chs. 26–28) often sounds a great deal like what Zophar would say. Critics have commonly assumed that this apparent disarrangement results from textual problems, but, if so, these corruptions must have happened well before any text of Job—Hebrew or otherwise—was preserved in its current form. The discussion, therefore, is largely redaction-critical, and according to some, Job's figure in the third cycle was transformed from a sufferer to a teacher by a threefold redaction (Witte 1994). Interestingly, similar problems with content and identification of speakers characterize the end of the Babylonian Theodicy (Foster 2005, 921 n. 3).

In chapters 26 and 27, Job continues to declare the foolishness of his friends' "wisdom" (26:3), and he refuses to yield his claim to be in the right (27:6). Yet, strangely, his speeches begin to emphasize God's power in bringing order out of chaos. Particularly problematic for many interpreters is chapter 28, which, because of its reflective mood, is often characterized as a "hymn" to wisdom. Though the chapter's location in the book's current form suggests that it is Job's, it is often re-assigned to others, including Zophar (Fox 2018), Elihu (Greenstein 2003b; Clines 2004), or even "a disembodied voice" (Newsom 2003, 259), perhaps of the author himself. Some, however, have argued that it may still be read as Job's speech (Lo 2003). Even the topic of chapter 28 is contested, and I have argued extensively that much of the chapter is modeled on ancient Near Eastern epics of heroes who explore distant lands to obtain precious treasure (Jones 2009).

In chapters 29–31, Job once again offers a monologue, as he did at the outset of the book's poetic section in chapter 3. His memory turns now to his former life, well before his suffering began. These chapters contain "a judicial complaint against wrongful conduct by someone in a position of power" that has affinities with the Yavneh Yam inscription (Seow 2013, 60). Job was a wise and just judge, respected by all those who heard his counsel (29:7–25). But now he has become an object of taunting by those who once honored him (30:9), and like dust and ashes to God (30:19). Job is now completely isolated, the companion only to strange and dangerous animals beyond the reaches of civilization (30:29). Job asks that he be weighed on a scale so that he may be found to have integrity (31:6). He recounts his just and merciful deeds in every stratum of society and, one last time, imagines himself in a legal hearing with the Almighty, now wearing a written record of his indictment as if it were a garland gracing his flayed body (31:35).

32.8 Two Answers (Job 32–42:6)

With the onset of chapter 32, we learn that a fourth friend, Elihu, was standing there all along, who has until now been silent. He waited for Eliphaz, Bildad, and Zophar to finish out of respect for their age (32:4, 6), but their inability to answer Job made him so angry that he can now no longer restrain himself. Full of words, he feels he will burst if he does not let them out (32:18–19). Despite his relative youth, Elihu argues that he is filled with the spirit of God and so is qualified to answer when they cannot (32:7–10). He hopes to be the vindicator Job has been longing for and to be able to declare Job righteous (33:32). Yet he also wants to justify God (36:3). Thus Elihu's speeches are a theodicy (e.g., 34:10–15). God disciplines, he says, in order to change human actions (33:16–17). Elihu responds to Job's suffering by emphasizing total transcendence: God is greater than humans (33:12; 36:22, 26), and humans do not affect God (35:5–8). After a poem about God's might in creation, including the storm (37:9), Elihu closes his speeches by stating that no human can see God (37:24). YHWH then appears to Job in the following verse (38:1).

Though some have regarded Elihu's speeches as being essential to the theology of the book, others have viewed him as a braggart who can be readily dismissed (see overview in Wahl 1993, 1–35). Already in the Testament of Job, the author characterizes Elihu as being "inspired by Satan" (T. Job 41:5), and even includes a hymn of imprecation against him (T. Job 43:1–17). Elihu is not mentioned in Job 42:9 along with the other friends, and the Testament concludes that this is because Elihu was not forgiven by God (T. Job 43:1–2).

On the whole, modern scholars have continued to advance this negative evaluation of Elihu's usefulness. Several studies have concluded that the Elihu speeches were written by a later author or even by the book's redactor, who was dissatisfied with the current state of the book and sought to correct it (e.g., Wahl 1993). Some have even proposed that much of the rest of the book was re-worked in light of the Elihu speeches (Mende 1990). More recently, however, Choon Leong Seow (2011b) has proposed that the Elihu speeches are critical for the argument and movement of the book from chapters 29–31 to chapters 38–41. For Seow, the Elihu speeches represent a mediated revelation through dreams and visions (e.g., 33:14–16), such as that which is common to traditions about the god El, while the divine speeches that follow represent the unmediated revelation of a storm theophany characteristic of traditions relating to YHWH.

Immediately upon the close of Elihu's monologue, YHWH appears to Job in a storm-wind (סערה; 38:1), and Job sees YHWH with his own eyes (cf. 42:5). After rebuking Job for speaking out of ignorance, YHWH offers what most interpreters have viewed as YHWH's answer to Job and the key to interpreting the book. On the face of it, one must admit, however, YHWH's response does not seem to answer Job's complaints at all.

YHWH takes Job on a tour of the far reaches of the cosmos and the wonders of the animal kingdom (chs. 38–39), and then parades out two strange and wonderful monsters for Job's consideration (chs. 40–41). Is this really just an overly long lecture in the natural sciences? As Clines (2003, 250) notes of the final speech on Leviathan, "[I]f everything in the book has been tending towards it, its significance has to be more than crocodiles." Interpreters have hardly been united about the nature of this "answer." For example, some have interpreted the divine speeches as both correction and invitation to restoration and flourishing (Janzen 2009, 99–104). Others have portrayed them as an aggressive attack by a hostile and self-centered deity (Greenstein 2009, 353). The second speech about Behemoth and Leviathan is a special quandary. It is common to interpret these creatures as representing evil and chaos that God must defeat, as in other *Chaoskampf* texts in ancient Near Eastern literature, though others emphasize YHWH's care and even admiration for them (see discussion in Fox 2013, 9–13).

My own view is that the first divine speech is aimed at de-centering Job and more accurately re-describing his place in the cosmos, while the second speech about Behemoth and Leviathan intends to inspire Job to re-imagine himself as one who is honored and whom YHWH cares for (Jones 2013, 854–863). Job can only be answered outside of the framework from which he posed his complaints and questions, for that frame itself is flawed. The divine speeches expose those flaws and offer another one for him to adopt—one in which God does not view Job merely as "dust and ashes" (30:19) nor as "insignificant" (40:3). Like Leviathan, he is powerful and glorious, but his strength and pride must know their proper limits within the bounds of God's cosmos.

32.9 THE AFTERMATH, AND A HAPPY ENDING (JOB 42:7–17)

So what does Job make of all this? Aside from one brief interjection between the two divine speeches (40:3–5), Job has not spoken since the end of his final monologue in 31:40. Job now concedes that he spoke ignorantly and that YHWH may indeed run the cosmos according to a plan that he was ignorant of (42:2–4). Now having encountered YHWH directly, rather than just through hearsay, he changes his mind about characterizing God as one who views him as mere dust and ashes (42:5–6; cf. 30:19).

The translation and interpretation of Job 42:6 is hotly contested, with the verb נחם at the heart of the debate. Interpretations range from Job taking comfort regarding his finite humanity to repenting in dust and ashes to offering a bold and impious statement of loathing and contempt for God. And even if he did "repent," this is now commonly understood as ironic or disingenuous (surveys in Krüger 2007; Fox 2013, 18–20). To my mind, the most cogent interpretation includes a sincere change in Job—one that leads YHWH to allow him to be effective once again as a priestly intercessor, now for his three friends (42:8–10; cf. 1:5). Additionally, some debate exists over the meaning of YHWH's pronouncement that Job has spoken truthfully (נכונה), while the three friends have not (42:7–8). If, as most translations render the phrase, Job spoke truthfully *about* God, then how does one square Job's apparent blasphemies throughout the book with YHWH's evaluation of his speech? Does this mean that YHWH is conceding that Job was correct about the deity's unjust governance of the universe (Krüger 2018); that Job has spoken truthfully *to* God, not merely *about* God, as the three friends did (Oeming 2000); that he used his theology constructively while the friends used theirs abusively (Cooper 1997, 241); or perhaps simply that Job's recent "repentance" in 42:6 was speaking truth?

In 42:11–17, the book returns to a prose narrative much like the one that opened the book. Notably, however, in their current state, these two prose tales do not make a complete story, and 42:7 suggests that the whole has been edited so as to comport with the ending of the poetic dialogues (Ngwa 2005). The epilogue makes no comment on the outcome of the Joban experiment, and the Adversary is entirely absent. Job 42:10 employs prophetic language of "restoring Job's fortunes," and his possessions lost in the prologue are now doubled. Where Job formerly had 11,000 animals, he now has 22,000. Job's ten children who died in 1:13–19 are replaced by ten new children, though now his three daughters—Dove, Cinnamon, and Little Makeup-Box—are given more emphasis, even receiving an inheritance alongside their brothers (42:15; cf. Num 27:7). Strikingly, however, Job's new wife goes unnamed in the Hebrew text, and the restoration of his body is not mentioned. In early Jewish interpretation, these two apparent gaps are filled in, as the Testament of Job identifies Job's wife as "Sitis" (remarkably close to Job's place of origin in the Greek text, "Ausitis"; cf. LXX Job 1:1; 42:17). Further, it specifies that Job was healed by magical girdles which became the inheritance he passed on to his daughters (T. Job 47). Like the patriarchs Abraham (Gen 25:8) and Isaac (Gen 35:29), Job dies "old and sated with years" (42:17), a precursor, as the Septuagint would have it, to his eventual resurrection: "It is written, 'He will rise again with those whom the Lord raises up'" (LXX Job 42:17).

Works Cited

Attridge, Harold W. 2013. "Testament of Job." Pages 1872–1899 in vol. 2 of *Outside the Bible: Ancient Jewish Writings Related to Scripture*. Edited by Louis H. Feldman et al. 3 vols. Philadelphia, PA: The Jewish Publication Society.

Balentine, Samuel E. 2015. *Have You Considered My Servant Job? Understanding the Biblical Archetype of Patience*. Columbia, SC: The University of South Carolina Press.

Baskin, Judith R. 1983. *Pharaoh's Counsellors: Job, Jethro, and Balaam in Rabbinic and Patristic Tradition*. BJS 47. Chico, CA: Scholars.

Baskin, Judith R. 1992. "Rabbinic Interpretations of Job." Pages 101–110 in *The Voice from the Whirlwind: Interpreting the Book of Job*. Edited by Leo Perdue and W. Clark Gilpin. Nashville, TN: Abingdon.

Breed, Brennan W. 2014. *Nomadic Text: A Theory of Biblical Reception History*. Bloomington, IN: Indiana University Press.

Breytenbach, C., and P.L. Day. 1999. "Satan, שׂטן, Σατάν, Σατανᾶς." Pages 726–732 in *Dictionary of Deities and Demons*. Edited by Karel van der Toorn, Bob Becking, and Pieter W. van der Horst. 2nd ed. Grand Rapids, MI: Eerdmans.

Brown, Ken. 2015. *The Vision in Job 4 and its Role in the Book*. FAT II 4. Tübingen: Mohr Siebeck.

Burrell, David B. 2008. *Deconstructing Theodicy: Why Job Has Nothing to Say to the Puzzle of Suffering*. Grand Rapids, MI: Brazos Press.

Clines, D.J.A. 1985. "False Naivety in the Prologue to Job." *HAR* 9:127–136.

Clines, D.J.A. 1994. "Why Is There a Book of Job, and What Does It Do to You If You Read It?" Pages 1–20 in *The Book of Job*. Edited by W.A.M. Beuken. BETL 114. Leuven: Peeters.

Clines, D.J.A. 2003. "On the Poetic Achievement of the Book of Job." Pages 243–252 in *Palabra, prodigio, poesía: In memoriam P. Luis Alonso Schökel, SJ*. Edited by Vicente Collado Bertomeu. AnBib 151. Rome: Pontifical Biblical Institute.

Clines, D.J.A. 2004. "Putting Elihu in His Place: A Proposal for the Relocation of Job 32–37." *JSOT* 29:243–253.

Cooper, Alan. 1990. "Reading and Misreading the Prologue to Job." *JSOT* 46:67–79.

Cooper, Alan. 1997. "The Sense of Job." *Proof* 17:227–244.

Dell, Katharine J. 1991. *The Book of Job as Sceptical Literature*. BZAW 197. Berlin: de Gruyter.

Erickson, Amy. 2013. "'Without My Flesh I Will See God': Job's Rhetoric of the Body." *JBL* 132:295–313.

Foster, Benjamin. 2005. *Before the Muses: An Anthology of Akkadian Literature.* 3rd ed. Bethesda, MD: CDL Press.

Fox, Michael V. 2011. "Reading the Tale of Job." Pages 145–162 in *A Critical Engagement: Essays on the Hebrew Bible in Honour of J. Cheryl Exum.* Edited by D.J.A. Clines and Ellen van Wolde. HBM 38. Sheffield: Sheffield Phoenix.

Fox, Michael V. 2013. "God's Answer and Job's Response." *Bib* 94:1–23.

Fox, Michael V. 2018. "The Speaker in Job 28." Pages 21–38 in Jones and Yoder 2018.

Gillmayr-Bucher, Susanne. 2007. "Rahmen und Bildträger: Der mehrsichtige Diskurs in den Prosatexten des Ijobbuchs." Pages 139–164 in *Das Buch Ijob: Gesamtdeutungen— Einzeltexte—Zentrale Themen.* Edited by Theodor Seidl and Stephanie Ernst. ÖBS 31. Frankfurt am Main: Peter Lang.

Ginsberg, Harold Louis. 1967. "Job the Patient and Job the Impatient." *Conservative Judaism* 21:12–28.

Ginsberg, Harold Louis. 1971. "Job, The Book of." *EncJud* 10:111–129.

Greenstein, Edward L. 2003a. "The Language of Job and Its Poetic Function." *JBL* 122:651–666.

Greenstein, Edward L. 2003b. "The Poem on Wisdom in Job 28 in Its Conceptual and Literary Contexts." Pages 253–280 in *Job 28: Cognition in Context.* Edited by Ellen van Wolde. BibInt 64. Leiden: Brill.

Greenstein, Edward L. 2007a. "Features of Language in the Poetry of Job." Pages 81–96 in Krüger et al. 2007.

Greenstein, Edward L. 2007b. "'On My Skin and in My Flesh': Personal Experience as a Source of Knowledge in the Book of Job." Pages 63–77 in *Bringing the Hidden to Light: The Process of Interpretation. Studies in Honor of Stephen A. Geller.* Edited by Kathryn F. Kravitz and Diane M. Sharon. Winona Lake, IN: Eisenbrauns.

Greenstein, Edward L. 2009. "The Problem of Evil in the Book of Job." Pages 333–362 in *Mishneh Todah: Studies in Deuteronomy and Its Cultural Environment in Honor of Jeffrey H. Tigay.* Edited by Nili S. Fox et al. Winona Lake, IN: Eisenbrauns.

Hoffman, Yair. 1996. *A Blemished Perfection: The Book of Job in Context.* Translated by J. Chipman. JSOTSup 213. Sheffield: Sheffield Academic Pres

Illman, Karl-Johan. 2003. "Theodicy in Job." Pages 304–333 in *Theodicy in the World of the Bible.* Edited by Antti Laato and Johannes C. de Moor. Leiden: Brill.

Janzen, J. Gerald. 2009. *At the Scent of Water: The Ground of Hope in the Book of Job.* Grand Rapids, MI: Eerdmans.

Janzen, J. Gerald. 2018. "Blessing and Justice in Job: In/commensurable?" Pages 51–69 in Jones and Yoder 2018.

Jones, Scott C. 2009. *Rumors of Wisdom: Job 28 as Poetry.* BZAW 397. Berlin: de Gruyter.

Jones, Scott C. 2013. "Corporeal Discourse in the Book of Job." *JBL* 132:845–863.

Jones, Scott C. 2015. "Job the Nazi Warrior." *Marginalia Review of Books.* Online: http://marginalia.lareviewofbooks.org/job-nazi-warrior-scott-c-jones/.

Jones, Scott C., and Christine Roy Yoder, eds. 2018. *"When the Morning Stars Sang": Essays in Honor of Choon Leong Seow on the Occasion of His Sixty-Fifth Birthday.* BZAW 500. Berlin: de Gruyter.

Kramer, Samuel Noah. 1960. "'Man and His God': A Sumerian Variation on the 'Job' Motif." Pages 170–182 in *Wisdom in Israel and in the Ancient Near East: Presented to Harold Henry Rowley by the Editorial Board of Vetus Testamentum in Celebration of His 65th Birthday, 24 March 1955.* Edited by Martin Noth and D. Winton Thomas. VTSup 3. Leiden: Brill.

Krüger, Thomas. 2007. "Did Job Repent?" Pages 217–229 in Krüger et al. 2007.

Krüger, Thomas. 2018. "Job Spoke the Truth About God (Job 42:7–8)." Pages 71–80 in Jones and Yoder 2018.

Krüger, Thomas, Manfred Oeming, Konrad Schmid, and Chris Uehlinger, eds. 2007. *Das Buch Hiob und seine Interpretationen: Beiträge zum Hiob-Symposium auf dem Monte Verità vom 14.–19. August 2005*. ATANT 88. Zurich: TVZ.

Kynes, Will. 2015. "The Modern Scholarly Wisdom Tradition and the Threat of Pan-Sapientialism: A Case Report." Pages 11–38 in *Was There a Wisdom Tradition? New Prospects in Israelite Wisdom Studies*. Edited by Mark R. Sneed. AIL 23. Atlanta, GA: SBL.

Lambert, W.A. 1960. *Babylonian Wisdom Literature*. Oxford: Clarendon.

Leibniz, Gottfried Wilhelm. 1710. *Essais de théodicée sur la bonté de Dieu, la liberté de l'homme et l'origene du mal*. Amsterdam: Troyel.

Lewalski, Barbara K. 1966. *Milton's Brief Epic: The Genre, Meaning, and Art of "Paradise Regained."* Providence, RI: Brown University Press.

Linafelt, Tod. 1996. "The Undecidability of ברך in the Prologue to Job and Beyond." *BibInt* 4:154–172.

Linafelt, Tod, and Andrew R. Davis. 2013. "Translating חנם in Job 1:9 and 2:3: On the Relationship between Job's Piety and His Interiority." *VT* 63:627–639.

Lo, Alison. 2003. *Job 28 as Rhetoric: An Analysis of Job 28 in the Context of Job 22–31*. VTSup 97. Leiden: Brill.

Low, Katherine. 2013. *The Bible, Gender, and Reception History: The Case of Job's Wife*. LHBOTS 586. London: Bloomsbury T&T Clark.

Luther, Martin. 1960. "Preface to the Book of Job." Pages 251–253 in *Luther's Works*, vol. 35: *Word and Sacrament I*. Edited by E. Theodore Bachmann. Philadelphia, PA: Fortress.

Mattingly, Gerald L. 1990. "The Pious Sufferer: Mesopotamia's Traditional Theodicy and Job's Counselors." Pages 305–348 in *The Bible in the Light of Cuneiform Literature: Scripture in Context 3*. Edited by William W. Hallo et al. ANETS 8. Lewiston, NY: Mellen.

Mende, Theresia. 1990. *Durch Leiden zur Vollendung: Die Elihureden im Buch Ijob (Ijob 32–37)*. TThSt 49. Trier: Paulinus.

Mies, Françoise. 2003. "Le genre littéraire du livre de Job." *RB* 110:336–369.

Mies, Françoise. 2006. *L'espérance de Job*. BETL 193. Leuven: Peeters.

Moran, William L. 2002. "The Babylonian Job." Pages 182–200 in *The Most Magic Word*. Edited by Ronald S. Hendel. CBQMS 35. Washington, D.C.: The Catholic Biblical Association of America.

Newsom, Carol A. 2002. "Narrative Ethics, Character, and the Prose Tale of Job." Pages 121–134 in *Character and Scripture: Moral Formation, Community, and Biblical Interpretation*. Edited by William P. Brown. Grand Rapids, MI: Eerdmans.

Newsom, Carol A. 2003. *The Book of Job: A Contest of Moral Imaginations*. Oxford: Oxford University Press.

Newsom, Carol A. 2016. "Plural Versions and the Challenge of Narrative Coherence in the Story of Job." Pages 236–244 in *The Oxford Handbook of Biblical Narrative*. Edited by Danna Nolan Fewell. Oxford: Oxford University Press.

Ngwa, Kenneth Numfor. 2005. *The Hermeneutics of the "Happy" Ending in Job 42:7–17*. BZAW 354. Berlin: de Gruyter.

Oeming, Manfred. 2000. "Ihr habt nicht recht von mir geredet wie mein Knecht Hiob." *EvT* 60:103–116.

Oeming, Manfred. 2018. "The Kerygma of the Book of Job." Pages 81–98 in Jones and Yoder 2018.

Oshima, Takayoshi. 2014. *Babylonian Poems of Pious Sufferers: Ludlul Bēl Nēmeqi and the Babylonian Theodicy*. ORA 14. Tübingen: Mohr Siebeck.

Raeder, Siegfried. 2008. "The Exegetical and Hermeneutical Work of Martin Luther." Pages 363–406 in *Hebrew Bible/Old Testament: The History of Its Interpretation*, vol. 2: *From the Renaissance to the Enlightenment*. Edited by Magne Sæbø. Göttingen: Vandenhoeck & Ruprecht.

Roberts, J.J.M. 1973. "Job's Summons to Yahweh: The Exploitation of a Legal Metaphor." *ResQ* 16:159–165.

Sarna, Nahum. 1957. "Epic Substratum in the Prose of Job." *JBL* 76:13–25.

Seow, Choon Leong. 2007. "Job's Wife, with Due Respect." Pages 351–373 in Krüger et al. 2007.

Seow, Choon Leong. 2010. "Hope in Two Keys: Musical Impact and the Poetics of Job 14." Pages 495–510 in *Congress Volume, Ljubljana 2007*. Edited by André Lemaire. VTSup 133. Leiden: Brill.

Seow, Choon Leong. 2011a. "Orthography, Textual Criticism, and the Poetry of Job." *JBL* 130:63–85.

Seow, Choon Leong. 2011b. "Elihu's Revelation." *ThTo* 68:253–271.

Seow, Choon Leong. 2013. *Job 1–21: Interpretation and Commentary*. Grand Rapids, MI: Eerdmans.

Skehan, Patrick W., Eugene Ulrich, and Judith E. Sanderson. 1992. *Qumran Cave 4.IV: Palaeo-Hebrew and Greek Biblical Manuscripts*. DJD 9. Oxford: Clarendon.

Snell, Daniel C. 2011. *Religions of the Ancient Near East*. Cambridge: Cambridge University Press.

Stordalen, Terje. 2006. "Dialogue and Dialogism in the Book of Job." *SJOT* 20:18–37.

Szpek, Heidi M. 2005. "On the Influence of Job on Jewish Hellenistic Literature." Pages 357–370 in *Seeking Out the Wisdom of the Ancients: Essays Offered to Michael V. Fox on the Occasion of His Sixty-Fifth Birthday*. Edited by Ronald L. Troxel et al. Winona Lake, IN: Eisenbrauns.

Tsevat, Matitiahu. 1966. "The Meaning of the Book of Job." *HUCA* 37:73–106.

Uzzane, Octave. 1892. "Conversations and Opinions of Victor Hugo. From Unpublished Papers Found at Guernsey." *Scribner's Magazine* 12:558–576.

Wahl, Harald-Martin. 1993. *Der gerechte Schöpfer: Eine redaktions- und theologiegeschichtliche Untersuchung der Elihureden—Hiob 32–37*. BZAW 207. Berlin: de Gruyter.

Weinberg, Joanna. 1994. "Job versus Abraham: The Quest for the Perfect God-Fearer in Rabbinic Tradition." Pages 281–296 in *The Book of Job*. Edited by W.A.M. Beuken. BETL 114. Leuven: Peeters.

Weinfeld, Moshe. 1988. "Job and Its Mesopotamian Parallels—A Typological Analysis." Pages 217–226 in *Text and Context: Old Testament and Semitic Studies for F.C. Fensham*. Edited by Walter T. Claassen. JSOTSup 48. Sheffield: JSOT Press.

Weiss, Meir. 1983. *The Story of Job's Beginning: Job 1–2: A Literary Analysis*. Jerusalem: Magnes.

Witte, Markus. 1994. *Vom Leiden zur Lehre: Der dritte Redegang (Hiob 21–27) und die Redaktionsgeschichte des Hiobbuches*. BZAW 230. Berlin: de Gruyter.

Zuckerman, Bruce. 1991. *Job the Silent: A Study in Historical Counterpoint*. Oxford: Oxford University Press.

CHAPTER 33

....

SONG OF SONGS

....

ANSELM C. HAGEDORN

SONG of Songs is not a Wisdom book! A generation ago such a statement would not have been controversial. In Gerhard von Rad's famous and ground-breaking study on the wisdom of ancient Israel, Song of Songs is only mentioned once—in a footnote (von Rad 1971, 168 n. 29), drawing attention to the use of the term "sister" in Song 4:9–10, 12 and 5:1 in relation to texts like Prov 7:4. In his discussion of "intellectual love" (von Rad 1971, 166–176) Song of Songs is absent. This absence reflects the interpretative paradigm of modernity, which has been rightfully described as a liberation of Song of Songs from the clutches of allegory (Staubli 1997).

In the wake of J.G. Herder (1744–1803), Song of Songs has been seen as a collection of profane love songs, emphasizing the love between man and woman (Gaier 1990, 431–522; Gaier 2005, 317–337), similar to descriptions of love in ancient Egypt and Arabic wedding poetry. This modern consensus is most clearly stated in the opening sentence of Othmar Keel's (1994, 1) magnificent commentary: "If one encountered the Song anywhere but in the Bible, one would hardly hesitate to call it a collection of love songs— which of course would be basically correct" (cf. Müller 1992, 8; Exum 2005a, 1). The interpretative insights gained from a historical-critical as well as a religion-historical perspective are challenged by an increasing number of studies that either reclassify Song of Songs as sapiential (Dell 2005; Kingsmill 2009; Andruska 2019) or attempt to resurrect an allegorical reading of the text (Schwienhorst-Schönberger 2016; Schwienhorst-Schönberger 2018). Both approaches are guided by an understanding of intertextuality that superimposes a sapiential or theological meaning by interpreting a biblical text within its late canonical setting ignoring the vexing problem of the status of "Bible" in the early phases of interpretation (Mroczek 2016).

33.1 Song of Songs—Some Introductory Remarks

The Song of Songs is a carefully crafted anthology of secular love poems celebrating the sensual, sexual and erotic love between man and woman. To characterize the collection as an anthology allows the individual character of the poems to be maintained while at the same time recognizing overarching structures and larger units of composition. In the Hebrew Bible, the Song is part of the Megilloth and used in Jewish tradition as part of the Passover liturgy.

Dating the collection is notoriously difficult. Some poems (e.g., 1:9–11; 6:4–7) may stem from the pre-exilic period, but a detailed linguistic analysis shows that the Hebrew belongs to a late stage already on the path towards the Mishnah. The possible Greek and Persian loan words in 3:9 (אפריון) and 4:13 (פרדס) are just one indication here. The familiarity with Greek (pastoral) lyric and the frequent use of luxury vocabulary point to a compilation during the Hellenistic period (Hagedorn 2016, 90–106).

The *Sitz im Leben* is equally difficult to determine. The oft-proposed context of a (sacred) marriage ritual cannot be sustained. Rather, the lovers of Song of Songs should be seen as archetypes for all lovers. Due to the manifold allusions to other literary texts from the ancient Near East and the Greek world, it appears unlikely that the poems originated in a rural setting. Instead the Song seems to imitate this setting.

Ever since Friedrich Horst's (1935) influential study, discussion of the different literary genres in Song of Songs has been quite prevalent. Though the list of genres can be expanded further and further, the following are particularly notable and clearly distinguishable:

1. Description of physical charms (Arab. *waṣf*), which can be used for both the woman (2:2; 4:1–7, 12–15) and the man (2:3, 8–19; 5:10–16, see also 3:9–11);
2. Song of admiration (of the woman: 1:9–11, 15; 3:6–8; 4:1–7, 9–11; 6:4–7, 10; 7:1–7, 8–10; of the man: 1:16–17 and 2:1–3);
3. Songs of yearning (of the woman: 1:2–4; 2:4–16; 7:12–13; 8:1–2, 6–7; of the man: 8:13–14);
4. Self-description (1:5–6; 2:1; 8:10).

The absence of God in Song of Songs (אש שלהבתיה in Song 8:6 should be seen as superlative ["great flame"] rather than an abbreviated reference to Yahweh) and celebration of several practices that are criticized elsewhere in the Hebrew Bible (Song 1:16–17; cf. Hos 4:13; Song 4:9; cf. Isa 3:16; Song 1:13 and 4:14; cf. Prov 7:17) have puzzled interpreters and prompted the rise of Jewish and Christian allegorical interpretation transforming the text into a sublime document of religious belief. The absence of God does not mean that the divine (and magic) sphere is absent (Hagedorn 2015, 23–41). The lovers describe each other using theomorphism, in which they imbue each other with divine aspects and love itself seems to have magic qualities.

The love in Song of Songs celebrates the body as both object of desire and source of delight. It is a love undisturbed by rivalry and jealousy. "The lovers are always present for each other because they are always speaking or being spoken about; in other words, they are continually desiring and desired" (Exum 2005a, 6). When describing their love, both protagonists speak differently about the beloved. The woman tends to tell stories while the man describes what he sees metaphorically. The motifs and metaphors employed to describe the other are more than simple descriptions of outer appearances. Especially in the comparisons of body parts with animals it becomes apparent that the dynamic aspect connected to the animal is important (Keel 1984).

33.2 SONG OF SONGS AS PART OF A "SOLOMONIC COLLECTION"?

The anthology of love poems now forming Song of Songs is attributed to Solomon in Song 1:1. This superscription is a secondary addition as it uses the relative particle אשר instead of the usual ש found throughout the body of the text. The attribution to Solomon is often seen as being "the first commentary on the Song and declares that the work, being recognizably sapiential, is to be ascribed or dedicated to the biblical metaphor for wisdom—Solomon" (Kingsmill 2016, 314). Further, it has been argued that the Song, "though not a didactic composition in any obvious sense, was seen to contain a message which the sages wished to recommend with all the authority of an age-old tradition" (Blenkinsopp 1995a, 3). Such an interpretation finds support in the canonical order of the Septuagint, which groups Proverbs, Qoheleth, and Song of Songs together as part of the Wisdom books. Thomas Krüger (2004, 28) has observed that "one reads the book of Qoheleth after the book of Proverbs as a critical reflection of the 'wisdom' developed there…, just as Canticles is the realization of the exhortation to enjoy life in the book of Qoheleth." Jewish tradition groups the books in a similar way (b. B. Bat. 14b; Stone 2013, 103–105), but resists a hasty connection to wisdom when Canticles Rabbah reads the books attributed to Solomon biographically connecting the individual writings to phases of his life: "When a man is young, he composes songs; when he grows up, he speaks proverbs; when he gets old he speaks of vanities" (Cant. Rab. 1:6; Neusner 1989, 54). Even if the Rabbis had Solomon's wisdom in mind here, we have to remember that the wisdom "associated with the ancient grouping is different than that later used to define the Wisdom category" (Kynes 2019, 72).

There is no doubt that Solomon is connected to wisdom in the Hebrew Bible, which presents it as a gift from YHWH. When God appears to him in a dream at Gibeah offering to give him whatever he requests (שאל מה אתן לך [1 Kgs 3:5]), the king replies:

> Grant, then, your servant a listening heart (לב שמע) to judge (שפט) your people, to distinguish between good and evil (להבין בין טוב לרע); for who is able to judge this vast people of yours?   (1 Kgs 3:9)

The authors of 1 Kings make it clear that Solomon's humility finds divine approval and 1 Kgs 3:6–9 may be the first step towards an identification of wisdom and Torah. Though Solomon himself never asks directly for wisdom, YHWH's reply in 3:12 clarifies that this is meant when the deity states that Solomon was given a wise and understanding heart (לב חכם ונבון). As the Solomonic narrative unfolds, it becomes apparent that the wisdom of the king is twofold. He possesses both judicial wisdom and—according to 1 Kgs 5:9–14 [ET 4:29–34]—"Solomon is endowed with analytical and practical wisdom of the kind that could be found in many quarters of the Near East" (Cogan 2000, 221). Solomon is described, then, as possessing wisdom that enables him to compose songs and to utter proverbs. This picture of Solomon as the archetypal sage is the reason why books like Proverbs and Ecclesiastes are attributed to him and their references to royal themes can be reconciled more or less with an imagined Solomonic setting. The multifaceted portrait of Solomon in the Hebrew Bible, however, precludes the reader from a simplistic reading that exclusively focuses on the sapiential aspect. Solomon is also seen as the archetypal lover and 1 Kgs 11:1–13 states that his love for many (foreign) women provokes YHWH's punishment.

Besides the superscription, the name Solomon appears five times in the Song of Songs (1:5; 3:7, 9, 11; 8:11). These occurrences are supplemented by the use of מלך in 1:4, 12; 3:9, 11; 7:6 and probably by השולמית ("the Shulammite") in 7:1 [ET 6:13], which may be understood as an allusion to a female counterpart of Solomon. The references to Solomon are scattered throughout the text and generally refer more to his riches than his wisdom. In Song of Songs itself, Solomon is only present in the things that belong to him and these objects are not connected to the king elsewhere in the Hebrew Bible.[1] Even if one argues on the basis of 1:1 that Song of Songs should be connected to Wisdom, the open eroticism of the following verses may trigger different associations. It has, therefore, been suggested that references to Solomon are part of a later redaction of Song of Songs that wants to shift the focus away from a more common eroticism towards a chaste love-play between Solomon and his bride (Loretz 2004, 806). As a result, Solomon's introduction into Song of Songs contributes to the confusion of the reader because the existence of Solomon seems to double the actors. This confusion is enlarged by the lack of reference in Song of Songs to the positive aspects of Solomon in 1 Kings 1–11, and it has been argued that the portrait of Solomon in the Song is more a critique of a passive king who is seen in opposition to the active lovers (Birnbaum 2017, 233–264).

This ambiguity in the picture of Solomon makes it very difficult to propose a royal setting in analogy to ancient Near Eastern texts (Heereman 2018). As a result, the reference to Solomon in Song 1:1 cannot be used as an obvious interpretative key, which allows a

---

[1] "Curtains of Solomon" (יריעות שלמה, 1:5); "litter of Solomon" (מטתו שלשלמה, 3:7); "palanquin King Solomon made for himself" (אפריון עשה לו המלך שלמה, 3:9); "look…at King Solomon, at the crown" (ראינה...במלך שלמה בעטרה, 3:11); "vineyard which belonged to Solmon" (כרם היה לשלמה, 8:11).

clear classification of the character of the following chapters. Though it is tempting to identify Solomon (and the fictitious Shulammite) as the two protagonists in Song of Songs, we have to remember that the "song's lovers are archetypal lovers—composite figures, types of lovers rather than any specific lovers" (Exum 2005a, 8). Furthermore, to read Song of Songs in light of the Wisdom tradition so prominently assigned to Solomon in Proverbs (and Ecclesiastes) is only possible—if one wants to maintain a non-allegorical reading—when one assumes that Song of Songs is about marriage. Such a view, however, is difficult to connect to the portrait of Solomon elsewhere in the Hebrew Bible. He is simply not an icon of marital fidelity.

33.3 WISDOM ELEMENTS IN SONG OF SONGS

Any reader who approaches Song of Songs with a more detailed knowledge of the sapiential books of the Hebrew Bible will be disappointed. Despite a recent awareness of a certain fluidity of genre and a lack of well-defined boundaries in which "a text's participation in one genre by no means precludes participation in another" (Brown 2014, 16), it cannot be denied that prevalent topics from the "classic" Wisdom books of the Hebrew Bible do not appear. Linguistic evidence lends support to such a view. Most obviously, the term "wisdom" (חכמה)—occurring frequently in other Wisdom books—is never mentioned in Song of Songs. The same can be said of the antonym "folly" (סכלות) and further terms generally connected to the Wisdom genre, such as "righteousness" (צדקה), "knowledge" (דעת), and "wickedness" (רשע). Similarly, Song of Songs is simply not interested in acts and consequences so prevalent in other didactic literature of the Hebrew Bible. "Like its two lovers, the Song as a whole is not concerned with morals or consequences of people's behavior" (Schellenberg 2016, 395). This is especially striking as Song of Songs sometimes describes consequences (Song 1:6; 5:7; 8:1) but never does so by alluding to any social norms. Song 1:6b is a case in point:

> My mother's sons were angry (חרה ni.) with me;
> they placed me as keeper (נטרה) of the vineyards,
> but my own vineyard I have not kept (נטר).

The verse is a fine example that with the Song, "it is never one meaning or the other, for multiple levels of meaning and erotic double entendre are everywhere" (Exum 2005a, 106). Instead of offering an evaluative comment on the woman's behavior—as one would expect in a Wisdom setting—the verse, as well as Song 1:7, seems to defy traditional male authority by asserting the woman's erotic independence.

A similar strategy is at play in Song 8:1:

> If only you were like a brother to me,
> sucking the breasts of my mother,

I would find you in the street and kiss you
and no one would disdain (בז) me.

Again, the social reality seems accidental and so seem the allusions to Proverbs. בז occurs frequently in Proverbs (1:7; 6:30; 11:12; 13:13; 14:21; 23:9, 22; 30:17), but never in the context of sexual relationships. Though it is tempting to read Song 8:1–4 in the context of Temple theology and Wisdom (Kingsmill 2009, 276–277), such a reading ignores the emphasis such passages in the Song place on the "shift from the world in which social expectations influence behaviour... to the world the lovers inhabit... where they are so completely wrapped up in each other that they give little thought to convention" (Exum 2005a, 247).

Though emphasis is placed in Wisdom Literature (Proverbs, Ben Sira) on the dangers of sexuality and eroticism, "sporadic statements on the erotic show that wisdom authors were familiar with the positive aspects of eroticism" (Schellenberg 2018, 256). Proverbs 30:18–19 lists the way of a man with a young woman (ודרך גבר בעלמה) amongst the things that are too wondrous to behold (פלא/ידע) but fails to expand on the joys of such a way. Instead, Prov 30:20 reverts immediately back to the more common warning against the adulteress (אשה מנאפת). Similarly, Prov 5:18 stresses the delight in the woman of one's youth (ושמח מאשת נעורך) only to incorporate such delight in the warnings against a foreign woman. In Prov 5:19, however, the young man is advised to remain faithful to his wife, and the sages employ language quite similar to Song of Songs. "In the love language of the poem, the wife is portrayed as unique, like no one else, to be treasured for herself alone, to be shared with no other" (Clifford 1999, 71–72).

Though Song of Songs is primarily concerned with the ideal beloved, she can be envisaged as a future ideal wife in some passages (Hagedorn 2010), but this should not lead to the assumption that "it is best to interpret it as a book celebrating that marriage, as intended by God" (Kaiser 2000, 114). Song of Songs takes a different path. Neither love nor the sexual encounter between man and woman is seen as potentially dangerous. Rather, love is seen as a force per se, it "is personified as something that has a will of its own" (Exum 2005a, 118; cf. Hagedorn 2015, 32–34). It might not be surprising then that the two sentences that could be classified as sapiential in Song of Songs address the nature of love (2:7 [cf. 3:5; 8:4] and 8:6–7).

I adjure you, daughters of Jerusalem,
by the gazelles (צבאות) and the hinds (אילות) of the fields
do not arouse or awaken (עור) Love (האהבה),
until it pleases (חפץ).

The woman offers general advice about love to the daughters of Jerusalem, telling them that "its arousal drives one into unanticipated and even unknown experiences" (Murphy 1990, 147). Due to the recurring nature of the admonition, it is classified as didactic, serving the purpose of advice to be passed on to future generations. "And just as parental advice, from father to son, was used as a literary convention in instructions in

the ancient world, provocatively in the Song of Songs, it is passed down from the female
lover to the daughters of Jerusalem" (Andruska 2019, 114). The lack of trans-generational
issues in Song of Songs remains, of course, which is a hindrance to such an interpretation,
as are the manifold ambiguities in the wording (Schellenberg 2016, 402–404). The
"wisdom" Song of Songs wants to disperse reminds its readers that "love has its laws
which society ought to respect because love is not a social invention" (Barbiero 2011, 94).

In fact, love seems to be regarded as an independent force that engages with the male
and female protagonist (Hagedorn 2015, 33). In other words, love "is personified as
something that has a will of its own" (Exum 2005a, 118). Since the love in Song of Songs is
mutual and neither devious nor adulterous, the man and the woman are never in danger
of falling into the traps outlined by other Wisdom Literature. Additionally, a classification of the refrain as didactic and thus part of a sapiential setting ignores the first couplet
with its reference to a more polytheistic setting (Müller 1976; Keel 1994, 92–94)—something that would be difficult to reconcile with the generally theological thrust of biblical
wisdom.

The same problem persists in Song 8:6–7, a text often linked to the *mashal*-genre of
ancient Near Eastern Wisdom (Andruska 2019, 113 following Weeks 2010, 3–4), and the
lynchpin for any classification of Song of Songs as sapiential, since the verses teach "a
general truth about love, which the entire book displays through the actions of its characters" (Andruska 2019, 113). There is no doubt that the verses are central to the message
of Song of Songs as a whole (Exum 2005b, 78–79), but the Song nowhere else explicitly explains the nature or meaning of love. In contrast, classic Wisdom books sometimes expound on the nature of love when the relationship between man and woman is
described to stress harmony (Prov 19:13–14; 21:9, 19; 24:24), and set love in opposition to
hate (e.g. Prov 10:12; Eccl 9:1, 9) or use love to emphasize the importance of friendship
(Prov 17:9; 25:5). What we can learn from these verses in Song of Songs, however, is that
older mystical or numinous elements are transmitted as part of love-poetry and that
older divinities such as "death" continue to exist in this genre and are only domesticated
in the course of reception history (Kaplan and Wilson-Wright 2018).

In a similar vein, the exhortation in Song 5:1b encourages a different behavior than
that known from Wisdom texts: "Eat, friends, drink (שתה) and be drunk (שכר) with (the)
joys of love (דודים)." There can be no doubt that the exhortation reminds the reader of
similar expressions in Prov 5:5–20 (Schellenberg 2018, 260–261), where drinking is used
as a metaphor for sex (Fox 2000, 199–200; Kingsmill 2016, 318–319). The encouragement to find satisfaction in one's wife (Prov 5:19), who is a "lovely deer" (אילת אהבים) and
a "graceful doe" (יעלת חן), undoubtedly evokes similar images from the Song of Song, and
it is tempting to place these similarities within the larger framework of Lady Wisdom
(Andruska 2019, 131–135). Such an identification, however, overlooks significant differences. First of all, Song of Songs never likens the woman to a "doe" or "deer" as such comparisons are reserved for the man (Song 2:9, 17; 8:14; Keel 1984, 78–81). In regard to the
woman, these animals are used to describe her breasts (Song 4:5; 7:4), emphasizing agil-
ity and youth within a general description of female beauty. As such they signify one
physical aspect and not a person as a whole. Most striking, however, is the use of the

terminology for love. דודים in Song 5:1 makes it clear that sexual love is intended (cf. Song 1:4; 4:10; 5:1; 7:13) and the invitation "to be drunk with (the) joys of love" is addressed to everybody (Schellenberg 2018, 261). Proverbs only uses the term once (7:18), describing adulterous behavior. In Prov 5:19, when the intimate relationship with one's wife is described, the broader term אהבה is employed, and the setting within the framework of marriage and the opposition to the foreign woman restricts any erotic pleasures to a legalized and socially sanctioned union.

Nevertheless, it has often been observed that Song of Songs and Proverbs 7 utilize similar erotic language, imagery, and themes, so it is apparent that both texts recognize the power of sexuality. Since the current trend of classifying Song of Songs as sapiential generally looks at the text through the lenses of classic Wisdom, such as Proverbs, it is fruitful to turn this interpretative direction onto its head. If the traditional direction of reading is maintained, Song of Songs becomes a tractate of Wisdom for young Jewish women, which hopes to guard them against the disappointments of "adolescent pursuits of love" and prepare them for the fulfillment that can only happen in marriage (Sparks 2008). Such an approach reveals more about the modern author's fear of sexuality than the intention of the text. Especially so as only women seem to be advised to strive towards marriage.

Proverbs 7:6–20 is part of the last of four lectures addressing the issue of the Strange Woman (2:16–22; 5:1–23; 6:20–35; 7:1–27). After an introduction urging the son to call wisdom (חכמה) his sister and understanding (בינה) his friend in 7:1–5, verses 6–20 focus on the seductive and alluring power of the foreign woman. Verses 21–23 describe the fate of the one devoid of sense before verses 24–27 return to the warning and exhortative tone that opened the chapter. In contrast to other passages in Proverbs, the teacher does not speak in imperatives but rather "relies on his descriptive powers and his ability to reconstruct imaginatively the woman's stratagems and seductive conversation" (McKane 1970, 332).

Proverbs 7:6 describes the acts of the foreign woman from a male perspective, that of the teacher who addresses his pupil in 7:1. The passage is a clear warning against adultery. While sexual intercourse with a woman married to another man is punished by the death of both participants in Deut 22:22, Proverbs 7 only stresses the dangers for the young man. Later (7:27) it will be highlighted that the desire for her "is to take the road to Sheol and to arrive at the point of no return." The concluding verse emphasizes that a correction of the youth's ways is no longer possible and that the entry into the house of the woman equates with entry into the underworld.

The behavior of the woman tends to puzzle (male) interpreters. Such puzzlement is probably intended by the authors, who want us to adhere to the strict separation of male from female space—a concept that simply expresses an ideal state that can never be achieved. We have to remember that "Prov 7:10 does not say that the Strange Woman *is* a harlot or even that she intends to look like one, but that her harlot-like garb gives her a harlotrous appearance" (Fox 2000, 243). It seems that Proverbs 7 uses a common literary topos explaining the dangers threatening a man who is away from home, leaving his wife to act adulterously, endanger the marriage, and shame the husband (e.g. Aristophanes,

Peace 979–985). In other words, it is the danger that the adulterous behavior of the married woman that endangers the marriage, i.e. shaming the husband. In Prov 7:14–20 the woman herself "verbalizes the dangers she presents to the untutored young man" (Yee 1989, 62). We have to note that such verbalization is done through a male lens within a society that views "independent female eroticism and unrestrained sexuality…to endanger the family structure" (Arbel 2015, 128). When reading the description of the foreign woman in Proverbs, suddenly her physical attractiveness is mentioned, something that is never done when speaking about Wisdom. That beauty is dangerous becomes apparent when the teacher warns his pupil in Prov 6:25:

> Do not be infatuated by her beauty,
> and do not let her take you captive with her glances.

Despite these warnings, the author of Proverbs seems to transfer his hidden (and forbidden) desires onto the foreign woman in much the same way as modern Europeans transferred their unbridled sexual desire to an orientalist setting. Perhaps we can argue that he is well aware of the possibilities of sexuality and love and struggles with the chosen disapproval. As a result, he arrives at a portrait of Wisdom as a woman who accepts and respects male honor and submits to the traditional male construction of society, while the foreign woman "is made to embrace aspects of femininity that are culturally adverse, including unbound sexuality, eroticism, seduction, and pleasure" (Arbel 2015, 132).

Numerous textual links can be uncovered between Proverbs 7 and Song of Songs:

צפן Prov 7:1 / Song 7:14; חלון Prov 7:6 / Song 2:9; שקף Prov 7:6 / Song 6:10; שוק Prov 7:8 / Song 3:2; המה Prov 7:11 / Song 5:4; בחוץ Prov 7:12 / Song 8:1; ברחבות Prov 7:12 / Song 3:2; בשוק/בשוים Prov 7:8 / Song 3:2; נשק Prov 7:13 / Song 1:2; 8:1; ערש Prov 7:16, 17 / Song 1:16; משכב Prov 7:16, 17 / Song 3:1; מר, אהלים/אהלות/קנמון Prov 7:17 / Song 4:14; הלך Prov 7:18 / Song 7:12; דדים Prov 7:18 / Song 5:1; צרור Prov 7:20 / Song 1:13.

These verbal parallels are supplemented by the similar setting of the chapter to Song 3:1–5 (and 5:2–8), which may have served as a *Vorlage* for Proverbs 7. It can indeed be debated whether Proverbs 7, as well as Prov 31:10–31, can be understood as a conservative response to the Song of Songs (Zakovitch 2019, 89–99).

We have to note, however, that—despite the obvious allusions—Proverbs 7 introduces several different aspects that are alien to Song of Songs. First of all, the (young) man is regarded as being in danger. He has to be protected from the temptations provided by the foreign woman. He is easily distracted (הטתו ברב לקחה [7:21]) and follows the woman on an impulse (הולך אחריה פתאם), as his behavior is likened to the ox that will be slaughtered and the bird that is trapped (7:22). "The youth…is as ignorant of where he is heading as these dumb animals are" (Fox 2000, 250). In contrast, the man in the Song of Songs is never in danger. "As he presents himself, he is not unlike other biblical male characters, especially when we take into account that our picture of him comes from a love poem" (Exum 2015, 123). The vulnerability he displays is triggered by his response to the woman whom he desires. Such desire is a vastly different feeling than the surrender of the young man in Proverbs 7. Despite his desire and his response to the invitation of the woman, the man of Song of Songs remains in control. True, the woman in Proverbs 7 exerts the same dominance and presence that has been observed for the female protagonist in Song of Songs (Landy 2011, 60), but the free reciprocity that constitutes the encounter of the sexes in Song of Songs is missing, adding to the man's victim status. Furthermore, the exclusiveness of the love described in Song of Songs is missing. Both lovers describe themselves as unique (2:16; 3:1, 2, 3, 4; 6:8–9), while in Proverbs 7 the woman uses the phrase, "to seek you eagerly, and I have found you!" (לשחר פניך ואמצאך) in 15b as part of her strategy to lure the man into disaster as 7:26 stresses, and it has been observed that "[t]he ideal against which she is so judged is the ideal of the Song of Songs—mutuality" (Clifford 1999, 87). In contrast to Song of Songs, the objects of her desire are exchangeable and her goal seems to be sexual intercourse (Prov 7:18)—this is not excluded from Song of Songs albeit with a different connotation.

Secondly, Proverbs 7 changes the playing field by transforming the male-female encounter into an illegal meeting. There may have been some emotional distance between the woman and her husband, whom she simply calls "the man" (7:19), but there can be no doubt that she is a legitimate wife. Her status is asserted by her husband, rendering any encounter with a male person outside her family illegal. Since marriage is not an issue in Song of Songs, neither are adultery or marital infidelity. Though Song 8:8–10 (as well as 2:15–16; 3:6–11) could be understood as an indirect allusion to marriage (Müller 1992, 86–87), Song of Songs makes it clear "when desire burns like a raging flame (8:6), when it pleases love to be roused (2:7; 3:5; 8:4), social expectations and values are irrelevant" (Exum 2005a, 256). Thus, the advice Proverbs 7 wants to offer is irrelevant to the man of Song of Songs.

This irrelevancy characterizes much of the intertextual allusions between Song of Song and Wisdom texts as the book does not emphasize values, which are primary in Wisdom thought (contra Murphy 1981, xiii). Complicated as it may be to locate the social milieu of biblical Wisdom (Schipper 2019, 11–24), we realize that sapiential thinking moves for the most part on the father-son or teacher-disciple axis. Within such a system, women need to be controlled. "A teaching of this kind, which gives so much attention to self-control, social maintenance, and property rights, has slight interest in affirming the erotic and expansive possibilities in human relations" (Blenkinsopp 1995b, 48). By contrast, Song of Songs propagates a view of love that is determined by exclusiveness and reciprocity (Song 2:16). The text trusts its readers to be able to distinguish between love and sexual wantonness. Since the latter is never addressed and since there are hardly any intruders into the togetherness of the lovers, one gets the impression that Song of Songs describes a more mature approach to human sexuality. Part of Song of Songs' maturity is the expression of independence from traditional social norms. This behavior is justified because of the quasi-sapiential insight that love is a force of its own and thus beyond human control. Despite this almost numinous character of love, it never intrudes upon the relationship with the divine, which is simply ignored. If Song of Songs really wants to "teach" or convey any wisdom, it does so by telling the reader how thrilling and delightful love can be, and it might be possible that Song of Songs is more successful in doing so than Wisdom texts will ever be.

33.4 Love Lyrics in a Sapiential and Theological Environment

If we recognize that Song of Songs is not overtly sapiential, we are confronted with the question of its function in a "literary society" that places significant importance on didactic and theological issues. In other words, what is the role of love poetry in the society portrayed in the Hebrew Bible and how does its interpretation and reception effect the structure and value system of such a society? Here we have to remember Jonathan Culler's (2015, 301) observation on the transcendental nature of the lyric:

> One of the things that lyrics may do is to project a distinction between the immediate historical, communicative situation and the level at which the work operates in its generality of address and its openness to being articulated by readers who will be differently situated.

Despite its rootedness in the socio-historical setting of its authors (Keel 1984; Hagedorn 2010) it is part of the character of poetry to move beyond such settings, creating a world apart from the world of its origin. As Culler (2015, 305) observes:

> Lyric language doubtless works subliminally, and much of its social efficacy may depend on its ability to embed itself in the mind of readers, to invade and to occupy it, to be taken in, introjected, or housed as instances of alterity that can be repeated, considered, treasured, or ironically cited.

It is this ability to adapt as well as the openness to interpretation and engagement that displays poetry's contribution to the construction of a community. "Writing as it spatializes language fixes it in materiality, and thus gives it substance that may be touched, pointed to and returned to, conceptualized" (Dobbs-Allsopp 2015, 221). These theoretical observations help to describe and evaluate the obvious intertextual links between Song of Songs and the Wisdom texts of the Hebrew Bible. I would propose that Song of Songs provides a register for erotic discourse. Like the didactic literature, this poetry is international in outlook (Hagedorn 2016; Nissinen 2016) and not completely devoid of theological allusions. Notions of the divine permeate the Song, but they never determine the actions of the protagonists of the individual poems. Instead, the force of the divine realm is acknowledged and in turn never encroaches upon the human relationship (Hagedorn 2015). "If sex and love can be considered the highlights of human experience, they also serve as ideal metaphors to feed the readers' imagination of the divine-human relationship, hence religious readings of love poetry easily merge even without explicit references to divine beings" (Nissinen 2011, 276). Song of Songs only provides the start-ing point for such a reading but never moves in this direction. Instead, it counters tradi-tional values and constructions of society by proposing that the love between man and woman is able to overcome the established order generally justified by divine legitima-tion. It is this "wisdom" that connects Song of Songs to the sapiential thrust of the non-Priestly primeval history in Genesis 2–3 (Gertz 2018, 127). The paradisal existence has not simply vanished but it is covered by negativity, and love, not matrimony, enables the human person to return to a quasi-state normally reserved to the primeval period characterized by an undisturbed existence of male and female. The love undisturbed by external and social factors, advocated in Song of Songs finds a parallel in Gen 2:24 and Franz Rosenzweig can later advocate that "love is perforce sensuous and thus neutralizes the existential sting of our finitude" (Mendes-Flohr 2009, 315).

As traditional wisdom supports (traditional) order, such a view on the relationship of the sexes must be domesticated. This is explicitly done by allusions to the poems of Song of Songs in Proverbs (Schipper 2019, 215). In modeling the foreign woman and Woman Wisdom on the portrait of the beloved woman in Song of Songs, the authors of Proverbs "clarified that the intoxicating eroticism described in the Song must only be experienced in spiritualized form, being too dangerous and morally unacceptable in ordinary life" (Schellenberg 2018, 266). The powerful lyric is employed to create the wise construc-tion of the world imagined. The reshaping of the views of love in Song of Songs by other Wisdom texts is a strong indication that they were originally read as erotic literature, since a more allegorical understanding would not have been a problem for the authors of Wisdom Literature.

33.5 CONCLUSION

Yair Zakovitch (2019, 42) has stressed that "laughter and general optimism are a fitting accompaniment to love"; it is this optimism that drives the "wisdom" of Song of Songs. The result is a powerful lyric creation of a counter-world, where sentiments—other-wise carefully veiled—can be freely expressed in a "modest discourse of detachment balanced by a poetic discourse of attachment and deep feeling" (Abu-Lughod 1988, 209). It is this emotional world that significantly contributes to a deeper understand-ing of the complexities of negotiating identity in the Hebrew Bible. Subsuming such complexity hastily under the rubrics of Wisdom or didactic literature would not only limit the impact of Song of Songs but also deprive the biblical authors of their ability to create new genres and convictions that do not necessarily comply with the received view of biblical literature. To return to the opening statement: Song of Songs is (still) not a Wisdom book but a form of poetic and erotic literature that deeply impacted a developing sapiential corpus and whose language enabled other authors to create their own discourses about sexual relationships. If emotion is indeed "a touchstone of cul-tural value, a sluggish barometer of social change" as anthropologists have observed

(Beatty 2019, 7), the above-mentioned domestication of eroticism is one of the first steps towards an understanding of Song of Songs as a *mashal* written by Solomon to be the hermeneutic key to unlock Torah (Boyarin 1990). The rich tradition of allegorical reading and the philosophical conviction that in the Song of Songs "the word of God and the word of humanity meet each other" (Benjamin 2009, 62) make the Song of Songs a unique text that influences concepts originally alien to the biblical text. Song of Songs continues to challenge our perception of love and of wisdom and it does so by refraining from offering any strict guidelines, but rather instilling in the reader a notion of immediacy (Exum 1999, 48), as it extends the invitation, to eat, drink, and be drunk with (the) joys of love.

WORKS CITED

Abu-Lughod, Lila. 1988. *Veiled Sentiments: Honor and Poetry in a Bedouin Society*. Berkeley, CA: University of California Press.

Andruska, Jennifer L. 2019. *Wise and Foolish Love in the Song of Songs*. OTS 75. Leiden: Brill.

Arbel, Daphna V. 2015. "'The Most Beautiful Woman,' 'Woman Wisdom,' and 'The Strange Woman': On Femininity in the Song of Songs." Pages 125–140 in *Poets, Prophets, and Texts in Play: Study in Biblical Poetry and Prophecy in Honour of Francis Landy*. Edited by Ehud Ben Zvi, Claudia V. Camp, David M. Gunn, and Aaron W. Huges. LHBOTS 597. London: Bloomsbury T&T Clark.

Barbiero, Gianni. 2011. *Song of Songs: A Close Reading*. VTSup 144. Leiden: Brill.

Beatty, Andrew. 2019. *Emotional Worlds: Beyond and Anthropology of Emotion*. New Departures in Anthropology. Cambridge: Cambridge University Press.

Benjamin, Mara H. 2009. *Rosenzweig's Bible: Reinventing Scripture for Jewish Modernity*. Cambridge: Cambridge University Press.

Birnbaum, Elisabeth. 2017. "'Just Call Me Salomo?': Hld 3,6–11 und 8,11–12 als Fallbeispiele der Hohliedinterpretation." Pages 233–264 in *Das Hohelied im Konflikt der Interpretationen*. Edited by Ludger Schwienhorst-Schönberger. ÖBS 47. Frankfurt a.M.: Peter Lang.

Blenkinsopp, Joseph. 1995a. *Wisdom and Law in the Old Testament: The Ordering of Life in Israel and Early Judaism*. OBS. Rev. ed. Oxford: Oxford University Press.

Blenkinsopp, Joseph. 1995b. *Sage, Priest, Prophet: Religious and Intellectual Leadership in Ancient Israel*. LAI. Louisville, KY: Westminster John Knox.

Boyarin, Daniel. 1990. *Intertextuality and the Reading of Midrash*. ISBL. Bloomington, IN: Indiana University Press.

Brown, William P. 2014. "The Psalms: An Overview." Pages 1–23 in *The Oxford Handbook of the Psalms*. Edited by William P. Brown. Oxford: Oxford University Press.

Clifford, Richard J. 1999. *Proverbs: A Commentary*. OTL. Louisville, KY: Westminster John Knox.

Cogan, Mordechai. 2000. *1 Kings: A New Translation with Introduction and Commentary*. AB 10. New York, NY: Doubleday.

Culler, Jonathan. 2015. *Theory of the Lyric*. Cambridge, MA: Harvard University Press.

Dell, Katharine J. 2005. "Does the Song of Songs Have Any Connections to Wisdom?" Pages 8–26 in Hagedorn 2005.

Dobbs-Allsopp, F.W. 2015. *On Biblical Poetry*. Oxford: Oxford University Press.

Exum, J. Cheryl. 1999. "How Does the Song of Songs Mean? On Reading the Poetry of Desire." *SEÅ* 64:47–63.

Exum, J. Cheryl. 2005a. *Song of Songs*. OTL. Louisville, KY: Westminster John Knox.

Exum, J. Cheryl. 2005b. "The Poetic Genius of the Song of Songs." Pages 78–95 in Hagedorn 2005.

Exum, J. Cheryl. 2015. "The Man in the Song of Songs." Pages 107–124 in *Poets, Prophets, and Texts in Play: Studies in Biblical Poetry and Prophecy in Honour of Francis Landy*. Edited by Ehud Ben Zvi, Claudia V. Camp, David M. Gunn, and Aaron W. Hughes. LHBOTS 597. London: Bloomsbury T&T Clark.

Fox, Michael V. 2000. *Proverbs 1–9: A New Translation with Introduction and Commentary*. AB 18A. New Haven, CT: Yale University Press.

Gaier, Ulrich. 1990. *Johann Gottfried Herder: Volkslieder, Übertragungen, Dichtungen*. BdK 60. Frankfurt a.M.: Deutscher Klassiker Verlag.

Gaier, Ulrich. 2005. "Lieder der Liebe: Herders Hohelied-Interpretation." Pages 317–337 in Hagedorn 2005.

Gertz, Jan Christian. 2018. *Das erste Buch Moses (Genesis): Die Urgeschichte Gen 1–11*. ATD 1. Göttingen: Vandenhoeck & Ruprecht.

Hagedorn, Anselm C., ed. 2005. *Perspectives on the Song of Songs—Perspektiven der Hoheliedauslegung*. BZAW 346. Berlin: de Gruyter

Hagedorn, Anselm C. 2010. "Die Frau des Hohenlieds zwischen babylonisch-assyrischer Morphoskopie und Jacques Lacan (Teil I und II)." *ZAW* 122:417–430, 593–607.

Hagedorn, Anselm C. 2015. "Erotische und theologische Aspekte der Liebe im Hohelied." *JBTh* 29:23–41.

Hagedorn, Anselm C. 2016. "What Kind of Love Is It? Egyptian, Hebrew, or Greek?" *WO* 46:90–106.

Heereman, Nina Sophie. 2018. "'Where Is Wisdom to Be Found?' Rethinking the Song of Songs' Solomonic Setting." *ZAW* 130:418–435.

Horst, Friedrich. 1935. "Die Formen des althebräischen Liebesliedes." Pages 43–54 in *Orientalische Studien: Enno Littmann zu seinem 60. Geburtstag am 16. September 1933*. Edited by R. Paret. Leiden: Brill.

Kaiser, Walter C. 2000. "True Marital Love in Proverbs 5:15–23 and the Interpretation of Song of Songs." Pages 106–116 in *The Way of Wisdom: Essays in Honor of Bruce K. Waltke*. Edited by James I. Packer and Sven K. Soderlund. Grand Rapids, MI: Zondervan.

Kaplan, Jonathan, and Aren M. Wilson-Wright. 2018. "How Song of Songs Became a Divine Love Song." *BibInt* 26:334–351.

Keel, Othmar. 1984. *Deine Blicke sind Tauben: Zur Metaphorik des Hohen Liedes*. SBS 114/115. Stuttgart: Katholisches Bibelwerk.

Keel, Othmar. 1994. *The Song of Songs*. CC. Minneapolis, MN: Fortress.

Kingsmill, Edmée. 2009. *The Song of Songs and the Eros of God: A Study in Biblical Intertextuality*. Oxford: Oxford University Press.

Kingsmill, Edmée. 2016. "The Song of Songs: A Wisdom Book." Pages 310–335 in *Perspectives on Israelite Wisdom: Proceedings of the Oxford Old Testament Seminar*. Edited by John Jarick. LHBOTS 618. London: Bloomsbury T&T Clark.

Krüger, Thomas 2004. *Qoheleth: A Commentary*. Hermeneia. Minneapolis, MN: Fortress.

Kynes, Will. 2019. *An Obituary for "Wisdom Literature": The Birth, Death, and Intertextual Reintegration of a Biblical Corpus*. Oxford: Oxford University Press.

Landy, Francis. 2011. *Paradoxes of Paradise: Identity and Difference in the Song of Songs*. Classic Reprints. 2nd ed. Sheffield: Phoenix.

Loretz, Oswald. 2004. "*Enjambement, versus* und 'salomonische' Königstravestie im Abschnitt Canticum canticorum 3,6–11." Pages 805–816 in *Gott und Mensch im Dialog: Festschrift für Otto Kaiser zum 80. Geburtstag Vol. II*. Edited by Markus Witte. BZAW 345/II. Berlin: de Gruyter.

McKane, William. 1970. *Proverbs: A New Approach*. OTL. London: SCM.

Mendes-Flohr, Paul. 2009. "Between Sensual and Heavenly Love: Franz Rosenzweig's Reading of the Song of Songs." Pages 310–318 in *Scriptural Exegesis: The Shapes of Culture and the Religious Imagination (Essays in Honour of Michael Fishbane)*. Edited by Deborah A. Green and Laura S. Lieber. Oxford: Oxford University Press.

Mroczek, Eva. 2016. *The Literary Imagination in Jewish Antiquity*. Oxford: Oxford University Press.

Müller, Hans-Peter. 1976. "Die lyrische Reproduktion des Mythischen im Hohenlied." *ZTK* 73:23–41.

Müller, Hans-Peter. 1992. *Das Hohelied*. ATD 16/2. Göttingen: Vandenhoeck & Ruprecht.

Murphy, Roland E. 1981. *Wisdom Literature: Job, Proverbs, Ruth, Canticles, and Esther*. FOTL 13. Grand Rapids, MI: Eerdmans.

Murphy, Roland E. 1990. *The Song of Songs*. Hermeneia. Minneapolis, MN: Fortress Press.

Neusner, Jacob. 1989. *Song of Songs Rabbah: An Analytical Translation Volume One (Song of Songs Rabbah to Song Chapters One Through Three)*. BJS 197. Atlanta, GA: Scholars Press.

Nissinen, Martti. 2011. "Is God Mentioned in the Song of Songs? Flame of Yahweh, Love, and Death in Song of Songs 8.6–7a." Pages 273–287 in *A Critical Engagement: Essays on the Hebrew Bible in Honour of J. Cheryl Exum*. Edited by David J.A. Clines and Ellen van Wolde. HBM 38. Sheffield: Phoenix.

Nissinen, Martti. 2016. "Akkadian Love Poetry and the Song of Songs: A Case of Cultural Interaction." Pages 145–170 in *Zwischen Zion und Zaphon: Studien zum Gedenken and den Theologen Oswald Loretz (14.01.1928–12.04.2014)*. Edited by Ludger Hiepel and Marie-Theres Wacker. AOAT 436. Münster: Ugarit Verlag.

Rad, Gerhard von. 1971. *Wisdom in Israel*. London: SCM.

Schellenberg, Annette. 2016. "Questioning the Trend of Classifying the Song of Songs as Sapiential." Pages 393–407 in *Nächstenliebe und Gottesfurcht: Beiträge aus alttestamentlicher und altorientalischer Wissenschaft für Hans-Peter Mathys zum 65. Geburtstag*. Edited by Hanna Jenni and Markus Saur. AOAT 439. Münster: Ugarit Verlag.

Schellenberg, Annette. 2018. "'May Her Breasts Satisfy You at All Times' (Prov 5:19): On the Erotic Passages in Proverbs and Sirach and the Question of How They Relate to the Song of Songs." VT 68:252–271.

Schipper, Bernd U. 2019. *Proverbs 1–15: A Commentary on the Book of Proverbs 1:1–15:33*. Hermeneia. Minneapolis: Fortress.

Schwienhorst-Schönberger, Ludger. 2016. "The Song of Songs as Allegory: Methodological and Hermeneutical Considerations." Pages 1–50 in *Interpreting the Song of Songs—Literal or Allegorical?* Edited by Annette Schellenberg and Ludger Schwienhorst-Schönberger. BTS 26. Leuven: Peeters.

Schwienhorst-Schönberger, Ludger. 2018. "Traces of an Original Allegorical Meaning of the Song of Songs." Pages 317–330 in *"When the Morning Stars Sang": Essays in Honor of Choon Leong Seow on the Occasion of His Sixty-Fifth Birthday*. BZAW 500. Berlin: de Gruyter.

Sparks, Kenton. 2008. "The Song of Songs: Wisdom for Young Jewish Women." *CBQ* 70:277–299.

Staubli, Thomas. 1997. "Von der Heimführung des Hoheliedes aus der babylonischen gefangenschaft der Allegorese." *BL* 70:91–99.

Stone, Timothy J. 2013. *The Compilational History of the Megilloth: Canon, Contoured Intertextuality and Meaning in the Writings*. FAT II 59. Tübingen: Mohr Siebeck.

Weeks, Stuart. 2010. *An Introduction to the Study of Wisdom Literature*. London: T&T Clark.

Yee, Gale A. 1989. "'I Have Perfumed My Bed with Myrrh': The Foreign Woman (*'iššâ zārâ*) in Proverbs 1–9." *JSOT* 43:53–68.

Zakovitch, Yair. 2019. *The Song of Songs: Riddle of Riddles*. LHBOTS 673. London: T&T Clark.

CHAPTER 34

WISDOM PSALMS

W.H. BELLINGER, JR.

STUDY of the Psalms in the twentieth century was dominated by a form-critical approach initiated with the work of Hermann Gunkel.[1] Gunkel moved the beginning points of Psalms study away from a personal/historical approach in which a context in a person's life or an event in the nation's history was the impetus for the psalm and so its interpretive key. With Gunkel's form-critical approach, the starting point was the comparison of psalms in the Psalter, in the wider biblical canon, and in the ancient Near East. With attention to literary structures, vocabulary, and religious feeling, interpreters could consider the psalm type (hymn, thanksgiving, lament, royal psalm, etc.) and the setting in ancient Israel's social and religious life (*Sitz im Leben*) from which the type (and psalm) originated (Bellinger 2012, 15–27). It has been traditional in modern Psalms scholarship that one of the categories of psalm types is "Wisdom psalms."

One of the difficulties is the matter of definition of Wisdom psalms. That issue has perplexed Psalms scholars for the last century and is central to this essay. Gunkel used the term *Gattung* for his psalm categories. It is a broad term and is not limited to a literary type but is a category of a particular definition. While Gunkel does not categorize Wisdom psalms as a distinctive *Gattung*, I will consider in this essay what constitutes a Wisdom psalm and what criteria we might use to determine the categorization. I will also consider the question of the *Sitz im Leben* of the category and whether that is related to the cult in ancient Israel. There have been many and varied responses to these questions, and some interesting creative suggestions in recent scholarship. I will also consider theological issues and themes in these psalms. In addition, the essay will come to the question of what these psalms add to our understanding of Wisdom in the Hebrew Bible as well as the place of Wisdom in the "shape and shaping" of the Hebrew Psalter.

---

[1] Chwi-Woon Kim has contributed valuable assistance as Research Assistant in preparing this essay. My thanks to him.

34.1 FORM-CRITICAL APPROACHES

In his *Einleitung*, Gunkel (Gunkel and Begrich 1998 [1933], 293–305) uses the term "wisdom poetry" as an indication that these texts created by the wise did not follow literary conventions as do the more common psalm types of praise and lament. The same would be true of "royal psalms," those associated with settings in the life of the Davidic king. According to Gunkel, Wisdom poetry centered on themes and forms characteristic of the Wisdom books (Proverbs, Job, Ecclesiastes, Ben Sira, Wisdom of Solomon) and likely arose from Wisdom circles. Gunkel lists Psalms 49, 127 (vv. 3–5), and 133 as early Wisdom poetry on universal human themes. This poetry, he argues, was later brought into Israel's religious life. Psalms 1, 91, 112, and 128 constitute meditation with a focus on Israel's doctrine of reward and retribution. Later doubt emerged about such theodicy issues, reflected in Psalms 37 and 73 as well as in Job and other texts. These texts use the following Wisdom terms: wisdom (37:30; 49:4), instruction (78:1), riddle (49:5), and proverb (49:5). They address learners with positive admonitions and negative warnings (299–300). Gunkel lists a small number of Wisdom poems, but he also suggests that Wisdom elements influenced other *Gattungen* (297–298). Wisdom elements were strongly present in psalms Gunkel labels as mixed types. Just this brief summary of Gunkel's view of Wisdom poetry raises many issues in defining the category of Wisdom psalms.

Not unlike Gunkel, Sigmund Mowinckel (1962, 2:104–125) finds Wisdom poetry as originating in non-cultic settings, particularly in the circle of Wisdom schools. According to Mowinckel, the wise developed a newer type of literature—Wisdom poetry—to serve educational purposes, and this private psalmography was adopted in the Psalter. He lists the following psalms as Wisdom poems: Psalms 1, 19B, 34, 37, 49, 78, 105, 106, 111, 112, and 127. The work of Gunkel and Mowinckel alone as the primary progenitors of the form-critical approach to the Psalms shows that the category of Wisdom psalms is difficult to define. Most scholars who use the category appeal in one way or another to similarity to other Wisdom texts such as Proverbs, Job, and Ecclesiastes in terms of style, themes, vocabulary, and setting in life (Jacobson 2014, 148).[2] A number of scholars have followed this trail.

Roland Murphy (1963, 156–167) considers style, structure, recurrent motifs, and life setting. He includes אשרי ("blessed") formulas, numerical sayings, "better" sayings, a teacher's address to a "son," alphabetic structure, simple comparisons, and admonitions in style and structures. He includes the contrast between righteous and wicked, the two ways, the problem of retribution, practical advice on conduct, and fear of the Lord as themes. Murphy simply speaks of the sapiential milieu for the *Sitz im Leben*. He considers cultic settings for Wisdom psalms: "As the testimony took on more and more a

---

[2] Gerhard von Rad (1972, 48) generally takes the same path as Gunkel and Mowinckel in describing Wisdom psalms as "a type of school poetry which, in the post-exilic period, was delivered to an audience of pupils."

didactic character, the role of wisdom within the cult would have been secured, and with it the independence of the wisdom psalm form" (161). Murphy's list of Wisdom psalms is Psalms 1, 32, 34, 37, 49, 112, and 128. He also speaks of Wisdom elements in other Psalms genres. Kenneth Kuntz (1974, 186–222) takes a similar view in light of rhetorical elements, vocabulary, themes, and forms, and sees interaction between cult and Wisdom. He adds Psalms 127 and 133 (and later 73) to Murphy's list. He highlights Wisdom vocabulary and similar themes to those of Murphy. Avi Hurvitz (1988, 41–51) focuses on terminology and suggests that frequency of appearance be combined with importance in Proverbs, Job, and Ecclesiastes to form the criteria for terms and phrases that appear as markers of Wisdom texts. He identifies but two terms, i.e., הון ("wealth") and סור מרע ("turn away from evil"). The question of Wisdom vocabulary and its importance in identifying Wisdom psalms is an important part of the story of this genre debate.

The question of the relationship of the Wisdom tradition and the cult is also central to the story. Leo Perdue (1977, 261–343) notes the relationship between Wisdom and cult and suggests that some Wisdom psalms come from the cult but not others. Similar to Murphy and Kuntz, Perdue attends to forms, themes, language, and structure in identifying psalms from the sages, with focus on texts centered on proverbs, אשרי formulas, and riddles. He understands the texts to have originated from instructional settings, perhaps schools, but some may have also been part of worship. In Perdue's 2008 volume, he continues to argue for the usefulness of categorizing Wisdom psalms, indicating that didactic psalms use sapiential vocabulary, shared semantics, and themes related to Wisdom texts. This recent work primarily associates didactic psalms with scribal activities appearing in various loci, such as the temple and administrative as well as private milieu in the Persian period. In his commentary on Psalms, Gerstenberger (1988, 20–21, 257–258) similarly notes that didactic texts were part of the cult from the beginning of Israel's worship. He suggests that Wisdom discourse was primarily related to educational settings outside the cult, but that liturgy came to include instruction of the community. For Gerstenberger, the intersection between cult and school correlates with Israel's loss of hope in the exilic and post-exilic contexts. In his recent work, Gerstenberger (2014, 338–349) highlights that the didactic texts reflect the shift from emphasis on sacrifice to emphasis on Torah in worship during the Persian period.

34.2 Responses to the Form-Critical Views

All of these scholars see a place for the category of Wisdom psalms among the *Gattungen* in a form-critical approach to the Psalms. Kuntz's categories of rhetorical elements, vocabulary, themes, and forms provide a common way to think about the criteria for the category. Not all Psalms scholars would take that view today. A major voice of dissent comes from James Crenshaw (2000, 9–17), who particularly critiques Kuntz's 1974 article.[3] He notes the small number of psalms classified as Wisdom, and casts doubt on the hope of distinguishing Wisdom terms from prophetic and priestly terms as well as common language. According to Crenshaw, the themes Kuntz associates with Wisdom also occur in prophetic and priestly texts and together do not appear in any given Wisdom psalm. Crenshaw also notes the differences between the lists of Wisdom psalms articulated by form critics. Thus, he suggests that classifying Wisdom psalms as a form-critical category is both obscure and confusing. Kuntz (2003, 145–154) responds by defending the form-critical category and objecting that Crenshaw's need to find all things about wisdom in one text is unreasonable and that the number of Wisdom psalms is not a particularly relevant issue. Both Crenshaw and Kuntz note that there are didactic elements in the Psalms. The issues are defining those elements and categorizing them. Crenshaw (2003, 155–158) then responds to Kuntz by saying that matters of quantification are important to the argument and casting doubt on several of the forms and terms Kuntz suggests mark Wisdom texts. If I were to follow Crenshaw's lead, this essay would be very brief indeed!

Others focus on a modified understanding of genre. Raymond Van Leeuwen (2003, 72) notes that "the…question of the relation of genres to putative *Sitz im Leben* has proven especially intractable, largely because we lack the data needed to settle such questions reliably." While valuing the form-critical insight that literary genre shares the cognitive ground between authors and readers, Van Leeuwen recognizes that the literary adaptations of genres may differ from their original settings. Here, he refers to the notion of family resemblance between complex forms to highlight various modifications of literary genres. He illustrates with the paired Psalms 111 and 112. They share acrostic structures, terms, and theology. There are two genres but one *Sitz im Leben*. This example reflects a single scribe's use of multiple genres and life settings in a literary context. Van Leeuwen applies such a flexible understanding of genre to Wisdom psalms. He further suggests that the Wisdom genre is tied to the task of education and can take place in cultic and non-cultic settings. Similarly, Mark Sneed (2011, 50–71) critiques the standard understanding of genre in both Gunkel's work and Crenshaw's. Sneed understands the texts often categorized as Wisdom psalms as "texts that reflect some of the themes in the Hebrew wisdom literature" (67). The category helps readers understand these psalms geared toward instruction of persons and likely more studied than sung. A rigid understanding of genres and their boundaries is not helpful hermeneutically; genres have a heuristic function.

The comparison between psalms and biblical Wisdom books has usually been part of the study of Wisdom psalms. William Brown (2005, 85–102) explores didactic psalms in light of their parallels with Proverbs. A didactic psalm for Brown is one that is meant for instruction as indicated by form and/or language. Psalms and texts from Wisdom Literature share language, motifs, and metaphors. For Brown, the issue is not categorizing a unique category of Wisdom psalms, but identifying the rhetorical aims of these texts, sometime shared and sometimes not (85–86). Kent Reynolds (2010) is very spe-

---

[3] See also Crenshaw's (2001, 94) comment: "My own research in the Psalter leads me to question the very category of wisdom psalms." See also his list of Wisdom psalms according to various scholars (94–95); compare Jacobson's (2014, 150) list.

cific in comparing the language in Psalm 119 with the language in Wisdom Literature. He does not classify Psalm 119 as a Wisdom psalm but suggests that its role is in shaping character formation. This psalm is a type unto itself. The writer appropriates language and themes from Wisdom Literature. The psalm emphasizes Torah above wisdom. So while Reynolds's work is specifically on Psalm 119, it depends on comparison of the psalm with Wisdom books and also shows how complicated the form-critical issues are.

Others attend to the task of refining the criteria to be used in classifying Wisdom psalms, tasks Murphy and Kuntz had already begun in their form-critical work. For example, Tova Forti (2015, 205–220) suggests four criteria: themes, language and style, Wisdom vocabulary, and figurative features. Susan Gillingham (2015, 285–302) describes three dimensions of the category: a mode of writing (vocabulary, style, form); a mode of thinking (admonitions, practical wisdom, retribution, righteous contrasted with wicked, cosmic order in creation, fear of YHWH); a mode of living (advising in the royal court, practical wisdom for daily life, scribes who challenged traditional wisdom as in Job). The second criterion (a mode of thinking) leads Gillingham to understand the Wisdom tradition to be both multi-cultural and extensive, in contrast to Crenshaw. Reviewing different groups within the Wisdom tradition in light of the third criterion (a mode of living), she also notes that royal, familial, and intellectual sages relate to only a few psalms (301). Building on Mowinckel's notion of "learned psalmographer," she argues that the "Levitical Temple singers" represent "the group who preserved and ordered and taught and sang the psalms" (302). For Gillingham, therefore, Psalms are liturgical songs, and they also have a didactic function.

In his recent monograph, Simon Chi-chung Cheung (2015) offers a new set of criteria to define Wisdom and Wisdom psalms by way of a variety of recent methodologies. Cheung points out that a form-critical approach fails because it builds a rigid connection between forms and settings. Wisdom psalms are mixed types, according to Gunkel, and so do not fit categories that are tied to particular settings in life. As a result, the content, form, tone, and rhetoric of the texts get little attention. Raising this issue, Cheung prefers the flexibility of the genre theory of family resemblance (note the discussion of Van Leeuwen above). Here Proverbs and Ecclesiastes serve as prototypical members of the Wisdom genre with Job as a "cousin." To determine core and peripheral groups of Wisdom psalms, Cheung proposes three categories: first, "a ruling wisdom thrust" that displays a Wisdom-related theme that consolidates other themes; second, "an intellectual tone" that conveys communicative intent through stylistic devices and Wisdom terms; and third, "a didactic intention" that serves the speech's teaching purpose rather than its origin.

To discern "a didactic intention" of the speech, Cheung further adopts speech-act theory, introduced by J.L. Austin and further developed by J.R. Searle. Among other types of speech acts, he focuses on illocutionary acts.[4] Following Searle's types of illocution-

---

[4] Speech-act theory lists three types of speech acts: Locutionary acts (saying something, such as, "There is a bear over there"), illocutionary acts (performing an act through saying something, such as giving a warning), and perlocutionary acts (producing particular effects with speech, such as creating fear).

ary acts, Cheung adds that indirect speech can also imply a request, such as the lament psalms requesting divine deliverance (47).[5] At a literary level, the task of identifying a speech intention requires examining the integral relationship among different illocutions within the text in order to find the ruling illocution that governs the whole text. In light of this creative set of criteria, Cheung analyzes seven psalms: Psalms 37, 49, 73, 128, 32, 39, and 19. He does not pursue a closed set of Wisdom psalms but a grouping by family resemblance, asking how the parts of the psalm contribute to a didactic intention. He suggests that non-Wisdom themes in Psalms 37 and 49 reinforce a didactic intention and so these psalms are the prototypical Wisdom psalms. In Psalm 73, however, the Wisdom themes reinforce themes of thanksgiving and trust. Cheung goes on to suggest that Psalms 128, 39, and 19 are similar to Psalm 73 in that their resemblance is in the extended family arena rather than the heart of Wisdom. He also classifies Psalm 32 as a thanksgiving psalm, with only verses 8–10 related to Wisdom.

For Cheung, theme, tone, and speech intention need to connect to Wisdom in some way to include the psalm in the category. Otherwise the family resemblance does not hold. Genre is flexible for Cheung. That could be a strength or weakness for those reviewing his work. Cheung's approach to questions of genre and the relationships between genre is helpful as is his emphasis on the wisdom (didactic) intention of a psalm. His is an important current attempt to meaningfully discuss the question of Wisdom psalms. An alternative would be to focus on the primary genres in the Psalter (lament and praise) and their relationships. Texts often categorized as Wisdom psalms might well fit with these two major genres, while at the same time articulating didactic purposes (see below, 34.4 Theological Themes, for my discussion of Catherine Petrany [2015]).

34.3 THE SHAPE AND SHAPING OF THE PSALTER

As noted in the introduction, contemporary Psalms scholarship also emphasizes questions related to the shape of the Psalter as a whole and how that shape came to be. This interest goes back to Brevard Childs's (1979, 504–525) emphasis on canon and especially Gerald Wilson's (1985) volume on the editing of the Hebrew Psalter. This methodological shift characterizes a number of recent Psalms studies. James Mays (1987, 3–12) notes the move from form-critical and cult-functional categories to the reading of the Psalter as a whole. Mays also suggests that Psalms 1, 19, and 119 be understood as Torah Psalms that are important in the shape of the Psalter. He explores the connections of these psalms to each other and to other texts in the Psalter and to Wisdom. J. Clinton McCann (1992, 121)

[5] Cheung refers to five types of illocutionary acts from Searle's work: assertive, expressing the speaker's belief; directive, expressing the speaker's desire; commissive, expressing the speaker's commitment to the action; expressive, expressing the speaker's feeling or attitude; and declarative, expressing the speaker's intent to change things (45–46).

views the Psalter as "God's word to humans—as torah, 'instruction.'" He suggests that different psalm genres offer lessons and thus serve as instruction. For example, psalms of praise teach divine intervention for humans and the world, while laments call attention to the pain of life as well as the voices of complaint and trust in life. McCann suggests that didactic elements pervade nearly every genre in the Psalms.[6]

Gerald Wilson's (1993, 72–82) well-known essay arguing for a Wisdom frame for the Psalter also needs mention in this context. He understands Psalm 1, with its attention to individual meditation, as a hermeneutical introduction to the book of Psalms. Wilson also suggests that Pss 107:42–43 and 145:19–20 represent Wisdom teaching. Ps 90:11–12 represents the Wisdom theme in the transition from Books I–III to Books IV–V, with Psalm 73 also part of that transition. These editorial pieces exhibit the centrality of the didactic function of the Psalter.

Samuel Terrien (1993, 51–72) also considers the Wisdom tradition in the Psalter. He indicates that sages and musicians were not isolated from each other. He notes evolution in the use of the term torah from divine instruction in the pre-exilic era to a written Torah after the exile. He further suggests that psalms of praise and lament reflect the views of orthodox wisdom with the use of "the fear of YHWH" and that Psalms 49, 73, and 139 exhibit similarities to Job.

Norman Whybray has been one of the major critics of the trend to consider the shape and shaping of the Psalter; he is not persuaded by the proposals for reading the Psalms as a book. He has also had an interesting journey with the question of Wisdom psalms. In Whybray's 1995 essay he become the first of several interpreters to use the metaphor of making bricks without straw to describe the state of seeking some kind of consensus on the identification of Wisdom psalms (152–160). He proposes to use but one criterion—significant terms that are shared with Proverbs, Job, and Ecclesiastes. At the same time, he notes that אשרי appears more in the Psalms than in these three Wisdom books and is likely of cultic origin (158–159). Whybray's 1996 volume recognizes a greater presence of Wisdom psalms. Here he suggests considering Wisdom ways of thinking in the biblical Wisdom books as central to the task of identifying Wisdom elements in the Psalms. He uses a variety of expressions to characterize such thinking: reflection on personal experience and on the implications of faith and on the human condition, attention to the concerns of the Wisdom books, and the attempt to editorially portray the Psalms as a Wisdom or Torah Psalter. In so doing, he does not follow the form-critical route of prioritizing literary form or didactic tone. He lists a number of "pure Wisdom and Torah Psalms": Psalms 8, 14/53, 25, 34, 39, 49, 73, 90, 112, 127, 131, and 139. He categorizes Psalms 1 and 119 as "Torah Psalms" and suggests that a variety of additional poems exhibit Wisdom elements: Psalms 18, 27, 32, 86, 92, 94, 105, 107, 111, 144, and 146. He suggests that Wisdom scribes were active in the redaction of the Psalms and thus the move toward the Psalter.

---

[6] Cf. Anthony Ceresko (1990, 217–230), who understands the authors of the Psalter to be sages, post-exilic scholars and scribes who both participate in the cult and revere Torah.

In his influential treatment of Book V of the Psalter, Erich Zenger (1998, 77–102) builds on Wilson's work and suggests that the final book of the Psalter has a concentric structure centered on Psalm 119. He notes, "Psalm 119 is a prayer for a life lived according to the Torah which is the precondition for the advent of the universal reign of the God of the Exodus and of Zion celebrated in the fifth book of psalms (God of the Exodus: Psalms 113–118; God of Zion: Psalms 120–136, 137)" (98). He takes the sequence of Psalm 113–118, 119, and 120–136 as a meditation on "the canonical history of the origin of Israel (Psalms 113–118: the Exodus; Psalm 119: Sinai; Psalms 120–135: entry into the Promised Land with Zion/Jerusalem as the heart of the land)" (100–101).[7] He concludes that the ordering of this middle portion of Book V suggests a spiritual pilgrimage.

Psalm 119 is also at the center of David Noel Freedman's work (1999); he attends to the poetic artistry of the psalm and concludes that the poem has a symmetrical structure based on the alphabet with a series of refinements, elaborations, and deviations from established norms. Building on the work of Mays (1987) and McCann (1992), he suggests that the writer of Psalm 119 was aware of other acrostic psalms (9–10, 25, 34, 37, 111, 112, 145) and worked from the context of understanding the Psalter as a book.

Similarly, David Firth (2015, 63–82) focuses, as have other interpreters, on the significance of Psalm 119. He understands the lengthy text as not only a Torah psalm but also a theological center that relates to other parts of the Psalter. Noting that the psalm's terms related to law appear throughout the Psalter, he explores how these terms relate to divine instruction to Israel, the king, and individuals (74). According to Firth, Psalms 78, 105, and 106 review Israel's story in relation to law and covenant. Psalms 18, 89, and 132 relate to divine instruction to the king. Psalms 25 and 111 present divine law as the basis for individual identity and life. This treatment relates linguistic and theological elements of Torah. That is particularly true of the royal psalms included, all related to David in content and in superscription.

While recognizing the importance of Torah, Manfred Oeming (2008, 161) further suggests that the shape of the Psalter exhibits a Wisdom orientation with Wisdom psalms at the junctures of the five books. At the center of the Psalter is a psalm attributed to Solomon as "the ideal wise man and the model king." Acknowledging the lack of consensus on identifying Wisdom psalms, he suggests that interpreters could use narrower or broader criteria and thus produce smaller and larger lists. Oeming (2008, 157) refers to levels of criteria deriving from Hubert Irsigler (1984): those most commonly accepted (Psalms 1, 37, 49, and 112); those less than unanimous but constructed with Wisdom aphorisms (73, 127, and 128); those disputed that are Torah psalms (19B, 34, 119, and 133); and those with less consideration (32, 78, 91, and 111). Other psalms may include some typical Wisdom language. Oeming locates Wisdom psalms in the context of the change in vocabulary from Mowinckel's non-cultic origins to post-cultic origins. He understands Wisdom psalms to be mixed forms and thus written texts rather than initially oral poetry for the cult (159). While referring to Zenger's view that the Jerusalem Wisdom

---

[7] Weber (2012, 289–306) follows Zenger's lead and interprets Psalms 1–3 as a Wisdom theology prologue for the Psalter announcing themes throughout the Psalter. See also Bellinger 2007, 114–126.

school completed the redaction of the Psalter in the second century BCE, Oeming suggests that the final editing took place in the first century BCE, since the Wisdom elements of the Psalms are similar to Qumran texts and the Odes of Solomon.

In Markus Saur's (2015, 181–204) contribution to the collection of essays *Was There a Wisdom Tradition?* (Sneed 2015), he argues that the Psalter presents a theology of the Hebrew Bible *in nuce* since it originates over the course of centuries and reflects various theological perspectives of that time. He ties that view to the redaction of the Psalter by various hands and with various collections. He suggests that there are in the Psalms a broad range of Wisdom topics with parallels in other traditional Wisdom texts in the Hebrew Scriptures. He then lists Psalms 37, 49, and 73 as representative Wisdom psalms among the plurality of voices in the Psalter.

Much of the scholarship I have reviewed is concerned with categorizing psalms and in particular determining which psalms, if any, qualify as Wisdom psalms. The other area of research related to the topic is how these psalms and Wisdom elements in other texts help to shape the Psalter as a whole. Mowinckel suggested that the "learned psalmographers" were the editors of the Psalter. Recent work on the Psalms has greatly expanded this topic, and Wisdom psalms are part of that picture. The Psalms are purposefully arranged and Wisdom psalms have strategic placements in the shape of the Hebrew Psalter. Psalm 1 plays a strategic role as the introductory text of the book and "invites us to see the Psalter as more than a prayer book or a loose collection of hymns; the Psalter is also a book of instruction" (Jacobson 2014, 155). A number of interpreters have noted the connection between these crucially placed Wisdom texts and royal psalms. The works summarized above from McCann, Wilson, and Zenger emphasize the didactic character of the shape of the Hebrew Psalter. A survey of the five-book structure of the Psalter supports that view.

Psalm 1 introduces the purpose of the Psalter as part of divine instruction to be meditated upon as a source of life. Psalms 3–14 bring together a sequence of lament psalms that serve as model prayers. The same could be said for Psalms 25–34. Psalms 15, 19, and 24 in different ways articulate torah or divine instruction and its significance for the life of faith. The first book of Psalms (Psalms 1–41) as a collection does seem to serve didactic purposes. The second book (Psalms 42–72) comes to themes of exile and how the divine presence relates to that experience of alienation. The concluding psalm of the book is associated with the patron of wisdom in Israel, Solomon. Book III (Psalms 73–89) begins with a lengthy and engaging reflection on the problems of theodicy, a theme central to the Psalms of Asaph. Questions of justice, especially in an exilic setting, pervade Book III. With Book IV (Psalms 90–106) the turn is to the divine king as the one who holds a future for the singing and reading community. In the final book of the Psalter (Psalms 107–150), the dominant Psalm 119 focuses on torah, and the Psalms of Ascents (Psalms 120–134) also include texts often associated with Wisdom. These texts are central to Zenger's view articulated above that this concluding book of the Psalter serves as a spiritual pilgrimage to Zion, the place of the presence of the divine king and teacher of torah. The collection we have come to call the Hebrew Psalter seems to move in the didactic direction of teaching for the pilgrimage of faith. Its shape betrays a Wisdom purpose.

Questions on the shape and shaping of the Psalter stand now as an established part of Psalms scholarship, though interpreters deal with these questions in a variety of ways. Didactic purposes do seem to be important in the canonical shape of the Psalter and thus related to Wisdom emphases.

34.4 THEOLOGICAL THEMES

Some recent studies, while interacting with the scholarship noted above, have also emphasized theological themes in Psalms texts often tied to Wisdom. Stephan Geller (2002) traces a move from "Old Wisdom" to "New Wisdom," from natural and moral order reflected in צדק and אמת and Egyptian *maʿat* to a new wisdom in the eighth and seventh centuries with the emergence of Deuteronomic law and a corresponding interest in divine retribution. He suggests that Psalms 8, 19, 104, and 139 reflect Old Wisdom with their references to nature but not to problems of theodicy. These psalms move toward the place of humans in covenant/torah piety and the implications thereof.

Katharine Dell (2004, 445–458) suggests that Israel's early theology of creation shapes a worldview and that creation order is a central theme for Wisdom texts.[8] The connection between creation theology and Wisdom leads Dell to suggest that Wisdom has a place in the pre-exilic Israelite cult rather than pursuing a Wisdom setting in the post-exilic era that influenced the shape of the Psalter. She also has a different view of mixed psalm types; they bring together cult and Wisdom traditions rather than suggesting later dates for these texts. In light of the link between cult and Wisdom, she suggests both a narrower list of Wisdom psalms and a broader list. Psalms 1, 34, 37, 39, 49, and 73 form the narrower group and Psalms 1, 14, 19, 25, 32, 34, 36, 37, 39, 49, 51, 53, 62, 73, 78, 90, 92, 94, 104, 105, 106, 111, 112, 119, 127, and 128 the broader one (452). Dell understands pre-exilic settings for cult and Wisdom to be possible.

Adele Berlin (2005, 71–83) focuses on Wisdom thought in the Psalms and the relationship of Wisdom to Torah. She suggests that the only real difference between Wisdom psalms and Torah psalms is the use of the term "torah." She argues that "the topic of creation is never an end in itself in Psalms but always a trope or subtheme that supports a psalm's main theme" (74). Psalm 104 is her test case. While Geller understands this psalm as an example of Old Wisdom with its theme of creation and nature, Berlin understands creation and torah to be together in the text. The term "torah" is not used, but Berlin suggests that the psalm's accounts of creation reflect Genesis 1–3 and thus knowledge of the Torah.

Stuart Weeks (2005, 292–307) seeks to define Wisdom not by way of genres or forms but in terms of the content of texts. He begins with the traditional Wisdom books of Proverbs, Job, and Ecclesiastes. He suggests that Wisdom Literature is mostly concerned

---

[8] For this suggestion, Dell refers to Zimmerli 1964, 146–158; Crenshaw 1982, 190; Schmid 1984, 102–117; Levenson 1988.

with how individuals are able to shape life and their future and how they receive reliable guidance (or wisdom) for that task. The issue for Wisdom is how individuals survive and thrive and follow wisdom for living. That is different than a concern with the relationship of Israel as a whole with God. This content is typically in poetic form and associated with certain literary genres. Therefore, literary form and subject matter correspond. This observation leads Weeks to suggest two groups of Wisdom psalms. One commends the benefits of righteous living—Psalms 1, 19B, 25, 32, 34, 37, 52, 112, 125, 128; the other deals with problems tied to such life style or its benefits—Psalms 10, 14, 49, 73, 90, 94.

John Kartje (2014) examines "an epistemological progression" among Psalms 1, 73, 90, and 107, all of which sit in critical places in the Psalter. According to Kartje, "the moral paradox" of the Psalter is "that the righteous can suffer, while the wicked can prosper" (171). The paradox is absent in Psalm 1, recognized with some resolution in Psalm 73, more actively resolved in Psalm 90. In Psalm 107, YHWH responds to the psalm's appeal. Therefore, the Psalter invites readers to follow this epistemological path.

Two recent contributions focus on the relationship between the speaker in the psalm and God and the relationship between the voice in the text and its audience. Carleen Mandolfo (2002) argues that when interpreters attend to grammar and rhetoric, psalms include a variety of voices such as a petitioning voice, divine voice, or didactic voice. She understands the didactic voice to interrupt the divine-human communication as a way to encourage inner dialogue for those lamenting in a cultic setting. She concentrates on several lament psalms and two thanksgiving psalms, noting the grammatical features that distinguish the various voices. She then characterizes the cultic settings in light of conflicts between dissenting voices; her focus is the rhetoric and ideology in these social settings. Her contribution to Wisdom is the emphasis on the didactic in cultic settings.

Catherine Petrany (2015) advances Mandolfo's work by attending to the Psalter as a whole and examining how psalmic speech invites addressees to join in the speaker's prayer and praise to the deity in the cult. She understands traditional Wisdom Literature to address horizontal relationships between humans while the Psalms address both horizontal and vertical dimensions of speech with the deity. By attending to the divine and human voices in the Psalms, therefore, she searches for the pedagogical function of the Psalms. Petrany notes that Proverbs presents speech between humans; an "I" addresses a "Thou." The book moves in the direction of the addressee maturing in wisdom. In the Psalms, she considers pedagogical speeches in non-Wisdom psalms (Psalms 25, 62, 92, and 94). Here the interaction between parent/teacher and child/student invites the participants into both horizontal (teaching) and vertical activity (reflection, supplication, and praise). For Petrany, the Wisdom psalms (1, 37, and 49) individually address character formation and thus horizontal pedagogy but their immediate contexts move the teaching to the call for addressing the divine with petition. For example, Petrany locates the context of the pedagogical Psalm 37 as the cluster of Psalms 35–41. The section begins with supplication and moves with Psalm 39 to the wisdom of prayer. Psalms 40 and 41 offer thanksgiving. In the context of the Psalter, she follows Brueggemann in seeing Psalm 73 as the pivot of the Psalter ultimately leading to the conclusion of praise in Psalms 146–150 (193). She also connects Psalm 73 with Psalms

1, 37, and 49 by way of lexical and thematic parallels concerning the righteous and the wicked. She suggests that the praise and description of God in Psalm 73 teach the addressees to join the speaker in addressing God (204). Therefore, Psalmic pedagogy invites the audience to prayer and praise.

34.5 CONCLUSION

Much of the scholarship on Wisdom psalms has related to Gunkel's form-critical agenda. When I wrote an introductory textbook on the Psalms, I included a brief chapter on the Wisdom psalms and indicated that they used forms and themes from the Wisdom books, primarily Proverbs, Job, and Ecclesiastes (Bellinger 2012, 129–140). That is the traditional type-analytical view. More recent work in this vein contributes to the newer form-critical perspective in which lines between categories are more flexible. Most interpreters of the Psalms would argue that there are Wisdom elements in the Psalms, and those elements are the focus of a relatively small number of psalms. Crenshaw and some others would eliminate the category as confusing.[9] Recent work on these texts has brought to light intriguing accounts of the relationship of Wisdom elements to torah and particularly to the didactic purposes of these texts. Careful attention to who is speaking and who is addressed in the texts are enlightening. Proverbs and Ecclesiastes exhibit didactic purposes. Job is a bit more indirect with its narrative setting and lengthy dialogue but it also takes a didactic stance in the divine speeches and in the pronouncement that Job is the one who has spoken "what is right" (Job 42:7). The Psalms also seem to operate from didactic purposes. At the same time, the addressee in the Psalms is both human and divine. The connection to the cult is important in these texts. The Wisdom elements could well function in that setting also. Didactic purposes in worship seem to have been present in the ancient cult even as they continue to be in worship today. The Psalter is a compendium of much of ancient Israel's faith. It thus intertwines a variety of elements: priestly, prophetic, and didactic. Diane Jacobson (2014, 155) may well be right that "not much is settled about wisdom language in the Psalms. We end with more questions than answers." I think we have, however, learned helpful insights into the didactic functions of this language and the contributions of this language to the shape of the Hebrew Psalter as a whole. The Psalms in delicate but explicit ways bring wisdom into the realm of worship.

WORKS CITED

Bellinger, W.H., Jr. 2007. "Reading from the Beginning (Again): The Shape of Book I of the Psalter." Pages 114–126 in *Diachronic and Synchronic: Reading the Psalms in Real Time:*

---

[9] Bellinger 2014, 321–323. While many Psalms scholars would agree that the Psalter is dominated by praise and lament, they retain the categories of royal psalms and Wisdom psalms.

Proceedings of the Baylor Symposium on the Book of Psalms. Edited by Joel S. Burnett, W. H. Bellinger, Jr., and W. Dennis Tucker, Jr. LHBOTS 488. New York, NY: T&T Clark.

Bellinger, Jr., W.H. 2012. *Psalms: A Guide to Studying the Psalter.* 2nd ed. Grand Rapids, MI: Baker Academic.

Bellinger, Jr., W.H. 2014. "Psalms and the Question of Genre." Pages 313–325 in *The Oxford Handbook of the Psalms.* Edited by William P. Brown. Oxford: Oxford University Press.

Berlin, Adele. 2005. "The Wisdom of Creation in Psalm 104." Pages 71–83 in *Seeking Out the Wisdom of the Ancients: Essays Offered to Honor Michael V. Fox on the Occasion of His Sixty-Fifth Birthday.* Edited by Ronald L. Roxel, Kelvin G. Friebel, and Dennis R. Magary. Winona Lake, IN: Eisenbrauns.

Brown, William P. 2005. "'Come, O Children...I Will Teach You the Fear of the LORD' (Psalm 34:12): Comparing Psalms and Proverbs." Pages 85–102 in *Seeking Out the Wisdom of the Ancients: Essays Offered to Honor Michael V. Fox on the Occasion of His Sixty-Fifth Birthday.* Edited by R.L. Troxel, Kelvin G. Friebel, and Dennis R. Magary. Winona Lake, IN: Eisenbruans.

Ceresko, Anthony. 1990. "The Sage in the Psalms." Pages 217–230 in *The Sage in Israel and the Ancient Near East.* Edited by John G. Gammie and Leo G. Perdue. Winona Lake, IN: Eisenbrauns.

Cheung, Simon Chi-chung. 2015. *Wisdom Intoned: A Reappraisal of the Genre "Wisdom Psalms"* LHBOTS 613. New York, NY: Bloomsbury T&T Clark.

Childs, Brevard S. 1979. *Introduction to the Old Testament as Scripture.* Philadelphia, PA: Fortress.

Crenshaw, James L. 1982. *Old Testament Wisdom: An Introduction.* London: SCM.

Crenshaw, James L. 2000. "Wisdom Psalms?" *CurBS* 8:9–17.

Crenshaw, James L. 2001. *The Psalms: An Introduction.* Grand Rapids, MI: Eerdmans.

Crenshaw, James L. 2003. "Gold Dust or Nuggets: A Brief Response to J. Kenneth Kuntz." *CurBR* 1:155–158.

Dell, Katharine J. 2004. "'I Will Solve My Riddle to the Music of the Lyre' (Psalm 49:4[5]): A Cultic Setting for Wisdom Psalms?" *VT* 54:445–458.

Firth, David G. 2015. "More than Just Torah: God's Instruction in the Psalms." *STR* 6:63–82.

Forti, Tova L. 2015. "*Gattung* and *Sitz im Leben*: Methodological Vagueness in Defining Wisdom Psalms." Pages 205–220 in *Was There a Wisdom Tradition? New Prospects in Israelite Wisdom Studies.* Edited by Mark R. Sneed. AIL 23. Atlanta, GA: SBL.

Freedman, David Noel. 1999. *Psalm 119: The Exaltation of Torah.* BJSUCSD 6. Winona Lake, IN: Eisenbrauns.

Geller, Stephan A. 2002. "Wisdom, Nature and Piety in Some Biblical Psalms." Pages 101–121 in *Riches Hidden in Secret Places: Ancient Near Eastern Studies in Memory of Thorkild Jacobsen.* Edited by Tzvi Abusch. Winona Lake, IN: Eisenbrauns.

Gerstenberger, Erhard S. 1988. *Psalms, Part I, with an Introduction to Cultic Poetry.* FOTL 14. Grand Rapids, MI: Eerdmans.

Gerstenberger, Erhard S. 2014. "Non-Temple Psalms: The Cultic Setting Revisited." Pages 338–349 in *The Oxford Handbook of the Psalms.* Edited by William P. Brown. Oxford: Oxford University Press.

Gillingham, Susan E. 2015. "'I Will Incline My Ear to a Proverb; I Will Solve My Riddle to the Music of the Harp' (Psalm 49:4): The Wisdom Tradition and the Psalms." Pages 277–309 in *Perspectives on Israelite Wisdom: Proceedings of the Oxford Old Testament Seminar.* Edited by John Jarick. LHBOTS 618. New York, NY: Bloomsbury T&T Clark.

Gunkel, Hermann, and Joachim Begrich. 1998 [German orig. 1933]. *An Introduction to the Psalms: The Genres of the Religious Lyric of Israel.* Translated by James D. Nogalski. Macon, GA: Mercer University Press.

Hurvitz, Avi. 1988. "Wisdom Vocabulary in the Hebrew Psalter: A Contribution to the Study of 'Wisdom Psalms.'" *VT* 38:41–51.

Irsigler, Hubert. 1984. *Psalm 73—Monolog Eines Weisen: Text, Programm, Struktur.* St. Ottilien: EOS Verlag.

Jacobson, Diane. 2014. "Wisdom Language in the Psalms." Pages 147–157 in *The Oxford Handbook of the Psalms.* Edited by William P. Brown. Oxford: Oxford University Press.

Kartje, John. 2014. *Wisdom Epistemology in the Psalter: A Study of Psalms 1, 73, 90, and 107.* BZAW 472. Berlin: de Gruyter.

Kuntz, J. Kenneth. 1974. "The Canonical Wisdom psalms of Ancient Israel: Their Rhetorical, Thematic, and Formal Dimensions." Pages 186–222 in *Rhetorical Criticism.* Edited by J. Jackson and M. Kessler. Pittsburgh, PA: Pickwick.

Kuntz, J. Kenneth. 2003. "Reclaiming Biblical Wisdom Psalms: A Response to Crenshaw." *CurBR* 1:145–154.

Levenson, Jon D. 1988. *Creation and the Persistence of Evil: The Jewish Drama of Divine Omnipotence.* San Francisco, CA: Harper & Row.

Mandolfo, Carleen. 2002. *God in the Dock: Dialogic Tension in the Psalms of Lament.* JSOTSup 357. Sheffield: Sheffield Academic.

Mays, James L. 1987. "The Place of the Torah Psalms in the Psalter." *JBL* 106:3–12.

McCann, J. Clinton, Jr. 1992. "The Psalms as Instruction." *Int* 46:117–128.

Mowinckel, Sigmund. 1962. *The Psalms in Israel's Worship.* 2 vols. New York, NY: Abingdon.

Murphy, Roland. 1963. "A Consideration of the Classification 'Wisdom Psalms.'" Pages 156–167 in *Congress Volume: Bonn 1962.* Edited by J.A. Emerton. VTSup 9. Leiden: Brill.

Oeming, Manfred. 2008. "Wisdom as a Hermeneutical Key to the Book of Psalms." Pages 154–162 in *Scribes, Sages, and Seers: The Sage in the Eastern Mediterranean World.* Edited by Leo G. Perdue. FRLANT 219. Göttingen: Vandenhoeck & Ruprecht.

Perdue, Leo G. 1977. *Wisdom and Cult: A Critical Analysis of the Views of Cult in the Wisdom Literature of Israel and the Ancient Near East.* SBLDS 30. Missoula, MT: Scholars Press.

Perdue, Leo G. 2008. *The Sword and the Stylus: An Introduction to Wisdom in the Age of Empires.* Grand Rapid, MI: Eerdmans.

Petrany, Catherine. 2015. *Pedagogy, Prayer, and Praise: The Wisdom of the Psalms and Psalter.* FAT II 83. Tübingen: Mohr Siebeck.

Rad, Gerhard von. 1972. *Wisdom in Israel.* New York, NY: Abingdon.

Reynolds, Kent A. 2010. *Torah as Teacher: The Exemplary Torah Student in Psalm 119.* VTSup 137. Leiden: Brill.

Saur, Markus. 2015. "Where Can Wisdom Be Found? New Perspectives on the Wisdom Psalms." Pages 181–204 in *Was There a Wisdom Tradition? New Perspectives in Israelite Wisdom Studies.* Edited by Mark R. Sneed. AIL 23. Atlanta, GA: SBL.

Schmid, H.H. 1984. "Creation, Righteousness, and Salvation: 'Creation Theology' as the Broad Horizon of Biblical Theology." Pages 102–117 in *Creation in the Old Testament.* Edited by B.W. Anderson. Philadelphia, PA: Fortress.

Sneed, Mark S. 2011. "Is the 'Wisdom Tradition' a Tradition?" *CBQ* 73:50–71.

Sneed, Mark S., ed. 2015. *Was There a Wisdom Tradition? New Prospects in Israelite Wisdom Studies.* AIL 23. Atlanta: SBL.

Terrien, Samuel. 1993. "Wisdom in the Psalter." Pages 51–72 in *In Search of Wisdom: Essays in Memory of John G. Gammie*. Edited by Leo G. Perdue, Bernard Brandon Scott, and William Johnston Wiseman. Louisville, KY: Westminster John Knox.

Van Leeuwen, Raymond C. 2003. "Form Criticism, Wisdom, and Psalms 111–112." Pages 65–84 in *The Changing Face of Form Criticism for the Twenty-First Century*. Edited by Marvin A. Sweeney and Ehud Ben Zvi. Grand Rapids, MI: Eerdmans.

Weber, Beat. 2012. "'Like a Bridge over Troubled Water…': Weisheitstheologische Wegmarkierungen im Psalter." Pages 289–306 in *Ex oriente Lux: Studien zur Theologie des Alten Testaments. Festschrift für Rüdiger Luz zum 65. Geburststag*. Edited by A. Berlejung and R. Heckl. ABG 39. Leipzig: Evangelische Verlagsanstalt.

Weeks, Stuart. 2005. "Wisdom Psalms." Pages 292–307 in *Temple and Worship in Biblical Israel*. Edited by John Day. New York, NY: T&T Clark.

Whybray, R. Norman. 1995. "The Wisdom Psalms." Pages 152–160 in *Wisdom in Ancient Israel: Essays in Honour of J.A. Emerton*. Edited by John Day, Robert P. Gordon, and H.G. M. Williamson. Cambridge: Cambridge University Press.

Whybray, R. Norman. 1996. *Reading the Psalms as a Book*. JSOTSup 22. Sheffield: Sheffield University Press.

Wilson, Gerald Henry. 1985. *The Editing of the Hebrew Psalter*. SBLDS 76. Chico, CA: Scholars Press.

Wilson, Gerald Henry. 1993. "Shaping of the Psalter: A Consideration of Editorial Linkages in the Book of Psalms." Pages 72–82 in *The Shape and Shaping of the Psalter*. Edited by J. Clinton McCann, Jr. JSOTSup 159. Sheffield: JSOT.

Zenger, Erich. 1998. "The Composition and Theology of the Fifth Book of Psalms, Psalms 107–145." *JSOT* 80:77–102.

Zimmerli, Walther. 1964. "The Place and Limit of the Wisdom in the Framework of the Old Testament Theology." *SJT* 17:146–158.

CHAPTER 35

....

BEN SIRA

....

BENJAMIN G. WRIGHT III

THE Wisdom of Ben Sira (or Sirach), a Wisdom text composed by a Jewish scribe/sage in the early part of the second century BCE, is the paradigmatic example of Wisdom Literature in the Second Temple period. Like other Wisdom texts, Ben Sira gives counsel on a range of practical subjects to students whom he is training for their own careers, but he also devotes considerable attention to existential matters, especially focusing on a triad of broadly related topics—fear of the Lord, fulfilling the commandments, gaining wisdom—that will enable his students to live a life pleasing to God and that will assure them of a lasting post-mortem legacy of a good name and reputation. Ben Sira lived in a period before the Hasmonean Revolt, and his book offers important clues for reconstructing his social location and for understanding how at least one elite Jew constructed a Jewish identity within a larger Hellenistic world.

35.1 TRANSMISSION HISTORY OF THE BOOK

....

The language that one employs in speech or in writing plays an important role in how a person constructs an identity, and thus, the complicated nature of the textual transmission of Sirach has a direct bearing on what conclusions can be drawn about its author's social location, his Jewish identity, and how he engaged the imperial context in which he lived and worked. Sirach was originally composed in Hebrew, but that version fell into obscurity in all likelihood because the book was not accepted into the canon of Hebrew Scripture. A translator who calls himself the author's grandson rendered the book into Greek, the *lingua franca* of the Hellenistic Mediterranean, in the latter part of the second century BCE, and this version became its primary vehicle of transmission, since it became part of the Christian Old Testament. Two other important translations were made into Syriac, based on a Hebrew parent text, and Latin, based on a Greek parent. As part of Christian Scripture, Ben Sira also was translated into other daughter languages of Christian communities for whom it was Scripture.[1]

A complete text of the Hebrew has not survived. Before the end of the nineteenth century, the only Hebrew that was known came in citations attributed to Ben Sira or his book in rabbinic literature and in the work of Saadya Gaon (tenth century) (Wright 1999; Labendz 2006; Wright 2018). In 1896, Solomon Schechter identified a leaf of a Hebrew manuscript brought to England by Agnes Lewis and Margaret Gibson from a synagogue Genizah in Cairo as a passage of Ben Sira in Hebrew (Schechter and Taylor 1899). Eventually six fragmentary medieval manuscripts of Ben Sira in Hebrew dating from the tenth to twelfth centuries, designated A–F, came to light in the Cairo Genizah materials. Five of them are running texts of the book and one, MS C, is an anthology, excerpting proverbs on practical topics such as relationships with women and friends. In 1952, Maurice Baillet identified two small fragments of about thirty Hebrew letters as coming from chapter 6, dating from the second half of the first century BCE (2Q18; Baillet, Milik, de Vaux 1962, 75–77). In 1956, James A. Sanders published the Cave 11 Psalms scroll, which dates from the first part of the first century CE and contains sections of Sirach 51 (11QPsᵃ; Sanders 1965, 79–85). Finally, in 1964, Yigael Yadin discovered at Masada a scroll of Ben Sira preserving portions of 39:27–44:17, dating from the first part of the first century BCE (Mas1h; Yadin 1965). Recently additional leaves of MSS C and D from the Genizah have been identified, and some offset letters in MS A have provided a bit more text from that manuscript (Elitzur 2006–2007; Elitzur 2010; Elitzur and Rand 2011; Reymond 2015; Karner 2015). Currently about 70 percent of the book survives in the Hebrew manuscripts, although all of the Hebrew manuscripts, including the earliest ones, contain scribal errors and interventions.

The book's complex transmission history, particularly of the Hebrew and its translation into Greek, complicates any attempts to reconstruct Ben Sira's Hebrew and thus to talk about what "Ben Sira" the person said. Right from the beginning, the Hebrew text suffered from changes. Even the Masada scroll, which preserves the earliest Hebrew text of any consequence, offers evidence that changes in the text of Ben Sira began at a very early stage. So, for example, in 41.16b Masada reads לא כל בשת נאוה לבוש, "it is not proper to be ashamed of every shame." However, in the place of the Hebrew infinitive בוש ("to be ashamed"), the Greek has διαφυλάξαι ("to guard"), resulting in the clause "for it is not good to guard against every shame." This reading agrees with the Genizah manuscripts B and C, both of which have the infinitive לשמר, "to guard." Whether the scribe who copied the Masada text (or his exemplar) changed the text to create the word play with the noun and the infinitive or whether the parent text of the Greek (as in MS B and MS C) already had modified the text from "be ashamed" to "to guard" cannot be determined with certainty. What we can say, however, is that almost from the beginning of Ben Sira's transmission history, the Hebrew text underwent modifications—and in the case of Masada

---

[1] For more details on these various translations, see "4.1 Textual History of Ben Sira" in Henze and Feder, 191–194.

or the Greek parent text, this occurred within sixty to a hundred years or so of the book's composition.

Moreover, the book underwent periodic expansions that range from individual words and phrases to entire cola and bi-cola, resulting in differing versions:

1. The earliest form of the Hebrew (HI);
2. The grandson's translation (GI);
3. A Hebrew text that had been expanded with additional proverbs (HII);
4. An expanded Greek version (GII).

No single major language tradition preserves all of the expanded material. The Genizah Hebrew manuscripts transmit some expanded proverbs, whereas in Greek, GII readings are most prominent in the Origenic and Lucianic manuscripts, particularly the Lucianic miniscule 248. The Syriac translation shares proverbs with GII, but it also has seventy-four cola unique to itself. The Latin translation preserves more additional material than any GII witness. The expanded version(s) of Ben Sira are often called a second *recension*, although Jason Gile (2011) has argued persuasively that the additional material more likely represents additions from a variety of sources expanded at different times rather than any systematic recensional activity.

After the Judean Desert Ben Sira manuscripts, the Hebrew text of Ben Sira effectively disappears from our view until the tenth century, except for the rabbinic citations. How the text of Ben Sira circulated during this hiatus remains a mystery. Alexander Di Lella (1966, 78–105), building on previous suggestions by Paul Kahle and others about the relationship between the Cairo Genizah and some Dead Sea Scroll texts, argued that Ben Sira was part of discoveries mentioned by Timothy I of Baghdad in the early ninth century. This hypothesis does not account sufficiently for the presence of Ben Sira manuscripts in the Genizah, however. The widespread knowledge, and indeed popularity, of Ben Sira in the early medieval period points to a continuous transmission of the text, even if its specific mechanisms are not altogether clear (Labendz 2006; Reif 2011; Rey 2017).

35.2 Author, Date, and Provenance

In its various language traditions, Ben Sira is known by several different titles. In Greek manuscripts, one generally finds "The Wisdom of Jesus son of Sirach" (σοφία Ἰησοῦ υἱοῦ σ[ε]ιράχ), although sometimes manuscripts have a shorter title like "Wisdom of Sirach" or just "Sirach." The Vulgate usually has a similar title, *liber hiesu filii Sirach* ("The Book of Jesu son of Sirach"), or *Ecclesiasticus*, which means something like "the Church's book." The latter title is frequent in Latin churches. None of the Hebrew manuscripts preserve the beginning of the book, and thus if a title stood there, it is now lost. MS B from the Genizah has a three-line subscription at the end of the book that reads like two separate titles before a final blessing.

עד הנה דברי שמעון בן ישוע שנקרא בן סירא
חכמת שמעון בן ישוע בן אלעזר בן סירא
יהי שם ייי מבורך מעתה ועד עולם

> Until here are the sayings of Shimon son of Yeshua who is called son of Sira.
> The Wisdom of Shimon son of Yeshua son of Elazar son of Sira.
> May the name of the Lord be blessed from now until forever.[2]

Syriac manuscripts most often have the title as either "The Wisdom of Bar Sira"
(ܚܟܡܬܐ ܕܒܪ ܣܝܪܐ) or "The Book of Yeshua Bar Asira" (ܟܬܒܐ ܕܒܪ ܐܣܝܪܐ).

Most scholars accept that the author's name was ישוע in Hebrew. The grandson/trans-
lator calls him Ἰησοῦς (Jesus, the Greek equivalent of the Hebrew name) in a prologue
to the Greek translation. The Hebrew and Greek traditions differ on his entire name,
however, which both versions have in 50:27. In Greek the name is given as a self-reference:
"Instruction and understanding and knowledge I have inscribed in this book, Jesus
son of Sirach, Eleazar the Jerusalemite."[3] In Cairo MS B, the only Hebrew manuscript
that preserves 50:27, the author's name is given as Shimon ben Yeshua ben Elazar ben
Sira (שמעון בן ישוע בן אלעזר בן סירא).[4] While both the Hebrew and Greek traditions include
Elazar (Gk Ἐλεαζαρ) as part of his name, the Greek has it as an appositive, making Sirach
the author's father, whereas the Hebrew has Elazar as Ben Sira's father and Sira as his
grandfather. The reason for this confusion is not immediately apparent.

The work's date can be established with relative security based on internal evidence
from both the Hebrew and Greek versions. In chapter 50, Ben Sira praises the high priest
Simon II (219–196 BCE). The description of Simon and his position as the culmination
of Ben Sira's list of Israelite heroes in chapters 44–50 suggest that Ben Sira lived during his tenure as high priest, perhaps writing after his death as the phrases בדורו ("in his
generation") and בימיו ("in his days") in 50:1 might indicate. Moreover, Ben Sira betrays
no knowledge of the problematic events under the Seleucid ruler Antiochus IV (175–164
BCE) that resulted in the Hasmonean Revolt in the 160s. These considerations would
place the book somewhere between 196 BCE and the early 170s BCE. The evidence of the
prologue to the Greek translation coincides with this date range. In line 26, the grand-
son/translator calls the author "my grandfather" (ὁ πάππος μου; l. 7) and says that he (i.e.,
the translator) arrived in Egypt "in the thirty-eighth year of Euergetes" (l. 27), referring
to the reign of Ptolemy VIII Euergetes II, which would have been 132 BCE. In line 28,

---

[2] The name Shimon is unique to this manuscript, and it matches the name of the author given in MS
B at 50:27. See the discussion in the following paragraph below.

[3] Joseph Ziegler's critical Göttingen edition has the third-person singular verb ἐχάραξεν in 50:27. The
first-person verb ἐχάραξα is found in most of the Greek manuscript tradition and much of the Latin
(Ziegler 1980), and in my estimation, this reading reflects the best text of the verse. All translations
of the Greek are taken from *A New English Translation of the Septuagint* (NETS; Pietersma and
Wright 2007).

[4] The name Shimon might have come mistakenly from 50:24, where the high priest Simon II
(Shimon in Hebrew) is mentioned (Skehan and Di Lella 1987, 557). The Syriac of 50:27 omits the name
altogether, whereas the Latin follows the Greek.

he comments that he had "stayed a while" (συγχρονίσας) in Egypt before undertaking his translation. If we reckon backwards from a period toward the end of Ptolemy VIII's reign (d. 117 BCE) and from grandson to grandfather, we would arrive at a date sometime in the first quarter of the second century BCE.[5]

Most scholars place the composition of the book in Jerusalem, although the evidence for this provenance is mostly circumstantial. The Greek translation designates Ben Sira as "the Jerusalemite" (50:27), and if the translator was indeed a relative of the author, then we ought to take that evidence seriously. The Hebrew of MS B lacks the designation. Otherwise, Ben Sira's description of Simon II and his ministrations in the Temple combined with his clear preference for the Jerusalemite priesthood lend support to a Jerusalemite origin for Ben Sira.

35.3 BEN SIRA AND A WISDOM GENRE

Although Ben Sira is often regarded as the Second Temple period Wisdom text *par excellence*, it pushes the genre boundaries of Wisdom when compared to Wisdom texts, such as Proverbs, in the Hebrew Bible. Contemporary scholarship has struggled with how to define Wisdom as a genre of literature, and some scholars recently have questioned whether we can even speak of a Wisdom genre in any meaningful way (Weeks 2010; Kynes 2016). Inasmuch as Ben Sira evinces some generic relationship to a core group of Wisdom prototypes, we can usefully call it a Wisdom text (Wright 2010). For the most part, Ben Sira relies on the staple of Wisdom Literature, the mashal, which he puts together in bi-cola and then builds into poems on the traditional subjects of practical wisdom, such as speech, friends, or women. Yet, Ben Sira stretches the category of Wisdom by incorporating sub-genres that rarely appear in earlier Wisdom texts like Proverbs. So, for example, we find the sage employing the prophetic "Woe," as in 2:12–14 or the prayer of petition/lament in 36:1–22. Ben Sira departs most distinctively from other Wisdom texts in chapters 44–50, the "Praise of the Ancestors," the largest single section of the work. Though Israel's history is largely absent from earlier Wisdom texts, here Ben Sira praises a series of exemplary figures from Israel's past, culminating with the recent high priest, Simon II. He introduces the section in 44:1–15, where he highlights categories of persons who deserve praise (vv. 3–6). These verses prominently display important themes in Ben Sira's thought: the importance of a good name that persists through time and the value of progeny who will carry on one's legacy. Beginning in 44:16, he identifies specific figures from Israel's past, starting with the prediluvian Enoch, moving to Noah, then to Abraham and through to Nehemiah.[6] He concludes the

---

[5] This reckoning assumes that the translator was, in fact, the author's grandson. The Greek could also refer to an ancestor more generally.

[6] The Masada manuscript does not have 44:16 on Enoch, which might suggest that it was a secondary addition, but the omission more likely results from a scribal error (see Wright 2008b, 120–121).

list of ancestors with a return to Enoch and finally to Adam, before moving to his praise of Simon II in chapter 50. We see a similar use of historical exemplars in 16:6–10 where Ben Sira lists paradigmatic sinners that God did not fail to punish.

35.4 Ben Sira, Torah, and Sapiential Pedagogy

Ben Sira's inclusion of the Praise of the Ancestors points to a larger development in Wisdom Literature in the Second Temple period, that is, the increasing importance of the Torah and the Israelite literary heritage more generally as one source of wisdom among others (Schipper and Teeter 2013). This development emerges most clearly in personified Wisdom's self-praise in chapter 24 in which Ben Sira locates Lady Wisdom, who has traversed creation (24:3–6), has settled in Israel (24:8–9), and has ministered in the temple (24:10), in the Torah: "All these things [i.e., what has been said about Wisdom] are the book of the Most High God, a law that Moses commanded us, an inheritance for the gatherings of Jacob" (Gk). Torah, as the embodiment of Wisdom in Israel, now falls under the purview of the sage. Ben Sira also knows texts other than those connected with Moses. The Praise of the Ancestors, especially, reveals his familiarity with texts and traditions that would become part of the Hebrew Bible.

Yet, all of this textual tradition serves the agenda of Ben Sira's pedagogy in which he employs inherited texts, the traditional wisdom of the sages, and the lessons drawn from observation of nature to create a "figured world" for his students to inhabit.[7] All three of these sources of wisdom he absorbs into his own teaching, and so, unlike later texts, such as the *pesharim* from Qumran, Ben Sira does not quote or otherwise distinguish the texts he employs from his own use of them. He explicitly refers to the "Law of the Most High" as authoritative (even if it is a somewhat vague category), but ultimately *his* teaching must be authoritative. As one who had learned these texts and who almost certainly made his students learn them, he absorbed their language into his own teaching, and thereby they functioned to confer authority on his instruction (Wright 2013).

Ben Sira then links this relatively new source of wisdom with two other more traditional themes, fear of the Lord and acquiring wisdom, to create an encompassing agenda for his students to pursue. Fear of the Lord (יראת יהוה) forms the basis for gaining knowledge and wisdom in previous Wisdom texts (e.g., Prov 1:7; 2:1–15; 15:33; cf. also Ps 110:10). Ben Sira's incorporation of fulfillment of Torah witnesses to the growing importance of the doing of the Law in the Wisdom curriculum, as we can see in 19:20: "The whole of wisdom is fear of the Lord, and in all wisdom there is the fulfillment of the Law" (Gk).

In this vein, we return to the critical chapter 24 that sits at the center of the book. Since Wisdom resides in the Torah, Ben Sira's use of the language of Torah implicitly makes

---

[7] For the phrase "figured world" and its implications, see Newsom 2004, 92–95.

the connection between Ben Sira and his pedagogy and primordial Wisdom herself. At the end of the chapter, he employs a detailed metaphor of water that makes the connection between him and Wisdom unmistakable. In vv. 30–31, he compares himself to a canal that turns into a river and then into a sea. This last body of water recalls v. 29: "The first man did not complete knowing her [i.e., Wisdom], and so the last one did not track her out; for her thought was filled from the sea and her counsel from the great abyss." Ben Sira, then, is directly connected to Wisdom. In v. 33 he takes all of this one step farther. The Greek translator uses the verb ἐκχέω, to pour out, in order to invoke prophecy: "I will again pour out teaching like prophecy, and I will leave it behind for generations of eternity."[8] The continuing use of language connected with water maintains Ben Sira's link to Wisdom, who was "from the beginning" with God (24:9) and who infuses Torah, but he now compares his own teaching to prophecy and thus to revelation. In his instruction, then, he speaks for God. All of his appeals coalesce into a broad claim to his authority as a sage and as a teacher, and before this authority his students must submit in order to become wise.

35.5 BEN SIRA'S SOCIAL LOCATION

Due to Wisdom Literature's often practical and seemingly timeless instruction, these texts have sometimes been read as if they did not originate in specific historical, social, and cultural locations. The recent trend in studying this literature, however, has been to take more into consideration the particular contexts of these texts, as much as they can be determined (Perdue 2008). For Ben Sira, understanding his historical, social, and cultural context has a significant impact on how we might read the book. The time in which Ben Sira lived was one of political uncertainty, especially in the contest between the Ptolemaic and Seleucid kingdoms. Ben Sira almost certainly experienced the change of rule from the Ptolemies to the Seleucids that occurred at the turn of the third to the second century BCE.[9] It seems as if, in this international competition, the high priest Simon II led a pro-Seleucid faction of the Judean elite (Tcherikover 1982, 79–82; VanderKam 2004, 182). In Ben Sira's later years, under Simon's son Onias III, some of those sympathies might have changed, as Seleucus IV raised funds to pay an indemnity imposed by the Romans after Antiochus III's defeat at Magnesia (Wright 2008c, 129; Marttila 2012, 151).

Ben Sira would not have been a disinterested observer of these political events. Indeed, the inclusion of a long section at the end of the book (chs. 44–50) that reviews selected heroes of Israel's past suggests that Ben Sira possessed a sense of the significance

---

[8] No Hebrew is extant for this verse. In all but one instance where Hebrew does survive, the Greek verb renders שפך, "to pour out."

[9] For more details on the relationship between the two kingdoms and the Jews, see Tcherikover 1982; Gera 1998.

of history for interpreting his own time. His strong support of the Jerusalem priesthood and the temple cult, especially the way that his praise of Simon in chapter 50 reflects his praise of Aaron in 44:6–22 and Wisdom in chapter 24, points to his agreement with Simon's political leanings. Indeed, he might well have thought Simon to be the leader who would free God's people from foreign rule, a condition that Ben Sira found intolerable, as we can see in the nationalistic prayer for God's deliverance of his people in 36:1–22 (Wright 2008c). So, in chapter 50, Ben Sira emphasizes Simon's dual roles as secular ruler and religious leader. In his political capacity, Ben Sira notes how Simon repaired and fortified the temple (50:1–2), provided a water supply (50:3), and "was concerned for his people against calamity and strengthened his city against distress" (50:4). In 50:5–21, Ben Sira paints a glorious picture of Simon as he ministered at the temple. Simon's time must have represented for Ben Sira a possible renewal of the glory of a bygone Israel. Things did not work out that way, however, and we do not know Ben Sira's reaction to events subsequent to Simon's rule.

Ben Sira's loyalty to Simon II and the Jerusalem priestly elite also stems from his own dependence on them for his livelihood. Ben Sira belonged to a class of retainers whom we might call scribes/sages, who occupied a sort of middle position between the wealthy, primarily priestly, elites for whom they labored and the Jewish common folk (Horsley and Tiller 2002). Throughout the book, he betrays his dependence on his social and economic superiors, and he instructs his students about the caution that they must exercise when dealing with the rich and powerful. He warns his charges about the hazards of relations with those more powerful than they: "Do not contend with a powerful person, lest you fall into his hands. Do not quarrel with a rich person, lest he pay out the price of your downfall" (8:1–2). He counsels his students about the risks inherent in becoming a judge: "Do not seek to become a judge, or you may be unable to root out injustice; you may be partial to the powerful and so mar your integrity" (7:6). In two substantial sections, 31:12–18 and 32:1–9, Ben Sira instructs his students about how to behave when banqueting with powerful people or when asked to preside over a banquet. Ben Sira knew how to navigate the difficult waters of relating to the rich and powerful, and the number of passages in the book that deal with them witness to how critical he thought those relationships would be for his students' success.

Yet, Ben Sira did not rank himself among the poor or the destitute. In fact, he encouraged his students both to advocate for the poor and to provide material support for them, all the while demonstrating an awareness about how fragile their own positions remained. So, in 13:4–7, he explains how the rich and powerful act out of their own self-interest and how they will exploit those below them. He frequently admonishes his students to perform acts of charity (צדקה/ἐλεημοσύνη), connecting assistance to the needy with fulfilling the Law and making acceptable sacrifice: so, for example, "A blazing fire water will extinguish; thus, charity will atone for sin" (3:30; MS A); "Nevertheless with a lowly person be patient, and do not make him wait for charity. On account of the commandment, assist a needy person, and according to his need do not turn him away empty" (29:8–9; Gk); "And he who does an act of charity is one who makes a sacrifice of praise" (35:4; Gk).

35.6 BEN SIRA'S SCRIBAL AND JEWISH IDENTITIES

Ben Sira experiences some cognitive dissonance as he finds himself in this middling status, since for him the scribe/sage ought to occupy the highest rung on the social ladder because of his expertise in the Law (Camp and Wright 2002, 168–172). His valuation of the scribe/sage is nowhere more obvious than in his praise of the scribe/sage in 38:34c–39:11, a passage that follows his remarks on tradespersons and laborers in 38:24–34b. Already in 38:24, Ben Sira contrasts the scribe/sage with farmers (38:25–26), artisans (38:27), smiths (38:28), and potters (38:29–30): "The wisdom of the scribe increases wisdom, and whoever lacks business will become wise" (MS B).[10] He remarks that tradespersons enable cities to be inhabited, but they will not serve on councils or become judges, nor will they ever "shed light on instruction and judgment" (38:33; Gk). The scribe/sage is different because he engages in the study of the tradition, serves among nobles, and travels to foreign lands (39:1–4). Even more, God will fill him with "a spirit of understanding" so that "he will direct counsel and knowledge, and on his [i.e., God's] hidden things he will think. He will illuminate the instruction of his teaching, and in the law of the Lord's covenant he will boast" (39:7–8). In this way the sage's name "will live for generations of generations" (39:9), and "he will leave a name greater than a thousand" (39:11).

Ben Sira reconciles the difference between his social position and his idealization of the scribe/sage by proposing a different hierarchy of values that positions the scribe/sage at the top. Instead of wealth and social and political power, Ben Sira contends that proper fear of the Lord, a prevalent theme of the book, actually determines status in the eyes of God (Camp and Wright 2002, 168). Fear of the Lord constitutes the primary criterion for receiving honor, the primary social value for Ben Sira. "What kind of offspring is worthy of honor? Those who fear the Lord" (10:19; Gk).[11] The quintessential statement of the worth of fear of the Lord comes in 25:10–11: "How great is he who finds wisdom, but there is none above him who fears the Lord" (Gk). Of course, who is positioned best to cultivate and perfect fear of the Lord (along with fulfilling the commandments and acquiring wisdom)? The scribe/sage, the one who has the leisure to study the secrets of the tradition and the Law, as Ben Sira has set out in 38:24c–39:11.

Along with Ben Sira's need to negotiate his status within Jerusalemite society he also had to contend with a rapidly changing cultural context. As someone who worked in the employ of the priestly elites, he likely had a front-row seat to view the interactions between ruling-class Jews, like Simon II, and the Hellenistic empires that exerted con-

---

[10] The Greek translation reads here, "A scribe's wisdom is in the opportunity for leisure, and he who does less business, it is he who will become wise."

[11] These lines are missing in Cairo MS A, likely due to homoioarchton, since each line of the verse begins with the same Hebrew word, ‏זרע‎.

trol over Judea. In a similar manner that he occupied a middle position between the ruling elites and laborers, artisans, and the poor, he might well have found himself in a middle position between service to his superiors and his commitment to the governance of God. On the one hand, his expertise as a scribe might well have found him serving the imperial powers, at least indirectly, and the totalizing discourses on which that power was based, but, on the other hand, resisting those same powers and those same discourses, since for Ben Sira, God was the only legitimate king over Israel and all foreign rule was illegitimate (Himmelfarb 2000, 94–95; Wright 2008a, 78–80).

Scholars have frequently interpreted Ben Sira's book through the lens of his location, Jerusalem in the early second-century BCE, as a contest between reified Judaism and Hellenism, primarily in a cultural sense. Alexander Di Lella, for example, comments, "In his travels, Ben Sira must have seen the baneful effects of Hellenization on the Jewish people.... His purpose was not to engage in a systematic polemic against Hellenism but rather to convince Jews and even well-disposed Gentiles that true wisdom is to be found in Jerusalem and not in Athens, more in the inspired books of Israel than in the clever writings of Hellenistic humanism" (Skehan and Di Lella 1987, 16). Similarly, Martin Hengel (1974, 134) comments, "Thus with Ben Sira two tendencies are in conflict: on the one side political-religious engagement, protest against the arrogance of the liberal aristocracy which was probably already predominantly molded by the spirit of Hellenism, and on the other side the traditional caution of the wise, which counseled silence and subjection before the powerful." Yet, a closer examination of Ben Sira's book indicates that his argument was not against Hellenistic culture per se. Several factors suggest that instead Ben Sira was polemicizing against foreign imperial domination of God's people in which culture (broadly construed) comprised one of the tools, or even weapons, of imperialism and colonialism (Wright 2017).[12]

I briefly outlined above how Ben Sira thought that foreign rule over God's people was illegitimate, but what is Ben Sira's attitude toward Hellenistic culture? The question of whether Ben Sira favored or rejected Hellenistic culture is the wrong one to ask, but rather we should be asking how Ben Sira interacts with Hellenistic culture and for what purpose. The *locus classicus* for those who see Ben Sira as polemicizing against Greek culture is 3:21–24 (Hengel 1974, 139–140; Skehan and Di Lella 1987, 160–161):

> Things too wondrous for you do not seek, and things too strong for you do not scrutinize. The things that have been prescribed for you think about these, for you have concern for hidden matters. With matters greater than your affairs do not meddle, for more than enough has been shown. For many are the thoughts of human beings, evil and erring fantasies.   (MS A)

Rather than a polemic against "the futility of Greek learning" (Skehan and Di Lella 1987, 160), a more likely target of these thoughts is Jewish apocalyptic speculation like that found in the Enochic *Book of the Watchers* or the *Astronomical Book* (Wright 2008b).

---

[12] For a more positive assessment on Ben Sira's attitudes toward foreign nations, see Marttila 2012.

Several factors point in this direction rather than to Hellenistic culture. As a general observation, Ben Sira and the Enochic texts treat the same themes—revelation, creation, and judgment—articulating them in ways that are similar but that suggest differences in approach (Argall 1995). Ben Sira admonishes his students to avoid speculating about פלאות, "things too wondrous," a term that he uses elsewhere to refer to the secrets of creation (cf. 42:17; 43:32), and about נסתרות, "hidden matters," which elsewhere in Sirach denotes what the future holds (cf. 42:19; 48:25). In addition, Ben Sira inveighs against relying on dreams and visions (34:1–8), and he seems to follow a calendar governed by the moon rather than the sun, which serves as the basis for texts like the *Astronomical Book* (Wright 2008b, 110–114). The cumulative effect of this evidence indicates that Ben Sira's warnings are directed at an inner-Jewish debate about scribal and priestly legitimacy.

The case for Ben Sira's interactions with Hellenistic culture can be made more positively, however. In short, Ben Sira adopted and adapted Hellenistic cultural resources to the extent that he could martial them in the service of his own wisdom teaching. Theophil Middendorp (1973), who argued that Ben Sira composed a Hellenistic school book, has made the most thoroughgoing case that Ben Sira relied heavily on Hellenistic sources, and he identifies dozens of passages that in his view influenced our sage. Both Jack Sanders (1983) and Volker Kieweler (1992) have made persuasive arguments that Middendorp was overly optimistic about how much Ben Sira relied on Greek sources. But Middendorp's study does raise important questions about the extent to which (a) Ben Sira used Greek sources and (b) he might have had enough education in Greek to become acquainted with them. With respect to Ben Sira's use of Greek sources, the most convincing example comes in Sir 6:5–17, a poem on friendship. These verses contain a dense series of similarities between Ben Sira and the Greek gnomic poet Theognis, which point to Ben Sira knowledge of at least Theognis's poems on friendship (Sanders 1983, 30–36; Wright 2016, 83–85). One other passage, a much more difficult one to assess, might come from a Greek source. Sirach 14:18 reads, "As leaves grow upon a tree, so this one fades and one grows, thus are the generations of flesh and blood, one dies and another ripens" (MS A). Jack Sanders (1983) has pointed out the linguistic overlaps between this verse and the *Iliad* 6.148–149, and it seems likely that the proverb in Ben Sira originated in Homer, even if Ben Sira did not know it from that source.[13] In both of these cases, the likelihood that these texts were available in a Hebrew translation seems low, and thus, if Ben Sira did know them, he probably read them in Greek.[14]

---

[13] James Aitken has shown that the grandson seems to have recognized the reference, and the Greek version reflects some aspects of the Homeric proverb not present in the Hebrew. Moreover, the proverb might well have circulated divorced from its source, and it seems to have been somewhat popular in antiquity. Both of these observations indirectly offer evidence for Ben Sira's knowledge of it. See the discussion in Aitken 2017, 124–127.

[14] The issue of whether Ben Sira knew Stoic philosophy has been debated. I hesitate to include such knowledge as evidence here, although I think some acquaintance with Stoic ideas probable on Ben Sira's part. On the positive side, see Winston 1989; Collins 1997, 85; Wicke-Reuter 2002. On the negative, see Mattila 2000.

Of course, this raises the question of whether Ben Sira knew Greek and how well. Given his social location and occupation, Ben Sira likely had some facility with the Greek language. If his comments about traveling in 34:9–12 and 39:4 reflect personal experience, then he would have known sufficient Greek to get around, but that is a far cry from being educated in literary Greek in order to engage Greek literature. While the evidence is circumstantial, one can paint a picture of fairly widespread knowledge of Greek in Judea and its environs at the time of Ben Sira and immediately after him with several strands of evidence converging to enable the conclusion that Ben Sira would have had access to institutions where he could have learned Greek and have been exposed to Greek literature.[15]

If we read some passages in Ben Sira through this wider lens of knowledge of Greek and the possibility of Greek education in Judea and surrounding areas, then some passages in Sirach can be read as indications that Ben Sira was open to whatever resources would help him to construct his own thought. Of course, traditional Jewish literary sources were primary, but in the light of the discussion above, we can read 39:1–4, for instance, in a broader sense than it has generally been read:

> He [i.e., the scribe/sage] will seek out the wisdom of *all* the ancients, and he will be occupied with prophecies. He will preserve the narrative of famous men [cf. chs. 44–50], and he will penetrate into the twists of illustrations. He will seek out the obscurities of proverbs, and he will be engaged with the riddles of illustrations. He will serve among nobles, and he will appear in front of rulers. He will travel in the land of foreign nations, for he has tested the good and bad things in people.   (Gk)

The terms used here are not those that usually appear in Ben Sira for the Law. While Ben Sira has a relatively new source of wisdom to incorporate into his sapiential teaching, the Israelite literary tradition, these verses hark back to the traditional activities of sages, studying the wisdom of *all* the ancients in order to discover wisdom, and in the second century BCE, those sources included the wisdom of the Greeks (Wright 2016, 81).

If Ben Sira knew Greek and used Greek sources, if he worked in an environment where he, and presumably his students, would have to know Greek, then his decision to write his book in Hebrew requires some examination. He belonged to an elite stratum of society that "sought to carve out a moderate accommodationist position that cooperated with the Seleucid empire in the political realm but at the same time claimed a high level of continuity with ancestral traditions and identified both the city of Jerusalem and the Jerusalem cult as key loci of Jewish identity" (Portier-Young 2011, 112). As we have seen, Ben Sira's negotiation involved appropriating Hellenistic literature and ideas that helped to realize his agenda while at the same time rejecting foreign imperial authority over God's people in favor of a "continuity with ancestral traditions." In the face of imperial discourses and ideologies, language is one area where the subordinated can exercise some sover-

---

[15]   For more detail on the argument about Judean knowledge of and access to Greek learning, see Wright 2016. Middendorp (1973, 17–34) spends more time discussing Ben Sira's exposure to Greek thought, although he thinks that Ben Sira knew Greek and read Greek texts.

eignty, one of the areas in which the identity of the "nation thing" can be constructed; it also marks cultural difference from the dominant power.[16] Ben Sira's choice to write in Hebrew rather than Greek resisted the use of Greek to categorize people on the one hand—the Greek distinction between Greeks and barbarians based on language—and it contributed to the construction of a Jewish identity based on the discourse of a Jewish "nation thing" on the other (Wright 2017). Moreover, Ben Sira was an early contributor to a broader movement in this period to reclaim Hebrew as the national language of the Jews, the prime example being Jubilees 12:25–27 from a slightly later time:

> And the Lord God said to me [i.e., the Angel of the Presence], "Open his [i.e., Abram's] mouth and his ears so that he might hear and speak with his mouth the language which is revealed because it ceased from the mouth of all of the sons of men from the day of the Fall." And I opened his mouth and his ears and his lips, and I began to speak with him in Hebrew, in the tongue of creation. And he took his father's books—and they were written in Hebrew—and he copied them. And he began studying them thereafter.

Several aspects of Ben Sira's book can be read in this light. So, for example, the connection in 24:23–29 of Wisdom's embodiment in the Torah (written in Hebrew) and Ben Sira's own teaching (also in Hebrew) recalls both Moses's revelation and Wisdom's presence at the creation. Moreover, as with the Praise of the Ancestors, which culminates in the praise of Simon II in Ben Sira's own time, this claim links an ideal past with Ben Sira's present (Wright 2017).

On this reading, Ben Sira's decision to write in Hebrew was ideological. Through his use of Hebrew, Ben Sira expressed his Jewish identity and contributed to the discourse of the Jewish "nation thing." In the face of imperial domination, writing in Hebrew allowed him to speak openly to his students about their own relationships to foreign powers while at the same time hiding this act of resistance from those same powers in what James Scott (1990) has called a "hidden transcript."[17]

While Ben Sira indeed might be regarded as the second-temple Wisdom book *par excellence*, to read his book, or any Wisdom text, for that matter, as if it can be divorced from its various contexts—historical, social, cultural, or religious—is to miss readings of the text that have the potential to illuminate it in new ways. To see Ben Sira only as theologically rejecting foreign rule over God's people is to get only part of the story. The theology of divine kingship established a basis on which Ben Sira could participate in active resistance against foreign rule. Of course, his book is not *only* about such resistance. Nothing is ever so simple. Yet, even though he might not have taken the same path as

[16] The phrase comes from Gayatri Chakravorty Spivak (2012, 279), who writes, "I say nation thing rather than nationalism because something like nations, collectivities bound by birth, that allowed strangers in gingerly, have been in existence long before nationalism came around."

[17] For the implications for Ben Sira, see Wright 2017. Ironically, the translation of Ben Sira's book into Greek, its primary language of transmission, and the subsequent receding of the Hebrew text obscures that aim.

those, such as apocalypticists, whose writings more obviously reject and resist foreign oppressors by envisioning their demise at the hands of divine forces, Ben Sira also worked against those foreign powers by training students whose identities were rooted in a Jewish "nation thing" over which their God ruled and held sway.

WORKS CITED

Aitken, James A. 2017. "The Literary and Linguistic Subtlety of the Greek Version of Sirach." Pages 115–140 in *Texts and Contexts of the Book of Sirach/Texte und Kontexte des Sirachbuches*. Edited by Gerhard Karner, Frank Ueberschaer, and Burkard M. Zapff. SBLSCS 66. Atlanta, GA: SBL.

Argall, Randal A. 1995. *1 Enoch and Sirach: A Comparative Literary and Conceptual Analysis of the Themes of Revelation, Creation and Judgment*. SBLEJL 8. Atlanta, GA: Scholars Press.

Baillet, M., J.T. Milik, and R. de Vaux, with a contribution by H.W. Baker. 1962. *Les "Petites Grottes" de Qumran: Exploration de la falaise Les Grottes 2Q, 3Q, 5Q, 7Q, à 10Q Les rouleu de cuivre* Textes*. DJD III. Oxford: Clarendon Press.

Camp, Claudia V., and Benjamin G. Wright. 2002. "'Who Has Been Tested by Gold and Found Perfect?' Ben Sira's Discourse of Riches and Poverty." *Henoch* 23:153–174.

Collins, John J. 1997. *Jewish Wisdom in the Hellenistic Age*. OTL. Louisville, KY: Westminster John Knox.

Di Lella, Alexander A. 1966. *The Hebrew Text of Sirach: A Text-Critical and Historical Study*. The Hague: Mouton.

Elitzur, Shulamit. 2006–2007. קטע חדש מהנוסח העברי של ספר בן סירא. *Tarbiz* 76:17–28.

Elizur, Shulamit. 2010. "Two New Leaves of the Hebrew Version of Ben Sira." *DSD* 17:13–29.

Elizur, Shulamit, and Michael Rand. 2011. "A New Fragment of the Book of Ben Sira." *DSD* 18:200–205.

Gera, Dov. 1998. *Judaea and Mediterranean Politics, 219 to 161 B.C.E.* BSJS 8. Leiden: Brill.

Gile, Jason. 2011. "The Additions to Ben Sira and the Book's Multiform Textual Witness." Pages 237–256 in *The Texts and Versions of the Book of Ben Sira: Transmission and Interpretation*. Edited by Jan Joosten and Jean-Sébastien Rey. JSJSup 150. Leiden: Brill.

Hengel, Martin. 1974. *Judaism and Hellenism: Studies in Their Encounter in Palestine in the Early Hellenistic Period*. Translated by John Bowden. Philadelphia, PA: Fortress.

Henze, Matthias, and Frank Feder, eds. 2019. *Textual History of the Hebrew Bible: The Deuterocanonical Scriptures*, vol. 2B. Leiden: Brill.

Himmelfarb, Martha. 2000. "The Wisdom of the Scribe, the Wisdom of the Priest, and the Wisdom of the King According to Ben Sira." Pages 89–99 in *For a Later Generation: The Transformation of Tradition in Israel, Early Judaism and Early Christianity*. Edited by Randal A. Argall, Beverly A. Bow, and Rodney A. Werline. Harrisburg, PA: Trinity Press International.

Horsley, Richard A., and Patrick Tiller. 2002. "Ben Sira and the Sociology of the Second Temple." Pages 74–107 in *Second Temple Studies III: Studies in Politics, Class and Material Culture*. Edited by Philip R. Davies and John M. Halligan. JSOTS 340. Sheffield: Sheffield Academic.

Karner, Gerhard. 2015. "Ben Sira Ms A Fol. I Recto and Fol. VI Verso (T-S 12.863), Revisited." *RevQ* 27:177–203.

Kieweler, Volker. 1992. *Ben Sira zwischen Judentum und Hellenismus. Eine Auseinandersetzung mit Th. Middendorp*. BEATAJ 30. Frankfurt: Peter Lang.

Kynes, Will. 2016. "The Nineteenth-Century Beginnings of 'Wisdom Literature,' and Its Twenty-First-Century End?" Pages 83–108 in *Perspectives on Israelite Wisdom: Proceedings of the Oxford Old Testament Seminar*. Edited by John Jarick. LHBOTS 618. London: Bloomsbury T&T Clark.

Labendz, Jenny R. 2006. "The Book of Ben Sira in Rabbinic Literature." *AJSR* 39:347–392.

Marttila, Marko. 2012. *Foreign Nations in the Wisdom of Ben Sira: A Jewish Sage between Opposition and Assimilation*. DCLS 13. Berlin: de Gruyter.

Mattila, Sharon Lea. 2000. "Ben Sira and the Stoics: A Reexamination of the Evidence." *JBL* 119:473–501.

Middendorp, Theophil. 1973. *Die Stellung Jesu Ben Siras zwischen Judentum und Hellenismus*. Leiden: Brill.

Newsom, Carol A. 2004. *The Self as Symbolic Space: Constructing Identity and Community at Qumran*. STDJ 52. Leiden: Brill.

Perdue, Leo. 2008. *The Sword and the Stylus: An Introduction to Wisdom Literature in the Age of Empires*. Grand Rapids, MI: Eerdmans.

Pietersma, Albert, and Benjamin G. Wright. 2007. *A New English Translation of the Septuagint and the Other Greek Translations Traditionally Included under That Title*. New York, NY: Oxford University Press.

Portier-Young, Anathea. 2011. *Apocalypse Against Empire: Theologies of Resistance in Early Jewish Literature*. Grand Rapids, MI: Eerdmans.

Reif, Stefan. 2011. "The Genizah and the Dead Sea Scrolls: How Important and Direct Is the Connection?" Pages 673–691 in *The Dead Sea Scrolls in Context: Integrating the Dead Sea Scrolls in the Study of Ancient Texts, Languages, and Cultures*. Edited by Armin Lange, Emanuel Tov, and Mathias Weigold in association with Bennie H. Reynolds III. Vol. 2. VTSup 140. Leiden: Brill.

Rey, Jean-Sébastien. 2017. "Scribal Practices in the Ben Sira Hebrew Manuscript A and Codicological Remarks." Pages 99–114 in *Texts and Contexts of the Book of Sirach/Texte und Kontexte des Sirachbuches*. Edited by Gerhard Karner, Frank Ueberschaer, and Burkard M. Zapff. SBLSCS 66. Atlanta, GA: SBL.

Reymond, Eric D. 2015. "New Hebrew Text of Ben Sira Chapter 1 in MS A (T-S 12.863)." *RevQ* 27:83–98.

Sanders, Jack T. 1983. *Ben Sira and Demotic Wisdom*. SBLMS 28. Chico, CA: Scholars Press.

Sanders, James A. 1965. *The Psalms Scroll of Qumran Cave 11 (11QPs^a)*. DJD 4. Oxford: Clarendon Press.

Schechter, Solomon, and Charles Taylor. 1899. *The Wisdom of Ben Sira: Portions of The Book of Ecclesiasticus from Hebrew Manuscripts in the Cairo Genizah Collections Presented to the University of Cambridge by the Editors*. Cambridge: Cambridge University Press.

Schipper, Bernd U., and D. Andrew Teeter, eds. 2013. *Wisdom and Torah: The Reception of "Torah" in the Wisdom Literature of the Second Temple Period*. JSJSup 163. Leiden: Brill.

Scott, James C. 1990. *Domination and the Arts of Resistance*. New Haven, CT: Yale University Press.

Skehan, Patrick W., and Alexander A. Di Lella. 1987. *The Wisdom of Ben Sira*. AB 39. New York, NY: Doubleday.

Spivak, Gayatri Chakravorty. 2012. "Nationalism and Imagination." Pages 274–300 in *An Aesthetic Education in the Era of Globalization*. Edited by Gayatri Chakravorty Spivak. Cambridge, MA: Harvard University Press.

Tcherikover, Victor. 1982. *Hellenistic Civilization and the Jews*. New York, NY: Atheneum.

VanderKam, James C. 2004. *From Joshua to Caiaphas: High Priests after the Exile.* Minneapolis, MN: Fortress.

Weeks, Stuart. 2010. *An Introduction to the Study of Wisdom Literature.* New York, NY: T&T Clark International.

Wicke-Reuter, Ursel. 2002. "Ben Sira und die Frühe Stoa. Zum Zusammenhang von Ethik und dem Glauben an eine göttliche Providenz." Pages 268–281 in *Ben Sira's God: Proceedings of the International Ben Sira Conference Durham—Ushaw College 2001.* BZAW 321. Berlin: de Gruyter.

Winston, David. 1989. "Theodicy in Ben Sira and Stoic Philosophy." Pages 239–249 in *Of Scholars, Savants, and Their Texts: Studies in Philosophy and Religious Thought. Essays in Honor of Arthur Hyman.* Edited by Ruth Link-Salinger, Sol Roth, and Robert Herrera. New York, NY: Peter Lang.

Wright, Benjamin G. 1999. "B. Sanhedrin 100b and Rabbinic Knowledge of Ben Sira." Pages 41–50 in *Treasures of Wisdom: Studies in Ben Sira and the Book of Wisdom; Festschrift M. Gilbert.* Edited by N. Calduch-Benages and J. Vermeylen. BETL 143. Leuven: Peeters.

Wright, Benjamin G. 2008a. "Ben Sira on Kings and Kingship." Pages 76–91 in *Jewish Perspectives on Hellenistic Rulers.* Edited by Tessa Rajak et al. HCS 50. Berkeley, CA: University of California Press.

Wright, Benjamin G. 2008b. "Fear the Lord and Honor the Priest: Ben Sira as Defender of the Jerusalem Priesthood." Pages 97–126 in *Praise Israel for Wisdom and Instruction: Essays on Ben Sira and Wisdom, The Letter of Aristeas and the Septuagint.* Edited by Benjamin G. Wright. JSJSup 131. Leiden: Brill.

Wright, Benjamin G. 2008c. "'Put the Nations in Fear of You': Ben Sira and the Problem of Foreign Rule." Pages 127–146 in *Praise Israel for Wisdom and Instruction: Essays on Ben Sira and Wisdom, The Letter of Aristeas and the Septuagint.* Edited by Benjamin G. Wright. JSJSup 131. Leiden: Brill.

Wright, Benjamin G. 2010. "Joining the Club: A Suggestion about Genre in Early Jewish Texts." *DSD* 17:289–314.

Wright, Benjamin G. 2013. "Torah and Sapiential Pedagogy in the Book of Ben Sira." Pages 157–186 in *Wisdom and Torah: The Reception of "Torah" in the Wisdom Literature of the Second Temple Period.* Edited by Bernd U. Schipper and D. Andrew Teeter. JSJSup 163. Leiden: Brill.

Wright, Benjamin G. 2016. "Ben Sira and Hellenistic Literature in Greek." Pages 71–88 in *Tracing Sapiential Traditions in Ancient Judaism.* Edited by Hindy Najman, Jean-Sébastien Rey, and Eibert Tigchelaar. JSJSup 174. Leiden: Brill.

Wright, Benjamin G. 2017. "What Does India Have to Do with Jerusalem? Ben Sira, Language, and Colonialism." Pages 136–156 in *Jewish Cultural Encounters in the Mediterranean and Near Eastern World.* Edited by Mladen Popovic, Myles Schoonover, and Marijn Vandenberghe. JSJSup 178. Leiden: Brill.

Wright, Benjamin G. 2018. "The Persian Glosses and the Text of Manuscript B Revisited." Pages 125–145 in *Discovering, Deciphering and Dissenting: Ben Sira Manuscripts after 120 Years.* Edited by J.K. Aitken, R. Egger-Wenzel, and S.C. Reif. ISDCL Yearbook. Berlin: de Gruyter.

Yadin, Yigael. 1965. *The Ben Sira Scroll from Masada.* Jerusalem: The Israel Exploration Society and The Shrine of the Book.

Ziegler, Joseph. 1980. *Septuaginta Vetus Tesamentum Graecum Auctoritate Academiae Scientiarum Gottingensis editum,* vol. XII/2: *Sapientia Iesu Filii Sirach.* 2nd ed. Göttingen: Vandenhoeck & Ruprecht.

CHAPTER 36

....

THE WISDOM OF SOLOMON

....

JAMES K. AITKEN AND EKATERINA MATUSOVA

36.1 TITLE AND PLACE WITHIN WISDOM LITERATURE

....

THE Wisdom of Solomon is a book that draws upon Greek philosophical traditions, Jewish sources, and the biblical texts to recount the eschatological fate of humans. The distinctive fates of the godly and the ungodly are expounded (Wisdom 1–6), and these are closely tied to the review of Israel's past, wherein the Israelites and the Egyptians suffer differing consequences (Wisdom 10–19). The central section praises Wisdom (Wisdom 7–9).

The attribution to Solomon appears in the early codices (S* B A) and in the Vetus Latina tradition, based upon the apparent but unnamed association of the author with Solomon (Wisdom 7). While in Jewish tradition a number of works attributed to the Wisdom genre are associated with Solomon (Proverbs, Ecclesiastes, Song of Songs; see Mazzinghi 2019, 17), there is no reason to think this was the author's intention here, since anonymity and the potential it offers for universalization of the message seem to be an important strategy for the writer.

How far the work can be placed within anything that might be termed a Wisdom tradition is debatable. The Greek term σοφία ("wisdom") appears thirty times in the book, alongside the concept of φρόνησις "understanding" (ten times), while Wisdom is partially personified (Wis 7:22–30; 9:9; 10:4) in the manner of other Wisdom books (e.g., Proverbs 8; Sirach 24). Yet, the themes and focus of the book are distinctive. The opening words, "Love righteousness, you rulers of the earth," are derived from Ps 2:10 (Dimant 1988, 410), a verse that is picked up again in Wis 6:1 ("Listen therefore, O kings, and understand; learn, O judges of the ends of the earth"). That God will judge the earth is also a theme of the Psalms (e.g., Ps 95[96]:13; 97[98]:9). Thus, the book is structured around Psalmic language, even if the Psalms and Proverbs also share terminology. By addressing kings, the book may be an indirect polemic against Hellenistic kingship, although there is a longer biblical tradition of advice to kings (cf. Prov 8:15–16).

Focus upon the first-person speech (perhaps of Solomon) in chapter 7 has obscured the importance of Solomonic themes from 1 Kings and Proverbs that are already to be found in chapter 1, and throughout chapters 6–9. The author apparently already knows the Septuagint versions of these books, and, as he is writing in Greek, adopts their vocabulary. In the idealized portrait of Solomon in 1 Kings (LXX 3 Kingdoms) God grants Solomon both "wisdom" ($\sigma o \phi \acute{\iota} a$) and "understanding" ($\phi \rho \acute{o} \nu \eta \sigma \iota s$, 3 Kgdms 5:9), the two key terms in Wisdom. In 3 Kgdms 3:28 Solomon exercises "justice" ($\delta \iota \kappa a \acute{\iota} \omega \mu a$) with "divine understanding" ($\phi \rho \acute{o} \nu \eta \sigma \iota s \ \theta \epsilon o \hat{\upsilon}$) and is said to exceed all the kings of the earth (3 Kgdms 10:23; cf. address to "rulers of the earth," Wis 1:1; 6:1), who in turn listen to his "understanding" ($\phi \rho \acute{o} \nu \eta \sigma \iota s$, 3 Kgdms 10:23) and "wisdom" ($\sigma o \phi \acute{\iota} a$, 3 Kgdms 5:14). The subservience of other kings and judges to Solomon is echoed in Wisdom 6, where the kings ($\beta a \sigma \iota \lambda \epsilon \hat{\iota} s$), judges ($\delta \iota \kappa a \sigma \tau a \acute{\iota}$), and rulers ($o \acute{\iota} \ \kappa \rho a \tau o \hat{\upsilon} \nu \tau \epsilon s \ \pi \lambda \acute{\eta} \theta o \upsilon s$, Wis 6:1–2) fail in the rule given them by God (Wis 6:3–4). A connection with Proverbs is also apparent here since Solomon teaches the kings wisdom, as personified Wisdom does in Proverbs (Prov 8:15–16).

Other aspects of the portrayal of Solomon are subtly drawn out. In the biblical account, Solomon becomes a glorious warrior and victor whose very name inspires fear in all peoples (3 Kgdms 8:43, "so that all the peoples [$\lambda a o \acute{\iota}$] of the earth may know your name [$\acute{o} \nu o \mu a$] and fear [$\phi o \beta \hat{\omega} \nu \tau a \iota$] you"). The unnamed speaker in Wisdom 8 likewise has, thanks to Wisdom, "obtained immortality" ($\acute{a} \theta a \nu a \sigma \acute{\iota} a$) and an "everlasting memorial" ($\mu \nu \acute{\eta} \mu \eta \nu \ a \acute{\iota} \acute{\omega} \nu \iota o \nu$, Wis 8:13). As a result, he declares (Wis 8:14–15):

> [14] I shall govern peoples ($\lambda a o \acute{\upsilon} s$),
> and nations will be subject to me;
> [15] dread monarchs will be afraid ($\phi o \beta \eta \theta \acute{\eta} \sigma o \nu \tau a \iota$) of me when they hear of me;
> among the people I shall show myself capable, and courageous in war ($\acute{\epsilon} \nu \ \pi o \lambda \acute{\epsilon} \mu \omega$ $\acute{a} \nu \delta \rho \epsilon \hat{\iota} o s$).

Solomon asks wisdom from God (3 Kgdms 3:7–9; cf. Wis 8:21) so that he can judge (using Greek $\delta \iota a \kappa \rho \acute{\iota} \nu \epsilon \iota \nu$ and $\kappa \rho \acute{\iota} \nu \epsilon \iota \nu$) the people (3 Kgdms 7:9). Similar sentiments are expressed in Wis 9:12 ($\delta \iota a \kappa \rho \iota \nu \hat{\omega}$). Likewise, there is a passing mention of the building of the Temple in Wisdom (9:8; cf. 3 Kingdoms 7).

The first-person speaker in Wisdom is modeled upon Proverbs, where Solomon also speaks in the first person. In Proverbs he refers to his human nature (Prov 4:3), a tradition going back to 1 Kings but also adopted by the speaker in Wisdom (Wis 7:1, "I also am mortal…and in the womb of a mother I was molded into flesh"). Thus, the image of Solomon is based on carefully chosen elements from Proverbs and Kings, permeating the narrative in chapters 6–9. It also ties together the opening chapters 1–6 with the

"Solomonic" speech in chapters 7–9, providing a significant degree of structure to the work.

Scholars have drawn attention to lexical and thematic consistency between the various parts of the book, implying it was composed as a unit (Reese 1970, 122–145; Gilbert 1986, 88–91; Grabbe 1997, 24–25). However, another aspect should be taken into account: the work throughout, and not only in the second half (chs. 10–19), can be seen as a commentary on earlier biblical texts, already a feature of Wisdom discourse in Sirach (chs. 44–50). Such commentary as a form of derivation of Wisdom is to be found in various branches of the Jewish tradition in the second and first centuries BCE. In the Alexandrian tradition, the philosophers Aristobulus and Philo write commentaries on the biblical text, while the *pesharim*, Hebrew commentaries on the Prophets, express the exquisite inspired wisdom of the commentators (1QpHab 7:3–8). We also have commentaries on the past history of Israel in the Admonition section of the Damascus Document, which is introduced as a demonstration of the wisdom of the Teacher of Righteousness, who is said to reveal the truth (CD 1:11–12; 3:1–21). Another Wisdom text, 4QInstruction, formulates the idea that understanding the events of the past is the expression of wisdom:

> [1]…you, enlightened one…[2]…behold, [and you will understand the awesome] secrets of the wonders [of God]…[3]…and behold [the secret of the way things are, and the deeds of old, why they came to be and what they were.] (4Q417 fr. 1 col. 1 + 4Q418 43–45)

We will see later on that these three texts (CD, 4QInstruction, and Sirach) are very important for the understanding of certain ideas in Wisdom and were most probably among the author's sources. The second half of Wisdom (chs. 10–19), as a commentary on the biblical history of Israel, accords well with the first (chs. 1–9) as a demonstration of the wisdom of Solomon.

36.2 DEPENDENCE ON EARLIER WISDOM TRADITIONS

The dependence upon earlier Wisdom books is an important indicator that the author of Wisdom sees himself within a tradition found in biblical and early Jewish writers. As we will show, he sets himself in a complex dialectical relationship with other books that engage the wisdom theme. He draws upon them, but in a critical, sometimes polemical, manner. Despite this, the differences between Wisdom and, for example, Proverbs, are more often noted than the parallels (e.g., Collins 2005, 143–144).

A rich engagement with the Greek version specifically of Proverbs can be observed. From the very opening the author demonstrates a strong dependence, where he explores the relation of thought to speech and recognizes that even the innermost thoughts are known to God:

> For wisdom is a kindly spirit,
> but will not free blasphemers from the guilt of their words (ἀπὸ χειλέων αὐτοῦ);
> because God is witness of their inmost feelings,
> and a true observer of their hearts (καρδίας αὐτοῦ ἐπίσκοπος), and a hearer of their
> tongues.   (Wis 1:6)

The crucial importance of utterance, using the notion of χείλη "lips," in Wis 1:6 derives from Proverbs (4:24; 8:7, 12; 12:13–14, 22; 13:3; 14:3–4; 17:4), as does the divine knowledge of humans, using the verb σκοπεύω (Prov 5:21; 15:3; 20:12, 27; 22:12; 24:12). The idea of God's "castigating" (ἐλέγχω) in Wis 1:3 is associated with God's ἔλεγχοι from Proverbs (Prov 1:23, 25, 30; 3:11), and the false utterances leading to death (Wis 1:11) comes from Prov 18:6; 21:6. In addition, the general context of 1:10–20, where the causality of sin and death is stressed, is connected to Prov 1:17–19; 2:12–18; 8:36. Finally, the appeal not to join sinners/sin (Wis 1:12) has clear parallels in Proverbs (1:10–15; 4:14–16; 24:1–2).

In Wisdom chapter 2 the associations continue. The speech of the wicked who are plotting to kill the righteous (2:10–20) has a clear connection to Prov 1:11–14, as well as the general opposition between the wicked and righteous, with righteousness (Wis 1:15 = Prov 10:2) and the righteous connected to life (Wis 3:4; 5:15; cf. Prov 3:22; 4:22–23; 8:35; 10:2–3, 10–17, 25; 11:30). The theme that the righteous have to be "tested" (δοκιμάζω) and "disciplined" (παιδεύω) by God (Wis 3:5–6) has a clear parallel in Prov 3:11–12; 5:12; 17:3.

These are not mere parallel notions; Wisdom is responding to the words of Proverbs directly. In distinction to the MT, which speaks of the wicked, Prov 11:7 LXX indicates that when the righteous person (ἀνδρὸς δικαίου) dies, hope (ἐλπίς) is not lost. Wisdom expands on this by explaining that the righteous (δικαίων, 3:1) find hope (ἐλπίς) in immortality (ἀθανασία, Wis 3:4). In Proverbs the wicked reject wisdom and teaching (σοφίαν δὲ καὶ παιδείαν ἀσεβεῖς ἐξουθενήσουσιν, 1:7), leading to Wisdom's minor rephrasing that the one who rejects them is "wretched" (σοφίαν γὰρ καὶ παιδείαν ὁ ἐξουθενῶν ταλαίπωρος, Wis 3:11). Examples such as this, where theme and vocabulary coincide, could be multiplied.

A particular area of connection between the two texts is the wisdom theme itself. Proverbs depicts wisdom as being generally available to all: on the streets, at the thresholds of the mighty people, loving those who love her, and easily found (Prov 8:1–3, 17, 20). The wording and imagery used by Proverbs (particularly in its Greek version) strongly evoke the image of a prostitute. The author of Wisdom adopts the imagery and vocabulary of a woman available to those who love her (Wis 6:12–13), sitting on thresholds (Wis 6:14), and looking for people on the streets (Wis 6:16). However, the author is aware of the potential for a negative erotic association from Proverbs and therefore averts a possible negative interpretation by noting Wisdom is "undefiled" (ἀμάραντος Wis 6:12), using a word that can have a sexual connotation. He also opts for the verb θεωρέομαι "to be seen" (contrast ὁράω in Prov 3:13), a technical term in Platonism for intellectual "contemplation," elevating the discussion to a philosophical plane and subtly creating a link to the Platonic image of wisdom ($\sigma o\varphi i a$) as the object of erotic love. However, this is only a secondary allusion, since the image of wisdom as a beloved woman is explicit in Proverbs (4:6: $\dot{\epsilon}\rho\acute{a}\sigma\theta\eta\tau\iota$ $a\dot{v}\tau\hat{\eta}s$; cf. Wis 8:2) and Proverb' discourse on the good and bad woman is closely linked to notions of $\dot{a}\varphi\rho o\sigma\acute{v}\nu\eta$ and $\pi a\iota\delta\epsilon\acute{\iota}a$ upon which Wisdom builds his image of wisdom-wife (Prov 4:5–9; 5:1–8 and Wis 8:2, 9–10, 16). Other elements from Proverbs shape Wisdom's view of $\sigma o\varphi\acute{\iota}a$: wisdom is given by God (Prov 2:5–6; Wis 7:16–17), consists of the knowledge of turns and puzzles ($\sigma\tau\rho o\varphi a\grave{\iota}$ $\lambda\acute{o}\gamma\omega\nu$ and $a\grave{\iota}\nu\acute{\iota}\gamma\mu a\tau a$, Prov 1:3, 6; Wis 8:8), is more precious than precious stones (Prov 3:16; 8:10–11, 18–19, 21; Wis 7:8–12, 8:5); is compared to a "tree of life" ($\xi\acute{v}\lambda o\nu$ $\zeta\omega\hat{\eta}s$, Prov 3:18, alluded to in Wis 10:4); and, is an instrument of divine creation (Prov 3:19–20 and Wis 9:1–2). A detailed description of wisdom's origins in Prov 8:21–31 inspires a briefer one in Wisdom (6:22).

The introduction of corrective elements show that the author of Wisdom was freely elaborating on the material in Proverbs and distancing himself from it when necessary. Some of these we have already remarked upon, but one of the best indicators is his avoidance of certain terms used in Proverbs. The philosophically updated notion of $\lambda\acute{o}\gamma os$ "reason" (Wis 9:1) replaces the "words" ($\lambda\acute{o}\gamma ous$) of $\varphi\rho\acute{o}\nu\eta\sigma\iota s$ (Prov 1:2), expressing mere sensible spoken words, while the word $a\ddot{\iota}\sigma\theta\eta\sigma\iota s$, used systematically as an intellectual term in Proverbs is avoided (3:20; contrast Wis 9:1–2, where the context but not the word is adopted). In Proverbs $a\ddot{\iota}\sigma\theta\eta\sigma\iota s$ occurs twenty-three times (Hebrew נערת), and yet never appears in Wisdom ($\dot{\epsilon}\pi\iota\sigma\tau\acute{\eta}\mu\eta$ is used instead, which never appears in Proverbs). This is a conscious avoidance of a word that could have a neutral meaning in everyday language ("sense"), but which also had a precise philosophical denotation. From at least Plato on, it referred to sense-perception that in the Platonic tradition was a fallacious source of knowledge ("perception"). In Aristotelianism and especially in Stoicism it still held some value. Hence, Wisdom's complete avoidance is a sign of the influence of Platonism (see below, 36.4 Relation to Greek Philosophy).

In sum we can see that Wisdom is heavily indebted to the tradition of Proverbs, and yet modifies its lexical choices and its lack of precision in philosophical vocabulary. At the same time Wisdom deviates from Proverbs in several important ways that suggests it is responding to it. To do this, Wisdom draws upon other sources within the tradition.

36.2.1 Qoheleth on the Wicked

Among the elements that distinguish Wisdom from Proverbs is the fate of the wicked. In Proverbs the wicked will be punished and perish; nothing good is in their lives (Prov 4:16–17, 19; 10:27, 30; cf. the punishment of the unrighteous in Prov 1:26–32; 13:23; 14:11). In Wisdom we see an emphasis upon the wicked prospering until old age without receiving punishment explicitly during their lifetime (Wis 3:10–19). This accords with the pessimistic statements in Qoh 4:1; 7:15; 8:10–14. Although it might have been present in a wider range of sources, the clear influence of Qoh 5:17–19 and 9:5–10 is visible in Wis 2:1–11 (cf. especially Wis 2:11 and Qoh 9:10), as well as in statements on the destiny of souls (Qoh 12:7) that might have influenced the philosophical elaborations of Wisdom (15:8 and possibly 16:14).

36.2.2 Immortality after Death in 4QInstruction

In Proverbs, although the wicked will tempt and attack them, the righteous will not fall foul of anything bad. Building upon these themes (cf. Wis 3:10–19), the author of Wisdom depicts the assault on the righteous as leading to martyrdom through death (3:1–9). However, this death is "full of hope for immortality" (Wis 3:4; 5:15–16). Although the alternative fates for the sinners (death) and the righteous (life) are also typical of Proverbs, there they are metaphorical. The distinctive difference is that Wisdom speaks about future immortality in concrete rather than metaphorical terms. More precisely, it implies, at least in some passages (Wis 3:4; 5:15–16), the possibility of life despite (or after) physical death brought about by persecution at the hands of the wicked.

Martyrdom and eternal life are combined themes typical of a variety of Second Temple sources (e.g., Dan 12:2–3; 2 Macc 7:23; 14:46; 1QS 1:17–18; 4:7; CD 3:20). In Hebrew it can correspond to the notion of "life eternal [עולם]" (4Q418 69ii, l. 7; Dan 12:2) or "life everlasting [נצח]" (CD 3:20; 1QS 4:7; 4Q228 f1:9 [Hodayot]; 4Q257 5:5 [Community Rule]; 6Q18 2:2). The Septuagint equivalents for these Hebrew expressions (ζωή/ζῶσι and αἰών/αἰώνιος) appear in Wis 5:15. Strikingly, the discourse in Wisdom is similar to 4QInstruction (as stressed also by Puech 2005, 132–134), which not only speaks about eternal life, rising from the dead, and triumph over the sinners who will then disappear from the earth, but pointedly puts all these elements in the context of wisdom and the search for wisdom. The Qumran context has occasionally been noted (e.g., Dubarle 1953, 425; Delcor 1955, 614; Larcher, 1969, 112–129), but the connection with 4QInstruction has the strongest parallels, even though its fragmentary preservation limits our ability to identify precise correspondences.

In both 4QInstruction and Wisdom the righteous are pitted against the wicked (4Q418 69ii 4–15 and Wis 3:4–11), and it seems that in 4QInstruction, too, the wicked have killed the righteous, since retribution is postponed to the day of judgment. The righteous, who will have eternal life and will judge the wicked, are endowed with wisdom and truth (cf. Rey 2009, 252). The wicked, on the contrary, are devoid of these attributes:

> But that which exists eternally (וכול נהיה עולם), those who seek truth, will awaken to give judgment...[8] they will destroy those who are foolish of heart, and the children of evil will no longer exist, and all who cling to wickedness will be bewildered...[9] at your judgment the pillars of the sky-dome will be shattered, and all the [host of heaven] will thunder...[10] But you, O chosen of truth, who earnestly follow...seek[ers of insight...and] the watchful[11] for all knowledge. How can you say, We are weary of insight, and we have been careful to pursue true knowledge...[12] and untiring in all the years of eternity. Indeed, he will take delight in truth forever

and knowledge [eternally] will serve him; and [the sons of][13] heaven, whose
inheritance is eternal life, will they truly say, We are weary of deeds of truth, we
worked hard...[14] of every era. Indeed, in eternal light they will wa[lk]...glory
and great honor you...[15] in the sky...council of the divinities all.... But you,
O [enlightened] son....   (4Q418 69ii 4–15)

There are two places in Wis (3:4–11 and 5:4–5, 15–23) that particularly correspond to this
fragment. Wisdom 5:15–23 opens with the statement that the righteous will live forever
(ϵἰς τὸν αἰῶνα ζῶσιν) before speaking about God's judgment ("impartial judgment," Wis
5:18; "at your judgment," fr. l. 9). The fragment mentions the involvement of the whole
cosmos (l. 9), and Wisdom elaborates on that extensively ("and creation will join with
him to fight against his frenzied foes," Wis 5:20–23); finally, both texts speak about the
annihilation of evil along with the wicked (l. 9; cf. Wis 5:23).

In both sources the wise are addressed as "son" (fr. l. 15; παῖς, Wis 2:13; υἱός, Wis 2:18),
as well as "firstborn" in 4QInstruction (4Q416 fr. 2 col. ii l. 13; fr. 81–81a). In Wisdom the
designation of the righteous as the Lord's child is associated with knowledge (2:18), precisely as in 4Q418. Concepts of inheritance in heaven (Wis 5:5; fr. ll. 12–13) and eternal
light (Wis 5:6; l. 14) are also shared.

These and other elements from this fragment in 4QInstruction are also reflected
in Wis 3:4–11, a passage on the hope of immortality. The hope full of immortality
(ἀθανασία, Wis 3:4; cf. 5:15) is expressed through the allusion to Prov 11:7 discussed
above, but thematically corresponds to the theme of eternal life that runs throughout
the fragment (ll. 7, 12, 13). Similar concepts of truth (Wis 1:7, 10, 12; 3:9), judgment
(Wis 3:8; fr. l. 7) and election (Wis 3:9, ἐκλεκτοῖς; fr. l. 18 "O chosen of truth") are
apparent, and the theme of light (fr. l. 14) might be reflected in the description of the
righteous as shining forth and running like sparks (Wis 3:7). The notion of visitation
(ἐπισκοπή, Wis 3:7) is the traditional rendering of Hebrew פקדה, the day of visitation,
and one of the important notions in 4QInstruction (see 4Q417 I i, l.14). In both the
visitation is for the righteous, rather than to the sinners (Wis 3:13; 4:15). Finally, the
mystery of God as used in Wis 2:22 (as something which eludes the understanding of
the wicked and is connected to eternal life and divine judgment) is a direct equivalent of the Hebrew רז "mystery" (as Dan 2:18, 19, 27, 28, 29, 30, 47 shows), one of the
key notions in 4QInstruction. It appears thirty times (Rey 2009, 286), in particular
in this very context of the day of visitation and retribution and eternal life (4Q417 fr.
1 col. i; fr. 2 col. i 10–11).

Thus, not only the notion of eternal life in Wisdom, but also its associated imagery
and concepts, find their precise counterparts in 4QInstruction. It is plausible that this
text was one of the author's immediate sources for the development of the theme of
eternal life in the context of a Wisdom discourse. This corresponds with the suggestion of many that 4QInstruction was not a sectarian composition, but belonged to
"the common Jewish wisdom tradition" (Strugnell and Harrington 1999, 31; see also
Harrington 2006, 122).

36.2.3 Procreation and Sirach

The traditional Jewish blessing on children (Prov 14:26; 17:6) is reversed in Wisdom: the wicked may have (wicked) children (Wis 3:12; 4:3–6), whereas it is sometimes better for the righteous to die childless (Wis 3:13–14; 4:1). The thought clearly finds its inspiration from Sir 16:1–4 ("Do not desire a multitude of worthless children, and do not rejoice in ungodly offspring"), although there may be a Greek influence as well (see below, 36.4 Relation to Greek Philosophy). Both Wisdom and Sirach use the same nomenclature for Wisdom terms and in a more careful way than we see in LXX Proverbs. Other influences from Sirach include the notion that God is not the cause of evil (Sir 15:11–20; Wis 1:13–15), the female personification of Wisdom (Sir 15:1–6), her availability (24:16–22), and the reasoning ascribed to sinners (Wisdom 2; Sir 23:16–18; 29:21–25).

36.3 Response to Earlier Wisdom
Traditions

When borrowing themes from Sirach, the author of Wisdom sometimes takes a distinctively corrective position toward them (even stronger than he does toward Proverbs). At times this attitude can be defined as polemical. Thus, the author not only speaks about immortality ($\dot{a}\theta a\nu a\sigma\acute{\iota}a/\dot{a}\varphi\theta a\rho\sigma\acute{\iota}a$) and eternal life (Wis 5:15), but he finds it necessary to make a statement that death is not created by God and originally humans were not meant to die (Wis 1:13–15). The strong denial implies the author was responding to something. It is well known that Sirach has no concept of immortality (see Goff 2007, 125–130). On the contrary, it has a fatalistic idea of death as predestined from God (Sir 14:17; cf. 41:3–4). The key passage appears to be Sir 17:30–32, which emphasizes "human beings are not immortal" but mere "dust and ashes." In modern editions this is the end of the section. If, however, one reads the first line of Sirach 18 as a continuation of the previous pericope ("He who lives forever created [$\check{\epsilon}\kappa\tau\iota\sigma\epsilon\nu$] all together [$\tau\grave{a}\ \pi\acute{a}\nu\tau a\ \kappa o\iota\nu\hat{\eta}$]"), a picture emerges of God creating death together with the cosmos. In this case, Wisdom's denial of death as created by God can be explained as a polemic against this statement. The author of Wisdom not only denies that God created death, but also asserts that he created ($\check{\epsilon}\kappa\tau\iota\sigma\epsilon\nu$) the world ($\tau\grave{a}\ \pi\acute{a}\nu\tau a$) to be eternal, which is the antithesis of the thought in Sirach that the sun will cease, and declares that man is like God in his immortality, an antithesis of Sirach's view that he is "dust and earth."

A polemic against a trend in Jewish thought is found in Wis 11:23–25 when compared to CD II, 2–16. The words of Wisdom are striking:

> [23] But you are merciful to all, for you can do all things,
> and you overlook people's sins, so that they may repent.
> [24] For you love all things that exist,

and detest none of the things that you have made,
for you would not have made anything if you had hated it.
²⁵ How would anything have endured if you had not willed it?
Or how would anything not called forth by you have been preserved?

If we compare these lines with column 2 of CD, we see that CD contains two relevant thoughts. First, God's punishment is very severe. God eradicated certain people from the earth as sinners, "leaving them neither remnant nor survivors" (CD 2:7). Second, God had such an aversion to sinners at creation that his hatred led to their misbehavior: "For God did not choose them *primordially*.... And he *despised* the generations (in which) they [st]ood.... But those whom he *hated* he caused to stray" (CD 2:7–8, 13). There is a parallel in 1QS 3:25–4:1 with the difference that the subject is the two spirits rather than the righteous and sinners. God's hatred and abhorrence form a theological picture (in contrast to the biblical metaphorical usage in Deut 1:27; 9:28; 16:22; Ps 5:5; Prov 6:16) and are placed into a creation context (cf. Matusova forthcoming). The two words used of hating in CD (תעב and שנא), have standard LXX equivalents βδελύττω and μισέω, both attested in Wis 11:24. Therefore, the passage should be taken as a clear rejection of this thought. God does not despise anyone and nothing originated or was caused by his hatred. The phrase, "For you love all the things that are" (Wis 11:24) can be taken as its antithesis or, specifically, an antithesis of the idea of the selective love of God that is found in 1QS. The polemical connection to CD, however, seems to be clearer because the opening lines of the Wisdom passage also form a polemical counterpart to the thought in CD 2:6–8 that God eradicated the sinners from the earth:

> You have mercy on all, because you can do all things,
>   and you overlook the sins of the human beings that they may repent.   (Wis 11:23)

This thought is clearly developed in Wisdom 12, which immediately follows, although borrowings from this ideology in CD are also present in this chapter (which is a matter for further study).

36.4 RELATION TO GREEK PHILOSOPHY

Given the fragmentary character of Qumran sources, it is not possible to say with certainty whether intentional polemics against ideas known to us primarily from CD should be ascribed to the author of Wisdom, as seems likely in his response to Sirach on creation. The alternative is that they were borrowed from a pre-existing Jewish source stressing God's goodness and mercy (similar to elements in 1QS XI 14; 1QHª V 22; 1QHª XV 30; XVIII 16; XIX 9, 31; XX 21, or even 4QInstruction). However, what is clear is that every idea he directs against Sirach and CD have been aligned with currents in Greek philosophical and political thought. The author successfully combines his Jewish heritage and reading of his predecessors with distinct strands in Greek thought.

The picture of God as a merciful, loving ruler, instead of a wrathful deity whose hatred predestines the wicked for extermination, is built to a significant degree upon Hellenistic ethics of kingship (Reese 1970). The heavenly and the earthly king operate in tandem, showing mercy and love toward all people (φιλανθρωπία, a Greek notion very important in Wis 1:6; 7:23; 12:19). This philosophy probably goes back to the peripatetic work *De mundo*, which draws an analogy between the great king of Persia and the king in heaven. It is further developed in the treatise *On Kingship* written by Ekphantos, a pseudo-Pythagorean author. If we compare Ekphantos with Wisdom, we find several parallels. God does not punish people severely, but affords them a place and time to improve (Ekphantos 80, 25 Thesleff and Wis 12:20; see also Ekphantos 82, 1–3; 83, 18–20 Thesleff).

These polemics on creation are very much in accord with Platonism, which claims that the only cause of creation is the goodness of God (Plato, *Tim.* 29d–30); that the cosmos is meant to be eternal, although it is created (*Tim.* 41a7–b6); and that God cannot be the cause of any evil thing, deed, or feeling (*Rep.* 379b1; *Rep.* 379c2–7). A specific Platonic influence can be seen in Wisdom's view that the envy (φθόνος) of the devil was responsible for the origin of death (Wis 1:24). This striking interpretation does not derive from the biblical text, but is a response to the Platonic denial of φθόνος to God (*Tim.* 29d). Indeed, Wis 11:25 ("How would anything have endured if you had not willed it?") corresponds to the Platonic idea of the world being created and imperishable by the will of God (*Tim.* 41a: "Gods of gods, those works whereof I am framer and father, you came into being by me, but you *are indissoluble as I am unwilling*").

A clue to the philosophical context is the term κόσμος "world," used sixteen times in Wisdom but never used with this meaning in the LXX (where it denotes "order" or "jewelry"). Although important in all currents of Greek thought, the notion is particularly linked to Plato's philosophy of creation. The idea of creating the world (Wis 9:9, ἐποίεις τὸν κόσμον) uses a typically Platonic phrasing. In Wis 11:17, which describes creation from formless matter, we find a Hellenistic understanding of the *Timaeus* (Plut., *De an. procr.* 1013a1–b5; 1014a9–b6, c5–10), while Wis 13:1 uses a Platonic word, "the fashioner" (τεχνίτης [sc. of the world]).

Further Platonic influence is visible in reference to the four cardinal "virtues" (ἀρεταί) as explained in Wis 8:7: self-control and understanding, righteousness and courage, familiar from Plato (e.g., *Phaed.* 69b) and later handbooks (Alcinous, *Did.* 1.4; 29.1). The verb θεωρέω is borrowed from Platonic language and applied to wisdom ("she is discerned," Wis 6:12). The Platonic influence is also distinctive in 8:19–20, which describes the soul entering the body of Solomon since he was gifted and undefiled (reaffirmed by Sterling 2017, 202–203). It is notable that the terms in 8:19, "As a child I was naturally gifted, and I obtained (ἔλαχον) a good soul," correspond once more to ideas in Sir 6:4: "an evil soul destroys those who obtain it (τὸν κτησάμενον αὐτήν)." The verbs λαγχάνω and κτάομαι can be used as synonyms. Importantly, the author signals his interpretative technique, since after v. 19 he inserts the word "rather" (μᾶλλον, 8:20), denoting a specification or modification. Verse 20 then provides a Platonic reformulation of the thought borrowed in v. 19 from Sirach ("or rather, being good, I entered an undefiled body"). This accords with Wisdom's response to and polemics against Sirach on death.

Platonic influence is evident in Wis 6:17–19, a philosophical elaboration on the acquisition of wisdom leading to immortality (ἀφθαρσία and ἀθανασία). Both Greek terms are distinctive philosophical terms, although used elsewhere in Wisdom for the idea of "eternal life" in the Jewish sense. In Diotima's speech in the *Symposium* (204a–212a), Plato explains wisdom (σοφία, φιλοσοφία) as desire (ἐπιθυμία) and love (ἔρως), which enable a human being to reach immortality (ἀθανασία). Wisdom epitomizes this chain of thoughts precisely, with the only differences being that ἀγάπη replaces ἔρως and the idea of observing the law is brought in. It is a well-thought out and subtle adjustment of Platonism to Jewish themes, similar to the idea of God not being the cause of death.

Although some themes are shared by the author and the first-century CE Jewish philosopher Philo, his philosophical understanding of the Bible in Platonic terms is, in comparison to Philo, rudimentary. For instance, in Wis 10:1 the expression "the father of the world" is applied to Adam rather than God. This is a spontaneous use of the word, which neglects the philosophical significance of the term in Platonism. Philo already has it as a term designating God-creator (e.g., *Opif.* 2), in full accord with how Plato uses the term and the tendencies featured in the Bible.

The idea that the κόσμος was created from "formless matter" (11:17) is a typical Hellenistic understanding of the Platonic creation account in the *Timaeus* (Arist., *De caelo* 279b34; Philo, *Aet.* 13; Plut., *De an. procr.* 1013a1–b5; 1014a9–b6, c5–10). Philo reflects Jewish attempts to correct this understanding toward the idea of creation from nothing when speaking about the biblical creation (*Somn.* 1.76–77). The same tendency to deviate from typical Hellenistic understandings of Plato can be seen in other branches of Judaism (see Matusova 2020). The author of Wisdom knows nothing of it. His use of λόγος in the creational sense is also rudimentary. In Wis 9:1–2 the instrumental use of ἐν "by" reflects the use of Proverbs (3:19–20) and Sirach (43:26, ἐν λόγῳ). He has no idea of the prepositional metaphysics of creation developed by Philo, in which only "through" (διά + genitive) is possible on philosophical grounds (cf. Philo, *Cher.* 125–127).

Wisdom reflects on some philosophical notions introduced in Judaism by the earlier Jewish philosopher Aristobulus. In Wis 1:3, 7 he refers to God as δύναμις "power," a use attested in Aristobulus, where it is based on the theology of the Pseudo-Aristotelian treatise *De mundo* (Matusova 2017, 64–65). Along similar lines God is called "the one who holds all things together" (Wis 1:7, τὸ συνέχον τὰ πάντα). The use of the neuter is entirely Greek (cf. Aristobulus apud Eus., *Pr. ev.* 13.12.3–4). Generally, like Aristobulus, the author of Wisdom also shows his familiarity with *De mundo* (as noted by Reese 1970, although not all his parallels are unequivocal), but in a peculiar way.

Despite the author's undoubted adaptation of Platonism, he combines this with many instances of an incorrect or negligent use of Greek philosophical elements. One of the clearest examples is his use of the treatise *De mundo*. In Wis 13:1–9 the author blames certain people who deify elements of nature or stars for not knowing God. The argument seems to be directed against Greek philosophy, where elements of nature were considered divine by the Presocratics, and the stars were treated similarly in Aristotelianism and Platonism. Apparently, when accusing these people for being unable to reach the idea of God *by analogy*, he borrows all of his argument from the treatise *De mundo* (which uses analogy in nature for coming to know God; *De mundo* 398b1–10; 399a30–32; 399b10–23). Although Wisdom admits that these people have come to the idea of eternity (taken from *De mundo*), he says that they have not come to the idea of God. This is a blatant contradiction of what the treatise actually says, since having bestowed divinity upon the stars and having spoken about eternity, it does speak about coming to the idea of God. The author's strategy is to affirm that Jewish wisdom prevails over the wisdom of the people (see below, 36.6 Setting and Date), and to indicate his turn to Platonism. Anyway, the use of the argument from the *De mundo* is incorrect.

An odd use of Platonic elements appears in Wis 9:15: "and this earthy tent burdens the much-caring (πολυφρόντιδα) mind." The image is Platonic, but the word "much-caring" would never be used of mind in a positive sense in Platonism. On the contrary, "many cares" is the trouble caused by the body to the soul; a properly thinking mind should never have *many* objects. Perhaps the epithet is used here in the "final" sense of what the mind becomes in the case it is attached to body, but this seems an unlikely reading of the passage. Similarly, the Platonic word θεωρέω in reference to Wisdom in 6:12 appears amid a blatantly non-Platonic context: that one can with ease find wisdom is distinctively non-Platonic since this is the most difficult task in Platonism. It is instead adopted from Proverbs with support from Sirach.

Similarly, in Wis 7:17–21 Greek philosophical notions are inserted into a passage of such a non-philosophical character (from the viewpoint of Greek philosophy) that one is justifiably puzzled how these two layers coexist. Thus, the author claims to have gained "knowledge of what is" (τῶν ὄντων γνῶσιν, 7:17), and knows "the composition of the world" (σύστασιν κόσμου καὶ ἐνέργειαν στοιχείων), using vocabulary from physical philosophy (but cf. Sir 1:2–3). He then switches to a fantasized list of skills reminiscent of an oriental magician (7:18–21). Equally, epithets given to Wisdom in 7:22–23 are listed like elements of a magical spell, as found in the Greek magical papyri (PGM) with their characteristic homoioteleuton: καὶ διὰ πάντων χωροῦν πνευμάτων // νοερῶν καθαρῶν λεπτοτάτων.

36.5 VOCABULARY AND THOUGHT

The author's oscillation between two worlds—the Jewish and the Greek—manifests itself in the use of vocabulary. The philosophical vocabulary has already been noted, which reflects both independence from the Septuagint and at the same time adaptation of Jewish predecessors to philosophical norms. For instance, the Greek words ἀφθαρσία/ἀθανασία "immortality" may express both Greek and distinctively non-Greek notions. They reflect in Wis 2:23 and 3:4–8 the concept of eternal life in Jewish terms (as found in Qumran and the New Testament), but then in Wis 4:1 and 8:13 refer to the idea of immortality in the memory of the future generations (which is a traditional

Greek understanding of immortality) and in Wis 6:18–19 a Platonic philosophical idea of immortality. The author therefore uses one Greek notion, but progresses and changes the ideas that it expresses. This makes it difficult to speak about one ideological/theological system that underlies the narrative and explains why scholars can argue for a rigorous Jewish understanding of eternal life in the sense of bodily resurrection (Puech 2005) similar to 1 Corinthians 15, while others suppose the opposite, a Greek understanding in terms of immortality of the soul (Collins 2005, 148–149). This inconsistency of usage is clear in the author's application of the word μυστήριον. In Wis 2:22 it is a clear translation of the Jewish notion of רז (see above 36.2.2 Immortality after Death in 4QInstruction), and thus used in the positive sense. In Wis 14:15, 23 it is used in the standard Greek meaning of a mystery cult, and thus in the negative.

Generally speaking, the author of Wisdom delights in playing on the multiple meanings of one and the same word, which is a Greek stylistic device. He uses the word ἀναλύω in the intransitive sense in 2:1 ("to return"), but in the transitive sense ("to release," a completely different meaning!) in a very similar context in 16:14. He uses the word παιδεία ("education, discipline") in all possible meanings (both specifically Greek and those created by the LXX translation). Thus, παιδεία refers to wisdom (1:5; 3:11; 7:14), education (2:12; 6:11; 6:25 [2]), and discipline (3:5; 11:9; 12:22).

As for the word σοφία, it mainly means an abstract wisdom in Wisdom. The other meaning of "craft, skill" is used very often in the LXX and appears in Wis 7:21; 14:2 (with this connotation also in 8:5, 7; 9:2). This sense is clearly expressed in 7:16 (although the word σοφία is not used in this place). In Proverbs σοφία appears with the meaning of a skill only once in Proverbs (24:3), once more suggesting Wisdom is independent from Proverbs and consciously crafts LXX vocabulary in a more sophisticated way than Proverbs (cf. Sir 38:3).

36.6 SETTING AND DATE

It has been common in scholarship to identify sociological circumstances in which the book was written from the imagery contained within it. Many have advocated the reign of Caligula (37–41 CE) as the most likely explanation for the image of persecution of the righteous (Winston 1979, 20–25). Others point more generally to its condemnation of idolatry and portrayal of the destruction of the Egyptians as a form of polemic against the author's Hellenistic environment. The philosophical language is seen as a strategy to win back young Jews to their faith and away from philosophy (Reese 1970; Winston 1979). Such conclusions are unwarranted without analysis of and sufficient attention given to the book's relation to its literary sources and patterns, as we have tried to show.

It has been noted correctly that the narrative of the Exodus includes the notion of Egypt as "oppressing" (θλίβω) the Jews (a theme developed in Wisdom using the vocabulary of Exodus; cf. Pearce 2007, 84). The dependence on books within the

Wisdom tradition, especially on Proverbs and 4QInstruction, is sufficient to explain the themes of opposition between the righteous and sinners. However, a closer look at 4QInstruction sheds an even more interesting light on the anti-Egyptian and anti-Greek expressions of the book and the desire to prove that both the Greeks and the Egyptians are devoid of wisdom. In 4Q418 fr. 80+81a a division between "the human race" and "the whole world" on the one hand, and "the holy of holies" and God's "portion and inheritance" on the other is emphasized. This division corresponds to the division between "the sons of Seth" and "spiritual people" in 4Q417 I i 13–18. "The sons of Seth" is a category which occurs in Qumran texts and most probably derives from Num 24:17, where it refers to a people to be expelled from the promised land (Goff 2003, 89–92; Rey 2009, 296–297). In Numbers it refers to non-Jews *tout court* and nothing prevents understanding it in this sense in 4QInstruction as well, particularly given the distinction between them and "spiritual people" (עם רוח, 4Q417 I i l.16). The same interpretation is possible for the opposition in 4Q418. Whatever these opposites originally meant in their Hebrew context, they could have acquired a precise specification once translated, or interpreted, into Greek among Alexandrian Jews. In Hellenistic Egypt the long opposition between Egyptians and Jews would have made this easier. Remarkably, Seth in Egyptian mythology is the evil deity with whom all foreigners and opponents are identified; in Ptolemaic Egypt the Greeks are included in the same notion, when necessary, and even a particular expression "the son of Seth" is used of a Hellenistic king in one inscription from Edfu (Edfu III, 132; see Huss 1994, 170 n. 651). In Egypt, "the sons of Seth" could be taken as an idiomatic expression referring to foreigners (used even by Greek authors: Aelian, *Nat. an.* X 28; Plutarch, *De Is. et Os.* 363BC; Dio Chrysost., *Or.* 32,101), whose adversary in the text was clearly the Jewish people. This would have increased the possibility of understanding the opposition in terms of the Jews against all other pagans, in particular in their relation to wisdom. There is a good chance that the text of 4QInstruction or its themes in some Greek form was known to Philo, who describes Egypt as σῶμα ("body") in opposition to the Jews who are associated with the ψυχή ("soul") (e.g., *Leg.* 2.59, 77; *Sacr.* 48, 139; *Post.* 62). This reflects the distinction in 4Q417 I i 13–18, where "spiritual people" (עם רוח) are opposed to "the spirit of the body" (רוח בשר), identified with the "sons of Seth" (l.17). If Philo's distinction goes back to this text, it confirms our suggestion that the "sons of Seth" could be identified with Egypt from a Jewish viewpoint.

If the author of Wisdom read 4QInstruction this way, it not only explains the contrasting of Israel for their wisdom and righteousness to the Egyptians and Greeks (chs. 10–19; sometimes merged into one opponent, as in Wis 19:16), but also the promise to the righteous that they will judge "nations and peoples" (Wis 3:8: κρινοῦσιν ἔθνη καὶ κρατήσουσιν λαῶν), where the gentiles appear in place of the otherwise unspecified sinners. It is to be noted that this part of Wisdom particularly contains parallels with 4QInstruction. The identification of the sinners with the pagans is a very clear indication of how the author of Wisdom may have understood the message of 4QInstruction. The negative statements in Wisdom, therefore, against other nations are not to be taken as proof of any one particular social context, but further evidence of a complex interpretative tradition behind the book.

Philological arguments for pinpointing the date of Wisdom have often been imprecise. According to Scarpat (1967) and others, the term κράτησις "rule" in Wis 6:3 refers to the Roman conquest of Egypt. However, in the literary context, the verb κρατέω derives from the LXX where it refers to various kings and rulers, as it does in many Hellenistic sources. This passage in Wisdom recounts themes from 3 Kingdoms (the "kings of the earth" come to hear Solomon's wisdom, 5:14) and Prov 8:16 ("through me kings rule the earth," κρατοῦσι γῆς). Another argument, that the term διάγνωσις refers to the trial of Caesar and is first attested in Philo (*Flacc.* 100) and Acts (25:21) cannot stand since several Ptolemaic papyri testify to its use of the trial of the king as early as the third century BCE (pAmh 2 29; pHib 1 93).

Conformity to pre-existing literary themes and patterns does not exclude, of course, the possibility of reference to an actual political context. However, its importance should not be overestimated. One argument from an actual political context has been developed by Baslez (2005, 34–45; on a suggestion by Larcher 1969, 159–160). She pinpoints Wis 19:16 ("those who had already shared the same rights"), which is an actualizing interpretation of the Exodus, and according to her refers to civil rights of which the Jews were deprived. She connects it with the salt-tax decree, dated to 27 (24–23?) BCE, in which the Jews were reduced to the level of a people λαός (i.e. the Egyptians), having previously been classed as Hellenes ("Greeks").

The term δίκαια can refer to civil rights, as Philo (*Flacc.* 53) uses the term. However, there is no evidence that the term implies distinctive rights rather than a general term for rights. For instance, the Jewish participation at the Gymnasium was also a matter of discussion starting from the time of Octavian, at least (CPJ I 38–39, 59; II 53), and 3 Maccabees refers to similar troubles, tracing them back to the second century BCE. However, the salt-tax decree is our first historical document containing such information. Baslez is very resolute in dating the book to around 20 BCE.

The argument from philosophy offers greater possibilities for dating the book, since the author shows a clear turn to Platonism. Jewish Alexandrian writers do not show any trace of Platonic influence until a certain point (*Aristeas* and Aristobulus are familiar with Aristotle rather than Plato; see Matusova 2017; Matusova 2019). Nevertheless, several elements show that the author is unfamiliar with the adaptation of Platonism in Philo (in particular, his reference to the creational λόγος is rudimentary). On the contrary, Philo can be read as alluding to the text of Wisdom at certain points (see for instance, Wis 2:22–24 probably reflected by Philo in *Opif.* 154–155; Wis 7:14 and *Deus* 6–7; Wis 8:20 and *Cher.* 114). The revival of Platonism in Alexandria is traditionally connected with the activity of the school of Eudorus (fl. ca. 50–25 BC). Consequently, Wisdom is likely to have been written some time from the second half of the first century BCE and before Philo's *floruit*. The combined arguments on the deprivation of rights and on philosophy place the work in this period, possibly after 27–24 BCE, if one is inclined to see an allusion to the salt-tax decree in Wis 19:6.

36.7 CONCLUSIONS

We have shown how much the author of Wisdom places his own work in dialogue with and dissent from his Jewish sources. He is aware of Proverbs and Sirach in their Greek versions and has knowledge of traditions in Qoheleth, which might not have been translated by his time. He also appears to be aware of other Hebrew sources, known from Qumran, that helped to shape his theology and his narrative. Further research is needed to identify precisely the sources he uses and how he differs from them. Hebrew sources or traditions found within them appear to have been available among Greek-speaking Jews in Alexandria (cf. Matusova 2017) and the exchange of ideas between Hebrew and Greek works needs to be examined further.

At the same time, sources of Wisdom include Greek philosophical works, from within the Platonic tradition. He engages with his Jewish sources through an interpretative method that utilizes Platonism to interrogate those sources. At times it is merely a superficial use of vocabulary, but at other times there is a deep combination of Jewish and Hellenistic philosophical ideas. His work demonstrates the complexity of the cultural context of ancient Alexandria and therefore it does not permit straightforward answers to the questions of date or purpose. The rich and subtle use of sources still requires sustained investigation before we can reach precise conclusions on the purpose, meaning and context of this book.

WORKS CITED

Baslez, Marie-Françoise. 2005. "The Author of Wisdom and the Cultured Environment of Alexandria." Pages 33–52 in Passaro and Bellia 2005.

Collins, John J. 2005. "The Reinterpretation of the Apocalyptic Traditions in the Wisdom of Solomon." Pages 143–158 in Passaro and Bellia 2005.

Delcor, Mathias. 1955. "L'immortalité de l'âme dans le livre de la Sagesse et dans les documents de Qumran." *NRTh* 77:614–630.

Dimant, Devorah. 1988. "Use and Interpretation of Mikra in the Apocrypha and Pseudepigrapha." Pages 379–419 in *Mikra*. Edited by J. Mulder. Assen: van Gorcum.

Dubarle, André-Marie. 1953. "Une source du livre de la Sagesse." *RSPT* 37:425–443.

Gilbert, Maurice. 1986. "Sagesse de Salomon (ou Livre de la Sagesse)." *DBS* 11:88–91.

Goff, Matthew J. 2003. *The Worldly and Heavenly Wisdom of 4QInstruction*. Leiden: Brill.

Goff, Matthew J. 2007. *Discerning Wisdom: The Sapiential Literature of the Dead Sea Scrolls*. Leiden: Brill.

Grabbe, Lester L. 1997. *Wisdom of Solomon*. Sheffield: Sheffield Academic.

Harrington, Daniel J. 2006. "Recent Study of 4QInstruction." Pages 105–123 in *From 4QMMT to Resurrection: Mélanges qumraniens en hommage à Émile Puech*. Edited by Florentino García Martínez, Annette Steudel, and Eibert Tigchelaar. Leiden: Brill.

Huss, Werner. 1994. *Der makedonische König und die ägyptischen Priester: Studien zur Geschichte des ptolemäischen Ägyptens*. Stuttgart: Franz Steiner.

Larcher, Claude. 1969. *Études sur le Livre de la Sagesse*. Paris: J. Gabalda.

Matusova, Ekaterina. 2017. "'Seeing' God in Alexandrian Exegesis of the Bible: From Aristobulus to Philo." Pages 63–86 in *Gottesschau-Gotteserkentnis*. Edited by E. Dafni. WUNT 387. Tübingen: Mohr Siebeck.

Matusova, Ekaterina. 2019. "Genesis 1–2 in *De opificio mundi* and Its Exegetical Context." *SPhiloA* 31:57–94.

Matusova, Ekaterina. 2020. "A New Translation of Ps 78:2 (LXX 77:2) in Matt 13:35." Pages 271–287 in *History and Theology in the Gospels*. Edited by Tobias Nicklas, Karl-Wilhelm Niebuhr, and Mikhail Seleznev. WUNT. Tübingen: Mohr Siebeck.

Matusova, Ekaterina. Forthcoming. "The Making of the Theme of Immortality in the Wisdom of Solomon." In *Bookish Circles: Social Contexts of Literacy in the Greco-Roman Mediterranean*. Edited by J.D.H. Norton, L.A. Askin, and G.V. Allen. London: T&T Clark.

Mazzinghi, Luca. 2019. *Wisdom*. IECOT. Stuttgart: Kohlhammer.

Passaro, Angelo, and Giuseppe Bellia, eds. 2005. *The Book of Wisdom in Modern Research: Studies on Tradition, Redaction, and Theology*. Berlin: de Gruyter.

Pearce, Sarah. 2007. *The Land of the Body*. Tübingen: Mohr Siebeck.

Puech, Émile. 2005. "The Book of Wisdom and the Dead Sea Scrolls: An Overview." Pages 117–141 in Passaro and Bellia 2005.

Reese, James M. 1970. *Hellenistic Influence on the Book of Wisdom and Its Consequences*. Rome: Biblical Institute Press.

Rey, Jean-Sébastien. 2009. *4QInstruction: Sagesse et eschatology*. Leiden: Brill.

Scarpat, Giuseppe. 1967. "Ancora sull'autore del Libro della Sapienza." *RivB* 15:171–189.

Sterling, Gregory. 2017. "The Love of Wisdom: Middle Platonism and Stoicism in the Wisdom of Solomon." Pages 198–213 in *From Stoicism to Platonism: The Development of Philosophy, 100 BCE–100 CE*. Edited by T. Engberg-Pedersen. Cambridge: Cambridge University Press.

Strugnell, John, and Daniel J. Harrington. 1999. *Qumran Cave 4. 24: Sapiential Texts. Part 2, 4QInstruction (Mûsār lĕ Mēvîn): 4Q415 ff*. DJD 34. Oxford: Clarendon Press.

Winston, David. 1979. *The Wisdom of Solomon: A New Translation with Introduction and Commentary*. AB 43. Garden City, NY: Doubleday.

CHAPTER 37

···

THE PURSUIT OF WISDOM AT QUMRAN

Assessing the Classification "Wisdom Literature" and Its Application to the Dead Sea Scrolls

···

MATTHEW GOFF

WISDOM is a polysemous term that resists overly prescribed or narrow definitions (Goff 2018).[1] The term can denote knowledge necessary to understand the world (i.e., the revelation Enoch received from angels [e.g., 1 En. 82:2]), an intellectual capacity or aptitude (the ability to understand the world), social categories of learning or pedagogy (i.e., "wisdom" teachers or sages), or a literary category—Wisdom texts. The latter is the core topic of this article.

In recent years, there has been a trend in scholarship to argue that the genre designation Wisdom creates more problems than it solves and should be retired from our scholarly lexicon. The most vocal proponent of this position is Will Kynes (2015; 2016), who likens the Wisdom category to a disease that infects, as it were, biblical studies. In different ways, and with less acerbic language, Stuart Weeks (2015; 2016; cf. 2010) and Mark Sneed (2011; 2015a) have also questioned the utility of Wisdom as a literary category.

Wisdom traditionally functions as a classification for a group of biblical texts—Proverbs, Ecclesiastes, and Job in the Hebrew Bible, and in the Apocrypha or deuterocanonical literature, Ben Sira and the Wisdom of Solomon. As Kynes (2015, 12–18) observes, in the twentieth century, this designation was expanded to other texts, including other parts of the Hebrew Bible, such as the Joseph novella or various psalms (e.g., Psalms 1 and 37), and instructional literature from elsewhere in the ancient world, above all Mesopotamia and Egypt. Texts from these areas, such as the Instruction of Amenemope, attest an established type of instructional literature (*sbꜣyt*) which contains teaching on how to lead an ethical and prosperous life (Fox 2015, 79–80). The Wisdom label has also

[1] I thank Giancarlo Angulo for his helpful feedback on this essay.

been applied to various texts of the Dead Sea Scrolls—a large corpus of Jewish writings that in general date to the second and first centuries BCE which constitute a core subject of the present essay. Kynes warns menacingly of "the threat of pan-sapientialism." Despite this hyperbole, the expansion of a predominantly biblical category to non-biblical texts merits methodological and taxonomic reflection. Moreover, the new Wisdom minimalism creates a new context to re-examine an old problem—the viability of Wisdom as a category of scholarly analysis. An overriding question is: what do new texts do to old textual categories?

It has become common since the 1990s to designate a core group of Qumran texts as Wisdom Literature, chief among them 4QInstruction (1Q26, 4Q415–418, 4Q423), the book of Mysteries (1Q27, 4Q299–301), the Wiles of the Wicked Woman (4Q184), 4QSapiential Work (4Q185), and 4QBeatitudes (4Q525; for surveys, see Goff 2007; Kampen 2011). Articulating a category of literature should involve not only identifying the shortcomings or problems inherent in such an intellectual endeavor (such as how diversity among members of the set should be explained). One should also assess how the category can assist interpreters of texts—to use Thomas Beebee's (1994, 7, 14) terminology, the pragmatic "use-value" of the genre (cf. Najman 2012, 309). Describing some compositions from Qumran as Wisdom Literature is an etic and heuristic designation, a convention of reading, that is intellectually valuable insofar as it draws attention to their affinities, in terms of theme, form, and content, with biblical texts conventionally classified as Wisdom Literature. It is a way to highlight that these texts are instructional and thematize the acquisition of knowledge, and that they have a degree of continuity with earlier literature categorized as Wisdom (or sapiential). This continuity should be understood in terms of the pedagogy of ancient Israel and Second Temple Judaism.

I first address recent challenges to the viability of Wisdom as a literary category and then turn to the problems and value of applying this category to the Dead Sea Scrolls.

37.1 WISDOM AND ITS DISCONTENTS: THE NEW SAPIENTIAL MINIMALISM

Will Kynes has rung the death knell of Wisdom Literature. He describes Wisdom Literature as an "ill-defined, circularly justified, modernly developed, and extrinsically imposed corpus" (2016, 100). According to him, scholars have simply imposed their own concerns upon the canvas of ancient Israel. The whole category is an invention of nineteenth-century German scholars, he alleges, in particular Johann Bruch, who argued that Wisdom Literature is a type of universalistic, humanistic Hebrew philosophy that should be distinguished from the particularism of Israel's cultus (2016, 96). This dialectic between religion and "secular" philosophy is a product of the intellectual climate in Germany at the time, and yet the modern Teutonic origins of Wisdom Literature over time, he argues, became lost. The category has since thrived illegitimately as something thought to exist in ancient Israel and as such has been detrimental to scholarship. Efforts in the twentieth century to describe Wisdom Literature are guilty of circular reasoning, since they proceed from the assumption that there is such a thing called Wisdom Literature and then try to define it. Removal of the category would liberate biblical books so classified (Kynes stresses in particular the book of Job) and allow for types of intertexts and relationships with other books to be explored.

Stuart Weeks dismisses the value of genres as taxonomic categories (2015, 174). Drawing on genre theory, he understands genres primarily as tools of communication—sets of "intertextual relations" that occur between types of writing recognizable by the reader—"micro-genres," one can say, such as proverbs, riddles, or genealogical lists of ancestors—as opposed to genre in the sense of literary categories. Weeks stresses that genres, in the sense he advocates, through their combination and interplay allow a text to produce meaning when it is read (Weeks 2015, 162; cf. Frow 2006, 29–40; Najman 2012, 308). He argues for using the metaphor of family resemblance—a theory developed by Wittgenstein and applied to genres by Fowler (1982, 42) that is a popular way to explain diversity and variation within members of a given genre set—to understand Wisdom Literature (Weeks 2015, 163; cf. Najman 2012, 313; Dell 2015, 156). In this metaphor (examined below, 37.2 Wisdom as a Category of Biblical Literature), texts classified together have similarities and differences, sometimes great differences, but they are all part of the same group, like members of a biological family.

Weeks (2016) also questions what scholarship on Wisdom Literature has accomplished. He critiques the study of the subject in the twentieth century as imposing more meaning on the core Wisdom texts than they can bear. Wisdom texts were often on the margins of post-WWII scholarship, and the field as a whole was preoccupied with grand theological constructs of salvation history (evident in von Rad's early tradition criticism). This shaped, Weeks argues, the emergence of Wisdom Literature essentially as a type of ancient Israelite religion, with its own theology (a non-revelatory Yahwism) and adherents (courtly sages) (11–12). It is not difficult with this perspective to understand the sages as rivals to priests and prophets, with each representing a distinct thought-world of ancient Israel. This for Weeks illustrates the problems with lumping the Wisdom books together—reification of the literary category created a social category (the sages) that in turn loomed large in reconstructions of ancient Israel. He questions the value of the label and speculates that we should stop using it (2016, 22). It follows that he disapproves that the category is now being applied to the Dead Sea Scrolls (more on this below, 37.3 Wisdom and the Dead Sea Scrolls).

Sneed distinguishes, following Kenton Sparks, two types of genre theories—genre realism and genre nominalism (2015a, 40). In the former, genres are considered as real, static ontological categories, while the latter approach, which he endorses, acknowledges that they (quoting Sparks) are fluid, inherently "arbitrary," and "essentially taxonomic inventions" (Sneed 2015a, 40). He argues for the latter while accusing major scholars of Wisdom, such as James Crenshaw, of being genre realists (43). For Sneed (2011, 50), the dynamic nature of genres makes it difficult to sustain the long-held view that Wisdom texts attest a common "sapiential worldview" (defined in part by Crenshaw [2010, 11] as a search for order in the world and human experience). Reifying the genre into an ontological category, he argues, has contributed to the scholarly opinion that Wisdom is a distinct tradition, with its own adherents (the sages), who were opposed to and in tension with other ancient segments of Israelite society such as prophets or priests, a point Weeks also critiqued. Sneed (2011, 57) insists that we should not make rigid boundaries between Wisdom Literature and other kinds of biblical literature. He prefers not to think of the scribes or sages who produced Wisdom texts as a distinct group, a view that von Rad (1993) famously articulated. Rather, these scribes were also involved in the production of other types of biblical literature (Sneed 2011, 62–63). He thus promulgates a minimalist view of Wisdom as a distinct tradition to reach maximalist conclusions—those who produced Wisdom Literature essentially produced the literature of the Hebrew Bible.

37.2 Wisdom as a Category of Biblical Literature

Some scholars do indeed give the impression that the existence of Wisdom as a category is assumed before analysis begins. Crenshaw's influential definition of Wisdom Literature (2010, 12) reads like a summary of the main themes of Wisdom Literature, as Kynes recognizes (2015, 17). The prodding of the minimalists prompts the important reminder that Wisdom is not an ontological category that existed in ancient Israel but one that readers of Scripture have created. This realization runs counter to the form-critical heritage of the field which holds that, as Gunkel argued, particular social settings produced particular types of literature. It would follow from this position that the genres scholars identify were, as it were, part of the landscape of ancient Israel. Studies of genre in biblical studies generally agree today that how we understand genre should be flexible and allow for diversity and variation (e.g., Newsom 2005; Wright 2010; Najman 2012; Sneed 2015a). The complaint that biblical scholars are genre realists, to use Sneed's terminology, has more validity as a critique of earlier scholarship than as an identification of a flaw in scholarship today.

The intellectual challenge today is not just to admit that diversity and ambiguity are inherent in our categories but also to articulate how this makes us re-envision them (Zahn 2012, 276–278). Some scholars, like Ben Wright, turn to prototype theory (2010; cf. Collins 2010, 394–396). This approach draws on cognitive science and is based on how the mind forms categories (Lakoff 1987, 39–48; Bowker and Star 1999, 62; Sinding 2002; Newsom 2005). In this model, categories are extrapolated primarily from core exempla. They have a metonymic function on the basis of which, pars pro toto, the categories to which they should be assigned are deduced. A key implication is that justification for a given category does not require a rigid epistemological policing of its boundaries. The category can remain fuzzy and ill-defined in many ways, as long as it has a discernable core. There is probably something to prototype theory. For many scholars, the lack of agreement regarding whether various texts (such as some of the psalms) should be classified as sapiential has not led them to question the viability of Wisdom Literature as a category, because it is nevertheless defined by core exempla such as Proverbs.

Many scholars, like Weeks, explain the inherent messiness of our categories through appeal to the metaphor of family resemblance (so too Dell 2015; Sneed 2015a, 59; note also Collins 2010, 393). But while this metaphor does provide aptly a characterization of genre that allows for diversity among texts understood as examples of the same kind of literature, I question the value of this metaphor. It presumes that a given text is, as it were, part of the family. The metaphor allows for the easy slippage to the view that genres are autonomous ontological entities rather than creations of readers. It is a biological metaphor, analogous to conceptualizing genres as species (Fishelov 1993, 53–83; Beebee 1994, 252–253).

Contemporary genre theory, however, resists the idea that texts should be conceptualized as belonging to genres, whereas individuals do belong to particular families. For Derrida, texts do not belong to genres but participate in them (Derrida and Ronell 1980; Frow 2006, 22–28; cf. Duff 2000, 219–231). There are established conventions regarding modes of speech and writing, and texts "participate" in these forms. A given text performs, one can say, a particular genre type, giving expression to linguistic conventions that are crucial in terms of how a reader makes the text she is reading intelligible. Genres are semiotic acts. They constitute a sort of "social organisation of knowledge" (Frow 2006, 4). In this regard, Bakhtin has immensely enriched our understanding of genre (Boer 2007). In his nomenclature, "primary" genres are macro-categories (Wisdom would be an example of this) that are constituted by the ecology of "secondary" genres, such as riddles or genealogies, that interact and transform when they are used (Weeks [2015] focuses on genre in the latter sense; cf. Duff 2000, 82–97). The proverb (*mashal*) would be a "secondary" genre that is critical in Proverbs, and so is the admonition form. Their use in Proverbs shows that they were established linguistic conventions (neither the *mashal* nor the admonition were invented by the producers of Proverbs), even if the full range of those conventions are lost to us. The attribution of this material to Solomon, and the re-combination of proverbs into anthologies (Proverbs essentially being an anthology of anthologies) are processes that change those secondary genres, as would be evident if one could compare them with how they were used elsewhere in ancient Israel (as discernible, perhaps, through the use of the proverb form in Ezekiel 18). Genres do not simply have fuzzy boundaries. They are multivocal, fluid, and relational.

While it is possible to be cognizant of the diversity and fluidity of our textual categories, Kynes in his critique nevertheless asks a good question: why should one of our literary categories be something called Wisdom? For him, Wisdom is not simply an etic category—it is one that hinders our analysis of biblical literature. We cannot see that, he opines, because of our circular reasoning: we assume the category and then try to define it. Scholars are certainly capable of circular logic and specialists of Wisdom Literature are no exception. But good scholarship is characterized by critical inquiry, regardless of what is being scrutinized. One should, with regard to any literary category, assess not only its problems and weaknesses but also its value. The core value of Wisdom, as a category of biblical literature, is a pragmatic one: it helps highlight key affinities between particular texts—affinities with regard to literary form, theme, and function. If one analyzes Proverbs, Job, and Ecclesiastes without classifying them as Wisdom texts, it would still be clear that these three texts have more similarities, despite their extensive differences, with each other than with other books of the Hebrew Bible (Collins forthcoming). Both Job and Ecclesiastes critique the conventional view that having wisdom (in the sense of being ethical and acting with righteousness) will allow one to attain this-worldly rewards, a view prominently espoused in Proverbs. The office of teacher is paramount in Ecclesiastes, like Proverbs, and lists of proverbs are prominent in the book, again like Proverbs. Major literary forms in Job, such as dialogue and lament, are quite different from the predominant forms in Proverbs and Ecclesiastes, and the language of Job is famously idiosyncratic. But much of what the friends tell Job is in general reminiscent of Proverbs. If, for example, Bildad's statement in Job 18:5 ("Surely the light of the wicked is put out, and the flame of their fire does not shine") were in Proverbs it would not strike observers as out of place. The famous poem in Job 28 about the inaccessibility of wisdom (in the sense of knowledge necessary to understand and succeed in the world) critiques a prominent theme in Proverbs, that to have wisdom one must simply want it, as evident from Woman Wisdom calling out in the streets, inviting people to partake of her wisdom (e.g., 8:1–9). The core of the Wisdom designation is recognition of the basic fact that these books have extensive affinities and that each engages themes found throughout these books.

Contra Kynes, readers of Scripture have long recognized—long before the nineteenth century—that some books in the Bible should be grouped together in a way that roughly approximates our modern category of Wisdom Literature. Josephus, in his famous summary of the twenty-two books that comprise the Jewish Scriptures, after enumerating the books that constitute the Law and the Prophets states that the "remaining four books contain hymns to God and precepts (ὑποθήκας) for the conduct of human life" (1.40). He does not name the three books at issue (aside from the "hymns to God," likely an allusion to the Psalter) but they must surely include Proverbs and Ecclesiastes. Josephus observes a major rationale upon which the modern category of biblical Wisdom Literature is based—that some books, which are not in the Torah or the prophets, are characterized by ethical advice.

That earlier readers of Scripture had a category that is close to our designation of Wisdom Literature is also evident in the late antique and medieval biblical category of "Solomonic books." This grouping includes the Song of Songs and, pointedly, not Job. Several canon lists also regard Ben Sira and the Wisdom of Solomon as "Solomonic." The canon list of the Council of Hippo (393 CE), for example, identifies these texts (Proverbs, Ecclesiastes, Song of Songs, Ben Sira, Wisdom of Solomon) as the "five books of Solomon." This attribution likely emerged as a way to rationalize the affinities readers could discern throughout this "Solomonic" corpus. There are also early modern classifications of sapiential books, as Weeks (2016, 4–6) helpfully demonstrates.

37.3 Wisdom and the Dead Sea Scrolls

If Wisdom is valid as a category for biblical literature, does it follow that it can be legitimately applied to other ancient texts, in particular the Dead Sea Scrolls? My own answer to this is yes, but it is an answer that must be qualified with hesitations and concerns that help us reach a more transparent understanding of Wisdom Literature as an etic and constructed category (Najman and Tigchelaar 2014).

In the early days of Qumran research, it was observed that some of the available Dead Sea Scrolls had affinities with biblical Wisdom Literature. This was the case, for example, with the Hodayot and the Damascus Document (Bardtke 1956; Romaniuk 1978). There was an unpublished dissertation completed in 1968 by John Worrell on "Concepts of Wisdom in the Dead Sea Scrolls." An interest in Wisdom Literature vis-à-vis the Dead Sea Scrolls increased dramatically in the 1990s, with the publication of *DJD 20* (Elgvin et al. 1997), which identifies itself as an edition of sapiential texts, and the appearance of the official edition of 4QInstruction in *DJD 34* (Strugnell and Harrington 1999), which is also entitled by its editors as *Musar le-Mevin* ("Instruction for a Student"). It was the last lengthy text of the Dead Sea Scrolls to be published.

4QInstruction, which prior to its official edition was referred to as Sapiential Work A, is a Hebrew text that is generally dated to the second century BCE (Goff 2013). It was immediately recognizable as having themes and forms that scholars use to identify Wisdom Literature. It is a self-consciously pedagogical composition. The implied speaker is a teacher who gives instruction to a student, who is typically addressed in the singular. He is called a *mebin* or "understanding one." The text has admonitions, with use of the imperative form, that encourage the *mebin* to study and acquire knowledge. He is told, for example: "Improve greatly in understanding and from all of your teachers get ever more learning" (4Q418 81 17)—a statement that would not appear out of place if it were in Proverbs. Moreover, much of the ethical advice covers topics found throughout Proverbs—advice that is important for everyday life, engaging issues such as marriage, family ethics, borrowing money, and the repayment of debts. To underscore the importance of paying off debts, 4QInstruction uses the same imagery employed by Proverbs (6:4) to make this point—that one should go without sleep until the debt is paid off ("[let there be n]o slumber for your eyes until you carry out [his directives]"; 4Q416 2 ii 9–10; Goff 2013, 79). In terms of content, literary form, function, and setting (pedagogy/the instruction of students), 4QInstruction has clear affinities with Proverbs. Scholars have in general considered 4QInstruction a Wisdom text in terms of genre and the best example of a Wisdom text preserved among the Dead Sea Scrolls.

Other texts from Qumran also resemble biblical Wisdom Literature in terms of theme, literary form, and function. 4QBeatitudes derives its modern title from its sequence of beatitudes which encourages the pursuit of wisdom. This passage reads in part:

> Happy are those who cling to her statutes and do not cling to the ways of iniquity.
> Hap[py] are those who rejoice in her and do not burst out upon the ways of folly.

Happy are those who seek her with pure hands and do not search for her with a deceitful heart. Happy is the man who has obtained wisdom, follows the Torah of the Most High, sets his heart toward her ways, controls himself with her disciplines and takes pleasure alw[ays] in her chastisements. (4Q525 2 ii + 3 1–4; Goff 2007, 198–229; Uusimäki 2016)

This passage encourages ethical righteousness and the search for wisdom. In Proverbs, this theme is connected to personified wisdom which one should seek and embrace, a metaphor for one's devotion to a life characterized by study and ethical comportment. This is probably also the case in 4QBeatitudes. The voice of the composition is uttered by a teacher figure who encourages the student addressee to heed his words: "And now, understanding one, listen to me and set your heart to the w[ords of my mouth]" (4Q525 14 ii 18). As a way to encourage him to study, this same passage urges the student to envision his own future death, after he has himself become a teacher, mourned by his own students who are resolved to continue his memory and carry on his teaching (ll. 14–17). The key material is fragmentary, but 4QBeatitudes likely expresses the importance of following a teacher, like Proverbs, through the theme of personification of wisdom as a woman. Fragment 24 ii begins "tr]uly she pours out (תביע) her speech." The same verb is used in Prov 1:23 to signify the speech of Woman Wisdom, which she employs to encourage people to heed her teachings. Line 2 of the fragment reads, "Pay attention to me," a statement that should perhaps be understood as the voice of Woman Wisdom. It is evident that the speaker has a house, a theme prominently associated with personified wisdom in Proverbs 9. The composition probably combines the personified wisdom known from Proverbs with Torah piety—a development that is also prominent in Ben Sira and Baruch (e.g., Sir 24; Bar 3:9–4:4; Uusimäki 2014). This is implicit in the use of feminine pronouns in 4Q525 2 ii + 3, denoting what the (male) addressee should be devoted to (ḥokmah and torah being both grammatically feminine; cf. also 4Q525 5). Calling 4QBeatitudes a Wisdom text helps highlight not simply its affinity with Proverbs but also that the text constitutes additional evidence for a trend long discerned in the study of Wisdom Literature: that later Wisdom texts (Ben Sira and the Wisdom of Solomon) combine themes and terminology from Proverbs with the national traditions of Israel.

One can identify further textual evidence from Qumran for this combination of language from Proverbs with Torah piety and the (scriptural) history of Israel. 4Q185 is routinely called a Wisdom text (Goff 2007, 122–145). No extended portrait of personified wisdom survives in this text, but, like 4QBeatitudes, feminine pronouns are prominent in it, along with the beatitude form, to denote what the addressee should study (e.g., 4Q185 1–2 ii 13). This likely denotes a combination of personified wisdom and the Torah. Line 12 of this column describes one of the rewards of this study as "length of days" (a partially reconstructed phrase), which is also evoked by Woman Wisdom in Prov 3:16. 4Q185 encourages devotion to the Torah as well—"listen to me, my sons, and do not rebel against the words of YHWH" (1–2 ii 3). Moreover, the composition draws moral lessons from the history of Israel, as presented in the Torah. 4Q185 1–2 i 13–ii 2, for example, encourages people to tremble before God and do his "wi[ll]" by reminding them of the miracles he carried out in Egypt, invoking the Exodus.

Other Qumran texts also resonate with biblical Wisdom Literature. 4Q184 encourages its addressees to be ethical by encouraging them to avoid a wicked woman. The text's description of her resonates with regard to both theme and terminology with the "foreign woman" of Proverbs 7, who attempts to seduce unsuspecting men (compare, for example, 4Q184 1 12 and Prov 7:12). 4Q424 provides instruction about types of people whom one should not trust to carry out tasks and also about positive types, such as the "man of generosity" who gives to the poor (4Q424 3 9). The advice of the composition, with its focus on success in practical, this-worldly affairs, is fully compatible with Proverbs 10–31. 4Q424 urges one to avoid negative types of people that Proverbs also warns about. 4Q424 1 12, for example, recommends that one stay away from "a short-temp[ered] man" ([ם] קצר אפֿׂ; literally "short of nose"; Goff 2007, 181). Proverbs 14:17 uses this same expression when urging people to avoid those who lose patience (cf. Sir 8:16).

While some Qumran texts have strong affinities, in terms of theme, terminology, literary form, and function (pedagogy), with writings traditionally defined as Wisdom texts, in particular Proverbs and Ben Sira, there are several issues that problematize the conclusion that Wisdom Literature is a coherent category for the Dead Sea Scrolls (Goff 2010). The fragmentary nature of the Dead Sea Scrolls complicates the task of genre classification. The editor of 4Q455 (4QDidactic Work C), Esther Chazon, asserts, for example, that it could be a sapiential text but so little of the composition survives, the value of such a designation is limited (Pfann et al. 2000, 351–352). There is disagreement as to which Qumran texts should be classified as sapiential. Drawnel (2004) has argued that the Aramaic Levi Document, which provides extensive instruction on priestly affairs, should be classified as a Wisdom text. The famous Treatise of the Two Spirits from the Community Rule, which gives instruction on the nature of humankind, is explicitly didactic and composed for students. Should it be considered a Wisdom text? Normally it is not included in surveys of Qumran Wisdom. *DJD 20*, the only volume of the series that purports to be devoted to Wisdom texts, includes several compositions that are generally not considered in scholarly analysis of Early Jewish Wisdom Literature (e.g., 4Q413). These differing opinions illustrate the ambiguity in the application of the criteria that define the Wisdom category. Pedagogical function for example is important for identifying Wisdom Literature but arguably most if not all of the Dead Sea Scrolls are intended to teach something. Because of issues like this, there is not and cannot be a comprehensive or exhaustive list of Qumran Wisdom texts upon which all commentators would agree.

Moreover, the Qumran texts generally classified as Wisdom Literature demonstrate a striking degree of diversity, both when compared to each other and the core biblical specimens of Wisdom Literature. Major hallmarks of biblical Wisdom are by and large not found at Qumran. No Qumran text identified as sapiential is attributed to Solomon and this monarch does not play a significant role in the Dead Sea Scrolls in general. There are no major collections of proverbs among the Qumran Wisdom texts. The term משל is not prominent in the Dead Sea Scrolls, sapiential or otherwise (occurring eleven times, including reconstructed instances). The only text in which the term appears repeatedly is the Book of Mysteries, an important text for our discussion (more on this below; see 4Q300 1 a ii–b 1; 4Q301 2b 2; cf. 4Q424 3 8). The books of Job and Ecclesiastes do not play a significant role in the Qumran sapiential corpus or the Dead Sea Scrolls as a whole, although the corpus does include two targums of Job (4Q157; 11Q10), an indication that there was some interest at the time in reading this book (and that people needed assistance when doing so!).

Major themes in the Qumran Wisdom texts are alien to traditional sapiential literature. The parade example of this is 4QInstruction, which is generally identified as the key exemplar of Qumran Wisdom. The pedagogy of the document revolves around the study of revealed wisdom—the *raz nihyeh*, which is generally translated "the mystery that is to be." The *mebin* is repeatedly told to reflect and contemplate this "mystery" (e.g., 4Q416 2 iii 14; 4Q417 1 i 6–7). He has the potential to learn a great deal from this intellectual labor, such as the knowledge of good and evil and the eschatological fate of humans. The *raz nihyeh* signifies how God structured history and creation (Najman 2017). Also, one can attain this comprehensive knowledge ("wisdom" one could say) by studying this "mystery." *Raz* is an Aramaic loanword that denotes supernatural revelation in Early Jewish apocalypses (Dan 2:29; 4QEnᶜ 5 ii 26–27 [1 En. 106:19]). It denotes esoteric knowledge possessed by the *mebin*, who belongs to a group with elect status defined to a large extent by their possession of the *raz nihyeh*; it is not universally available knowledge. The presentation of heavenly revelation as the key to obtaining knowledge is not a feature of traditional sapiential literature. Proverbs dismisses "a revealer of secrets" (גולה סוד) as someone who gossips (20:19). 4QInstruction also envisages eschatological judgment, as do some other Qumran Wisdom texts, another significant departure from biblical wisdom (4Q418 69 ii; 4Q185 1–2 i 8–9). 4QInstruction, because of the prominence of the themes of eschatological judgment and supernatural revelation in it, can be said to have an apocalyptic worldview. Wisdom literature, insofar as it attested at Qumran, can incorporate various worldviews, even those that are starkly different from biblical Wisdom. Scholars have often defined biblical Wisdom Literature as having a common worldview, as discussed above (37.1 Wisdom and Its Discontents: The New Sapiential Minimalism). The Dead Sea Scrolls prompt scholars to acknowledge that Wisdom Literature can accommodate diverse perspectives towards the world (Collins 1997).

It should not be concluded on the basis of 4QInstruction that Qumran Wisdom Literature is characterized by the incorporation of themes of eschatology and transcendental revelation. In this sense, 4QInstruction, the best-known exemplar of Qumran Wisdom Literature, is not very representative of the category (a fact that does not square well with prototype theory). While there are some eschatological elements in Qumran Wisdom texts, aside from 4QInstruction eschatology is not a major theme in this material. No other Wisdom text thematizes the *raz nihyeh* as the key to the acquisition of knowledge. The particular pedagogy of 4QInstruction is not found in other Qumran Wisdom texts. Supernatural revelation is not a major theme in these other compositions aside from 4QInstruction.

There is a major exception to this assessment—the Book of Mysteries (Goff 2007, 69–103; Kister 2004). The central passage of this composition, a composite text based on 1Q27 1 i, 4Q299 1 and 4Q300 3, is a scene of eschatological judgment:

> ... in order that they might know the difference between good and evil, and between falsehood and truth, [because] the mysteries of transgression.... But they do not know the mystery that is to be (רז נהיה) and the former things they do not understand. They do not know what will happen to them. They will not save their lives from the mystery that is to be (מרז נהיה). And this shall be the sign to you that it is taking place: when those begotten of iniquity are locked up, wickedness will disappear before righteousness, as darkness disappears before light. As smoke vanishes and is no more, so will wickedness vanish forever. Righteousness will be revealed like the sun (throughout) the measure of the world and all those who hold fast to mysteries [of wickedness] will be no more.   (Goff 2007, 73)

The *raz nihyeh* here is not revelation to be studied, as in 4QInstruction. Rather it is more directly associated with eschatological judgment. Mysteries describes its addressees as having access to supernatural revelation (4Q299 8 6). Mysteries and 4QInstruction have much in common. It is reasonable to posit some sort of continuity between them. Whoever produced one had perhaps read the other or the elect communities envisaged in these texts may have had some sort of connection. But the clear parallels 4QInstruction has with Proverbs are not found in the Book of Mysteries. Ethical advice on family or finances that echoes with Proverbs is not prominent in this composition. Mysteries does however have forms of rhetoric which indicate that the text is pedagogical. The intended addressees are likely called "those who pursue knowledge" (4Q299 8 7). The didactic mode of the composition is characterized by open-ended questions that the addressees were supposed to contemplate. 4Q299 3c 3–4, for example, asks "Listen: for what is hidden wisdom?" (cf. 4Q299 3a ii-b 3–4; 4Q300 7 1).

Mysteries can be, and often is, called a Wisdom text. But, as sketched out above, the work does not have much to do with traditional Wisdom, as represented by Proverbs. Mysteries has general similarities with Proverbs, such as the thematization of the pursuit of knowledge and a pedagogical function, but, unlike 4QInstruction or 4QBeatitudes, it does not engage specific themes and tropes that resonate directly with Proverbs, such as personified wisdom. The designation of Mysteries as a Wisdom text draws more on its affinities with 4QInstruction than Proverbs. I have argued, and still hold, that Mysteries can be called a Wisdom text but the case is not "clear-cut" (Goff 2010, 300). The issue of classifying this text as sapiential forces us to admit that our categories, while they have integrity through core criteria and exempla, have fuzzy boundaries, such that it can be debated whether a particular genre label should be applied to a particular text. This problem is not unique to the Wisdom genre. As discussed above (37.2 Wisdom as a Category of Biblical Literature), genres are by nature subjective, and theorists of genre recognize that genres which have fuzzy boundaries are a common phenomenon.

37.4 THE FRAGILITY AND VITALITY OF WISDOM

The category Wisdom Literature, utilized primarily for the analysis of biblical texts, can be applied to the Dead Sea Scrolls. At one level, this involves articulating criteria used to define Wisdom Literature and then applying this definition to Qumran texts. But there is more at stake. It is an intellectual act that forces us to acknowledge what sort of category is being envisioned and its limitations. This results, I think, in a more nuanced understanding of the category, as it is applied to both the Hebrew Bible and the Dead Sea Scrolls. There are various criteria on the basis of which texts identified as Wisdom Literature are similar, despite their myriad differences—terminology, literary forms, thematic content, and social settings. But one should be cognizant that it is a category which is etic and constructed. By way of contrast, while scholars can debate the diversity and nuances of Egyptian texts marked at their outset as *sbyʾt* ("instruction") literature, the texts with this heading have a common focus in teaching and ethics, allowing us to understand *sbyʾt* as an emic, ancient classification of texts. "Wisdom" is not used analogously as a marker or heading that shows texts were understood by ancient Jewish scribes as exempla of the same kind of literature (but note the use of "Wisdom of Solomon" as a title; one medieval Hebrew manuscript of Ben Sira concludes by describing the words of the sage as the "Wisdom" of Ben Sira [B; 51:30] but there is no ancient evidence for this usage and it is likely a later development). Wisdom is a metadiscursive textual category, developed by readers of Scripture rather than the ancients who produced this material (cf. Frow 2006, 69). It should be understood as an intertextual entity, a creation produced through the interface between reader and text. Applying this category to texts outside of the Bible spurs interpreters not only to recognize the variety and diversity encompassed by texts classified as Wisdom but also, one can say, the fragility of Wisdom, as a literary category.

It is important not only to acknowledge the constructed nature of the categories we employ but also what this act of classification entails. Problematizing this effort, the study of genre is beset by a confusion of terms (Duff 2000, 17). To this end I identify three general ways people understand genre that are germane for the articulation of the Wisdom category and its use-value.

1. Genre(s) as tools of communication that give semantic potency to texts. Bakhtin's "secondary genres." Here genre denotes discrete conventional modes of speech and writing, such as the proverb, the nature of which changes over time and depending on its interaction with other (secondary) genres. There is an implicit understanding on the part of producers of such genres that readers or listeners are familiar with them. The writers of such texts do not need to know how genres, in this sense of the term, function as taxonomic criteria for categories devised by later readers of these same texts. An important issue for genres in this

sense is the relationship between texts and the occasions/contexts in which they are produced. The issues discussed above regarding etic constructs pertain less to genres, so understood.

2. Genre as a convention of reading (Beebee 1994, 3). This can be understood as akin to Bakhtin's "primary" genres. The conceptualization of Wisdom as an etic, constructed category pertains to genre in this sense of the word. It is not an ontological category. Texts do not "belong" to the Wisdom genre in an exclusivist sense (in which case inclusion in the category would prevent its members from being classified in other ways; see Reed 2017; note also the concern expressed in Najman 2017, 460). The category is produced when readers, as I have done in this article, discern affinities between the texts so categorized. Wisdom as a genre in this sense provides use-value as a hermeneutic tool (more on this below).

3. Genre as taxonomy. Here genre denotes a literary category primarily as a tool of macro-classification. Theorists of genre often reject this neo-Aristotelian dimension of genre "as a prescriptive taxonomy and as a constraint on textual energy" (Frow 2006, 26). But classification is a core and basic act of the human mind (Bowker and Star 1999, 1). It should be acknowledged rather than dismissed. Wisdom here has value as part of a scheme of macro-classification, used to provide a general or introductory orientation of the Hebrew Bible to modern readers. The work as a whole is understood by the generic classification of the books of which it is composed. The same logic applies to the Dead Sea Scrolls—a basic understanding of the vast corpus of texts as a whole can be acquired by a delineation of the categories of literature that comprise it (as one can see in the organization of all the Qumran scrolls in *DJD* 39 according to genre [Tov 2002]). Here the sense of genre as a literary category is rather fixed. Texts belong to such literary categories, so understood. And they in general will belong to only one.

While Weeks urges us to focus on the first category of genre, I encourage readers to concentrate on the latter two or rather to distinguish between them. The potential of Wisdom as a hermeneutic tool should not be limited to the fact that Wisdom can be and is used in macro-taxonomic schemes with regard to the Hebrew Bible or the Dead Sea Scrolls. One should not only be attentive to problems or ambiguities in our categories but also what they can accomplish. Affiliating Wisdom texts together on the basis of their affinities, with regard to literary form, theme, and/or function, has pragmatic value for interpreters of these texts. In principle, one does not need a Wisdom category when comparing, for example, 4QInstruction with Proverbs. But the construct Wisdom Literature helps modern readers recognize what texts are important in the interpretation of the material so classified. As examined above, with regard to several Qumran texts, including 4QInstruction, 4Q184, 4Q424, and 4QBeatitudes, it is helpful to elucidate their main themes and key details by comparing them with Proverbs. Similarly, it is critical to understand Job and Ecclesiastes in relation to major themes in Proverbs or to recognize that Ben Sira and the Wisdom of Solomon develop and refashion macro-themes of this book. Using the category is a way to highlight that particular texts have affinities with others. As such the Wisdom label has pragmatic value for scholars. The affinities between biblical texts and the Dead Sea Scrolls sketched above, in my estimation, also illustrate that it can be useful to apply the label Wisdom to the Qumran corpus, despite being initially developed as a category of biblical literature.

Affiliating Wisdom texts with this etic category also makes it easier to discern that they are part of a common pedagogical discourse, a loose "codification of discursive properties," to use the language of Tzvetan Todorov (1990, 18), that informed the production of these texts. Teachers produced instructional texts (without a rigid or fixed sense of genre) that were, not surprisingly, shaped by the education they themselves received, which included instructional or didactic texts (Vayntrub 2016). One can also describe this as the pedagogical transmission of a "constellation" of texts with common features or elements (Najman 2012, 316). Positing this helps not only explain why the content of didactic texts is similar but also why writings classified as sapiential are united by the fact that in various ways they thematize the pursuit of knowledge. These writings do not just teach students discrete epistemes but also instill in them a desire to learn and study. The Wisdom category, articulated as a convention of reading rather than a rigid taxonomic schema, can help us better understand the pedagogy of ancient Judaism as a context in which texts were studied, transmitted, and produced.

The Dead Sea Scrolls themselves provide an important example of this phenomenon (Brooke 2016). The regulations of the Dead Sea sect mandate constant study and learning, in particular of the Torah (e.g., 1QS 6:6–8). It can be reasonably classified as a pedagogical community. The Qumran Wisdom texts have no explicit markers of being products of the Dead Sea sect, such as references to the Teacher of Righteousness. The only key exception is 4Q298, entitled 4QWords of the Maśkil to all the Sons of Dawn; the Maśkil is an important pedagogical office in the Dead Sea sect (e.g., 1QS 3:13; 9:12–26). The composition consists of exhortations to acquire knowledge and live with righteousness, without instruction on specific topics (Goff 2007, 146–159). It is written in a cryptic form of Hebrew, suggesting that its moral teachings were circulated only within the sect. The scribal transmission of this work and other Wisdom texts by the Dead Sea sect suggest that they were read and studied by this community. The likely possibility that they copied pedagogical texts they did not compose implies that these writings had some sort of reputation or known value as material that they should be esteemed by people devoted to education. One can understand the study of Wisdom texts, with their emphasis on learning and the acquisition of knowledge, as helping group members maintain pedagogical discipline. Understanding authors of key sectarian texts as familiar with (non-sectarian) Wisdom texts can also help explain, for example, the use of the term *raz nihyeh* to describe supernatural revelation in 1QS 11:3–4, or the extensive similarities between 4QInstruction and the Hodayot (Goff 2004).

The realization that Wisdom texts were transmitted and studied also provides a coherent approach to an issue that Kynes derides as "pan-sapientialism"—the assertion that affinities of non-Wisdom texts with Wisdom texts (as has been claimed, for example, with the Joseph novella) should be explained as "Wisdom" influence. This characterization of the issue sets it up in form-critical terms, and this helps explain the methodological problems that Kynes justly critiques (if a given psalm has affinities to Wisdom Literature should it then be also considered Wisdom Literature?). This approach privileges Wisdom as a genre in the sense of my third category (genre as taxonomy), stressing that various texts should also be identified as "belonging" to Wisdom. It is important to recognize that virtually all ancient Jewish texts are the products of people who received some sort of education, including not only written literacy but also inculcation in a body of traditional lore and texts, including the Torah (a focal point of Jewish education in the late Second Temple period) and also what we call Wisdom texts (Goff 2017). People as part of their intellectual training were steeped in some of this material. So, it should not be surprising that in various writings one sees points of similarity with what we call Wisdom texts.

37.5 CONCLUSION

A characteristic feature of Wisdom Literature is a critique of wisdom itself, as evident in the complaints of Job and Ecclesiastes. Contemporary scholarship, in its own way, is currently undergoing something similar—some question the value of Wisdom as a valid category of biblical literature. As I have tried to show, the label Wisdom can be understood as a legitimate category of biblical literature. This label can be applied to the Dead Sea Scrolls, not only because some Qumran texts attest the same core elements found in biblical Wisdom Literature, but also because these texts often have clear and direct links to these texts, above all Proverbs. This is not "circular reasoning." I am not assuming the category and then figuring out how to justify it. I adopt this scholarly convention when interpreting particular Qumran texts because I find it useful when performing this intellectual task, as I have delineated above. We should also keep in mind the constructed and etic nature of this textual category, and that genre categories inevitably have fuzzy boundaries and ambiguities. We need to acknowledge the limitations of our categories and be aware how they can potentially hinder analysis. Understanding the constructed nature of our categories can help recognize that affiliating a set of texts with a single textual category does not in principle force us to reject other schemas of classification or prevent us from comparing them with texts outside of this set. But one should ask not only what are the problems or limitations inherent to Wisdom as a literary category but also assess its value. As I have tried to show, the Wisdom genre, as a convention of reading, can provide insights not only into the affinities between texts so classified but also the importance of these writings in ancient Jewish pedagogy. Developing sensitivity to the categories we develop and utilize as hermeneutic tools is, one can say, a sign of wisdom.

WORKS CITED

Bardtke, Hans. 1956. "Considérations sur les Cantiques de Qumrân." *RB* 63:220–233.

Beebee, Thomas O. 1994. *The Ideology of Genre: A Comparative Study of Generic Instability.* University Park, PA: The Pennsylvania State University Press.

Boer, Roland, ed. 2007. *Bakhtin and Genre Theory in Biblical Studies.* SemeiaSt 63. Atlanta, GA: SBL.

Bowker, Geoffrey C., and Susan Leigh Star. 1999. *Sorting Things Out: Classification and Its Consequences.* Cambridge, MA: MIT Press.

Brooke, George J. 2016. "The Place of Wisdom in the Formation of the Movement behind the Dead Sea Scrolls." Pages 20–33 in *Goochem in Mokum, Wisdom in Amsterdam. Papers on Biblical and Related Wisdom Read at the Fifteenth Joint Meeting of the Society for Old Testament Study and the Oudtestamentisch Werkgezelschap, Amsterdam, July 2012.* Edited by George J. Brooke and Pierre Van Hecke. OTS 68. Leiden: Brill.

Collins, John J. 2010. "Epilogue: Genre Analysis and the Dead Sea Scrolls." *DSD* 17:389–401.

Collins, John J. Forthcoming. "Wisdom as Genre and as Tradition in the Book of Ben Sira." In *The Pursuit of Wisdom and Human Flourishing: The Book of Sirach and Its Contexts.* Edited by Samuel L. Adams, Greg Goering, and Matthew Goff. JSJSup XXX. Leiden: Brill.

Collins, John J. 1997. "Wisdom Reconsidered, in Light of the Scrolls." *DSD* 4:265–281.

Crenshaw, James L. 2010. *Old Testament Wisdom: An Introduction.* 3rd ed. Louisville, KY: Westminster John Knox.

Dell, Katharine J. 2015. "Deciding the Boundaries of Wisdom: Applying the Concept of Family Resemblance." Pages 145–160 in Sneed 2015b.

Derrida, Jacques, and Avital Ronell. 1980. "The Law of Genre." *Critical Inquiry* 7:55–81.

Drawnel, Henryk. 2004. *An Aramaic Wisdom Text from Qumran: A New Interpretation of the Levi Document.* JSJSup 86. Leiden: Brill.

Duff, David, ed. 2000. *Modern Genre Theory.* Essex: Longman.

Elgvin, Torleif, et al. 1997. *Qumran Cave 4.XV: Sapiential Texts, Part 1.* DJD 20. Oxford: Clarendon.

Fishelov, David. 1993. *Metaphors of Genre: The Role of Analogies in Genre Theory.* University Park, PA: The Pennsylvania State University Press.

Fowler, Alastair. 1982. *Kinds of Literature: An Introduction to the Theory of Genres and Modes.* Oxford: Clarendon.

Fox, Michael V. 2015 "Three Theses on Wisdom." Pages 69–86 in Sneed 2015b.

Frow, John. 2006. *Genre.* London: Routledge.

Goff, Matthew. 2013. *4QInstruction.* WLAW 2. Atlanta, GA: SBL.

Goff, Matthew. 2007. *Discerning Wisdom: The Sapiential Literature of the Dead Sea Scrolls.* VTSup 116. Leiden: Brill.

Goff, Matthew. 2004. "Reading Wisdom at Qumran: 4QInstruction and the Hodayot." *DSD* 11:263–288.

Goff, Matthew. 2010. "Qumran Wisdom Literature and the Problem of Genre." *DSD* 17:315–335.

Goff, Matthew. 2017. "Students of God in the House of Torah: Education in the Dead Sea Scrolls." Pages 71–89 in *Second Temple Jewish "Paideia" in Context.* Edited by Jason Zurawski and G. Boccaccini. BZNW 228. Berlin: de Gruyter.

Goff, Matthew. 2018. "Wisdom." Pages 449–456 in *T&T Clark Companion to the Dead Sea Scrolls.* Edited by Charlotte Hempel and George Brooke. London: Bloomsbury T&T Clark.

Kampen, John. 2011. *Wisdom Literature.* Grand Rapids, MI: Eerdmans.

Kister, Menahem. 2004. "Wisdom Literature and Its Relation to Other Genres: From Ben Sira to Mysteries." Pages 13–47 in *Sapiential Perspectives: Wisdom Literature in Light of the Dead Sea Scrolls. Proceedings of the Sixth International Symposium of the Orion Center, 20–22 May 2001.* Edited by John J. Collins, Gregory E. Sterling, and R.A. Clements. STDJ 51. Leiden: Brill.

Kynes, Will. 2015. "The Modern Scholarly Wisdom Tradition and the Threat of Pan-Sapientialism: A Case Report." Pages 11–38 in Sneed 2015b.

Kynes, Will. 2016. "The Nineteenth-Century Beginnings of 'Wisdom Literature,' and its Twenty-First-Century End?" Pages 83–108 in *Perspectives on Israelite Wisdom: Proceedings of the Oxford Old Testament Seminar.* Edited by John Jarick. London: Bloomsbury T&T Clark.

Lakoff, George. 1987. *Women, Fire, and Dangerous Things: What Categories Reveal about the Mind.* Chicago, IL: University of Chicago Press.

Najman, Hindy. 2012. "The Idea of Biblical Genre: From Discourse to Constellation." Pages 307–321 in *Prayer and Poetry in the Dead Sea Scrolls and Related Literature: Essays in Honor of Eileen Schuller on the Occasion of Her Sixty-Fifth Birthday.* Edited by Jeremey Penner, Ken M. Penner, and Cecilia Wassen. STDJ 98. Leiden: Brill.

Najman, Hindy. 2017. "Jewish Wisdom in the Hellenistic Period: Towards the Study of a Semantic Constellation." Pages 459–472 in *Is There a Text in This Cave? Studies in the Textuality of the Dead Sea Scrolls in Honour of George J. Brooke.* Edited by Ariel Feldman, Maria Cioată, and Charlotte Hempel. STDJ 119. Leiden: Brill.

Najman, Hindy, and Eibert Tigchelaar. 2014. "A Preparatory Study of Nomenclature and Text Designation in the Dead Sea Scrolls." *RevQ* 26:305–325.

Newsom, Carol A. 2005. "Spying Out the Land: A Report from Genology." Pages 437–450 in *Seeking Out the Wisdom of the Ancients: Essays Offered to Honor Michael V. Fox on the Occasion of His Sixty-Fifth Birthday.* Winona Lake, IN: Eisenbrauns.

Pfann, Stephen J., et al. 2000. *Qumran Cave 4.XXVI: Cryptic Texts and Miscellanea,* Part 1. DJD 36. Oxford: Clarendon.

Rad, Gerhard von. 1993. *Wisdom in Israel.* Translated by James D. Martin. London: SCM Press Ltd; Valley Forge, PA: Trinity Press International.

Reed, Annette Yoshiko. 2017. "Categorization, Collection, and the Construction of Continuity: *1 Enoch* and *3 Enoch* in and Beyond 'Apocalypticism' and 'Mysticism.'" *MTSR* 29:268–311.

Romaniuk, Casimir. 1978. "Le Thème de la sagesse dans les documents de Qumran." *RevQ* 9:429–435.

Sinding, Michael. 2002. "After Definitions: Genre, Categories, and Cognitive Science." *Genre* 35:181–220.

Sneed, Mark R. 2011. "Is the 'Wisdom Tradition' a Tradition?" *CBQ* 73:50–71.

Sneed, Mark R. 2015a. "'Grasping after the Wind': The Elusive Attempt to Define and Delimit Wisdom." Pages 39–67 in Sneed 2015b.

Sneed, Mark R., ed. 2015b. *Was There a Wisdom Tradition? New Prospects in Israelite Wisdom Studies.* AIL 23. Atlanta, GA: SBL.

Strugnell, John, and Daniel J. Harrington. 1999. *Qumran Cave 4.XXIV: Sapiential Texts, Part 2. 4QInstruction (Mûsār Lĕ Mēbîn): 4Q415ff. With a Re-edition of 1Q26.* Oxford: Clarendon.

Todorov, Tzvetan. 1990. *Genres in Discourse.* Translated by Catherine Porter. Cambridge: Cambridge University Press.

Tov, Emanuel, ed. 2002. *The Texts from the Judaean Desert: Indices and an Introduction to the Discoveries in the Judaean Desert Series.* Oxford: Clarendon.

Uusimäki, Elisa. 2014. "'Happy Is the Person to Whom She Has Been Given': The Continuum of Wisdom and Torah in '4QSapiential Admonitions B' (4Q185) and '4QBeatitudes' (4Q525)." *RevQ* 26:345–359.

Uusimäki, Elisa. 2016. *Turning Proverbs towards Torah: An Analysis of 4Q525*. STDJ 117. Leiden: Brill.

Vayntrub, Jacqueline. 2016. "The Book of Proverbs and the Idea of Ancient Israelite Education." *ZAW* 128:96–114.

Weeks, Stuart. 2010. *An Introduction to the Study of Wisdom Literature*. London: T&T Clark.

Weeks, Stuart. 2016. "Is 'Wisdom Literature' a Useful Category?" Pages 3–23 in *Tracing Sapiential Traditions in Ancient Judaism*. Edited by Hindy Najman, Jean-Sébastien Rey, and Eibert J.C. Tigchelaar. JSJSup 174. Leiden: Brill.

Weeks, Stuart. 2015. "Wisdom, Form and Genre." Pages 161–177 in Sneed 2015b.

Wright, Benjamin G. 2010. "Joining the Club: A Suggestion about Genre in Early Jewish Texts." *DSD* 17:260–285.

Worrell, John. 1968. "Concepts of Wisdom in the Dead Sea Scrolls." Ph.D. diss., Claremont Graduate School.

Zahn, Molly M. 2012. "Genre and Rewritten Scripture: A Reassessment." *JBL* 131:271–288.

Author Index

Scriptural and Ancient Texts

For the benefit of digital users, indexed terms that span two pages (e.g. 52–53) may, on occasion, appear on only one of those pages.

Proverbs (*Continued*)